User's Guide

SPSS X™

Coming Features in SPSS^X

SPSS^X™ is growing to keep pace with its users' needs. New features are constantly being developed, and some are being tested even as the first release, documented in this manual, begins its general distribution. Look for the following enhancements in the next release of SPSS^X:

Table and Report Builders. Two new procedures produce tables and reports suitable for publication. TABLE BUILDER gives current users of CROSSTABS the same kind of added power that REPORT gave to users of BREAKDOWN. REPORT BUILDER produces reports with case listings from a sorted file. Current users of REPORT will be delighted with the additional capabilities to produce enhanced reports with the REPORT BUILDER.

Data Verification and Updating. Two new facilities, CLEAN and UPDATE, provide data checking and updating capabilities. In CLEAN, you can specify permissible values for all variables and relational and/or mathematical contingencies among variables. The cleaning specification commands use the same syntax as the SPSS^X transformation commands. The facility produces detailed reports of variables and cases in error. In UPDATE, you can replace values for specified variables and cases.

USERPROC Facility. The SPSS^X USERPROC facility allows you to write your own procedure within the SPSS^X system or easily incorporate an existing program into SPSS^X. USERPROC supplies a subroutine library containing all the necessary service facilities and many statistical subroutines to incorporate a program written in a standard high-level language. You can also use the USERPROC facility to interface stand-alone programs directly with SPSS^X to take full advantage of the data and file management capabilities of SPSS^X.

PROBIT Analysis. Probit analysis models the relationship between a dichotomous response variable and one or more independent variables—for example, survival of rats after administration of varying doses of poison. The PROBIT procedure applies the probit transformation to the dependent variable and calculates maximum likelihood estimates of the coefficients for the independent variables, as well as some ancillary statistics.

MATRIX Procedure. The MATRIX procedure provides a complete matrix language for performing a wide variety of matrix manipulations and calculations. You can use the transformation structures, DO IF—END IF and LOOP, along with matrix calculation statements. In addition, the MATRIX procedure reads and writes data files and SPSS^X system files.

User's Guide

SPSS X™

McGRAW-HILL BOOK COMPANY

New York St. Louis San Francisco Auckland Bogotá Hamburg
Johannesburg London Madrid Mexico Montreal New Delhi
Panama Paris São Paulo Singapore Sydney Tokyo Toronto

SPSS Inc.

Suite 3000
444 North Michigan Avenue
Chicago, Illinois 60611

For information about the SPSSˣ™ system, SPSS® Graphics, SCSS™, and other software produced and distributed by SPSS Inc., please write or call

Marketing Department
SPSS Inc.
Suite 3300
444 North Michigan Avenue
Chicago, IL 60611
(312) 329-2400

5 6 7 8 9 0 SMSM 89 8 7 6 5

ISBN 0-07-046550-9

Library of Congress Catalog Card No.: 82-062808

Preface

While this manual documents the first release of the SPSS^{X}™ Batch System, both the manual and the system it documents are products of over seventeen years of program development and interaction with users. We have created SPSS^{X} based on the experiences of nine releases of the SPSS Batch System and have written this manual based on feedback from two editions plus two updates of the SPSS manual. Therefore, SPSS^{X} is the most fully refined data analysis system of its kind and this manual is the most user-designed document in the industry.

This manual is both a reference to all SPSS^{X} facilities and a guide to their use. We have included the following features to make it as quick and complete a guide as possible.

- Turn to introductory Chapters 1 and 2 for an outline of SPSS^{X} facilities, for a discussion of the kinds of input and output files the system uses, and for the general rules for SPSS^{X} commands.
- Use the table of contents, the index, and the thumb index with its guide on the back cover to locate the information you need quickly.
- Consult the outline at the beginning of each chapter for an overview of topics discussed.
- Use the syntax summary at the beginning of each chapter as an overview of the commands discussed in the chapter and as a quick reference to available specifications.
- Look for annotated examples set off on separate, shaded pages in each chapter which place the facility being discussed in the context of a complete SPSS^{X} job. Also look for examples throughout the chapter and for suggestions on when and how to apply the facilities.
- If you are familiar with SPSS, turn to Appendix A, "Help for Old Friends," for an outline of differences and for suggestions on how you can move easily to SPSS^{X}.
- Tear out the pocket-sized reference card provided at the back of the manual to carry with you as a reminder of syntax requirements and options.

$SPSS^X$ is supported by other manuals that supplement this document in the areas of statistics and applications. The following manuals will be available soon:

$SPSS^X$ Basics
SPSS Inc.

This manual will get new $SPSS^X$ users off to a quick but solid start. It introduces the $SPSS^X$ system through a series of progressive tasks, starting simply with the mechanics of submitting an $SPSS^X$ job to the computer and obtaining the output. The tasks are designed to be simple but to generalize readily to the kinds of jobs you want to get done.

$SPSS^X$ Introductory Statistics Guide
Marija J. Norusis, Rush-Presbyterian-St. Luke's Medical Center

This text features introductions to statistics with instructions for performing sample analyses with $SPSS^X$. It is intended as a supplementary guide for teaching and for personal use. It carries the reader from basic statistics through multiple regression. Examples come from research in a variety of fields, and each is supported by explanations of $SPSS^X$ output, the commands used to create the output, and review questions and computer exercises designed to reinforce the concepts.

$SPSS^X$ Advanced Statistics Guide
Marija J. Norusis, Rush-Presbyterian-St. Luke's Medical Center

Designed for researchers and for the multivariate statistics course, this text takes up where *$SPSS^X$ Introductory Statistics Guide* leaves off. For people who use this manual without the introductory volume, a preliminary chapter presents the operations of $SPSS^X$ and an appendix provides summaries of data management facilities and statistical procedures not discussed in depth.

$SPSS^X$ Data Management
SPSS Inc.

This manual provides information useful to people whose applications of $SPSS^X$ involve more than routine data definition and management: researchers in universities or private research organizations, planners using census data to develop profiles of geographical areas, and companies maintaining inventory, sales, or employee files. It shows, in detailed examples, how to define a variety of complex files, check files for record sequence, aggregate data within a file, match files with common variables, and add data to existing files.

$SPSS^X$ Analysis of United States Census Data
SPSS Inc.

$SPSS^X$ provides both the data management and statistical facilities needed to use the data distributed by the United States Census Bureau. This book will show actual applications, including merging census data with the user's own data files, deriving demographic statistics for a local area such as a school district, and producing formatted tables and graphs to display the results.

SPSS^X Analysis of SMF Data
SPSS Inc.

This manual shows how to use SPSS^X to read IBM System Maintenance Facilities (SMF) data and do system performance evaluation. With the file definition and labeling capabilities and extensive statistical, tabulating, and reporting facilities available in SPSS^X, access to SMF information becomes convenient and flexible for anyone who has to monitor the performance of the computer.

Like its predecessor, SPSS^X is constantly undergoing enhancements. Therefore, you should look for information about additional applications documents and updates to the system itself via the INFO command documented in Chapter 2. This is one way you keep up with developments at SPSS Inc. The other way to keep current is to fill out and mail the McGraw-Hill reader reply card included in this manual (or to call or write SPSS Inc. at the address shown on the copyright page). Once we know who you are, you can expect to share in the full support of SPSS^X provided both by SPSS Inc. and by a very active group of data processors, researchers, and instructors.

Acknowledgments

A project the size of SPSS^X involves legions of people contributing at many levels. However, there are those who deserve individual recognition for their accomplishments, without which SPSS^X could never have been contemplated, much less executed. Those responsible for the overall design and implementation of the system are:

Jonathan Fry, *general system architecture*
C. Hadlai Hull, *general system architecture*
William Arendt, *transformations implementation*
Jean Jenkins, *procedures conversion*
Andrew Walaszek, *procedures conversion*
Keith Sours, *language design and documentation*
Nancy Morrison, *language design and documentation*
ViAnn Beadle, *procedure design and documentation*
Robert Gruen, *documentation design and production*

In addition, SPSS^X could never have come to fruition without the efforts of the following people, who had specific responsibilities in the design or implementation of the system:

Anthony Babinec
David Farb
Jeffrey A. Mlynarczyk
Marija Norusis
Sanford Stein
Kenneth Stehlik-Barry
C. Ming Wang

All SPSS Inc. staff members deserve credit for their contributions to SPSS^X, its documentation, and its technical support. Among the many who worked directly on the project, I would like to mention the following individuals:

Elisabeth Adams
Mark Barton
Kathleen M. Bonell
Douglas G. Chene
Leonid Feygin
Pamela K. Hecht
David Nayer
James C. Person
Sarah Sample
David Silkey

Finally, the literally thousands of names we cannot list are our steadfast and loyal users who have given us criticism and encouragement throughout the years. Specifically, we are fortunate to have had the opportunity to exchange ideas through the activities of ISSUE Inc., our user group, under the presidency of Marcia Tolbert for the past five years. I would also like to express gratitude to our special test sites who have given the system and preliminary versions of this manual the thorough workover that only our most sophisticated and dedicated users can provide. It is to our user community that we dedicate this manual.

Norman H. Nie
President, SPSS Inc.

Contents

Chapter 1 Introduction 1

1.1 A SAMPLE JOB 2
1.2 FILES USED IN SPSS^X 6
 1.3 Multiple Files and the Active File 7
1.4 DATA DEFINITION 7
 1.5 Cases and Variables 7
  1.6 Missing Values 1.7 Labels 1.8 Format
 1.9 Defining Complex Files 9
1.10 MANIPULATING VARIABLES 9
 1.11 Manipulating Numeric Variables 10
 1.12 Manipulating String Variables 10
 1.13 Conditional Transformations 10
 1.14 Transformation Utilities 11
1.15 FILE MANAGEMENT 11
 1.16 Combining Files 11
 1.17 Splitting, Sorting, and Aggregating Files 11
 1.18 System Files 12
 1.19 Procedure Output 12
1.20 OTHER UTILITIES FOR CONTROLLING THE JOB 12
1.21 PRINTING AND WRITING CASES 13
1.22 TABLES AND REPORTS 14
1.23 GRAPHICS 14
1.24 STATISTICAL PROCEDURES 14
 1.25 Frequency Distributions and Descriptive Statistics 14
 1.26 Relationships Between Two or More Variables 15
 1.27 Correlation Coefficients and Scatterplots 15
 1.28 Multiple Regression Analysis 15
 1.29 Factor Analysis 15
 1.30 Discriminant Analysis 15
 1.31 Survival Analysis 16
 1.32 Analysis of Additive Scales 16
 1.33 Nonparametric Statistics 16
 1.34 Log-linear Models 16
 1.35 Univariate and Multivariate Analysis of Variance 16
 1.36 Box-Jenkins Analysis of Time Series Data 17

Chapter 2 The SPSS^X Language 19

2.1 PREPARING SPSS^X COMMANDS 19
 2.2 Commands and Specifications 19
 2.3 Names 20
  2.4 The TO Conventions
 2.5 Keywords 21
  2.6 Truncation
 2.7 Numbers and Literals 22
 2.8 Arithmetic Operators and Delimiters 22
 2.9 Notation Used to Describe SPSS^X Commands 23
2.10 THE ORDER OF SPSS^X COMMANDS 23
2.11 THE INFO COMMAND 24
 2.12 Selecting the Type of Information 25
 2.13 Specifying Releases 25
 2.14 Writing Information to an External File 26
 2.15 Truncation 26

Chapter 3 Defining Data 29

3.1 INTRODUCTION TO DATA DEFINITION 29
3.2 THE FILE HANDLE COMMAND 30
3.3 The Active File 30
3.4 FILE DEFINITION ON DATA LIST 31
3.5 The FILE Subcommand 31
3.6 Keywords FIXED, FREE, and LIST 32
3.7 The RECORDS Subcommand 32
3.8 The TABLE and NOTABLE Subcommands 32
3.9 VARIABLE DEFINITION ON DATA LIST 33
3.10 Specifying the Record Number 33
3.11 Naming the Variables 33
3.12 Indicating Column Locations 34
3.13 Specifying Multiple Records 34
3.14 Specifying Multiple Variables 34
3.15 Indicating Decimal Places 35
3.16 The Default Format Type 35
3.17 N and E Format Types 3.18 String Variables 3.19 Other Format Types
3.20 FREE and LIST Variable Definition 37
3.21 Specifying Format Types
3.22 Undefined Data Values 38
3.23 Printing and Writing Formats 38
3.24 MISSING VALUES 39
3.25 The MISSING VALUES Command 39
3.26 Referencing Several Variables 3.27 Specifying Ranges of Missing Values
3.28 Missing Values for String Variables 41
3.29 Redefining Missing Values 41
3.30 VARIABLE AND VALUE LABELS 41
3.31 The VARIABLE LABELS Command 42
3.32 The VALUE LABELS Command 42
3.33 INPUT DATA IN THE COMMAND FILE 43
3.34 The BEGIN DATA and END DATA Commands 43
3.35 FORTRAN-LIKE FORMAT SPECIFICATIONS ON DATA LIST 45
3.36 Format Elements 45
3.37 The T and X Format Elements 3.38 Mixing Styles
3.39 Skipping Records 47

Chapter 4 Job Utilities and Error Messages 51

4.1 TITLES AND SUBTITLES 51
4.2 COMMENTS IN SPSS^X COMMANDS 52
4.3 THE FINISH COMMAND 52
4.4 NUMBERED AND UNNUMBERED COMMAND LINES 53
4.5 THE SET AND SHOW COMMANDS 53
4.6 Summary of SET and SHOW Commands 53
4.7 Blanks and Undefined Input Data 54
4.8 Maximum Errors and Loops 55
4.9 Printed Output 55
4.10 Samples and Random Numbers 57
4.11 Scratch File Compression 57
4.12 Additional Information from SHOW 57
4.13 NOTES, WARNINGS, AND ERROR MESSAGES 60
4.14 Notes 4.15 Warnings 4.16 Errors
4.17 EDIT JOBS 61

Chapter 5 SPSS^X System Files 65

5.1 INTRODUCTION TO SYSTEM FILES 65
5.2 THE GET COMMAND 66
5.3 The FILE Subcommand 66
5.4 The MAP Subcommand 67
5.5 The RENAME Subcommand 67
5.6 The DROP Subcommand 68
5.7 The KEEP Subcommand 69
5.8 Reordering Variables
5.9 Multiple Subcommands 70
5.10 THE SAVE COMMAND 70
5.11 The OUTFILE Subcommand 71
5.12 The MAP Subcommand 71
5.13 The RENAME Subcommand 72
5.14 The DROP and KEEP Subcommands 72
5.15 Reordering Variables
5.16 The COMPRESSED and UNCOMPRESSED Subcommands 76
5.17 SYSTEM FILE UTILITIES 76
5.18 The FILE LABEL Command 76
5.19 The DOCUMENT Command 76
5.20 The DISPLAY Command 77
5.21 The VARIABLES Subcommand
5.22 STRUCTURE OF A SYSTEM FILE 79
5.23 Binary Storage 79
5.24 Upper and Lower Case 79
5.25 Limitations 80

Chapter 6 Numeric Transformations 83

6.1 INTRODUCTION TO DATA TRANSFORMATIONS 83
6.2 Printing and Writing Formats 84
6.3 THE RECODE COMMAND 84
6.4 Specifying Numeric Values 85
6.5 Keywords THRU, LOWEST, and HIGHEST 6.6 Keyword ELSE
6.7 Keywords MISSING and SYSMIS 6.8 Value Ranges
6.9 Keyword INTO 86
6.10 Keyword COPY
6.11 THE COMPUTE COMMAND 87
6.12 Computing Numeric Variables 87
6.13 Missing Values 90
6.14 NUMERIC EXPRESSIONS 90
6.15 Arithmetic Operations 91
6.16 Numeric Constants 6.17 The Order of Operations
6.18 Numeric Functions 92
6.19 Arithmetic Functions 6.20 Statistical Functions 6.21 Missing-Value Functions 6.22 The Across-Case LAG Function 6.23 Logical Functions 6.24 Other Functions 6.25 Using Logical Functions 6.26 Using the YRMODA Function 6.27 Complex Numeric Arguments
6.28 Logical Expressions 95
6.29 Missing Values 96
6.30 Missing Values in Arguments 6.31 Domain Errors
6.32 THE COUNT COMMAND 100
6.33 Initialization and Missing Values 101
6.34 TRANSFORMATION UTILITIES 101
6.35 The LEAVE Command 101
6.36 Scratch Variables 102
6.37 The TEMPORARY Command 103
6.38 The NUMERIC Command 104
6.39 The DO REPEAT Utility 104
6.40 Replacement Variable and Value Lists 6.41 The PRINT Subcommand
6.42 System Variables 106

6.43 EXECUTING DATA TRANSFORMATIONS 107
6.44 Data Definition Commands 107
6.45 The Active File 107

Chapter 7 String Transformations 109

7.1 INTRODUCTION TO STRING VARIABLES 109
7.2 The STRING Command 110
7.3 Literals 110
7.4 Missing Values 111
7.5 THE RECODE COMMAND 111
7.6 Specifying String Values 112
7.7 Keywords INTO, ELSE, and COPY
7.8 Changing Variable Types 114
7.9 Keyword CONVERT
7.10 STRING EXPRESSIONS 114
7.11 Computing String Variables 114
7.12 Constructing String Expressions 115
7.13 Logical Expressions 115
7.14 String Functions 116
7.15 Padding and Trimming Strings 7.16 Indexing and Substrings 7.17 The NUMBER Function
7.18 The Third Argument of INDEX 7.19 Nesting Functions

Chapter 8 Conditional Transformations 121

8.1 THE IF COMMAND 121
8.2 THE DO IF—END IF STRUCTURE 122
8.3 The DO IF and END IF Commands 122
8.4 DO IF—END IF Compared with IF
8.5 The ELSE Command 123
8.6 ELSE Compared with IF
8.7 The ELSE IF Command 124
8.8 Multiple ELSE IF Commands
8.9 Missing Values and the DO IF Structure 125
8.10 Nested DO IF Structures 125
8.11 Summary 126
8.12 LOGICAL EXPRESSIONS 127
8.13 Logical Variables 128
8.14 Relational Operators 128
8.15 The AND and OR Logical Operators 129
8.16 The NOT Logical Operator 129
8.17 The Order of Evaluation 129
8.18 Missing Values 132
8.19 Missing Values and Logical Operators

Chapter 9 Listing and Writing Cases 135

9.1 THE PRINT COMMAND 135
9.2 Variable Specifications 136
9.3 Specifying Formats 9.4 Printing Multiple Lines per Case 9.5 Using Literals
9.6 Creating Column Headings
9.7 File and Table Specifications 139
9.8 Features and Limitations 140
9.9 THE PRINT EJECT COMMAND 140
9.10 THE PRINT SPACE COMMAND 140
9.11 Specifying the Number of Blank Lines 141
9.12 THE WRITE COMMAND 141
9.13 Variable Specifications 142
9.14 File and Table Specifications 142

9.15 PRINT AND WRITE FORMAT COMMANDS 143
9.16 The PRINT FORMATS Command 144
9.17 The WRITE FORMATS Command 144
9.18 The FORMATS Command 144
9.19 THE LIST PROCEDURE 144
9.20 The VARIABLES Subcommand 145
9.21 The CASES Subcommand 146
9.22 The FORMAT Subcommand 146
9.23 LIST and Case Selection 147

Chapter 10 Selecting, Sampling, and Weighting Cases 151

10.1 THE SELECT IF COMMAND 151
10.2 Logical Expressions 151
10.3 Missing Values 152
10.4 SELECT IF and $CASENUM 152
10.5 Multiple SELECT IF Commands 153
10.6 THE SAMPLE COMMAND 153
10.7 Multiple SAMPLE Commands 153
10.8 THE N OF CASES COMMAND 154
10.9 THE WEIGHT COMMAND 154
10.10 Turning Off or Changing Weights 155
10.11 How Procedures Use Weights 155
10.12 Tests of Significance 157
10.13 PLACEMENT OF SAMPLE, SELECT IF, AND WEIGHT 157
10.14 Temporary Sampling, Selecting, and Weighting 157
10.15 SELECT IF, SAMPLE, and Other Transformations 158
10.16 SAMPLE and SELECT IF with DO IF

Chapter 11 Defining Complex File Structures 161

11.1 INTRODUCTION TO COMPLEX FILES 161
11.2 TYPES OF FILES 162
11.3 FILE TYPE MIXED 162
11.4 The FILE Subcommand 163
11.5 The RECORD Subcommand 163
11.6 The WILD Subcommand 164
11.7 The RECORD TYPE Command for FILE TYPE MIXED 164
11.8 Keyword OTHER 11.9 The SKIP Subcommand
11.10 FILE TYPE GROUPED 166
11.11 The RECORD Subcommand 167
11.12 The CASE Subcommand 167
11.13 The WILD Subcommand 168
11.14 The DUPLICATE Subcommand 168
11.15 The MISSING Subcommand 168
11.16 The ORDERED Subcommand 169
11.17 The RECORD TYPE Command for FILE TYPE GROUPED 169
11.18 The SKIP Subcommand 11.19 The CASE Subcommand
11.20 The DUPLICATE and MISSING Subcommands
11.21 FILE TYPE NESTED 171
11.22 The RECORD Subcommand 172
11.23 The CASE Subcommand 173
11.24 The WILD Subcommand 173
11.25 The DUPLICATE Subcommand 173
11.26 The MISSING Subcommand 174
11.27 The RECORD TYPE Command for FILE TYPE NESTED 175
11.28 The CASE Subcommand 11.29 The SPREAD Subcommand
11.30 SUMMARY OF FILE DEFINITIONS 179
11.31 THE REPEATING DATA COMMAND 179
11.32 The INPUT PROGRAM—END INPUT PROGRAM Structure 181
11.33 The STARTS Subcommand 182

11.34 The OCCURS Subcommand 183
11.35 The DATA Subcommand 184
11.36 The NOTABLE Subcommand 184
11.37 The FILE Subcommand 184
11.38 The LENGTH Subcommand 185
11.39 The CONTINUED Subcommand 185
11.40 The ID Subcommand 186

Chapter 12 Input Programs 189

12.1 THE LOOP AND END LOOP COMMANDS 190
12.2 The Indexing Clause for the LOOP Command 190
12.3 Keyword BY
12.4 The IF Clause for the END LOOP Command 191
12.5 The IF Clause for the LOOP Command 192
12.6 Missing Values and the LOOP Structure 192
12.7 Nesting LOOP Structures 193
12.8 The BREAK Command 193
12.9 THE VECTOR COMMAND 193
12.10 The VECTOR Command Short Form 194
12.11 Using VECTOR Outside a LOOP Structure 195
12.12 INPUT PROGRAM and END INPUT PROGRAM 195
12.13 The Input State 196
12.14 The END CASE Command 196
12.15 END CASE and Other Commands
12.16 The END FILE Command 198
12.17 END FILE and END CASE 12.18 Creating Data
12.19 The REREAD Command 202
12.20 Keyword COLUMN
12.21 Predetermining Variable Order 203
12.22 CONTROL STRUCTURES AND DEFINING FILES 203
12.23 The DO IF Structure 203
12.24 The LOOP Structure 204

Chapter 13 Sorting and Splitting Files 207

13.1 THE SORT CASES COMMAND 207
13.2 Ascending or Descending Order 207
13.3 Multiple Variable Specifications 207
13.4 String Variables 208
13.5 SORT CASES and Other Commands 209
13.6 THE SPLIT FILE COMMAND 212
13.7 Keyword BY 212
13.8 Placement of SPLIT FILE 212
13.9 SPLIT FILE and Other Commands 213

Chapter 14 AGGREGATE 215

14.1 OVERVIEW 215
14.2 OPERATION 216
14.3 The OUTFILE Subcommand 216
14.4 The BREAK Subcommand 217
14.5 Creating AGGREGATE Variables 217
14.6 Labels and Formats 14.7 AGGREGATE Functions 14.8 Function Arguments
14.9 Missing Data 220
14.10 The MISSING Subcommand 14.11 Including Missing Values
14.12 Comparing Missing-Value Treatments

Chapter 15 Combining System Files 225

15.1 THE MATCH FILES COMMAND 225
15.2 Parallel Files 226
15.3 The FILE Subcommand 15.4 Specifying the Active File 15.5 The MAP Subcommand
15.6 The RENAME Subcommand 15.7 The DROP and KEEP Subcommands
15.8 Reordering Variables
15.9 Nonparallel Files 230
15.10 The FILE and BY Subcommands 15.11 Common Variables 15.12 The IN Subcommand
15.13 Tables and Files 234
15.14 The FILE, TABLE, and BY Subcommands 15.15 The FIRST and LAST Subcommands
15.16 The FIRST and LAST Subcommands on One File 238
15.17 THE ADD FILES COMMAND 238
15.18 Concatenating Files 238
15.19 The FILE Subcommand 15.20 Optional Subcommands
15.21 Interleaving Files 241
15.22 The FILE and BY Subcommands 15.23 Optional Subcommands

Chapter 16 File Interfaces 245

16.1 THE SCSS INTERFACE 245
16.2 The SAVE SCSS Command 245
16.3 The OUTFILE Subcommand 16.4 The KEEP and DROP Subcommands
16.5 The RENAME Subcommand 16.6 The Display Output
16.7 The GET SCSS Command 248
16.8 The MASTERFILE Subcommand 16.9 The WORKFILE Subcommand
16.10 The VARIABLES Subcommand
16.11 TRANSPORTING SPSS^X SYSTEM FILES 250
16.12 Considerations for Portable Files 250
16.13 Characteristics of Portable Files 251
16.14 Character Translation
16.15 The EXPORT Command 251
16.16 The KEEP and DROP Subcommands 16.17 The RENAME Subcommand
16.18 The MAP Subcommand 16.19 The DIGITS Subcommand
16.20 The IMPORT Command 253
16.21 The KEEP and DROP Subcommands 16.22 The RENAME Subcommand
16.23 The MAP Subcommand

Chapter 17 Using Procedures in SPSS^X 257

17.1 WHAT IS A PROCEDURE? 257
17.2 PROCEDURE PLACEMENT 258
17.3 The EXECUTE Command 258
17.4 The BEGIN DATA and END DATA Commands 259
17.5 OPTIONS AND STATISTICS COMMANDS 259
17.6 SAVING CASEWISE RESULTS 260
17.7 PROCEDURES AND OUTPUT FILES 260
17.8 The PROCEDURE OUTPUT Command 260
17.9 Matrix Materials 261
17.10 Writing Matrix Materials 17.11 The INPUT MATRIX Command
17.12 The N OF CASES Command 17.13 Passing Matrix Materials among Procedures
17.14 Split-File Processing

Chapter 18 FREQUENCIES 265

18.1 OVERVIEW 265
18.2 OPERATION 266
18.3 The VARIABLES Subcommand 266
18.4 General vs. Integer Mode
18.5 The FORMAT Subcommand 267
18.6 Table Formats 18.7 The Order of Values 18.8 Suppressing Tables 18.9 Index of Tables
18.10 Writing Tables to a File
18.11 Bar Charts and Histograms 269
18.12 The BARCHART Subcommand 18.13 The HISTOGRAM Subcommand
18.14 The HBAR Subcommand

18.15 Percentiles and Ntiles 273
18.16 The PERCENTILES Subcommand 18.17 The NTILES Subcommand
18.18 The STATISTICS Subcommand 276
18.19 Missing Values 276
18.20 LIMITATIONS 277

Chapter 19 **CONDESCRIPTIVE 279**

19.1 OVERVIEW 279
19.2 OPERATION 279
19.3 The Variable List 279
19.4 Statistics 280
19.5 *Z* Scores 281
19.6 Missing Values 282
19.7 Formatting Options 282
19.8 LIMITATIONS 284

Chapter 20 **CROSSTABS 287**

20.1 OVERVIEW 287
20.2 OPERATION 288
20.3 General Mode 288
20.4 Integer Mode 291
20.5 The VARIABLES Subcommand 20.6 The TABLES subcommand
20.7 Cell Contents 293
20.8 Percentages 20.9 Expected Values and Residuals
20.10 Optional Statistics 294
20.11 Missing Values 295
20.12 Formatting Options 297
20.13 Indexing Tables 297
20.14 Writing and Reproducing Tables 297
20.15 Writing Tables to a File 20.16 The Output File 20.17 Reproducing Tables
20.18 LIMITATIONS 299

Chapter 21 **MULT RESPONSE 303**

21.1 INTRODUCTION TO MULTIPLE RESPONSE ITEMS 303
21.2 Constructing Group Variables 304
21.3 Crosstabulations 305
21.4 OVERVIEW 307
21.5 OPERATION 307
21.6 The GROUPS Subcommand 308
21.7 The VARIABLES Subcommand 309
21.8 The FREQUENCIES Subcommand 309
21.9 The TABLES Subcommand 311
21.10 Paired Crosstabulations
21.11 Cell Contents and Percentages 315
21.12 Missing Values 315
21.13 Formatting Options 316
21.14 Stub and Banner Tables 316
21.15 LIMITATIONS 317

Chapter 22 **BREAKDOWN 321**

22.1 OVERVIEW 321
22.2 OPERATION 321
22.3 General Mode 322
22.4 Integer Mode 324
22.5 The VARIABLES Subcommand 22.6 The TABLES Subcommand
22.7 The CROSSBREAK Alternate Display Format

22.8 Optional Statistics 326
22.9 Missing Values 327
22.10 Formatting Options 328
22.11 LIMITATIONS 329

Chapter 23 REPORT 333

23.1 INTRODUCTION 333
23.2 Page Layout 334
23.3 Columns 23.4 Rows
23.5 Breaks and Break Variables 335
23.6 Command Overview 336
23.7 A Company Report 337
23.8 THE FORMAT SUBCOMMAND 338
23.9 The LIST Keyword 338
23.10 Page Dimensions 339
23.11 Vertical Spacing 339
23.12 The MISSING Keyword 339
23.13 FORMAT Summary 339
23.14 THE VARIABLES SUBCOMMAND 340
23.15 Column Contents 340
23.16 Column Widths 341
23.17 Column Heads 341
23.18 Positioning Columns under Heads 342
23.19 Intercolumn Spacing 342
23.20 VARIABLES Summary 343
23.21 THE STRING SUBCOMMAND 346
23.22 Variables within Strings 346
23.23 Literals within Strings 347
23.24 Using Strings 347
23.25 STRING Specifications 347
23.26 The Company Report Using Strings 348
23.27 THE BREAK SUBCOMMAND 349
23.28 Column Heads, Contents, and Width 349
23.29 One- and Two-Break Reports with Two Variables
23.30 Keyword (TOTAL) and Multiple Break Reports 23.31 Reports with No Breaks
23.32 BREAK Summary 354
23.33 THE SUMMARY SUBCOMMAND 354
23.34 Basic Specifications 354
23.35 REPORT Statistics 355
23.36 Composite Functions 355
23.37 Multiple Aggregate Functions 355
23.38 Summary Titles 356
23.39 Spacing Summary Lines 357
23.40 Summary Titles in Break Columns 23.41 Print Formats for Summaries 23.42 Using Composite Functions 23.43 Nested Composite Functions
23.44 Multiple Summary Statistics on One Line 364
23.45 Repeating Summary Specifications 365
23.46 SUMMARY Summary 366
23.47 TITLES AND FOOTNOTES 367
23.48 THE MISSING SUBCOMMAND 368
23.49 REPORTS WITH NO BREAKS 369
23.50 SUBCOMMAND ORDER 370
23.51 Limitations 370
23.52 Trial Runs 371
23.53 Split-File Processing 371
23.54 Sorting Cases 371
23.55 REPORT Compared with Other Procedures 372
23.56 Producing CROSSBREAK-like Tables 23.57 Producing CROSSTABS-like Tables
23.58 REPORT and Other $SPSS^X$ Commands 374

Chapter 24 SPSS Graphics 377

24.1 OVERVIEW 377
- 24.2 Overview of the PIECHART Procedure 378
- 24.3 Overview of the BARCHART Procedure 379
- 24.4 Overview of the LINECHART Procedure 380

24.5 THE PIECHART PROCEDURE 381
- 24.6 The PLOT Subcommand 382
  - 24.7 Keyword BY 24.8 Selectors
- 24.9 The FORMAT Subcommand 383
- 24.10 The TITLE, FOOTNOTE, and COMMENT Subcommands 384
- 24.11 Controlling the Segments 384
  - 24.12 The SEGMENT LABELS Subcommand 24.13 The EXPLODE Subcommand 24.14 The ORDER Subcommand 24.15 The COLORS Subcommand
- 24.16 The FONT Subcommand 387
- 24.17 The XPAGE and YPAGE Subcommands 387
- 24.18 The MISSING Subcommand 387
- 24.19 Multiple PLOT Subcommands 390
- 24.20 Special Plotting Applications 391
  - 24.21 Anticipating Multiple Plots per Page 24.22 Entering Aggregate Data for Plots

24.23 THE BARCHART PROCEDURE 392
- 24.24 The PLOT Subcommand 393
  - 24.25 The Function and WITH Specifications 24.26 Keyword BY 24.27 Selectors 24.28 Multiple Variables 24.29 Cross-Products
- 24.30 The FORMAT Subcommand 397
- 24.31 The TITLE, FOOTNOTE, and COMMENT Subcommands 399
- 24.32 Controlling the Axes and the Bars 399
  - 24.33 The BASE AXIS Subcommand 24.34 The SIDE AXIS Subcommand 24.35 The LEGEND TITLE and LEGEND LABELS Subcommands 24.36 The ORDER Subcommand 24.37 The COLORS Subcommand
- 24.38 The FONT Subcommand 404
- 24.39 The XPAGE and YPAGE Subcommands 404
- 24.40 The MISSING Subcommand 404
- 24.41 Multiple PLOT Subcommands 407

24.42 THE LINECHART PROCEDURE 408
- 24.43 The PLOT Subcommand 408
  - 24.44 The Function and WITH Specifications 24.45 Keyword BY 24.46 Selectors 24.47 Multiple Functions 24.48 Superimposing Line Charts
- 24.49 The FORMAT Subcommand 412
- 24.50 The TITLE, FOOTNOTE, and COMMENT Subcommands 412
- 24.51 Controlling the Axes and the Curves 413
  - 24.52 The X AXIS Subcommand 24.53 The Y AXIS Subcommand 24.54 The CURVES Subcommand 24.55 The LEGEND TITLE and LEGEND LABELS Subcommands 24.56 The ORDER Subcommand 24.57 The COLORS Subcommand
- 24.58 The FONT Subcommand 418
- 24.59 The XPAGE and YPAGE Subcommands 418
- 24.60 The MISSING Subcommand 418
- 24.61 Multiple PLOT Subcommands 419
- 24.62 LINECHART Applications 420
  - 24.63 Plotting Regression Lines 24.64 Shaded Line Charts

24.65 THE TELL-A-GRAF INTERFACE 422

24.66 THE GRAPHICS OUTPUT COMMAND 425

24.67 THE SPSS GRAPHICS POSTPROCESSOR 425

Chapter 25 **T-TEST 431**

25.1 OVERVIEW 431
25.2 OPERATION 431
25.3 Independent Samples 431
25.4 The GROUPS Subcommand 25.5 The VARIABLES Subcommand
25.6 Paired Samples 434
25.7 Independent and Paired Designs 435
25.8 One-Tailed Significance Levels 435
25.9 Missing Values 435
25.10 Formatting Options 436
25.11 LIMITATIONS 436

Chapter 26 **ANOVA 439**

26.1 OVERVIEW 439
26.2 OPERATION 440
26.3 Specifying Full Factorial ANOVA Models 440
26.4 Cell Means
26.5 Suppressing Interaction Effects 443
26.6 Specifying Covariates 443
26.7 Order of Entry of Covariates 26.8 Regression Coefficients for the Covariates
26.9 Methods for Decomposing Sums of Squares 444
26.10 Summary of Analysis Methods 448
26.11 Multiple Classification Analysis 449
26.12 Missing Values 450
26.13 Formatting Options 450
26.14 LIMITATIONS 450

Chapter 27 **ONEWAY 453**

27.1 OVERVIEW 453
27.2 OPERATION 454
27.3 Specifying the Design 454
27.4 The POLYNOMIAL Subcommand 454
27.5 The CONTRAST Subcommand 455
27.6 The RANGES Subcommand 456
27.7 User-Specified Ranges 27.8 Harmonic Means
27.9 Optional Statistics 459
27.10 Missing Values 459
27.11 Formatting Options 459
27.12 Matrix Materials 460
27.13 Writing Matrices 27.14 Reading Matrices
27.15 LIMITATIONS 461

Chapter 28 **MANOVA: General Linear Models 465**

28.1 OVERVIEW 465
28.2 OPERATION 466
28.3 The MANOVA Specification 466
28.4 Dependent Variable List 28.5 Factor List 28.6 Covariate List
28.7 The ANALYSIS Subcommand 468
28.8 The DESIGN Subcommand 469
28.9 Simple Main Effects 28.10 Interaction Terms 28.11 Single-Degree-of-Freedom Effects
28.12 Keyword CONTIN 28.13 Interactions Between Factors and Interval Variables
28.14 Nested Designs 28.15 Lumped Effects 28.16 Keyword CONSPLUS 28.17 Error Terms
28.18 Keyword CONSTANT 28.19 Keyword MWITHIN
28.20 The WSFACTORS Subcommand 473
28.21 The WSDESIGN Subcommand 474
28.22 The ANALYSIS Subcommand for Repeated Measures Designs 475

28.23 The MEASURE Subcommand 476
28.24 The TRANSFORM Subcommand 476
28.25 Keyword REPEATED 28.26 Keyword POLYNOMIAL 28.27 Keyword SPECIAL
28.28 Multiple Variable Lists
28.29 The RENAME Subcommand 479
28.30 The METHOD Subcommand 480
28.31 Keyword MODELTYPE 28.32 Keyword ESTIMATION 28.33 Keyword SSTYPE
28.34 The PARTITION Subcommand 481
28.35 The CONTRAST Subcommand 482
28.36 The SETCONST Subcommand 486
28.37 The ERROR Subcommand 486
28.38 The PRINT and NOPRINT Subcommands 487
28.39 Keyword CELLINFO 28.40 Keyword HOMOGENEITY 28.41 Keyword DESIGN
28.42 Keyword PRINCOMPS 28.43 Keyword ERROR 28.44 Keyword SIGNIF
28.45 Keyword DISCRIM 28.46 Keyword PARAMETERS 28.47 Keyword OMEANS
28.48 Keyword PMEANS 28.49 Keyword POBS 28.50 Keyword TRANSFORM
28.51 Keyword FORMAT
28.52 The PLOT Subcommand 493
28.53 Matrix Materials 497
28.54 The WRITE Subcommand 28.55 The READ Subcommand
28.56 Missing Values 499
28.57 EXAMPLES OF COMMON DESIGNS 499
28.58 Univariate Analysis of Variance 499
28.59 Specifying a Model with the DESIGN Subcommand 28.60 Specifying the ERROR Term
28.61 Using DESIGN and ERROR 28.62 Partitioning the Sum of Squares 28.63 Contrasts
28.64 Randomized Block Designs 501
28.65 Complete Randomized Block Designs
28.66 Balanced Incomplete (Randomized) Block Designs (BIB)
28.67 Partially Balanced Incomplete Block Designs (PBIB)
28.68 Latin and Other Squares 502
28.69 Nested Designs 502
28.70 MANOVA EXAMPLES 509
28.71 Example 1: Analysis of Covariance Designs 509
28.72 Example 2: Multivariate One-Way ANOVA 513
28.73 Example 3: Multivariate Multiple Regression, Canonical Correlation 519
28.74 Example 4: Repeated Measures 529
28.75 Example 5: Repeated Measures with a Constant Covariate 527
28.76 Example 6: Repeated Measures with a Varying Covariate 531
28.77 Example 7: A Doubly Multivariate Repeated Measures Design 532
28.78 Example 8: Profile Analysis 536

Chapter 29 LOGLINEAR 541

29.1 OVERVIEW 541
29.2 OPERATION 542
29.3 The LOGLINEAR Specification 542
29.4 The Logit Model 29.5 Specifying Covariates
29.6 The DESIGN Subcommand 544
29.7 Specifying Main Effects Models 29.8 Specifying Interactions: Keyword BY
29.9 Specifying Covariates 29.10 Single-Degree-of-Freedom Partitions
29.11 The CWEIGHT Subcommand 545
29.12 The GRESID Subcommand 546
29.13 The PRINT and NOPRINT Subcommands 547
29.14 The PLOT Subcommand 547
29.15 The CONTRAST Subcommand 548
29.16 Contrasts for a Multinomial Logit Model 29.17 Contrasts for a Linear Logit Model
29.18 Contrasts for a Logistic Regression Model
29.19 The CRITERIA Subcommand 554
29.20 The WIDTH Subcommand 554
29.21 Missing Values 554
29.22 LOGLINEAR EXAMPLES 555
29.23 Example 1: A General Log-linear Model 555
29.24 Example 2: A Multinomial Logit Model 558
29.25 Example 3: Frequency Table Models 558
29.26 Example 4: A Linear Logit Model 560

29.27 Example 5: Logistic Regression Model 562
29.28 Example 6: Multinomial Response Models 564
29.29 Example 7: A Distance Model 567

Chapter 30 SCATTERGRAM 571

30.1 OVERVIEW 571
30.2 OPERATION 571
30.3 Specifying the Design 572
30.4 Default Scatterplot
30.5 Scaling 573
30.6 Setting Bounds 30.7 Integer Scaling
30.8 Optional Statistics 576
30.9 Missing Values 577
30.10 Formatting Options 577
30.11 Random Sampling 577
30.12 LIMITATIONS 577

Chapter 31 PEARSON CORR 579

31.1 OVERVIEW 579
31.2 OPERATION 579
31.3 Specifying the Design 580
31.4 Two-Tailed Significance Levels 581
31.5 Optional Statistics 581
31.6 Missing Values 584
31.7 Formatting Options 584
31.8 Writing Matrix Materials 585
31.9 LIMITATIONS 586

Chapter 32 PARTIAL CORR 589

32.1 OVERVIEW 589
32.2 OPERATION 590
32.3 Specifying the Design 590
32.4 Correlation List 32.5 Control List and Order Values 32.6 Specifying Multiple Analyses
32.7 Two-Tailed Significance Levels 593
32.8 Optional Statistics 593
32.9 Missing Values 594
32.10 Formatting Options 594
32.11 Matrix Materials 595
32.12 Reading Matrices 32.13 Indexing Matrices 32.14 Writing Matrices
32.15 LIMITATIONS 597

Chapter 33 REGRESSION 601

33.1 OVERVIEW 601
33.2 OPERATION 602
33.3 Minimum Required Syntax 602
33.4 The VARIABLES Subcommand 33.5 The DEPENDENT Subcommand
33.6 The Method Subcommands
33.7 VARIABLES Subcommand Modifiers 606
33.8 The MISSING Subcommand 33.9 The DESCRIPTIVES Subcommand
33.10 The SELECT Subcommand
33.11 Equation Control Modifiers 608
33.12 The CRITERIA Subcommand 33.13 The STATISTICS Subcommand
33.14 Regression through the Origin

33.15 Analysis of Residuals 612
33.16 The Temporary Variables 33.17 The RESIDUALS Subcommand
33.18 The CASEWISE Subcommand 33.19 The SCATTERPLOT Subcommand
33.20 The PARTIALPLOT Subcommand 33.21 The SAVE Subcommand
33.22 Matrix Materials 619
33.23 The READ Subcommand 33.24 The WRITE Subcommand
33.25 The WIDTH Subcommand 621

Chapter 34 DISCRIMINANT 623

34.1 OVERVIEW 623
34.2 OPERATION 624
34.3 The GROUPS Subcommand 624
34.4 The VARIABLES Subcommand 625
34.5 The ANALYSIS Subcommand 626
34.6 Variable Selection 627
34.7 The METHOD Subcommand 34.8 Inclusion Levels 34.9 The MAXSTEPS Subcommand
34.10 Statistical Controls
34.11 The FUNCTIONS Subcommand 632
34.12 Optional Statistics for the Analysis Phase 633
34.13 The SELECT Subcommand 634
34.14 Rotation Options 634
34.15 Display Options 634
34.16 Classifying Cases 634
34.17 The PRIORS Subcommand 34.18 The Classification Results Table 34.19 Classification Plots
34.20 Printed Discriminant Scores 34.21 Classification Options
34.22 Using Classification Coefficients
34.23 Missing Values 641
34.24 The SAVE Subcommand 641
34.25 Matrix Materials 642
34.26 Writing Matrices 34.27 Reading Matrices
34.28 Summary of Syntax Rules 644
34.29 LIMITATIONS 645

Chapter 35 FACTOR 647

35.1 OVERVIEW 647
35.2 OPERATION 648
35.3 The Variable Selection Block 648
35.4 The VARIABLES Subcommand 35.5 The MISSING Subcommand
35.6 The WIDTH Subcommand
35.7 The Extraction Block 649
35.8 The ANALYSIS Subcommand 35.9 The EXTRACTION Subcommand
35.10 The PRINT Subcommand 35.11 The FORMAT Subcommand 35.12 The PLOT Subcommand
35.13 The CRITERIA Subcommand 35.14 The DIAGONAL Subcommand
35.15 The ROTATION Subcommand 654
35.16 The SAVE Subcommand 655
35.17 Matrix Materials 660
35.18 The READ Subcommand 35.19 The WRITE Subcommand
35.20 LIMITATIONS AND SUMMARY OF SYNTAX 661

Chapter 36 NONPAR CORR 663

36.1 OVERVIEW 663
36.2 OPERATION 663
36.3 Specifying the Design 664
36.4 Types of Coefficients 665
36.5 Two-Tailed Significance Tests 665
36.6 Missing Values 665
36.7 Formatting Options 668
36.8 Random Sampling 668
36.9 Writing Matrix Materials 669
36.10 LIMITATIONS 669

Chapter 37 NPAR TESTS 671

37.1 INTRODUCTION TO NONPARAMETRIC TESTS 671
37.2 OVERVIEW 671
37.3 OPERATION 672
37.4 One-Sample Tests 672
37.5 One-Sample Chi-Square Test 37.6 Kolmogorov-Smirnov One-Sample Test 37.7 Runs Test
37.8 Binomial Test
37.9 Tests for Two Related Samples 678
37.10 McNemar Test 37.11 Sign Test 37.12 Wilcoxon Matched-Pairs Signed-Ranks Test
37.13 Tests for *k* Related Samples 682
37.14 Cochran *Q* Test 37.15 Friedman Test 37.16 Kendall Coefficient of Concordance
37.17 Tests for Two Independent Samples 684
37.18 Two-Sample Median Test 37.19 Mann-Whitney *U* Test
37.20 Kolmogorov-Smirnov Two-Sample Test 37.21 Wald-Wolfowitz Runs Test
37.22 Moses Test of Extreme Reactions
37.23 Tests for *k* Independent Samples 691
37.24 *k*-Sample Median Test 37.25 Kruskal-Wallis One-Way Analysis of Variance
37.26 Optional Statistics 694
37.27 Missing Values 694
37.28 Random Sampling 695
37.29 Aliases for Subcommand Names 695
37.30 LIMITATIONS FOR NPAR TESTS 695

Chapter 38 BOX-JENKINS 697

38.1 OVERVIEW 697
38.2 OPERATION 698
38.3 The VARIABLE Subcommand 698
38.4 Step-of-Analysis Subcommands 698
38.5 Plotting the Series
38.6 Transformation Subcommands 700
38.7 The LOG and POWER Subcommands
38.8 Differencing Subcommands 701
38.9 The DIFFERENCE Subcommand 38.10 The SDIFFERENCE and PERIOD Subcommands
38.11 The LAG Subcommand 702
38.12 Parameters Subcommands 703
38.13 Estimation Subcommands 704
38.14 Keywords CONSTANT and NCONSTANT 38.15 Keywords CENTER and NCENTER
38.16 The ITERATE Subcommand 38.17 The BFR Subcommand 38.18 Keywords TEST and NTEST
38.19 The FPR Subcommand 38.20 Perturbation Increment Subcommands
38.21 Tolerance Subcommands 38.22 Initial Estimates Subcommands
38.23 Forecast Subcommands 712
38.24 The ORIGIN Subcommand 38.25 The LEAD Subcommand 38.26 The CIN Subcommand
38.27 Final Estimates Subcommands
38.28 The PRINT Subcommand 714
38.29 The PLOT Subcommand 714

Chapter 39 RELIABILITY 717

39.1 INTRODUCTION TO RELIABILITY MODELS 717
39.2 OVERVIEW 718
39.3 OPERATION 719
39.4 The VARIABLES Subcommand 719
39.5 The SCALE Subcommand 719
39.6 The MODEL Subcommand 720
39.7 Optional Statistics 721

39.8 Analysis of Variance 723
39.9 Tests for the Violation of Assumptions 39.10 Friedman's Analysis of Variance for Ranked Data
39.11 Analysis of Variance of Dichotomous Data
39.12 Matrix Materials 728
39.13 Matrix Input 39.14 Matrix Output 39.15 The FORMAT Subcommand
39.16 Alternative Computing Methods 731
39.17 Missing Values 732
39.18 Suppressing Variable Labels 732
39.19 LIMITATIONS 732

Chapter 40 SURVIVAL 735

40.1 OVERVIEW 735
40.2 OPERATION 736
40.3 The TABLES Subcommand 737
40.4 The INTERVALS Subcommand 737
40.5 The STATUS Subcommand 738
40.6 Life Table Output 738
40.7 Survival Functions 40.8 Suppressing Life Tables
40.9 The PLOTS Subcommand 740
40.10 The COMPARE Subcommand 741
40.11 Pairwise Comparisons 40.12 Approximate Comparisons 40.13 Obtaining Comparisons Only
40.14 Entering Aggregated Data 743
40.15 Missing Values 746
40.16 Writing Out Survival Tables 746
40.17 Format 40.18 Record Order
40.19 LIMITATIONS 747

Appendix A Help for Old Friends 749

A.1 SUMMARY OF CHANGES 749
A.2 DATA DEFINITION COMMANDS 751
A.3 DATA LIST 751
A.4 File Definition A.5 Variable Definition A.6 Format Types
A.7 Other Definitions 752
A.8 INPUT MEDIUM A.9 VARIABLE LIST and INPUT FORMAT A.10 PRINT FORMATS
A.11 VARIABLE LABELS and VALUE LABELS A.12 MISSING VALUES A.13 N OF CASES
A.14 READ INPUT DATA and END INPUT DATA
A.15 UTILITY COMMANDS 753
A.16 Job Utilities 753
A.17 ALLOCATE A.18 LIST ERRORS A.19 NUMBERED A.20 RUN NAME and TASK NAME
A.21 PAGESIZE A.22 PRINT BACK A.23 SEED
A.24 Listing and Writing Cases 754
A.25 LIST CASES A.26 WRITE CASES A.27 WRITE FILEINFO A.28 Print and Write Formats
A.29 Sorting Cases and Splitting Files 755
A.30 SORT CASES A.31 Subfiles A.32 Automatic Sequence Variable
A.33 FILE UPDATE COMMANDS 755
A.34 ADD DATA LIST and ADD VARIABLES 755
A.35 MERGE FILES 755
A.36 ADD CASES and ADD SUBFILES 756
A.37 SYSTEM FILE COMMANDS 756
A.38 Reading SPSS System Files 756
A.39 REFORMAT 757
A.40 Other System File Commands 758
A.41 DELETE VARS and KEEP VARS A.42 REORDER VARS A.43 Archive Files A.44 Subfiles
A.45 LIST FILEINFO A.46 FILE NAME
A.47 File Interfaces 758
A.48 GET SCSS A.49 SAVE SCSS
A.50 DATA SELECTION COMMANDS 759
A.51 SELECT IF 759
A.52 N OF CASES 759
A.53 WEIGHT 759

A.54 DATA TRANSFORMATIONS 759
A.55 Temporary Transformations 759
A.56 Numeric Transformations 759
A.57 Initialization A.58 ASSIGN MISSING A.59 Functions A.60 LAG A.61 RECODE
A.62 Recoding Blanks A.63 COMPUTE A.64 COUNT A.65 DO REPEAT and END REPEAT
A.66 String Transformations 761
A.67 Conditional Transformations 761
A.68 Logical Expressions
A.69 PROCEDURE COMMANDS 761
A.70 AGGREGATE 762
A.71 FREQUENCIES 762
A.72 CONDESCRIPTIVE 763
A.73 CROSSTABS 763
A.74 New Options List
A.75 MULT RESPONSE 764
A.76 BREAKDOWN 764
A.77 REPORT 764
A.78 Keyword Changes
A.79 GRAPHICS 766
A.80 T-TEST 766
A.81 ANOVA 767
A.82 ONEWAY 767
A.83 MANOVA 767
A.84 WRITE and READ A.85 Repeated Measures A.86 Other Changes
A.87 SCATTERGRAM 768
A.88 PEARSON CORR 768
A.89 PARTIAL CORR 768
A.90 REGRESSION 768
A.91 DISCRIMINANT 769
A.92 New Options and Statistics List
A.93 NONPAR CORR 770
A.94 NPAR TESTS 770
A.95 FACTOR 770
A.96 BOX-JENKINS 770
A.97 RELIABILITY 770
A.98 SURVIVAL 771
A.99 EXAMPLE 771

Appendix B Command Order 774

B.1 PROGRAM STATES 774
B.2 DETERMINING COMMAND ORDER 775
B.3 Unrestricted Utility Commands 778
B.4 File Definition Commands 778
B.5 Input Program Commands 778
B.6 Transformation Commands 778
B.7 Restricted Transformations 778
B.8 Procedures 779

Appendix C IMPORT/EXPORT Character Sets 780

Appendix D Writing User Programs 784

D.1 THE MATRIX PROCEDURE 784
D.2 ADDING USER PROCEDURES 785

References 786

Index 789

1

A SAMPLE JOB, **1.1**
FILES USED IN SPSS^X, **1.2**
Multiple Files and the Active File, **1.3**
DATA DEFINITION, **1.4**
Cases and Variables, **1.5**
Missing Values, **1.6**
Labels, **1.7**
Format, **1.8**
Defining Complex Files, **1.9**
MANIPULATING VARIABLES, **1.10**
Manipulating Numeric Variables, **1.11**
Manipulating String Variables, **1.12**
Conditional Transformations, **1.13**
Transformation Utilities, **1.14**
FILE MANAGEMENT, **1.15**
Combining Files, **1.16**
Splitting, Sorting, and Aggregating Files, **1.17**
System Files, **1.18**
Procedure Output, **1.19**
OTHER UTILITIES FOR CONTROLLING THE JOB, **1.20**
PRINTING AND WRITING CASES, **1.21**
TABLES AND REPORTS, **1.22**
GRAPHICS, **1.23**
STATISTICAL PROCEDURES, **1.24**
Frequency Distributions and Descriptive Statistics, **1.25**
Relationships Between Two or More Variables, **1.26**
Correlation Coefficients and Scatterplots, **1.27**
Multiple Regression Analysis, **1.28**
Factor Analysis, **1.29**
Discriminant Analysis, **1.30**
Survival Analysis, **1.31**
Analysis of Additive Scales, **1.32**
Nonparametric Statistics, **1.33**
Log-linear Models, **1.34**
Univariate and Multivariate Analysis of Variance, **1.35**
Box-Jenkins Analysis of Time Series Data, **1.36**

Chapter 1 Introduction

The SPSS$^{X™}$ Batch System is a comprehensive tool for managing, analyzing, and displaying data. Its capabilities include

- Input from almost any type of data file.
- File management, including sorting, splitting, and aggregating files, match-merging multiple files, and saving fully defined system files.
- Data management, including sampling, selecting, and weighting cases, recoding variables, and creating new variables using extensive numeric and string functions.
- Tabulation and statistical analysis—from describing single variables to performing complex multivariate analyses.
- Report writing.
- Device-independent graphics.

This manual describes the operations of the SPSS^X system. It tells how to get results, not how to interpret them. If you are unfamiliar with the statistical procedures the system makes available, you might begin with *SPSS^X Introductory Statistics Guide,* where the most frequently used procedures are presented with overviews of the statistics they calculate.

Two types of information not included in this manual are available through the INFO command documented in Chapter 2. These are information specific to the computer, operating system, and installation at which you use SPSS^X and information about new features and changes to SPSS^X since publication of this manual. The INFO command is both an integral part of SPSS^X documentation and a guide to system developments available on your computer.

This first chapter gives an overview of SPSS^X. The sample job in Section 1.1 illustrates how individual commands work together in an SPSS^X job and shows some of the printed output the job creates. Sections 1.2 and 1.3 describe the types of files used in SPSS^X, and Sections 1.4 through 1.9 review data definition facilities. Sections 1.10 through 1.14 introduce facilities for revising and creating variables, and Sections 1.15 through 1.19 briefly summarize file management facilities. Sections 1.20 through 1.23 describe utilities for controlling the environment of an SPSS^X job, for printing and writing cases, and for generating tables, reports, and high-quality graphs. Finally, Sections 1.24 through 1.36 summarize the statistical procedures available in SPSS^X.

1.1 A SAMPLE JOB

The SPSS^X job shown in Figure 1.1a analyzes data stored in a file named BANKDATA. The SPSS^X commands, each of which is discussed briefly in the following list, accomplish a set of tasks typical in analyzing data: naming and locating a data file; naming, locating, and labeling variables; computing a new variable from the values of existing variables; printing the values of selected cases; obtaining graphs and statistics describing certain variables; performing a statistical analysis (a rather straightforward description of subgroups in this case); and saving the fully defined data in a system file.

Figure 1.1a Sample SPSS^X job with data in a separate file

```
UNNUMBERED
TITLE  BANK EMPLOYMENT STUDY

FILE HANDLE  BANKDATA  NAME='BANKDATA DATA M'
FILE HANDLE  BANK      NAME='BANK SPSSXSF A'
DATA LIST  FILE=BANKDATA/
   ID 1-4  SALBEG 6-10  SEX 12  TIME 14-15  AGE 17-20 (2)
   SALNOW 22-26  EDLEVEL 28-29  WORK 31-34 (2)
   JOBCAT,MINORITY 36-37
VARIABLE LABELS
   ID        'EMPLOYEE CODE'
   SALBEG    'BEGINNING SALARY'
   SEX       'SEX OF EMPLOYEE'
   TIME      'JOB SENIORITY'
   AGE       'AGE OF EMPLOYEE'
   SALNOW    'CURRENT SALARY'
   EDLEVEL   'EDUCATIONAL LEVEL'
   WORK      'WORK EXPERIENCE'
   JOBCAT    'EMPLOYMENT CATEGORY'
   MINORITY  'MINORITY CLASSIFICATION'
VALUE LABELS
   SEX      0 'MALES' 1 'FEMALES'/
   JOBCAT   1 'CLERICAL' 2 'OFFICE TRAINEE' 3 'SECURITY OFFICER'
            4 'COLLEGE TRAINEE' 5 'EXEMPT EMPLOYEE' 6 'MBA TRAINEE'
            7 'TECHNICAL'/
   MINORITY 0 'WHITE' 1 'NONWHITE'
MISSING VALUES  SALBEG,TIME TO EDLEVEL,JOBCAT (0)/
                SEX, MINORITY (9)
PRINT FORMATS  SALBEG SALNOW (DOLLAR11.2)

COMPUTE  AVGRAISE = (SALNOW-SALBEG)/TIME
VARIABLE LABELS  AVGRAISE 'AVERAGE MONTHLY RAISE'
PRINT FORMATS  AVGRAISE (DOLLAR9.2)

DO IF AVGRAISE GT 300 OR AVGRAISE LT 30
PRINT  / ID 'BEG: ' SALBEG  'NOW: ' SALNOW  'MONTHS: ' TIME
       'RAISE: ' AVGRAISE  'JOBCAT: ' JOBCAT
END IF

FREQUENCIES  VARIABLES=SALBEG SALNOW AVGRAISE/
             FORMAT=NOTABLE/ STATISTICS/ HISTOGRAM/
BREAKDOWN  TABLES=SALBEG SALNOW AVGRAISE BY MINORITY BY SEX
SAVE OUTFILE=BANK
```

UNNUMBERED tells SPSS^X not to look for sequence numbers in the SPSS^X command file. (See Chapter 4.)

TITLE assigns the title "BANK EMPLOYMENT STUDY," which will appear at the top of each page of printed output. (See Chapter 4.)

FILE HANDLE relates a handle (a brief name) to the information the computer needs to identify the file. This example shows the identifying information needed for an IBM/CMS operating system. The file named BANKDATA contains the data to be analyzed. The file named BANK will be created by the SAVE command. (See Chapter 3.)

DATA LIST tells SPSS^X how to read file BANKDATA. It assigns a name to each variable to be read, specifies the column or range of columns in which the data for each variable are located, and specifies that variables AGE and WORK have an implied decimal point two places from the right. (See Chapter 3.)

VARIABLE LABELS assigns labels to the variables. These optional labels appear in printed output to further identify each variable. (See Chapter 3.)

VALUE LABELS assigns labels to the specific values of the variables SEX, JOBCAT, and MINORITY. For example, the values 0 and 1 for SEX will be labeled "MALES" and "FEMALES" on printed output. (See Chapter 3.)

MISSING VALUES declares that the value 0 for variables SALBEG, TIME, AGE, SALNOW, EDLEVEL, and JOBCAT represents missing information and should be treated differently from other values in data transformations and analyses. The value 9 represents missing data for variables SEX and MINORITY. (See Chapters 3 and 6.)

PRINT FORMATS instructs SPSS^X to print the values of SALBEG and SALNOW in dollar format (with dollar signs and commas) in an 11-column field with two decimal places. The second PRINT FORMATS command does the same for AVGRAISE, though it specifies a width of 9 rather than 11 characters. (See Chapter 9.)

COMPUTE creates the new variable AVGRAISE as the difference between current salary and beginning salary, divided by months of employment. Once created, the variable is assigned a label and a new print format. (See Chapter 6.)

DO IF and **END IF** enclose commands that are executed for a particular case only if the conditions on the DO IF command are met. In this example, the PRINT command is executed only for those cases for which AVGRAISE is either greater than $300 per month or less than $30 per month. (See Section 1.13 and Chapter 8.)

PRINT prints out the values of the specified variables as the data are being read during the first procedure. Mixed with the variables are *literals*, enclosed in apostrophes, which will be included in the printed output to identify the variables. (See Section 1.21 and Chapter 9.)

FREQUENCIES is generally used to print tables showing the frequencies and percentages of individual values for selected variables. Here, since the variables (salaries) can have many different values, the NOTABLE keyword on the FORMAT subcommand suppresses the table, and only descriptive statistics and histograms are requested (see Chapter 18). The histogram and statistics for AVGRAISE are shown in Figure 1.1c.

BREAKDOWN requests tables showing the mean and other statistics for the three variables SALBEG, SALNOW, and AVGRAISE, within categories defined by minority classification and by sex within minority classification (see Chapter 22). The table for AVGRAISE is given in Figure 1.1d.

SAVE tells SPSS^X to save a permanent copy of the current *active file* in a file associated with file handle BANK. The active file is the file as defined by DATA LIST and other data definition commands and as altered by the data transformation commands (so, AVGRAISE is included on the active file). All data definition information, such as labels and missing-value flags, is included in the saved system file. To rerun the same job from the system file, you need only the following commands:

```
UNNUMBERED
TITLE  BANK EMPLOYMENT STUDY
FILE HANDLE  BANK  NAME='BANK SPSSXSF A'
GET  FILE BANK
DO IF AVGRAISE GT 300 OR AVGRAISE LT 30
PRINT  / ID ' BEG:' SALBEG  ' NOW:' SALNOW  ' MONTHS: ' TIME
         ' RAISE:' AVGRAISE  ' JOBCAT: ' JOBCAT
END IF
FREQUENCIES  VARIABLES=SALBEG SALNOW AVGRAISE/
             FORMAT=NOTABLE/ STATISTICS/ HISTOGRAM/
BREAKDOWN  TABLES=SALBEG SALNOW AVGRAISE BY MINORITY BY SEX
```

Figures 1.1b through 1.1e show printed output generated by the sample job. As shown in Figure 1.1b, commands are printed back with two columns of SPSSˣ-generated numbers to their left. The first column gives the sequence numbers of the command lines, and the second column gives level-of-control numbers. The level-of-control numbers indicate when a set of commands is under the control of another command. In the example, most commands are at the first level, indicated by a *0*. The *1*s in lines 37–40 indicate that these commands are under control of the DO IF in line 36. With the FREQUENCIES command in line 41, control returns to the first level. These indicators can be particularly helpful in checking transformations if you have nested several levels of DO IF or LOOP structures.

Figure 1.1b Printback of SPSSˣ commands with DATA LIST correspondence table and output from the PRINT command

```
09 NOV 82 SPSS-X RELEASE 0 LEVEL 1 ALPHA TEST (29 JUL 82) FOR VM/CMS                                          PAGE   1

   1 0          UNNUMBERED
   2 0          TITLE  BANK EMPLOYMENT STUDY
   3 0
   4 0          FILE HANDLE  BANKDATA   NAME='BANKDATA DATA M'
   5 0          FILE HANDLE  BANK       NAME='BANK SPSSXSF A'
   6 0
   7 0          DATA LIST  FILE=BANKDATA/
   8 0             ID 1-4  SALBEG 6-10  SEX 12  TIME 14-15  AGE 17-20 (2)
   9 0             SALNOW 22-26  EDLEVEL 28-29  WORK 31-34 (2)
  10 0             JOBCAT,MINORITY 36-37

THE ABOVE DATA LIST STATEMENT WILL READ   1 RECORDS FROM FILE BANKDATA.

          VARIABLE  REC   START    END          FORMAT  WIDTH  DEC

          ID          1       1      4          F           4    0
          SALBEG      1       6     10          F           5    0
          SEX         1      12     12          F           1    0
          TIME        1      14     15          F           2    0
          AGE         1      17     20          F           4    2
          SALNOW      1      22     26          F           5    0
          EDLEVEL     1      28     29          F           2    0
          WORK        1      31     34          F           4    2
          JOBCAT      1      36     36          F           1    0
          MINORITY    1      37     37          F           1    0

END OF DATALIST TABLE.

  11 0          VARIABLE LABELS
  12 0             ID        'EMPLOYEE CODE'
  13 0             SALBEG    'BEGINNING SALARY'
  14 0             SEX       'SEX OF EMPLOYEE'
  15 0             TIME      'JOB SENIORITY'
  16 0             AGE       'AGE OF EMPLOYEE'
  17 0             SALNOW    'CURRENT SALARY'
  18 0             EDLEVEL   'EDUCATIONAL LEVEL'
  19 0             WORK      'WORK EXPERIENCE'
  20 0             JOBCAT    'EMPLOYMENT CATEGORY'
  21 0             MINORITY  'MINORITY CLASSIFICATION'
  22 0          VALUE LABELS
  23 0             SEX        0 'MALES' 1 'FEMALES'/
  24 0             JOBCAT     1 'CLERICAL' 2 'OFFICE TRAINEE' 3 'SECURITY OFFICER'
  25 0                        4 'COLLEGE TRAINEE' 5 'EXEMPT EMPLOYEE' 6 'MBA TRAINEE'
  26 0                        7 'TECHNICAL'/
  27 0             MINORITY 0 'WHITE' 1 'NONWHITE'
  28 0          MISSING VALUES  SALBEG,TIME TO EDLEVEL,JOBCAT (0)/
  29 0                          SEX, MINORITY (9)
  30 0          PRINT FORMATS  SALBEG SALNOW (DOLLAR11.2)
  31 0
  32 0          COMPUTE  AVGRAISE = (SALNOW-SALBEG)/TIME
  33 0          VARIABLE LABELS  AVGRAISE 'AVERAGE MONTHLY RAISE'
  34 0          PRINT FORMATS  AVGRAISE (DOLLAR9.2)
  35 0
  36 0          DO IF AVGRAISE GT 300 OR AVGRAISE LT 30
--------------------------------------------------------------------------------------------------------------------
09 NOV 82 BANK EMPLOYMENT STUDY                                                                               PAGE   2

  37 1          PRINT  / ID ' BEG:' SALBEG  ' NOW:' SALNOW  ' MONTHS: ' TIME
  38 1                 ' RAISE:' AVGRAISE  ' JOBCAT: ' JOBCAT
  39 1          END IF
  40 1
  41 0          FREQUENCIES  VARIABLES=SALBEG SALNOW AVGRAISE/
  42 0                       FORMAT=NOTABLE/ STATISTICS/ HISTOGRAM/

THERE ARE    19016 BYTES OF MEMORY AVAILABLE.
THE LARGEST CONTIGUOUS AREA HAS    19016 BYTES.

 ***** GIVEN WORKSPACE ALLOWS FOR   864 VALUES AND    216 LABELS PER VARIABLE FOR 'FREQUENCIES' *****

 786  BEG:  $6,300.00  NOW: $32,000.00  MONTHS: 82  RAISE:  $313.41  JOBCAT: 2
 951  BEG: $12,500.00  NOW: $36,250.00  MONTHS: 65  RAISE:  $365.38  JOBCAT: 5
 965  BEG:  $8,700.00  NOW: $33,500.00  MONTHS: 79  RAISE:  $313.92  JOBCAT: 4
1005  BEG: $11,004.00  NOW: $41,500.00  MONTHS: 97  RAISE:  $314.39  JOBCAT: 5
 754  BEG:  $3,900.00  NOW:  $6,480.00  MONTHS: 92  RAISE:   $28.04  JOBCAT: 1
 869  BEG:  $4,080.00  NOW:  $6,480.00  MONTHS: 82  RAISE:   $29.27  JOBCAT: 1
 948  BEG: $17,640.00  NOW: $40,000.00  MONTHS: 66  RAISE:  $338.79  JOBCAT: 5
```

Figure 1.1b also includes the output from the DATA LIST and PRINT commands. The DATA LIST command produces a table showing the variables defined, their formats, and their locations in the data file. The output from the PRINT command appears on page 2 of the printed output. Note that it follows the printback of the FREQUENCIES command and related diagnostics. This happens because PRINT is not one of the *procedure* commands that cause SPSS^X to read the data. Instead, the printing takes place as the data are being read to execute the first procedure. The values are printed in the print formats established through the DATA LIST or assigned through PRINT FORMATS. In this case, the values are printed in dollar format, as specified in the PRINT FORMATS command.

The output from the FREQUENCIES procedure appears on pages 3–5 of the printed output. Figure 1.1c shows one of the three histograms from this procedure. Page 6 of the output (not shown) contains the diagnostics from the BREAKDOWN procedure. The tables from this procedure occupy output pages 7–9, of which the last is shown in Figure 1.1d.

Figure 1.1c A histogram and statistics from the sample job

```
09 NOV 82 BANK EMPLOYMENT STUDY                                                                    PAGE   5

FILE:

AVGRAISE  AVERAGE MONTHLY RAISE

    COUNT   MIDPOINT    ONE SYMBOL EQUALS APPROX.        4.00 OCCURRENCES

       21         27  *****
       83         44  *********************
      126         61  ********************************
       89         78  **********************
       46         95  ************
       28        112  *******
       19        129  *****
       17        146  ****
        5        163  *
       11        180  ***
        7        197  **
        6        214  **
        5        231  *
        1        248
        3        265  *
        1        282
        1        299
        3        316  *
        1        333
        0        350
        1        367
                     I....+....I....+....I....+....I....+....I....+....I
                     0        40        80       120       160       200
                               HISTOGRAM FREQUENCY

MEAN           86.291       STD DEV       53.235       MINIMUM       28.043
MAXIMUM       365.385

VALID CASES       474       MISSING CASES      0
```

Figure 1.1d Breakdown of AVGRAISE

```
09 NOV 82 BANK EMPLOYMENT STUDY                                                                    PAGE   9
FILE:

- - - - - - - - - - - - - - - -  D E S C R I P T I O N   O F   S U B P O P U L A T I O N S  - - - - - - - - - - - - - - -
CRITERION VARIABLE   AVGRAISE   AVERAGE MONTHLY RAISE
    BROKEN DOWN BY   MINORITY   MINORITY CLASSIFICATION
                BY   SEX        SEX OF EMPLOYEE
- - - - - - - - - - - - - - - - - - - - - - - - - - - - - - - - - - - - - - - - - - - - - - - - - - - - - - - - - - - - -

VARIABLE                 CODE      VALUE LABEL                 SUM          MEAN       STD DEV      VARIANCE         N

FOR ENTIRE POPULATION                                   40901.7413       86.2906       53.2352     2833.9867    (  474)


MINORITY                   0.      WHITE                33615.2736       90.8521       55.1150     3037.6637    (  370)
   SEX                     0.      MALES                21756.9268      112.1491       63.0232     3971.9291    (  194)
   SEX                     1.      FEMALES              11858.3468       67.3770       31.1066      967.6233    (  176)

MINORITY                   1.      NONWHITE              7286.4677       70.0622       42.3221     1791.1609    (  104)
   SEX                     0.      MALES                 5145.2716       80.3949       50.4940     2549.6414    (   64)
   SEX                     1.      FEMALES               2141.1961       53.5299       12.5029      156.3228    (   40)

  TOTAL CASES =      474
```

The printed information from the SAVE command, on page 10 of this output (see Figure 1.1e), includes the number of cases and the number of variables on the file. More information is available via subcommands to SAVE, as described in Chapter 5.

Figure 1.1e Diagnostic information from SAVE command

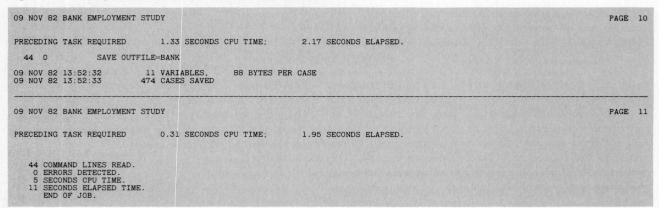

```
09 NOV 82 BANK EMPLOYMENT STUDY                                                                         PAGE  10

PRECEDING TASK REQUIRED        1.33 SECONDS CPU TIME;        2.17 SECONDS ELAPSED.

  44  0            SAVE OUTFILE=BANK

09 NOV 82 13:52:32          11 VARIABLES,      88 BYTES PER CASE
09 NOV 82 13:52:33         474 CASES SAVED
------------------------------------------------------------------------------------------------------------------
09 NOV 82 BANK EMPLOYMENT STUDY                                                                         PAGE  11

PRECEDING TASK REQUIRED        0.31 SECONDS CPU TIME;        1.95 SECONDS ELAPSED.

    44 COMMAND LINES READ.
     0 ERRORS DETECTED.
     5 SECONDS CPU TIME.
    11 SECONDS ELAPSED TIME.
       END OF JOB.
```

Had the job contained errors, error messages would have been included in the printed output. SPSS^X error handling and messages are discussed in Chapter 4.

1.2 FILES USED IN SPSS^X

Operating SPSS^X means dealing with files. Depending on the complexity of your job, you may have one or more of each of the following types of files:

- *Command file* (one per job): Contains your SPSS^X commands. The rules for creating these commands are discussed in Chapter 2.
- *Input data file:* Contains your data in almost any format. This file can be included within your SPSS^X command file, or it can be a separate file on tape or disk. The facilities for defining input data are summarized in Sections 1.4 through 1.9.
- *Display file:* Contains the tabular output from the SPSS^X procedures you have requested, diagnostic information about your job, and output from any PRINT or WRITE commands for which you have not specified a separate output file. This file is formatted for listing at a terminal or on a line printer.
- *Output file:* Contains data formatted to be read by a computer. Some procedures create output files containing matrix or other materials (see Chapter 17), and the WRITE command produces a data file to your specifications.
- *SPSS^X system file:* A file specifically formatted for use by SPSS^X, containing both data and the *dictionary* that defines the data to the system (see Section 1.4). System files speed processing and are required as input for combining files.

Conventions for naming, printing, deleting, or permanently saving files, and for submitting command files for processing differ considerably from one computer and operating system to another. Use the INFO command and look for other documentation at your site for information about handling files outside SPSS^X.

1.3 Multiple Files and the Active File

Because you can read and write a number of files within a single SPSS^X job, you must let your computer's operating system know which files are to be read or created. Commands such as DATA LIST, GET, and MATCH FILES take a FILE specification that includes a *file handle*. The file handle identifies to your operating system the file you want to access. (For IBM/OS systems, the file handle must match the DD name; for most other systems, the file handle is assigned with the FILE HANDLE command discussed in Chapter 3.) A file handle can also specify an output file. The SAVE command requires an OUTFILE specification naming an output file. Such commands as PRINT and WRITE can also take an OUTFILE specification indicating an output file other than the display file.

Most SPSS^X commands, however, do not take a FILE subcommand. They simply act upon the *active file*, which is the file most recently defined by a DATA LIST command, called by a GET command, or defined by some other input program. Thus you get what you expect: after you define a file or access a system file, subsequent transformations modify that file and subsequent procedures analyze that file.

The active file is not actually created until SPSS^X encounters a procedure command—one that causes it to read the data. This allows the data to be read and transformed and the first procedure processed with only one pass through the original file. It also ensures that the system will not use computer resources to read data and perform transformations before it has received syntactically correct instructions to produce some kind of output. When the system does encounter a procedure command, it executes all of the preceding data definition and transformation commands and performs whatever action the procedure calls for. The active file is then available for further transformations and procedures, and it remains available until the end of the job or until it is specifically replaced. Some of the facilities available for modifying the active file are discussed in Section 1.23.

1.4 DATA DEFINITION

Data definition means telling SPSS^X how to read and interpret your data. This involves naming the variables you want to analyze, specifying their location and their format within the data for each case, informing the system of any values that represent missing data, and supplying any labels you want included in your printed output. SPSS^X uses data definition specifications to build a *dictionary* that describes the variables on the active file. SPSS^X looks to this dictionary whenever it needs such information to carry out an operation. For example, if you use a WRITE command to write out the values of a variable and do not specify the output format, SPSS^X looks to the dictionary for the write format assigned to that variable.

1.5 Cases and Variables

A data file contains the values of certain *variables* measured for a set of *cases*: the names, ages, and test scores of individuals; the populations and average incomes for cities; the energy requirements and vibration levels of electric generators, and so on. The case can be almost any unit of analysis: an individual, a family, or a country; a sale, a customer, a product line, or an industry; a time interval or a geographical area. A variable could be a measurement such as income in dollars, response time in hundredths of a second, or resistance in ohms; or it could be a set of categories such as sex or response to a multiple-choice questionnaire; or it could be a unique identifier for each case, such as an account or social security number. In short, it can be anything for which a value can be assigned to a case.

Although SPSS^X can accept complex data structures as input, its statistical and tabulation procedures operate on a *rectangular* data file—one in which each case contains one and only one value for each variable and in which the case is the same unit of analysis throughout the entire file.

If the data you want to analyze are already in a rectangular file, you can probably define it with one DATA LIST command, on which you give the names, locations, and formats of every variable you want SPSS^X to read and place in the active file (see Chapter 3). If your file has a more complex structure or if you want to check for missing or duplicate records, you can use some of the facilities outlined in Section 1.9.

1.6 Missing Values

If your data contain values that indicate missing data, you can specify those values on a MISSING VALUES command. SPSS^X procedures give you options for handling missing values in an analysis, and you can use the keyword MISSING in data transformations to refer to missing values. If your data include blanks, these are automatically set to a system-defined missing value unless you specify otherwise via the BLANKS subcommand to the SET command. See Chapter 3 for information about missing and system-missing values and Chapter 4 for information about the SET command.

1.7 Labels

The VARIABLE LABELS command allows you to assign labels to appear on your output along with the variable name or, in some cases, in lieu of the variable name. Similarly, the VALUE LABELS command allows you to specify labels for the values of a specified variable or list of variables. You can assign different labels to the values of different variables. Variable and value labels are discussed in Chapter 3.

1.8 Format

The format of a variable can be both the way the values of that variable are represented to the computer and the way those values are printed on output. SPSS^X accepts data in a wide variety of machine-readable formats and allows you to control the format of both printed output and machine-readable output.

Data in SPSS^X can be either *string* (alphanumeric) or *numeric.* String variables can contain numbers, letters, and special characters and can be up to 255 characters long. SPSS^X further differentiates between long strings and short strings. Long strings can be printed out by some procedures and by the PRINT command, and they can be used as "break" variables to define subgroups in REPORT, but they cannot be tabulated as long strings in procedures such as CROSSTABS and cannot have values declared as missing. Short strings, on the other hand, can be tabulated and can have missing values. The maximum length of a short string depends on the computer and operating system you are using; the maximum is 8 in IBM/OS. See Chapters 3 and 7 for information about defining and manipulating string variables, and see the sections within the chapters on SPSS^X procedures for how a specific procedure handles long and short strings.

Numeric variables vary in width, number of decimal places, and the way they are represented to the computer. You specify these format items when you define input data, and you can (with certain limitations) change the format SPSS^X uses for a numeric variable in a display file or an output data file. Some of the formats available are comma (for variables coded with commas), dollar (with dollar sign and commas), zoned decimal, and others depending upon your computer and operating system. For a full list, see Chapter 3.

Some SPSS^X procedures and the PRINT and WRITE commands use dictionary formats for listing the values of variables. When you supply the format of a variable on your DATA LIST command, SPSS^X enters both a write format and a print format in the dictionary for that variable. The write format is always the format in which the variable is read. The print format will be the same as the write format if that is a printable format; otherwise SPSS^X chooses an appropriate printable format. Variables you create within the transformation language are assigned default print and write formats, which you can also control with the SET command. You can change the print and write formats for individual variables or lists of variables using the PRINT FORMATS and WRITE FORMATS commands, or you can change both formats at once with a FORMATS command. See Chapter 9 for information about how formats are assigned and how to change them.

1.9 Defining Complex Files

If your data are not arranged conveniently for a single DATA LIST command, or if you have multiple records per case and you want SPSS^X to check that all records are present and in the right order, you can take advantage of additional file definition capabilities within SPSS^X. For most types of files, you can specify on a FILE TYPE command whether the records are *mixed* (one record per case, but different types of records within the file); *grouped* (multiple records per case, some of which might be duplicated or missing); or *nested* (hierarchical structures with different types of records for different levels in the hierarchy). You can then enter a RECORD TYPE command and associated DATA LIST for each type of record, and SPSS^X will build a file containing, for every case, all of the variables you have defined.

If, on the other hand, you have the same variables for more than one case recorded on a single input record, you can define the data with the REPEATING DATA command. If some of the information on the record applies to all the cases defined by the repeating data, SPSS^X will spread the data automatically. See Chapter 11 for details on defining complex files with the FILE TYPE/RECORD TYPE and REPEATING DATA commands.

If your data do not conform to one of the available file types, or if they lack a type identifier on each record, you can use data definition and transformation commands to construct your own INPUT PROGRAM. This means, for example, that you can place DATA LIST commands within DO IF structures to define individual records based on one or more conditions having to do with that record or previous records. The REREAD command allows you to read an individual record as often as necessary to determine how it should be defined and to assign values to all the variables being defined for that record. Operations to be repeated in defining a record can be specified in a LOOP—END LOOP structure. These commands and other utilities within the data transformation language give you considerable power to read your data file. See Chapter 12 for full discussions.

1.10 MANIPULATING VARIABLES

Data frequently do not come in the form needed for analysis or display. Age may be recorded in years, but you want a variable that assigns each case to one of three age groups. Several test scores may be recorded for each individual, but you want one variable that contains the average score. Or you might want to compute bonuses for employees based on department, length of service, and current salary. SPSS^X provides facilities for revising existing variables and creating new variables. It allows you to transform both numeric and string variables and to do so for every case or only for cases that meet one or more conditions.

1.11 Manipulating Numeric Variables

Data manipulation in SPSS^X begins with three basic commands: RECODE, COMPUTE, and COUNT. RECODE allows you to revise the coding structure of one or more variables. You can use it to collapse a variable such as age or income into categories or, if your file has yes and no answers coded differently for different variables, to make them consistent. You can either alter the values of the existing variable or store the results of the recoding in a new variable, leaving the existing variable unchanged.

COMPUTE creates a new variable from an expression made up of existing variables, constants, and functions. A simple example is computing average salary increase from variables giving employees' salaries at the end of each year. A number of functions are available for computing new variables. These include arithmetic functions, such as rounding, truncating, or taking the square root of a value; statistical functions, such as the sum, mean, or variance of a set of values; functions that test for missing values; functions that generate random numbers with uniform or normal distributions; a function that converts dates to day numbers for use in computations; and many others.

Finally, COUNT creates a variable whose value is the number of times a particular value or group of values occurs across a list of variables. You might, for example, want to create an uncertainty index by counting the number of times each respondent answered "Don't know" to a series of questionnaire items.

See Chapter 6 for a discussion of the RECODE, COMPUTE, and COUNT commands and the functions available for numeric transformations.

1.12 Manipulating String Variables

The same commands used for manipulating numeric variables can also be used with string variables. Special functions are available for concatenating strings, padding them on the left or right with your choice of characters, trimming characters from the left or right, and converting strings to numbers or numbers to strings. Other functions allow you to take substrings and to index the locations of substrings within strings. Using these functions, you can, for example, insert hyphens within social security numbers, sort names by last name first but print them with first name first, or identify from a list of drugs all those that end in "ene."

One restriction in dealing with strings is that you must declare a new string variable and its length before you can assign it a value with a transformation. To create new variables not defined on a DATA LIST command, a STRING command is provided.

The facilities for manipulating strings are documented in Chapter 7.

1.13 Conditional Transformations

The COMPUTE, COUNT, and RECODE commands operate on every case in the file. If you want a command to affect only certain cases, you can use the IF command or a DO IF—END IF structure. The IF command executes an operation such as a COMPUTE command only if a case meets a certain condition. That condition could be a simple test on a single variable (if variable AGE is greater than 65) or a complex expression involving functions and multiple conditions joined by AND or OR (if variable AGE is greater than 65 and the sum of three income variables is within the range 10,000–15,000).

Like the IF command, the DO IF command establishes a condition, but it applies that condition to any number of subsequent transformation commands. This can save your time in coding multiple IF commands and the computer's time in evaluating those commands. You can also build multiple conditions by enclosing IF commands or DO IF—END IF structures within DO IF—END IF structures. You can also use ELSE IF and ELSE commands to establish a full range of conditional executions.

Examples of IF commands and of DO IF—END IF structures can be found in Chapter 8.

1.14 Transformation Utilities

SPSS^X provides a number of utilities to simplify coding and to give you added control over the execution of data transformations. DO REPEAT saves coding by performing the same set of transformations on a set of variables. TEMPORARY makes all transformations between the place it appears in the command file and the first procedure that follows it apply only to that one procedure. And LEAVE retains the values of specified variables from one case to the next, allowing you to build cumulative indexes or spread data across cases. (See Chapter 6.)

1.15 FILE MANAGEMENT

SPSS^X provides commands for combining multiple files into a single analysis file, for splitting the active file into subgroups for processing, sorting, and aggregating the active file, and for saving and retrieving efficient system files.

1.16 Combining Files

To combine files, you can use ADD FILES or MATCH FILES. ADD FILES combines the cases of two or more files, either by simply attaching the cases from one file to the end of the other or by interleaving the cases according to the values of a key variable. Thus, if you have two or more files sorted by name or ID number, you can combine them in sequence—a much more efficient operation than adding cases to the end of the file and resorting. MATCH FILES combines the variables of two or more files into one file, keeping the same cases wherever possible. If you specify a key variable or variables, SPSS^X combines the cases with matching keys. If some of the files have more than one case with the same key, you can instruct SPSS^X to spread the data from one file to all cases with the same key in the other files. For example, if you have one file containing information about individual hospital patients and other files containing information on surgical operations (each with a patient number, and more than one for some patients), you can create a file of operations with information about the patient added to each case. The many ways in which you can use ADD FILES and MATCH FILES are discussed in Chapter 15.

1.17 Splitting, Sorting, and Aggregating Files

Neither the active file nor the SPSS^X system file maintains a subfile structure. You can, however, use the SPLIT FILE command to segment your file for processing in groups defined by one or more variables (see Chapter 13).

SORT CASES orders the active file according to the values of one or more variables. You can specify ascending or descending order for each of the variables you name as sort keys. You can sort on numeric variables, short strings, and long strings; but when sorting string variables you may need to pay attention to the collating sequence on your computer. See Chapter 13 for information on sorting cases.

The AGGREGATE procedure builds a new file containing summary statistics for subgroups within the original file and allows you to choose whether to write this file to an external file or replace the active file. See Chapter 14 for details and examples.

1.18 System Files

If you plan to analyze a data file several times, consider saving it as an SPSS^X system file. The system file is essentially a copy of the active file as it exists when the SAVE command is encountered (though you can specify on the SAVE command that some variables are to be dropped or renamed). Because the system file contains the dictionary built from data definition commands, you can omit those commands when you retrieve a system file with a GET command, as illustrated in Section 1.1. In addition, you can use the DOCUMENT command to store any information you choose along with the system file so that you can later recover a record of how the information in the file was gathered, how variables were measured, and so on. You can retrieve this information, as well as dictionary information such as the names, positions, labels, and formats of variables, via the DISPLAY command. Finally, because the system file is stored in a more efficient format than most input data files, using it can save considerably on computer resources. (See Chapter 5.)

System files are required as input to ADD FILES and MATCH FILES. You will find it very easy to save and retrieve files when you need them within a single SPSS^X job.

1.19 Procedure Output

In addition to the tabular or graphical display, SPSS^X procedures create a variety of output data: *Z* scores; residuals, predicted values, and other values from regression; correlation matrices; aggregated files; and so on. In general, when scores are calculated for each case in the active file, these are simply added to the current active file. Thus, when you use CONDESCRIPTIVE to calculate standardized scores for one or more variables, the scores are simply added as new variables on your active file. To save them on a permanent file, you must use either the SAVE command to include them in a system file or the WRITE command to place them in an output data file. The same is true of residuals, predicted values, and other scores from REGRESSION.

On the other hand, when a procedure generates a matrix or new file structure, the current active file is not affected, and a new output file is created. In this case, you must specify the handle of the new file on the PROCEDURE OUTPUT command. This is explained in more detail in Chapter 17.

1.20 OTHER UTILITIES FOR CONTROLLING THE JOB

Besides the information contained in the data dictionary, SPSS^X maintains a number of other values that establish such things as the length and width of pages in the display file, whether variable and value labels should be in upper and lower case, how blanks in the input file should be handled, how many times a loop may be executed, and how many errors should be tolerated before the job is aborted. All of these parameters have preset values, which may differ from installation to installation. You can display them with the SHOW command and change them with the SET command. It is worth your while to read through the list in Chapter 4. You may find several ways to suit the job to your needs.

Other commands that may help develop the SPSS^X job include TITLE and SUBTITLE, which label the whole job and its parts, and COMMENT, which allows you to include explanatory text within the command file. As an alternative to the COMMENT command, you can enclose comments between the symbols /* and */. Comments will be included within the printback of SPSS^X commands on the display file.

If your computer system numbers the lines in your command file, the NUMBERED command tells SPSS^X that certain columns of the command lines are reserved for these numbers. The numbers will be included on the printback of commands in the display file.

Finally, by inserting an EDIT command at the start of the command file, you can instruct SPSS^X to check your commands without reading data or executing procedures. An edit job requires a minimum of computer resources and does not require that the data file be made available, thereby saving the inconvenience and charges often incurred in making substantial data files available.

1.21 PRINTING AND WRITING CASES

To obtain a listing of cases, you can choose among the PRINT command and the LIST and REPORT procedures. If the case listing is the only output you want from an SPSS^X job, then the choice depends only on which facility creates the output in the form you want. But if you include any other procedure in your job, you can avoid an extra pass through the data by using PRINT, which prints the data as they are being read for the first procedure.

With the PRINT command you can specify both the variables whose values you want to list and literal strings that will be reproduced for every case. You can specify starting columns and formats for variables, or you can allow SPSS^X to format the listing using dictionary formats. PRINT operates as one of the transformation commands, so you can enclose it in control structures and specify it more than once for a single case (for example, to print the values of variables before and after some complex transformations). By adding PRINT SPACE and PRINT EJECT commands, you can create carefully formatted case listings. You can also take advantage of dollar, comma, and other special formats. Using the LEAVE command (Section 1.14) you can even add summary statistics. However, you should then consider whether the REPORT procedure will give you what you want more easily.

To produce a machine-readable case listing, you could also choose the WRITE command. WRITE differs from PRINT primarily in that WRITE uses by default the write format for each variable while PRINT uses the print format. WRITE also introduces no space between columns, while PRINT by default leaves a blank column.

As tranformation commands, PRINT and WRITE are not executed until SPSS^X executes a procedure command. If you want to execute PRINT or WRITE in the absence of a procedure designed to produce other output, use the EXECUTE command. For details about using the PRINT and WRITE commands and the commands for establishing formats, see Chapter 9.

The LIST procedure is easy to specify—only the command name is required if you want to list all cases for all variables on your active file. It allows you to select variables and to limit the cases to be printed. It automatically labels columns with variable names and optionally numbers the cases (within split-file groups if SPLIT FILE is in effect). (See Chapter 9.)

The REPORT procedure lists cases if you specify FORMAT=LIST. Since REPORT is designed to produce aggregate statistics for subgroups within a file, it is particularly useful if you want to combine a case listing with group summaries. REPORT also allows you to specify headings, special formatting, and other features such as printing value labels rather than values for selected variables. (See Chapter 23.)

1.22 TABLES AND REPORTS

The FREQUENCIES procedure produces frequency tables for single variables, plus optional bar charts and histograms. The CROSSTABS procedure produces two-way to *n*-way crosstabulations. The BREAKDOWN procedure produces tables of means in a choice of three formats. All of these procedures also produce a variety of statistics, as described in Sections 1.25 and 1.26.

For questionnaire or other data in which each case might have more than one value for a single item (for example, "Which of the following periodicals do you read regularly?"), the MULT RESPONSE procedure produces both univariate tables and crosstabulations with ordinary variables or with other multiple response items.

The REPORT procedure calculates a wide variety of summary statistics for subgroups defined by one or more variables and prints them in a format you can control. You can obtain most of the statistics available in FREQUENCIES, and you can obtain them for groups defined at multiple levels (for example, grade within school within district within state). You can also obtain composite statistics calculated on group summaries, such as the average of the means for several variables. And you can control almost every part of the report format: dimensions, column widths, spacing, titles, footnotes, labels, and so on.

1.23 GRAPHICS

For those many occasions when a well-constructed graph can convey information more quickly and forcefully than columns of numbers, the three SPSS Graphics procedures, PIECHART, BARCHART, and LINECHART, produce high-quality plots directly from your data. The procedures obey SPSS^X syntax rules and offer both flexibility in specifying titles, patterns, colors, and so forth, and they are easy to use via defaults for most specifications. They produce a graphics file, which you identify on the GRAPHICS OUTPUT command. You can then access this file with the Graphics Postprocessor and produce your plots on a wide variety of graphic terminals and plotters. You can also preview plots on one device before producing them on another. Examples of SPSS Graphics output can be found on the inside covers of this manual and in Chapter 24.

SPSS Graphics is an optional addition to the SPSS^X system. It is produced by SPSS Inc. and ISSCO, Inc.

1.24 STATISTICAL PROCEDURES

The SPSS^X statistical procedures described in the following sections provide for a wide variety of analyses. Using these procedures properly requires an understanding not only of the SPSS^X operations described in this manual but also of the statistical techniques and of the data to which they are being applied. The procedures themselves have little ability to distinguish between proper and improper application. For suggestions about using the procedures, check one of the statistics guides described in the preface to this manual and the bibliographies within those guides.

1.25 Frequency Distributions and Descriptive Statistics

The FREQUENCIES procedure calculates a variety of descriptive statistics, such as the mean, median, mode, range, variance, measures of skewness and kurtosis, and percentiles. Barcharts and frequency tables of the individual values of a variable can be displayed. Histograms are available for variables that have many distinct values. The CONDESCRIPTIVE procedure calculates many of the same measures of central tendency and dispersion as does FREQUENCIES. However, since it does not sort the observations, it does not compute the median and mode. CONDESCRIPTIVE calculates standardized (*Z*) scores for cases and adds them to your active file for use in other procedures.

1.26 Relationships Between Two or More Variables

The CROSSTABS procedure produces two-way to *n*-way crosstabulations for variables that have a limited number of distinct values. The observed frequencies in each cell can be expressed as a percentage of the row total, column total, or table total. A variety of statistics which measure the strength of association between the variables, such as lambda, gamma, and Kendall's tau *b*, can be computed. The chi-square test of independence and associated residuals and expected values are also available.

Another technique for examining the relationship between two or more variables using a table format is provided by the BREAKDOWN procedure, which computes the means, standard deviations, and variances of a criterion or dependent variable for subgroups of cases. You can enter up to six variables into a single BREAKDOWN table. BREAKDOWN optionally computes a one-way analysis of variance table including a test for linearity.

1.27 Correlation Coefficients and Scatterplots

The PEARSON CORR procedure calculates the Pearson product-moment correlation coefficient, while the NONPAR CORR procedure computes two coefficients, the Spearman and Kendall coefficients, based on the ranks of the observations. The output from the procedures includes the coefficients, sample sizes, and observed significance levels for selected pairs or lists of variables. In addition, correlation matrices can be written on a file and used as input to other procedures.

The SCATTERGRAM procedure prints a two-dimensional plot of data points where the coordinates of the points are the values of two variables. Correlation coefficients, as well as bivariate regression statistics, can also be computed. Options are available to control handling of missing values, positioning of grid lines, and scaling of axes.

1.28 Multiple Regression Analysis

The REGRESSION procedure can be used to study the relationship between a dependent variable and a set of independent variables. Regression coefficients, as well as a variety of statistics and plots that evaluate how well the model fits and the contribution of the individual variables, are also calculated. Forward-inclusion, backward-elimination, and stepwise-selection algorithms are available for selecting the independent variables to be included in the equation. Extensive facilities for analyzing residuals and influential cases are included. Residuals and other statistics computed for the cases can be added to your active file for use in other procedures.

1.29 Factor Analysis

The FACTOR procedure can be used to summarize the information available in a correlated set of variables. Initial factors can be extracted using principal components, principal axis factoring, unweighted or generalized least squares, and maximum likelihood algorithms. Several methods for orthogonal and oblique rotations are available. Factor scores can be computed and added to the active file.

1.30 Discriminant Analysis

The DISCRIMINANT procedure calculates linear combinations of variables which can be used to distinguish among members of different groups. All variables may be included in the functions, or a stepwise algorithm using one of several possible entry and removal criteria may be used for variable selection. A classification table which contains the number of cases classified correctly using the derived functions is printed. A variety of statistics and plots useful for discriminant analysis are available. For each case, discriminant scores and probabilities of group membership can be printed and stored on the active file.

1.31 Survival Analysis

The SURVIVAL procedure analyzes the time interval between two events. It produces life tables, graphs of survival functions, and comparisons of the survival distributions for various subgroups. The procedure allows censored observations, cases for which the second event has not occurred. Output from procedure SURVIVAL can be written onto an external file.

1.32 Analysis of Additive Scales

A variety of coefficients which evaluate the reliability of additive scales can be calculated using the RELIABILITY procedure. In addition, RELIABILITY calculates basic summary statistics including item means, standard deviations, inter-item covariance and correlation matrices, scale means, and item-to-scale correlations. The procedure can perform a repeated measures design analysis of variance, a two-way factorial analysis of variance with one observation per cell, Tukey's test for additivity, Hotelling's T^2 test for equality of means in repeated measures designs, and Friedman's two-way analysis of variance on ranks.

1.33 Nonparametric Statistics

A variety of nonparametric tests can be computed using the NPAR TESTS procedure. The tests available include the sign test, the runs test, the Wilcoxon signed-ranks test, McNemar's test, the Kruskal-Wallis one-way analysis of variance, and the Kolmogorov-Smirnov test. Quantile values for the variables are also available.

1.34 Log-linear Models

The LOGLINEAR procedure models multi-way contingency tables using the multinomial response model (following Haberman, 1978, 1979). LOGLINEAR can fit hierarchical or nonhierarchical models, quasi-independence models, and models with structural zeros. You can choose from available contrasts or specify your own contrasts. You can enter the data as tables or counts, or you can build the table from variables in your SPSS^X file. Output includes parameter estimates, their standard errors, standardized estimates, the covariance matrix of the estimates, and the likelihood-ratio statistic. LOGLINEAR also produces observed and expected counts, as well as observed and expected cell probabilities. Residuals output includes unstandardized residuals, standardized residuals, adjusted residuals, and a normal probability plot of the adjusted residuals.

1.35 Univariate and Multivariate Analysis of Variance

The ONEWAY procedure calculates a one-way analysis of variance, as well as a variety of multiple comparison procedures. The T-TEST procedure calculates a test for the equality of two means for independent or paired samples.

The ANOVA procedure can be used for univariate analysis of variance. Several different methods for assessing main effects and interactions are available. A multiple classification analysis table can also be calculated.

The MANOVA procedure is a generalized multivariate analysis of variance and covariance program which will perform univariate and multivariate linear estimation and tests of hypotheses for any crossed and/or nested design with or without covariates. You have complete control of the model specification. Special features include a variety of graphical displays, the ability to collapse and specify multiple error terms, partitioning degrees of freedom, and specification of contrasts and orthogonal polynomials.

Tests of significance for a multivariate analysis of variance model include hypotheses and error matrices, four multivariate test criteria, dimension reduction analysis, univariate *F* tests, and step-down analysis. In addition, principal components analysis and discriminant analysis can be requested.

MANOVA enables you to analyze a large class of repeated measures designs. The observation can be either single-valued or vector-valued. Covariates, varying or constant across repeated measures, can also appear in the model.

1.36 Box-Jenkins Analysis of Time Series Data

The BOX-JENKINS procedure is used to fit and forecast time series data by means of a general class of statistical models. The procedure is designed to provide for easy and flexible model identification, estimation, and forecasting. Several models can be examined in a single invocation of the procedure. Parameter estimates, forecasts, and plots of the autocorrelation function, partial autocorrelation function, and forecasts at different leads can be included in the output.

2

```
INFO [OUTFILE = handle]
     [OVERVIEW]
     [LOCAL]
     [FACILITIES]
     [PROCEDURES]
     [ALL]
     [procedure name] [/procedure name . . . ]
     [SINCE release number]
```


PREPARING SPSS^X COMMANDS, **2.1**
- Commands and Specifications, **2.2**
- Names, **2.3**
  - The TO Conventions, **2.4**
- Keywords, **2.5**
  - Truncation, **2.6**
- Numbers and Literals, **2.7**
- Arithmetic Operators and Delimiters, **2.8**
- Notation Used to Describe SPSS^X Commands, **2.9**

THE ORDER OF SPSS^X COMMANDS, **2.10**

THE INFO COMMAND, **2.11**
- Selecting the Type of Information, **2.12**
- Specifying Releases, **2.13**
- Writing Information to an External File, **2.14**
- Truncation, **2.15**

Chapter 2 The SPSS^X Language

To use SPSS^X, you need to become familiar with its language. For the most part, this is easily done, since every attempt has been made to keep the language natural and straightforward. This chapter sets forth the general characteristics or *syntax* of the SPSS^X language; the specific format of each command is explained in the following chapters.

Within this manual and in the enclosed reference card, certain conventions have been adopted for setting out the generalized format of commands. Section 2.9 enumerates these conventions.

2.1 PREPARING SPSS^X COMMANDS

Every SPSS^X command begins in column 1 of a command line and continues for as many lines as needed. All continuation lines are indented at least one column. Except within literals (Section 2.7), you can add space or break lines at any point where a single blank is allowed, including around special delimiters such as a slash, parenthesis, or equals sign. The maximum length of an input line is usually 80 characters but may vary by type of computer and operating system.

Enter commands in any case you wish. SPSS^X preserves upper and lower case within labels and literals but translates keywords and names to upper case before processing. You can use the SET command to control translation of labels and messages to upper case on output (see Chapter 4). Some installations may not recognize lower case and will automatically translate all input to upper case. For information on how your installation handles case translation consult the local documentation available via the INFO command (see Section 2.11).

2.2 Commands and Specifications

Each command begins with a *command keyword* (which may contain more than one word). A few commands, such as EDIT and BEGIN DATA, are complete in themselves; but most require specifications. *Specifications* are made up of names, keywords, numbers, literals, arithmetic operators, special delimiters, and spacing as needed to separate these elements. Many specifications include *subcommands*, such as the FILE, RENAME, DROP, KEEP, and MAP subcommands on the SAVE command, many of which require additional specifications.

Command keywords begin in column 1. Specifications begin at least one space after the command keyword and continue for as many lines as necessary. Continuation lines must be indented at least one column and can be indented as much as you want. The command

```
VALUE LABELS
   SEX     0 'MALES'
           1 'FEMALES' /
   JOBCAT  1 'CLERICAL'
           2 'OFFICE TRAINEE'
           3 'SECURITY OFFICER'
           4 'COLLEGE TRAINEE'
           5 'EXEMPT EMPLOYEE'
           6 'MBA TRAINEE'
           7 'TECHNICAL' /
```

is equivalent to

```
VALUE LABELS SEX 0 'MALES' 1 'FEMALES'
 /JOBCAT 1 'CLERICAL' 2 'OFFICE TRAINEE' 3 'SECURITY OFFICER'
 4 'COLLEGE TRAINEE' 5 'EXEMPT EMPLOYEE' 6 'MBA TRAINEE' 7 'TECHNICAL'/
```

The difference is merely one of style.

If you wish to indent commands to indicate level of control (or for any other reason), place one of the symbols +, −, or . in column 1 and then indent the command keyword as much as you wish, as in:

```
DO IF (REGION EQ 8)
+  IF (SEX = 1) WT = .8
+  IF (SEX = 2) WT = 1.2
END IF
```

2.3 Names

Both in defining data and in creating variables through COMPUTE, IF, RECODE, COUNT, and other transformation commands, you assign *names* to your variables. These names must be no longer than eight characters. They must begin with one of the 26 letters A–Z or with one of the three additional characters @, #, or $. See the following paragraphs about variable names beginning with # or $. The remaining characters in the name can be any letter, any digit, a period, @, #, or $. Some keywords are reserved to SPSS^X and cannot be used as variable names (see Section 2.5). The following are all valid variable names: LOCATION, LOC#5, @2.5, X.1, A#######, OVER$500, and #32 (but see the next paragraph before using a name that begins with #).

If you begin a variable name with the character #, SPSS^X understands that this is a *scratch variable* to be used only for convenience in defining the file or in transforming the data. Scratch variables are not available in procedures and are not saved on system files. You might, for example, want to read in a string variable as a scratch variable in preparation for recoding that variable into a new, numeric variable. The string variable disappears when the active file is created.

SPSS^X provides several *system variables* that you can use in transformation commands. They allow you to refer to the current date, page dimensions, the system-missing value, or the sequence number of the current case. System variable names begin with a dollar sign, as in $CASENUM. See Chapter 6 for more information on system variables.

2.4 The TO Conventions

You can both create and refer to a set of variable names by using keyword TO.

Generating Variable Names. When you are assigning new names, as in DATA LIST specifications, ITEM1 TO ITEM5 is equivalent to five names: ITEM1, ITEM2, ITEM3, ITEM4, and ITEM5. The prefix can be any valid name and the numbers can be any integers, so long as the first number is smaller than the second and the full variable name, including the number, does not exceed eight characters. Note that the number is a part of the variable name, not a subscript. If you include leading zeros in the number, they are preserved in the variable name. X1 TO X100 and X001 TO X100 both generate 100 variable names, but the first 99 names are not the same in the two lists. X01 TO X9 is not valid.

Referring to Variables. When you are referring to variables, as in a list of variables to be analyzed by a procedure, VARA TO VARD refers to VARA, VARD, and any variables that fall between VARA and VARD on the active file. If the active file contains the variables SCORE3, AGE, SEX, SCORE1, SCORE2, SCORE4, the variable list AGE TO SCORE4 includes AGE, SEX, SCORE1, SCORE2, and SCORE4 but not SCORE3. You can use TO in variable lists everywhere except where explicitly stated in this manual.

The order of the variables on the active file is the order in which the variables are defined by the DATA LIST, STRING, and NUMERIC commands or created by the COMPUTE, IF, RECODE, and COUNT commands. If you want to place variables on the active file in a particular order and you can't define or create them in the order you want, you can use STRING and NUMERIC commands to declare the variables before you name them on a DATA LIST or transformation command (see Chapter 12). When dealing with system files, you can use the KEEP subcommand on the SAVE, GET, MATCH FILES, and ADD FILES commands to reorder the variables (see Chapters 5 and 15).

2.5 Keywords

Keywords have special meaning to SPSS^X. Besides the command keywords that identify commands, almost every command has associated keywords that may be included in its specifications. For example, the SPLIT FILE command used to divide a file into two or more separate files for analysis uses keyword OFF to return to processing the file as a whole, as in:

```
SPLIT FILE OFF
```

For the most part, the SPSS^X language is structured so that keywords cannot be confused with variable names or file handles. Therefore, you don't have to worry about whether you use one of these keywords as one of your variable names or file handles. For example, the SPLIT FILE command requires keyword BY before a variable name, so you could have a variable named OFF and use that variable in the SPLIT FILE command. But some keywords can occur where a name also can be used, such as ALL in:

```
FREQUENCIES VARIABLES=ALL
```

These are *reserved keywords* (Table 2.5): do not use them as variable names.

Table 2.5 SPSS^X reserved keywords

ALL	EQ	LE	NOT	TO
AND	GE	LT	OR	WITH
BY	GT	NE	THRU	

2.6 Truncation

The first word of every command keyword must be spelled out in full. All subsequent keywords that make up the command and most other keywords can be truncated to a minimum of three characters. The exceptions are the reserved keyword WITH and all specifications to the INFO command.

2.7 Numbers and Literals

Numbers and literals are frequent components of specifications. They may refer to the values of variables, or they may serve other purposes such as constants in numeric transformations or literals in string functions. Enter numbers, either integers or decimal numbers, with or without leading zeros, as in:

```
SELECT IF (AMOUNT GT 0.05)
```

The SELECT IF command tests each case to see if numeric variable AMOUNT is greater than 0.05. The zero before the decimal point is optional.

Enclose literals within apostrophes, as in:

```
SELECT IF (STATE EQ 'IL')
```

This command tests each case to see if the string variable STATE is equal to the literal IL. If you need to break a literal across input lines, enclose the first line of the literal in apostrophes, end the first line with a plus sign, and begin the second line of the literal with an apostrophe, as in this TITLE subcommand to REPORT:

```
TITLE='SELLINGSWORTH COUNTY COMMISSION FOR EMERGENCY PREPAREDNESS'+
       'AND DISASTER SERVICES'/
```

You can enclose literals in quotation marks instead of apostrophes, so long as you do not begin with one and end with the other. Within a literal demarcated by quotation marks, apostrophes are valid characters. Within a literal demarcated by apostrophes, quotation marks are valid characters. Within a literal demarcated by quotation marks, two quotation marks entered without separation are interpreted as a single, valid quotation mark. Similarly, within a literal demarcated by apostrophes, two contiguous apostrophes are interpreted as a single, valid apostrophe. The following are equivalent specifications for a title within REPORT:

```
TITLE='Murphy''s Sports Shop' '1982 Sales by Division'/
   or
TITLE="Murphy's Sports Shop" "1982 Sales by Division'/
   or
TITLE="Murphy's Sports Shop"'1982 Sales by Division'/
```

The space between the two lines of the title is required in the first two examples but optional in the third. See Chapter 7 for more information on literals and string variables

2.8 Arithmetic Operators and Delimiters

Five arithmetic operators occur in SPSS^X specifications: addition (+), subtraction (−), multiplication (*), division (/), and exponentiation (**). The equals sign (=), is also used to show equivalence in many expressions. These operators are self-delimiting; insert space around them if you wish, but none is required. VARA+VARB is equivalent to VARA + VARB.

Special delimiters in SPSS^X include parentheses, apostrophes, quotation marks, the slash, and the equals sign. These characters set apart certain elements in specifications, as shown in the general syntax for each command (see Section 2.9). You can insert blanks before and after special delimiters, but none is required.

- **Parentheses** enclose arguments to functions, value ranges in some procedures, keywords that could otherwise be confused with variable names, and certain expressions such as (value list = value) in RECODE specifications and RENAME = (old variable list = new variable list) in GET and SAVE specifications.
- **Apostrophes** and **quotation marks** set off literals. See Section 2.7 for a discussion of literals.

- The **slash** is used primarily to separate subcommands and lists such as multiple analysis lists in many procedures. Although slashes are sometimes optional, entering them as shown in the syntax diagrams is good practice.
- The **equals sign** is used between a subcommand and its specifications, as in FILE=handle, and to show equivalence, as in (old variable list = new variable list). Equals signs following subcommands are frequently optional, but it is best to enter them.

Where no arithmetic operator or special delimiter is required between elements within a specification, use either one or more blanks or one or more commas or a combination of the two. In arguments to functions described in Chapters 6 and 7, single commas are required and a blank is not a valid substitute.

2.9 Notation Used to Describe SPSS^{X} Commands

Use the following rules to create commands according to the general formats shown throughout this manual:

- Elements in capital letters are keywords. Enter them exactly as they appear, or truncate them as discussed in Section 2.6. In Figure 2.9, OUTFILE, MISSING, COLUMNWISE, and BREAK are keywords. AGGREGATE, the command keyword, cannot be truncated.
- Elements in lower case describe specifications you should provide. For example, replace *file handle* with the appropriate file handle.
- Enter special delimiters as they appear, and use blanks or commas to separate keywords, names, labels, and numbers from each other. In Figure 2.9, the slashes following each subcommand are required.
- Elements enclosed in square brackets [ ] are optional. In Figure 2.9, subcommand MISSING is optional. But where brackets would confuse the format, they are omitted and the accompanying text explains what specifications are required or optional.
- Braces { } indicate a choice between the elements they enclose. For the file handle in procedure AGGREGATE, you have the choice between the symbol * to refer to the active file and a file handle that writes the aggregated file to a disk or tape. If there is a default specification (the instruction understood by SPSS^{X} if you specify nothing), that specification is shown in bold.

Figure 2.9 General format for procedure AGGREGATE

```
                        {handle}
AGGREGATE   OUTFILE =   {*     }

      [/MISSING = COLUMNWISE]
      /BREAK = varlist
      /aggvar ['label'] aggvar ['label'] . . . = function arguments) [/aggvar . . . ]
```

2.10 THE ORDER OF SPSS^{X} COMMANDS

There is little formal precedence order for SPSS^{X} commands. Most ordering of commands will come from your understanding of how SPSS^{X} works so you can instruct it in the right order.

There is a required order for some commands. A variable must be defined before it or its values can be labeled. STATISTICS and OPTIONS commands must follow immediately after the procedure command.

Besides formal precedence order, you must keep in mind the logical outcome of the order in which your commands are processed. Although data definitions and transformations are not carried out until a procedure command (including a SAVE command) causes the data to be read, the result is as though the commands were executed when encountered. Thus you can control the logic of calculations by the sequence of commands.

Finally, there are some commands that can appear only in an *input program* where the cases are being created and other commands that operate only in the *transformation program* after the cases have been created. For example, commands REREAD and END CASE are used only to read data records and create cases, and the SELECT IF command works only after the cases are created. On the other hand, the COMPUTE command is used both to create and to transform cases and can appear in either program. For a discussion of these *program states* and command order, see Appendix B.

2.11 THE INFO COMMAND

The INFO command makes available or tells you how to obtain two kinds of documentation not included in this manual: local and update.

Local documentation concerns the environment in which you are running SPSS^X:

- Commands or job control language for running SPSS^X. Of course, you will need some basic instructions before you can obtain documentation from the INFO command.
- Conventions for specifying files. These are especially important for the FILE HANDLE command, which tells your computer's operating system how to access or create a particular file.
- Conventions for handling tapes and other input/output devices.
- Data formats. The formats that SPSS^X reads and writes may differ from one computer and operating system to another (see Chapter 3).
- Default values for parameters controlled by the SET command (see Chapter 4). Such parameters as translation to upper case or compression of scratch files can be set at your installation. You can use the SHOW command to discover the values in effect on a given run, and local documentation may contain more information on why you should prefer a particular setting.
- Other information specific to your your computer and operating system or to your individual installation.

Update documentation includes changes to existing procedures and facilities made after publication of this manual, new procedures and facilities, and corrections to this manual. Specifications to the INFO command allow you to choose update documentation for facilities (all SPSS^X commands except procedures), for all procedures, or for individual procedures. You can also request documentation produced since a particular release of SPSS^X.

While the INFO command provides a handy mechanism for obtaining local and update information, SPSS^X requires more computer resources than most printing utilities. Your installation may provide an alternative method for printing the documentation. In that case, the INFO command may simply give you instructions for using the preferred documentation facility.

2.12 Selecting the Type of Information

To select the type of information you want, enter one or more of the following specifications:

OVERVIEW *Overview of available documentation.* This overview includes a table of contents for the documentation available via the INFO command, along with information about documentation available in print.

LOCAL *Local documentation,* as described in Section 2.11.

FACILITIES *Update information for SPSS^X facilities.* This documentation covers all differences, except in procedures, between the system as documented in this manual and the system as installed on your computer—whether those differences result from updates to the system, revisions required for conversions to particular operating systems, or errors in this manual. However, unless you use keyword SINCE to specify the SPSS^X release documented in this manual, you will receive updates only for the most current release (see Section 2.13).

PROCEDURES *Update information for procedures.* This includes full documentation for procedures new in the current release and update information for procedures that existed prior to the current release.

procedure *Documentation for the procedure named.* This is the same information as that printed by the PROCEDURES keyword, but limited to the procedure named. Follow every procedure name with a slash.

ALL *All available documentation.* ALL is equivalent to OVERVIEW, LOCAL, FACILITIES, and PROCEDURES.

You can enter as many of these keywords as you wish. If you specify overlapping sets of information, only one copy is printed. The order of specifications is not important and does not affect the order in which the documentation is printed. The following commands produce an overview and documentation for any changes made to system facilities and to the FREQUENCIES and CROSSTABS procedures:

```
INFO  OVERVIEW FACILITIES FREQUENCIES / CROSSTABS
```

Because of possible conflict with procedure names, all keywords in the INFO command must be spelled out in full.

2.13 Specifying Releases

Releases of SPSS^X are numbered by integers, with decimal digits indicating maintenance releases between major releases (so Release 1.1 would be a maintenance release with few changes from Release 1). The release number appears in the heading to each SPSS^X job. Each SPSS^X manual is identified on the title page by the number of the release it documents. This manual documents Release 1.

By default, the INFO command produces update information only for the current major release and subsequent maintenance releases. Documentation for earlier releases may also be available, and that fact will be indicated in the overview. To obtain information for earlier releases or to limit the information to maintenance releases since the last major release, use keyword SINCE followed by a release number.

SINCE n *Print documentation for all releases since Release* n.

The following commands print documentation for all changes to system facilities and procedures FREQUENCIES and CROSSTABS since the first release (the release documented in this manual):

```
INFO OVERVIEW FACILITIES FREQUENCIES / CROSSTABS SINCE 1
```

SINCE is not inclusive—SINCE 2 does not include changes made to the system in Release 2, though it does include any changes made in Release 2.1 (if a Release 2.1 occurs). To identify a maintenance release, enter the exact number, with decimal, as in 1.1.

2.14 Writing Information to an External File

By default, the output from the INFO command is included in the display file. If you prefer to send the output to another file, use the OUTFILE subcommand, naming the handle of the file you want to create. The following commands create a file of text comprising an overview, local documentation, changes, and new procedures since Release 1:

```
FILE HANDLE SPSSXDOC / file specifications
INFO OUTFILE=SPSSXDOC ALL SINCE 1
```

The characteristics of the output file produced by the INFO command may vary by computer type. As implemented at SPSS Inc., the file includes carriage control, with the maximum length of a page determined by the LENGTH subcommand to the SET command. A printer width of 132 characters is assumed for some examples, though the text is generally much narrower.

2.15 Truncation

Three-character truncation does *not* apply to INFO command specifications. Spell all keywords out in full. For procedure names, spell the first word out in full and subsequent words through at least the first three characters.

3

DATA LIST [FIXED / FREE / LIST] [FILE = handle] [RECORDS = {1 / n}] [{TABLE / NOTABLE}]

/ [1 / rec #] varlist {col location [(format)] / (format list)} [varlist . . .]

[/ [2 / rec #] . . .] [/ . . .]

Available Formats:

Format	FORTRAN-like Format	Data type
(d)	Fw.d	Numeric (default)
(N)	Nw	Restricted numeric
(E,d)	Ew.d	Scientific notation
(COMMA,d)	COMMAw.d	Numeric with commas
(DOLLAR,d)	DOLLARw.d	Numeric with commas and dollar sign
(Z,d)	Zw.d	Zoned decimal
(A)	Aw	String
(AHEX)	AHEXw	Hexadecimal character
(IB,d)	IBw.d	Integer binary
(P,d)	Pw.d	Packed decimal
(PIB,d)	PIBw.d	Unsigned integer binary
(PIBHEX)	PIBHEXw	Hexadecimal unsigned integer binary
(PK,d)	PKw.d	Unsigned packed decimal
(RB)	RBw	Floating point binary
(RBHEX)	RBHEXw	Hexadecimal floating point binary

Some formats may not be available on all implementations of SPSS^X.

MISSING VALUES varlist (value list) [/varlist . . .]

Keywords available for numeric value lists:
LOW LOWEST HI HIGHEST THRU

VARIABLE LABELS varname 'label' [/varname . . .]

VALUE LABELS varlist value 'label' value 'label' . . .
[/varlist . . .]

BEGIN DATA
lines of data
END DATA

INTRODUCTION TO DATA DEFINITION, **3.1**

THE FILE HANDLE COMMAND, **3.2**
The Active File, **3.3**

FILE DEFINITION ON DATA LIST, **3.4**
The FILE Subcommand, **3.5**
Keywords FIXED, FREE, and LIST, **3.6**
The RECORDS Subcommand, **3.7**
The TABLE and NOTABLE Subcommands, **3.8**

VARIABLE DEFINITION ON DATA LIST, **3.9**
Specifying the Record Number, **3.10**
Naming the Variables, **3.11**
Indicating Column Locations, **3.12**
Specifying Multiple Records, **3.13**
Specifying Multiple Variables, **3.14**
Indicating Decimal Places, **3.15**
The Default Format Type, **3.16**
N and E Format Types, **3.17**
String Variables, **3.18**
Other Format Types, **3.19**
FREE and LIST Variable Definition, **3.20**
Specifying Format Types, **3.21**
Undefined Data Values, **3.22**
Printing and Writing Formats, **3.23**

MISSING VALUES, **3.24**
The MISSING VALUES Command, **3.25**
Referencing Several Variables, **3.26**
Specifying Ranges of Missing Values, **3.27**
Missing Values for String Variables, **3.28**
Redefining Missing Values, **3.29**

VARIABLE AND VALUE LABELS, **3.30**
The VARIABLE LABELS Command, **3.31**
The VALUE LABELS Command, **3.32**

INPUT DATA IN THE COMMAND FILE, **3.33**
The BEGIN DATA and END DATA Commands, **3.34**

FORTRAN-LIKE FORMAT SPECIFICATIONS ON DATA LIST, **3.35**
Format Elements, **3.36**
The T and X Format Elements, **3.37**
Mixing Styles, **3.38**
Skipping Records, **3.39**

Chapter 3 Defining Data

Data files consist of *values* recorded in *variables* for a set of *cases*. Data files can be organized in a variety of ways, but data definition discussed here assumes that your input data file is a rectangular, case-ordered file. More complex types of data files, such as hierarchical files, are discussed in Chapter 11.

A file is *rectangular* if, for every case, a value is recorded for each variable—always in the same order. Each case is defined as the same unit of analysis. For example, if you start out defining a case as an individual sale, you cannot include in the same file cases defined as individual customers. A single case can be entered on one or more *records* of any length. If the cases require more than one record, each case must contain the same number of records, which must be in the same order within each case. The values can be punched on 80-column punched cards or stored on some machine-readable medium such as a tape or disk. Data records can be included in the same file as your SPSS^X commands (the command file) or stored in a separate file.

3.1 INTRODUCTION TO DATA DEFINITION

SPSS^X data definition requires two parts: *file definition* provides basic information about the data file, and *variable definition* provides specific information about the location, structure, and meaning of the data on the file. You define the file on the FILE HANDLE and DATA LIST commands, and you define variables beginning on the DATA LIST command and continuing on optional variable definition commands such as VARIABLE LABELS, MISSING VALUES, and so forth. The commands

```
FILE HANDLE BALLOONS/ file specifications
DATA LIST  FILE=BALLOONS/ COLOR 1
VARIABLE LABELS  COLOR 'COLOR OF DELIVERY'
VALUE LABELS COLOR 1 'BLUE' 2 'RED' 3 'GREEN' 4 'YELLOW' 5 'ORANGE'
            8 'POPPED' 9 'DEFLATED'
MISSING VALUES COLOR (8,9)
```

define the *file handle* BALLOONS on the FILE HANDLE command (Section 3.2) to the data file and reference the file handle on the DATA LIST command, implicitly telling SPSS^X that the file is a simple fixed-format file with one record per case. These two commands, along with the operating-system commands needed to define BALLOONS at your computer installation, complete file definition.

The variable definition portion of the DATA LIST command begins with a slash and names variable COLOR to be read from column 1 of each record on file BALLOONS. Variable COLOR is implicitly understood to be numeric without decimal places.

Once a variable is identified on a DATA LIST command, you can use optional variable definition commands for assigning labels (the VARIABLE LABELS and VALUE LABELS commands) and for declaring specific values representing missing information (the MISSING VALUES command). Information provided via data definition commands is stored in a dictionary and can be saved along with the data values in an SPSS^X system file, which can be retrieved on subsequent SPSS^X jobs without repeating data definitions (see Chapter 5).

3.2 THE FILE HANDLE COMMAND

Since SPSS^X can read and write more than one file in a single job, each file must be assigned a unique *file handle* to identify it. The file handle is used only during the SPSS^X job to reference the data file on SPSS^X commands. It is never saved as part of a system file. The file handle can be no longer than eight characters and must begin with an alphabetic character (A–Z) or a $, #, or @. It can also contain numeric characters (0–9). No embedded blanks are allowed.

In most implementions of SPSS^X, you use the FILE HANDLE command to define the file handle for each file and to supply the necessary operating-system specifications for the file. The FILE HANDLE command is used for all files read and written by SPSS^X, including data files, system files, and special files of matrix materials or statistical results. For example, to assign the file handle BALLOONS to your data file, specify:

```
FILE HANDLE BALLOONS/ file specifications
```

The first specification on the FILE HANDLE command is the file handle. The remaining specifications are specific to the type of computer and operating system that you run SPSS^X on. For example, in the DIGITAL VAX version of SPSS^X, the file specification is a full VAX file specification, which supplies the device, directory, filename, filetype, and version number of each file. In the IBM/CMS version, the file specification section is the subcommand NAME, which supplies the filename, filetype, and filemode:

```
FILE HANDLE BALLOONS/NAME='BALL DATA A'
```

Throughout this manual, examples of the FILE HANDLE command are shown with the general notation, *file specifications*. For details on writing the file specifications section of the FILE HANDLE command, refer to the documentation available with the keyword LOCAL on the INFO command (see Chapter 2).

In the IBM/OS version of SPSS^X, the FILE HANDLE command is not used. Rather, the file handle is automatically equated to the DDNAME of the JCL command, which provides operating-system-specific information about the file such as the file name, record length, blocksize, storage location, and so forth. The specification

```
DATA LIST FILE=BALLOONS/ COLOR 1
```

tells SPSS^X to look for the JCL command

```
//BALLOONS DD DSN= ...
```

which provides operating-system information about the file. For additional information on writing JCL commands, see the documentation available with the keyword LOCAL on the INFO command (see Chapter 2).

If your input data are included as lines in your SPSS^X command file, the default file handle INLINE is assigned. Section 3.33 discusses the BEGIN DATA and END DATA commands used for this special method of data input.

3.3 The Active File

The DATA LIST command does not read the data; it gives SPSS^X information on the location and format of the data. Data are read when a procedure or other data-reading command is executed (see Chapter 17).

Once SPSS^X reads your data according to the DATA LIST command, it creates an *active file* which consists of the data and a *dictionary* containing variable definitions such as variable names, labels, printing and writing formats, and missing-value flags. The active file is the file that you modify using the transformation language (Chapters 6, 7, and 8), that you analyze using any of the procedures, and that you save as an SPSS^X system file (Chapter 5).

Once SPSS^X has an active file, refer to it with an asterisk (*) as the file handle on other commands. The file handle named on the DATA LIST still references the input data file.

3.4 FILE DEFINITION ON DATA LIST

The file definition portion of the DATA LIST command points SPSS^X to the data file and indicates the format of the file and the number of records SPSS^X should read per case from fixed-format data files. You can specify four pieces of information describing the data file on the DATA LIST command:

The FILE Subcommand. FILE indicates the file handle of the file described by the DATA LIST command. (See Sections 3.2 and 3.5.)

Keywords FIXED, FREE, and LIST. FIXED, the default, indicates that the data are recorded in fixed format. FREE indicates that the data are recorded in freefield format, and LIST indicates that the data are in freefield format with one case recorded on each record. (See Section 3.6.)

The RECORDS Subcommand. RECORDS indicates the number of records per case for fixed-format files. (See Section 3.7.)

The TABLE and NOTABLE Subcommands. TABLE, the default for fixed-format files, prints a summary table describing file and and variable definitions. NOTABLE suppresses the summary table. (See Section 3.8.)

The commands

```
FILE HANDLE BALLOONS/ file specifications
DATA LIST  FILE=BALLOONS,FIXED RECORDS=1 TABLE/ COLOR 1 COUNT 2-5
```

define file handle BALLOONS, indicate fixed-format data, tell SPSS^X to expect one record per case, and request a summary table describing the DATA LIST specifications.

- Equals signs after the FILE and RECORDS subcommands are optional.
- FILE, FIXED, RECORDS, and TABLE specifications are separated by at least one blank or comma.
- FILE, FIXED, RECORDS, and TABLE specifications can appear in any order.

The FILE HANDLE and DATA LIST commands along with any operating-system commands are all you need to describe the file.

3.5 The FILE Subcommand

Use the FILE subcommand to specify the file handle for the data described by the DATA LIST command. The specification

```
FILE HANDLE HUBDATA/ file specifications
DATA LIST  FILE=HUBDATA RECORDS=3
  /1 YRHIRED 14-15 DEPT82 19 SEX 20
```

indicates that file HUBDATA is being described. You can omit the FILE subcommand only when the data are included with the SPSS^X commands (see Section 3.33).

3.6 Keywords FIXED, FREE, and LIST

Use one of the following keywords to indicate the format of the data:

FIXED *Fixed-format data.* Each variable is recorded in the same location on the same record for each case in the data. FIXED is the default.

FREE *Freefield-format data.* The variables are recorded in the same order for each case, but not necessarily in the same locations. You can enter multiple cases on the same record with each value separated by one or more blanks or commas.

LIST *Freefield data with one case on each record.* The variables are recorded in freefield format as described for keyword FREE except the variables for each case must be recorded on one record.

For example, to indicate explicitly that the HUBDATA file is in fixed format, specify:

```
FILE HANDLE HUBDATA/ file specifications
DATA LIST FILE=HUBDATA FIXED RECORDS=3
  /1 YRHIRED 14-15 DEPT82 19 SEX 20
```

Sections 3.7 and 3.8 describe two other file definition specifications on the DATA LIST command, the RECORDS, TABLE, and NOTABLE subcommands, which can be used only with fixed-format data. The variable definition specifications for fixed-format data are described in Sections 3.10 through 3.19. The variable definition specifications for FREE and LIST format data are described in Sections 3.20 and 3.21.

3.7 The RECORDS Subcommand

Use the RECORDS subcommand with fixed-format data to specify the number of records per case. The specification

```
FILE HANDLE HUBDATA/ file specifications
DATA LIST  FILE=HUBDATA RECORDS=3
  /1 YRHIRED 14-15 DEPT82 19 SEX 20
```

tells SPSS^X to expect three records per case in file HUBDATA.

By default, SPSS^X assumes one record per case for fixed-format data. Therefore, you must use the RECORDS subcommand if there are more. You should not use the RECORDS subcommand with freefield data (keywords LIST and FREE).

To maintain compatibility with earlier releases of SPSS, the number of records enclosed in parentheses is also acceptable syntax.

3.8 The TABLE and NOTABLE Subcommands

By default for fixed-format data, SPSS^X displays a table that summarizes your variable definitions immediately following your DATA LIST command (see Figure 3.8). The table includes the number of records per case along with the following information on each variable: the variable name, the record number, the starting and ending columns, the format, the width, and the number of decimal places. To suppress this table, specify subcommand NOTABLE, as in:

```
FILE HANDLE TESTDATA/ file specifications
DATA LIST  FILE=TESTDATA NOTABLE / X 1-2
```

Figure 3.8 DATA LIST summary table

```
 1 0          DATA LIST  FILE=TESTDATA / X 1-2
THE ABOVE DATA LIST STATEMENT WILL READ   1 RECORDS FROM FILE TESTDATA.
        VARIABLE  REC   START    END         FORMAT  WIDTH  DEC
        X           1       1      2         F           2    0
END OF DATALIST TABLE.
```

You can request explicitly the default summary table with the TABLE subcommand. Summary tables are not available with freefield data.

3.9 VARIABLE DEFINITION ON DATA LIST

Use the variable definition portion of the DATA LIST command to assign a name to each variable you intend to analyze and, depending on the format of your file, to provide information about the location and format of the individual variables. For fixed-format data, specify the record number, name, column location, and type of each variable as described in Sections 3.10 through 3.19. For FREE or LIST format data, specify the name and type of each variable as described in Sections 3.20 and 3.21.

3.10 Specifying the Record Number

Variable definition on the DATA LIST command begins with a slash. Following this slash, specify the sequence number of the first record from which you are defining variables. The specification

```
FILE HANDLE HUBDATA/ file specifications
DATA LIST  FILE=HUBDATA RECORDS=3
  /1 YRHIRED 14-15 DEPT82 19 SEX 20
```

indicates that the variables being defined are located on the first of the three records for each case. If you do not specify the record number, SPSS^X assumes that you are defining variables on the first (or only) record of each case.

You can omit the sequence number of the record and use the slash alone to define the record location. Each slash means "skip to the next record." In the above example, the record sequence number is not needed because variables defined after the first slash are located on the first record. Variables defined after the second slash are located on the second record, and so forth. See Section 3.39 for additional discussion of using slashes to skip records.

3.11 Naming the Variables

Assign a *variable name* to each variable that you describe. The specification

```
FILE HANDLE HUBDATA/ file specifications
DATA LIST  FILE=HUBDATA RECORDS=3
  /1 YRHIRED 14-15 DEPT82 19 SEX 20
```

defines three variables: year hired, department in 1982, and sex for each case on the file.

Variable names are used on all other SPSS^X commands to refer to the data values. Variable names have a maximum length of eight characters, the first of which must be an alphabetic letter or the characters @, #, or $. A # character in the first position of a variable name defines a scratch variable. A $ indicates the variable is a system variable. Scratch variables can be defined on the DATA LIST and used on the transformation commands but cannot be used by procedure commands or saved permanently on a system file. System variables cannot be named on the DATA LIST command and are not available for procedures. See Chapter 6 for a description of the use of scratch and system variables. All other rules and conventions for constructing names must be followed for variable names (see Chapter 2).

The name you give to a variable cannot duplicate that of any other variable named on the same DATA LIST command. You should select variable names that reflect the nature of the variables being named. For example, suppose that your data file contains information for individuals on income, occupation, and age. You could use the variable names INCOME, OCCUP, and AGE for these variables. Note that OCCUPATION cannot be used as a variable name since it is longer than eight characters.

The order in which variable names are mentioned on the DATA LIST command determines their order in the variable *dictionary*. If you save your active file as a system file, the variables will be saved in this order unless you explicitly reorder them (see Chapter 5).

3.12 Indicating Column Locations

Follow the name of the variable with its column location. If the variable is one column wide, specify the number of the column. If the variable is two or more columns wide, specify the number of the first column followed by a dash (–) and the number of the last column, as in:

```
FILE HANDLE HUBDATA/ file specifications
DATA LIST  FILE=HUBDATA RECORDS=3
  /1 YRHIRED 14-15 DEPT82 19 SEX 20
```

This command defines three variables on the first record of a data file with three records per case: variable YRHIRED is found in columns 14 and 15, DEPT82 in column 19, and SEX in column 20.

You do not need to define all of the variables in the data file—only those that you intend to use. SPSS^X ignores the data in columns and on records that you do not mention.

3.13 Specifying Multiple Records

Once you've specified variables from one record, enter a slash, followed by the record number of the next record to be read and the variable definitions for that record.

```
FILE HANDLE HUBDATA/ file specifications
DATA LIST  FILE=HUBDATA RECORDS=3
  /1 YRHIRED 14-15 DEPT82 19 SEX 20
  /2 SALARY82 21-25
```

Three variables, YRHIRED, DEPT82, and SEX, are located on the first record of the data file. One variable, SALARY82, will be read from columns 21 through 25 on the second record. The total number of records per case is specified as three, even though no variables are defined on the third record.

Define all variables you want to read from a given record before you proceed to the next record. However, within a record, you can define the same column location(s) as two different variables, and variables need not be defined in the same sequence as they are recorded on the file, as in:

```
FILE HANDLE HUBDATA/ file specifications
DATA LIST  FILE=HUBDATA RECORDS=3
  /1 DEPT82 19 SEX 20 YRHIRED 14-15 MOHIRED 12-13 HIRED 12-15
  /2 SALARY82 21-25
```

The first two defined variables are DEPT82 and SEX located in columns 19 and 20, respectively, on record 1. The next three variables, YRHIRED, MOHIRED, and HIRED, are also located on the first record. YRHIRED will be read from columns 14 and 15, MOHIRED from columns 12 and 13, and HIRED from columns 12 through 15. The HIRED variable is a four-column variable with the first two columns representing the month when an employee was hired (the same as the MOHIRED variable) and the last two columns representing the year of employment (the same as YRHIRED). The order of the variables in the dictionary is the order in which they are defined on the DATA LIST command, not their sequence on the input data file.

3.14 Specifying Multiple Variables

If several variables are recorded in adjacent columns of the same record and have the same width and format type, they can be defined on the DATA LIST in an abbreviated format. List all of the variable names followed by the beginning column location of the first variable in the list, a dash, and the ending column location of the last variable in the list, as in

```
FILE HANDLE HUBDATA/ file specifications
DATA LIST  FILE=HUBDATA RECORDS=3
  /1 DEPT82 19 SEX 20 MOHIRED YRHIRED 12-15
  /2 SALARY82 21-25
```

where MOHIRED and YRHIRED form a list of variables followed by the column specification for both. The DATA LIST command divides the total number of columns specified equally among the variables in the list. If the total number of columns is not an even multiple of the number of variables listed, SPSS^X prints an error message and continues scanning the commands that follow DATA LIST for syntax errors but does not read the data file.

The list of variable names can include both specific variable names and variable names defined using the TO keyword. For example, ITEM1 TO ITEM5 is equivalent to five names: ITEM1, ITEM2, ITEM3, ITEM4, and ITEM5. The prefix can be any valid name and the numbers can be any integers, so long as the first number is smaller than the second and the full variable name, including the number, does not exceed eight characters. Note that the number is a part of the variable name, not a subscript. If you include leading zeros in the number, they are preserved in the variable name. X1 TO X100 and X001 TO X100 both generate 100 variable names, but the first 99 names are not the same in the two lists. X01 TO X9 is not valid.

You can include both individual variable names and inclusive lists of variable names on a single DATA LIST command, as in:

```
FILE HANDLE HUBDATA/ file specifications
DATA LIST  FILE=HUBDATA RECORDS=3
  /1 MOHIRED YRHIRED 12-15 DEPT79 TO DEPT82 SEX 16-20
  /2 SALARY79 TO SALARY82 6-25
```

DEPT79, DEPT80, DEPT81, DEPT82, and SEX are defined as single-column variables located in columns 16 through 20 on the first record. SALARY79, SALARY80, SALARY81, and SALARY82 are defined as five-column variables located in columns 6 through 25 on the second record.

3.15 Indicating Decimal Places

By default, DATA LIST assumes that the data format type is numeric and either that the numbers are integer or that the decimal point has been recorded on the data file. To indicate noninteger values when the decimal point is not actually coded in the data, specify the number of *implied* decimal places in parentheses following the column specification. The specification

```
FILE HANDLE HUBDATA/ file specifications
DATA LIST  FILE=HUBDATA RECORDS=3
  /1 MOHIRED YRHIRED 12-15 DEPT79 TO DEPT82 SEX 16-20
  /2 SALARY79 TO SALARY82 6-25 HOURLY81 HOURLY82 42-53(2)
```

locates the variables that records the hourly wage of an employee for 1981 and 1982 in columns 42 through 47 and 48 through 53 on record two. The last two digits of both HOURLY81 and HOURLY82 will be stored as decimal positions. Any coded decimal point found in the data overrides the number of implied places defined on the DATA LIST command.

3.16 The Default Format Type

Only numeric values can be read with the default variable format type. The numeric values can be either signed or unsigned numbers and either integer or noninteger. All alphabetic characters and punctuation characters, except the decimal point and leading plus and minus signs, are considered undefined, and SPSS^X assigns the system-missing value when one of these characters is encountered (see Chapter 2). Blanks to the left or right of a number are ignored; embedded blanks are in error. By default, SPSS^X assigns the system-missing value to a completely blank field. You can change the value assigned to blank fields by specifying the subcommand BLANKS on the SET command (see Chapter 4).

Table 3.16 illustrates how values are interpreted for a four-column variable defined as the default format type (integer) and as the default format type with two decimal places defined.

Table 3.16 Default format type: values read by SPSS^X

Values in the data file	Integer (default)	Two decimal places
2001	2001	20.01
201	201	2.01
-201	-201	-2.01
2	2	.02
20	20	.20
2.2	2.2	2.2
.201	.201	.201
2 01	Undefined	Undefined

3.17 N and E Format Types

Two additional numeric formats that are commonly used are the N and E formats. The N, or restricted numeric, format reads unsigned integers. Leading, trailing, and embedded blanks are not allowed. Decimal points, either implied or coded in the data, are not allowed. This restricted numeric format is useful for reading and checking values that you know can be only integers with leading zeros.

The E, or scientific notation, format reads all forms of scientific notation numbers. The E or D preceding the exponent is not necessary if a sign is coded before the exponent. For example, the value 1−1 is read under E format as 1.0E−1. You can not code decimal points in the exponent portion of the number. However, decimal points can be coded in the number preceding the exponent. You can also specify implied decimal points.

3.18 String Variables

Another type of variable found in many data files is the *string variable*, also known as the alphanumeric or character variable. The format type specification for a string variable is the letter A enclosed in parentheses following the column specification, as in:

```
FILE HANDLE HUBDATA/ file specifications
DATA LIST  FILE=HUBDATA RECORDS=3
  /1 MOHIRED YRHIRED 12-15 DEPT79 TO DEPT82 SEX 16-20
  /2 SALARY79 TO SALARY82 6-25 HOURLY81 HOURLY82 42-53(2)
  /3 NAME 25-48 (A) NAMEFOUR 25-28 (A)
```

Two string variables are defined on the third record, NAME is the 24-character name of the employee and NAMEFOUR is the first four characters only of the name. On all computers, NAME would be considered a *long string variable* and NAMEFOUR a *short string variable*.

SPSS^X recognizes these two kinds of string variables based on the length of the variable. Names of individuals or places are usually long string variables. On the other hand, a variable SEX coded as M for male and F for female is a short string variable. The maximum length of short string variables depends on the computer at your installation. For example, short string variables have a maximum of 8 characters on an IBM computer and a maximum of 10 characters on a DEC 10 or DEC 20 computer. Any string variable longer than the maximum length allowed for short strings is considered a long string variable. The maximum length of a long string variable is 255 columns for most implementations of SPSS^X.

3.19 Other Format Types

Several format types are available on the DATA LIST command. Table 3.36a lists the most commonly used format types (shown in FORTRAN-like style). Additional format types that are available only for specific operating systems are described in supplemental documentation available with keyword LOCAL on the INFO command (see Chapter 2). All of the format types shown in Table 3.36a are implemented on the IBM/OS and IBM/CMS systems.

When you use the column style shown up to this point in this chapter (as opposed to the FORTRAN style shown in Sections 3.35 through 3.39), the default numeric format is F. You can specify any of the other format types enclosed in parentheses following the column specification. For example, the Z format is specified:

```
FILE HANDLE TESTDATA/ file specifications
DATA LIST FILE=TESTDATA/ ZTEST 3-6 (Z,2)
```

The 2 following the Z format type is the number of implied decimal places.

3.20 FREE and LIST Variable Definition

If you specify FREE or LIST in the file definition portion of your DATA LIST command, SPSS^X expects freefield-format data. Therefore, you do not specify the location of the variables on the variable definition portion of DATA LIST. Rather SPSS^X reads the values sequentially in the order that the variables are named on the DATA LIST command. The values must be separated in your data by at least one blank or comma.

Use the keyword FREE to read freefield-format data with multiple cases recorded on one record or with one case recorded on more than one record. Use the keyword LIST to read data with one case recorded on each record. If all of the values in your data are numeric, you simply list the variable names in the order that the values are recorded, as in:

```
FILE HANDLE WINS/ file specifications
DATA LIST FILE=WINS FREE/POSTPOS NWINS
```

Figure 3.20a shows the data in file WINS. All of the data are recorded on one record. The first two values build the first case in the active file. The value 2 is assigned to variable POSTPOS, and the value 19 to NWINS. The second case is built from the next two values in the data, and so forth. Eight cases are built on the active file.

Figure 3.20a Data in FREE format

```
2 19 7 5 10 25 5 17 8 11 3 18 6 8 1 29
```

In FREE format, the end of a data record is the same as a blank or comma. That is, a value cannot be split across records. However, multiple blank columns at the end of a record are interpreted as one delimiter between values.

Figure 3.20b shows the same data recorded in LIST format. Each case is recorded on a separate record. To read this data, specify the keyword LIST, as in:

```
FILE HANDLE WINSL/ file specifications
DATA LIST FILE=WINSL LIST/POSTPOS NWINS
```

Figure 3.20b Data in LIST format

```
2 19
7 5
10 25
5 17
8 11
3 18
6 8
1 29
```

The LIST format requires more records in your data file than the FREE format. However, it is less prone to errors in data entry. Since FREE format reads the data as one long series of numbers, if you leave out a value in the data, the values after the missing value are assigned to the incorrect variable for all remaining cases. Since LIST format reads a case from each record, the missing value will affect only the one case.

You cannot use a blank value to indicate missing information in FREE or LIST formatted data. Rather you must assign a value to the missing information and declare the value missing with the MISSING VALUES command (see Section 3.25).

3.21 Specifying Format Types

You can specify any of the FORTRAN-like format specifications described in Section 3.36 that are available on your implementation of SPSS^X. A specified format type applies only to the variable immediately preceding the format specification. If you specify a format type for any variable, you must specify an asterisk for all variables that you want read with the default format type. The asterisk applies to all variables named preceding it. For example, to explicitly specify the default format for variables POSTPOS and NWINS, specify:

```
FILE HANDLE WINS/ file specifications
DATA LIST FILE=WINS FREE/POSTPOS NWINS *
```

To specify a string variable, you must specify the format type A and the maximum length occurring in your data enclosed in parentheses after the name of the string variable, as in:

```
FILE HANDLE WINS/ file specifications
DATA LIST FILE=WINS FREE/POSTPOS NWINS * POSNAME (A24)
```

The variable POSNAME is specified as a 24-character string. The asterisk specifies that the variables POSTPOS and NWINS are to be read with the default format type.

If the string in your data is longer than the specified length, the string is truncated and a warning message is printed. If the string in your data is shorter, it is right-padded with blanks, and no warning message is printed. You must enclose the string in your data in apostrophes or quotation marks if the string contains a blank or a comma. Otherwise, the blank or comma is treated as a delimiter between values. You can include apostrophes in a string enclosed in quotation marks, or quotation marks in a string enclosed in apostrophes.

3.22 Undefined Data Values

When SPSS^X encounters a value that it cannot read according to the format type specified, it must consider the value undefined and must assign the system-missing value. SPSS^X prints a warning message when an undefined value is encountered and continues reading the file. The default limit is 80 undefined values per job. However, you can use the MXWARNS subcommand on the SET command to change this limit and the UNDEFINED subcommand to suppress the warning messages (see Chapter 4).

3.23 Printing and Writing Formats

For every permanent variable in your file, SPSS^X stores in the variable dictionary formats that are then used to print and write out the values. The default dictionary formats are based on the format type used on the DATA LIST command to read the data, and this is usually what you want. If you use the default numeric format on FREE or LIST, the print and write format is set to F8.2 or the format indicated by the FORMAT subcommand on the SET command (see Chapter 4). If you have decimal points coded in your data, you may need to change the dictionary formats depending on the format that you used to read the variable. To change the dictionary formats, use the PRINT FORMATS command to change the printing format, the WRITE FORMATS command to change the writing format, and the FORMATS command to change both (see Chapter 9).

3.24 MISSING VALUES

Very often, your data file lacks complete information on some cases for some variables. Monitoring equipment can malfunction, interviewers can forget to ask a question or record an answer, respondents can refuse to answer, data can be entered incorrectly, and so forth. *Missing* does not always mean the same as unknown or absent. In order to distinguish why information is missing, you can instruct SPSS^X to consider more than one value missing for each variable. For example, if you code the value 9 for "Refused to answer" and the value 0 for "No answer reported," you might want to specify both of these values as missing.

The MISSING VALUES command declares the missing values for certain variables in your file. The values defined as missing values are never changed on the data; they are simply flagged in the dictionary of the active file and, if the active file is saved as a system file, in the dictionary of the system file. The SPSS^X statistical procedures and transformation commands recognize this flag, and those cases that contain a user-defined missing value are handled specially. Although all SPSS^X statistical procedures provide options for handling cases with missing values, the exact nature of the options depends on the statistical procedure.

User-missing values defined on the MISSING VALUES command are distinguished from the *system-missing value*. SPSS^X assigns the system-missing value when a value in your data is undefined according to the format type that you have specified (Section 3.22), when a numeric field is blank for the default format type (Section 3.16), or when a value resulting from a transformation command like COMPUTE is undefined (Chapter 6).

3.25 The MISSING VALUES Command

The MISSING VALUES command consists of the command keywords MISSING VALUES followed by a variable name or variable list and the specified missing value or values, as in:

```
DATA LIST  FILE=BALLOONS/ COLOR 1 COUNT 2-5
MISSING VALUES COUNT(9999) COLOR(8,9)
```

This command names 9999 as the missing value for variable COUNT and 8 and 9 for variable COLOR.

- You can specify missing values for any variable previously defined on a DATA LIST command or a transformation command, except long strings (Section 3.18) and scratch variables (Chapter 6).
- You can specify a maximum of three individual values for each variable.
- Enclose the values that you want to define as missing for a variable in parentheses and separate the values from each other by a comma or blank.

For example, if you conduct a survey and ask the respondents to report their income level, some respondents may refuse to answer the question, others may indicate that they do not know, and some respondents may simply neglect to fill in an answer. In this instance, you might code 9 for "Refused to answer," 8 for "Don't know," and 0 for "No answer." To declare all of these values as missing data for the variable INCOME, specify:

```
MISSING VALUES  INCOME (0,8,9)
```

To declare a large number of values as missing, you can either specify a range as shown in Section 3.27 or use the transformation language to change the values to a single value and declare that value missing, as in:

```
RECODE X(LO THRU 0=0)
MISSING VALUES X (0)
```

The RECODE command recodes negative values to 0 (Chapter 6) and the MISSING VALUES command declares 0 missing.

3.26 Referencing Several Variables

You can define missing values for more than one variable on a MISSING VALUES command either by specifying a variable list when the missing values are the same for all variables in the list or by specifying several sets of variable names and missing-value specifications when the values are different.

To define the same missing values for several variables, list all of the variables followed by the missing-value specification. Consecutive variables on your active file as defined on the DATA LIST command can be referenced using the keyword TO. For example, to declare the value 0 as missing for all the variables defined on the DATA LIST beginning with DEPT79 through SALARY82 and for the variable AGE, specify:

```
FILE HANDLE HUBDATA/ file specifications
DATA LIST  FILE=HUBDATA RECORDS=3
  /1 MOHIRED YRHIRED 12-15 DEPT79 TO DEPT82 SEX 16-20
  /2 SALARY79 TO SALARY82 6-25 HOURLY81 HOURLY82 42-53(2)
     AGE 54-55 RAISE82 66-70
  /3 JOBCAT 6
MISSING VALUES  DEPT79 TO SALARY82, AGE (0)
```

To define different missing values for other variables in your file, specify the additional variables and their missing-value specifications, as in:

```
FILE HANDLE HUBDATA/ file specifications
DATA LIST  FILE=HUBDATA RECORDS=3
  /1 MOHIRED YRHIRED 12-15 DEPT79 TO DEPT82 SEX 16-20
  /2 SALARY79 TO SALARY82 6-25 HOURLY81 HOURLY82 42-53(2)
     AGE 54-55 RAISE82 66-70
  /3 JOBCAT 6
MISSING VALUES  DEPT79 TO SALARY82, AGE (0)
  HOURLY81, HOURLY82, RAISE82 (-999) JOBCAT (9)
```

You can continue this process of specifying variables and missing values on one or more MISSING VALUES commands.

To declare the same missing values for all of the variables on your active file, specify the keyword ALL followed by the missing-value specification, as in:

```
MISSING VALUES  ALL (0)
```

Note that all your variables must be numeric or all must be string; otherwise keyword ALL will cause errors since the value specified will inevitably not correspond to one type or the other.

If you accidentally name the same variable on two MISSING VALUES commands, the second specification overrides the first (see Section 3.29).

3.27 Specifying Ranges of Missing Values

You can specify a range of values as missing for numeric variables but not for string variables. Use keyword THRU to indicate an inclusive list of values. For example, 0 THRU 1.5 includes the values 0 through (and including) 1.5. The values must be separated from THRU by at least one blank space. Use keywords HIGHEST and LOWEST with THRU to indicate the highest and lowest values of a variable. The command

```
MISSING VALUES  RAISE82 (LOWEST THRU 0)
```

defines all negative values and 0 as missing for variable RAISE82.

- Keywords HIGHEST and LOWEST can be abbreviated to HI and LO, respectively.
- Only one THRU specification can be used for each variable list.
- The THRU specification can be combined with one individual value in each missing-value specification, as in:

```
MISSING VALUES RAISE82 (LO THRU 0, 999)
```

Only three values, including the values on each side of the keyword THRU and the keywords HIGHEST and LOWEST, can be specified.

3.28 Missing Values for String Variables

You can define missing values for short string variables but not for long strings. To specify a value of a short string variable, enclose the value in apostrophes or quotation marks. The command

```
MISSING VALUES  STRING1 ('X','Y')
```

specifies the values X and Y as missing for a single-column string variable STRING1.

The exact value of the string including blanks must be enclosed in apostrophes or quotation marks. For example, to indicate the value X recorded in the right-most position of a three-column string variable, specify the value as ' X'. A value longer or shorter than the length of the variable will not match.

Value ranges cannot be specified for short string variables. You cannot use the keywords THRU, HIGHEST, or LOWEST with missing-value specifications for string variables.

3.29 Redefining Missing Values

After saving a system file that includes missing-value flags for some variables, you may decide that you want to change these definitions for some variables. You can define new missing values or delete the flags for all previously defined missing values using the MISSING VALUES command.

To delete the flags for all previously defined missing values, specify no values in the missing-value specification. For example, to delete all the flags for previously defined missing values for the variables SALARY79 TO SALARY82, specify:

```
MISSING VALUES  SALARY79 TO SALARY82 ()
```

Missing-value specifications for a variable on a MISSING VALUES command replace all of the previously defined missing values for that variable. For example, the command

```
MISSING VALUES ALL(0)
```

declares 0 as the *only* user-missing value for all variables, overriding all previous declarations.

3.30 VARIABLE AND VALUE LABELS

Although you can construct variable names to represent what the variable actually measures, it is sometimes difficult to fully describe a variable in an eight-character name. Likewise, values of variables sometimes have no apparent meaning by themselves. Use one or more VARIABLE LABELS commands to assign labels to variables in your file, and one or more VALUE LABELS commands to assign labels to values of variables. SPSS^X displays these variable and value labels on the output produced by the procedures and saves them in the dictionary of the active file.

Labels in SPSS^X are specified as *literals*. In the command

```
VARIABLE LABELS  SALARY82 'SALARY IN 1982'
```

the label for variable SALARY82 is specified as the literal "SALARY IN 1982."

- Enclose literals within apostrophes or quotation marks, using the same symbol to begin and end the literal.
- Enter an apostrophe as part of a label by enclosing the literal in quotation marks or by entering the apostrophe twice with no separation.

For example, the command

```
VARIABLE LABELS  SALARY82 "EMPLOYEE'S YEARLY SALARY IN 1982"
```

is the same as

```
VARIABLE LABELS  SALARY82 'EMPLOYEE''S YEARLY SALARY IN 1982'
```

Quotation marks are entered in a label in the same manner. A label cannot be continued from one command line to the next as the same literal. However, literals can be concatenated using the plus sign, where

```
VARIABLE LABELS  SALARY82 'EMPLOYEE''S YEARLY SALARY IN'
   + ' 1982' YRHIRED 'YEAR OF FIRST HIRING'
```

assigns labels to variables SALARY82 and YRHIRED. The label for the first variable is the result of concatenating two literals with the plus sign. The blank between IN and 1982 must be included in the first or second literal to be included in the label.

3.31 The VARIABLE LABELS Command

Use the VARIABLE LABELS command to assign an extended descriptive label to variables. Specify the variable name followed by at least one comma or blank and the associated label enclosed in apostrophes or quotation marks, as in:

```
VARIABLE LABELS  YRHIRED 'YEAR OF FIRST HIRING'
  DEPT82 'DEPARTMENT OF EMPLOYMENT IN 1982'
  SALARY82 'YEARLY SALARY IN 1982'
  JOBCAT 'JOB CATEGORIES'
```

This command assigns variable labels to the variables YRHIRED, DEPT82, SALARY82, and JOBCAT.

- A variable label applies to only one variable.
- The variable must have been previously defined, either on a DATA LIST command or on a transformation command.
- Each variable label can be up to 40 characters long and can include blanks and any character.

To maintain compatibility with earlier releases of SPSS, the command VAR LABELS is accepted and the label need not be enclosed in apostrophes. If you use this syntax, the variable name must be separated from the label by at least one blank space or comma, and each variable and its label must be separated from the next variable and its label by a slash. The variable label specified in this manner cannot contain slashes and cannot begin with a quotation mark or an apostrophe.

3.32 The VALUE LABELS Command

Use the VALUE LABELS command to provide descriptive labels for values. The VALUE LABELS command is followed by a variable name, or variable list, and a list of the values with their associated labels. The command

```
VALUE LABELS  DEPT82  0 'NOT REPORTED' 1 'ADMINISTRATIVE'
         2 'PROJECT DIRECTORS' 3 'CHICAGO OPERATIONS'
         4 'ST LOUIS OPERATIONS'/
```

assigns labels to the values 0, 1, 2, 3, and 4 of DEPT82.

- You can assign labels to values of any previously defined variable.
- Enclose each value label in apostrophes or quotation marks.
- Value labels cannot exceed 20 characters and can contain any characters including blanks.

Value labels are automatically displayed on the output from many procedures and are saved in the dictionary of a system file. It is not necessary to enter value labels for all of the variables or values in your file. In some instances, the value itself is completely descriptive, such as the values for SALARY82.

Although the maximum length for a value label is 20 characters, some procedures print fewer than 20 characters for each label. See especially the CROSSTABS procedure in Chapter 20.

To assign the same labels to the same values of several variables, list all of the variables followed by the values and associated labels. Also, additional sets of variable names and value labels can be specified on the same command, as in:

```
VALUE LABELS  DEPT79 TO DEPT82  0 'NOT REPORTED' 1 'ADMINISTRATIVE'
         2 'PROJECT DIRECTORS' 3 'CHICAGO OPERATIONS'
         4 'ST LOUIS OPERATIONS'/
  SEX 1 'MALE' 2 'FEMALE'/
  JOBCAT 1 'OFFICIALS & MANAGERS' 2 'PROFESSIONALS' 3 'TECHNICIANS'
         4 'OFFICE AND CLERICAL' 5 'CRAFTSMEN' 6 'SERVICE WORKERS'
```

The slash is required to separate value labels for one variable or variable list from the next variable or variable list.

You can assign value labels to short string variables but not to long string variables. To specify a value of a short string variable, enclose the value in apostrophes. For example, to assign labels to the values for string variable JOBGRADE, specify:

```
FILE HANDLE CHIGHOME/ file specifications
DATA LIST  FILE=CHIGHOME/JOBGRADE 43 (A)
VALUE LABELS JOBGRADE 'X' 'SALES STAFF'   'S' 'SUPERVISORY STAFF'
                      'M' 'MANAGERIAL STAFF'  'C' 'SUPPORT STAFF'
```

The exact alphanumeric value, including blanks, must be enclosed in apostrophes.

If you assign value labels to any variable that already has value labels assigned to it, the new assignment completely replaces the old assignment. Value labels specifications are not additive.

To maintain compatibility with earlier releases of SPSS, the value can be enclosed in parentheses and the label need not be enclosed in apostrophes. If you use this syntax, the slash separating the sets of value labels is required, and slashes or parentheses cannot be included in the label.

3.33 INPUT DATA IN THE COMMAND FILE

If your input data are included as lines in your SPSS^X command file, you can omit the FILE subcommand on the DATA LIST command or specify the default FILE=INLINE. Two additional SPSS^X commands are required to separate lines containing data from lines containing SPSS^X commands: BEGIN DATA and END DATA.

3.34 The BEGIN DATA and END DATA Commands

The BEGIN DATA command must be entered immediately before the first line of in-line data and the END DATA command must be entered immediately after the last line of data. Figure 3.34a shows a complete SPSS^X command file with the data included in the file.

Figure 3.34a Input data in the SPSS^X command file

```
DATA LIST /NTCPRI NTCSAL NTCPUR RENT 5-16 WORLD 18 CONT 20
  NAME 24-37 (A)
VARIABLE LABELS NTCPRI 'NET PRICE LEVEL'
  NTCSAL 'NET SALARY'
  NTCPUR 'NET PURCHASING LEVEL'
  RENT 'NORMAL RENT'
  WORLD 'ECONOMIC CLASS FOR COUNTRY'
  CONT 'CONTINENT'
VALUE LABELS  WORLD 1 '1ST WORLD' 2 'PETROWORLD' 3 '3RD WORLD'/
  CONT 1 'N EUROPE' 2 'S EUROPE' 3 'MEDITERRANEAN'
   4 'MIDEAST' 5 'ASIA' 6 'AFRICA' 7 'AUSTRALIA'
   8 'N AMERICA' 9 'S AMERICA'
MISSING VALUES NTCPRI TO CONT (0)

CROSSTABS VARIABLES=WORLD BY CONT
OPTIONS 3,4

BEGIN DATA
01   125 46 27403 2 4   ABU DHABI
02    79 68 86 76 1 1   AMSTERDAM
03    78 34 32 97 3 3   ATHENS
04   124 49 29440 2 4   BAHRAIN
 .
 .
 .
44    78 59 75 40 1 1   VIENNA
45   100100100100 1 1   ZURICH
END DATA
```

In Figure 3.34a, the file definition portion of the DATA LIST command is not needed because the data are contained in the default format of one record per case. In this case, the first specification on the DATA LIST command must be the slash that begins variable definitions.

You can use the BEGIN DATA command followed by the lines of data and the END DATA command without a procedure command. If used without a procedure command, the BEGIN DATA command causes SPSS^X to read the data. If SPSS^X procedure commands are included in the job, the BEGIN DATA command followed by the lines of data and the END DATA command should follow the first SPSS^X procedure command and any associated OPTIONS and STATISTICS commands. In the example in Figure 3.34a, the CROSSTABS procedure is used. However, any of the statistical procedures documented in Chapters 18 through 40 can be used. Additional transformation and procedure commands can follow the END DATA command.

Figure 3.34b Display output produced by Figure 3.34a

```
- - - - - - - - - - - - - - - -  C R O S S T A B U L A T I O N   O F   - - - - - - - - - - - - - - - -
   WORLD      ECONOMIC CLASS FOR COUNTRY                     BY  CONT       CONTINENT
- - - - - - - - - - - - - - - - - - - - - - - - - - - - - - - - - - - - - - - - - - - -  PAGE  1 OF  1

                  CONT
         COUNT   |
        ROW PCT  |N EUROPE MEDITERR MIDEAST  ASIA     AFRICA   AUSTRALI N AMERIC S AMERIC   ROW
        COL PCT  |         ANEAN                               A        A        A          TOTAL
                 |       1|       3|       4|       5|       6|       7|       8|       9|
WORLD    --------+--------+--------+--------+--------+--------+--------+--------+--------+
             1   |    13  |     1  |     1  |     2  |     1  |     1  |     6  |        |     25
  1ST WORLD      |  52.0  |   4.0  |   4.0  |   8.0  |   4.0  |   4.0  |  24.0  |        |   55.6
                 |  92.9  |  20.0  |  20.0  |  33.3  | 100.0  | 100.0  | 100.0  |        |
                 +--------+--------+--------+--------+--------+--------+--------+--------+
             2   |        |        |     4  |     1  |        |        |        |     2  |      7
  PETROWORLD     |        |        |  57.1  |  14.3  |        |        |        |  28.6  |   15.6
                 |        |        |  80.0  |  16.7  |        |        |        |  28.6  |
                 +--------+--------+--------+--------+--------+--------+--------+--------+
             3   |     1  |     4  |        |     3  |        |        |        |     5  |     13
  3RD WORLD      |   7.7  |  30.8  |        |  23.1  |        |        |        |  38.5  |   28.9
                 |   7.1  |  80.0  |        |  50.0  |        |        |        |  71.4  |
                 +--------+--------+--------+--------+--------+--------+--------+--------+
          COLUMN      14        5        5        6        1        1        6        7        45
           TOTAL    31.1     11.1     11.1     13.3      2.2      2.2     13.3     15.6     100.0

NUMBER OF MISSING OBSERVATIONS =        0
```

Figure 3.34b shows the display output produced by the CROSSTABS command in the SPSS^X command file in Figure 3.34a. Notice that the variable and value labels assigned to WORLD and CONT are automatically displayed on the table. See Chapter 20 for a detailed description of the CROSSTABS procedure.

3.35 FORTRAN-LIKE FORMAT SPECIFICATIONS ON DATA LIST

An optional syntax for the variable definition portion of the DATA LIST command describes the format type and location of each variable using FORTRAN-like format definitions enclosed in parentheses. The column syntax described in Sections 3.9 through 3.19 is more straightforward and easier to use, but the FORTRAN-like formats may be more convenient in some situations.

The variable names are constructed in the same way as described in Section 3.11 and the order of the variable names on the DATA LIST command determines their sequence in the active file. The type and location of each variable are described using FORTRAN-like format elements rather than directly specifying the column location and format type. The number of variables named must be equal to the number of data format elements.

3.36 Format Elements

Each format element defines the type of variable, the width of the variable, and, if applicable, the number of decimal places. The format types are described here in their FORTRAN style, but they can also be used in the column style as shown in Section 3.19. Table 3.36a lists the format elements available in the IBM/OS and IBM/CMS implementations of SPSS^X and the maximum total width and decimal width available for each. Most of these formats are available for most implementations of SPSS^X. See the supplemental documentation available with the LOCAL subcommand on the INFO command for a description of the formats available and the width and decimal ranges for your computer (see Chapter 1).

Two special positioning format elements, T and X (available only in FORTRAN-like format specifications), skip columns in the data records and are necessary to describe the location of variables when you do not want to read the entire record. The T and X elements are discussed in Section 3.37.

The F format element is equivalent to the default format type in the column syntax described earlier in this chapter. The syntax for the F element is F*w.d*, where *w* specifies the width of the variable and *d* specifies the number of implied decimal places. For example, the format element F2.0 defines a two-column integer variable and F2.1 defines a two-column variable with one implied decimal position. The *d* specification is optional for integer variables—F2 is equivalent to F2.0. Any decimal coded in the data overrides the number of places defined by the format element. For example,

```
FILE HANDLE BALLOONS/ file specifications
DATA LIST  FILE=BALLOONS/ COLOR (F1)
```

defines variable COLOR as a one-column numeric variable coded in column 1.

The syntax of the format elements for all printable numeric format types is the same as for the F format element. For formats IB, PIB, P, and PK, the total width is specified in bytes and the decimal positions in digits. The format elements A and AHEX for string variables and the RB, PIBHEX, and RBHEX formats for numeric variables do not permit the specification of implied decimal positions. Blank fields read with any of the printable numeric formats are set to system-missing by default or to the value

Table 3.36a Data formats

Description	Format	Width range	Decimal range	Input blank
Printable numeric formats				
Standard numeric	Fw.d, Fw	1-40	d<min(w,17)	SET
Restricted numeric	Nw	1-40		SET
Scientific notation	Ew.d	1-40	d<min(w,17)	SET
	Ew	1-40	d=0	SET
Commas in numbers	COMMAw.d	1-40	d<min(w,17)	SET
	COMMAw	1-40	d=0	SET
Dollar sign, comma	DOLLARw.d	1-40	d<min(w,17)	SET
	DOLLARw	1-40	d=0	SET
Hexadecimal of PIB	PIBHEXw	2-8(even)		SET
Hexadecimal of RB	RBHEXw	4-16(even)		SET
Zoned decimal	Zw.d	1-40	d<min(w,17)	SET
	Zw	1-40	d=0	SET
Nonprintable numeric formats				
Integer binary	IBw.d	1-8	d<10	value
	IBw	1-8	d=0	value
Positive integer binary	PIBw.d	1-8	d<10	value
	PIBw	1-8	d=0	value
Packed decimal	Pw.d	1-16	d<min(2w-1,17)	SET
	Pw	1-16	d=0	SET
Unsigned packed	PKw.d	1-16	d<min(2w,17)	value
	PKw	1-16	d=0	value
Real binary	RBw	2-8(even)		64/255
String formats				
Standard character	Aw	1-255		
Hexadecimal character	AHEXw	1-510		

specified on the BLANK subcommand on the SET command (see Chapter 4). For many of the unprintable numeric formats, a blank field is read as as a valid value.

If two or more variables are recorded in adjacent columns of the same record and have the same format type, width, and number of implied decimal places, they can be defined by specifying the number of adjacent variables before the format element. For example, to define 20 adjacent single-column integer variables, specify 20F1.0.

Several format elements can be combined into a *format list* within the same set of parentheses to define a list of variables. The variable list can include individual variable names and variable names defined using the TO keyword (see Section 3.14). The format element or format list enclosed in parentheses follows the variable name or variable list to which it applies. For example, to define the variables, MOHIRED, YRHIRED, and DEPT79 through DEPT82, specify:

```
FILE HANDLE HUBDATA/ file specifications
DATA LIST  FILE=HUBDATA RECORDS=3
  /MOHIRED, YRHIRED, DEPT79 TO DEPT82 (T12,2F2.0,4F1.0)
```

All of the defined variables are located on record 1. The T12 format element in the format list positions the next data format element in column 12 (see Section 3.37). The first variable, MOHIRED, is a two-column integer variable located in columns 12 and 13. The second variable, YRHIRED, also a two-column integer variable, is located in columns 14 and 15. The next four variables, DEPT79 through DEPT82, are single-column variables located in columns 16 through 19.

3.37 The T and X Format Elements

Use the T and X format elements to skip columns that you do not want to define. The element T*n* tabs to the column number specified by *n*. The next format element defines the variable to be read beginning in that column. For example, to define a variable MOHIRED located in columns 12 and 13, specify:

```
FILE HANDLE HUBDATA/ file specifications
DATA LIST  FILE=HUBDATA RECORDS=3
  /MOHIRED (T12,F2.0)
```

The element *n*X skips *n* columns. The next format element defines the variable to be read beginning with the column *following* the skip. The above DATA LIST can be specified using the X element, as in:

```
FILE HANDLE HUBDATA/ file specifications
DATA LIST  FILE=HUBDATA RECORDS=3
  /MOHIRED (11X,F2.0)
```

The T format element can be used to move backward and forward within the same record, as in:

```
FILE HANDLE HUBDATA/ file specifications
DATA LIST  FILE=HUBDATA RECORDS=3
  /DEPT82 (T19,F1.0) MOHIRED (T12,F2.0)
```

The first defined variable is DEPT82 located in column 19 on record 1. The second variable is MOHIRED located in columns 12 and 13 on record 1.

3.38 Mixing Styles

You can mix FORTRAN-like and column format specifications in the same DATA LIST, as in:

```
FILE HANDLE HUBDATA/ file specifications
DATA LIST FILE=HUBDATA RECORDS=3
  /DEPT82 (T19,F1.0) YRHIRED 14-15
```

One style might be convenient for one set of variables and not for another. For example, if you have a repeating pattern that causes you to skip columns, the FORTRAN-like formats may help, as in

```
FILE HANDLE TESTDATA/ file specifications
DATA LIST FILE=TESTDATA
  /SCORE1 TO SCORE5 (T10,5(F2.0,1X))
```

which reads variable SCORE1 from columns 10 and 11, SCORE2 from columns 13 and 14, and so forth, skipping columns 12, 15, and so forth.

3.39 Skipping Records

If your data file has multiple records per case, you can use the slash to skip to the next record, rather than explicitly specifying the record sequence number. For example, to define the variable YRHIRED located on record 1 and the variable NAME located on record 3, specify:

```
FILE HANDLE HUBDATA/ file specifications
DATA LIST  FILE=HUBDATA RECORDS=3
  /YRHIRED 14-15 //NAME 25-48 (A)
```

Format elements can be used with slashes to define these variables, as in:

```
FILE HANDLE HUBDATA/ file specifications
DATA LIST  FILE=HUBDATA RECORDS=3
  /YRHIRED (T14,F2.0)// NAME (T25,A24)
```

Alternatively, the complete format list can follow the list of variables, as in:

```
FILE HANDLE HUBDATA/ file specifications
DATA LIST  FILE=HUBDATA RECORDS=3
  /YRHIRED NAME (T14,F2.0//T25,A24)
```

ANNOTATED EXAMPLE FOR DATA DEFINITIONS

The task developed in Sections 3.5 through 3.32 is to define the variables of interest and to produce basic tables from a personnel file for the fictitious Hubbard Consultants Inc.

```
FILE HANDLE HUBDATA/NAME='HUBDATA DATA A'
DATA LIST  FILE=HUBDATA RECORDS=3
  /1 EMPLOYID 1-5 MOHIRED YRHIRED 12-15 DEPT79 TO DEPT82 SEX 16-20
  /2 SALARY79 TO SALARY82 6-25 HOURLY81 HOURLY82 42-53(2) PROMO81 72
     AGE 54-55 RAISE82 66-70
  /3 JOBCAT 6 NAME 25-48 (A)

MISSING VALUES  DEPT79 TO SALARY82, AGE (0)
  HOURLY81, HOURLY82, RAISE82 (-999) JOBCAT (9)

VARIABLE LABELS  YRHIRED 'YEAR OF FIRST HIRING'
  DEPT82 'DEPARTMENT OF EMPLOYMENT IN 1982'
  SALARY82 'YEARLY SALARY IN 1982'
  JOBCAT 'JOB CATEGORIES'

VALUE LABELS  DEPT79 TO DEPT82  0 'NOT REPORTED' 1 'ADMINISTRATIVE'
        2 'PROJECT DIRECTORS' 3 'CHICAGO OPERATIONS'
        4 'ST LOUIS OPERATIONS'/
  SEX 1 'MALE' 2 'FEMALE'/
  JOBCAT 1 'OFFICIALS & MANAGERS' 2 'PROFESSIONALS' 3 'TECHNICIANS'
        4 'OFFICE AND CLERICAL' 5 'CRAFTSMEN' 6 'SERVICE WORKERS'

FREQUENCIES  VARIABLES=DEPT82,SEX,JOBCAT
```

- The FILE HANDLE command assigns the file handle HUBDATA to the data file and supplies the necessary operating-system specifications for the file. This example uses the IBM/CMS file specifications (see Section 3.2).
- The first line of the DATA LIST command names the HUBDATA file handle pointing to the data file (see Sections 3.2 and 3.5). The RECORDS subcommand tells SPSS^X to expect three records per employee (see Section 3.7).
- The second line of the DATA LIST command defines variables from the first record (see Section 3.10). The employee identification number is found in the first five columns. Variables MOHIRED and YRHIRED, for month and year of hiring, are found in columns 12 through 15, which SPSS^X understands to mean that MOHIRED is in columns 12 and 13 of record 1 and YRHIRED is in columns 14 and 15 (see Section 3.14). Variable DEPT79, implied variables DEPT80 and DEPT81, variable DEPT82, and variable SEX are single-column variables found in columns 16 through 20.
- The DATA LIST command continues with record 2 which names nine variables. First are four salary variables of five columns each. The next two variables, HOURLY81 and HOURLY82 (representing hourly wages), are in columns 42 through 47 and 48 through 53. The last two positions of HOURLY81 and HOURLY82 are to be considered decimal places (see Section 3.15). The final three variables defined on the second record are PROMO81 in column 72, AGE in columns 54 through 55, and RAISE82 in columns 66 through 70.
- The last line of the DATA LIST command defines two variables: a single-numeric job-category variable in column 6 of record 3, and the employee name, which is in the 24 columns from 25 through 48, and is alphanumeric. The latter is a long string variable in SPSS^X (see Section 3.18).
- The first line of the MISSING VALUES command flags 0 as the missing value for variables defined between DEPT79 and SALARY82 and for SEX (see Sections 3.25 through 3.27). The second line flags -999 as missing for HOURLY81, HOURLY82, and RAISE82, and 9 as missing for job category.

- The VARIABLE LABELS command assigns labels to four variables (see Section 3.31), and the VALUE LABELS command assigns labels to the values of the four department variables, sex, and job category (see Section 3.32).
- The FREQUENCIES command requests tables for three variables (see Chapter 18). These tables are shown in Figure B. The labels assigned for the variables are displayed in the tables. Value 0 for DEPT82 is marked as a missing value.

Figure A shows the first display page from SPSS^{X}. In particular, notice the summary table produced from the DATA LIST command (see Section 3.8). The F format item indicates the default numeric format.

A Display results from definition commands

```
1 0        FILE HANDLE HUBDATA/NAME='HUBDATA DATA A'
2 0        DATA LIST  FILE=HUBDATA RECORDS=3
3 0          /1 EMPLOYID 1-5 MOHIRED YRHIRED 12-15 DEPT79 TO DEPT82 SEX 16-20
4 0          /2 SALARY79 TO SALARY82 6-25 HOURLY81 HOURLY82 42-53(2) PROMO81 72
5 0             AGE 54-55 RAISE82 66-70
6 0          /3 JOBCAT 6 NAME 25-48 (A)
7 0
```

THE ABOVE DATA LIST STATEMENT WILL READ 3 RECORDS FROM FILE HUBDATA .

VARIABLE	REC	START	END	FORMAT	WIDTH	DEC
EMPLOYID	1	1	5	F	5	0
MOHIRED	1	12	13	F	2	0
YRHIRED	1	14	15	F	2	0
DEPT79	1	16	16	F	1	0
DEPT80	1	17	17	F	1	0
DEPT81	1	18	18	F	1	0
DEPT82	1	19	19	F	1	0
SEX	1	20	20	F	1	0
SALARY79	2	6	10	F	5	0
SALARY80	2	11	15	F	5	0
SALARY81	2	16	20	F	5	0
SALARY82	2	21	25	F	5	0
HOURLY81	2	42	47	F	6	2
HOURLY82	2	48	53	F	6	2
PROMO81	2	72	72	F	1	0
AGE	2	54	55	F	2	0
RAISE82	2	66	70	F	5	0
JOBCAT	3	6	6	F	1	0
NAME	3	25	48	A	24	

END OF DATALIST TABLE.

B FREQUENCIES tables

DEPT82 DEPARTMENT OF EMPLOYMENT IN 1982

VALUE LABEL	VALUE	FREQUENCY	PERCENT	VALID PERCENT	CUM PERCENT
ADMINISTRATIVE	1	34	12.4	23.4	23.4
PROJECT DIRECTORS	2	22	8.0	15.2	38.6
CHICAGO OPERATIONS	3	60	21.8	41.4	80.0
ST LOUIS OPERATIONS	4	29	10.5	20.0	100.0
NOT REPORTED	0	130	47.3	MISSING	
	TOTAL	275	100.0	100.0	

VALID CASES 145 MISSING CASES 130

SEX

VALUE LABEL	VALUE	FREQUENCY	PERCENT	VALID PERCENT	CUM PERCENT
MALE	1	83	30.2	30.2	30.2
FEMALE	2	192	69.8	69.8	100.0
	TOTAL	275	100.0	100.0	

VALID CASES 275 MISSING CASES 0

JOBCAT JOB CATEGORIES

VALUE LABEL	VALUE	FREQUENCY	PERCENT	VALID PERCENT	CUM PERCENT
OFFICIALS & MANAGERS	1	48	17.5	17.5	17.5
PROFESSIONALS	2	62	22.5	22.5	40.0
TECHNICIANS	3	98	35.6	35.6	75.6
OFFICE AND CLERICAL	4	67	24.4	24.4	100.0
	TOTAL	275	100.0	100.0	

VALID CASES 275 MISSING CASES 0

4

TITLE ['] text [']

SUBTITLE ['] text [']

COMMENT text

FINISH

{**NUMBERED** | **UNNUMBERED**}

SET [BLANKS = {**SYSMIS** | value}] [CASE = {**UPPER** | UPLOW}] [COMPRESSION = {**OFF** | ON}]

[FORMAT = {**F8.2** | format}] [LENGTH = {**59** | integer | NONE}] [MXERRS = {**40** | integer}]

[MXLOOPS = {**40** | integer}] [MXWARNS = {**80** | integer}] [PRINTBACK = {**YES** | NO}]

[SEED = {**2000000** | integer}] [UNDEFINED = {**WARN** | NOWARN}] [WIDTH = {**132** | integer}]

Defaults may differ at your installation.

SHOW [BLANKS] [CASE] [COMPRESSION] [FORMAT] [LENGTH]
[MXERRS] [MXLOOPS] [MXWARNS] [N] [PRINTBACK] [SEED]
[SYSMIS] [UNDEFINED] [WEIGHT] [WIDTH] [$VARS] [ALL]

TITLES AND SUBTITLES, **4.1**

COMMENTS IN SPSS^X COMMANDS, **4.2**

THE FINISH COMMAND, **4.3**

NUMBERED AND UNNUMBERED COMMAND LINES, **4.4**

THE SET AND SHOW COMMANDS, **4.5**
- Summary of SET and SHOW Commands, **4.6**
- Blanks and Undefined Input Data, **4.7**
- Maximum Errors and Loops, **4.8**
- Printed Output, **4.9**
- Samples and Random Numbers, **4.10**
- Scratch File Compression, **4.11**
- Additional Information from SHOW, **4.12**

NOTES, WARNINGS, AND ERROR MESSAGES, **4.13**
- Notes, **4.14**
- Warnings, **4.15**
- Errors, **4.16**

EDIT JOBS, **4.17**

Chapter 4 Job Utilities and Error Messages

This chapter describes a set of SPSS^X commands that allow you to control some of the general characteristics of your output and of the environment under which your job is processed. You can use TITLE and SUBTITLE (Section 4.1) to label the pages of your display file. To insert comments into your command file, you can choose between the COMMENT command and comments enclosed between the symbols /* and */ (Section 4.2). The FINISH command (Section 4.3) is useful for signaling the end of a job, and the NUMBERED and UNNUMBERED commands (Section 4.4) tell SPSS^X whether or not your command file includes line numbers.

With the SET command (Sections 4.5 through 4.11) you can establish the way SPSS^X treats blanks and undefined values in your input data, the starting values for random sampling, the maximum executions of a loop, and the number of errors or warnings to be accepted before a job is terminated. You can also set the maximum length and width of the printed output page as well as the default print and write formats for numeric variables created by transformation commands. And you can specify whether you want labels and error messages to print in upper case only or in upper and lower case. The SHOW command (Sections 4.5, 4.6, and 4.12) allows you to display the current settings of all those parameters and several others.

Sections 4.13 through 4.16 provide an overview of the way SPSS^X handles errors. Section 4.17 presents the EDIT command, which allows you to check your job for syntax errors without processing the data.

4.1 TITLES AND SUBTITLES

SPSS^X places a heading that includes the date, a title, and the page number at the top of each page in the display file. At the start of the job, the title is assigned by SPSS^X and indicates the version of the system being used. To replace this title on subsequent pages with one of your own, use the TITLE command, as in:

```
TITLE "Running Shoe Study from Runner's World Data"
```

The title can be up to 60 characters long and can contain any characters valid on your computer. The usual SPSS^X rules for specifying literals apply: If you enclose the title in apostrophes, double apostrophes within the string will print as single apostrophes and quotation marks are valid characters; if you enclose the title in quotation marks, double quotation marks will print as single quotation marks and apostrophes are valid characters. The following title is equivalent to the one above:

```
TITLE 'Running Shoe Study from Runner''s World Data'
```

You can insert as many TITLE commands as you wish, so long as you do not place them between a procedure command and its associated OPTIONS and STATISTICS commands, between a procedure command and BEGIN DATA when data are in-line, or within the data records. Each command overrides the previous one and takes effect on the next page in the display file (the command does not cause a page eject). Only the title portion of the heading is changed. The date and page number remain.

The SUBTITLE command follows the same rules as the TITLE command. It prints on the line immediately under the title, which is blank in the absence of a SUBTITLE command. For example,

```
SUBTITLE 'Training Shoes Only'
```

along with the title specified above produces the heading shown in Figure 4.1.

Figure 4.1 Output from TITLE and SUBTITLE commands

```
18 MAR 82  Running Shoe Study from Runner's World Data                    PAGE   2
           Training Shoes Only
```

TITLE and SUBTITLE are independent; you can change either without changing the other.

4.2 COMMENTS IN SPSS^X COMMANDS

Comments can help you and others review what you intend to accomplish with individual commands and blocks of commands within an SPSS^X job. You can insert comments in one of two ways: by using the COMMENT command or by enclosing the comment within the symbols /* and */ in any command line. Comments are included in the command printback on the display file. They do not become part of the information saved on a system file. To include commentary in the dictionary of a system file, use the DOCUMENT command (see Chapter 5).

The COMMENT command takes as its specification any message you wish, as in:

```
COMMENT Create uniform distribution for testing computations
```

As with specifications to other SPSS^X commands, the message can be continued on as many lines as necessary.

Alternatively, you can use /* and */ to set off comments wherever a blank would be valid (leaving the blank in place before the comment) except within literals. A comment demarcated by /* and */ cannot be continued on the next line. The most reasonable place for the comment is at the end of the line, in which case the closing */ is optional, as in:

```
IF (RACE EQ 1 AND SEX EQ 1) SEXRACE = 1 /*WHITE MALES
```

4.3 THE FINISH COMMAND

The FINISH command terminates an SPSS^X job. Its format is simply

```
FINISH
```

FINISH is optional, and it takes no specifications. Its primary use is to mark the end of a job. Its appearance on the printback of commands on the display file indicates that the job has been completed. FINISH causes SPSS^X to stop reading commands, so anything following it in the command file is ignored. Placing it within a DO IF structure to end a job conditionally doesn't work: FINISH is not subject to DO IF and will end the job unconditionally.

4.4 NUMBERED AND UNNUMBERED COMMAND LINES

It is common practice to reserve columns 73–80 of each input line for line numbers; and if you or your computer system numbers lines this way, SPSS^{X} includes the line numbers on the printback of commands on the display file (see Chapter 2). The NUMBERED command instructs SPSS^{X} to check just the first 72 columns for command specifications, and the UNNUMBERED command instructs SPSS^{X} to check all 80 columns. Neither command takes any specifications, so their format is simply

```
NUMBERED
```

or

```
UNNUMBERED
```

The default may vary by installation. You use the SHOW command to ascertain what is in effect, or check local documentation available with the INFO command (see Chapter 2).

4.5 THE SET AND SHOW COMMANDS

The SET command allows you to choose optional treatments of data on input, properties of the display file, compression of scratch files, the starting point for random number generation, and so on. The SHOW command displays the current settings of those options as well as additional information about the values of system variables, the system-missing value, the variable used to weight cases, and the number of cases currently in the active file.

4.6 Summary of SET and SHOW Commands

Specifications for SET are subcommands of the form

SET keyword = value / keyword = value / ...

as in:

```
SET BLANKS=0/UNDEFINED=NOWARN/MXWARNS=200
```

The slashes between subcommands are optional, but if you omit them, leave at one blank.

SHOW takes specifications of the form

SHOW keyword / keyword / ...

as in:

```
SHOW BLANKS/UNDEFINED/MXWARNS
```

The slashes between keywords are optional.

The following alphabetical list gives the keywords available for SET and SHOW along with acceptable arguments.

BLANKS *Value to which blanks read under numeric format should be translated.* The default is the system-missing value. (See Section 4.7.)

CASE *Case capability for display of labels and error messages.* Specifications are UPPER (the default) and UPLOW. The default may vary by installation. (See Section 4.9.)

COMPRESSION *Compression of scratch files.* Specifications are ON and OFF (alias YES and NO). The default is set by the individual installation. (See Section 4.11.)

FORMAT *Default print and write formats for numeric variables created by transformations.* The specification can be any F format. The initial setting is F8.2. (See Section 4.9.)

LENGTH *Page length for printed output.* The specification can be any integer in the range 40 through 999,999 inclusive or NONE to suppress page ejects altogether. The default is 59. (See Section 4.9.)

MXERRS *Maximum number of errors permitted before job is terminated.* The default is 40. (See Section 4.8.)

MXLOOPS *Maximum executions of a loop on a single case.* The default is 40. (See Section 4.8.)

MXWARNS *Maximum number of warnings and errors permitted, collectively, before job is terminated.* The default is 80. (See Section 4.8.)

N *Unweighted number of cases on the active file.* Available for SHOW only. Prints UNKNOWN if no active file has been created yet. (See Section 4.12.)

PRINTBACK *Printing of SPSS^X commands in the display file.* Specifications are YES (the default) and NO. (See Section 4.9.)

SEED *Seed for the random number generator.* The specification is a large integer. The default is 2,000,000 but may vary by machine. (See Section 4.10.)

SYSMIS *The system-missing value.* Available for SHOW only. (See Section 4.12.)

UNDEFINED *Warning message for undefined data.* Specifications are WARN (the default) and NOWARN. NOWARN suppresses messages but does not alter the count of warnings toward the MXWARNS total. (See Section 4.7.)

WEIGHT *The name of the variable used to weight cases.* Available for SHOW only. (See Section 4.12.)

WIDTH *Maximum page width for the display file.* The specification can be any integer from 80 through 255. The default is 132 columns. (See Section 4.9.)

$VARS *Values of system variables.* Available for SHOW only. (See Section 4.12.)

ALL *Available for SHOW only.* Displays the settings of all elements available to SHOW.

4.7 Blanks and Undefined Input Data

As it reads a data file defined by a DATA LIST command or a REPEATING DATA command, SPSS^X usually assigns the system-missing value whenever it encounters a completely blank field for a numeric variable (see Chapter 3 for exceptions). If you want blanks translated to a number, use the BLANKS subcommand, as in:

```
SET BLANKS = 0
```

Since the command applies only to numeric variables (blanks in strings are taken literally), only numbers are valid specifications.

When SPSS^X encounters anything other than a number or a blank as the value for a numeric format item, it assigns the system-missing value and issues a warning, as in:

```
>WARNING   652
>AN INVALID NUMERIC FIELD HAS BEEN FOUND.  THE RESULT HAS BEEN SET TO THE SYSTEM
>MISSING VALUE.
SOURCE CARD NUMBER -       3
STARTING COLUMN NUMBER -    2, CONTENTS OF FIELD: *
```

This message is printed for each conversion of an alphanumeric symbol to the system-missing value. To suppress the message, specify:

```
SET UNDEFINED = NOWARN
```

If you want to reestablish such warning messages later in the job, you can specify SET UNDEFINED = WARN.

Suppressing the warning message does not stop the counting of warnings toward the maximum allowed before job termination. To control the number of conversions of undefined data permitted within a job, use the MXWARNS subcommand, as described in Section 4.8.

SET UNDEFINED does not allow you to recode alphanumeric values to numbers. To accomplish that, define the variable as alphanumeric and then recode it into a numeric variable, as discussed in Chapter 7.

4.8 Maximum Errors and Loops

Certain errors, such as faulty syntax on a procedure command, cause SPSS^X to disregard the command on which the error occurred but to continue processing. By default, the system allows 40 such errors before it decides that the job is unredeemable and ought to be discontinued. To raise or lower that number, use the MXERRS subcommand, as in:

```
SET MXERRS = 5
```

SPSS^X also keeps track of the number of warnings issued and terminates the job when the number exceeds the maximum. Initially, the maximum is set to 80; you can change that number with the MXWARNS subcommand, as in:

```
SET MXWARNS = 200
```

All errors are included with warnings in the count toward the MXWARNS limit. Notes are not. See Section 4.13 through 4.16 for descriptions of error messages and warnings in SPSS^X.

The LOOP and END LOOP commands (Chapter 12) execute a set of transformation and data definition commands repeatedly for a single case or input record. It is possible to set up a loop such that the conditions for ending it are never met. To cut short such infinite loops, SPSS^X counts the number of times a loop is executed on each case and terminates the loop when a limit is reached. That limit is initially 40. To change this limit, use the MXLOOPS subcommand, as in:

```
SET MXLOOPS = 10
```

4.9 Printed Output

The SET command has subcommands that allow you to control the page length and width for the display file and the print and write formats for numeric variables created by transformation commands. It also has subcommands to establish whether lower-case letters in labels and error messages are to be translated to upper case in the display file and whether your commands are to be printed back along with other output from your SPSS^X job.

LENGTH. The LENGTH subcommand establishes the maximum length for a printed output page. Initially, the length is set to 59 lines. You can change that to any length from 40 to 999,999 lines with the LENGTH subcommand, as in:

```
SET LENGTH = 50
```

The length includes the lines from the first printed line on the page to the last that can be printed. The printer you use most likely includes a margin at the top; that margin is not included in the length used by SPSS^X. SPSS^X may occasionally print one line beyond the number specified by LENGTH, so the default 59 lines allows for a ½-inch margin at top and bottom of an 11-inch page printed with 6 lines per inch or an 8½-inch page printed with 8 lines per inch.

If you specify a long page length, SPSS^X will continue to give page ejects and titles at the start of each procedure and at logical points in the display, such as between crosstabulation tables. If you want to suppress page ejects altogether, use the NONE keyword, as in:

```
SET LENGTH=NONE
```

SPSS^X will then continue to insert titles at logical points in the display, but the display will not jump to the top of the page when a title is inserted.

WIDTH. The WIDTH subcommand allows you to set the maximum width of the display file to any number of characters from 80 through 255, as in:

```
SET WIDTH = 80
```

The specified width does not include the carriage control character. The default width is 132.

CASE. SPSS^X accepts variable labels and value labels in upper and lower case and maintains the case distinction on the active file and on system files. However, the system may translate these labels to upper case before sending them to the display file, depending on the default at your installation. To have them printed in the case in which they were entered, use the CASE subcommand:

```
SET CASE = UPLOW
```

You can set the case to all upper case by specifying SET CASE=UPPER. Use the SHOW command to display your installation's default.

Error messages will appear in upper and lower case if CASE=UPLOW is set, otherwise in upper case only.

The printback of commands, however, is not affected by the case established by SET CASE. Commands are printed back in the case in which they were entered. The same is true of titles. The reason for this is that commands and titles must be entered as part of the command file, and it is assumed that they will be entered in the case appropriate for the device that will print the output. Labels, however, may come from a system file, and it is handy to have a mechanism within SPSS^X for translating these before printing.

Lower-case letters within string variables are not translated to upper case. Thus the results of PRINT and WRITE are not translated even if they are directed to the display file.

PRINTBACK. The PRINTBACK subcommand controls whether SPSS^X includes your commands in the display file. By default, commands are printed. If you know that your commands are syntactically correct and do not want them included in your display, specify:

```
SET PRINTBACK = NO
```

If you also want to suppress the table indicating how SPSS^X is reading your data from a DATA LIST, see the NOTABLE keyword to that command, as discussed in Chapter 3.

FORMAT. The FORMAT subcommand establishes the print and write formats for numeric variables created by transformation commands or read in with the default format on a DATA LIST command specifying LIST or FREE formatted data. The specification must be a simple F format, as in:

```
SET FORMAT = F3.0
```

The default is F8.2. The format established by the FORMAT subcommand applies to all numeric variables created by transformation commands and to numeric variables read on a DATA LIST command with LIST or FREE specified, unless the format is specified. You can use the PRINT FORMATS, WRITE FORMATS, and FORMATS commands to specify the print and write formats for individual variables (see Chapter 9). It is important to note that the actual value maintained on the active file and saved in a system file is not affected by the print or write format.

4.10 Samples and Random Numbers

The pseudo random number generator that SPSS^X uses in selecting random samples or in creating uniform or normal distributions of random numbers begins with a *seed*, a large integer. Starting with the same seed, the system will repeatedly produce the same sequence of numbers and will select the same sample from a given data file. At the start of each job, the seed is set by SPSS^X to a value that may vary or may be fixed, depending on the implementation. You can set the seed yourself via the SEED subcommand to the SET command, as in:

```
SET SEED = 987654321
```

The argument can be any integer, preferably a large one, less than 2,000,000,000, which approaches the limit on some machines. The command sets the seed for the next time the random number generator is called. Thus you can reset it following each procedure command in a job if you want to repeat the same random distribution. In the absence of the SEED subcommand, SPSS^X will not reset the seed within a job, so all distributions and samples within the same job will be different.

4.11 Scratch File Compression

Compressing scratch files saves disk space at some expense in processing resources. The better choice between compressing scratch files or not depends upon which resources are more readily available at your installation and upon the contents of your file: files containing many variables with small integer values will gain more from compression than will files with primarily large integer or noninteger variables. Your installation will have selected whether scratch files should be compressed by default. (You can use the SHOW command, Section 4.12, to determine what has been set.) If you want to override that choice, use the COMPRESSION subcommand, as in:

```
SET COMPRESSION = YES
```

ON is a synonym for YES, and either NO or OFF specifies the reverse. The command takes effect the next time a scratch file is written and stays in effect until SET COMPRESSION is specified again or until the end of the job.

4.12 Additional Information from SHOW

The SHOW command displays the current settings of options that can be selected by the SET command. SHOW accepts five additional keywords: $VARS, SYSMIS, N, WEIGHT, and ALL. SHOW $VARS displays the values of all system variables such as $CASENUM and $DATE. See Chapter 6 for a discussion of system variables. SHOW SYSMIS displays the number used for the system-missing value. SHOW N gives the unweighted number of cases in the active file. If the active file has not yet been created (the data have not been read because no procedure command has been encountered), N is given as UNKNOWN. SHOW WEIGHT displays the name of the variable used to weight the cases on the file. SHOW ALL displays the current values of all items available to SHOW.

ANNOTATED EXAMPLE FOR RUN UTILITIES

The following job uses most of the general utilities available for controlling an SPSS^X job. It also contains a number of errors to illustrate how SPSS^X handles errors of varying severity.

```
EDIT
UNNUMBERED
TITLE "1981 U. S. Almanac Data"
SUBTITLE "Percent Growth for Fifty Largest Cities
FILE HANDLE CITYDATA NAME='CITYDATA DATA B'  /*On TECHSVC disk 192
SET CASE=UPLOW/WIDTH=72/MXWARNS=5
SHOW COMPRESSION
DATA LIST  FILE=CITYDATA  RECORDS=3
  /1 CITY 6-18 STATE 19-38(A) POP70 44-50 POP80 54-60
COMPUTE PCTGROW = RND((POP80-POP70)/POP70)*100)
VARIABLE LABELS POP70 'Population in 1970'
                POP89 'Population in 1980'
                PCTGROW 'Percent Population Growth 1970-1980'
PRINT FORMATS POP70 POP80(COMMA9.0)/PCTGROW(F3.0)
SORT CASES PCTGROW (D)
PRINT /CITY TO PCTGROW
CONDESCRIPTIVE POP70 POP89 PCTGROW
SAVE OUTFILE=CITYSF
FINISH
```

- The EDIT command directs SPSS^X to scan the command file for errors but not to read the data or process any procedures (see Section 4.17).
- The UNNUMBERED command instructs SPSS^X to interpret any data in columns 73-80 of the command line as part of the command rather than as a line number (see Section 4.4).
- The TITLE and SUBTITLE commands assign titles to each display page. In the display file these titles begin on the second page (see Section 4.1). The closing quotation mark is omitted from the SUBTITLE specification. This error receives a warning along with information about the action taken by SPSS^X.
- The FILE HANDLE command identifies the CITYDATA file (see Chapter 3). The specifications shown here are for an IBM/CMS system.
- The comment following /* in the FILE HANDLE command is inserted as a reminder of where the data are stored (see Section 4.2).
- The SET command sets case to upper and lower, so error messages print in upper and lower case, as seen in the display. It also calls for a width of 72 characters—an error, since the minimum is 80. Note in the output that this error causes SPSS^X to cease processing, since it cannot operate according to the specifications.
- The SET command also sets the maximum combined number of errors and warnings to 5. The job exceeds that limit and is terminated with the message near the bottom of the display (see Sections 4.5 through 4.12).
- The SHOW command requests information about compression of scratch files, perhaps to decide whether to alter the default in a subsequent job (see Section 4.11).
- The DATA LIST command contains a single error—CITY is an alphanumeric variable but is not specified as such. SPSS^X cannot detect this error during the EDIT job, though it would begin issuing warnings as soon as it began reading the data and discovered non-numeric characters (see Section 4.7). However, the DATA LIST table in the printed output shows that CITY will be read in F format.
- The COMPUTE command, designed to create a new variable for percentage growth of cities, lacks one of three parentheses that should follow RND. The error message flags the final parenthesis as the error, since the syntax is correct up to that point. If the final parenthesis were also omitted, the command would not be in error, though the outcome would not be the desired one. If this error were the first of its severity in the job, a message would be printed to indicate that processing ceases.

- The VARIABLE LABELS command includes a label for POP89 instead of the correct name POP80. As a result, SPSS^X ignores the label and issues a warning.
- The PRINT FORMATS, SORT CASES, and PRINT commands correctly establish a listing of the cities in order from highest growth rate to most rapid decline.
- The CONDESCRIPTIVE command names POP89 instead of POP80 and is flagged with an error that causes the procedure to be skipped.
- The SAVE command names a file handle that has not been defined. At this point, the limit of five errors and warnings has been exceeded.
- The FINISH command at the end of the job does not appear on the output because the job terminated before it was reached.

Output from the EDIT job

```
17 NOV 82 SPSS-X RELEASE 0 LEVEL 1 ALPHA TEST (29 JUL 82) FOR VM/CMS                                            PAGE   1

   1  0          EDIT
   2  0          UNNUMBERED
   3  0          TITLE "1981 U. S. Almanac Data"
   4  0          SUBTITLE "Percent Growth for Fifty Largest Cities

>WARNING   208  LINE   4, COLUMN 10, TEXT: Percent Growth for F
>NO CLOSING QUOTE FOR A QUOTED STRING.  QUOTED STRINGS MAY NOT CONTINUE ACROSS
>LINES.  THE END OF LINE IS ASSUMED TO BE THE END OF THE STRING.

   5  0          FILE HANDLE CITYDATA NAME='CITYDATA DATA B'  /*On TECHSVC disk 192
   6  0          SET CASE=UPLOW/WIDTH=72/MXWARNS=5

>ERROR     804  LINE   6, COLUMN 22, TEXT: 72
>The WIDTH subcommand of the SET command specified an invalid page width.  The
>allowable range is 80 thru 255 inclusive.
>NO FURTHER COMMANDS WILL BE EXECUTED.  ERROR SCAN CONTINUES.

   7  0          SHOW COMPRESSION

COMPRESSION = OFF  (WORKFILES ARE NOT COMPRESSED)

   8  0          DATA LIST  FILE=CITYDATA  RECORDS=3
   9  0            /1 CITY 6-18 STATE 19-38(A) POP70 44-50 POP80 54-60

THE ABOVE DATA LIST STATEMENT WILL READ   3 RECORDS FROM FILE CITYDATA.

          VARIABLE  REC   START    END        FORMAT  WIDTH  DEC

          CITY        1      6     18         F         13    0
          STATE       1     19     38         A         20
          POP70       1     44     50         F          7    0
          POP80       1     54     60         F          7    0

END OF DATALIST TABLE.


  10  0          COMPUTE PCTGROW = RND((POP80-POP70)/POP70)*100)

>ERROR    4020  LINE  10, COLUMN 47, TEXT: )
>Unbalanced parenthesis.

  11  0          VARIABLE LABELS POP70 'Population in 1970'
  12  0                          POP89 'Population in 1980'

>WARNING  4461  LINE  12, COLUMN 17, TEXT: POP89
>An unknown variable name was specified on the VARIABLE LABELS command.  The name
>and the label will be ignored.

  13  0                          PCTGROW 'Percent Population Growth 1970-1980'
  14  0          PRINT FORMATS POP70 POP80(COMMA9.0)/PCTGROW(F3.0)
  15  0          SORT CASES PCTGROW (D)


  16  0          PRINT /CITY TO PCTGROW
  17  0          CONDESCRIPTIVE POP70 POP89 PCTGROW
-------------------------------------------------------------------------------------------------------------------
17 NOV 82 1981 U. S. Almanac Data                                                                              PAGE   2
Percent Growth for Fifty Largest Cities

>ERROR     701  LINE  17, COLUMN 22, TEXT: POP89
>Undefined variable name, or a scratch or system variable was specified in a
>variable list which accepts only standard variables.  Check spelling, verify
>the existence of this variable.


  18  0          SAVE OUTFILE=CITYSF

>ERROR    5306  LINE  18, COLUMN 11, TEXT: CITYSF
>Undefined file handle on the SAVE command.
>THE LIMIT OF    5 WARNINGS PLUS ERRORS HAS BEEN EXCEEDED.
>SPSSX CANNOT CONTINUE.


   19 COMMAND LINES READ.
    4 ERRORS DETECTED.
    1 SECONDS CPU TIME.
    4 SECONDS ELAPSED TIME.
      END OF JOB.
```

4.13 NOTES, WARNINGS, AND ERROR MESSAGES

When SPSS^X encounters a peculiarity or error in your job, it issues a message to the display file and takes some action appropriate to the kind of problem. The message appears immediately following where the error was detected and always includes what action the system is taking. These messages and actions can be organized into five categories:

- Notes, which call attention to peculiarities in the job that have no effect on output.
- Warnings, which indicate problems that do affect the output but that are probably not serious.
- Errors that cause a command to be skipped but allow processing to continue.
- Errors that cause processing to cease but allow continued scanning of commands for syntax errors.
- Errors that cause immediate termination of the job.

There are limits to the number of errors and to the combined number of errors and warnings that are permitted before the job is terminated. See the MXERRS and MXWARNS subcommands to the SET command in Section 4.8.

If CASE=UPLOW has been set, messages will print in upper case (see Section 4.9). In any case, the messages print on as many lines as necessary to identify the error as fully as possible and to suggest some solutions to the most common causes of the error.

4.14 Notes

Typical of the kind of information provided by notes is the message issued when SORT CASES is specified and the file contains only one case:

```
 11  0    17. SORT CASES PCTGROW (D)

>NOTE     5802
>SORT CASES did nothing because the file has fewer than 2 cases.
```

Notes do not count toward the total number of warnings or errors that cause a job to terminate.

4.15 Warnings

Misspelling a variable name on the VARIABLE LABELS command causes just the label for that variable to be skipped, with a warning such as:

```
  7  0   13. VARIABLE LABELS POP70 'Population in 1970'
   8  0   14.                  POP89 'Population in 1980'

>WARNING  4461  LINE   8, COLUMN 17, TEXT: POP89
>An unknown variable name was specified on the VARIABLE LABELS command. The name
>and the label will be ignored.
```

Warnings often result from "undefined" data: values encountered in the input data that do not conform to the defined type of variable, such as alphanumeric characters in data defined as numeric. In this case, SPSS^X changes the code to the system-missing value and issues a warning message:

```
>WARNING   652
>An invalid numeric field has been found.  The result has been set to the system
>missing value.

SOURCE CARD NUMBER -      4
  STARTING COLUMN NUMBER -    1, CONTENTS OF FIELD: Albuquerque
```

You can suppress the warning message for undefined data with the UNDEFINED subcommand on the SET command (Section 4.7), but each occurrence of an undefined value will count toward the maximum number of warnings permitted in a job (Section 4.8).

A similar warning message can be issued when SPSS^X assigns the system-missing value because of missing data records in a grouped or nested file (Chapter 11) or because of domain errors in computations (Chapter 6).

4.16 Errors

Some errors force SPSS^X to skip an entire command but allow processing to continue for subsequent commands. Frequently this involves a procedure command, such as an error in the variable list for the BREAKDOWN procedure:

```
 43  0          BREAKDOWN  TABLES=SALBEG SALNOW AVERAISE BY MINORITY BY SEX

>ERROR      701  LINE  43, COLUMN 33, TEXT: AVERAISE
>Undefined variable name, or a scratch or system variable was specified in a
>variable list which accepts only standard variables.  Check spelling, verify
>the existence of this variable.
>THIS COMMAND NOT EXECUTED.
```

Errors that are likely to affect the results of later commands force SPSS^X to cease processing. For example, an error on the COMPUTE command causes SPSS^X to assume that later processing would most likely be meaningless. Thus processing ends, though the system continues to check for other errors that might be caught in the same job:

```
 6  0     6. COMPUTE PCTGROW = RND((POP80-POP70)/POP70)*100)

>ERROR     4020  LINE    6, COLUMN 47, TEXT: )
>Unbalanced parenthesis.
>NO FURTHER COMMANDS WILL BE EXECUTED.  ERROR SCAN CONTINUES.
```

Occasionally SPSS^X is forced to terminate a job immediately. This typically happens when the MXERRS or MXWARNS limit is exceeded or when errors occur in accessing files, as in:

```
120S INPUT  ERROR 003 ON BANKDATA,

>ERROR      334
>An I/O error has occurred.  The causes could include a damaged medium such as
>a tape, an improper DCB specification, an attempt to read a file which was
>never written, an attempt to read a BCD file as an SPSS system file, etc.
>THIS IS A CATASTROPHIC ERROR FROM WHICH SPSSX CANNOT RECOVER.
>SPSSX CANNOT CONTINUE.
```

No further error checking is done when this type of error is encountered.

4.17 EDIT JOBS

At times you may want to have SPSS^X check the syntax of your commands without actually reading and processing the data. This can save on costly jobs that terminate before completion and on mounting charges for data files on tape or other off-line media. It can allow you to do your checking in a quick, high-priority job while you wait and then submit a lower-priority job to process a large data file.

The EDIT command causes SPSS^X to evaluate your job without reading the data file. Its format is simply

```
EDIT
```

EDIT can appear anywhere in your command file. Commands following the EDIT command are checked for syntax, and variable names are checked against the DATA LIST and other commands that create variables to ensure that they have been defined. Note, however, that some SPSS^X procedures create variables such as standard scores and residuals and add them to the active file. The EDIT facility does not know about these variables and issues error messages when it encounters them in later commands.

Since EDIT checks variable names, if you are using a system file in your job you will have to make it available so that SPSS^X can read the dictionary. Alternatively, you can replace the GET command with a DATA LIST or with NUMERIC and STRING commands within INPUT PROGRAM and END INPUT PROGRAM for the EDIT job. The DATA LIST does not need to correspond exactly to the data, though it must name all the variables to be used in the remainder of the job in the same order as on the system file and with the same format type.

If your job contains data in the command file, you must remove both the data and the BEGIN DATA and END DATA commands for an EDIT job.

The EDIT facility does not detect every possible error. For example, if you name a defined variable, but the wrong one, in a COMPUTE command, the system will not recognize that the computation is impossible or not what you intend. It will, however, report on a string variable used where a numeric variable is required and vice versa. It will not know whether your DATA LIST defines your data correctly, only whether it obeys the syntax rules.

5

```
GET  FILE = handle

  [/KEEP = {ALL    }]  [/DROP = varlist]
           {varlist}

  [/RENAME = (old varlist = new varlist) . . . ]

  [/MAP]
```

```
SAVE  OUTFILE = handle

  [/KEEP = {ALL    }]  [/DROP = varlist]
           {varlist}

  [/RENAME = (old varlist = new varlist) . . . ]

  [/MAP]  [/{COMPRESSED  }]
            {UNCOMPRESSED}
```

```
FILE LABEL  label
```

```
DOCUMENT  text
```

```
DISPLAY DOCUMENTS

                 {DICTIONARY}
DISPLAY [SORTED] {INDEX     } [/VARIABLES = varlist]
                 {VARIABLES }
                 {LABELS    }
```


INTRODUCTION TO SYSTEM FILES, **5.1**

THE GET COMMAND, **5.2**
- The FILE Subcommand, **5.3**
- The MAP Subcommand, **5.4**
- The RENAME Subcommand, **5.5**
- The DROP Subcommand, **5.6**
- The KEEP Subcommand, **5.7**
  - Reordering Variables, **5.8**
- Multiple Subcommands, **5.9**

THE SAVE COMMAND, **5.10**
- The OUTFILE Subcommand, **5.11**
- The MAP Subcommand, **5.12**
- The RENAME Subcommand, **5.13**
- The DROP and KEEP Subcommands, **5.14**
  - Reordering Variables, **5.15**
- The COMPRESSED and UNCOMPRESSED Subcommands, **5.16**

SYSTEM FILE UTILITIES, **5.17**
- The FILE LABEL Command, **5.18**
- The DOCUMENT Command, **5.19**
- The DISPLAY Command, **5.20**
  - The VARIABLES Subcommand, **5.21**

STRUCTURE OF A SYSTEM FILE, **5.22**
- Binary Storage, **5.23**
- Upper and Lower Case, **5.24**
- Limitations, **5.25**

Chapter 5 SPSS^{X} System Files

Once you have defined your data file in SPSS^{X}, you do not need to repeat the data definition process. Information on the data definition commands described in Chapter 3 can be permanently saved along with the data on a specially formatted file called the SPSS^{X} *system file*. Variables created or altered by data transformations and the descriptive information for these variables can also be saved on a system file. You can access the system file on subsequent SPSS^{X} jobs or later in the same job without respecifying variable locations, formats, missing values, or variable and value labels. You can update the system file, altering the descriptive information or modifying the data, and you can save the updated version in a new system file.

5.1 INTRODUCTION TO SYSTEM FILES

An SPSS^{X} system file is a self-documented file containing data and descriptive information. The part of the file containing descriptive information is called the *dictionary*. It contains variable names, their printing and writing formats, and optional extended variable labels, value labels, and missing-value indicators. The dictionary also contains the file label from the FILE LABEL command, the date and time the file was created, and optional additional documentation supplied on the DOCUMENT command. The FILE LABEL and DOCUMENT commands are described in Sections 5.18 and 5.19.

The data in a system file are stored in binary format, which reduces the time required to read and interpret the data values. This form of data representation looks quite different from the character form usually used to enter data. You should never list an SPSS^{X} system file at a terminal or print it on a line printer. You cannot change the information in a system file through another program, package, utility, or text editor; only SPSS^{X} reads and modifies this file.

Two SPSS^{X} commands save and read system files: the SAVE command and the GET command. The only specification required on the SAVE command is the OUTFILE subcommand, and the only specification required on the GET command is the FILE subcommand. These subcommands specify the file handle of the system file to be saved or read. The command

```
SAVE OUTFILE=HUBEMPL
```

saves the active file as a system file designated by file handle HUBEMPL. (Use the FILE HANDLE command described in Chapter 3 to define the file handle to the operating system.) To read the previously saved system file, specify:

```
GET FILE=HUBEMPL
```

Optional subcommands on SAVE and GET rename variables, select a subset of variables, and reorder the variables. The GET command is discussed in Sections 5.2 through 5.9, and the SAVE command in Sections 5.10 through 5.16.

Once you read a system file, you can add variables created or altered by transformations and procedures, and you can change descriptive information in the dictionary. Changes are not made directly to a system file. Instead, modifications are made on the active file and are saved on a new system file. See Chapters 2 and 3 for discussions of the active file. You can also display descriptive information from the dictionary using the DISPLAY command (see Section 5.20).

Other facilities in SPSS^X allow you to modify and combine system files by merging two or more system files into one (Chapter 15), by saving aggregated data as a new system file (Chapter 14), and by sorting the cases on any variables in the file (Chapter 13).

5.2 THE GET COMMAND

The GET command reads a previously created system file. Variable names, labels, and missing-value indicators are retrieved from the system file. The only specification required is the FILE subcommand, which identifies the file handle of the system file that you want to use (see Section 5.3). Additional subcommands on the GET command are

The RENAME Subcommand. Use RENAME to change the names of variables (see Section 5.5).

The DROP and KEEP Subcommands. Use DROP and KEEP to save computer resources by accessing only a subset of variables in the system file (see Sections 5.6 and 5.7). KEEP also reorders variables (see Section 5.8).

The MAP Subcommand. Use MAP to display the names of the variables in the active file after any renaming, subsetting, or reordering, along with their corresponding names in the system file (see Section 5.4).

Operations are performed as the system file is copied to the active file; the original system file is not changed.

You can use the optional subcommands RENAME, KEEP, DROP, and MAP more than once on a GET command. Separate each subcommand from the other subcommands with a slash. A subcommand acts on the results of all the previous subcommands on the GET command. For example, if you use a KEEP subcommand followed by a RENAME subcommand, you can rename only the variables that you subset with KEEP.

The GET command cannot be used inside the DO IF structure described in Chapter 8 nor the LOOP structure described in Chapter 12.

5.3 The FILE Subcommand

The FILE subcommand is required and must be the first specification on the GET command. The FILE subcommand specifies the file handle of the system file. The file handle must first be defined on a FILE HANDLE command (see Chapter 3). In the IBM/OS environment, the FILE HANDLE command is unnecessary. Rather, the file handle must correspond to a DDNAME of the same name in a JCL DD statement. In the example,

```
FILE HANDLE SHOES/ file specifications
GET FILE=SHOES
```

the FILE HANDLE command defines the file handle SHOES and associates it with a disk or tape file, and the GET command retrieves all variables and descriptive information from a system file containing the 1980 *Runner's World* rating data on running shoes.

5.4 The MAP Subcommand

If you use the RENAME, DROP, or KEEP subcommands to tailor your file, you may find it difficult to keep track of what you have done. To check the results of these subcommands, use the MAP subcommand immediately following the subcommand you want mapped. The command

```
FILE HANDLE SHOES/ file specifications
GET FILE=SHOES/MAP
```

reads the system file dictionary and displays a list of all variables, in this case those containing the 1980 *Runner's World* shoe ratings data. Since no renaming, reordering, or subsetting of variables is specified on the GET command, the resulting variables are identical to the variables from file SHOES. The output displayed by the MAP subcommand is shown in Figure 5.4.

Figure 5.4 Output display of MAP subcommand

```
FILE CALLED SHOES    :
  LABEL: 1980 RUNNER'S WORLD SHOE SURVEY DATA
  CREATED 12 APR 82 13:55:22        14 VARIABLES

FILE MAP

RESULT    SHOES       RESULT    SHOES
------    ------      -------   -----
RATING79  RATING79    FOREIMP   FOREIMP
RATING80  RATING80    FLEX      FLEX
PREFER    PREFER      SOLEWEAR  SOLEWEAR
TYPE      TYPE        REARCONT  REARCONT
MAKER     MAKER       SOLETRAC  SOLETRAC
QUALITY   QUALITY     WEIGHT    WEIGHT
REARIMP   REARIMP     SHOE      SHOE
```

Usually, you use the MAP subcommand after other subcommands in order to verify the results of complicated sets of subcommands. See the following sections for examples.

5.5 The RENAME Subcommand

Use the RENAME subcommand to change the names of variables as they are copied from the system file. Variable names are changed only on the active file, not on the system file. You cannot rename variables to scratch variables. See Chapter 6 for a description of scratch variables.

To rename variables, specify the keyword RENAME followed by an optional equals sign and the rename specification enclosed in parentheses in the form (*old=new*), as in:

```
FILE HANDLE SHOES/ file specifications
GET FILE=SHOES/
  RENAME= (RATING79=TOTRAT79)
```

This command changes the name of the variable RATING79 to TOTRAT79. You can omit the parentheses when renaming a single variable.

If you rename more than one variable on a RENAME subcommand, you can specify several sets of individual variable specifications, as in:

```
FILE HANDLE SHOES/ file specifications
GET FILE=SHOES/
  RENAME= (RATING79=TOTRAT79) (RATING80=TOTRAT80)
```

Or you can specify a list of variable names and a corresponding list of new names, as in:

```
FILE HANDLE SHOES/ file specifications
GET FILE=SHOES/
  RENAME= (RATING79 RATING80=TOTRAT79 TOTRAT80)
```

Both commands rename RATING79 as TOTRAT79 and RATING80 as TOTRAT80.

If you specify lists, both lists must name the same number of variables and the entire specification must be enclosed in parentheses. The first variable listed on the left side of the equals sign is changed to the first name listed on the right side of the equals sign, the second variable listed on the left to the second name on the right, and so forth. You do not need to list the old variable names in the same order as their sequence in the system file.

Name changes take place in one operation for a given RENAME subcommand. Therefore, you can exchange the names of two variables. The command

```
FILE HANDLE READERS/ file specifications
GET FILE=READERS/
  RENAME= (TIME=NEWSWEEK) (NEWSWEEK=TIME)
```

exchanges the names of variables TIME and NEWSWEEK.

You can use keyword TO both to refer to consecutive variables to be renamed (on the left side of the equals sign) or to generate new variable names (on the right side of the equals sign). Keyword TO used in the old variable list refers to consecutive variables in the system file. The command

```
FILE HANDLE SHOES/ file specifications
GET FILE=SHOES/
  RENAME= (REARIMP TO FLEX=RIMPACT FIMPACT FLEXIBLE)
```

renames the consecutive variables REARIMP, FOREIMP, and FLEX to RIMACT, FIMPACT, and FLEXIBLE.

To generate new variable names, specify an alphabetic prefix and an inclusive range of associated sequence numbers. This method of defining multiple variable names is discussed in detail in Chapter 2. The variable names implied by the inclusive list are assigned sequentially to the variables referenced in the old variable list. The command

```
FILE HANDLE SHOES/ file specifications
GET FILE=SHOES/
  RENAME= (REARIMP TO FLEX=TEST1 TO TEST3) /MAP
```

renames the same variables as in the above example to TEST1, TEST2, and TEST3. Figure 5.5 shows the output displayed by the MAP subcommand. Note the change in names for the three variables specified on the RENAME subcommand.

Figure 5.5 Output display of MAP after RENAME

```
FILE CALLED SHOES   :
  LABEL: 1980 RUNNER'S WORLD SHOE SURVEY DATA
  CREATED 12 APR 82 13:55:22      14 VARIABLES

FILE MAP

RESULT     SHOES      RESULT     SHOES
-------    ------     -------    ------
RATING79   RATING79   TEST2      FOREIMP
RATING80   RATING80   TEST3      FLEX
PREFER     PREFER     SOLEWEAR   SOLEWEAR
TYPE       TYPE       REARCONT   REARCONT
MAKER      MAKER      SOLETRAC   SOLETRAC
QUALITY    QUALITY    WEIGHT     WEIGHT
TEST1      REARIMP    SHOE       SHOE
```

The RENAME subcommand does not reorder variables. Variables assigned new names created with the TO keyword are not consecutive on the active file unless they were consecutive on the system file or unless you reorder them using the KEEP subcommand.

After the RENAME subcommand, use the new names to refer to the variables.

5.6 The DROP Subcommand

When your system file includes variables that you do not want, you can use the DROP subcommand to specify variables you want dropped when SPSS^X creates an active file from the system file. For example, an SPSS^X system file containing all data from the 1980 General Social Survey has 1500 respondents (cases) and 325 variables. The command

```
FILE HANDLE GSS80/ file specifications
GET FILE=GSS80/
  DROP=MARITAL TO CUTSPDFG
```

retains only the first seven variables since MARITAL is the eighth variable in the system file GSS80 and CUTSPDFG is the last variable. You would obviously have to know this information ahead of time from a codebook or from a previous job using the DISPLAY command (see Section 5.20).

You do not need to list the variable names on the DROP subcommand in the same order as their sequence in the system file. However, variables retained are always copied in the same sequence as they are in the system file. If you want to reorder the variables, use the KEEP subcommand described in Section 5.8.

After the DROP subcommand, the active file contains only the variables not named on the DROP subcommand.

5.7 The KEEP Subcommand

When your system file has many variables and you want to use only a few, use the KEEP subcommand to select a subset of variables, as in:

```
FILE HANDLE GSS80/ file specifications
GET FILE=GSS80/
  KEEP=EDUC INCOME AGE CONFINAN TO CONARMY /MAP
```

This command keeps the variables for education, income, age, and the thirteen consecutive variables recording the measure of confidence in people in charge of different institutions. Figure 5.7 shows the map of the resulting active file.

Figure 5.7 Output display of MAP after KEEP

```
FILE CALLED GSS80    :
  LABEL: GENERAL SOCIAL SURVEY 1980(N=500)
  CREATED 29 MAR 82 09:54:58      323 VARIABLES

FILE MAP

RESULT     GSS80          RESULT     GSS80
------     -----          ------     -----
EDUC       EDUC           CONLABOR   CONLABOR
INCOME     INCOME         CONPRESS   CONPRESS
AGE        AGE            CONMEDIC   CONMEDIC
CONFINAN   CONFINAN       CONTV      CONTV
CONBUS     CONBUS         CONJUDGE   CONJUDGE
CONCLERG   CONCLERG       CONSCI     CONSCI
CONEDUC    CONEDUC        CONLEGIS   CONLEGIS
CONFED     CONFED         CONARMY    CONARMY
```

The variables are copied from the system file in the order they are listed on the KEEP subcommand. If you do not want the variables reordered, list the variables in the same order as their sequence on the system file. If you name a variable more than once on the KEEP subcommand, only the first mention of the variable is observed; all subsequent references to the variable are ignored.

After the KEEP subcommand, the active file contains only the variables named on the KEEP subcommand.

5.8 Reordering Variables

On many SPSS^X commands, you can use the TO keyword to specify consecutive variables in your active file. Therefore, you may want to reorder the variables so that you can more conveniently reference them with the TO keyword on subsequent SPSS^X commands. Use the KEEP subcommand to reorder variables in your file. You can either list the names of all the variables in the order that you want them, or you can simply list the names of the variables that you want at the beginning of the file in the desired order, followed by the keyword ALL. Keyword ALL places all the unnamed variables in the same sequence as they appear in the system file. Keyword

ALL must be the last specification on the KEEP subcommand, as in:

```
FILE HANDLE SHOES/ file specifications
GET FILE=SHOES/
  KEEP=SHOE MAKER TYPE ALL /MAP
```

This command reorders variables in the 1980 *Runner's World* shoe ratings file so that the first three variables are SHOE, MAKER, and TYPE, followed by the remaining variables in the same sequence as in the system file. Figure 5.8 shows the map of the reordered file. Notice the different order of the variables compared with the original order as shown in Figure 5.4.

Figure 5.8 Output display of MAP after KEEP with ALL

```
FILE CALLED SHOES    :
  LABEL: 1980 RUNNER'S WORLD SHOE SURVEY DATA
  CREATED 12 APR 82 13:55:22        14 VARIABLES

FILE MAP

RESULT     SHOES       RESULT     SHOES
------     -----       ------     -----
SHOE       SHOE        REARIMP    REARIMP
MAKER      MAKER       FOREIMP    FOREIMP
TYPE       TYPE        FLEX       FLEX
RATING79   RATING79    SOLEWEAR   SOLEWEAR
RATING80   RATING80    REARCONT   REARCONT
PREFER     PREFER      SOLETRAC   SOLETRAC
QUALITY    QUALITY     WEIGHT     WEIGHT
```

5.9 Multiple Subcommands

Use only one FILE subcommand on the GET command, and specify it first. Then use the RENAME, DROP, KEEP, and MAP subcommands in any order and as many times as you wish. Each subcommand refers to the results of previous subcommands. Thus, any variables renamed on the RENAME subcommand must be referred to by their new names on subsequent KEEP or DROP subcommands. Similarly, only variables retained on the active file as the result of KEEP or DROP can be specified on a subsequent RENAME subcommand. If the KEEP subcommand reorders the variables, the keyword TO on subsequent subcommands will refer to the reordered sequence.

For example, to rename the subset of variables selected in Section 5.7, specify:

```
FILE HANDLE GSS80/ file specifications
GET FILE=GSS80/
  KEEP=EDUC INCOME AGE CONFINAN TO CONARMY/
  RENAME=(CONFINAN TO CONARMY=CONF1 TO CONF13) /MAP
```

The map of the resulting active file is shown in Figure 5.9.

Figure 5.9 Output display of MAP after KEEP and RENAME

```
FILE CALLED GSS80    :
  LABEL: GENERAL SOCIAL SURVEY 1980(N=500)
  CREATED 29 MAR 82 09:54:58        323 VARIABLES

FILE MAP

RESULT     GSS80       RESULT     GSS80
------     -----       ------     -----
EDUC       EDUC        CONF6      CONLABOR
INCOME     INCOME      CONF7      CONPRESS
AGE        AGE         CONF8      CONMEDIC
CONF1      CONFINAN    CONF9      CONTV
CONF2      CONBUS      CONF10     CONJUDGE
CONF3      CONCLERG    CONF11     CONSCI
CONF4      CONEDUC     CONF12     CONLEGIS
CONF5      CONFED      CONF13     CONARMY
```

5.10 THE SAVE COMMAND

The SAVE command saves the active file as a system file. All data-descriptive information is stored in the system file dictionary. New variables created by transformations and procedures previous to the SAVE command are included in the new system file, and variables altered by transformations are saved in their modified form. Results of any temporary transformations immediately preceding the SAVE command are included in the system file; scratch variables are not. See Chapter 6 for the discussion of temporary transformations and scratch variables.

The only specification required on the SAVE command is the OUTFILE subcommand identifying the file handle of the system file (see Section 5.11). Additional subcommands on the SAVE command are

The RENAME Subcommand. Use RENAME to change the names of variables (see Section 5.13).

The DROP and KEEP Subcommands. Use DROP and KEEP to save a subset of variables (see Section 5.14). You can also use the KEEP subcommand to reorder variables (see Section 5.15).

The MAP Subcommand. Use MAP to display the names of the variables saved in the system file after any renaming, subsetting, or reordering, along with their corresponding names in the active file (see Section 5.12).

The COMPRESSED and UNCOMPRESSED Subcommands. Use COMPRESSED and UNCOMPRESSED to instruct SPSS^X to save the system file in compressed or uncompressed form (see Section 5.16).

All of these operations are executed as the active file is copied to the system file; the active file is not changed.

After the OUTFILE subcommand, specify the RENAME, DROP, KEEP, and MAP subcommands in any order and as many times as you need, separated by slashes. As with the GET command, if you use multiple subcommands on the SAVE command, each operation refers to the results of all previous subcommands.

5.11 The OUTFILE Subcommand

The OUTFILE subcommand is required and must be the first specification on the SAVE command. The OUTFILE subcommand specifies the file handle of the output system file. The file handle must be previously defined on a FILE HANDLE command (see Chapter 3). In the IBM/OS environment, the FILE HANDLE command is unnecessary. Rather, the file handle must correspond to a DDNAME on a JCL DD command. In the commands

```
FILE HANDLE HUBEMPL/ file specifications
SAVE OUTFILE=HUBEMPL
```

the FILE HANDLE command defines file handle HUBEMPL and associates it with an output file on tape or disk, and the SAVE command saves the current active file as a system file identified by the file handle HUBEMPL. See the annotated SAVE example for the complete job.

5.12 The MAP Subcommand

If you use the optional subcommands RENAME, DROP, or KEEP, you may want to print the names of the variables that you are saving in order to verify the results. Use the MAP subcommand to print a list of the variables on the system file and their corresponding names on the active file, as in:

```
FILE HANDLE HUBEMPL/ file specifications
SAVE OUTFILE=HUBEMPL/MAP
```

This command displays a list of all the variables saved in the system file HUBEMPL. Since no renaming, reordering, or deletion of variables is requested, the variables are identical to those in the active file.

5.13 The RENAME Subcommand

The RENAME subcommand changes the names of variables as they are copied into the system file. The command

```
FILE HANDLE HUBEMPL/ file specifications
SAVE OUTFILE=HUBEMPL/
  RENAME=(AGE=AGE80) (JOBCAT=JOBCAT82) /MAP
```

renames variables AGE and JOBCAT to AGE80 and JOBCAT82. Figure 5.13 shows the output from the MAP subcommand. If you rename only one variable, the parentheses enclosing the specification are optional.

Figure 5.13 MAP of the variables in the system file

```
OUTPUT FILE MAP

RESULT                      RESULT
------                      ------
EMPLOYID  EMPLOYID          SALARY81  SALARY81
MOHIRED   MOHIRED           SALARY82  SALARY82
YRHIRED   YRHIRED           HOURLY81  HOURLY81
DEPT79    DEPT79            HOURLY82  HOURLY82
DEPT80    DEPT80            PROMO81   PROMO81
DEPT81    DEPT81            AGE80     AGE
DEPT82    DEPT82            RAISE82   RAISE82
SEX       SEX               JOBCAT82  JOBCAT
SALARY79  SALARY79          NAME      NAME
SALARY80  SALARY80

12 APR 82 16:53:05              19 VARIABLES,    168 BYTES PER CASE
12 APR 82 16:53:08             275 CASES SAVED
```

To rename more than one variable, specify several sets of individual variable specifications (as shown above), or specify a list of variable names and a list of new names, as in:

```
FILE HANDLE HUBEMPL/ file specifications
SAVE OUTFILE=HUBEMPL/
  RENAME=(AGE JOBCAT=AGE80 JOBCAT82) /MAP
```

If you specify variable lists, the same number of variables must be named in both lists, and the entire specification must be enclosed in parentheses. The first variable listed on the left side of the equals sign is changed to the first name on the right side of the equals sign, the second variable listed on the left to the second name on the right, and so forth. You do not need to list the old variable names in the same order as their sequence in the file.

Name changes take place in one operation for a given RENAME subcommand. Therefore, you can exchange the names of two variables, as in:

```
FILE HANDLE MAGS/ file specifications
SAVE OUTFILE=MAGS/
  RENAME= (TIME=NEWSWEEK) (NEWSWEEK=TIME)
```

This command exchanges the names of variables TIME and NEWSWEEK on the new system file.

Keyword TO can be used both to refer to consecutive variables to be renamed (on the left side of the equal sign) and to generate new variable names (on the right side of the equal sign). See Section 5.5 for examples of RENAME subcommands using TO.

5.14 The DROP and KEEP Subcommands

Your active file may contain variables you do not need to save on a system file. To select a subset of variables, use the KEEP subcommand to specify those you want to save or the DROP subcommand to specify those you do not want to save. Depending upon the number of variables you want to save and their sequence, one or the other will probably be easier.

Specify the DROP subcommand followed by an optional equals sign and the list of variables you do not want to save. The variable list can include individual variable names and consecutive variables referenced by the keyword TO.

You can list the variable names on the DROP subcommand in any sequence. However, the variables retained are always saved in the system file in the same sequence as they are in the active file. If you want to reorder the variables, use the KEEP subcommand (see Section 5.15).

Specify the KEEP subcommand followed by an optional equals sign and the list of variables that you want to save. The variable list can include individual variable names and consecutive variables referenced by the keyword TO. The order of the variable names on the KEEP subcommand determines their sequence on the system file. If you name a variable more than once on a KEEP subcommand, only the first mention of the variable is recognized, and the variable is written on the system file in the sequence of the first mention of the name.

For example, assume that you have saved the system file (as shown in the annotated example of the SAVE command) containing the Hubbard employee data. In your next SPSSX job, suppose you read the system file, run a BREAKDOWN procedure on the variables RAISE82 by DEPT82, and then save a new system file containing only the variables SEX, DEPT79 TO DEPT82, and SALARY79 TO SALARY82, as in:

```
FILE HANDLE HUBEMPL/ file specifications
GET FILE=HUBEMPL
BREAKDOWN  RAISE82 BY DEPT82
FILE HANDLE SUBHUB/ file specifications
SAVE OUTFILE=SUBHUB/
    KEEP=SEX, DEPT79 TO DEPT82, SALARY79 TO SALARY82/MAP
```

The new system file is saved on a file identified by the file handle SUBHUB. Figure 5.14 shows the map of the new system file. Note that the variables are saved on the new system file SUBHUB in the order that they are listed on the KEEP subcommand. The original system file HUBEMPL is not changed or deleted.

Figure 5.14 MAP of the new system file SUBHUB

```
OUTPUT FILE MAP

RESULT
------
SEX        SEX
DEPT79     DEPT79
DEPT80     DEPT80
DEPT81     DEPT81
DEPT82     DEPT82
SALARY79   SALARY79
SALARY80   SALARY80
SALARY81   SALARY81
SALARY82   SALARY82

25 SEP 81 14:19:07          9 VARIABLES,      72 BYTES PER CASE
25 SEP 81 14:19:10        275 CASES SAVED
```

5.15 Reordering Variables

If you have created new variables with transformations or procedures, the new variables are added to the end of your active file. If you want to save these variables in a different order in your system file, perhaps to reference them with the TO keyword on SPSSX commands in later jobs, use the KEEP subcommand. You can either list every variable name in the order that you want them saved, or you can list the names of the variables that you want to be at the beginning of the system file in the desired order, followed by the keyword ALL. Keyword ALL must be the last specification on the KEEP subcommand since it implies all the variables not previously named, as in:

```
FILE HANDLE HUBEMPL/ file specifications
FILE HANDLE REORHUB/ file specifications
GET FILE=HUBEMPL
SAVE OUTFILE=REORHUB/ KEEP=SEX, AGE, ALL
```

This command reads the system file containing the Hubbard employee data and saves a new system file with SEX and AGE as the first two variables, followed by the remaining variables in the same sequence as in the original system file.

ANNOTATED EXAMPLE FOR SAVE

The job developed in Sections 5.10 through 5.19 is to save an SPSS^X system file from the Hubbard Consultants Inc. employment data. The object is to document the data completely in order to create a self-documenting file. The SPSS^X commands are

```
FILE HANDLE HUBDATA/ file specifications
TITLE  SAVE A SYSTEM FILE OF THE HUBBARD EMPLOYEE DATA
DATA LIST  FILE=HUBDATA RECORDS=3
  /1 EMPLOYID 1-5 MOHIRED YRHIRED 12-15 DEPT79 TO DEPT82 SEX 16-20
  /2 SALARY79 TO SALARY82 6-25 HOURLY81 HOURLY82 42-53(2) PROMO81 72
     AGE 54-55 RAISE82 66-70
  /3 JOBCAT 6 NAME 25-48 (A)

MISSING VALUES  DEPT79 TO SALARY82, AGE (0)
  HOURLY82, RAISE82 (-999) JOBCAT (9)

VAR LABELS  YRHIRED 'YEAR OF FIRST HIRING'
  DEPT82 'DEPARTMENT OF EMPLOYMENT IN 1982'
  SALARY82 'YEARLY SALARY IN 1982'
  JOBCAT 'JOB CATEGORIES'

VALUE LABELS  DEPT79 TO DEPT82 1 'ADMINISTRATIVE' 2 'PROJECT DIRECTORS'
  3 'CHICAGO OPERATIONS' 4 'ST LOUIS OPERATIONS' 0 'NOT REPORTED'/
 SEX 1 'MALE' 2 'FEMALE'/
 JOBCAT 1 'OFFICIALS & MANAGERS' 2 'PROFESSIONALS' 3 'TECHNICIANS'
  4 'OFFICE AND CLERICAL' 5 'CRAFTSMEN' 6 'SERVICE WORKERS'

FILE HANDLE HUBEMPL/ file specifications
FILE LABEL  HUBBARD INDUSTRIAL CONSULTANTS INC. EMPLOYEE DATA
DOCUMENT  THIS FILE CONTAINS EMPLOYEE RECORDS FOR HUBBARD
          INDUSTRIAL CONSULTANTS, INC. A CONSULTING FIRM
          WITH HEADQUARTERS IN CHICAGO AND A BRANCH OFFICE
          IN ST. LOUIS.
          THE FILE INCLUDES ALL INDIVIDUALS EMPLOYED IN 1980
          WITH INFORMATION FOR THOSE EMPLOYEES FOR 1979 THROUGH
          1982.
SAVE  OUTFILE=HUBEMPL/
  RENAME=(AGE=AGE80)(JOBCAT=JOBCAT82)/
  KEEP=EMPLOYID TO MOHIRED SEX AGE80 NAME JOBCAT82 ALL/ MAP

BREAKDOWN  RAISE82 BY JOBCAT
```

- The TITLE command provides a title for each page of display output from this job (see Chapter 4).
- The FILE HANDLE commands define the file handles for the data file described with the DATA LIST command and for the system file saved with the SAVE command (see Chapter 3).
- The DATA LIST command describes the employment data accessed with file handle HUBDATA (see Chapter 3).
- The MISSING VALUES, VARIABLE LABELS, and VALUE LABELS commands complete definition of the variables (see Chapter 3).
- The FILE LABEL command provides a label that is printed on the display output for this job and, since it is stored on the system file, for any future job from the system file (see Section 5.18).
- The DOCUMENT command saves a block on the system file (see Section 5.19). This text is displayed in response to the DISPLAY command in any future job from the system file (see Section 5.20).
- The SAVE command saves the employment data and all the definitions, file labels, and documentation in a system file. HUBEMPL is the file handle for the new system file (see Section 5.10).
- The RENAME subcommand renames two of the variables (see Section 5.13). The old names remain in effect for the rest of this job, but the variables are saved on the system file with the new names.
- The KEEP subcommand is used here to reorder the variables (see Section 5.15). Keyword ALL tells SPSS^X to keep the rest of the variables in their original order.

- The MAP subcommand is used to provide a record of what variables were saved, in what order, and with what names (see Section 5.12).
- The BREAKDOWN command asks for a means breakdown of the employees' raises in 1982 by their job categories (see Chapter 22). Note that the RENAME subcommand of the SAVE command had no effect on the JOBCAT variable since the active file is unchanged.

In any subsequent job, you would enter the commands

```
FILE HANDLE HUB/ file specifications
GET FILE=HUB
```

to read the system file containing the employment data, variable names, labels, missing-value flags, and the file label and documentation (see Section 5.2).

The MAP display

```
  29  0           SAVE FILE=HUBEMPL/
  30  0             RENAME=(AGE=AGE80)(JOBCAT=JOBCAT82)/
  31  0             KEEP=EMPLOYID TO YRHIRED SEX AGE80 NAME JOBCAT82 ALL/ MAP
  32  0

OUTPUT FILE MAP

RESULT                      RESULT
------                      ------

EMPLOYID  EMPLOYID          DEPT82     DEPT82
MOHIRED   MOHIRED           SALARY79   SALARY79
YRHIRED   YRHIRED           SALARY80   SALARY80
SEX       SEX               SALARY81   SALARY81
AGE80     AGE               SALARY82   SALARY82
NAME      NAME              HOURLY81   HOURLY81
JOBCAT82  JOBCAT            HOURLY82   HOURLY82
DEPT79    DEPT79            PROMO81    PROMO81
DEPT80    DEPT80            RAISE82    RAISE82
DEPT81    DEPT81

14 JUN 82 09:00:06            19 VARIABLES,     168 BYTES PER CASE
14 JUN 82 09:00:10           275 CASES SAVED
```

5.16 The COMPRESSED and UNCOMPRESSED Subcommands

Although the binary form of storing data in a system file is efficient in processing time, it sometimes requires a large amount of storage. For example, if your data file contains mostly variables with small integer values, the system file can require significantly more storage space than the original data file. For this type of file, it may be to your advantage to store the system file in *compressed* form. Compression maximizes the number of variables stored in each computer word and thus reduces the storage requirements for files with mostly small integer values (see Section 5.22 for a discussion of the structure of system files). However, the processing time for saving and retrieving compressed files is greater than for uncompressed files.

Either the COMPRESSED or UNCOMPRESSED keyword can be specified on a SAVE command. If neither is specified, the default is used. The default will usually be COMPRESSED, but it may be different at your installation. Use the INFO command to check the default available at your installation (see Chapter 2). However, you can always specify explicitly the form that you want.

If you are saving a very large data file, check with your local consultants for advice on whether storage and input/output operations are more expensive at your installation than the processing time needed to compress a file.

Once the system file is saved, you need not remember whether it was saved in compressed or uncompressed form. The system file will be accessed automatically in the correct form by the GET command and all other commands that access system files.

5.17 SYSTEM FILE UTILITIES

Two utilities store documentary information on a system file. The FILE LABEL command stores a label that prints automatically whenever the system file is accessed. The DOCUMENT command stores a block of text that can be accessed at any later date via the DISPLAY command (see Section 5.20).

5.18 The FILE LABEL Command

Use the FILE LABEL command to provide a descriptive label for your data file. The file label is printed on the first line of each page of output displayed by SPSS^X and is included in the dictionary of the system file. The command

```
FILE HANDLE HUBEMPL/ file specifications
FILE LABEL  HUBBARD INDUSTRIAL CONSULTANTS INC. EMPLOYEE DATA
SAVE OUTFILE=HUBEMPL/
  RENAME=(AGE JOBCAT=AGE80 JOBCAT82) /MAP
```

assigns a file label to the Hubbard Consultants Inc. employee data saved in the system file.

A file label can be up to 60 characters long. If it is longer, SPSS^X will truncate the label to 60 characters without warning.

5.19 The DOCUMENT Command

Use the DOCUMENT command to save a block of text of any length on your system file. The command

```
FILE HANDLE HUBEMPL/ file specifications
FILE LABEL  HUBBARD INDUSTRIAL CONSULTANTS INC. EMPLOYEE DATA
DOCUMENT   THIS FILE CONTAINS EMPLOYEE RECORDS FOR HUBBARD INDUSTRIAL
   CONSULTANTS, INC.--A CONSULTING FIRM WITH HEADQUARTERS IN CHICAGO
   AND A BRANCH OFFICE IN ST. LOUIS.  THE FILE INCLUDES ALL INDIVIDUALS
   EMPLOYED IN 1980 WITH INFORMATION FOR THOSE EMPLOYEES FOR 1979
   THROUGH 1982.
SAVE OUTFILE=HUBEMPL/
  RENAME=(AGE JOBCAT=AGE80 JOBCAT82) /MAP
```

provides information describing the Hubbard data. This block of text is saved on the system file and is available via the DISPLAY command whenever you or someone else needs to know more about the system file (see Section 5.20).

You can use the DOCUMENT command to add documentation to an existing system file. The new documentation and the date it was entered are saved along with any existing documentation when the new system file is saved.

5.20 The DISPLAY Command

The dictionary of a system file is available at any time via the DISPLAY command for exploring an unfamiliar or forgotten system file or for producing a printed archive document for a system file. In addition, the DISPLAY utility can be used during any SPSS^X job to display the data definitions that are being applied to the active file, even if a system file is neither being read nor saved.

For example, to display DOCUMENT information and information supplied on the DATA LIST, VARIABLE LABELS, VALUE LABELS, and MISSING VALUES commands, specify:

```
FILE HANDLE HUB/ file specifications
GET FILE=HUB
DISPLAY DOCUMENTS
DISPLAY DICTIONARY
```

These commands display the documentation and the dictionary from the system file defined by the HUB file handle. No procedure is needed to read the data from the system file since DISPLAY gets its information from the dictionary alone. Figure 5.20 shows the results of DISPLAY DOCUMENTS.

Figure 5.20 Display of documentary information

```
DOCUMENT ENTERED 12 APR 82
   THIS FILE CONTAINS EMPLOYEE RECORDS FOR HUBBARD INDUSTRIAL
   CONSULTANTS, INC.—A CONSULTING FIRM WITH HEADQUARTERS IN CHICAGO
   AND A BRANCH OFFICE IN ST. LOUIS.  THE FILE INCLUDES ALL INDIVIDUALS
   EMPLOYED IN 1980 WITH INFORMATION FOR THOSE EMPLOYEES FOR 1979
   THROUGH 1982.
```

The following keywords can be specified on the DISPLAY command:

DOCUMENTS *Display the text provided by the DOCUMENT command.* No error message is issued if there is no documentary information on the system file.

DICTIONARY *Display complete dictionary information for variables.* Information includes the variable names, labels, sequential position of each variable in the file, print and write formats, missing values, and value labels.

INDEX *Display the variable names and positions.*

VARIABLES *Display the variable names, positions, print and write formats, and missing values.*

LABELS *Display the variable names, positions, and variable labels.*

Only one of the above keywords can be specified per DISPLAY command, but you can use as many DISPLAY commands as necessary to obtain the desired information.

In addition, you can use keyword SORTED to display information alphabetically by variable name. SORTED can precede keywords DICTIONARY, INDEX, VARIABLES, or LABELS, as in:

```
FILE HANDLE HUB/ file specifications
GET FILE=HUB
DISPLAY DOCUMENTS
DISPLAY SORTED DICTIONARY
```

The first DISPLAY command displays the document information, and the second displays complete dictionary information for variables sorted alphabetically by variable name.

SORTED *Alphabetize the display by variable name.* Use with DICTIONARY, INDEX, VARIABLES, or LABLES.

5.21 The VARIABLES Subcommand

To limit the display to certain variables, follow any specification other than DOCUMENTS with a slash, the VARIABLES subcommand, an optional equals sign, and a list of variables, as in:

```
FILE HANDLE HUB/ file specifications
GET FILE=HUB
DISPLAY DOCUMENTS
DISPLAY SORTED DICTIONARY/
  VARIABLES=DEPT82, SALARY82, SEX TO JOBCAT
```

This specification produces dictionary information only for the variables mentioned (or implied by keyword TO) in the variable list, and sorts them alphabetically by variable name. Without keyword SORTED, information is displayed in the order variables are stored on the system file regardless of the order you name them on the VARIABLES subcommand. Compare the results in Figure 5.21 with the original job that created the system file in the annotated SAVE example.

Figure 5.21 Display of dictionary information

```
FILE:     HUBBARD INDUSTRIAL CONSULTANTS INC. EMPLOYEE DATA

                LIST OF VARIABLES ON THE ACTIVE FILE

      NAME                                                     POSITION

      AGE80                                                          5
                     PRINT FMT:  F2.0
                     WRITE FMT:  F2.0
                     MISSING VALUES:  0

      DEPT82    DEPARTMENT OF EMPLOYMENT IN 1982                    13
                     PRINT FMT:  F1.0
                     WRITE FMT:  F1.0
                     MISSING VALUES:  0

               VALUE    LABEL

                    0 M  NOT REPORTED
                    1    ADMINISTRATIVE
                    2    PROJECT DIRECTORS
                    3    CHICAGO OPERATIONS
                    4    ST LOUIS OPERATIONS

      JOBCAT82  JOB CATEGORIES                                       9
                     PRINT FMT:  F1.0
                     WRITE FMT:  F1.0
                     MISSING VALUES:  9

               VALUE    LABEL

                    1    OFFICIALS & MANAGERS
                    2    PROFESSIONALS
                    3    TECHNICIANS
                    4    OFFICE AND CLERICAL
                    5    CRAFTSMEN
                    6    SERVICE WORKERS

      NAME                                                           6
                     PRINT FMT:  A24
                     WRITE FMT:  A24

      SALARY82  YEARLY SALARY IN 1982                               17
                     PRINT FMT:  F5.0
                     WRITE FMT:  F5.0
                     MISSING VALUES:  0

      SEX                                                            4
                     PRINT FMT:  F1.0
                     WRITE FMT:  F1.0
                     MISSING VALUES:  0

               VALUE    LABEL

                    1    MALE
                    2    FEMALE
```

5.22 STRUCTURE OF A SYSTEM FILE

An SPSS^X system file is a fully integrated file containing the data and all descriptive information. The part of the file containing the descriptive information—called the *dictionary*—contains the variable names, their printing and writing formats, and optional extended variable labels, value labels, and missing-value indicators. Descriptive information is supplied on the data definition commands described in Chapter 3. The dictionary also contains the file label from the FILE LABEL command, additional documentation supplied on the DOCUMENT command, and the date and time the file was created. The FILE LABEL and DOCUMENT commands are described in Sections 5.18 and 5.19.

5.23 Binary Storage

When data are initially entered on a machine-readable device, the values are usually recorded in character format. In character format, each character is stored in a single column. Data in a system file are stored in binary format. This form of data representation reduces the time required for SPSS^X to read and interpret the data values. In binary format, each value, regardless of the number of columns it occupies externally, is stored internally in units of storage called *words*. The actual size of a computer word depends on the type of computer. On most computers, SPSS^X stores all values except long string variables in two computer words. Thus, numeric values in SPSS^X are double-precision values. Values of long string variables are stored in as many computer words as are necessary to accurately represent the string.

Many values in a typical data file can be stored in much less than a double word. Therefore, you can instruct SPSS^X to store the system file in *compressed* form (see Section 5.16). Compression reduces the storage requirements for files that contain mostly small integer values.

5.24 Upper and Lower Case

SPSS^X accepts commands in any case but interprets keywords and names as upper case. However, labels, literals, and information from the DOCUMENT command are stored on the active file and system file in the case in which they are entered. SPSS^X prints labels, literals, and DOCUMENT information in mixed case if you specify CASE=UPLOW on the SET command, or it will translate them to upper case with CASE=UPPER (see Chapter 4). Therefore, if you have access to a printer with upper- and lower-case capabilities, you can specify upper and lower case when using the DISPLAY command, as in:

```
FILE HANDLE HUBLOW/ file specifications
SET CASE=UPLOW
GET FILE=HUBLOW
DISPLAY DICTIONARY/
  VARIABLES=SEX, DEPT82, JOBCAT82
```

These commands display the dictionary information for variables SEX, DEPT82, and JOBCAT82. If this information was originally provided in upper and lower case, DISPLAY will observe the SET command and print in mixed case as shown in the display output in Figure 5.24.

Figure 5.24 DISPLAY output in mixed case

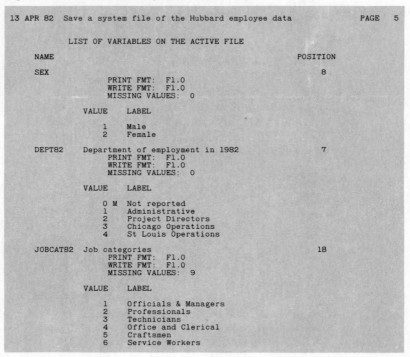

```
13 APR 82  Save a system file of the Hubbard employee data              PAGE  5

           LIST OF VARIABLES ON THE ACTIVE FILE

     NAME                                                         POSITION

     SEX                                                              8
                    PRINT FMT:  F1.0
                    WRITE FMT:  F1.0
                    MISSING VALUES:  0

               VALUE    LABEL

                   1    Male
                   2    Female

     DEPT82    Department of employment in 1982                       7
                    PRINT FMT:  F1.0
                    WRITE FMT:  F1.0
                    MISSING VALUES:  0

               VALUE    LABEL

                   0 M  Not reported
                   1    Administrative
                   2    Project Directors
                   3    Chicago Operations
                   4    St Louis Operations

     JOBCAT82  Job categories                                        18
                    PRINT FMT:  F1.0
                    WRITE FMT:  F1.0
                    MISSING VALUES:  9

               VALUE    LABEL

                   1    Officials & Managers
                   2    Professionals
                   3    Technicians
                   4    Office and Clerical
                   5    Craftsmen
                   6    Service Workers
```

5.25 Limitations

The number of cases or the number of variables that can be saved in an SPSS^X system file is virtually unlimited. Limitations on the size of variables are machine dependent. While there is no fixed limit to the width of a numeric variable, there is a practical limit to the number of digits that can be stored precisely. SPSS^X stores numeric values in double-precision on most computers. For example, the last digit of numbers larger than sixteen digits in the IBM/OS and IBM/CMS environments may be inaccurate. Values of long string variables are limited to 255 characters. The maximum length of a short string variable is defined by the computer you are using and may be as few as eight characters.

6

For numeric variables:

RECODE varlist (value list = value) . . . (value list = value)
[INTO varlist] [/varlist . . .]

Keywords available for input value lists:
LOW LOWEST HI HIGHEST
THRU ELSE MISSING SYSMIS

Keywords available for output values:
COPY SYSMIS

COMPUTE target variable = expression

Arithmetic Operators:

+	Addition	-	Subtraction
*	Multiplication	/	Division
**	Exponentiation		

Arithmetic Functions:

ABS	Absolute value	RND	Round
TRUNC	Truncate	MOD	Modulus
SQRT	Square root	EXP	Exponential
LG10	Base 10 logarithm	LN	Natural logarithm
ARSIN	Arcsin	ARTAN	Arctangent
SIN	Sine	COS	Cosine

Statistical Functions:

SUM[.n]	Sum of arguments	MEAN[.n]	Mean of arguments
SD[.n]	Standard deviation of args.	VARIANCE[.n]	Variance of arguments
		MIN[.n]	Minimum of arguments
CFVAR[.n]	Coef. of variation of args.	MAX[.n]	Maximum of arguments

Missing Value Functions:

VALUE	Ignore user-missing	MISSING	True if missing
SYSMIS	True if system-missing	NMISS	Number of missing arguments
NVALID	No. of valid arguments		

Cross-case Function:

LAG	Lag

Other Numeric Functions:

UNIFORM	Uniform pseudo random number	NORMAL	Normal pseudo random number
CDFNORM	Standard normal cumulative distribution	PROBIT	Inverse of standard normal cumulative distribution
YRMODA	Date function		

Logical Functions:

RANGE	True, if value is within range	ANY	True if any value matches

String functions:

CONCAT	Concatenate	LPAD	Pad left
RPAD	Pad right	LTRIM	Trim left
RTRIM	Trim right	SUBSTR	Substring
INDEX	Index	STRING	Convert to a string
NUMBER	Convert to a number		

COUNT varname = varlist (value list) [/varname = . . .]

Keywords available for numeric value lists:
LO LOWEST HI HIGHEST THRU MISSING SYSMIS

LEAVE varlist

TEMPORARY

NUMERIC varlist [(format)] [/varlist . . .]

DO REPEAT stand-in var = {varlist | value list}

[/stand-in var = . . .]

transformation commands

END REPEAT [PRINT]

INTRODUCTION TO DATA TRANSFORMATIONS, **6.1**
Printing and Writing Formats, **6.2**

THE RECODE COMMAND, **6.3**
Specifying Numeric Values, **6.4**
Keywords THRU, LOWEST, and HIGHEST, **6.5**
Keyword ELSE, **6.6**
Keywords MISSING and SYSMIS, **6.7**
Value Ranges, **6.8**
Keyword INTO, **6.9**
Keyword COPY, **6.10**

THE COMPUTE COMMAND, **6.11**
Computing Numeric Variables, **6.12**
Missing Values, **6.13**

NUMERIC EXPRESSIONS, **6.14**
Arithmetic Operations, **6.15**
Numeric Constants, **6.16**
The Order of Operations, **6.17**
Numeric Functions, **6.18**
Arithmetic Functions, **6.19**
Statistical Functions, **6.20**
Missing-Value Functions, **6.21**
The Across-Case LAG Function, **6.22**
Logical Functions, **6.23**
Other Functions, **6.24**
Using Logical Functions, **6.25**
Using the YRMODA Function, **6.26**
Complex Numeric Arguments, **6.27**
Logical Expressions, **6.28**
Missing Values, **6.29**
Missing Values in Arguments, **6.30**
Domain Errors, **6.31**

THE COUNT COMMAND, **6.32**
Initialization and Missing Values, **6.33**

TRANSFORMATION UTILITIES, **6.34**
The LEAVE Command, **6.35**
Scratch Variables, **6.36**
The TEMPORARY Command, **6.37**
The NUMERIC Command, **6.38**
The DO REPEAT Utility, **6.39**
Replacement Variable and Value Lists, **6.40**
The PRINT Subcommand, **6.41**
System Variables, **6.42**

EXECUTING DATA TRANSFORMATIONS, **6.43**
Data Definition Commands, **6.44**
The Active File, **6.45**

Chapter 6 Numeric Transformations

The ability to transform data before you analyze it or after preliminary analysis is often as important as the analysis itself. You may want to perform simple data-cleaning checks, correct coding errors, or adjust an inconvenient coding scheme. Or you may want to construct an index from several variables or rescale several variables prior to analysis. The SPSS^{X} transformation language provides these and many other possibilities.

This chapter describes the major components of the SPSS^{X} transformation language, with emphasis on manipulating numeric variables. For additional information on string transformations, see Chapter 7. For conditional data transformations, see Chapter 8.

6.1 INTRODUCTION TO DATA TRANSFORMATIONS

Two commands are the core of the transformation language: RECODE and COMPUTE. The RECODE command, documented in Sections 6.3 through 6.10, changes the coding scheme of an existing variable on a value-by-value basis or for ranges of values. For example, to change the coding order for three questionnaire items from 0 for "Agree," 1 for "No opinion," and 2 for "Disagree" to 1, 0, and −1, respectively, specify:

```
RECODE ITEM1,ITEM2,ITEM3 (0=1) (1=0) (2=-1)
VALUE LABELS ITEM1 TO ITEM3 -1 'DISAGREE' 0 'NO OPINION' 1 'AGREE'
```

The three values are recoded as shown for each of the variables in the variable list and labels are provided for the new values.

The COMPUTE command, documented in Sections 6.11 through 6.13, computes a new variable as some combination or transformation of one or more existing variables. For example, to build a simple index averaging the three questionnaire items just recoded, specify:

```
COMPUTE      INDEXQ = (ITEM1 + ITEM2 + ITEM3)/3
VARIABLE LABELS INDEXQ 'SUMMARY INDEX OF QUESTIONS'
```

For each case, the three items are added together, the sum is divided by 3, and the result is stored in new variable INDEXQ, which is then given a label.

You can make execution of data transformations conditional on other information in the data via the IF command or the DO IF—END IF structure, both documented in Chapter 8. For example, to establish a dichotomous (two-valued) variable indicating cities that are classified as poor based on median family income, specify:

```
COMPUTE POOR=0
IF (FAMINC LE 10000) POOR=1
VARIABLE LABELS POOR 'CITIES WITH FAMILY INCOME UNDER $10,000'
```

The COMPUTE command initializes variable POOR to 0 for all cities, and the IF command changes POOR to 1 for cities with values for FAMINC less than or equal to $10,000.

The COUNT command, a specialized version of the COMPUTE command, is documented in Sections 6.32 and 6.33. To create a simple index that counts the number of times a respondent answered "Agree" to the items recoded above, specify:

```
COUNT    AGREE=ITEM1, ITEM2, ITEM3 (1)
VARIABLE LABELS AGREE 'NUMBER OF POSITIVE RESPONSES'
```

The COUNT command initializes new variable AGREE to 0 for all cases and changes it to 1 for cases with value 1 for any one of the three items; to 2 for cases with value 1 for any two items; or to 3 for cases with value 1 for all three items.

6.2 Printing and Writing Formats

By default, SPSS^X assigns print and write formats of F8.2 (or the format you specify using the SET command described in Chapter 4) for new numeric variables created by the RECODE, COMPUTE, or COUNT commands. If the default format is not appropriate, use PRINT FORMATS, WRITE FORMATS, or FORMATS to reset it, as in:

```
COMPUTE INCOME=WAGES + BONUS + INTEREST + OTHERINC
COMPUTE PCTWAGES = RND((WAGES/INCOME)*100)
PRINT FORMATS INCOME (DOLLAR10.2)/ PCTWAGES (F3.0)
VARIABLE LABELS INCOME 'INDIVIDUAL INCOME FROM ALL SOURCES'/
        PCTWAGES 'WAGES AS A PERCENTAGE OF TOTAL INCOME'
```

These commands specify a dollar printing format for variable INCOME and a three-digit, no-decimal format for PCTWAGES. The write format is not changed. See Chapter 9 for a complete discussion of print and write utilities.

6.3 THE RECODE COMMAND

The most direct data transformation is the RECODE command, which tells SPSS^X to change the code for a variable as the data are being read. The command

```
RECODE X (0=9)
```

instructs SPSS to change all zeros found for variable X to nines.

The variable or variables to be recoded must already exist and must precede the value specifications. You can specify as many value specifications as needed, enclosing each specification within parentheses, as in:

```
RECODE ITEM1 (0=1) (1=0) (2=-1)
```

You can use multiple input values in a single specification but only one output value following the equals sign, as in:

```
RECODE RESPONSE (8,9=1) (4 THRU 7=2) (1,2=3)
```

The RECODE command is evaluated left to right, and the values for a case are recoded only once per RECODE command. For example, if a case has an input value of 0 for variable ITEM1, the command

```
RECODE ITEM1 (0=1) (1=0) (2=-1)
```

recodes ITEM1 to 1 and SPSS^X then moves on to the next command. The value is *not* recoded back to 0 by the second value specification. Input values not mentioned in the RECODE command are left unchanged.

You can name multiple variables for the same value specifications, as in:

```
RECODE ITEM1 TO ITEM3 (0=1) (1=0) (2=-1)
```

In addition, you can specify different values for different variables on the same RECODE command by separating the recode specifications with a slash, as in:

```
RECODE AGE (0=9)/ ITEM1 TO ITEM3 (0=1) (1=0) (2=-1)
```

These rules apply to both numeric and short string variables. See Chapter 7 if your variable is a short string or if you want to recode a numeric variable into a string variable.

6.4 Specifying Numeric Values

There are several keyword utilities available for recoding numeric variables. They are

Keyword THRU. Use THRU to specify value ranges, as in 0 THRU 99. (See Section 6.5.)

Keywords LOWEST and HIGHEST. Use LOWEST and HIGHEST to specify the lowest and highest values encountered in a range. (See Section 6.5.)

Keyword ELSE. Use ELSE to recode all values not explicitly mentioned. (See Section 6.6.)

Keywords MISSING and SYSMIS. Use MISSING to reference missing values on input, and SYSMIS to reference missing values on both input and output. (See Section 6.7.)

Keyword INTO. Use INTO to create a new variable as a recoded version of an old one. (See Section 6.9.)

Keyword COPY. Use COPY to copy input values unchanged. (See Section 6.10.)

Blank fields for numeric variables are handled according to the BLANKS specification on the SET command (Chapter 4) prior to any recode specifications.

6.5 Keywords THRU, LOWEST, and HIGHEST

To recode ranges of values for numeric variables into a single value, use keyword THRU. Use keyword LO (LOWEST) or HI (HIGHEST) to specify the lowest or highest input value for the variable. For example, to recode all individuals below the United States voting age to 0 and leave all other ages unchanged, specify:

```
RECODE AGE (LO THRU 17=0)
```

You can also use these keywords to collapse variable AGE into gross categories, perhaps for tabular display, as in:

```
RECODE AGE (LO THRU 20=1)(20 THRU 25=2)(25 THRU 30=3)(30 THRU 35=4)
       (35 THRU 40=5)(40 THRU 45=6)(45 THRU 50=7)(50 THRU 55=8)
       (55 THRU 60=9)(60 THRU 65=10)(65 THRU HI=11)

VARIABLE LABELS AGE 'EMPLOYEE AGE CATEGORIES'
VALUE LABELS AGE 1 'Up to 20' 2 '20 to 25' 3 '25 to 30' 4 '30 to 35'
       5 '35 to 40' 6 '40 to 45' 7 '45 to 50' 8 '50 to 55'
       9 '55 to 60' 10 '60 to 65' 11 '65 and older'
```

Keywords LOWEST and HIGHEST do not include the system-missing value. However, user-missing values are included.

6.6 Keyword ELSE

To recode all values not previously mentioned into a single catchall category, use the keyword ELSE. For example, to recode AGE to a dichotomous (two-valued) variable with 0 representing individuals below the voting age and 1 representing potential voters, specify:

```
RECODE AGE (LO THRU 17=0) (ELSE=1)
```

ELSE should be the last specification for the variable. Otherwise all subsequent value specifications for that variable are ignored. Keyword ELSE *does* include the system-missing value.

You can also use keyword ELSE on the RECODE command as a data-cleaning device, as in:

```
RECODE ITEM1 TO ITEM3 (0=1) (1=0) (2=-1) (9=9) (ELSE=SYSMIS)
```

Input values 0, 1, 2, and 9 (user-missing value) are recoded, while remaining values, known to be illegal codes, are recoded to the system-missing value. In this example, it is unnecessary to redeclare 9 as missing for each variable.

6.7 Keywords MISSING and SYSMIS

To recode a variable that may have missing values defined in the system file or resulting from data input errors, computations, or a MISSING VALUES command, use keyword MISSING or SYSMIS. For example, if −98 and −99 were declared missing for variable AGE, the command

```
RECODE AGE (MISSING=9)
```

recodes −98, −99, and any system-missing values (perhaps from input errors) for variable AGE to 9. The command

```
RECODE AGE (MISSING=SYSMIS)
```

recodes all missing values to the system-missing value.

You can use keyword MISSING only as an input value. MISSING references all missing values including the system-missing value. The output value from a MISSING input specification is not automatically missing; use the MISSING VALUES command to declare the new value missing (see Chapter 3). You can use keyword SYSMIS for either input or output. As an input value, SYSMIS references only system-missing values. As an output value specification, SYSMIS recodes all values named on the left side of the equals sign to the system-missing value.

6.8 Value Ranges

Value ranges include the end points. For variables with noninteger values, values can escape recoding unless you explicitly include them in a range. For instance, you might have calculated variable AGE using a COMPUTE command and the YRMODA function to subtract an individual's birth date from the current date (see Section 6.26). Thus, AGE could be noninteger. If you specify

```
RECODE AGE (MISSING=9) (LO THRU 17=0) (18 THRU HI=1)
```

value 17.01 escapes recoding. (Or worse, unrecoded noninteger values may fall into a catchall ELSE category.) To cover all possibilities, specify the same end point values on two recode specifications, as in:

```
RECODE AGE (MISSING=9) (18 THRU HI=1) (LO THRU 18=0)
```

The specification 18 THRU HI precedes LO THRU 18 so that cases with age exactly equal to 18 are recoded to 1 rather than 0.

6.9 Keyword INTO

To recode the values of one variable and store them in another variable, use the keyword INTO, as in:

```
RECODE AGE (MISSING=9) (18 THRU HI=1) (0 THRU 18=0) INTO VOTER
```

The recoded AGE values are stored in *target variable* VOTER, leaving AGE unchanged.

You can store values for several input variables in one command, as in:

```
RECODE ITEM1 TO ITEM3 (0=1) (1=0) (2=-1) INTO DEFENSE WELFARE HEALTH
```

The number of target variables must equal the number of input variables. Target variables can be existing or new variables. If you use an existing variable, cases with values not mentioned in the recode specification are not changed. If you use a new variable, cases with values not specified for recoding are assigned the initialized system-missing values for that variable. For example, if a case in the example above has a value less than 0 for variable AGE, new variable VOTER is system-missing. As shown in Section 6.6, you can recode all such wild values using keyword ELSE. The command

```
RECODE AGE (MISSING=9) (18 THRU 110=1) (0 THRU 18=0) (ELSE=8)
     INTO VOTER
```

recodes any case with an AGE value below zero and over 110 to value 8 for variable VOTER.

New numeric variables have default print and write formats of F8.2 (Section 6.2) or the format you specify using the SET command (Chapter 4).

6.10 Keyword COPY

To recode a variable into a new variable or to use keyword ELSE as a cleanup category, you may want to retain a set of input values. The command

```
RECODE ITEM1 TO ITEM3 (0=1) (1=0) (2=-1) (ELSE=COPY)
                     INTO DEFENSE WELFARE HEALTH
```

creates three new variables with values 1, 0, and −1. Input values other than 0, 1, or 2 are retained. In other words, if a case has value 9 for variable ITEM1, it will have value 9 for variable DEFENSE, and so forth.

Keyword COPY is an output specification only. Input values to be copied can be a range of values, keywords SYSMIS or MISSING, or keyword ELSE. User-missing values are copied, but their missing-value status is not. In the example above, value 9 should be redeclared missing for new variables DEFENSE, WELFARE, and HEALTH. System-missing is copied as system-missing.

6.11 THE COMPUTE COMMAND

Often, you want to create a new variable or transform an existing variable using information from other variables on your file. The COMPUTE command generates a variable on your active file that is constructed on a case-by-case basis as an arithmetic or logical transformation of existing variables and constants. For example, the command

```
COMPUTE INCOME=WAGES + BONUS + INTEREST + OTHERINC
```

assigns the sum of four existing variables to variable INCOME for each case on your active file.

To compute a variable, specify the *target variable* on the left of the equals sign and the *expression* on the right. You can compute one target variable per command. The expression must be *numeric* (return a number) if the target variable is numeric and *string* (return a string) if the target is a string variable. Facilities for computing numeric variables are described in Sections 6.12 through 6.31. String variables are described in Chapter 7.

6.12 Computing Numeric Variables

The command

```
COMPUTE X=1
```

assigns the value 1 to variable X for every case. Numeric variable X is the target and 1 is the numeric expression.

The target variable can be an existing variable or a new variable defined by the COMPUTE command itself. If the target variable already

ANNOTATED EXAMPLE FOR RECODE

The job developed in Sections 6.3 through 6.10 is to change all values known to be outside the expected range to system-missing for three ITEM variables and to create a new dichotomous (two-valued) variable from AGE that flags individuals who are eligible to vote in the United States (18 years of age or older). The SPSS^{X} commands are

```
TITLE  PILOT FOR COLLEGE SURVEY
FILE HANDLE TESTDATA/ file specifications
DATA LIST  FILE=TESTDATA
  /AGE 1-3 ITEM1 TO ITEM3 5-7
VARIABLE LABELS  ITEM1 'OPINION ON LEVEL OF DEFENSE SPENDING'
  ITEM2 'OPINION ON LEVEL OF WELFARE SPENDING'
  ITEM3 'OPINION ON LEVEL OF HEALTH SPENDING'
VALUE LABELS  ITEM1 TO ITEM3 -1 'DISAGREE' 0 'NO OPINION' 1 'AGREE'
MISSING VALUES  AGE(-99,-98) ITEM1 TO ITEM3 (9)

RECODE  ITEM1 TO ITEM3 (0=1) (1=0) (2=-1) (9=9) (ELSE=SYSMIS)

RECODE  AGE (MISSING=9) (18 THRU HI=1) (LO THRU 18=0) INTO VOTER
PRINT /$CASENUM 1-2 AGE 4-6 VOTER 8-10

VARIABLE LABELS  VOTER 'ELIGIBLE TO VOTE'
VALUE LABELS  VOTER 0 'UNDER 18' 1 '18 OR OVER'
MISSING VALUES  VOTER (9)
PRINT FORMATS VOTER(F1.0)
FREQUENCIES VARIABLES=VOTER,ITEM1 TO ITEM3
```

- The TITLE command supplies a title for the top of each page of display from this job (see Chapter 4).
- The DATA LIST command names the input data file and defines the variables (see Chapter 3).
- The VARIABLE LABELS, VALUE LABELS, and MISSING VALUES commands complete the variable definitions (see Chapter 3).
- The first RECODE command recodes input values 0, 1, and 2 to 1, 0, and −1, respectively, for the three ITEM variables and preserves missing value 9 by recoding it to itself. Keyword ELSE can then be used to change all unmentioned values to the system-missing value in order to clean up the coding (see Sections 6.3, 6.6, and 6.7).
- The second RECODE command recodes missing values for AGE (−99 and −98) to 9, values 18 through the highest to 1 (eligible voters), and values less than 18 to 0 (not eligible). The results are stored in new variable VOTER (see Sections 6.5, 6.7 and 6.8).
- The PRINT command provides a check on the recoding of AGE by printing the values for AGE and VOTER (see Chapter 9). System variable $CASENUM supplies a case number on the printed results (see Section 6.42). The printed output is shown in Figure A.
- The VARIABLE LABELS, VALUE LABELS, and MISSING VALUES commands complete the definition of new variable VOTER (see Chapter 3).
- The PRINT FORMATS command provides a one-digit printing format with no decimal places for VOTER (see Chapter 9). The default for new variables is F8.2.
- The FREQUENCIES command produces frequency tables as a complete check on the new variable and on the ITEM variables including labels and missing values (see Chapter 18). The output from the FREQUENCIES command is shown in Figure B. Notice that variable ITEM1 has two cases with the system-missing value (denoted with the period), indicating that two cases were miscoded and should probably be corrected.

A PRINT values for variables AGE and VOTER

```
 1  22   1
 2   0   9
 3  34   1
 4  17   0
 5  17   0
 6  21   1
 7 -99   9
 8  18   1
 9  18   1
10  19   1
11  16   0
12  21   1
13  20   1
```

B FREQUENCIES for new variable VOTER

05 OCT 82 PILOT FOR COLLEGE SURVEY

FILE:

VOTER ELIGIBLE TO VOTE

VALUE LABEL	VALUE	FREQUENCY	PERCENT	VALID PERCENT	CUM PERCENT
UNDER 18	0	3	23.1	27.3	27.3
18 OR OVER	1	8	61.5	72.7	100.0
	9	2	15.4	MISSING	
	TOTAL	13	100.0	100.0	

VALID CASES 11 MISSING CASES 2

- -

ITEM1 OPINION ON LEVEL OF DEFENSE SPENDING

VALUE LABEL	VALUE	FREQUENCY	PERCENT	VALID PERCENT	CUM PERCENT
DISAGREE	-1	3	23.1	27.3	27.3
NO OPINION	0	5	38.5	45.5	72.7
AGREE	1	3	23.1	27.3	100.0
	.	2	15.4	MISSING	
	TOTAL	13	100.0	100.0	

VALID CASES 11 MISSING CASES 2

exists when SPSS^{X} encounters the command, the old values are replaced. If the target variable does not exist, it is created by the COMPUTE command. New numeric variables are initialized to the system-missing value unless the LEAVE command is used (Section 6.35) and are assigned a default print and write format of F8.2 (Section 6.2).

Once computed, the variable exists on your active file in its new form and can be labeled, analyzed, and stored on a new system file along with all other variables on your active file. If it is a new variable, it is added to the end of the dictionary on your active file. Scratch variables, described in Section 6.36, are not added to your active file and are not saved on a new system file.

The expression to the right of the equals sign can be composed of existing variables, arithmetic operators such as + and −, arithmetic or statistical functions such as SQRT or MEAN, logical functions such as ANY and SYSMIS, system variables, numeric constants, and so forth. For example, the command

```
COMPUTE PCTWAGES=(WAGES/INCOME)*100
```

creates PCTWAGES as a percentage of INCOME through use of the slash for division, the asterisk for multiplication, and the parentheses to clarify the order of operations (see Section 6.17). The command

```
COMPUTE SCALE=MEAN(Q1,Q2,Q3)
```

constructs variable SCALE from three variables using the MEAN function (see Section 6.20). Facilities for handling numeric expressions are documented in Sections 6.14 through 6.31.

6.13 Missing Values

If a case is missing on any of the variables used in an expression when the COMPUTE command is executed, SPSS^{X} nearly always returns the system-missing value since the operation is indeterminate. For example, in the command

```
COMPUTE PAYHOURS = WORKDAYS * 7.5
```

variable PAYHOURS cannot be computed for any case missing on variable WORKDAYS.

SPSS^{X} also returns missing values when the expression itself is undefined. In the command

```
COMPUTE PCTWAGES=(WAGES/INCOME)*100
```

variable PCTWAGES is considered indeterminate for a case when the value for INCOME is 0, since division by 0 is not defined (see Section 6.31).

If these rules do not fit your application, you should be able to specify exactly what you want using one or more of the functions described in Section 6.21. A complete discussion of missing values in numeric expressions appears in Sections 6.29 through 6.31.

6.14 NUMERIC EXPRESSIONS

While numeric expressions are commonly used with the COMPUTE command, they can be used as part of a logical expression for commands such as IF, DO IF, LOOP IF, SELECT IF, and so forth (Chapter 8). Arithmetic expressions can also appear in the index portion of a LOOP command (Chapter 12), on the REPEATING DATA command (Chapter 11), and on the PRINT SPACES command (Chapter 9).

Facilities for numeric expressions are

Arithmetic Functions. These functions allow you to round or truncate a variable, take the square root or the log of a variable, and so forth. (See Section 6.19.)

Statistical Functions. Statistical functions allow you to compute statistics such as the mean or variance across variables for each case. (See Section 6.20.)

Missing-Value Functions. Missing-value functions are used to control the propagation of missing values in numeric and logical expressions. (See Section 6.21.)

The LAG Function. LAG is a special function that provides access to across-case information. (See Section 6.22.)

Logical Functions. Logical functions check the logic of an expression and yield the result 1 when the expression is true and 0 when it is false. (See Section 6.23.)

Other Functions. Specialized functions for handling dates, pseudo random numbers, and normal cumulative distributions are also available (see Section 6.22).

Numeric expressions can also be composed of arithmetic operations and numeric constants (see Sections 6.15 and 6.16).

6.15 Arithmetic Operations

Arithmetic operators and their meanings are

- + *Addition.* See also the SUM function described in Section 6.20.
- − *Subtraction.*
- * *Multiplication.*
- / *Division.*
- ** *Exponentiation.* See also the SQRT function for taking the square root described in Section 6.19.

No two operators can appear consecutively. You cannot specify VAR1+*VAR2, but VAR1*−VAR2 is valid because the minus sign is also used to represent a negative number. In addition, you cannot imply arithmetic operators. For example, you cannot specify (VAR1)(VAR2) in place of VAR1*VAR2.

The arithmetic operators and the parentheses serve as delimiters. You can insert blanks (not commas) before and after an operator to improve readability, as in:

```
COMPUTE PCTWAGES = (WAGES / INCOME) * 100
```

6.16 Numeric Constants

Constants used in numeric expressions or as arguments to functions can be integer or noninteger, depending on the application or the function. You can specify as many digits in a constant as needed, as long as you understand the precision restrictions of your computer. Numeric constants can be signed (+ or −) but cannot contain any other special characters such as the comma or dollar sign. You can use the alternative exponential format by specifying E and a signed exponent after a number, as in:

```
COMPUTE X = Y * 5.1E+5
```

This command returns the value 510,000.0 for a case with value 1 for variable Y. This is also known as scientific notation.

6.17 The Order of Operations

You can use variables, constants, and functions with arithmetic operators to form complex expressions. The order in which SPSS^X executes the operations of a COMPUTE command when the data are read and the target variable is constructed is (1) functions; (2) exponentiation; (3) multiplication, division, and unary −; and (4) addition and subtraction. Thus, in the command

```
COMPUTE X = SQRT(Y1) / SQRT(Y2) + SQRT(Y3)
```

the square root operations are executed first, then the division, and then the addition.

You can control the order of operations by enclosing in parentheses the operation you want to execute first. The command

```
COMPUTE X = SQRT(Y1) / (SQRT(Y2) + SQRT(Y3))
```

returns a different value than the previous example since the square roots of Y2 and Y3 are summed before the division takes place.

The order of execution for operations at the same level unspecified by parentheses is left to right. Thus, the command

```
COMPUTE TESTVAR = (X/Y*Z)+1
```

returns 3 for a case with a value of 2 for X, Y, and Z since 2 (variable X) divided by 2 (variable Y) is 1, times 2 (variable Z) is 2, plus 1 is 3. However, the command

```
COMPUTE TESTVAR = (X/(Y*Z))+1
```

returns 1.5 for the same case since the expression (2/(2*2)) returns .5 when the parentheses alter the order of execution.

If you are ever unsure of the order of execution, use parentheses to make the order explicit—even if you specify the order SPSS^X would use anyway.

6.18 Numeric Functions

You can use the functions described below in any numeric expression on IF, SELECT IF, DO IF, ELSE IF, LOOP IF, END LOOP IF, and COMPUTE. Numeric functions always return numbers (or the system-missing value whenever the result is indeterminate). The expression to be transformed by a function is called the *argument*. Most functions have a variable name or a list of variable names as arguments. For example, to generate the square root of variable X, specify variable X as the argument to the SQRT function, as in SQRT(X). Enclose arguments in parentheses, as in

```
COMPUTE INCOME = TRUNC(INCOME)
```

where the TRUNC function returns the integer portion of variable INCOME. Separate multiple arguments with commas, as in

```
COMPUTE SCALE=MEAN(Q1,Q2,Q3)
```

where the MEAN function returns the mean of variables Q1, Q2, and Q3.

These functions, their arguments, their applications, and how they handle missing values are discussed in Sections 6.19 through 6.31.

6.19 Arithmetic Functions

ABS(arg) *Absolute value.* ABS(−4.7) is 4.7; ABS(4.7) is 4.7.

RND(arg) *Round the absolute value to an integer (and reaffix the sign).* RND(−4.7) is −5.

TRUNC(arg) *Truncate to an integer.* TRUNC(−4.7) is −4.

MOD(arg,arg) *Remainder (modulo) of the first argument divided by the second.* MOD(1983,100) is 83.

SQRT(arg) *Square root.*

EXP(arg) *Exponential.* e is raised to the power of the argument.

LG10(arg) *Base 10 logarithm.*

LN(arg) *Natural or Naperian logarithm (base* e*).*

ARSIN(arg) *Arcsine.* The result is given in radians (alias ASIN).

ARTAN(arg)	*Arctangent.* The result is given in radians (alias ATAN).
SIN(arg)	*Sine.* The argument must be specified in radians.
COS(arg)	*Cosine.* The argument must be specified in radians.

All arithmetic functions except MOD have single arguments; MOD has two. Arguments can be numeric expressions as in RND(A**2/B).

6.20 Statistical Functions

SUM(arg list)	*Sum of the values across the argument list.*
MEAN(arg list)	*Mean of the values across the argument list.*
SD(arg list)	*Standard deviation of the values across the argument list.*
VARIANCE(arg list)	*Variance of the values across the argument list.*
CFVAR(arg list)	*Coefficient of variation of the values across the argument list.* The coefficient of variation is the standard deviation divided by the mean.
MIN(arg list)	*Minimum value across the argument list.*
MAX(arg list)	*Maximum value across the argument list.*

You can use the *.n* suffix described in Section 6.30 with all statistical functions to specify the number of valid arguments you consider acceptable. For example, MEAN.2(A,B,C,D) returns the mean of the valid values for variables A, B, C, and D only if at least two of the variables have valid values. You can also use the TO keyword to reference a set of variables in the argument list.

6.21 Missing-Value Functions

VALUE(arg)	*Ignore user-defined missing values.* The argument must be a variable name. (See Section 6.30.)
MISSING(arg)	*Return 1 if the value is missing and 0 otherwise.* (See Section 6.25.)
SYSMIS(arg)	*Return 1 if the value is system-missing and 0 otherwise.* (See Section 6.25.)
NMISS(arg list)	*Count of the number of missing values in the argument list.*
NVALID(arg list)	*Count of the number of valid values in the argument list.*

You can use the keyword TO to reference a set of variables in the argument list for functions NMISS and NVALID. For example, NMISS(A TO D) returns a count of the number of variables with missing values in the list from A through D.

6.22 The Across-Case LAG Function

LAG(arg,n)	*The value of the variable* n *cases before.* The argument must be a numeric variable. LAG(GNP,4) returns the value of GNP for the fourth case before the current one.

If you are selecting cases from a file (Chapter 10), LAG returns the value for the *n*th case previously selected.

6.23 Logical Functions

RANGE(arg,arg list)	*Return 1 if the value of the first argument is in the inclusive range(s), otherwise, return 0.* The first argument is usually a variable, and the list usually contains pairs of values. RANGE(AGE,1,17,62,99) returns 1 for ages 1 through 17 and 62 through 99 inclusive.
ANY(arg,arg list)	*Return 1 if the value of the first argument matches one of the arguments in the list, otherwise, return 0.* The first argument is usually a variable. ANY(PROJECT,3,4,7,9) returns 1 if the value for variable PROJECT is 3, 4, 7, or 9.

See the discussion on using logical functions in Section 6.25.

6.24 Other Functions

UNIFORM(arg) *A uniform pseudo random number.* The random number is uniformly distributed with values varying between 0 and the value of the argument.

NORMAL(arg) *A normal pseudo random number.* The random number is randomly distributed with a mean of 0 and a standard deviation equal to the argument.

CDFNORM(arg) *Standard normal cumulative distribution.* This function returns the probability that a random variable with a normal distribution falls below the value of the argument.

PROBIT(arg) *Inverse of the standard normal cumulative distribution.* The value of the argument must be greater than 0 and less than 1. The argument is the probability that a normally distributed random variable will be less than the value returned.

YRMODA(arg list) *Convert year, month, and day to a day number.* With this function you must specify the year, month, and day, in that order. The number returned is the number of days since October 15, 1582 (Day 1 of the Gregorian calendar). (See Section 6.26.)

6.25 Using Logical Functions

Functions MISSING and SYSMIS (Section 6.21) and RANGE and ANY (Section 6.23) are logical functions. Logical functions are useful short cuts to more complicated specifications on the IF, DO IF, and other conditional commands. For example,

```
IF ANY(DEPT82,1,2) BONUS = .16*SALARY82
```

is equivalent to

```
IF  (DEPT82 EQ 1 OR DEPT82 EQ 2)  BONUS = .16*SALARY82
```

To set an individual's bonus to 0 if the department code is missing, specify:

```
IF MISSING(DEPT82) BONUS = 0
```

You can also use logical functions in COMPUTE applications to create *logical variables*, which have values 0, 1, or missing (see Section 6.28). For example, to dichotomize an age variable to indicate those likely to be in the adult work force, you could specify

```
COMPUTE WORKERS = RANGE(AGE,18,65)
```

instead of the commands

```
IF  (AGE GE 18 AND AGE LE 65)  WORKERS = 1
IF  (AGE LT 18 OR AGE GT 65)   WORKERS = 0
```

In both examples, WORKERS is 1 for cases with AGE from 18 to 65, 0 for all other valid values, and system-missing for cases with a missing value for AGE.

Or to create a dichotomous (two-valued) variable that records 1 for individuals who gave the same response to two agree-disagree questions (assuming the same coding scheme), specify

```
COMPUTE QSAME=ANY(Q1,Q2)
```

where QSAME is 1 whenever Q1 equals Q2.

In the RANGE and ANY examples, a missing value for the first argument always returns the system-missing value. However, missing values in the argument list for ANY and RANGE do not always return the system-missing value (see Section 6.30).

6.26 Using the YRMODA Function

To calculate the number of days between dates, use the YRMODA function to convert to a day number and subtract. The command

```
COMPUTE AGE=($JDATE - YRMODA(YRBIRTH,MOBIRTH,DABIRTH))/365.25
```

calculates an individual's age by converting birth date to a day number using the YRMODA function and subtracting that number from the current date using the $JDATE system variable (see Section 6.42).

The YRMODA function returns the number of days since the first day of the Gregorian calendar, which is October 15, 1582. The expression YRMODA(1582,10,15) returns 1, and YRMODA(1800,1,1) returns 79337, which means that January 1, 1800, was 79,336 days after the beginning of the Gregorian calendar.

The YRMODA function has three arguments. Arguments can be variables, as above, constants, or any other type of expression, and they must yield integers.

- The first argument can be any year from 1582 to 47516. Or if you specify a number between 00 and 99, SPSS^X will assume 1900 through 1999.
- The second argument is the month from 1 through 13. Month 13 allows the use of Day 0 to refer to the last day of the year, as in YRMODA(YEAR,13,0). Or to indicate the first month of the coming year, specify YRMODA(YEAR,13,DA).
- The final argument is the day from 0 through 31. Day 0 is the last day of the previous month regardless of whether it is 28, 29, 30, or 31. Thus, YRMODA(YEAR,MONTH + 1,0) is the last day of variable MONTH.

You may want to enclose expressions in parentheses for readability, as in YRMODA(YEAR,(MONTH + 1),0).

6.27 Complex Numeric Arguments

Except where explicitly noted, you can construct complex expressions by nesting functions and arithmetic operators as arguments to functions. For example, to ensure that the result of a numeric expression returns an integer value, specify:

```
COMPUTE PCTWAGES = RND((WAGES/INCOME)*100)
```

Likewise, to determine the minimum square root across a list of variables, specify:

```
COMPUTE QMINSQRT = SQRT(MIN(Q1,Q2,Q3,Q4))
```

SPSS^X evaluates complex numeric arguments in the same order described in Section 6.17. Parentheses can be used to control the order of execution. For example,

```
COMPUTE TESTVAR = TRUNC(SQRT(X/Y)) * .5
```

returns .5 for a case with value 2 for X and Y since 2 divided by 2 (X/Y) is 1, the square root of 1 is 1, truncating 1 returns 1, and 1 times .5 is .5. However,

```
COMPUTE TESTVAR = TRUNC(SQRT(X/Y) * .5)
```

returns 0 since SQRT(X/Y) is 1, 1 times .5 is .5, and truncating .5 returns 0.

6.28 Logical Expressions

As described in Chapter 8, logical expressions can be composed of logical variables, relations comparing two or more values, or a compound expression. Logical expressions are either true, false, or missing. Because SPSS^X actually returns a numeric 1, 0, or system-missing value, logical expressions are numeric expressions and are not limited to commands involving

IF expressions. Therefore, you can use logical expressions in a COMPUTE command. For example, the command

```
COMPUTE ELIGIBLE = AGE GE 18
```

returns 1 for cases 18 or over (eligible voters in the United States), 0 for cases under 18, and system-missing if AGE is missing. If you want variable ELIGIBLE to be 1 for those 18 or older who are registered to vote and if you have variable REGISTRD with 1 for "yes" and 0 for "no," specify:

```
COMPUTE ELIGIBLE = AGE GE 18 AND REGISTRD
```

To use REGISTRD in this manner, it must be a *logical variable*, which is a variable with values 0, 1, and missing only. For a logical variable, SPSS^X accepts 1 as true, 0 as false, and system- or user-missing values as missing. All other values cause warning messages and are forced to false. Therefore, REGISTRD EQ 1 would produce the same results as above but would not generate warnings.

You can use logical variables with computation language to construct complex variables. For example, to create a dummy variable with values 1, 0, and −1 (typically used in multiple regression analysis), specify

```
COMPUTE RELIG5 = (RELIG EQ 5) - (RELIG EQ 3)
```

which returns 1 if RELIG equals 5 (1−0), −1 if RELIG equals 3 (0−1), and 0 for all other valid categories.

6.29 Missing Values

Missing values arise in numeric expressions for reasons other than when SPSS^X encounters missing values in variables. Certain arithmetic operations, such as division by zero, produce the system-missing value (see Section 6.31). SPSS^X also returns system-missing for operations that involve functions with arguments that cannot be evaluated (see Section 6.30).

Some arithmetic operations involving 0 produce the same results regardless of what values are used. In these cases, SPSS^X evaluates the operation even when the variables have missing values. These operations are presented in Table 6.29.

Table 6.29 Missing-value exceptions in numeric expressions

Expression	Result
0 * missing	= 0
0 / missing	= 0
missing ** 0	= 1
0 ** missing	= 0
MOD(0,missing)	= 0

6.30 Missing Values in Arguments

SPSS^X tries to evaluate a function using all the information it has and returns the system-missing value only when it doesn't have enough information (see Table 6.30). For example, the ANY and RANGE functions follow the same exceptions described for AND and OR in Chapter 8. Thus, the expression ANY(X,Y,0) returns true if variable X is equal to 0 even if Y is missing. Likewise, the expression RANGE(X,0,Y) is false if X is −1 even if Y is missing.

Table 6.30 Missing values in arguments to functions

Function	Returns system-missing if
ABS (x) ARSIN (x) ARTAN (x) CDFNORM (x) COS (x) EXP (x) LG10 (x) LN (x) NORMAL (x) PROBIT (x) RND (x) SIN (x) SQRT (x) TRUNC (x) UNIFORM (x)	x is missing
VALUE (x)	x is system-missing
YRMODA (x1,x2,x3)	any x is missing
MOD (x1,x2)	x1 is missing, or x2 is missing and x1 is not 0
MAX.n (x1,x2,...xk) MEAN.n (x1,x2,...xk) MIN.n (x1,x2,...x1) SUM.n (x1,x2,...xk)	fewer than n arguments are valid (NVALID (x1,x2,...xk) < n) default n is 1
CFVAR.n (x1,x2,...xk) SD.n (x1,x2,...xk) VARIANCE.n (x1,x2,...xk)	fewer than n arguments are valid (NVALID (x1,x2,...xk) < n) default n is 2
LAG (x,n)	x is missing n cases previously (and always for the first n cases)
ANY (x,x1,x2,...xk)	x or all of x1,x2,...xk are missing
RANGE (x,x1,x2,...xk)	x or all of pairs x1,x2, etc. are missing
MISSING (x) NMISS (x1,x2,...xk) NVALID (x1,x2,...xk) SYSMIS (x)	never

Arithmetic functions that take only one argument cannot be evaluated if that argument is missing. However, statistical functions are evaluated if a sufficient number of arguments are valid. For example, to sum the values of three variables, you could use arithmetic operators, as in:

```
COMPUTE FACTOR = SCORE1 + SCORE2 + SCORE3
```

With this command, variable FACTOR is assigned the system-missing value for any case with a missing value for any one (or more) of the score variables. On the other hand, the SUM function is executed even if only one of the arguments has valid information, as in:

```
COMPUTE FACTOR = SUM(SCORE1 TO SCORE3)
```

With this command, a valid value is assigned to FACTOR by summing any two valid score values or by simply assigning the single valid score. FACTOR is missing if all variables are missing.

You can use the *.n* suffix with the statistical functions SUM, MEAN, MIN, MAX, SD, VARIANCE, and CFVAR to specify the number of valid arguments you consider acceptable. For example, to compute FACTOR only

ANNOTATED EXAMPLES FOR COMPUTE

The following examples represent most of the applications of the COMPUTE command.

Arithmetic Operations. A complete list of arithmetic operators appears in Section 6.15.

To initialize variable POOR to 0 for all cases (Section 6.1), specify:

```
COMPUTE  POOR=0
```

To compute variable PCTWAGES a percentage of variable INCOME (Section 6.12), specify:

```
COMPUTE  PCTWAGES=(WAGES/INCOME)*100
```

Numeric Functions. A complete list of available numeric functions appears in Sections 6.19 through 6.24. See Section 6.17 for information on the order of operations in complex numeric expressions.

To compute variable PCTWAGES as a percentage of INCOME and round the percentage to an integer (Section 6.27), specify:

```
COMPUTE  PCTWAGES=RND((WAGES/INCOME)*100)
```

To create a scale that is the mean of three variables (Section 6.12), specify:

```
COMPUTE  SCALE=MEAN(Q1,Q2,Q3)
```

To truncate values of a variable with decimal places to integers (Section 6.19), specify:

```
COMPUTE  INCOME=TRUNC(INCOME)
```

To divide the square root of Y1 by the square root of Y2 and then add the square root of Y3 (Section 6.17), specify:

```
COMPUTE  X=SQRT(Y1) / SQRT(Y2) + SQRT(Y3)
```

To find the minimum square root value of variables Q1, Q2, Q3, and Q4 (Section 6.27), specify:

```
COMPUTE  QMINSQRT=SQRT(MIN(Q1,Q2,Q3,Q4))
```

Missing Values. Methods for handling missing values in numeric expressions are described in Sections 6.29 through 6.31.

To compute the sum of three variables only for cases with valid values for all three variables (Section 6.30), specify:

```
COMPUTE  FACTOR=SCORE1 + SCORE2 + SCORE3
```

On the other hand, to compute the sum of three variables for cases with a valid value for any one or more of the three (Section 6.30), specify:

```
COMPUTE  FACTOR=SUM(SCORE1 TO SCORE3)
```

To compute the sum of three variables for cases with valid values for any two or more of the three variables, use the *.n* suffix (Section 6.30), as in:

```
COMPUTE  FACTOR=SUM.2(SCORE1 TO SCORE3)
```

To compute the sum of three variables for cases and include cases with user-defined missing values for any of the three variables (Section 6.30), specify:

```
COMPUTE  FACTOR=VALUE(SCORE1) + VALUE(SCORE2) + VALUE(SCORE3)
```

Logical Operations. Logical functions are described in Sections 6.23 and 6.25. The use of other types of logical expressions with the COMPUTE command is described in Section 6.28.

To create a logical variable WORKERS with value 1 for cases with AGE between 18 and 65 inclusive, value 0 for all other ages, and missing if AGE is missing (Section 6.25), specify:

```
COMPUTE  WORKERS=RANGE(AGE,18,65)
```

To create a logical variable with value 1 when two variables are equal, 0 when they are not, and missing when one or the other is missing (Section 6.25), specify:

```
COMPUTE  QSAME=ANY(Q1,Q2)
```

To create a logical variable with value 1 when AGE is 18 or greater, 0 when AGE is less than 18, and missing when AGE is missing (Section 6.28), specify:

```
COMPUTE  ELIGIBLE=AGE GE 18
```

Across-Case Operations. The across-case LAG function is described in Section 6.22 The LEAVE command is documented in Section 6.35.

To set the value of variable RATE4 to the value of RATE for the fourth previous case (Section 6.22), specify:

```
COMPUTE  RATE4=LAG(RATE,4)
```

To accumulate the sum of salaries across cases where TSALARY is the value of SALARY82 for the current case plus the sum of SALARY82 for all cases already read (Section 6.35), specify:

```
COMPUTE  TSALARY=TSALARY+SALARY82
LEAVE  TSALARY
```

if a case has valid information for at least two scores, use the *.n* suffix with the SUM function, as in:

```
COMPUTE FACTOR = SUM.2(SCORE1 TO SCORE3)
```

This command instructs SPSS^X to sum any two or more valid scores and to return missing otherwise.

To override the definition for user-missing values, use the VALUE function, as in:

```
COMPUTE FACTOR = VALUE(SCORE1) + VALUE(SCORE2) + VALUE(SCORE3)
```

This command instructs SPSS^X to treat all user-missing values as valid and to use them in constructing the target variable. (You cannot override system-missing values in this way.) This will produce different results from the SUM command above, which constructs FACTOR when at least one score is valid but does not sum the user-missing values for the other variables.

6.31 Domain Errors

Domain errors occur when numeric expressions are mathematically undefined or are numerically unrepresentable on the computer for reasons other than missing data. Two common examples are division by zero and the square root of a negative number. When SPSS^X detects a domain error in an expression, it returns the system-missing value for that expression. For example, the command

```
COMPUTE TESTVAR = TRUNC(SQRT(X/Y) * .5)
```

returns system-missing if X or Y is negative or if Y is 0.

The following are domain errors in numeric expressions:

**	A negative number to a noninteger power.
/	A divisor of 0.
MOD	A divisor of 0.
SQRT	A negative argument.
EXP	An argument that produces a result too large to be represented on the computer.
LG10	A negative or 0 argument.
LG	A negative or 0 argument.
ARSIN	An argument whose absolute value exceeds 1.
ARTAN	An argument whose absolute value exceeds 1.
NORMAL	A negative or 0 argument.
YRMODA	Arguments that do not form a valid date (see Section 6.25).
PROBIT	A negative argument, zero, or an argument 1 or greater.

6.32 THE COUNT COMMAND

The COUNT command is a special data transformation utility used to create a numeric variable that, for each case, counts the occurrences of the same value (or list of values) across a list of numeric or string variables. For example,

```
COUNT  READER=NEWSWEEK,TIME,USNEWS (2)
```

creates a simple index READER that indicates the number of times the value 2 (those who read each magazine) is recorded for the three variables for a case. Thus, the value of reader will be either 0, 1, 2, or 3. You can enter more than one criterion variable list and more than one criterion value enclosed in parentheses, as in

```
COUNT  READER=NEWSWEEK,TIME,USNEWS (2)
              NYTIMES,WPOST,CHIGTRIB,LATIMES (3,4)
```

which adds four more news sources to the previous index. This time, SPSS^X increases the count for a case by 1 whenever it encounters either value 3 (Sunday only) or 4 (daily plus Sunday) for each newspaper variable.

You can specify a variable more than once in the variable list to increase the count by more than one for that variable, thus giving it more weight. You can also use the TO keyword to list your variables and the THRU, LOWEST, and HIGHEST keywords in the value list. You can also create more than one variable on a COUNT command by separating the specifications with a slash, as in:

```
COUNT  LOWCOUNT = Q1 TO Q10 (LOWEST THRU 5)
      /HICOUNT = Q1 TO Q10 (11 THRU HIGHEST)
```

6.33 Initialization and Missing Values

The COUNT command ignores the missing-value status of user-missing values. In other words, the COUNT command counts a value even if that value has been previously declared as missing. In the command

```
COUNT LOWCOUNT=Q1 TO Q10(LOWEST THRU 5)
```

target variable LOWCOUNT is increased for a case with value 0 for variables Q1, Q2, and so forth, even if 0 was declared user-missing for the Q variables.

COUNT will not propagate missing values automatically. In other words, the target variable will never be system-missing. However, you can use the MISSING VALUES command to declare missing values for the target variable.

You can use keyword MISSING to count all missing values and keyword SYSMIS to count system-missing values. Specify these keywords in parentheses in the value list, as in:

```
COUNT  QMISS = Q1 TO Q10 (MISSING)
      /QSYSMIS= Q1 TO Q10 (SYSMIS)
```

This command creates one variable (QMISS) that counts the number of missing values for the criterion variables and a second variable (QSYSMISS) that counts only system-missing values.

6.34 TRANSFORMATION UTILITIES

SPSS^X provides various utilities to assist in manipulating your data. In general, the basic transformation language without these features can solve your problems. However, your work will be easier if you learn to use scratch variables (Section 6.36), temporary transformations (Section 6.37), the NUMERIC command (Section 6.38), and the DO REPEAT—END REPEAT structure (Section 6.39). The VECTOR command, another utility, is most closely associated with the LOOP structure and is documented in Chapter 12. Finally, the LEAVE command (Section 6.35) is very important since it provides access to information from previous cases and controls how a new variable is initialized.

6.35 The LEAVE Command

Normally, SPSS^X reinitializes a numeric or string variable each time it reads a new case. To leave a variable at its value for the previous case as each new case is read, specify the variable on a LEAVE command. Numeric variables named on a LEAVE command are initialized to 0 for the first case and string variables are initialized to blanks. For example, to keep a running total of salaries across all cases, specify

```
COMPUTE TSALARY=TSALARY+SALARY82
LEAVE TSALARY
FORMAT TSALARY (DOLLAR8)/ SALARY82 (DOLLAR7)
PRINT /SALARY82 TSALARY
EXECUTE
```

where SALARY82 is the variable containing the employee's 1982 salary and TSALARY is the new variable containing the cumulative salaries for all previous cases. The results of the PRINT command are shown in Figure 6.35a.

Figure 6.35a Accumulating the sum across all variables

```
$10,733  $10,733
 $9,767  $20,500
$11,983  $32,483
$12,888  $45,371
$13,803  $59,174
$24,222  $83,396
$22,111 $105,507
$25,223 $130,730
$27,223 $157,953
$20,100 $178,053
$28,888 $206,941
$21,800 $228,741
$22,338 $251,079
$34,880 $285,959
$28,000 $313,959
$28,888 $342,847
```

To accumulate a sum across groups of cases (time intervals, departments, and so forth), use the IF command described in Chapter 8, as in:

```
SORT CASES DEPT82
IF DEPT82 NE LAG(DEPT82,1) TSALARY=0 /*INITIALIZE FOR NEW DEPT
COMPUTE TSALARY=TSALARY+SALARY82     /*SUM SALARIES
LEAVE TSALARY                        /*PREVENT INITIALIZATION EACH CASE
FORMAT TSALARY (DOLLAR8)/ SALARY82 (DOLLAR7)
EXECUTE
```

The results of this PRINT command are shown in Figure 6.35b. The sum is reset each time the value of DEPT82 changes. This example assumes that the data are sorted in order of DEPT82.

Figure 6.35b Accumulating sums across groups of variables

```
1 $10,733  $10,733
1  $9,767  $20,500
1 $11,983  $32,483
1 $12,888  $45,371
1 $13,803  $59,174
1 $24,222  $83,396
1 $22,111 $105,507
2 $25,223  $25,223
2 $27,223  $52,446
2 $20,100  $72,546
2 $28,888 $101,434
3 $21,800  $21,800
3 $22,338  $44,138
3 $34,880  $79,018
3 $28,000 $107,018
3 $28,888 $135,906
```

You can name more than one variable on a LEAVE command and can use the TO keyword to reference a list of consecutive variables. The variables named on the LEAVE command must already exist and cannot be scratch variables (see Section 6.36). If you name a variable that is being read from a system file via GET, for example, the LEAVE command has no effect. However, the LEAVE command can be helpful in conjunction with DATA LIST (see Chapters 11 and 12).

6.36 Scratch Variables

To create a *scratch variable*, use the # character as the first character of the numeric or string variable name. Use scratch variables to read or create variables that you want to use in defining files or in other transformations but that you do not want to analyze or to save on a system file. For example, to create a permanent variable that measures an individual's age, you might want to define day, month, and year variables as scratch variables for use with the YRMODA function (Section 6.24), as in:

```
FILE HANDLE HUBDATA/ file specifications
DATA LIST FILE=HUBDATA RECORDS=3
  /1 #MOBIRTH #DABIRTH #YRBIRTH 6-11
COMPUTE    AGE=($JDATE - YRMODA(#YRBIRTH,#MOBIRTH,#DABIRTH))/365.25
VARIABLE LABELS AGE 'EMPLOYEE''S AGE'
```

The #MOBIRTH, #DABIRTH, and #YRBIRTH variables are read from the data file and used as arguments to the YRMODA function. System variable $JDATE is the current date in YRMODA format (see Section 6.42). Division by 365.25 transforms the result from days into years (with an approximate adjustment for leap year).

- Scratch variables are unavailable for procedures and cannot be saved on a system file.
- You cannot assign missing values, variable labels, or value labels for scratch variables.
- Scratch variables are initialized to 0 for numeric variables or blank for string variables for the first case and are "left" across cases (see Section 6.35).
- Scratch variables can be created between procedures but are always discarded as the next procedure begins.
- You cannot use the keyword TO to refer to scratch variables and permanent variables at the same time.
- You cannot name scratch variables on a WEIGHT command (see Chapter 10).

6.37 The TEMPORARY Command

Use the TEMPORARY command to signal the beginning of temporary transformations that are in effect only for the next procedure. New numeric or string variables created after the TEMPORARY command are *temporary variables*. Any modifications made to existing variables after the TEMPORARY command are also temporary. The commands

```
DATA LIST FILE=HUBDATA RECORDS=3
  /1 #MOBIRTH #DABIRTH #YRBIRTH 6-11 DEPT82 19
COMPUTE      AGE=($JDATE - YRMODA(#YRBIRTH,#MOBIRTH,#DABIRTH))/365.25
VARIABLE LABELS AGE 'EMPLOYEE''S AGE'
           DEPT82 'DEPARTMENT CODE IN 1982'

TEMPORARY
RECODE AGE (LO THRU 20=1)(20 THRU 25=2)(25 THRU 30=3)(30 THRU 35=4)
       (35 THRU 40=5)(40 THRU 45=6)(45 THRU 50=7)(50 THRU 55=8)
       (55 THRU 60=9)(60 THRU 65=10)(65 THRU HI=11)
VARIABLE LABELS AGE 'EMPLOYEE AGE CATEGORIES'
VALUE LABELS AGE 1 'Up to 20' 2 '20 to 25' 3 '25 to 30' 4 '30 to 35'
       5 '35 to 40' 6 '40 to 45' 7 '45 to 50' 8 '50 to 55'
       9 '55 to 60' 10 '60 to 65' 11 '65 and older'

FREQUENCIES VARIABLES=AGE
BREAKDOWN AGE BY DEPT82
```

temporarily recode the AGE variable computed in Section 6.36. FREQUENCIES then uses the temporary version of variable AGE with the temporary variable and value labels. BREAKDOWN uses the unrecoded values of AGE and the permanent variable label. You can use the following commands after the TEMPORARY command:

- Transformation commands COMPUTE, RECODE, IF, and COUNT, and the DO REPEAT utility.
- The LOOP and DO IF control structures.
- Print and write commands PRINT, PRINT EJECT, PRINT SPACE, and WRITE.
- Format declarations PRINT FORMATS, WRITE FORMATS, and FORMATS.
- Data selection commands SELECT IF, SAMPLE, and WEIGHT.
- Variable declarations NUMERIC, STRING, and VECTOR.
- Labeling commands VARIABLE LABELS and VALUE LABELS, and the MISSING VALUES command.

- SPLIT FILE.
- All procedure commands.

You cannot use SORT CASES, MATCH FILES, or ADD FILES after the TEMPORARY command without an intervening procedure. In addition, you cannot use the TEMPORARY command inside the DO IF—END IF or LOOP—END LOOP structures.

You can use the TEMPORARY command after the first procedure to make additional transformations temporary. Otherwise, transformations between procedures are permanent and cause SPSS^X to rewrite the permanent dictionary.

Since SAVE is a procedure, any temporary transformations between the TEMPORARY and SAVE commands without an intervening procedure are saved on the system file.

6.38 The NUMERIC Command

Use the NUMERIC command to declare new numeric variables. While you can also create new numeric variables directly with COMPUTE, IF, RECODE, and COUNT, you may need to refer to a numeric variable in the transformation language before it is created. For example, you might want to add a series of variables to your active file in a fixed order so you can use the TO keyword to reference variables on procedure commands. The specification

```
NUMERIC SCALE79 IMPACT79 SCALE80 IMPACT80 SCALE81 IMPACT81 SCALE82
          IMPACT82
```

declares variables SCALE79 through IMPACT82. Then, regardless of the order in which you actually store values in them, the variables remain in that order on the active file.

The default format for variables named on a NUMERIC command is F8.2 (or whatever you specify using the SET command), but you can declare variables using any simple FORTRAN-like format (Chapter 3) in parentheses following the variable name or names, as in:

```
NUMERIC X(F4.0)/Y(F1.0)
```

Permanent or temporary variables are initialized to the system-missing value and scratch variables are initialized to 0.

You can also use the NUMERIC command along with the STRING command to predetermine the order of variables in the dictionary (see Chapter 12).

6.39 The DO REPEAT Utility

If you are doing the same basic transformation on a large set of variables, you can reduce the number of commands by using DO REPEAT—END REPEAT. This utility does not reduce the number of commands SPSS^X executes, just the number of commands you enter.

The specification on the DO REPEAT utility is the stand-in variable. The *stand-in variable* stands for a list of numeric variables, string variables, constants, or literals and is used in one or more transformation commands within the DO REPEAT—END REPEAT structure. For example, to initialize a set of five variables to 0 without entering five COMPUTE commands, specify:

```
DO REPEAT R=REGION1 TO REGION5
COMPUTE R=0
END REPEAT
```

The commands between DO REPEAT and END REPEAT are repeated once for each variable in the replacement list. Thus, five COMPUTE commands are generated, one for each REGION variable (see keyword PRINT in Section 6.41).

Stand-in variables (R in this example) do not exist outside of the DO REPEAT—END REPEAT utility. You can use any valid variable name you wish—permanent, temporary, scratch, system, and so forth. The stand-in variable has no effect on any variable with the same name. However, you cannot have two stand-in variables with the same name in the same DO REPEAT structure.

You can use the following commands within the DO REPEAT—END REPEAT structure:

- Data transformations COMPUTE, RECODE, IF, COUNT, and SELECT IF.
- Data declarations VECTOR, STRING, NUMERIC, and LEAVE.
- Data definitions DATA LIST and MISSING VALUES (but not VARIABLE LABELS or VALUE LABELS).
- LOOP structure commands LOOP, END LOOP, and BREAK.
- DO IF structure commands DO IF, ELSE IF, ELSE, and END IF.
- Print and write commands PRINT, PRINT EJECT, PRINT SPACE, and WRITE.
- Format commands PRINT FORMATS, WRITE FORMATS, and FORMATS.

6.40 Replacement Variable and Value Lists

A replacement variable list can be a list of new or existing variable names and can be string or numeric. You can use the TO keyword both to name consecutive existing variables and to create a set of new variables (see Chapter 2). If the new variables are string, they must be declared on a STRING command before being named on the DO REPEAT command (see Chapter 7). All replacement variable and value lists must have the same number of items.

A replacement value list can be a list of literals or numeric values, or it can be of the form n_1 TO n_2, where n_1 is less than n_2 and both are integers. (Note that the keyword is TO, not THRU.) The commands

```
DO REPEAT R=REGION1 TO REGION5/ X=1 TO 5
COMPUTE R=0
IF (REGION EQ X) R=1
END REPEAT
```

create dummy variables REGION1 to REGION5 that measure 1 or 0 for each of 5 regions, perhaps for use in procedure REGRESSION or REPORT (see Chapters 23 and 33).

If you use the PRINT keyword on the END REPEAT command (Section 6.41), SPSS^X prints the commands it generated, as shown in Figure 6.40. The plus signs mark the generated commands.

Figure 6.40 Commands generated by DO REPEAT

```
 2 0     DO REPEAT R=REGION1 TO REGION5/ X=1 TO 5
 3 0     COMPUTE R=0
 4 0     IF (REGION EQ X) R=1
 5 0     END REPEAT PRINT

 6 0    +COMPUTE REGION1=0
 7 0    +IF (REGION EQ 1) REGION1=1
 8 0    +COMPUTE REGION2=0
 9 0    +IF (REGION EQ 2) REGION2=1
10 0    +COMPUTE REGION3=0
11 0    +IF (REGION EQ 3) REGION3=1
12 0    +COMPUTE REGION4=0
13 0    +IF (REGION EQ 4) REGION4=1
14 0    +COMPUTE REGION5=0
15 0    +IF (REGION EQ 5) REGION5=1
```

6.41 The PRINT Subcommand

To see the commands that SPSS^{X} generates from the DO REPEAT utility, use the PRINT subcommand on the END REPEAT command. For example, to initialize one set of variables to 0 and another set to 1, specify:

```
DO REPEAT Q=Q1 TO Q5/ R=R1 TO R5
COMPUTE Q=0
COMPUTE R=1
END REPEAT PRINT
```

The output from the PRINT subcommand on the END REPEAT command is shown in Figure 6.41.

Figure 6.41 Display from the PRINT keyword

```
 2  0        DO REPEAT Q=Q1 TO Q5/ R=R1 TO R5
 3  0        COMPUTE Q=0
 4  0        COMPUTE R=1
 5  0        END REPEAT PRINT

 6  0       +COMPUTE Q1=0
 7  0       +COMPUTE R1=1
 8  0       +COMPUTE Q2=0
 9  0       +COMPUTE R2=1
10  0       +COMPUTE Q3=0
11  0       +COMPUTE R3=1
12  0       +COMPUTE Q4=0
13  0       +COMPUTE R4=1
14  0       +COMPUTE Q5=0
15  0       +COMPUTE R5=1
```

Use the PRINT subcommand to verify the order in which your commands are executed. In this example, notice that the COMPUTE commands are executed such that variables are created in alternating order: Q1, R1, Q2, R2, and so forth. If you plan to use the TO convention to refer to Q1 TO Q5 later, you should use two separate DO REPEAT utilities; otherwise, Q1 TO Q5 will include four of the five R variables. Or you can use the NUMERIC command as explained in Section 6.38 to predetermine the order.

Alternatively, you can specify a series of constants as a stand-in value list and create the Q and R value lists in order, as in:

```
DO REPEAT Q=Q1 TO Q5,R1 TO R5/ N=0,0,0,0,0,1,1,1,1,1
COMPUTE Q=N
END REPEAT PRINT
```

6.42 System Variables

Special *system variables* are used in data transformations to determine the number of cases read by the system, compare the system-missing value, obtain the current date, and so forth. The names of these variables begin with a dollar sign. You cannot modify a system variable and you cannot alter its print and write formats. Except for these restrictions, you can use system variables anywhere a normal variable is used in the transformation language. System variables are not available for procedures.

$CASENUM *Number of cases read.* For each case, $CASENUM is the number of cases read up to and including that case. The format is F8.0.

$SYSMIS *System-missing value.* The format is F1.0 so that it will always print as a period (.).

$JDATE *Current date in YRMODA format.* The format is F6.0. See Section 6.26 for the discussion of the YRMODA function.

$DATE *Current date.* The format is A9 in the form *dd mmm yy.*

$LENGTH *The current page length.* The format is F11.0. See the SET command in Chapter 4 for more information.

$WIDTH *The current page width.* The format is F3.0. See the SET command in Chapter 4 for more information.

6.43 EXECUTING DATA TRANSFORMATIONS

Execution of transformation commands is straightforward. When the data are read, each transformation command is evaluated and executed in order. This means that the order in which you give your transformations to SPSS^X may be important. With the commands

```
RECODE   ITEM1 TO ITEM3 (0=1) (1=0) (2=-1) (9=9) (ELSE=SYSMIS)
COUNT    AGREE=ITEM1 TO ITEM3 (1)
```

the order of execution is critical since the COUNT command assumes that the RECODE has already been executed.

Transformations do not actually take place until the data are read. Unless you use a procedure or other command that instructs SPSS^X to read the data, your transformations are not executed. Likewise, unless you save a system file or write out the data in some other manner, the transformations are in effect only for that single run of SPSS^X.

6.44 Data Definition Commands

You can use the data definition commands VARIABLE LABELS, VALUE LABELS, MISSING VALUES, and so forth, to fully define any variable created or altered by data transformations. For example, once a new variable is created, you may want to add a complete set of definitions, as in:

```
RECODE  ITEM1 TO ITEM3 (0=1) (1=0) (2=-1) (9=9) (ELSE=SYSMIS)
COUNT   AGREE=ITEM1 TO ITEM3 (1)
FORMATS AGREE (F1)
VARIABLE LABELS AGREE 'LEVEL OF AGREEMENT WITH SPENDING'
VALUE LABELS AGREE 3 'AGREE A LOT' 2 'AGREE' 1 'AGREE A LITTLE'
                   0 'DISAGREE'
```

The only requirement for using data definition commands with transformations is that the variable being defined must already exist on your active file. In other words, the data definitions must follow the transformation commands that create the variable.

6.45 The Active File

Data transformations are made to your active file. Unless you submit a command that causes SPSS^X to read the data, there is no active file. Also, unless you save the active file as a new system file, new variables do not exist, altered variables are unchanged in the data, and new data definitions disappear. In the commands

```
FILE HANDLE TESTDATA/ file specifications
DATA LIST  FILE=TESTDATA
  /AGE 1-3 ITEM1 TO ITEM3 5-7
VARIABLE LABELS  ITEM1 'OPINION ON LEVEL OF DEFENSE SPENDING'
  ITEM2 'OPINION ON LEVEL OF WELFARE SPENDING'
  ITEM3 'OPINION ON LEVEL OF HEALTH SPENDING'
VALUE LABELS  ITEM1 TO ITEM3 -1 'DISAGREE' 0 'NO OPINION' 1 'AGREE'
MISSING VALUES  AGE(-99,-98) ITEM1 TO ITEM3 (9)

RECODE  ITEM1,ITEM2,ITEM3 (0=1) (1=0) (2=-1) (9=9) (ELSE=SYSMIS)

RECODE  AGE (MISSING=9) (18 THRU HI=1) (LO THRU 18=0) INTO VOTER
PRINT /$CASENUM 1-2 AGE 4-6 VOTER 8-10

VARIABLE LABELS  VOTER 'ELIGIBLE TO VOTE'
VALUE LABELS  VOTER 0 'UNDER 18' 1 '18 OR OVER'
MISSING VALUES  VOTER (9)
PRINT FORMATS VOTER(F1.0)
FREQUENCIES VARIABLES=VOTER,ITEM1 TO ITEM3

FILE HANDLE NEWDATA/ file specifications
SAVE OUTFILE=NEWDATA
```

the data are read from file TESTDATA when SPSS^X encounters the FREQUENCIES command. At that point, SPSS^X applies the transformations and definitions and constructs the frequencies table.

The SAVE FILE command saves a new system file with file handle NEWDATA that contains the data and dictionary information on the variables read from TESTDATA plus the new variable VOTER.

STRING varlist (An) [/varlist . . .]

For string variables:

RECODE varlist ('string' ['string' . . .] = 'string') . . . ('string' . . .) [INTO varlist]
[/varlist . . .]

Keywords valid for input value lists:
CONVERT ELSE

Keyword valid for output value lists:
COPY

7

INTRODUCTION TO STRING VARIABLES, **7.1**
The STRING Command, **7.2**
Literals, **7.3**
Missing Values, **7.4**

THE RECODE COMMAND, **7.5**
Specifying String Values, **7.6**
Keywords INTO, ELSE, and COPY, **7.7**
Changing Variable Types, **7.8**
Keyword CONVERT, **7.9**

STRING EXPRESSIONS, **7.10**
Computing String Variables, **7.11**
Constructing String Expressions, **7.12**
Logical Expressions, **7.13**
String Functions, **7.14**
Padding and Trimming Strings, **7.15**
Indexing and Substrings, **7.16**
The NUMBER Function, **7.17**
The Third Argument of INDEX, **7.18**
Nesting Functions, **7.19**

Chapter 7 String Transformations

You can manipulate string variables in SPSS^X using most of the same commands described in Chapter 6 for numeric variables. While you cannot treat strings with a full range of mathematical operations and functions, you can modify strings, split them apart and put them back together, and combine them with literals and other string variables using the RECODE and COMPUTE commands. The RECODE command is specifically discussed in Sections 7.5 through 7.9. A generalized discussion of string expressions is presented in Sections 7.10 through 7.19. Of particular interest are the special string functions described in Section 7.14.

For the complete range of possibilities with string variables, you should also consult Chapter 6 for the following topics:

- String variables can be used in the criterion list of a COUNT command.
- String variables can be named on a LEAVE command.
- Scratch variables can be strings.
- String manipulations specified after a TEMPORARY command follow the same rules given for numeric variables.
- Variables used in the DO REPEAT utility can be strings and constants can be literals.

7.1 INTRODUCTION TO STRING VARIABLES

The principal difference between string variables and numeric variables in data transformations is that you must always keep track of the length of strings. Only rarely will SPSS^X not allow a requested transformation because one string is longer or shorter than another or because you are referencing a value that is longer or shorter than the length specified for the variable. However, you must keep track of length to be certain that SPSS^X does what you want. In fact, you must know the length of a new string variable before you create it using the required STRING command as shown in Section 7.2.

Another length consideration is the difference between short and long strings. The exact definition of a short string is machine dependent (see Chapter 3). Short strings can have missing values which have general implications for transformations discussed in Section 7.4 and specific implications for RECODE discussed in Section 7.5.

String variables also differ from numeric variables in that there are no range specifications. Keywords LOWEST, HIGHEST, and THRU are not defined for strings in any data transformations.

7.2 The STRING Command

A string variable must be declared before it can be used as a target variable in data transformations. If a string variable does not already exist on the active file, you must use the STRING command to declare it. The STRING command keyword is followed by the name of the new variable and its simple format in parentheses, as in:

```
STRING   SSNUMBER (A11)
```

- New string variables are initialized as blanks unless the LEAVE command is used (see Chapter 6).
- The length of a string variable is fixed by the format given when it is declared and cannot be changed.
- You cannot use the STRING command to redefine an existing variable.
- String variables cannot have zero length (format A0).

More than one string variable can be declared on a STRING command either by specifying a variable list when the format is the same, as in

```
STRING   ALPHA1 TO ALPHA6 (A8)
```

or by separating the definitions with a slash, as in

```
STRING   ALPHA1 TO ALPHA6 (A8)/ALPHA7,ALPHA10 (A16)
```

All implementations of SPSS^X allow the A format. There may be other valid string formats available on the computer at your installation. Also, the definition of a long string depends on which machine you are using. See the INFO command for local documentation.

The STRING command can also be used with the NUMERIC command to predetermine the order of variables in the dictionary. See Chapter 12 for a complete discussion.

7.3 Literals

References to values of string variables within SPSS^X are called *literals*. In the COMPUTE command, literals can be assigned to string variables or can appear as arguments to functions, depending on the application and the function. In the RECODE command, literals are the old or new values specified for recoding. In the command

```
RECODE STATE ('IO'='IA')
```

values IO and IA are both literals.

- Literals are enclosed within apostrophes or quotation marks. The same symbol must be used to begin and end the literal.
- A literal must be contained on a single command line; it cannot be continued to the next line, except by concatenation as described below.
- You can concatenate literals using the plus sign, as in

  ```
  RECODE NAME ('Georgianne Baxter Birney' = 'Georgianne Baker'
    +' Baxter')
  ```

  which restores Georgianne Baxter Birney to her birth name.
- An apostrophe can be entered as part of a literal if the literal is enclosed in quotation marks or if the apostrophe is entered twice with no separation. For example,

  ```
  COMPUTE BAR='Harry''s'
  ```

  and

  ```
  COMPUTE BAR="Harry's"
  ```

both assign Harry's to variable BAR. A quotation mark can be entered in a similar manner, as in

```
COMPUTE  RESPONSE='"Ouch!"'
```

which assigns value "Ouch!" to variable RESPONSE.

Literals must agree in length with the variable to which they are assigned. If not, they are usually trimmed or padded to the correct length, or SPSS^X generates an error. These rules are described for each command.

7.4 Missing Values

The transformation language does not propagate missing values for short strings (long strings cannot have missing values). If a string variable for which missing values have been defined appears in an assignment specification for a COMPUTE or IF command, the assignment is made without regard to the missing-value status of any strings. For example,

```
STRING NEWALPHA(A8)
COMPUTE NEWALPHA=ALPHA
```

returns a string of eight blanks for a case with an all-blank value for variable ALPHA, even if a blank string is considered missing for ALPHA. To make a blank string also missing for variable NEWALPHA, use the MISSING VALUES command.

If a string variable for which missing values have been defined appears in a logical expression for an IF, SELECT IF, DO IF, or other conditional command, the comparison is made without regard to the missing-value status of any strings. For example,

```
MISSING VALUES ALPHA ('XA')
SELECT IF ALPHA EQ 'XA' OR ALPHA EQ 'XB'
```

selects cases with ALPHA equal to XA even though XA is a missing value.

Functions MISSING and SYSMIS are not available for string variables.

7.5 THE RECODE COMMAND

To transform strings, you can use the RECODE command to change one code for a variable to another as the data are being read. The command

```
RECODE STATE ('IO'='IA')
```

instructs SPSS^X to change all cases coded IO to IA, the correct Postal Service abbreviation for Iowa.

- You can recode both short and long strings.
- Variables to be recoded must be named first and must already exist (see the STRING command in Section 7.2).
- Values must be enclosed in apostrophes.
- You can include as many value specifications as needed, containing each within parentheses.
- You can include multiple input values in a single specification but only one output value after the equals sign, as in:

  ```
  RECODE STATE ('IO','IW'='IA')
  ```

- The RECODE command is evaluated left to right. If SPSS^X encounters the current case's value in an input value list, that case is recoded and the rest of the recode specifications are ignored. In the command

  ```
  RECODE STATE ('MI'='MN') ('MN'='MI')
  ```

  SPSS^X recodes a case with value MI for variable STATE to MN and then proceeds to the next command. The value is *not* recoded back to MI by the second specification.

- All input values not mentioned on the RECODE command are left unchanged.
- You can name multiple variables for the same value specifications. You can also recode multiple variables differently on the same command by separating the variables with a slash. For example,

```
RECODE STATE ('IO'='IA')/ Q1 TO Q5 ('X'='Y') ('A'='B')
```

recodes STATE and the list of Q variables in the same command.

7.6 Specifying String Values

If you are recoding more than one variable using the same specifications, all variables in the list must have the same length. The rules for specifying values are

- Values must be specified as literals (enclosed in apostrophes or quotation marks).
- Blanks are significant characters in values of string variables.
- If the input or output literal is shorter than the variable, the literal is right-padded with blanks to the length of the variable being recoded.
- If the input or output literal is longer than the variable, it is an error.

Assuming S1 is a two-character string variable, the command

```
RECODE S1 ('M'='MM') (ELSE='X')
```

is not an error, but SPSS^X is actually looking for "M " (M followed by a blank) in the first specification and will change all other values to "X " in the second.

Keywords THRU, HIGHEST, and LOWEST are not available for specifying value ranges for string variables, and keywords MISSING and SYSMIS are not valid.

7.7 Keywords INTO, ELSE, and COPY

You can use keyword INTO to specify a target variable for recoding a string variable, but the variable named must already exist. Usually, you use the STRING command (Section 7.2) to declare a new variable, as in:

```
STRING STATE1 (A2)
RECODE STATE ('IO'='IA') (ELSE=COPY) INTO STATE1
```

In this example, keywords ELSE and COPY are used to copy the other state codes over unchanged. Variables STATE and STATE1 are identical except for cases with original input value IO.

If you are recoding multiple variables with the same specifications, the number of target variables following the INTO keyword must be the same as the number of variables in the input list. All target variables must already exist, and they must all be the same length, although they needn't be the same length as the input variables.

If the original and target variables have different lengths, the criterion for input values is the length of the input variable, and the criterion for output values is the length of the target variable. Otherwise, the same rules apply:

- It is an error if the input literal is longer than the input variable or if the output literal is longer than the target variable.
- If the input literal is shorter than the input variable, the literal is right-padded with blanks to the length of the input variable.
- If the output literal is shorter than the target variable, the literal is right-padded with blanks to the length of the target variable.

ANNOTATED EXAMPLE FOR STRING TRANSFORMATIONS

This job corrects known recording errors in the Postal Service's two-letter state abbreviations. The SPSS^X commands are

```
FILE HANDLE TESTDATA/ file specifications
FILE HANDLE NEWDATA/ file specifications
GET FILE=TESTDATA
PRINT /STATE
RECODE STATE ('IO'='IA') ('KA'='KS') ('VE'='VT') ('  '='XX')
MISSING VALUES STATE ('XX')
PRINT /STATE (1X,A2)
SAVE OUTFILE=NEWDATA
```

- The FILE HANDLE command defines the file handle TESTDATA to the system (see Chapter 3).
- The GET command names the input system file (see Chapter 5).
- The first PRINT command provides a check on each case by printing the value of STATE as the cases are being read, before any transformations are performed (see Chapter 9).
- The RECODE command first corrects the abbreviation codes for Iowa, Kansas, and Vermont. Then any codes that are entirely blank are recoded to XX.
- The MISSING VALUES command declares the literal XX missing for variable STATE (see Chapter 3).
- The second PRINT command provides a check on the RECODE command by printing the value for STATE after the RECODE command is executed. The recoded value is indented one column to distinguish the results from the first PRINT command.
- The SAVE command defines the output system file (see Chapter 5).

The output from the two PRINT commands prints the value of STATE for each case twice as they are being read, once for each command. The output for the first eight cases is

```
IL
 IL
AZ
 AZ
IO
 IA
NJ
 NJ
IL
 IL

 XX
NY
 NY
UT
 UT
```

The first four lines show the values for the first two cases which are correct and are within the valid range and are therefore copied unchanged. The fifth and sixth lines show that the code for Iowa is changed from IO to IA. The blank code for the sixth case is changed to XX.

7.8 Changing Variable Types

You cannot change a variable from string to numeric or from numeric to string by recoding it into itself. You must use keyword INTO to specify a new variable name (see Section 7.7). The command

```
RECODE SEX ('M'=1) ('F'=2) INTO NSEX
```

recodes variable SEX from a string variable into a numeric variable called NSEX. Any value other than M or F becomes system-missing.

To recode a variable into a string variable, use the STRING command to declare it before naming it with the INTO keyword, as in:

```
STRING SMONTH (A3)
RECODE MONTH(1='JAN')(2='FEB')(3='MAR')(4='APR')(5='MAY')(6='JUN')
 (7='JUL')(8='AUG')(9='SEP')(10='OCT')(11='NOV')(12='DEC') INTO SMONTH
```

Since string variables are initialized to blanks, if a case has a value other than 1 through 12 for variable MONTH, it will be blank for variable SMONTH. If you specify an output literal longer than the length of the output string variable, it is an error. If you specify a literal shorter than the string, it is right-padded with blanks.

7.9 Keyword CONVERT

Use keyword CONVERT to recode the string representation of numbers to their numeric representation. The command

```
RECODE #JOB (CONVERT) ('-'=11) ('&'=12) INTO JOB
```

first recodes all numbers in string variable #JOB (read as a scratch variable) to numbers for target variable JOB and then specifically recodes the minus sign (the "eleven" punch) to 11 and the ampersand (or "twelve" punch in EBCDIC) to 12. Keyword CONVERT is specified first as an efficiency measure to recode cases with numbers immediately.

- SPSS^{X} converts numbers as if the variable were being reread using the F format described in Chapter 3.
- If SPSS^{X} encounters a field that cannot be converted, it scans the remaining recode specifications.
- If a code cannot be converted and there is no specific recode specification for that code, the target variable is unchanged.

7.10 STRING EXPRESSIONS

Expressions involving string variables can be used in COMPUTE commands and in logical expressions on commands such as IF, DO IF, LOOP IF, SELECT IF, and so forth. For example, the simplest string expression is a literal, as in

```
SELECT IF STATE EQ 'IL'
```

where string variable STATE is compared to the expression IL.

A string expression can be a literal composed of a single string enclosed in apostrophes (Section 7.3), a special string function (Section 7.14), or another string variable.

7.11 Computing String Variables

When you compute string variables, the expression on the right of the equals sign in the COMPUTE command must return a string, and the target variable named on the left of the equals sign must be an existing variable. Thus, the target variables must have been defined on a DATA LIST command or exist on the system file as a string variable. Alternatively, you can use the STRING command to declare a new string variable (Section 7.2), as in:

```
STRING  S(A2)
COMPUTE S='NA'
```

The STRING command declares string variable S with a length of two characters and COMPUTE sets S to the literal NA for every case.

The length of a string variable is established when it is declared and cannot be altered by data transformations. To change the length, declare a new variable with the desired length.

7.12 Constructing String Expressions

An expression must return a string if the target variable is string. A string expression can simply be a literal, as in:

```
STRING   DRUG (A)
COMPUTE DRUG='A'
```

In this example, the one-character variable DRUG is assigned a value of A for every case, perhaps to initialize it in preparation for further transformations. String expressions can also be complex string operations using the special string functions documented in Section 7.14, as in

```
STRING   SSNUMBER (A11)
COMPUTE  SSNUMBER = CONCAT(SS1,'-',SS2,'-',SS3)
```

where variable SSNUMBER is constructed by concatenating (joining) the three portions of a social security number and separating these portions with hyphens. Presumably, variables SS1, SS2, and SS3 exist and are strings of length 3, 2, and 4, respectively.

The string returned by a string expression does not have to be the same length as the target variable, but no warning messages are issued if the lengths are not the same. If the target variable in a COMPUTE command is shorter, the result is right-trimmed. If the target variable is longer, the result is right-padded. String functions are available for padding (LPAD, RPAD), trimming (LTRIM, RTRIM), and selecting a portion of strings (SUBSTR) so you can control the lengths yourself.

If variables SS1, SS2, and SS3 are numeric instead of string, converting them to a string with the hyphens is more difficult (see Section 7.19).

7.13 Logical Expressions

String variables, like numeric variables, can be tested in logical expressions. The rules are

- You cannot compare string variables and numeric variables.
- You can compare strings of different lengths using EQ and NE. The shorter string or literal is right-padded with blanks to equal the length of the longer.
- You can compare the "magnitude" of strings using LT, GT, and so forth, but the success or failure of the comparison depends on the sorting sequence of the particular computer. Use with caution.

For example, to check for a particular state code, specify:

```
SELECT IF (STATE EQ 'IL')
```

If variable STATE has an A2 format, the comparison is direct. If for some reason STATE has an A4 format, the comparison is true only for cases with value "IL " for STATE since the literal "IL" is right-padded with blanks for the comparison. It will not be true for cases with value "ILL " or "ILLI." If you want to check only the first two characters, use the SUBSTR function (Section 7.14), as in:

```
SELECT IF (SUBSTR(STATE,1,2) EQ 'IL')
```

7.14 String Functions

Except where otherwise noted, the target variable for each of these functions must be a string and must have already been declared. Multiple arguments in a list must be separated by commas.

CONCAT(arg list) *Concatenate the arguments into a string.* String variables and literals can be intermixed as arguments. CONCAT(A,'**') creates the string ABCD** for a case with value ABCD for string variable A.

LPAD(a_1,a_2,a_3) *Pad left.* Pad the beginning of a_1 up to the length specified by a_2 using the optional single-character a_3 as the pad character. a_2 must be a positive integer from 1 to 255. The default pad character is a blank. LPAD(ALPHA1,10) adds four leading blanks to the target variable if ALPHA1 has an A6 format. a_3 can be any character enclosed in apostrophes or any single-character expression.

RPAD(a_1,a_2,a_3) *Pad right.* Pad the end of a_1 up to the length of a_2 using the optional single-character a_3 as the pad character. a_2 must be a positive integer from 1 to 255. The default pad character is a blank. RPAD(ALPHA2,8,'*') adds two trailing asterisks to the target variable if ALPHA2 has an A6 format. a_3 can be any character enclosed in apostrophes or any single-character expression.

LTRIM(a_1,a_2) *Trim left.* Trim the character a_2 from the beginning of a_1. LTRIM(ALPHA3,'0') trims leading zeroes from variable ALPHA3. a_2 can be any character enclosed in apostrophes or any single-character expression. The default a_2 is a blank.

RTRIM(a_1,a_2) *Trim right.* Trim the character a_2 from the end of a_1. RTRIM(ALPHA4,'*') trims trailing asterisks from variable ALPHA4. a_2 can be any character enclosed in apostrophes or any single-character expression. The default a_2 is a blank.

SUBSTR(a_1,a_2,a_3) *Substring.* Return the substring of a_1 beginning with the position in a_2 and optionally for a length of a_3. a_2 can be a positive integer from 1 to the length of a_1. a_3, when added to a_2, should not exceed the length of a_1. If a_3 is not specified, the substring is returned up to the end of a_1. SUBSTR(ALPHA6,3) returns the last four characters of ALPHA6 if it has an A6 format. SUBSTR(ALPHA6,3,1) returns the third character of ALPHA6.

INDEX(a_1,a_2,a_3) *Return a number that indicates the position of the first occurrence of a_2 in a_1.* a_1 is the string which will be searched. a_2 is the string variable or literal which will be used in the search. If a_3 is not specified, all of a_2 will be used. INDEX(ALPHA6,'**') returns 2 for a case with value X***** for variable ALPHA6. The optional a_3 is the number of characters used to divide a_2 into separate strings to be used for searching (see Section 7.18). a_3 must be a positive integer and must divide evenly into the length of a_2.

STRING(arg,format) *Convert the argument into a string using the format.* The argument is numeric and the format is a numeric format, but the result is a string. The number is converted from internal representation according to the format and then stored as a string. STRING(INCOME,DOLLAR8) converts the numeric variable INCOME to the dollar format and returns it as a string value. If the result is shorter than the string variable, it is right-justified. If the result is longer than the string variable, it is right-trimmed.

NUMBER(arg,format) *Convert the argument into a number using the format.* The argument is string and the format is a numeric format, but the result is numeric. The string is essentially reread using the format and returned as a number. NUMBER(XALPHA,F3.1) converts the string XALPHA to a number using the F3.1 format.

7.15 Padding and Trimming Strings

Padding and trimming operations can easily be nullified if you don't keep track of the length of the target variable and what SPSS^{X} is doing. For example, if you use RTRIM to trim trailing blanks from a string and name a target variable the same length as the original string, SPSS^{X} left-justifies the trimmed string and right-pads it back with the same number of blanks just trimmed. To right-justify a string in a target variable, you can nest functions to instruct SPSS^{X} to execute the operations simultaneously, as in

```
COMPUTE NAME=LPAD(RTRIM(NAME),24)
```

where all trailing blanks are trimmed from the right of string variable NAME and then the result is left-padded with blanks out to a length of 24. Thus, the string

```
"Georgianne Baker        "
```

becomes

```
"        Georgianne Baker"
```

Variable NAME must have a length of 24 since you cannot alter the length of string variables once they have been declared.

If the length argument (which can be an expression) is illegal or missing, the result is a null string. If the pad or trim is the only operation, the string is then padded to its entire length with blanks. If the operation is nested, the null string is passed to the next nested level.

7.16 Indexing and Substrings

The INDEX and SUBSTR functions can be used to pull out substrings of varying position and length. For example, if you have recorded people's first name followed by a blank and the last name in a field of length 24, you may want to separate the last name, perhaps for sorting, as in:

```
STRING    LAST (A18)
COMPUTE LAST=SUBSTR(NAME,INDEX(NAME,' ')+1)
```

The expression INDEX(NAME,' ') returns the position of the first blank in variable NAME. For Georgianne Baker, that position is 11. Then, when you add 1 and use it as the second argument to the SUBSTR function, SPSS^{X} returns everything following the first blank up to the end of the string, which should be the last name. In other words, the command says, "Make LAST equal to the substring of NAME starting with the first character after the first blank through the rest of the string." For Georgianne Baker, it says to take the name starting at the 12th character, which is the *B* in Baker.

If the result of the SUBSTR function is shorter than LAST, the string is left-justified and padded with blanks. Thus, for Georgianne Baker, the value of LAST is:

```
"Baker             "
```

If the result of the operation is longer than LAST, it is right-trimmed to 18 characters.

If a numeric argument to SUBSTR is illegal or missing, the result is a null string. If SUBSTR is the only operation, the string is then padded to its entire length with blanks. If the operation is nested, the null string is passed to the next nested level. If a numeric argument to INDEX is illegal or missing, the result is system-missing.

7.17 The NUMBER Function

The NUMBER function is similar to the CONVERT keyword for the RECODE command (see Section 7.9). For example, the command

```
RECODE  STRING1 (CONVERT) INTO X
```

yields the same results for new numeric variable X as the command

```
COMPUTE X=NUMBER(STRING1,F8)
```

In both examples, values that cannot be converted become system-missing.

7.18 The Third Argument of INDEX

The third argument of INDEX is helpful when you need to look for more than one character or set of characters in a string. For example, the expression INDEX('MISSISSIPPI','LLSS',2) looks for either LL or SS. If the number of characters in the second string is not evenly divisible by the third argument, it is an error. If INDEX finds more than one string, it returns the smallest index value. For example, the function INDEX('MISSISSIPPI','PPSS',2) returns 3, not 9.

The most useful application of the third argument of INDEX is looking for one among several special characters. For example, if two variables have been recorded in two columns separated by either a blank, a comma, or a semicolon, you could separate the variables by reading the data as a string and separating it into numeric variables, as in:

```
DATA LIST  NOTABLE/#VAR (A5)

COMPUTE #DELIM=INDEX(#VAR,' ,;',1)
COMPUTE VAR1=NUMBER(SUBSTR(#VAR,1,#DELIM-1),F2)
COMPUTE VAR2=NUMBER(SUBSTR(#VAR,#DELIM+1),F2)

PRINT /VAR1 VAR2 (F2,1X,F2)
BEGIN DATA
1 3
1,4
3,4
4,3
6;3
10 2
11;4
4 10
END DATA
```

#VAR is a scratch variable (Chapter 6) used to read the first five columns of data as a single alphanumeric variable, and #DELIM is a scratch variable that stores the position of the delimiter character. In the COMPUTE command for variable VAR1, SUBSTR(#VAR,1,#DELIM−1) says, "Return the substring of #VAR starting in the first position and ending one position before a blank, comma, or semicolon." Then SUBSTR(#VAR,#DELIM+1) returns the substring starting one position after any of these characters to the end of the string. The two substrings are converted to numbers using the NUMBER function (see Section 7.17). The PRINT display output is shown in Figure 7.18.

Figure 7.18 PRINT output for the new variables

```
 1  3
 1  4
 3  4
 4  3
 6  3
10  2
11  4
 4 10
```

As you develop these transformations, it might be helpful to make several trial runs against a small subset of your data to make certain SPSS^X

is generating the desired results. It is also helpful to use the PRINT command to display intermediate results (see Chapter 9).

7.19 Nesting Functions

Functions can be nested to the degree required by your application. Several examples of nesting string functions to two levels have been shown in Sections 7.12 through 7.17. An example of nesting functions to four levels involves reconstructing a social security number into a string when the three components are numbers (see Section 7.12). The successive levels from inside out are (1) the STRING function to convert the numbers to strings; (2) the LTRIM function to trim off leading blanks generated when the converted number should have leading zeros in the string; (3) the LPAD function to add the leading zeros; and (4) the CONCAT function to concatenate the three variables plus the hyphens into one string.

```
STRING SSN(A11)
COMPUTE SSN=CONCAT(
  LPAD(LTRIM(STRING(SS1,F3)),3,'0'),'-',
  LPAD(LTRIM(STRING(SS2,F2)),2,'0'),'-',
  LPAD(LTRIM(STRING(SS3,F4)),4,'0')
```

Without nesting LTRIM within LPAD to restore leading zeros, social security number 911030555 would come out 911- 3- 555.

The sequence for generating the 03 is as follows: the number 3 is first converted to the string " 3" (3 right-justified into the F2 format); next, the leading blank is left-trimmed from the 3; then a zero is left-padded onto the 3; finally, the result is concatenated into the result string variable with the literals and other variables. The TRIM and PAD functions must be nested in the same command because, by itself, LTRIM(' 3') first takes the blank off and then puts one back if the next step is to store the result in a two-character variable. Therefore, it must be trimmed and padded in a simultaneous operation.

8

IF [(] logical expression [)] target variable = expression

The following relational and logical operators are available:

EQ or =	Equal to	NE or ¬ = or < >	Not equal to
LT or <	Less than		
GT or >	Greater than	LE or < =	Less than or equal to
AND		GE or > =	Greater than or equal to
NOT or ¬		OR	

DO IF, ELSE IF, ELSE, END IF

```
DO IF [(] logical expression [)]
  transformations
[ELSE IF [(] logical expression [)]]
  transformations
[ELSE IF [(] logical expression [)]]
  .
  .
  .
[ELSE]
  transformations
END IF
```

THE IF COMMAND, **8.1**

THE DO IF—END IF STRUCTURE, **8.2**
- The DO IF and END IF Commands, **8.3**
  - DO IF—END IF Compared with IF, **8.4**
- The ELSE Command, **8.5**
  - ELSE Compared with IF, **8.6**
- The ELSE IF Command, **8.7**
  - Multiple ELSE IF Commands, **8.8**
- Missing Values and the DO IF Structure, **8.9**
- Nested DO IF Structures, **8.10**
- Summary, **8.11**

LOGICAL EXPRESSIONS, **8.12**
- Logical Variables, **8.13**
- Relational Operators, **8.14**
- The AND and OR Logical Operators, **8.15**
- The NOT Logical Operator, **8.16**
- The Order of Evaluation, **8.17**
- Missing Values, **8.18**
  - Missing Values and Logical Operators, **8.19**

Chapter 8 Conditional Transformations

In certain situations, you may want to construct or alter variables one way for one subset of cases and other ways for other subsets. You can instruct SPSS^X to execute data transformations conditionally via the IF command or the DO IF—END IF structure. The IF command, which executes a single COMPUTE-like assignment based on the truth of a single logical expression, is documented in Section 8.1. The DO IF—END IF structure, which conditionally executes one or more data definitions and transformations based on one or more logical expressions, is documented in Sections 8.2 through 8.11. The use of logical expressions is described in Sections 8.12 through 8.19.

8.1 THE IF COMMAND

The IF command makes COMPUTE-like transformations contingent upon logical conditions found in the data. The IF command is followed by a *logical expression*, described Sections 8.12 through 8.19, and an *assignment expression*, which has the same syntax described for the COMPUTE command in Chapter 6. For example, the command

```
IF (X EQ 0) Y=1
```

assigns the value 1 to variable Y only for cases with value 0 for variable X. The logical expression is X EQ 0 and the assignment expression is Y=1. The parentheses around the logical expression are optional.

The assignment expression follows all of the rules and possibilities described for the COMPUTE command (see Chapter 6). The assignment is executed only if the logical expression is true. The command

```
IF (DEPT82 EQ 2) BONUS = .14*SALARY82
```

creates variable BONUS (an employee's salary bonus) as 0.14 times salary in 1982 only for cases with value 2 for variable DEPT82 (those in Department 2 as of 1982).

If a logical expression is false or indeterminate because of missing values, the assignment is not made and the target variable remains unchanged from its previous value. If the target variable is being created as a new variable, it retains the initialized system-missing value. If the target variable already exists, it is simply unchanged.

8.2 THE DO IF—END IF STRUCTURE

You can execute one or more conditional transformations on the same subset of cases via the the DO IF—END IF structure. The DO IF—END IF structure must begin with the DO IF command and end with the END IF command. For example, the commands

```
DO IF (X EQ 1)
RECODE Y(1=2)(2=1)
RECODE Z(3=4)(4=3)
END IF
```

tell SPSS^X to execute the RECODE commands only for cases with value 1 for variable X.

The structure can be further defined with the ELSE (Section 8.5) and ELSE IF commands (Sections 8.7 and 8.8). You can also nest DO IF—END IF structures as long as you include an END IF command for each DO IF command (Section 8.10).

The DO IF—END IF structure transforms data on subsets of cases defined by the logical expressions on the DO IF and ELSE IF commands. You might compare this structure with the LOOP—END LOOP structure described in Chapter 12, which performs repeated transformations on the same case. Like the LOOP—END LOOP structure, the DO IF—END IF structure can encompass transformations such as the DATA LIST, END CASE, END FILE, and REREAD commands, which define complex file structures. See Chapter 12 for examples.

8.3 The DO IF and END IF Commands

The DO IF and END IF commands by themselves (without ELSE IF or ELSE) are most frequently used to execute RECODE, COUNT, and multiple COMPUTE transformations conditionally. For example, to reverse the coding order of variable RACE for those individuals hired before 1980, specify:

```
DO IF (YRHIRED LT 80)
RECODE RACE(1=5)(2=4)(4=2)(5=1)
END IF
```

The logical expression on the DO IF command specifies individuals hired before 1980. Thus, the RACE variable for individuals hired in 1980 or later is not recoded.

The DO IF command marks the beginning of the control structure and END IF marks the end. The specification on the DO IF command is a logical expression of the form described in Sections 8.12 through 8.19. The parentheses enclosing the logical expression are optional.

- Commands like MISSING VALUES, VARIABLE LABELS, VALUE LABELS, and so forth specified within a DO IF structure take effect as if they were specified for the entire variable.
- Commands SELECT IF, SAMPLE, and WEIGHT specified within a DO IF structure take effect unconditionally.
- Commands like SET, DISPLAY, SHOW, and so forth specified within a DO IF structure are invoked once when they are encountered in the command file.

8.4 DO IF—END IF Compared with IF

You can express a single conditional COMPUTE command more efficiently with a simple IF command. For example, the commands

```
DO IF (X EQ 0)
COMPUTE Y=1
END IF
```

are equivalent to

```
IF (X EQ 0) Y=1
```

However, you should generally replace multiple IF commands testing the same condition with a DO IF structure in order to reduce processing time. For instance, suppose the day and month of birth on an employee file are recorded in reversed order for individuals hired before 1980. To exchange the values of MOBIRTH and DABIRTH depending on year hired, you might specify

```
IF (YRHIRED LT 80) #HOLD=MOBIRTH
IF (YRHIRED LT 80) MOBIRTH=DABIRTH
IF (YRHIRED LT 80) DABIRTH=#HOLD
```

where scratch variable #HOLD holds the value of month of birth for the exchange. When these IF commands are executed, SPSS^X evaluates logical expressions three times for every case before the complete set of transformations can be accomplished. However, in the commands

```
DO IF (YRHIRED LT 80)
COMPUTE #HOLD=MOBIRTH
COMPUTE MOBIRTH=DABIRTH
COMPUTE DABIRTH=#HOLD
END IF
```

if the logical expression is false, control is passed to the first command after the END IF. Thus, processing of cases with values 80 or greater for YRHIRED is greatly reduced.

8.5 The ELSE Command

Use the ELSE command to execute one or more transformations when the logical expression on the DO IF command is not true, as in:

```
DO IF (X EQ 0)
COMPUTE Y=1
ELSE
COMPUTE Y=2
END IF
```

In this structure, Y is set to 1 for all cases with value 0 for X, and Y is set to 2 for cases with any other valid value for X. The value of Y is not set to anything by this structure if X is missing (see Section 8.9).

If the logical expression on the DO IF command is true, SPSS^X executes the transformation command or commands immediately following the DO IF up to the next ELSE (or ELSE IF; see Section 8.7). Then control passes to the command following the END IF command. If the result of the logical expression is false, then control passes to ELSE (or ELSE IF).

8.6 ELSE Compared with IF

With the IF command, SPSS^X executes each transformation for each case regardless of what has been executed before and what will be executed. For example, one IF command can change the value of a variable that was set by a previous IF command. If you specify

```
IF (DEPT82 EQ 1) BONUS = .12*SALARY82
IF (DEPT82 EQ 2) BONUS = .14*SALARY82
IF (DEPT82 EQ 3) BONUS = .1*SALARY82
IF (DEPT82 EQ 4) BONUS = .08*SALARY82
IF (YRHIRED GT 80) BONUS = 0
```

the BONUS value is set for each case according to the department and then reset for cases with a value greater than 80 for YRHIRED. To prevent these unnecessary operations, you can use the ELSE command, as in:

```
DO IF (YRHIRED GT 80)
COMPUTE           BONUS = 0
ELSE
IF (DEPT82 EQ 1) BONUS = .12*SALARY82
IF (DEPT82 EQ 2) BONUS = .14*SALARY82
IF (DEPT82 EQ 3) BONUS = .1*SALARY82
IF (DEPT82 EQ 4) BONUS = .08*SALARY82
END IF
```

In this structure, if an individual was hired since 1980, the bonus is set to 0 and control passes out of the structure. Otherwise, control passes to the series of IF commands following ELSE.

8.7 The ELSE IF Command

You can further control the flow of execution by using the ELSE IF command. The structure

```
DO IF (X EQ 0)
COMPUTE Y=1
ELSE IF (X LE 9)
COMPUTE Y=9
ELSE
COMPUTE Y=2
END IF
```

sets Y equal to 1 when X equals 0; Y equal to 9 when X is less than 9 but not equal to 0; and Y to 2 for all valid values of X greater than 9. The value of Y is not set at all by this structure if X is missing (see Section 8.9).

Once a case satisfies a logical expression on a DO IF, ELSE IF, or ELSE command, the transformations are made up to the next structure command and control is passed out of the structure. For cases in the example above with value 0 for X, Y is set to 1 and control passes out of the structure. Such cases are not reevaluated by the ELSE IF command, even though 0 is less than 9. However, when the logical expression is false, control passes to the ELSE IF command, where the second COMPUTE is executed only for cases with X less than or equal to 9. Then control passes out of the structure. If the logical expressions on both the DO IF and ELSE IF commands are false, control passes to ELSE, where the third COMPUTE is executed.

For example, to increase the bonuses for individuals in certain departments who have been with the organization for a number of years, specify:

```
DO IF (YRHIRED GT 80)
COMPUTE           BONUS = 0
ELSE IF ((DEPT82 EQ 1 OR DEPT82 EQ 2) AND YRHIRED LE 75)
COMPUTE           BONUS = .16*SALARY82
ELSE
IF (DEPT82 EQ 1) BONUS = .12*SALARY82
IF (DEPT82 EQ 2) BONUS = .14*SALARY82
IF (DEPT82 EQ 3) BONUS = .1*SALARY82
IF (DEPT82 EQ 4) BONUS = .08*SALARY82
END IF
```

If an individual was hired after 1980, the bonus is set to 0 and control passes out of the structure. Otherwise, control passes to ELSE IF, where the second COMPUTE is executed only for those individuals in Departments 1 or 2 who were hired before 1976. Control then passes out of the structure. For all other individuals, control passes to ELSE, where the IF commands are evaluated.

Thus, a number of cases are processed without having to pass through the series of four IF commands following ELSE. Also, a value is set for new variable BONUS only once per case.

8.8 Multiple ELSE IF Commands

In the previous example, cases that do not meet the conditions on the DO IF or ELSE IF commands are evaluated by all four IF commands following ELSE. To pass control out of the structure as soon as the expression on an IF command is true, substitute ELSE IF and COMPUTE commands for each IF command, as in:

```
DO IF (YRHIRED GT 80)
COMPUTE              BONUS = 0
ELSE IF  ((DEPT82 EQ 1 OR DEPT82 EQ 2) AND YRHIRED LE 75)
COMPUTE              BONUS = .16*SALARY82
ELSE IF  (DEPT82 EQ 3)
COMPUTE              BONUS = .1*SALARY82
ELSE IF  (DEPT82 EQ 1)
COMPUTE              BONUS = .12*SALARY82
ELSE IF  (DEPT82 EQ 4)
COMPUTE              BONUS = .08*SALARY82
ELSE IF  (DEPT82 EQ 2)
COMPUTE              BONUS = .14*SALARY82
END IF
```

As soon as SPSS^X processes a case with value 3 for DEPT82 (and hired before 1980), control passes out of the structure. The other three ELSE commands are not evaluated for that case.

Note that the order of departments differs from previous examples. If Department 3 were the largest, Department 1 the next largest, and so forth, control will pass out of the structure more quickly for many cases. If you have a large number of cases or if your SPSS^X job will be executed frequently, these efficiency considerations can be important.

8.9 Missing Values and the DO IF Structure

If SPSS^X encounters a case with a missing value for the logical expression on the DO IF command, control passes to the first command after END IF. If a case has a missing value for the conditional expression on any subsequent ELSE IF command, control also passes to the first command after END IF. In the structure

```
DO IF (X EQ 0)
COMPUTE Y=1
ELSE IF (Z EQ 0)
COMPUTE Y=2
ELSE
COMPUTE Y=3
END IF
```

the entire structure is skipped (control passes to END IF) for any case with a missing value for X. Even if 0 is a missing value for variable X, Y is never 1. For cases with valid values other than 0 for X, the ELSE IF is evaluated and, if Z is missing, the rest of the structure is skipped.

In the example in Section 8.7, the DO IF—END IF structure is skipped for any case with a missing value for YRHIRED. In the absence of any other transformations, BONUS will remain at the initialized system-missing value. Likewise, if YRHIRED is less than or equal to 80 and DEPT82 is missing, control passes out of the structure and BONUS is system-missing.

8.10 Nested DO IF Structures

To perform transformations involving logical tests on two variables, you can use nested DO IF—END IF structures. For example, to create a single variable that indicates both the sex and minority status of an individual, you might specify:

```
DO IF (RACE EQ 5)                          /*DO WHITES
.  DO IF (SEX EQ 2)                            /*WHITE FEMALE
.  COMPUTE SEXRACE=3                           /*WHITE FEMALE
.  ELSE                                        /*WHITE MALE
.  COMPUTE SEXRACE=1                           /*WHITE MALE
.  END IF                                      /*WHITES DONE
ELSE IF (SEX EQ 2)                         /*NONWHITE FEMALE
COMPUTE SEXRACE=4                          /*NONWHITE FEMALE
ELSE                                       /*NONWHITE MALE
COMPUTE SEXRACE=2                          /*NONWHITE MALE
END IF                                     /*NONWHITES DONE
```

An optional period (or plus or minus sign) in column one allows you to indent commands to emphasize the nested nature of the structures (see Chapter 2).

8.11 Summary

The DO IF—END IF case control structure, which involves the DO IF, ELSE IF, ELSE, and END IF commands, can be used according to the following rules:

- The DO IF command marks the beginning of the structure and the END IF command marks its end.
- The ELSE IF command is optional and can be repeated as many times as desired within the structure.
- The ELSE command is optional. It can be used only once and must follow any ELSE IF commands.
- The END IF command must follow any ELSE IF or ELSE commands.
- Logical expressions are mandatory on the DO IF and ELSE IF commands. Do not use logical expressions on the ELSE and END IF commands.

The flow of control operates according to the following rules:

- Missing values returned by the logical expression on the DO IF command or on any ELSE IF commands causes control to pass outside of the structure at that point.
- If the logical expression on the DO IF command is true, the commands immediately following the DO IF are executed up to the next ELSE IF or ELSE in the structure. Control then passes to the first statement following the END IF for that structure.
- If the expression on the DO IF command is false, control passes to the first ELSE IF where the logical expression is evaluated. If this expression is true, commands following the ELSE IF are executed up to the next ELSE IF or ELSE command, and control passes to the first statement following the END IF for that structure.
- If the expressions on the DO IF and the first ELSE IF commands are both false, control passes to the next ELSE IF, where that logical expression is evaluated. If none of the expressions are true on any of the ELSE IF commands, commands following the ELSE command are executed and control falls out of the structure.
- If none of the expressions on the DO IF command or the ELSE IF commands are true and there is no ELSE command, then a case falls through the entire structure with no change.

DO IF—END IF control structures can be nested to any level permitted by available memory. Also, DO IF—END IF control structures can be nested within LOOP—END LOOP control structures or LOOP structures within DO IF structures (see Chapter 12).

8.12 LOGICAL EXPRESSIONS

SPSS^X evaluates a logical expression as true or false, or as missing if it is indeterminate. A logical expression returns 1 if the expression is true, 0 if it is false, or system-missing if it is missing. Thus, logical expressions can be any expressions that yield this three-valued logic. The logical expression

```
SELECT IF (X GE 5)
```

is true if X is 5 or greater, false if X is less than 5, and missing if X is missing. The parentheses around the logical expression are optional.

Logical expressions can be simple logical variables or relations, or they can be complex logical tests involving variables, constants, functions, relational operators, logical operators, and nested parentheses to control the order of evaluation.

Logical expressions can appear on the IF, SELECT IF, DO IF, ELSE IF, LOOP, END LOOP, and COMPUTE commands.

IF. A logical expression on an IF command that is true causes the assignment expression to be executed. A logical expression that returns missing has the same effect as one that is false: the value of the target variable is not altered. The command

```
IF (X EQ 5) Y=3
```

sets Y to 3 when the expression is true, but does not set or alter the value of Y when the expression is false or when X is missing. (See Section 8.1.)

The DO IF—END IF Structure. If a logical expression on a DO IF command is true, SPSS^X executes the commands immediately following the DO IF up to the next ELSE IF, ELSE, or END IF. A false logical expression on a DO IF command causes SPSS^X to look for the next ELSE IF or ELSE command. A logical expression on a DO IF command that returns missing causes the entire structure to be skipped. The structure

```
DO IF (X GE 5)
RECODE Z (1=2)
ELSE
RECODE Z (0=2)
END IF
```

recodes value 1 for variable Z to 2 when the logical expression is true. When the logical expression is false, value 0 for variable Z is recoded to 2. For cases with missing values for X, variable Z is not changed. (See Sections 8.2 through 8.11.)

SELECT IF. If the logical expression on a SELECT IF command is true, the case is selected. A logical expression that returns missing has the same effect as one that is false: the case is not selected. The command

```
SELECT IF (X GE 5)
```

selects cases when the expression is true and rejects cases when it is false or when X is missing. (See Chapter 10.)

The LOOP—END LOOP Structure. If an IF logical expression on a LOOP command is true, looping begins (or continues). An IF logical expression on a LOOP command that returns missing has the same effect as one that is false: the structure is skipped. On the END LOOP command, if an IF logical expression is *false,* control returns to the LOOP command for that structure and looping continues. If it is true, looping stops and the structure is terminated. An IF command that returns missing has the same effect as one that is true: the structure is terminated. The structure

```
LOOP IF (X GE 5)
COMPUTE Y=Y+1
END LOOP IF (Y GE 10)
```

begins looping and adding 1 to Y only when the expression X GE 5 is true. Looping never begins if X is missing. Looping terminates either when the expression Y GE 10 is true or when Y is missing. (See Chapter 12.)

COMPUTE. A logical expression on a COMPUTE command returns 1 if the expression is true, 0 if it is false, and missing if is missing. In the command

```
COMPUTE Y=(X GE 5)
```

Y equals 1 if the logical expression is true, 0 if it is false, and missing if X is missing. (See Chapter 6.)

8.13 Logical Variables

The simplest logical expression is a logical variable. A logical variable is any variable that takes on values 1, 0, or system-missing. For example, the expression

```
DO IF PROMO81
```

is true if PROMO81 is 1 (employee promoted in 1981), false if it is 0 (employee not promoted in 1981), or missing if the value of PROMO81 is missing. Any other value for PROMO81 causes a warning message, and SPSS^X evaluates the expression for that case as 0 and false.

Logical variables cannot be strings.

8.14 Relational Operators

A relation is a logical expression that compares two values using a *relational operator*. In the command

```
IF (X EQ 0) Y=1
```

variable X and 0 are expressions that yield the values to be compared by the EQ relational operator. Relational operators are

EQ *Equal to.* Returns true if the expression on the left is exactly equal to the expression on the right.

NE *Not equal to.* Returns true if the expression on the left does not equal the expression on the right.

LT *Less than.* Returns true if the expression on the left is less than the expression on the right.

LE *Less than or equal to.* Returns true if the expression on the left is less than or equal to the expression on the right.

GT *Greater than.* Returns true if the expression on the left is greater than the expression on the right.

GE *Greater than or equal to.* Returns true if the expression on the left is greater than or equal to the expression on the right.

You can specify either the relational operators above or their symbolic equivalents: = (EQ), ¬= or <> (NE), < (LT), > (GT), <= (LE), and >= (GE).

The expressions in a relation can be variables, constants, or more complicated arithmetic expressions, as in

```
IF (W+Y GT X+Z) NEWX=1
```

which assigns the value 1 to NEWX if the sum of W and Y is greater than the sum of X and Z. Or you can use one or more of the functions described for the COMPUTE command, as in

```
IF MEAN(Q1 TO Q5) LE 5 INDEX=1
```

which assigns the value 1 to INDEX if the mean of variables Q1 through Q5 is less than or equal to 5.

You must use blanks (not commas) to separate the relational operator from the expressions, but you are free to introduce more blanks and parentheses in order to make the command more readable, as in:

```
IF (MEAN (Q1 TO Q5) LE 5) INDEX=1
```

8.15 The AND and OR Logical Operators

You can join two or more relations logically using the *logical operators* AND and OR, as in:

```
IF (X EQ 0 AND Z LT 2) Y=2
```

This command assigns value 2 to variable Y only for cases with X equal to zero and Z less than two. The AND logical operator means that both relations must be true. Logical operators combine relations according to the following rules:

AND *Both relations must be true.*

OR *Either relation can be true.*

You can use only one logical operator to combine two relations; AND/OR is invalid. However, you can combine many relations into a complex logical expression. Regardless of the number of relations and logical operators used to build a logical expression, the result is either true, false, or indeterminate because of missing values (see Section 8.18). The command

```
IF (DEPT82 EQ 2 AND YRHIRED LE 75) BONUS = .16*SALARY82
```

assigns the value .16*SALARY82 to BONUS only for those cases where the value of DEPT 82 is 2 and YRHIRED is less than or equal to 75. Similarly,

```
IF (DEPT82 EQ 3 OR YRHIRED GT 80) BONUS = .08*SALARY82
```

assigns the value .08*SALARY82 to BONUS for cases with either 3 for variable DEPT82 or a value greater than 80 for variable YRHIRED.

Operators or expressions cannot be implied. For example, you cannot specify X EQ 1 OR 2 in place of X EQ 1 OR X EQ 2. You can use the ANY and RANGE functions to simplify complex expressions (see Chapter 6), as in:

```
SELECT IF ANY(X,1,2)
```

8.16 The NOT Logical Operator

The NOT logical operator reverses the true/false outcome of the expression that immediately follows. For example,

```
IF NOT(X EQ 0) Y=3
```

assigns value 3 to Y for all cases with values other than 0 for variable X.

The NOT operator affects only the expression that immediately follows, unless more than one expression is enclosed in parentheses. The expression

```
SELECT IF (NOT X EQ 0 AND Z LT 2)
```

is true for cases where X *is not* 0 and Z *is* less than 2. The expression

```
SELECT IF  NOT(X EQ 0 OR Z EQ 2)
```

is equivalent to

```
 SELECT IF (X NE 0 AND Z NE 2)
```

because the only way the first logical expression can be true is for the parenthetical expression to be false.

The ¬ symbol is a valid substitute for the NOT keyword.

8.17 The Order of Evaluation

When arithmetic operators and functions are used in a logical expression, the order of operations is exactly the same as for the COMPUTE command as described in Chapter 6. Functions and arithmetic operations are evaluated first, then relational operators, then NOT, then AND, and then OR. In the expression NOT VARB/5 GT 10, the value of VARB is divided by 5, the result is compared to 10, and the logical result is reversed by NOT.

ANNOTATED EXAMPLE FOR CONDITIONAL TRANSFORMATIONS

The task developed in Sections 8.2 through 8.9 is to compute a company bonus based on an individual's salary, department, and tenure with the company. In addition, this example writes out the computed information onto a file, perhaps for input to a check-writing program, and produces a breakdown analysis of mean bonus by department. The SPSS^X commands are

```
FILE HANDLE HUBEMPL/ file specifications
GET FILE=HUBEMPL

DO IF (YRHIRED GT 80)
+ COMPUTE            BONUS = 0
ELSE IF ((DEPT82 EQ 1 OR DEPT82 EQ 2) AND YRHIRED LE 75)
+ COMPUTE            BONUS = .16*SALARY82
ELSE
+ IF (DEPT82 EQ 1) BONUS = .12*SALARY82
+ IF (DEPT82 EQ 2) BONUS = .14*SALARY82
+ IF (DEPT82 EQ 3) BONUS = .1*SALARY82
+ IF (DEPT82 EQ 4) BONUS = .08*SALARY82
END IF

SORT CASES EMPLOYID
FORMAT BONUS(DOLLAR9.2)

FILE HANDLE BONUS/ file specifications
DO IF (BONUS NE 0)
WRITE OUTFILE=BONUS /EMPLOYID NAME BONUS
END IF

BREAKDOWN BONUS BY DEPT82
```

- The FILE HANDLE command (see Chapter 3) defines the file handle for the system file to be read by the GET command.
- The GET command reads the SPSS^X system file containing the personnel data (see Chapter 5).
- The first control structure defined by the DO IF and END IF commands assigns no bonus to individuals hired after 1980 (YRHIRED GT 80) (see Section 8.3). Plus signs are used in column 1 so commands can be indented to improve readability (see Chapter 2).
- The ELSE IF command assigns a special bonus to individuals from Departments 1 and 2 who have been with the company since at least 1975 (see Section 8.7).
- The series of IF commands following the ELSE command set the bonuses for everyone else (see Sections 8.1, 8.5, and 8.6).
- The SORT CASES command sorts the cases according to employee identification number (see Chapter 13). FORMAT provides a printing and writing format for the bonus variable (see Chapter 9).
- The second FILE HANDLE command defines the file handle for the WRITE command that follows.
- The second DO IF—END IF structure limits the WRITE command to those who are eligible for the bonus (see Chapter 9). Figure A shows a listing of the first 20 cases from the file created by the WRITE command.
- The BREAKDOWN command asks for a breakdown of the bonus variable by department (see Chapter 22). The output is shown in Figure B.

A Data from the WRITE command

```
1801CONNIE E. JANNSEN       $1,560.00
2211MARY CHAFEE               $804.00
2690HOLLY C. BRADSHAW       $3,016.00
2821JACKIE HAMILTON           $887.20
3061KARIN HEGEL             $2,275.00
3091C. M. BROWN             $1,310.40
3171VERA D. LOGGINS         $1,446.64
3261LUCINDA JACKSON           $984.00
3390ANITA PULASKI           $1,232.80
4381REUBEN D. CROSS         $3,078.40
4981TANI PATEL              $2,215.20
5402PETER D. GAMINO         $4,133.92
5601LUCIA DELMONICO         $2,838.50
6061ROSE C. LANDA           $1,513.80
6151BESSIE D. GRAVES        $1,789.28
6161SUZANNE RADFORD         $2,412.80
6241SEAN D. MCGILLICUDDY    $1,366.40
6251DIANNE HARRINGTON         $816.20
6351BRIAN M. CURTIS         $1,638.56
6402JOANNA C. DRESSLER      $3,120.00
```

B The BREAKDOWN results

```
- - - - - - - - - - - - - - - - -   D E S C R I P T I O N   O F   S U B P O P U L A T I O N S   - - - - - - - - - - - - - - - - -
CRITERION VARIABLE   BONUS
    BROKEN DOWN BY   DEPT82     DEPARTMENT CODE IN 1982
- - - - - - - - - - - - - - - - - - - - - - - - - - - - - - - - - - - - - - - - - - - - - - - - - - - - - - - - - - - - - - - - -
```

VARIABLE	CODE	VALUE LABEL	SUM	MEAN	STD DEV	VARIANCE	N
FOR ENTIRE POPULATION			271897.5800	1875.1557	1102.8420	1216260.4506	(145)
DEPT82	1.	ADMIN	71327.2400	2097.8600	1026.4519	1053603.4389	(34)
DEPT82	2.	PROJECT DIRECTORS	56142.1000	2551.9136	1536.0324	2359395.4578	(22)
DEPT82	3.	CHICAGO OPERATIONS	104029.6000	1733.8267	1011.3238	1022775.9274	(60)
DEPT82	4.	ST LOUIS OPERATIONS	40398.6400	1393.0566	620.5001	385020.4134	(29)

```
  TOTAL CASES =    275
MISSING CASES =    130 OR  47.3 PCT.
```

When more than one logical operator is used, AND is evaluated before OR. For example, in the command

```
IF (DEPT82 EQ 2 AND YRHIRED GT 80 OR PROMO81 EQ 0)
   BONUS = .08*SALARY82
```

the logical expression is true if a case has either value 2 for DEPT82 and a value greater than 80 for YRHIRED, or if the case has 0 for PROMO81 (the individual was not promoted in 1981) regardless of department or year hired. In other words, the command above is equivalent the the following command using parentheses to clarify the order of evaluation:

```
IF ((DEPT82 EQ 2 AND YRHIRED GT 80) OR PROMO81 EQ 0)
   BONUS = .08*SALARY82
```

You can change the order of evaluation with parentheses. For example, in the command

```
IF (DEPT82 EQ 2 AND (YRHIRED GT 80 OR PROMO81 EQ 0))
   BONUS = .08*SALARY82
```

the expression is true only for cases with value 2 for DEPT82 that also have either a value greater than 80 for YRHIRED or 0 for PROMO81.

8.18 Missing Values

If the logic of an expression is indeterminate because of missing values, the expression returns missing and the command is not executed. In a simple relation, the logic is indeterminate if the expression on either side of the relational operator is missing. For example, in the command

```
IF (X GT Z) Y=Y**2
```

SPSS^X cannot tell whether one variable is greater or less than the other for any case where X and/or Z are missing. In this example, SPSS^X would not evaluate the assignment specification and the case's value for variable Y would not change. Since Y already exists in this example (i.e., it also appears to the right of the equals sign), it retains its previous value. If Y were being defined by this IF command, it would remain at the initialized system-missing value.

8.19 Missing Values and Logical Operators

When two or more relations are joined by logical operators AND and OR, SPSS^X always returns missing if all of the relations in the expression are missing. However, if any one of the relations can be determined, SPSS^X tries to return true or false according to the logical outcomes shown in Table 8.19. The asterisk flags expressions where SPSS^X can evaluate the outcome with incomplete information.

Table 8.19 Logical outcome

Expression	Outcome	Expression	Outcome
true AND true	= true	true OR true	= true
true AND false	= false	true OR false	= true
false AND false	= false	false OR false	= false
true AND missing	= missing	true OR missing	= true*
missing AND missing	= missing	missing OR missing	= missing
false AND missing	= false*	false OR missing	= missing

When two relations are joined with the AND operator, the logical expression can never be true if one of the relations is indeterminate. The expression can, however, be false. Consider the DO IF command in the following structure:

```
DO IF (X EQ 2 AND Y LE 7)
COMPUTE Z=1
ELSE IF (X EQ 0)
COMPUTE Z=2
ELSE
COMPUTE Z=0
END IF
```

For any case with a missing value for both X and Y, the logical expression on the DO IF command is missing and the entire structure is skipped, leaving Z unaltered. Likewise, if X equals 2 but Y is missing, or if Y is less than or equal to 7 but X is missing, the logical expression is missing and the structure is skipped because AND means that both relations must be true.

However, if one of the relations is false and the other is missing, the logical expression is evaluated as false and only the DO IF command is skipped. For example, if X is 0 and Y is missing, SPSS^X does not set Z equal to 1 but evaluates the logical expression on the ELSE IF command. Because X is 0, SPSS^X sets Z equal to 2.

When two relations are joined with the OR operator, the logical expression can never be false if one relation returns missing. In the command

```
IF (DEPT82 EQ 3 OR YRHIRED GT 80) BONUS = .08*SALARY82
```

the logical expression is true if DEPT82 equals 3 or YRHIRED is greater than 80, even if one of these two relations evaluates as missing. In other words, SPSS^X can determine the truth of the expression if it finds a case of someone hired in 1981—even if the case has missing information for department—since the logical expression specifies that only one relation needs to be true.

```
PRINT  [OUTFILE = handle]  [RECORDS = {1}]  [{NOTABLE}]
                                      {n}     {TABLE  }

  / {1    } varlist [ {col location [(format)]} ]  [varlist . . . ]
    {rec #}           {(format list)          }
                      {*                      }

  [/ {2    } . . . ]
     {rec #}

PRINT EJECT  [OUTFILE = handle]
             [RECORDS = {1}]  [{NOTABLE}]
                        {n}     {TABLE  }

  / {1    } varlist [ {col location [(format)]} ]  [varlist . . . ]
    {rec #}           {(format list)          }
                      {*                      }

  [/ {2    } . . . ]
     {rec #}

PRINT SPACE  [OUTFILE = handle]  [numeric expression]

WRITE  [OUTFILE = handle]  [RECORDS = {1}]  [{NOTABLE}]
                                      {n}     {TABLE  }

  / {1    } varlist [ {col location [(format)]} ]  [varlist . . . ]
    {rec #}           {(format list)          }
                      {*                      }

  [/ {2    } . . . ]
     {rec #}

PRINT FORMATS  varlist (format) [varlist . . . ]

WRITE FORMATS  varlist (format) [varlist . . . ]

FORMATS  varlist (format) [varlist . . . ]

LIST  [VARIABLES = {ALL    }]
                   {varlist}

  [/CASES = [FROM {1}]  [TO {eof}]  [BY {1}]]
                  {n}       {n  }       {n}

  [/FORMAT = [{WRAP  }]  [{UNNUMBERED}]]
              {SINGLE}     {NUMBERED  }
```


THE PRINT COMMAND, **9.1**
- Variable Specifications, **9.2**
  - Specifying Formats, **9.3**
  - Printing Multiple Lines per Case, **9.4**
  - Using Literals, **9.5**
  - Creating Column Headings, **9.6**
- File and Table Specifications, **9.7**
- Features and Limitations, **9.8**

THE PRINT EJECT COMMAND, **9.9**

THE PRINT SPACE COMMAND, **9.10**
- Specifying the Number of Blank Lines, **9.11**

THE WRITE COMMAND, **9.12**
- Variable Specifications, **9.13**
- File and Table Specifications, **9.14**

PRINT AND WRITE FORMAT COMMANDS, **9.15**
- The PRINT FORMATS Command, **9.16**
- The WRITE FORMATS Command, **9.17**
- The FORMATS Command, **9.18**

THE LIST PROCEDURE, **9.19**
- The VARIABLES Subcommand, **9.20**
- The CASES Subcommand, **9.21**
- The FORMAT Subcommand, **9.22**
- LIST and Case Selection, **9.23**

Chapter 9 Listing and Writing Cases

There are occasions when you want to see the actual contents of cases. You may want to see that a DATA LIST command is defining your data as you intend, or you may want to verify results of transformations or examine cases you suspect have coding errors. The PRINT and LIST commands allow you to display the values of variables for each case in your data file (see Sections 9.1 through 9.8 and 9.19 through 9.23, respectively).

You may also want to write the values of variables to an output file, for example to send data to another organization or to use another program to analyze the data. The WRITE command writes values to an output file in nearly any format you wish (see Sections 9.12 through 9.13).

Both PRINT and WRITE are not actually executed until the data are read. SPSS^X stores your specifications and executes them as data are read by a procedure. LIST, on the other hand, acts like a procedure and reads the data immediately.

By default, the PRINT and LIST commands use the associated print formats stored in the dictionary for each variable and WRITE uses the associated write formats. You can specify formats on the PRINT or WRITE commands, or you can change the dictionary formats. You must change the dictionary print format to affect LIST. You may want to change formats for other reasons, such as to display values in DOLLAR format in procedure REPORT. Three commands allow you to change dictionary formats—PRINT FORMATS, WRITE FORMATS, and FORMATS—described in Sections 9.16 through 9.18.

9.1 THE PRINT COMMAND

The PRINT command is designed to be simple enough for a quick check on reading and transforming data and yet flexible enough for formatting simple reports. As a quick check on data values, the simplest PRINT command begins with a slash followed by the list of variables to be printed, as in:

```
PRINT / MOHIRED YRHIRED DEPT82 SALARY82 NAME
FREQUENCIES VARIABLES=DEPT82
```

Values are printed on the display file as the data are read, but appear before the output of the first procedure (see Figure 9.1). PRINT uses the dictionary print formats assigned when the variables are defined on a DATA LIST command, on a PRINT FORMATS, or FORMATS command, or assigned when the variables are created with transformation commands. PRINT is executed as the data are being read, once for each case constructed from your data file. Values for each case are displayed with a blank space between each value. Figure 9.1 shows 10 cases of display from the above PRINT command.

Figure 9.1 PRINT results using defaults

```
8 69 3 15600 CONNIE E. JANNSEN
3 80 4 10050 MARY CHAFEE
2 74 1 18850 HOLLY C. BRADSHAW
7 79 2 16250 KARIN HEGEL
6 79 1 10920 C. M. BROWN
4 80 4 18083 VERA D. LOGGINS
9 79 3  9840 LUCINDA JACKSON
4 79 3 12328 ANITA PULASKI
1 74 1 19240 REUBEN D. CROSS
7 79 1 18460 TANI PATEL
```

If PRINT is not followed by a procedure command that causes the data to be read, SPSS^X does nothing. To execute the PRINT command anyway, use the EXECUTE command documented in Chapter 17. See the LIST procedure described in Section 9.19 for an alternative.

9.2 Variable Specifications

Specify the variable names following a slash. The first slash begins definition of the first (and possibly only) line per case of your PRINT output (see Section 9.4). Variables named must already exist, but they can be numeric, string, scratch, temporary, or system variables. You can use the TO convention for naming consecutive variables, as in:

```
PRINT / MOHIRED YRHIRED DEPT82 SALARY79 TO SALARY82 NAME
```

If you specify more variables than can be printed in 132 columns or within the width you specify using the WIDTH subcommand of SET (Chapter 4), the line will be wrapped starting in the second column of the next line. Lines will still wrap if you override dictionary formats up to the set page width. However, you cannot override dictionary formats that reference positions beyond the set page width. See Section 9.4 for an alternative.

9.3 Specifying Formats

You can specify formats for some or all variables you want printed. Use an asterisk to distinguish those variables that you want printed using dictionary formats from those variables for which you have provided format specifications. A format specification following a list of variables without formats applies to all variables in the list. There must be one format for each variable in the list, as in:

```
PRINT / MOHIRED YRHIRED DEPT82 *
        SALARY79 TO SALARY82 (4(DOLLAR8,1X))
        NAME
```

When you specify a format, the automatic blank following the variable or variables affected is suppressed. If you want a blank between variables, you must specify it in the format, as shown in both examples above. Use a literal, an extra column, or X or T format elements (see Chapter 3) to insert blanks between variables for which you specify formats on the PRINT command.

The asterisk is a special format that tells SPSS^X to use the dictionary format. The automatic blank following the variable is preserved for variables specified with an asterisk format. An asterisk following a variable list with no formats applies to all variables in the list. For example, in the command

```
PRINT   / MOHIRED YRHIRED DEPT82 * SALARY82 (DOLLAR8,1X) NAME *
EXECUTE
```

the asterisk following the first three variables tells SPSS^X to print them using their dictionary print formats, each separated by a single blank. SALARY82 is printed using the DOLLAR format, followed by a blank specified with the 1X format. DOLLAR8 allows the printing of values up to $999,999. Variable NAME is a string variable with a dictionary print format of 24 characters. The asterisk following variable NAME is optional since the default would be to use the dictionary format. See Figure 9.3 for 10 cases of the display from this command.

- Format specifications can be either column-style or FORTRAN-style.
- Printable numeric formats are F, COMMA, DOLLAR, PIBHEX, RBHEX, and Z. Printable string formats are A and AHEX. See Chapter 3 for details.
- Format specifications are in effect only for the output of the PRINT command. They do not change the dictionary print formats.

Figure 9.3 PRINT results specifying a format

```
8 69 3  $15,600 CONNIE E. JANNSEN
3 80 4  $10,050 MARY CHAFEE
2 74 1  $18,850 HOLLY C. BRADSHAW
7 79 2  $16,250 KARIN HEGEL
6 79 1  $10,920 C. M. BROWN
4 80 4  $18,083 VERA D. LOGGINS
9 79 3   $9,840 LUCINDA JACKSON
4 79 3  $12,328 ANITA PULASKI
1 74 1  $19,240 REUBEN D. CROSS
7 79 1  $18,460 TANI PATEL
```

9.4 Printing Multiple Lines per Case

You can use the PRINT command to display variables on more than one line for each case. Specifications for each line of output must begin with a slash. Optionally, an integer can follow the slash, indicating on which line the values are to be printed. For example, to display the values of an individual's department and salary in 1981 on one line, the department and salary in 1982 on the next line, the employee identification number on both lines, followed by a completely blank third line, specify:

```
PRINT  /EMPLOYID DEPT81 SALARY81
       /EMPLOYID DEPT82 SALARY82
       /
EXECUTE
```

The display output for 10 cases in this example is shown in Figure 9.4.

The command above is equivalent to the following:

```
PRINT /1 EMPLOYID DEPT81 SALARY81 /2 EMPLOYID DEPT82 SALARY82 /3
```

Figure 9.4 PRINT results with three lines per case

```
1801 3 14300
1801 3 15600

2211 4  8840
2211 4 10050

2690 1 16250
2690 1 18850

3061 2 14300
3061 2 16250

3091 1  9750
3091 1 10920

3171 4 16900
3171 4 18083

3261 3  8866
3261 3  9840

3390 3  9750
3390 3 12328

4381 1 16575
4381 1 19240

4981 3 12480
4981 1 18460
```

9.5 Using Literals

You can include literals with your variable specifications on the PRINT command. Literals must be enclosed in apostrophes or quotation marks. In the following example, literals are used to label the values being printed and to insert a slash between the month hired (MOHIRED) and the year hired (YRHIRED) to create a composite hiring date.

```
PRINT / NAME * 'HIRED=' MOHIRED(F2) '/' YRHIRED *
              '  SALARY82=' SALARY82 (DOLLAR8)
EXECUTE
```

In this example, the F2 format is supplied for variable MOHIRED in order to suppress the blank that would follow it if the dictionary format were used. The asterisks following variables NAME and YRHIRED are actually optional since formats do not refer back across literals to other variables without formats. That is, a literal terminates a variable list. Figure 9.5 shows the display with literals.

Figure 9.5 PRINT results with literals

```
CONNIE E. JANNSEN         HIRED= 8/69  SALARY82= $15,600
MARY CHAFEE               HIRED= 3/80  SALARY82= $10,050
HOLLY C. BRADSHAW         HIRED= 2/74  SALARY82= $18,850
KARIN HEGEL               HIRED= 7/79  SALARY82= $16,250
C. M. BROWN               HIRED= 6/79  SALARY82= $10,920
VERA D. LOGGINS           HIRED= 4/80  SALARY82= $18,083
LUCINDA JACKSON           HIRED= 9/79  SALARY82=  $9,840
ANITA PULASKI             HIRED= 4/79  SALARY82= $12,328
REUBEN D. CROSS           HIRED= 1/74  SALARY82= $19,240
TANI PATEL                HIRED= 7/79  SALARY82= $18,460
```

9.6 Creating Column Headings

You can use literals to include column headings to identify the variables that you are displaying. This can be done using the DO IF—END IF structure discussed in Chapter 8, as in:

```
DO IF $CASENUM EQ 1
PRINT /'    NAME ' 1 'DEPT' 25 'HIRED' 30 '   SALARY' 35
END IF
PRINT / NAME DEPT82 *
        MOHIRED 30-31 '/' YRHIRED *
        SALARY82 35-42(DOLLAR)
EXECUTE
```

The above PRINT commands produce the listing shown in Figure 9.6. The values are printed with column headings that identify the variables. Since PRINT is executed once for each case in your data file, you must enclose the PRINT command that specifies column headings within the DO IF—END IF structure. DO IF $CASENUM EQ 1 causes the PRINT command that defines the column heads to be executed only once, as the first case is processed. END IF closes the structure.

The second PRINT command specifies the variables to be printed. It is executed once for each case in your data file. To align the column headings with the list of values, you should specify the format for the printing of the variables rather than relying on the defaults. In this example, the T format element could be used to align the variables and the column headings. For example, specifying MOHIRED (T30,F2) begins the printing of the values for the variable MOHIRED in column 30 in order to line up the composite hiring date under the title HIRED. See Section 9.3 for a discussion of format specifications on the PRINT command.

Figure 9.6 PRINT results with literals as column heads

```
    NAME                     DEPT HIRED  SALARY
CONNIE E. JANNSEN             3    8/69 $15,600
MARY CHAFEE                   4    3/80 $10,050
HOLLY C. BRADSHAW             1    2/74 $18,850
KARIN HEGEL                   2    7/79 $16,250
C. M. BROWN                   1    6/79 $10,920
VERA D. LOGGINS               4    4/80 $18,083
LUCINDA JACKSON               3    9/79  $9,840
ANITA PULASKI                 3    4/79 $12,328
REUBEN D. CROSS               1    1/74 $19,240
TANI PATEL                    1    7/79 $18,460
```

9.7 File and Table Specifications

Two specifications are allowed on the PRINT command before the first slash.

The OUTFILE Subcommand. OUTFILE specifies the file handle of the target file for the output from the PRINT command. By default, the PRINT command sends the results to the display file, which is usually what you want. If you use the OUTFILE subcommand, you must define the file to the host operating system using the FILE HANDLE command (see Chapter 3).

The TABLE Subcommand. TABLE requests a format table on the display file showing how the variable information is formatted. NOTABLE is the default.

To send output from a PRINT command to a file other than the display file and to tell SPSS^X to print a table describing the format of that file, specify:

```
FILE HANDLE PRINTOUT/ file specifications
PRINT OUTFILE=PRINTOUT TABLE / EMPLOYID DEPT82 SALARY82 NAME
EXECUTE
```

The OUTFILE subcommand names PRINTOUT as the file on which the values specified will be written (see Figure 9.7a). The equals signs after the OUTFILE subcommand is optional. TABLE requests a summary table describing the PRINT specifications. The table is printed on the display file (see Figure 9.7b). The file and table specifications can appear in any order and both are optional.

Figure 9.7a PRINT results to an output file

```
1801 3 15600 CONNIE E. JANNSEN
2211 4 10050 MARY CHAFEE
2690 1 18850 HOLLY C. BRADSHAW
3061 2 16250 KARIN HEGEL
3091 1 10920 C. M. BROWN
3171 4 18083 VERA D. LOGGINS
3261 3  9840 LUCINDA JACKSON
3390 3 12328 ANITA PULASKI
4381 1 19240 REUBEN D. CROSS
4981 1 18460 TANI PATEL
```

Figure 9.7b TABLE output

```
THE TABLE FOR THE ABOVE PRINT   COMMAND IS:

            VARIABLE  REC   START    END         FORMAT  WIDTH  DEC

            EMPLOYID   1       1      5          F          5    0
            DEPT82     1       7      7          F          1    0
            SALARY82   1       9     13          F          5    0
            NAME       1      15     38          A         24
```

If you specify an output file, you must provide the necessary operating-system information on a FILE HANDLE command. See the INFO command (Chapter 2) for documentation on how to construct the FILE HANDLE command at your installation. The output from the PRINT command cannot be longer than 255 characters, even if the external file is defined with a longer record length.

As shown in Figure 9.7b, the table lists the variable names and the locations of the variables on the output file. REC refers to the number of the record on which the variable is located. START and END give you the first and last positions, respectively, of the variable. FORMAT, WIDTH, and DEC give you the print format type of each variable to be printed, the column width, and the number of decimal places.

9.8 Features and Limitations

- User-defined missing values are printed like any other value for a variable specified on a PRINT command.
- System-missing values are represented by a period.
- Lines of output on a PRINT command cannot exceed 255 characters (if WIDTH is set to the maximum). Lines over 132 characters are continued on the next line starting in column 2.

9.9 THE PRINT EJECT COMMAND

The PRINT EJECT command prints the information requested on the command at the top of a new page of your output or display file each time it is executed. If the PRINT EJECT command is not in a DO IF—END IF structure, it is executed for each case and prints the values each time on a separate page. The syntax for PRINT EJECT is identical to the PRINT command. You can use PRINT EJECT to insert titles and column headings by using the DO IF—END IF structure (see Chapter 8). For example, to force the display output shown in Figure 9.6 to begin on a new page, specify:

```
DO IF $CASENUM EQ 1
PRINT EJECT /'   NAME ' 1 'DEPT' 25 'HIRED' 30 '  SALARY' 35
END IF
PRINT / NAME DEPT82 *
        MOHIRED(T30,F2) '/' YRHIRED *
        SALARY82 (T35,DOLLAR8)
EXECUTE
```

In this example, the DO IF—END IF structure controls the PRINT EJECT command, allowing it to be executed only once when the system variable $CASENUM is equal to 1 (see Chapter 6).

9.10 THE PRINT SPACE COMMAND

The only function of the PRINT SPACE command is to print blank lines. PRINT SPACE with no specifications prints one blank line on the display file. The PRINT SPACE command has two optional specifications, the number of blank lines (the default is 1) and the output file handle. There are no variable specifications. The command

```
DO IF $CASENUM EQ 1
PRINT EJECT /'   NAME ' 1 'DEPT' 25 'HIRED' 30 '  SALARY' 35
PRINT SPACE
END IF
PRINT / NAME DEPT82 *
        MOHIRED(T30,F2) '/' YRHIRED *
        SALARY82 (T35,DOLLAR8)
EXECUTE
```

prints a blank line following the headings as shown in Figure 9.10.

Figure 9.10 PRINT SPACE used to set off headings

```
   NAME                   DEPT HIRED  SALARY

CONNIE E. JANNSEN          3    8/69 $15,600
MARY CHAFEE                4    3/80 $10,050
HOLLY C. BRADSHAW          1    2/74 $18,850
KARIN HEGEL                2    7/79 $16,250
C. M. BROWN                1    6/79 $10,920
VERA D. LOGGINS            4    4/80 $18,083
LUCINDA JACKSON            3    9/79  $9,840
ANITA PULASKI              3    4/79 $12,328
REUBEN D. CROSS            1    1/74 $19,240
TANI PATEL                 1    7/79 $18,460
```

Use an OUTFILE subcommand on a PRINT SPACE command when you want to insert blank lines in the output of a PRINT or WRITE command that is directed to a file other than the display file.

9.11 Specifying the Number of Blank Lines

You can use a numeric expression with the PRINT SPACE command to specify the number of blank lines. The numeric expression can simply be an integer or it can be a more complex expression.

An example of using a complex expression with PRINT SPACE might be when you have a variable number of input records for each name and address that you want printed in a fixed number of lines for mailing labels. The goal is to know when you have printed the last line for each address, how many lines you have printed, and therefore how many blank records to print. Assuming there is already one blank line between each address on input and that you want to print eight lines per label, specify:

```
FILE HANDLE ADDRESS/ file specifications
FILE HANDLE LABELS/ file specifications

DATA LIST FILE=ADDRESS/RECORD 1-40 (A)    /*READ A RECORD
COMPUTE #LINES=#LINES+1                   /*BUMP COUNTER AND PRINT
WRITE OUTFILE=LABELS /RECORD

DO IF RECORD EQ ' '                       /*BLANK BETWEEN ADDRESSES?
+  PRINT SPACE OUTFILE=LABELS 8-#LINES    /*PRINT EXTRA BLANK #LINES
+  COMPUTE #LINES=0
END IF

EXECUTE
```

Variable #LINES is the key to this example. #LINES is intialized to 0 as a scratch variable. Then it is incremented for each record written (see Section 9.12 for the WRITE command). When SPSS^X encounters a blank line (RECORD EQ ' '), PRINT SPACE prints a number of blank lines equal to 8 minus the number already printed, and #LINES is then reset to 0. The first three mailing labels from file LABELS are shown in Figure 9.11.

Figure 9.11 PRINT SPACE with a variable number of lines

```
Dr. Theodore Thomson, Superintendent
Central Offices
Northfield School District 29
Room 101-B
525 Sunset Ridge Road
Northfield, IL  60093

Dr. Susan J. Lewis, Superintendent
Dolton School District 149
15141 Dorchester Avenue
Dolton, IL  60419



Mr. Larry A. Bannes, Superintendent
Kenilworth School District 38
Room 596
542 Abbotsford Road
Kenilworth, IL  60043
```

9.12 THE WRITE COMMAND

The WRITE command is basically the same as the PRINT command except that it is designed for writing data to be read by other software rather than by people. The WRITE command operates the same as the PRINT command except that no blank columns are inserted automatically between variables when you use dictionary formats, the system-missing value is represented by blanks, and you can write lines longer than 255 characters. With WRITE, the dictionary format for a variable is the dictionary write format, not the print format.

9.13 Variable Specifications

You can specify formats for some or all variables you want written, you can write more than one record per case, and you can write out literals as well as values of variables. For example, the command

```
FILE HANDLE NEWHUB/ file specifications
WRITE OUTFILE=NEWHUB TABLE
  /EMPLOYID '1' MOHIRED YRHIRED SEX AGE JOBCAT NAME
  /EMPLOYID '2' DEPT79 TO DEPT82 SALARY79 TO SALARY82 *
                HOURLY82(F5.2)
```

specifies two records per input case, one literal on each record ('1' and '2'), and a format for variable HOURLY82 to override the F7.2 dictionary format.

Formats. Format specifications can be column-style, FORTRAN-style, or the special asterisk symbol that specifies the dictionary format. In addition to the print formats described in Section 9.3, write formats in IBM/OS can be IB, PIB, P, PK, and RB. See Chapter 3 for a complete discussion of formats. Format specifications are in effect only for the output of the WRITE command. They do not change the dictionary write formats.

Multiple Records. You can use the WRITE command to write variables on more than one record for each case. Specifications for each record of output must begin with a slash. Optionally, an integer can follow the slash, indicating on which record the values are to be written.

Literals. You can include literals with your variable specifications on the WRITE command. Literals must be enclosed in apostrophes or quotation marks. In the example above, literals are used to assign the constant 1 to record 1 of each case and 2 to record 2 to provide record identifiers in addition to the case identifier EMPLOYID.

If you are writing data, you should consider taking advantage of all of these features of the WRITE command, including the ability to write records longer than 255 characters. Within the same machine environment, some data types are more convenient than others. If you are going across machines, you should take into account that some data types cannot be read on another machine. Seek advice at your local installation.

If long records are less convenient than multiple records per case with shorter record lengths, you can take advantage of the ability to write out a case identifier and to insert a literal as a record identification number. The software at the other end might then be able to check for missing record numbers should something happen to the data in transit.

9.14 File and Table Specifications

Two specifications are allowed on the WRITE command before the first slash.

The OUTFILE Subcommand. The OUTFILE subcommand specifies the file handle of the target file for the output from the WRITE command. By default, the WRITE command sends the results to the display file, which is usually not what you want. If you use the OUTFILE subcommand, you must define the file to the host operating system using the FILE HANDLE command (see Chapter 3).

The TABLE Subcommand. TABLE requests a format table on the display file showing how the variable information is formatted. NOTABLE is the default.

To write a subset of your data to a file other than the display file and to tell SPSS^X to print a table on the display file describing the format of the external file, specify:

```
FILE HANDLE NEWHUB/ file specifications
WRITE OUTFILE=NEWHUB TABLE
  /EMPLOYID '1' MOHIRED YRHIRED SEX AGE JOBCAT NAME
  /EMPLOYID '2' DEPT79 TO DEPT82 SALARY79 TO SALARY82 * HOURLY82(F5.2)
EXECUTE
```

Ten cases written to the file defined by the NEWHUB file handle are shown in Figure 9.14a.

Figure 9.14a WRITE output

```
1801 8692443CONNIE E. JANNSEN
   23333111801300014300015600 8.00    1801
2211 3802264MARY CHAFEE
   20444     0 8190 884010050 5.15    2211
2691 2742331HOLLY C. BRADSHAW
   21111137151449516250188 50 9.67    2690
3061 7792322KARIN HEGEL
   20222     010140143001625 0 8.33    3061
3091 6791251C. M. BROWN
   20111     0 8450 975010920 5.60    3091
3171 4802334VERA D. LOGGINS
   20444     0135201690018083 9.27    3171
3261 9792333LUCINDA JACKSON
   20333     0 8060 8866 9840 5.05    3261
3391 4792453ANITA PULASKI
   23333 7605 8255 975012328 6.32    3390
4381 1741491REUBEN D. CROSS
   2111114397152751657519240 9.87    4381
4981 7792283TANI PATEL
   20331     0101401248018460 9.47    4981
```

The table showing the format of this file is produced only if you specify the TABLE subcommand (see Figure 9.14b). The table lists the variable names and their location on the output file. REC indicates the number of the record on which the variable is located. START and END give you the first and last positions, respectively, of the variable. FORMAT, WIDTH, and DEC give you the format of the variable to be written, the column width, and the number of decimal places.

Figure 9.14b Format table for the data in Figure 9.14a

THE TABLE FOR THE ABOVE WRITE COMMAND IS:

VARIABLE	REC	START	END	FORMAT	WIDTH	DEC
EMPLOYID	1	1	5	F	5	0
'1 '	1	6	6			
MOHIRED	1	7	8	F	2	0
YRHIRED	1	9	10	F	2	0
SEX	1	11	11	F	1	0
AGE	1	12	13	F	2	0
JOBCAT	1	14	14	F	1	0
NAME	1	15	38	A	24	
EMPLOYID	2	1	5	F	5	0
'2 '	2	6	6			
DEPT79	2	7	7	F	1	0
DEPT80	2	8	8	F	1	0
DEPT81	2	9	9	F	1	0
DEPT82	2	10	10	F	1	0
SALARY79	2	11	15	F	5	0
SALARY80	2	16	20	F	5	0
SALARY81	2	21	25	F	5	0
SALARY82	2	26	30	F	5	0
HOURLY82	2	31	35	F	5	2

9.15 PRINT AND WRITE FORMAT COMMANDS

SPSS^X stores your data in binary format. However, for most applications you do not want variable values that appear in the results of your SPSS^X job to be displayed or written in this form. So, for each variable defined using SPSS^X there is a print and write format stored on the dictionary associated with your data file. These formats control the form in which values are displayed (when you use a procedure or PRINT command) or written (when you use the WRITE command). These print and write formats are assigned differently depending on how the variables are defined. If you define your variables using a DATA LIST command, the dictionary print and write formats are generally those specified on the variable definition portion of the DATA LIST command.

If you use a GET command to access variables from a system file, the default print and write formats are those stored on the dictionary of the system file.

When you use the transformation language to create a new numeric variable, the dictionary print and write formats are both F8.2 or the format specified on the FORMAT subcommand of SET. Default formats for string variables created using the SPSS^X transformation language are those specified on the STRING command that creates the variable.

9.16 The PRINT FORMATS Command

The PRINT FORMATS command changes the print formats for the variables specified on the command. To change print formats, specify the variable name or variable list followed by the new format specification in parentheses, as in:

```
PRINT FORMATS SALARY79 TO SALARY82 (DOLLAR8)
```

This specification sets a dollar print format with eight positions including the dollar sign and comma when appropriate (the number 11550 is printed as $11,550 for example).

The same command can specify different formats for different variables. Separate the specifications for each variable or variable list with a slash, as in:

```
PRINT FORMATS SALARY79 TO SALARY82 (DOLLAR8)/
              HOURLY82 (DOLLAR7.2)
```

The print formats available include the F, COMMA, DOLLAR, Z, and A format types. In addition, AHEX, PIB, HEX, and RBHEX format types are available on IBM/OS systems. The hexadecimal format types print in hexadecimal notation. For a complete discussion of format elements see Chapter 3.

The formats specified on a PRINT FORMATS command are in effect for the duration of the SPSS^X job. The specified print formats can be saved by using a subsequent SAVE command to create a new system file in which the new print formats become the dictionary formats.

9.17 The WRITE FORMATS Command

The WRITE FORMATS command operates exactly like the PRINT FORMATS command except that it changes only the write formats of variables specified on the command. There are also additional format types available for write formats that are not available as print formats. These include various packed decimal and binary formats. For further discussion of these format types see Chapter 3.

9.18 The FORMATS Command

The FORMATS command operates exactly like the PRINT FORMATS and WRITE FORMATS commands except that it redefines both the print and the write formats for the variables specified.

9.19 THE LIST PROCEDURE

The LIST procedure displays the values of variables for cases in the active file in an automatic format. The simplest LIST command is the command alone, as in:

```
FILE HANDLE HUBDATA/ file specifications
DATA LIST  FILE=HUBDATA RECORDS=3
  /1 MOHIRED YRHIRED 12-15 DEPT82 19
  /2 SALARY79 TO SALARY82 6-25
  /3 NAME 25-48 (A)

LIST
```

Values are printed on the display file when the LIST command is encountered (see Figure 9.19). Listing includes by default every permanent and temporary numeric and string variable in the active file in dictionary order. LIST uses the dictionary print formats assigned when the variables are defined on a DATA LIST, PRINT FORMATS, or FORMATS command, or the formats assigned when the variables are created with transformation commands.

Figure 9.19 LIST results using defaults

```
MOHIRED YRHIRED DEPT82 SALARY79 SALARY80 SALARY81 SALARY82 NAME

    8      69      3     11180    13000    14300    15600  CONNIE E. JANNSEN
    9      79      0         0     6337        0        0  ESTHER MARX
    3      80      4         0     8190     8840    10050  MARY CHAFEE
    2      74      1     13715    14495    16250    18850  HOLLY C. BRADSHAW
   10      78      3      6370     7410        0     8872  JACKIE HAMILTON
    9      74      0     20150    20800        0        0  RAY J. LUKE
   10      78      0      8450     9880        0        0  ANNETTE JONES
    1      79      0      6987     7410        0        0  EILEEN WOO
    7      79      2         0    10140    14300    16250  KARIN HEGEL
    9      79      0         0    19500        0        0  DOROTHY CAROLE OSBORNE
    .
    .
    .
```

LIST may require more than one line to display each case within the 132-character page width or the width you have established using the SET command (see Chapter 4). (See Figure 9.22a for the wrapped format when the page width will not accommodate the entire variable list.) Values for each case are always displayed with a blank space between the variables. If a long string variable cannot be listed within the entire page width, it is truncated.

Each execution of LIST begins at the top of a new page. If SPLIT FILE is in effect (Chapter 13), each split also begins at the top of a new page.

9.20 The VARIABLES Subcommand

The default specification for the VARIABLES subcommand is keyword ALL. You can limit the listing to specific variables using the VARIABLES subcommand, as in:

```
FILE HANDLE HUBDATA/ file specifications
DATA LIST  FILE=HUBDATA RECORDS=3
  /1 EMPLOYID 1-5 MOHIRED YRHIRED 12-15 DEPT79 TO DEPT82 SEX 16-20
  /2 SALARY79 TO SALARY82 6-25 HOURLY81 HOURLY82 40-53(2) PROMO81 72
     AGE 54-55 RAISE82 66-70
  /3 JOBCAT 6 NAME 25-48 (A)

LIST VARIABLES=MOHIRED YRHIRED DEPT82 NAME
```

Variables named must already exist. Because LIST is a procedure, variables named cannot be scratch or system variables (see PRINT for an alternative). You can use the TO convention for naming consecutive variables, as in:

```
LIST VARIABLES=MOHIRED YRHIRED DEPT82 SALARY79 TO SALARY82 NAME
```

If you specify more variables than can be printed in 132 columns, or within the width you specify using the WIDTH subcommand of SET (Chapter 4), the line will be wrapped according to the format shown in Figure 9.22a. If all the variables fit on a single line, SPSSˣ prints a heading using the variable name and prints a single line per case as shown in Figure 9.19. When the variable name is longer than the print width, SPSSˣ centers numeric variables in the column. When all variables fit on a line width, LIST first tries to reserve columns according to the length of the variable name or the print width, whichever requires more space. If this format becomes too wide, LIST then begins reducing column widths by printing variable names vertically.

9.21 The CASES Subcommand

Use the CASES subcommand to limit the number and pattern of cases listed. Subcommand CASES must be followed by at least one of the keywords FROM, TO, or BY.

FROM n *The case number of the first case to be listed.* The specification CASES FROM 100 starts listing cases at the 100th sequential case. If LIST is preceded by SAMPLE or SELECT IF, it is the 100th case selected. The default is 1, which means listing begins with the first selected case.

TO n *Upper limit on the cases to be listed.* The specification CASES TO 1000 limits listing to the 1000th selected case or the end of the file, whichever comes first. The default is to list until the end of the file. If LIST encounters the CASE subcommand followed by a single number, TO is assumed. That is, CASES 100 is interpreted as CASES TO 100.

BY n *Increment used to choose cases for listing.* The specification CASES BY 5 lists every fifth selected case. The default is 1, which means every case is listed.

You need only specify one of these keywords, but you can specify any two or all three, as in:

```
LIST VARIABLES=MOHIRED YRHIRED DEPT82 SALARY79 TO SALARY82 NAME/
  CASES FROM 50 TO 100 BY 5
```

The output from this command is shown in Figure 9.22c. Note particularly how the LIST numbering (Section 9.22) shows the pattern of cases listed as a result of the CASES specification.

If SPLIT FILE is in effect, case selections specified via the CASE subcommand are restarted for each split.

9.22 The FORMAT Subcommand

The default specifications for the FORMAT subcommand are WRAP and UNNUMBERED. If the page width cannot accommodate your entire variable list, keyword WRAP wraps the listing in multiple lines per case as shown in Figure 9.22a, which was generated by the following commands:

```
SET WIDTH=80
FILE HANDLE HUBDATA/ file specifications
DATA LIST  FILE=HUBDATA RECORDS=3
  /1 EMPLOYID 1-5 MOHIRED YRHIRED 12-15 DEPT79 TO DEPT82 SEX 16-20
  /2 SALARY79 TO SALARY82 6-25 HOURLY81 HOURLY82 40-53(2) PROMO81 72
     AGE 54-55 RAISE82 66-70
  /3 JOBCAT 6 NAME 25-48 (A)

LIST
```

Figure 9.22a LIST in wrapped format

```
EMPLOYID:  1801  8 69 3 3 3 3 2 11180 13000 14300 15600      7.33      8.00 0 44
 RAISE82:  1300 3 CONNIE E. JANNSEN

EMPLOYID:  2191  9 79 0 3 0 0 2     0  6337     0     0  -999.00   -999.00 9 20
 RAISE82:  -999 3 ESTHER MARX

EMPLOYID:  2211  3 80 0 4 4 4 2     0  8190  8840 10050     4.53      5.15 0 26
 RAISE82:  1210 4 MARY CHAFEE

EMPLOYID:  2690  2 74 1 1 1 1 2 13715 14495 16250 18850     8.33      9.67 0 33
 RAISE82:  2600 1 HOLLY C. BRADSHAW

EMPLOYID:  2821 10 78 3 3 0 3 2  6370  7410     0  8872  -999.00      4.55 9 53
 RAISE82:  -999 3 JACKIE HAMILTON
```
. . .

When the list requires more than one line per case, SPSS^X prints the name of the first variable listed in that line. To locate the values of a particular variable, consult the table produced before the listing, as shown in Figure 9.22b.

Figure 9.22b Variable table

```
THE VARIABLES ARE LISTED IN THE FOLLOWING ORDER:

LINE   1: EMPLOYID MOHIRED YRHIRED DEPT79 DEPT80 DEPT81 DEPT82 SALARY79 SEX
             SALARY80 SALARY81 SALARY82 HOURLY81 HOURLY82 PROMO81 AGE

LINE   2: RAISE82 JOBCAT NAME
```

If there is enough space, keyword WRAP implies one line per case. To tell SPSSX to use the single-line format only, specify the keyword SINGLE, as in:

```
LIST VARIABLES=MOHIRED YRHIRED DEPT82 SALARY79 TO SALARY82 NAME/
  CASES FROM 50 TO 100 BY 5/ FORMAT=SINGLE
```

If there is not enough room within the line width, SPSSX issues an error message and does not execute the listing. Therefore, use SINGLE only when you want one line per case or nothing.

If you want LIST to number the cases that are being listed, specify keyword NUMBERED, as in:

```
LIST VARIABLES=MOHIRED YRHIRED DEPT82 SALARY79 TO SALARY82 NAME/
  CASES FROM 50 TO 100 BY 5/ FORMAT=SINGLE,NUMBERED
```

Figure 9.22c shows the output from this command. LIST calculates the width for printing the numbers based on the value you specify using TO on the CASES subcommand. In the above example, LIST chooses a print width of 3 (plus the blank between columns) based on the TO 100 specification. If you specify no TO value, LIST uses a width of 6.

Figure 9.22c LIST using the CASES subcommand and NUMBERED

	MOHIRED	YRHIRED	DEPT82	SALARY79	SALARY80	SALARY81	SALARY82	NAME
50	1	79	0	14300	14300	15730	0	EVA ELDER
55	6	79	0	0	15600	0	0	EDWARD GREEN
60	12	79	0	0	8840	9503	0	LOVEY E. HUDSON
65	5	80	0	0	13520	0	0	PATRICIA SMITH
70	8	79	0	0	8255	0	0	HELEN D. SMITH
75	10	70	4	14300	18850	21450	26182	MONICA C. RIVERS
80	1	79	0	0	7442	0	0	THOMAS P. JOHNSON
85	4	80	3	0	18200	18395	19682	ANN JOHNSON
90	10	79	0	0	5720	0	0	CHRISTINA P. NORRIS
95	5	79	0	7670	9490	0	0	M. ELLIOT KRAFT
100	2	70	3	11830	12545	13799	18083	FANNIE SMITH

If SPLIT FILE is in effect, numbering restarts at each split. If you want sequential numbering regardless of splits, set a variable equal to the system variable $CASENUM and name that variable as the first variable on your VARIABLES list. Don't forget to override the new variable's print format to whatever you think is appropriate, as in:

```
COMPUTE SEQ=$CASENUM
PRINT FORMATS SEQ (F3)

SORT CASES BY DEPT82
SPLIT FILE BY DEPT82
LIST VARIABLES=SEQ MOHIRED YRHIRED DEPT82 SALARY79 TO SALARY82 NAME
```

9.23 LIST and Case Selection

The automatic numbering in LIST is based on the cases that are seen by LIST. Therefore, the numbering is established for each case *after* the case has been selected. For example, if you want to look at only employees in a particular department, you might specify:

```
FILE HANDLE HUBDATA/ file specifications
DATA LIST  FILE=HUBDATA RECORDS=3
  /1 EMPLOYID 1-5 MOHIRED YRHIRED 12-15 DEPT79 TO DEPT82 SEX 16-20
  /2 SALARY79 TO SALARY82 6-25 HOURLY81 HOURLY82 40-53(2) PROMO81 72
     AGE 54-55 RAISE82 66-70
  /3 JOBCAT 6 NAME 25-48 (A)

SELECT IF DEPT82 EQ 4
LIST VARIABLES=MOHIRED YRHIRED DEPT82 SALARY79 TO SALARY82 NAME/
  FORMAT=NUMBERED
```

In this example, numbering would start with 1 for the first employee with DEPT82 equal to 4. If you want to know the sequential number of the case before selection, you can create a sequence variable with the transformation language prior to selecting, as in:

```
COMPUTE  CASESEQ=CASESEQ+1
LEAVE CASESEQ
PRINT FORMATS CASESEQ (F3)

SELECT IF DEPT82 EQ 4
LIST VARIABLES=CASESEQ MOHIRED YRHIRED DEPT82
   SALARY79 TO SALARY82 NAME/ FORMAT=NUMBERED
```

This example computes a new variable, CASESEQ, containing the sequence number of each case. You must use the LEAVE command (Chapter 6) so CASESEQ is not reinitialized for every case. You should also provide an appropriate print format for LIST to use. The partial listing from this command is shown in Figure 9.23. Compare the automatic numbering with the listing of variable CASESEQ.

Figure 9.23 Using your own sequence variable

```
   CASESEQ MOHIRED YRHIRED DEPT82 SALARY79 SALARY80 SALARY81 SALARY82 NAME

 1     3       3      80      4        0     8190     8840    10050  MARY CHAFEE
 2    14       4      80      4        0    13520    16900    18083  VERA D. LOGGINS
 3    39       1      79      4     8450     8450     9490    10627  CAROL LAVENDER
 4    43       8      79      4        0     8190     9230    10780  MARIA PROVENZA
 5    74       7      79      4        0     9490    11050    14309  CLEVELAND SMITH
 6    75      10      70      4    14300    18850    21450    26182  MONICA C. RIVERS
 7    78       6      80      4        0    12350    12740    15132  ROSE C. SHUMWAY
 8   106       7      76      4    12480    13292    14690    16900  CYNTHIA RILEY
 9   121       5      72      4    14560    18850    21450    25577  LINDA IVERSON
10   130      11      68      4    15860    19500    21710    25577  SILVIA KUDIRKA
11   132       9      73      4    12220    14950    16640    18599  MARY HAINES
12   133       4      80      4        0     9750    10790    15608  MAUREEN J. WAYNE
 .
 .
 .
```

```
SELECT IF   [(] logical expression [)]

SAMPLE   {percentage}
         {n FROM m  }

N OF CASES   n

WEIGHT   {BY varname}
         {OFF       }
```


THE SELECT IF COMMAND, **10.1**
- Logical Expressions, **10.2**
- Missing Values, **10.3**
- SELECT IF and $CASENUM, **10.4**
- Multiple SELECT IF Commands, **10.5**

THE SAMPLE COMMAND, **10.6**
- Multiple SAMPLE Commands, **10.7**

THE N OF CASES COMMAND, **10.8**

THE WEIGHT COMMAND, **10.9**
- Turning Off or Changing Weights, **10.10**
- How Procedures Use Weights, **10.11**
- Tests of Significance, **10.12**

PLACEMENT OF SAMPLE, SELECT IF, AND WEIGHT, **10.13**
- Temporary Sampling, Selecting, and Weighting, **10.14**
- SELECT IF, SAMPLE, and Other Transformations, **10.15**
  - SAMPLE and SELECT IF with DO IF, **10.16**

Chapter 10 Selecting, Sampling, and Weighting Cases

SPSS^X allows you to control the number and groups of cases used in analysis or reporting by selecting, sampling, or differentially weighting cases. Four commands are used to control cases analyzed by procedures. The SELECT IF command selects cases for analysis based upon logical criteria. The SAMPLE command randomly selects cases. With the SAMPLE command, you can specify a proportional or exact-sized sample. The N OF CASES command controls the number of cases built. The WEIGHT command assigns case weights or turns off weighting. Weighting is usually used to compensate for over- or undersampling, or to weight a sample or aggregated file up to population size.

10.1 THE SELECT IF COMMAND

The SELECT IF command selects cases based on logical criteria. For example, the command

```
SELECT IF (SEX EQ 'M')
```

selects cases for which variable SEX has the value M. The syntax of the logical expression for the SELECT IF command is the same as for the IF and DO IF commands. The logical expression does not have to be enclosed in parentheses and can be as simple as a logical variable, as in:

```
SELECT IF INVAR
```

This command selects cases for which INVAR is equal to 1 (see Section 10.2). The expression can be as complex as a comparison of arithmetic expressions, as in:

```
SELECT IF ((YRMODA(81,13,0) - YRMODA(STARTYR,STARTMO,STARTDA)) LE 60)
```

This command selects cases dated for the last 60 days in 1981.

10.2 Logical Expressions

The specification field for SELECT IF is a logical expression that can be evaluated as true, false, or missing. See Chapter 8 for a complete discussion of logical expressions. Logical expressions can be any of the following:

A Logical Variable. A logical variable takes on values 0 or 1, where 0 is false and 1 is true. INVAR in Section 10.1 is a logical variable.

A Relation. A relation compares two values using a relational operator. The values can be variables, constants, or arithmetic expressions. Valid relational operators are EQ, NE, LT, LE, GT, and GE (and their symbolic equivalents). SEX EQ 'M' in the example in Section 10.1 is a relation between a variable and a constant. The example using the YRMODA function above is a relation between an arithmetic expression and a constant.

A Compound Expression. A compound expression is composed of two or more relations and/or logical variables joined by logical operators AND and OR. If the expression has more than two relations, AND has precedence over OR. For example, A AND B OR C is evaluated as (A AND B) OR C. However, parentheses can be used to control the order of the evaluation, such as in A AND (B OR C).

If a logical expression is true, the case is selected; if it is false or missing, the case is not selected. There are no programmed restrictions on the complexity of logical expressions used with SELECT IF. Strings can be used according to rules documented in Chapter 7.

10.3 Missing Values

If the logic of the expression is indeterminate because of missing values, the case is not selected. In a simple relational expression, the logic is indeterminate if the expression on either side of the relational operator is missing. For example,

```
SELECT IF (VSAT GT MSAT)
```

selects only cases for which both VSAT and MSAT are valid and VSAT is greater than MSAT. If either VSAT or MSAT is missing, the logic of the expression is indeterminate and the case is not selected.

If you use a compound expression in which relations are joined by the logical operator OR, as in

```
SELECT IF (VSAT GT 600 OR MSAT GT 600)
```

the case is selected if either relation is true, even if the other is missing.

To select cases with missing values for the variables within the expression, use the missing-value functions described in Chapter 6. For example,

```
SELECT IF MISSING(X)
```

selects all cases missing for variable X. The MISSING function returns 1, which is true, if X is missing. To include cases with values that have been declared user-missing along with other cases, use the VALUE function, as in:

```
SELECT IF VALUE(X) GT 100
```

This expression is true if X is greater than 100, even if 999 was defined as missing on the MISSING VALUES command (see Chapter 3). The VALUE function does not include the system-missing value, so the above SELECT IF does not select cases for which X is system-missing.

10.4 SELECT IF and $CASENUM

System variable $CASENUM is the sequence number of the case in the active file (see Chapter 6). It is established for each case *after* the case has been selected. Although it is syntactically correct to use $CASENUM on SELECT IF, it does not produce the expected results. If you wish to select a set of cases based on their sequence in a file, create your own sequence variable with the transformation language prior to selecting, as in:

```
COMPUTE  #CASESEQ=#CASESEQ+1
SELECT IF (MOD(#CASESEQ,2)=0)
```

This example computes a scratch variable, #CASESEQ, containing the sequence numbers for each case, and it selects every other case beginning with the second. It is important that the sequence number variable (#CASESEQ in this example) be a scratch variable so that it is not reinitialized for every case. (See the LEAVE command described in Chapter 6 for an alternative.)

10.5 Multiple SELECT IF Commands

If you use multiple SELECT IF commands in your job, they must all be true for a case to be selected. For example, the commands

```
SELECT IF (SEX EQ 'M')
SELECT IF RANGE(AGE,18,65)
```

select all males between the ages of 18 and 65.

The SELECT IF command permanently selects cases, unless preceded by the TEMPORARY command (see Section 10.14). Unless you are careful when you use more than one SELECT IF, you might select no cases. For example, consider the following commands:

```
FILE HANDLE GSS80/ file specifications
GET  FILE=GSS80/KEEP SEX PRESTIGE SPPRES
SELECT IF (SEX EQ 1)     /*THIS COMMAND SHOULD FOLLOW A TEMPORARY COMMAND
FREQUENCIES  VARIABLES=PRESTIGE SPPRES/FORMAT=CONDENSE/
STATISTICS=MEDIAN
SELECT IF (SEX EQ 2)
FREQUENCIES  VARIABLES=PRESTIGE SPPRES/FORMAT=CONDENSE/
STATISTICS=MEDIAN
```

The second FREQUENCIES command has no cases to analyze since a case cannot have SEX equal to both 1 and 2. As indicated by the comment, a TEMPORARY command should precede the first SELECT IF. The preferred solution in this example is to use SPLIT FILE since the FREQUENCIES specifications are the same for the two groups (see Chapter 13).

10.6 THE SAMPLE COMMAND

The SAMPLE command selects a random sample of cases. To select an approximate percentage of cases, specify a decimal value between 0 and 1, as in:

```
SAMPLE .25
```

This command samples approximately 25% of the cases in the active file. When you specify a proportional sample, you usually won't obtain the exact proportion specified. If you know exactly how many cases are in the active file, you can obtain an exact-sized random sample by specifying the number of cases to be sampled from the size of the active file, as in:

```
SAMPLE 60 FROM 200
```

In this example, the active file must have exactly 200 cases to obtain a random sample of 60 cases. If the file has fewer than 200 cases, proportionally fewer cases are sampled. If the file has more, the sample is drawn from only the first 200 cases. Note that any SELECT IF commands occurring prior to the SAMPLE command will affect the size of the active file.

10.7 Multiple SAMPLE Commands

The SAMPLE command permanently samples the active file unless a TEMPORARY command precedes it (see Section 10.14). Thus, if you use two SAMPLE commands, the second takes a sample of the first, as in:

```
SAMPLE .50
CONDESCRIPTIVE  SALARY79 TO SALARY82
SAMPLE .50
CONDESCRIPTIVE  SALARY79 TO SALARY82
```

In this example, the first CONDESCRIPTIVE command computes statistics for approximately 50% of the cases, and the second CONDESCRIPTIVE command computes statistics for approximately 50% of those cases, or 25% of the original cases.

10.8 THE N OF CASES COMMAND

You can use the N OF CASES command to build the first *n* cases from a file. For example, if you have a data file containing 1,000 cases but want to use only the first 100 cases to test your SPSS^X commands, specify:

```
FILE HANDLE DATA/ file specifications
DATA LIST  FILE=DATA NOTABLE/1 NAME 1-20(A) TOTPOP 21-30 MEDSAL70
                  MEDSAL75 MEDSAL80 31-60
N OF CASES  100
```

The N OF CASES command follows the DATA LIST command. You can also use the N OF CASES command to control the reading of cases from SPSS^X system files, as in:

```
FILE HANDLE CITY/ file specifications
GET  FILE=CITY
N OF CASES  40
```

In addition, you can use the N OF CASES command to control the number of cases built when using a FILE TYPE—END FILE TYPE structure to define complex files (see Chapter 11). However, you should bear in mind that N OF CASES controls the building of cases, not the reading of records. For example, when you use FILE TYPE NESTED, cases are built from the lowest level record type defined. The number of cases specified on the N OF CASES command applies to the cases built, not to records read.

If you use SAMPLE or SELECT IF with N OF CASES, SPSS^X reads as many records as required to build the specified *n*. For example, assume each case is built from one record and you have specified a 50% sample. If you specify N OF CASES 100 for a file with 1,000 records, approximately 200 records are read to obtain the 100 cases. It makes no difference whether the N OF CASES precedes or follows the SAMPLE or SELECT IF. Specifying more cases than actually can be built is not an error. Instead, SPSS^X obtains as many cases as possible.

Only one N OF CASES command can be used in a job. It can be placed after a DATA LIST command, after a FILE TYPE or INPUT PROGRAM command, or after a GET command. It can also be placed following a procedure command. In this instance it behaves like a permanent SELECT IF and limits the number of cases analyzed by subsequent procedures.

10.9 THE WEIGHT COMMAND

The WEIGHT command is used to weight cases differentially for analysis. For example, if you have a sample from a population for which some substratum has been over- or undersampled, you can apply weights to obtain population estimates. Or you may simply want to weight the sample up to population size for reporting purposes. Or you may want to replicate an example from a table or other aggregated data as shown for the CROSSTABS procedure in Chapter 20. Name the variable following the keyword BY, as in:

```
WEIGHT BY WTFACTOR
```

This command tells SPSS^X to use the value of variable WTFACTOR to weight cases.

- Only one variable can be specified.
- The variable must be numeric and cannot be a scratch or system variable.
- Weight values need not be integer.
- Missing or negative values are treated as if they were 0.
- Weighting is permanent during a job unless TEMPORARY is in effect.
- A file saved when weighting is in effect maintains the weighting.

The variable can be a weighting factor already precoded when the data file was prepared, or it can be computed with the transformation language. For example, assume your file contains a sample of households in which rural households were oversampled by a factor of 2. To compensate for oversampling, you can weight the rural households by one half, as in:

```
COMPUTE WT=1
IF (LOCATE EQ 'RURAL') WT=.5
WEIGHT BY WT
```

Variable WT is initialized to 1 with the COMPUTE command and then changed to .5 with the IF command for cases where the value of LOCATE equals RURAL. Be sure to initialize the weighting variable to 1 when creating it with IF commands. Otherwise, cases not covered by IF commands will be missing and will have a zero weight.

10.10 Turning Off or Changing Weights

Unless you precede the WEIGHT command with a TEMPORARY command, weighting stays in effect. To turn off weighting, simply use a WEIGHT command with the keyword OFF, as in:

```
WEIGHT  OFF
```

To change the weight, use another WEIGHT command specifying a different variable. Weighting is not cumulative. That is, a second weight command changes the weight; it does not weight the weight. For example, in the following job,

```
FILE HANDLE CITY/ file specifications
GET FILE CITY
WEIGHT BY POP81
CONDESCRIPTIVE  ALL
WEIGHT BY POP82
CONDESCRIPTIVE  ALL
```

the first CONDESCRIPTIVE command computes summary statistics based on cases weighted by POP81, and the second CONDESCRIPTIVE command computes summary statistics based on cases weighted by POP82.

10.11 How Procedures Use Weights

SPSS^X does not physically replicate cases when weighting is in effect. Rather, it arithmetically replicates them. For example, if you use CROSSTABS, the counts in the cells are actually the sums of the case weights. CROSSTABS then rounds cell counts when printing the tables.

Most procedures can handle noninteger weights. Those that cannot are SCATTERGRAM (Chapter 30), NONPAR CORR (Chapter 36), and NPAR TESTS (Chapter 37). An alternative weighting scheme is used for these procedures. In this scheme, a case is replicated as many times as the integer portion of the weight indicates. The fractional portion of the weight represents the probability that the case will be weighted to the next integer. For example, a case with a weight of 2.3 has a 30% probability of being weighted to 3. To do this, SPSS^X compares a random number generated by SPSS^X for each case with the fractional portion of the weight. If the random number is smaller than the proportion, the case is weighted up. Since, by default, the seed value used to generate the random number is the same across jobs, you can replicate a job. If you specify a different seed value using the SEED subcommand on the SET command (Chapter 4), cases are weighted differently for those procedures requiring integer weights.

ANNOTATED EXAMPLE FOR SELECT IF AND WEIGHT

This job analyzes a file of the fifty largest cities in the United States, based on data from a 1981 almanac. The job contains a frequency distribution of people by region for cities that ranked higher in population in 1980 than in 1970. The SPSS^X commands are

```
FILE HANDLE ALMANAC/ file specifications
GET  FILE=ALMANAC/KEEP REGION RANK70 RANK80 POP80

SELECT IF (RANK80 GT RANK70)
WEIGHT BY POP80

FREQUENCIES  VARIABLES=REGION
```

- The FILE HANDLE (Chapter 3) and GET commands (Chapter 5) define the data to SPSS^X and retain only the variables of interest.
- The SELECT IF command selects cities that ranked higher in population in 1980 than in 1970.
- The WEIGHT command weights the selected cities by their population in 1980.
- The FREQUENCIES command computes the frequency distribution for regions (see Chapter 18).

Frequencies on a selected and weighted file

FILE: 50 LARGEST CITIES IN THE U.S.; 1981 ALMANAC DATA

REGION REGION OF THE UNITED STATES

VALUE LABEL	VALUE	FREQUENCY	PERCENT	VALID PERCENT	CUM PERCENT
NEW ENGLAND	1	562994	5.1	5.1	5.1
MIDDLE ATLANTIC	2	1111056	10.2	10.2	15.3
EAST NORTH CENTRAL	3	3854272	35.2	35.2	50.6
WEST NORTH CENTRAL	4	1583876	14.5	14.5	65.0
SOUTH ATLANTIC	5	1849448	16.9	16.9	82.0
EAST SOUTH CENTRAL	6	582864	5.3	5.3	87.3
WEST SOUTH CENTRAL	7	557482	5.1	5.1	92.4
PACIFIC	9	833134	7.6	7.6	100.0
	TOTAL	10935126	100.0	100.0	

VALID CASES 1.1E+07 MISSING CASES 0

10.12 Tests of Significance

Tests of statistical significance usually are based on the weighted sample size. If the weighted number of cases exceeds the sample size, tests of significance are inflated; if it is smaller, they are deflated. See Moser and Kalton (1972) for further information on the use of significance tests with weighted samples.

To avoid inflated or deflated tests of significance, you may consider using a weight factor which, when summed, is the same as the unweighted number of cases. For example, you can use AGGREGATE (Chapter 14) to compute the sum of weights and number of cases. Then, match these numbers back to the file with MATCH FILES (Chapter 15), and use them to adjust the weight factor, as in:

```
COMPUTE  WTFACTOR=1
IF  (LOCATE='RURAL') WTFACTOR=5
COMPUTE  CONSTANT=1  /* Set up a constant variable for the BREAK

AGGREGATE  OUTFILE=TEMP1/BREAK=CONSTANT/
           MEANWT=MEAN(WTFACTOR)

MATCH FILES  TABLE=TEMP1/FILE=*/BY CONSTANT

COMPUTE  WTFACTOR=WTFACTOR/MEANWT
WEIGHT BY WTFACTOR
```

This set of commands readjusts the weight so that the sum of weights equals the number of cases. AGGREGATE builds one case with two variables, MEANWT and CONSTANT. The aggregated file is written to disk (file handle TEMP1). MATCH FILES then spreads the variables from the aggregated file back to every case in the active file, so that the adjustment to WTFACTOR can be accomplished with the COMPUTE command.

10.13 PLACEMENT OF SAMPLE, SELECT IF, AND WEIGHT

SAMPLE, SELECT IF, and WEIGHT cannot be placed in an input program defined by the FILE TYPE—END FILE TYPE structure or by the INPUT PROGRAM—END INPUT PROGRAM structure. They can be placed nearly anywhere following these commands in a transformation program. See Appendix B for a discussion of the program states in SPSS^{X} and the placement of commands.

10.14 Temporary Sampling, Selecting, and Weighting

As transformations, SAMPLE, SELECT IF, and WEIGHT are permanent, unless a TEMPORARY command is in effect (see Chapter 6). TEMPORARY operates exactly the same way with these commands as with COMPUTE, IF, RECODE, and so forth. If a SELECT IF, SAMPLE, or WEIGHT command follows a TEMPORARY command, it is in effect only for the next procedure. For example, in the commands

```
TEMPORARY
SAMPLE .25
PEARSON CORR  X1 TO X5
FREQUENCIES  VARIABLES=SCALE1
```

the 25% sample applies only to the PEARSON CORR command. FREQUENCIES uses all the cases in the active file. Since SAVE is a procedure, a temporary SAMPLE or SELECT IF affects the number of cases saved on the file only if the SAVE command is the first procedure following the TEMPORARY command.

10.15 SELECT IF, SAMPLE, and Other Transformations

SELECT IF and SAMPLE operate on realized cases. That is, they operate only on cases that are built from DATA LIST, GET, FILE TYPE, INPUT PROGRAM, and so forth. Use SAMPLE or SELECT IF only in a transformation program (see Chapter 12).

SAMPLE and SELECT IF are executed in the order they occur in a job. If a SAMPLE command follows a SELECT IF command, it samples only cases selected by the SELECT IF. For efficiency considerations, you should place SAMPLE and SELECT IF commands prior to other transformations. For example, if you are going to modify extensively a file that you are sampling, sample first, then modify.

10.16 SAMPLE and SELECT IF with DO IF

You can use SELECT IF and SAMPLE inside a DO IF—END IF control structure. For example, assume you want to select males with prestige scores above 50 and females with prestige scores above 45. You can use one compound SELECT IF, as in:

```
SELECT IF ((SEX EQ 'M' AND PRESTIGE GT 50) OR (SEX EQ 'F' AND
  PRESTIGE GT 45))
```

Or you can use two SELECT IF commands inside a DO IF—END IF, as in:

```
DO IF  SEX EQ 'M'
. SELECT IF PRESTIGE GT 50
ELSE IF  SEX EQ 'F'
. SELECT IF PRESTIGE GT 45
END IF
```

In this example, the optional period in column 1 indents the SELECT IF commands for readability.

Similarly, SAMPLE commands can be placed inside a DO IF—END IF structure to sample substrata differentially. Assume you have a survey of 10,000 people in which 80% of the sample is male, while the known universe is 48% male. To obtain a sample that corresponds to the known universe and that maximizes the size of the sample, 1,846 of the 8,000 (48/52*2000) males and all of females must be sampled. The DO IF is used to restrict the sampling process to the males:

```
DO IF  SEX EQ 'M'
SAMPLE 1846 FROM 8000
END IF
```

```
FILE TYPE  MIXED [FILE = handle]
           RECORD = [varname] {col loc } [WILD = {NOWARN}]
                              {(format)}         {WARN  }

FILE TYPE  GROUPED [FILE = handle]
           RECORD = [varname] {col loc } CASE = [varname] {col loc }
                              {(format)}                  {(format)}

   [WILD = {WARN  }]  [DUPLICATE = {WARN  }]
           {NOWARN}                {NOWARN}

   [MISSING = {WARN  }]  [ORDERED = {YES}]
              {NOWARN}              {NO }

FILE TYPE  NESTED [FILE = handle]
           RECORD = [varname] {col loc } CASE = [varname] {col loc }
                              {(format)}                  {(format)}

   [WILD = {NOWARN}]  [MISSING = {NOWARN}]
           {WARN  }              {WARN  }

                 {NOWARN}
   [DUPLICATE =  {WARN  }]
                 {CASE  }


For FILE TYPE MIXED
   RECORD TYPE {value list} [SKIP]
               {OTHER     }

For FILE TYPE GROUPED
   RECORD TYPE {value list} [SKIP]  [CASE = {col loc }]
               {OTHER     }                 {(format)}

   [DUPLICATE = {WARN  }]  [MISSING = {WARN  }]
                {NOWARN}              {NOWARN}

For FILE TYPE NESTED
   RECORD TYPE {value list} [SKIP]  [CASE = {col loc }]
               {OTHER     }                 {(format)}

   [SPREAD = {YES}]  [MISSING = {WARN  }]
             {NO }              {NOWARN}


END FILE TYPE


REPEATING DATA  [FILE = handle] /STARTS = beg pos[-end pos]

   /OCCURS = {value  } [/LENGTH = {value  }]
             {varname}            {varname}

   [/CONTINUED [= beg pos [-end pos]]]

   [/ID = {col loc} = varname]  [{TABLE  }]
          {format }               {NOTABLE}

   DATA = data list specifications
```

11

INTRODUCTION TO COMPLEX FILES, **11.1**

TYPES OF FILES, **11.2**

FILE TYPE MIXED, **11.3**
- The FILE Subcommand, **11.4**
- The RECORD Subcommand, **11.5**
- The WILD Subcommand, **11.6**
- The RECORD TYPE Command for FILE TYPE MIXED, **11.7**
- Keyword OTHER, **11.8**
  - The SKIP Subcommand, **11.9**

FILE TYPE GROUPED, **11.10**
- The RECORD Subcommand, **11.11**
- The CASE Subcommand, **11.12**
- The WILD Subcommand, **11.13**
- The DUPLICATE Subcommand, **11.14**
- The MISSING Subcommand, **11.15**
- The ORDERED Subcommand, **11.16**
- The RECORD TYPE Command for FILE TYPE GROUPED, **11.17**
  - The SKIP Subcommand, **11.18**
  - The CASE Subcommand, **11.19**
  - The DUPLICATE and MISSING Subcommands, **11.20**

FILE TYPE NESTED, **11.21**
- The RECORD Subcommand, **11.22**
- The CASE Subcommand, **11.23**
- The WILD Subcommand, **11.24**
- The DUPLICATE Subcommand, **11.25**
- The MISSING Subcommand, **11.26**
- The RECORD TYPE Command for FILE TYPE NESTED, **11.27**
  - The CASE Subcommand, **11.28**
  - The SPREAD Subcommand, **11.29**

SUMMARY OF FILE DEFINITIONS, **11.30**

THE REPEATING DATA COMMAND, **11.31**
- The INPUT PROGRAM—END INPUT PROGRAM Structure, **11.32**
- The STARTS Subcommand, **11.33**
- The OCCURS Subcommand, **11.34**
- The DATA Subcommand, **11.35**
- The NOTABLE Subcommand, **11.36**
- The FILE Subcommand, **11.37**
- The LENGTH Subcommand, **11.38**
- The CONTINUED Subcommand, **11.39**
- The ID Subcommand, **11.40**

Chapter 11 Defining Complex File Structures

Many data files are not organized into the rectangular, case-ordered structure described in Chapter 3. You may have *mixed files*, which contain several types of records that define different types of cases; hierarchical or *nested files*, which contain several types of records with a defined relationship among the record types; or *grouped files*, which contain several records for each case with some records missing or duplicated. Or your data file may contain records with *repeated groups* of information.

SPSS^X has utilities for handling all of these complex types of files. You can define mixed or nested files using FILE TYPE, RECORD TYPE, and END FILE TYPE with the DATA LIST command. Or you can use these commands to read a grouped file with missing records or check for duplicated records. Finally, you can use the REPEATING DATA command to read repeated groups and build cases for each repeated group.

All of these commands and the files they define are documented in this chapter. In addition to the file definition commands discussed here, you can use the data transformation language discussed in Chapter 12 to define complex files.

11.1 INTRODUCTION TO COMPLEX FILES

To define complex files, use the FILE TYPE, RECORD TYPE, and DATA LIST commands. On the FILE TYPE command, specify the type of file, the location of the record type identifier, and optional information on the handling of duplicate, missing, or invalid record types. Include a RECORD TYPE and a DATA LIST command for each type of record that you want to define. At the end of the file definition commands, specify the END FILE TYPE command. The resulting file, the active file, is always a rectangular file.

For example, to define the Hubbard employee data used in Chapter 3 with a FILE TYPE command in order to check for missing or duplicate records, specify:

```
FILE HANDLE HUBDATA/ file specifications
FILE TYPE GROUPED FILE=HUBDATA RECORD=#RECID 80 CASE=ID 1-5
RECORD TYPE 1
DATA LIST   /MOHIRED YRHIRED 12-15 DEPT79 TO DEPT82 SEX 16-20
RECORD TYPE 2
DATA LIST   /SALARY79 TO SALARY82 6-25 HOURLY81 HOURLY82 42-53 (2)
             PROMO81 72  AGE 54-55 RAISE82 66-70
RECORD TYPE 3
DATA LIST   /JOBCAT 6 NAME 25-48 (A)
END FILE TYPE
 .
 Additional Data Definition Commands
 .
FILE HANDLE HUBEMPL/ file specifications
SAVE     OUTFILE=HUBEMPL
```

The FILE HANDLE command associates file handle HUBDATA with the appropriate file specifications necessary for your operating system to access the data. In the IBM/OS environment, this command is unnecessary and file handle HUBDATA points directly to the //HUBDATA DD command. Otherwise, consult documentation available via the INFO command described in Chapter 2.

The FILE TYPE command specifies a grouped file type (one record of each type for each case), the record identifier (#RECID) and its location (column 80 of each case), and the case identifier (ID) and its location (columns 1 through 5). All records with the value 1 on #RECID are defined by the DATA LIST command following the RECORD TYPE 1 command. Records with the value 2 on #RECID are defined by the second DATA LIST command, and records with value 3 by the third DATA LIST command. Records with other values on #RECID are reported as errors. If a case has a duplicate record type or if a record type is missing for a case, a warning message is printed. The HUBEMPL file saved as a system file is identical to the file saved in Chapter 5.

11.2 TYPES OF FILES

The file type keyword is the first specification on the FILE TYPE command. This keyword defines the structure of your data file. There are three file type keywords: MIXED, GROUPED, and NESTED. The MIXED file type defines a file in which each record type defines a case. Some information may be the same for all record types but is recorded in different locations. Other information may be recorded only for specific record types. For example, a data file maintained by a hospital may contain a record for each treatment administered to cancer patients, with different data recorded for each type of treatment.

The GROUPED file type defines a file in which cases are defined by grouping together record types with the same identification number. Each case usually has one record of each type. The HUBDATA file in Section 11.1 is a GROUPED data file.

The NESTED file type defines a file in which the record types are related to each other hierarchically. Usually, the last record type defined—the lowest level of the hierarchy—defines a case. For example, in a file containing household records and records for each person living in the household, each person record defines a case. However, information from previous record types may be *spread* to each case. For example, you might want to include a variable from the household record, such as location (CITY), on the person record. The value for CITY for a particular household can be spread to the records for each person in the household.

The specifications on the FILE TYPE and RECORD TYPE commands differ for each file type. Therefore, each file type is discussed in separate sections of this chapter. A summary of the specifications and defaults for all file types are presented in Section 11.30.

11.3 FILE TYPE MIXED

FILE TYPE MIXED builds a file in which each of the record types named on a RECORD TYPE command defines a case. You do not need to define all types of records on the file. In fact, FILE TYPE MIXED is very useful when you are reading only one type of record because SPSS^X can decide whether to execute the DATA LIST for a record by simply reading the variable that identifies the record type. Four types of information are specified on the FILE TYPE command for FILE TYPE MIXED.

The MIXED Keyword. Keyword MIXED is required. It indicates that the file being defined is a mixed file type.

The FILE Subcommand. FILE lists the file handle of the file to be defined and is required unless your data are included in the command file (see Section 11.4).

The RECORD Subcommand. RECORD names the variable and specifies the column location of the record type identifier. The record type identifier must be located in the same column(s) on all records. The value on this variable determines the type of each record (see Section 11.5).

The WILD Subcommand. WILD tells SPSS^X how to handle any undefined record types encountered in your file. By default, SPSS^X skips records that are not defined (see Section 11.6).

11.4 The FILE Subcommand

Use the FILE subcommand to specify the file handle of the file you are defining. For example, the commands

```
FILE HANDLE TREATMNT/ file specifications
FILE TYPE  MIXED FILE=TREATMNT RECORD=RECID 1-2
```

define a mixed file type identified by the handle TREATMNT. The record identifier is recorded in columns 1 and 2 of each record. Figure 11.4 shows the first 10 records of the hospital treatment data stored in the file identified by the handle TREATMNT.

Figure 11.4 Hospital treatment data file

```
21  145010 1
22  257200 2
25  235  250  2
35  167            300    3
24  125150 1
23  272075 1
21  149050 2
25  134  035  3
30  138            300    3
32  229            500    3
```

You must specify the FILE subcommand unless the data are included in the SPSS^X command file.

11.5 The RECORD Subcommand

Each record type must be identified by a unique code and the value must be coded in the same location on all records. However, you do not need to sort the records according to type.

Use the RECORD subcommand to define the variable name and the column location of the record identifier. To define the record identifier as variable RECID located in columns 1 and 2 of the hospital treatment data file, specify:

```
FILE HANDLE TREATMNT/ file specifications
FILE TYPE  MIXED FILE=TREATMNT RECORD=RECID 1-2
```

If you do not want to save the record type variable, you can assign a scratch variable name by using the # character as the first character of the variable name. If you do not specify a variable name on the RECORD subcommand, the record identifier is defined as the scratch variable ####RECD.

The record identifier variable can be any of the format types listed in Chapter 3, and you can use the FORTRAN-like format specification or the column format specification. If you use the FORTRAN-like format specification, you must enclose the entire format in parentheses. For example,

```
RECORD=ID 3-4
```

is equivalent to

```
RECORD=ID (T3,F2.0)
```

11.6 The WILD Subcommand

By default, SPSS^X simply skips all record types not mentioned on the RECORD TYPE commands and does not print warning messages. To request the default explicitly, specify WILD=NOWARN. If you want SPSS^X to report as errors all records that are not mentioned, specify:

```
FILE HANDLE TREATMNT/ file specifications
FILE TYPE  MIXED FILE=TREATMNT RECORD=RECID 1-2 WILD=WARN
```

A warning message and the first 80 characters of the record are printed for each record type that is not mentioned on a RECORD TYPE command. Use this specification only when you have explicitly defined all of the possible record types on the RECORD TYPE commands. You cannot use the WARN specification on the WILD subcommand if you use the keyword OTHER on your last RECORD TYPE command to indicate all other record types (see Section 11.8). Use the SKIP subcommand on the RECORD TYPE command to skip specific record types (see Section 11.9).

11.7 The RECORD TYPE Command for FILE TYPE MIXED

The RECORD TYPE command determines the processing for each type of record in the file. You must include a RECORD TYPE command for each type of record that you want to process. The first specification on the RECORD TYPE command is the value of the record type variable defined on the RECORD subcommand of the FILE TYPE command. If the record type variable is a string variable, you must enclose the value in apostrophes or quotation marks. Next, specify a DATA LIST command following the RECORD TYPE command indicating the variables that you want to read.

For example, you might want to read only the records for chemotherapy treatment where Drug A was administered. These records are coded 23 on RECID, the record identifier variable. In addition, you might be interested only in the sex and age of the patients, the dosage of Drug A, and the results. To define this record, specify the FILE TYPE, RECORD TYPE for record type 23, and the DATA LIST command specifying the variables SEX, AGE, DOSAGE, and RESULT from these records, as in:

```
FILE HANDLE TREATMNT/ file specifications
FILE TYPE  MIXED FILE=TREATMNT RECORD=RECID 1-2
.     RECORD TYPE 23
.     DATA LIST    /SEX 5 AGE 6-7 DOSAGE 8-10 RESULT 12
END FILE TYPE
```

By default, SPSS^X skips all other record types on the file. The active file contains only variables SEX, AGE, DOSAGE, and RESULT for all type 23 records.

You can also specify a list of values on the RECORD TYPE command. Separate the values from each other with either a blank or a comma. All record types specified in the value list are defined using the DATA LIST command that follows. For example, to read all of the chemotherapy treatment records, record types 21 through 24, specify:

```
FILE HANDLE TREATMNT/ file specifications
FILE TYPE  MIXED FILE=TREATMNT RECORD=RECID 1-2
.     RECORD TYPE 21,22,23,24
.     DATA LIST    /SEX 5 AGE 6-7 DOSAGE 8-10 RESULT 12
END FILE TYPE
```

All variables defined on the DATA LIST command must be located in the same columns on all record types listed on the RECORD TYPE command.

If the record types have different variables or if they have the same variables recorded in different locations, separate RECORD TYPE and DATA LIST commands are required for each record type. For example, if the DOSAGE and RESULT variables are recorded in different columns on record type 25, separate RECORD TYPE and DATA LIST commands are required for the type 25 records, as in:

```
FILE HANDLE TREATMNT/ file specifications
FILE TYPE  MIXED FILE=TREATMNT RECORD=RECID 1-2
.      RECORD TYPE 21,22,23,24
.      DATA LIST   /SEX 5 AGE 6-7 DOSAGE 8-10 RESULT 12
.      RECORD TYPE 25
.      DATA LIST   /SEX 5 AGE 6-7 DOSAGE 10-12 RESULT 15
END FILE TYPE
```

The variable DOSAGE is read from columns 8–10 on record types 21, 22, 23, and 24 and from columns 10–12 on record type 25. RESULT is read from column 12 on type 21, 22, 23, and 24 records and from column 15 on type 25 records. The active file contains the values for all variables defined on the DATA LIST commands for record types 21 through 25. All other record types are skipped.

If the same variable is defined for more than one record type, the format type and length of the variable should be defined the same on all DATA LIST commands. SPSS^X refers to the *first* DATA LIST command that defines a variable for the print and write formats to be included in the dictionary of the active file. If different variables are defined for different record types, the variables are assigned the system-missing value for those record types on which the variable is not defined.

You cannot define a record type on more than one RECORD TYPE command. If you do, SPSS^X uses the DATA LIST for the first occurrence and ignores all others.

11.8 Keyword OTHER

The keyword OTHER on the RECORD TYPE command specifies all record types that have not been mentioned on previous RECORD TYPE commands. You can specify OTHER only on the last RECORD TYPE command in the file definition. For example, if all other record types on the file are recorded in the same format, specify:

```
FILE HANDLE TREATMNT/ file specifications
FILE TYPE  MIXED FILE=TREATMNT RECORD=RECID 1-2
.      RECORD TYPE 21,22,23,24
.      DATA LIST   /SEX 5 AGE 6-7 DOSAGE 8-10 RESULT 12
.      RECORD TYPE 25
.      DATA LIST   /SEX 5 AGE 6-7 DOSAGE 10-12 RESULT 15
.      RECORD TYPE OTHER
.      DATA LIST   /SEX 5 AGE 6-7 DOSAGE 18-20 RESULT 25
END FILE TYPE
```

If you specify WILD=WARN on the FILE TYPE command, you cannot specify OTHER on the RECORD TYPE command.

11.9 The SKIP Subcommand

The SKIP subcommand on the RECORD TYPE command tells SPSS^X to skip all records of the type listed on the command. By default for MIXED file types, SPSS^X skips all records that are not specified on one of the RECORD TYPE commands. To specify explicitly that all other records are to be skipped, you can specify:

```
FILE HANDLE TREATMNT/ file specifications
FILE TYPE  MIXED FILE=TREATMNT RECORD=RECID 1-2
.      RECORD TYPE 21,22,23,24
.      DATA LIST   /SEX 5 AGE 6-7 DOSAGE 8-10 RESULT 12
.      RECORD TYPE 25
.      DATA LIST   /SEX 5 AGE 6-7 DOSAGE 10-12 RESULT 15
.      RECORD TYPE OTHER SKIP
END FILE TYPE
```

If WILD=WARN is specified on the FILE TYPE command, you may want to skip only selected record types. Specify the values for the types that you want to skip followed by the SKIP subcommand, as in:

```
FILE HANDLE TREATMNT/ file specifications
FILE TYPE  MIXED FILE=TREATMNT RECORD=RECID 1-2 WILD=WARN
.       RECORD TYPE 21,22,23,24
.         DATA LIST    /SEX 5 AGE 6-7 DOSAGE 8-10 RESULT 12
.       RECORD TYPE 25
.         DATA LIST    /SEX 5 AGE 6-7 DOSAGE 10-12 RESULT 15
.       RECORD TYPE   30,32 SKIP
END FILE TYPE
```

Record types 21 through 24 are read using the first DATA LIST command, and record type 25 using the second DATA LIST command. Record types 30 and 32 are skipped. The WILD=WARN specification on the FILE TYPE command prints a warning message for all other record types encountered.

11.10 FILE TYPE GROUPED

FILE TYPE GROUPED builds a file in which all record types are grouped together for each case identification number. All records for a single case must be together in your file. By default, SPSS^X assumes that the records are in the same sequence within each case. Use the ORDERED=NO subcommand specification if the records are not in the same sequence within each case (see Section 11.16). Case identification numbers do not have to be in sequence. For example, the following file is sorted in a correct order for a grouped file:

```
CASEID  RECID
 001      1
 001      2
 001      3
 003      1
 003      2
 003      3
 002      1
 002      2
 002      3
```

Four types of information are required on the FILE TYPE command for grouped file types.

The GROUPED Keyword. GROUPED indicates that the file being described is a grouped file type.

The FILE Subcommand. FILE names the file handle of the file to be defined and is required unless your data are included in the command file.

The RECORD Subcommand. RECORD names the variable and specifies the column location of the record type identifier. The record type identifier must be located in the same column(s) on all records. The value on this variable determines the type of each record (see Section 11.11).

The CASE Subcommand. CASE names the variable and specifies the column location of the case identifier. Each case must contain a unique value on this variable. The records for each case identification number are grouped together to define a case on the active file (see Section 11.12).

Optionally, you can specify the following subcommands on the FILE TYPE command.

The WILD Subcommand. WILD indicates the action that SPSS^X is to take if an undefined record type is encountered in your file. If this subcommand is not specified, SPSS^X issues a warning message for each undefined record encountered in your file and does not include the record in the active file (see Section 11.13).

The DUPLICATE Subcommand. DUPLICATE tells SPSS^X how to handle any duplicate records of the same type encountered within a case. By default, SPSS^X issues a warning message for each duplicate record encountered and builds the case in the active file using the *last* duplicate record (see Section 11.14).

The MISSING Subcommand. MISSING tells SPSS^X how to handle missing record types within a case. By default, SPSS^X issues a warning message for each missing record and builds the case in the active file assigning the system-missing value to those variables from the missing record (see Section 11.15).

The ORDERED Subcommand. ORDERED specifies whether the records are in the same sequence within all cases. By default, SPSS^X assumes that the records are in the same sequence for all cases and issues a warning message if a record is out of sequence (see Section 11.16).

The example in Section 11.1 shows the file definition commands for the Hubbard employee data file. Only the required subcommands on the FILE TYPE command are included.

11.11 The RECORD Subcommand

Each record type must be identified by a unique code, and the value must be coded in the same location on all records. Use the RECORD subcommand to define the variable name and the column location of the record identifier. The specification for the RECORD subcommand is the same as described in Section 11.5. For example, to define the HUBDATA as a grouped file with the record identifier variable #RECID in column 80 of each record, specify:

```
FILE HANDLE HUBDATA/ file specifications
FILE TYPE GROUPED FILE=HUBDATA RECORD=#RECID 80 CASE=ID 1-5
```

If you do not specify a variable name on the RECORD subcommand, SPSS^X assigns the scratch variable name ####RECD to the record identifier variable. The record identifier can have any of the format types listed in Chapter 3, and you can use the FORTRAN-like format specification or the column format specification. If you use the FORTRAN-like format specification, you must enclose the entire format in parentheses.

11.12 The CASE Subcommand

The CASE subcommand is required for FILE TYPE GROUPED. It defines the variable name and the column location of the case identifier. The value on the case identification variable defines a case in the active file. For example, to define the variable ID located in columns 1–5 as the case identifier variable, specify:

```
FILE HANDLE HUBDATA/ file specifications
FILE TYPE GROUPED FILE=HUBDATA RECORD=#RECID 80 CASE=ID 1-5
```

If you do not want to save the case identification variable, you can assign a scratch variable name, using the # character as the first character of the variable name. If you specify no variable name on the CASE subcommand, the case identifier is defined as the scratch variable ####CASE.

The case identification variable can be defined with any of the format types listed in Chapter 3, and you can use the FORTRAN-like format specification or the column format specification to indicate the location and format type of the variable. If you use the FORTRAN-like format specification, you must enclose the entire format in parentheses. For example,

```
FILE HANDLE HUBDATA/ file specifications
FILE TYPE GROUPED FILE=HUBDATA RECORD=RECID 80 CASE=ID 1-5
```

is equivalent to

```
FILE HANDLE HUBDATA/ file specifications
FILE TYPE GROUPED FILE=HUBDATA RECORD=RECID 80 CASE=ID (F5)
```

If the case identification number is not coded in the same columns on all record types, use the CASE subcommand on the RECORD TYPE command (see Section 11.19).

11.13 The WILD Subcommand

The specification for the WILD subcommand can be either WARN or NOWARN. The default specification for FILE TYPE GROUPED is WARN. SPSS^X issues a warning message whenever it encounters a record that is not defined as a valid record type on the RECORD TYPE commands. The undefined record is not included in the active file. If you specify WILD= NOWARN, no warning message is issued; but the undefined record is still not included in the active file. For example, if you do not want warning messages issued for undefined records, specify:

```
FILE HANDLE HUBDATA/ file specifications
FILE TYPE GROUPED FILE=HUBDATA RECORD=#RECID 80 CASE=ID 1-5
          WILD=NOWARN
```

You cannot use the keyword OTHER on your last RECORD TYPE command when the default specification WILD=WARN is in effect. To explicitly specify that all other records be skipped, use the specification WILD= NOWARN on the FILE TYPE command and the keywords OTHER and SKIP on the RECORD TYPE command. See Section 11.18 for a discussion of these subcommands.

11.14 The DUPLICATE Subcommand

The specification on the DUPLICATE subcommand can be either WARN or NOWARN. The default specification for FILE TYPE GROUPED is WARN. Regardless of whether you specify WARN or NOWARN, only the *last* record from a set of duplicates is included in the active file; other records in the set are skipped. With the default DUPLICATE=WARN, SPSS^X issues a warning message whenever it encounters more than one record of the same type within a case. The first 80 characters of the last record of the duplicate set are also displayed. If you specify keyword NOWARN, no warning message is issued.

For example, suppose that Case 1 of the HUBDATA file contains two type 1 records. If you specify

```
FILE HANDLE HUBDATA/ file specifications
FILE TYPE GROUPED FILE=HUBDATA RECORD=#RECID 80 CASE=ID 1-5
        DUPLICATE=NOWARN
RECORD TYPE 1
DATA LIST    /MOHIRED YRHIRED 12-15 DEPT79 TO DEPT82 SEX 16-20
RECORD TYPE 2
DATA LIST    /SALARY79 TO SALARY82 6-25 HOURLY81 HOURLY82 40-53 (2)
              PROMO81 72 AGE 54-55 RAISE82 66-70
RECORD TYPE 3
DATA LIST    /JOBCAT 6 NAME 25-48 (A)
END FILE TYPE
```

no warning message is issued, and the active file contains only the values from the second type 1 record for Case 1.

11.15 The MISSING Subcommand

The specification for the MISSING subcommand can be either WARN or NOWARN. The default specification for FILE TYPE GROUPED is WARN. SPSS^X issues a warning message if a record type is missing within a case identification number and builds the case in the active file with system-missing values for the variables defined on the missing record.

If you do not expect all cases in your file to have each record type, use the keyword NOWARN. If you specify NOWARN, SPSS^X does not issue a warning message but still builds the case assigning system-missing values to the variables defined on the missing record. For example, suppose your data file contains one record for each of four tests administered to a student. However, not all students took all tests. To define this file and allow for missing records for each case, specify:

```
FILE HANDLE STUDENTS/ file specifications
FILE TYPE GROUPED FILE=STUDENTS RECORD=5 CASE=STUDNUM 1-4
  MISSING=NOWARN
RECORD TYPE 1
DATA LIST  /IQ 6-9
RECORD TYPE 2
DATA LIST /READING 6-10 (2)
RECORD TYPE 3
DATA LIST /MATH 6-10 (2)
RECORD TYPE 4
DATA LIST /ACT 6-8
END FILE TYPE
```

All students are included in the active file. If a student did not take a test, the record is missing in the input file, and the system-missing value is assigned to the variable for the missing test in the active file. No warning messages are issued for missing records.

11.16 The ORDERED Subcommand

The specification for the ORDERED subcommand indicates whether the records are in the same order within each case identification number in your file. The default is YES, indicating that the record order within each case is the same as defined on the RECORD TYPE commands. For example, if the first RECORD TYPE command specifies record type 1, and the second RECORD TYPE command specifies record type 2, SPSS^X expects that the type 1 record is the first record for each case and the type 2 record is the second record.

If the records are not in the same order within each case identification number, specify ORDERED=NO. SPSS^X builds cases on the active file with the records in the same order as defined on the RECORD TYPE commands, regardless of the order of the records on the data file.

11.17 The RECORD TYPE Command for FILE TYPE GROUPED

You must include one RECORD TYPE command for each record that contains data that you want to include in your active file. The first specification on the RECORD TYPE command is the value of the record-type variable defined on the RECORD subcommand on the FILE TYPE command. You must also specify a DATA LIST command following the RECORD TYPE command for each record you want to read. For example, the SPSS^X job in Section 11.1 includes three RECORD TYPE commands. The DATA LIST command following each RECORD TYPE command describes the variables to be read from the record type specified on the previous RECORD TYPE command.

For FILE TYPE GROUPED, you can specify a single value or a list of values indicating the record type(s). You can also specify keyword OTHER on the last RECORD TYPE command to include all other record types not described on previous RECORD TYPE commands. The keyword OTHER is usually used with the SKIP subcommand (see Section 11.18).

11.18 The SKIP Subcommand

Use the SKIP subcommand on the RECORD TYPE command to skip the record type specified on the command. By default, SPSS^X issues a warning message for all record types not defined on a RECORD TYPE command. For example, to read variables from type 1 records and skip all other types, specify:

```
FILE HANDLE HUBDATA/ file specifications
FILE TYPE GROUPED FILE=HUBDATA RECORD=#RECID 80 CASE=ID 1-5
                                       WILD=NOWARN
RECORD TYPE 1
DATA LIST    /MOHIRED YRHIRED 12-15 DEPT79 TO DEPT82 SEX 16-20
RECORD TYPE OTHER SKIP
END FILE TYPE
```

Keyword OTHER cannot be used when the default WILD=WARN specification is in effect. To suppress the warning messages for undefined record types, use the WILD=NOWARN specification as shown above.

To skip only selected record types, specify the values for the types that you want to skip followed by the SKIP subcommand, as in:

```
FILE HANDLE HUBDATA/ file specifications
FILE TYPE GROUPED FILE=HUBDATA RECORD=#RECID 80 CASE=ID 1-5
RECORD TYPE 1
DATA LIST    /MOHIRED YRHIRED 12-15 DEPT79 TO DEPT82 SEX 16-20
RECORD TYPE 2,3 SKIP
END FILE TYPE
```

Record type 1 is defined for each case, and record types 2 and 3 are skipped. Since WARN is the default specification for the WILD subcommand on the FILE TYPE command for GROUPED files, a warning message is issued for all other record types. Even though record types 2 and 3 are skipped, no warning message is printed for them because they are explicitly specified on a RECORD TYPE command.

11.19 The CASE Subcommand

Sometimes, the case identification number defined with the CASE subcommand on the FILE TYPE command is not recorded in the same location on all of the record types. Use the CASE subcommand on the RECORD TYPE command to specify the location of the case identification number for a record type. This specification overrides the location specified on the FILE TYPE command for only that record type. For example, assume that the case identification number is located in columns 1–5 for record types 1 and 2 and in columns 75–79 for record type 3. To indicate this change in location for record type 3, specify:

```
FILE HANDLE HUBDATA/ file specifications
FILE TYPE GROUPED FILE=HUBDATA RECORD=#RECID 80 CASE=ID 1-5
RECORD TYPE 1
DATA LIST    /MOHIRED YRHIRED 12-15 DEPT79 TO DEPT82 SEX 16-20
RECORD TYPE 2
DATA LIST    /SALARY79 TO SALARY82 6-25 HOURLY81 HOURLY82 40-53 (2)
               PROMO81 72  AGE 54-55 RAISE82 66-70
RECORD TYPE 3  CASE=75-79
DATA LIST    /JOBCAT 6 NAME 25-48 (A)
END FILE TYPE
```

The format type of the case identification variable must be the same on all of the records. For example, if the case identification variable is defined as format type "A" on the FILE TYPE command, you cannot change the format type to "F" (default format type) on the RECORD TYPE command.

If the case identification number is in the same location on all record types, the CASE subcommand on the RECORD TYPE commands is unnecessary.

11.20 The DUPLICATE and MISSING Subcommands

You can also specify the DUPLICATE and MISSING subcommands on the RECORD TYPE command. The specifications for these subcommands are the same as described in Sections 11.14 and 11.15. If specified on a RECORD TYPE command, DUPLICATE and MISSING override the specification or default on the FILE TYPE command for that record type specified on the RECORD TYPE command. For example, you might want SPSS^X to skip missing records for type 3, but to report all missing records for types 1 and 2. The default specification for MISSING is WARN—report all missing record types. To override this default for only record type 3, include the MISSING subcommand on the RECORD TYPE command for record type 3, as in:

```
FILE HANDLE HUBDATA/ file specifications
FILE TYPE GROUPED FILE=HUBDATA RECORD=#RECID 80 CASE=ID 1-5
RECORD TYPE 1
DATA LIST    /MOHIRED YRHIRED 12-15 DEPT79 TO DEPT82 SEX 16-20
RECORD TYPE 2
DATA LIST    /SALARY79 TO SALARY82 6-25 HOURLY81 HOURLY82 40-53 (2)
              PROMO81 72 AGE 54-55 RAISE82 66-70
RECORD TYPE 3 MISSING=NOWARN
DATA LIST    /JOBCAT 6 NAME 25-48 (A)
END FILE TYPE
```

11.21 FILE TYPE NESTED

FILE TYPE NESTED defines a file in which the record types are related to each other hierarchically. The record types are grouped together by a case identification number that identifies the highest level—the first record type—of the hierarchy. The last record type described defines a case on the active file. For example, a data file recording information about automobile accidents contains three types of records related to each other hierarchically. Figure 11.21a shows the structure of this file. The highest level of the hierarchical structure is the accident record. The accident record includes information about the accident, such as weather conditions, location, date, and so forth. For each accident record, there is one vehicle record for each vehicle involved in the accident. The vehicle record contains information about the vehicle, such as type of vehicle, age of vehicle, state of registration, and so forth. The lowest level of the hierarchy is the person record—one record for each person in a vehicle. This record contains information about each person, such as type of injury, hospital costs, position in car, and so forth.

Figure 11.21a Structure of accident file

```
Accident Record (Type 1)
Vehicle Record  (Type 2)
Person Record   (Type 3)
Person Record
Vehicle Record  (Type 2)
Person Record   (Type 3)

Accident Record (Type 1)
Vehicle Record  (Type 2)
Person Record   (Type 3)
      .
      .
      .
```

Each record in the file contains a record number identifying the record type and an accident identification number identifying the accident each record relates to. Figure 11.21b shows the set of records for one accident. The accident number is recorded in positions 1 through 4 of each record, and the record identifier in position 6. As the figure shows, the first accident involved three vehicles (three records with the value 2 recorded in position 6). One person was in the first vehicle (one type 3 record), three people in the second, and one person in the third.

Figure 11.21b Records from accident file

```
0001 1  322 180/ 3/ 3 330
0001 2     1 4IL4 134M
0001 3     1134M1FR 776
0001 2     2 1IL6 322F
0001 3     2122F1FR 463
0001 3     2035M1FR1011
0001 3     2059M1FR 421
0001 2     3 4IL2 146M
0001 3     3146M0FR   0
```

Using FILE TYPE NESTED, you can define an active file with each case representing one person and information from the accident and vehicle records spread to each case.

Three types of information are required on the FILE TYPE command for NESTED file types.

The NESTED Keyword. NESTED indicates that the file being defined is a nested or hierarchical file type.

The FILE Subcommand. FILE names the file handle of the file to be defined and is required unless your data are included in the command file.

The RECORD Subcommand. RECORD names the variable and specifies the column location of the record type identifier. The record type identifier must be located in the same column(s) on all records. The value on this variable determines the type of each record (see Section 11.22).

Optionally, you can specify the following subcommands on the FILE TYPE command.

The CASE Subcommand. CASE names the variable and specifies the column location of the case identifier. The case identifier uniquely identifies the highest level of the hierarchy. If you specify the CASE subcommand, SPSS^X issues a warning message for each record with a case identification number not equal to the case identification number on the last highest level record and builds the case using the record with the invalid case number (see Section 11.23).

The WILD Subcommand. WILD tells SPSS^X how to handle undefined record types encountered in your file. By default, SPSS^X does not issue a warning message for an undefined record (see Section 11.24).

The DUPLICATE Subcommand. DUPLICATE tells SPSS^X how to handle duplicate records of the same type (other than the last defined record) encountered within a case. SPSS^X checks for duplicate records as it builds the case on the active file. By default, SPSS^X does not build a new case on the active file for each duplicate record (see Section 11.25).

The MISSING Subcommand. MISSING tells SPSS^X how to handle missing record types within a case defined by the lowest level record of the hierarchy. By default, SPSS^X skips missing record types (see Section 11.26).

11.22 The RECORD Subcommand

Each record type in a nested file must be identified by a unique code and the value must be coded in the same location on all records. The RECORD subcommand defines the variable name and the column location of the record identifier. The specification for the RECORD subcommand is the same as for MIXED and GROUPED files (see Sections 11.5 and 11.11). For example, to define the ACCIDENT file as a nested file with record identifier variable #RECID in column 6 of each record, specify:

```
FILE HANDLE ACCIDENT/ file specifications
FILE TYPE  NESTED FILE=ACCIDENT RECORD=#RECID 6
```

If you do not specify a variable name, the record identifier is defined as the scratch variable ####RECD. The record identifier variable can be any of the format types listed in Chapter 3, and you can use the FORTRAN-like format specification or the column format specifications. If you use the FORTRAN-like format specification, the entire format must be enclosed in parentheses.

11.23 The CASE Subcommand

The CASE subcommand is optional for FILE TYPE NESTED. If used, it specifies the case identifier, which uniquely identifies the highest level record of the hierarchy. SPSS^X issues a warning message for each record with a case identification number not equal to the case identification number on the last highest level record and builds the case using the record with the invalid case number. The specification for the CASE subcommand is the same as for the FILE TYPE GROUPED (see Section 11.12). For example, to define the variable ACCID located in columns 1–4 of each record as the case identifier variable, specify:

```
FILE HANDLE ACCIDENT/ file specifications
FILE TYPE  NESTED FILE=ACCIDENT RECORD=#RECID 6 CASE=ACCID 1-4
```

As each case is built, the value of the variable ACCID is checked against the value of ACCID on the last highest level record (record type 1). If the values do not match, a warning message is issued. However, the record is used in building the case.

If you do not specify a variable name, the case identifier is defined as the scratch variable ####CASE. The case identifier can be defined as any of the format types listed in Chapter 3. You can use the FORTRAN-like format specification or the column format specification to indicate the location and the type of the variable. If you use the FORTRAN-like format specification, you must enclose the entire format in parentheses.

If the case identification number is not recorded in the same location on all record types, use the CASE subcommand on the RECORD TYPE command (see Section 11.29).

11.24 The WILD Subcommand

The specification for the WILD subcommand can be either WARN or NOWARN. The default specification for FILE TYPE NESTED is NOWARN. SPSS^X does not issue a warning message when it encounters a record type that is not defined on one of the RECORD TYPE commands. However, the undefined record is not included in the active file. If you specify WARN, SPSS^X issues a warning message for each undefined record type encountered. For example, to receive warning messages for all undefined records encountered in the ACCIDENT file, specify:

```
FILE HANDLE ACCIDENT/ file specifications
FILE TYPE  NESTED FILE=ACCIDENT RECORD=#RECID 6 CASE=ACCID 1-4
          WILD=WARN
```

11.25 The DUPLICATE Subcommand

As a case is built for nested files, SPSS^X checks for consecutive duplicate record types for all levels except the last record type defined. In other words, SPSS^X determines that it has one and only one record of each type for the case that is being built. For example, suppose that the records for an accident included one accident record (type 1), two vehicle records (type 2), followed by three person records (type 3). This series of records is shown in Figure 11.25a.

Figure 11.25a Accident file with duplicate records

```
0001 1   322 180/ 3/ 3 330
0001 2     1 4IL4 134M
0001 2     2 1IL6 322F
0001 3     2122F1FR 463
0001 3     2035M1FR1011
0001 3     2059M1FR 421
```

If each person record (type 3) defines a case in the active file, the two consecutive type 2 records are considered duplicate records. The DUPLICATE subcommand provides you with three ways to handle this kind of structure.

The specification for DUPLICATE can be NOWARN, WARN, or CASE. The default specification for FILE TYPE NESTED is NOWARN. SPSS^X does not issue a warning message and uses only the *last* record of the duplicate set to build the case; the other record is skipped. Using the default, SPSS^X builds three cases on the active file from the file in Figure 11.25a; one for each type 3 record, using only the information from the second type 2 record, and the information from the type 1 record. The first type 2 record is quietly skipped.

To receive a warning message when a duplicate record is encountered in building a case, specify WARN. SPSS^X issues a warning message whenever duplicate records are encountered and prints the first 80 characters of the last record of the duplicate set. Cases are built in the same way as with the default specification, NOWARN.

To build a case on the active file for the duplicate record, specify CASE. SPSS^X then builds a case on the active file spreading the information from any higher level records and assigning system-missing values to the variables defined on the lower level records. For example, if you specify

```
FILE HANDLE ACCIDENT/ file specifications
FILE TYPE NESTED FILE=ACCIDENT RECORD=#RECID 6 CASE=ACCID 1-4
          DUPLICATE=CASE
RECORD TYPE 1
DATA LIST   /WEATHER 12-13
RECORD TYPE 2
DATA LIST /STYLE 16
RECORD TYPE 3
DATA LIST /INJURY 16
END FILE TYPE
```

four cases are built on the active file: one for the first type 2 record, with system-missing for the variable INJURY defined from the type 3 record, and one case for each of the three type 3 records. The cases built on the active file are shown in Figure 11.25b.

Figure 11.25b Cases built with DUPLICATE=CASE

```
0001 01 4 .
0001 01 6 1
0001 01 6 1
0001 01 6 1
```

11.26 The MISSING Subcommand

After a case is built for nested files, SPSS^X verifies that each defined case includes one record of each type. If a record type is missing, SPSS^X assigns system-missing values to the variables defined on the missing record. For example, suppose that the records for an accident included one accident record (type 1), no vehicle records (type 2), and three person records (type 3). These records are shown in Figure 11.26. If a case is defined for each person record, SPSS^X will build three cases with a missing record type 2 for each case.

Figure 11.26 Accident file with missing records

```
0001 1  322 180/ 3/ 3 330
0001 3     2122F1FR 463
0001 3     2035M1FR1011
0001 3     2059M1FR 421
```

The MISSING subcommand has two specifications, NOWARN or WARN. The default for FILE TYPE NESTED is NOWARN. SPSS^X does not issue a warning message if a record type is missing for a defined case and builds the case in the active file assigning system-missing values to the variables defined on the missing record.

To receive a warning message for every case built with a missing record, specify WARN. The cases are built in the same way as with the default specification NOWARN. For example, to request warning messages for the cases with missing records shown in Figure 11.26, specify:

```
FILE HANDLE ACCIDENT/ file specifications
FILE TYPE NESTED FILE=ACCIDENT RECORD=#RECID 6 CASE=ACCID 1-4
        MISSING=WARN
RECORD TYPE 1
DATA LIST   /WEATHER 12-13
RECORD TYPE 2
DATA LIST /STYLE 16
RECORD TYPE 3
DATA LIST /INJURY 16
END FILE TYPE
```

The MISSING=WARN subcommand specification prints the following warning messages:

```
>WARNING  518
>A RECORD IS MISSING FROM THE INDICATED CASE.  THE DATA HAS BEEN SET TO THE
>SYSTEM MISSING VALUE.

RECORD IDENTIFIER:2
CASE IDENTIFIER :   1
CURRENT CASE NUMBER:      1, CURRENT SPLIT FILE NUMBER:      1.

>WARNING  518
>A RECORD IS MISSING FROM THE INDICATED CASE.  THE DATA HAS BEEN SET TO THE
>SYSTEM MISSING VALUE.

RECORD IDENTIFIER:2
CASE IDENTIFIER :   1
CURRENT CASE NUMBER:      2, CURRENT SPLIT FILE NUMBER:      1.

>WARNING  518
>A RECORD IS MISSING FROM THE INDICATED CASE.  THE DATA HAS BEEN SET TO THE
>SYSTEM MISSING VALUE.

RECORD IDENTIFIER:2
CASE IDENTIFIER :   1
CURRENT CASE NUMBER:      3, CURRENT SPLIT FILE NUMBER:      1.
```

and builds the following three cases:

```
0001 01 . 1
0001 01 . 1
0001 01 . 1
```

11.27 The RECORD TYPE Command for FILE TYPE NESTED

You must include a RECORD TYPE command and a DATA LIST command for each record that contains data that you want to include in your active file. The only required specification on RECORD TYPE is the value of the record type variable defined on the RECORD subcommand on the FILE TYPE command. The order of the RECORD TYPE commands defines the hierarchical structure of the file. The first RECORD TYPE command defines the highest level record type, the next RECORD TYPE command the next highest level record, and so forth. The last RECORD TYPE command defines a case in the active file. For example, to build a case for each person

ANNOTATED EXAMPLE FOR FILE TYPE NESTED

The job in this example is to crosstabulate type of injury with weather conditions and with type of vehicle, using information from an accident file. The file has three types of records: accident, vehicle, and person. Weather conditions are recorded on the accident record, type of vehicle is recorded on the vehicle record, and injury is recorded on the person record. To create these crosstabulation tables, we must define a rectangular file with one case for each person in the accident, spreading information from all levels of the hierarchy to the appropriate person. The SPSS^X commands to read the accident file in this way and run the crosstabulation tables are

```
FILE HANDLE ACCIDENT/ file specifications
FILE TYPE  NESTED FILE=ACCIDENT RECORD=#RECID 6 CASE=ACCID 1-4

.  RECORD TYPE 1          /* ACCIDENT RECORD
.  DATA LIST /WEATHER 12-13

.  RECORD TYPE 2          /* VEHICLE RECORD
.  DATA LIST /STYLE 16

.  RECORD TYPE 3          /* VICTIM RECORD
.  DATA LIST /INJURY 16

END FILE TYPE

VARIABLE LABELS WEATHER 'WEATHER CONDITIONS AT TIME OF ACCIDENT'
                STYLE 'TYPE OF VEHICLE'
                INJURY 'TYPE OF INJURY'

VALUE LABELS  WEATHER 1 'CLEAR' 2 'RAIN' 3 'SLEET'
       4 'LIGHT SNOW' 5 'HEAVY SNOW' 6 'BLIZZARD'/
       STYLE 1 'SUBCOMPACT' 2 'COMPACT' 3 'MIDSIZE'
       4 'FULLSIZE' 5 'PICKUP' 6 'SMALL TRUCK' 7 'VAN'
       8 'LARGE TRUCK'/
       INJURY 0 'NONE' 1 'MINOR' 2 'MAJOR' 3 'DOA'/

COMMENT  TABULATE TYPE OF INJURY AGAINST WEATHER
         AND STYLE OF VEHICLE

CROSSTABS     INJURY BY WEATHER STYLE
```

- The FILE TYPE command begins the file definition for this hierarchical file and the END FILE TYPE command indicates the end of the definitions. The FILE TYPE command specifies a NESTED file type, indicates that the data are stored in a file identified by the handle ACCIDENT, and defines the variable names and locations for the record identifier and the case identification number.
- The three RECORD TYPE and DATA LIST commands tell SPSS^X which record types and variables to read. The period in column 1 of the RECORD TYPE and DATA LIST commands allows them to be indented to set them off from the other commands in the job.
- The DATA LIST command for record type 1 defines one variable, WEATHER, located in positions 12–13 of the accident record.
- The second RECORD TYPE and DATA LIST commands define the variable STYLE on the vehicle record (record type 2).
- The last set of RECORD TYPE and DATA LIST commands define the variable INJURY on the person record (record type 3). Each person record represents one case in the defined file. Variables WEATHER and STYLE from the accident and vehicle records are spread to the related person record.
- The VARIABLE LABELS and VALUE LABELS commands assign labels to the variables and values.
- The CROSSTABS command requests two two-way crosstabulation tables: type of injury by weather conditions and type of injury by style of vehicle. Figure 11.41 shows the crosstabulation of type of injury by weather conditions.

Table of type of injury by weather conditions

```
- - - - - - - - - - - - - - - - - -  C R O S S T A B U L A T I O N   O F  - - - - - - - - - - - - - - - - - -
   INJURY    TYPE OF INJURY                                      BY  WEATHER   WEATHER CONDITIONS AT TIME OF ACCIDENT
- - - - - - - - - - - - - - - - - - - - - - - - - - - - - - - - - - - - - - - - - - - - - - - - - PAGE  1 OF  1

                      WEATHER
            COUNT   |
                    |CLEAR    RAIN      SLEET     LIGHT SN   ROW
                    |                             OW         TOTAL
                    |       1|       2|       3
INJURY      --------+--------+--------+--------+
                0   |    49  |    29  |    22  |
  NONE              |        |        |        |
                    +--------+--------+--------+
                1   |    66  |    51  |    35  |
  MINOR             |        |        |        |
                    +--------+--------+--------+
                2   |    36  |    27  |    10  |
  MAJOR             |        |        |        |
                    +--------+--------+--------+
                3   |    13  |    11  |     7  |
  DOA               |        |        |        |
                    +--------+--------+--------+
           COLUMN      164      118       74       118        474
            TOTAL     34.6     24.9     15.6      24.9      100.0

NUMBER OF MISSING OBSERVATIONS =        0
```

record that includes the values of the variable WEATHER from the accident record, the variable STYLE from the vehicle record, and the variable INJURY from the person record, specify:

```
FILE HANDLE ACCIDENT/ file specifications
FILE TYPE NESTED FILE=ACCIDENT RECORD=#RECID 6 CASE=ACCID 1-4
RECORD TYPE 1           /*ACCIDENT RECORD
DATA LIST   /WEATHER 12-13
RECORD TYPE 2           /*VEHICLE RECORD
DATA LIST /STYLE 16
RECORD TYPE 3           /*PERSON RECORD
DATA LIST /INJURY 16
END FILE TYPE
```

You can specify a single value or a list of values indicating the record type(s) to be read by the following DATA LIST command. If the record type variable is defined as a string variable on the RECORD subcommand of the FILE TYPE command, you must enclose each value in apostrophes or quotation marks.

The first record in the file should be the type specified on the first RECORD TYPE command—the highest level record of the hierarchy. If the first record in the file is not the highest level type, SPSS^X skips all records until it encounters a record of the highest level type. If the MISSING or DUPLICATE subcommands have been specified on the FILE TYPE command, these records may produce warning messages but will not be used to build a case on the active file.

11.28 The CASE Subcommand

You can specify the variable name, format type, and location of a case identification number on the CASE subcommand on the FILE TYPE command (see Section 11.23). However, the case identification number may not be recorded in the same location on all record types. To specify the location of the case identification number for a record type, use the CASE subcommand on the RECORD TYPE command. Do not specify the CASE subcommand on RECORD TYPE unless you have specified the CASE subcommand on the FILE TYPE command. The format type of the case identification variable must be the same on all records; you cannot specify a different format type on the FILE TYPE command and on the RECORD TYPE command.

11.29 The SPREAD Subcommand

Use the SPREAD subcommand to indicate if the values for variables defined for a record type should be spread to all the built cases related to that record. The default specification for the SPREAD subcommand is the keyword YES—all variables defined for the record type are automatically spread to all cases built from the last record type defined. If you specify the keyword NO, the variables defined on the record type are spread only to the *first* case built from the set of records related to that record type. All other cases built from the same record are assigned the system-missing value for the variables defined on the record type.

For example, suppose that the first person record (type 3) related to each vehicle record (type 2) in the accident file is the driver of the vehicle. To spread the variable STYLE from the vehicle record to only the case built for the driver, specify:

```
FILE HANDLE ACCIDENT/ file specifications
FILE TYPE NESTED FILE=ACCIDENT RECORD=#RECID 6 CASE=ACCID 1-4
RECORD TYPE 1                     /*ACCIDENT RECORD
DATA LIST   /WEATHER 12-13
RECORD TYPE 2 SPREAD=NO           /*VEHICLE RECORD
DATA LIST /STYLE 16
RECORD TYPE 3                     /*PERSON RECORD
DATA LIST /INJURY 16
END FILE TYPE
PRINT /ACCID WEATHER STYLE INJURY
EXECUTE
```

Figure 11.29 displays the cases built from the records in the accident file shown in Figure 11.21b. The first vehicle record (type 2) has one related person record (type 3), and the value for STYLE is spread to the case built for the person record. The second vehicle record has three related person records, and the value for STYLE is spread to only the case built from the first person record. The other two persons have the system-missing value for STYLE. The third vehicle record has one related person record, and the value for STYLE is spread to the person.

Figure 11.29 Cases built with SPREAD=NO for record type 2

```
1  1 4 1
1  1 6 1
1  1 . 1
1  1 . 1
1  1 2 0
```

11.30 SUMMARY OF FILE DEFINITIONS

Table 11.30 shows the default values for each FILE TYPE subcommand for the three types of files. The notation "Not App." indicates that the subcommand is not available for that type of file. The RECORD subcommand is always required, and the FILE subcommand is required unless your data are included in the command file.

Table 11.30 Summary of defaults for FILE TYPE subcommands

Subcommand	MIXED	GROUPED	NESTED
FILE	Conditional	Conditional	Conditional
RECORD	Required	Required	Required
CASE	Not App.	Required	Optional
WILD	NOWARN	WARN	NOWARN
DUPLICATE	Not App.	WARN	NOWARN
MISSING	Not App.	WARN	NOWARN
ORDERED	Not App.	YES	Not App.

You can also specify the CASE, DUPLICATE, and MISSING subcommands on the RECORD TYPE command for file type GROUPED. You can specify the CASE and MISSING subcommands on the RECORD TYPE command for file type NESTED. If you specify any of these subcommands on a RECORD TYPE command, the default or specification on the FILE TYPE command is overridden only for the record types listed on that RECORD TYPE command. The default or FILE TYPE specification applies to all other record types.

11.31 THE REPEATING DATA COMMAND

Use the REPEATING DATA command to read and generate cases from repeating groups of data from the same input record. Each repeated group contains the same information, and a case is built on the active file for each repeated group. The number of repeated groups often varies for each record. Each input record may also include information that is common to all of the repeated groups that you want *spread* to each case built on the active file. In this respect, a file with a repeating data structure is like a hierarchical file with both levels of information recorded on one record rather than on separate record types.

For example, suppose you have a data file with each record representing a household. Information about the household, such as total number of persons living in the house and number of vehicles owned by the household is recorded on each record. Each record also includes a group of information about each vehicle, such as make of vehicle, model, and number of cylinders. Figure 11.31 shows the first three records from this data file.

Figure 11.31 Vehicle information file

```
1001 02 02 FORD     T8PONTIAC C6
1002 04 01 CHEVY    C4
1003 02 03 CADILAC C8FORD     T6VW        C4
```

The first field of numbers (columns 1–4) for each record is an identification number unique to each record. The next two fields of numbers are number of persons in household and number of vehicles. The remaining portion of the record are the repeated groups—one for each vehicle.

You can use the REPEATING DATA command only within an input program that is explicitly specified with the INPUT PROGRAM and END INPUT PROGRAM commands, or within a FILE TYPE—END FILE TYPE file definition structure for MIXED or NESTED file types. The REPEATING DATA command cannot be used with FILE TYPE GROUPED. See Section 11.32 for a discussion of the INPUT PROGRAM and END INPUT PROGRAM commands.

Because the REPEATING DATA command creates cases, you must define all fixed-format data on a given record before the REPEATING DATA command, even if the fixed-format data follow the repeating data structure. This is not a common construction since most repeating groups are recorded at the end of records rather than within them, but you may encounter the problem in data structures such as IBM SMF and RMF records.

The following three subcommands are required on the REPEATING DATA subcommand.

The STARTS Subcommand. STARTS specifies the beginning position of the repeating data segments. Optionally, you can also specify the ending position of the last repeating group. If you do not specify an ending position, SPSS^X scans to the end of the record or to the value on the OCCURS subcommand looking for repeating data groups (see Section 11.33).

The OCCURS Subcommand. OCCURS specifies the number of repeating groups on each record. You can specify a number if the number of repeating groups is the same for each record. Otherwise, specify the name of a previously defined variable whose value for each record indicates the number of repeating groups on that record (see Section 11.34).

The DATA Subcommand. DATA lists the variable name, location within the repeated group, and the type for each variable to be read from the repeated groups. The specifications for the DATA subcommand are the same as for the variable definition portion of the DATA LIST command (see Chapter 3). The DATA subcommand must be the last subcommand on the REPEATING DATA command (see Section 11.35).

Optionally, you can specify the following subcommands on the REPEATING DATA command.

The NOTABLE Subcommand. NOTABLE suppresses the printing of the summary table that lists the variable names, locations, and format types of the variables specified on the DATA subcommand. This table has the same format as the table printed by the DATA LIST command. The default is TABLE (see Section 11.36).

The FILE Subcommand. FILE specifies the file handle of the input data file that you are defining with the REPEATING DATA command. If you do not specify a FILE subcommand, REPEATING DATA defines the file specified on the previous DATA LIST command (see Section 11.37).

The LENGTH Subcommand. LENGTH specifies the length of each repeating group on the record. Use the LENGTH subcommand if you do not want to read all variables in each repeating group or if the length of each repeating group varies by record. If you do not specify the LENGTH subcommand, SPSS^X uses the specifications on the DATA subcommand to determine the length of each repeating group (see Section 11.38).

The CONTINUED Subcommand. CONTINUED indicates that the repeating groups may be continued on successive records. Optionally, you can specify the beginning position and the ending position of the repeating data groups on the continuation records (see Section 11.39).

The ID Subcommand. Use ID with the CONTINUED subcommand only. ID compares the value of an identification variable across records of the same input case. If the values are not equal for all records of an input case, SPSS^X prints an error message and stops reading data (see Section 11.40).

11.32 The INPUT PROGRAM—END INPUT PROGRAM Structure

When you submit your job for execution, SPSS^X builds the active file dictionary as it encounters commands that create and define variables. At the same time, SPSS^X builds an *input program* that constructs cases and an optional *transformation program* that modifies cases prior to analysis or display. By the time SPSS^X encounters a procedure command that tells it to read the data, the active file dictionary is ready and the programs that construct and modify the active file cases are built. The active file dictionary is described in Chapter 3 and the commands and applications that make up the transformation program are discussed in Chapters 6, 7, 8, and 10.

The input program is usually built from either a single DATA LIST command (Chapter 3) or any of the commands that read or combine system files (the GET command in Chapter 5 or the MATCH FILES and ADD FILES commands in Chapter 15). The input program can also be built from the FILE TYPE—END FILE TYPE structure used to define nested or mixed files (Sections 11.3 through 11.21). The third type of input program is one that you specify yourself using the INPUT PROGRAM and END INPUT PROGRAM commands documented in Chapter 12.

The REPEATING DATA command can appear only in a FILE TYPE—END FILE TYPE structure or in an input program explicitly specified with the INPUT PROGRAM and END INPUT PROGRAM commands. Use a DATA LIST command to define the variables on each record that you want spread to each case built from the repeated groups and the REPEATING DATA command to define the variables in each repeating group. You must place the DATA LIST, REPEATING DATA, and any transformation commands used to build the cases between the INPUT PROGRAM command and the END INPUT PROGRAM command.

To read the data shown in Figure 11.31 and build an active file with each case representing one vehicle and the information about the household spread to each of the vehicles, specify:

```
FILE HANDLE VEHICLE/ file specifications
INPUT PROGRAM
DATA LIST FILE=VEHICLE/SEQNUM 2-4 NUMPERS 6-7 NUMVEH 9-10
REPEATING DATA STARTS=12/OCCURS=NUMVEH/
                DATA=MAKE 1-8 (A) MODEL 9 (A) NUMCYL 10
END INPUT PROGRAM
```

The INPUT PROGRAM command indicates the beginning of your data definition commands, DATA LIST reads the variables from the household portion of the record, REPEATING DATA reads the information from the repeating groups and builds the new cases, and END INPUT PROGRAM indicates the end of your data definition program. These commands produce six cases.

The first record shown in Figure 11.31 contains information on two vehicles producing two cases on the active file. One case is built from the second record which contains information on one vehicle, and three cases are built from the third record. The values of the variables defined on the DATA LIST command are spread to every case built on the active file.

11.33 The STARTS Subcommand

The STARTS subcommand is required. Use this subcommand to indicate the beginning location of the repeating data segment of each record. The specification on the STARTS subcommand is either a number or a variable name. If the repeating groups begin in the same position on each record, specify the starting location with a number. To indicate that the repeating groups begin in column 12 of each record of the vehicle file, specify:

```
FILE HANDLE VEHICLE/ file specifications
INPUT PROGRAM
DATA LIST FILE=VEHICLE/SEQNUM 2-4 NUMPERS 6-7 NUMVEH 9-10
REPEATING DATA STARTS=12/OCCURS=NUMVEH/
               DATA=MAKE 1-8 (A) MODEL 9 (A) NUMCYL 10
END INPUT PROGRAM
```

If the repeating groups begin in a different location on different records, you can specify the name of a previously defined variable whose value for each record indicates the beginning location of the repeating segment of the record. You can define this variable on the DATA LIST command before the REPEATING DATA command if it is already recorded on each record. Otherwise, you may need to create the variable with transformation commands before the REPEATING DATA command.

For example, suppose that in the vehicle file the repeating groups begin in column 12 for all records with sequence numbers 1 through 100 and in column 15 for all records with sequence numbers greater than 100. To specify the beginning position of the repeating groups for this file, create a new variable that specifies the beginning position for each record and specify the new variable on the STARTS subcommand, as in:

```
FILE HANDLE VEHICLE/ file specifications
INPUT PROGRAM
DATA LIST FILE=VEHICLE/SEQNUM 2-4 NUMPERS 6-7 NUMVEH 9-10
.    DO IF    (SEQNUM LE 100)
.    COMPUTE FIRST=12
.    ELSE IF (SEQNUM GT 100)
.    COMPUTE FIRST=15
.    END IF
REPEATING DATA STARTS=FIRST/OCCURS=NUMVEH/
               DATA=MAKE 1-8 (A) MODEL 9 (A) NUMCYL 10
END INPUT PROGRAM
```

The sequence number is defined as variable SEQNUM on the DATA LIST command for each record. The DO IF—END IF structure and the COMPUTE commands create the variable FIRST with the value 12 for records with sequence numbers through 100 and the value 15 for records with sequence numbers greater than 100. The variable FIRST is specified on the STARTS subcommand. The value for FIRST then indicates the beginning position of the repeating data groups for each record.

If the repeating groups are continued on successive records, you can specify on the STARTS command the ending position of the last possible repeating group on the first record. Separate the beginning position and the ending position specifications by a dash. You can specify the ending position with a number or a variable name. The values of the variable used to define the ending position must be valid values and must be larger than the starting value. If the value of the variable specified as the ending position is undefined or missing, SPSS^X prints a warning message and builds no cases from that record. If the value of the variable specified as the ending position is less than the value specified for the starting position, SPSS^X builds one case from the continuation record but does not print a warning message. You must also use the CONTINUED subcommand (see Section 11.39).

11.34 The OCCURS Subcommand

The OCCURS subcommand specifies the number of repeating groups on each record. You can specify a number if the number of groups is the same on all records or a variable if the number of groups varies across records. The variable must be defined on a previous DATA LIST command or created with the transformation commands.

For example, in the vehicle file, some households may own two vehicles, others may own three, and some none. The number of vehicles per household is recorded on each record. To specify the number of repeating groups, first define a variable for the number of vehicles on the DATA LIST command, and then specify this variable on the OCCURS subcommand, as in:

```
FILE HANDLE VEHICLE/ file specifications
INPUT PROGRAM
DATA LIST FILE=VEHICLE/SEQNUM 2-4 NUMPERS 6-7 NUMVEH 9-10
REPEATING DATA STARTS=12/OCCURS=NUMVEH/
               DATA=MAKE 1-8 (A) MODEL 9 (A) NUMCYL 10
END INPUT PROGRAM
```

In this example, the value on variable NUMVEH from columns 9 and 10 indicates the number of repeating groups for each record. A case is built on the active file for each occurrence of a repeating group. For the records shown in Figure 11.31, NUMVEH has the value 2 on the first record, 1 on the second record, and 3 on the third. Thus, six cases are built from these records. If the value of NUMVEH is zero, no cases are built from that record.

If the number of repeating groups is the same for each record or if you want to read the same number of repeating groups from each record, specify the number on the OCCURS subcommand. For example, to read only the first repeating group from each record, specify:

```
FILE HANDLE VEHICLE/ file specifications
INPUT PROGRAM
DATA LIST FILE=VEHICLE/SEQNUM 2-4 NUMPERS 6-7 NUMVEH 9-10
REPEATING DATA STARTS=12/OCCURS=1/
               DATA=MAKE 1-8 (A) MODEL 9 (A) NUMCYL 10
END INPUT PROGRAM
```

One case is built from the first repeating group on each record regardless of the total number of repeating groups actually recorded on the record.

SPSS^X scans to the end of the record or the value specified on the OCCURS subcommand looking for repeating data groups. If the value specified on the OCCURS subcommand is higher than the actual number of repeating groups on the record, SPSS^X will continue to create cases for repeating groups until the end of record is detected. Under these circumstances, some cases generated will include system-missing or other values from your data. If you are in doubt about the accuracy of the value of the variable specified on the OCCURS subcommand, include commands to check the value.

11.35 The DATA Subcommand

Use the DATA subcommand to specify the variable names, location within each repeating group, and the format type of all variables you want to read from each repeating group. If the LENGTH subcommand is not specified, the total specifications on the DATA subcommand define the length of each repeating data group. The specifications for the DATA subcommand are the same as for the DATA LIST command (see Chapter 3). The specified location of the variables is their location within each repeating group—*not* the location within the record. The DATA subcommand is required and must be the last subcommand on the REPEATING DATA command. For example, to read all of the variables recorded for each vehicle, specify:

```
FILE HANDLE VEHICLE/ file specifications
INPUT PROGRAM
DATA LIST FILE=VEHICLE/SEQNUM 2-4 NUMPERS 6-7 NUMVEH 9-10
REPEATING DATA STARTS=12/OCCURS=NUMVEH/
                      DATA=MAKE 1-8 (A) MODEL 9 (A) NUMCYL 10
END INPUT PROGRAM
PRINT /SEQNUM TO NUMCYL
EXECUTE
```

The variable MAKE is a string variable read from positions 1 through 8 of each repeating group; MODEL is a single-character string variable read from position 9; and NUMCYL is a one-digit numeric variable read from position 10. The DATA subcommand defines a total length of ten for each repeating group.

The variables SEQNUM, NUMPERS, and NUMVEH defined on the DATA LIST command for each record are spread to each case built from the repeating groups for the record. Figure 11.35 shows the cases built on the active file from the three records shown in Figure 11.31.

Figure 11.35 Cases built with REPEATING DATA

```
1  2  2 FORD      T 8
1  2  2 PONTIAC   C 6
2  4  1 CHEVY     C 4
3  2  3 CADILAC   C 8
3  2  3 FORD      T 6
3  2  3 VW        C 4
```

You can use any of the format types listed in Chapter 3 on the DATA subcommand. You can also use the FORTRAN-like format specifications as well as the column format specifications.

11.36 The NOTABLE Subcommand

By default, SPSS^X prints a summary table for all variables defined on the DATA subcommand. The summary table lists the names, locations, and format types of the variables. The format of the summary table is identical to the summary table printed by the DATA LIST command. To suppress the printing of this table, specify the subcommand NOTABLE, as in:

```
FILE HANDLE VEHICLE/ file specifications
INPUT PROGRAM
DATA LIST FILE=VEHICLE/SEQNUM 2-4 NUMPERS 6-7 NUMVEH 9-10
REPEATING DATA STARTS=12/OCCURS=NUMVEH/NOTABLE/
                      DATA=MAKE 1-8 (A) MODEL 9 (A) NUMCYL 10
END INPUT PROGRAM
```

To specify explicitly the default, use the subcommand TABLE.

11.37 The FILE Subcommand

REPEATING DATA must be used with a DATA LIST or FILE TYPE NESTED or MIXED commands. The REPEATING DATA command reads the file specified on the previous DATA LIST or FILE TYPE command if the FILE subcommand is not specified. To specify explicitly the file handle of the file you want to read, use the FILE subcommand on the REPEATING DATA, as in:

```
FILE HANDLE VEHICLE/ file specifications
INPUT PROGRAM
DATA LIST FILE=VEHICLE/SEQNUM 2-4 NUMPERS 6-7 NUMVEH 9-10
REPEATING DATA FILE=VEHICLE/STARTS=12/OCCURS=NUMVEH/
               DATA=MAKE 1-8 (A) MODEL 9 (A) NUMCYL 10
END INPUT PROGRAM
```

11.38 The LENGTH Subcommand

The LENGTH subcommand specifies the length of each repeating data group. If you do not specify the LENGTH subcommand, the length of each repeating group is determined by the last specification on the DATA subcommand. Use the LENGTH subcommand if the last variable specified on the DATA subcommand is not read from the last position of each repeating group or if the length of the repeating groups varies by record. For example, to read only the variable MAKE for each vehicle, specify:

```
FILE HANDLE VEHICLE/ file specifications
INPUT PROGRAM
DATA LIST FILE=VEHICLE/SEQNUM 2-4 NUMPERS 6-7 NUMVEH 9-10
REPEATING DATA STARTS=12/OCCURS=NUMVEH/LENGTH=10/
               DATA=MAKE 1-8 (A)
END INPUT PROGRAM
```

The LENGTH subcommand indicates that each repeating group is 10 positions long. The DATA subcommand specifies that MAKE is to be read from positions 1 through 8 of each repeating group. Thus, positions 9 and 10 of each repeating group are skipped.

The specification for the LENGTH subcommand can be a number, as above, or the name of a previously defined variable. If the length of the repeating groups varies by record, you need to define a variable on a previous DATA LIST command or create a variable with transformation commands whose value is the length of the repeating groups on the record. Specify the name of this variable on the LENGTH subcommand. If the value of the variable specified on the LENGTH subcommand is an undefined or missing value, SPSS^X prints a warning message and builds one case for that record.

11.39 The CONTINUED Subcommand

If the repeating groups are continued onto more than one record, you must specify the CONTINUED subcommand. Each repeating group must be contained on a single record: in other words, a repeating group cannot be split across records. You can specify on the CONTINUED subcommand the beginning and ending positions of the repeating data groups on the continuation records. If you do not specify the beginning and ending positions, SPSS^X assumes that the repeating groups begin in column 1 of continuation records and scans to the end of the record or to the value specified by the OCCURS subcommand looking for repeating groups.

Figure 11.39 shows the first four records from a mail-order file. The length of each record is defined to the computer as 50 positions long.

Figure 11.39 Records from mail-order file

```
10020 04 45-923-89 001  25.9923-899-56 100 101.99
10020 63-780-32 025  13.9554-756-90 005  56.75
20030 03 45-781-43 010  10.9789-236-54 075 105.95
20030 32-569-38 015  75.00
```

The order number is recorded in columns 1 through 5 of each record. The first two records apply to the same order, and the next pair of records represent a second order. The second field of numbers on the first record for each pair indicates the total number of items ordered. The repeating groups begin in column 10 of the first record and column 7 of the second record. Each repeating data group represents information on one item ordered and contains three variables—the item inventory number, the quantity ordered, and the price of the item—a total of 20 positions for each item.

To define all of the repeating groups on this file, use the CONTINUED subcommand. Since the repeating groups begin in position 7 of the continuation records, you must also specify the beginning position of the repeating groups on the continuation records, as in:

```
INPUT PROGRAM
FILE HANDLE ORDERS/ file specifications
DATA LIST FILE=ORDERS/ORDERID 1-5 NITEMS 7-8
REPEATING DATA STARTS=10/OCCURS=NITEMS/
               CONTINUED=7/
               DATA=ITEM 1-9 (A) QUANTITY 11-13 PRICE 15-20 (2)
END INPUT PROGRAM
```

The DATA LIST command defines variables ORDERID and NITEMS on the *first record* of each input case. The STARTS subcommand on REPEATING DATA indicates that the repeating groups begin in position 10 of the first record of each input case. OCCURS indicates that the total number of repeating groups for each input case is the value of NITEMS. The CONTINUED subcommand indicates that the repeating groups may be continued onto successive records and that the beginning position of the repeated groups on the continuation records is position 7. The DATA subcommand defines variables ITEM, QUANTITY, and PRICE for each repeating data group.

If each record were defined to the computer as 80 positions long, and the data were actually recorded only in the first 49 positions, the ending column position must be specified on the STARTS subcommand. Otherwise, SPSS^X will read positions 50 through 69 of the first record for each input case as a repeating group and build a case with system-missing values for the variables defined on the DATA subcommand since these columns are blank. For example,

```
INPUT PROGRAM
FILE HANDLE ORDERS/ file specifications
DATA LIST FILE=ORDERS/ORDERID 1-5 NITEMS 7-8
REPEATING DATA STARTS=10-50/OCCURS=NITEMS/CONTINUED=7/
               DATA=ITEM 1-9 (A) QUANTITY 11-13 PRICE 15-20 (2)
END INPUT PROGRAM
```

indicates that SPSS^X is to scan only the first 50 positions of the first record of each input case looking for repeating data groups. It will scan all columns of subsequent records until the value specified on the OCCURS subcommand is reached.

11.40 The ID Subcommand

Use the ID subcommand with the CONTINUED subcommand to compare the value of an identification variable across records of the same input case. If the values are not equal for all records of an input case, SPSS^X prints an error message and stops reading data. The identification variable must be defined on a previous DATA LIST command and must be recorded on all records in the file.

The ID subcommand has two specifications, the location of the variable on the continuation records and the name of the variable defined on the DATA LIST command for the first record of each input case. The specifications must be separated from each other by an equals sign. The format type and length of the variable must be specified the same as for the variable defined on the first record.

For example, in the data shown in Figure 11.39, the order number is recorded in positions 1–5 of each record. To tell SPSS^X to compare the order number for all records in the same input case, specify:

```
INPUT PROGRAM
FILE HANDLE ORDERS/ file specifications
DATA LIST FILE=ORDERS/ORDERID 1-5 NITEMS 7-8
REPEATING DATA STARTS=10-50/OCCURS=NITEMS/
               CONTINUED=7/ID=1-5=ORDERID/
               DATA=ITEM 1-9 (A) QUANTITY 11-13 PRICE 15-20 (2)
END INPUT PROGRAM
```

In this example, ORDERID is defined on the DATA LIST command as a five-digit integer variable. The first specification on the ID subcommand must therefore specify a five-digit integer variable. Only the location of the identification number can be different on continuation records.

LOOP [varname = n TO m [BY {1 / n}]] [IF [)] logical expression [)]]
transformations
END LOOP [IF [(] logical expression [)]]

BREAK
LOOP . . .

DO IF [(] logical expression [)]
BREAK
END IF

END LOOP

VECTOR {vector name = varlist / vector name (n)} [/vector name . . .]

• **INPUT PROGRAM**
commands to create cases
END INPUT PROGRAM

END CASE

END FILE

REREAD [COLUMN = expression]

THE LOOP AND END LOOP COMMANDS, **12.1**
The Indexing Clause for the LOOP Command, **12.2**
Keyword BY, **12.3**
The IF Clause for the END LOOP Command, **12.4**
The IF Clause for the LOOP Command, **12.5**
Missing Values and the LOOP Structure, **12.6**
Nesting LOOP Structures, **12.7**
The BREAK Command, **12.8**

THE VECTOR COMMAND, **12.9**
The VECTOR Command Short Form, **12.10**
Using VECTOR Outside a LOOP Structure, **12.11**

INPUT PROGRAM and END INPUT PROGRAM, **12.12**
The Input State, **12.13**
The END CASE Command, **12.14**
END CASE and Other Commands, **12.15**
The END FILE Command, **12.16**
END FILE and END CASE, **12.17**
Creating Data, **12.18**
The REREAD Command, **12.19**
Keyword COLUMN, **12.20**
Predetermining Variable Order, **12.21**

CONTROL STRUCTURES AND DEFINING FILES, **12.22**
The DO IF Structure, **12.23**
The LOOP Structure, **12.24**

Chapter 12 Input Programs

When you submit a job for execution, SPSS^X builds the active file dictionary as it encounters commands that create and define variables. At the same time, SPSS^X builds an *input program* that will construct the cases and an optional *transformation program* that will modify the cases prior to analysis or display. By the time SPSS^X encounters a procedure command that tells it to read the data, the active file dictionary is ready and the programs that construct and modify the cases in the active file are built. The active file dictionary is described in Chapter 3, and the commands and applications that make up the transformation program are discussed in Chapters 6, 7, 8, and 10.

The input program is usually built from either a single DATA LIST command (Chapter 3) or any of the commands that read or combine system files (the GET command described in Chapter 5, the MATCH FILES and ADD FILES commands described in Chapter 15, or the GET SCSS and IMPORT commands described in Chapter 16). The input program can also be built from the FILE TYPE—END FILE TYPE structure used to define nested, grouped, or mixed files (see Chapter 11). Or you may in special instances need to specify the input program using the INPUT PROGRAM and END INPUT PROGRAM commands documented in this chapter.

The INPUT PROGRAM and END INPUT PROGRAM commands enclose data definition and transformation commands that build cases from input records. These commands establish flow of control with one or more DO IF or LOOP structures and usually include the REPEATING DATA command, multiple DATA LIST commands, the END CASE or END FILE command, or the REREAD command.

The DO IF—END IF structure (Chapter 8) selects subsets of cases on which one or more transformation commands are executed. The LOOP—END LOOP structure discussed in this chapter controls the execution of commands on a single case or on a single input record containing information on multiple cases. In this chapter, the LOOP structure is documented first in general, mechanical terms (Sections 12.1 through 12.8 and then in applications for defining files. Applications of LOOP appear throughout the rest of the chapter in conjuction with explanations of other commands (see particularly Section 12.24).

This chapter also documents several utility commands designed primarily for creating input programs. END CASE and END FILE (Sections 12.14 through 12.18) signal that a case or a file is complete. REREAD (Sections 12.19 and 12.20) instructs SPSS^X to read the same record again—usually to define data in light of information gleaned from a previous reading of the record. VECTOR (Sections 12.9 through 12.11) is a shorthand reference to a number of variables. Though the VECTOR command has other uses within the transformation language, its power is most fully exploited in conjunction with LOOP structures.

12.1 THE LOOP AND END LOOP COMMANDS

The LOOP command defines the beginning of a LOOP structure and the END LOOP command defines its end. Every LOOP structure must have both a LOOP and an END LOOP command, as in:

```
SET MXLOOPS=10
COMPUTE X=0
LOOP                              /*LOOP WITH NO LIMIT
COMPUTE X=X+1
END LOOP
```

The SET MXLOOPS command limits the number of times the loop is executed to 10. The first COMPUTE command initializes the value of X to 0; otherwise it would be initialized to system-missing (see Chapter 6). The first iteration for the first case sets the value of X to 0 plus 1. Then control returns to the LOOP command and the value of X is set to 1 plus 1. After 10 iterations, as specified in the SET command, control is passed to the first command after the END LOOP command. Thus, the value of X is 10 for every case.

In addition to MXLOOPS, you can control the number of trips SPSS^X makes through the LOOP structure by an optional indexing clause on the LOOP command or by the IF clause on the END LOOP command. You can also terminate a trip before it is complete with the BREAK command (see Section 12.8). Or you can use the IF clause on the LOOP command to control entry into the loop. Without one of these controls, the upper limit on the number of trips is the SPSS^X default limit of 40 iterations (see the MXLOOPS subcommand of the SET command in Chapter 4).

When specified within a LOOP structure, definition commands like MISSING VALUES and VARIABLE LABELS, case selection commands like SELECT IF and SAMPLE, and utility commands like SET and SHOW are invoked once when they are encountered in the command file.

12.2 The Indexing Clause for the LOOP Command

If you know exactly how many times you want to iterate through a LOOP structure, you can include an indexing clause on the LOOP command. The simplest form is

```
COMPUTE X=0
LOOP #I=1 TO 5                    /*LOOP FIVE TIMES
COMPUTE X=X+1
END LOOP
```

where scratch variable #I (the indexing variable) is set to the *initial value* of 1, and increased by 1 each time the loop is executed for a case. The last trip through the loop is when #I reaches or surpasses the *terminal value,* which is 5. Thus, the value of X will be 5 for every case.

- The indexing variable can have any valid variable name.
- Unless you specify a scratch variable, the indexing variable is treated as a permanent variable and is saved on your active file.
- If you give the indexing variable the same name as an existing variable, the values of the existing variable are altered by the LOOP structure as it is executed and the original values are lost.

The initial and terminal values of the indexing clause can be numeric expressions of the type described in Chapter 6 and can therefore be noninteger and negative. For example, the terminal value is frequently a numeric variable from the data, perhaps the number of records SPSS^X should expect per case (see Section 12.9).

- If the expression for the initial value is greater than the terminal value, no interations of the loop are executed. #J=X TO Y is a zero-trip loop if X is 0 and Y is −1.

- If the expressions for the initial and terminal values are equal, the loop is executed once. #J=0 TO Y is a one-trip loop when Y is 0.

In the structure

```
COMPUTE X=0
LOOP #I=1 TO Y                 /*LOOP TO THE VALUE OF Y
COMPUTE X=X+1
END LOOP
```

the number of iterations for a case depends on the value of variable Y for the case. For a case with value 0 for variable Y, the loop is not executed and X is 0. For a case with value 1 for variable Y, the loop is executed once and X is 1.

Altering the value of the indexing variable within the structure has no effect on the iterations. At the end of the structure, the indexing variable is restored to its value at the beginning of the iteration before it is incremented again for the next iteration.

12.3 Keyword BY

By default, SPSS^X increases the indexing variable by 1 for each iteration. You can override this increment using keyword BY, as in

```
LOOP #I=2 TO 10 BY 2           /*LOOP FIVE TIMES BY 2'S
COMPUTE X=X+1
END LOOP
```

where #I starts at 2 and increments by 2 for each of 5 iterations until it equals 10 for the last iteration. Order is unimportant: 2 BY 2 TO 10 is equivalent to 2 TO 10 BY 2.

- The *increment value* can be a numeric expression and can therefore be noninteger or negative. Zero causes a warning and results in a zero-trip loop.
- If the initial value is greater than the terminal value and the increment is positive, the loop is never entered. #I=1 TO 0 BY 2 is a zero-trip loop.
- If the initial value is less than the terminal value and the increment is negative, the loop is never entered. #I=1 TO 2 BY −1 is a zero-trip loop.
- If the initial value plus a positive increment value is greater than the terminal value, the loop is entered once. #I=1 TO 5 BY 5 is a one-trip loop since #I becomes 6 after the first trip.
- If the initial value plus a negative increment value is less than the terminal value, the loop is entered once. #I=−1 TO −5 BY −5 is a one-trip loop since #I becomes −6 after the first trip.

In the structure

```
COMPUTE X=0
LOOP #I=1 TO Y BY Z            /*LOOP TO Y INCREMENTING BY Z
COMPUTE X=X+1
END LOOP
```

the loop is executed once for a case with Y equal to 2 and Z equal to 2, because #I is 3 after one loop. The loop is executed twice if Y is 3 and Z is 2.

12.4 The IF Clause for the END LOOP Command

Frequently it is more logical to control the iterations using an IF clause on the END LOOP command. The structure

```
COMPUTE X=0
LOOP
COMPUTE X=X+1
END LOOP IF (X EQ 5)           /*LOOP UNTIL X IS 5
```

sets the value of X to 5 for each case. Iterations continue until the logical expression on the END LOOP is true, which for every case is when X equals 5.

12.5 The IF Clause for the LOOP Command

You can control the number of trips through a LOOP structure using the IF clause on the LOOP command, as in:

```
COMPUTE X=0
LOOP IF (X LT 5)                  /*LOOP UNTIL X IS 5
COMPUTE X=X+1
END LOOP
```

The IF clause is evaluated each trip through the structure, so looping stops once X is 5.

Or if you want to execute transformations within the LOOP structure to be executed only for a subset of cases, specify

```
COMPUTE X=0
LOOP IF (Y GT 10)                 /*LOOP ONLY FOR CASES WITH Y GT 10
COMPUTE X=X+1
END LOOP IF (X EQ 5)              /*LOOP UNTIL X IS 5
```

where X will be 5 for cases with values greater than 10 for variable Y. Variable X is 0 for all other cases.

If you need both an indexing and an IF clause on the LOOP command, specify the indexing clause first, as in:

```
COMPUTE X=0
LOOP #I=1 TO 5  IF (Y GT 10)   /*LOOP TO X=5 ONLY FOR CASES Y GT 10
COMPUTE X=X+1
END LOOP
```

This structure produces the same results as the previous structure.

12.6 Missing Values and the LOOP Structure

If SPSS^X encounters a case with a missing value for the initial, terminal, or increment expressions in an indexing clause, or if the conditional expression on the LOOP command returns missing, a zero-trip loop results and control is passed to the first command after the END LOOP command. In the structure

```
COMPUTE X=0
LOOP #I=1 TO Z  IF (Y GT 10)   /*LOOP TO X=Z ONLY FOR CASES Y GT 10
COMPUTE X=X+1
END LOOP
```

the value of X remains at 0 for cases with a missing value for Y or a missing value for Z (or if Z is less than 1; see Section 12.2).

If a case has a missing value for the conditional expression on an END LOOP command, all iterations of the loop are terminated for that case. In the structure

```
MISSING VALUES X(5)
COMPUTE X=0
LOOP
COMPUTE X=X+1
END LOOP IF (X GE 10)          /*LOOP UNTIL X IS AT LEAST 10 OR MISSING
```

looping is terminated when the value of X reaches 5 because 5 is the missing value for X and the logical expression on the END LOOP command returns missing. The value of X is 5 for every case.

To prevent cases with missing values on any of the variables used in the LOOP structure from ever entering the loop, use the IF clause on the LOOP command, as in:

```
COMPUTE X=0
LOOP IF NOT MISSING(Y)         /*LOOP ONLY WHEN Y ISN'T MISSING
COMPUTE X=X+Y
END LOOP IF (X GE 10)          /*LOOP UNTIL X IS AT LEAST 10
```

In this structure, X is 0 for cases with a missing value for Y since the loop is never entered.

12.7 Nesting LOOP Structures

LOOP structures can be nested within other LOOP structures or within DO IF structures, and vice versa. The structure

```
COMPUTE X=0
LOOP #I=1 TO 5                    /*LOOP FIVE TIMES
+ LOOP #J=1 TO 5                  /*INNER LOOP FIVE TIMES
+ COMPUTE X=X+1
+ END LOOP
END LOOP
```

sets the value of variable X to 25 for every case. The outer loop executes 5 times and the inner loop executes 5 times, so the result of adding 1 each trip is 25. The optional plus signs (or periods or minus signs) in column one allow indentation of the nested structure so it is easily distinguished.

The indexing variables can be the same for all levels since each structure operates on its own version of the indexing variable. Thus, in the example above, #J could be named #I without affecting the results.

12.8 The BREAK Command

If you cannot fully control looping with the IF clauses on the LOOP and END LOOP commands, you may have to resort to the BREAK command inside a DO IF—END IF structure. The expression on the DO IF command specifies the condition in which the BREAK is executed. For example, in the structure

```
COMPUTE X=0
LOOP #I=1 TO 5                    /*LOOP FIVE TIMES
+ LOOP #J=1 TO 5                  /*INNER LOOP FIVE TIMES
+     DO IF (#J EQ 4)             /*BREAK INNER LOOP BEFORE COMPLETE
+     BREAK
+     END IF
+ COMPUTE X=X+1
+ END LOOP
END LOOP
```

the inner loop terminates when the scratch variable #J equals 4.

- You must enclose the BREAK command within a LOOP structure. Otherwise, an error results.
- A BREAK command inside a LOOP structure but not inside a DO IF structure terminates the first iteration of the loop for all cases, since no conditions for the BREAK are specified.

A BREAK command within an inner loop terminates only iterations in that structure, not in any outer loop structures. In the example above, the outer loop always repeats five times, while the inner loop is "broken" when the indexing variable reaches 4. Thus, the value of X in the example is 20 for each case.

12.9 THE VECTOR COMMAND

The VECTOR command is designed for use with a LOOP structure, though it can be used in data transformations wherever you find an application. The VECTOR command defines a *vector*, which references a list of permanent or temporary numeric variables to be used in other transformations. For example, if you want to define a vector as referencing a list of ten existing numeric variables measuring children's ages, specify:

```
VECTOR AGES=AGEKID1 TO AGEKID10
```

In this command, vector AGES has 10 *elements*, AGES(1), AGES(2), and so forth up to AGES(10), which correspond to AGEKID1, AGEKID2, and so forth up to AGEKID10 from the original variable list.

- Variables specified on a VECTOR command must already exist on your active file.

- Variables specified must be consecutive and must be from the same dictionary, permanent or scratch. Thus, you must specify the variables using the TO convention (see Chapter 2).
- The vector can have the same name as any variable in your active file, but this is not recommended. The vector can also have the name of one of the functions, although you will then lose access to that function.
- You can use vectors in transformations but not in procedures.
- The vector name can never appear without a subscript in parentheses.
- The VECTOR command is in effect only until the first procedure that follows it. The vector must be redeclared to be reused between procedures.

For example, you can use vector AGES to search for teenage children in any of variables AGEKID1, AGEKID2, and so forth. To find the first teenage child in a file on parents, specify

```
VECTOR AGES=AGEKID1 TO AGEKID10

LOOP #I=1 TO KIDS
COMPUTE #TEENAGE=RANGE(AGES(#I),13,19)   /*FIND A TEENAGER
END LOOP IF #TEENAGE                     /*END IF ONE IS FOUND

PRINT /#TEENAGE (F2,2X) AGEKID1 TO AGEKID10
SELECT IF #TEENAGE
```

where KIDS is a variable containing the number of children per case and scratch variable #TEENAGE is used to terminate the loop and then to select only parents of teenagers. As SPSS^{X} executes the loop, the subscript #I for vector AGES is incremented until either the number of children is reached (the LOOP command) or a teenage child is found (the END LOOP command). That is, the first loop tests AGES(1), the first element of the vector which corresponds to variable AGEKID1. IF the value for AGES(1) is not between 13 and 19, the loop repeats, testing the age of each child until all elements are tested or the loop terminates upon finding an age between 13 and 19. See the display from the PRINT command in Figure 12.9.

Figure 12.9 PRINT variable #TEENAGE and elements of vector AGES

```
1   8 11 15
0   4  8
0   2
0
1  11 12 14 16 20
0   4  4
0  20 22
1  14 21
1  14 14 18
1   4  4  9 11 12 15 17 20 22
```

Multiple vectors can be created on the same command using the slash to separate specifications.

12.10 The VECTOR Command Short Form

You can use an alternative form of the VECTOR command to create simultaneously a list of new numeric variables and the vector that refers to them. Simply give a prefix of alphabetic characters followed by the number of variables you want to create in parentheses, as in:

```
VECTOR #WORK(10)
```

SPSS^{X} creates vector #WORK, which references 10 scratch variables: #WORK1, #WORK2, and so on, through #WORK10. Thus element #WORK(5) of the vector is variable #WORK5.

The new variable names must not conflict with existing variables. They are created according to the rules for scratch variables if the prefix is given a # character, or otherwise according to the rules for permanent and temporary variables.

You can create more than one vector of the same length by naming two or more prefixes before the length specification. The command

```
VECTOR X,Y(5)
```

creates vectors X and Y defining new variables X1 through X5 and Y1 through Y5, respectively.

12.11 Using VECTOR Outside a LOOP Structure

The VECTOR command is most commonly associated with the LOOP structure since the index variable for LOOP can be used as the subscript. However, the subscript can come from elsewhere, including from the data. Consider a file of scores on tests recorded in separate cases along with a subject identification number and a test number. To create a single case for each subject, you can use the test number as a subscript to a vector to assign the test score to the right test variable, as in:

```
FILE HANDLE FILEC/ file specifications
GET FILE=FILEC
PRINT /ID SCORE TESTNUM

VECTOR RESULT(4)
COMPUTE RESULT(TESTNUM)=SCORE
AGGREGATE OUTFILE=*/BREAK=ID/
          RESULT1 TO RESULT4=MAX(RESULT1 TO RESULT4)

PRINT FORMATS RESULT1 TO RESULT4 (F2.0)
PRINT /ID RESULT1 TO RESULT4
```

Figure 12.11a PRINT before aggregating

```
1 10 1
1 20 2
1 30 3
1 40 4
2 15 2
2 25 3
3 40 1
3 55 3
3 60 4
```

In this example, there are four possible tests for three subjects. Not all subjects took every test. The first PRINT command shows the data before the new cases are created (see Figure 12.11a). Vector RESULT creates variables RESULT1 through RESULT4, and COMPUTE assigns SCORE values to these variables, depending on the value of TESTNUM. Aggregating by variable ID creates new cases as shown by the results of the second PRINT command (see Figure 12.11b). The MAX function in AGGREGATE returns the maximum value across cases with the same value for ID.

Figure 12.11b PRINT output after aggregating

```
1 10 20 30 40
2  . 15 25  .
3 40  . 55 60
```

12.12 INPUT PROGRAM and END INPUT PROGRAM

When a single DATA LIST command does not allow you to define your data and the general file definition facilities described in Chapter 11 are not applicable, you can use one or more DATA LIST commands, transformation commands, and the utility commands documented in this chapter to build your own input program. When you do, you must begin your input program with the INPUT PROGRAM command and end it with the END INPUT PROGRAM command, as illustrated in the examples throughout the remainder of the chapter.

The following utilities are available for use within input programs:

END CASE. Use the END CASE command to write your own end-of-case processing (see Sections 12.14 and 12.15).

END FILE. Use the END FILE command to terminate processing of a data file before the actual end of the file (see Sections 12.16 and 12.17) or to define the end of the file when you are creating data (see Section 12.18).

REREAD. Use the REREAD command to reread the current record using a different DATA LIST (see Sections 12.19 and 12.20).

REPEATING DATA. Use the REPEATING DATA command to read repeating groups of data from the same input record (see Chapter 11).

12.13 The Input State

There are four program states in SPSS^X: the *initialization state,* where the active file dictionary is initialized; the *input state,* where cases are created from the input file; the *transformation state,* where cases are transformed; and the *procedure state,* where procedures are executed. While these states are generally of no real importance to you, when specifying either FILE TYPE—END FILE TYPE or INPUT PROGRAM—END INPUT PROGRAM you must pay attention to which commands are allowed within the input state, which commands can appear *only* within the input state, and which are not allowed within the input state. See Appendix B for a discussion of the four program states, command precedence, and a table that describes what happens to each command when it is encountered in each of the four states.

12.14 The END CASE Command

Use the END CASE command whenever you change the case structure of your file by building a single case from several cases or by building several cases from a single case. END CASE terminates execution of your SPSS^X commands and delivers a case to the next procedure. For example, consider the following data matrix:

```
2 1 1
3 5 1
```

The task is to make each data item into a single case, thereby creating six cases out of two. First, read the three data items into three scratch variables: #X1, #X2, and #X3. Then use a LOOP structure to create a new permanent variable from each scratch variable in turn and an END CASE command to build three new cases from each old one.

```
INPUT PROGRAM
FILE HANDLE  TESTDATA/ file specifications
DATA LIST  FILE=TESTDATA /#X1 TO #X3 (3(F1,1X))

VECTOR V=#X1 TO #X3

LOOP #I=1 TO 3
COMPUTE X=V(#I)
END CASE
END LOOP
END INPUT PROGRAM
```

The VECTOR command creates vector V with the original scratch variables as its three elements (see Section 12.9). The indexing expression on the LOOP command increments variable #I three times to control the number of iterations per input case and to provide the index for vector V (see Section 12.2). The COMPUTE command then sets X to each of the scratch variables, and the END CASE command tells SPSS^X to build a case. Thus, the first loop for the first case sets X equal to the first element of vector V. Since V(1) references #X1, and #X1 is 2, the value of X is 2. END CASE then builds the case. The END LOOP returns control to the LOOP command since the indexing is not complete. SPSS^X then sets X to #X2, which is 1, and builds the second case. The third iteration sets X equal to #X3, which is also 1, builds the third case, and terminates the loop. At this point, control is returned to the DATA LIST for the next input case. The six new cases are therefore

```
2
1
1
3
5
1
```

12.15 END CASE and Other Commands

The END CASE command tells SPSS^X that it has built a case and to pass it immediately to the procedure. When you use END CASE in an input program, SPSS^X abandons its default end-of-case processing and gives you total control. In the absence of instructions to the contrary, transformations such as COMPUTE, definitions such as VARIABLE LABELS, and utilities such as PRINT that follow an END CASE inside an input program are executed while a case is being initialized, not when it is complete. For definition commands like VARIABLE LABELS, MISSING VALUES, and PRINT FORMATS, this has no effect since these are merely written into the dictionary. However, for commands that act on the data itself, such as COMPUTE and PRINT, it makes a big difference.

A PRINT command that follows an END CASE command and precedes the END INPUT PROGRAM command prints the cases at initialization using system-missing values for permanent numeric variables, zero for scratch variables, and blanks for string variables. While the printed information is useless, it does not affect the outcome of the variable once the data are read. However, a COMPUTE that is executed at initialization does affect the outcome. For instance, if you specify PRINT and COMPUTE after the END CASE command in Section 12.14, as in

```
INPUT PROGRAM
FILE HANDLE  TESTDATA/ file specifications
DATA LIST  FILE=TESTDATA /#X1 TO #X3 (3(F1,1X))

VECTOR V=#X1 TO #X3

LOOP #I=1 TO 3
COMPUTE X=V(#I)
END CASE
END LOOP

COMPUTE Y=X**2
VARIABLE LABELS X 'TEST VARIABLE' Y 'SQUARE OF X'
PRINT FORMATS X Y (F2)
PRINT /X Y
END INPUT PROGRAM

FREQUENCIES VARIABLES=X Y
```

no error or warning is issued, but SPSS^X prints only two lines with two periods each. These periods are the initialized system-missing values of X and Y for the two original cases. After the data are read and the six cases are created, the VARIABLE LABELS and PRINT FORMATS commands have their desired effects, as shown in the FREQUENCIES table in Figure 12.15. However, because Y is computed from the initialized value of X, it is always system-missing.

Figure 12.15 FREQUENCIES output

```
X          TEST VARIABLE

                                                    VALID      CUM
 VALUE LABEL                VALUE FREQUENCY  PERCENT  PERCENT  PERCENT

                                1         3     50.0     50.0     50.0
                                2         1     16.7     16.7     66.7
                                3         1     16.7     16.7     83.3
                                5         1     16.7     16.7    100.0
                                    -------  -------  -------
                            TOTAL         6    100.0    100.0

VALID CASES      6       MISSING CASES      0
- - - - - - - - - - - - - - - - - - - - - - - - - - - - - - - - - - - -

Y          SQUARE OF X

                                                    VALID      CUM
 VALUE LABEL                VALUE FREQUENCY  PERCENT  PERCENT  PERCENT

                                .         6    100.0  MISSING
                                    -------  -------  -------
                            TOTAL         6    100.0    100.0
```

One solution is to specify PRINT and COMPUTE before the END CASE command. The preferred solution is to specify these commands in the transformation program after the END INPUT PROGRAM command, since they operate on the cases created by the input program.

12.16 The END FILE Command

The END FILE command tells SPSS^X to stop reading data before it actually encounters the end of the file. You can also use END FILE to indicate the end of the file when you are generating data (see Section 12.18). Consider a historical study of price increases for a product taken from magazine advertisements in the United States, sorted by date. To instruct SPSS^X to stop reading the file when it first encounters data collected in 1881 (when the product was changed and essentially became a new product), specify:

```
FILE HANDLE  PRICES/ file specifications
INPUT PROGRAM
DATA LIST FILE=PRICES /YEAR 1-4 QUARTER 6 PRICE 8-12(2)

DO IF (YEAR GE 1881)          /*STOP READING BEFORE 1881
END FILE
END IF
END INPUT PROGRAM

PRINT FORMATS PRICE (DOLLAR7.2)
PRINT /YEAR QUARTER PRICE
```

Figure 12.16 shows the display output from the PRINT command. Notice that the case for 1881 that caused the end of the file is not included.

Figure 12.16 PRINT output for END FILE

```
1867 2  $11.49
1867 4  $11.49
1868 1  $11.49
1869 2  $11.99
1869 3  $12.49
1869 4  $12.99
1870 2  $14.99
1871 2  $15.99
1871 3  $16.99
1872 3  $20.99
1873 1  $27.99
1874 1  $28.99
1874 2  $29.99
1875 1  $31.99
1876 3  $35.49
1877 2  $41.99
1877 3  $43.99
1877 4  $43.99
1878 4  $45.49
1879 2  $52.99
1879 4  $52.99
1880 3  $55.49
```

If you know the exact number of cases you want SPSS^X to create, you can use the N OF CASES command (see Chapter 10). You can also use a SELECT IF (also Chapter 10) to select cases before 1881, but then SPSS^X would unnecessarily read the rest of the file.

12.17 END FILE and END CASE

The END FILE command excludes the case it creates to determine the end of the file. If you want SPSS^X to include this case, use the END CASE command, as in:

```
FILE HANDLE  PRICES/ file specifications
INPUT PROGRAM
DATA LIST FILE=PRICES /YEAR 1-4 QUARTER 6 PRICE 8-12(2)

DO IF (YEAR GE 1881)        /*STOP READING AT 1881
END CASE                    /*CREATE CASE 1881
END FILE

ELSE
END CASE                    /*CREATE CASES

END IF
END INPUT PROGRAM

PRINT FORMATS PRICE (DOLLAR7.2)
PRINT /YEAR QUARTER PRICE
```

Notice that there are *two* END CASE commands. The first END CASE forces SPSS^X to include the last case. Once SPSS^X encounters the END CASE command, it abandons automatic end-of-case processing. Thus, you must include the second END CASE command following the ELSE command to create all cases previous to the first case in 1881.

12.18 Creating Data

To create data without any data input, use a LOOP structure and an END CASE command within an input program, as in:

```
INPUT PROGRAM
LOOP #I=1 TO 20
COMPUTE AMOUNT=RND(UNIFORM(5000))/100
END CASE
END LOOP
END FILE
END INPUT PROGRAM

PRINT FORMATS AMOUNT (DOLLAR6.2)
PRINT /AMOUNT
EXECUTE
```

This example creates 20 cases with a single variable AMOUNT, a uniformly distributed number between 0 and 5000, rounded to a an integer and divided by 100 to provide a variable in dollars and cents (see Figure 12.18).

The END FILE command is required to terminate processing once the LOOP structure is complete.

Figure 12.18 Printing generated cases

```
$32.64
$28.81
$32.22
$13.19
$23.74
$18.63
$11.62
$21.69
$40.58
$39.59
 $7.75
$37.21
$34.61
$11.05
$13.50
$19.33
$38.41
$18.62
$15.08
$23.75
```

ANNOTATED EXAMPLE FOR INPUT PROGRAM

Consider a file, each record of which has an invoice number, a series of book codes, and quantities of books ordered. Five example records are

```
1045 182 2 155 1 134 1 153 5
1046 155 3 153 5 163 1
1047 161 5 182 2 163 4 186 6
1048 186 2
1049 155 2 163 2 153 2 074 1 161 1
```

Invoice 1045 is for nine books of four different titles: two copies of book 182, one copy each of 155 and 134, and five copies of book 153. The task is to break each individual book order into a record, preserving the order number on each new case. The SPSS^X commands are

```
FILE HANDLE SPORTSBK/ file specifications
INPUT PROGRAM
DATA LIST  FILE=SPORTSBK
  /ORDER 1-4 #X1 TO #X24 (1X,12(F3.0,F2.0,1X))

LEAVE ORDER
VECTOR BOOKS=#X1 TO #X24

LOOP #I=1 TO 24 BY 2
- COMPUTE ISBN=BOOKS(#I)
- COMPUTE QUANTITY=BOOKS(#I+1)
- END CASE
END LOOP IF SYSMIS(BOOKS(#I+2))
END INPUT PROGRAM

SORT CASES ISBN

DO IF $CASENUM EQ 1
- PRINT EJECT /'Order ISBN Quantity'
- PRINT SPACE
END IF

FORMATS ISBN (F3)/ QUANTITY (F2)
PRINT /' ' ORDER ' ' ISBN '  ' QUANTITY

EXECUTE
```

- The FILE HANDLE command defines file handle SPORTSBK to the operating system. The file specifications are machine-dependent (see Chapter 3).
- The INPUT PROGRAM and END INPUT PROGRAM commands begin and end the block of commands that build cases from the input file (see Section 12.12). They are required because the END CASE command is used to create multiple cases from single input records.
- The DATA LIST command names SPORTSBK as the data file, specifies ORDER as a permanent variable, and defines 24 scratch variables to hold the alternating 12 maximum possible book numbers and 12 quantities (see Chapter 3).
- The LEAVE command preserves the value of variable ORDER across the new cases to be generated (see Chapter 6).
- The VECTOR command sets up vector BOOKS such that the first element is #X1, the second is #X2, and so forth (see Section 12.9).

- The LOOP command initiates the LOOP structure that moves through vector BOOKS picking off the book numbers and quantities (see Section 12.1). The indexing clause initiates the indexing variable #I at 1, to be increased by 2 to a maximum of 24 (see Section 12.2).
- The first COMPUTE command sets variable ISBN equal to the element in vector BOOKS indexed by #I, which is the current book number. The second COMPUTE sets variable QUANTITY equal to the next element in vector BOOKS, which is the quantity associated with the book number now stored in variable ISBN (see Chapter 6 for the COMPUTE command).
- The END CASE command tells $SPSS^X$ to write out a case with the current values of ORDER, ISBN, and QUANTITY (see Section 12.14).
- The END LOOP command terminates the loop structure if the next element in vector BOOKS is missing (see Section 12.4). Otherwise, control is returned to the LOOP command where #I is increased by 2 and looping continues (until #I reaches 24).
- The SORT CASES command sorts the new cases by book number in preparation for printing (see Chapter 13).
- The DO IF structure encloses a PRINT EJECT command and a PRINT SPACE command to set up titles for the printed output (see Chapter 9).
- The PRINT FORMATS command establishes dictionary print formats for new variables ISBN and QUANTITY. See the output from the PRINT command.
- The EXECUTE command is shown here as the procedure that processes the cases for printing; any procedure will do (see Chapter 17).

PRINT output showing new cases

```
Order ISBN Quantity

 1049   74     1
 1045  134     1
 1045  153     5
 1046  153     5
 1049  153     2
 1045  155     1
 1046  155     3
 1049  155     2
 1047  161     5
 1049  161     1
 1046  163     1
 1047  163     4
 1049  163     2
 1045  182     2
 1047  182     2
 1047  186     6
 1048  186     2
```

12.19 The REREAD Command

Use the REREAD command when you need to obtain information from a record to tell you how to read the remaining portion of the record. Suppose a company that manufactures automobile parts receives orders recorded in different formats for different automobiles. Two of the records may look like the following:

```
111295100FORD
11       CHEVY 295015
```

The name of the automobile appears in columns 10 through 15, but the rest of the information may or may not be in the same place depending on the automobile. In this example, the part number appears in columns 1 and 2 for both types of automobiles, but the price and quantity appear in columns 3 through 9 for the Ford and in columns 15 through 21 for the Chevrolet. To read this file, specify:

```
FILE HANDLE  CARPARTS/ file specifications
INPUT PROGRAM
DATA LIST FILE=CARPARTS/KIND 10-14 (A)

DO IF (KIND EQ 'FORD')
REREAD
DATA LIST /PARTNO 1-2 PRICE 3-6 (DOLLAR,2) QUANTITY 7-9
END CASE

ELSE IF (KIND EQ 'CHEVY')
REREAD
DATA LIST /PARTNO 1-2 PRICE 15-18 (DOLLAR,2) QUANTITY 19-21
END CASE
END IF
END INPUT PROGRAM
```

The first DATA LIST defines variable KIND for testing in the DO IF and ELSE IF commands. Since each execution of a DATA LIST command causes a new record to be read, you must use the REREAD command to tell SPSS^X to set the pointer back to the current record. This example is developed in Section 12.23.

12.20 Keyword COLUMN

Use keyword COLUMN to specify the beginning column for the REREAD command if the pointer should be placed in a column other than column 1. You can specify a numeric expression for the column, as described in Chapter 6. For example, suppose you do not want to read the part number in the above parts file. Notice that price and quantity for Chevrolets are 12 columns away from price and quantity for Fords. Therefore, you could apply the same DATA LIST to both types of automobiles, as in:

```
FILE HANDLE  CARPARTS/ file specifications
INPUT PROGRAM
DATA LIST FILE=CARPARTS/KIND 10-14 (A)
COMPUTE #COL=1
IF (KIND EQ 'CHEVY') #COL=13

DO IF (KIND EQ 'CHEVY' OR KIND EQ 'FORD')
REREAD COLUMN #COL
DATA LIST /PRICE 3-6 (DOLLAR,2) QUANTITY 7-9
END CASE
END IF
END INPUT PROGRAM
```

Scratch variable #COL is set to 13 for Chevrolets and left at 1 for all other automobiles. Thus, for Fords, the DATA LIST begins in column 1 and variable PRICE is read from columns 3 through 6. When the record is a Chevrolet, the DATA LIST begins in column 13, forcing variable PRICE to be read from columns 15 through 18 (15 is 3, 16 is 4, and so forth).

12.21 Predetermining Variable Order

You can use the VECTOR short form or the NUMERIC and STRING commands to establish the dictionary order of a group of variables before they are defined on a DATA LIST command. The VECTOR, NUMERIC, or STRING command and the DATA LIST must be enclosed within INPUT PROGRAM and END INPUT PROGRAM, as in:

```
INPUT PROGRAM
VECTOR X(4)
DATA LIST / X4 X3 X2 X1 1-4
END INPUT PROGRAM

PRINT /X1 TO X4
BEGIN DATA
4321
4321
4321
END DATA
```

This job sets up variables X1, X2, X3, and X4 so they can be referenced using the TO convention even though they are read from the input record in the reverse order.

The ability to predetermine the order of variables is most helpful when you are forced to read variables out of order, such as when they are on different records. The NUMERIC and STRING commands (Chapters 6 and 7) are a more generalized solution to this problem since you can assign any names and formats to the variables, as in:

```
FILE HANDLE POPDATA/ NAME= 'DUMMY DATA'

INPUT PROGRAM
STRING CITY (A24)
NUMERIC POP81 TO POP83 (F9)/ REV81 TO REV83(F10)
DATA LIST FILE=POPDATA RECORDS=3
  /1 POP81 22-30 REV81 31-40
  /2 POP82 22-30 REV82 31-40
  /3 POP83 22-30 REV83 31-40
  /4 CITY 1-24(A)
END INPUT PROGRAM
```

You should specify the formats you want on the NUMERIC command as shown in this example. Otherwise, SPSS^X will take the default numeric format (F8.2) from the NUMERIC command for the dictionary format, even though it will use the format on the DATA LIST to read the data (that is, the dictionary formats are the first formats SPSS^X encounters).

12.22 CONTROL STRUCTURES AND DEFINING FILES

You may be confronted with data that cannot be handled by the file definition facilities described in Chapter 11. Using combinations of DO IF —END IF and LOOP—END LOOP structures and utilities such as REREAD, VECTOR, END CASE, and LEAVE, you can program your own definitions.

12.23 The DO IF Structure

Frequently, defining a complex file structure is simply a matter of imbedding more than one DATA LIST command inside a DO IF structure. Suppose you have a data file that has been collected from various sources. The information from each source is basically the same, but it is simply in different places on the records. For example, suppose an automobile part number always appears in columns 1 and 2, and the automobile manufacturer always appears in columns 10 through 14. Otherwise, the location of other information such as the price and quantity depends on both the part number and the type of automobile. The sample data records are

```
111295100FORD       CHAPMAN AUTO SALES
121199005VW    MIDWEST VOLKSWAGEN SALES
11 395025FORD       BETTER USED CARS
11       CHEVY 195005          HUFFMAN SALES & SERVICE
11       VW    595020          MIDWEST VOLKSWAGEN SALES
11       CHEVY 295015          SAM'S AUTO REPAIR
12       CHEVY 210 20          LONGFELLOW CHEVROLET
 9555032 VW                    HYDE PARK IMPORTS
```

To simplify this example, only the data for Part 11 will be displayed.

Since you must use more than one DATA LIST, you first have to obtain information from each record to determine which DATA LIST applies to which record. Record type 11 has only two formats, one for Fords and one for both Chevrolets and Volkswagens. Thus, three DATA LISTS are required, one to determine which type of record is being read, and one each to reread the two types of records.

```
TITLE  READING DATA FOR PART TYPE 11

FILE HANDLE  CARPARTS/ file specifications
INPUT PROGRAM
DATA LIST FILE=CARPARTS/PARTNO 1-2 KIND 10-14 (A)

DO IF (PARTNO EQ 11 AND KIND EQ 'FORD')
REREAD
DATA LIST /PRICE 3-6 (2) QUANTITY 7-9 BUYER 20-43 (A)
END CASE

ELSE IF (PARTNO EQ 11 AND (KIND EQ 'CHEVY' OR KIND EQ 'VW'))
REREAD
DATA LIST /PRICE 15-18 (2) QUANTITY 19-21 BUYER 30-53 (A)
END CASE
END IF
END INPUT PROGRAM

PRINT FORMATS PRICE (DOLLAR6.2)
PRINT /PARTNO TO BUYER
WEIGHT BY QUANTITY
CONDESCRIPTIVE PRICE
```

The first DATA LIST extracts the part number and the type of automobile. Then, depending on the information from the first DATA LIST, the records are reread using one or another format, pulling the price, quantity, and buyer from different places. The two END CASE commands limit the active file to only those cases with Part 11 and automobile type Ford, Chevrolet, or Volkswagen (see Section 12.14). Without the END CASE commands, cases would be created on the active file for other part numbers and automobile types with missing values for price, quantity, and buyer.

The results of the PRINT command are shown in Figure 12.23.

Figure 12.23 Printed information for Part 11

```
11 FORD  $12.95 100 CHAPMAN AUTO SALES
11 FORD   $3.95  25 BETTER USED CARS
11 CHEVY  $1.95   5 HUFFMAN SALES & SERVICE
11 VW     $5.95  20 MIDWEST VOLKSWAGEN SALES
11 CHEVY  $2.95  15 SAM'S AUTO REPAIR
```

12.24 The LOOP Structure

You may encounter a file structure that is read by looping on the same DATA LIST command a variable number of times in order to "spread" information from one or more header records to individual records. Suppose you have a header record that tells you how many individual records follow.

The information might look like this:

```
1 AC
91
2 CC
35
43
0 XX
1 BA
34
3 BB
42
96
37
```

The 1 in the first column of the first header record (AC), says that only one individual record (91) follows. The 2 in the first column of the second header record (CC) says that two individual records (35 and 43) follow. The next header record has no individual records, indicated by the 0 in column 1, and so on.

To define these cases, read the header record, keep any information you need to spread to multiple individual records, and then loop on reading and creating individual records up to the expected number.

```
INPUT PROGRAM
DATA LIST  /#RECS 1 HEAD1 HEAD2 3-4(A)      /*READ HEADER INFO
LEAVE  HEAD1 HEAD2

LOOP  #I=1 TO #RECS
DATA LIST  /INDIV 1-2(1)                    /*READ INDIVIDUAL INFO
PRINT  /#RECS HEAD1 HEAD2 INDIV
END CASE                                    /*CREATE COMBINED CASE
END LOOP
END INPUT PROGRAM
```

The first DATA LIST reads the expected number of individual records for each header record into temporary variable #RECS. #RECS is then used as the terminal value in the LOOP command to read the correct number of individual records using the second DATA LIST. Variables HEAD1 and HEAD2 are the information in columns 3 and 4, respectively, in the header records. The LEAVE command retains HEAD1 and HEAD2 so that this information can be spread to the individual records. Variable INDIV is the information from the individual record. INDIV is then combined with #RECS, HEAD1, and HEAD2 to create the new case (see Section 12.14). Notice in the output from the PRINT command in Figure 12.24 that no case is created for the header record with 0 as #RECS.

Figure 12.24 Printed information for individual records

```
1 A C 9.1
2 C C 3.5
2 C C 4.3
1 B A 3.4
3 B B 4.2
3 B B 9.6
3 B B 3.7
```

13

```
SORT CASES  [BY] varlist [({A})]  [varlist . . . ]
                           {D}

SPLIT FILE  {BY varlist}
            {OFF       }
```

THE SORT CASES COMMAND, **13.1**
Ascending or Descending Order, **13.2**
Multiple Variable Specifications, **13.3**
String Variables, **13.4**
SORT CASES and Other Commands, **13.5**

THE SPLIT FILE COMMAND, **13.6**
Keyword BY, **13.7**
Placement of SPLIT FILE, **13.8**
SPLIT FILE and Other Commands, **13.9**

Chapter 13 Sorting and Splitting Files

In managing and analyzing data, you may want to group cases or reorder their sequence in your data file by sorting the cases according to the values of one variable or a set of variables in your file. Sections 13.1 through 13.5 discuss the SORT CASES procedure.

Once your cases are in a desired sequence on the active file, you may want to perform analyses on subgroups of the data. The SPLIT FILE utility allows you to split your file by a specified variable or set of variables. See Sections 13.6 through 13.9 for discussion of the SPLIT FILE command.

13.1 THE SORT CASES COMMAND

The SORT CASES procedure reorders the sequence of cases in the active file. Reordering is controlled by the variable or variables specified on the SORT CASES command following the optional keyword BY, as in:

```
FILE HANDLE HUBEMPLX/ file specifications
GET FILE=HUBEMPLX
SORT CASES BY SEX
```

You can name any permanent numeric or string variable as the sort variable (see Section 13.4). You cannot name scratch or temporary variables as sort keys with SORT CASES.

13.2 Ascending or Descending Order

You can sort cases in either ascending or descending order. Ascending sequence—cases with the smallest values for the sort variable or variables at the front of the file—is the default. You can specify the default by following the variable name with (A) or (UP). To sort cases in descending order—cases with the largest values for the sort variable or variables at the front of the file—specify either (D) or (DOWN) after the variable name, as in:

```
FILE HANDLE HUBEMPLX/ file specifications
GET FILE=HUBEMPLX
SORT CASES BY SEX(D)
```

In this example, if SEX is coded 1 for males and 2 for females, the data for women will sort first, followed by the data for men.

The order of the cases within a sort group remains the same. For example, if the file above is already sorted by age, the cases will be sorted by age within each sex after the SORT CASES command.

13.3 Multiple Variable Specifications

You can specify several variables as sort variables with SORT CASES, as in:

```
FILE HANDLE HUBEMPLX/ file specifications
GET FILE=HUBEMPLX
SORT CASES BY DEPT82 SEX SALARY82
```

This command sorts by department, by sex within department, and by salary within sex, all in ascending order.

To mix the order, specify the desired order in parentheses after each sort variable, as in:

```
FILE HANDLE HUBEMPLX/ file specifications
GET FILE=HUBEMPLX
SORT CASES BY DEPT82(D) SEX(A) SALARY82(D)

DO IF YRHIRED GE 80 AND DEPT82 NE 0
PRINT /DEPT82 SEX * SALARY82 (DOLLAR8)
END IF

EXECUTE
```

This command sorts first on department in descending order with Department 4 first, then on sex in ascending order, and then on salary, with the highest salary first within each sex-department grouping. Figure 13.3 shows the results of the PRINT command executed only for those employees hired since 1980 who are still working in the company (a department other than 0). See Chapter 9 for the PRINT command and Chapter 8 for the DO IF structure.

Figure 13.3 Mixed sort order

```
4 1   $9,750
4 2  $18,083
4 2  $15,608
4 2  $15,132
4 2  $12,438
4 2  $11,240
4 2  $10,050
3 1  $17,051
3 2  $39,000
3 2  $19,682
3 2  $13,650
3 2   $9,777
3 2   $9,507
3 2   $8,872
3 2   $8,239
1 1  $35,750
1 1  $17,111
1 1  $13,910
```

An order specification in parentheses applies to all variables to its left that are unspecified. For example, the command

```
FILE HANDLE HUBEMPLX/ file specifications
GET FILE=HUBEMPLX
SORT CASES BY DEPT82 SEX SALARY82(D)
```

sorts cases in descending order for all three variables.

13.4 String Variables

You can use both short and long string variables as sort keys with SORT CASES, as in:

```
FILE HANDLE CITIES/ file specifications
GET FILE=CITIES
SORT CASES BY CITY
PRINT /CITY STATE POP80
EXECUTE
```

In this example, SORT CASES reorders the cases in alphabetical order by CITY, which is a 14-character string variable. Figure 13.4 displays the results of the PRINT command for the first 20 cases.

The sort sequence of string variables depends on the character set in use at your installation. With EBCDIC character sets, most special characters are sorted first, followed by lower-case alphabetic characters, upper-case alphabetic characters, and, finally, numbers. The order is almost exactly reversed with ASCII character sets. Numbers are sorted first, followed by upper-case alphabetic characters and lower-case alphabetic characters. In addition, special characters are sorted between the other character types. Consult documentation available via the INFO command for information on the character set in use at your installation and the exact sort sequence.

Figure 13.4 Sorting cases by city name

Albuquerque	New Mexico	331,767
Atlanta	Georgia	425,022
Austin	Texas	345,496
Baltimore	Maryland	786,775
Birmingham	Alabama	284,413
Boston	Massachusetts	562,994
Buffalo	New York	357,870
Charlotte	North Carolina	314,447
Chicago	Illinois	3,005,061
Cincinnati	Ohio	385,457
Cleveland	Ohio	573,822
Columbus	Ohio	564,871
Dallas	Texas	904,078
Denver	Colorado	491,396
Detroit	Michigan	1,203,339
El Paso	Texas	425,259
Fort Worth	Texas	385,141
Honolulu	Hawaii	365,048
Houston	Texas	1,594,086
Indianapolis	Indiana	700,807

13.5 SORT CASES and Other Commands

Several facilities or procedures within SPSS^X require that cases be in a particular order. In addition, the display of some facilities is enhanced if cases are sorted.

REPORT. Since REPORT processes cases in the active file sequentially and reports summary statistics when the value of the break variable or variables changes, the file should be grouped by break variable or variables. The SORT CASES command is the most direct means of reorganizing a file for REPORT. Specify the SORT CASES command before the REPORT command, and list the break variables in the same order on each, as in:

```
SORT CASES BY EDUC SEX
REPORT VARS=SCORE1 TO SCORE5/
       BREAK=EDUC/
       SUMMARY= MEAN/
       BREAK=SEX/
       SUMMARY=MEAN/
```

See Chapter 23 for a discussion of the REPORT command.

AGGREGATE. AGGREGATE assumes that cases are sorted in ascending order on the break variable or variables. If your cases are not in this sequence, you can reorder them with a SORT CASES command prior to running AGGREGATE. See Chapter 14 for a discussion of the AGGREGATE command.

ADD FILES. You can use SORT CASES in conjunction with the BY keyword in ADD FILES to interleave cases with the same variables but from different files. See Chapter 15 for a discussion of interleaving cases with ADD FILES.

MATCH FILES. Cases must be sorted in the same order for all files you combine using MATCH FILES. See Chapter 15 for a discussion of the types of matches that can be done in SPSS^X.

PRINT. The PRINT command is not an executable command and must be followed by a procedure or EXECUTE. Thus, to use the PRINT command to check the results of a SORT CASES command, you must specify EXECUTE. See Chapter 9 for a discussion of the PRINT command.

ANNOTATED EXAMPLE FOR SORT CASES AND SPLIT FILE

The following job sorts cases in ascending order by sex, splits the file by sex, and produces two barcharts summarizing the distribution of personal income for each sex. The data for this example come from the 1980 General Social Survey. The SPSS^X commands are

```
FILE HANDLE GSS80/ file specifications
GET FILE=GSS80/KEEP SEX RINCOME
SORT CASES BY SEX
SPLIT FILE BY SEX
FREQUENCIES VARIABLES=RINCOME/BARCHART PERCENT(45)/STATS=DEFAULTS/
           FORMAT=NOTABLE/
```

- The GET command accesses the data file, keeping only the variables used in this job (see Chapter 5).
- The SORT CASES command sorts the cases in ascending order according to the values of the variable SEX for each case.
- The SPLIT FILE command splits the file into two subgroups according to the values for the variable SEX.
- The FREQUENCIES command requests a barchart for respondent's personal-income category (RINCOME). The horizontal axis is scaled in percentages with a maximum value of 45%. The frequencies table is suppressed and the default statistics are printed. One barchart is produced for each split in the file (see Chapter 18).

Barcharts from a sorted and split file

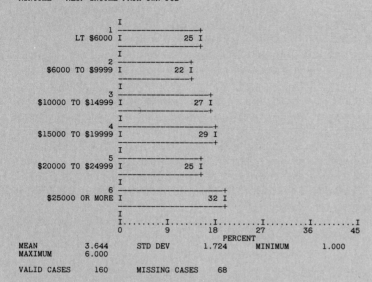

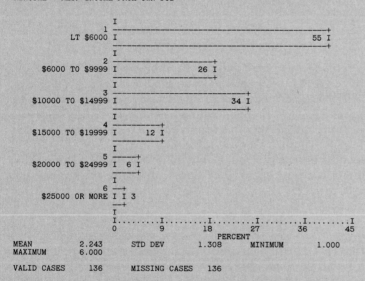

```
FILE LABEL:  GENERAL SOCIAL SURVEY 1980(N=500)
SEX:  1   MALE
RINCOME   RESP INCOME FROM OWN JOB

                 I
               1 -----------------+
        LT $6000 I             25 I
                 -----------------+
                 I
               2 ---------------+
    $6000 TO $9999 I           22 I
                 ---------------+
                 I
               3 -------------------+
 $10000 TO $14999 I               27 I
                 -------------------+
                 I
               4 --------------------+
 $15000 TO $19999 I                29 I
                 --------------------+
                 I
               5 -----------------+
 $20000 TO $24999 I             25 I
                 -----------------+
                 I
               6 ----------------------+
   $25000 OR MORE I                  32 I
                 ----------------------+
                 I
                 I.........I.........I.........I.........I.........I
                 0         9        18        27        36        45
                                      PERCENT
MEAN          3.644      STD DEV        1.724      MINIMUM        1.000
MAXIMUM       6.000

VALID CASES     160      MISSING CASES    68

FILE LABEL:  GENERAL SOCIAL SURVEY 1980(N=500)
SEX:  2   FEMALE
RINCOME   RESP INCOME FROM OWN JOB

                 I
               1 ---------------------------------------------+
        LT $6000 I                                         55 I
                 ---------------------------------------------+
                 I
               2 ---------------------+
    $6000 TO $9999 I                 26 I
                 ---------------------+
                 I
               3 ----------------------------+
 $10000 TO $14999 I                        34 I
                 ----------------------------+
                 I
               4 ----------+
 $15000 TO $19999 I      12 I
                 ----------+
                 I
               5 -----+
 $20000 TO $24999 I  6 I
                 -----+
                 I
               6 --+
   $25000 OR MORE I I 3
                 --+
                 I
                 I.........I.........I.........I.........I.........I
                 0         9        18        27        36        45
                                      PERCENT
MEAN          2.243      STD DEV        1.308      MINIMUM        1.000
MAXIMUM       6.000

VALID CASES     136      MISSING CASES   136
```

13.6 THE SPLIT FILE COMMAND

During the analysis of a data file, you may want to perform separate analyses on subgroups of your data. You can use the SPLIT FILE command to split the active file into subgroups that can be analyzed separately by SPSS^X. These subgroups or splits are sets of adjacent cases on the file that have the same values for the split variable or variables.

For example, in analyzing attitudes toward abortion, you may want to perform separate analyses for men and women because you suspect the dimensions are very different for each group. Use the SPLIT FILE command to split the active file into subgroups of men and women. When you split the file, each sex is considered a break group. Cases within a break group must be grouped together on the active file. When a procedure is requested while split-file processing is in effect, the file is processed sequentially. A change or "break" in values on any one of the split variables signals the end of one break group and the beginning of the next. Thus, if you split the file by sex, two splits are created as long as all the cases for men and all the cases for women are grouped together.

If your cases are not grouped together according to the split variable or variables, use SORT CASES to sort them in the proper order before specifying SPLIT FILE. See Sections 13.1 through 13.4 for discussion of the SORT CASES procedure.

13.7 Keyword BY

Use the BY keyword followed by a variable list to specify the variable or variables that control split-file processing, as in:

```
SORT CASES BY SEX
SPLIT FILE BY SEX
```

This command splits the file according to the values for each case for the variable SEX. When SPSS^X encounters a command that causes your file to be read, SPLIT FILE creates a new subgroup each time it reads a case with a different value for SEX than on the previous case. Thus, if SEX is coded 1 for males and 2 for females, SPLIT FILE creates two subgroups for your analyses, assuming that your cases are sorted by SEX.

You can specify or imply up to eight variables on a SPLIT FILE command. You can use both temporary transformations and long string variables as break variables. Scratch variables and system variables cannot be used with SPLIT FILE.

13.8 Placement of SPLIT FILE

SPLIT FILE is in effect for all procedures in a job unless you limit it with a TEMPORARY command, turn it off, or override it with a new SPLIT FILE command. To apply SPLIT FILE to only one procedure, use the TEMPORARY command, as in:

```
SORT CASES BY SEX
TEMPORARY
SPLIT FILE BY SEX
FREQUENCIES VARS=RINCOME/STATISTICS=MEDIAN/
FREQUENCIES VARS=RINCOME/STATISTICS=MEDIAN/
```

With these commands, SPLIT FILE applies to the first procedure only. Thus, the first FREQUENCIES procedure gives you the median income for men and women separately. The second FREQUENCIES procedure gives you the median income for both sexes.

Alternatively, you can specify:

```
SORT CASES BY SEX
SPLIT FILE BY SEX
FREQUENCIES VARS=RINCOME/STATISTICS=MEDIAN/
SPLIT FILE OFF
FREQUENCIES VARS=RINCOME/STATISTICS=MEDIAN/
```

Here, SPLIT FILE applies to the first procedure only because it is turned off after the first FREQUENCIES procedure. This set of commands produces the same results as the example above.

In addition, you can control split-file processing by overriding a SPLIT FILE command with a new SPLIT FILE command, as in:

```
SORT CASES BY SEX RACE
SPLIT FILE BY SEX
FREQUENCIES VARS=RINCOME/STATISTICS=MEDIAN/
SPLIT FILE BY SEX RACE
FREQUENCIES VARS=RINCOME/STATISTICS=MEDIAN/
```

The command SPLIT FILE BY SEX RACE turns off the SPLIT FILE BY SEX command, and the file is now split by sex and race. This split is in effect for the second FREQUENCIES procedure.

13.9 SPLIT FILE and Other Commands

There are several considerations when you use SPLIT FILE with other SPSS^X procedures and facilities.

AGGREGATE. AGGREGATE ignores the SPLIT FILE command. To split files using AGGREGATE, name the variable or variables used to split the file as break variables ahead of any other break variables. AGGREGATE still produces one file, but the aggregated cases are in the same order as the splits. See Chapter 14 for a complete discussion of AGGREGATE.

Split-File Processing and Matrices. If you use a procedure to write matrices while SPLIT FILE is in effect, SPSS^X writes one set of matrix materials for every split. If you use multiple sets of matrix materials as input to a procedure, the procedure automatically detects the presence of multiple sets. If you use the SPLIT FILE command naming any variable defined by the NUMERIC command, SPSS^X prints page headings indicating the split-file grouping. See Chapter 17 for a discussion of matrix input and output.

AGGREGATE OUTFILE = {handle | *} [/MISSING = COLUMNWISE]

/BREAK = varlist

/aggvar ['label'] aggvar ['label'] . . . = function (arguments) [/aggvar . . .]

The following functions are available:

SUM	Sum	MEAN	Mean
SD	Standard deviation	MAX	Maximum
MIN	Minimum	PGT	% of cases greater than value
PLT	% of cases less than value	PIN	% of cases between values
POUT	% of cases not in range	FGT	Fraction greater than value
FLT	Fraction less than value	FIN	Fraction between values
FOUT	Fraction not in range	N	Weighted n
NU	Unweighted n	NMISS	Weighted n of missing
NUMISS	Unweighted n of missing	FIRST	First nonmissing
LAST	Last nonmissing		

OVERVIEW, **14.1**

OPERATION, **14.2**

The OUTFILE Subcommand, **14.3**

The BREAK Subcommand, **14.4**

Creating AGGREGATE Variables, **14.5**

Labels and Formats, **14.6**

AGGREGATE Functions, **14.7**

Function Arguments, **14.8**

Missing Data, **14.9**

The MISSING Subcommand, **14.10**

Including Missing Values, **14.11**

Comparing Missing-Value Treatments, **14.12**

14

Chapter 14 AGGREGATE

Procedure AGGREGATE computes summary measures such as sum and mean across groups of cases and produces an $SPSS^X$ system file containing one case for each group. The variables on this *aggregated file* are the summary measures. For example, consider a file of employees in which each employee is assigned to a specific department. You can aggregate the employee file to create a department file containing items such as total wages within the department, number of employees within the department, and percentage of female employees within the department. In the new file, each case is a department with aggregated information on employees.

AGGREGATE often is used in conjunction with the MATCH FILES facility (Chapter 15) to perform many of the operations available in relational or hierarchical data-base systems. For example, you could add state information to a file of counties so that each case contains median family income for both the county and for the state. See the annotated example in Chapter 15 for an example using AGGREGATE with MATCH FILES.

14.1 OVERVIEW

To use the AGGREGATE procedure, you must specify three sets of information: the aggregated file, the variable(s) that define the aggregate groups, and the functions that create the new aggregate variables.

The Aggregated File. AGGREGATE produces a system file or a new active file with variable names, optional variable labels, and printing and writing formats. Once this file is created, you can analyze it with any of the procedures in $SPSS^X$, perform transformations on it, or combine it with any other file using the MATCH FILES facility. In other words, you can use the aggregated file as you would any system file. For example, if you need nested composite functions which are not provided by procedure REPORT, use AGGREGATE to perform the grouping function of the BREAK subcommand in REPORT, use the transformation language to calculate the variables, and then use the PRINT command (Chapter 9) or the REPORT procedure (Chapter 23) to write your own formatted report.

Break Groups. AGGREGATE summarizes groups of cases. A *break group* is a set of adjacent cases on the file that have the same values for a variable or set of variables. For example, in a file of philanthropic organizations, each case is an organization and includes variables for location, source of funding, and primary purpose, among other attributes. Each of these variables can be used individually or jointly to group the organizations. If you were to aggregate by location, all the New York organizations would constitute one group, all the Chicago organizations another, and so on. If you were to aggregate by location and primary purpose, all the New York organizations providing funding to medical research would be in one group, all the New York organizations providing funding to day-care centers would be in another, all the Chicago organizations providing funding to community action groups would be in another, and so forth. Each set of organizations is a break group.

Each break group defines a case on the new aggregated file. The concept of a break group is integral to the correct operation of AGGREGATE. Cases within a break group must reside together in sequence on the file. AGGREGATE processes the file sequentially and a change or "break" in values on any one of the grouping variables signals the end of one break group and the beginning of the next. If your cases are not grouped together according to the grouping variables, you should use SORT CASES to sort them in the proper order (see Chapter 13). For a further discussion of the concept of breaks, see Chapter 23 on the REPORT procedure which also depends upon a grouped file and the concept of breaks.

AGGREGATE Functions. An aggregate function summarizes the values of one variable across the cases in a break group. Functions include sum, mean, standard deviation, percentages, and fractions.

Missing Values. AGGREGATE computes statistics across cases. If a case has a missing value for a particular source variable, it is not used to compute the statistic. If all the cases in a group have missing values for a particular source variable (or all but one for some functions such as the standard deviation), the target variable is missing. Two additional options are available. To force the target variable to be missing if any case in the group is missing, use the MISSING subcommand (see Section 14.10). To include missing values in functions, use a special form of the function keyword (see Section 14.11).

14.2 OPERATION

The AGGREGATE procedure is operated via subcommands. The OUTFILE subcommand specifies a file handle for the aggregated output file or an asterisk to specify the active file (see Section 14.3). The BREAK subcommand names the variable or variables that define the aggregate groups (see Section 14.4). The MISSING subcommand sets the target aggregate variable to system-missing if any case in the group is missing (see Section 14.10). Following these subcommands, name the variables being created, their source variables, and the functions being applied to the source variables (see Section 14.5). Function keywords such as SUM or MEAN are specified as if they were subcommands. All subcommands are terminated with a slash. The OUTFILE and BREAK subcommands are required. The MISSING subcommand is optional.

14.3 The OUTFILE Subcommand

The OUTFILE subcommand is required and must be first. It specifies the handle of the output aggregated file. There are two possible specifications: the file handle or an asterisk. If you want to create and save a system file, specify a file handle on the OUTFILE subcommand. You must define the file handle on a FILE HANDLE command before the AGGREGATE procedure (see Chapter 3). Use the INFO command to get a complete description of file handles on your version of SPSS^X (see Chapter 2). Assume that you are creating an aggregated file from the Hubbard employee file. The sequence of commands is:

```
FILE HANDLE HUBEMPL/ file specifications
FILE HANDLE AGGEMP/ file specifications
GET FILE=HUBEMPL
AGGREGATE OUTFILE=AGGEMP
    /BREAK=DEPT82
    /AVGSAL=MEAN(SALARY82)
```

In this example, the new aggregated system file is written to the file defined by AGGEMP, and the active file remains unchanged. To replace the active file with the aggregated file, specify an asterisk in place of the file handle on the OUTFILE subcommand, as in:

```
FILE HANDLE HUBEMPL/ file specifications
GET FILE=HUBEMPL
AGGREGATE OUTFILE=*
   /BREAK=DEPT82
   /AVGSAL=MEAN(SALARY82)
```

When you specify the asterisk rather than a file handle, the file is not permanently saved unless you use the SAVE command (see Chapter 5).

14.4 The BREAK Subcommand

The BREAK subcommand follows the OUTFILE subcommand and names the grouping variables. To name variable DEPT82 as the grouping variable, specify:

```
FILE HANDLE HUBEMPL/ file specifications
FILE HANDLE AGGEMP/ file specifications
GET FILE=HUBEMPL
AGGREGATE OUTFILE=AGGEMP
   /BREAK=DEPT82
   /AVGSAL=MEAN(SALARY82)
```

The variable list can be as long as you want. You can use the keyword TO to reference a set of consecutive variables on the file. Each unique combination of values on the break variables defines a group. Cases on the input file must be grouped by the break variables. AGGREGATE warns you if the file is not sorted in ascending order on the grouping variables. If your active file is not correctly grouped, use SORT CASES to sort the file on the grouping variables, as in:

```
FILE HANDLE HUBEMPL/ file specifications
FILE HANDLE AGGEMP/ file specifications
GET FILE=HUBEMPL
SORT CASES DEPT82
AGGREGATE OUTFILE=AGGEMP
   /BREAK=DEPT82
   /AVGSAL=MEAN(SALARY82)
```

See Chapter 13 for a discussion of the SORT CASES command.

All break variables specified on the BREAK subcommand are saved on the aggregated file with their existing names and dictionary information. If your break variable is DEPT82, the aggregated file includes the value of DEPT82 for each group.

AGGREGATE ignores split-file processing (see Chapter 13). To achieve the same effect, name the variable or variables used to split the file as break variables before any other break variables. AGGREGATE produces one file, but the aggregated cases are in the same order as the split files.

14.5 Creating AGGREGATE Variables

Each variable on the aggregated file is created by applying an aggregate function to a variable on the active file. The simplest form of subcommand used to create aggregated variables is the *target variable list* followed by an equals sign, the function keyword, and a parenthetical list of *source variables*. For example,

```
FILE HANDLE HUBEMPL/ file specifications
FILE HANDLE AGGEMP/ file specifications
GET FILE=HUBEMPL
SORT CASES DEPT82
AGGREGATE OUTFILE=AGGEMP
     /BREAK=DEPT82
     /AVGSAL=MEAN(SALARY82)
```

creates new variable AVGSAL as the mean of variable SALARY82 for each department. The target and source variable lists must be of equal length, as in:

```
FILE HANDLE HUBEMPL/ file specifications
FILE HANDLE AGGEMP/ file specifications
GET FILE=HUBEMPL
SORT CASES DEPT82
AGGREGATE OUTFILE=AGGEMP
     /BREAK=DEPT82
     /AVGSAL AVGRAISE=MEAN(SALARY82 RAISE82)
```

You can use the keyword TO in both the target variable list and the source variable list. For example, to create averages for four salary years, specify:

```
FILE HANDLE HUBEMPL/ file specifications
FILE HANDLE AGGEMP/ file specifications
GET FILE=HUBEMPL
SORT CASES DEPT82
AGGREGATE OUTFILE=AGGEMP
     /BREAK=DEPT82
   /AVGSAL79 TO AVSAL82=MEAN(SALARY79 TO SALARY82)
```

Any number of function subcommands can be used to create variables. Separate them with slashes, as in:

```
FILE HANDLE HUBEMPL/ file specifications
FILE HANDLE AGGEMP/ file specifications
GET FILE=HUBEMPL
SORT CASES DEPT82
AGGREGATE OUTFILE=AGGEMP
   /BREAK=DEPT82
    /AVGSAL AVGRAISE=MEAN(SALARY82 RAISE82)
    /SUMSAL SUMRAISE = SUM(SALARY82 RAISE82)
```

14.6 Labels and Formats

With the exception of functions MAX, MIN, FIRST, and LAST, which copy complete dictionary information from the source variable, new variables are created by procedure AGGREGATE with no labels and with default dictionary print and write formats described in Section 14.7. To label a new variable, place the label in apostrophes immediately following its name, as in:

```
FILE HANDLE HUBEMPL/ file specifications
FILE HANDLE AGGEMP/ file specifications
GET FILE=HUBEMPL
SORT CASES DEPT82
AGGREGATE OUTFILE=AGGEMP
     /BREAK=DEPT82
     /AVGSAL 'AVERAGE SALARY' AVGRAISE 'AVERAGE RAISE' = MEAN(SALARY2
RAISE82)/
```

The label applies only to the immediately preceding variable.

If you are specifying the aggregated file as the new active file, you can also use the VARIABLE LABELS command to add labels to your file, as in:

```
FILE HANDLE HUBEMPL/ file specifications
GET FILE=HUBEMPL
SORT CASES DEPT82
AGGREGATE OUTFILE=*
     /BREAK=DEPT82
     /AVGSAL AVGRAISE = MEAN(SALARY82 RAISE82)
VARIABLE LABELS AVGSAL 'AVERAGE SALARY'/
                   AVGRAISE 'AVERAGE RAISE'
```

Use the PRINT FORMATS, WRITE FORMATS, or FORMATS commands to change dictionary formats for an active file created from AGGREGATE, as in:

```
FILE HANDLE HUBEMPL/ file specifications
GET FILE=HUBEMPL
SORT CASES DEPT82
AGGREGATE OUTFILE=*
   /BREAK=DEPT82
   AVGSAL AVGRAISE = MEAN(SALARY82 RAISE82)/
VARIABLE LABELS AVGSAL 'AVERAGE SALARY'/
            AVGRAISE 'AVERAGE RAISE'
PRINT FORMATS AVGSAL (DOLLAR10.2)/AVGRAISE (DOLLAR9.2)
```

The printing formats for AVGSAL and AVGRAISE are changed to DOLLAR formats of the appropriate width.

14.7 AGGREGATE Functions

The examples above use functions MEAN and SUM to demonstrate the construction of function subcommands. The following functions are available:

SUM(varlist) *Sum across cases.* Dictionary formats are F8.2.

MEAN(varlist) *Mean across cases.* Dictionary formats are F8.2.

SD(varlist) *Standard deviation across cases.* Dictionary formats are F8.2.

MAX(varlist) *Maximum value across cases.* Complete dictionary information is copied from the source variables to the target variables.

MIN(varlist) *Minimum value across cases.* Complete dictionary information is copied from the source variables to the target variables.

PGT(varlist,value) *Percentage of cases greater than value.* Dictionary formats are F5.1.

PLT(varlist,value) *Percentage of cases less than value.* Dictionary formats are F5.1.

PIN(varlist,value1,value2) *Percentage of cases between value1 and value2 inclusive.* Dictionary formats are F5.1.

POUT(varlist,value1,value2) *Percentage of cases not between value1 and value2 exclusive.* Dictionary formats are F5.1.

FGT(varlist,value) *Fraction of cases greater than value.* Dictionary formats are F5.3.

FLT(varlist,value) *Fraction of cases less than value.* Dictionary formats are F5.3.

FIN(varlist,value1,value2) *Fraction of cases between value1 and value2 inclusive.* Dictionary formats are F5.3.

FOUT(varlist,value1,value2) *Fraction of cases not between value1 and value2 exclusive.* Dictionary formats are F5.3.

N(varlist) *Weighted number of cases in break group.* Dictionary formats are F7.0 for unweighted files, F8.2 for weighted files.

NU(varlist) *Unweighted number of cases in break group.* Dictionary formats are F7.0.

NMISS(varlist) *Weighted number of missing cases.* Dictionary formats are F7.0 for unweighted files, F8.2 for weighted files.

NUMISS(varlist) *Unweighted number of missing cases.* Dictionary formats are F7.0.

FIRST(varlist) *First nonmissing observed value in break group.* Complete dictionary information is copied from the source variables to the target variables.

LAST(varlist) *Last nonmissing observed value in break group.* Complete dictionary information is copied from the source variables to the target variables.

14.8 Function Arguments

Functions PGT, PLT, PIN, POUT, FGT, FLT, FIN, and FOUT have special numeric arguments. PGT, PLT, FGT, and FLT have one numeric argument; PIN, POUT, FIN, and FOUT have two numeric arguments. For example, the specification

```
LOVAC,LOSICK = PLT (VACDAY SICKDAY,10)
```

assigns the percentage of cases with values less than 10 for VACDAY to LOVAC, and SICKDAY to LOSICK. The specification

```
COLLEGE = FIN(EDUC,13,16)
```

assigns the fraction of cases having 13 to 16 years of education to COLLEGE. The first argument should be lower than the second argument for functions PIN, POUT, FIN, and FOUT. If the first argument is higher, AGGREGATE automatically reverses them and prints a warning message.

The percentage functions return values between 0 and 100 inclusive; the fraction functions return values between 0 and 1 inclusive.

Only numeric variables can be used with SUM, MEAN, and SD. Both short and long string variables can be used with all other functions. To obtain the percentage of females when SEX is coded M and F, specify either

```
PCTFEM = PLT(SEX,'M')
```

or

```
PCTFEM = PIN(SEX,'F','F')
```

Blanks and commas can be used interchangeably to delimit arguments to functions.

The N and NU functions do not require arguments. Without arguments, they return the number of weighted and unweighted cases in a break group. If you supply a variable list, they return the weighted and unweighted number of valid cases for the variables specified.

14.9 Missing Data

By default, if the source variable used in a function has a missing value for a case, the case is not included in the computation of the function. If all cases in a break group have missing values for a variable, the function returns the system-missing value. You can override this rule by including missing values in calculations (Section 14.11) or by forcing the target variable to missing if any case in a break group has a missing value for the source variable (Section 14.10).

Considerations for missing values do not apply to break variables. Even if a break variable has a system-missing value, cases in that group are processed and the break variable is saved on the file with the system-missing value. Use SELECT IF if you want to eliminate cases with missing values on the break variables.

14.10 The MISSING Subcommand

To force target variables to system-missing if any of the cases in the group are missing on the source variable, use the MISSING subcommand. The MISSING subcommand has one keyword specification, COLUMNWISE.

The MISSING subcommand, when used, follows the OUTFILE subcommand, as in:

```
FILE HANDLE HUBEMPL/ file specifications
FILE HANDLE AGGEMP/ file specifications
GET FILE=HUBEMPL
SORT CASES DEPT82
AGGREGATE OUTFILE=AGGEMP
    /MISSING=COLUMNWISE
    /BREAK=DEPT82
    /AVGSAL 'AVERAGE SALARY' AVGRAISE 'AVERAGE RAISE'
    = MEAN(SALARY82 RAISE82)
```

The MISSING subcommand has no effect on the N, NU, NMISS, or NUMISS functions. For example, N(AGE) returns the same result for the default and for columnwise deletion.

14.11 Including Missing Values

To force a function to ignore user-missing values, follow the function name with a period, as in:

```
LOVAC = PLT.(VACDAY,10)
```

This function sets new variable LOVAC to the percentages of cases within the group with values less than 10 for VACDAY even if some of the values are defined as missing.

To obtain the first value of AGE in a break group whether it is missing or not, specify:

```
FIRSTAGE = FIRST.(AGE)
```

If the first case in a break group has a missing value on AGE, FIRSTAGE is set to that value and, since variables created with FIRST have the same dictionary information as their source variables, that value is still treated as missing on the aggregated file.

The period is ignored when used with N, NU, NMISS, and NUMISS if these functions have no argument. On the other hand, NMISS.(AGE) gives the number of cases on which AGE has the system-missing value. The rationale for the special missing treatment for N, NU, NMISS, and NUMISS is illustrated by the following identities:

N = N. = N(AGE)+NMISS(AGE) = N.(AGE)+NMISS.(AGE)

NU = NU. = NU(AGE)+NUMISS(AGE) = NU.(AGE)+NUMISS.(AGE)

That is, the function N (the same as N. with no argument) is equal to the sum of cases with valid and with missing values for AGE, which is also equal to the sum of cases with either valid or user-missing values and with system-missing values for AGE. The same identities hold for the NU, NMISS, and NUMISS functions.

14.12 Comparing Missing-Value Treatments

Table 14.12 demonstrates the effects of the MISSING subcommand and of the period missing-value convention. Each entry in the table is the number of cases used to compute the specified function for variable EDUC, which has 10 nonmissing cases, 5 user-missing cases, and 2 system-missing cases for the group. Note that columnwise treatment produces the same results as the default for every function except the MEAN function.

Table 14.12 Alternative missing-value treatments

Function	Default	Columnwise
N	17	17
N.	17	17
N(EDUC)	10	10
N.(EDUC)	15	15
MEAN(EDUC)	10	0
MEAN.(EDUC)	15	0
NMISS(EDUC)	7	7
NMISS.(EDUC)	2	2

ANNOTATED EXAMPLE FOR AGGREGATE

In the following example, the Hubbard Consultants Inc. personnel file is aggregated to produce one case for each combination of values of LOCATN82 and DEPT82. The mean and sum of employee salaries and raises in 1982, percent black, and percent white are calculated for each group. The variable RACE on this file has codes 1 and 5, where 1=black and 5=white. The SPSS^X commands are

```
FILE HANDLE HUBEMPL/ file specifications
GET FILE=HUBEMPL
        /KEEP=LOCATN82 DEPT82 SALARY82 RAISE82 RACE
SORT CASES LOCATN82 DEPT82

AGGREGATE OUTFILE=*
    /BREAK=LOCATN82 DEPT82
    /COUNT=N
    /AVGSAL AVGRAISE = MEAN(SALARY82 RAISE82)
    /SUMSAL SUMRAISE = SUM(SALARY82 RAISE82)
    /BLACKPCT 'PERCENTAGE BLACK' = PIN(RACE,1,1)
    /WHITEPCT 'PERCENTAGE WHITE' = PIN(RACE,5,5)

FILE LABEL AGGREGATED HUBBARD EMPLOYEE DATA
VARIABLE LABELS AVGSAL 'AVERAGE 1982 SALARY'/
                AVGRAISE 'AVERAGE 1982 RAISE'/
                SUMSAL  'TOTAL 1982 SALARY'/
                SUMRAISE 'TOTAL 1982 RAISE'

PRINT FORMATS AVGSAL (DOLLAR10.2)/ AVGRAISE (DOLLAR9.2)/
              SUMSAL (DOLLAR13.2)/ SUMRAISE (DOLLAR11.2)

DO IF $CASENUM EQ 1
PRINT /'LOC DEP NUM'1 'AVGSAL'16 'AVGRAISE'25 'SUMSAL'38 'SUMRAISE'50
      '%B'62 '%W'68
END IF
PRINT /LOCATN82 DEPT82 COUNT (3(F3,1X)) AVGSAL TO WHITEPCT
EXECUTE
```

- The FILE HANDLE command defines the handle HUBEMPL to the SPSS^X system file with the Hubbard employee data (see Chapter 3).
- The GET command reads the system file with the Hubbard employee data keeping only variables needed for this job (see Chapter 5).
- The SORT CASES command sorts the data in order by location and department so these variables can be used as break variables in AGGREGATE (see Chapter 13).
- The OUTFILE subcommand on the AGGREGATE command uses the asterisk to indicate that the new file will replace the active file (see Section 14.3).
- The BREAK subcommand names the variables indicating the employee's location and department, the combination of which form the groups for aggregation (see Section 14.4).
- The first aggregate function creates a new variable COUNT which is equal to the function N, the number of cases in each group (see Sections 14.5 and 14.7).
- The next two aggregate functions create two new variables each: AVGSAL, the group mean for salary; AVGRAISE, the group mean for raise; SUMSAL, the group total for salary; and SUMRAISE, the group total for raise.

- The final two functions create two new variables using the PIN function to create BLACKPCT or the percentage black in each group and WHITEPCT or the percentage white. Since black is coded 1 for variable RACE, the percentage between 1 and 1 inclusive is the percentage black. Labels are assigned to these new variables within procedure AGGREGATE (see Section 14.6).
- FILE LABEL provides a label for the new active file created by AGGREGATE (see Chapter 5).
- The VARIABLE LABELS command provides labels to four other new variables (see Chapter 3). PRINT FORMATS overrides the default dictionary print formats for the four new variables that are measured in dollars (see Chapter 9). The default dictionary formats for the other new variables are appropriate (see Section 14.7).
- The DO IF structure enclosing the first PRINT sets up titles and the second PRINT displays the values of the seven new variables and the two break variables (see Chapter 9).
- The EXECUTE command reads the active file for the PRINT. Alternatively, you could use the LIST procedure to list the values of the variables (see Chapter 9).

The output produced by this job includes the following:

AGGREGATE Messages. AGGREGATE prints the messages shown in Figure A. The aggregated file contains nine variables: LOCATN82, DEPT82, COUNT, AVGSAL, AVGRAISE, SUMSAL, SUMRAISE, BLACKPCT, and WHITEPCT. The message also tells you that the aggregated file replaced the active file.

PRINT Output. Figure B shows the PRINT output. Note that SPSS^X prints periods for the system-missing values for each of the four dollar variables that are missing for all cases in the group represented by 0 for location and 0 for department.

A AGGREGATE messages

```
'AGGREGATE' PROBLEM REQUIRES      453 BYTES OF MEMORY.

A NEW (AGGREGATED) ACTIVE FILE HAS REPLACED THE EXISTING ACTIVE FILE.
IT CONTAINS     9 VARIABLES AND       6 CASES.
```

B PRINT output of the aggregated file

```
LOC DEP NUM     AVGSAL   AVGRAISE       SUMSAL       SUMRAISE    %B    %W
  0   0 130          .          .            .              .  30.0  63.1
  1   1  34 $15,257.47 $1,704.24   $518,754.00    $57,944.00  55.9  35.3
  1   2  17 $18,339.29 $1,450.19   $311,768.00    $23,203.00  11.8  82.4
  1   3  60 $17,918.22 $3,218.22 $1,075,093.00   $177,002.00  33.3  65.0
  5   2   5 $15,565.40   $464.20    $77,827.00     $2,321.00    .0 100.0
  5   4  29 $17,413.21 $2,573.39   $504,983.00    $72,055.00  24.1  65.5
```

```
MATCH FILES {FILE } = {handle}
            {TABLE}   {*     }

  [/RENAME = (old varlist = new varlist) . . . ]
  [/IN = varname]
     [/ {FILE } = . . . ]
        {TABLE}
  [/BY varlist]
  [/MAP]
  [/KEEP = {ALL    }] [/DROP = varlist]
           {varlist}
  [/FIRST = varname] [/LAST = varname]
```

```
ADD FILES FILE = {handle}
                 {*     }

  [/RENAME = (old varlist = new varlist) . . . ]
  [/IN = varname]
     [/FILE = . . . ]
  [/BY varlist]
  [/MAP]
  [/KEEP = {ALL    }] [/DROP = varlist]
           {varlist}
  [/FIRST = varname] [/LAST = varname]
```


THE MATCH FILES COMMAND, **15.1**
- Parallel Files, **15.2**
  - The FILE Subcommand, **15.3**
  - Specifying the Active File, **15.4**
  - The MAP Subcommand, **15.5**
  - The RENAME Subcommand, **15.6**
  - The DROP and KEEP Subcommands, **15.7**
  - Reordering Variables, **15.8**
- Nonparallel Files, **15.9**
  - The FILE and BY Subcommands, **15.10**
  - Common Variables, **15.11**
  - The IN Subcommand, **15.12**
- Tables and Files, **15.13**
  - The FILE, TABLE, and BY Subcommands, **15.14**
  - The FIRST and LAST Subcommands, **15.15**
- The FIRST and LAST Subcommands on One File, **15.16**

THE ADD FILES COMMAND, **15.17**
- Concatenating Files, **15.18**
  - The FILE Subcommand, **15.19**
  - Optional Subcommands, **15.20**
- Interleaving Files, **15.21**
  - The FILE and BY Subcommands, **15.22**
  - Optional Subcommands, **15.23**

Chapter 15 Combining System Files

Two SPSS^X commands, MATCH FILES and ADD FILES, allow you to combine information from two or more files into a single active file. The MATCH FILES command combines variables from parallel, nonparallel, and table lookup files into one file. The ADD FILES command combines cases from two or more files by concatenating or interleaving the cases.

The MATCH FILES and ADD FILES facilities operate much like transformation commands. The data files are not read and the result file is not created when the MATCH FILES or ADD FILES command is encountered. SPSS^X simply reads the dictionaries of the files and sets up the internal specifications. The result file is built when the data are read by one of the procedure commands or the EXECUTE, SAVE, or SORT CASES commands.

The MATCH FILES command is documented in Sections 15.1 through 15.16, and the ADD FILES command is documented in Sections 15.17 through 15.23.

15.1 THE MATCH FILES COMMAND

The MATCH FILES command combines variables from parallel, nonparallel, and table lookup files. In the simplest match, you can combine two *parallel files,* which have the same cases in the same order but different variables (see Sections 15.2 through 15.5). For example, you can combine file TEST1, containing results for a set of subjects from the first testing period, and file TEST2, containing results for the same set of subjects from the second testing period, as in:

```
MATCH FILES  FILE=TEST1/FILE=TEST2
```

Nonparallel files have more or less overlapping sets of cases. For example, a company may maintain separate payroll files for each quarter, where some employees did not work during all quarters and are not recorded on all files. MATCH FILES can perform an unequal match-merge on nonparallel files if there is a key that uniquely identifies each case (see Sections 15.9 through 15.12). A *table lookup file* contains information at one level that can be "spread" across groups of cases on another file. For example, you may have survey information on households recorded on one file that you want spread to individuals within the households recorded on another file. You can spread information from a table lookup file to case files provided the files have key variables (see Sections 15.13 through 15.15).

In all three applications, you specify the file handles of all files to be matched and whether the file is to be used as a table lookup file. For nonparallel and table lookup matches, you also specify the key variables. One of the input files can be the active file, but the others must be SPSS^X system files. You can rename variables on the input files, and you can drop or reorder variables in the result file. You can also create special variables that indicate the first and last case within each group defined by the key variable(s) and that indicate which input file or files contributed data to each case.

The result file of the match is the new active file. It contains complete dictionary information copied from the input files, including variable names, labels, print and write formats, and missing-value indicators.

15.2 Parallel Files

Parallel files have the same cases in the same order but different variables. One file may contain measures across a set of observations for one time period, and another file may contain measures across the same set of observations for another time period. Or, one file may contain one type of test results across a set of observations and another file a different set of test results for the same observations.

For a parallel match, a FILE subcommand for each input file is the only required specification on the MATCH FILES command. Four optional subcommands can be used with parallel matches.

The RENAME Subcommand. To rename variables on any of the input files before matching, specify the RENAME subcommand. Otherwise, the result file will retain the variable names from the input files. Use RENAME if different variables have the same name on two or more of the input files or if a single variable has several different names (see Section 15.6).

The DROP and KEEP Subcommands. Use DROP and KEEP to include only a subset of variables in the result file. By default, all variables from the matched files are included in the result file (see Section 15.7). KEEP also reorders variables in the result file. By default, all variables are included in the result file in their original order, with variables from the first specified file at the beginning of the result file, those from the second file next, and so forth (see Section 15.8).

The MAP Subcommand. Use MAP to display the names of the variables in the files being matched and the names of the variables being kept in the result file after any renaming, subsetting, or reordering (see Section 15.5).

15.3 The FILE Subcommand

FILE is the only subcommand required for matching parallel files. Use one FILE subcommand for each file in the match. For example, suppose one monitoring device at each reporting station measures particulates in the air, and another device measures various gas pollutants, such as ozone and carbon monoxide. Particulate measures for each reporting station are recorded in one SPSS^X system file, and measures of gas pollutants in another. The same reporting stations are included in each file in the same order. The two files are shown in Table 15.3a.

Table 15.3a Parallel pollution files

Particulate file		Gas file			
STATION	PARTIC	STATION	OZONE	CO	SULFUR
1	15	1	5	2	3
2	1	2	2	1	1
3	4	3	5	3	4
100	8	100	6	3	5

To combine these two files, specify:

```
FILE HANDLE PARTICLE/ file specifications
FILE HANDLE GAS/ file specifications
MATCH FILES  FILE=PARTICLE/FILE=GAS
```

In this example, file handles PARTICLE and GAS are defined on the FILE HANDLE commands and are associated with SPSS^X system files. The resulting active file contains five variables: the station number and the four measures. The PARTICLE file and GAS file are matched case by case. The cases are constructed by first including the variables from the first case in the PARTICLE file (STATION and PARTIC) and then appending the variables for the first case in file GAS. Since STATION is a common variable on both files, only the value from file PARTICLE is included on the result file (see Section 15.11). The process continues until all cases have been read. If the files do not have the same number of cases, the shorter file is extended with system-missing values. Table 15.3b shows the file built from the two files in Table 15.3a.

Table 15.3b The pollution result file

STATION	PARTIC	OZONE	CO	SULFUR
1	15	5	2	3
2	1	2	1	1
3	4	5	3	4
100	8	6	3	5

You can combine up to fifty SPSS^X system files on one MATCH FILES command. You must specify one FILE subcommand for each file being matched. The specification for the FILE subcommand is the file handle of the input system file or an asterisk for the active file (see Section 15.4). Do not include GET commands for the system files that you specify on the FILE subcommands.

15.4 Specifying the Active File

If you want to add variables from a data file to an existing system file, use the DATA LIST command to define the data file as the active file and the MATCH FILES command to combine the active file with the system file. In the following example, PARTICLE is a previously saved system file, and GASDATA is the data obtained from the device measuring gases.

```
FILE HANDLE GASDATA/ file specifications
FILE HANDLE PARTICLE/ file specifications
DATA LIST FILE=GASDATA/1 OZONE 10-12 CO 20-22 SULFUR 30-32

VARIABLE LABELS OZONE 'LEVEL OF OZONE'
  CO 'LEVEL OF CARBON MONOXIDE'
  SULFUR 'LEVEL OF SULFUR DIOXIDE'

MATCH FILES  FILE=PARTICLE/FILE=*

SAVE  OUTFILE=POLLUTE
```

The GASDATA file is defined on the DATA LIST command and variable labels are assigned on the VARIABLE LABELS command. The subcommand FILE=* on the MATCH FILES command specifies the active file, which is now the gas data. FILE=PARTICLE specifies the PARTICLE system file. In this example, the resulting active file is then saved as a system file with the file handle POLLUTE.

To match two data files, first use the DATA LIST command to define the first file and then save it temporarily as a system file using the SAVE command (see Chapter 5). Next, use the DATA LIST command to define the second data file as the active file. Finally use MATCH FILES to combine the two.

Do not use the TEMPORARY command with any active file used as an input file with MATCH FILES (see Chapter 6).

15.5 The MAP Subcommand

For complicated matches or files containing large numbers of variables, the status of the active file can be difficult to ascertain. To list the names of variables on the active file, their order, and the file from which they were obtained, use the MAP subcommand, as in:

```
FILE HANDLE PARTICLE / file specifications
FILE HANDLE GAS / file specifications
MATCH FILES FILE=PARTICLE/
  FILE=GAS/MAP
```

The output displayed by this MAP command is shown in Figure 15.5. Variables are listed in the order they exist in the result file. If variables are renamed, their original names are shown in the source file and the new name appears in the result file. Variables created by IN, FIRST, and LAST are not included in the map since they are automatically attached to end of the file and cannot be dropped (see Sections 15.12 and 15.15).

Figure 15.5 MAP of a simple match

```
MAP OF THE RESULT FILE

RESULT    PARTICLE GAS
------    -------- ---
STATION   STATION  STATION
PARTIC    PARTIC
OZONE              OZONE
CO                 CO
SULFUR             SULFUR
```

The MAP subcommand has no specification field and must be placed after all FILE and RENAME subcommands. It reports the current status of the active file. If you place the MAP subcommand before a KEEP or DROP subcommand, the results of the KEEP or DROP will not be reflected on the MAP. You cannot obtain a map for a match of more than 12 files; the display page is not wide enough.

If you are not sure what the result of a MATCH FILES will be, you can obtain a map on an SPSS^X EDIT job without actually reading the data and executing the match (see Chapter 4).

Usually, you use the MAP subcommand to verify the results of complicated sets of subcommands. See the following sections for examples.

15.6 The RENAME Subcommand

Variables with the same name on two or more of the files being matched are called *common variables*. For parallel matches, MATCH FILES automatically uses the values from the first file named for a common variable. MATCH FILES uses the dictionary information from the first file that has labels or missing-value indicators for the common variable. If the first file named has no such information, MATCH FILES checks the second file, and so forth, searching for dictionary information.

To obtain the values of common variables, use the RENAME subcommand to make all variable names unique across all files being matched. You can also use RENAME to clarify the meaning of variables in the result file even though they are not common variables. The RENAME subcommand must follow the FILE subcommand naming the file that contains the variables you want to rename.

Specify the subcommand RENAME followed by an optional equals sign and the rename specification. To rename one variable, specify the old variable name followed by an equals sign and the new variable name. For example, to rename the variable PARTIC to POLLUTE1, specify:

```
MATCH FILES FILE=PARTICLE/
    RENAME=(PARTIC=POLLUTE1)/
    FILE=GAS/
```

PARTIC is the old name; POLLUTE1 is the new name. When you specify one variable, the parentheses enclosing the specification are optional.

You can rename more than one variable on a RENAME subcommand either by specifying a list of variable names and a list of their new names or by specifying several sets of individual variable specifications. For example, to rename the variables OZONE and CO, specify either

```
MATCH FILES FILE=PARTICLE/
    RENAME=(PARTIC=POLLUTE1)/
  FILE=GAS/
    RENAME=(OZONE=POLLUTE2)(CO=POLLUTE3)
```

or

```
MATCH FILES FILE=PARTICLE/
    RENAME=(PARTIC=POLLUTE1)/
  FILE=GAS/
    RENAME=(OZONE CO=POLLUTE2 POLLUTE3)
```

When you specify lists of variables, the specification must be enclosed in parentheses, and the two variable lists must name or imply the same number of variables. You can use the keyword TO both to refer to consecutive variables to be renamed (on the left side of the equals sign) and to generate new names (on the right side of the equals sign). For example, the RENAME subcommand

```
MATCH FILES FILE=PARTICLE/
    RENAME=(PARTIC=POLLUTE1)/
  FILE=GAS/
    RENAME=(OZONE TO SULFUR=POLLUTE2 TO POLLUTE4)/MAP
```

renames OZONE to POLLUTE2, CO to POLLUTE3, and SULFUR to POLLUTE4 (see Figure 15.6). See Chapter 2 for more information on the distinction between using keyword TO to refer to existing variables and to define new variables.

Figure 15.6 MAP of a match with renamed variables

```
MAP OF THE RESULT FILE

RESULT     PARTICLE GAS
------     -------- ---
STATION    STATION  STATION
POLLUTE1   PARTIC
POLLUTE2            OZONE
POLLUTE3            CO
POLLUTE4            SULFUR
```

You can use more than one RENAME subcommand to rename variables on one file. All renaming specifications in one RENAME subcommand are executed in one operation and a variable is renamed only once. Thus, you can switch variable names, as in:

```
RENAME=(A=B) (B=A)
```

You cannot rename variables to scratch variables (see Chapter 6). After the RENAME subcommand, refer to a renamed variable by its new name.

15.7 The DROP and KEEP Subcommands

By default, all variables from the files being matched are included in the result file. MATCH FILES first copies the variables in order from the first file, then the variables in order from the second file, and so on. Use either the KEEP or DROP subcommands to select a subset of variables. These subcommands apply to the result file and must follow all FILE and RENAME subcommands.

Specify the subcommand DROP or KEEP followed by an optional equals sign and a list of variables. KEEP saves the variables named, and DROP saves the variables not named. The variable list can include individual variable names or variables implied by the keyword TO. If you have renamed variables, specify the new names on the DROP and KEEP subcommands. For example, to exclude the renamed variable POLLUTE4 from the result file, specify:

```
MATCH FILES FILE=PARTICLE/
    RENAME=(PARTIC=POLLUTE1)/
  FILE=GAS/
    RENAME=(OZONE TO SULFUR=POLLUTE2 TO POLLUTE4)/
    DROP=POLLUTE4
```

You cannot use the DROP subcommand with variables created by the IN, FIRST, or LAST subcommand (see Sections 15.12 and 15.15). With the KEEP subcommand, variables are kept in the order they are listed on the subcommand. If you name a variable more than once on the KEEP subcommand, only the first mention of the variable is in effect; all subsequent references to that variable name are ignored.

15.8 Reordering Variables

You may want to reorder the variables in the result file so that you can more conveniently refer to them with the TO keyword on subsequent SPSS^X commands. Since KEEP saves variables in the order they are named, it can be used to reorder variables.

To reorder variables, you can either list the names of all the variables in the order that you want them, or simply list the names of the variables that you want at the beginning of the file in the desired order, followed by the keyword ALL. Keyword ALL must be the last specification on the KEEP subcommand, and it implies all the variables not previously named on the KEEP subcommand. You can use KEEP to reorder variables and DROP to delete variables in the same MATCH FILES command, as in:

```
MATCH FILES FILE=PARTICLE/
    RENAME=(PARTIC=POLLUTE1)/
  FILE=GAS/
    RENAME=(OZONE TO SULFUR=POLLUTE2 TO POLLUTE4)/
    DROP=POLLUTE4/
    KEEP=POLLUTE1 POLLUTE2 POLLUTE3 ALL/MAP
```

The map of the result file produced by this MATCH FILE command is shown in Figure 15.8.

Figure 15.8 MAP from a parallel match

```
MAP OF THE RESULT FILE

RESULT    PARTICLE GAS
------    -------- ---
POLLUTE1  PARTIC
POLLUTE2           OZONE
POLLUTE3           CO
STATION   STATION  STATION
```

15.9 Nonparallel Files

There are two reasons why files may not have a parallel one-to-one case structure: cases in one file may be missing from another; or, cases may be duplicated in one or the other files. MATCH FILES can handle most of these problems if there is a *key*. The key is a variable or set of variables that identifies the cases. As long as the files are sorted in ascending order on the key, cases can be properly matched.

The two subcommands required for nonparallel MATCH FILES are FILE and BY (see Section 15.10). The following subcommands are optional:

The RENAME Subcommand. To rename variables on any of the input files before matching, specify the RENAME subcommand (see Section 15.6).

The DROP and KEEP Subcommands. Use DROP and KEEP to include only a subset of variables in the result file (see Section 15.7). KEEP also reorders the variables in the result file (see Section 15.8).

The MAP Subcommand. Use MAP to display the names of the variables in the files being matched and in the result file after any renaming, subsetting, or reordering (see Section 15.5).

The IN Subcommand. IN creates a logical variable in the result file that flags whether a case was present in the input file. The IN subcommand is associated with the FILE subcommand for each input file (see Section 15.12).

15.10 The FILE and BY Subcommands

To properly match cases from nonparallel files, specify one or more variables as keys for the match. Use the BY subcommand to specify the variables to be used as the keys. You can use any type of variable, including long string variables. When BY is used to name the key variables, cases from one file are matched only with cases from other files having the same values for the key variables.

Table 15.10a Nonparallel employee files

Week 10 file		Week 11 file	
EMPID	HOURS10	EMPID	HOUR11
34	38.5	34	41.5
50	18.5	50	36.5
50	20.5	61	25.0
61	25.0	1015	40.0
1015	35.0	1150	40.0
1150	40.0	4003	15.0
1212	40.0		

For example, consider the two payroll files in Table 15.10a. Each employee has the same identification number in both files. The first file contains hours worked during the tenth week of the quarter. The second file contains hours worked during the eleventh week of the quarter. The employee identification number is the key to the match. Note that Employee 4003 did not work during the tenth week, and Employee 1212 did not work during the eleventh week. In addition, two time cards were submitted for Employee 50 for the tenth week. To combine the files shown in Table 15.10a, specify:

```
MATCH FILES  FILE=WEEK10/FILE=WEEK11/BY=EMPID
```

Table 15.10b shows the combined employee file after matching by EMPID. A period indicates that the system-missing value has been supplied.

Table 15.10b The combined employee file

EMPID	HOURS10	HOURS11
34	38.5	41.5
50	18.5	36.5
50	20.5	.
61	25.0	25.0
1015	35.0	40.0
1150	40.0	40.0
1212	40.0	.
4003		15.0

If a case is missing on one of the files being matched, the variables for that case are set to the system-missing value for numeric variables and to blanks for strings. Employee ID 4003 does not exist in the file for the tenth week, and variable HOURS10 is assigned the system-missing value in the result file for that case.

If several cases in the files have the same value for the key variable(s), they are matched sequentially, and unmatched cases are assigned system-missing values or blanks. For example, the file for the tenth week contains two cases for Employee 50, and the file for the eleventh week contains only one case. Table 15.10b shows that the result file contains two cases for Employee 50, and the second case is assigned a system-missing value for variable HOURS11. In addition, SPSS^{X} prints a warning when duplicate keys are encountered in one or more of the files being matched.

All files must be sorted in ascending order on the key variables, and the key variables must have the same name on all files. There is no way to tell from the data whether the right matches have been made. The matches are right only if the sequence of cases acts as a correct key. If your files are not already sorted, use the SORT CASES command prior to MATCH FILES (see Chapter 13). You can use the RENAME subcommand on MATCH FILES to rename the variables if they do not have the same name on all of your files (see Section 15.6).

Missing values on the key variables are handled the same as valid values. You can match a case with a missing value for the key variable with a case from another file with the same value (whether or not the value is missing on the second file). The BY subcommand must follow the FILE subcommands and any associated RENAME and IN subcommands.

15.11 Common Variables

Variables with the same name on two or more of the files being matched are called common variables. For the values of common variables, MATCH FILES automatically uses the values from the first file named in which a case exists for that variable. It uses the dictionary information from the first file containing value labels, missing values, or a variable label for the common variable. If the first file has no such information, MATCH FILES checks the second file, and so on, seeking dictionary information. You should be certain that the first file with a common variable contains the appropriate dictionary information; otherwise the value of the common variable can come from one file while the dictionary information can come from another.

Table 15.11a shows two files with the common variable B. To combine the files without renaming the common variable B, specify:

```
MATCH FILES  FILE=FIRST/FILE=SECOND/BY=ID
```

Table 15.11b shows the result file. A period indicates that a system-missing value has been supplied. For case identifiers 1, 2, 4, and 5, the value for variable B comes from the first file since it is named first on the MATCH FILES command. For case identifier 3, the value for variable B comes from the second file since that case does not exist on the first file.

Table 15.11a Files with a common variable

File FIRST

ID	A	B
1	5	3
2	1	6
4	4	9
5	2	.

File SECOND

ID	B	C
2	3	4
3	2	5
4	1	7
5	9	8

Table 15.11b Result file from files with a common variable

ID	A	B	C
1	5	3	.
2	1	6	4
3	.	2	5
4	4	9	7
5	2	.	8

To combine the files in Table 15.11a and retain the values for variable B from both files, use the RENAME subcommand to rename variable B on one of the files, as in:

```
MATCH FILES  FILE=FIRST/
  FILE=SECOND/RENAME=B=BB/BY=ID
```

The result file after renaming is shown in Table 15.11c. The result file contains five variables: A and B from the first file, and BB (the renamed B variable) and C from the second file.

Table 15.11c Result file after renaming

ID	A	B	BB	C
1	5	3	.	.
2	1	6	3	4
3	.	.	2	5
4	4	9	1	7
5	2	.	9	8

15.12 The IN Subcommand

When you match nonparallel files, some cases in the result file do not come from all files. For example, in the combined employee file shown in Table 15.10b, the last case is missing on the first file, WEEK10. The system-missing value is supplied on the result file for the variable HOUR10 from that file. Use the IN subcommand to create a new variable on the result file that indicates whether a case was contained on the associated input file. The IN subcommand is optional and applies to the previously named file on the FILE subcommand. The variable created by the IN subcommand has the value 1 for every case where the associated input file contains a case, or the value 0 if no matching case was found on the input file. The IN subcommand has one specification, the name of the flag variable, as in:

```
MATCH FILES  FILE=WEEK10/FILE=WEEK11/IN=INWEEK11/BY=EMPID
```

The IN subcommand creates the variable INWEEK11, which has the value 1 for all cases in the result file that had values in the input file WEEK11 and the value 0 for those cases that were not in file WEEK11.

The variable name for the variable created by the IN subcommand must be different from any other name in the result file, including after renaming, keeping, or dropping variables. When the files are matched, the new variable is added to the result file after all the variables supplied from the input files. The variable created by subcommand IN can be used to screen partially missing cases for subsequent analyses. For example,

```
MATCH FILES  FILE=WEEK10/FILE=WEEK11/IN=INWEEK11/BY=EMPID
SELECT IF  (NOT INWEEK11)
```

selects only the cases in the result file for which there are no matching cases in file WEEK11. Since IN variables have either the value 1 or 0, they can be used as logical expressions where 1=true and 0=false. See Chapter 8 for the use of logical expressions and Chapter 10 for the use of the SELECT IF command.

15.13 Tables and Files

Parallel and nonparallel matches combine files with the same kinds of observations or units of analysis. That is, a case in one file corresponds to a case in another. You can also use MATCH FILES to transfer information from a table lookup file to another file with a different unit of analysis. For example, you can match information about households with persons in the household, unit prices with shipping records to produce billing information, schoolwide reading scores with student records, and so on. In all these examples, a key is used to look up information in the table file and transfer it to the case file. In the household example, each individual in the person file has a variable identifying the household to which she or he belongs. This key variable corresponds to a variable identifying each household in the household file. When the files are matched, information on a household is spread to the cases in the person file with the same value for the key variable.

The TABLE, FILE, and BY subcommands are required to specify a table lookup MATCH FILES (see Section 15.14). The following subcommands are optional:

The RENAME Subcommand. To rename variables on any of the input files before matching, specify the RENAME subcommand (see Section 15.6).

The DROP and KEEP Subcommands. Use DROP and KEEP to include only a subset of variables on the result file (see Section 15.7). KEEP also reorders the variables in the result file (see Section 15.8).

The MAP Subcommand. Use MAP to display the names of the variables in the files being matched and in the result file after any renaming, subsetting, or reordering (see Section 15.5).

The IN Subcommand. IN creates a logical variable that flags in the result file whether each case was present in a particular input file. The IN subcommand is associated with the FILE subcommand for each input file (see Section 15.12).

The FIRST and LAST Subcommands. FIRST and LAST create logical variables that flag the first or last case of a group of cases with the same value on the BY variables (see Section 15.15).

15.14 The FILE, TABLE, and BY Subcommands

Two subcommands are used to name input files for table lookup. Use the FILE subcommand to refer to a file containing cases and the TABLE subcommand to refer to a table lookup file containing information to be supplied to the cases on the case file. Each subcommand has one specification, either the file handle of the file or an asterisk to indicate the active file. You must specify each file to be matched on a separate FILE or TABLE subcommand.

For example, Table 15.14a contains two files. The catalog file contains the supplier name and the unit prices for each product. The orders file contains the number of units shipped. Both files contain the product name, which will be specified as the key in the BY subcommand. The command

```
MATCH FILES  TABLE=CATALOG/FILE=ORDERS/BY=PRODUCT
```

transfers unit price information from the catalog file (the table lookup file) to the order file (the case file). Table 15.14b shows the result file.

Table 15.14a A table and case file

Catalog file

Product	Supplier	Price
Corn Oil	General Products	$1.10
Cottage Cheese	Foods Inc.	$1.95
Cracked Wheat	ABD Dist.	$2.01
Dried Peas	ABD Dist.	$1.45
Sunflower Oil	General Products	$2.98

Orders file

Product	Qty
Cottage Cheese	1200
Dried Peas	1440
Cows Milk	4800
Sunflower Oil	900

Table 15.14b A matched shipping order file

Product	Supplier	Price	Qty
Cottage Cheese	Foods Inc.	$1.95	1200
Dried Peas	ABD Dist.	$1.45	1440
Cows Milk		.	4800
Sunflower Oil	General Products	$2.98	900

As Table 15.14b demonstrates, MATCH FILES treats table lookup files differently from case files. An entry in a table file not matched with an entry in a case file is ignored. For example, cases for corn oil and cracked wheat are not included in the result file shown in Table 15.14b.

A table file cannot have duplicate keys. For example, there is only one entry for each product (the key) in the table file displayed in Table 15.14a. Note also that there is no entry for cows milk in the table file. Thus, blanks are used in place of the supplier's name in the result file.

15.15 The FIRST and LAST Subcommands

You may have files in which several cases have the same values on the key variables. For example, if you are matching individuals with household information (a case file with a table file), more than one individual will usually have the same household identifier. It is sometimes useful to identify either the first or last case in a group sharing a common set of values for the key variables. For example, you may want to do a transformation contingent upon a case being the first case in a group, or you may want to write a specialized report "breaking" on the first or last case in a group.

The FIRST subcommand creates a variable with the value 1 for the first case of each group and the value 0 for all other cases. The LAST subcommand creates a variable with the value 1 for the last case of each group and the value 0 for all other cases. For example, if you are adding household information to a person file, you may want to indicate the first person in each household as the head of the household, as in:

```
MATCH FILES  TABLE=HOUSE/FILE=PERSONS/
  BY=HOUSEID/FIRST=HEAD
```

The variable HEAD contains the value 1 for the first person in each household and the value 0 for all other persons. Assuming that the person file is sorted with the head of household as the first case for each household, variable HEAD identifies the case for the head of household.

The FIRST and LAST subcommands are associated with the result file and must be placed after all FILE and TABLE subcommands and their associated RENAME and IN subcommands. The variable names for the variables created by the FIRST and LAST subcommands must be different from any other names in the result file, including after renaming, keeping, or dropping variables. When the files are matched, the new variables are added to the result file after the variables supplied from the input files and the variables created with IN subcommands.

ANNOTATED EXAMPLE FOR MATCH FILES

In Chapter 14, the Hubbard Consultants Inc. personnel file was aggregated by department. The job below transfers the information in the aggregated file to the employee file, computes the ratios of each employee's salary and raise to the department averages, and runs a breakdown analysis on these ratios by sex of the employee. The SPSS^X commands are

```
FILE HANDLE HUBEMPL/ file specifications
FILE HANDLE AGGFILE/ file specifications
GET FILE  HUBEMPL/KEEP=LOCATN82 DEPT82 HOURLY82 RAISE82 SEX
SORT CASES BY LOCATN82 DEPT82

AGGREGATE  OUTFILE=AGGFILE/
  BREAK=LOCATN82 DEPT82/
  AVGHOUR 'AVERAGE HOURLY WAGE'
  AVGRAISE 'AVERAGE RAISE'=MEAN(HOURLY82 RAISE82)

MATCH FILES  TABLE=AGGFILE/
  FILE=*/BY LOCATN82 DEPT82/
  KEEP AVGHOUR AVGRAISE LOCATN82 DEPT82 SEX HOURLY82 RAISE82/MAP
FILE LABEL COMBINED FILE WITH DEPARTMENT INFORMATION

COMPUTE  HOURDIF=HOURLY82/AVGHOUR
COMPUTE  RAISEDIF=RAISE82/AVGRAISE
BREAKDOWN  HOURDIF RAISEDIF BY SEX
```

- The GET command reads the HUBEMPL system file and keeps the variables LOCATN82, DEPT82, HOURLY82, RAISE82, and SEX in the active file (see Chapter 5).
- The SORT CASES command sorts cases on the variables LOCATN82 and DEPT82 in ascending order (see Chapter 13).
- The AGGREGATE command creates a file aggregated by LOCATN82 and DEPT82 with the two new variables, AVGHOUR and AVGRAISE, indicating the means by location and department for HOURLY82 and RAISE82. The aggregated file is saved as the system file AGGFILE (see Chapter 14).
- The MATCH FILES command specifies a table lookup match with the AGGFILE system file as the table file and the active file (the sorted and subsetted HUBEMPL file) as the case file (see Section 15.14).
- The BY subcommand indicates that the keys for the match are the same variables used for the break variables in AGGREGATE: LOCATN82 and DEPT82 (see Section 15.10).
- The KEEP subcommand specifies the subset and order of variables to be retained on the result file (see Sections 15.7 and 15.8).
- The MAP subcommand provides a listing of the variables in the result file and the two input files (see Section 15.5). The map display is shown in Figure A.
- The FILE LABEL command prints a new label at the top of each page of SPSS^X display output after this command is encountered (see Chapter 5).
- The COMPUTE commands calculate the ratios of each employee's hourly wage and raise to the department averages for wage and raise. The results are stored in the variables HOURDIF and RAISEDIF (see Chapter 6).
- The BREAKDOWN command displays a means breakdown of the ratio variables by sex of employee to determine if there are observed differences between men and women (see Chapter 22). The BREAKDOWN tables are shown in Figure B.

A MAP display from MATCH FILES

```
MAP OF BY VARIABLES

RESULT    AGGFILE  *
-------   -------  -
LOCATN82  LOCATN82 LOCATN82
DEPT82    DEPT82   DEPT82

MAP OF THE RESULT FILE

RESULT    AGGFILE  *
-------   -------  -
AVGHOUR   AVGHOUR
AVGRAISE  AVGRAISE
LOCATN82  LOCATN82 LOCATN82
DEPT82    DEPT82   DEPT82
SEX                SEX
HOURLY82           HOURLY82
RAISE82            RAISE82
```

B BREAKDOWN table display

```
FILE LABEL:  COMBINED FILE WITH DEPARTMENT INFORMATION

------------------ D E S C R I P T I O N   O F   S U B P O P U L A T I O N S -------------
CRITERION VARIABLE   HOURDIF
   BROKEN DOWN BY    SEX          EMPLOYEE'S SEX
------------------------------------------------------------------------------------------

VARIABLE                  CODE    VALUE LABEL              SUM        MEAN      STD DEV     VARIANCE        N

FOR ENTIRE POPULATION                                 145.0000      1.0000       0.4941       0.2442   (   145)

SEX                        1.     MALE                 42.6111      1.1213       0.6747       0.4552   (    38)
SEX                        2.     FEMALE              102.3889      0.9569       0.4070       0.1656   (   107)

  TOTAL CASES =      275
MISSING CASES =      130 OR   47.3 PCT.

FILE LABEL:  COMBINED FILE WITH DEPARTMENT INFORMATION

------------------ D E S C R I P T I O N   O F   S U B P O P U L A T I O N S -------------
CRITERION VARIABLE   RAISEDIF
   BROKEN DOWN BY    SEX          EMPLOYEE'S SEX
------------------------------------------------------------------------------------------

VARIABLE                  CODE    VALUE LABEL              SUM        MEAN      STD DEV     VARIANCE        N

FOR ENTIRE POPULATION                                 138.0000      1.0000       1.6816       2.8279   (   138)

SEX                        1.     MALE                 34.8771      0.9178       2.7326       7.4673   (    38)
SEX                        2.     FEMALE              103.1229      1.0312       1.0578       1.1190   (   100)

  TOTAL CASES =      275
                                  MISSING CASES =      137 OR   49.8 PCT.
```

15.16 The FIRST and LAST Subcommands on One File

You may have one file that has several cases with a single value on a key variable(s), and you want to create a variable that flags the first or last case of the group. To create flag variables for a single file, use the FIRST and LAST subcommands on the MATCH FILES command, as in:

```
MATCH FILES  FILE=PERSONS/BY HOUSEID/FIRST=HEAD
SELECT IF  (HEAD EQ 1)
CROSSTABS  JOBCAT BY SEX
```

The MATCH FILES command replaces the GET command and reads the system file PERSONS. The BY and FIRST subcommands identify the key variable (HOUSEID) and create the variable HEAD with the value 1 for the first case in each household and value 0 for all other cases. The SELECT IF command selects only the cases with value 1 for HEAD, and the CROSSTABS procedure is run on these cases.

15.17 THE ADD FILES COMMAND

The ADD FILES command combines cases from two to fifty SPSS^{X} system files by concatenating or interleaving the cases. For example, you may maintain a separate file for each of three schools with information on students attending that school. To analyze all students in the school, you can combine the cases by concatenating the school files, as in:

```
ADD FILES  FILE=SCHOOL1/FILE=SCHOOL2/FILE=SCHOOL3
```

If the files have keys, ADD FILES can interleave the cases by the key. For example, you may have four files recording information for each employee for each quarter of the fiscal year. You can combine the cases from these files by interleaving the cases according to employee identification number. See Sections 15.18 through 15.20 for a description of concatenating files, and Sections 15.21 through 15.23 for interleaving files.

The syntax for the ADD FILES command is the same as for the MATCH FILES command except the TABLE subcommand is not allowed. A FILE subcommand is required for each input file. For each input file, you can also rename variables and create a variable that indicates whether the case in the result file came from that file. You can select a subset of variables and reorder variables in the result file. The result file is the new active file, and it contains complete dictionary information, including variable names, labels, print and write formats, and missing-value indicators, copied from the input files.

15.18 Concatenating Files

To *concatenate* two or more files, that is, add the cases from one file to the end of the other, use the ADD FILES command. A FILE subcommand for each input file to be concatenated is the only required specification on the ADD FILES command (see Section 15.19). Each FILE subcommand specifies the file handle of the input system file or an asterisk to indicate the active file.

Optional subcommands are the RENAME subcommand, the DROP and KEEP subcommands, the MAP subcommand, and the IN subcommand (see Section 15.20).

15.19 The FILE Subcommand

The FILE subcommand is the only required ADD FILES subcommand when you are concatenating files. For example, suppose you have two SPSS^{X} system files on two schools, each containing test scores for students.

These two files are shown in Table 15.19a. To concatenate these files, specify:

```
FILE HANDLE SCHOOL1/ file specifications
FILE HANDLE SCHOOL2/ file specifications
ADD FILES FILE=SCHOOL1/FILE=SCHOOL2
```

The result file contains three variables: the student identification number, reading scores, and math scores. The result file contains all the cases from the SCHOOL1 file followed by all the cases from the SCHOOL2 file. Table 15.19b shows the result file. To save the result file (the new active file) as a permanent system file, you must use a SAVE command (see Chapter 5).

Table 15.19a School files

School1 file

STUDENT	READ	MATH	GRADE
25	350	425	7
27	425	375	8
30	475	485	8
35	375	400	9

School2 file

STUDENT	READ	MATH	GRADE
20	250	300	7
25	325	225	9
27	300	375	9

Table 15.19b Concatenated school files

STUDENT	READ	MATH	GRADE
25	350	425	7
27	425	375	8
30	475	485	8
35	375	400	9
20	325	300	7
25	325	335	9
27	300	375	9

You can combine up to fifty SPSS^X system files on one ADD FILES command. You must specify one FILE subcommand for each file being added. The specification for the FILE subcommand is the file handle of the input system file or an asterisk for the active file. Do not include GET commands for the system files that you specify on the FILE subcommand. The TEMPORARY command cannot be used with any active file that is used as input with ADD FILES (see Chapter 6).

If you want to add cases from a data file to an existing system file, use the DATA LIST command to define the data file as the active file and the ADD FILES command to combine the active file with the system file.

15.20 Optional Subcommands

In addition to the required FILE subcommand, you can use optional subcommands to rename variables, save a subset of variables, reorder variables, create a variable indicating whether a case came from a particular input file, or produce a map of the result file and the source files. All of these subcommands are the same as those used on the MATCH FILES command.

The RENAME Subcommand. Like MATCH FILES, ADD FILES takes the dictionary information for a common variable from the first file that has labels or missing-value indicators for that variable. The value for the variable always comes from the file where each case resides; however, the dictionary information can come from another file.

Usually, most or all of the variables in the files being combined with ADD FILES will be common variables. However, if the same variable does not have the same name on all input files, or if different variables have the same name, you can use the RENAME subcommand to rename the variables. For example, suppose that the variable measuring reading scores was named VERBAL on the SCHOOL1 file. The command

```
ADD FILES FILE=SCHOOL1/RENAME=(VERBAL=READ)/
  FILE=SCHOOL2
```

renames the variable VERBAL to READ on file SCHOOL1. The result file is the same as the one shown in Table 15.19b. See Section 15.6 for a complete discussion of the syntax for the RENAME subcommand.

The DROP and KEEP Subcommands. By default, all variables from the files being combined are included in the result file. If a variable is not common across all files, the cases that do not reside on the file containing the variable are assigned the system-missing value on the variable. You may want to delete those variables that are not common across all files being combined or to select a subset of common variables. Use either the DROP or KEEP subcommand to select a subset of variables to be retained on the result file. DROP and KEEP must follow the FILE and RENAME subcommands on the ADD FILES command. See Section 15.7 for a complete discussion of the DROP and KEEP subcommands.

Reordering Variables. By default, all variables from the files being added are included in the result file in the same order as in the input files. Use the KEEP subcommand to reorder variables on the result file. If variables are not in the same order across files to be concatenated, use KEEP to reorder them (see Section 15.8). For example, if variable MATH was recorded before READ on the SCHOOL2 file, you would specify:

```
ADD FILES FILE=SCHOOL1/RENAME=(VERBAL=READ)/
  FILE=SCHOOL2/KEEP=STUDENT READ MATH GRADE
```

The MAP Subcommand. Use the MAP subcommand to describe the result file. The map lists the names of the variables on the result file, their order, their source file, and their original names. For example, to produce a map of the result file for the combined SCHOOL file, specify:

```
ADD FILES FILE=SCHOOL1/RENAME=(VERBAL=READ)/
  FILE=SCHOOL2/KEEP=STUDENT READ MATH GRADE/MAP
```

The map is shown in Figure 15.20.

Figure 15.20 MAP of the concatenated school files

```
MAP OF THE RESULT FILE

RESULT    SCHOOL1   *
------    -------   -
STUDENT   STUDENT   STUDENT
READ      VERBAL    READ
MATH      MATH      MATH
GRADE     GRADE     GRADE
```

You must place the MAP subcommand after the FILE and RENAME subcommands. If you place it before a KEEP or DROP subcommand, the results of the KEEP or DROP will not be reflected on the MAP. You cannot obtain a map for an ADD FILES of more than 12 files; the display page is not wide enough. You can use the MAP subcommand on an SPSS^{X} EDIT job to check the result of renaming, reordering, or subsetting before running the job with your data (see Chapter 4).

The IN Subcommand. When you combine files using the ADD FILES command, you might want to identify whether a case came from a particular file. Use the IN subcommand to create a variable on the result file that flags whether a case was contained on the associated input file. The IN subcommand applies to the previously named file on the FILE subcommand and creates a variable that has the value 1 for every case that came from the associated input file and the value 0 if the case was not in that file. For example, to create the variable INSCH1 that has the value 1 for all students in SCHOOL1 and the value 0 for all students in SCHOOL2, specify:

```
ADD FILES FILE=SCHOOL1/IN=INSCH1/
  FILE=SCHOOL2/MAP
```

The variable name for the variable created by the IN subcommand must be different from any other name in the result file, including after renaming, keeping, or dropping variables. The new variable is added to the result file after variables supplied from the input files.

15.21 Interleaving Files

You may want to combine cases from two or more files by interleaving the cases according to the values of a *key*. The key variable(s) must exist on all files being combined and the cases must be sorted in ascending order on the values of this variable in all files being combined. Two subcommands, FILE and BY, are required to interleave cases from two or more files. Optional subcommands are RENAME, KEEP, DROP, MAP, IN, FIRST, and LAST.

15.22 The FILE and BY Subcommands

The two ADD FILES subcommands required for interleaving files are FILE and BY. FILE specifies each file being interleaved, and BY lists the key variables. For example, consider the two files in Table 15.19a. The students in each file are identified by their grade in school and the files are sorted in ascending order on this variable. To interleave the cases in the school files by the grade in school of each student, specify:

```
ADD FILES FILE=SCHOOL1/FILE=SCHOOL2/
  BY GRADE
```

Table 15.22 shows the combined file using GRADE as the key variable. The cases and variables in the file are the same as in Table 15.19b, the result of concatenating the files. However, when combining the files with the key variable, the cases in the result file are ordered by GRADE. All cases from the first file with a value on the key variable are included on the result file followed by cases from the second file with the same value, then all cases from the first file with the next value on the key variable, and so forth, interleaving the cases from the input files according to the values of the key variable. For example, Student 25 in grade 7 from SCHOOL1 file is the first case in the result file, followed by the first case from the SCHOOL2 file, Student 20 also with the value 7 for GRADE. Then the two students from SCHOOL1 file in grade 8 are included in the result file, followed by the case from SCHOOL1 and the two cases from SCHOOL2 in grade 9.

Table 15.22 Interleaved school files

STUDENT	READ	MATH	GRADE
25	350	425	7
20	250	300	7
27	425	375	8
30	475	485	8
35	375	400	9
25	325	225	9
27	300	375	9

You can specify multiple key variables on the BY subcommand as long as all key variables have the same name on all files being combined, and all input files are sorted in ascending order on the key variables. If your files are not already sorted, use the SORT CASES command prior to ADD FILES (see Chapter 13). You can use the RENAME subcommand on ADD FILES to rename the variables if they do not have the same name on all of your files.

The BY subcommand must follow all FILE subcommands and any associated RENAME and IN subcommands.

15.23 Optional Subcommands

In addition to the required FILE and BY subcommands, you can use the following optional subcommands when interleaving files.

The RENAME Subcommand. Usually the files that you are interleaving with ADD FILES will have all or most of the variables as common variables. However, if the same variable is stored under different names on one or more files, use RENAME to rename them to a common variable. For example, suppose that the grade-level variable was named LEVEL in the SCHOOL2 file. You would need to change the name of the variable to GRADE before you can use it as a key variable, as in:

```
ADD FILES FILE=SCHOOL1/FILE=SCHOOL2/RENAME=(LEVEL=GRADE)/
    BY GRADE
```

See Section 15.6 for a complete discussion of RENAME.

The DROP and KEEP Subcommands. By default, all variables from the files being combined are included in the result file. If a variable is not common across all files, cases that do not reside on the file containing the variable are assigned the system-missing value on that variable. Use either DROP or KEEP to delete those variables that are not common across all files being interleaved or to select a subset of common variables (see Section 15.7).

Reordering Variables. The KEEP subcommand can also be used to reorder variables on the result file. If variables are not in the same order across files to be interleaved, you can use KEEP on one or more of the files to reorder them (see Section 15.8).

The MAP Subcommand. Use the MAP subcommand to describe the result file. The map lists the names of the variables on the result file, their order, the file from which they came, and their original names (see Section 15.5).

The IN Subcommand. Use IN to identify whether a case came from a particular file. The IN subcommand applies to the previously named file on the FILE subcommand and creates a variable that has the value 1 for every case that came from the associated input file and the value 0 if the case was not in that file. For example, you might want to create a variable using the IN subcommand that indicates whether a student is enrolled in SCHOOL1 or SCHOOL2 (see Section 15.20).

The FIRST and LAST Subcommands. Occasionally, the result file from an ADD FILES using the BY subcommand will have more than one case for each value or combination of values for the key variable(s). For example, the combined school file has two students in grade 7, three students in grade 8, and two students in grade 9 (see Table 15.22).

It is sometimes useful to identify the first or last case of a group sharing a common value for the key variable(s). For example, the first student listed in each grade in the SCHOOL1 file may be the highest scoring student for the entire school district. Use the FIRST or LAST subcommand to create a logical variable that flags, respectively, the first or last case in each group identified by a particular value for the key variable. For example, to create the variable HISCORE in the combined school file, specify:

```
ADD FILES FILE=SCHOOL1/FILE=SCHOOL2/
    BY GRADE/FIRST=HISCORE
```

The new variable HISCORE is added to the result file after all variables from the input files and has the value 1 for the first case in each grade in the result file and the value 0 for all other cases.

The FIRST and LAST subcommands are associated with the result file. They must be placed after all FILE subcommands and any associated RENAME and IN subcommands.

ANNOTATED EXAMPLE FOR ADD FILES

The following set of commands adds the cases from the raw data file, SCHOOL2, to the system file, SCHOOL1. The result file is a system file, SCHOOL. The SPSS^X commands are

```
TITLE ADDING SCHOOL2 DATA TO SCHOOL1 SYSTEM FILE
FILE HANDLE SCHOOL/ file specifications
FILE HANDLE SCHOOL1/ file specifications
FILE HANDLE SCHOOL2/ file specifications
DATA LIST FILE=SCHOOL2/STUDENT 1-2 MATH 7-9 READ 4-6 GRADE 11

ADD FILES FILE=SCHOOL1/RENAME=(VERBAL=READ)/
  FILE=*/KEEP=STUDENT READ MATH GRADE/MAP

SAVE OUTFILE=SCHOOL
```

- The TITLE command prints a title at the top of each page of output.
- The FILE HANDLE commands assign handles to refer to the input and output files for this job.
- The DATA LIST command defines the variables for the raw data file SCHOOL2.
- The ADD FILES command adds the cases from the active file to the system file. The first FILE subcommand refers to the system file SCHOOL1. The RENAME subcommand instructs SPSS^X to rename the variable VERBAL to READ on file SCHOOL1.
- The second FILE subcommand refers to the active file (*) defined by the previous DATA LIST command. The KEEP subcommand requests that the four variables STUDENT, READ, MATH, and GRADE be included in the result file.
- The MAP subcommand requests a map of the result file.
- The SAVE command saves the result file into the system file SCHOOL.

MAP of the result file

```
MAP OF THE RESULT FILE

RESULT    SCHOOL1   *
-------   -------   -
STUDENT   STUDENT   STUDENT
READ      VERBAL    READ
MATH      MATH      MATH
GRADE     GRADE     GRADE
```

SAVE SCSS OUTFILE = handle

[/KEEP = {**ALL** | varlist}] [/DROP = varlist]

[/RENAME = (old varlist = new varlist)]

GET SCSS MASTERFILE = handle [/WORKFILE = handle]

[/VARIABLES = {**ALL** | varlist | $varlist | $ALL | (old varlist = new varlist)}]

EXPORT OUTFILE = handle

[/KEEP = {**ALL** | varlist}] [/DROP = varlist]

[/RENAME = (old varlist = new varlist) . . .]

[/MAP]

[/DIGITS = number]

IMPORT FILE = handle

[/KEEP = {**ALL** | varlist}] [/DROP = varlist]

[/RENAME = (old varlist = new varlist) . . .]

[/MAP]

THE SCSS INTERFACE, **16.1**
- The SAVE SCSS Command, **16.2**
  - The OUTFILE Subcommand, **16.3**
  - The KEEP and DROP Subcommands, **16.4**
  - The RENAME Subcommand, **16.5**
  - The Display Output, **16.6**
- The GET SCSS Command, **16.7**
  - The MASTERFILE Subcommand, **16.8**
  - The WORKFILE Subcommand, **16.9**
  - The VARIABLES Subcommand, **16.10**

TRANSPORTING SPSS^X SYSTEM FILES, **16.11**
- Considerations for Portable Files, **16.12**
- Characteristics of Portable Files, **16.13**
  - Character Translation, **16.14**
- The EXPORT Command, **16.15**
  - The KEEP and DROP Subcommands, **16.16**
  - The RENAME Subcommand, **16.17**
  - The MAP Subcommand, **16.18**
  - The DIGITS Subcommand, **16.19**
- The IMPORT Command, **16.20**
  - The KEEP and DROP Subcommands, **16.21**
  - The RENAME Subcommand, **16.22**
  - The MAP Subcommand, **16.23**

Chapter 16 File Interfaces

SPSS^X provides two types of file interfaces. You can interface with the SCSS™ Conversational System via the GET SCSS and SAVE SCSS commands. The SAVE SCSS command saves an SPSS^X system file in an SCSS masterfile format (see Sections 16.10 through 16.6). The GET SCSS command reads SCSS masterfiles and workfile/masterfile combinations. This command is discussed in Section 16.7 through 16.10. In addition, you can write a portable file that includes all of the information of an SPSS^X system file, including the dictionary and the data. This portable file can be read by SPSS^X on another computer. The EXPORT command writes portable files and the IMPORT command reads portable files. These commands are discussed in Sections 16.11 through 16.14.

16.1 THE SCSS INTERFACE

The interface between SPSS^X and the SCSS™ Conversational System is entirely through SCSS files written and read by SPSS^X. Use the SAVE SCSS command to create an SCSS masterfile from SPSS^X and the GET SCSS command to read an SCSS masterfile (or workfile and masterfile) into SPSS^X. SCSS neither reads nor writes SPSS^X system files.

The following documentation assumes a knowledge of the SCSS system, including workfiles, masterfiles, variable types, variable masks, and so forth.

16.2 The SAVE SCSS Command

You can save an SCSS masterfile at any point after you have created your SPSS^X active file. For example, to save the file defined in Chapter 3 as an SCSS masterfile, specify:

```
FILE HANDLE HUBDATA/ file specifications
DATA LIST  FILE=HUBDATA RECORDS=3
  /1 EMPLOYID 1-5 MOHIRED YRHIRED 12-15 DEPT79 TO DEPT82 SEX 16-20
  /2 SALARY79 TO SALARY82 6-25 HOURLY81 HOURLY82 42-53(2) PROMO81 72
     AGE 54-55 RAISE82 66-70
  /3 JOBCAT 6 NAME 25-48 (A)

MISSING VALUES  DEPT79 TO SALARY82, AGE (0)
  HOURLY81, HOURLY82, RAISE82 (-999) JOBCAT (9)

VARIABLE LABELS  YRHIRED 'YEAR OF FIRST HIRING'
  DEPT82 'DEPARTMENT OF EMPLOYMENT IN 1982'
  SALARY82 'YEARLY SALARY IN 1982'
  JOBCAT 'JOB CATEGORIES'

VALUE LABELS  DEPT79 TO DEPT82  0 'NOT REPORTED' 1 'ADMINISTRATIVE'
          2 'PROJECT DIRECTORS' 3 'CHICAGO OPERATIONS'
          4 'ST LOUIS OPERATIONS'/
  SEX 1 'MALE' 2 'FEMALE'/
  JOBCAT 1 'OFFICIALS & MANAGERS' 2 'PROFESSIONALS' 3 'TECHNICIANS'
          4 'OFFICE AND CLERICAL' 5 'CRAFTSMEN' 6 'SERVICE WORKERS'

FREQUENCIES VARIABLES=SEX

COMPUTE PCTRAISE=RAISE82/SALARY82*100

FILE HANDLE HUBOUT/ file specifications
SAVE SCSS OUTFILE=HUBOUT
```

The OUTFILE subcommand is discussed in Section 16.3. The display output from the SAVE SCSS command, including the DROP and RENAME subcommands discussed in Sections 16.4 and 16.5, is shown in Section 16.6.

Since SAVE SCSS saves the current active file, it saves the dictionary information and the data in their form at the point SAVE SCSS is encountered. This includes all permanent transformations and any temporary transformations made just prior to the SAVE SCSS command.

- SCSS does not support string variables and they are not saved. SPSS^X informs you which variables will not be saved (see Figure 16.6a).
- The system-missing value for numeric variables is recoded to a value at one end of the range (usually the highest value plus one) for each variable. Look in the variable-by-variable listing in your SPSS^X display output for the missing value selected for each variable (see Figure 16.6b).
- In converting from double precision in SPSS^X to single precision in SCSS, numeric values are usually truncated (SPSS^X actually does a mixed mode assignment which may result in rounding in some operating-system environments).
- SCSS has some reserved keywords that are not reserved in SPSS^X, so variables with the names AGAINST, ON, SPSS, and SPSS0001 will not be saved. They can be renamed using the RENAME subcommand (see Section 16.5).

16.3 The OUTFILE Subcommand

The OUTFILE subcommand is required and must be first. It specifies the file handle of the masterfile to be saved. You must define the file to your operating system on a FILE HANDLE command, the specifications for which depend on your machine and operating system (see the INFO command in Chapter 2).

16.4 The KEEP and DROP Subcommands

Following the OUTFILE subcommand, you can specify a list of variables to be kept or dropped before saving your file. For example, to drop a list of variables before saving the masterfile, specify:

```
FILE HANDLE HUBOUT/ file specifications
SAVE SCSS OUTFILE=HUBOUT/
  DROP=DEPT79 TO DEPT81, SALARY79 TO SALARY81, HOURLY81
```

The DROP and KEEP subcommands affect only the file written with the SAVE SCSS command. Variables dropped (or variables not kept) within the SAVE SCSS procedure are still available on the active file. Slashes are required between subcommands.

In addition, you can use the KEEP subcommand to control the order in which variables are written onto the SCSS masterfile. If you use a KEEP subcommand, variables are written onto the masterfile in the order named. You can name a subset of the variables followed by the keyword ALL. This will write the variables specifically named in the order specified followed by the rest of the variables in the active file in their order on the active file.

16.5 The RENAME Subcommand

To rename variables saved on the SCSS masterfile, use the RENAME subcommand, as in:

```
FILE HANDLE HUBOUT/ file specifications
SAVE SCSS OUTFILE=HUBOUT/
  DROP=DEPT79 TO DEPT81, SALARY79 TO SALARY81, HOURLY81/
  RENAME=(DEPT82,SALARY82,HOURLY82,PROMO81=DEPT,SALARY,HOURLY,PROMO)
```

This subcommand renames DEPT82 to DEPT, SALARY82 to SALARY, and so forth. The format of the RENAME command is *old names = new names* enclosed in parentheses. If you use variable lists the lists on each side of the equals signs must specify the same number of variables. Both lists can employ TO conventions, the old variable list implying a list of consecutive variables from the SCSS file and the new variable list creating a set of names, as in VAR01 TO VAR99.

Alternatively, you can rename variables one at a time, each pair enclosed in optional parentheses, as in:

```
FILE HANDLE HUBOUT/ file specifications
SAVE SCSS OUTFILE=HUBOUT/
  DROP=DEPT79 TO DEPT81, SALARY79 TO SALARY81, HOURLY81/
  RENAME=(DEPT82=DEPT) (SALARY82=SALARY) (HOURLY82=HOURLY)
  (PROMO81=PROMO)
```

Variables that have been renamed retain their variable and value labels. Renaming variables within the SAVE SCSS procedure does not rename them on the active file. However, if you rename a variable and then list it on a subsequent KEEP or DROP subcommand on SAVE SCSS, use the new name. Subcommands must be separated by slashes.

16.6 The Display Output

The first piece of information displayed as a result of the SAVE SCSS command shown in Section 16.5 is shown in Figure 16.6a. SPSS^X tells you which string variables are not going to be saved, the number of variables to be saved, and the total number of variables possible given the memory available.

Figure 16.6a SAVE SCSS messages

```
 27  0          FILE HANDLE HUBOUT/NAME='HUBEMPL SCSSMF'
 28  0          SAVE SCSS OUTFILE=HUBOUT/
 29  0            DROP=DEPT79 TO DEPT81, SALARY79 TO SALARY81, HOURLY81/
 30  0            RENAME=(DEPT82,SALARY82,HOURLY82,PROMO81=DEPT,SALARY,HOURLY,PROMO)

'NAME     ' IS A STRING VARIABLE AND WILL NOT BE SAVED.


WORKSPACE ALLOWS FOR 1425 VARIABLES.   12 VARIABLES ARE TO BE KEPT.
```

SPSS^X then produces a table of variable names that are to be saved, their SCSS type (DISCRETE or CONTINUOUS), the number of cases that can be compressed per word, the valid cases, minimum and maximum values encountered reading the data, and the value selected to replace the SPSS^X system-missing value (see Figure 16.6b).

Figure 16.6b Table of variables

VARIABLE	LABEL	TYPE	CASES /WORD	VALID CASES	MINIMUM	MAXIMUM	SYSMISS RESULT
EMPLOYID		DISCRETE	2	275	1801.00	43902.00	
MOHIRED		DISCRETE	4	275	1.00	12.00	
YRHIRED	YEAR OF FIRST HIRING	DISCRETE	4	275	48.00	81.00	
DEPT	DEPARTMENT OF EMPLOYMENT IN 1982	DISCRETE	4	145	0.0	4.00	
SEX		DISCRETE	4	275	1.00	2.00	
SALARY	YEARLY SALARY IN 1982	DISCRETE	2	145	0.0	50700.00	
HOURLY		CONTINUOUS	1	145	-999.00	26.00	
PROMO		DISCRETE	4	275	0.0	9.00	
AGE		DISCRETE	4	272	0.0	69.00	
RAISE82		DISCRETE	2	138	-5739.00	11700.00	
JOBCAT	JOB CATEGORIES	DISCRETE	4	275	1.00	4.00	
PCTRAISE		CONTINUOUS	1	138	-98.44	50.00	50.00

Finally, SPSS^X tells you if the file was saved and the internal file name (see Figure 16.6c). It also repeats the number of cases and the variable names in alphabetical order (including special SCSS variables SPSS and SPSS0001), and tells you if any additional numeric variables were dropped because alphanumeric or extreme values were encountered when the data were read.

Figure 16.6c File messages

```
SCSS MASTERFILE 'MO2NOV82' SAVED WITH    275 CASES.
SORTED LIST OF VARIABLES SAVED:

 9 AGE           4 DEPT           1 EMPLOYID       7 HOURLY        11 JOBCAT
 2 MOHIRED      13 PCTRAISE       8 PROMO         10 RAISE82        6 SALARY
 5 SEX           0 SPSS          14 SPSS0001       3 YRHIRED

 0 VARIABLES WITH ALPHA OR EXTREME VALUES WERE DROPPED.
```

16.7 The GET SCSS Command

You can read an SCSS masterfile or a workfile/masterfile combination in SPSS^{X} using the GET SCSS command, as in:

```
FILE HANDLE HUBIN/ file specifications
GET SCSS MASTERFILE=HUBIN
FREQUENCIES VARIABLES=MOHIRED TO SEX, JOBCAT
```

This set of commands retrieves the SCSS masterfile saved in Sections 16.2 through 16.6. The MASTERFILE subcommand is discussed in Section 16.8. The frequency table for variable SEX from this command is shown in Figure 16.7a.

Figure 16.7a Frequency table from the SCSS masterfile

```
FILE: FILE BUILT VIA GET SCSS

SEX

                                                              VALID      CUM
 VALUE LABEL                   VALUE  FREQUENCY  PERCENT    PERCENT  PERCENT

MALE                               1         83     30.2       30.2     30.2
FEMALE                             2        192     69.8       69.8    100.0
                                          -------  -------    -------
                               TOTAL        275    100.0      100.0

VALID CASES      275       MISSING CASES      0
```

SPSS^{X} can encounter problems with missing values because SPSS^{X} and SCSS handle missing values differently. First, SCSS allows more than three missing values. In addition, SCSS variables can have missing-value ranges that include valid values. Also, SCSS can use alphabetical ranges to declare missing values. Problem numeric values will be recoded to the system-missing value and problem alphabetical values will be recoded to blanks. Furthermore, in SCSS a value can be missing for some cases (via value revision) and not for other cases. SPSS^{X} considers such a value missing for all cases when the file is read using GET SCSS. In any case, SPSS^{X} informs you what has been done, as shown in Figure 16.7b.

Figure 16.7b Missing-value message

```
          MIS VAL          RESULT
VARIABLE  PROBLEM           VALUE  OBSERVED VALUES

AGE       TOO MANY            . M      69.00
```

The print and write formats for numeric variables are based on the length of the values. Variables copied with original alphanumeric values have print and write formats of A1, A2, or A4 for variables with three or four characters. (Alphanumeric values cannot occur in a variable in a masterfile created using the SAVE SCSS command in SPSS^{X} but can occur in a masterfile defined directly in SCSS where the original values are alphanumeric but were revised as the masterfile was created.)

16.8 The MASTERFILE Subcommand

The MASTERFILE subcommand specifies the file handle of the masterfile to be read. You must define the file to your operating system on a FILE HANDLE command. The specifications depend on your machine and operating system (see the INFO command in Chapter 2). If you specify the masterfile alone, only masterfile information is copied. Revisions or additions kept on any of the workfiles that point to that masterfile are not available to SPSS^X unless you also specify a WORKFILE subcommand. See Section 16.9 for the additional specification of a workfile.

16.9 The WORKFILE Subcommand

Optionally, you can use the WORKFILE subcommand to specify the file handle of a workfile associated with the masterfile you are reading, as in:

```
FILE HANDLE MHUBIN/ file specifications
FILE HANDLE WHUBIN/ file specifications
GET SCSS WORKFILE=WHUBIN/ MASTERFILE=MHUBIN
FREQUENCIES VARIABLES=MOHIRED TO SEX, JOBCAT
```

You must define the workfile to your operating system on a FILE HANDLE command.

If you specify the workfile in addition to the masterfile, SPSS^X builds the active file to reflect changes recorded on the workfile including labels, revisions to existing variables, and computed variables. For example, variable SEX was revised in SCSS by assigning new labels and by changing the value for females from 2 to 0. Value 0 was labeled WOMEN and value 1 was labeled MEN. Compare the table produced from workfile information (Figure 16.9) with the table produced from the masterfile alone (Figure 16.7a).

Figure 16.9 Frequency table from the SCSS workfile

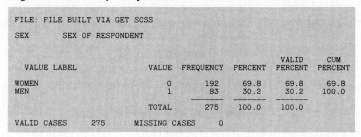

```
FILE: FILE BUILT VIA GET SCSS
SEX       SEX OF RESPONDENT

                                                          VALID      CUM
  VALUE LABEL                 VALUE  FREQUENCY  PERCENT  PERCENT  PERCENT

WOMEN                             0        192     69.8     69.8     69.8
MEN                               1         83     30.2     30.2    100.0
                                      --------  -------  -------
                              TOTAL        275    100.0    100.0

VALID CASES       275       MISSING CASES     0
```

You can specify the WORKFILE and MASTERFILE subcommands in any order. The slash between these subcommands is optional. If you specify the workfile alone, SPSS^X will try to locate the masterfile but will not always succeed (depending on the completeness of the specification on the workfile and on your operating system).

16.10 The VARIABLES Subcommand

To limit the number of variables SPSS^X copies from the SCSS files, use the VARIABLES subcommand, as in:

```
FILE HANDLE MHUBIN/ file specifications
FILE HANDLE WHUBIN/ file specifications
GET SCSS WORKFILE=WHUBIN/ MASTERFILE=MHUBIN/
  VARIABLES=MOHIRED TO SEX, JOBCAT
FREQUENCIES VARIABLES=ALL
```

- Variables are copied in the order specified on the VARIABLES subcommand.

- Variable name THRU is allowed in SCSS but not SPSS^X, so it must be renamed.
- Keywords ALL and $ALL are recognized. Keyword ALL is the default if a workfile is specified. Keyword $ALL specifies the unrevised masterfile version of all of the variables.

If you also want to rename the variables you are reading, use the *old name = new name* format enclosed in optional parentheses, as in:

```
FILE HANDLE MHUBIN/ file specifications
FILE HANDLE WHUBIN/ file specifications
GET SCSS WORKFILE=WHUBIN/ MASTERFILE=MHUBIN/
  VARIABLES=MOHIRED TO SEX ($SEX=SEX$) JOBCAT
FREQUENCIES VARIABLES=ALL
```

This example shows use of the dollar sign to signal to SCSS that you want the unrevised masterfile version of variable SEX. Since variable names beginning with dollar signs are not allowed in SPSS^X, the variable has to be renamed.

If you have a list of variables you want to rename in a single specification, the parentheses are required, as in:

```
VARIABLES=(DEPT,SALARY,HOURLY,PROMO=DEPT82,SALARY82,
           HOURLY82,PROMO81)
```

Variable DEPT is renamed DEPT82, SALARY is renamed SALARY82, and so forth. The lists must contain the same number of variables. Both lists can employ TO conventions, the old variable list implying a list of consecutive variables from the SCSS file and the new variable list creating a set of names, such as VAR01 TO VAR99.

16.11 TRANSPORTING SPSS^X SYSTEM FILES

You can read and write portable data files with SPSS^X. A portable file contains all of the data and dictionary information stored in the system file from which it is created. Use portable files to transport data from SPSS^X system files created on one machine to another conversion of SPSS^X. If you are sending data to an installation using the same machine, send an SPSS^X system file. A system file is cheaper to process than a portable file. To write portable files, use the EXPORT command (see Sections 16.15 through 16.19). To read portable files, use the IMPORT command (see Sections 16.20 through 16.14).

16.12 Considerations for Portable Files

When you plan to send a data file to another installation, the portable file format will take care of most potential problems. However, before you write your portable file you should know certain standards for tapes at the installation where the portable file will be read.

If you are sending data on magnetic tape, make sure that the tape drives can read the tape you are sending. You should know the following characteristics of tapes before writing the portable file:

- The number of tracks—either 7 or 9.
- The tape density—200, 556, 800, 1600, or 6250 bits per inch (BPI).
- Parity—even or odd. You need to know this only if you are writing a 7-track tape.
- Tape labels—labeled or unlabeled. Check whether the site can use tape labels. Also make sure that the site has the ability to read multivolume tape files if the file you are writing will use more than one tape.
- Blocksize—the maximum blocksize the receiving installation can accept.

If you do not know these characteristics, a tape written with the following characteristics can be read at most installations: 9-track, 1600 BPI, unlabeled, and with a blocksize of 3200 characters. We do not guarantee that a tape written with these characteristics will be read successfully by the receiving installation. The best policy is to know the acceptable characteristics at the receiving installation.

16.13 Characteristics of Portable Files

Portable files contain all the information in an SPSS^X system file, including both the dictionary and the data. The dictionary contains variable and value labels, missing-value flags, and printing and writing formats for each variable. Also included on the portable file is the file label, the name of the originating installation, the name, release, and version of the originating software, and the date and time the portable file was created. Portable files have 80-character record lengths so that they can be transmitted over data links. Portable files are character files, not binary files.

You can check that the tape you have received is an SPSS^X portable file by dumping the first few records. If you have a copy of a portable file, one of these records will contain the words "SPSS^X Portable File." Portable files never need character translation. However, a portable file will still be readable after character translation, but depending on the character set in use, some characters in labels and in string data may be lost. For example, if you transport a file from an installation using a seven-bit ASCII character set to an installation using a six-bit ASCII character set, there may be characters on the file for which there are no matching characters in six-bit ASCII (see Section 16.14).

16.14 Character Translation

Your installation may not use the same character set as the installation where the portable file was written. Where possible, SPSS^X translates characters from the portable file to the character set in use at your installation. If there is no matching character, SPSS^X will generate an appropriate nonprintable character (the null character for most character sets). For a complete display of the character set translations available with the IMPORT and EXPORT commands, see Appendix C. A blank space in the table means that there is no matching character for that character set, and an appropriate nonprintable character will be generated by SPSS^X when you import the file.

16.15 The EXPORT Command

Use the EXPORT command to create a portable file. An SPSS^X portable file is a file that can be read on a machine other than the one on which it was created. The EXPORT command is very much like the SAVE command. It can occur in the same position in the command file as the SAVE command and saves the current active file. This includes the results of all permanent transformations and any temporary transformations made just prior to the EXPORT command. The active file is unchanged after the EXPORT command.

The OUTFILE subcommand is the only required specification on the EXPORT command, as in:

```
FILE HANDLE HUBOUT/ file specifications
EXPORT OUTFILE=HUBOUT
```

These commands save the active file as a portable file referred to by file handle HUBOUT.

In addition, you can use optional subcommands to restrict the number of variables saved, to rename variables, to get a map of the variables, and to control the minimum precision to be used in representing numbers. The subcommands must be separated by slashes.

16.16 The KEEP and DROP Subcommands

Use the KEEP and DROP subcommands to save a subset of variables on the exported file. For example, to drop a list of variables before writing the portable file, specify:

```
FILE HANDLE HUBOUT/ file specifications
EXPORT OUTFILE=HUBOUT/
  DROP=DEPT79 TO DEPT81, SALARY79 TO SALARY81, HOURLY81
```

The DROP and KEEP subcommands affect only the portable file created by the EXPORT command. These subcommands do not change the active file.

16.17 The RENAME Subcommand

Use the RENAME subcommand to rename variables being written onto the portable file, as in:

```
FILE HANDLE HUBOUT/ file specifications
EXPORT OUTFILE=HUBOUT/
  DROP=DEPT79 TO DEPT81, SALARY79 TO SALARY81, HOURLY81/
  RENAME=(DEPT82,SALARY82,HOURLY82,PROMO81=DEPT,SALARY,HOURLY,PROMO)
```

In this example, the RENAME subcommand renames variable DEPT82 to DEPT, variable SALARY82 to SALARY, and so forth. The format of the RENAME subcommand is *old name = new name*, enclosed in parentheses. If you use variable lists, the same number of variables must be specified on both sides of the equals sign. Both lists can employ the TO convention, the old variable list implying a list of consecutive variables on the active file and the new variable list creating a set of names, such as VAR01 TO VAR99, on the portable file.

Alternatively, you can rename variables one at a time, with each pair enclosed in optional parentheses, as in:

```
FILE HANDLE HUBOUT/ file specifications
EXPORT OUTFILE HUBOUT/
  DROP=DEPT79 TO DEPT81, SALARY79 TO SALARY81, HOURLY81/
  RENAME=(DEPT82=DEPT) (SALARY82=SALARY)
        (HOURLY82=HOURLY) (PROMO81=PROMO)
```

Variables that are renamed on the EXPORT command retain any variable and value labels. Using the RENAME subcommand does not rename variables on the active file. However, if you rename a variable and then list it on a subsequent DROP or KEEP subcommand on the EXPORT command, use the new name.

16.18 The MAP Subcommand

If you use the RENAME, DROP, or KEEP subcommands to tailor your file, you may find it difficult to keep track of what you have done. To check the results of these subcommands, use the MAP subcommand immediately following the subcommand you want mapped, as in:

```
FILE HANDLE HUBOUT/ file specifications
EXPORT OUTFILE HUBOUT/
  DROP=DEPT79 TO DEPT81, SALARY79 TO SALARY81, HOURLY81/MAP/
  RENAME=(DEPT82=DEPT)(SALARY82=SALARY)(HOURLY82=HOURLY)
  PROMO81=PROMO)/MAP
```

In this example, the first MAP subcommand gives you a map of the variables after the DROP subcommand has dropped the specified variables. The second MAP subcommand displays the results following the renaming of a set of variables. Since this is the last subcommand specified, the second map displays the variables that are written onto the portable file.

16.19 The DIGITS Subcommand

The EXPORT command encodes the number on the portable file to ensure that the receiving machine sees the same number the sending machine saw. The methods used work perfectly for integers that are not too large and for fractions whose denominators are products of 2, 3, and 5 (meaning all decimals, quarters, eighths, sixteenths, thirds, thirtieths, sixtieths, and so forth.) For other fractions and for integers too large to be represented exactly in the active file (usually more than 9 digits, often 15 or more), the representation used in the active file contains some error already, so no exact way of sending these numbers is possible. SPSS^X sends enough digits to get very close. The number of digits sent in these cases depends on the originating program: on the IBM versions of SPSS^X, it is the equivalent of 15 decimal digits (in integer and fractional parts combined).

If many numbers on a file require this treatment, the file can grow quite large. These numbers take a great deal of space. If you do not need the full precision normally used, you can save some space on the portable file by using the DIGITS subcommand.

The DIGITS subcommand has the general form DIGITS=*n*, where *n* is the number of decimal digits of precision you want. Specifying DIGITS=6, for example, means you will be satisfied if 1.23456789087654 is rounded to 1.23457 on the portable file. Since the number base used is not 10, the actual representation used will be different, but the rounding error will not exceed that of a six-decimal-digit representation. The DIGITS subcommand specification is applied to all numbers for which no exact representation in a reasonable number of digits is possible. It cannot be different for different variables, so it should be set according to the requirements of the variable that needs the most precision.

16.20 The IMPORT Command

Use the IMPORT command to read SPSS^X portable files created with the EXPORT command. For example, if you are at an IBM installation you can use the IMPORT command to read a portable file created with the EXPORT command at a DIGITAL VAX site. The only required subcommand is the FILE subcommand followed by an optional equals sign and a file handle defined on a previous FILE HANDLE command that refers SPSS^X to the location of the portable file, as in:

```
FILE HANDLE HUBIN/ file specifications
IMPORT FILE=HUBIN
```

These commands create an active file of the portable file referred to by file handle HUBIN.

You can use additional subcommands to restrict the number of variables brought into the active file from the portable file, to rename variables on the active file, and to get a map of the variables on the active file.

16.21 The KEEP and DROP Subcommands

Use the KEEP and DROP subcommands to retain a subset of variables on the active file. For example, to drop a list of variables read from the portable file, specify:

```
FILE HANDLE HUBIN/ file specifications
IMPORT FILE=HUBIN/
  DROP=DEPT79 TO DEPT81, SALARY79 TO SALARY81, HOURLY81
```

The DROP and KEEP subcommands affect only the active file created by the IMPORT command. They do not change the portable file.

16.22 The RENAME Subcommand

Use the RENAME subcommand to rename variables being read from the portable file, as in:

```
FILE HANDLE HUBIN/ file specifications
IMPORT FILE=HUBIN/
  DROP=DEPT79 TO DEPT81, SALARY79 to SALARY81, HOURLY81/
   RENAME=(DEPT82,SALARY82,HOURLY82,PROMO81=DEPT,SALARY,HOURLY,PROMO)
```

In this example, the RENAME subcommand renames variable DEPT82 to DEPT, variable SALARY82 to SALARY, and so forth. The format of the RENAME subcommand is *old name = new name*, enclosed in parentheses. If you use variable lists, the same number of variables must be specified on both sides of the equals sign. Both lists on the RENAME subcommand can employ the TO convention, the old variable list implying a list of consecutive variables on the portable file and the new variable list creating a set of names, such as VAR01 TO VAR99.

Alternatively, you can rename variables one at a time, with each pair enclosed in optional parentheses, as in:

```
FILE HANDLE HUBIN/ file specifications
IMPORT FILE HUBIN/
  DROP=DEPT79 TO DEPT81, SALARY79 TO SALARY81, HOURLY81/
   RENAME=(DEPT82=DEPT) (SALARY82=SALARY)
   (HOURLY82=HOURLY) (PROMO81=PROMO)
```

Variables that are renamed on the IMPORT command retain any variable and value labels. If you rename a variable and then list it on a subsequent DROP or KEEP subcommand on the IMPORT command, use the new name.

16.23 The MAP Subcommand

If you use the RENAME, DROP, or KEEP subcommands to tailor your file, you may find it difficult to keep track of what you have done. To check the results of these subcommands, use the MAP subcommand immediately following the subcommand you want mapped, as in:

```
FILE HANDLE HUBIN/ file specifications
IMPORT FILE HUBIN/
  DROP=DEPT79 TO DEPT81, SALARY79 TO SALARY81, HOURLY81/MAP/
  RENAME=(DEPT82=DEPT)(SALARY82=SALARY)(HOURLY82=HOURLY)
  (PROMO81=PROMO)/MAP
```

In this example, the first MAP subcommand gives you a map of the variables after the DROP subcommand has dropped the specified variables. The second MAP subcommand displays the results following the renaming of a set of variables. Since this is the last subcommand specified, the second map displays the variables that are currently on the active file.

EXECUTE

OPTIONS option numbers

STATISTICS {statistics numbers | ALL}

PROCEDURE OUTPUT OUTFILE = handle

INPUT MATRIX [FILE = handle] [/FREE]

WHAT IS A PROCEDURE?,**17.1**

PROCEDURE PLACEMENT,**17.2**
- The EXECUTE Command,**17.3**
- The BEGIN DATA and END DATA Commands, **17.4**

OPTIONS AND STATISTICS COMMANDS,**17.5**

SAVING CASEWISE RESULTS,**17.6**

PROCEDURES AND OUTPUT FILES,**17.7**
- The PROCEDURE OUTPUT Command,**17.8**
- Matrix Materials,**17.9**
  - Writing Matrix Materials,**17.10**
  - The INPUT MATRIX Command,**17.11**
  - The N OF CASES Command,**17.12**
  - Passing Matrix Materials among Procedures, **17.13**
  - Split-File Processing,**17.14**

Chapter 17 Using Procedures in SPSS^X

SPSS^X is both a data management and analysis program. You use definition and transformation commands to define and manage data and procedures to analyze data. This chapter describes in general how to use procedures in SPSS^X, including the use of OPTIONS and STATISTICS commands, the placement of procedures within SPSS^X jobs, and the writing and reading of matrix materials.

17.1 WHAT IS A PROCEDURE?

A *procedure* is defined as any command that actually reads data. This definition distinguishes a procedure from transformations used to define a file, the PRINT and WRITE utilities used to display a file, GET used to obtain the dictionary from a saved system file, and ADD FILES or MATCH FILES used to combine dictionaries from active files and system files. Table 17.1 lists procedures within SPSS^X, what they do, and the chapter in which they are documented.

Table 17.1 SPSS^X procedures

Command	Function	Chapter
AGGREGATE	Save an aggregated file	14
ANOVA	Factorial analysis of variance	26
BARCHART	Bar charts	24
BOX-JENKINS	Time series analysis	38
BREAKDOWN	Subpopulation means	22
CONDESCRIPTIVE	Univariate descriptive statistics	19
CROSSTABS	Contingency table analysis	20
DISCRIMINANT	Discriminant analysis	34
EXECUTE	Read data file	17
EXPORT	Save transportable system file	16
FACTOR	Factor analysis	35
FREQUENCIES	Frequency tables	18
LINECHART	Line charts	24
LIST	List cases	9
LOGLINEAR	Loglinear analysis	29
MANOVA	General linear models	28
MULT RESPONSE	Multiple response tables	21
NONPAR CORR	Nonparametric correlations	36
NPAR TESTS	Nonparametric tests	37
ONEWAY	One-way analysis of variance	27
PARTIAL CORR	Partial correlations	32
PEARSON CORR	Pearson correlations	31
PIECHART	Pie charts	24
REGRESSION	Multiple regression analysis	33
RELIABILITY	Item analysis	39
REPORT	Report writer	23
SAVE	Save system file	5
SCATTERGRAM	Bivariate scatterplots	30
SORT CASES	Sort cases	13
SURVIVAL	Life table analysis	40
T-TEST	t tests	25

All procedures in SPSS^X read data from the *active file*. Although you may be defining or manipulating several files during one job, only one file is active at any given point. In the following example, two files are analyzed using two different procedures for each.

```
FILE HANDLE AGENTS/ file specifications
FILE HANDLE ACCTS/ file specifications
GET FILE=AGENTS/KEEP JUNE JULY AUG TYPE
FREQUENCIES  VARIABLES=JUNE JULY AUG TYPE/
             FORMAT=LIMIT(20)/HBAR
BREAKDOWN  JUNE JULY AUG BY TYPE
GET FILE=ACCTS/KEEP REGION TYPE SIZE
FREQUENCIES  VARIABLES=SIZE/FORMAT=NOTABLE/
             HISTOGRAM
BREAKDOWN  SIZE BY REGION TYPE
FINISH
```

The first GET command makes the file referenced by AGENTS the active file. The first FREQUENCIES and BREAKDOWN procedures analyze this file. The second GET command replaces the active file with the file referenced by ACCTS, and the second set of procedures analyzes this file. For further discussion of the active file, see Chapters 1 and 3.

If you make a syntax error on a procedure command, usually that procedure is skipped and subsequent procedures are executed. However, since some procedures save variables on the active file, a subsequent procedure that analyzes the variables you intended to save with an earlier procedure is also in error.

17.2 PROCEDURE PLACEMENT

Procedures operate on files defined by commands such as DATA LIST, COMPUTE, RECODE, GET, MATCH FILES, and ADD FILES. In fact, procedures execute transformations. Thus, procedures follow blocks of transformations in a job. You can interleave blocks of transformations and procedures. For example, you can define a file, run a procedure, transform that file, and run another procedure on the transformed file, as in:

```
DATA LIST  /1 SEX 1 SCORE1 TO SCORE10 10-39 GPA 40-42(1)
MISSING VALUES SCORE1 TO SCORE10 (-1)
PEARSON CORR SCORE1 TO SCORE10
BEGIN DATA
data records
END DATA
COMMENT  TRICHOTOMIZE SCORE VARIABLES FOR CROSSTABS
RECODE  SCORE1 TO SCORE10 (0 THRU 33=1)(34 THRU 67=2)(68 THRU 100=3)
VALUE LABELS SCORE1 TO SCORE10 (1) 'LOWER THIRD' (2) 'MIDDLE THIRD'
              (3) 'UPPER THIRD'
CROSSTABS  SCORE1 TO SCORE10 BY SEX
OPTIONS    5
STATISTICS 1
FREQUENCIES  VARIABLES=SCORE1 TO SCORE10
FINISH
```

In this example, PEARSON CORR uses the unrecoded values of variables SCORE1 to SCORE10, while CROSSTABS and FREQUENCIES tabulate the recoded values of the variables. Transformations apply to all subsequent procedures analyzing the active file unless you use the TEMPORARY command (see Chapter 6). If you use the TEMPORARY command, all transformations placed between it and the next procedure command are executed only for the next procedure. For example, if TEMPORARY was placed before the RECODE in the above example, FREQUENCIES would have tabulated the original values of the SCORE variables.

17.3 The EXECUTE Command

As noted by their absence in Table 17.1, facilities such as ADD FILES, MATCH FILES, PRINT, and WRITE are not procedures. Thus, these commands are not executed unless followed by one of the procedures listed in Table 17.1. For this reason, SPSS^{X} has a special procedure, EXECUTE, which does nothing but force the reading of the data file. The EXECUTE command contains no subcommands or specifications. For example,

```
FILE HANDLE RAWDATA/ file specifications
FILE HANDLE SMITHS/ file specifications
TITLE  'A Simple EXECUTE Example'
DATA LIST  FILE=RAWDATA/1 LNAME 1-13 (A) FNAME 15-24 (A)
           MMAIDENL 40-55
VAR LABELS  MMAIDENL 'MOTHER''S MAIDEN NAME'
DO IF (MMAIDENL EQ 'Smith')
WRITE OUTFILE=SMITHS/LNAME FNAME
END IF
EXECUTE
FINISH
```

writes the last and first names of all people whose mother's maiden name was Smith to the file referenced by SMITHS. The EXECUTE command reads the data and executes all of the preceding transformation commands.

17.4 The BEGIN DATA and END DATA Commands

The BEGIN DATA command signals the beginning of data lines in the command file, and the END DATA command signals the end of the data lines. You usually place BEGIN DATA, data lines, and END DATA immediately following the first procedure in your job. If your job contains no procedures, BEGIN DATA behaves as a procedure and forces the reading of the data. See Chapter 3 for a discussion of the BEGIN DATA and END DATA commands.

17.5 OPTIONS AND STATISTICS COMMANDS

There are two types of syntax for procedures in SPSS^{X}. Some procedures are entirely self-contained. In these procedures, you use subcommands to specify analyses, formatting options, missing-data options, additional statistics, and so forth. REGRESSION is an example of a subcommand-driven procedure. Other procedures use associated OPTIONS and STATISTICS commands to produce nondefault output. For example, to obtain listwise deletion of missing data from PEARSON CORR, you must use an OPTIONS command, since by default PEARSON CORR deletes cases on an analysis-by-analysis basis.

The OPTIONS and STATISTICS commands, when used, immediately follow the procedure command to which they apply. They can be specified in either order. The specification field for either command contains one or more numbers corresponding to specific options or statistics available for the procedure. In addition, you can use the keyword ALL on the STATISTICS command to request all optional statistics. The following example demonstrates the use and placement of OPTIONS and STATISTICS commands with procedure SCATTERGRAM to obtain scatterplots with integer scaling (Option 7), Pearson's *r* (Statistic 1), and the intercept with the vertical axis (Statistic 5):

```
FILE HANDLE HUBEMPL/ file specifications
GET FILE=HUBEMPL/KEEP RAISE81 RAISE82 RAISE83
SCATTERGRAM  ALL
STATISTICS   1 5
OPTIONS      7
FINISH
```

Some options and statistics are not available in combination with other options or statistics. If you specify an illegal combination of options or statistics, SPSS^{X} usually overrides the conflict and prints a warning message indicating the action taken.

17.6 SAVING CASEWISE RESULTS

Several procedures in SPSS^X compute and save new variables on the active file that can be analyzed in subsequent procedures. For example, CONDESCRIPTIVE computes standardized variables with a mean of 0 and a standard deviation of 1. When a variable cannot be computed for a case, SPSS^X supplies the system-missing value.

Once the procedure saves new variables on the active file, you can use them just like any other variables on the file. If you save the active file with the SAVE command, variables added by procedures are saved unless explicitly dropped with the KEEP or DROP subcommand. In the following example, CONDESCRIPTIVE creates standardized variables that are then used in transformations and subsequently analyzed by the CROSSTABS command:

```
FILE HANDLE SURVEY/ file specifications
DATA LIST  FILE=SURVEY/1 FAMINC 6-15 (DOLLAR) EDOFR 16-17 EDSPOUSE 18-19
                          CARSTYLE 20
CONDESCRIPTIVE  FAMINC(INCZ) EDOFR(EDZ1) EDSPOUSE(EDZ2)
OPTIONS 3
COMPUTE  SESZ=MEAN(INCZ,EDZ1,EDZ2)
RECODE   SESZ (LO THRU -1=-1)(-1 THRU 0=0)(0 THRU HI=1)
CROSSTABS  SESZ BY CARSTYLE
STATISTICS  ALL
FINISH
```

Option 3 on CONDESCRIPTIVE computes standardized variables INCZ, EDZ1, and EDZ2 and adds them to the end of the active file. The COMPUTE command creates variable SESZ, which is the mean of these three variables. RECODE recodes SESZ into three values for use with the CROSSTABS command.

17.7 PROCEDURES AND OUTPUT FILES

Some procedures in SPSS^X write output files whose organization prevents them from being added directly to the active file. Included among these files are cell totals from CROSSTABS and various types of matrix materials. Table 17.7 lists procedures that create output files. The graphics procedures, BARCHART, LINECHART, and PIECHART, write an output plotting file. See Chapter 24 for a discussion of this special file.

Table 17.7 Procedures writing output files

Procedure	Type of file
CROSSTABS	Cell counts
DISCRIMINANT	Matrix materials
FACTOR	Matrix materials
FREQUENCIES	Display file
MANOVA	Matrix materials
NONPAR CORR	Matrix materials
PARTIAL CORR	Matrix materials
PEARSON CORR	Matrix materials
REGRESSION	Matrix materials
RELIABILITY	Matrix materials
SURVIVAL	Life table records

17.8 The PROCEDURE OUTPUT Command

When a procedure writes a file, you must specify the PROCEDURE OUTPUT command before the procedure. PROCEDURE OUTPUT has one subcommand, OUTFILE, which names the file handle to which the output is directed. You must also specify the file handle on a previous FILE HANDLE command (see Chapter 3). In the IBM/OS environment, the file handle is the DDNAME of the JCL statement defining the output file. For example, to save the cell totals from CROSSTABS on the file referenced by CELLS, specify:

```
FILE HANDLE GSS80/ file specifications
FILE HANDLE CELLS/ file specifications
GET FILE=GSS80
PROCEDURE OUTPUT  OUTFILE=CELLS
CROSSTABS  ABNOMORE BY ABHEALTH
OPTIONS   10
FINISH
```

The FILE HANDLE command assigns the handle CELLS to the output file. Option 10 specifies that the cell counts are to be saved on an output file, and the PROCEDURE OUTPUT command specifies the file handle of the output file (see Chapter 20).

After the procedure writes results to the file referenced by the PROCEDURE OUTPUT command, SPSS^X closes and rewinds the file. If several procedures write results to the same file, only the results from the last procedure are saved. Thus, if you are writing out results from more than one procedure, you must specify different file handles using a PROCEDURE OUTPUT command for each procedure.

17.9 Matrix Materials

Many of the correlational-based procedures in SPSS^X read and write various types of matrix materials. For example, procedures PEARSON CORR and PARTIAL CORR write matrices of correlations and *n*'s. If you specify listwise deletion of missing data, the matrix is followed by a record containing the number of cases upon which the matrix was computed. If you specify pairwise deletion of missing data, the matrix of coefficients is followed by a matrix containing the pairwise *n*'s upon which the matrix is computed.

Several procedures are able to read the matrix materials written by other procedures. For example, you can use the matrix materials written by procedure REGRESSION as input to procedure FACTOR. You can also use matrices that you have entered in freefield format.

17.10 Writing Matrix Materials

Matrices are not saved on the active file. Rather, they are written to the file referenced by the PROCEDURE OUTPUT command. The following example saves the matrix materials written by REGRESSION on the file referenced by REGMAT:

```
FILE HANDLE CITYFILE/ file specifications
FILE HANDLE RGMAT/ file specifications
GET FILE=CITYFILE
PROCEDURE OUTPUT OUTFILE = RGMAT
REGRESSION  WRITE CORR N/
            VARIABLES=NTCPRI TO FSALES/DEPENDENT=NTCPRI/
            STEP/
FINISH
```

The WRITE subcommand on REGRESSION specifies that the number of cases and the correlation matrix are to be saved on an output file (see Chapter 33).

The types of matrix materials produced vary greatly from procedure to procedure. You can explicitly request different types of matrix output in REGRESSION and FACTOR. Other procedures are not so flexible. If you use pairwise deletion in PEARSON CORR (the default) and specify matrix output, PEARSON CORR writes two matrices, one of correlations and one of *n*'s. If you specify listwise deletion of missing data, PEARSON CORR writes one record containing the number of cases following the records containing the matrix. The matrix materials written by DISCRIMINANT are designed to be read by DISCRIMINANT and are unlikely to be used as input to any other procedure in SPSS^X.

17.11 The INPUT MATRIX Command

Some procedures accept matrix materials in place of actual cases, and some procedures accept matrix materials along with cases. You can insert matrix materials in the command file or read them from a separate file. The matrix materials that procedures write are formatted. For example, correlation matrices are written with a 8F10.7 format. See the individual chapters for each procedure for the types of matrix materials read and their formats.

Use the INPUT MATRIX command to read matrix materials and the FILE subcommand to specify the handle of the file containing the matrix materials. If you are using only matrix materials in your job, you must use the NUMERIC command to provide variable names and must enclose the NUMERIC and INPUT MATRIX commands in an INPUT PROGRAM—END INPUT PROGRAM structure. The commands should immediately precede the procedure command to which they apply. For example, to use matrix materials on the file referenced by file handle REGMAT as input to REGRESSION, specify:

```
FILE HANDLE REGMAT/ file specifications
INPUT PROGRAM
NUMERIC NTCPRI FOOD SERVICE RENT
INPUT MATRIX FILE=REGMAT
END INPUT PROGRAM
REGRESSION READ CORR N/
   VARIABLES=NTCPRI FOOD SERVICE RENT/DEPENDENT=NTCPRI/
   STEP/
FINISH
```

The FILE HANDLE command defines the file handle for the file containing the matrix materials. The INPUT PROGRAM and END INPUT PROGRAM commands enclose the commands defining the matrix file. The NUMERIC command defines variable names for the variables in the matrix, and the INPUT MATRIX command indicates that the matrix materials are to be read from the file referenced by handle REGMAT. The READ subcommand on the REGRESSION command specifies that a correlation matrix and number of cases are to be used as input (see Chapter 33).

You can use both matrix materials and a file of cases as input to DISCRIMINANT and REGRESSION procedures. If you use both types of files, you should not use the INPUT PROGRAM—END INPUT PROGRAM structure with the INPUT MATRIX command. See Chapters 33 and 34 for examples.

If matrix materials are included in the command file and are formatted, use the INPUT MATRIX command with no specifications and place the materials between a BEGIN DATA and an END DATA command following the procedure using them.

Procedures can read freefield-format matrices, in which elements are separated by blanks and each row of the matrix or each vector begins on a new record. Use the keyword FREE on the INPUT MATRIX command to read freefield-format matrix materials. For example, to use FACTOR to analyze a correlation matrix from a journal article, specify:

```
INPUT PROGRAM
NUMERIC      X1 TO X5
INPUT MATRIX  FREE
END INPUT PROGRAM
FACTOR       VARIABLES=X1 TO X5/
             READ CORRELATION/
             PRINT DET INV EXTRACTION ROTATION/
             EXTRACTION ML/
             ROTATION QUARTIMAX
BEGIN DATA
1.0 -.020 .181 .418 .246
-.020 1.0 -.112 -.156 -.064
.181 -.112 1.0 .333 -.174
.418 -.156 .333 1.0 .022
.246 -.064 -.174 .022 1.0
END DATA
```

The NUMERIC command defines arbitrary variable names for use in the FACTOR procedure. The INPUT MATRIX command signals freefield input and, since no file handle is provided, in-line data. The READ subcommand on the FACTOR command signals that a correlation matrix is being used as input.

If matrix materials are stored on a file, they can be used by several different procedures in a job. If matrix materials are placed in-line, they apply only to the previous procedure.

17.12 The N OF CASES Command

Most procedures in SPSS^X write the *n*'s on the file with matrix materials. If you do not include the *n* with the matrix materials, you can specify the number of cases on an N OF CASES command. If you use the N OF CASES command, you must specify listwise deletion of missing-data for the procedure using the matrix materials as input.

17.13 Passing Matrix Materials among Procedures

You can produce matrix materials with one procedure and then read those materials with other procedures in the same job, as long as the subsequent procedures read the same type of matrix materials as the first procedure produces. Use the PROCEDURE OUTPUT command to name the file being written and the INPUT MATRIX command to name the file for reading.

17.14 Split-File Processing

If you use the SPLIT FILE command (Chapter 13) to subdivide your file when writing matrix materials, SPSS^X writes one set of matrix materials for each split-file group. To signal split-file processing when reading matrix materials, use the SPLIT FILE command with any variable defined on the NUMERIC command, as in:

```
FILE HANDLE PEARMAT/ file specifications
INPUT PROGRAM
NUMERIC  Y,X1 TO X10
INPUT MATRIX  FILE=PEARMAT
SPLIT FILE  BY Y
END INPUT PROGRAM
FACTOR  VARIABLES=X1 TO X10/READ CORRELATION/
        PRINT DET INV EXTRACTION ROTATION
```

The procedure produces as many analyses as sets of matrix materials it reads. In other words, if split-file processing produced five sets of matrix materials, the procedure reading the materials prints five sets of results, one for each set of matrix materials read. Each set of results is identified by a heading giving the sequential number of the split group.

```
FREQUENCIES  VARIABLES = varlist [(min, max)]  [varlist . . . ]

 [/FORMAT = [{CONDENSE}]  [{NOTABLE }]  [NOLABELS]  [WRITE]
             {ONEPAGE }     {LIMIT(n)}

            {DVALUE}
           [{AFREQ }]  [DOUBLE]  [NEWPAGE]  [INDEX]]
            {DFREQ }

 [/MISSING = INCLUDE]

 [/BARCHART = [MINIMUM(n)]  [MAXIMUM(n)]  [{FREQ(n)   }]]
                                           {PERCENT(n)}

 [/HISTOGRAM = [MINIMUM(n)]  [MAXIMUM(n)]  [{FREQ(n)   }]
                                            {PERCENT(n)}

               [{NONORMAL}]  [INCREMENT(n)]]
                {NORMAL  }

 [/HBAR = same as HISTOGRAM]

 [/NTILES = n]

 [/PERCENTILES = value list]

 [/STATISTICS = [DEFAULT]  [MEAN]  [STDDEV]  [MINIMUM]
                [MAXIMUM]  [SEMEAN]  [VARIANCE]  [SKEWNESS]
                [SESKEW]  [KURTOSIS]  [SEKURT]  [RANGE]  [MODE]
                [MEDIAN]  [SUM]  [ALL]  [NONE]]
```


OVERVIEW, **18.1**

OPERATION, **18.2**

- The VARIABLES Subcommand, **18.3**
  - General vs. Integer Mode, **18.4**
- The FORMAT Subcommand, **18.5**
  - Table Formats, **18.6**
  - The Order of Values, **18.7**
  - Suppressing Tables, **18.8**
  - Index of Tables, **18.9**
  - Writing Tables to a File, **18.10**
- Bar Charts and Histograms, **18.11**
  - The BARCHART Subcommand, **18.12**
  - The HISTOGRAM Subcommand, **18.13**
  - The HBAR Subcommand, **18.14**
- Percentiles and Ntiles, **18.15**
  - The PERCENTILES Subcommand, **18.16**
  - The NTILES Subcommand, **18.17**
- The STATISTICS Subcommand, **18.18**
- Missing Values, **18.19**

LIMITATIONS, **18.20**

Chapter 18 FREQUENCIES

Procedure FREQUENCIES produces a table of frequency counts and percentages for the values of individual variables. Optionally, you can obtain bar charts for discrete variables, histograms for continuous variables, univariate summary statistics, and percentiles. To produce only statistics on interval-level data, you can also use procedure CONDESCRIPTIVE (see Chapter 19).

18.1 OVERVIEW

FREQUENCIES produces a table of values and the corresponding number of cases for numeric or short string variables. FREQUENCIES operates in two modes: general and integer. General mode can be used with both numeric and short string variables. Integer mode operates on numeric variables only. With integer mode, you must specify the range of values to be tabulated. You can specify all optional subcommands with either mode.

Table Formats. By default, FREQUENCIES prints as many single-spaced tables with complete labeling information as fits on a page. You can use the FORMAT subcommand to suppress tables or to request double-spaced tables, no labeling, one table per page, or condensed tables. (See Sections 18.6 and 18.8.)

Order of Values. By default, FREQUENCIES orders tables by values in ascending order. You can use the FORMAT subcommand to request tables ordered by values in descending order, by frequencies in ascending order, or by frequencies in descending order. (See Section 18.7.)

Index of Tables. You can use the FORMAT subcommand to request an index of the tables printed by FREQUENCIES. (See Section 18.9.)

Writing Tables to a File. You can use the WRITE keyword on the FORMAT subcommand to write the frequency tables to a separate file on disk or tape. (See Section 18.10.)

Bar Charts and Histograms. You can print a bar chart or histogram for all variables via the BARCHART or HISTOGRAM subcommands, respectively. Or, you can request bar charts for variables that fit on one page and histograms for all others via the HBAR subcommand. (See Sections 18.11 through 18.14.)

Percentiles and Ntiles. You can use the PERCENTILES or NTILES subcommand to print percentiles or ntiles for each variable. (See Sections 18.15 through 18.17.)

Statistics. You can use the STATISTICS subcommand to print optional statistics for each variable. Available statistics are mean, median, mode, standard deviation, variance, skewness, kurtosis, sum, and so forth. (See Section 18.18.)

Missing Values. By default, cases with missing values are shown in the frequency table but are deleted from statistics calculations. Use the MISSING subcommand to include user-missing values in statistics calculations. (See Section 18.19.)

18.2 OPERATION

The FREQUENCIES procedure operates via subcommands. Each subcommand begins with a subcommand keyword, followed by an optional equals sign and subcommand specifications. Subcommands can be named in any order and are separated from each other by a slash. With the exception of PERCENTILES and NTILES, each subcommand can be used only once per FREQUENCIES command. The only required subcommand is VARIABLES, which specifies the variables being analyzed. All other subcommands are optional.

18.3 The VARIABLES Subcommand

The VARIABLES subcommand names the variables to be analyzed. It is the only required subcommand. The specification on the VARIABLES subcommand depends on whether you want to use the *integer* or *general* mode to build tables. In integer mode, you specify the dimensions of the table, and FREQUENCIES sorts cases into the elements of the table. In general mode, FREQUENCIES dynamically builds the table, setting up one cell for each unique value encountered in the data. You cannot mix integer and general modes on the VARIABLES subcommand.

To use FREQUENCIES in general mode, simply list the variable names on the VARIABLES subcommand, as in:

```
FREQUENCIES VARIABLES=POLVIEWS RES16
```

Figure 18.3 shows the table for POLVIEWS produced by this command. The variable and value labels are printed, if available, followed by the value and the number of cases that have the value. The percentage is based on all the observations, and the valid and cumulative percentages are based on those cases that have valid values. The number of valid and missing observations is also provided.

Figure 18.3 A default frequency table

POLVIEWS THINK SELF LIBERAL OR CONSERVATIVE

VALUE LABEL	VALUE	FREQUENCY	PERCENT	VALID PERCENT	CUM PERCENT
EXTREMELY LIBERAL	1	17	3.4	3.5	3.5
LIBERAL	2	38	7.6	7.7	11.2
SLIGHTLY LIBERAL	3	80	16.0	16.3	27.4
MODERATE	4	190	38.0	38.6	66.1
SLGHTLY CONSERVATIVE	5	88	17.6	17.9	83.9
CONSERVATIVE	6	68	13.6	13.8	97.8
EXTRMLY CONSERVATIVE	7	11	2.2	2.2	100.0
DK	8	5	1.0	MISSING	
NA	9	3	.6	MISSING	
	TOTAL	500	100.0	100.0	

VALID CASES 492 MISSING CASES 8

You can use the keyword ALL to name all the variables on the file or the keyword TO to reference a set of consecutive variables on the active file.

General mode tabulates any type of variable, including numeric variables with decimal positions and string variables. However, long strings are truncated to short strings in the tabulation. In other words, only the short-string portion of the variable is actually tabulated. For a discussion of short and long strings, see Chapter 3.

To use FREQUENCIES in integer mode, you must specify in parentheses the value range for each variable following the variable name, as in:

```
FREQUENCIES  VARIABLES=POLVIEWS(0,9) RES16(1,6)
```

The value range for POLVIEWS is 0 through 9, and the range for RES16 is 1 through 6. You must specify a value range for every variable listed. If several variables have the same range, you can specify the range once at the end of the variable list, as in:

```
FREQUENCIES  VARIABLES=SEX(1,2) TVHOURS(0,24) SCALE1 TO SCALE5(1,7)
```

In this example, the value range for SCALE1, SCALE2, and so on through SCALE5 is 1 through 7.

Only observations with values within the range are included in the frequency table. Integer mode truncates values with decimal positions when tabulating. For example, 2.46, 2.59, and 2.73 are all counted as value 2. Values outside the range are grouped into an out-of-range category and are considered missing for calculation of percents and statistics. You can specify a more generous range than actually occurs in the data, but this will needlessly increase the amount of memory needed to store the table. If the variables being tabulated are sparsely distributed within the specified range (that is, there are many empty categories), use the general mode or recode the values to consecutive values with the RECODE command (see Chapter 6).

18.4 General vs. Integer Mode

All optional specifications are available with either integer or general mode. However, you should consider the following points when choosing between the two modes.

- Integer mode usually takes less computation time. However, it is impossible to predict savings on time since the amount of time required for general mode depends upon the range of values and the order in which they are read.
- Integer mode requires less memory than does general mode, except when variables are sparsely distributed.
- In integer mode, you can use the value range specification to eliminate extremely low or high values.
- Since integer mode truncates decimal positions, you can obtain grouped frequency tables for continuous variables without having to recode them to integers. On the other hand, general mode tabulates short strings and does not truncate nonintegers.

18.5 The FORMAT Subcommand

Several formatting options are available via the FORMAT subcommand. The FORMAT subcommand applies to all variables named on the VARIABLES subcommand. You can control the formatting of tables and the order in which values are sorted within the table, suppress tables, produce an index of the tables, and write the FREQUENCIES display to another file via keywords on the FORMAT subcommand.

You can specify as many formatting options as desired on the FORMAT subcommand. For example,

```
FREQUENCIES  VARIABLES=POLVIEWS PRESTIGE/
       FORMAT=ONEPAGE DVALUE/
```

specifies conditional condensed formatting of the tables (keyword ONEPAGE) with values sorted in descending order (keyword DVALUE). Keywords on the FORMAT subcommand are described in Sections 18.6 through 18.10.

18.6 Table Formats

The following keywords on the FORMAT subcommand control the formatting of tables:

NOLABELS *Do not print variable or value labels.* By default, FREQUENCIES prints variable and value labels defined by the VARIABLE LABELS and VALUE LABELS commands (see Chapter 3).

DOUBLE *Double-space frequency tables.*

NEWPAGE *Begin each table on a new page.* By default, FREQUENCIES prints as many tables on a page as fit.

CONDENSE *Condensed format.* This format prints frequency counts in three columns. It does not print value labels and percentages for all cases, and it rounds valid and cumulative percentages to integers. Figure 18.6 shows an example of a condensed frequency table.

ONEPAGE *Conditional condensed format.* Keyword ONEPAGE uses the condensed format for tables that would require more than one page with the default format. All other tables are printed in default format. If you specify both CONDENSE and ONEPAGE, all tables are printed in condensed format.

Specify these keywords following the FORMAT subcommand and an optional equals sign, as in:

```
FREQUENCIES  VARIABLES=PRESTIGE/FORMAT=CONDENSE
```

Figure 18.6 shows the condensed frequency table for PRESTIGE.

Figure 18.6 Condensed frequency table

```
PRESTIGE  RESP'S OCCUPATIONAL PRESTIGE SCORE

                   CUM                        CUM                        CUM
  VALUE   FREQ PCT PCT     VALUE   FREQ PCT PCT     VALUE   FREQ PCT PCT

     12      5   1   1        33     10   2  34        52      1   0  87
     14      2   0   2        34     14   3  37        54      2   0  88
     16      9   2   3        35      3   1  38        55      2   0  88
     17      8   2   5        36     30   7  44        56      7   2  90
     18      7   2   7        37      6   1  45        57     12   3  92
     19      4   1   8        38      4   1  46        58      1   0  93
     20     13   3  10        39      9   2  48        60      8   2  94
     21      1   0  11        40     12   3  51        61      2   0  95
     22      9   2  13        41     15   3  54        62      5   1  96
     23      4   1  13        42      9   2  56        63      4   1  97
     24      1   0  14        43      3   1  57        67      2   0  97
     25     17   4  17        44      4   1  57        68      1   0  97
     26     14   3  20        45     19   4  62        69      2   0  98
     27      5   1  21        46     33   7  69        71      1   0  98
     28      5   1  23        47     14   3  72        72      2   0  98
     29     15   3  26        48     18   4  76        76      4   1  99
     30      2   0  26        49      4   1  77        78      3   1 100
     31      5   1  27        50     39   8  85
     32     20   4  32        51     10   2  87

                         M I S S I N G   D A T A
  VALUE   FREQ             VALUE   FREQ                 VALUE   FREQ

            39

VALID CASES     461       MISSING CASES     39
```

18.7 The Order of Values

By default, frequency tables are printed in ascending order of values. You can override this order with one of three sorting options on the FORMAT subcommand.

AFREQ *Sort categories in ascending order of frequency.*

DFREQ *Sort categories in descending order of frequency.*

DVALUE *Sort categories in descending order of values.*

If you specify more than one sorting option, FREQUENCIES uses the last one specified.

18.8 Suppressing Tables

You might be using FREQUENCIES to obtain univariate statistics not available in other procedures, or to print histograms or bar charts, and thus may not be interested in the frequency tables themselves. Or you might want to suppress tables for variables with a large number of values. Two options are available for suppressing tables.

LIMIT(n) *Do not print tables with more categories than the specified value.*
NOTABLE *Suppress all frequency tables.*

If you specify both NOTABLE and LIMIT, NOTABLE overrides LIMIT and no tables are printed. FREQUENCIES displays the number of missing and valid cases for the variable when the table is suppressed.

18.9 Index of Tables

To obtain both a positional index of frequency tables and an index arranged alphabetically by variable name, use the INDEX keyword on the FORMAT subcommand.

INDEX *Index of tables.*

18.10 Writing Tables to a File

Use the WRITE keyword on the FORMAT subcommand to write the FREQUENCIES display to a separate output file. When you write the display to a separate file, you must use a PROCEDURE OUTPUT command before the FREQUENCIES command to specify the file handle of the output file (see Chapter 17). Also, you usually need to use a FILE HANDLE command to define the file handle of the output file (see Chapter 3). When you use WRITE, no tables, statistics, histograms, or bar charts are printed.

This is a useful option for producing a machine-readable codebook. For example,

```
FILE HANDLE  CODEBOOK/  file specifications
PROCEDURE OUTPUT  OUTFILE=CODEBOOK
FREQUENCIES  VARIABLES=ALL/
  FORMAT=ONEPAGE WRITE/
```

writes a relatively compact codebook to the file referenced by CODEBOOK.

WRITE *Direct display to another file.*

18.11 Bar Charts and Histograms

Bar charts and histograms are graphic representations of frequency distributions. Figure 18.11a is an example of a bar chart, and Figure 18.11b is an example of a histogram for the same variable.

Each bar in a bar chart corresponds to a value, and the length of the bar is determined by the number of cases having the value. Each bar is labeled with the value and value label, if a label has been defined. Bars are not displayed for empty categories. In Figure 18.11a, GOVSPEND has no cases with values 2 through 5 and 7. Therefore, the bar for value 1 is next to the bar for value 6. Compare this to the histogram in Figure 18.11b. Since the vertical axis has a scale on the histogram, the missing categories are quite apparent.

A histogram is useful for examining the distribution of a variable with many values. Values are tabulated into intervals of equal width, depending upon the range of values and the number of intervals defined. Each row of asterisks represents the number of cases with values in the interval. If the range of values fits within the default of 21 intervals, the collection process is not used and each value has its own bar, as in Figure 18.11b. The histogram in Figure 18.13 displays a variable with value range of 12 to 78 collapsed into 21 intervals. In a histogram, the vertical axis has a scale, and empty categories within the range implied by the minimum and maximum are identified by the absence of rows of asterisks.

You can request both bar charts and histograms on one FREQUENCIES command. Use the BARCHART subcommand to produce bar charts for all variables named on the VARIABLES subcommand (see Section 18.12) and the HISTOGRAM subcommand to produce histograms for all variables (see Section 18.13). Or use the HBAR subcommand to produce bar charts for variables that fit on one page (11 individual categories for the default page length) and histograms for other variables (see Section 18.14). You can specify only one of these three subcommands on each FREQUENCIES command. If you specify more than one, FREQUENCIES assumes HBAR.

Figure 18.11a A barchart produced by FREQUENCIES

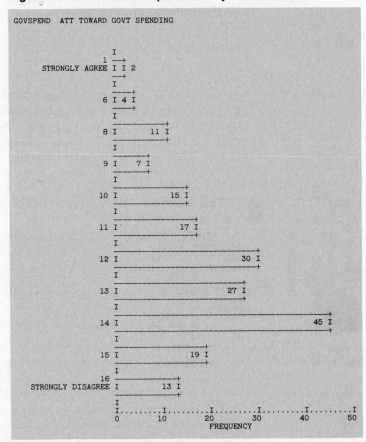

```
GOVSPEND   ATT TOWARD GOVT SPENDING

                     I
                   1 --+
      STRONGLY AGREE I I 2
                     --+
                     I
                     ----+
                   6 I 4 I
                     ----+
                     I
                     -----------+
                   8 I       11 I
                     -----------+
                     I
                     -------+
                   9 I    7 I
                     -------+
                     I
                     ---------------+
                  10 I           15 I
                     ---------------+
                     I
                     -----------------+
                  11 I             17 I
                     -----------------+
                     I
                     ------------------------------+
                  12 I                          30 I
                     ------------------------------+
                     I
                     ---------------------------+
                  13 I                       27 I
                     ---------------------------+
                     I
                     ---------------------------------------------+
                  14 I                                         45 I
                     ---------------------------------------------+
                     I
                     -------------------+
                  15 I               19 I
                     -------------------+
                     I
                  16 -------------+
   STRONGLY DISAGREE I         13 I
                     -------------+
                     I
                     I.........I.........I.........I.........I.........I
                     0        10        20        30        40        50
                                        FREQUENCY
```

Figure 18.11b A histogram produced by FREQUENCIES

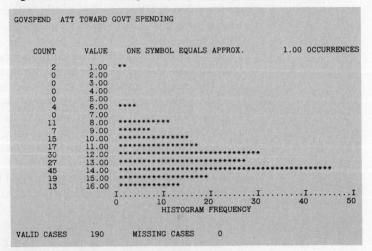

```
GOVSPEND   ATT TOWARD GOVT SPENDING

  COUNT      VALUE    ONE SYMBOL EQUALS APPROX.        1.00 OCCURRENCES

      2       1.00   **
      0       2.00
      0       3.00
      0       4.00
      0       5.00
      4       6.00   ****
      0       7.00
     11       8.00   ***********
      7       9.00   *******
     15      10.00   ***************
     17      11.00   *****************
     30      12.00   ******************************
     27      13.00   ***************************
     45      14.00   *********************************************
     19      15.00   *******************
     13      16.00   *************
                     I.........I.........I.........I.........I.........I
                     0        10        20        30        40        50
                                   HISTOGRAM FREQUENCY

VALID CASES      190      MISSING CASES      0
```

18.12 The BARCHART Subcommand

The BARCHART subcommand produces bar charts. No specifications are required for the BARCHART subcommand, as in:

```
FREQUENCIES  VARIABLES=POLVIEWS/
             BARCHART/
```

In the default bar chart format, all tabulated values are plotted, and the horizontal axis is scaled in frequencies. The scale is determined by the frequency count of the largest single category plotted. You can specify minimum and maximum bounds for plotting and can request a horizontal scale labeled with percentages or frequency counts via the following optional specifications on subcommand BARCHART:

MIN(n) *Lower bound.* Values below the specified minimum are not plotted.

MAX(n) *Upper bound.* Values above the specified maximum are not plotted.

PERCENT(n) *Horizontal axis scaled in percentages.* The *n* specifies the preferred maximum and is not required. If you do not specify an *n* or your *n* is too small, FREQUENCIES chooses 5, 10, 25, 50 or 100, depending on the percentage for the largest category.

FREQ(n) *Horizontal axis scaled in frequencies.* While FREQ is the default scaling method, you can use this specification if you want to specify a maximum frequency *(n)* for the scale. If you do not specify an *n* or your *n* is too small, FREQUENCIES chooses 10, 20, 50, 100, 200, 500, 1000, 2000, and so forth, depending on the frequency count for the largest category.

You can enter optional specifications in any order, as in

```
FREQUENCIES  VARIABLES=SIBS/
         BARCHART=PERCENT MAX(10)
```

which requests a bar chart on SIBS with values through 10 plotted and the horizontal axis scaled in percentages.

18.13 The HISTOGRAM Subcommand

The HISTOGRAM subcommand produces histograms. No specifications are required for the HISTOGRAM subcommand, as in:

```
FREQUENCIES  VARIABLES=PRESTIGE/
             HISTOGRAM/
```

In the default histogram format, all tabulated values are included, and the horizontal axis is scaled by frequencies. The scale is determined by the frequency count of the largest category plotted. The number of intervals plotted is 21 (or fewer if the range of values is less than 21).

Figure 18.13 shows the histogram produced by previous specification. Since the variable PRESTIGE ranges from 12 to 78, values are collapsed into the 21 bars. The midpoint of each interval is printed.

Figure 18.13 A default histogram

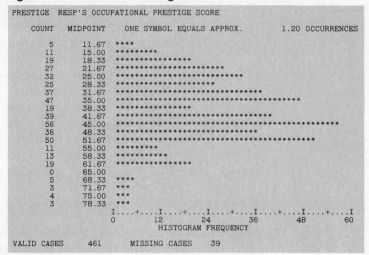

```
PRESTIGE  RESP'S OCCUPATIONAL PRESTIGE SCORE

  COUNT   MIDPOINT    ONE SYMBOL EQUALS APPROX.        1.20 OCCURRENCES

      5      11.67  ****
     11      15.00  *********
     19      18.33  ****************
     27      21.67  ***********************
     32      25.00  ***************************
     25      28.33  *********************
     37      31.67  *******************************
     47      35.00  ***************************************
     19      38.33  ****************
     39      41.67  *********************************
     56      45.00  ***********************************************
     36      48.33  ******************************
     50      51.67  ******************************************
     11      55.00  *********
     13      58.33  ***********
     19      61.67  ****************
      0      65.00
      5      68.33  ****
      3      71.67  ***
      4      75.00  ***
      3      78.33  ***
                    I....+....I....+....I....+....I....+....I....+....I
                    0         12        24        36        48        60
                              HISTOGRAM FREQUENCY

VALID CASES     461      MISSING CASES     39
```

You can use all of the formatting options available with BARCHART on the HISTOGRAM subcommand. In addition, you can specify the interval width and superimpose a normal curve on the histogram. The following specifications are optional on subcommand HISTOGRAM:

MIN(n) *Lower bound.* Values below the specified minimum are not plotted.

MAX(n) *Upper bound.* Values above the specified maximum are not plotted.

PERCENT(n) *Horizontal axis scaled in percentages.* The *n* specifies the preferred maximum and is not required. If you do not specify an *n* or your *n* is too small, FREQUENCIES chooses 5, 10, 25, 50 or 100, depending on the percentage for the largest category.

FREQ(n) *Horizontal axis scaled in frequencies.* While FREQ is the default scaling method, you can use this specification if you want to specify a maximum frequency *(n)* for the scale. If you do not specify an *n* or your *n* is too small, FREQUENCIES chooses 10, 20, 50, 100, 200, 500, 1000, 2000, and so forth, depending on the frequency count for the largest category.

INCREMENT(n) *Interval width.* By default, values are collected into 21 intervals for plotting. You can override the default by specifying the actual interval width. For example, if a variable ranges from 1 to 100 and you specify INCREMENT(2), the width of each interval will be 2, which will produce 50 intervals. If the variable has a range less than 21, a common divisor producing integer multiples of a common difference is used to produce a "nice" interval width.

NORMAL *Superimpose the normal curve.* The normal curve is based on all valid values for the variable and includes values excluded by MIN and MAX. The default is NONORMAL.

You can enter the optional specifications in any order, as in

```
FREQUENCIES  VARIABLES=PRESTIGE/
         HISTOGRAM=NORMAL INCREMENT(4)
```

which produces a histogram of PRESTIGE with a superimposed normal curve and an interval width of four.

18.14 The HBAR Subcommand

The HBAR subcommand produces either bar charts or histograms depending upon the number of values encountered in the data. If a bar chart for a variable fits on a page, HBAR produces a bar chart; otherwise, it produces a histogram. For the default page length of 59, a barchart will be displayed for variables with fewer than 12 categories. Histograms will be displayed for all other variables specified on the VARIABLES subcommand. You can use the SET command to change the page length (see Chapter 4). All of the specifications for HISTOGRAM and BARCHART will also work with HBAR.

18.15 Percentiles and Ntiles

You can use either the PERCENTILES or NTILES subcommands to specify the printing of percentiles for all variables specified on the VARIABLES subcommand. If more than one PERCENTILES and NTILES subcommands are specified, FREQUENCIES prints one table with the variable values for all requested percentiles.

18.16 The PERCENTILES Subcommand

Percentiles are the values below which a given percentage of cases fall. Use the PERCENTILES subcommand followed by an optional equals sign and a list of percentiles between 0 and 100 to print the variable values for each percentile. For example, to request the values for percentiles 10, 25, 33.3, 66.7, and 75 for variable PRESTIGE, specify:

```
FREQUENCIES VARIABLES=PRESTIGE/
         PERCENTILES=10 25 33.3 66.7 75/
```

The five values of PRESTIGE associated with these percentiles are shown in Figure 18.16.

Figure 18.16 PERCENTILES subcommand output

```
PERCENTILE     VALUE      PERCENTILE     VALUE      PERCENTILE     VALUE

  10.00       20.000        25.00       29.000        33.30       33.000
  66.70       46.000        75.00       48.000

VALID CASES      461      MISSING CASES      39
```

18.17 The NTILES Subcommand

Ntiles are the variable values that divide the sample into groups of equal numbers of cases. To print the variable values for each *n*tile, use the NTILES subcommand followed by an optional equals sign and one integer value specifying the number of subgroups. For example, to request quartiles for PRESTIGE, specify:

```
FREQUENCIES VARIABLES=PRESTIGE/NTILES=4/
```

Figure 18.17 shows the printed output from the NTILES subcommand. Note that SPSS^X prints one less percentile than the number specified on the NTILES subcommand. If a requested percentile cannot be calculated, SPSS^X prints a period (.) as the value associated with that percentile.

Figure 18.17 NTILES subcommand output

```
PERCENTILE     VALUE      PERCENTILE     VALUE      PERCENTILE     VALUE

  25.00       29.000        50.00       40.000        75.00       48.000

VALID CASES      461      MISSING CASES      39
```

ANNOTATED EXAMPLE FOR FREQUENCIES

The following example demonstrates the use of FREQUENCIES to do some preliminary checks on a newly defined file. The file is based on employment data from Hubbard Consultants Inc. Variables include date employee was hired, employee's department, salary, job category, name, age, and sex, as well as salary increases from 1980 to 1982. The $SPSS^X$ commands are

```
FILE HANDLE HUBDATA/ file specifications
FILE TYPE  GROUPED FILE=HUBDATA RECORD=#RECID 80 CASE=ID 1-4

RECORD TYPE 1
DATA LIST   /MOHIRED YRHIRED 12-15 DEPT79 TO DEPT82 SEX 16-20

RECORD TYPE 2
DATA LIST   /SALARY79 TO SALARY82 6-25
             AGE 54-55 RAISE80 TO RAISE82 56-70

RECORD TYPE 3
DATA LIST   /JOBCAT 6 EMPNAME 25-48 (A)

END FILE TYPE

MISSING VALUES  DEPT79 TO SALARY82 AGE (0)
                RAISE80 TO RAISE82 (-999) JOBCAT (9)

VARIABLE LABELS  SALARY79 'SALARY IN 1979'
                 SALARY80 'SALARY IN 1980'
                 SALARY81 'SALARY IN 1981'
                 SALARY82 'SALARY IN 1982'
                 JOBCAT 'JOB CATEGORIES'
VALUE LABELS  SEX 1 'MALE' 2 'FEMALE'/
              JOBCAT 1 'OFFICIALS & MANAGERS' 2 'PROFESSIONALS'
              3 'TECHNICIANS' 4 'OFFICE & CLERICAL' 5 'CRAFTSMEN'
              6 'SERVICE WORKERS'

FREQUENCIES  VARIABLES=SALARY79 TO SALARY82 SEX AGE JOBCAT/
             FORMAT=LIMIT(10)/
             STATISTICS=DEFAULT MEDIAN
FINISH
```

- Since there are three records per case, FILE TYPE GROUPED is used to check for duplicate or missing records (see Chapter 11).
- MISSING VALUES, VARIABLE LABELS, and VALUE LABELS complete the file definition (see Chapter 3).
- FREQUENCIES displays frequency tables for variables having 10 or fewer categories and statistics for all the variables named. The default statistics are the mean, standard deviation, minimum, and maximum.

Figure 18.21 is the FREQUENCIES display produced by this job.

FREQUENCIES display

```
SALARY79  SALARY IN 1979

MEAN       12247.323       MEDIAN    10140.000       STD DEV     6665.182
MINIMUM     6337.000       MAXIMUM   45500.000

VALID CASES      158       MISSING CASES   117

- - - - - - - - - - - - - - - - - - - - - - - - - - - - - - - - - - - - -

SALARY80  SALARY IN 1980

MEAN       12123.725       MEDIAN    10400.000       STD DEV     6316.356
MINIMUM     5720.000       MAXIMUM   48100.000

VALID CASES      273       MISSING CASES     2

- - - - - - - - - - - - - - - - - - - - - - - - - - - - - - - - - - - - -

SALARY81  SALARY IN 1981

MEAN       15096.212       MEDIAN    12359.500       STD DEV     8074.387
MINIMUM     7605.000       MAXIMUM   52000.000

VALID CASES      160       MISSING CASES   115

- - - - - - - - - - - - - - - - - - - - - - - - - - - - - - - - - - - - -

SALARY82  SALARY IN 1982

MEAN       17161.552       MEDIAN    15132.000       STD DEV     8695.734
MINIMUM     5830.000       MAXIMUM   50700.000

VALID CASES      145       MISSING CASES   130

- - - - - - - - - - - - - - - - - - - - - - - - - - - - - - - - - - - - -

SEX

                                                             VALID     CUM
  VALUE LABEL                VALUE  FREQUENCY  PERCENT  PERCENT  PERCENT

MALE                             1         83     30.2     30.2     30.2
FEMALE                           2        192     69.8     69.8    100.0
                                       -------  -------  -------
                             TOTAL        275    100.0    100.0

MEAN           1.698       MEDIAN        2.000       STD DEV         .460
MINIMUM        1.000       MAXIMUM       2.000

VALID CASES      275       MISSING CASES     0

- - - - - - - - - - - - - - - - - - - - - - - - - - - - - - - - - - - - -

AGE

MEAN          37.158       MEDIAN       34.000       STD DEV       11.335
MINIMUM       20.000       MAXIMUM      69.000

VALID CASES      272       MISSING CASES     3

- - - - - - - - - - - - - - - - - - - - - - - - - - - - - - - - - - - - -

JOBCAT    JOB CATEGORIES

                                                             VALID     CUM
  VALUE LABEL                VALUE  FREQUENCY  PERCENT  PERCENT  PERCENT

OFFICIALS & MANAGERS             1         48     17.5     17.5     17.5
PROFESSIONALS                    2         62     22.5     22.5     40.0
TECHNICIANS                      3         98     35.6     35.6     75.6
OFFICE & CLERICAL                4         67     24.4     24.4    100.0
                                       -------  -------  -------
                             TOTAL        275    100.0    100.0

MEAN           2.669       MEDIAN        3.000       STD DEV        1.030
MINIMUM        1.000       MAXIMUM       4.000

VALID CASES      275       MISSING CASES     0
```

18.18 The STATISTICS Subcommand

The STATISTICS subcommand specifies univariate statistics for all variables named on the VARIABLES subcommand. If you are using the integer mode, only cases with values in the specified range are used in the computation of statistics. The available statistics and their keywords are:

MEAN *Mean.*

SEMEAN *Standard error of the mean.*

MEDIAN *Median.* The median is defined as the value below which half the cases fall. If there are an even number of cases, the median is the average of the (*n*th/2) and (*n*th/2+1) cases when the cases are sorted in ascending order. The median is not available if you specify AFREQ or DFREQ on the FORMAT subcommand.

MODE *Mode.*

STDDEV *Standard deviation.*

VARIANCE *Variance.*

SKEWNESS *Skewness.*

SESKEW *Standard error of the skewness statistic.*

KURTOSIS *Kurtosis.*

SEKURT *Standard error of the kurtosis statistic.*

RANGE *Range.*

MINIMUM *Minimum.*

MAXIMUM *Maximum.*

SUM *Sum.*

DEFAULT *Mean, standard deviation, minimum, and maximum.* You can use DEFAULT jointly with other statistics.

ALL *All available statistics.*

NONE *No statistics.*

You can specify as many keywords as you wish on the STATISTICS subcommand. For example,

```
FREQUENCIES  VARIABLES=PRESTIGE POLVIEWS/
   STATISTICS=MEDIAN DEFAULT/
```

prints the median and the default statistics (the mean, standard deviation, minimum, and maximum). The annotated example shows the output produced by this STATISTICS subcommand. If you use the STATISTICS subcommand with no specifications, the default statistics are printed.

18.19 Missing Values

FREQUENCIES recognizes three types of missing values: user-missing, system-missing, and in integer mode, out-of-range values. Both user- and system-missing values are included in frequency tables. They are labeled as missing and are not included in the valid and cumulative percentages. Missing values are not used in the calculation of descriptive statistics, nor do they appear in bar charts and histograms.

One optional missing-value treatment is available. To include user-missing values as valid values, use the MISSING subcommand, which has one specification, INCLUDE. For example,

```
MISSING VALUES  SATFAM TO HAPPY(8,9)
FREQUENCIES  VARIABLES=SATFAM HAPPY (0,9)/
             BARCHART/
             MISSING=INCLUDE
```

includes values 8 and 9 (which were previously defined as missing with the MISSING VALUES command) in the bar charts.

18.20 LIMITATIONS

The following limitations apply to FREQUENCIES:

- A maximum of 500 variables total per FREQUENCIES command.
- A maximum value range of 32,767 for a variable in integer mode.
- A maximum of 32,767 observed values over all variables.

CONDESCRIPTIVE:
CONDESCRIPTIVE varname [(zname)] [varname . . .]

OPTIONS:
1 Include missing values.
2 Suppress variable labels.
3 Compute *Z*-scores.
4 Reference indexes.
5 Exclude missing values listwise.
6 Serial-style formatting.
7 Narrow formatting.

STATISTICS:
1 Mean.
2 Standard error of mean.
5 Standard deviation.
6 Variance.
7 Kurtosis.
8 Skewness.
9 Range.
10 Minimum.
11 Maximum.
12 Sum.
13 Default statistics: mean, standard deviation, minimum, and maximum.

OVERVIEW, **19.1**
OPERATION, **19.2**
The Variable List, **19.3**
Statistics, **19.4**
Z Scores, **19.5**
Missing Values, **19.6**
Formatting Options, **19.7**
LIMITATIONS, **19.8**

Chapter 19 CONDESCRIPTIVE

Procedure CONDESCRIPTIVE computes univariate summary statistics and standardized variables which are saved on the active file. Although it computes statistics also available in procedure FREQUENCIES (Chapter 18), CONDESCRIPTIVE computes descriptive statistics for continuous variables more efficiently because it does not sort values into a frequencies table.

19.1 OVERVIEW

CONDESCRIPTIVE calculates the mean, standard deviation, minimum, and maximum for numeric variables. You can request optional statistics and *Z*-score transformations. CONDESCRIPTIVE has alternative formats and methods of handling missing data.

Statistics. In addition to the default statistics, you can obtain the standard error of the mean, variance, kurtosis, skewness, range, and sum. CONDESCRIPTIVE does not compute the median or mode. (See Section 19.4.)

Z Scores. You can request standardized scores for variables named or implied on the CONDESCRIPTIVE command. These transformed variables are stored as new variables on the active file. (See Section 19.5.)

Missing Values. By default, CONDESCRIPTIVE excludes cases with missing values on a variable-by-variable basis. Optionally, you can request that missing values be handled as if they were valid or that cases with missing values be deleted listwise. (See Section 19.6.)

Formatting Options. You can suppress the printing of variable labels, produce reference indexes, print statistics in serial-style format, and restrict the output to an 80-character width. (See Section 19.7.)

19.2 OPERATION

The CONDESCRIPTIVE command operates via a variable list and associated OPTIONS and STATISTICS commands. You can request statistics and compute the *Z*-score form for the variables on the list. CONDESCRIPTIVE computes summary statistics for *numeric* variables only. It skips string variables and prints a warning message.

19.3 The Variable List

To request the default summary statistics, specify a simple list of variables, as in:

```
CONDESCRIPTIVE  NTCPRI FOOD RENT
```

You can use the keyword TO for consecutive variables, as in:

```
CONDESCRIPTIVE  NTCPRI TO COOK
```

You can also use the keyword ALL to specify all variables in the active file. For example,

```
CONDESCRIPTIVE ALL
```

produces the display in Figure 19.3. This output includes the mean, standard deviation, minimum, maximum, number of valid cases, and variable labels. CONDESCRIPTIVE always displays the number of valid cases that would be available if listwise deletion of missing values had been selected (see Section 19.6).

Figure 19.3 Default statistics

NUMBER OF VALID OBSERVATIONS (LISTWISE) = 38.00

VARIABLE	MEAN	STD DEV	MINIMUM	MAXIMUM	VALID N	LABEL
NTCPRI	81.378	20.238	46.000	141.000	45	NET PRICE LEVEL
NTCSAL	50.341	24.295	8.000	100.000	44	NET SALARY LEVEL
NTCPUR	58.705	28.806	10.000	110.000	44	NET PURCHASING LEVEL
FOOD	70.467	18.744	40.000	130.000	45	AVG FOOD PRICES
WCLOTHES	80.711	30.195	21.000	174.000	45	MEDIUM-PRICED WOMEN'S CLOTHES
MCLOTHES	87.044	26.192	22.000	147.000	45	MEDIUM-PRICED MEN'S CLOTHES
RENT	120.089	94.225	27.000	440.000	45	NORMAL RENT
APPL	78.178	22.255	54.000	165.000	45	PRICE FOR APPLIANCES
SERVICE	73.089	19.007	42.000	113.000	45	PRICE FOR SERVICES
TEACHER	38.318	25.182	4.000	108.000	44	TEACHER'S GROSS SALARY
MECHANIC	50.705	30.746	5.000	115.000	44	MECHANIC'S GROSS SALARY
CONSTRUC	64.114	74.722	5.000	476.000	44	CONSTRUCTION WORKER'S GROSS SALARY
LATHE	41.814	24.353	4.000	100.000	43	LATHE WORKER'S GROSS SALARY
COOK	64.659	30.279	13.000	137.000	44	COOK'S GROSS SALARY
MANAGER	53.659	25.074	11.000	100.000	44	MANAGER'S GROSS SALARY
ENGINEER	60.045	26.175	8.000	114.000	44	ENGINEER'S GROSS SALARY
TELLER	42.636	24.123	7.000	100.000	44	TELLER'S GROSS SALARY
SECRET	48.841	22.230	8.000	100.000	44	SECRETARY'S GROSS SALARY
FSALES	48.182	27.127	5.000	100.000	44	FEMALE SALESWORKER'S GROSS SALARY
FTEX	50.718	31.195	3.000	111.000	39	FEMALE TEXTILE WORKER'S GROSS SALARY
CASWGT	1.000	0.0	1.000	1.000	45	

You can specify only one variable list with CONDESCRIPTIVE, but there is no limit to the number of variables named or implied on one command. If you separate variable lists with slashes, the variables on all the lists will be displayed as if a single list had been supplied. Variables named more than once will appear in the output more than once. If there is insufficient space to process all the requested variables, CONDESCRIPTIVE truncates the variable list.

19.4 Statistics

By default, CONDESCRIPTIVE prints the mean, standard deviation, minimum, and maximum. To control the printing of statistics, use the STATISTICS command, specifying the number(s) of the requested statistic(s). The available statistics and their corresponding numbers are

STATISTIC 1 *Mean.*

STATISTIC 2 *Standard error of the mean.*

STATISTIC 5 *Standard deviation.*

STATISTIC 6 *Variance.*

STATISTIC 7 *Kurtosis.* Also prints standard error.

STATISTIC 8 *Skewness.* Also prints standard error.

STATISTIC 9 *Range.*

STATISTIC 10 *Minimum.*

STATISTIC 11 *Maximum.*

STATISTIC 12 *Sum.*

STATISTIC 13 *Mean, standard deviation, minimum, and maximum.* These are the default statistics.

If you do not use the STATISTICS command, CONDESCRIPTIVE prints Statistics 1, 5, 10, and 11. If you do use it, CONDESCRIPTIVE prints *only* those statistics requested. You can use the keyword ALL to obtain all statistics. When requesting additional statistics, you can specify Statistic 13 to obtain the default statistics without having to name Statistics 1, 5, 10, and 11.

Note that Statistics 3 and 4, corresponding to the median and mode available in FREQUENCIES, are not available in CONDESCRIPTIVE. These statistics require that values be sorted, and CONDESCRIPTIVE does not sort values. CONDESCRIPTIVE ignores statistic numbers not listed above.

The number of columns needed to display the statistics controls the manner in which they are printed. The maximum column width for skewness, kurtosis, and their standard error is 10; the maximum width for mean, standard error of the mean, minimum, maximum, and range is 11; the maximum width for standard deviation is 12; the maximum width for variance is 13; and the maximum width for sum is 14. These widths include a blank between statistics. CONDESCRIPTIVE prints all statistics with three positions to the right of the decimal point if it can fit them into the space allocated within the maximum width. Large numbers are rounded to fit the column width. If the integer portion still exceeds the column width, CONDESCRIPTIVE uses scientific notation. Extremely small numbers are also printed with scientific notation.

19.5 Z Scores

The *Z*-score variable transformation standardizes variables with different observed scales to the same scale. CONDESCRIPTIVE generates new variables, each with a mean of 0 and a standard deviation of 1, and stores them on the active file. To obtain one *Z*-score variable for each variable specified on the CONDESCRIPTIVE variable list, use Option 3. For example, the commands

```
CONDESCRIPTIVE  ALL
OPTIONS  3
```

produce the table of old variables and new *Z*-score variables shown in Figure 19.5.

OPTION 3 *Compute Z scores.* Calculates standardized variables for all variables specified with CONDESCRIPTIVE and stores them on the active file.

CONDESCRIPTIVE automatically supplies variable names and labels for the new variables. The new variable name is created by prefixing the letter Z to the first seven characters of the variable name. For example, ZNTCPRI is the *Z*-score variable for NTCPRI. When CONDESCRIPTIVE creates new *Z*-score variables, it prints a table containing the source variable name, new variable name, its label, and the number of cases for which it is computed.

Figure 19.5 Z-score correspondence table

```
THE FOLLOWING Z-SCORE VARIABLES HAVE BEEN SAVED ON YOUR ACTIVE FILE:

FROM       TO                                                        WEIGHTED
VARIABLE   Z-SCORE     LABEL                                          VALID N
--------   -------     -----                                          -------

NTCPRI     ZNTCPRI     ZSCORE:  NET PRICE LEVEL                            45
NTCSAL     ZNTCSAL     ZSCORE:  NET SALARY LEVEL                           44
NTCPUR     ZNTCPUR     ZSCORE:  NET PURCHASING LEVEL                       44
FOOD       ZFOOD       ZSCORE:  AVG FOOD PRICES                            45
WCLOTHES   ZWCLOTHE    ZSCORE:  MEDIUM-PRICED WOMEN'S CLOTHES              45
MCLOTHES   ZMCLOTHE    ZSCORE:  MEDIUM-PRICED MEN'S CLOTHES                45
RENT       ZRENT       ZSCORE:  NORMAL RENT                                45
APPL       ZAPPL       ZSCORE:  PRICE FOR APPLIANCES                       45
SERVICE    ZSERVICE    ZSCORE:  PRICE FOR SERVICES                         45
TEACHER    ZTEACHER    ZSCORE:  TEACHER'S GROSS SALARY                     44
MECHANIC   ZMECHANI    ZSCORE:  MECHANIC'S GROSS SALARY                    44
CONSTRUC   ZCONSTRU    ZSCORE:  CONSTRUCTION WORKER'S GROSS SAL            44
LATHE      ZLATHE      ZSCORE:  LATHE WORKER'S GROSS SALARY                43
COOK       ZCOOK       ZSCORE:  COOK'S GROSS SALARY                        44
MANAGER    ZMANAGER    ZSCORE:  MANAGER'S GROSS SALARY                     44
ENGINEER   ZENGINEE    ZSCORE:  ENGINEER'S GROSS SALARY                    44
TELLER     ZTELLER     ZSCORE:  TELLER'S GROSS SALARY                      44
SECRET     ZSECRET     ZSCORE:  SECRETARY'S GROSS SALARY                   44
FSALES     ZFSALES     ZSCORE:  FEMALE SALESWORKER'S GROSS SALA            44
FTEX       ZFTEX       ZSCORE:  FEMALE TEXTILE WORKER'S GROSS S            39
CASWGT     ZCASWGT     ZSCORE(CASWGT)                                       0
```

If you want Z scores for a subset of the variables on the list, specify the name of the new variable in parentheses following the source variable and *do not use Option 3*. For example,

```
CONDESCRIPTIVE  NTCSAL NTCPUR (PURCHZ) NTCPRI (PRICEZ)
```

creates PURCHZ and PRICEZ. If you both use Option 3 and specify new names, CONDESCRIPTIVE creates one new variable for each variable in the list, using the default names for variables not explicitly assigned names. When you specify the name of the new variable yourself, you can use any acceptable eight-character variable name, including any of the default variable names, that is not already part of the active file.

If CONDESCRIPTIVE cannot use the default naming convention because it would produce duplicate names, it uses an alternative naming convention: first ZSC001 through ZSC099, then STDZ01 through STDZ09, then ZZZZ01 through ZZZZ09, then ZQZQ01 through ZQZQ09. For example,

```
CONDESCRIPTIVE  SALARY80 SALARY81 SALARY82
OPTIONS  3
```

creates ZSALARY8, ZSC001, and ZSC002.

CONDESCRIPTIVE automatically supplies variable labels for the new variables by prefixing *ZSCORE:* to the first 31 characters of the source variable's label. If it uses a name like ZSC001, it prefixes *ZSCORE(varname)* to the first 31 characters of the source variable's label. If the source variable has no label, it uses *ZSCORE(varname)* for the label.

19.6 Missing Values

By default, CONDESCRIPTIVE deletes cases with missing values on a variable-by-variable basis. A case missing on a variable will not be included in the summary statistics for that variable but the case *will* be included for variables where it is not missing. Two missing-value options are available.

OPTION 1 *Include missing values.* User-missing values are included in the analysis.

OPTION 5 *Exclude missing values listwise.* Cases missing on any variable named are excluded from the computation of summary statistics for all variables.

When you use the default missing-value treatment, CONDESCRIPTIVE reports the number of valid cases for each variable. It always displays the number of cases that would be available if listwise deletion of missing values had been selected.

19.7 Formatting Options

By default, CONDESCRIPTIVE prints the statistics and a 40-character variable label for each variable on one line, as shown in Figure 19.3. Use Option 2 to suppress the printing of variable labels. With Option 4, you can obtain a reference index that shows the page location in the output of the statistics for each variable. The variables are listed by their position in the active file and alphabetically. Option 6 requests serial-style format, with the requested statistics printed below each variable name. This format provides larger field widths and permits more decimal digits for very large or very small numbers. CONDESCRIPTIVE automatically forces this format if the number of statistics requested does not fit in the column format. Option 7 restricts CONDESCRIPTIVE output to 80 columns and is useful if you are examining displays on short-carriage terminals. However, the number of columns for statistics is severely restricted. If you use Option 2 to suppress variable labels, more space is available for statistics. Also, if you specify listwise deletion of missing values with Option 5, the column for valid number of cases is suppressed, providing additional space for statistics.

OPTION 2 *Suppress variable labels.*

OPTION 4 *Reference indexes.* Print a positional and an alphabetic reference index following the statistical display.

OPTION 6 *Serial-style format.* Print statistics below the variable name.

OPTION 7 *Narrow formatting.* Print with an 80-character width.

The following commands request reference indexes and print the statistics in serial-style format with an 80-column width:

```
CONDESCRIPTIVE  TEACHER FTEX FSALES SECRET
STATISTICS    ALL
OPTIONS  4 6 7
```

See the display in Figure 19.7.

Figure 19.7 Serial format and reference indexes

```
NUMBER OF VALID OBSERVATIONS (LISTWISE) =          38.00

VARIABLE  TEACHER    TEACHER'S GROSS SALARY

MEAN              38.318                 S.E. MEAN          3.796
STD DEV           25.182                 VARIANCE         634.129
KURTOSIS            .249                 S.E. KURT          1.963
SKEWNESS            .727                 S.E. SKEW           .357
RANGE            104.000                 MINIMUM            4.000
MAXIMUM          108.000                 SUM             1686.000

VALID OBSERVATIONS -        44         MISSING OBSERVATIONS -        1

- - - - - - - - - - - - - - - - - - - - - - - - - - - - - - - - -

VARIABLE  FTEX       FEMALE TEXTILE WORKER'S GROSS SALARY

MEAN              50.718                 S.E. MEAN          4.995
STD DEV           31.195                 VARIANCE         973.103
KURTOSIS          -1.102                 S.E. KURT          1.959
SKEWNESS            .218                 S.E. SKEW           .378
RANGE            108.000                 MINIMUM            3.000
MAXIMUM          111.000                 SUM             1978.000

VALID OBSERVATIONS -        39         MISSING OBSERVATIONS -        6

- - - - - - - - - - - - - - - - - - - - - - - - - - - - - - - - -

VARIABLE  FSALES     FEMALE SALESWORKER'S GROSS SALARY

MEAN              48.182                 S.E. MEAN          4.090
STD DEV           27.127                 VARIANCE         735.873
KURTOSIS          -1.055                 S.E. KURT          1.963
SKEWNESS            .185                 S.E. SKEW           .357
RANGE             95.000                 MINIMUM            5.000
MAXIMUM          100.000                 SUM             2120.000

VALID OBSERVATIONS -        44         MISSING OBSERVATIONS -        1

- - - - - - - - - - - - - - - - - - - - - - - - - - - - - - - - -

VARIABLE  SECRET     SECRETARY'S GROSS SALARY

MEAN              48.841                 S.E. MEAN          3.351
STD DEV           22.230                 VARIANCE         494.183
KURTOSIS           -.417                 S.E. KURT          1.963
SKEWNESS            .200                 S.E. SKEW           .357
RANGE             92.000                 MINIMUM            8.000
MAXIMUM          100.000                 SUM             2149.000

VALID OBSERVATIONS -        44         MISSING OBSERVATIONS -        1


POSITIONAL INDEX

 VARIABLE  PAGE    VARIABLE  PAGE    VARIABLE  PAGE    VARIABLE  PAGE

 TEACHER      5    SECRET       5    FSALES       5    FTEX         5


ALPHABETIC INDEX

 VARIABLE  PAGE    VARIABLE  PAGE    VARIABLE  PAGE    VARIABLE  PAGE

 FSALES       5    FTEX         5    SECRET       5    TEACHER      5
```

19.8 LIMITATIONS

There are no specific limitations. If there is insufficient workspace to process all the requested variables, CONDESCRIPTIVE will truncate the variable list.

ANNOTATED EXAMPLE FOR CONDESCRIPTIVE

This example analyzes 1979 prices and earnings in 45 cities around the world, compiled by the Union Bank of Switzerland. The variables are

- NTCPUR—the city's net purchasing power level, calculated as the ratio of labor expended (measured in number of working hours) to the cost of more than 100 goods and services, weighted by consumer habits. NTCPUR is expressed as a percentage above or below that of Zurich, where Zurich equals 100%.
- FOOD—the average net cost of 39 different food and beverage items in the city, expressed as a percentage above or below that of Zurich, where Zurich equals 100%.
- RENT—the average gross monthly rent in the city, expressed as a percentage above or below that of Zurich, where Zurich equals 100%.
- APPL—the average cost of six different household appliances, expressed as a percentage above or below that of Zurich, where Zurich equals 100%.
- SERVICE—the average cost of 28 different goods and services in the city, expressed as a percentage above or below that of Zurich, where Zurich equals 100%.
- WCLOTHES—the cost of medium-priced women's clothes, expressed as a percentage above or below that of Zurich, where Zurich equals 100%.
- MCLOTHES—the cost of medium-priced men's clothes, expressed as a percentage above or below that of Zurich, where Zurich equals 100%.
- CLOTHES—the average cost of medium-priced women's and men's clothes, expressed as a percentage above or below that of Zurich, where Zurich equals 100%.

In this example, we obtain univariate summary statistics about purchasing power and the costs of various goods and services in cities and generate standardized variables for the costs of men's and women's clothes. The SPSS^{X} commands are

```
FILE HANDLE  CITY/ file specifications
GET  FILE=CITY/KEEP NTCPUR TO SERVICE
COMPUTE  CLOTHES=(WCLOTHES + MCLOTHES)/2
VAR LABELS  CLOTHES, AVERAGE COST OF W AND M CLOTHES
CONDESCRIPTIVE  NTCPUR, FOOD, RENT TO SERVICE, WCLOTHES (ZWWEAR),
   MCLOTHES (ZMWEAR), CLOTHES (ZCLOTHES)
STATISTICS  6 13
OPTIONS  5
FINISH
```

- The FILE HANDLE identifies the CITY data file and gives the operating-system specifications (see Chapter 3).
- The GET command defines the data to SPSS^X and selects the variables needed for analysis (see Chapter 5).
- The COMPUTE command creates the variable CLOTHES by adding the values for WCLOTHES and MCLOTHES and dividing by 2 (see Chapter 6).
- The VAR LABELS command assigns a label to the new variable CLOTHES (see Chapter 3).
- The CONDESCRIPTIVE command requests statistics for all the variables outside parentheses and computes *Z* scores for a subset of variables, WCLOTHES, MCLOTHES, and CLOTHES. The new standardized variables are named ZWWEAR, ZMWEAR, and ZCLOTHES (see Sections 19.3 and 19.5).
- Statistic 6 requests the variance for each variable. Statistic 13 requests the default statistics: mean, standard deviation, minimum, and maximum (see Section 19.4).
- Option 5 specifies listwise deletion of missing values. A case missing on any variable specified on the CONDESCRIPTIVE command is excluded from the computation of statistics for all variables (see Section 19.6).
- Since no formatting option is specified, CONDESCRIPTIVE displays the statistics and variable labels for each variable on one line and can use more than 80 columns (see Section 19.7).

Output from CONDESCRIPTIVE

NUMBER OF VALID OBSERVATIONS (LISTWISE) =   44.00

VARIABLE	MEAN	STD DEV	VARIANCE	MINIMUM	MAXIMUM	LABEL
NTCPUR	58.705	28.806	829.794	10.000	110.000	NET PURCHASING LEVEL
FOOD	71.000	18.612	346.419	40.000	130.000	AVG FOOD PRICES
RENT	121.750	94.646	8957.773	27.000	440.000	NORMAL RENT
APPL	78.705	22.227	494.027	54.000	165.000	PRICE FOR APPLIANCES
SERVICE	73.682	18.801	353.478	42.000	113.000	PRICE FOR SERVICES
WCLOTHES	81.205	30.360	921.701	21.000	174.000	MEDIUM-PRICED WOMEN'S CLOTHES
MCLOTHES	87.864	25.906	671.097	22.000	147.000	MEDIUM-PRICED MEN'S CLOTHES
CLOTHES	84.534	26.749	715.505	21.500	160.500	AVERAGE COST OF W AND M CLOTHES

THE FOLLOWING Z-SCORE VARIABLES HAVE BEEN SAVED ON YOUR ACTIVE FILE:

FROM VARIABLE	TO Z-SCORE	LABEL	WEIGHTED VALID N
WCLOTHES	ZWWEAR	ZSCORE: MEDIUM-PRICED WOMEN'S CLOTHES	44
MCLOTHES	ZMWEAR	ZSCORE: MEDIUM-PRICED MEN'S CLOTHES	44
CLOTHES	ZCLOTHES	ZSCORE: AVERAGE COST OF W AND M CLOTHES	44

General Mode:

CROSSTABS [TABLES =] varlist BY varlist [BY . . .] [/varlist . . .]

Integer Mode:

CROSSTABS VARIABLES = varlist (min, max) [varlist . . .]
/TABLES = varlist BY varlist [BY . . .] [/varlist . . .]

OPTIONS:

1 Include missing values.
2 Suppress variable and value labels.
3 Print row percentages.
4 Print column percentages.
5 Print total percentages.
6 Suppress value labels.
7 Report missing values in table (integer mode only).
8 Print rows ordered on highest to lowest values.
9 Print index of tables.
10 Write cell count for nonempty cells to a file.
11 Write cell count for all cells to a file (integer mode only).
12 Suppress tables.
13 Suppress cell counts.
14 Print expected frequencies.
15 Print residuals.
16 Print standardized residuals.
17 Print adjusted standardized residuals.
18 Print all cell information.

STATISTICS:

1 Chi-square.
2 Phi for 2 x 2 tables, Cramer's *V* for larger tables.
3 Contingency coefficient.
4 Lambda.
5 Uncertainty coefficient.
6 Kendall's tau-*b*.
7 Kendall's tau-*c*.
8 Gamma (partial for three-way to *n*-way table in integer mode only).
9 Somers' *d*.
10 Eta.
11 Pearson's *r*.

OVERVIEW, **20.1**

OPERATION, **20.2**
- General Mode, **20.3**
- Integer Mode, **20.4**
  - The VARIABLES Subcommand, **20.5**
  - The TABLES Subcommand, **20.6**
- Cell Contents, **20.7**
  - Percentages, **20.8**
  - Expected Values and Residuals, **20.9**
- Optional Statistics, **20.10**
- Missing Values, **20.11**
- Formatting Options, **20.12**
- Indexing Tables, **20.13**
- Writing and Reproducing Tables, **20.14**
  - Writing Tables to a File, **20.15**
  - The Output File, **20.16**
  - Reproducing Tables, **20.17**

LIMITATIONS, **20.18**

Chapter 20 CROSSTABS

Procedure CROSSTABS produces tables that are the joint distribution of two or more variables that have a limited number of distinct values. The frequency distribution of one variable is subdivided according to the values of one or more variables. The unique combination of values for two variables defines a cell, the basic element of all tables. CROSSTABS can operate in either general or integer mode, similar to FREQUENCIES (Chapter 18) and BREAKDOWN (Chapter 22). If you want to analyze contingency tables using a general linear model approach, see procedure LOGLINEAR (Chapter 29).

20.1 OVERVIEW

CROSSTABS produces two-way to *n*-way crosstabulations for variables that have a limited number of numeric or string values. In addition to cell counts, you can obtain cell percentages, expected values, residuals, and optional measures of association. You can also alter the handling of missing values, produce measures of association without printing tables, request an index of tables, and write the cell frequencies to a file.

Methods for Building Tables. CROSSTABS operates in two different modes: *general* and *integer*. General mode requires fewer specifications (see Section 20.3). Integer mode requires that you specify the minimum and maximum values for the variables and builds tables more efficiently (see Section 20.4).

Cell Contents. By default, CROSSTABS prints only the number of cases in each cell. You can request row, column, and total percentages, expected values, and residuals (see Section 20.7).

Statistics. In addition to the tables, you can obtain summary statistics for each subtable (see Section 20.10).

Missing Values. By default, CROSSTABS excludes cases with missing values on a table-by-table basis. You can request that missing values be included in the tables and in the calculation of statistics or only in the tables (see Section 20.11).

Formatting Options. You can control the order of values for the row variables and suppress the printing of variable labels, value labels, and the table itself (see Section 20.12).

Index of Tables. You can print a list of the tables produced by the CROSSTABS command with the page number where each table begins (see Section 20.13).

Writing and Reproducing Tables. CROSSTABS can write cell frequencies to a file and reproduce the original tables (see Section 20.14).

20.2 OPERATION

Procedure CROSSTABS operates via subcommands and associated OPTIONS and STATISTICS commands. The specifications for these commands depend on whether you want to use the *general mode* or the *integer mode* to build tables. Each method has advantages and disadvantages in computational efficiency, available statistics, and additional options.

- General mode permits string or noninteger variables. You do not have to specify ranges for variables, which makes general mode more convenient. You can reference any defined SPSS^X variable. The order of the variables in the active file determines the positional order of variables in the tables list. (See Section 20.3.)
- Integer mode builds tables more quickly. However, it requires more space if the table has many empty cells. By specifying the appropriate ranges, you can select a subset of values for processing. You can include missing values in tables while excluding them from the calculation of statistics and percentages. Partial and zero-order gammas are available only in integer mode. The order of the variables on the VARIABLES subcommand determines the positional order of the variables on the TABLES subcommand. (See Section 20.4.)

20.3 General Mode

To run CROSSTABS in general mode, use the TABLES subcommand followed by a list of one or more variables, the keyword BY, and another list of one or more variables. For example, the command

```
CROSSTABS TABLES=FEAR BY SEX
```

produces a bivariate table displayed in Figure 20.3a. The variable FEAR defines the rows of the table and the variable SEX defines the columns. In general mode you can specify numeric and string variables. However, long strings are truncated to short strings for purposes of defining categories (see Chapter 3).

Figure 20.3a A bivariate crosstabulation using general mode

```
- - - - - - - - - - - - - - - - - - -  C R O S S T A B U L A T I O N   O F   - - - - - - - - - - - - - - - - -
   FEAR       AFRAID  TO WALK AT NIGHT IN NEIGHBORHOOD      BY  SEX
- - - - - - - - - - - - - - - - - - - - - - - - - - - - - - - - - - - - - - - - - - - - - - - -  PAGE  1 OF  1

                      SEX
           COUNT     |
                     |MALE      FEMALE      ROW
                     |                      TOTAL
                     |       1|       2|
FEAR        ---------+--------+--------+
               1     |    55  |   180  |     235
  YES                |        |        |    47.4
                     +--------+--------+
               2     |   172  |    89  |     261
  NO                 |        |        |    52.6
                     +--------+--------+
           COLUMN        227      269        496
            TOTAL       45.8     54.2      100.0

NUMBER OF MISSING OBSERVATIONS =          4
```

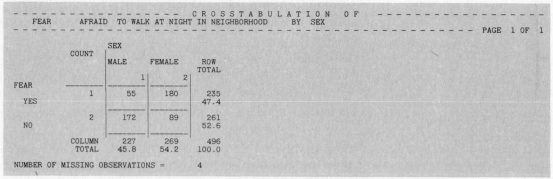

The keyword TABLES appears only once in a CROSSTABS command, but it is not required to operate CROSSTABS in general mode. For example, the following commands produce identical displays:

```
CROSSTABS  TABLES=FEAR BY SEX
```

```
CROSSTABS  FEAR BY SEX
```

However, if you use the keyword TABLES for general mode, as shown in the examples in this section, you must also include the equals sign.

A maximum of 10 dimensions can be specified on a tables list in general mode. A list of one or more variables can be specified for each dimension. Separate each list with the keyword BY. The first variables list is the list of *row variables* and the variables list following the first BY keyword is the list of *column variables*. Subsequent variables lists following BY keywords specify orders of *control variables*. For example,

```
CROSSTABS  TABLES=FEAR BY SEX BY RACE
```

crosstabulates FEAR by SEX, controlling for RACE. Figure 20.3b shows the output from this command. In each subtable, FEAR is the row variable and SEX is the column variable. The first subtable crosstabulates FEAR by SEX within the first category of RACE. This category has the value 1 and the label WHITE. The second subtable also crosstabulates FEAR by SEX, but for the next category of RACE, which has the value 2 and the value label NONWHITE. When you use control variables, a subtable is produced for each value of the control variable.

Figure 20.3b A crosstabulation with two subtables

```
- - - - - - - - - - - - - - - - - -  C R O S S T A B U L A T I O N   O F   - - - - - - - - - - - - - - - - - -
   FEAR      AFRAID  TO WALK AT NIGHT IN NEIGHBORHOOD      BY  SEX
CONTROLLING FOR..
   RACE                                                    VALUE =         1.  WHITE
- - - - - - - - - - - - - - - - - - - - - - - - - - - - - - - - - - - - - - - - - - - - - - -  PAGE  1 OF  1

                   SEX
          COUNT   |
                  |MALE      FEMALE      ROW
                  |                      TOTAL
                  |       1|       2|
FEAR      --------+--------+--------+
               1  |    48  |   149  |    197
   YES            |        |        |    46.5
                  +--------+--------+
               2  |   153  |    74  |    227
   NO             |        |        |    53.5
                  +--------+--------+
          COLUMN      201      223        424
           TOTAL     47.4     52.6      100.0


- - - - - - - - - - - - - - - - - -  C R O S S T A B U L A T I O N   O F   - - - - - - - - - - - - - - - - - -
   FEAR      AFRAID  TO WALK AT NIGHT IN NEIGHBORHOOD      BY  SEX
CONTROLLING FOR..
   RACE                                                    VALUE =         2.  NONWHITE
- - - - - - - - - - - - - - - - - - - - - - - - - - - - - - - - - - - - - - - - - - - - - - -  PAGE  1 OF  1

                   SEX
          COUNT   |
                  |MALE      FEMALE      ROW
                  |                      TOTAL
                  |       1|       2|
FEAR      --------+--------+--------+
               1  |     7  |    31  |     38
   YES            |        |        |    52.8
                  +--------+--------+
               2  |    19  |    15  |     34
   NO             |        |        |    47.2
                  +--------+--------+
          COLUMN       26       46         72
           TOTAL     36.1     63.9      100.0

NUMBER OF MISSING OBSERVATIONS =         4
```

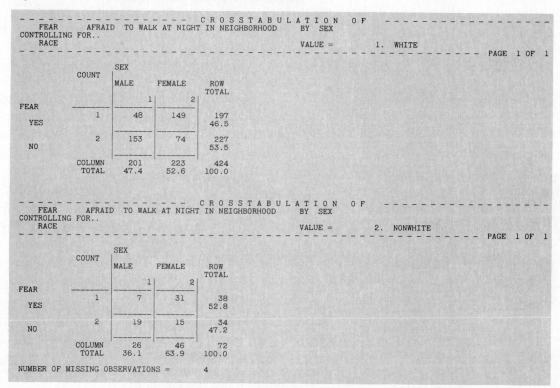

In CROSSTABS, the value of the first control variable changes most quickly and the value of the last control variable changes most slowly. For example, you might add another order of control to the previous example:

```
CROSSTABS  TABLES=FEAR BY SEX BY RACE BY DEGREE
```

The variable DEGREE has two values: 1=high school or less and 2=college or more. This command produces the four subtables shown in Figure 20.3c. The first subtable crosstabulates FEAR by SEX, controlling for the first value of RACE and the first value of DEGREE; the second subtable controls for the second value of RACE and the first value of DEGREE; the third subtable controls for the first value of RACE and the second value of DEGREE; and the fourth subtable controls for the second value of RACE and the second value of DEGREE.

You can specify more than one variable in each dimension. Use the keyword TO to name a set of adjacent variables in the active file, as in:

```
CROSSTABS  TABLES=CONFINAN TO CONARMY BY SEX TO REGION
```

This command will produce CROSSTABS tables for all the variables between and including CONFINAN and CONARMY by all the variables

Figure 20.3c A crosstabulation with four subtables

```
- - - - - - - - - - - - - - - - - -  C R O S S T A B U L A T I O N   O F  - - - - - - - - - - - - - - - - -
    FEAR      AFRAID  TO WALK AT NIGHT IN NEIGHBORHOOD      BY  SEX
CONTROLLING FOR..
    RACE                                                    VALUE =         1.  WHITE
BY  DEGREE     HIGHEST DEGREE,RESP                          VALUE =         1.  LE HS
- - - - - - - - - - - - - - - - - - - - - - - - - - - - - - - - - - - - - - - - - - - - - - -  PAGE  1 OF  1

                      SEX
            COUNT   |
                    |MALE      FEMALE      ROW
                    |                      TOTAL
                    |       1|        2|
FEAR        --------+--------+--------+
               1    |   39   |   126  |    165
  YES               |        |        |    47.7
                    +--------+--------+
               2    |  114   |    67  |    181
  NO                |        |        |    52.3
                    +--------+--------+
            COLUMN      153       193       346
             TOTAL     44.2      55.8     100.0


- - - - - - - - - - - - - - - - - -  C R O S S T A B U L A T I O N   O F  - - - - - - - - - - - - - - - - -
    FEAR      AFRAID  TO WALK AT NIGHT IN NEIGHBORHOOD      BY  SEX
CONTROLLING FOR..
    RACE                                                    VALUE =         2.  NONWHITE
BY  DEGREE     HIGHEST DEGREE,RESP                          VALUE =         1.  LE HS
- - - - - - - - - - - - - - - - - - - - - - - - - - - - - - - - - - - - - - - - - - - - - - -  PAGE  1 OF  1

                      SEX
            COUNT   |
                    |MALE      FEMALE      ROW
                    |                      TOTAL
                    |       1|        2|
FEAR        --------+--------+--------+
               1    |    5   |    27  |     32
  YES               |        |        |    50.0
                    +--------+--------+
               2    |   17   |    15  |     32
  NO                |        |        |    50.0
                    +--------+--------+
            COLUMN       22        42        64
             TOTAL     34.4      65.6     100.0


- - - - - - - - - - - - - - - - - -  C R O S S T A B U L A T I O N   O F  - - - - - - - - - - - - - - - - -
    FEAR      AFRAID  TO WALK AT NIGHT IN NEIGHBORHOOD      BY  SEX
CONTROLLING FOR..
    RACE                                                    VALUE =         1.  WHITE
BY  DEGREE     HIGHEST DEGREE,RESP                          VALUE =         2.  COLLEGE
- - - - - - - - - - - - - - - - - - - - - - - - - - - - - - - - - - - - - - - - - - - - - - -  PAGE  1 OF  1

                      SEX
            COUNT   |
                    |MALE      FEMALE      ROW
                    |                      TOTAL
                    |       1|        2|
FEAR        --------+--------+--------+
               1    |    9   |    23  |     32
  YES               |        |        |    41.0
                    +--------+--------+
               2    |   39   |     7  |     46
  NO                |        |        |    59.0
                    +--------+--------+
            COLUMN       48        30        78
             TOTAL     61.5      38.5     100.0


- - - - - - - - - - - - - - - - - -  C R O S S T A B U L A T I O N   O F  - - - - - - - - - - - - - - - - -
    FEAR      AFRAID  TO WALK AT NIGHT IN NEIGHBORHOOD      BY  SEX
CONTROLLING FOR..
    RACE                                                    VALUE =         2.  NONWHITE
BY  DEGREE     HIGHEST DEGREE,RESP                          VALUE =         2.  COLLEGE
- - - - - - - - - - - - - - - - - - - - - - - - - - - - - - - - - - - - - - - - - - - - - - -  PAGE  1 OF  1

                      SEX
            COUNT   |
                    |MALE      FEMALE      ROW
                    |                      TOTAL
                    |       1|        2|
FEAR        --------+--------+--------+
               1    |    2   |     4  |      6
  YES               |        |        |    75.0
                    +--------+--------+
               2    |    2   |        |      2
  NO                |        |        |    25.0
                    +--------+--------+
            COLUMN        4         4         8
             TOTAL     50.0      50.0     100.0

NUMBER OF MISSING OBSERVATIONS =         4
```

between and including SEX and REGION. You can use similar variables lists to request higher order CROSSTABS tables. The values of the variables to the right of the last BY keyword change most slowly. Within lists separated by the keyword BY, variables rotate from left to right. For example,

```
CROSSTABS  TABLES=CONFINAN TO CONARMY BY SEX BY RACE,REGION
```

will produce CROSSTABS tables for all the variables between and including CONFINAN and CONARMY by SEX, controlling for RACE, and for all the variables between and including CONFINAN and CONARMY, controlling for REGION. If there are five variables implied by the first variables list, the command produces 10 crosstabulations. The first table is CONFINAN by SEX by RACE and the second table is CONFINAN by SEX by REGION. The last table produced is CONARMY by SEX by REGION. The number of values encountered for the control variables determines the total number of subtables. If RACE has two values and REGION has three values, the output from the command will have a total of 25 subtables.

You can specify up to 20 tables lists on one CROSSTABS command. A maximum of 200 variables can be named or implied by all the tables lists. Use a slash to separate tables lists on one CROSSTABS command. For example,

```
CROSSTABS  TABLES=FEAR BY SEX/RACE BY REGION
```

specifies two bivariate tables, FEAR by SEX and RACE by REGION. If you omit a slash between tables lists, CROSSTABS includes the variables as if one tables list had been supplied. If the preceding command had no slash, as in

```
CROSSTABS  TABLES=FEAR BY SEX RACE BY REGION
```

it would produce two three-dimensional tables, FEAR by SEX by REGION and FEAR by RACE by REGION.

20.4 Integer Mode

To run CROSSTABS in integer mode, the values of all the variables must be integers. Two subcommands are required. The VARIABLES subcommand specifies all the variables to be used in the CROSSTABS procedure and the minimum and maximum values for building tables. The TABLES subcommand specifies the tables lists. In integer mode, the equals sign following the VARIABLES and TABLES subcommands is optional.

Integer mode can produce more tables in a given amount of core storage space than general mode, and the processing is faster. The values supplied as variable ranges do not have to be as wide as the range of the variables; thus, you have control from within CROSSTABS over the tabulated ranges of the variables. Some options and statistics are available only in integer mode.

20.5 The VARIABLES Subcommand

The VARIABLES subcommand is followed by a list of variables to be used in the crosstabulations. Specify the lowest and highest values in parentheses after each variable. These values must be integers. For example, the command

```
CROSSTABS  VARIABLES=FEAR (1,2) MOBILE16 (1,3)/
   TABLES=FEAR BY MOBILE16
```

produces a table where FEAR has a range from 1 to 2 and MOBILE16 has a range from 1 to 3. Noninteger values are truncated. The final range must be followed by a slash. A maximum of 100 variables can be named or implied by the VARIABLES subcommand.

You must specify a range for each variable to be used in the CROSSTABS procedure and several variables can have the same range. For example,

```
CROSSTABS  VARIABLES=FEAR SEX RACE (1,2) MOBILE16 (1,3)/
   TABLES=FEAR BY SEX MOBILE16 BY RACE
```

defines 1 as the lowest value and 2 as the highest value for FEAR, SEX, and RACE. Variables may appear in any order. However, the order in which you place them on the VARIABLES subcommand affects their implied order on the TABLES subcommand as described in Section 20.6.

CROSSTABS uses the ranges you specify to allocate tables. One cell is allocated for each possible combination of values of the row and column variables for a requested table before the data are read. Therefore, if you specify more generous ranges than the variables actually have, you are wasting some space. If the table is sparse because the variables do not have values falling throughout the range specified, you might consider using the general mode or recoding the variables. If, on the other hand, the values of the variables fall outside the range you specify, cases with these values are considered missing and are not used in the computation of the table.

20.6 The TABLES Subcommand

The TABLES subcommand names the tables list. It has the same syntax as the TABLES subcommand in general mode described in Section 20.3. For example,

```
CROSSTABS  VARIABLES=FEAR (1,2) MOBILE16 (1,3)/
   TABLES=FEAR BY MOBILE16
```

produces the table in Figure 20.6. Variables named on the TABLES subcommand must have been previously named or implied on the VARIABLES subcommand.

You can name multiple tables lists separated by slashes, but the TABLES subcommand appears only once in a CROSSTABS command. Like general mode, integer mode can process up to 20 tables lists. However, you can specify only up to 100 tables over all the lists together, and you can name or imply only up to 100 variables on all the tables lists. Also, tables can have a maximum of only eight dimensions in integer mode.

Figure 20.6 A crosstabulation using integer mode

```
- - - - - - - - - - - - - - - - -  C R O S S T A B U L A T I O N   O F  - - - - - - - - - - - - - - - -
   FEAR      AFRAID  TO WALK AT NIGHT IN NEIGHBORHOOD     BY  MOBILE16  GEOGRAPHIC MOBILITY SINCE AGE 16
- - - - - - - - - - - - - - - - - - - - - - - - - - - - - - - - - - - - - - - - - - - - - - - PAGE  1 OF  1

                    MOBILE16
            COUNT
                   |SAME CIT DIF CITY    ROW
                   |Y         OR STAT   TOTAL
                   |       1|       2|
FEAR       --------+--------+--------+
              1    |    97  |   136  |    233
  YES              |        |        |   47.4
                   +--------+--------+
              2    |   112  |   147  |    259
  NO               |        |        |   52.6
                   +--------+--------+
           COLUMN       209      283       492
            TOTAL      42.5     57.5     100.0

NUMBER OF MISSING OBSERVATIONS =      8
```

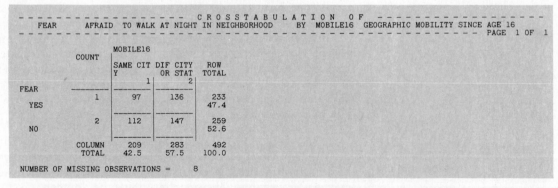

There is one important difference between the tables request in integer mode and the tables request in general mode. In integer mode, the order of the variables implied on the TABLES subcommand is established by the order of the variables named or implied on the VARIABLES subcommand. In general mode, the order of variables implied on the tables lists is established by their order in the active file.

20.7 Cell Contents

By default, CROSSTABS prints only the number of cases in each cell. You can request the printing of other types of information in the cells with the OPTIONS command. To print row, column, or total percentages, see Section 20.8. To print expected values and residuals, see Section 20.9. These items are calculated separately for each bivariate table or subtable.

If you want to print any of the optional cell information without cell counts, specify Option 13. You must also request at least one other option pertaining to cell content. For example,

```
CROSSTABS  TABLES=FEAR BY SEX
OPTIONS  4 13
```

requests column percentages with Option 4 and suppresses cell counts with Option 13. If you specify Option 13 alone, no table is printed. You can request all cell information with Option 18.

OPTION 13 *Suppress cell counts.* You must specify at least one other option pertaining to cell content.

OPTION 18 *Print all cell information.* Print cell count; row, column, and total percentages; expected values; residuals; standardized residuals; and adjusted standardized residuals.

If you specify both Option 13 and Option 18, only Option 18 is in effect and cell counts are printed along with all the other cell information.

20.8 Percentages

You can print any or all of the following percentages in the cells of the CROSSTABS table:

OPTION 3 *Print row percentages.* Print the number of cases in each cell in a row expressed as a percentage of all cases in that row.

OPTION 4 *Print column percentages.* Print the number of cases in each cell in a column expressed as a percentage of all cases in that column.

OPTION 5 *Print two-way table total percentages.* Print the number of cases in each cell of a subtable expressed as a percentage of all cases in that subtable.

For example, the following commands print row and column percentages in the cells:

```
CROSSTABS  TABLES=FEAR BY SEX
OPTIONS  3 4
```

Figure 20.8 displays this table. The key located at the top left corner of the table describes the information contained in each cell. If you request only percentages and cell counts, the percentages are printed without a percent sign and blanks are printed instead of zero values for counts and percents. If you request percentages and any of the expected values or residuals, the percent sign appears next to the percentage and zero values are printed as zeros.

Figure 20.8 Requesting cell percentages with Options 3 and 4

```
- - - - - - - - - - - - - - - - -  C R O S S T A B U L A T I O N   O F  - - - - - - - - - - - - - - - - -
   FEAR     AFRAID  TO WALK AT NIGHT IN NEIGHBORHOOD        BY  SEX
- - - - - - - - - - - - - - - - - - - - - - - - - - - - - - - - - - - - - - - - - - - - - -  PAGE  1 OF  1

                    SEX
            COUNT   |
          ROW PCT   |MALE      FEMALE      ROW
          COL PCT   |                      TOTAL
                    |       1|        2|
FEAR       ---------+--------+---------+
               1    |    55  |   180   |    235
  YES               |  23.4  |  76.6   |   47.4
                    |  24.2  |  66.9   |
                    +--------+---------+
               2    |   172  |    89   |    261
  NO                |  65.9  |  34.1   |   52.6
                    |  75.8  |  33.1   |
                    +--------+---------+
            COLUMN      227      269        496
             TOTAL     45.8     54.2      100.0

NUMBER OF MISSING OBSERVATIONS =          4
```

20.9 Expected Values and Residuals

Use Option 14 to print expected frequencies which are the number of cases expected in each cell if the two variables were independent. Option 15 prints residuals, the value of the observed cell count minus the expected value. Options 16 and 17 produce standardized residuals and adjusted standardized residuals (Haberman, 1978). Use the following options to request expected frequencies and residuals:

OPTION 14 *Print expected frequencies.* Print the number of cases expected in each cell if the two variables in the subtable were statistically independent.

OPTION 15 *Print residuals.* Print the value of the observed cell count minus the expected value.

OPTION 16 *Print standardized residuals.*

OPTION 17 *Print adjusted standardized residuals.*

20.10 Optional Statistics

You can request a number of summary statistics for each subtable with the STATISTICS command. By default, these measures of association are calculated for the cases with valid values included in the subtable. If you specify a range in integer mode that excludes cases, the excluded cases are *not* used in the calculation of the statistics. If you include missing values with Option 1, cases with values defined as missing are included in the tables as well as in the calculation of statistics. The following statistics are available for CROSSTABS:

STATISTIC 1 *Chi-square.* Fisher's exact test is computed using the rounded values of the cell entries when there are fewer than 20 cases in a 2 × 2 table that does not result from missing rows or columns in a larger table; Yates' corrected chi-square is computed for all other 2 × 2 tables.

STATISTIC 2 *Phi for 2 × 2 tables, Cramer's* V *for larger tables.*

STATISTIC 3 *Contingency coefficient.*

STATISTIC 4 *Lambda, symmetric and asymmetric.*

STATISTIC 5 *Uncertainty coefficient, symmetric and asymmetric.*

STATISTIC 6 *Kendall's tau*-b.

STATISTIC 7 *Kendall's tau*-c.

STATISTIC 8 *Gamma.* Partial and zero-order gammas for 3-way to 8-way tables are available in integer mode only. Zero-order gammas are printed for 2-way tables and conditional gammas are printed for 3-way to 10-way tables in general mode.

STATISTIC 9 *Somers'* d, *symmetric and asymmetric.*

STATISTIC 10 *Eta.* Available for numeric data only.

STATISTIC 11 *Pearson's* r. Available for numeric data only.

If you omit the STATISTICS command, no statistics are calculated or printed. To request all available statistics, use the keyword ALL, as in:

```
CROSSTABS  FEAR BY SEX
STATISTICS  ALL
```

Figure 20.10 shows these statistics, which are associated with the crosstabulation in Figure 20.3a. For chi-square, the output shows the degrees of freedom, the significance level, the smallest expected frequency, and the number of cells with an expected frequency less than 5. For lambda, the uncertainty coefficient, Somers' *d*, and eta, SPSS^X prints the symmetric value and both asymmetric values. The remaining statistics display the value of the statistic and the significance level when appropriate.

Figure 20.10 Statistics available with CROSSTABS

```
 CHI-SQUARE     D.F.        SIGNIFICANCE         MIN E.F.        CELLS WITH E.F.< 5
 ----------     ----        ------------         --------        ------------------

   88.26870       1            0.0000            107.550            NONE
   89.97266       1            0.0000            ( BEFORE YATES CORRECTION )

                                                   WITH FEAR             WITH SEX
          STATISTIC                 SYMMETRIC      DEPENDENT             DEPENDENT
          ---------                 ---------      -------------         -------------

LAMBDA                                0.37662         0.38723               0.36564
UNCERTAINTY COEFFICIENT               0.13624         0.13602               0.13646
SOMERS'S D                           -0.42591        -0.42685              -0.42496
ETA                                                   0.42591               0.42591
          STATISTIC                 VALUE          SIGNIFICANCE
          ---------                 -----          ------------

PHI                                 0.42591
CONTINGENCY COEFFICIENT             0.39185
KENDALL'S TAU B                    -0.42591           0.0000
KENDALL'S TAU C                    -0.42379           0.0000
PEARSON'S R                        -0.42591           0.0000
GAMMA                              -0.72696

NUMBER OF MISSING OBSERVATIONS =          4
```

20.11 Missing Values

By default, CROSSTABS deletes cases with missing values on a table-by-table basis. A case missing on any of the variables specified for a table is not used either in the printed table or in the calculation of the statistics. When you separate tables requests with a slash, missing values are handled separately for each list. The number of missing cases is always printed at the end of the table, following the last subtable and after any requested statistics.

Two missing-value options are available. Option 7 reports missing values in the table but excludes them from the calculation of percentages and statistics. Option 7 is available only in integer mode. If the missing values are not included in the range specifications on the VARIABLES subcommand, they are excluded from the table regardless of the option. The following commands produce the output in Figure 20.11a:

```
CROSSTABS  VARIABLES=FEAR (1,8) SEX (1,2)/
   TABLES=FEAR BY SEX
STATISTICS  1
OPTIONS  7
```

Missing rows and columns appear at the bottom and the right of the table. The letter *M* indicates that the cases in these cells are missing. In Figure 20.11a, four cases have the user-defined missing-value code of 8. Only the

Figure 20.11a Reporting missing values in the table with Option 7

```
- - - - - - - - - - - - - - - -  C R O S S T A B U L A T I O N   O F  - - - - - - - - - - - - - - - -
   FEAR       AFRAID  TO WALK AT NIGHT IN NEIGHBORHOOD      BY  SEX
- - - - - - - - - - - - - - - - - - - - - - - - - - - - - - - - - - - - - - - - - - - - -   PAGE  1 OF  1

                     SEX
             COUNT  |
                    |MALE      FEMALE       ROW
                    |                       TOTAL
                    |      1|       2|
FEAR       ---------+-------+--------+
                  1 |    55 |    180 |      235
  YES               |       |        |      47.4
                    +-------+--------+
                  2 |   172 |     89 |      261
  NO                |       |        |      52.6
                    +-------+--------+
                  8 |    1M |     3M |       4M
  DK                |       |        |      0.0
                    +-------+--------+
             COLUMN     227      269        496
              TOTAL    45.8     54.2      100.0

CHI-SQUARE     D.F.        SIGNIFICANCE         MIN E.F.        CELLS WITH E.F.< 5
----------     ----        ------------         --------        ------------------

  88.26868       1            0.0000            107.550            NONE
  89.97266       1            0.0000            ( BEFORE YATES CORRECTION )

NUMBER OF MISSING OBSERVATIONS =          4
```

valid cases appear in the row, column, and total percentages. The statistics also include only the valid cases. For example, the chi-square statistics in Figure 20.11a are identical to those in Figure 20.10, which uses the default treatment for missing values.

Option 1 handles user-defined missing values as if they were not missing. Cases with values defined as missing are included in the tables as well as the calculation of statistics. For example, the commands

```
CROSSTABS  TABLES=FEAR BY SEX
STATISTICS  1
OPTIONS  1
```

produce the crosstabulation in Figure 20.11b of FEAR by SEX which includes missing values in the table and in the statistics. Option 1 can be specified while using either general mode or integer mode. When you use Option 1 with integer mode, remember to include the missing values in the range specification on the VARIABLES subcommand.

OPTION 1 *Include missing values.*

OPTION 7 *Report missing values in the tables.* This option includes missing values in tables but not in the calculation of percentages or statistics. This option is available only in integer mode.

Figure 20.11b Including missing values with Option 1

```
- - - - - - - - - - - - - - - - - -   C R O S S T A B U L A T I O N   O F   - - - - - - - - - - - - - - - - - -
   FEAR      AFRAID  TO WALK AT NIGHT IN NEIGHBORHOOD     BY  SEX
- - - - - - - - - - - - - - - - - - - - - - - - - - - - - - - - - - - - - - - - - - - - - - - -  PAGE  1 OF  1

                         SEX
               COUNT    |
                        |MALE      FEMALE      ROW
                        |                      TOTAL
                        |       1|        2|
FEAR           ---------+--------+---------+
                     1  |     55 |     180 |    235
  YES                   |        |         |   47.0
                        +--------+---------+
                     2  |    172 |      89 |    261
  NO                    |        |         |   52.2
                        +--------+---------+
                     8  |      1 |       3 |      4
  DK                    |        |         |     .8
                        +--------+---------+
               COLUMN        228       272      500
                TOTAL       45.6      54.4    100.0

 CHI-SQUARE    D.F.        SIGNIFICANCE          MIN E.F.         CELLS WITH E.F.< 5
 ----------    ----        ------------          --------         ------------------

   90.71444       2            0.0000               1.824         2 OF     6 ( 33.3%)

NUMBER OF MISSING OBSERVATIONS =          0
```

20.12 Formatting Options

By default, CROSSTABS prints tables and subtables with variable labels and value labels when they are available. Although value labels can be up to 20 characters long in SPSS^X, CROSSTABS uses only the first 16 characters. The value labels for the columns print on two lines with eight characters per line. If the format of the labels is an important consideration in your table, you can redefine the value labels to fit the columns as shown in the annotated example for CROSSTABS. Alternatively, you can suppress the printing of value labels with Option 6 or suppress the printing of both the variable labels and the value labels with Option 2.

The default output also prints tables with the values for the row variables in order from lowest to highest. Use Option 8 to print the rows in order from highest to lowest.

Option 12 suppresses printed tables. If you use the STATISTICS command and specify Option 12, only the statistics are printed. If you do not use the STATISTICS command and specify Option 12, the CROSSTABS command produces no output. Use Option 12 when you write the tables to a file with Options 10 or 11 and you do not want the printed tables.

OPTION 2 *Suppress variable and value labels.*
OPTION 6 *Suppress value labels, but print variable labels.*
OPTION 8 *Print row variables ordered from highest to lowest.*
OPTION 12 *Suppress tables.*

20.13 Indexing Tables

Use Option 9 to print an index of tables. The index lists all tables produced by the CROSSTABS command and the page number where each table begins. The index follows the last page of tables produced by the tables list.

OPTION 9 *Print an index of tables.*

20.14 Writing and Reproducing Tables

CROSSTABS can write cell frequencies to a file for subsequent use by either SPSS^X or some other program. It can also use cell frequencies as input to reproduce tables and compute statistics.

20.15 Writing Tables to a File

CROSSTABS has two options for producing an output file of cell frequencies. You can write out all the cells of the table or only the nonempty cells. The file contains one record for each cell; each record contains a split-file group number and a table number, which identify the table, and the cell frequency and values, which identify the cell.

Use Option 10 to write only nonempty cells. Combinations of values that include a missing value are not written to the output file. If you include missing values in the tables with Option 1, no values are considered missing and all nonempty cells will be written.

Option 11 writes out all defined cells and is available only with integer mode. A record for each combination of values defined by the TABLES subcommand is written to the output file. If you include missing values in the tables with Option 1 or Option 7, all defined cells are written whether or not a missing value is involved. If you exclude missing values on a table-by-table basis (the default), no records are written for combinations of values that include a missing value.

OPTION 10 *Write the cell count for nonempty cells to a file.*
OPTION 11 *Write the cell count for all cells to a file.* Available only in integer mode.

If you specify both Option 10 and Option 11, only Option 10 is in effect and only the contents of the nonempty cells will be written to a file.

20.16 The Output File

When you write tables to a file, you must supply a FILE HANDLE command and a PROCEDURE OUTPUT command to define the output file for the cell records (see Chapter 17). For example,

```
FILE HANDLE  GSS80/ file specifications
GET FILE  GSS80
FILE HANDLE  CELLDATA/ file specifications
PROCEDURE OUTPUT  OUTFILE=CELLDATA
CROSSTABS  VARIABLES=FEAR SEX (1,2)/
  TABLES=FEAR BY SEX
OPTIONS  11
```

writes a record for each cell in the table FEAR by SEX to the file CELLDATA. Figure 20.16 shows the contents of the CELLDATA file.

Figure 20.16 Cell output records

```
1  1     55     1     1
1  1    172     2     1
1  1    180     1     2
1  1     89     2     2
```

The output record from each cell contains the following information:

Columns	Contents
1–4	Split-file group number, numbered consecutively from 1. Note that this is not the value of the variable or variables used to define the splits.
5–8	Table number. A table is defined by taking one variable from each of the variable lists separated by the keyword BY.
9–16	Cell frequency. The number of times this combination of variable values occurred in the data, or, if case weights are used, the sum of case weights for cases having this combination of values.
17–24	The value of the row variable (the one named before the first BY).
25–32	The value of the column variable (the one named after the first BY).
33–40	The value of the first control variable (the one named after the second BY).
41–48	The value of the second control variable (the one named after the third BY).
49–56	The value of the third control variable (the one named after the fourth BY).
57–64	The value of the fourth control variable (the one named after the fifth BY).
65–72	The value of the fifth control variable (the one named after the sixth BY).
73–80	The value of the sixth control variable (the one named after the seventh BY).

The split-file group number, table number, and frequency are written as integers. If the integer mode of CROSSTABS is used, the values of variables are also written as integers. If the general mode is used, the values are written in accordance with the PRINT FORMAT specified for each variable. Alphanumeric values are written at the left end of any field in which they occur.

Within each table, the records are written in the following order:

the value of the row variable, within
the value of the column variable, within
the value of the first control variable, within
. . .
the value of the fifth control variable

This order implies that the records are written from one column of the table at a time and the value of the last control variable changes most slowly.

If you specify multiple tables, the tables are written in the same order as they are printed. The variable in the row variables list changes the slowest and the variable in the last control variables list change the fastest. For example, the following commands write a set of records for each table to the XTABDATA output file:

```
FILE HANDLE  XTABDATA/ file specifications
PROCEDURE OUTPUT  OUTFILE=XTABDATA
CROSSTABS  TABLES=V1 TO V3 BY V4 BY V10 TO V15
OPTIONS  10
```

All of the records for the table V1 BY V4 BY V10 are written first, the records for V1 BY V4 BY V11 second, and the records for V3 BY V4 BY V15 last.

20.17 Reproducing Tables

You can use the file created by Option 10 or 11 in a subsequent SPSS^X job to reproduce a table and compute statistics for it. Each record in the file contains all the information used to build the original table. For example, if you read the CELLDATA file created by the commands in Section 20.15, you can reproduce the table displayed in Figure 20.3a and calculate statistics for it. The following commands read the cell frequency as a weighting factor (WGHT), the value of the row variable (FEAR), and the value of the column variable (SEX):

```
FILE HANDLE  CELLDATA/ file specifications
DATA LIST FILE=CELLDATA
   /WGHT 9-16 FEAR 17-24 SEX 25-32
VARIABLE LABELS  FEAR 'AFRAID TO WALK AT NIGHT IN NEIGHBORHOODS'
VALUE LABELS  FEAR 1 'YES' 2 'NO'/ SEX 1 'MALE' 2 'FEMALE'
WEIGHT  BY WGHT
CROSSTABS  TABLES=FEAR BY SEX
STATISTICS  ALL
```

The WEIGHT command recreates the sample size by weighting each of the four cases (cells) by the cell frequency (see Chapter 10). You can also use the WEIGHT command to reproduce tables and compute statistics for published tables where you do not have the original data. Each cell in the table becomes a case and each record should include the cell frequency for weighting, the row and column variables, and any control variables. For example, the following commands also reproduce the table in Figure 20.3a:

```
DATA LIST  /FEAR 1 SEX 3 WGHT 5-7
VARIABLE LABELS  FEAR 'AFRAID TO WALK AT NIGHT IN NEIGBORHOOD'
VALUE LABELS  FEAR 1 'YES' 2 'NO'/ SEX 1 'MALE' 2 'FEMALE'
WEIGHT  BY WGHT
CROSSTABS  TABLES=FEAR BY SEX
STATISTICS  ALL
BEGIN DATA
1 1  55
2 1 172
1 2 180
2 2  89
END DATA
```

You can define the variables for the cell frequency, row value, and column value in any order.

20.18 LIMITATIONS

The following limitations apply to CROSSTABS in *general mode*:

- A maximum of 200 variables total per CROSSTABS command.
- A maximum of 250 nonempty rows or columns printed for each variable.
- A maximum of 20 tables lists per CROSSTABS command.
- A maximum of 10 dimensions per table.
- A maximum of 250 value labels printed on any single table.

The following limitations apply to CROSSTABS in *integer mode*:

- A maximum of 100 variables named or implied with the VARIABLES subcommand.
- A maximum of 100 variables named or implied with the TABLES subcommand.
- A maximum of 200 nonempty rows or columns printed for each variable.
- A maximum of 200 rows per subtable.
- A maximum of 200 columns per table.
- A maximum of 20 tables lists per CROSSTABS command.
- A maximum of 8 dimensions per table.
- No more than 20 rows or columns of missing values can be printed with Option 7.
- The largest range that can be implied on the minimum-maximum range specification on the VARIABLES subcommand is 32,766.

ANNOTATED EXAMPLE FOR CROSSTABS

The example illustrating CROSSTABS analyzes a 500-case sample from the 1980 General Social Survey. The variables are AGE, the respondent's age recoded to four categories, and DRUNK, the response to the question, Did you ever drink too much? This task examines how respondents in different age groups answer a question on alcohol-drinking habits. The following SPSS^X commands produce a crosstabulation of these two numeric variables and print several summary statistics:

```
FILE HANDLE  GSS80/ file specifications
GET FILE GSS80
RECODE  AGE (LOW THRU 29=1) (29 THRU 40=2) (40 THRU 58=3)
   (58 THRU HI=4)/ DRUNK (MISSING=8)
VARIABLE LABELS  AGE 'AGE IN FOUR CATEGORIES'
VALUE LABELS  AGE 1 'YOUNGESTQUARTER' 4 'OLDEST  QUARTER'/
   DRUNK 1 'YES' 2 'NO' 8 "DON'T DRINK/NA"
CROSSTABS  VARIABLES=DRUNK (1,8) AGE (1,4)/ TABLES=DRUNK BY AGE
OPTIONS  3,4,7
STATISTICS  1,4,6,7,8,9
FINISH
```

- The FILE HANDLE identifies the GSS80 data file and gives the operating-system specifications (see Chapter 3).
- The GET command defines the data to SPSS^X (see Chapter 5).
- The RECODE command redefines the variable AGE into four categories and recodes all missing values for the variable DRUNK to one missing value (see Chapter 6).
- The VARIABLE LABELS command defines a new variable label for AGE and the VALUE LABELS command defines value labels for AGE and DRUNK (see Chapter 3). The value labels for AGE are formatted to print appropriate labels for a column variable. Note that the label YOUNGEST-QUARTER has no blanks between the words and the label OLDEST QUARTER has two blanks separating the words (see Section 20.12).
- The CROSSTABS command uses integer mode to set up the table. The VARIABLES subcommand specifies the variables and their minimum and maximum values, including the missing values that will be displayed (see Section 20.5). The TABLES subcommand specifies variable DRUNK as the row variable and AGE as the column variable (see Sections 20.3 and 20.6).
- Options 3 and 4 request row and column percents (see Section 20.8). Option 7 reports missing values in the table but does not include them in calculating percentages and statistics (see Section 20.11).
- The STATISTICS command requests chi-square, lambda, Kendall's tau-*b*, Kendall's tau-*c*, gamma, and Somers' *d*. Although the table reports missing cases, they are not included in the calculation of statistics (see Section 20.10).

Output from the CROSSTABS command

```
- - - - - - - - - - - - - - - - - - - -   C R O S S T A B U L A T I O N   O F - - - - - - - - - - - - - - - - -
   DRUNK      EVER DRINK TOO MUCH                                          BY  AGE       AGE IN FOUR CATEGORIES
- - - - - - - - - - - - - - - - - - - - - - - - - - - - - - - - - - - - - - - - - - - - - - - - - - PAGE  1 OF  1

                          AGE
                COUNT    |
                ROW PCT  |YOUNGEST                     OLDEST     ROW
                COL PCT  |QUARTER                      QUARTER    TOTAL
                         |       1|       2|       3|       4|
DRUNK           ---------+--------+--------+--------+--------+
                     1   |    62  |    33  |    36  |    16  |    147
  YES                    |  42.2  |  22.4  |  24.5  |  10.9  |   38.5
                         |  57.9  |  34.7  |  37.9  |  18.8  |
                         +--------+--------+--------+--------+
                     2   |    45  |    62  |    59  |    69  |    235
  NO                     |  19.1  |  26.4  |  25.1  |  29.4  |   61.5
                         |  42.1  |  65.3  |  62.1  |  81.2  |
                         +--------+--------+--------+--------+
                     8   |   17M  |   27M  |   31M  |   43M  |    118M
  DON'T DRINK/NA         |        |        |        |        |    0.0
                         |        |        |        |        |
                         +--------+--------+--------+--------+
                COLUMN       107       95       95       85       382
                 TOTAL      28.0     24.9     24.9     22.3     100.0

 CHI-SQUARE    D.F.       SIGNIFICANCE       MIN E.F.       CELLS WITH E.F.< 5
 ----------    ----       ------------       --------       ------------------

   31.57228      3           0.0000           32.709          NONE

                                                       WITH DRUNK          WITH AGE
        STATISTIC                        SYMMETRIC     DEPENDENT           DEPENDENT
        ---------                        ---------     -------------       -------------

LAMBDA                                     0.09716         0.11565            0.08727
SOMERS'S D                                 0.23546         0.19222            0.30381

        STATISTIC                          VALUE        SIGNIFICANCE
        ---------                          -----        ------------

KENDALL'S TAU B                          0.24165           0.0000
KENDALL'S TAU C                          0.28768           0.0000
GAMMA                                    0.39632

NUMBER OF MISSING OBSERVATIONS =    118
```

MULT RESPONSE GROUPS = grpname ['label']

(itemlist ({value 1, value 2 | value})) . . . [grpname . . .]

/VARIABLES = itemlist (min, max) [itemlist . . .]

/FREQUENCIES = itemlist

/TABLES = itemlist BY itemlist . . .
[BY itemlist] [(PAIRED)] [/itemlist BY . . .]

OPTIONS:
1 Include missing values.
2 Exclude missing values listwise for multiple dichotomy groups.
3 Exclude missing values listwise for multiple response groups.
4 Suppress value labels.
5 Percentage on responses rather than respondents.
6 Narrow formatting.
7 Condensed-format frequency table.
8 Conditional condensed-format frequency table.

STATISTICS:
1 Row percents.
2 Column percents.
3 Total percents.

INTRODUCTION TO MULTIPLE RESPONSE ITEMS, **21.1**
Constructing Group Variables, **21.2**
Crosstabulations, **21.3**
OVERVIEW, **21.4**
OPERATION, **21.5**
The GROUPS Subcommand, **21.6**
The VARIABLES Subcommand, **21.7**
The FREQUENCIES Subcommand, **21.8**
The TABLES Subcommand, **21.9**
Paired Crosstabulations, **21.10**
Cell Contents and Percentages, **21.11**
Missing Values, **21.12**
Formatting Options, **21.13**
Stub and Banner Tables, **21.14**
LIMITATIONS, **21.15**

Chapter 21 MULT RESPONSE

Procedure MULT RESPONSE displays multiple response items in univariate tables and multivariate crosstabulations. *Multiple response items* are questions that can have more than one value for an individual case. For example, survey questions often ask respondents to indicate which magazines they read or to rank in importance a list of political issues. Variables that record these responses cannot be handled directly by procedures like FREQUENCIES and CROSSTABS but are conveniently displayed in MULT RESPONSE tables.

21.1 INTRODUCTION TO MULTIPLE RESPONSE ITEMS

The example in this section illustrates the use of multiple response items in a marketing research survey. The data in these tables are fictitious and should not be interpreted as real.

An airline might survey passengers flying a particular route to evaluate competing carriers. In this example, American Airlines wants to know about its passengers' use of other airlines on the Chicago–New York route and the relative importance of schedule and service in selecting an airline. The flight attendant hands each passenger a brief questionnaire upon boarding which looks like Figure 21.1. The first question is a multiple response question because the passenger can circle more than one airline. However, this question cannot be coded directly because an SPSS^X variable can have only one value for each case. You must use several variables to map the responses to this question. There are two ways to do this. One is to define a variable corresponding to each of the choices (i.e., AMERICAN, UNITED, TWA, EASTERN, OTHER). If the passenger circles United, the UNITED variable is assigned a code of 1, otherwise 0. This is the *multiple dichotomy method* of mapping variables.

Figure 21.1 An in-flight questionnaire

> Circle *all* airlines that you have flown at least one time in the last six months on this route:
>
> American United TWA Eastern Other:____________
>
> Which is more important in selecting a flight?
>
> Schedule Service
>
> *(Circle only one.)*
>
> Thank you for your cooperation.

The other way to map the responses is the *multiple response method*, in which you estimate the maximum number of possible responses to the question and set up the same number of variables, with codes used to specify the airline flown. By perusing a sample of the questionnaires, you might discover that no user has flown more than three different airlines on this route in the last six months. Further, you find that, due to the deregulation of airlines, 10 other airlines are named in the OTHER category. Using the multiple response method, you would define three variables, coded as 1=American, 2=United, 3=TWA, 4=Eastern, 5=Republic, 6=USAir, and so on. If a given passenger circles TWA and American, the first variable has a code of 1, the second has a code of 3, and the third variable has some missing-value code. Another passenger might have circled American and entered USAir. Thus, the first variable has a code of 1, the second a code of 6, and the third a missing-value code. If you use the multiple dichotomy method, you end up with 14 separate variables to map no more than three responses per passenger. Although either method of mapping multiple answers is feasible for this survey, the method you choose depends upon the distribution of responses.

21.2 Constructing Group Variables

Each variable created from the survey question about airlines is an *elementary variable*. To analyze a multiple response item, you must combine the elementary variables into *groups*. The specific technique for grouping variables depends on whether you have defined multiple dichotomy variables or multiple response variables. For example, if the airline survey asks only about three airlines (American, United, TWA) and you use multiple dichotomies to account for multiple responses, the separate frequency tables would resemble Table 21.2a. When you create a multiple dichotomy group, each of the three variables becomes a category of the group variable. The tabulated values represent the "Have flown" category of each elementary variable. Table 21.2b shows the frequencies for this multiple dichotomy group. The 75 people using American Airlines are the 75 cases with code 1 for the variable representing American Airlines in Table 21.2a. Because some people circled more than one response, 120 responses are recorded for 100 respondents.

Table 21.2a Dichotomies tabulated separately

American

Category Label	Code	Frequency	Relative Frequency
Have flown	1	75	75.0
Have not flown	0	25	25.0
	Total	100	100.0

United

Category Label	Code	Frequency	Relative Frequency
Have flown	1	30	30.0
Have not flown	0	70	70.0
	Total	100	100.0

TWA

Category Label	Code	Frequency	Relative Frequency
Have flown	1	15	15.0
Have not flown	0	85	85.0
	Total	100	100.0

Table 21.2b Multiple dichotomies tabulated as a group

Airlines
(Tabulating 1)

Variable		Frequency	Relative Frequency
American		75	62.5
United		30	25.0
TWA		15	12.5
	Total	120	100.0

If you discover that no respondent mentioned more than two airlines, you could create two multiple response variables, each having three codes, one for each airline. The frequency tables for these elementary variables would resemble Table 21.2c. When you create a multiple response group, the values are tabulated by adding the same codes in the elementary variables together. The resulting set of values is the same as those for each of the elementary variables. Table 21.2d shows the frequencies for this multiple response group. For example, the 30 responses for United are the sum of the 25 United responses for the multiple response item Airline 1 and the five United responses for Airline 2.

Table 21.2c Multiple response items tabulated separately

Airline 1

Category Label	Code	Frequency	Relative Frequency
American	1	75	75.0
United	2	25	25.0
	Total	100	100.0

Airline 2

Category Label	Code	Frequency	Relative Frequency
United	2	5	5.0
TWA	3	15	15.0
Missing	99	80	80.0
	Total	100	100.0

Table 21.2d Multiple response items tabulated as a group

Airlines

Category Label	Code	Frequency	Relative Frequency
American	1	75	62.5
United	2	30	25.0
TWA	3	15	12.5
	Total	120	100.0

21.3 Crosstabulations

Both multiple dichotomy and multiple response groups can be crosstabulated with other variables in MULT RESPONSE. In the airline passenger survey, the airline choices can be crosstabulated with the question asking why people choose different airlines. If you have organized the first question into dichotomies as in Table 21.2a, the three crosstabulations of the dichotomy variables with the schedule/service question would resemble Table 21.3a. If you had chosen the multiple response group method and created two multiple response variables, the two crosstabulations would resemble Table 21.3b. With either method, the crosstabulation of the elementary variable and the group variable would resemble Table 21.3c. Each row in Table 21.3c is the "Have flown" row for the three dichotomy variables. Like codes are added together for the multiple response group. For example, 21 respondents have flown United and think schedule is most important in selecting a flight. The 21 cases are a combination of 20 people who flew United as Airline 1 and circled Schedule plus one person who flew United as Airline 2 and circled Schedule.

Table 21.3a Dichotomies crosstabulated separately

American	Schedule	Service	Row Total
Have flown	41	34	75
Have not flown	20	5	25
Column Total	61	39	100

United	Schedule	Service	Row Total
Have flown	21	9	30
Have not flown	40	30	70
Column Total	61	39	100

TWA	Schedule	Service	Row Total
Have flown	8	7	15
Have not flown	53	32	85
Column Total	61	39	100

Table 21.3b Multiple response variables crosstabulated separately

Airline 1	Schedule	Service	Row Total
American	41	34	75
United	20	5	25
Column Total	61	39	100

Airline 2	Schedule	Service	Row Total
United	1	4	5
TWA	8	7	15
Missing	52	28	80
Column Total	61	39	100

Table 21.3c A group crosstabulated

Airlines	Schedule	Service	Row Total
American	41	34	75
United	21	9	30
TWA	8	7	15
Column Total	61	39	100

21.4 OVERVIEW

MULT RESPONSE combines elementary variables into multiple dichotomy groups and multiple response groups to produce univariate tables and multivariate crosstabulations for these groups and elementary SPSS^X variables. In addition to the tables, you can specify percentaging, formatting, and missing-value options and create stub and banner tables.

Cell Contents and Percentages. By default, crosstabulations do not include any percentages. You can request row, column, and total table percentages. Optionally, you can also base percentages on responses instead of respondents. (See Section 21.11.)

Missing Values. By default, MULT RESPONSE excludes cases with missing values on a table-by-table basis. Optionally, you can request that missing values be handled as if they were not missing or that cases be deleted listwise from the tabulation of group variables. (See Section 21.12.)

Formatting Options. You can suppress the printing of value labels, print tables on an 8½-by-11-inch page, and request condensed-format frequency tables. (See Section 21.13.)

Stub and Banner Tables. With appropriate data transformations, you can create tables with more than one variable in each dimension. (See Section 21.14.)

21.5 OPERATION

Procedure MULT RESPONSE operates via subcommands and associated OPTIONS and STATISTICS commands. All subcommands begin with a subcommand keyword followed by an optional equals sign and terminate with a slash. MULT RESPONSE has four subcommands:

- The GROUPS subcommand names groups of multiple response items to be analyzed and determines how the variables will be combined (see Section 21.6).
- The VARIABLES subcommand identifies all elementary variables to be analyzed (see Section 21.7).
- The FREQUENCIES subcommand requests frequency tables for items identified by the GROUPS and VARIABLES subcommands (see Section 21.8).
- The TABLES subcommand requests the crosstabulation of items identified by the GROUPS and VARIABLES subcommands (see Section 21.9).

To operate MULT RESPONSE you must use at least two subcommands: either the GROUPS subcommand to define one or more groups or the VARIABLES subcommand to define elementary variables, and either the FREQUENCIES or TABLES subcommand to request tables. You must specify those subcommands you use in the following order: GROUPS, VARIABLES, FREQUENCIES, TABLES. You can also use three or all four subcommands, but you can have only one set of subcommands per MULT RESPONSE command.

21.6 The GROUPS Subcommand

The GROUPS subcommand defines both *multiple dichotomy* and *multiple response* groups. You must specify a name for the group, with an optional label, followed by a list of the elementary variables in the group and the value(s) to be used in the tabulation. Enclose the variable list in parentheses and enclose the values in an inner set of parentheses following the last variable in the list. The elementary variables must have integer values. You can specify up to 20 groups. You can name or imply up to 100 elementary variables on the GROUPS and VARIABLES subcommands together.

For example, assume that you have data from a survey on magazine readership. Since a respondent may read several different magazines, readership is a multiple response question. This question can be coded as a series of dichotomies about specific magazines. Alternatively, you may give the respondent a list of magazines and ask which ones are read. If the magazines are coded as a series of dichotomies, you can use the elementary variables as controls in crosstabulation or as selection variables. On the other hand, if the list is lengthy (for example, 100 magazines plus open-ended items) and the average number of magazines read is moderate, you may choose the multiple response coding scheme. If the most well-read respondent reads five different magazines, then the coding scheme must allow for five variables representing magazines read. In the following command, the GROUPS subcommand creates MAGS, a *multiple dichotomy group*:

```
MULT RESPONSE  GROUPS=MAGS 'MAGAZINES READ' (TIME TO STONE (2))/
   FREQUENCIES=MAGS/
```

The group label, 'MAGAZINES READ', is optional and can be up to 40 characters in length, including imbedded blanks. For compatability with other types of SPSS^X labels, apostrophes are used to delimit the label, but they are not required. The group MAGS is tabulated from all the variables between and including TIME and STONE. Use the keyword TO to name an adjacent set of variables in the active file. To define a multiple dichotomy group, specify only one tabulating value following the variable list. Each elementary variable becomes a value of the group variable and the number of cases that have the tabulating value becomes the frequency. However, if no case has the tabulating value for a given component variable, that variable does not appear in the tabulation.

A *multiple response group* requires minimum and maximum values to define the inclusive range for the elementary variables in the group. In this case the group variable takes on the same range of values as the elementary variables. The frequencies for these values are tabulated across all the elementary variables in the list. For example, the command

```
MULT RESPONSE  GROUPS=PROBS 'PERCEIVED NATIONAL PROBLEMS'
   (PROB1 TO PROB3 (1,9))/
   FREQUENCIES=PROBS/
```

defines the multiple response group PROBS using the elementary variables between and including PROB1 and PROB3. Values from 1 to 9 are used to tabulate the group variable. Totally empty categories are not printed in either frequency or crosstabular tables.

MULT RESPONSE builds tables in the same manner as the integer mode in procedures FREQUENCIES (Chapter 18) and CROSSTABS (Chapter 20). Therefore, if you define a multiple response group with a very wide range, the tables require substantial amounts of workspace. If the component variables are sparsely distributed, you might consider recoding them to minimize the workspace required.

You can use any valid SPSS^X variable name for the group. The group name should be unique; however, you may reuse an existing variable name, provided both the elementary variable and group variable are not specified in the same MULT RESPONSE command. The group names and labels exist only during the execution of MULT RESPONSE and disappear once MULT RESPONSE has been executed. Reference to the group names in other procedures results in errors.

21.7 The VARIABLES Subcommand

The VARIABLES subcommand names elementary variables used in frequencies tables and crosstabulations. The VARIABLES subcommand follows the GROUPS subcommand. The following example uses the VARIABLES subcommand to name variables SEX and EDUC so they can be used in a frequencies table:

```
MULT RESPONSE  GROUPS=MAGS 'MAGAZINES READ' (TIME TO STONE (2))/
   VARIABLES SEX(1,2) EDUC(1,3)/
   FREQUENCIES=MAGS SEX EDUC/
```

The VARIABLES subcommand has the same specification field in MULT RESPONSE as in FREQUENCIES (Chapter 18), CROSSTABS (Chapter 20), and BREAKDOWN (Chapter 22). Each variable is followed by a minimum and maximum value in parentheses. To provide the same minimums and maximums for a set of variables, specify a variable list followed by a range specification. You can also use the keyword TO to name a set of adjacent variables on the active file. The minimums and maximums allocate cells for tables that use the elementary variables named on the VARIABLES subcommand. You can specify any numeric variables with the VARIABLES subcommand, but nonintegers are truncated.

The items named by the GROUPS subcommand can be used in frequencies tables and crosstabulations, but you must name them again with the VARIABLES subcommand, along with a range for the values. For example, to use the variable TIME as an item in a group and also use it in a table, specify:

```
MULT RESPONSE  GROUPS=MAGS 'MAGAZINES READ' (TIME TO STONE (2))/
   VARIABLES=EDUC (1,3) TIME (1,2)/
   TABLES=MAGS BY EDUC TIME/
```

You do not have to respecify the items in the groups if they will not be used in any tables.

You may wish to use MULT RESPONSE only to produce crosstabulations of elementary variables in order to take advantage of its special formatting options. In that case, the GROUPS subcommand is not required and the VARIABLES subcommand becomes the first subcommand.

21.8 The FREQUENCIES Subcommand

The FREQUENCIES subcommand requests frequency tables for groups and elementary variables. All groups must be created by the GROUPS subcommand and all elementary variables must be named on the VARIABLES subcommand. The following commands produce a frequency table for a multiple dichotomy group:

```
MULT RESPONSE  GROUPS=MAGS 'MAGAZINES READ' (TIME TO STONE (2))/
   FREQUENCIES=MAGS
```

Figure 21.8a shows the frequencies for the "2" or "Yes" responses to the four dichotomy variables comprising the multiple dichotomy group MAGS. The category labels come from the variable labels defined for the four elementary variables. The NAME column gives the names of variables in the group. The first column of percentages is based on the number of responses and always sums to 100. The second column of percentages is based on the number of respondents or valid cases. These percentages may sum to as high as $n \times 100$, where n is the number of elementary variables comprising the group, since each case can contribute n times to the frequencies. If you want the percentage of cases based upon the survey sample size, include a category to account for cases missing on all dichotomy variables. If an individual reads none of the four magazines, the case is missing for the group.

Figure 21.8a A multiple dichotomy frequency table

```
GROUP MAGS        MAGAZINES READ
    (VALUE TABULATED =      2)

                                                                PCT OF   PCT OF
DICHOTOMY LABEL                         NAME          COUNT  RESPONSES   CASES

READS TIME REGULARLY                    TIME            177     26.0      45.7

READS NEWSWEEK REGULARLY                NEWSWEEK        191     28.1      49.4

READS U.S. NEWS & WORLD REPORT REGULARLY U.S.NEWS       181     26.6      46.8

READS ROLLING STONE REGULARLY           STONE           131     19.3      33.9
                                                      -----    -----     -----
                              TOTAL RESPONSES           680    100.0     175.7

     78 MISSING CASES          387 VALID CASES
```

These commands produce a frequency table for a multiple response group:

```
MULT RESPONSE  GROUPS=PROBS 'NATIONAL PROBLEMS MENTIONED' (PROB1 TO
    PROB3 (1,9))/ FREQUENCIES=PROBS
```

The frequencies in Figure 21.8b are summed for each value across the component variables in the PROBS multiple response group. The category labels come from the value labels attached to the *first* variable in the group. If categories are missing for the first variable but are present for other variables in the group, define a value label for the missing catgories. Percentages based on responses and respondents are printed. A case is missing for the group if it is missing for *all* the component variables in the group.

Figure 21.8b A multiple response frequency table

```
GROUP PROBS       NATIONAL PROBLEMS MENTIONED
                                                                PCT OF   PCT OF
CATEGORY LABEL                            CODE        COUNT  RESPONSES   CASES

RECESSION                                    1          119     12.0      26.5

INFLATION                                    2          144     14.6      32.1

LACK OF RELIGION                             3          150     15.2      33.4

WATERGATE                                    4          129     13.1      28.7

RACIAL CONFLICT                              5           92      9.3      20.5

UNIONS TOO STRONG                            6            9      0.9       2.0

BIG BUSINESS                                 7          141     14.3      31.4

COMMUNIST AGGRESSION                         8          138     14.0      30.7

WEATHER                                      9           66      6.7      14.7
                                                      -----    -----     -----
                              TOTAL RESPONSES           988    100.0     220.0

     16 MISSING CASES          449 VALID CASES
```

You can use the keyword TO only to imply a set of adjacent items *of the same type* whose order is determined by the order in which they were named on either the GROUPS or VARIABLES subcommands. For example, the command

```
MULT RESPONSE  GROUPS=MAGS 'MAGAZINES READ' (TIME TO STONE (2))
    PROBS 'PERCEIVED NATIONAL PROBLEMS' (PROB1 TO PROB3 (1,9))
    MEMS 'SOCIAL ORGANIZATION MEMBERSHIPS' (VFW AMLEG ELKS (1))/
    VARIABLES SEX(1,2) EDUC(1,3)/
    FREQUENCIES=MAGS TO MEMS SEX EDUC
```

specifies frequency tables for MAGS, PROBS, MEMS, SEX, and EDUC. You cannot specify MAGS TO EDUC because SEX and EDUC are elementary variables, while MAGS, PROBS, and MEMS are group variables.

21.9 The TABLES Subcommand

The TABLES subcommand names the crosstabulations to be produced by MULT RESPONSE and follows the FREQUENCIES subcommand (when used). The TABLES subcommand specification field is exactly the same as the TABLES subcommands for CROSSTABS (Chapter 20) and BREAKDOWN (Chapter 22). Both elementary and group items can be tabulated together. You can specify up to five dimensions for a table. Use the keyword BY to separate the dimensions. The first item list defines the rows of the tables; the next item list defines the columns of the tables. Subsequent item lists define controls producing subtables.

The following commands produce a crosstabulation of an elementary variable by a multiple dichotomy group:

```
MULT RESPONSE  GROUPS=MAGS 'MAGAZINES READ' (TIME TO STONE (2))/
   VARIABLES=EDUC (1,3)/TABLES=EDUC BY MAGS
STATISTICS  1 2 3
```

In Figure 21.9a, the rows correspond to categories of the variable EDUC and the columns correspond to the components of the multiple dichotomy group MAGS. The labels for the group variable include the elementary variable name and its variable label. The value labels for the columns print on three lines with eight characters per line. To avoid splitting words, you can reverse the row and column variables or redefine the variable labels. Although Figure 21.9a appears to be a standard crosstabulation, the relationship between cells and marginals is less straightforward. Row and column marginals are *respondents*, but cell frequencies are *responses.* Because MAGS is a group variable, a case may appear in more than one cell within a row. In this example the row frequencies for people with a high-school education sum to 258 (46+60+37+115). However, only 145 respondents have a high-school education (as indicated by the row marginal). Therefore, the average high-school graduate must read more than one of the four magazines. Note also that the column marginals sum to more than 371. Because EDUC is an elementary variable, column frequencies sum to the column total. By default, MULT RESPONSE bases percentages on respondents (cases). Thus, some of the row percentages also sum to over 100. You may choose to base percentages on responses (see Section 21.11).

Figure 21.9a A dichotomy group tabulated with a simple variable

```
* * *  C R O S S T A B U L A T I O N  * * *

  EDUC      HIGHEST EDUCATIONAL ATTAINMENT OF RESP
BY MAGS     (TABULATING      2) MAGAZINES READ


                      MAGS

            COUNT   IREADS TI READS NE READS U. READS RO
            ROW PCT IME REGUL WSWEEK R S. NEWS  LLING ST   ROW
            COL PCT IARLY      EGUL     & WO     ONE       TOTAL
            TAB PCT ITIME     INEWSWEEKIU.S.NEWSISTONE   I
EDUC        --------I---------I---------I---------I---------I
                  1 I     23  I     23  I      0  I      0  I     46
  GRADE SCHOOL      I   50.0  I   50.0  I    0.0  I    0.0  I   12.4
                    I   13.0  I   12.0  I    0.0  I    0.0  I
                    I    6.2  I    6.2  I    0.0  I    0.0  I
                    I---------I---------I---------I---------I
                  2 I     46  I     60  I     37  I    115  I    145
  HIGH SCHOOL       I   31.7  I   41.4  I   25.5  I   79.3  I   39.1
                    I   26.0  I   31.4  I   20.4  I  100.0  I
                    I   12.4  I   16.2  I   10.0  I   31.0  I
                    I---------I---------I---------I---------I
                  3 I    108  I    108  I    144  I      0  I    180
  COLLEGE           I   60.0  I   60.0  I   80.0  I    0.0  I   48.5
                    I   61.0  I   56.5  I   79.6  I    0.0  I
                    I   29.1  I   29.1  I   38.8  I    0.0  I
                    I---------I---------I---------I---------I
             COLUMN      177       191       181       115       371
              TOTAL     47.7      51.5      48.8      31.0     100.0

PERCENTS AND TOTALS BASED ON RESPONDENTS

   371 VALID CASES             94 MISSING CASES
```

The following commands tabulate a multiple dichotomy group with a multiple response group, shown in Figure 21.9b:

```
MULT RESPONSE  GROUPS=MAGS 'MAGAZINES READ' (TIME TO STONE (2))
   PROBS 'NATIONAL PROBLEMS MENTIONED' (PROB1 TO PROB3 (1,9))/
   TABLES=MAGS BY PROBS
STATISTICS  1 2 3
```

Because both the row and column variables are groups, neither row nor column totals sum to the sample size, and percentages exceed 100. This table also includes table percentages within the cells.

Figure 21.9b Two groups tabulated together

```
                  * * *  C R O S S T A B U L A T I O N  * * *

   MAGS      (TABULATING     2) MAGAZINES READ
BY PROBS     (GROUP) NATIONAL PROBLEMS MENTIONED


                         PROBS

                  COUNT  IRECESSIO INFLATIO LACK OF  WATERGAT RACIAL C UNIONS T BIG BUSI COMMUNIS WEATHER
                ROW PCT  IN        N        RELIGION E        ONFLICT  OO STRON NESS     T AGGRES            ROW
                COL PCT  I                                             G                 SION               TOTAL
                TAB PCT  I     1   I    2   I    3   I    4   I    5   I    6   I    7   I    8   I    9   I
MAGS            ---------I---------I--------I--------I--------I--------I--------I--------I--------I--------I
             TIME        I    23   I   55   I   72   I  102   I    0   I    9   I   43   I   84   I   27   I   177
  READS TIME REGULARLY   I  13.0   I 31.1   I 40.7   I 57.6   I  0.0   I  5.1   I 24.3   I 47.5   I 15.3   I  47.7
                         I  20.9   I 38.2   I 56.7   I 79.1   I  0.0   I100.0   I 39.4   I 60.9   I 54.0   I
                         I   6.2   I 14.8   I 19.4   I 27.5   I  0.0   I  2.4   I 11.6   I 22.6   I  7.3   I
                         I---------I--------I--------I--------I--------I--------I--------I--------I--------I
             NEWSWEEK    I    37   I   32   I  109   I   72   I   23   I    9   I   27   I   54   I   50   I   191
  READS NEWSWEEK REGUL   I  19.4   I 16.8   I 57.1   I 37.7   I 12.0   I  4.7   I 14.1   I 28.3   I 26.2   I  51.5
                         I  33.6   I 22.2   I 85.8   I 55.8   I100.0   I100.0   I 24.8   I 39.1   I100.0   I
                         I  10.0   I  8.6   I 29.4   I 19.4   I  6.2   I  2.4   I  7.3   I 14.6   I 13.5   I
                         I---------I--------I--------I--------I--------I--------I--------I--------I--------I
             U.S.NEWS    I    64   I   27   I  100   I   72   I    0   I    0   I   27   I   99   I   27   I   181
  READS U.S. NEWS & WO   I  35.4   I 14.9   I 55.2   I 39.8   I  0.0   I  0.0   I 14.9   I 54.7   I 14.9   I  48.8
                         I  58.2   I 18.8   I 78.7   I 55.8   I  0.0   I  0.0   I 24.8   I 71.7   I 54.0   I
                         I  17.3   I  7.3   I 27.0   I 19.4   I  0.0   I  0.0   I  7.3   I 26.7   I  7.3   I
                         I---------I--------I--------I--------I--------I--------I--------I--------I--------I
             STONE       I    60   I   78   I   37   I    0   I   23   I    0   I   55   I    0   I    0   I   115
  READS ROLLING STONE    I  52.2   I 67.8   I 32.2   I  0.0   I 20.0   I  0.0   I 47.8   I  0.0   I  0.0   I  31.0
                         I  54.5   I 54.2   I 29.1   I  0.0   I100.0   I  0.0   I 50.5   I  0.0   I  0.0   I
                         I  16.2   I 21.0   I 10.0   I  0.0   I  6.2   I  0.0   I 14.8   I  0.0   I  0.0   I
                         I---------I--------I--------I--------I--------I--------I--------I--------I--------I
                COLUMN        110      144      127      129       23        9      109      138       50       371
                 TOTAL       29.6     38.8     34.2     34.8      6.2      2.4     29.4     37.2     13.5     100.0

PERCENTS AND TOTALS BASED ON RESPONDENTS

   371 VALID CASES          94 MISSING CASES
```

Each cell in a MULT RESPONSE crosstabulation is created by adding together the individual cells of a number of component crosstabulations. Cells corresponding to the tabulated values are combined to build the printed table. Multiple response groups are formed by adding the cells for like values. Thus, when a multiple response group is crosstabulated, MULT RESPONSE adds together the cells from the components to produce the printed table containing multiple response groups. For example, in Figure 21.9b, the cell in the upper-left corner of the crosstabulation has 23 cases. This is the number of respondents who read *Time* regularly and named "Recession" as PROB1, PROB2, or PROB3.

If you crosstabulate two groups, MULT RESPONSE tabulates all components of the first group with all components of the second group, pooling the responses. Alternatively, you can pair the first variable in the first group with the first variable in the second group, the second variable in the first group with the second variable in the second group, and so on. Section 21.10 describes paired crosstabulations.

To produce more than one table, name one or more items for each dimension of the tables. Use the keyword TO to imply a set of adjacent variables of the same type, as described for the FREQUENCIES subcommand. The following example specifies two crosstabulations:

```
MULT RESPONSE  GROUPS=MAGS 'MAGAZINES READ' (TIME TO STONE (2))
   MEMS 'SOCIAL ORGANIZATION MEMBERSHIPS' (VFW AMLEG ELKS (1))/
   VARIABLES EDUC (1,3)/TABLES=MEMS MAGS BY EDUC
```

You can specify up to 10 tables lists on one MULT RESPONSE command. By using both the FREQUENCIES subcommand and all the tables lists on the TABLES subcommand, you can name or imply a maximum of 100 groups and elementary variables. Use a slash to separate each tables list, as in

```
MULT RESPONSE  GROUPS=MAGS 'MAGAZINES READ' (TIME TO STONE (2))/
   VARIABLES SEX (1,2) EDUC (1,3)/
   TABLES=MAGS BY EDUC SEX/EDUC BY SEX
```

which produces two tables from the first tables list and one table from the second tables list.

21.10 Paired Crosstabulations

By default, when MULT RESPONSE tabulates one multiple response group with another, it tabulates each variable in the first group with each variable in the second group and sums the counts for each cell. In the example above about magazine readership, this kind of tabulation gives useful cell frequencies. However, other types of problems may require a more selective crosstabulation. For example, a file about pregnancies, where each case is a mother, contains information for up to three pregnancies. P1SEX, P2SEX, and P3SEX are variables for the sex of each child born to the mother. P1AGE, P2AGE, and P3AGE are variables for the age of the mother at the onset of each pregnancy, recoded into four categories. The following MULT RESPONSE command defines two multiple response groups, PSEX and PAGE:

```
MULT RESPONSE  GROUPS=PSEX 'SEX OF CHILD'  (P1SEX P2SEX P3SEX (1,2))
   PAGE 'AGE OF ONSET OF PREGNANCY' (P1AGE P2AGE P3AGE (1,4))/
   TABLES=PSEX BY PAGE/
```

If you tabulate PSEX with PAGE, a case with information on three pregnancies would occur in nine component tables,

P1SEX BY P1AGE
P1SEX BY P2AGE
P1SEX BY P3AGE
.
.
.
P3SEX BY P3AGE

and would produce the crosstabulation in Figure 21.10a. If a mother had two boys and two pregnancies between ages 20 and 24, she would appear four times in the summed table. This may not be the information you desire. Rather, you might be interested in the number of male births occurring for pregnancies beginning between ages 20 and 24. In effect, this table is the sum of three tables:

P1SEX BY P1AGE
P2SEX BY P2AGE
P3SEX BY P3AGE

To produce this type of table for two multiple response groups, use the special keyword PAIRED in parentheses on the TABLES subcommand following the last variable named for a specific tables list. The command

```
MULT RESPONSE  GROUPS=PSEX 'SEX OF CHILD' (P1SEX P2SEX P3SEX (1,2))
   PAGE 'AGE OF ONSET OF PREGNANCY' (P1AGE P2AGE P3AGE (1,4))/
   TABLES=PSEX BY PAGE (PAIRED)/
```

produces a paired crosstabulation of PSEX by PAGE, shown in Figure 21.10b.

Figure 21.10a A crosstabulation of two groups

```
 * * *  C R O S S T A B U L A T I O N  * * *

   PSEX        (GROUP) , SEX OF CHILD
 BY PAGE       (GROUP) , AGE OF ONSET OF PREGNANCY

                         PAGE

                  COUNT  ILESS THA 20 THRU  25 THRU  OVER 30
                         IN 20      24       30                 ROW
                         I                                     TOTAL
                         I     1 I     2 I     3 I     4 I
PSEX             --------I-------I-------I-------I-------I
                      1  I    72 I    71 I   147 I    62 I    160
  MALE                   I       I       I       I       I   76.6
                         I-------I-------I-------I-------I
                      2  I    72 I   131 I   250 I    55 I    240
   FEMALE                I       I       I       I       I  114.8
                         I-------I-------I-------I-------I
                 COLUMN       72     116     173      39      209
                  TOTAL     34.4    55.5    82.8    18.7    100.0

 PERCENTS AND TOTALS BASED ON RESPONDENTS

    209 VALID CASES           256 MISSING CASES
```

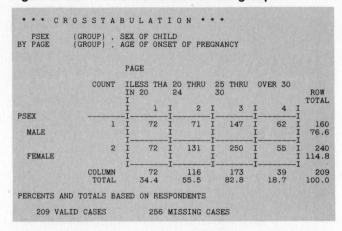

Figure 21.10b A crosstabulation of two paired groups

```
 * * *  C R O S S T A B U L A T I O N  * * *

   PSEX        (PAIRED GROUP) , SEX OF CHILD
 BY PAGE       (PAIRED GROUP) , AGE OF ONSET OF PREGNANCY

                         PAGE

                  COUNT  ILESS THA 20 THRU  25 THRU  OVER 30
                         IN 20      24       30                 ROW
                         I                                     TOTAL
                         I     1 I     2 I     3 I     4 I
PSEX             --------I-------I-------I-------I-------I
                      1  I    27 I    53 I    62 I     0 I    142
  MALE                   I       I       I       I       I   49.5
                         I-------I-------I-------I-------I
                      2  I    18 I    45 I    43 I    39 I    145
   FEMALE                I       I       I       I       I   50.5
                         I-------I-------I-------I-------I
                 COLUMN       45      98     105      39      287
                  TOTAL     15.7    34.1    36.6    13.6    100.0

 PERCENTS AND TOTALS BASED ON RESPONSES

    209 VALID CASES           256 MISSING CASES
```

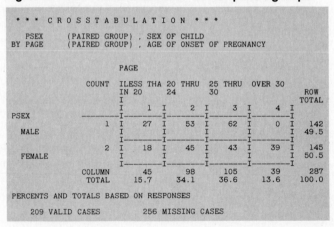

When you request paired crosstabulations, the order of the elementary variables on the GROUPS subcommand determines the construction of the table. For example, the group PSEX could legitimately be defined with the elementary variables P1SEX and P2SEX reversed on the GROUPS subcommand, as in:

```
MULT RESPONSE  GROUPS=PSEX 'SEX OF CHILD' (P2SEX P1SEX P3SEX (1,2))
   PAGE 'AGE OF ONSET OF PREGNANCY' (P1AGE P2AGE P3AGE (1,4))/
   TABLES=PSEX BY PAGE (PAIRED)/
```

However, pairing PSEX with PAGE would then result in a table where the cells were based on the frequencies for P2SEX paired with P1AGE and P1SEX paired with P2AGE.

A paired table request can also contain elementary variables and multiple dichotomy groups. However, only items within multiple response groups are paired. For example, the following command, in which EDUC is a simple variable, pairs only PSEX with PAGE:

```
MULT RESPONSE  GROUPS=PSEX 'SEX OF CHILD' (P1SEX P2SEX P3SEX (1,2))
   PAGE 'AGE OF ONSET OF PREGNANCY' (P1AGE P2AGE P3AGE (1,4))/
   VARIABLES=EDUC (1,3)/
   TABLES=PSEX BY PAGE BY EDUC (PAIRED)
```

The paired option also applies to a multiple response group used as a controlling variable in a three-way or higher order table.

Paired tables are identified in the output by the adjective PAIRED GROUP in the table header. Percentages in paired tables are always based upon responses rather than respondents.

21.11 Cell Contents and Percentages

Frequency tables always report percentages based upon both responses and respondents (see Figure 21.8a). By default, crosstabulations do not include any percentages. The STATISTICS command controls the printing of percentages:

STATISTIC 1 *Print row percentages.*

STATISTIC 2 *Print column percentages.*

STATISTIC 3 *Print two-way table total percentages.*

Figures 21.9a and 21.9b display tables with all of these statistics.

With Option 5 you can obtain cell percentages based on responses rather than respondents. If you request paired tables, Option 5 will be in effect by default.

OPTION 5 *Base cell percentages on responses.* Table marginals are responses.

The following commands use Option 5 to produce table marginals based on responses, shown in Figure 21.11.

```
MULT RESPONSE  GROUPS=PROBS 'NATIONAL PROBLEMS MENTIONED'
   (PROB1 TO PROB3 (1,9))/VARIABLES=EDUC (1,3)/
   TABLES=EDUC BY PROBS
STATISTICS  1 2
OPTIONS  5
```

Figure 21.11 A table with cell percentages based on responses

```
 * * *  C R O S S T A B U L A T I O N  * * *

   EDUC     HIGHEST EDUCATIONAL ATTAINMENT OF RESP
BY PROBS    (GROUP) NATIONAL PROBLEMS MENTIONED


                      PROBS

                 COUNT  IRECESSIO INFLATIO LACK OF  WATERGAT RACIAL C UNIONS T BIG BUSI COMMUNIS WEATHER
               ROW PCT IN         N        RELIGION E        ONFLICT  OO STRON NESS     T AGGRES           ROW
               COL PCT I                                              G                 SION              TOTAL
                       I      1 I      2 I      3 I      4 I      5 I      6 I      7 I      8 I      9 I
EDUC                   --------I--------I--------I--------I--------I--------I--------I--------I--------I
                     1 I    32  I     0  I    23  I     0  I    69  I     0  I    32  I     0  I    39  I   195
  GRADE SCHOOL         I  16.4  I   0.0  I  11.8  I   0.0  I  35.4  I   0.0  I  16.4  I   0.0  I  20.0  I  19.7
                       I  26.9  I   0.0  I  15.3  I   0.0  I  75.0  I   0.0  I  22.7  I   0.0  I  59.1  I
                       I--------I--------I--------I--------I--------I--------I--------I--------I--------I
                     2 I    60  I   108  I    37  I    30  I    23  I     0  I    55  I    30  I     0  I   343
  HIGH SCHOOL          I  17.5  I  31.5  I  10.8  I   8.7  I   6.7  I   0.0  I  16.0  I   8.7  I   0.0  I  34.7
                       I  50.4  I  75.0  I  24.7  I  23.3  I  25.0  I   0.0  I  39.0  I  21.7  I   0.0  I
                       I--------I--------I--------I--------I--------I--------I--------I--------I--------I
                     3 I    27  I    36  I    90  I    99  I     0  I     9  I    54  I   108  I    27  I   450
  COLLEGE              I   6.0  I   8.0  I  20.0  I  22.0  I   0.0  I   2.0  I  12.0  I  24.0  I   6.0  I  45.5
                       I  22.7  I  25.0  I  60.0  I  76.7  I   0.0  I 100.0  I  38.3  I  78.3  I  40.9  I
                       I--------I--------I--------I--------I--------I--------I--------I--------I--------I
                COLUMN     119      144      150      129       92        9      141      138       66      988
                 TOTAL    12.0     14.6     15.2     13.1      9.3      0.9     14.3     14.0      6.7    100.0

PERCENTS AND TOTALS BASED ON RESPONSES

    449 VALID CASES          16 MISSING CASES
```

21.12 Missing Values

By default, MULT RESPONSE deletes cases with missing values on a table-by-table basis for both elementary variables and groups. Also, values falling outside the specified range are not tabulated and are included in the missing category. Therefore, specifying a range that excludes missing values is equivalent to the default treatment of missing values. Use Option 1 to include cases with user-defined missing values.

OPTION 1 *Include missing values.* User-defined missing values are included in tables if they are implied by the range specification on the GROUPS or VARIABLES subcommands.

A case is considered missing for a multiple dichotomy group if none of its component variables contain the tabulating value. For example, if the multiple dichotomy group consists of three elementary variables with the tabulating value of 1, at least one of the three variables must have the value

1 for a given case to be tabulated. A case is considered missing for a multiple response group if none of its components have valid values falling within the tabulating range. Thus cases with missing or excluded values on some but not all of the components of a group are included in tabulations of the group variable. Two missing-value options are available to delete cases from a group if any of the components are missing:

OPTION 2 *Exclude missing values listwise for multiple dichotomy groups.* Cases missing on any elementary dichotomy variable are excluded from the tabulation of the multiple dichotomy group.

OPTION 3 *Exclude missing values listwise for multiple response groups.* Cases missing on any elementary variable are excluded from the tabulation of the multiple response group.

21.13 Formatting Options

By default, MULT RESPONSE prints the value labels defined for variables in frequency and crosstabulation tables. Use Option 4 to suppress the printing of value labels for multiple response groups and elementary variables. You cannot suppress the printing of variable labels used as value labels for multiple dichotomy groups.

The default output also prints tables with up to 10 column categories across a page. Option 6 limits the page width to 75 characters and prints tables on an 8½-by-11-inch page. For frequencies tables, MULT RESPONSE uses more than one page to print frequencies with more than 20 categories. Use Option 7 to print a three-up condensed-format frequency table for all multiple response groups and elementary variables with more than 20 categories and print items with fewer categories in the default format. Options 7 and 8 do not apply to multiple dichotomy groups.

OPTION 4 *Suppress value labels.* This option applies to multiple response groups and elementary variables but not to multiple dichotomy groups.

OPTION 6 *Print tables in 8½-by-11-inch page.* The page is 75 characters wide.

OPTION 7 *Print a condensed-format frequency table.* Prints frequency tables in a three-up condensed format for multiple response groups and elementary variables.

OPTION 8 *Print a conditional condensed-format frequency table.* Prints frequency tables in a three-up condensed format if the multiple response group or elementary variable has more than 20 categories. Prints items with fewer categories in the default format.

21.14 Stub and Banner Tables

Although the method of combining variables within MULT RESPONSE is probably indicated by the coding scheme used, you may want to group together in a table a series of items which do not have parallel codes. Since MULT RESPONSE combines elementary variables on one dimension of a table, with appropriate data transformations, you can create tables with more than one variable across the top and more than one variable down the side. Such tables are commonly called stub and banner tables. The following commands produce a stub and banner table:

```
COUNT  MALE=SEX(1)/FEMALE=SEX(2)/HIGHSCH=EDUC(1,2)/COLLEGE=EDUC(3)
MULT RESPONSE  GROUPS=VITAMINS 'USE NUTRITIONAL SUPPLEMENTS'
  (C TO NONE(1)) DEMOGRAP 'DEMOGRAPHICS' (MALE FEMALE HIGHSCH
  COLLEGE(1))/
  TABLES=VITAMINS BY DEMOGRAP
STATISTICS  2
```

Figure 21.14 displays this crosstabulation of two dichotomy groups, VITAMINS and DEMOGRAP. VITAMINS is a standard dichotomy group based on series of questions about nutritional supplements. DEMOGRAP places together two very different types of variables, sex and educational level. Because a multiple dichotomy only tabulates one value for a variable, transformations are used to map all the categories for one variable into several variables. Although this can be done in a variety of ways, this computation uses the COUNT command. To keep the table relatively simple, people with grade-school educations were combined with people with high-school educations.

The elementary variable NONE is included in the tabulation to account for cases missing on all the other dichotomy variables and to obtain correct percentaging. The row total shows the higher number of cases for the two original variables, SEX and EDUC, used to create the elementary variables for the group DEMOGRAP. For example, the row labeled "MULTI" in Figure 21.14 shows 40 males and 33 females, or a total of 73 cases, and 40 people with high school and 27 people with college, or a total of 67 cases. The row total is 73, reflecting the higher number of cases over the two variables.

Figure 21.14 A MULT RESPONSE stub and banner table

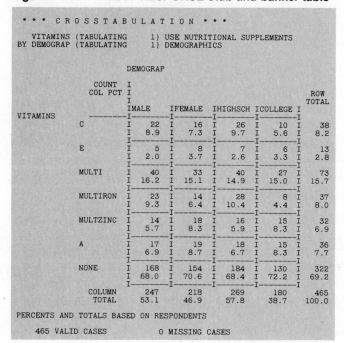

```
 * * *  C R O S S T A B U L A T I O N  * * *

   VITAMINS (TABULATING      1) USE NUTRITIONAL SUPPLEMENTS
BY DEMOGRAP (TABULATING      1) DEMOGRAPHICS


                    DEMOGRAP

              COUNT I
            COL PCT I                                             ROW
                    I                                           TOTAL
                    IMALE     IFEMALE  IHIGHSCH ICOLLEGE I
VITAMINS    --------I--------I--------I--------I--------I
          C         I    22  I    16  I    26  I    10  I      38
                    I   8.9  I   7.3  I   9.7  I   5.6  I     8.2
                    I--------I--------I--------I--------I
          E         I     5  I     8  I     7  I     6  I      13
                    I   2.0  I   3.7  I   2.6  I   3.3  I     2.8
                    I--------I--------I--------I--------I
          MULTI     I    40  I    33  I    40  I    27  I      73
                    I  16.2  I  15.1  I  14.9  I  15.0  I    15.7
                    I--------I--------I--------I--------I
          MULTIRON  I    23  I    14  I    28  I     8  I      37
                    I   9.3  I   6.4  I  10.4  I   4.4  I     8.0
                    I--------I--------I--------I--------I
          MULTZINC  I    14  I    18  I    16  I    15  I      32
                    I   5.7  I   8.3  I   5.9  I   8.3  I     6.9
                    I--------I--------I--------I--------I
          A         I    17  I    19  I    18  I    15  I      36
                    I   6.9  I   8.7  I   6.7  I   8.3  I     7.7
                    I--------I--------I--------I--------I
          NONE      I   168  I   154  I   184  I   130  I     322
                    I  68.0  I  70.6  I  68.4  I  72.2  I    69.2
                    I--------I--------I--------I--------I
             COLUMN     247      218      269      180        465
              TOTAL    53.1     46.9     57.8     38.7      100.0

PERCENTS AND TOTALS BASED ON RESPONDENTS

   465 VALID CASES                 0 MISSING CASES
```

21.15 LIMITATIONS

The following limitations apply to MULT RESPONSE:

- One set of subcommands per MULT RESPONSE command.
- A maximum of 100 elementary variables named or implied by the GROUPS and VARIABLES subcommands together.
- A maximum of 20 groups defined on the GROUPS subcommand.
- A maximum of 32,767 categories for a multiple response group or an elementary variable.
- A maximum of 10 tables lists on the TABLES subcommand.
- A maximum of 5 dimensions per table.
- A maximum of 100 groups and elementary variables named or implied on the FREQUENCIES and TABLES subcommands together.
- A maximum of 200 nonempty rows in a single table.
- A maximum of 200 nonempty columns in a single table.
- MULT RESPONSE stores category labels in WORKSPACE. If there is insufficient space to store the labels after the tables are built, the labels are not printed.

ANNOTATED EXAMPLE FOR MULT RESPONSE

This example analyzes a 465-case sample from a survey about magazine readership and organizational memberships. The variables are

- TIME, NEWSWEEK, U.S.NEWS, STONE, REPUBLIC—dichotomous variables which show whether the respondent regularly read *Time, Newsweek, U.S. News and World Report, Rolling Stone,* or *New Republic* magazines.
- PROB1, PROB2, PROB3—elementary variables created from a multiple response item asking the respondent to name three national problems from a list of nine problems.
- EDUC—the respondent's education, coded in three categories.
- SEX—the respondent's sex, coded 1=male, 2=female.

This example examines the distribution of magazine readership and national problems by education and sex. The SPSS^X commands are

```
FILE HANDLE  MRESFILE/ file specifications
GET  FILE=MRESFILE
MULT RESPONSE  GROUPS=MAGS 'MAGAZINES READ' (TIME TO REPUBLIC (2))
   PROBS 'NATIONAL PROBLEMS MENTIONED' (PROB1 TO PROB3 (1,9))/
   VARIABLES=EDUC (1,3) SEX (1,2)/
   TABLES=EDUC SEX BY MAGS PROBS
STATISTICS  2
FINISH
```

- The FILE HANDLE identifies the MRESFILE data file and gives the operating-system specifications (see Chapter 3).
- The GET command defines the data to SPSS^X and selects the variables needed for analysis (see Chapter 5).
- The MULT RESPONSE command creates a multiple dichotomy group, MAGS, from the elementary variables between and including TIME and REPUBLIC, and creates a multiple response group, PROBS, from the elementary variables between and including PROB1 and PROB3. Two other elementary variables, EDUC and SEX, are referenced on the VARIABLES subcommand. The TABLES subcommand requests four crosstabulations: EDUC by MAGS, EDUC by PROBS, SEX by MAGS, and SEX by PROBS.
- Statistic 2 requests column percentages in the tables.

Output from the MULT RESPONSE command

```
  * * *  C R O S S T A B U L A T I O N  * * *

    EDUC     HIGHEST EDUCATIONAL ATTAINMENT OF RESP
 BY MAGS     (TABULATING     2) MAGAZINES READ


                    MAGS

               COUNT  IREADS TI READS NE READS U. READS RO READS RE
             COL PCT  IME REGUL WSWEEK R S. NEWS  LLING ST PUBLIC R   ROW
                      IARLY     EGUL     & WO     ONE      EGUL      TOTAL
                      ITIME    INEWSWEEKIU.S.NEWSISTONE   IREPUBLICI
EDUC          --------I--------I--------I--------I--------I--------I
                   1  I    23  I    23  I     0  I     0  I     0  I     46
  GRADE SCHOOL        I  13.0  I  12.0  I   0.0  I   0.0  I   0.0  I   12.4
                      I--------I--------I--------I--------I--------I
                   2  I    46  I    60  I    37  I   115  I    30  I    145
  HIGH SCHOOL         I  26.0  I  31.4  I  20.4  I 100.0  I  32.3  I   39.1
                      I--------I--------I--------I--------I--------I
                   3  I   108  I   108  I   144  I     0  I    63  I    180
  COLLEGE             I  61.0  I  56.5  I  79.6  I   0.0  I  67.7  I   48.5
                      I--------I--------I--------I--------I--------I
              COLUMN      177      191      181      115       93      371
               TOTAL     47.7     51.5     48.8     31.0     25.1    100.0

 PERCENTS AND TOTALS BASED ON RESPONDENTS

     371 VALID CASES          94 MISSING CASES
```

* * * C R O S S T A B U L A T I O N * * *

EDUC HIGHEST EDUCATIONAL ATTAINMENT OF RESP
BY PROBS (GROUP) NATIONAL PROBLEMS MENTIONED

PROBS

EDUC	COUNT / COL PCT	RECESSIO IN 1	INFLATIO N 2	LACK OF RELIGION 3	WATERGAT E 4	RACIAL C ONFLICT 5	UNIONS T OO STRON G 6	BIG BUSI NESS 7	COMMUNIS T AGGRES SION 8	WEATHER 9	ROW TOTAL
GRADE SCHOOL	1	32	0	23	0	69	0	32	0	39	124
		26.9	0.0	15.3	0.0	75.0	0.0	22.7	0.0	59.1	27.6
HIGH SCHOOL	2	60	108	37	30	23	0	55	30	0	145
		50.4	75.0	24.7	23.3	25.0	0.0	39.0	21.7	0.0	32.3
COLLEGE	3	27	36	90	99	0	9	54	108	27	180
		22.7	25.0	60.0	76.7	0.0	100.0	38.3	78.3	40.9	40.1
	COLUMN TOTAL	119	144	150	129	92	9	141	138	66	449
		26.5	32.1	33.4	28.7	20.5	2.0	31.4	30.7	14.7	100.0

PERCENTS AND TOTALS BASED ON RESPONDENTS

449 VALID CASES 16 MISSING CASES

* * * C R O S S T A B U L A T I O N * * *

SEX OBSERVED SEX OF RESPONDENT
BY MAGS (TABULATING 2) MAGAZINES READ

MAGS

SEX	COUNT / COL PCT	READS TIME REGULARLY TIME	READS NEWSWEEK REGUL NEWSWEEK	READS U.S. NEWS & WO U.S.NEWS	READS ROLLING STONE STONE	READS REPUBLIC REGUL REPUBLIC	ROW TOTAL
MALE	1	82	119	64	92	66	208
		46.3	62.3	35.4	70.2	71.0	53.7
FEMALE	2	95	72	117	39	27	179
		53.7	37.7	64.6	29.8	29.0	46.3
	COLUMN TOTAL	177	191	181	131	93	387
		45.7	49.4	46.8	33.9	24.0	100.0

PERCENTS AND TOTALS BASED ON RESPONDENTS

387 VALID CASES 78 MISSING CASES

* * * C R O S S T A B U L A T I O N * * *

SEX OBSERVED SEX OF RESPONDENT
BY PROBS (GROUP) NATIONAL PROBLEMS MENTIONED

PROBS

SEX	COUNT / COL PCT	RECESSIO IN 1	INFLATIO N 2	LACK OF RELIGION 3	WATERGAT E 4	RACIAL C ONFLICT 5	UNIONS T OO STRON G 6	BIG BUSI NESS 7	COMMUNIS T AGGRES SION 8	WEATHER 9	ROW TOTAL
MALE	1	37	78	87	84	62	9	93	66	39	231
		31.1	54.2	58.0	65.1	67.4	100.0	66.0	47.8	59.1	51.4
FEMALE	2	82	66	63	45	30	0	48	72	27	218
		68.9	45.8	42.0	34.9	32.6	0.0	34.0	52.2	40.9	48.6
	COLUMN TOTAL	119	144	150	129	92	9	141	138	66	449
		26.5	32.1	33.4	28.7	20.5	2.0	31.4	30.7	14.7	100.0

PERCENTS AND TOTALS BASED ON RESPONDENTS

449 VALID CASES 16 MISSING CASES

22

General mode:

BREAKDOWN [TABLES =] varlist BY varlist [BY . . .] [/varlist . . .]

Integer mode:

BREAKDOWN VARIABLES = varlist ({min, max | LOWEST, HIGHEST}) [varlist . . .]

/{TABLES | CROSSBREAK} = varlist BY varlist [BY . . .] [/varlist . . .]

OPTIONS:
1 Include missing values.
2 Exclude missing values for dependent variables only.
3 Suppress variable and value labels.
4 Tree format (general mode only).
5 Suppress cell frequencies (CROSSBREAK only).
6 Suppress cell sums (CROSSBREAK only).
7 Suppress cell standard deviations (CROSSBREAK only).
8 Suppress value labels (CROSSBREAK only).

STATISTICS:
1 One-way analysis of variance.
2 Test of linearity.

OVERVIEW, **22.1**

OPERATION, **22.2**
- General Mode, **22.3**
- Integer Mode, **22.4**
  - The VARIABLES Subcommand, **22.5**
  - The TABLES Subcommand , **22.6**
  - The CROSSBREAK Alternate Display Format, **22.7**
- Optional Statistics, **22.8**
- Missing Values, **22.9**
- Formatting Options, **22.10**

LIMITATIONS, **22.11**

Chapter 22 BREAKDOWN

BREAKDOWN calculates means and variances for a criterion or dependent variable over subgroups of cases defined by independent or control variables. This operation is similar to crosstabulation, where each mean and standard deviation summarizes the distribution of a complete row or column of a contingency table.

22.1 OVERVIEW

BREAKDOWN displays means, sums, standard deviations, and variances for a dependent variable across groups defined by one or more independent variables. You can operate BREAKDOWN in either general or integer mode, request optional statistics, alter the handling of missing values, and obtain crosstabular and tree formats.

Methods for Building Tables. BREAKDOWN operates in two different modes: *general* and *integer*. General mode requires fewer specifications and offers an optional tree format for the output (see Section 22.3). Integer mode requires that you specify the minimum and maximum values for the variables and builds tables more efficiently (see Section 22.4).

Optional Statistics. In addition to the statistics displayed for groups, you can obtain a one-way analysis of variance and test of linearity (see Section 22.8).

Missing Values. By default, BREAKDOWN excludes cases with missing values on a tablewide basis. You can request that missing values be included or that cases missing only on the dependent variable be deleted (see Section 22.9).

Formatting Options. You can request a tree format with general mode and suppress labels in either mode (see Section 22.10). With integer mode you can obtain a crosstabular format and specify the contents of the cells (see Section 22.7).

22.2 OPERATION

Procedure BREAKDOWN operates via subcommands and associated OPTIONS and STATISTICS commands. The specifications for these commands depend on whether you want to use the *general mode* or the *integer mode* to build tables, and whether you request CROSSBREAK tables. Each of the three methods has advantages and disadvantages in computational efficiency, statistics, and additional options.

- General mode permits alphanumeric or noninteger control variables with no range specifications. It also provides the optional tree format (see Section 22.3).

- Integer mode builds breakdown tables more quickly. However, it requires more space if the matrix of control variables has many empty cells. By specifying the appropriate bounds, you can eliminate outliers for the criterion variable or select a subset of the values of the control variables (see Section 22.4).
- CROSSBREAK prints tables of two or more control variables in a crosstabular format and displays statistics for each of two variables controlling for the other. You can suppress the printing of cell counts, sums, and standard deviations from the breakdown table. The optional analysis of variance table and test of linearity are not available for CROSSBREAK (see Section 22.7).

22.3 General Mode

To run BREAKDOWN in general mode, use the TABLES subcommand followed by one or more dependent variables, the keyword BY, and one or more independent variables. For example, the command

```
BREAKDOWN  TABLES=PCTRAISE BY GRADE81
```

produces one table displayed in Figure 22.3a. PCTRAISE is the criterion variable, the variable to be summarized. This is the dependent variable and must be numeric. The values of GRADE81, the independent variable, define the groups. Independent variables can be numeric or strings. However, long strings are truncated to short strings for purposes of defining categories. Use the REPORT procedure to break down variables by long strings (see Chapter 23).

Figure 22.3a A one-way BREAKDOWN table

```
- - - - - - - - - - - - - - - - -  D E S C R I P T I O N   O F   S U B P O P U L A T I O N S  - - - - - - - - - - - - - - - - -
CRITERION VARIABLE    PCTRAISE
    BROKEN DOWN BY    GRADE81     JOB GRADE IN 1981
- - - - - - - - - - - - - - - - - - - - - - - - - - - - - - - - - - - - - - - - - - - - - - - - - - - - - - - - - - - - - - - -

VARIABLE                    CODE     VALUE LABEL                 SUM          MEAN        STD DEV       VARIANCE          N

FOR ENTIRE POPULATION                                         19.9900        0.1257        0.1034        0.0107     (   159)

GRADE81                       2.                               0.0157        0.0079        0.0111        0.0001     (     2)
GRADE81                       3.                               2.0050        0.0872        0.0536        0.0029     (    23)
GRADE81                       4.                               2.2133        0.0851        0.1077        0.0116     (    26)
GRADE81                       5.                               1.8286        0.1219        0.0648        0.0042     (    15)
GRADE81                       6.                               3.6132        0.1505        0.0742        0.0055     (    24)
GRADE81                       7.                               1.0326        0.1291        0.0518        0.0027     (     8)
GRADE81                       8.                               2.1087        0.1917        0.1253        0.0157     (    11)
GRADE81                       9.                               0.3262        0.1087        0.0205        0.0004     (     3)
GRADE81                      10.                               2.7435        0.1372        0.1184        0.0140     (    20)
GRADE81                      11.                               2.3820        0.1985        0.1771        0.0314     (    12)
GRADE81                      12.                               0.5847        0.0975        0.0602        0.0036     (     6)
GRADE81                      13.                               0.8049        0.1610        0.1454        0.0211     (     5)
GRADE81                      14.                               0.2505        0.0835        0.0522        0.0027     (     3)
GRADE81                      15.                               0.0811        0.0811        0.0           0.0        (     1)

  TOTAL CASES =       275
MISSING CASES =       116 OR  42.2 PCT.
```

The keyword TABLES is not required to operate BREAKDOWN in general mode. For example, the following commands produce identical displays:

```
BREAKDOWN  TABLES=SALARY82 BY YRHIRED

BREAKDOWN  SALARY82 BY YRHIRED
```

However, if you use the keyword TABLES for general mode, as shown in the examples in this section, you must also include the equals sign.

A maximum of six dimensions can be specified on an analysis list: one dependent variable and up to five independent variables separated by the keyword BY. For example,

```
BREAKDOWN  TABLES=RAISE81 BY DEPT81 BY GRADE81S
```

breaks down RAISE81 by DEPT81 and by GRADE81S within DEPT81. Figure 22.3b shows the output from this command. The first variable always becomes the dependent or criterion variable. The independent variables are entered into the table in the order in which they appear following the TABLES subcommand, proceeding from left to right. The values of the last variable change most quickly.

Although the BREAKDOWN tables list is the same as the CROSSTABS tables list (see Chapter 20), in CROSSTABS the values of the last variable change most slowly. BREAKDOWN prints subpopulation statistics for each category of the first independent variable. However, for subsequent variables, it prints statistics only for each category of the variable within a category of the preceding independent variable. For example, Figure 22.3b shows means for RAISE81 for categories of DEPT81 but shows means for GRADE81S only within categories of DEPT81, not for each grade. You can specify the order of controlling variables to obtain the most useful intermediate subpopulation statistics or use the CROSSBREAK format to display subpopulation statistics for two independent variables (see Section 22.7).

Figure 22.3b A two-way BREAKDOWN table

```
- - - - - - - - - - - - - - - - - - -  D E S C R I P T I O N   O F   S U B P O P U L A T I O N S  - - - - - - - - - - - - - - - - -
CRITERION VARIABLE   RAISE81    INCREASE IN SALARY OVER 1980
    BROKEN DOWN BY   DEPT81     DEPARTMENT CODE IN 1981
                BY   GRADE81S
- - - - - - - - - - - - - - - - - - - - - - - - - - - - - - - - - - - - - - - - - - - - - - - - - - - - - - - - - - - - - - - - - -

VARIABLE                   CODE     VALUE LABEL                   SUM          MEAN        STD DEV       VARIANCE          N

FOR ENTIRE POPULATION                                     258874.0000     1628.1384      1429.2467   2042746.1706     (    159)


DEPT81                       1.     ADMIN                  55941.0000     1472.1316      1113.9585   1240903.5228     (     38)
   GRADE81S                1.00                             8597.0000      716.4167       286.2629     81946.4470     (     12)
   GRADE81S                2.00                            18159.0000     1210.6000       495.5833    245602.8286     (     15)
   GRADE81S                3.00                            29185.0000     2653.1818      1354.6461   1835066.1636     (     11)

DEPT81                       2.     PROJECT DIRECTORS      50723.0000     1811.5357      2368.0374   5607600.9987     (     28)
   GRADE81S                1.00                             8281.0000      517.5625       857.3076    734976.3958     (     16)
   GRADE81S                2.00                             2730.0000      910.0000       343.9477    118300.0000     (      3)
   GRADE81S                3.00                            39712.0000     4412.4444      2500.8318   6254159.7778     (      9)

DEPT81                       3.     CHICAGO OPERATIONS     92065.0000     1484.9194      1072.1964   1149605.1245     (     62)
   GRADE81S                1.00                            15815.0000      988.4375       954.6331    911324.2625     (     16)
   GRADE81S                2.00                            21890.0000     1368.1250       389.3723    151610.7833     (     16)
   GRADE81S                3.00                            54360.0000     1812.0000      1270.4910   1614147.3103     (     30)

DEPT81                       4.     ST LOUIS OPERATIONS    60145.0000     1940.1613      1280.0114   1638429.2065     (     31)
   GRADE81S                1.00                             5538.0000      791.1429       339.8639    115507.4762     (      7)
   GRADE81S                2.00                            25065.0000     1928.0769       868.5525    754383.4103     (     13)
   GRADE81S                3.00                            29542.0000     2685.6364      1550.8244   2405056.4545     (     11)

  TOTAL CASES =      275
MISSING CASES =      116 OR  42.2 PCT.
```

You can specify more than one dependent variable and more than one independent variable in each dimension. Use the keyword TO to name a set of adjacent variables in the active file, as in:

```
BREAKDOWN  TABLES=RAISE79 TO RAISE81 BY DEPT TO AGE
```

This command will produce BREAKDOWN tables for all the variables between and including RAISE79 and RAISE81 by all the variables between and including DEPT and AGE. You can also use variable lists to request higher-order breakdowns. The variables to the right of the last BY change most quickly. Within lists separated with a BY, variables rotate from left to right. For example,

```
BREAKDOWN  TABLES=VAR1 TO VAR3 BY VAR4 VAR5 BY VAR6 TO VAR8
```

produces 18 tables. The first table is VAR1 by VAR4 by VAR6 and the second is VAR1 by VAR4 by VAR7. The combinations of VAR1 and VAR5 follow the combinations of VAR1 and VAR4. The last table produced is VAR3 by VAR5 by VAR8.

You can specify up to 30 tables lists on one BREAKDOWN command and up to 250 tables over all the lists together. A maximum of 200 variables can be named or implied by all the tables lists. Use a slash to separate tables lists on one BREAKDOWN command. For example,

```
BREAKDOWN  TABLES=RAISE82 BY GRADE/SALARY BY DEPT
```

specifies two tables, RAISE82 by GRADE and SALARY by DEPT. If you omit a slash between tables lists, BREAKDOWN includes the variables as if one analysis list had been supplied. If the preceding command had no slash, as in

```
BREAKDOWN  TABLES=RAISE82 BY GRADE SALARY BY DEPT
```

it would produce two tables, RAISE82 by GRADE by DEPT and RAISE82 by SALARY by DEPT.

22.4 Integer Mode

To run BREAKDOWN in integer mode, the values of all the independent variables must be integers. Two subcommands are required. The VARIABLES subcommand specifies all the variables to be used in the BREAKDOWN procedure and the minimum and maximum values for building tables. The TABLES subcommand specifies the tables lists. In integer mode, the equals sign following the VARIABLES and TABLES subcommands is optional.

Integer mode can produce more tables in a given amount of core storage space than general mode, and the processing is faster. In integer mode, you define the dimensions of the table with the independent variables, rather than having SPSS^X calculate the dimensions based on values encountered in your data. In addition, integer mode has an alternate CROSSBREAK display format (see Section 22.7).

22.5 The VARIABLES Subcommand

The VARIABLES subcommand is followed by a list of variables. Specify the lowest and highest values in parentheses after each variable. These values must be integers. For example, the command

```
BREAKDOWN  VARIABLES=DEPT81(1,4) EEO81(1,9) RAISE81(LO,HI)/
   TABLES=RAISE81 BY DEPT81 BY EEO81
```

produces the table in Figure 22.5 where RAISE81 has a range from the lowest to the highest value, DEPT81 has a range from 1 to 4, and EEO81 has a range from 1 to 9. The final variable or set of variables and their range must be followed by a slash. A maximum of 100 variables can be named or implied by the VARIABLES subcommand.

Figure 22.5 A two-way breakdown using integer mode

```
- - - - - - - - - - - - - - - -  D E S C R I P T I O N   O F   S U B P O P U L A T I O N S  - - - - - - - - - - - - - - - -
CRITERION VARIABLE   RAISE81    INCREASE IN SALARY OVER 1980
   BROKEN DOWN BY    DEPT81     DEPARTMENT CODE IN 1981
               BY    EEO81      E.E.O. CLASSIFICATION IN 1981
- - - - - - - - - - - - - - - - - - - - - - - - - - - - - - - - - - - - - - - - - - - - - - - - - - - - - - - - - - - - - -

VARIABLE                  CODE  VALUE LABEL                   SUM          MEAN      STD DEV      VARIANCE          N

FOR ENTIRE POPULATION                                   258874.0000     1628.1384    1429.2467  2042746.1706   (    159)

DEPT81                       1  ADMIN                    55941.0000     1472.1316    1113.9585  1240903.5228   (     38)
   EEO81                     1  OFF-MGR                  26845.0000     2684.5000    1413.1278  1996930.0556   (     10)
   EEO81                     2  PROF                      2470.0000     2470.0000       0.0           0.0       (      1)
   EEO81                     3  TECH                      4778.0000     1592.6667     622.8975   388001.3333   (      3)
   EEO81                     5  CLERICAL                 14064.0000      937.6000     467.2766   218347.4000   (     15)
   EEO81                     7  OPERTIVS                  1690.0000     1690.0000       0.0           0.0       (      1)
   EEO81                     9  SERVICE                   6094.0000      761.7500       2.1213        4.5000   (      8)

DEPT81                       2  PROJECT DIRECTORS        50723.0000     1811.5357    2368.0374  5607600.9987   (     28)
   EEO81                     2  PROF                     34125.0000     4875.0000    2567.7152  6593161.3333   (      7)
   EEO81                     3  TECH                      4160.0000     4160.0000       0.0           0.0       (      1)
   EEO81                     5  CLERICAL                 12438.0000      621.9000     805.6582   649085.1474   (     20)

DEPT81                       3  CHICAGO OPERATIONS       92065.0000     1484.9194    1072.1964  1149605.1245   (     62)
   EEO81                     1  OFF-MGR                  18739.0000     1561.5833     870.6716   758068.9924   (     12)
   EEO81                     2  PROF                      8158.0000     2719.3333    1190.4942  1417276.3333   (      3)
   EEO81                     3  TECH                      7839.0000     1959.7500    1326.5256  1759670.2500   (      4)
   EEO81                     5  CLERICAL                 57329.0000     1333.2326    1059.4303  1122392.6113   (     43)

DEPT81                       4  ST LOUIS OPERATIONS      60145.0000     1940.1613    1280.0114  1638429.2065   (     31)
   EEO81                     1  OFF-MGR                  25415.0000     3176.8750    1547.3501  2394292.4107   (      8)
   EEO81                     3  TECH                      3250.0000     1625.0000      91.9239     8450.0000   (      2)
   EEO81                     5  CLERICAL                 31480.0000     1499.0476     890.6131   793191.6476   (     21)

  TOTAL CASES =      275
MISSING CASES =      116 OR  42.2 PCT.
```

You do not have to specify an explicit range for dependent variables because they are usually continuous and are not assumed to be integers. However, you must provide bounds. Use the keywords LOWEST (or LO) and HIGHEST (or HI) for criterion variables. You can also use explicit bounds to eliminate outliers from the calculation of the summary statistics. Explicit numeric bounds must be specified as integers. For example, (0,HI) excludes nonnegative values. You can *not* use LOWEST, LO, HIGHEST, HI with independent variables.

You must specify a range for each variable to be used in the BREAKDOWN procedure and several variables can have the same range. For example,

```
BREAKDOWN  VARIABLES=DEPT80 DEPT81 DEPT82 (1,3) GRADE81S (1,4)
   SALARY82 (LO,HI)/
   TABLES=SALARY82 BY DEPT80 TO DEPT82 BY GRADE81S
```

defines 1 as the lowest value and 3 as the highest value for DEPT80, DEPT81, and DEPT82. Variables may appear in any order. However, the order in which you place them on the VARIABLES subcommand affects their implied order on the TABLES subcommand as described in Section 22.6.

BREAKDOWN uses the bounds you specify to allocate tables. One cell is allocated for each possible combination of values of the control variables for a requested table before the data are read. Therefore, if you specify more generous bounds than the control variables actually have, you are wasting some space. If the table is sparse because the control variables do not have values falling throughout the range specified, you might consider using the general mode or recoding the control variables. If, on the other hand, values of control variables fall outside the range you specify, cases with these values are considered missing and are not used in the computation of the table.

22.6 The TABLES Subcommand

The TABLES subcommand names the tables list. It has the same syntax as the TABLES subcommand in general mode described in Section 22.3 above. You can name multiple tables lists separated by slashes, but the subcommand appears only once in a BREAKDOWN command. Like general mode, integer mode can process up to 30 tables lists. However, you can specify only up to 100 tables over all the lists together, and you can name or imply only up to 100 variables on all the tables lists. Variables named on the TABLES subcommand must have been previously named or implied on the VARIABLES subcommand.

There is one important difference between the tables request in integer mode and the tables request in general mode. In integer mode, the order of the variables implied on the TABLES subcommand is established by the order of the variables named or implied on the VARIABLES subcommand. In general mode, the order of variables implied on the tables lists is established by their order in the active file.

22.7 The CROSSBREAK Alternate Display Format

To print tables in a crosstabular form when using the integer mode, use the CROSSBREAK subcommand in place of the TABLES subcommand. It has exactly the same specification field as the TABLES subcommand. The equals sign following the CROSSBREAK subcommand is optional. The following command produces the crossbreak table displayed in Figure 22.7:

```
BREAKDOWN  VARIABLES=RAISE81(LO,HI) DEPT81(1,4) EEO81(1,3)/
   CROSSBREAK=RAISE81 BY DEPT81 BY EEO81
```

Tables printed in crossbreak form resemble CROSSTABS tables, but their contents are considerably different. The cells contain means, counts, sums, and standard deviations for the dependent variable. The first independent variable defines the rows and the second independent variable defines the columns. The CROSSBREAK format is especially suited to breakdowns with two controlling variables. The CROSSBREAK subcommand prints separate subtables for each combination of values when you specify three or more dimensions.

By default, means, sums, standard deviations, and *n*'s are printed in the cells of the CROSSBREAK table. The cells are labeled with the value labels for the controlling variables when these have been defined. You can delete sums, standard deviations, *n*'s and value labels with the OPTIONS command. You cannot delete means from the CROSSBREAK table.

OPTION 5 *Suppress cell frequencies.*

OPTION 6 *Suppress cell sums.*

OPTION 7 *Suppress cell standard deviations.*

OPTION 8 *Suppress value labels.*

Note that the crossbreak table in Figure 22.7 displays overall means for each value of EEO81 in the column marginals and overall means for each value of DEPT81 in the row marginals.

Figure 22.7 A table in CROSSBREAK format

```
* * * * * * * * * * * * * * * * * * *  C R O S S---B R E A K D O W N   O F  * * * * * * * * * * * * * * * * * * *
   DEPT81    DEPARTMENT CODE IN 1981                          BY  EE081     E.E.O. CLASSIFICATION IN 1981
* * * * * * * * * * * * * * * * * * * * * * * * * * * * * * * * * * * * * * * * * * * * * * * * * * * * * * * * *
VARIABLE AVERAGED...     RAISE81   INCREASE IN SALARY OVER 1980
* * * * * * * * * * * * * * * * * * * * * * * * * * * * * * * * * * * * * * * * * * * * * * * * * * *  PAGE  1 OF  1

                EE081
          MEAN I
         COUNT I  OFF-MGR     PROF        TECH        CLERICAL   OPERTIVS   SERVICE       ROW
           SUM I                                                                         TOTAL
       STD DEV I        1 I        2 I        3 I        5 I        7 I        9 I
DEPT81  -------I----------I----------I----------I----------I----------I----------I
             1 I  2684.50 I  2470.00 I  1592.67 I   937.60 I  1690.00 I   761.75 I  1472.13
  ADMIN        I       10 I        1 I        3 I       15 I        1 I        8 I       38
               I 26845.00 I  2470.00 I  4778.00 I 14064.00 I  1690.00 I  6094.00 I 55941.00
               I  1413.13 I      0.0 I   622.90 I   467.28 I      0.0 I     2.12 I  1113.96
              -I----------I----------I----------I----------I----------I----------I
             2 I      0.0 I  4875.00 I  4160.00 I   621.90 I      0.0 I      0.0 I  1811.54
  PROJECT DIRECTOR I    0 I        7 I        1 I       20 I        0 I        0 I       28
               I      0.0 I 34125.00 I  4160.00 I 12438.00 I      0.0 I      0.0 I 50723.00
               I      0.0 I  2567.72 I      0.0 I   805.66 I      0.0 I      0.0 I  2368.04
              -I----------I----------I----------I----------I----------I----------I
             3 I  1561.58 I  2719.33 I  1959.75 I  1333.23 I      0.0 I      0.0 I  1484.92
  CHICAGO OPERATIO I   12 I        3 I        4 I       43 I        0 I        0 I       62
               I 18739.00 I  8158.00 I  7839.00 I 57329.00 I      0.0 I      0.0 I 92065.00
               I   870.67 I  1190.49 I  1326.53 I  1059.43 I      0.0 I      0.0 I  1072.20
              -I----------I----------I----------I----------I----------I----------I
             4 I  3176.87 I      0.0 I  1625.00 I  1499.05 I      0.0 I      0.0 I  1940.16
  ST LOUIS OPERATI I    8 I        0 I        2 I       21 I        0 I        0 I       31
               I 25415.00 I      0.0 I  3250.00 I 31480.00 I      0.0 I      0.0 I 60145.00
               I  1547.35 I      0.0 I    91.92 I   890.61 I      0.0 I      0.0 I  1280.01
              -I----------I----------I----------I----------I----------I----------I
   COLUMN TOTAL   2366.63    4068.45    2002.70    1164.76    1690.00     761.75     1628.14
                       30         11         10         99          1          8         159
                 70999.00   44753.00   20027.00  115311.00    1690.00    6094.00   258874.00
                  1403.33    2344.41    1131.10     950.99        0.0       2.12     1429.25

NUMBER OF MISSING OBSERVATIONS =       116
```

22.8 Optional Statistics

BREAKDOWN automatically computes sums, means, standard deviations, and variances for subpopulations. Optionally, you can obtain a one-way analysis of variance for each table as well as a test of linearity. To obtain these additional statistics, use an optional STATISTICS command.

STATISTIC 1 *Analysis of variance.* Prints a standard analysis of variance table, calculates *ETA* and ETA^2.

STATISTIC 2 *Test of linearity.* Calculates the sums of squares, degrees of freedom, and mean square associated with linear and nonlinear components, as well as the *F* ratio, Pearson's *r*, and r^2. Statistic 1 *must* be requested to obtain Statistic 2. Statistic 2 is ignored if the control variable is a short string.

If you specify a two-way or higher-order breakdown, the second and subsequent dimensions are ignored in the analysis of variance table. For example,

```
BREAKDOWN  TABLES=INCOME BY SEX BY RACE
STATISTICS  1
```

produces a breakdown of INCOME by RACE within SEX, but computes an analysis of variance only for INCOME by SEX. To obtain a two-way and higher analysis of variance, use procedure ANOVA (Chapter 26) or MANOVA (Chapter 28). Procedure ONEWAY (Chapter 27) calculates a one-way analysis of variance with multiple comparison tests. Statistics 1 and 2 are not available if you use the CROSSBREAK subcommand.

The following commands produce the optional statistics for the BREAKDOWN tables in Figure 22.3a.

```
BREAKDOWN  TABLES=PCTRAISE BY GRADE81
STATISTICS  1 2
```

Figure 22.8 displays these statistics.

Figure 22.8 Optional statistics

ANALYSIS OF VARIANCE

VARIABLE	CODE	VALUE LABEL	SUM	MEAN	STD DEV	SUM OF SQ	N
GRADE81	2.		0.0157	0.0079	0.0111	0.0001	(2)
GRADE81	3.		2.0050	0.0872	0.0536	0.0633	(23)
GRADE81	4.		2.2133	0.0851	0.1077	0.2900	(26)
GRADE81	5.		1.8286	0.1219	0.0648	0.0588	(15)
GRADE81	6.		3.6132	0.1505	0.0742	0.1265	(24)
GRADE81	7.		1.0326	0.1291	0.0518	0.0188	(8)
GRADE81	8.		2.1087	0.1917	0.1253	0.1570	(11)
GRADE81	9.		0.3262	0.1087	0.0205	0.0008	(3)
GRADE81	10.		2.7435	0.1372	0.1184	0.2664	(20)
GRADE81	11.		2.3820	0.1985	0.1771	0.3449	(12)
GRADE81	12.		0.5847	0.0975	0.0602	0.0181	(6)
GRADE81	13.		0.8049	0.1610	0.1454	0.0846	(5)
GRADE81	14.		0.2505	0.0835	0.0522	0.0055	(3)
GRADE81	15.		0.0811	0.0811	0.0	0.0	(1)
WITHIN GROUPS TOTAL			19.9900	0.1257	0.0995	1.4348	(159)

ANALYSIS OF VARIANCE

SOURCE	SUM OF SQUARES	D.F.	MEAN SQUARE	F	SIG.
BETWEEN GROUPS	0.253	13	0.019	1.968	0.0273
LINEARITY	0.075	1	0.075	7.566	0.0067
DEV. FROM LINEARITY	0.178	12	0.015	1.502	0.1297
	R = 0.2106	R SQUARED = 0.0444			
WITHIN GROUPS	1.435	145	0.010		
	ETA = 0.3873	ETA SQUARED = 0.1500			

22.9 Missing Values

By default, BREAKDOWN deletes cases with missing values on a tablewide basis. A case missing on any of the variables specified for a table is not used. Every case contained in a table will have a complete set of nonmissing values for all variables in that table. When you separate tables requests with a slash, missing values are handled separately for each list.

Two missing-value options are available. Option 1 handles user-defined missing values as if they were not missing. Option 2 deletes cases if they are missing on the dependent variable only. A case is included if it has a valid value for the dependent variable, although it may have missing values for the independent variables.

OPTION 1 *Include missing values.*

OPTION 2 *Exclude cases with missing values for the dependent variable only.* User-defined missing values are ignored for control variables.

22.10 Formatting Options

By default, BREAKDOWN prints the variable name, code, value label, and statistics for each category on one line. This always applies to general mode and applies to integer mode when you use the TABLES subcommand. You can print up to 200 value labels on a single table. You can suppress the variable labels and value labels in this format with Option 3. If you request the CROSSBREAK display format, you can suppress value labels with Option 8.

You can request a tree format for a BREAKDOWN table in general mode with Option 4. The individual cells of the BREAKDOWN table are printed as blocks. Figure 22.10 shows the tree format produced by the following commands:

```
BREAKDOWN  TABLES=PCTRAISE BY LOCATN81 BY GRADE81S
OPTIONS  4
```

The first column of blocks contains the statistics for PCTRAISE by the first independent variable, LOCATN81. The second column shows the breakdown for PCTRAISE by GRADE81S within LOCATN81.

OPTION 3 *Suppress variable and value labels.* This option is not available with the crossbreak format.

OPTION 4 *Print tables in tree format.* This option is available for general mode only.

OPTION 8 *Suppress value labels for crossbreak tables.*

22.11 LIMITATIONS

The following limitations apply to BREAKDOWN in general mode:

- A maximum of 200 variables total per BREAKDOWN command.
- A maximum of 250 tables.
- A maximum of 6 dimensions per table.
- A maximum of 30 tables lists per BREAKDOWN command.
- A maximum of 200 value labels printed on any single table.

The following limitations apply to BREAKDOWN in integer mode:

- A maximum of 100 variables named or implied with the VARIABLES subcommand.
- A maximum of 100 variables named or implied with the TABLES subcommand.
- A maximum of 100 tables.
- A maximum of 6 dimensions per table.
- A maximum of 30 tables lists per BREAKDOWN command.
- A maximum of 200 nonempty rows and columns in a CROSSBREAK table.

Figure 22.10 A tree-format BREAKDOWN table

```
- - - - - - - - - - - - - - - -  D E S C R I P T I O N   O F   S U B P O P U L A T I O N S  - - - - - - - - - - - - - - - -
CRITERION VARIABLE   PCTRAISE
    BROKEN DOWN BY   LOCATN81
                BY   GRADE81S
- - - - - - - - - - - - - - - - - - - - - - - - - - - - - - - - - - - - - - - - - - - - - - - - - - - - - - - - - - - - - -

FOR ENTIRE POPULATION
SUM             19.990
MEAN             0.126
STD DEV          0.103
VARIANCE         0.011
N           (     159)


VARIABLE   LOCATN81      VARIABLE   GRADE81S

CODE             1.      CODE           1.00
CHICAGO
SUM          15.356      SUM            3.595
MEAN          0.120      MEAN           0.082
STD DEV       0.109      STD DEV        0.091
VARIANCE      0.012      VARIANCE       0.008
N        (     128)      N         (     44)

                         CODE           2.00

                         SUM            4.038
                         MEAN           0.119
                         STD DEV        0.053
                         VARIANCE       0.003
                         N         (     34)

                         CODE           3.00

                         SUM            7.723
                         MEAN           0.154
                         STD DEV        0.139
                         VARIANCE       0.019
                         N         (     50)

CODE             5.      CODE           1.00
ST. LOUIS
SUM           4.634      SUM            0.640
MEAN          0.149      MEAN           0.091
STD DEV       0.070      STD DEV        0.038
VARIANCE      0.005      VARIANCE       0.001
N        (      31)      N         (      7)

                         CODE           2.00

                         SUM            2.436
                         MEAN           0.187
                         STD DEV        0.079
                         VARIANCE       0.006
                         N         (     13)

                         CODE           3.00

                         SUM            1.558
                         MEAN           0.142
                         STD DEV        0.043
                         VARIANCE       0.002
                         N         (     11)

  TOTAL CASES =     275
MISSING CASES =     116 OR  42.2 PCT.
```

ANNOTATED EXAMPLE FOR BREAKDOWN

The example illustrating BREAKDOWN analyzes personnel data from Hubbard Consultants Inc., a small industrial consulting firm with headquarters in Chicago and a branch office in St. Louis. This example examines salaries in 1981 by sex within departments and grades. The SPSS^{X} commands are

```
FILE HANDLE  HUB/ file specifications
GET  FILE=HUB
RECODE  GRADE81 (1 THRU 4=1) (5 THRU 7=2) (8 THRU 15=3) (ELSE=COPY)
   INTO GRADE81S/
VALUE LABELS  GRADE81S  (1) GRADES 1-4 (2) GRADES 5-7 (3) GRADES 8-15
MISSING VALUES  GRADE81S(0)
BREAKDOWN  SALARY81 BY DEPT81 BY GRADE81S BY SEX
FINISH
```

- The FILE HANDLE identifies the HUB data file and gives the operating-system specifications (see Chapter 3).
- The GET command defines the data to SPSS^{X} and selects the variables needed for analysis (see Chapter 5).
- The RECODE command creates the variable GRADE81S with three values which contain the 15 values of GRADE81 (see Chapter 6).
- The VALUE LABELS command assigns labels to the new variable GRADE81S (see Chapter 3).
- The MISSING VALUES command defines zero as the missing value for GRADE81S (see Chapter 3).
- The BREAKDOWN command specifies a three-way breakdown of salaries in general mode. SALARY81 is the dependent variable (see Section 22.3).
- Since no missing-value option is specified, BREAKDOWN deletes cases with missing values on a tablewide basis.

Output from BREAKDOWN

```
- - - - - - - - - - - - - - - - - - - D E S C R I P T I O N   O F   S U B P O P U L A T I O N S - - - - - - - - - - - - - - - -
CRITERION VARIABLE   SALARY81   YEARLY SALARY IN 1981
    BROKEN DOWN BY   DEPT81     DEPARTMENT CODE IN 1981
                BY   GRADE81S
                BY   SEX        EMPLOYEE'S SEX
- - - - - - - - - - - - - - - - - - - - - - - - - - - - - - - - - - - - - - - - - - - - - - - - - - - - - - - - - - - - - - - -
VARIABLE                   CODE     VALUE LABEL                    SUM          MEAN        STD DEV        VARIANCE          N

FOR ENTIRE POPULATION                                      2415394.0000    15096.2125      8074.3872  65195729.1747   (   160)

DEPT81                       1.     ADMIN                   590438.0000    15537.8421      9810.5522  96246934.6771   (    38)
   GRADE81S                1.00     GRADES 1-4              120922.0000    10076.8333      1685.2658   2840120.6970   (    12)
      SEX                    1.     MALE                    111172.0000    10106.5455      1764.2221   3112479.6727   (    11)
      SEX                    2.     FEMALE                    9750.0000     9750.0000        0.0             0.0      (     1)

   GRADE81S                2.00     GRADES 5-7              179291.0000    11952.7333      2019.7453   4079371.0667   (    15)
      SEX                    1.     MALE                     13910.0000    13910.0000        0.0             0.0      (     1)
      SEX                    2.     FEMALE                  165381.0000    11812.9286      2019.2662   4077435.9176   (    14)

   GRADE81S                3.00     GRADES 8-15             290225.0000    26384.0909     12759.5664 162806534.0909  (    11)
      SEX                    1.     MALE                    170625.0000    34125.0000     15498.1047 240191250.0000  (     5)
      SEX                    2.     FEMALE                  119600.0000    19933.3333      4858.3605  23603666.6667   (     6)
DEPT81                       2.     PROJECT DIRECTORS       428804.0000    15314.4286      8146.9522  66372830.4762   (    28)
   GRADE81S                1.00     GRADES 1-4              181449.0000    11340.5625      1999.6042   3998416.7958   (    16)
      SEX                    1.     MALE                    105839.0000    10583.9000      1143.2161   1306942.9889   (    10)
      SEX                    2.     FEMALE                   75610.0000    12601.6667      2566.9469   6589216.2667   (     6)

   GRADE81S                2.00     GRADES 5-7               38480.0000    12826.6667      2015.3494   4061633.3333   (     3)
      SEX                    2.     FEMALE                   38480.0000    12826.6667      2015.3494   4061633.3333   (     3)

   GRADE81S                3.00     GRADES 8-15             208875.0000    23208.3333     10558.8272 111488831.2500  (     9)
      SEX                    1.     MALE                    143065.0000    28613.0000     11587.9159 134279795.0000  (     5)
      SEX                    2.     FEMALE                   65810.0000    16452.5000      2953.7674   8724741.6667   (     4)
DEPT81                       3.     CHICAGO OPERATIONS      940294.0000    14925.3016      7705.3167  59371905.9237   (    63)
   GRADE81S                1.00     GRADES 1-4              168677.0000     9922.1765      1536.2349   2360017.7794   (    17)
      SEX                    1.     MALE                     20917.0000    10458.5000       836.5073    699744.5000   (     2)
      SEX                    2.     FEMALE                  147760.0000     9850.6667      1612.6409   2600610.6667   (    15)

   GRADE81S                2.00     GRADES 5-7              197356.0000    12334.7500      2190.5735   4798612.4667   (    16)
      SEX                    1.     MALE                     40924.0000    13641.3333      3333.0827  11109440.3333   (     3)
      SEX                    2.     FEMALE                  156432.0000    12033.2308      1903.0008   3621412.1923   (    13)

   GRADE81S                3.00     GRADES 8-15             574261.0000    19142.0333      9294.0232  86378866.9299   (    30)
      SEX                    1.     MALE                    142090.0000    28418.0000     15680.5949 245881057.5000  (     5)
      SEX                    2.     FEMALE                  432171.0000    17286.8400      6471.7384  41883398.5567   (    25)
DEPT81                       4.     ST LOUIS OPERATIONS     455858.0000    14705.0968      6624.5319  43884422.6237   (    31)
   GRADE81S                1.00     GRADES 1-4               66118.0000     9445.4286       680.5620    463164.6190   (     7)
      SEX                    1.     MALE                     18395.0000     9197.5000       873.2769    762612.5000   (     2)
      SEX                    2.     FEMALE                   47723.0000     9544.6000       679.0183    461065.8000   (     5)

   GRADE81S                2.00     GRADES 5-7              160420.0000    12340.0000      1925.6254   3708033.3333   (    13)
      SEX                    1.     MALE                     35100.0000    11700.0000      1357.2398   1842100.0000   (     3)
      SEX                    2.     FEMALE                  125320.0000    12532.0000      2087.3897   4357195.5556   (    10)

   GRADE81S                3.00     GRADES 8-15             229320.0000    20847.2727      7667.4707  58790106.8182   (    11)
      SEX                    1.     MALE                     21775.0000    21775.0000        0.0             0.0      (     1)
      SEX                    2.     FEMALE                  207545.0000    20754.5000      8075.7134  65217146.9444   (    10)

   TOTAL CASES =      275
 MISSING CASES =      115 OR  41.8 PCT.
```

23

```
REPORT [FORMAT = [TSPACE ({1|n})] [CHDSPACE ({1|n})]
   [BRKSPACE ({1|n})] [FTSPACE ({1|n})]
   [LENGTH ({1, 59|n, n})] [MARGINS ({1, 132|n, n})] [{NOLIST|LIST [(n)]}]
   [SUMSPACE ({1|n})] [MISSING {'.'|'s'}]]
 [/STRING = stringname (varname [(width)] [(BLANK)] 'literal' . . . )]
 /VARIABLES = varname ({VALUE|LABEL|DUMMY}) ['col head'] [(width)] [(OFFSET (n))] . . .
 [/MISSING = {VAR|NONE|LIST (varlist {1|n})}]
 [/TITLE = 'line 1' 'line 2' . . . ] [/FOOTNOTE = 'line 1' 'line 2' . . . ]
   or                                  or
 [/LTITLE = 'line 1' 'line 2' . . . ] [/LFOOTNOTE = 'line 1' 'line 2' . . . ]
 [/CTITLE = 'line 1' 'line 2' . . . ] [/CFOOTNOTE = 'line 1' 'line 2' . . . ]
 [/RTITLE = 'line 1' 'line 2' . . . ] [/RFOOTNOTE = 'line 1' 'line 2' . . . ]
 /BREAK {= varlist ['title'] [(width)] ({VALUE|LABEL}) ({NOTOTAL|TOTAL}) ({SKIP ({1|n})|PAGE})
          [(OFFSET ({0|n}))] ({NONAME|NAME})
        |= (NOBREAK) [(width)] [(SKIP ({1|n}))] [(OFFSET ({0|n}))]}
 [/SUMMARY {= {VALIDN|VARIANCE|SUM|MEAN|STDDEV|MIN|MAX|SKEWNESS|KURTOSIS|PCGT (n)|PCLT (n)|
               PCIN (n, m)|MEDIAN (min, max)|MODE (min, max)}
              [(varlist [(d)] [({PLAIN|DOLLAR|COMMA})]] ['title'] [(bc)]
            |{ABFREQ (min, max)|RELFREQ (min, max)}
            |{DIVIDE (agg ( ), agg ( ) [, factor])|PCT (agg ( ), agg ( ))|
              SUBTRACT (agg ( ), agg ( ))|ADD (agg ( ), agg ( ), . . . )|
              GREAT (agg ( ), agg ( ), . . . )|LEAST (agg ( ), agg ( ), . . . )|
              AVERAGE (agg ( ), agg ( ), . . . )|MULTIPLY (agg ( ), agg ( ), . . . )}
           [SKIP ({0|n})]
          |= PREVIOUS [({1|n})]}]
```


INTRODUCTION, **23.1**
- Page Layout, **23.2**
  - Columns, **23.3**
  - Rows, **23.4**
- Breaks and Break Variables, **23.5**
- Command Overview, **23.6**
- A Company Report, **23.7**

THE FORMAT SUBCOMMAND, **23.8**
- The LIST Keyword, **23.9**
- Page Dimensions, **23.10**
- Vertical Spacing, **23.11**
- The MISSING Keyword, **23.12**
- FORMAT Summary, **23.13**

THE VARIABLES SUBCOMMAND, **23.14**
- Column Contents, **23.15**
- Column Widths, **23.16**
- Column Heads, **23.17**
- Positioning Columns under Heads, **23.18**
- Intercolumn Spacing, **23.19**
- VARIABLES Summary, **23.20**

THE STRING SUBCOMMAND, **23.21**
- Variables within Strings, **23.22**
- Literals within Strings, **23.23**
- Using Strings, **23.24**
- STRING Specifications, **23.25**
- The Company Report Using Strings, **23.26**

THE BREAK SUBCOMMAND, **23.27**
- Column Heads, Contents, and Width, **23.28**
  - One- and Two-Break Reports with Two Variables, **23.29**
  - Keyword (TOTAL) and Multiple Break Reports, **23.30**
  - Reports with No Breaks, **23.31**
- BREAK Summary, **23.32**

THE SUMMARY SUBCOMMAND, **23.33**
- Basic Specifications, **23.34**
- REPORT Statistics, **23.35**
- Composite Functions, **23.36**
- Multiple Aggregate Functions, **23.37**
- Summary Titles, **23.38**
- Spacing Summary Lines, **23.39**
  - Summary Titles in Break Columns, **23.40**
  - Print Formats for Summaries, **23.41**
  - Using Composite Functions, **23.42**
  - Nested Composite Functions, **23.43**
- Multiple Summary Statistics on One Line, **23.44**
- Repeating Summary Specifications, **23.45**
- SUMMARY Summary, **23.46**

TITLES AND FOOTNOTES, **23.47**

THE MISSING SUBCOMMAND, **23.48**

REPORTS WITH NO BREAKS, **23.49**

SUBCOMMAND ORDER, **23.50**
- Limitations, **23.51**
- Trial Runs, **23.52**
- Split-File Processing, **23.53**
- Sorting Cases, **23.54**
- REPORT Compared with Other Procedures, **23.55**
  - Producing CROSSBREAK-like Tables, **23.56**
  - Producing CROSSTABS-like Tables, **23.57**
- REPORT and Other SPSS^X Commands, **23.58**

Chapter 23 REPORT

The SPSS^X REPORT procedure produces case listings and summary statistics and gives you considerable control over the appearance of the output. REPORT calculates all the univariate statistics available in CONDESCRIPTIVE, absolute and relative frequencies available in FREQUENCIES, subpopulation means and statistics available in BREAKDOWN, and statistics not directly available in any other SPSS^X procedure. It also allows you to specify column widths, titles, footnotes, spacing, and other elements.

23.1 INTRODUCTION

An SPSS^X report has a basic structure that you can modify with a variety of subcommands. The body of the report is formatted in rows and columns where the columns correspond to variables and the rows to individual cases or groups of cases. In the report shown in Figure 23.1, columns headed by AGE, TENURE IN COMPANY, TENURE IN GRADE, and ANNUAL SALARY are the variables and the rows labeled CARPETING, APPLIANCES, and so forth, represent groups of cases based on divisions within the company. The TOTAL row entries are the averages for the entire company.

Figure 23.1 A simple report

```
PERSONNEL REPORT (BASIC)                                              PAGE    1

PRODUCT            AGE    TENURE IN     TENURE IN          ANNUAL
DIVISION                    COMPANY         GRADE          SALARY

 CARPETING          33       4.14        3.47               14221

 APPLIANCES         34       4.29        3.94               15039

 FURNITURE          36       4.77        4.22               15894

 HARDWARE           35       4.54        4.18               15616

 TOTAL              34       4.47        4.00               15286
```

To format the output, REPORT provides full default specifications but allows you to control

- page lengths, margins, and column widths;
- vertical spacing between different types of information;
- page titles and footnotes; and
- labels for variables and statistics.

See Figure 23.2 for the page layout of the SPSS^X report as well as the special subcommand specifications to control its basic structure.

Finally, REPORT has two special features: a string function that concatenates variables and literals for display, and composite functions that perform arithmetic operations using two or more of the summary statistics calculated on single variables.

23.2 Page Layout

The complete page layout of the SPSS^{X} report and the subcommand specifications used to control the basic structure of the report are shown in Figure 23.2. Use this schematic report for reference as you read through this chapter and as you develop your own reports.

Figure 23.2 The report layout

```
------------------------------------top of page-----------------------------------
                                                                  <---- LENGTH
                ***************** TITLE ****************
                                                                  <---- TSPACE
BREAK HEAD           BREAK HEAD          COLUMN    COLUMN    COLUMN    COLUMN
                                         HEAD      HEAD      HEAD      HEAD
                                         [VAR]     [VAR]     [VAR]     [VAR]
                                                                  <---- CHDSPACE
BREAK A VALUE 1      BREAK B VALUE 1
                                                                  <---- BRKSPACE
                                         VALUE     VALUE     VALUE     VALUE
                                         VALUE     VALUE     VALUE     VALUE
                                                                  <---- LIST
                                         VALUE     VALUE     VALUE     VALUE
                                         VALUE     VALUE     VALUE     VALUE

                     SUMMARY TITLE        AGG.      AGG.      AGG.      AGG.
                                                                  <---- SKIP with SUMMARY
                     SUMMARY TITLE        AGG.      AGG.      AGG.      AGG.
                                                                  <---- SKIP with SUMMARY
                     BREAK B VALUE 2
                                                                  <---- BRKSPACE
                                         VALUE     VALUE     VALUE     VALUE
                                         VALUE     VALUE     VALUE     VALUE
                                                                  <---- LIST
                                         VALUE     VALUE     VALUE     VALUE
                                         VALUE     VALUE     VALUE     VALUE

                     SUMMARY TITLE        AGG.      AGG.      AGG.      AGG.<---- stats for B=2, A=1

                     SUMMARY TITLE        AGG.      AGG.      AGG.
                                                                  <---- SUMSPACE
SUMMARY TITLE                             AGG.      AGG.      AGG.      AGG.<---- stats for A=1

SUMMARY TITLE                             AGG.      AGG.      AGG.      AGG.
                                                                  <---- SKIP with BREAK
BREAK A VALUE 2      BREAK B VALUE 1
                                                                  <---- BRKSPACE
                                         VALUE     VALUE     VALUE     VALUE
                                         VALUE     VALUE     VALUE     VALUE
                                                                  <---- LIST
                                         VALUE     VALUE     VALUE     VALUE
                                         VALUE     VALUE     VALUE     VALUE

                     SUMMARY TITLE        AGG.      AGG.      AGG.      AGG.
                                                                  <---- SKIP
                     SUMMARY TITLE        AGG.      AGG.      AGG.      AGG.
                                                                  <---- SKIP with BREAK
                     BREAK B VALUE 2
                                                                  <---- BRKSPACE
                                         VALUE     VALUE     VALUE     VALUE
                                         VALUE     VALUE     VALUE     VALUE
                                                                  <---- LIST
                                         VALUE     VALUE     VALUE     VALUE
                                         VALUE     VALUE     VALUE     VALUE

                     SUMMARY TITLE        AGG.      AGG.      AGG.      AGG.

                     SUMMARY TITLE        AGG.      AGG.      AGG.      AGG.
                                                                  <---- SUMSPACE
SUMMARY TITLE                             AGG.      AGG.      AGG.      AGG.

SUMMARY TITLE                             AGG.      AGG.      AGG.      AGG.
                                                                  <---- FTSPACE
                ***************** FOOTNOTE ****************
                                                                  <---- LENGTH
----------------------------------bottom of page---------------------------------
|                                                                               |
left margin                                                          right margin
```

The maximum width of the report is controlled by the system-wide page width, which is specified with the SET command (see Chapter 4). You can decrease the overall width of the report and indent either the left or right margin of the report. For example, the report shown in Figure 23.1 has no left indent and has been assigned a right margin of 80 (the page number is in position 80). The top of the REPORT page begins at line 1 and ends at the bottom of the page whose length is specified by the SET command (see Chapter 4). The report shown in Figure 23.1 begins on the first line of the page with the title, PERSONNEL REPORT (BASIC), but is less than one page long. You can choose to print the top below the first line of the page and print the last line of the report above the bottom of the page (see Section 23.10).

Any number of lines of titles and footnotes can be placed on the page (see Section 23.47). The example in Figure 23.1, for instance, shows a single-line title. Titles and footnotes are repeated across pages, and pages can be numbered. You can control both the space between the title and body of the report and the space between the body of the report and any footnotes (see Section 23.11). In Figure 23.1, the space between the title and the column heads has been limited to one line. In fact, all the spacing indicated by the arrows in Figure 23.2 is subject to your control.

23.3 Columns

Columns in a report correspond to two sets of variables: break variables and report variables. *Break variables* define groups of cases. They function in the same way as BY variables in BREAKDOWN. Columns defined by break variables are placed on the left side of the report (e.g., the column headed PRODUCT DIVISION in Figure 23.1). Multiple break variables can be used to define groups, subgroups within groups, lower level subgroups within subgroups, etc. Both columns titled BREAK HEAD in Figure 23.2 are break columns: the left-hand break column (BREAK A) identifies groups; the right-hand break column (BREAK B) identifies subgroups within those groups.

Report variables are variables being listed in case listings or summarized with REPORT's set of statistical and arithmetic functions. They are identified in Figure 23.2 by the columns titled COLUMN HEAD. There are three basic types of report variables: actual SPSS^X variables (e.g., the four variables shown in Figure 23.1), variables created with the REPORT string function, and special placeholders termed *dummy variables* within the REPORT language.

23.4 Rows

The rows of a report contain case listings and summary statistics, identified by titles in the BREAK columns. For example, BREAK A VALUE 1 in Figure 23.2 labels the cases for the group with the value 1 on break variable A. The title SUMMARY TITLE labels the statistics being printed for the group. In Figure 23.1, CARPETING is the label for the first subgroup defined by the break variable. There is no summary title because the summary is placed on the same line as the break variable's labeled value.

23.5 Breaks and Break Variables

The concept of a break variable is central to generating a report. REPORT processes cases sequentially and at specified points prints a summary of cases processed since the last set of summary statistics was printed. The point at which it summarizes a set of cases is determined by the change, or "break," in the value of the break variable.

Break variables split a file into subpopulations or groups. For example, assume a file containing personnel information on a company organized into sales divisions. To produce a report that averages salaries by divisions, the file must contain a variable identifying the division. If the file is sorted on this variable, so that all employees working in one division are grouped together, REPORT reads through the file and stores the information required to compute average salary until the variable identifying the division changes. At this point, REPORT prints the average salary. It then continues to read the file, storing the information required for the next set of employees, then prints their average salary, etc. After it reads the last case in the file, it prints average salary for the last division. This is exactly what is reported in Figure 23.1.

Note that this design implies that a case cannot be in more than one group. A variable defines break groups, and each case has one and only one value for that variable.

REPORT permits breaks within breaks. Using the same example, assume that the file also contains information on which branch store the employee works in. Instead of just obtaining average salaries for employees within divisions, REPORT can be used to obtain average salaries for people within each division at each store. The mechanics of a multiple-break report are similar to those of the simple one-break report. Figure 23.5 is a sample data file for such a two-break report.

Figure 23.5 A sample file organized for a two-break report

```
388-55-1234        1    1
225-22-7242        1    1
455-55-0474        1    1
499-66-2235        1    2
526-62-2535        1    2
270-71-2262        1    2
811-12-3313        1    3
180-01-9205        1    3
424-44-3449        1    3
656-78-8443        1    4
244-22-9262        1    4
377-44-2393        1    4
     .                  .
     .                  .
     .                  .
577-72-2458        2    1
618-82-2320        2    1
277-33-2292        2    1
791-02-2955        2    2
200-22-5226        2    2
255-33-0272        2    2
299-33-4377        2    2
     .                  .
     .                  .
     .                  .
```

The first field in Figure 23.5 is a unique employee identification number (i.e., the United States social security number). The first single-column data item is the store (1 for suburban, 2 for downtown) and the second single column is the division within which the employee works (1 for carpeting, 2 for appliances, etc.). Other data columns and most of the cases have been removed for demonstration purposes. Note the way in which the file is organized: All employees within a store are grouped together and all employees within each store who work in the same division are grouped together. The file *must* be organized in this manner to ensure that the correct set of salaries is being averaged. For example, if not all employees in the same division are together in the file, they fall into different groups as the value of division changes from case to case and are not summarized together.

More than one variable can be used to define a break. For example, the file described in Figure 23.5 could be broken down into groups based on both store and division at the same break level. When the file is treated as divisions within stores, as first described, summary statistics are printed when the division changes as well as when the store changes. However, if divisions and stores are treated at the same break level, summary statistics are printed only when the division changes (see Section 23.29).

23.6 Command Overview

REPORT is an extremely flexible procedure with a large number of options. Flexibility implies some additional complexity in the language. However, the syntax required to produce reports that use the standard format is fairly simple. The REPORT command is divided into major subcommands controlling various parts of the display. Subcommands begin with a keyword followed by an optional equals sign and a set of specifications.

Subcommands are separated from each other by slashes. Four are basic:

FORMAT. The FORMAT subcommand specifies how the report is laid out on a page and whether case listings are to be presented. If the report uses only the default specifications, the FORMAT subcommand is not required. (See Section 23.8.)

VARIABLES. The VARIABLES subcommand specifies the report variables upon which statistics are computed and for which cases can be listed. The VARIABLES subcommand is required. (See Section 23.14.)

BREAK. The BREAK subcommand specifies the variables used to define groups. There can be more than one BREAK subcommand. It is required, even if the report is not breaking on groups. (See Section 23.27.)

SUMMARY. The SUMMARY subcommand specifies the statistics to be computed for report variables. Each SUMMARY subcommand defines one line of the summary section of the report. If the report contains more than one line of summary statistics, multiple SUMMARY subcommands are used. Sets of SUMMARY subcommands are paired with the BREAK subcommand. If there is more than one BREAK subcommand, there can be more than one set of SUMMARY subcommands. The SUMMARY is not required. However, if you do not specify case listings using the FORMAT subcommand, you must use a SUMMARY subcommand. Otherwise, your report has no content. (See Section 23.33.)

REPORT has no separate OPTIONS or STATISTICS commands. Statistics are specified with keywords, and the handling of missing values is controlled with the optional MISSING subcommand explained in Section 23.48.

Three special delimiters are used in REPORT subcommand specifications: apostrophes and parentheses (always in pairs) and the slash ending each subcommand. Note that apostrophes always enclose literals for titles or subtitles; parentheses enclose certain keywords and arguments associated with keywords. All keywords can be abbreviated to the first three characters.

23.7 A Company Report

Any report requires the VARIABLES and BREAK subcommands described above, and either the FORMAT subcommand specifying LIST or a SUMMARY subcommand.

Figure 23.7 The default report

```
PERSONNEL REPORT (BASIC)                                                                              PAGE     1

DIVISION         AGE   TENURE I    TENURE I    SALARY--
                       N COMPAN    N GRADE       ANNUAL
                              Y

       1

    MEAN     33.1489       4.14        3.47    14220.85

       2

    MEAN     33.9868       4.29        3.94    15039.28

       3

    MEAN     35.6625       4.77        4.22    15894.06

       4

    MEAN     34.5410       4.54        4.18    15615.82
```

Figure 23.7 is a report produced with default specifications. As individual subcommands are described in this chapter, this report is modified by overriding default subcommand specifications. The complete set of SPSS^X commands to produce the report in Figure 23.7 is as follows:

```
TITLE  PERSONNEL REPORT (BASIC)
DATA LIST  /1 S1 1-3 S2 4-5 S3 6-9
           LNAME 10-21(A) NAME 22-41(A)
           SEX 42 GRADE 43 (A) STORE 44 SALARY 45-49
           DIVISION 50 SHIFT 51 BDAY BMONTH BYEAR 52-57
           CMONTH CYEAR JMONTH JYEAR 58-65
COMPUTE  AGE=82-BYEAR
COMPUTE  TENURE=(12-CMONTH +(12*(82-CYEAR)))/12
COMPUTE  JTENURE=(12-JMONTH +(12*(82-JYEAR)))/12
PRINT FORMATS TENURE JTENURE (F2)
RECODE   GRADE('C'=4)('X'=1)('S'=2)('M'=3) INTO JOBGRADE/
VARIABLE LABELS JOBGRADE 'JOB GRADE'
           STORE 'BRANCH STORE'
           SALARY 'SALARY--ANNUAL'
           TENURE 'TENURE IN COMPANY'
           JTENURE 'TENURE IN GRADE'
VALUE LABELS   JOBGRADE 1 'SALES STAFF' 2 'SUPERVISORY STAFF'
                 3 'MANAGERIAL STAFF' 4 'SUPPORT STAFF'/
               SEX 1 'FEMALE' 2 'MALE'/
               STORE 1 'SUBURBAN' 2 'DOWNTOWN'/
               DIVISION 1 'CARPETING' 2 'APPLIANCES' 3 'FURNITURE'
                 4 'HARDWARE'/
               SHIFT 1 'FIRST' 2' SECOND' 3 'WEEKEND'/
SORT CASES  BY DIVISION
BEGIN DATA
388551234FORD          HARRIET L.          1C1 920011201155 4791080
419262235ZDEB          SUSAN E. A.         1C1´870021 5 362 780 780
534007333STANIK        ELIZABETH S.        1C2 92003118 862 679 980
     .
     .
     .
270622692WATSON        CLAUDETTE N.        1M2274004313 838 378 378
271552702SMITH         LEONARD H.          2M1420003310 23610761076
267562784COOK          MILT E.             2M2460002323 335 9751076
END DATA
REPORT  VARIABLES=AGE TENURE JTENURE SALARY/
        BREAK=DIVISION/
        SUMMARY=MEAN
```

This report uses one break variable, DIVISION, to split a personnel file into separate divisions. Data transformations are used to compute age, years at the company, and years within the job grade. The means for age, salary, tenure within the company, and tenure within the job grade are calculated for each division within the company. The file is sorted on DIVISION to ensure that cases are appropriately grouped.

23.8 THE FORMAT SUBCOMMAND

FORMAT specifications establish the physical dimensions of the report and vertical spacing around titles. The FORMAT subcommand is also used to specify case listings. FORMAT specifications can be named in any order.

23.9 The LIST Keyword

The keyword LIST instructs REPORT to print the contents of cases for variables named on the VARIABLES subcommand. LIST applies to all variables named on the VARIABLES subcommand. You cannot selectively specify variables to be listed. If you do not specify LIST, no case listings are printed: the default is NOLIST. Keyword LIST has an optional argument in parentheses which controls the spacing of cases. By default, no spaces are inserted between cases. An integer value in parentheses specifies a blank line after every *n* cases. For example, LIST(1) produces a double-spaced listing and LIST(3) lists cases in groups of three. Figure 23.31 demonstrates a double-spaced case listing. The count of lines within a group is reset at the beginning of a new break or a new page.

Although the FORMAT subcommand is not required, if you do not use the SUMMARY subcommand (Section 23.33) to specify any summary statistics, your report has no body, and REPORT issues an error message.

LIST(n) *List the contents of cases.* All variables named on the VARIABLES subcommand are listed. NOLIST is the default. A blank line is inserted after each *n* cases; by default, no lines are inserted.

23.10 Page Dimensions

Two keywords in the FORMAT subcommand control the dimensions and placement of the report within the page:

LENGTH(t,b) *The first and last printed lines on the page.* By default, REPORT uses 1 and the maximum page length as determined by the SET command (see Chapter 4). If you do not use the SET command the default page size is 59 lines and the default LENGTH specification is (1,59). You cannot specify a maximum longer than the system page length.

MARGINS(l,r) *The left and right margins.* The maximum width of a REPORT is limited by the system width, which defaults to 1 and 132. You can use MARGINS to decrease the report width; you cannot override the system width, which is controlled by the SET command (see Chapter 4).

23.11 Vertical Spacing

Five keyword specifications in the FORMAT subcommand control vertical spacing around titles (see Figure 23.2):

TSPACE(n) *The number of lines between the report title and the column heads* (the default is 1).

CHDSPACE(n) *The number of lines of space beneath the longest column head* (the default is 1).

BRKSPACE(n) *The number of lines of space beneath the break head and the case-listing* (when LIST is in effect) *or first summary line* (the default is 1). To place the first summary statistic requested on the same line as the break value or the first case listed, use BRKSPACE(−1).

SUMSPACE(n) *The number of lines of space between the last summary line at the lower break and the first summary line at the higher break when both are breaking simultaneously* (the default is 1). SUMSPACE also controls spaces between the last case listed and the first summary line.

FTSPACE(n) *The minimum number of lines of space between the last listing on the page and the footnote* (the default is 1).

23.12 The MISSING Keyword

The MISSING keyword changes the default missing-value indicator, a period (.), in case listings, break values, and summary statistics. Specify any one-character symbol (including a blank) in apostrophes following the keyword MISSING. For example,

```
FORMAT= LIST MISSING 'm'/
```

prints a lower-case *m* instead of the period.

MISSING 's' *Missing-value symbol.* The default symbol is a period.

23.13 FORMAT Summary

The default FORMAT specifications are as follows:

```
FORMAT= NOLIST LENGTH(1,system page length) MARGINS(1,132)
    TSPACE(1) SUMSPACE(1) CHDSPACE(1) BRKSPACE(1)
    FTSPACE(1) MISSING '.'/
```

- Formatting specifications can be named in any order.
- The FORMAT subcommand can be used only once, and when used must come first. If the FORMAT subcommand is omitted, all defaults are used.

Figure 23.13 The company report with formatting options

```
PERSONNEL REPORT (BASIC)                                                PAGE    1
DIVISION          AGE     TENURE I     TENURE I     SALARY--
                          N COMPAN     N GRADE        ANNUAL
                                 Y

       1     33.1489          4.14         3.47     14220.85

       2     33.9868          4.29         3.94     15039.28

       3     35.6625          4.77         4.22     15894.06

       4     34.5410          4.54         4.18     15615.82
```

Figure 23.13 illustrates the default report shown in Figure 23.7 modified with FORMAT specifications. The margins are reduced to 1 and 80 and the summary statistics are printed on the break label line. The following commands are required to produce the report in Figure 23.13:

```
REPORT   FORMAT=MARGINS (1,80) BRKSPACE(-1)/
         VARIABLES=AGE TENURE JTENURE SALARY/
         BREAK=DIVISION/
         SUMMARY=MEAN
```

23.14 THE VARIABLES SUBCOMMAND

The VARIABLES subcommand names the variables to be included in the report. It also has optional specifications for column heads and column widths and for controlling the contents of report columns. Break variables should not be included.

The minimum VARIABLES specification is a list of variables in the order in which they are to appear on the report. The variable list conforms to the conventional variable list in SPSS^X. REPORT also recognizes special placeholder variables (Section 23.15) and variables constructed within the procedure by the STRING subcommand (Section 23.21).

The number of variables that can be specified depends upon the width of the report, the width of the variable columns, and the number of BREAK subcommands.

23.15 Column Contents

When the LIST keyword is specified on the FORMAT subcommand, the contents of report columns are by default the actual values for cases. You can choose to list any defined value labels rather than actual values. The keyword LABEL in parentheses following a variable name lists value labels.

```
VARIABLES=SEX(LABEL).../
```

Value labels are left-justified in the column. If a given value does not have a defined value label, the value is printed. (LABEL) is ignored if no value labels have been defined for the variable. When you specify (LABEL) both values and value labels are printed left-justified in the column.

If the variable list contains a set of inclusive variables implied by the keyword TO, (LABEL) applies to the entire set of variables in the list. However, (LABEL) cannot be implied for a set of variables named individually. For example, in

```
VARIABLES=V1 TO V5(LABEL)/
```

(LABEL) applies to all variables implied by V1 TO V5. But in

```
VARIABLES=V1 V2 V3 V4 V5(LABEL)/
```

(LABEL) applies only to V5.

The keyword (DUMMY) can be used in place of (LABEL) to specify a variable that does not really exist but is used to define a column in the report. Dummy variable columns can be used to control spacing between columns or to reserve space for statistics computed upon other variables. A dummy variable cannot be an existing SPSS^X variable. The TO keyword cannot be used to generate multiple dummy variables within REPORT.

For completeness, (VALUE), which is the default, can be specified in parentheses following a variable name.

23.16 Column Widths

The default width for SPSS^X variables is 8 or the dictionary field width, whichever is greater. For dummy variables, it is 8. The default column width for variables created by the STRING subcommand is the length of the string. However, if (LABEL) has been specified for a variable, the default width of its column is 20, since the maximum length of a value label is 20 characters. Default widths can be overridden by a width specified in parentheses following a variable name, as in

```
VARIABLES=SEX(LABEL)(6)
```

which lists value labels in a column 6 characters wide, rather than one 20 characters wide.

Judicious use of the column width specification produces more compact reports and permits reports containing up to 60 columns. Some care must be taken to ensure that the specified column width is sufficient for the contents. If the column is not wide enough to print a case or a summary statistic with the appropriate number of decimal positions, REPORT first starts rounding the decimal digits. If the integer portion still cannot fit and the column is at least 7 characters wide, REPORT prints the number in scientific notation. If the column is less than 7 characters wide and the integer portion will not fit, REPORTS prints asterisks. Alphanumeric values, value labels, and REPORT-generated strings (Section 23.21), are truncated to fit specified column widths.

23.17 Column Heads

Every column has a column head. By default, REPORT uses the variable label if one has been defined on the VARIABLE LABELS command. Otherwise, REPORT uses the variable name. The column head is right-justified for a column defined by a numeric variable. If the variable is a string or you have specified (LABEL), the column head is left-justified. You can specify a column head consisting of one or more lines by enclosing a string in apostrophes, as in:

```
VARIABLES=HT 'HEIGHT'
```

If the column head is more than one line long, each line must be enclosed in apostrophes separated by at least one space. For example,

```
VARIABLES=HT 'HEIGHT' 'IN FEET'
```

produces a two-line column head. HT 'HEIGHT IN FEET' would be truncated in a column narrower than 14 characters. Trailing blanks can be inserted to center or left-align titles, as in:

```
VARIABLES=HT 'HEIGHT ' 'IN FEET'
```

Column heads cannot be wider than column widths. Specified titles that exceed the column width are truncated. Default titles (variable labels or variable names) wrap around for as many lines as required to print the entire label. For example, if VARIABLE LABELS assigns a label GRADE IN

1976 to variable GRADE76, the specification GRADE76(5) prints the following column head:

```
GRADE
 IN 1
  976
```

On the other hand, the specification GRADE76(5)'GRADE' 'IN' '1976' prints the column head:

```
GRADE
   IN
 1976
```

A blank title such as '' can be used to completely remove a column head from the report.

Titles such as column heads are permitted in several places within the report. They are always specified within apostrophes and may contain any string characters, including special symbols and lower-case letters. If your title contains an apostrophe, you can use one of two methods. Either enclose the string in quotation marks, as in

```
VARIABLES=AGE "Respondent's Age"
```

or use two apostrophes not separated by spaces, as in

```
VARIABLES=AGE 'Respondent''s Age'
```

Column heads are right-justified for numeric or dummy variables and left-justified for string variables or when (LABEL) is specified.

23.18 Positioning Columns under Heads

By default, REPORT either right- or left-justifies the column contents under the title defined by the VARIABLES or BREAK subcommand. If the variable is numeric the variable is right-justified. If it is a string variable or you have specified (LABEL) the contents are left-justified. You can use the OFFSET keyword in parentheses to offset the contents of case listings and computed summaries. Specify the number of offsetting spaces in parentheses, as in:

```
VARIABLES=SEX (3) (OFFSET(1)) AGE 'AGE OF' 'HEAD' (OFFSET(2))/
```

If SEX is a string variable, the contents are offset 1 space from the left, while the column defined by AGE is offset 2 spaces from the right. OFFSET permits you to center column contents within wide columns. See Figure 23.20, which uses (OFFSET(3)).

23.19 Intercolumn Spacing

The combination of report width, number of columns, and column widths determines intercolumn spacing. Given n columns on a report (including break columns), there are $n-1$ intercolumn spaces. REPORT calculates the number of print positions taken by all the columns and subtracts it from the width of the report. The remaining space is divided into equal intercolumns from 1 to 4 print positions wide. If the report is wide and the number of print positions required for the columns relatively small, the right side of the report is empty. Dummy variables can be defined to insert extra columns into the report and control spacing between columns. If the dummy variables are given blank column heads, REPORT "prints" empty columns, thus producing differential spacing between columns. Figure 23.20 uses this method.

23.20 VARIABLES Summary

The complete set of specifications for the VARIABLES subcommand is as follows:

VARIABLES= varname(VALUE|LABEL|DUMMY) ['column head'] [(width)] [(OFFSET(n))] [... varname ...] /

- The default width for short string variables or numeric variables is 8 or the dictionary width. The default width for long string variables is their length. If (LABEL) is specified, the default width is 20.
- The default column head is the variable label. If no label has been defined, the default is the variable name.
- The specifications following each variable or group of variables implied by the TO keyword apply only to that variable or group.
- Specifications are given in any order.

If a file contains the variables ID, SEX, JOBGRADE, STORE, SALARY, and DIVISION, and the variable labels EMPLOYEE IDENTIFICATION NUMBER, JOB GRADE, and BRANCH STORE have been defined, the following VARIABLES specification might be used for a report including a case listing:

```
REPORT   FORMAT=LIST/
         VARIABLES=ID 'EMPLOYEE' 'IDENTIFICATION' 'NUMBER'(14)
              SEX TO STORE (LABEL)(8)
              SALARY
              DIVISION 'PRODUCT' 'DIVISION'(LABEL)(9)/
         BREAK=(NOBREAK)
```

No column heads are provided for SEX to STORE (implying JOBGRADE) and SALARY so they have default column heads. No width is specified for SALARY so its width defaults to 8. ID and SALARY are printed as observed values while value labels are printed for SEX to STORE and DIVISION.

Figure 23.20 The company report with VARIABLES options

```
PERSONNEL REPORT (BASIC)                                                      PAGE    1

DIVISION    AGE    TENURE IN     TENURE IN              ANNUAL
                     COMPANY         GRADE              SALARY

       1     33      4.14           3.47                 14221

       2     34      4.29           3.94                 15039

       3     36      4.77           4.22                 15894

       4     35      4.54           4.18                 15616
```

Figure 23.20 is the company report modified with several VARIABLES specifications. The default column widths for AGE, TENURE, and JTENURE are overridden. SALARY is given a new column head and a shorter width, and a dummy variable named SPACE is inserted to separate SALARY from the tenure variables. OFFSET is used to center the TENURE and JTENURE values under the column heads. The following command produces Figure 23.20:

```
REPORT   FORMAT=MARGINS (1,80) BRKSPACE(-1)/
         VARIABLES=AGE(3) TENURE(9) (OFFSET(3)) JTENURE(9) (OFFSET(3))
           SPACE(DUMMY)' '(4)
            SALARY 'ANNUAL' 'SALARY'(6)/
         BREAK=DIVISION/
         SUMMARY=MEAN
```

ANNOTATED EXAMPLE OF REPORT USING LIST

This example produces a report using data from the October 1980 issue of *Runner's World* magazine. It lists the top-rated shoes in the survey organized by manufacturer. Measures used by the raters to determine an overall evaluation for each shoe are reported. The SPSS^X commands used to produce this report are

```
TITLE 'RUNNER''S WORLD 1980 SHOE SURVEY'
DATA LIST   /1 TYPE 1 MAKER 2-3 QUALITY 5-9
            REARIMP FOREIMP FLEX SOLEWEAR 10-29
            REARCONT SOLETRAC 31-40 WEIGHT 42-46 LASTYEAR 48
            PREFER 50-53 STARS 55 NAME 57-72 (A)
VALUE LABELS   MAKER (1)ADIDAS (2)AUTRY (3)BROOKFIELD (4)BROOKS
               (5)CONVERSE (6)REEBOK (7)NEW BALANCE (8)PUMA (9)OSAGA
               (10)PONY (11)ETONIC (12)NIKE (13)SAUCONY
               (14)WILSON-BATA (15)VOL SHOE CORP
               (16)SPECS INTERNATIONAL (17)POWER SPORT
               (18)THOM MCAN JOX (19)REGAL SHOES (20)SHOE CORP
               (21)ASICS (22)INTL FOOTWEAR (23)EB SPORT INTL
               (24)VAN DOREN/
               TYPE(1)MALE (2)FEMALE/
               STARS(6)****** (5)*****/
PRINT FORMATS  QUALITY (F5.3)/REARIMP FOREIMP SOLEWEAR (F4.1)/
               FLEX SOLETRAC (F4.2)/REARCONT WEIGHT (F5.1)/
               PREFER (F4.3)
SELECT IF     STARS GE 5
SORT CASES     MAKER STARS(D)
BEGIN DATA
1 4 3.965  8.3 11.0 1.33 10.0 -13.6  .55 232.4 5  .531 6 VANTAGE
1 4 3.965  8.5 10.9 1.31 10.0 -16.5  .58 239.1 5       6 VANTAGE SUPREME
 . . .
217 3.692 12.9 18.6 2.90  3.5   0.9  .68 280.6 0         LDT 138
221 4.920 13.2 17.6 2.34  2.1   8.6  .63 244.0 0 .026    TIGRESS 80
END DATA
REPORT  FORMAT=MISSING ' ' LIST(4)  BRKSPACE(-1)/
        VARIABLES=TYPE(LABEL)(6)' ' 'TYPE'
          SHOE(16)' ' 'SHOE'
          STARS(LABEL)(6)' ' 'RATING'
          SEP1(DUMMY)(1)' '
          REARIMP(8)'REARFOOT' 'IMPACT'
          FOREIMP(8)'FOREFOOT' 'IMPACT'
          FLEX(6)'FLEXI-' 'BILITY'
          SOLEWEAR(4)'SOLE' 'WEAR'
          REARCONT(8)'REARFOOT' ' CONTROL'
          SOLETRAC(8)'SOLE' 'TRACTION'
          WEIGHT(6)' ' 'WEIGHT'
          LASTYEAR(5)'1979' 'STARS'
          PREFER((10)'READER' 'PREFERENCE'/
        TITLE='RATINGS OF TRAINING SHOES'
          'RUNNER''S WORLD MAGAZINE - OCTOBER, 1980'/
        LFOOTNOTE='****** HIGHLY RECOMMENDED'
          '*****  RECOMMENDED'/
        RFOOTNOTE=' ' 'PAGE )PAGE'/
        BREAK=MAKER(LABEL)'MANUFACTURER'(12)
```

- The TITLE command supplies a title for the job (see Chapter 4).
- The DATA LIST command defines the variables to be used in the report. The data are in-line (see Chapter 3).
- The VALUE LABELS command supplies value labels for the manufacturer, type of shoe, and rating (see Chapter 3). These labels are used in the report.
- The PRINT FORMATS command overrides the default print formats. Since the data include decimal points, they were not supplied on the DATA LIST command, and the default print formats for the numeric variables are 0. The print formats are overriden to include decimal positions for the noninteger values (see Chapter 9 and Section 23.58).
- The SELECT IF command selects shoes with the top two ratings (see Chapter 10).
- The SORT CASES command sorts cases in descending order of ranking for each manufacturer. They are sorted by manufacturer since the report groups them by manufacturer. They are sorted by descending order of

ranking so that the top-rated shoes for the manufacturer are listed first (see Chapter 13 and Section 23.54).

- The BEGIN DATA command signals the beginning of the in-line data and the END DATA command signals the end of the data (see Chapter 3).
- The FORMAT subcommand specifies a case listing and places the first case for each break on the same line as the break value. The MISSING keyword prints a blank in place of the period for variables with missing values (see Section 23.8).
- The VARIABLES subcommand names all the SPSS^X variables being listed as well as a dummy column (SEP1) to separate the measures from the rating. Value labels are printed in place of values for variables TYPE and STAR (see Section 23.14).
- The TITLE subcommand prints a two-line centered title (see Section 23.47).
- The LFOOTNOTE subcommand prints a two-line left-justified footnote (see Section 23.47).
- The RFOOTNOTE subcommand prints a two-line right-justified footnote. The first line is blank; the second line uses the special keyword)PAGE to print page numbers (see Section 23.47).
- The BREAK subcommand groups the shoes by manufacturer, prints the manufacturers' names (which were supplied on the VALUE LABELS command) and restricts the break column to 12 characters.

Report on running-shoe data

RATINGS OF TRAINING SHOES
RUNNER'S WORLD MAGAZINE - OCTOBER, 1980

MANUFACTURER	TYPE	SHOE	RATING	REARFOOT IMPACT	FOREFOOT IMPACT	FLEXI- BILITY	SOLE WEAR	REARFOOT CONTROL	SOLE TRACTION	WEIGHT	1979 STARS	READER PREFERENCE
SAUCONY	MALE	TC84	******	9.3	15.1	1.56	6.5	5.2	.85	278.0		.028
	MALE	HORNET 84	******	9.9	13.1	2.65	7.6	3.0	.68	265.0	4	.097
	FEMALE	MS TRAINER	******	10.2	13.3	1.58	6.4	22.4	.86	237.7	5	.053
	MALE	JAZZ	*****	8.9	12.7	2.04	7.6	-7.0	.64	270.8		
	MALE	TRAINER 80	*****	10.5	14.5	2.18	4.1	11.5	.82	307.6	5	.232
	FEMALE	JAZZ	*****	9.0	12.2	1.86	6.1	-7.5	.63	223.0		.013
	FEMALE	TC 84	*****	9.3	14.6	1.46	7.5	1.3	.77	231.1		
	FEMALE	MS HORNET	*****	9.8	13.2	2.59	6.4	6.5	.67	224.0	4	.046
NIKE	MALE	DAYBREAK	******	10.8	15.4	2.17	3.7	7.8	.54	304.2	5	.602
	MALE	YANKEE	*****	10.9	13.7	1.93	2.0	9.8	.66	276.6		
	FEMALE	LIBERATOR	*****	10.6	14.7	2.20	5.8	6.5	.52	254.2	5	.503
ETONIC	MALE	ECLIPSE TRAINER	******	10.0	12.9	1.65	10.0	-2.6	.51	237.4		
	FEMALE	ECLIPSE TRAINER	******	9.6	12.8	1.78	10.0	1.4	.57	204.1		
	MALE	STABILIZER	*****	10.3	15.5	2.25	1.2	-.6	.53	283.1	4	.232
	MALE	STREETFIGHTER	*****	10.8	15.5	2.28	1.4	-.4	.61	266.1	4	.222
	FEMALE	STREETFIGHTER	*****	10.7	15.5	1.66	.7	-7.7	.70	214.1	4	.344
	FEMALE	STABILIZER	*****	10.8	14.4	2.09	2.6	-6.9	.67	235.3	4	.298
PONY	MALE	TARGA FLEX	******	9.6	14.3	1.32	2.5	-22.7	.86	253.0	3	
	MALE	SHADOW	*****	9.9	13.8	1.53	2.5	-17.9	.77	270.2		
	FEMALE	LADY SHADOW	*****	10.6	17.4	.91	3.0	-7.1	.90	211.8		
OSAGA	MALE	FAST RIDER	*****	10.5	14.0	2.48	4.9	1.9	.66	296.7	5	.025
	FEMALE	KT-26	*****	10.7	17.3	1.66	5.5	8.1	.60	223.1	2	
NEW BALANCE	MALE	420	*****	9.8	14.8	2.09	1.8	-17.7	.46	267.9		.516
	MALE	620	*****	12.0	14.6	2.73	1.1	-3.5	.41	242.0	5	.475
	FEMALE	420	*****	9.9	13.9	1.94	1.6	-.7	.46	219.3		.411
REEBOK	MALE	AZTEC	******	10.9	12.6	2.07	2.5	3.7	.65	260.8	5	.065
	MALE	SHADOW I	*****	10.7	13.1	1.79	1.9	-8.7	.63	253.0		
	FEMALE	SHADOW III	*****	10.2	12.9	1.63	2.4	-24.6	.66	212.8		
	FEMALE	AZTEC PRINCESS	*****	10.2	12.8	2.18	5.9	-20.3	.70	221.3	5	.033
CONVERSE	MALE	ARIZONA 84	*****	10.1	13.6	1.90	6.6	-5.1	.55	302.9	4	.006
	FEMALE	WORLD CLASS 84	*****	9.4	14.0	2.19	4.3	-.3	.65	234.7	3	.020
BROOKS	MALE	VANTAGE	******	8.3	11.0	1.33	10.0	-13.6	.55	232.4	5	.531
	MALE	VANTAGE SUPREME	******	8.5	10.9	1.31	10.0	-16.5	.58	239.1	5	
	MALE	HUGGER GT	******	8.5	11.2	1.32	9.4	-11.7	.60	234.5	5	.488
	MALE	NIGHTHAWK	******	8.7	13.5	1.57	3.1	-8.6	.45	216.7		
	MALE	SUPER VILLANOVA	******	10.0	14.1	1.07	10.0	14.4	.61	238.7	5	.155
	FEMALE	VANTAGE	******	8.1	11.0	1.27	10.0	-13.1	.58	199.9	5	.563
	FEMALE	HUGGER GT	******	8.2	11.1	1.28	10.0	-12.7	.60	203.8		.126
	FEMALE	VANTAGE SUPREME	******	8.2	11.1	1.34	10.0	.6	.62	201.4	3	.205

****** HIGHLY RECOMMENDED
***** RECOMMENDED

PAGE 1

23.21 THE STRING SUBCOMMAND

The STRING subcommand concatenates SPSS^X variables and literals to create new temporary variables that can be used in a report. It is not one of the four required subcommands. You can use it to manipulate string variables for use as temporary variables within REPORT instead of using the SPSS^X transformation language.

23.22 Variables within Strings

The simplest form of the STRING subcommand is as follows:

STRING=stringname (var var var...) [stringname ...] /

The name assigned to the string must be unique and must follow SPSS^X variable-naming conventions. Both string and numeric variables can be used in REPORT-defined strings and can be intermixed. The variables concatenated to form the string are listed in parentheses following the string variable name. If a file contains names stored as 4-character string variables NAME1 to NAME6, the string NAME can be defined as a single 24-character variable:

```
STRING=NAME(NAME1 NAME2 NAME3 NAME4 NAME5 NAME6)/
```

Note that the keyword TO cannot be used to specify an implied list of variables. There is no fixed limit to the length of a REPORT-defined string. However, if the string is extremely long, the amount of other information contained in the report is constrained by the limits on the total width of the report.

Each variable in a string can be limited to a character width specified in parentheses immediately following the variable name:

STRING=stringname(varname (width) ... varname (width))/

If a width is not specified, the default width is the dictionary print width. The width specified for a variable in a string must be sufficient to contain the largest value for that variable. Asterisks are printed in place of any numeric value that exceeds the specified width. A string value is right-truncated. If the specified width exceeds the width of a value, a variable with a print format of F is padded with zeros on the left and a string value is padded with blanks on the right. If a numeric variable has a DOLLAR or COMMA print format, it is left-padded with blanks. If VARA is a string variable with an A4 format and VARN is a numeric variable with an F8.0 format, the specification

```
STRING=STRING1(VARA VARN)/
```

prints the value of STRING1 as KJ 00000241 for the case containing values VARA=KJ and VARN=241. On the other hand, the specification

```
STRING=STRING1(VARA(2) VARN(3))/
```

prints the same values as KJ241. You can use the keyword BLANK to left-pad with blanks variables with a print format of F. For example,

```
STRING=STRING1(VARA(2) VARN(BLANK)(4))
```

prints as KJ 241.

The maximum width that can be specified for any of the numeric variables within a string is 16 characters, and 255 characters is the maximum width for any SPSS^X string variables within the string.

23.23 Literals within Strings

REPORT-defined strings can be composed entirely of literals, or literals can be intermixed with variables:

STRING=stringname('literal') stringname('literal' varname literal')…/

Literals are stored and printed exactly as spelled and spaced within the apostrophes. For example, assume that a file contains social security numbers stored as three variables, S1, S2, and S3 (see the example command file in Section 23.7). The social security number can be listed in its usual form, with hyphens, if it is defined by the following STRING subcommand:

```
STRING= ID(S1'-'S2'-'S3)/
```

The report shown in Figure 23.26 is a variation on the company report that uses REPORT-generated string variables and literals extensively.

23.24 Using Strings

REPORT-generated string variables can be used in VARIABLES and BREAK subcommands. In the VARIABLES subcommand they are used for case listings. When string variables are used on the VARIABLES subcommand, the default column width is the width of the string; and the default column head is the string name. In Figure 23.26, four strings are defined to accommodate social security number, surname, and two dates with a slash setting off month and year.

A constant string can be used to separate columns in a report with a column of special characters such as asterisks or vertical bars (if your printer has them). For example,

```
STRING=STAR('*')/
```

defines a string variable STAR equal to the constant "*'.

Strings can be used to define breaks. For example, a file of insurance policies can contain the agents' names as identifiers. If you want a report with no true break variable, you can use the (NOBREAK) keyword on the BREAK subcommand (Section 23.31), or you can define a string variable containing only literals and use it for the break variable. For example,

```
STRING=BREAK ('Total Population')/
  VARIABLES= .../
  BREAK=BREAK ' '/
  SUMMARY=.../
```

produces a report with a break column which is 16 characters wide and a blank break head. The string "Total Population" is printed as the break value.

The STRING subcommand can only be used to concatenate variables and literals. It cannot be used to extract substrings from numeric or SPSS^X string variables. For instance, if an SPSS^X string variable is 4 characters wide, specifying a width of 1 on the STRING subcommand does not affect the storage of the 4 characters, even though only the first character of the string is printed in the report. For more complex manipulations of string variables, use the transformation language outside of REPORT (see Chapter 7).

23.25 STRING Specifications

The complete syntax for the STRING subcommand is as follows:

STRING= stringname (varname [(BLANK)] [(width)] ['literal']
    [… varname (BLANK) (width) 'literal')] …
    [stringname (varname (BLANK) (width) 'literal')]/

- The default width for SPSS^X variables used in a string is determined by their print format in the dictionary.
- String variables are temporary variables specific to the the given REPORT command and disappear once the command has been executed.
- A STRING subcommand must be placed prior to any other subcommand referencing variables created with the STRING subcommand.

23.26 The Company Report Using Strings

Figure 23.26 is a report using four string variables as variables named in the VARIABLES subcommand. The following commands produce the report in Figure 23.26:

```
SELECT IF CYEAR LE 76
REPORT  FORMAT=MARGINS(1,80),BRKSPACE(0)LIST/
        STRING=ID(S1'-'S2'-'S3)
               CDATE(CMONTH(BLANK)'/'CYEAR)
               JDATE(JMONTH(BLANK)'/'JYEAR)/
        VARIABLES=ID ' ID NUMBER '
             LNAME 'LAST NAME'
             STORE (LABEL) (8) 'BRANCH' 'STORE'
             CDATE 'COMPANY' 'DATE' (7)
             JDATE 'JOB' 'DATE'
             SPACE(DUMMY) ' ' (4)
             SALARY 'ANNUAL' 'SALARY' (6)/
        BREAK=DIVISION'PRODUCT' 'DIVISION' (LABEL) (10) (SKIP(1))/
```

Figure 23.26 The company report using string variables

PERSONNEL REPORT (BASIC) PAGE 1

PRODUCT DIVISION	ID NUMBER	LAST NAME	BRANCH STORE	COMPANY DATE	JOB DATE	ANNUAL SALARY
CARPETING						
	356-33-0035	STONE	DOWNTOWN	4/75	12/76	19050
	497-56-0549	JANNSEN	DOWNTOWN	4/75	12/76	19050
	280-88-0100	WASILEWSKI	SUBURBAN	12/76	10/77	18500
	231-23-2272	GLENN	SUBURBAN	6/76	3/77	23450
	244-24-1472	TYGIELSKI	SUBURBAN	12/76	8/77	19500
APPLIANCES						
	317-22-3371	LEE	DOWNTOWN	2/76	8/77	17050
	340-22-2934	JACKSON	SUBURBAN	6/76	12/76	18000
	345-22-8834	PETEK	DOWNTOWN	2/76	6/76	18000
	412-51-0041	JOHNSON	SUBURBAN	6/76	6/76	18000
	485-59-3348	WAYNE	DOWNTOWN	2/76	7/76	18000
	597-82-3359	REICHI	DOWNTOWN	2/76	6/76	18000
	692-20-0069	YOUNG	SUBURBAN	6/76	6/76	18000
	200-88-2753	PARSONS	DOWNTOWN	11/76	4/78	19500
	230-81-5816	CHAN	SUBURBAN	6/76	6/77	23450
	233-43-2282	HOWELL	SUBURBAN	11/76	11/76	24500
	235-62-2302	CHOW	DOWNTOWN	10/75	3/77	24400
	255-88-2632	PINSKER	SUBURBAN	12/76	6/78	40000
	255-32-2642	BARKER	SUBURBAN	7/75	3/77	48000
	266-00-2652	BEST	SUBURBAN	12/75	10/76	42000
	267-56-2784	COOK	DOWNTOWN	9/75	10/76	46000
FURNITURE						
	424-41-3449	GALOBIC	SUBURBAN	2/76	3/77	12000
	485-52-2049	GRIMES	DOWNTOWN	4/75	5/76	12500
	642-02-2426	MILES	DOWNTOWN	2/76	8/77	12000
	312-27-2231	PRUITT	SUBURBAN	9/76	9/76	17050
	329-22-5533	KEY	DOWNTOWN	11/75	1/77	18000
	361-33-8623	JONES	DOWNTOWN	6/75	10/76	19050
	368-33-2236	OSBORNE	DOWNTOWN	4/75	4/75	21000
	502-55-4950	ASHRAI	DOWNTOWN	10/75	10/75	21000
	234-52-2292	POWELL	DOWNTOWN	5/76	8/77	24500
	244-00-2452	POOL	SUBURBAN	10/76	10/76	25500
	245-34-2492	SCOTT	SUBURBAN	7/75	10/76	29500
	255-61-2592	JONES	SUBURBAN	5/76	3/77	49400
	271-55-2702	SMITH	SUBURBAN	10/76	10/76	42000
HARDWARE						
	303-22-3043	COLEMAN	DOWNTOWN	10/76	10/76	17050
	324-22-4432	STARK	SUBURBAN	11/75	7/77	17000
	334-22-4633	COLE	DOWNTOWN	9/75	12/76	18050
	350-22-3735	REESE	DOWNTOWN	12/76	12/76	19050
	492-55-4519	CARLYLE	DOWNTOWN	12/76	12/76	19050
	280-48-0588	JABLONSKI	SUBURBAN	12/76	10/77	22500
	244-82-9830	POPE	SUBURBAN	12/76	10/77	22500
	255-30-2622	OSIECKI	SUBURBAN	12/76	12/76	37000

This report also uses the (LABEL) option in the VARIABLES subcommand for variable STORE to list the value labels instead of the values.

Only one STRING subcommand is permitted per REPORT command, but a maximum of 50 strings can be defined per REPORT command.

23.27 THE BREAK SUBCOMMAND

BREAK specifies the variable or set of variables that define a subpopulation within the report (Section 23.5). BREAK and the related SUMMARY (Section 23.33) are the two subcommands that can be issued more than once on the REPORT command. Each BREAK subcommand defines one break level, and the SUMMARY subcommands immediately following the BREAK specifications determine the set of statistics to be computed for the cases within that break level.

Because the BREAK subcommand specifies a column as does the VARIABLES subcommand, many of its specifications are parallel to the VARIABLES subcommand.

At least one break must be defined for each REPORT command. If you are reporting on subpopulations, name the break variable or set of break variables. The simplest specification for a report with breaks is as follows:

BREAK=varname ... varname/

If a change occurs in any one of the set of variables named, the aggregate statistics requested by the SUMMARY subcommands are calculated and printed.

Missing-value indicators are ignored for variables named on the BREAK subcommand.

If you are not reporting on subpopulations (that is, you have no breaks), use the keyword NOBREAK in parentheses:

```
BREAK=(NOBREAK)/
```

When you specify NOBREAK, certain spacing and layout conditions which apply to breaks operate differently. See Section 23.49 for formatting conditions which apply to NOBREAK.

23.28 Column Heads, Contents, and Width

The BREAK optional specifications include those that override defaults for columns in the same manner as VARIABLES optional specifications and an option which controls vertical breaks. The complete syntax for the BREAK subcommand is either

BREAK= varname ... varname ['break head'] [(width)]
    [(VALUE|LABEL)] [(NONAME|NAME)]
    [(PAGE|SKIP(n))] [(NOTOTAL|TOTAL)] [(OFFSET(n))]/

or

BREAK= (NOBREAK) [(width)] [(OFFSET(n))] [(SKIP(n))] /

'break head' *Title used as the head for the column occupied by the break variable.* By default, the variable label of the break variable is used. (If the break is defined by more than one variable, the label of the first is used.) The break head obeys the same rules as the report column head: multiple lines can be indicated with multiple sets of apostrophes; default titles wrap around within the column width. You cannot specify a break head with NOBREAK.

(width) *Width for the column assigned to the break variable.* Default widths are the maximum of 8, the dictionary width for SPSS^{X} variables, or the width of the string for variables created with the STRING subcommand. If (LABEL) is specified, the default width is 20. (See Section 23.21 for a discussion of the STRING subcommand.) If a break is defined by more than one variable, the value or value label for each variable is printed on a separate line, and the default column width is the longest of the default widths for any of the break variables. If you have specified (NOBREAK), by default no column is allocated. You may specify a width to allocate a column with NOBREAK in effect.

(VALUE|LABEL) *Print the value or the value label (but not both) for each value of the break variable.* VALUE is the default. The value is printed only once for each break change. It is not repeated at the top of each page for a multiple-page break group.

(NONAME|NAME) *Use* NAME *to print the name of the break variable alongside each value or value label.* If the variable name is STORE and one of the values is 1, NAME prints (STORE) 1. NAME can be used with LABEL. For example, if the variable name is SALARY and one of the value labels is OVER $25,000, NAME and LABEL print (SALARY)OVER $25,000. The NAME option requires 10 characters of column width (the maximum SPSS^X variable name plus two parentheses). If a column narrower than 11 characters is specified, NAME is ignored. If the column is 11 characters or wider but less than 10 plus the width of the value or label, the value or label is replaced by asterisks or truncated. A default column is extended to accommodate NAME. NONAME is the default.

(OFFSET(n)) *Offset the contents of the break column to the left for numeric quantities and to the right for strings.* The break column includes break values and summary titles.

(PAGE|SKIP(n)) *Override the vertical spacing between the last summary line for a break and the next break* (the default is 1). This vertical spacing can be overridden in one of two ways. If (PAGE) is specified, each break begins on a new page. If (SKIP(n)) is requested, each break begins following a skip of the number of lines specified. If you specify NOBREAK with a column width, SKIP is ignored. If you specify NOBREAK without a column width, summary titles are printed prior to the actual summaries, left-justified, and SKIP controls the number of blank lines between the last summary line and the next summary title.

(NOTOTAL|TOTAL) *Use* (TOTAL) *to request that summary statistics be computed across breaks as well as for each break.* If specified for the first BREAK subcommand, statistics are reported for the entire population.

(NOBREAK) *Define a report with no break variable.* When you use (NOBREAK), several of the optional specifications do not apply and others behave somewhat differently (see Section 23.49).

Since only one column is defined per BREAK subcommand, any optional specifications apply to all variables named on the command. That is, if (LABEL) is specified, it applies to all break variables. However, if no value labels have been defined for a variable, its values are printed instead.

Figure 23.28 is the company report further modified with BREAK specifications. The value label for DIVISION is printed in a break column 12 spaces wide and the break is given a two-line title. In addition, the summary for each break is printed one line below the break title. The following REPORT subcommands produce the report in Figure 23.28:

```
REPORT  FORMAT=MARGINS(1,80) BRKSPACE(-1)/
        VARIABLES=AGE(3) TENURE(9) (OFFSET(3)) JTENURE(9) (OFFSET(3))
          SPACE(DUMMY)' '(4)
          SALARY 'ANNUAL' 'SALARY' (6)/
        BREAK=DIVISION 'PRODUCT' 'DIVISION' (LABEL) (12) (OFFSET(1))
          (TOTAL)/
        SUMMARY=MEAN
```

Figure 23.28 The company report with BREAK modifications

```
PERSONNEL REPORT (BASIC)                                                  PAGE     1

PRODUCT            AGE    TENURE IN     TENURE IN            ANNUAL
DIVISION                    COMPANY         GRADE            SALARY

 CARPETING          33      4.14          3.47               14221

 APPLIANCES         34      4.29          3.94               15039

 FURNITURE          36      4.77          4.22               15894

 HARDWARE           35      4.54          4.18               15616

 TOTAL              34      4.47          4.00               15286
```

23.29 One- and Two-Break Reports with Two Variables

Figure 23.29a is the company report with two BREAK subcommands and the same summary request for each break level. The following commands produce this report:

```
SORT CASES  BY STORE DIVISION
REPORT   FORMAT=MARGINS(1,80) BRKSPACE(-1)/
         VARIABLES=AGE(3) TENURE(9) (OFFSET(3)) JTENURE(9) (OFFSET(3))
           SPACE(DUMMY)' '(4)
           SALARY 'ANNUAL' 'SALARY' (6)/
         BREAK=STORE 'BRANCH' 'STORE' (LABEL)(12)(OFFSET(1)) (TOTAL)/
         SUMMARY=MEAN/
         BREAK=DIVISION 'PRODUCT' 'DIVISION' (LABEL) (12) (OFFSET(1))
           (SKIP(0))/
         SUMMARY=MEAN
```

Figure 23.29a The company report using multiple breaks

```
PERSONNEL REPORT (BASIC)                                                      PAGE     1

BRANCH         PRODUCT           AGE    TENURE IN     TENURE IN              ANNUAL
STORE          DIVISION                   COMPANY         GRADE              SALARY

 SUBURBAN       CARPETING         32      4.07          3.52                 16004
                APPLIANCES        33      4.21          3.87                 16105
                FURNITURE         36      5.03          4.65                 18821
                HARDWARE          34      4.59          4.26                 16435

 MEAN                             34      4.51          4.13                 16881

 DOWNTOWN       CARPETING         33      4.17          3.45                 13465
                APPLIANCES        35      4.37          3.99                 14130
                FURNITURE         36      4.64          3.99                 14403
                HARDWARE          35      4.49          4.12                 14873

 MEAN                             35      4.44          3.90                 14232

 TOTAL                            34      4.47          4.00                 15286
```

Figure 23.29b is a report with one BREAK subcommand with two variables. The following commands produce this report:

```
SORT CASES  BY STORE DIVISION
REPORT   FORMAT=MARGINS (1,80) BRKSPACE (-1)/
         VARIABLES=AGE(3) TENURE (9) JTENURE (9)
           SPACE(DUMMY) ' ' (4)
           SALARY 'ANNUAL' 'SALARY'(6)/
         BREAK=STORE DIVISION 'STORE/' 'DIVISION' (LABEL) (12)
           (TOTAL)/
         SUMMARY=MEAN/
```

Figure 23.29b One break with two variables

```
PERSONNEL REPORT (BASIC)                                                  PAGE    1

STORE/          AGE     TENURE IN       TENURE IN             ANNUAL
DIVISION                  COMPANY           GRADE             SALARY

SUBURBAN
CARPETING        32          4.07            3.52              16004

SUBURBAN
APPLIANCES       33          4.21            3.87              16105

SUBURBAN
FURNITURE        36          5.03            4.65              18821

SUBURBAN
HARDWARE         34          4.59            4.26              16435

DOWNTOWN
CARPETING        33          4.17            3.45              13465

DOWNTOWN
APPLIANCES       35          4.37            3.99              14130

DOWNTOWN
FURNITURE        36          4.64            3.99              14403

DOWNTOWN
HARDWARE         35          4.49            4.12              14873

TOTAL            34          4.47            4.00              15286
```

23.30 Keyword (TOTAL) and Multiple Break Reports

The (TOTAL) specification on the BREAK subcommand prints summaries across all cases within the categories of the break. If it is used in the second or following BREAK subcommand, it produces redundant summaries. Figure 23.30 is the same report shown in 23.29a illustrating the effect of specifying (TOTAL) on both BREAK subcommands.

Figure 23.30 (TOTAL) and multiple breaks

```
PERSONNEL REPORT (BASIC)                                                        PAGE    1

BRANCH          PRODUCT            AGE     TENURE IN       TENURE IN                 ANNUAL
STORE           DIVISION                     COMPANY           GRADE                 SALARY

 SUBURBAN         CARPETING        32       4.07            3.52                      16004
                  APPLIANCES       33       4.21            3.87                      16105
                  FURNITURE        36       5.03            4.65                      18821
                  HARDWARE         34       4.59            4.26                      16435
                  TOTAL            34       4.51            4.13                      16881

 MEAN                              34       4.51            4.13                      16881

 DOWNTOWN         CARPETING        33       4.17            3.45                      13465
                  APPLIANCES       35       4.37            3.99                      14130
                  FURNITURE        36       4.64            3.99                      14403
                  HARDWARE         35       4.49            4.12                      14873
                  TOTAL            35       4.44            3.90                      14232

 MEAN                              35       4.44            3.90                      14232

 TOTAL                             34       4.47            4.00                      15286
```

In Figure 23.30, the summary line following the title "TOTAL" is produced by the TOTAL option. However, the same summary is computed automatically as the higher level break is summarized. To get only the summary for the entire population, the last line in Figure 23.30, specify (TOTAL) on only the *first* BREAK subcommand.

23.31 Reports with No Breaks

To produce a report with no breaks, specify:

```
BREAK=(NOBREAK) /
```

You can specify a column width to reserve space for summary titles. If you do not, summary titles are placed above the summary line to which they apply. Figure 23.31 is an example of a report with no breaks. For further discussion on the use of (NOBREAK), see Section 23.49. The following commands produce Figure 23.31:

```
SELECT IF  (STARS GE 5 AND TYPE = 1 AND NOT(MISSING(LASTYEAR)))
SORT CASES  BY STARS(D) LASTYEAR(D) PREFER(D)
REPORT  FORMAT=MISSING ' ' CHDSPACE(1) BRKSPACE(-1) LIST(1)/
              VARIABLES=MAKER(LABEL) 'MANUFACTURER'(12)
              NAME' ' 'SHOE'
              STARS(LABEL)(6)' ' 'RATING'
              SEP1(DUMMY)(1)' '
              REARIMP(8)'REARFOOT' 'IMPACT'
              FOREIMP 'FOREFOOT' 'IMPACT'
              FLEX(6)'FLEXI-' 'BILITY'
              SOLEWEAR(4)'SOLE' 'WEAR'
              REARCONT(8)'REARFOOT' 'CONTROL'
              SOLETRAC(8)'SOLE' 'TRACTION'
              WEIGHT(6)' ' 'WEIGHT'
              LASTYEAR(LABEL)(5)'1979' 'STARS'
              PREFER(LABEL)(10)'READER' 'PREFERENCE'/
              TITLE='RATINGS OF TRAINING SHOES'
                    'RUNNER''S WORLD MAGAZINE - OCTOBER, 1980'/
              LFOOT='INCLUDES ONLY MEN''S SHOES'
                    'RATED AS FIVE STARS OR BETTER'/
              RFOOT='LISTED IN ORDER OF LAST YEAR''S RANKINGS'/
              BREAK= (NOBREAK) /
              SUMMARY=MEAN 'Overall Means' (REARIMP FOREIMP FLEX
               SOLEWEAR REARCONT SOLETRAC WEIGHT)
```

Figure 23.31 A (NOBREAK) report

RATINGS OF TRAINING SHOES
RUNNER'S WORLD MAGAZINE - OCTOBER, 1980

MANUFACTURER	SHOE	RATING	REARFOOT IMPACT	FOREFOOT IMPACT	FLEXI- BILITY	SOLE WEAR	REARFOOT CONTROL	SOLE TRACTION	WEIGHT	1979 STARS	READER PREFERENCE
NIKE	DAYBREAK	******	10.8	15.4	2.17	3.7	7.8	.54	304.2	5	.602
BROOKS	VANTAGE	******	8.3	11.0	1.33	10.0	-13.6	.55	232.4	5	.531
BROOKS	HUGGER GT	******	8.5	11.2	1.32	9.4	-11.7	.60	234.5	5	.488
BROOKS	SUPER VILLANOVA	******	10.0	14.1	1.07	10.0	14.4	.61	238.7	5	.155
REEBOK	AZTEC	******	10.9	12.6	2.07	2.5	3.7	.65	260.8	5	.065
BROOKS	VANTAGE SUPREME	******	8.5	10.9	1.31	10.0	-16.5	.58	239.1	5	
SAUCONY	HORNET 84	******	9.9	13.1	2.65	7.6	3.0	.68	265.0	4	.097
PONY	TARGA FLEX	******	9.6	14.3	1.32	2.5	-22.7	.86	253.0	3	
NEW BALANCE	620	*****	12.0	14.6	2.73	1.1	-3.5	.41	242.0	5	.475
ADIDAS	MARATHON TRAINER	*****	13.0	17.2	2.75	10.0	14.5	.63	302.3	5	.315
SAUCONY	TRAINER 80	*****	10.5	14.5	2.18	4.1	11.5	.82	307.6	5	.232
ADIDAS	TRX TRAINER	*****	10.5	16.8	2.07	2.1	-.6	.72	309.0	5	.143
OSAGA	FAST RIDER	*****	10.5	14.0	2.48	4.9	1.9	.66	296.7	5	.025
AUTRY	CONCORDE	*****	9.2	13.2	2.41	2.0	-33.9	.61	261.7	5	.023
ETONIC	STABILIZER	*****	10.3	15.5	2.25	1.2	-.6	.53	283.1	4	.232
ETONIC	STREETFIGHTER	*****	10.8	15.5	2.28	1.4	-.4	.61	266.1	4	.222
CONVERSE	ARIZONA 84	*****	10.1	13.6	1.90	6.6	-5.1	.55	302.9	4	.006
AUTRY	MACH III	*****	8.7	13.0	2.13	3.0	-37.6	.66	250.2	4	
AUTRY	NEW JET	*****	9.1	14.5	1.88	4.0	-37.9	.69	242.4	4	
BROOKFIELD	COLT	*****	12.4	17.4	2.31	3.5	21.5	1.13	289.3	4	
Overall Means			10.180	14.120	2.0305	4.98	-5.290	.6545	269.05		

INCLUDES ONLY MEN'S SHOES
RATED AS FIVE STARS OR BETTER

LISTED IN ORDER OF LAST YEAR'S RANKINGS

Since BRKSPACE is set to −1, the summary title is printed on the same line as the summary statistics. This works because the first variable named has no summary statistics computed for it. You could not use BRKSPACE(−1) for this report if summary statistics were being requested for the leftmost column defined by the VARIABLES subcommand.

23.32 BREAK Summary

The following are the default specifications for the BREAK subcommand:

BREAK=varlist (VALUE) (NONAME) (SKIP(1)) (OFFSET(0))/

- At least one BREAK subcommand is required and must precede the first SUMMARY subcommand.
- BREAK specifications apply to all variables named on the BREAK subcommand.
- The default head is the variable label defined for the first variable used on the subcommand. If none is defined, the variable name is used.
- The default column width is the maximum of 8 and the width defined in the dictionary for numeric variables, and the length of the string for string variables. If (LABEL) is specified, the default width is 20.
- If you specify (NOBREAK), you cannot specify a title, (PAGE), or (TOTAL).
- Cases must be sorted by values of BREAK variables.

23.33 THE SUMMARY SUBCOMMAND

The SUMMARY subcommand prints one line of aggregated statistics using the variables named on the VARIABLES subcommand. The SUMMARY subcommand is directly tied to the BREAK subcommand that specifies the population upon which statistics are to be computed. SUMMARY subcommands following the BREAK subcommand apply to that break. If your report has multiple breaks for which you want the same sets of summaries, specify SUMMARY subcommands for the higher BREAK subcommand and use the special keyword (PREVIOUS) to imply the previous set of summary commands for the lower BREAK subcommand (see Section 23.45).

Summary arguments specify the statistic to be computed, the variables for which the statistic is computed, an optional summary title, the number of decimal digits to be printed for the summary statistic, and the break column in which the summary title is placed.

23.34 Basic Specifications

The basic SUMMARY subcommand includes an aggregated statistic and a set of variables on which that statistic is to be computed:

SUMMARY= agg (varname ... varname) /

The keyword TO cannot be used to imply a set of variables. If the function is to be performed on all variables included in the VARIABLES list, the variable list can be omitted.

The only statistic available for string variables is VALIDN, the valid number of cases. If you explicitly name a string variable on the SUMMARY subcommand with a numeric function, REPORT flags it with an error.

The company report in Figure 23.7 has a simple summary. One aggregate statistic, the mean, is specified without a variable list. Since the variable list is omitted, the mean is computed for all eligible variables named on the VARIABLES subcommand. The mean for each variable is printed in its corresponding column. The summary title MEAN is printed in the break column.

23.35 REPORT Statistics

Aggregate functions are specified by keywords (and, in some instances, arguments within parentheses). The following functions are available:

VALIDN	*Valid number of cases.*
VARIANCE	*Variance.*
SUM	*Sum of values.*
MEAN	*Mean.*
STDEV	*Standard deviation.*
MIN	*Minimum value encountered.*
MAX	*Maximum value encountered.*
SKEWNESS	*Skewness.*
KURTOSIS	*Kurtosis.*
PCGT(n)	*Percentage of cases with values greater than specified value.*
PCLT(n)	*Percentage of cases with values less than specified value.*
PCIN(n1,n2)	*Percentage of cases with values between specified values, including those with the specified values.*
ABFREQ(min,max)	*Frequency counts for all nonmissing values within range.*
RELFREQ(min,max)	*Percentages for all nonmissing values within the range.*
MEDIAN(min,max)	*Median value for all nonmissing values within the range.*
MODE(min,max)	*Modal value for all nonmissing values within the range.*

ABFREQ, RELFREQ, MEDIAN, and MODE are computed using the same algorithms used by procedure FREQUENCIES in *integer* mode. Consequently, noninteger values are truncated in computing these statistics. Commas between multiple arguments are required.

23.36 Composite Functions

Composite functions are computed upon simple aggregate functions. The following composite functions are available:

DIVIDE(agg() agg() [factor])	*Divide the first argument by the second and multiply by the optional factor.* The optional factor can be an integer or decimal number.
MULTIPLY (agg() ... agg())	*Multiply the arguments.*
PCT(agg() agg())	*Percentage of the first argument over the second.*
SUBTRACT(agg()agg())	*Subtract the second argument from the first argument.*
ADD(agg() ... agg())	*Add the arguments.*
GREAT(agg() ... agg())	*Give the maximum of the arguments.*
LEAST(agg() ... agg())	*Give the minimum of the arguments.*
AVERAGE(agg() ... agg())	*Give the average of the arguments.*

VALIDN, VARIANCE, SUM, MEAN, SD, MIN, MAX, SKEWNESS, and KURTOSIS as well as any numerical constants can be used in composite functions. The use of composite functions within reports is described in Section 23.42.

23.37 Multiple Aggregate Functions

Each SUMMARY subcommand prints one line of aggregated statistics. To request more than one aggregate function, use multiple SUMMARY subcommands. For example,

```
SUMMARY=VALIDN (VARA VARB VARC VARD)/
SUMMARY=SUM (VARA VARB VARC VARD)/
SUMMARY=MEAN (VARA VARB VARC VARD)
```

produces the valid number of cases, sum, and mean for variables VARA, VARB, VARC, and VARD.

Figure 23.37 is a report with four aggregate statistics requested: SUM, MEAN, RELFREQ, and MEDIAN. The following commands produce this report:

```
STRING   TOTPOP (A16)
COMPUTE  TOTPOP='TOTAL POPULATION'
REPORT   FORMAT=MARGINS(1,80) BRKSPACE(0) CHDSPACE(0)/
         VARIABLES= V1 TO V5/
         BREAK=TOTPOP/
         SUMMARY=SUM/
         SUMMARY=MEAN/
         SUMMARY=RELFREQ(0,9)/
         SUMMARY=MEDIAN(0,9)/
```

Figure 23.37 Multiple-summary simple report

```
DEMONSTRATE REPORT WITH MULTIPLE SUMMARIES                                     PAGE    1

TOTPOP                1ST VAR      2ND VAR      3RD VAR      4TH VAR      5TH VAR
TOTAL POPULATION
SUM                       534          523          486          477          469
MEAN                     5.56         5.28         5.01         5.02         5.04

RELFREQ

TOT FREQ               100.00       100.00       100.00       100.00       100.00
1                        4.17        14.14        13.40        11.58         6.45
2                       12.50         5.05        12.37        10.53        12.90
3                        8.33        10.10         8.25         5.26        17.20
4                        7.29        16.16        12.37        13.68         9.68
5                       11.46         8.08         8.25        14.74        10.75
6                       16.67         6.06         8.25        14.74         8.60
7                       13.54         9.09        11.34        10.53         8.60
8                       13.54        13.13        13.40         7.37        16.13
9                       12.50        18.18        12.37        11.58         9.68

MEDIAN                    6.0          5.0          5.0          5.0          5.0
```

23.38 Summary Titles

Each summary statistic has a title. By default, the keyword used to specify the statistic is printed in the column corresponding to the level of break being summarized. The summary title is left- or right-justified depending upon whether the break title is left- or right-justified. Summary titles are left-justified if the break column contains value labels or strings. If your report has no break column because you have specified NOBREAK on the BREAK subcommand, REPORT prints the summary title above the summary line at the left margin. See Section 23.49 for a discussion of special considerations for reports with no breaks. The default title can be overridden by a summary title defined as a literal in apostrophes or quotation marks. For example, the default summary title for VALIDN is VALIDN. To provide a summary title of "No. of Employees," specify:

```
SUMMARY=VALIDN 'No. of Employees'(GR78)/
```

A summary title wider than the break column is truncated. Leading blanks can be used to indent summary titles. Unlike other title strings in REPORT, a summary title can be only one line long. If more than one SUMMARY subcommand is used, a title can be continued from summary line to summary line to provide more extensive labeling. For example,

```
SUMMARY=SUM'SUMS AND AVERAGES'/
SUMMARY=MEAN'BASED ON 1980 5% SAMPLE'/
```

produces a two-line summary with a title continuing from the first to the second line. As with other titles in REPORT, a blank title can be used.

23.39 Spacing Summary Lines

If you specify multiple SUMMARY subcommands for a given BREAK subcommand, the lines are printed with no vertical spacing between them. The special keyword SKIP is used to specify spacing between summary lines for a break. Enclose the number of lines to be skipped before the summary line is printed in parentheses, as in

```
SUMMARY = MEAN 'Averages'/
SUMMARY = VALIDN 'Number of Cases' SKIP(1)/
```

which skips one line after printing the means. If you use the SKIP keyword on the first SUMMARY subcommand, it skips the specified lines before printing the first summary line beyond that specified for the BRKSPACE keyword used on the FORMAT subcommand. For example, if BRKSPACE is set to 2 and SKIP(5) is used on the first SUMMARY subcommand, REPORT skips 7 lines before printing the summary line. Note that the SKIP keyword used on the SUMMARY subcommand has a different function than its counterpart on the BREAK subcommand and is not enclosed in parentheses.

23.40 Summary Titles in Break Columns

By default, the summary title for a statistic is placed in the break column corresponding to the level of break for the group being summarized. It is possible to place the summary title in a different break column on a report that contains more than one BREAK subcommand. The column number for the break column placed in parentheses following the aggregate function overrides the default. To place the default title "VALIDN" in the second column regardless of the level of break being summarized, specify:

```
SUMMARY=VALIDN(2)/
```

To include a summary title, a column for the title, and the variables to be summarized, specify:

```
SUMMARY=VALIDN'No. of Employees'(2)(GR78 GR77 GR76)/
```

If you are using BRKSPACE(-1) to place the first summary on the same line as the break value, the title is not printed. If you specify a title in this situation, it is ignored.

The report in Figure 23.40 uses summary titles to produce a compact frequencies report. The following REPORT command produces this report:

```
REPORT  FORMAT=MARGINS(1,80) BRKSPACE (0) CHDSPACE(0)
              LENGTH(1,40)/
        VARIABLES=CITIES 'Aid to' 'Cities' (6)
              INFLATE 'Control' 'Inflation' (9)
              CIVIL 'Civil' 'Rights' (6)
              AID 'Foreign' 'Aid' (7)
              HIGHERED 'Higher' 'Educ' (6)
              MILITARY 'Defense' 'Spending'
              JOBS 'Increase' 'Jobs'/
        TITLE='Government Policy Priorities'/
        FOOT='Survey Conducted July, 1981'/
        BREAK=REGION 'Region' (LABEL) (SKIP(1))/
        SUMMARY=PCIN(1,1) 'Strongly Agree'/
        SUMMARY=PCIN(2,2) 'Agree'/
        SUMMARY=PCIN(3,3) 'Indifferent'/
        SUMMARY=PCIN(4,4) 'Disagree'/
        SUMMARY=PCIN(5,5) 'Strongly Disagree'/
        SUMMARY=PCIN(1,2) '  Favoring'/
        SUMMARY=PCIN(4,5) '  Opposed'/
        SUMMARY=VALIDN 'No. Respondents'
```

Figure 23.40 A multi-titled summary

```
                   Government Policy Priorities

Region             Aid to   Control  Civil Foreign Higher  Defense Increase
                   Cities Inflation Rights     Aid   Educ Spending     Jobs
East
Strongly Agree      22.73     17.31  24.69   20.39  18.75    14.65    20.89
Agree               20.78     27.56  19.14   23.03  20.00    24.84    22.15
Indifferent         24.03     17.95  20.99   23.68  25.63    21.02    20.89
Disagree            22.73     23.72  22.22   23.68  23.75    26.75    29.11
Strongly Disagree    9.74     13.46  12.96    9.21  11.88    12.74     6.96
  Favoring          43.51     44.87  43.83   43.42  38.75    39.49    43.04
  Opposed           32.47     37.18  35.19   32.89  35.63    39.49    36.08
No. Respondents       154       156    162     152    160      157      158

Middle West
Strongly Agree      27.73     22.12  20.54   17.70  25.00    20.83    23.21
Agree               19.33     22.12  17.86   31.86  21.55    26.67    18.75
Indifferent         18.49     25.66  24.11   17.70  21.55    20.83    22.32
Disagree            26.89     23.01  25.89   22.12  20.69    23.33    21.43
Strongly Disagree    7.56      7.08  11.61   10.62  11.21     8.33    14.29
  Favoring          47.06     44.25  38.39   49.56  46.55    47.50    41.96
  Opposed           34.45     30.09  37.50   32.74  31.90    31.67    35.71
No. Respondents       119       113    112     113    116      120      112

West
Strongly Agree      24.14     18.49  22.61   24.11  21.24    24.37    17.39
Agree               22.41     24.37  20.00   26.79  23.01    20.17    15.65
Indifferent         25.86     21.01  21.74   16.07  15.93    23.53    32.17
Disagree            18.10     23.53  23.48   18.75  17.70    21.01    20.00
Strongly Disagree    9.48     12.61  12.17   14.29  22.12    10.92    14.78
  Favoring          46.55     42.86  42.61   50.89  44.25    44.54    33.04
  Opposed           27.59     36.13  35.65   33.04  39.82    31.93    34.78
No. Respondents       116       119    115     112    113      119      115




                   Survey Conducted July, 1981
```

23.41 Print Formats for Summaries

Every aggregate function, either simple or composite, has a default print format for the number of decimal digits to be displayed. If the column is not wide enough to print the decimal digits for a given function, REPORT prints fewer. If the column is not wide enough to print the integer portion of the number, asterisks are printed. REPORT uses special conventions for printing true zero values in case listings, summary statistics, and for break values. Exactly zero is printed with one zero digit to the left of the decimal point and as many zero digits to the right as specified by the printing format. A very small number prints without a zero digit to the left of the decimal point. However, if the printing format is a DOLLAR-type format, very small numbers are printed with a zero digit to the left of the decimal point, as in $0.00. The default print formats by function are shown in Table 23.41.

In addition, MEAN, STDEV, MIN, MAX, MEDIAN, and MODE also print with COMMA or DOLLAR format if the variable being summarized has a COMMA or DOLLAR format. For example, if variable X has a format of DOLLAR5.2, MEAN prints with a format of DOLLAR7.4 provided that the column is wide enough.

Other print formats can be specified in parentheses immediately following the variable name. A digit implies an F, DOLLAR, or COMMA format with that number of decimal digits. For example,

```
SUMMARY=SUM (A(2) B(3))/
```

prints two decimal digits for the sum of variable A and three decimal digits for the sum of variable B. The keyword DOLLAR in parentheses prints the statistic with a DOLLAR format, irrespective of the variable's dictionary print format, while the keyword COMMA prints the statistic with a COMMA format. The keyword PLAIN overrides a DOLLAR or COMMA dictionary print format. You can jointly specify a keyword format and a decimal digit format to obtain the exact format desired. Both are enclosed

Table 23.41 Default print formats for functions

Function	Print format
VALIDN	0
VARIANCE	Column width – 1
SUM	Variable's print format
MEAN	Variable's print format + 2
STDEV	Variable's print format + 2
MIN	Variable's print format
MAX	Variable's print format
SKEWNESS	3
KURTOSIS	3
PCGT	2
PCLT	2
PCIN	2
MEDIAN	1
MODE	0
ABFREQ	0
RELFREQ	2
DIVIDE	Column width – 1
MULTIPLY	Column width – 1
PCT	2
SUBTRACT	Column width – 1
ADD	Column width – 1
GREAT	Column width – 1
LEAST	Column width – 1
AVERAGE	Column width – 1

in parentheses in either order following the variable name. For example, assume INCOME has a DOLLAR9.2 print format. The subcommand

```
SUMMARY=MEAN(INCOME(2))/
```

prints the mean with a dollar sign and two decimal digits. The subcommand

```
SUMMARY=MEAN(INCOME(PLAIN)(2))/
```

prints the mean without a dollar sign and two decimal digits.

Note that the specification modifies only the variable immediately preceding it and that the parentheses enclosing the print format go within the parentheses for the variable list.

23.42 Using Composite Functions

Section 23.36 describes the types of composite functions available within REPORT. This section describes the syntactical requirements and reasons for using composite functions.

Although the syntax for composite functions is similar to the syntax required for simple functions, the specifications are used in different ways. The general syntax for specifying a composite function is

agg ['title'] [(col #)] [(varname [(n)])]

where *agg* is the composite function and its arguments. For example,

```
SUMMARY=PCT(VALIDN(MALE) VALIDN(EMPLOY))
```

is a composite function producing the percentage of employees who are male. Note that this function computes only one result, unlike a simple function which computes results for each variable enclosed in parentheses following it. The purpose of the variable list following a composite function is to inform REPORT in which column to print the result. If the list is omitted, REPORT prints the results in the column defined by the first variable used as an argument to the composite function that is also named on the VARIABLES subcommand.

Any numeric SPSS^X variables can be used as arguments to composite functions. You do not have to name a variable on the VARIABLES subcommand to use it in a composite function. However, the target list following the composite function and its arguments must use variables defined on the

VARIABLES subcommand. Unlike simple functions, the composite function can be placed in any report column including those defined by dummy variables or string variables.

Because a composite function includes both the name of the functions and the arguments to the functions, a title specification must follow the arguments. A title cannot separate the function name from its arguments.

Print formats for composites are specified within parentheses following the name of the variable in whose column the result is to be printed, not within the arguments to the function. Since most composite functions have as a default print format the width of the column−1, it is usually advisable to specify the number of decimal digits to be printed, as in:

```
SUMMARY=DIVIDE(MEAN(CRIME)MEAN(POLICE))' '(RATIO(3))/
```

You cannot use a composite function as an argument to a composite function. Only simple functions, variables, and constants can be used. See Section 23.43 for a discussion of obtaining nested composites using AGGREGATE and MATCH FILES.

There are three basic reasons for using composite functions. First, a composite function can be used to place a summary statistic in a column other than the one for which it is calculated. For example, the sum of VARA is printed in the column corresponding to VARA. It can be placed in any other column with a composite such as

```
SUMMARY=ADD(SUM(VARA)) (VARB)
```

which adds VARA to nothing and places it in VARB's column. The SUBTRACT, GREAT, LEAST, and AVERAGE composite functions can achieve the same result.

Second, composite functions can be used to manipulate statistics and change the unit of analysis. Certain arithmetic operations between variables produce the same result at either the case level or the subpopulation level. You can subtract the sum of variable A from the sum of variable B and obtain the same answer as subtracting A from B for each case and summing the result. However, dividing the sum of A by the sum of B is not the same as dividing A by B for each case and averaging the results.

Third, composite functions are used to manipulate variables not defined on the VARIABLES subcommand. For example, you might want to adjust dollar figures by some index when printing means, but not to allocate a column for the index by naming it on the VARIABLES subcommand.

In Figure 23.42, the DIVIDE composite function is used to compute a grand mean. The specifications for the report are as follows:

```
REPORT   FORMAT=LIST BRKSPACE(0) MARGINS(1,103) TSPACE(1)CHDSPACE(1)/
           VARIABLES=PLAYER
                POSITION (OFFSET(3))
                ATBAT (7) 'TIMES' 'AT BAT' (OFFSET(2))
                RUNS (6) 'RUNS' 'SCORED' (OFFSET(2))
                HITS (4)
                 RBI (6) 'RUNS' 'BATTED' 'IN' (OFFSET(2))
                AVERAGE (7) 'BATTING' 'AVERAGE'(OFFSET(1)) /
           BREAK=LEAGUE(LABEL)(8)/
           SUM=MEAN (ATBAT(0) RUNS(0) HITS(0) RBI(0))
                 'AVERAGE FOR TEAM'
               DIVIDE (SUM(HITS)SUM(ATBAT))  (AVERAGE(3))/
           BREAK=TEAM(LABEL)
```

Figure 23.42 Report with composite function for grand mean

```
CHICAGO TEAMS VERSUS LEAGUE WINNERS, 1979                                                  PAGE    1

LEAGUE     TEAM                PLAYER        POSITION     TIMES     RUNS    HITS     RUNS   BATTING
                                                          AT BAT   SCORED           BATTED  AVERAGE
                                                                                      IN

NATIONAL   CHICAGO CUBS
                               DEJESUS          SS         636       92     180       52      .283
                               THOMPSON         RF         346       36     100       29      .289
                               BUCKNER          1B         591       72     168       66      .284
                               KINGMAN          LF         532       97     153       15      .288
                               MARTIN           CF         534       74     145       73      .272
                               ONTIVEROS        3B         519       58     148       57      .285
                               FOOTE             C         429       47     109       56      .254
                               DILLARD          2B         166       31      47       24      .283
                               REUSCHEL          P          79        8      13        6      .165

           PITTSBURGH PIRATES
                               MORENO           CF         695       10     196       69      .282
                               FOLI             SS         532       70     153       65      .288
                               PARKER           RF         622        9     193       94      .310
                               STARGELL         1B         424       60     119       82      .281
                               MADLOCK          3B         560       85     167       85      .298
                               MILNER           LF         326       52      90       60      .276
                               GARNER           2B         549       76     161       59      .293
                               OTT               C         403       49     110       51      .273
                               BLYLEVEN          P          70        1       9        3      .129

AVERAGE                                                    445       51     126       53      .282

AMERICAN   CHICAGO WHITE SOX
                               GARR             LF         331       34      89       39      .269
                               BANNISTER        DH         506       71     144       55      .285
                               WASHINGTON       RF         471       79     132       66      .280
                               JOHNSON          1B         479       60     148       74      .309
                               LEMON            CF         556       79     177       86      .318
                               ORTA             2B         325       49      85       46      .262
                               MORRISON         3B         240       38      66       35      .275
                               NAHORODNY         C         179       20      46       29      .257
                               PRYOR            SS         476       60     131       34      .275

           BALTIMORE ORIOLES
                               BUMBRY           CF         569       80     162       49      .285
                               DAUER            2B         479       63     123       61      .257
                               SINGLETON        RF         570       93     168       11      .295
                               MURRAY           1B         606       90     179       99      .295
                               ROENICKE         LF         376       60      98       64      .261
                               MAY              DH         456       59     116       69      .254
                               DECINCES         3B         422       67      97       61      .230
                               GARCIA           SS         417       54     103       24      .247
                               DEMPSEY           C         368       48      88       41      .239

AVERAGE                                                    435       61     120       52      .275
```

23.43 Nested Composite Functions

If your report requires a nested composite function, use AGGREGATE (Chapter 14) to compute the required information and then match it back to the active file with the MATCH FILES command (see Chapter 15). For example, assume you want to print the result of the arithmetic expression

(A/B)/(C/D)

for each break group. The sequence of commands is as follows:

```
FILE HANDLE  SYSFILE/ file specifications
GET FILE  SYSFILE
AGGREGATE  FILE=*/BREAK=GROUP/
           SUMA SUMB SUMC SUMD = SUM(A B C D)
COMPUTE  DIVIDE=(SUMA/SUMB)/(SUMC/SUMD)
MATCH FILES FILE=SYSFILE/TABLE=*/BY GROUP
REPORT  VARIABLES= A B C D/
        BREAK=GROUP/
        SUMMARY=MEAN/SUMMARY=ADD(MAX(DIVIDE)) (A(2))
```

AGGREGATE is used to sum A, B, C, and D for the break groups. This becomes the active file, so the COMPUTE command can be used to perform the transformation. MATCH FILES combines these results with the original file and REPORT simply moves the results into the appropriate column.

AGGREGATE and MATCH FILES are also required to carry information across breaks or perform pretotaling operations. See Figure 23.56 which requires pretotaling.

ANNOTATED EXAMPLE OF REPORT USING SUMMARIES

This example produces a report which summarizes information from a retail company's personnel file. It reports summary statistics for employees in each division of the company within each store. The SPSS^X commands are

```
FILE HANDLE CHIGDATA/NAME=file specifications
GET FILE=CHIGDATA
SET CASE=UPLOW

PRINT FORMATS SALARY(DOLLAR7.0)

SORT CASES  BY STORE DIVISION
REPORT FORMAT=MARGINS(1,72) LENGTH(1,22) BRKSPACE(-1)/
  VARIABLES=AGE ' ' 'Age' (3)
            TENURE(9) 'Tenure in' 'Company ' (OFFSET(2))
            JTENURE(9) 'Tenure in' 'Grade  ' (OFFSET(2))
            SPACE(DUMMY)' '(2)
            SALARY 'Annual' 'Salary' (7)/
  TITLE='Chicago Home Furnishing'/
  LFOOTNOTE='Tenure measured in months'/
  BREAK=STORE 'BRANCH' 'STORE' (LABEL)(8)/
    SUMMARY=MEAN 'AVERAGE:' (AGE TENURE(1) JTENURE(1) SALARY(0)) (2)/
    SUMMARY=VALIDN '  Count:' (2)(AGE)/
  BREAK=DIVISION 'Product' 'Division' (LABEL) (10) (SKIP(0))/
    SUMMARY=MEAN (AGE TENURE(1) JTENURE(1) SALARY(0))
```

- The FILE HANDLE command defines a file handle for the system file being reported (see Chapter 3).
- The GET command retrieves the system file containing information on the employees in the company (see Chapter 5). The handle refers back to the host information system supplied on the FILE HANDLE command.
- The SET command ensures that any variable or value labels which were defined in upper and lower case are printed in upper and lower case in the display file (see Chapter 4).
- The PRINT FORMATS command ensures that summaries on variable SALARY are printed with the dollar format (see Chapter 9).
- The SORT CASES command sorts the file into the major and minor breaks required for REPORT (see Chapter 13 and Section 23.54).
- The FORMAT subcommand sets the left margin at column 1 and right margin at column 72; the top of the report on the first line and the last line of the page on line 22; and the break group label on the first line of summary statistics (see Section 23.8).
- The VARIABLES subcommand defines four columns in the body of the report. AGE, TENURE, and JTENURE are SPSS^X variables while SPACE defines a dummy column for spacing purposes. The OFFSET keyword indents the summary statistics for TENURE and JTENURE under the column head. Column titles are defined for all columns (see Section 23.14).
- The TITLE subcommand defines a one-line centered title (see Section 23.47).
- The LFOOTNOTE subcommand defines a one-line left-justified footnote (see Section 23.47).
- The first BREAK subcommand defines the major break in this two-break report. Variable STORE breaks the file into two categories: the downtown store and the suburban store. Value labels for STORE are printed in the break column (see Section 23.28).
- The first two SUMMARY subcommands print two lines of summary statistics for each store. The first SUMMARY subcommand computes means for AGE, TENURE, and JTENURE. The second SUMMARY subcommand computes the number of employees in each store (see Section 23.33).

- The second BREAK subcommand breaks the file into divisions within each store. The SKIP specification suppresses blank lines between the summary for each division.
- The last SUMMARY subcommand computes means for AGE, TENURE, and JTENURE for each division.

A A summary report

Chicago Home Furnishing

BRANCH STORE	Product Division	Age	Tenure in Company	Tenure in Grade	Annual Salary
SUBURBAN	CARPETING	34	5.5	4.1	$16,004
	APPLIANCES	35	5.9	4.2	$16,105
	FURNITURE	38	6.7	5.0	$18,821
	HARDWARE	36	6.3	4.6	$16,435
	AVERAGE:	36	6.1	4.5	$16,881
	Count:	105			
DOWNTOWN	CARPETING	35	5.4	4.2	$13,465
	APPLIANCES	37	6.0	4.4	$14,130
	FURNITURE	38	6.0	4.6	$14,403
	HARDWARE	37	6.1	4.5	$14,873
	AVERAGE:	37	5.9	4.4	$14,232
	Count:	159			

Tenure measured in months

23.44 Multiple Summary Statistics on One Line

Most of the examples illustrated to this point have specified only one aggregate function and a single set of optional specifications on a SUMMARY subcommand: the variables on which the statistic is computed or the print column for a composite function, the print format, the summary title, and the break column for the summary title. In practice, you often want to print more than one such combination of functions and optional specifications on a summary line—for example, the VALIDN for VARA and the MEAN for VARB. You can use several functions on one SUMMARY subcommand as long as you do not try to print more than one statistic in any one column defined by the VARIABLES subcommand.

To place different sets of statistics on one summary line, you must provide variable arguments for simple aggregate functions. You *cannot* specify

```
SUMMARY=SUM MEAN /* error
```

because the default list of variables is all eligible variables named on the VARIABLES subcommand and this summary would try to print both the sum and the mean for each variable on the same line. This is flagged as an error because you specified overlapping summaries. However, you can specify

```
SUMMARY=SUM(VARA VARB) MEAN(VARC)
```

because each variable is used only once as an argument to the summary statistic.

Since ABFREQ and RELFREQ print multiple lines in a summary, neither of these functions can be used with any other function on one SUMMARY subcommand.

You may not have to specify target columns when using composite functions since, unlike simple functions, the composite function has only one default target column (the column defined by the leftmost variable used in the function). For example, the subcommand

```
SUMMARY=PCT(SUM(TIME0)SUM(AMOUNT))
        PCT(SUM(TIME1)SUM(AMOUNT))
```

is valid because the first PCT function prints the result in the column defined by TIME0 and the second PCT function prints the result in the column defined by TIME1, assuming both TIME0 and TIME1 are specified on the VARIABLES subcommand.

Since two different statistics are printed on the same line, you can specify a special summary title to identify the numbers more clearly. Otherwise, REPORT would use the name of the first function (SUM) as the summary title. The following commands produce the report in Figure 23.44a:

```
STRING  TOTPOP (A16)
COMPUTE  TOTPOP='TOTAL POPULATION'
REPORT  FORMAT=CHDSPACE(0) BRKSPACE(0) MARGINS(1,80)/
        VARIABLES=V1 TO V5/
        BREAK=TOTPOP/
        SUMMARY=SUM (V1 V2) MEAN (V3 V4 V5) 'SUM: 4 5 MEAN:6-8'/
```

Figure 23.44a Different functions on one summary

```
DIFF SUMS FOR DIFF VARS ON SAME LINE AND SUMMARY TITLE                    PAGE     1

TOTPOP                 1ST VAR     2ND VAR     3RD VAR     4TH VAR     5TH VAR
TOTAL POPULATION
SUM:4 5 MEAN:6-8           534         523        4.50        4.42        4.34
```

Figure 23.44b is a two-break report in which four different summary statistics are used on the SUMMARY subcommand. The following commands produce this report:

```
FILE HANDLE  P181/ file specifications
DATA LIST  FILE=P181
          /1 DIVISION 1 GROUP 2 SEX 3 SALARY 4-9
IF   (SEX EQ 1) MSALARY=SALARY
IF   (SEX EQ 2) FSALARY=SALARY
COMPUTE  LOWSAL=SALARY
VALUE LABELS  DIVISION 1 'Marketing' 2 'R & D'/
              GROUP 1 'New York' 2 'Boston' 3 'Philadelphia'
PRINT FORMATS  SALARY MSALARY FSALARY LOWSAL(DOLLAR7)
SORT CASES  BY DIVISION GROUP
REPORT  FORMAT=TSPACE(3)CHDSPACE(1)BRKSPACE(1)MARGINS(1,90)BRKSPACE(-1)/
        VARIABLES=SALARY 'Avg' 'Salary'
             LOWSAL '% of' 'Salaries' 'below 20k' (9)
             MAX(DUMMY) 'Max' 'Salary'
             MIN(DUMMY) 'Min' 'Salary'
             MSALARY 'Avg' 'Salary' 'Men'
             FSALARY 'Avg' 'Salary' 'Women'  /
          BREAK=DIVISION (LABEL) (10) (SKIP(2))(TOTAL)/
          SUMMARY=MEAN(2) 'For Division' (SALARY MSALARY FSALARY)
             PCLT(20000) (LOWSAL)
             ADD(MAX(SALARY)) (MAX(0)(DOLLAR))
             ADD(MIN(SALARY)) (MIN(0)(DOLLAR))/
           BREAK=GROUP (LABEL) (12)(SKIP(1))/
          SUMMARY=MEAN '' (SALARY MSALARY FSALARY)
             PCLT(20000) (LOWSAL)
             ADD(MAX(SALARY)) (MAX(0)(DOLLAR))
             ADD(MIN(SALARY)) (MIN(0)(DOLLAR))/
           TITLE='Analysis of Salaries within Division and Group'
```

Figure 23.44b Manipulating summaries

Analysis of Salaries within Division and Group

DIVISION	GROUP	Avg Salary	% of Salaries below 20k	Max Salary	Min Salary	Avg Salary Men	Avg Salary Women
Marketing	New York	$19,500	50.00	$28,000	$8,500	$18,100	$21,833
	Boston	$19,500	54.55	$32,000	$9,000	$21,000	$12,750
	Philadelphia	$22,000	43.75	$32,000	$9,000	$22,937	$21,062
	For Division	$20,643	48.57	$32,000	$8,500	$21,045	$19,962
R & D	New York	$17,750	66.67	$27,500	$9,000	$17,917	$17,583
	Boston	$21,900	33.33	$32,000	$10,500	$20,125	$23,929
	Philadelphia	$22,750	27.78	$32,000	$9,500	$23,812	$21,900
	For Division	$21,133	40.00	$32,000	$9,000	$20,864	$21,391
	TOTAL	$20,919	43.75	$32,000	$8,500	$20,955	$20,875

Each column of the report in Figure 23.44b is used to describe some aspect of the variable SALARY. Composite functions are used to move the minimum and maximum of SALARY into dummy columns. Data transformations are used to split SALARY into two groups (men and women) as described in Section 23.57. Since a composite cannot be used with the PCLT summary statistic, an exact copy of SALARY named LOWSAL is created with a COMPUTE command. The summary title for the higher level break is moved into the lower break column.

23.45 Repeating Summary Specifications

If you do not specify one or more SUMMARY subcommands following a BREAK subcommand, no summary statistics are printed for that break level. The special keyword PREVIOUS references a set of SUMMARY subcommands defined for a previous BREAK subcommand. For example,

```
REPORT  FORMAT=LIST/
        VARIABLES=NAME AGE CLAIMS/
        BREAK=DIVISION/
        SUMMARY=MEAN/
        SUMMARY=VALIDN(AGE)/
        BREAK=STORE/
        SUMMARY=PREVIOUS
```

prints means and the valid number of cases for AGE for each store within the DIVISION.

PREVIOUS accepts an optional argument in parentheses to point to the particular set of summaries to be copied. For example, PREVIOUS(1) copies all the SUMMARY subcommands applying to the first BREAK subcommand, and PREVIOUS(2) copies summary specifications for the second BREAK subcommand. No other specification can be used on a SUMMARY subcommand using PREVIOUS.

23.46 SUMMARY Summary

The complete syntax for the SUMMARY subcommand is

SUMMARY= agg ['summary title'] [(break column #)]
  [(varname [(decimal digits)] [(PLAIN)|(DOLLAR)|(COMMA)] ...)]
  [agg (varname...)] [SKIP(n)] /

or

SUMMARY=PREVIOUS(n)/

The following default specifications apply to the SUMMARY subcommand:

- If no variable list is specified, all numeric variables on the VARIABLES subcommand are summarized.
- Default print formats are used for printing summary statistics.
- The name of the summary statistic is used as the summary title.
- The summary title is printed in the break column corresponding to the break summarized.
- By default, PREVIOUS points to the last set of SUMMARY subcommands.

Figure 23.46 is the updated company report modified with optional summary specifications. Compare this report to the report in Figure 23.7. What began as a basically readable report has been iteratively transformed into a detailed report suitable for publication or presentation. Note that the report has been considerably compressed through the use of formatting options, but at the same time enhanced in its labeling through VARIABLES, BREAK, and SUMMARY options. This report can be further modified with additional titling information.

The following REPORT command produces the report in Figure 23.46:

```
REPORT  FORMAT=MARGINS(1,80) BRKSPACE(-1)/
        VARIABLES=AGE(3) TENURE(9) (OFFSET(3)) JTENURE(9) (OFFSET(3))
          SPACE(DUMMY)' '(4)
          SALARY 'ANNUAL' 'SALARY' (7)/
        BREAK=DIVISION 'PRODUCT' 'DIVISION' (LABEL) (12) (OFFSET(1))
          (TOTAL)/
        SUMMARY=MEAN(AGE TENURE(1) JTENURE(1) SALARY(DOLLAR)(0))/
        SUMMARY=VALIDN '     COUNT'(SALARY)
```

Figure 23.46 The company report with summary specifications

```
PERSONNEL REPORT (BASIC)                                                   PAGE      1

PRODUCT              AGE     TENURE IN      TENURE IN               ANNUAL
DIVISION                       COMPANY          GRADE               SALARY

 CARPETING            35         5.5            4.1                $14,221
     COUNT                                                              47

 APPLIANCES           36         5.9            4.3                $15,039
     COUNT                                                              76

 FURNITURE            38         6.2            4.8                $15,894
     COUNT                                                              80

 HARDWARE             37         6.2            4.5                $15,616
     COUNT                                                              61

 TOTAL                36         6.0            4.5                $15,286
     COUNT                                                             264
```

23.47 TITLES AND FOOTNOTES

Left, center, and right titles and footnotes can be placed on each page of the printed output. Each title or footnote can have as many lines as needed with each line specified by a string enclosed in apostrophes separated by at least one space, as in:

TITLE='line1' 'line 2' ... 'last line'/

To include an apostrophe in a title, either enclose the string in quotation marks or use double apostrophes not separated by a space. For an example, see Figure 23.31.

Any or all of the following can be specified:

```
LTITLE   ='      '/   Left-justified head
RTITLE   ='      '/   Right-justified head
CTITLE   ='      '/   Centered head
LFOOTNOTE='      '/   Left-justified foot
RFOOTNOTE='      '/   Right-justified foot
CFOOTNOTE='      '/   Centered foot
```

TITLE and FOOTNOTE are equivalent to CTITLE and CFOOTNOTE, except that TITLE cannot be used with LTITLE or RTITLE and FOOTNOTE cannot be used in combination with LFOOTNOTE or RFOOTNOTE. In addition to these exceptions, only one of each subcommand is permitted per REPORT command, although each subcommand can specify more than one title line. There is no fixed limit to the number of title and footnote lines on a report. These subcommands are optional and can be placed anywhere after the FORMAT subcommand. However, you cannot interleave title and footnote subcommands. All title subcommands should come first followed by footnote subcommands.

Titles and footnotes are repeated on each page of a multiple-page report. Centered titles and footnotes are placed exactly in the center of the page layout. Note that wide reports with few columns are offset to the left of the center since the maximum intercolumn width is four spaces. Centered titles on such reports appear to be offset to the right.

Two special arguments can be used in titles and footnotes:

)PAGE *Print the page number right-justified in a five-character field.*

)DATE *Print the current date in the form* dd/mmm/yy *right-adjusted in a nine-character field.*

The following are typical subcommands using these arguments:

```
LTITLE='PERSONNEL REPORT' 'PREPARED ON )DATE'/
RTITLE='Page )PAGE'/
```

If neither a title nor a footnote is specified, a default title is generated. If the width of the page is 15 or more characters, "PAGE   n" appears as a right-justified title. If the width is 60 or greater, the specification on the TITLE command (Chapter 4) is left-justified in the first 64 characters.

A blank title can be specified, producing an extra blank line at the top of every page of the report. There is no default footnote. Specifying a title or footnote longer than the report width generates an error.

Figure 23.47 The company report with title information

```
CHICAGO HOME FURNISHINGS                                                   Page     1
Personnel Report

BRANCH          PRODUCT            AGE     TENURE IN     TENURE IN               ANNUAL
STORE           DIVISION                    COMPANY          GRADE               SALARY

 SUBURBAN        CARPETING          32       4.07          3.52                   16004
                 APPLIANCES         33       4.21          3.87                   16105
                 FURNITURE          36       5.03          4.65                   18821
                 HARDWARE           34       4.59          4.26                   16435

 DOWNTOWN        CARPETING          33       4.17          3.45                   13465
                 APPLIANCES         35       4.37          3.99                   14130
                 FURNITURE          36       4.64          3.99                   14403
                 HARDWARE           35       4.49          4.12                   14873



Prepared on 21 NOV 82
```

Figure 23.47 is a final example of the company report modified through optional subcommand specifications demonstrating the use of titles and a footnote to build a final report. The following commands produce the report in Figure 23.47:

```
SORT CASES  BY STORE DIVISION
REPORT  FORMAT=MARGINS(1,80) LENGTH(1,20) BRKSPACE(-1)/
        VARIABLES=AGE(3) TENURE(9) (OFFSET(3)) JTENURE(9) (OFFSET(3))
          SPACE(DUMMY)' '(4)
          SALARY 'ANNUAL' 'SALARY' (6)/
        BREAK=STORE 'BRANCH' 'STORE' (LABEL)(12)(OFFSET(1)) (TOTAL)/
        BREAK=DIVISION 'PRODUCT' 'DIVISION' (LABEL) (12) (OFFSET(1))
          (SKIP(0))/
        SUMMARY=MEAN/
        LTITLE='CHICAGO HOME FURNISHINGS'
               'Personnel Report'/
        RTITLE='Page )PAGE'/
        LFOOT='Prepared on )DATE'/
```

Note the use of the LENGTH keyword in the FORMAT subcommand to force the footnote up to the bottom part of the report.

23.48 THE MISSING SUBCOMMAND

The treatment of missing values within REPORT is controlled by the MISSING subcommand. There are three options:

MISSING= VAR|NONE|LIST [(varname ... varname [n])] /

VAR *Indicates that missing values are treated separately for each variable named on the VARIABLES subcommand* (the default). Missing values are printed in case listings but are not included in summary statistics.

NONE *Specifies that user-missing values are handled as if they were not missing.*

LIST *Eliminates from case listings as well as from summaries any case with a specified number of missing values on a specified list of variables.*

For example, the subcommand

```
MISSING= LIST(GRADE74 GRADE75 GRADE76 2)/
```

deletes any case with missing values on two or more of the variables GRADE74, GRADE75, and GRADE76 from case listings and from summaries. If a case is missing for just one or for none of the variables listed, it is not deleted from case listings but is deleted from summaries for those variables for which it is missing. If no variables are specified with LIST, all variables and strings defined by the VARIABLES subcommand are assumed. If no *n* is specified, the default is 1.

MISSING specifications apply to REPORT-generated strings as well as to other variables. If one variable in a REPORT-generated string is missing, the string is missing.

Only variables named on the VARIABLES and SUMMARY subcommands are checked for missing values. A SELECT IF command must be used to eliminate cases missing on break variables.

Only one MISSING subcommand is permitted for each REPORT command. Since NONE applies to the entire set of variables named in the VARIABLES subcommand, it cannot be used to ignore missing-data indicators for some of the variables selectively. The MISSING VALUES command can be used to turn off previously defined missing values.

The MISSING subcommand must follow the VARIABLES subcommand and precede the BREAK subcommand. If it references a string created with the STRING subcommand, it must follow the STRING subcommand.

23.49 REPORTS WITH NO BREAKS

REPORT is designed to produce reports describing subpopulations. If your report has no breaks, you can use the (NOBREAK) specification on the BREAK subcommand. When you do this, special conventions apply to spacing and formatting and they differ depending upon whether a column is reserved for summary titles.

If you specify a width with (NOBREAK), a column is reserved for summary titles and REPORT observes the following formatting and spacing conventions:

- Because there is no break variable, there is no break head.
- SUMSPACE(n), TSPACE(n), and CHDSPACE(n) on the FORMAT subcommand operate as usual.
- BRKSPACE(n) is ignored.
- SKIP(n) on the SUMMARY subcommand operates as usual, but (SKIP(n)) on the BREAK subcommand is ignored.
- Summary titles are placed in the break column left-justified. You can use (OFFSET(n)) on the BREAK subcommand to offset them to the right.

If you do not specify a column width, the following formatting and spacing conventions apply:

- SUMSPACE(n), TSPACE(n), and CHDSPACE(n) on the FORMAT subcommand operate as usual.
- BRKSPACE(n) on the FORMAT subcommand controls the spacing between the extra line for the summary title and the associated line of summary figures. If you use BRKSPACE(−1) on the FORMAT subcommand and request a summary statistic for the leftmost report variable, the summary title overlays the statistic. You should only specify BRKSPACE(−1) if you are not computing statistics for the leftmost report variable.
- Summary titles are printed left-justified before the summary line.
- (SKIP(n)) on the BREAK subcommand controls the spacing between a prior summary line and the next extra line for the summary title.
- SKIP(n) on the SUMMARY subcommand is ignored.

If these conventions do not satisfy your formatting requirements, use a variable which never changes instead of specifying (NOBREAK). For example, you may want to place a title in the break title column. Section 23.24 describes a method of using a constant string for a report with no breaks.

23.50 SUBCOMMAND ORDER

The order of subcommands must correspond to the following rules:

- The FORMAT subcommand must be the first subcommand.
- The VARIABLES subcommand must precede the BREAK subcommand.
- The SUMMARY subcommand must immediately follow the first BREAK subcommand for which summary statistics are desired.
- The STRING subcommand must precede the VARIABLES subcommand.
- Title and footnote subcommands can appear anywhere after the FORMAT subcommand except between the BREAK and SUMMARY subcommands.
- The MISSING subcommand must follow the VARIABLES subcommand and precede the first BREAK subcommand.

Only the BREAK and SUMMARY subcommands must appear together in REPORT.

23.51 Limitations

The following formal limitations apply to the REPORT procedure:

- A maximum of 500 variables per VARIABLES subcommand.
- A maximum of 10 dummy variables per VARIABLES subcommand.
- A maximum of 50 strings per STRING subcommand.
- The maximum width of a printed report is set by the maximum width allowed on the SET command (see Chapter 4).
-)PAGE can occur only once in either the title or footnote.
- A maximum of 20 MODE, MEDIAN, ABFREQ, and RELFREQ requests per SUMMARY subcommand.
- A maximum of 20 PCGT, PCLT, and PCIN requests per SUMMARY subcommand.
- Workspace is required to store all labeling information; frequency counts if summaries request ABFREQ, RELFREQ, MEDIAN, or MODE; strings; and computed summary statistics. There should be enough workspace in 5000 bytes for a report of moderate size with a few strings, titles, and footnotes; two break levels; and simple descriptive statistics.

Memory requirements significantly increase if ABFREQ, RELFREQ, MEDIAN, or MODE is requested with variables having a wide range of values. The amount of workspace required can be calculated as follows:

20 + 8*(max−min+1) bytes per variable per function per break

If TOTAL is in effect, workspace requirements are almost doubled. If the same range is used for different statistics for the same variable, only one set of cells is collected. For example,

```
ABFREQ(1,100)(VARA) RELFREQ(1,100)(VARA)
```

requires only 820 bytes.

Memory requirements also increase if value labels are printed for variables with many value labels. The amount of workspace required can be calculated as follows:

4 + 24*nlabel per variable

For example, assume that the case listing contains value labels for the variable STATE and there are 51 value labels corresponding to state names and the District of Columbia. The amount of memory required to store the labels is 1228 bytes.

23.52 Trial Runs

Because REPORT is so flexible and the output has so many components, the first run of a complex report may not produce exactly the desired report. For example, the first attempt can reveal awkward column heads, truncated strings, printing overflows, etc.

To refine a report with a minimal cost in computer resources, you can run several REPORTs with different specifications using a small file until the intended format is obtained. The data file must be accessed because the EDIT facility only scans the REPORT command for syntax errors and does not display the report format. Obviously, the larger the file, the more important it is to access a small subset of that file in trying out various REPORT specifications. To process a subset of the file as inexpensively as possible, use one of the following techniques:

- The N OF CASES command can be used either when reading raw data or when accessing a system file to limit the number of cases read (see Chapter 10). SPSS^X does not attempt to read more cases than the number specified on the N OF CASES command. For example, assume that the file contains 10,000 cases. If the N OF CASES command specifies 10, only the first 10 cases are read.
- If the REPORT contains breaks, and the labeling and spacing of breaks are important considerations, a subset of the entire file containing cases from several breaks can be obtained using the SAMPLE command (see Chapter 10).

23.53 Split-File Processing

Use of SPLIT FILE (Chapter 13) with REPORT is equivalent to specifying the variables named on the SPLIT FILE command as the first break level with the BREAK subcommand. Specifying SPLIT FILE variables as the first BREAK instead of using the SPLIT FILE command has three distinct advantages:

- Less CPU time is required, because various arrays do not have to be reinitialized.
- The TOTAL option in the BREAK subcommand provides statistics over the total of split-file groups.
- The report can be more compact because new breaks begin on a new page only if the PAGE option has been selected.

23.54 Sorting Cases

Because REPORT processes cases in the file sequentially and reports summary statistics when the break variable(s) change in value, the file must be grouped by break variable(s). The SORT CASES command is the most direct means of reorganizing a file for REPORT. It can be inserted in the command file prior to the REPORT command and should list the BREAK variables in the order they appear within the REPORT command. For a report with a primary break on variable EDUC and a secondary break on variable SEX, the following sequence of commands is appropriate:

```
SORT CASES  BY EDUC SEX
REPORT VARIABLES=V1 TO V6/
       BREAK=EDUC/
       SUMMARY=MEAN/
       BREAK=SEX/
       SUMMARY=PREVIOUS
```

Variables can be sorted in descending or ascending order, but they must be grouped together. If a break contains more than one variable, the order in which the variables are named on the SORT CASES command is irrelevant to REPORT and depends solely on the preferred order of the groups for the report.

23.55 REPORT Compared with Other Procedures

Many of the features of REPORT can be found in part in other procedures in SPSS^X, and you may have to decide which is more appropriate for a particular job. Case listings can be obtained using PRINT or LIST; means, sum, variances, and standard deviations for subpopulations can be obtained using BREAKDOWN; descriptive statistics can be obtained by FREQUENCIES and CONDESCRIPTIVE; and aggregate files can be produced by AGGREGATE. The principal advantage of REPORT over other procedures producing essentially the same types of statistics is the compactness of the output produced and the flexibility in formatting and labeling that it provides.

There are some advantages for REPORT that are not so obvious:

- Frequency counts are printed with decimal digits if the default format is overridden. Therefore, if a file contains noninteger weights, the actual sum of the weights is printed, and not rounded as in FREQUENCIES.
- Subpopulation medians can be obtained without having to resort to multiple SELECT IFs, with a considerable savings in both command preparation and computer expenses.
- Composite functions such as the sum of one variable divided by the sum of another variable can be computed and printed easily.

There are also some REPORT limitations that other procedures producing the same kinds of output do not have:

- Subpopulations can be defined only once on the break variables. In BREAKDOWN they can be defined by several different variables. For example, one BREAKDOWN can define subpopulations first by SEX, then by AGE, etc.
- A limited number of variables can be analyzed on one REPORT command. The number of variables permitted is a function of report width and column widths.
- Frequencies, median, and mode are available only for integer variables.
- The file must be sorted on the break variable(s).

23.56 Producing CROSSBREAK-like Tables

Procedure BREAKDOWN optionally formats statistics for variables broken down by two or more variables into a tabular format when the keyword CROSSBREAK is used. REPORT can also produce such a table. In the CROSSBREAK format some of the columns in the report correspond to subsets of the file. Figure 23.56 is a more complicated version of a CROSSBREAK-like report. Variables TIME0, TIME1, TIME2, and TIME3 are created with COMPUTE commands executed conditionally based on TIME to subset AMOUNT. The file is first aggregated with the AGGREGATE command to obtain the TOTAL variable across all the cases (see Chapter 14). This variable is then spread back to the original file with the MATCH FILES command (see Chapter 15).

The following commands produce the report in Figure 23.56:

```
DO IF (TIME GE 90)
COMPUTE  TIME3=AMOUNT
ELSE IF (TIME GT 60)
COMPUTE  TIME2=AMOUNT
ELSE IF (TIME GT 30)
COMPUTE  TIME1=AMOUNT
ELSE
COMPUTE  TIME0=AMOUNT
END IF
PRINT FORMATS  TIME3 TO TIME0 (DOLLAR10.2)
COMPUTE CONST=1 /* Compute a constant for AGGREGATE*/
AGGREGATE  OUTFILE=HOLD/
           BREAK=CONST/
           TOTAL=SUM(AMOUNT)
MATCH FILES  TABLE=HOLD/FILE=*/BY CONST /* Place TOTAL back on file */

REPORT  FORMAT=BRKSPACE(-1) MARGINS(1,80) MISSING ' '
         CHDSPACE(1)/
        VARIABLES=AMOUNT'TOTAL' (10)
              TIME0 '0-30 DAYS' (10)
              TIME1 '31-60 DAYS' (10)
              TIME2 '61-90 DAYS' (10)
              TIME3 '90+ DAYS' (10)/
        TITLE='SUMMARY STATEMENT-ACCOUNTS RECEIVABLE' '(AGED)'
          ' ' 'APEX METAL FASTENERS' 'M.I.S. REPORT 2'/
        BREAK=INVTYPE(LABEL)(15)(TOTAL)/
        SUMMARY=SUM/
        SUMMARY=PCT(SUM(AMOUNT)SUM(AMOUNT))'  % OF TYPE'
                 PCT(SUM(TIME0)SUM(AMOUNT))
                 PCT(SUM(TIME1)SUM(AMOUNT))
                 PCT(SUM(TIME2)SUM(AMOUNT))
                 PCT(SUM(TIME3)SUM(AMOUNT))/
        SUMMARY=PCT(SUM(AMOUNT)MAX(TOTAL))'  % OF TOTAL'
                 PCT(SUM(TIME0)MAX(TOTAL))
                 PCT(SUM(TIME1)MAX(TOTAL))
                 PCT(SUM(TIME2)MAX(TOTAL))
                 PCT(SUM(TIME3)MAX(TOTAL))
```

Figure 23.56 A CROSSBREAK application with REPORT

```
                     SUMMARY STATEMENT-ACCOUNTS RECEIVABLE
                                    (AGED)

                             APEX METAL FASTENERS
                               M.I.S. REPORT 2

INVTYPE                  TOTAL   0-30 DAYS  31-60 DAYS  61-90 DAYS    90+ DAYS

Stove Bolts          $2,501.50     $346.11   $1,345.69     $403.86     $405.84
  % OF TYPE             100.00       13.84       53.80       16.14       16.22
  % OF TOTAL             18.06        2.50        9.72        2.92        2.93

Wood Screws          $3,417.60   $1,181.00   $1,244.58     $390.51     $601.51
  % OF TYPE             100.00       34.56       36.42       11.43       17.60
  % OF TOTAL             24.68        8.53        8.99        2.82        4.34

Metal Screws         $3,221.51                 $697.41   $1,982.59     $541.51
  % OF TYPE             100.00                   21.65       61.54       16.81
  % OF TOTAL             23.26                    5.04       14.32        3.91

Spring Washers       $2,429.97     $512.15     $206.81     $393.69   $1,317.32
  % OF TYPE             100.00       21.08        8.51       16.20       54.21
  % OF TOTAL             17.55        3.70        1.49        2.84        9.51

Other                $2,278.36     $354.77     $897.57     $579.70     $446.32
  % OF TYPE             100.00       15.57       39.40       25.44       19.59
  % OF TOTAL             16.45        2.56        6.48        4.19        3.22

TOTAL               $13,848.94   $2,394.03   $4,392.06   $3,750.35   $3,312.50
  % OF TYPE             100.00       17.29       31.71       27.08       23.92
  % OF TOTAL            100.00       17.29       31.71       27.08       23.92
```

23.57 Producing CROSSTABS-like Tables

REPORT can be used to produce CROSSTABS-like tables where columns correspond to the values of one or more variables. Transformations are required to split a variable into several variables, each one corresponding to a category of the original variable. The easiest means of creating such variables is to use the COUNT command (Chapter 6), as in:

```
COUNT MALE=SEX(1)/FEMALE=SEX(2)
```

In this example, all males on the file have a value of 1 for MALE and a value of 0 for FEMALE. Figure 23.57 is one example of such a CROSSTABS-like report.

The complete set of SPSSX commands required to produce the report in Figure 23.57 is as follows:

```
FILE HANDLE  HUB/ file specifications
GET  FILE=HUB
COMMENT  OBTAIN INTERSECTION OF NONMISSING ETHNIC AND SEX
IF (NOT(MISSING(RACE)) AND NOT(MISSING(SEX))) NOFCASES=1
COMMENT  SET UP VARIABLES COLUMNS
COUNT  MALE=SEX(1)/FEMALE=SEX(2)
MISSING VALUES  MALE FEMALE(0)
DO IF (SEX EQ 1)  /* SET UP COLUMNS FOR MALES
DO REPEAT  OUT=MNEGRO MORIENT MINDIAN MLATINO/
           VAL=2 TO 5
IF  (ETHNIC EQ VAL) OUT=1
END REPEAT
ELSE IF (SEX EQ 2) /* SET UP COLUMNS FOR FEMALES
DO REPEAT  OUT=FNEGRO FORIENT FINDIAN FLATINO/
           VAL=2 TO 5
IF  (ETHNIC EQ VAL) OUT=1
END REPEAT
END IF
SORT CASES  BY JOBGRADE
REPORT  FORMAT=TSPACE(3) BRKSPACE (-1) CHDSPACE (0) LENGTH (1,20)/
        VARIABLES=NOFCASES ' ' ' '  'TOTAL' ' (1)'(5)
        MALE ' ' ' '  'MALE' ' (2)'(5)
        FEMALE ' ' ' '  'FEMALE' '  (3)'(6)
        MNEGRO ' ' 'MALE' 'NEGRO' ' (4)'(5)
        MORIENT ' ' 'MALE' 'ORIENTAL' '   (5)'(8)
        MINDIAN ' ' 'MALE' 'INDIAN' '  (6)'(6)
        MLATINO 'MALE   ' 'SPANISH' 'SURNAME' '  (7)'(7)
        FNEGRO ' ' 'FEMALE' 'NEGRO' ' (8)'(6)
        FORIENT ' ' 'FEMALE' 'ORIENTAL' '   (9)'(8)
        FINDIAN ' ' 'FEMALE' 'INDIAN' ' (10)'(6)
        FLATINO 'FEMALE ' 'SPANISH' 'SURNAME' ' (11)'(7)/
        LTITLE='FORM T'/
        CTITLE='AFFIRMATIVE ACTION PROGRAM' ' '
        'QUARTERLY STATISTICAL REPORT'/
        RTITLE='ORGANIZATION UNIT:  ABCD'
        'LOCATION:  CHICAGO'
        'TIME PERIOD: 6/81 TO 9/81'/
        LFOOTNOTE='DATE OF SURVEY: )DATE'/
        RFOOTNOTE='PERSON PREPARING REPORT:  JANE BILANDIC'/
        BREAK=JOBCAT (LABEL)(TOTAL)/
        SUMMARY=VALIDN(NOFCASES MALE FEMALE MNEGRO
         MORIENT MINDIAN MLATINO FNEGRO FORIENT FINDIAN FLATINO)/
        SUMMARY=PCT(VALIDN(MALE)VALIDN(NOFCASES))'   PERCENTAGES'
        PCT(VALIDN(FEMALE)VALIDN(NOFCASES))
        PCT(VALIDN(MNEGRO)VALIDN(NOFCASES))
        PCT(VALIDN(MORIENT)VALIDN(NOFCASES))
        PCT(VALIDN(MINDIAN)VALIDN(NOFCASES))
        PCT(VALIDN(MLATINO)VALIDN(NOFCASES))
        PCT(VALIDN(FNEGRO)VALIDN(NOFCASES))
        PCT(VALIDN(FORIENT)VALIDN(NOFCASES))
        PCT(VALIDN(FINDIAN)VALIDN(NOFCASES))
        PCT(VALIDN(FLATINO)VALIDN(NOFCASES))
```

In this example, the IF commands required to produce the report are placed inside a DO REPEAT structure and executed conditionally based on the value of SEX.

23.58 REPORT and Other SPSSX Commands

REPORT interacts with other SPSSX commands. Data transformations are required for special types of reports described in previous sections. This section describes other commands that affect both the dimensions and the contents of reports.

The dictionary print formats defined by the PRINT FORMATS command for a variable instructs SPSSX how to print it. If a variable has a print format that includes no decimal places (F2.0 for example), no decimal digits are printed, even though the internal representation is a decimal number. Thus, misspecified print formats can produce misleading column contents in REPORT.

By default REPORT uses any label assigned using the VARIABLE LABELS command as the column head for report and break columns. To produce a nicely labeled column head, format the variable label to the

Figure 23.57 An affirmative action report

```
FORM T                     AFFIRMATIVE ACTION PROGRAM          ORGANIZATION UNIT:  ABCD
                                                                      LOCATION:  CHICAGO
                          QUARTERLY STATISTICAL REPORT        TIME PERIOD: 6/81 TO 9/81
```

JOB CATEGORIES	TOTAL (1)	MALE (2)	FEMALE (3)	MALE NEGRO (4)	MALE ORIENTAL (5)	MALE INDIAN (6)	MALE SPANISH SURNAME (7)	FEMALE NEGRO (8)	FEMALE ORIENTAL (9)	FEMALE INDIAN (10)	FEMALE SPANISH SURNAME (11)
OFFICIALS & MANAGER	48	19	29	7	0	0	0	18	4	0	0
PERCENTAGES		39.58	60.42	14.58	0.0	0.0	0.0	37.50	8.33	0.0	0.0
PROFESSIONALS	62	29	33	4	3	0	0	6	2	0	0
PERCENTAGES		46.77	53.23	6.45	4.84	0.0	0.0	9.68	3.23	0.0	0.0
TECHNICIANS	98	17	81	4	1	0	0	33	1	0	0
PERCENTAGES		17.35	82.65	4.08	1.02	0.0	0.0	33.67	1.02	0.0	0.0
OFFICE AND CLERICAL	67	18	49	3	1	0	0	12	2	0	3
PERCENTAGES		26.87	73.13	4.48	1.49	0.0	0.0	17.91	2.99	0.0	4.48
TOTAL	275	83	192	18	5	0	0	69	9	0	3
PERCENTAGES		30.18	69.82	6.55	1.82	0.0	0.0	25.09	3.27	0.0	1.09

```
DATE OF SURVEY: 01 MAR 82                      PERSON PREPARING REPORT:  JANE BILANDIC
```

column width. The VARIABLE LABELS command can also be used to produce empty column heads. SPSS^X permits a blank variable label, as in:

```
VARIABLE LABELS VARX' '/
```

In this example, VARX is given a blank variable label.

The length of a page in a report is determined by the SPSS^X page size. The SET command is used to override the default of 59 lines per page (see Chapter 4). The LENGTH specification on the FORMAT subcommand specifies actual line positions on the page. REPORT does not allow you to specify a page longer than system-set length. Thus, if you want a very long page, use the SET command to establish it. Similarly, the MARGINS specification only works within the system-set page width.

The number of cases "reported" is controlled by the number of cases being processed in a run. N OF CASES can be used to limit the number of cases processed (Section 23.52), as can SELECT IF and SAMPLE.

REPORT, unlike many other procedures in SPSS^X, actually begins printing your report as it reads through the data. Thus, if REPORT is the very first procedure in the run, warning messages concerning invalid data fields are interspersed with REPORT output. To avoid this possibility, use some other procedure such as SORT CASES or EXECUTE prior to the report when reading data using the DATA LIST command (Chapter 3) or turn off warning messages with the SET command (Chapter 4).

PRINT and WRITE are transformation utilities which can be used to print cases on the display file. Unless you are using the FILE subcommand on these commands to direct the display to an alternative file, do not use them immediately prior to your REPORT command. Otherwise, their results interleave with REPORT's results. If you are using either PRINT or WRITE in the same job with REPORT, you can avoid the interleaving effect by placing some other procedure between these commands and the REPORT command.

The SORT CASES command may be required to organize the file by break variables (see Section 23.54).

```
PIECHART PLOT varname [selector] [varname ... ]
              [BY varname [selector]]

                       {EQ} value list
                       {NE}
where selector is ( {LT             } )
                       {LE} value
                       {GE}
                       {GT}

[/[DEFAULT] FORMAT  [NO] {[{SIMPLE}] [COUNT   ]}]
                         {[{FANCY }] [PERCENT ]}
                         {           [SORT    ]}
                         {[COMBINE]  [DUMP    ]}

[/[DEFAULT] TITLE     'line1' ['line2' ['line3']]]*
[/[DEFAULT] FOOTNOTE  'line1' ['line2' ['line3']]]
[/[DEFAULT] COMMENT   'line1' ['line2' ['line3']]]

[/[DEFAULT] SEGMENT  LABELS  (value) 'label' ... ]*
[/[DEFAULT] EXPLODE  value list]

[/[DEFAULT] ORDER  {1, 2, 3 ... }]
                   {value list  }

[/[DEFAULT] COLORS  {0}]
                    {n}

[/[DEFAULT] FONT  {DUPLEX }]
                  {COMPLEX}
                  {TRIPLEX}
                  {GOTHIC }

[/[DEFAULT] XPAGE  {11   }]  [/[DEFAULT] YPAGE  {8.5  }]
                   {value}                      {value}

[/[DEFAULT] MISSING  {PIEWISE }]
                     {PLOTWISE}
                     {NONE    }

[/SAVE  name]
[/PLOT  ... ]
```

```
BARCHART PLOT function [function ... ] WITH varname [selector]
              [varname ... ] [BY varname [selector]] [varname ... ]

                    {COUNT                         }
                    {CCOUNT                        }
                    {PERCENT                       }
where function is   {CPERCENT                      }
                    {MEAN                          }
                    {SUM   } (varname [selector])  }
                    {CSUM                          }

                       {EQ} value list
                       {NE}
where selector is ( {LT             } )
                       {LE} value
                       {GE}
                       {GT}

[/[DEFAULT] FORMAT  {CLUSTERED} [NO] {[{SIMPLE}]     } [FRAME]
                    {STACKED  }      {[{FANCY }]     } [GRID ]
                    {HIDDEN   }      {[{VERTICAL  }] } [COUNT]
                                     {[{HORIZONTAL}] } [DUMP ]

[/[DEFAULT] TITLE     'line1' ['line2' ['line3']]]*
[/[DEFAULT] FOOTNOTE  'line1' ['line2' ['line3']]]
[/[DEFAULT] COMMENT   'line1' ['line2' ['line3']]]

[/[DEFAULT] BASE  AXIS  ['label']* {LABELED ['label' ... ]*}
                                   {LINEAR                 }
                                   {MONTHLY                }
                        [NAME 'label']*

                                              [RANGE min max ]
[/[DEFAULT] SIDE  AXIS  ['label']* {LINEAR}   [REFERENCE value]
                                   {LOG   }   [ROOT value     ]
                                              [NAME 'label'   ]*

[/[DEFAULT] LEGEND  TITLE  'title']*
[/[DEFAULT] LEGEND  LABELS  'label' ... ]*

[/[DEFAULT] ORDER  {1, 2, 3 ... }]
                   {value list  }

[/[DEFAULT] COLORS  {0}]
                    {n}

[/[DEFAULT] FONT  {DUPLEX }]
                  {COMPLEX}
                  {TRIPLEX}
                  {GOTHIC }

[/[DEFAULT] XPAGE  {11   }]  [/[DEFAULT] YPAGE  {8.5  }]
                   {value}                      {value}

[/[DEFAULT] MISSING  {BARWISE }]
                     {PLOTWISE}
                     {NONE    }

[/SAVE  name]
[/PLOT  ... ]
```

```
LINECHART PLOT function [function ... ] WITH varname
               [selector] [varname ... ]
               [BY varname [selector]] [varname ... ]

                    {COUNT                                          }
                    {CCOUNT                                         }
                    {PERCENT                                        }
                    {PROPORTION                                     }
                    {CPROPORTION                                    }
                    {MEAN                                           }
                    {SMEAN                                          }
                    {SD1                                            }
                    {SD2                                            }
where function is   {SD3                                            }
                    {SUM                                            }
                    {CSUM                                           }
                    {VALUES} (varname [selector] [varname ... ])    }
                    {REG                                            }
                    {M90                                            }
                    {I90                                            }
                    {M95                                            }
                    {I95                                            }
                    {M99                                            }
                    {I99                                            }

                       {EQ} value list
                       {NE}
where selector is ( {LT             } )
                       {LE} value
                       {GE}
                       {GT}

[/[DEFAULT] FORMAT  [NO] {[{SIMPLE}]          [FRAME ]}]
                         {[{FANCY }]          [GRID  ]}
                         {           [SHADE]  [XGRID ]}
                         {           [DUMP ]  [YGRID ]}

[/[DEFAULT] TITLE     'line1' ['line2' ['line3']]]*
[/[DEFAULT] FOOTNOTE  'line1' ['line2' ['line3']]]
[/[DEFAULT] COMMENT   'line1' ['line2' ['line3']]]

[/[DEFAULT] X  AXIS  ['label']* {LINEAR                } [RANGE min max  ]
                                {LOG                   } [REFERENCE value]
                                {LABELED ['label' ... ]} [NAME 'label' ...]*
                                {MONTHLY               }

[/[DEFAULT] Y  AXIS  ['label']* {LINEAR}  [RANGE min max  ]
                                {LOG   }  [REFERENCE value]
                                          [NAME 'label' ...]*

[/[DEFAULT] CURVES  {ALL       } {STRAIGHT} [value list ... ]]
                    {value list} {STEP    }
                                 {SPLINE  }
                    [[NO] MARKERS]

[/[DEFAULT] LEGEND  TITLE  'title']*
[/[DEFAULT] LEGEND  LABELS  'label' ... ]*

[/[DEFAULT] ORDER  {1, 2, 3 ... }]
                   {value list  }

[/[DEFAULT] COLORS  {0}]
                    {n}

[/[DEFAULT] FONT  {DUPLEX }]
                  {COMPLEX}
                  {TRIPLEX}
                  {GOTHIC }

[/[DEFAULT] XPAGE  {11   }]  [/[DEFAULT] YPAGE  {8.5  }]
                   {value}                      {value}

[/[DEFAULT] MISSING  {LINEWISE}]
                     {PLOTWISE}
                     {NONE    }

[/SAVE  name]
[/PLOT  ... ]
```

*Notes
TITLE, FOOTNOTE, COMMENT maximum line length 50
SEGMENT LABELS maximum length 20
BASE AXIS, SIDE AXIS, X AXIS, Y AXIS maximum label length 40
BASE AXIS, X AXIS maximum value label length 16
LEGEND TITLE and LEGEND LABELS maximum length 20

```
GRAPHICS OUTPUT  OUTFILE  handle
```


OVERVIEW, **24.1**
- Overview of the PIECHART Procedure, **24.2**
- Overview of the BARCHART Procedure, **24.3**
- Overview of the LINECHART Procedure, **24.4**

THE PIECHART PROCEDURE, **24.5**
- The PLOT Subcommand, **24.6**
  - Keyword BY, **24.7**
  - Selectors, **24.8**
- The FORMAT Subcommand, **24.9**
- The TITLE, FOOTNOTE, and COMMENT Subcommands, **24.10**
- Controlling the Segments, **24.11**
  - The SEGMENT LABELS Subcommand, **24.12**
  - The EXPLODE Subcommand, **24.13**
  - The ORDER Subcommand, **24.14**
  - The COLORS Subcommand, **24.15**
- The FONT Subcommand, **24.16**
- The XPAGE and YPAGE Subcommands, **24.17**
- The MISSING Subcommand, **24.18**
- Multiple PLOT Subcommands, **24.19**
- Special Plotting Applications, **24.20**
  - Anticipating Multiple Plots per Page, **24.21**
  - Entering Aggregate Data for Plots, **24.22**

THE BARCHART PROCEDURE, **24.23**
- The PLOT Subcommand, **24.24**
  - The Function and WITH Specifications, **24.25**
  - Keyword BY, **24.26**
  - Selectors, **24.27**
  - Multiple Variables, **24.28**
  - Cross-Products, **24.29**
- The FORMAT Subcommand, **24.30**
- The TITLE, FOOTNOTE, and COMMENT Subcommands, **24.31**
- Controlling the Axes and the Bars, **24.32**
  - The BASE AXIS Subcommand, **24.33**
  - The SIDE AXIS Subcommand, **24.34**
  - The LEGEND TITLE and LEGEND LABELS Subcommands, **24.35**
  - The ORDER Subcommand, **24.36**
  - The COLORS Subcommand, **24.37**
- The FONT Subcommand, **24.38**
- The XPAGE and YPAGE Subcommands, **24.39**
- The MISSING Subcommand, **24.40**
- Multiple PLOT Subcommands, **24.41**

THE LINECHART PROCEDURE, **24.42**
- The PLOT Subcommand, **24.43**
  - The Function and WITH Specifications, **24.44**
  - Keyword BY, **24.45**
  - Selectors, **24.46**
  - Multiple Functions, **24.47**
  - Superimposing Line Charts, **24.48**
- The FORMAT Subcommand, **24.49**
- The TITLE, FOOTNOTE, and COMMENT Subcommands, **24.50**
- Controlling the Axes and the Curves, **24.51**
  - The X AXIS Subcommand, **24.52**
  - The Y AXIS Subcommand, **24.53**
  - The CURVES Subcommand, **24.54**
  - The LEGEND TITLE and LEGEND LABELS Subcommands, **24.55**
  - The ORDER Subcommand, **24.56**
  - The COLORS Subcommand, **24.57**
- The FONT Subcommand, **24.58**
- The XPAGE and YPAGE Subcommands, **24.59**
- The MISSING Subcommand, **24.60**
- Multiple PLOT Subcommands, **24.61**
- LINECHART Applications, **24.62**
  - Plotting Regression Lines, **24.63**
  - Shaded Line Charts, **24.64**

THE TELL-A-GRAF INTERFACE, **24.65**

Chapter 24 SPSS Graphics

SPSS Graphics consists of three procedures—PIECHART, BARCHART, and LINECHART—that are fully integrated into the SPSS^X system. Pie, bar, and line charts produced by the SPSS Graphics procedures can be fully labeled, including titles, footnotes, and comments. They can be produced in two modes, depending on whether you want plots for testing and refining or for final publication and display. You can select colors and patterns according to the type of devices you have available. You can combine multiple charts on one page under a common title.

SPSS Graphics, like other SPSS^X procedures, works directly with your active file, and it takes advantage of the system's variable and value labeling facilities and missing-value declarations in setting defaults and providing you with choices. Only minimum specifications are needed to produce readable and informative plots. However, you have control over a wide range of format choices, labeling, functions, colors and patterns, shading, line markers, axis scaling, interpolation, missing-value treatment, and so forth.

SPSS Inc. recognizes the expense of producing high-quality plots for presentation and reproduction quality plots and understands the iterative nature of developing graphic displays. Therefore, the SPSS Graphics Postprocessor allows you to preview your plots and select those that you want plotted on a final production device. That is, you can sign on to one device—perhaps a black-and-white CRT graphics terminal—and inspect the plots produced by the three procedures, one at a time. As you view the plots, you can direct those that are satisfactory to a final plotting device—perhaps an eight-color pen plotter. SPSS Graphics also allows you to write out a file that can be accessed by the TELL-A-GRAF software package from ISSCO Inc. if you want to take advantage of its expanded facilities.

24.1 OVERVIEW

The SPSS Graphics procedures are driven by three command keywords, PIECHART, BARCHART, and LINECHART, and by a series of subcommands separated by slashes. Several subcommands are common to the three procedures. The only requirement for all three procedures is at least one PLOT subcommand which names the variables and functions to be plotted, as in:

```
PIECHART   PLOT=JOBGRADE,DIVISION,STORE,SHIFT/
BARCHART   PLOT=PERCENT WITH JOBGRADE/
LINECHART   PLOT=MEAN(SALARY) WITH TENURE BY JOBGRADE/
```

All three procedures have the following attribute subcommands to control various display options: FORMAT, TITLE, FOOTNOTE, COMMENT, COLORS, ORDER, XPAGE, YPAGE, and FONT; all have a MISSING subcommand to control missing-value treatment; and all have a SAVE subcommand to save a file acceptable to the TELL-A-GRAF plotting package (see Section 24.65).

Because the type of plot being generated is different, keyword specifications and defaults for the same subcommand may be different for each procedure. For example, PIECHART's FORMAT specifications include keywords SORT and PERCENT, which are not valid for the other two procedures because they describe the order and part of the labeling for the pie chart segments. BARCHART's unique FORMAT specifications include STACKED or CLUSTERED, which control how the bar sets are organized, and LINECHART's FORMAT specifications include XGRID, YGRID, and SHADE, which request additional display features. On the other hand, all three FORMAT subcommands can specify SIMPLE or FANCY, which control the plot quality.

Naturally, each procedure has unique subcommands that allow you to control attributes specific to the type of plot being produced. For example, PIECHART has a SEGMENT LABELS subcommand whereas BARCHART and LINECHART both have LEGEND LABELS subcommands. BARCHART has the BASE AXIS and SIDE AXIS subcommands and LINECHART has similar X AXIS and Y AXIS subcommands.

Because only one PLOT subcommand is required, all other subcommands have defaults. The defaults are appropriate to each procedure and may differ for the same subcommand. For example, the default TITLE is constructed from the PLOT specification and is likely to be different for each procedure because the PLOT specifications differ. Each new PLOT subcommand causes all attributes to return to the defaults. However, SPSS Graphics allows you to establish your own defaults by preceding the subcommand keyword or keywords with keyword DEFAULT.

Each procedure produces one or more sections of a file that either can be directly displayed on a plotting device you have selected or, if you have access to more than one device, can be previewed on one device and optionally directed to another for final production. During this preview using the SPSS Graphics Postprocessor, you can select which plots you want to be sent to the second device and you can direct multiple plots to appear on the same page.

Although the three procedures operate in a very similar fashion, each is described in this document separately, starting with an overview and an example default plot for each. Details regarding the complete operation of each procedure begin with Section 24.5 for PIECHART, Section 24.23 for BARCHART, and Section 24.42 for LINECHART.

To define the *intermediate file* written by the graphics procedures and accessed by the postprocessor, the GRAPHICS OUTPUT command is required (see Section 24.66). Operations of the SPSS Graphics Postprocessor are described beginning with Section 24.67.

24.2 Overview of the PIECHART Procedure

The SPSS Graphics PIECHART procedure produces a pie, with each "slice" representing the relative frequency of a category (or cell) of a variable. For example, consider a hypothetical company with a suburban and a downtown store. To produce a pie chart showing the employee distribution within job categories for the entire company, the simplest command would be

```
PIECHART  PLOT=JOBGRADE/
```

The plot produced by this command is shown in Figure 24.2. It shows that sales personnel make up over two-thirds of the staff (69.1%), whereas supervisory and managerial personnel account for the other third (22.0% and 8.9%, respectively).

Figure 24.2 A default pie chart

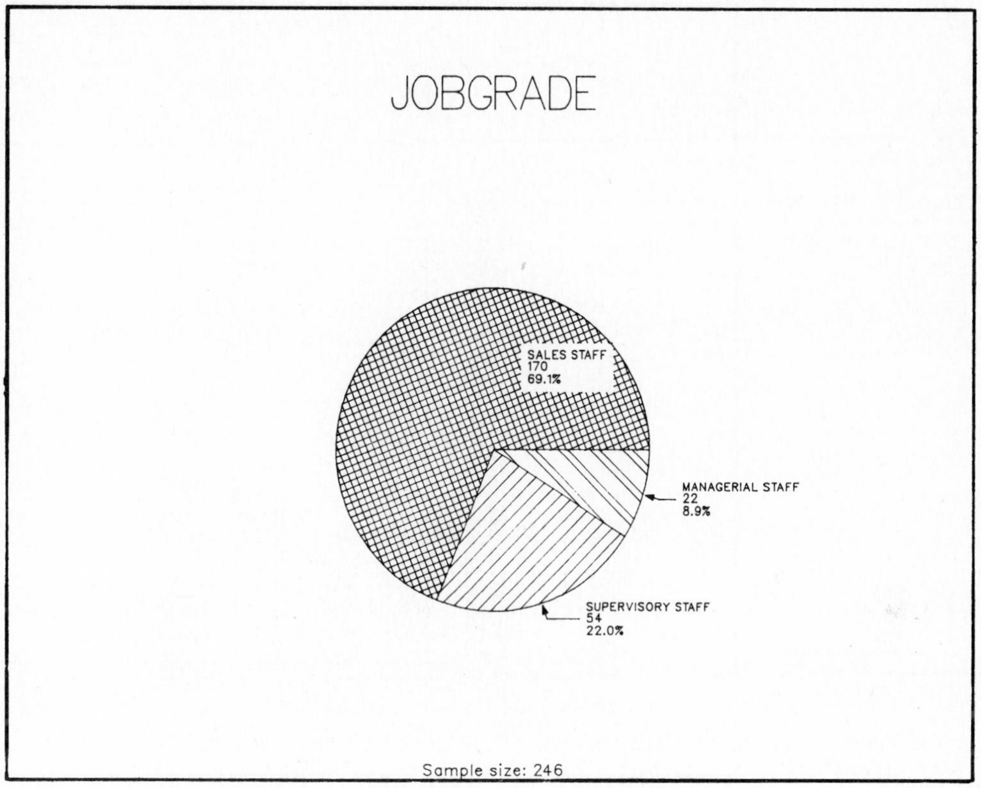

The pie chart in Figure 24.2 uses defaults for all user-controlled attributes such as pie segment order, titles, and labels. The title, for example, is constructed from the PLOT specification, which is simply the name of the variable being plotted in this case. The segment labels are the value labels associated with the variable. The default footnote describes the sample size. Any of these and several other default formatting options can be altered to make the plot exactly what you want. See Sections 24.5 through 24.22 for the complete range of options and how they affect the plot.

24.3 Overview of the BARCHART Procedure

The SPSS Graphics BARCHART procedure produces a plot with bars whose lengths represent the relative magnitude of a function within each category of a variable. The bar for each category of one variable can be divided further according to the values of a second variable. For example, to produce a bar chart showing the employee distribution within job categories for each shift, the command might be

```
BARCHART  PLOT=PERCENT WITH JOBGRADE BY SHIFT/
```

The plot produced by this command is shown in Figure 24.3. It shows not only that the sales category is by far the largest, but also that the percentage of sales personnel is smaller in the second and weekend shifts than in the first shift.

Figure 24.3 A default bar chart

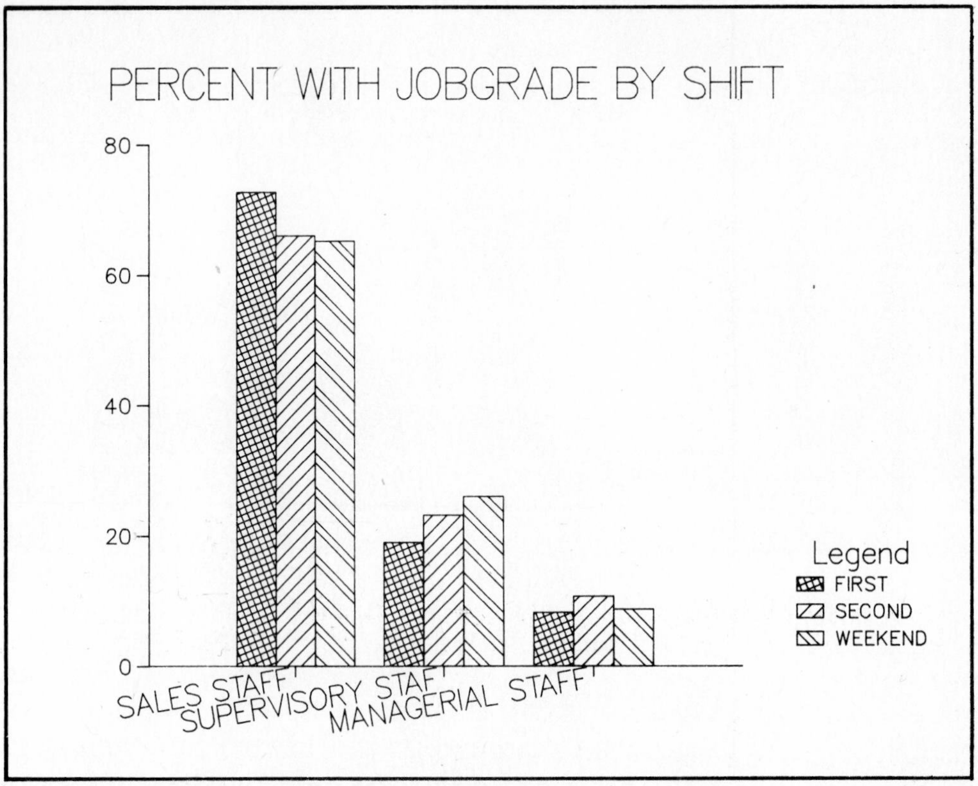

The bar chart in Figure 24.3 uses defaults for all user-controlled attributes such as bar organization, titles, and labels. The default bar organization is to display the bars vertically and to cluster them when there is more than one bar per category. As with the pie chart, the title is constructed from the PLOT specification. Any of these and several other default formatting options can be altered to make the plot display the information in the best possible manner. For instance, you might want to use the BASE AXIS subcommand to relabel the job categories. See Sections 24.23 through 24.41 for the complete range of options and how they affect the plot.

24.4 Overview of the LINECHART Procedure

The SPSS Graphics LINECHART procedure produces many kinds of plots depending on how you manipulate the functions and formats. However, the basic plot is a scatterplot of observed data points or a curve connecting the observed points (or functions such as the mean of the observed values) of cases on two variables. Also, one curve can be drawn for each value of an additional control variable. For example, to plot the mean salary of employees against time with the company for each job grade, specify:

```
LINECHART  PLOT=MEAN(SALARY) WITH TENURE BY JOBGRADE/
```

The plot produced by this command is shown in Figure 24.4. Variable TENURE is the number of months an employee has been with the company. The line chart shows that mean salary levels differ substantially for the three categories and that all tend to rise with length of tenure in the company.

Figure 24.4 A default line chart

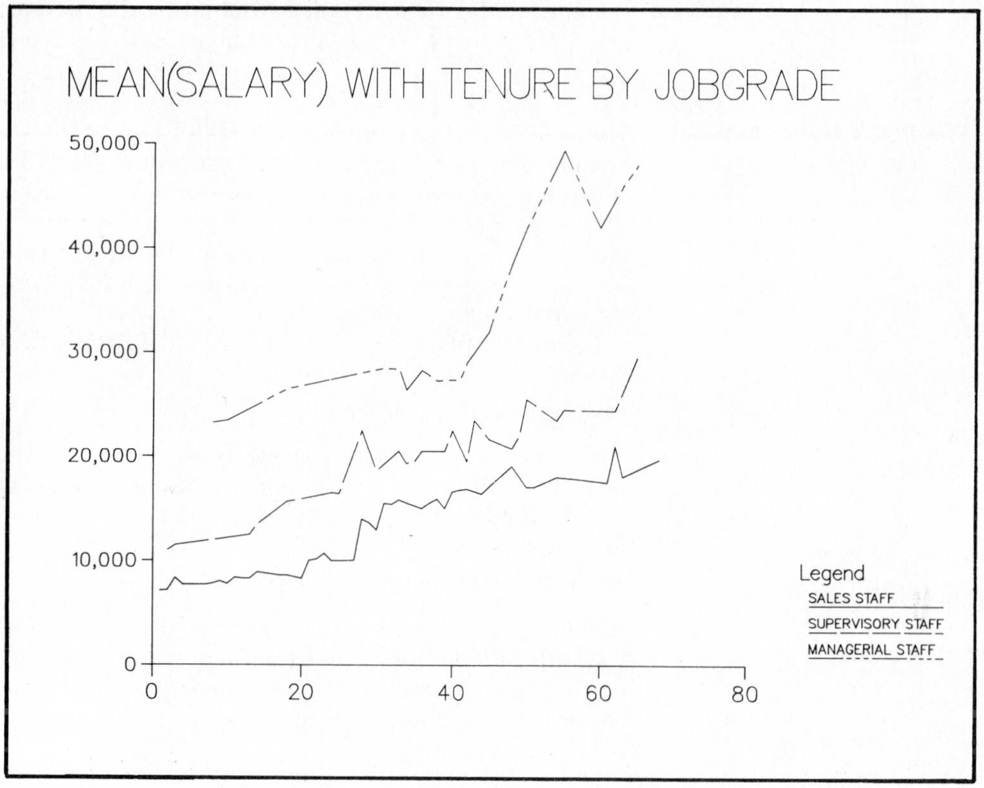

The line chart in Figure 24.4 uses defaults for all user-controlled attributes such as type of curve, axis measures, line markers, titles, and labels. As with the other procedures, the title is constructed from the PLOT specification. The default scales for the X and Y axis variables are based on the observed values and value ranges for the variables, but are unlabeled. Also by default, each point on the chart is connected with straight lines (of different patterns or colors if there is a control variable) and the points are not marked. The default plot attributes can be altered to enhance or change the plot in a number of ways. For instance, you might want to use the X AXIS and Y AXIS subcommands to describe the units. See Sections 24.42 through 24.64 for the complete range of options and how they affect the plot.

24.5 THE PIECHART PROCEDURE

The PIECHART command must include at least one PLOT subcommand to name the variable or variables to be plotted. In addition, PIECHART includes the FORMAT subcommand to control plot quality and contents; TITLE, FOOTNOTE, and COMMENT to control annotation; SEGMENT LABELS to alter default labels for the pie segments; EXPLODE to highlight one or more segments; COLORS and ORDER to select colors and patterns; XPAGE, YPAGE, and FONT to select plot dimensions and type style; MISSING to specify the missing-value treatment; and SAVE to save a file for input to the TELL-A-GRAF package. Subcommand keywords are followed in most cases by an optional equals sign and by specifications and are separated from other subcommands by slashes. Subcommands and their specifications are discussed beginning with the next section.

More than one PLOT subcommand can be specified in a PIECHART command. Unless otherwise altered, all subcommand specifications return to defaults with each new PLOT subcommand. You can establish your own default specifications for subcommands by prefacing the subcommand keyword with DEFAULT, thus eliminating the need for repetitive specifications. Multiple PLOT specifications are discussed in Section 24.19.

24.6 The PLOT Subcommand

The PLOT subcommand for PIECHART names the variables to be plotted, one plot for each variable in a simple variable list. PLOT must be the first subcommand specified. The TO convention for naming a series of variables is not accepted. The variables cannot be alphanumeric; they must be recoded to numeric. Variables need not be integer-valued but should have a limited number of possible values because PIECHART cannot accommodate more than 15 distinct values.

For example, to see the distribution of employees within job categories, specify:

```
PIECHART  PLOT=JOBGRADE/
```

The single pie chart produced by this command is shown in Figure 24.2. It accepts the default specifications for all other subcommands.

To display two pie charts, one for job categories and one for shift assignment, specify:

```
PIECHART  PLOT=JOBGRADE,SHIFT/
```

All changes to default labels, patterns, order, and so forth, described in the following sections are made subsequent to the PLOT subcommand and apply to both variables. For an alternative allowing you to define each plot separately, see the discussion of multiple PLOT subcommands beginning with Section 24.19.

24.7 Keyword BY

To request separate pie charts for each value of a control variable, use keyword BY. The BY keyword modifies all variables in the PLOT= list. For example, instead of a single pie chart for job categories for the whole company, you can display the same information for each of two stores:

```
PIECHART  PLOT=JOBGRADE BY STORE/
```

Figure 24.7 Pie charts from a control variable

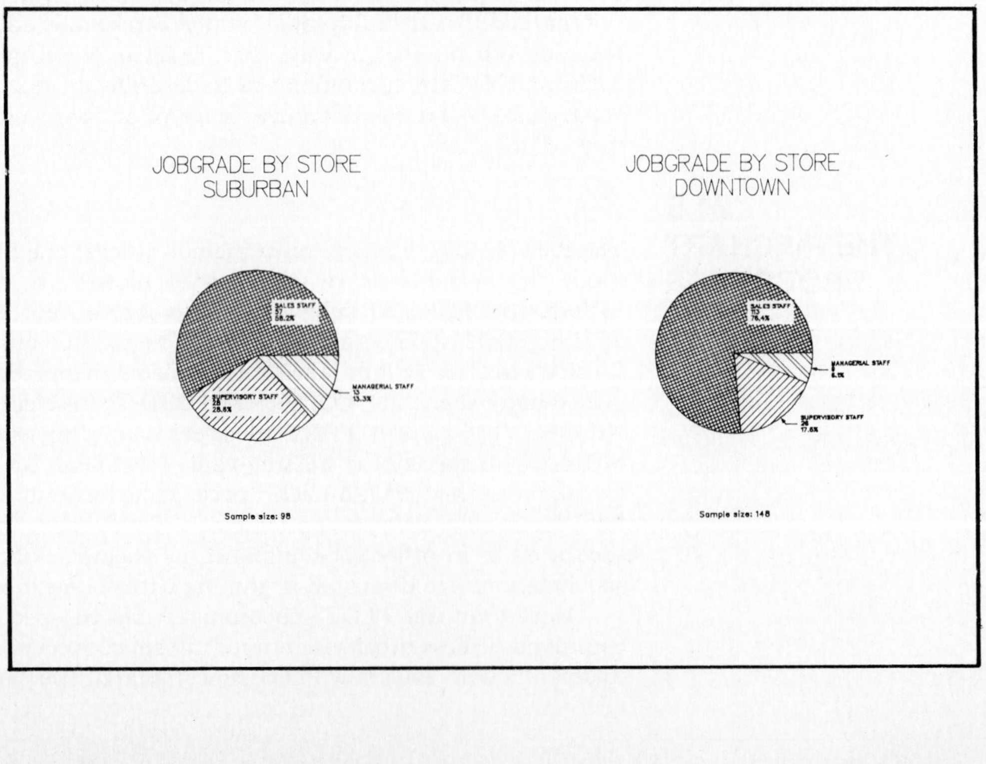

This command produces the two pie charts shown in Figure 24.7, the first for the suburban store (value 1 of STORE) and the second for the downtown store. The difference in the size of the managerial categories between the two stores becomes apparent. See Section 24.21 for a discussion of an alternative method of specifying these two pie charts to take advantage of the postprocessor.

24.8 Selectors

Each variable named in the PLOT subcommand can be followed by parentheses enclosing a selector which consists of a logical operator and a value or list of values, as in STORE(EQ 1). Relational operators are LT, LE, EQ, NE, GE, and GT, which mean respectively less than, less than or equal to, equal to, not equal to, greater than or equal to, and greater than. If you omit the logical operator, EQ is assumed. EQ and NE can be followed by a list of numbers where (EQ 1,2,3) means equal to 1, 2, or 3, and (NE 1,2,3) means not equal to 1, 2, and 3. All other operators are followed by a single value. If a case satisfies the condition, it is used in constructing the chart.

For example, to produce a pie chart showing the number and percentage of employees in each job category for just the first store, specify STORE(EQ 1), or, since EQ is assumed,

```
PIECHART  PLOT=JOBGRADE BY STORE(1)/
```

To limit the same pie chart to include only supervisors and managers (values 2 and 3), specify either JOBGRADE(EQ 2,3) or

```
PIECHART  PLOT=JOBGRADE(2,3) BY STORE(1)/
```

If you want to limit the plot to certain values of a control variable but produce a single plot rather than one for each value of the control variable, specify keyword COMBINE on the FORMAT subcommand (Section 24.9). For example, if STORE has several values and you want a single chart combining stores 1 and 2, specify:

```
PIECHART  PLOT=JOBGRADE BY STORE(1,2)/FORMAT=COMBINE/
```

24.9 The FORMAT Subcommand

You can specify the quality and contents of the pie charts using the FORMAT subcommand. Quality refers to the type of characters used, the density of certain lines drawn, and the first pattern used. You can also control the order in which the segments are displayed and whether percentages or counts for each segment are printed. If a keyword is preceded by NO, the opposite effect takes place. Valid keyword specifications (with defaults indicated with asterisks) for the FORMAT subcommand are

SIMPLE* *Produce a simple plot.* Single-stroke characters are drawn and pattern 1 is cross-hatched instead of solid (Section 24.14). Special fonts are not available. This is equivalent to NO FANCY.

FANCY *Produce a fancy plot.* Double-stroke characters are drawn by default and special fonts are available. Pattern 1 is solid. This is equivalent to NO SIMPLE.

PERCENT* *Display the percentage for each segment.* To turn percents off, specify NO PERCENT.

COUNT* *Display the frequency count for each segment.* To turn counts off, specify NO COUNT.

SORT *Display the segments in order of increasing frequency.* The segments are displayed smallest to largest starting from the three o'clock position moving counterclockwise. The default is NO SORT, which means that the segments are displayed in ascending value order.

COMBINE *Combine values specified in the selector for BY variables on the PLOT subcommand.* One pie chart is created combining all specified values rather than a separate pie chart for each value.

DUMP *Dump the data values to the file specified on the PROCEDURE OUTPUT command* (see Chapter 17). Each pie is a set of data and each data set is preceded by a record containing PIE *nn* starting in column 2, where *nn* is the number of the pie chart. The data set is composed of data pairs of segment number and segment count written in (1X,6G13.6) format. The default is NO DUMP.

Thus, the default pie chart is SIMPLE, PERCENT, COUNT, and NO SORT, as can be seen in Figure 24.2. To produce the same plot ordered by frequency count and with increased quality, specify:

```
PIECHART  PLOT=JOBGRADE/FORMAT=FANCY,SORT/
```

The effects of these format changes are shown in Figure 24.18.

24.10 The TITLE, FOOTNOTE, and COMMENT Subcommands

Three subcommands define the character strings displayed as text lines above the pie chart (TITLE), below the pie chart (FOOTNOTE), and vertically along the lower left edge of the plot (COMMENT). Each subcommand can specify up to three strings of 50 characters each according to the general SPSS^X rules for specifying literals (see Chapter 2). Each string defines one line in the title, footnote, or comment. As shown in Figure 24.2, the default title for a pie chart is taken from the PLOT subcommand specification. The default footnote is the sample size and the default comment is null. If you want to alter the default title and footnote, specify:

```
PIECHART  PLOT=JOBGRADE/ FORMAT=FANCY,SORT/
  TITLE='CHICAGO HOME FURNISHING'
        'Employee Study - Sales Department'/
  FOOTNOTE='As of December 1980'/
```

The effects of these subcommands are shown in Figure 24.18.

SPSS Graphics chooses the size and positioning of the annotation depending on the number and length of strings. These decisions are made for you so you won't have to repeatedly produce the same plot in order to arrive at an acceptable format. However, you can control the size and positioning by entering blank strings of various lengths before or after the one or two strings you want displayed, as long as you don't exceed three strings. For example, if you want the footnote to appear higher above the plot border than is shown in Figure 24.2, specify:

```
FOOTNOTE='As of December 1980' ' '/
```

If you intend to place multiple plots on the same page using the post-processor, see Section 24.21 for a discussion of how to use alternative labels.

24.11 Controlling the Segments

You can control how the pie segments are displayed by altering the default labels, by causing one or more of the segments to be "exploded" out from the center of the pie for emphasis, and by specifying the combination of pattern and color PIECHART uses for each segment.

24.12 The SEGMENT LABELS Subcommand

By default, PIECHART labels the pie chart segments with the value labels. If a value label is not available, the segment is labeled with the variable name followed by an equals sign and the value. To override those defaults specify each value in parentheses followed by a string of up to 20 characters according to SPSS^X rules for entering literals, as in:

```
PIECHART  PLOT=JOBGRADE/ FORMAT=FANCY,SORT/
  TITLE='CHICAGO HOME FURNISHING'
       'Employee Study - Sales Department'/
  FOOTNOTE='As of December 1980' ' '/
  SEGMENT LABELS=(1)'Salesclerks' (2)'Supervisors' (3)'Managers'/
```

The effect of altering the default segment labels is shown in Figure 24.18.

Along with the size of the segment and whether percents and/or counts are displayed (see Section 24.9), the length of the label affects PIECHART's decision to place annotation inside or outside the segment. The size of the pie drawn varies depending on how many labels must appear outside the segments.

24.13 The EXPLODE Subcommand

To emphasize one or more of the segments of a pie chart, indicate the value or values in the EXPLODE subcommand. PIECHART shifts the indicated segments outward along the radius of the pie. For example, to emphasize the relative size of the managerial job grade, specify:

```
PIECHART  PLOT=JOBGRADE/ FORMAT=FANCY,SORT/
  TITLE='CHICAGO HOME FURNISHING'
       'Employee Study - Sales Department'/
  FOOTNOTE='As of December 1980' ' '/
  SEGMENT LABELS=(1)'Salesclerks' (2)'Supervisors' (3)'Managers'/
  EXPLODE=3/
```

See Figure 24.18 for the result of exploding the segment corresponding to value 3 of variable JOBGRADE. By default, no segments are exploded.

24.14 The ORDER Subcommand

The ORDER subcommand controls the order in which PIECHART uses patterns from those shown in Figure 24.14. For FORMAT=FANCY, the patterns are the same as for SIMPLE except that pattern 1 is solid instead of cross-hatched. By default, patterns are applied in ascending numerical order to the variable values, also in ascending numerical order. Thus, specifying the SORT keyword in the FORMAT subcommand does not affect which segment gets which pattern, and patterns are consistent across multiple pie charts produced for values of a control variable (Section 24.7).

To choose your own patterns, use the ORDER subcommand to specify the pattern numbers in variable value order. For example, to apply patterns 5, 2, and 1 to the segments corresponding to values 1, 2, and 3 of variable JOBGRADE, specify:

```
PIECHART  PLOT=JOBGRADE/ FORMAT=FANCY,SORT/
  TITLE='CHICAGO HOME FURNISHING'
       'Employee Study - Sales Department'/
  FOOTNOTE='As of December 1980' ' '/
  SEGMENT LABELS=(1)'Salesclerks' (2)'Supervisors'
                 (3)'Managers'/
  EXPLODE=3/ ORDER=5,2,1/
```

Enter pattern numbers from 1 to 15 for the segments you want to alter, even if you might be respecifying the default value for a particular segment. If you specify fewer pattern numbers than there are segments, the remaining segments have the default patterns in the original sequence. That is, with ORDER=5,2,1, the next pattern numbers are 4,5,6, and so forth. If you specify more (up to 15 with COLORS=0), the remainder are not used. The effect of choosing a different pattern compared to the default patterns shown in Figure 24.2 is shown in Figure 24.18. You can select the same pattern for different segments by repeating its order number.

24.15 The COLORS Subcommand

To produce color plots, you must know how many colors the device supports in addition to black. A black-and-white device supports zero additional colors, an eight-pen plotter supports seven additional colors. The default specification for the COLORS subcommand is 0.

Figure 24.14 The PIECHART patterns

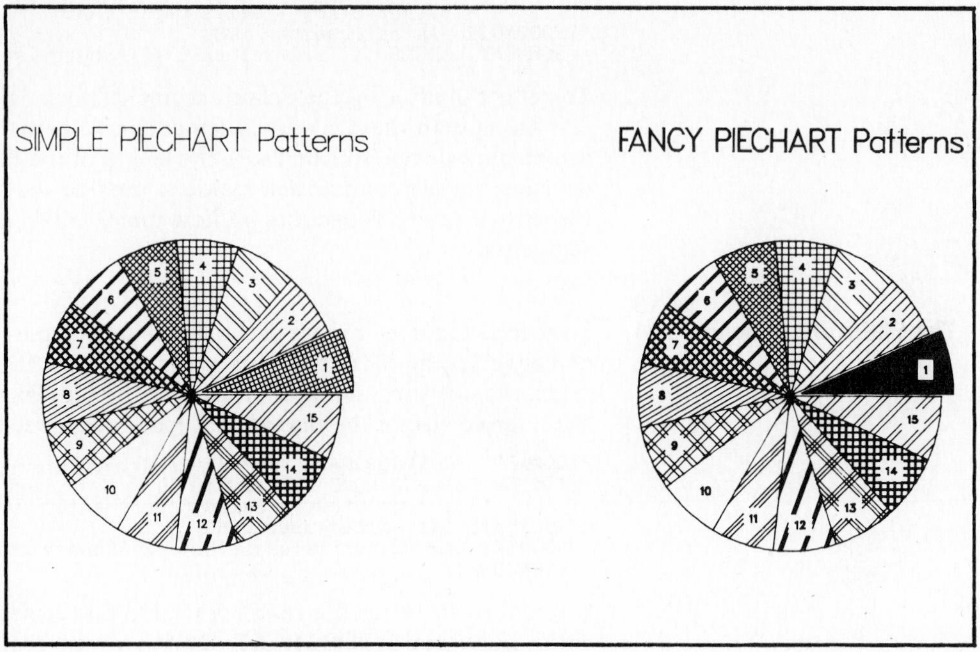

If you intend to produce your pie chart on a four-color device, to take advantage of the three additional colors, specify:

```
COLORS=3/
```

Table 24.15 The ORDER/COLORS interaction

COLORS=2	Pattern	COLORS=3	Pattern
	1 2 3 4 5 6 7 8 9...		**1 2 3 4 5 6 7 8 9...**
Red	1 3 5 7 9 11 13 15 17 . . .	**Red**	1 4 7 10 13 16 19 22 25 . . .
Green	2 4 6 8 10 12 14 16 18 . . .	**Green**	2 5 8 11 14 17 20 23 26 . . .
		Blue	3 6 9 12 15 18 21 24 27 . . .

If you specify more than zero colors, you can use ORDER numbers greater than 15. PIECHART uses the additional colors to draw the segments, generating patterns in an expanded order compared to that documented in Section 24.14. To determine the color/pattern associated with a given ORDER number, generate a matrix of order numbers with colors as the rows and patterns as the columns. For example, if you have COLORS=3 (red, green, blue), your matrix looks like the second matrix in Table 24.15. Note that pattern 1 is solid only for FORMAT=FANCY. Therefore, if you want the segments to begin with solid colors, you must request a FANCY plot (see Section 24.9).

For instance, look at the FANCY order of black-and-white patterns shown in Figure 24.14. Assume that you have three additional colors that correspond to red, green, and blue and that ORDER is left to the default order. The segment of a pie corresponding to the lowest value of the variable is drawn with the first additional color and the first pattern, thus making it solid red. The second and third segments corresponding to the second and third highest values of the variable are solid green and solid blue, respectively. The fourth, fifth, and sixth segments are drawn with red, green, and blue stripes, respectively, according to pattern 2. However, specifying ORDER=1,2,3,13,14,15 generates the same first three solid color segments, but selects pattern 5 for the fourth, fifth, and sixth segments (see Table 24.15). Therefore, on a color device, to predict the display pattern of a segment, you must know the order of the segment, the number and order of the additional colors, the order of the patterns, and whether the plot is FANCY or SIMPLE.

You can specify a pattern more than once in the ORDER subcommand if COLORS is greater than zero, but you must do it from your matrix of order numbers based on color and pattern. For example, with ORDER=1,2,1,2 and COLORS=2 (e.g., red and green), the first four segments are solid red, solid green, solid red, and solid green, respectively (with FORMAT=FANCY).

24.16 The FONT Subcommand

If you specify FORMAT=FANCY, you can choose among four fonts: DUPLEX, COMPLEX, TRIPLEX, and GOTHIC. Examples of these styles are in Figure 24.16. Your choice of font applies to all annotation in the graph except the comment line, which is always duplex when FORMAT=FANCY.

Figure 24.16 Optional fonts for FORMAT=FANCY

SPSS Graphics Duplex Font

SPSS Graphics Complex Font

SPSS Graphics Triplex Font

SPSS Graphics Gothic Font

24.17 The XPAGE and YPAGE Subcommands

SPSS Graphics constructs plots to fit on a page 8½ inches high by 11 inches wide, though the Graphics Postprocesser adjusts the actual size to fit the output device. To change the default page dimensions, use the XPAGE subcommand to control width and the YPAGE subcommand to control height. For example, to create your chart on a page 11 inches high by 8½ inches wide, specify:

```
YPAGE=11/XPAGE=8.5/
```

The proportions of the chart itself are not changed, though its size is adjusted to fit within the defined dimensions. The Graphics Postprocessor takes page dimensions into account when combining plots on one page.

24.18 The MISSING Subcommand

By default, PIECHART does not include a case in calculating the segments of a pie if the case has missing values on either the variable being plotted or the control variable. You can alter the default by using the MISSING subcommand with one of the following keyword specifications.

PIEWISE* *Omit cases with missing values on the plot or the control variable.* If more than one plot variable is specified in the PLOT subcommand, each is treated separately with regard to missing-value treatment. Therefore, each pie chart could be based on a different set of cases.

PLOTWISE *Omit cases with missing values on any plot variable or on the control variables.* All pie charts produced from the PLOT command are based on the same cases.

NONE *Include all cases regardless of missing values.*

For example, if you want PIECHART to ignore missing-data declarations for all variables specified in the PLOT subcommand, use keyword NONE. Clerical and other staff (JOBGRADE=4) are declared missing to SPSS and therefore were omitted from the pie chart shown in Figure 24.2, perhaps to separate support personnel from the rest of the staff. To include them in the final display, specify:

```
PIECHART  PLOT=JOBGRADE/ FORMAT=FANCY,SORT/
  TITLE='CHICAGO HOME FURNISHING'
       'Employee Study - Sales Department'/
  FOOTNOTE='As of December 1980' ' '/
  SEGMENT LABELS=(1)'Salesclerks' (2)'Supervisors'
                 (3)'Managers' (4)'Support'/
  EXPLODE=3/ ORDER=5,2,1,10/ MISSING=NONE/
```

The plot produced by this command is shown in Figure 24.18. Note that the additional segment label and the additional pattern were added to account for the inclusion of the missing value. If these additions were not specified, the segment label would have defaulted to the value label, as indicated in Section 24.12, and the pattern would have been pattern 4 from Figure 24.14 instead of the completely blank pattern selected with number 10.

Figure 24.18 An enhanced pie chart

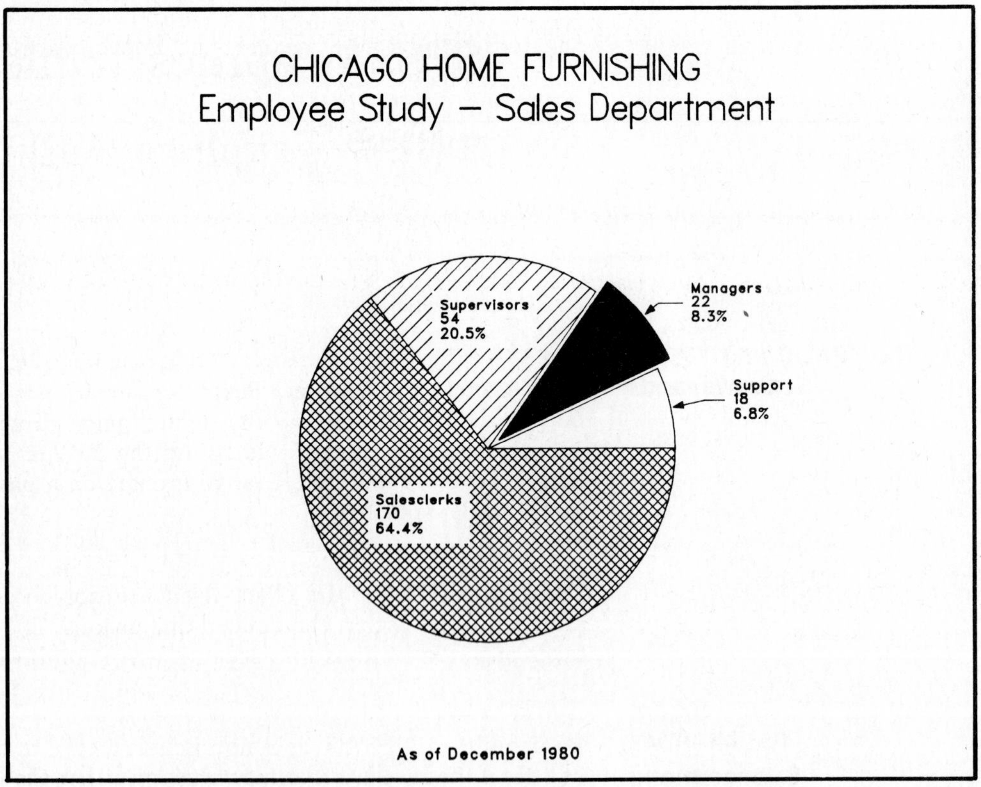

The difference between PIEWISE and PLOTWISE missing-value treatments arises only if you specify more than one plot variable on the PLOT subcommand. That is, if you specify:

```
PIECHART  PLOT=JOBGRADE,DIVISION,SHIFT/
```

ANNOTATED EXAMPLE FOR PIECHART

The data for this example come from an SPSS^X system file that contains information about 264 employees in a fictitious furniture sales company. The variable JOBGRADE assigns each employee to one of four categories: sales staff, supervisory staff, managerial staff, and support staff. The fourth category has been declared missing so that support staff will not appear in staff analyses unless specifically included with a missing-value specification. The task is to develop a presentation-quality plot of the number and percentage of employees in each of the four job categories.

```
FILE HANDLE  EMPLOYEE/ file specifications
GET  FILE=EMPLOYEE

FILE HANDLE  EMPPLOT1/ file specifications
GRAPHICS OUTPUT  OUTFILE=EMPPLOT1

PIECHART  PLOT=JOBGRADE/ FORMAT=FANCY,SORT/
  TITLE='CHICAGO HOME FURNISHING'
        'Employee Study - Sales Department'/
  FOOTNOTE='As of December 1980' ' '/
  SEGMENT LABELS=(1)'Salesclerks' (2)'Supervisors'
                 (3)'Managers' (4)'Support'/
  EXPLODE=3/ MISSING=NONE/
  COLORS=3/ ORDER=1,2,3,13/
```

- The first FILE HANDLE command defines the system file accessed by the GET command.
- The second FILE HANDLE command defines the output file named on the GRAPHICS OUTPUT command. This is the *intermediate file* to be accessed by the Graphics Postprocessor (see Section 24.66).
- The PLOT subcommand names the variable JOBGRADE, whose values define the segments of the pie chart. The relative frequency of each value determines the size of the segment for that value (see Section 24.6).
- The FORMAT subcommand specifies a fancy plot in which characters are double-stroked and the first shading pattern for each color is solid. The FORMAT subcommand also requests that the pie segments be sorted in order of frequency. Without the SORT specification, pie segments appear in the order of the values (see Section 24.9).
- The TITLE and FOOTNOTE subcommands define a two-line title and a two-line footnote for the chart. Each line is specified as a separate literal (see Chapter 2). The null second line of the footnote is specified simply to raise the first line higher above the frame of the plot (see Section 24.10).
- The SEGMENT LABELS subcommand assigns labels to each value of variable JOBGRADE and thus to each segment of the pie chart. By default PIECHART uses the value labels, if available, or else the variable name and value (see Section 24.12).
- The EXPLODE subcommand identifies a segment to be "exploded" out along the radius of the pie (see Section 24.13).
- The MISSING subcommand overrides the default missing-value treatment, which is to exclude cases with missing values (see Section 24.18).
- The COLORS subcommand specifies three colors, in addition to black, to be used to draw the plot. These are whatever colors are available as the first, second, and third colors on the graphics device—red, green, and blue in the case of the plotter used for this example (see Section 24.15).
- The ORDER subcommand selects the order in which combinations of color and pattern are applied to the segments (see Section 24.14).

The output from these commands is the pie chart on the inside front cover of this manual.

a plot is produced first for JOBGRADE with cases omitted if they are missing data for job grade, a second plot is produced for DIVISION with cases omitted with missing division information, and so forth. Instead, if you specify

```
PIECHART          PLOT=JOBGRADE,DIVISION,SHIFT/ MISSING=PLOTWISE
```

the three pie charts are produced, but this time cases are omitted if they are missing data on any of the three variables.

24.19 Multiple PLOT Subcommands

More than one PLOT subcommand can be specified in a PIECHART command. This is helpful particularly when some attributes are common to all plots. However, some attributes may be specific to each plot. Because a second and subsequent PLOT subcommand returns all other subcommands to their defaults, either you have to respecify all attributes following each PLOT subcommand or establish your own defaults and respecify only unique attributes. By specifying the keyword DEFAULT before any of the attribute subcommands FORMAT, TITLE, FOOTNOTE, COMMENT, EXPLODE, ORDER, COLORS, FONT, XPAGE, YPAGE, or MISSING, you establish the default specifications for the duration of the PIECHART command.

In the complete example shown in Section 24.18, you might want to add a PLOT command to generate a pie chart of the division to which each of the employees in the sales department is assigned. If you simply enter a PLOT=DIVISION subcommand following the last subcommand affecting the previous plot, the pie chart for the variable specified will look very much like the plot shown in Figure 24.2 because all other subcommands return to defaults. A better approach is to decide which of the subcommands for the first PLOT subcommand are also applicable to the second and then to make those the defaults. All other subcommands specific to the second plot (shown in Figure 24.19) are then specified.

Figure 24.19 The pie chart from the second PLOT subcommand

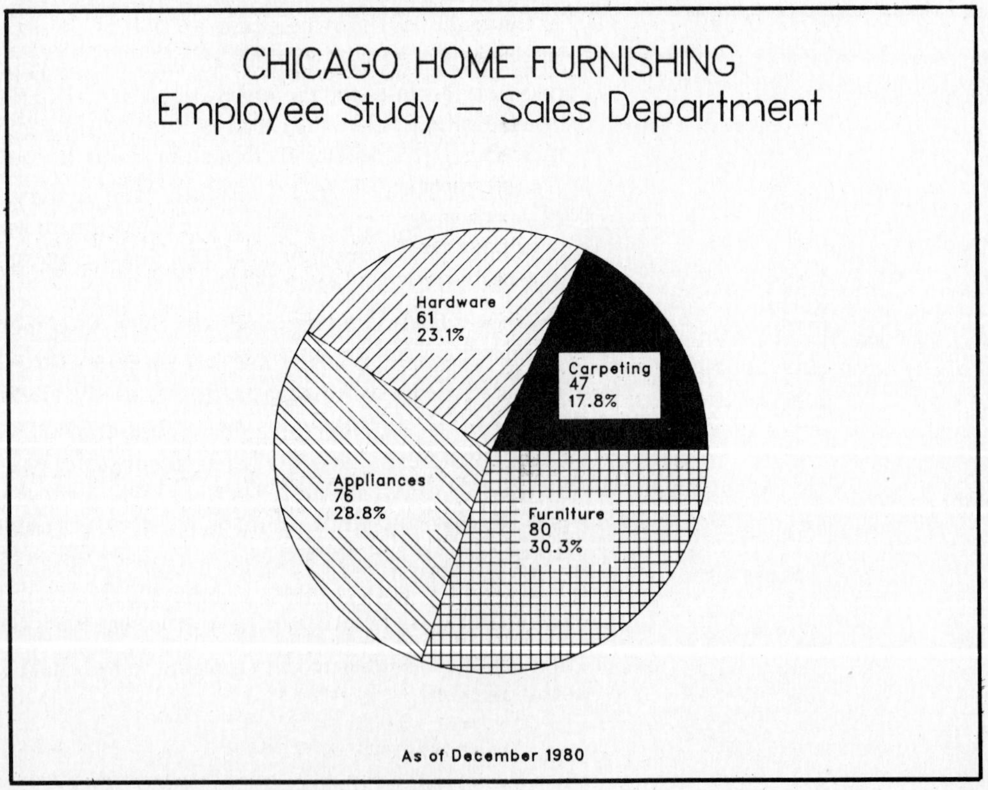

If you want the plot quality the same and also want the segments sorted, the first subcommand you want to establish as the default is the FORMAT subcommand. Because the company, store, department, and date produced are the same, the TITLE and FOOTNOTE specifications apply to both plots. Finally, because you want the other staff included in both parts, the MISSING=NONE specification should also apply to both plots (see the example command below).

For the second plot, you want to specify different segment labels. You prefer to have no segment exploded and want PIECHART to use the default segment patterns. Therefore, you specify SEGMENT LABELS following the second PLOT subcommand and leave out the EXPLODE and ORDER subcommands so they return to their defaults. Therefore, the complete command that produces both the plot shown in Figure 24.18 and the one shown in Figure 24.19 is

```
PIECHART  PLOT=JOBGRADE/ DEFAULT FORMAT=FANCY,SORT/
  DEFAULT TITLE='CHICAGO HOME FURNISHING'
        'Employee Study - Sales Department'/
  DEFAULT FOOTNOTE='As of December 1980' ' '/
  SEGMENT LABELS=(1)'Salesclerks' (2)'Supervisors'
                 (3)'Managers' (4)'Support'/
  EXPLODE=3/ ORDER=5,2,1,10/
  DEFAULT MISSING=NONE/
   PLOT=DIVISION/
   SEGMENT LABELS=(1)'Carpeting' (2)'Appliances'
                  (3)'Furniture' (4)'Hardware'/
```

24.20 Special Plotting Applications

There are some general considerations in deciding how to approach your plotting tasks that apply equally to PIECHART, BARCHART, and LINECHART, or to combinations of the three. Two of these considerations—anticipating multiple plots per page and entering aggregate data—are presented in the following sections.

24.21 Anticipating Multiple Plots per Page

If you intend to use the SPSS Graphics Postprocessor (Section 24.67) to place your plots on the same page, you might consider alternative ways of specifying the individual plots. The most obvious example is to use the TITLE subcommand to describe each plot and use the titling option in the postprocessor to assign the general title. With specific regard to pie charts, you would probably want to run separate PLOT subcommands for each value of the control variable in order to take advantage of TITLE or FOOTNOTE to describe the specific subpopulations. For example, to label the charts shown in Figure 24.7 and to enhance them fully as shown for the single pie chart in 24.18, specify:

```
PIECHART  PLOT=JOBGRADE BY STORE(1)/
  DEFAULT FORMAT=FANCY,SORT/
  TITLE='Sales Department' 'Suburban Store'/
  DEFAULT FOOTNOTE='As of December 1980' ' '/
  DEFAULT SEGMENT LABELS=(1)'Salesclerks'
          (2)'Supervisors' (3)'Managers' (4)'Support'/
  DEFAULT EXPLODE=3/
  DEFAULT ORDER=5,2,1,10/
  DEFAULT MISSING=NONE/
  PLOT=JOBGRADE BY STORE(2)/
  TITLE='Sales Department' 'Downtown Store'/
```

The plots are then put on the same page using the postprocessor, producing Figure 24.21.

Figure 24.21 Multiple plots on a page

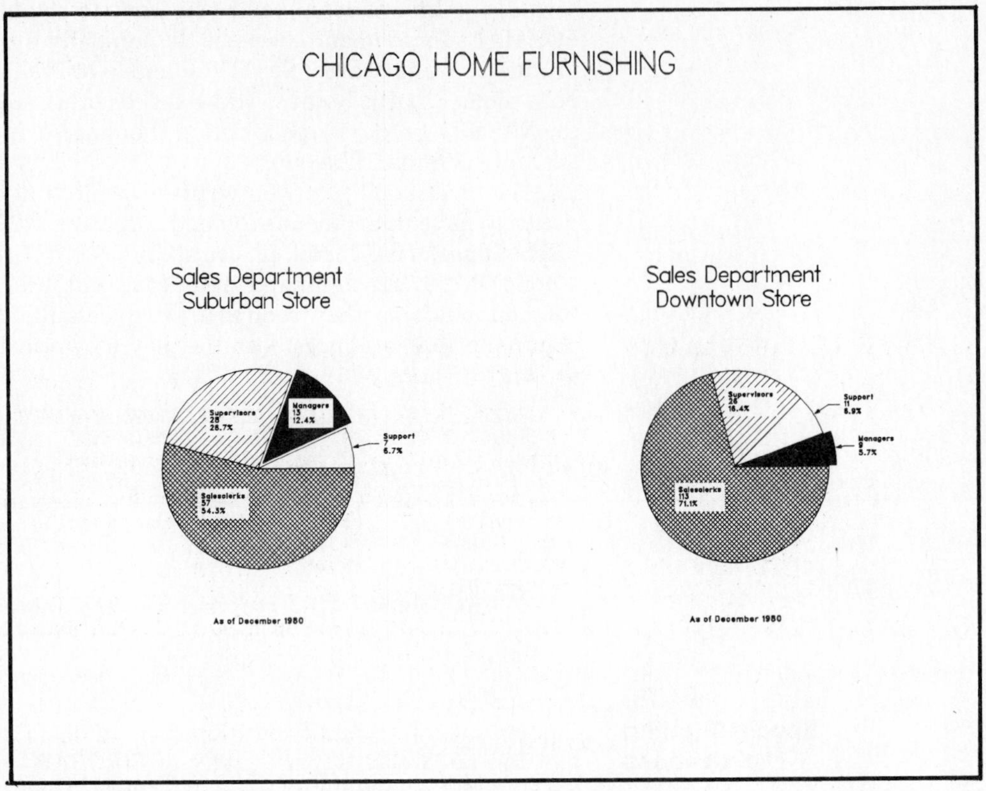

24.22 Entering Aggregate Data for Plots

Sometimes it may be more efficient to use already computed data rather than to go back to the raw data for presentation plots. You can enter computed values and use the WEIGHT command. For example, to reproduce the pie chart shown in Figure 24.18, enter one data line per segment. The complete SPSS command setup with the data is

```
TITLE  'ENTERING COMPUTED DATA'
DATA LIST  /1 JOBGRADE 1 JWEIGHT 3-5
WEIGHT BY JWEIGHT
PIECHART  PLOT=JOBGRADE/ FORMAT=FANCY,SORT/
  TITLE='CHICAGO HOME FURNISHING'
        'Employee Study - Sales Department'/
  FOOTNOTE='As of December 1980' ' '/
  SEGMENT LABELS=(1)'Salesclerks' (2)'Supervisors'
                 (3)'Managers' (4)'Support'/
  EXPLODE=3/ ORDER=5,2,1,10/
BEGIN DATA
1 170
2  54
3  22
4  18
END DATA
```

24.23 THE BARCHART PROCEDURE

The BARCHART command must include at least one PLOT subcommand to identify the function (count, percent, mean, and so forth) and to name the variable or variables to be plotted. In addition, BARCHART includes the FORMAT subcommand to control plot quality and contents; TITLE, FOOTNOTE, and COMMENT to control annotation; BASE AXIS and SIDE AXIS to label and define the axis parameters; LEGEND TITLE and LEGEND LABELS to provide a title and labels for the legend; COLORS and ORDER to control colors and patterns; XPAGE, YPAGE, and FONT to select plot dimensions and type style; and MISSING to select the missing-value treatment; and SAVE, which allows you to save a file for input to the TELL-A-GRAF package. Subcommand keywords are followed in most cases by an optional equals sign and by specifications and are separated from other subcommands by slashes.

More than one PLOT subcommand can be specified in a BARCHART command. Unless otherwise altered, all subcommand specifications return to defaults with each new PLOT subcommand. You can establish your own defaults by prefacing the subcommand keyword with DEFAULT, thus eliminating the need for repetitive specifications. Multiple PLOT specifications are discussed beginning with Section 24.41.

24.24 The PLOT Subcommand

The PLOT subcommand for BARCHART defines the function and names the variable or variables for which a bar chart is produced. The PLOT subcommand for BARCHART is divided into three parts:

- The required *function* part names the function (and the variable when appropriate) that determines the length of the bars, thus controlling the *side axis*.
- The required *WITH* part names the variable or variables whose categories determine the number of bars or bar sets, thus controlling the *base axis*.
- The optional *BY* part subdivides each bar into a set of bars according to the categories of a *control variable*.

In the example from Section 24.3,

```
BARCHART  PLOT=PERCENT WITH JOBGRADE BY SHIFT/
```

PERCENT is the function that determines the side axis scale and therefore the length of each bar. The actual number of bars is determined by the number of values in both JOBGRADE and SHIFT. JOBGRADE controls the number of sets of bars, and its values and labels form the base axis. SHIFT controls the number of bars in each set, and its values and labels appear in the legend. As the plot produced by this example shows in Figure 24.3, JOBGRADE is described in three sets of bars and SHIFT is described by three bars in each set.

PLOT must be the first subcommand specified. None of the variables named can be alphanumeric; they must be recoded to numeric. The base axis variable or variables named in the WITH part need not be integer-valued but should have a limited number of possible cells because each value or combination of values is represented by one bar (or set of bars in a controlled plot). In any case, BARCHART cannot accommodate more than 100 bars or sets of bars. Likewise, the variable or variables named in the BY part need not be integer-valued but can have no more than 15 possible values.

24.25 The Function and WITH Specifications

The first required part of the PLOT subcommand is the name of a function that establishes the side axis. If the function is a count or a percentage, there is no variable named. If the function is a mean or a sum, the name of the variable is enclosed in parentheses following the function keyword. Functions are

COUNT	*Plot cell frequencies.*
CCOUNT	*Plot the cumulative frequency across cells.*
PERCENT	*Plot cell percentages.*
CPERCENT	*Plot the cumulative percentage across cells.*
MEAN(varname)	*Plot cell means of the variable.*
SUM(varname)	*Plot cell sums of the variable.*
CSUM(varname)	*Plot the cumulative sum of the variable across cells.*

The function part is usually followed immediately by the keyword WITH and the name of the variable whose values form the cells and therefore determine the number of bars on the base axis. This completes the minimum required syntax of the PLOT subcommand in BARCHART. For example, to compare the mean length of time employees have been with the company, specify:

```
BARCHART  PLOT=MEAN(TENURE) WITH JOBGRADE/
```

The function selected is the MEAN and the dependent variable is TENURE, which is the length of time an employee has been with the company measured in months. The WITH part names variable JOBGRADE, which means that one bar is produced for each job grade. The plot produced by this example is developed in the next section by adding a control variable.

24.26 Keyword BY

Adding a control variable is simply a matter of specifying the keyword BY followed by the control variable, as in

```
BARCHART  PLOT=MEAN(TENURE) WITH JOBGRADE BY SHIFT/
```

The plot produced by this command is shown in Figure 24.26. It accepts defaults for all other BARCHART subcommands. To see this example fully developed as the discussion of altering the default specifications for the other subcommands progresses, pick up the discussion beginning with Section 24.30. To see the complete syntax possibilities for the PLOT subcommand, see the following sections on qualifying each variable named with a selector, on specifying multiple variables within each part, and on specifying cross-products.

Figure 24.26 A default bar chart with cell means

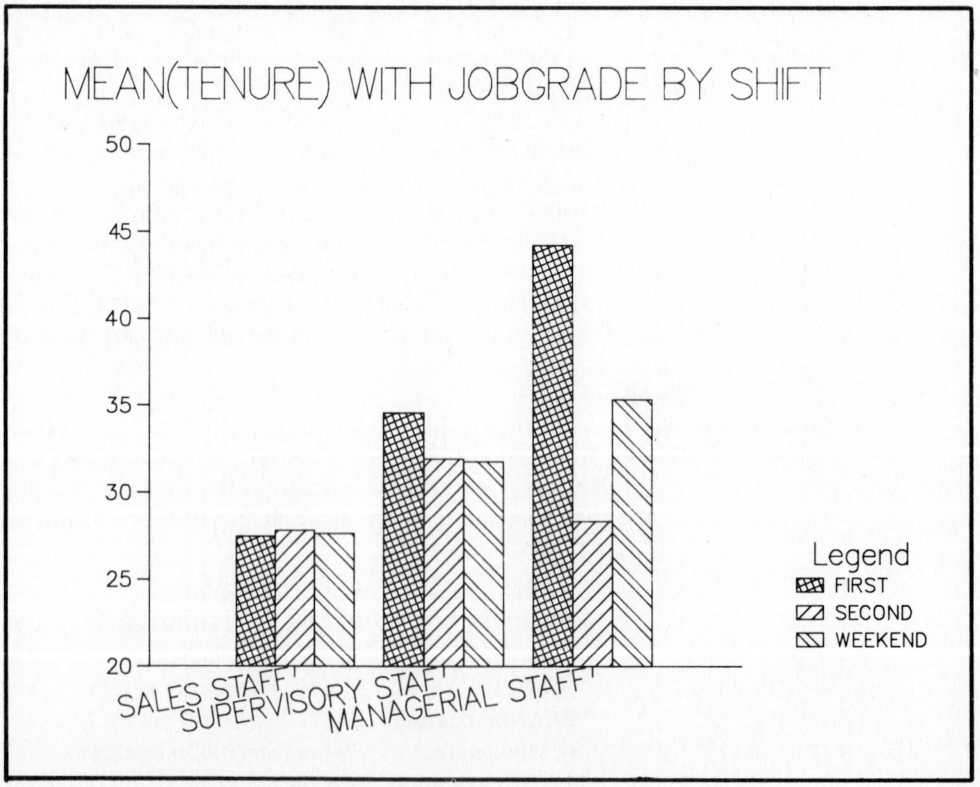

24.27 Selectors

Each variable named in the function, WITH, and BY parts of the PLOT subcommand can be followed by parentheses enclosing a selector which consists of a logical operator and a value or list of values, as in SHIFT(NE 3). Relational operators are LT, LE, EQ, NE, GE, and GT which mean respectively less than, less than or equal to, equal to, not equal to, greater than or equal to, and greater than. If you omit the logical operator, EQ is assumed. EQ and NE can be followed by a list of numbers where (EQ 1,2,3) means equal to 1, 2, or 3, and (NE 1,2,3) means not equal to 1, 2, and 3. All other operators are followed by a single value. If a case satisfies the condition, it is used in constructing the bar chart specified.

For example, to produce a bar chart of the mean tenure of only the first shift within job categories, specify SHIFT(EQ 1) in the BY part. Or, because the EQ operator is assumed if none is included in the parentheses, specify:

```
BARCHART  PLOT=MEAN(TENURE) WITH JOBGRADE BY SHIFT(1)/
```

To limit the same bar chart to include only supervisors and managers (values 2 and 3), specify either JOBGRADE(EQ 2,3) or

```
BARCHART  PLOT=MEAN(TENURE) WITH JOBGRADE(2,3) BY SHIFT(1)/
```

If you want the bar chart to be limited to those who have been with the company at least one year, specify:

```
BARCHART  PLOT=MEAN(TENURE(GE 12)) WITH JOBGRADE BY SHIFT/
```

Because the variable named in the function part is already enclosed in parentheses, the selector for that variable must be included within those parentheses as shown in this example.

24.28 Multiple Variables

The PLOT subcommand for BARCHART produces a single plot regardless of the number of variables named in the PLOT subcommand. That is, while more than one variable can be specified in the function and WITH parts (not the BY part) of the PLOT specification, multiple variables cause changes in the organization of a single plot; they do not produce multiple plots. For instance, the specification

```
BARCHART  PLOT=MEAN(TENURE) WITH JOBGRADE,DIVISION BY SHIFT/
```

produces a bar chart whose base axis is divided into two separated charts, the first for job categories and the second for the departmental divisions (see Figure 24.33).

You can use the multiple-variable feature to emphasize differences in categories of the base axis variable by introducing the selector. For example, you could cause office staff (value 3 for managers and missing-value 4 for support personnel) and floor staff (supervisors and managers) to be plotted in separate charts on the same plot by specifying

```
BARCHART  PLOT=PERCENT WITH JOBGRADE(GE 3) JOBGRADE(LE 2) BY SHIFT/
  MISSING=NONE/
```

(See Section 24.40 on including missing values.) Note that functions (PERCENT in this example) are calculated separately for the multiple variables. That is, the percents will total to 100 for office staff and for floor staff.

You can also name more than one function to be plotted on the same bar chart, as in PERCENT,CPERCENT WITH VAR1. This provision should be used with caution because the side axis scale must accommodate the minimum and maximum values for each function. That is, you could specify both count and percent for a base axis variable, but while the percent can only range from zero to 100, the count's minimum and maximum could be greater than 100, or very small. Likewise, you can specify that the mean of two dependent variables be plotted in the same bar chart, as in MEAN(VAR1,VAR2); but unless the two variables have similar values, the scales may be badly matched.

The result of multiple function specifications is represented in bar sets within categories of the base axis variable in the same manner as for a control variable. That is, the specification

```
BARCHART  PLOT=MEAN(TENURE,JTENURE) WITH JOBGRADE/
```

Figure 24.28 Multiple functions

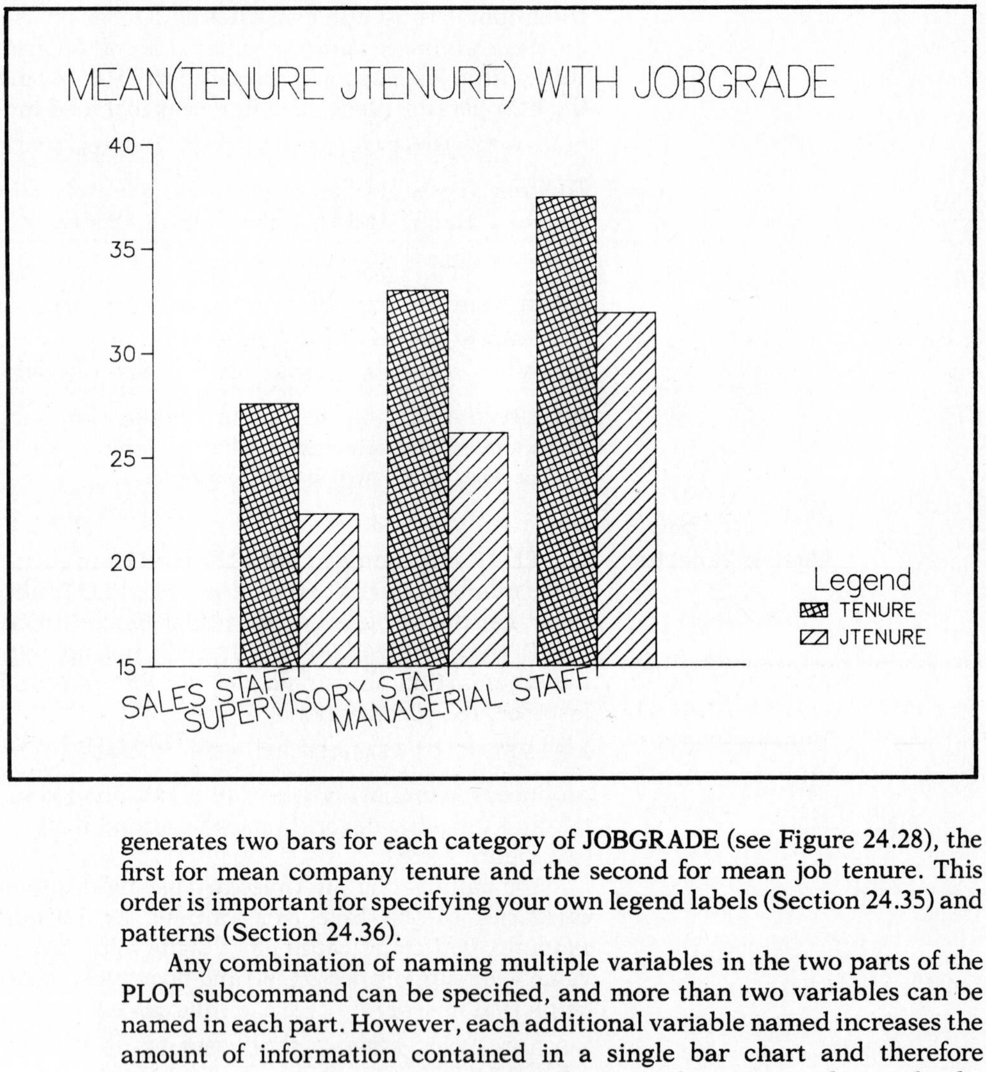

generates two bars for each category of JOBGRADE (see Figure 24.28), the first for mean company tenure and the second for mean job tenure. This order is important for specifying your own legend labels (Section 24.35) and patterns (Section 24.36).

Any combination of naming multiple variables in the two parts of the PLOT subcommand can be specified, and more than two variables can be named in each part. However, each additional variable named increases the amount of information contained in a single bar chart and therefore increases the detail. Complicated bar charts can become too cluttered to be readable. Consider the alternative of multiple plots discussed in Section 24.41, particularly as you can put them on the same page when you use the postprocessor discussed in Section 24.67.

24.29 Cross-Products

The cross-products of up to three variables can be specified in the WITH and BY parts of the PLOT subcommand for BARCHART. For instance, to combine the two store and the three shift categories into a single six-category BY variable in the same plot, specify:

```
BARCHART  PLOT=PERCENT WITH JOBGRADE BY STORE*SHIFT/
```

Figure 24.29 A cross-products control variable

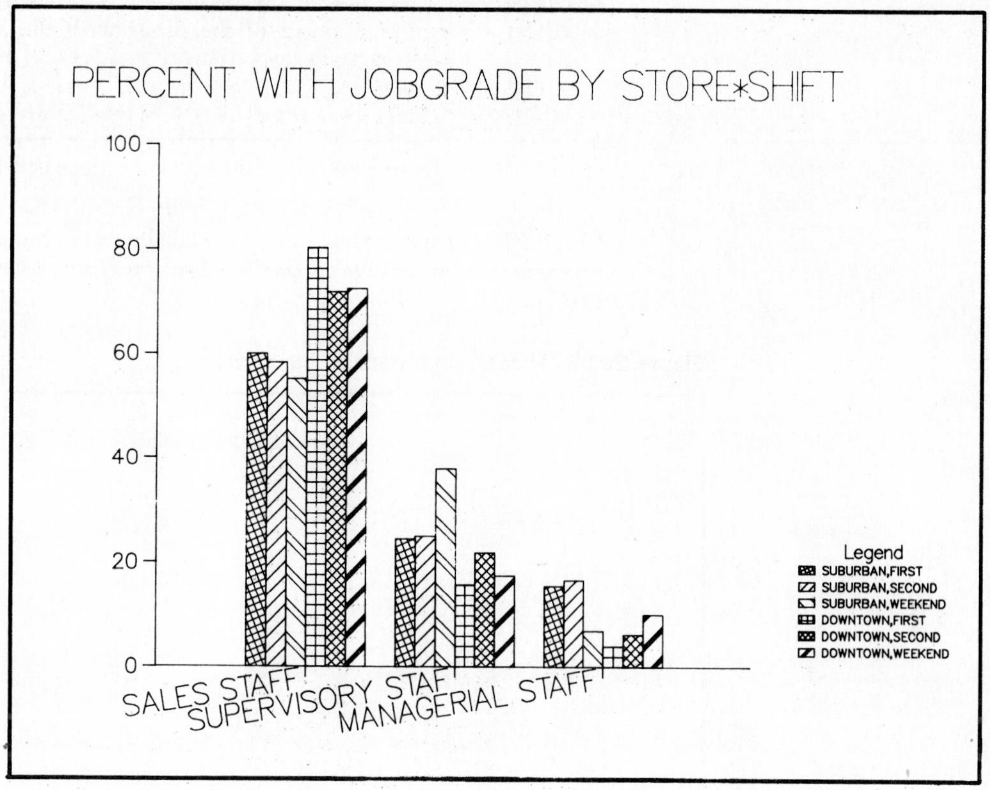

As can be seen in Figure 24.29, this specification causes the bars describing job grade percents to be plotted left to right in a vertical plot for the suburban first shift, the suburban second shift, the suburban weekend shift, the downtown first shift, the downtown second shift, and the downtown weekend shift. That is, the values of the first variable named in a cross-products specification rotate most slowly. This order is important for specifying your own legend labels (Section 24.35) and patterns (Section 24.36). If you specify

```
BARCHART  PLOT=MEAN(TENURE) WITH JOBGRADE*STORE BY SHIFT/
```

BARCHART produces a plot of mean tenure for each shift for suburban sales staff, downtown sales staff, suburban supervisors, downtown supervisors, and so forth. Again, the values of the first cross-products variable rotate most slowly.

You can specify cross-products of up to three variables in either the WITH or BY parts of the PLOT specification, but the cross-products cannot produce more than 15 cells. You cannot specify cross-products for dependent variables in the function part.

24.30 The FORMAT Subcommand

You specify the display quality and format of the bar charts using the FORMAT subcommand. You can ask that the display format be horizontal rather than vertical and that sets of bars be hidden or stacked rather than clustered. The format keywords are

VERTICAL* *Plot a vertical bar chart.* This is equivalent to NO HORIZONTAL.

HORIZONTAL *Plot a horizontal bar chart.* This is equivalent to NO VERTICAL and overrides the default VERTICAL plot.

CLUSTERED* *Plot clustered bar sets.*

HIDDEN *Plot hidden bar sets.* Bars in a set appear as if they are stacked one in front of the other with the smallest in front to the biggest in back. This overrides the default CLUSTERED format.

STACKED *Plot stacked bar sets.* Bars in a set are stacked one on top of the other. This generally requires a greater range of values along the side axis. Overrides the default CLUSTERED format.

As the previous examples show, the default format is VERTICAL and CLUSTERED when the chart includes bar sets. See the examples of hidden and stacked bar charts (placed on the same plot using the postprocessor) in Figure 24.30.

Figure 24.30 Hidden and stacked bar charts

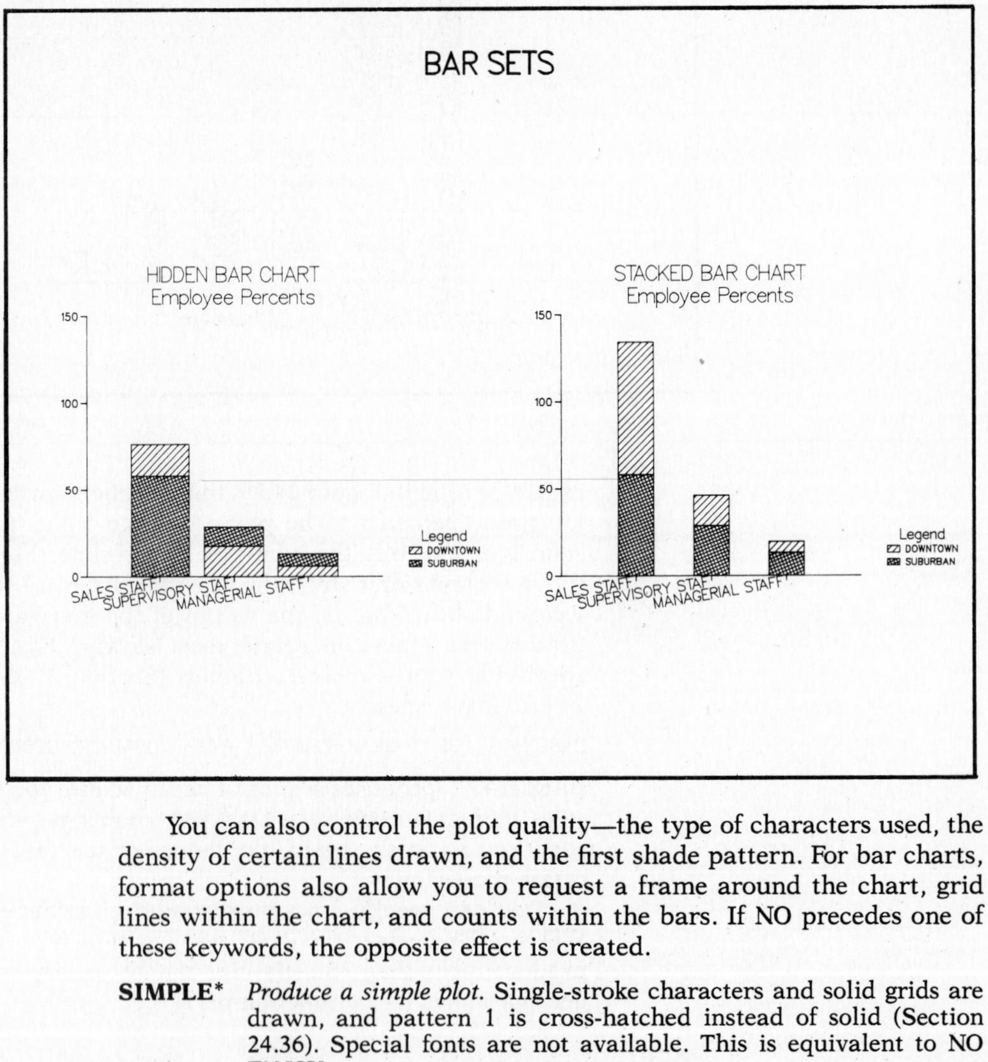

You can also control the plot quality—the type of characters used, the density of certain lines drawn, and the first shade pattern. For bar charts, format options also allow you to request a frame around the chart, grid lines within the chart, and counts within the bars. If NO precedes one of these keywords, the opposite effect is created.

SIMPLE* *Produce a simple plot.* Single-stroke characters and solid grids are drawn, and pattern 1 is cross-hatched instead of solid (Section 24.36). Special fonts are not available. This is equivalent to NO FANCY.

FANCY *Produce a fancy plot.* Double-stroke characters and dashed grid lines are drawn, and special fonts are available. Pattern 1 is solid. This is equivalent to NO SIMPLE.

COUNT *Display the frequency count for each bar.* The number of cases represented by each bar is displayed within the bar. The default is NO COUNT.

FRAME *Draw a frame around the chart.* The base and side axes lines are completed around the chart. The default is NO FRAME.

GRID *Draw grid lines within the chart.* Grid lines perpendicular to the bars are drawn across the chart. The default is NO GRID.

DUMP *Dump the data values to the file specified on the PROCEDURE OUTPUT command* (see Chapter 17). Each legend entry is a set of data and each data set is preceded by a record containing BARSET *nn* starting in column 2, where *nn* is the number of the legend entry. The data set is composed of data triples of base axis value, side axis value, and count written in (1X,6G13.6) format. The default is NO DUMP.

Thus, the default bar chart quality is SIMPLE, NO COUNT, NO FRAME, and NO GRID, as can be seen in any of the previous examples. For example, if you want to frame the chart started in Section 24.26 and make it horizontal with increased quality, specify:

```
BARCHART  PLOT=MEAN(TENURE) WITH JOBGRADE BY SHIFT/
  FORMAT=HORIZONTAL,FRAME,FANCY/
```

The effects of these format changes are shown in Figure 24.40.

24.31 The TITLE, FOOTNOTE, and COMMENT Subcommands

Three subcommands affect the text displayed along with your bar chart. These subcommands define the character strings displayed as lines of text above the chart (TITLE), below the chart (FOOTNOTE), and vertically along the lower left edge of the plot (COMMENT). They are specified according to the rules described in Section 24.10.

As shown in the previous figures, the default title for a bar chart is taken from the PLOT subcommand specification. The default footnote and comment are null. To alter each of these defaults, specify:

```
BARCHART  PLOT=MEAN(TENURE) WITH JOBGRADE BY SHIFT/
  FORMAT=HORIZONTAL,FRAME,FANCY/
  TITLE='CHICAGO HOME FURNISHING'
        'Employee Tenure - Sales Department'/
  FOOTNOTE='As of December 1980'/
  COMMENT='G.Wong, D.P.'/
```

The effects of these subcommands are shown in Figure 24.40.

24.32 Controlling the Axes and the Bars

You can control how the BARCHART base and side axes are scaled and labeled with the BASE AXIS and SIDE AXIS subcommands. The SIDE AXIS subcommand can also be used to establish a reference line or a root value, with the bars extending to either side. With the LEGEND TITLE and LEGEND LABELS subcommands, you can specify your own title and labels for the control variable or variables. Finally, you can control patterns or colors using the ORDER and COLORS subcommands.

24.33 The BASE AXIS Subcommand

By default, BARCHART does not provide a base axis label, but labels the axis divisions (see Figure 24.26), which can become quite complicated with more complex WITH specifications.

You can specify an axis label of up to 40 characters, following the general SPSS^X rules for specifying literals, either as the first specification in the BASE AXIS subcommand or immediately following the NAME keyword. To control the base axis divisions, use one of the following keywords, immediately after the axis label if one is specified.

LABELED* *Label the base axis divisions.* If no labels are provided, BARCHART labels the base axis divisions with the value labels. If a value label is not available, the division is labeled with the variable name followed by an equals sign and the value (depending on the complexity of the WITH specification). You can specify your own labels as literals up to 16 characters long following the LABELED keyword.

LINEAR *Divide the base axis linearly.* BARCHART computes the division marks based on the range of the base axis variable. This keyword can be used only with a single base axis variable.

MONTHLY *Give the base axis divisions monthly labels.* JAN corresponds to values 1, 13, 25, and so forth; FEB corresponds to 2, 14, and so forth. This keyword can be used only with a single base axis variable.

NAME 'label' *Assign this label to the base axis.* The base axis label is either the first BASE AXIS specification or follows the NAME keyword anywhere else in the specification field. This label can be up to 40 characters long and must be enclosed in apostrophes or quotation marks.

For example, to label the base axis and to give the divisions your own labels rather than the value labels, specify:

```
BARCHART  PLOT=MEAN(TENURE) WITH JOBGRADE BY SHIFT/
  FORMAT=HORIZONTAL,FRAME,FANCY/
  TITLE='CHICAGO HOME FURNISHING'
       'Employee Tenure - Sales Department'/
  FOOTNOTE='As of December 1980'/
  COMMENT='G.Wong, D.P.'/
  BASE AXIS='Job Category' LABELED 'Salesclerks'
            'Supervisors' 'Managers'/
```

The effect of altering the default base axis labels is shown in Figure 24.40.

Figure 24.33 A multiple variable bar chart

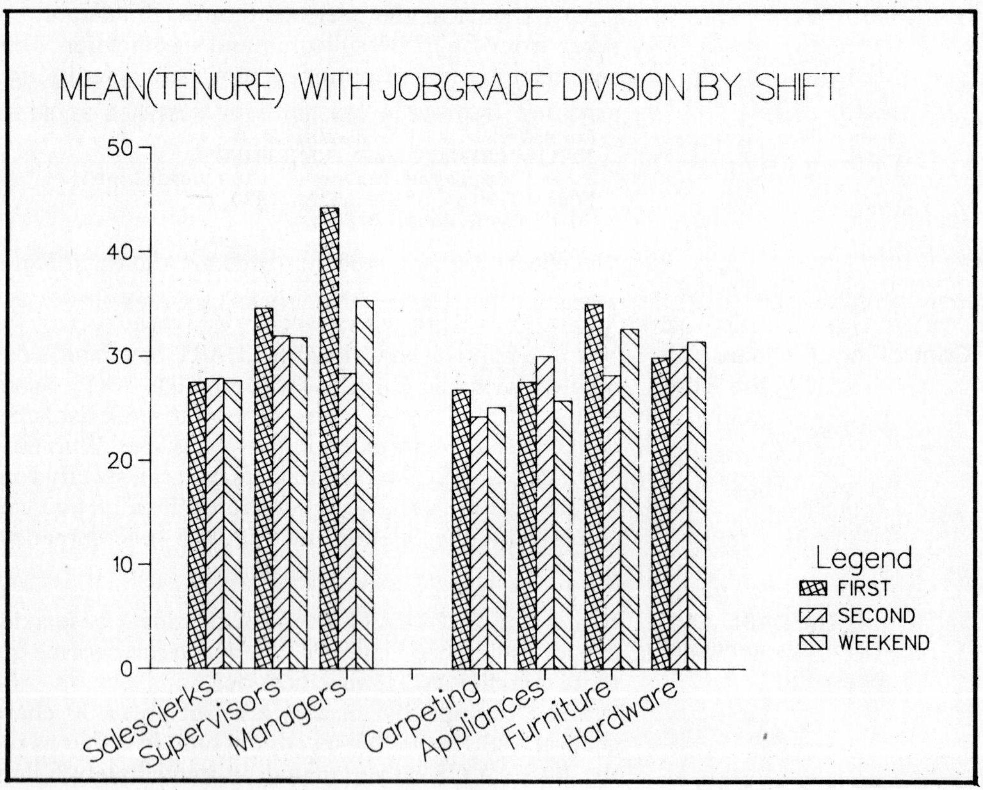

The alternative method of specifying a base axis label would be simply to use the NAME keyword, as in:

```
BASE AXIS=LABELED 'Salesclerks' 'Supervisors' 'Managers'
          NAME'Job Category'/
```

When you specify your own labels for a complex base axis specification, you must follow the order in which new categories are generated for cross-products and you must account for the space between multiple variables on the base axis. For cross-products, the new categories are generated with the first variable's values rotating most slowly. For example, the specification WITH STORE*JOBGRADE generates six categories, STORE=1 and JOBGRADE=1, STORE=1 and JOBGRADE=2, STORE=1 and JOBGRADE =3, STORE=2 and JOBGRADE=1, and so forth. For multiple variable specifications, you must add a label, usually ' ', for the space between the separate base axis variables. Take, for example, the specification

```
BARCHART  PLOT=MEAN(TENURE) WITH JOBGRADE,DIVISION BY SHIFT/
  BASE AXIS=LABELED 'Salesclerks' 'Supervisors' 'Managers'
          ' ' 'Carpeting' 'Appliances' 'Furniture' 'Hardware'/
```

The blank label accounts for the blank space on the base axis between JOBGRADE and DIVISION (see Figure 24.33).

24.34 The SIDE AXIS Subcommand

The SIDE AXIS subcommand defines the label and scale of the side axis, which is always parallel to the bars whether the chart is vertical or horizontal. The first specification can be an optional axis label of up to 40 characters in quotation marks or apostrophes. This label can be assigned alternatively following the NAME keyword documented below. The remainder of the SIDE AXIS specification defines the scale and the reference according to the following keywords:

LINEAR* *Divide the side axis on a linear scale.*

LOG *Divide the side axis on a logarithmic scale.* Overrides LINEAR.

RANGE min,max *Use these values for the scale.* The minimum and maximum default to the lowest and highest values resulting from the function part of the PLOT subcommand. These values may not be the exact scale limitations but are used to fit an appropriate scale. RANGE does not limit the bars, so it is possible for a bar to extend beyond the limits of the chart.

ROOT value *Extend the bars to either side of this value.* This is used to create a "hanging" bar chart. The root value must be within RANGE if RANGE is specified. The default root value is the same as the minimum. A reference line is drawn through the root value unless REFERENCE specifies a different value.

REFERENCE value *Draw a line through this value perpendicular to the bars.* The reference value must be within RANGE if RANGE is specified.

NAME 'label' *Assign this label to the side axis.* The side axis label is either the first SIDE AXIS specification or follows the NAME keyword anywhere else in the specification field. This label can be up to 40 characters long and must be enclosed in apostrophes or quotation marks.

For example, to label the side axis, provide your own range, and provide a reference line at the mean value for the data, specify:

```
BARCHART  PLOT=MEAN(TENURE) WITH JOBGRADE BY SHIFT/
  FORMAT=HORIZONTAL,FRAME,FANCY/
  TITLE='CHICAGO HOME FURNISHING'
        'Employee Tenure - Sales Department'/
  FOOTNOTE='As of December 1980'/
  COMMENT='G.Wong, D.P.'/
  BASE AXIS='Job Category' LABELED 'Salesclerks'
          'Supervisors' 'Managers'/
  SIDE AXIS='Mean Tenure in Months'
          RANGE 0,50 REFERENCE 29.7/
```

See the plot in Figure 24.40 for the results of this specification.

Figure 24.34 A hanging bar chart

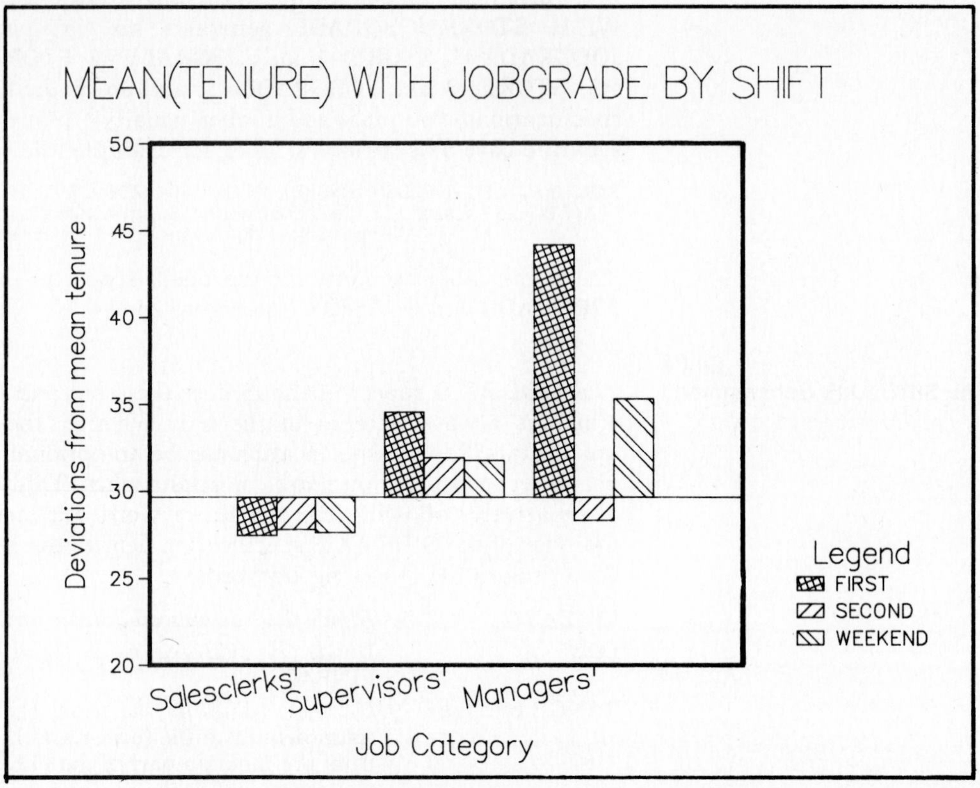

Hanging bar charts are particularly useful when you want to emphasize differences from some particular value. For example, to show how much on the average people deviated from the mean length of employment for the company, specify:

```
BARCHART  PLOT=MEAN(TENURE) WITH JOBGRADE BY SHIFT/
  FORMAT=FRAME/
  BASE AXIS=LABELED 'Salesclerks' 'Supervisors' 'Managers'
          NAME'Job Category'/
  SIDE AXIS=ROOT 29.7 NAME 'Deviations from mean tenure'/
```

See the plot generated by this command in Figure 24.34.

24.35 The LEGEND TITLE and LEGEND LABELS Subcommands

To specify a title up to 20 characters long for the legend that appears to the right of the bar chart describing the bar sets, use the LEGEND TITLE subcommand. The default title is LEGEND. To provide your own labels for the categories of the control variable or variables or multiple functions, use the LEGEND LABELS subcommand. These labels can also be up to 20 characters. For a single function and a single BY variable, the control variable's value labels are used by default; and if there are no value labels, the variable name followed by the value is used. For multiple functions and/or multiple control variables, combinations of the function keyword, value labels, and the variable name followed by the value are used. When the PLOT specification is complicated, however, you should probably provide your own labels, according to the order described in Section 24.29 for a cross-products control variable. If you have specified multiple functions, the functions rotate slowest.

If you provide your own legend labels, specify them as BARCHART displays them in the bar sets, left to right in a horizontal chart and bottom to top in a vertical chart. This order corresponds to ascending value order in the case of simple control variable specifications, or in the order the categories are generated in complex plot specifications. For example, to title the legend and provide your own labels for the control variable SHIFT, specify:

```
BARCHART  PLOT=MEAN(TENURE) WITH JOBGRADE BY SHIFT/
  FORMAT=HORIZONTAL,FRAME,FANCY/
  TITLE='CHICAGO HOME FURNISHING'
        'Employee Tenure - Sales Department'/
  FOOTNOTE='As of December 1980'/
  COMMENT='G.Wong, D.P.'/
  BASE AXIS='Job Category' LABELED 'Salesclerks'
          'Supervisors' 'Managers'/
  SIDE AXIS='Mean Tenure in Months'
          RANGE 0,50 REFERENCE 29.7/
  LEGEND TITLE='Shift'/
  LEGEND LABELS='Day' 'Evening' 'Weekend'/
```

24.36 The ORDER Subcommand

The ORDER subcommand controls the order in which BARCHART uses patterns from those shown in Figure 24.36. By default, patterns are applied in numerical order as the bars in a set are drawn. For sets of bars generated by cross-products, the patterns apply to the new categories in the same order as the legend labels discussed in Section 24.35.

Figure 24.36 The BARCHART patterns

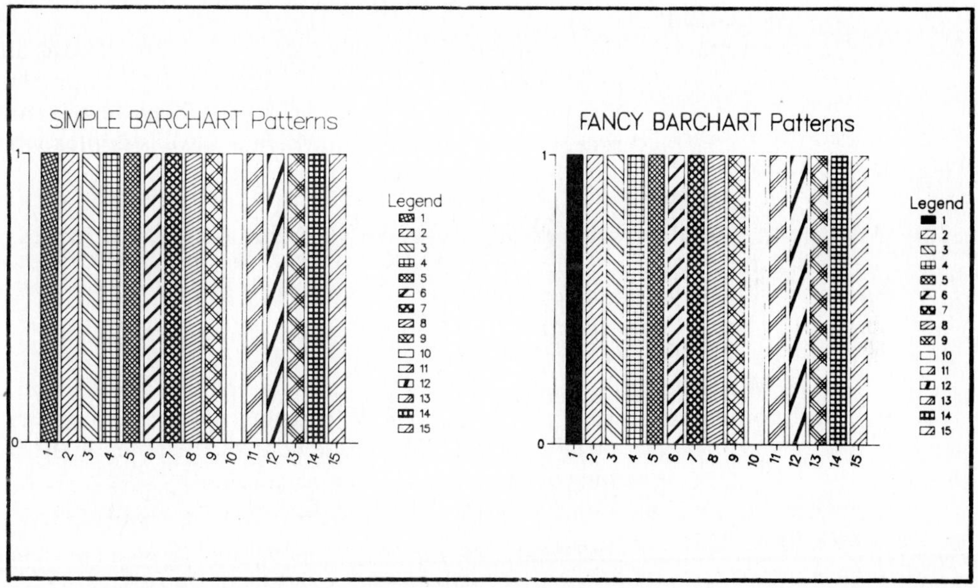

To choose your own patterns, use the ORDER subcommand to specify the corresponding numbers in variable value order for single control variables; or in generated order for complex plot specifications. For example, if you want patterns 1, 5, and 9 applied to the set of bars representing variable SHIFT, specify:

```
BARCHART  PLOT=MEAN(TENURE) WITH JOBGRADE BY SHIFT/
  FORMAT=HORIZONTAL,FRAME,FANCY/
  TITLE='CHICAGO HOME FURNISHING'
        'Employee Tenure - Sales Department'/
  FOOTNOTE='As of December 1980'/
  COMMENT='G.Wong, D.P.'/
  BASE AXIS='Job Category' LABELED 'Salesclerks'
          'Supervisors' 'Managers'/
  SIDE AXIS='Mean Tenure in Months'
          RANGE 0,50 REFERENCE 29.7/
  LEGEND TITLE='Shift'/
  LEGEND LABELS='Day' 'Evening' 'Weekend'/
  ORDER=1,5,9/
```

Enter pattern numbers from 1 to 15 for the bars you want to alter, even if you might be respecifying the default value for a particular bar. If you specify fewer pattern numbers than there are bars in each set, the remaining bars have the default patterns in the original sequence. If you specify more, the remainder are not used. The effect of choosing a different pattern is shown in Figure 24.40. To select the same pattern for different bars in a set, repeat the order number.

24.37 The COLORS Subcommand

To produce color plots, you must know how many colors the device supports in addition to black. A black-and-white device supports zero additional colors, an eight-pen plotter supports seven additional colors. The default specification for the COLORS subcommand is 0.

If you intend to produce your bar chart on a four-color device, to take advantage of the three additional colors, specify:

```
COLORS=3/
```

If you specify more than zero colors, BARCHART uses the additional colors to draw the bars in a set, using all available colors in one pattern before moving to the next pattern in the default order. To override the default color/pattern combinations, use the ORDER subcommand as described for PIECHART (see Section 24.15).

24.38 The FONT Subcommand

If you specify FORMAT=FANCY, you can choose among four fonts: DUPLEX, COMPLEX, TRIPLEX, and GOTHIC. Examples of these styles are in Figure 24.16. Your choice of font applies to all annotation in the graph except the comment line, which is always duplex when FORMAT=FANCY.

24.39 The XPAGE and YPAGE Subcommands

If the default page size, 11 inches wide by 8½ inches high, is not satisfactory, you can change it with the XPAGE and YPAGE commands documented in Section 24.17.

24.40 The MISSING Subcommand

By default, BARCHART does not include a case in calculating the set of bars within a base variable category if the case has missing values on the variable being plotted, the control variable, or the independent variables. You control missing-value treatment by using the MISSING subcommand with one of the following keyword specifications.

BARWISE* *Omit cases with missing values on the variable used in the bar being produced.* If you specify multiple variables in the function, WITH, or BY parts of the PLOT subcommand, cases are examined for missing values for each variable independently.

PLOTWISE *Omit cases with missing values on any variable named in the PLOT subcommand.* Bars of the same pattern produced from multiple variable specifications are based on the same cases.

NONE *Include all cases regardless of missing values.*

If you want BARCHART to ignore missing-data declarations for all variables specified in the PLOT subcommand, use keyword NONE. For example, clerical and other staff were omitted from the bar chart shown in Figure 24.36, perhaps to separate support personnel from the rest of the staff. To

Figure 24.40 An enhanced bar chart

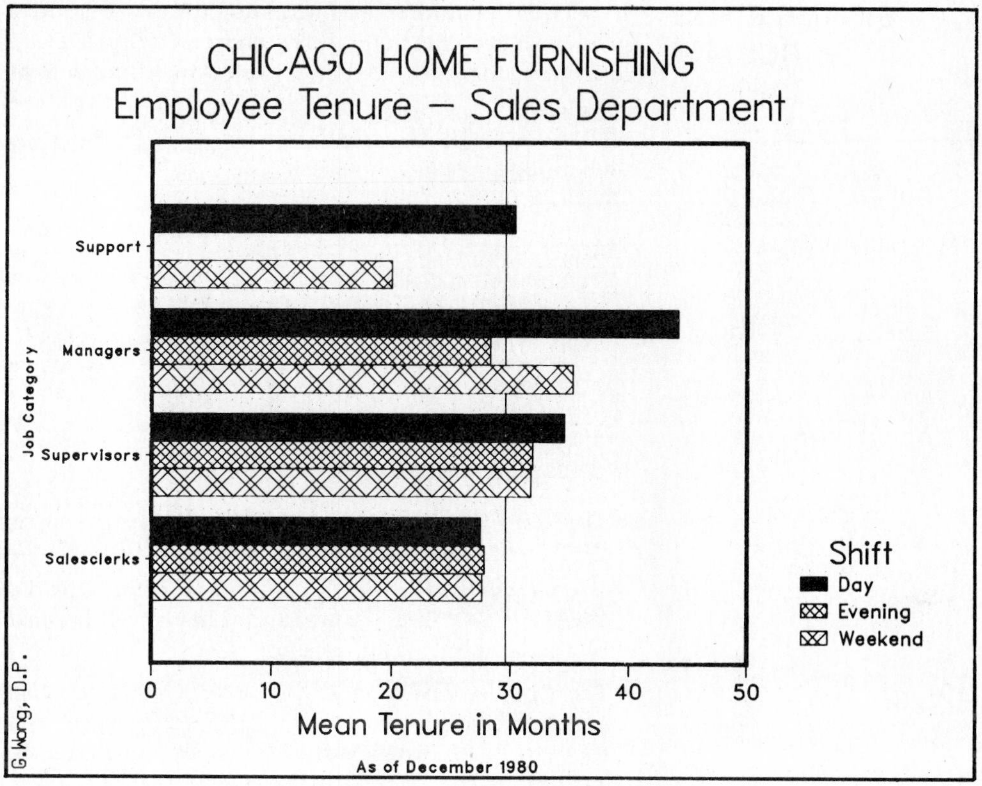

include them in the final display, specify:

```
BARCHART  PLOT=MEAN(TENURE) WITH JOBGRADE BY SHIFT/
  FORMAT=HORIZONTAL,FRAME,FANCY/
  TITLE='CHICAGO HOME FURNISHING'
       'Employee Tenure - Sales Department'/
  FOOTNOTE='As of December 1980'/
  COMMENT='G.Wong, D.P.'/
  BASE AXIS='Job Category' LABELED 'Salesclerks'
          'Supervisors' 'Managers' 'Support'/
  SIDE AXIS='Mean Tenure in Months'
            RANGE 0,50 REFERENCE 29.6/
  LEGEND TITLE='Shift'/
  LEGEND LABELS='Day' 'Evening' 'Weekend'/
  ORDER=1,5,9/
  MISSING=NONE/
```

The plot produced by this command is shown in Figure 24.40. The additional base axis category label and the different reference value were specified to account for the inclusion of the missing value. If these additions were not specified, the base axis category label would have defaulted to the value label and the reference line describing the grand mean would not have been correct for the full set of cases in the chart.

The difference between BARWISE and PLOTWISE missing-value treatments arises only if you specify more than one variable in any part of the PLOT subcommand, not if you specify only single variables or cross-products. That is, if you specify

```
BARCHART  PLOT=MEAN(TENURE) WITH JOBGRADE,DIVISION/
```

a chart is produced first for JOBGRADE with cases being omitted if they have missing data for job grade or tenure, a second chart is produced on the same base axis for DIVISION with cases omitted with missing division or

ANNOTATED EXAMPLE FOR BARCHART

The data for this example come from the same personnel file used for the PIECHART example and throughout this chapter. The task here is to produce a presentation-quality chart showing average job tenure in each of four job categories, further broken down into each of three shifts.

```
FILE HANDLE  EMPLOYEE/ file specifications
GET  FILE=EMPLOYEE

FILE HANDLE  EMPPLOT2/ file specifications
GRAPHICS OUTPUT  OUTFILE=EMPPLOT2

BARCHART  PLOT=MEAN(TENURE) WITH JOBGRADE BY SHIFT/
  FORMAT=HORIZONTAL,FRAME,FANCY/
  TITLE='CHICAGO HOME FURNISHING'
       'Employee Tenure - Sales Department'/
  FOOTNOTE='As of December 1980'/
  BASE AXIS='Job Category' LABELED 'Salesclerks'
           'Supervisors' 'Managers' 'Support'/
  SIDE AXIS='Mean Tenure in Months'
           RANGE 0,50 REFERENCE 29.6/
  LEGEND TITLE='Shift'/
  LEGEND LABELS='Day' 'Evening' 'Weekend'/
  COLORS=3/ MISSING=NONE/
```

- The first FILE HANDLE command defines the system file accessed by the GET command (see Chapters 3 and 5).
- The second FILE HANDLE command defines the output file named on the GRAPHICS OUTPUT command. This is the *intermediate file* to be accessed by the Graphics Postprocessor (see Section 24.66).
- The PLOT subcommand defines the function (MEAN), the variable on which the mean is calculated (TENURE), the variable whose values define the bars (JOBGRADE), and the control variable (SHIFT), which divides each of the bars for a value of JOBGRADE into a set of three bars, one for each shift (see Sections 24.24–24.29).
- The FORMAT subcommand specifies horizontal bars, a frame drawn on all sides of the plot, and a fancy format (see Section 24.30).
- The TITLE and FOOTNOTE subcommands define a two-line title and a one-line footnote (see Section 24.31).
- The BASE AXIS and SIDE AXIS subcommands override default specifications for the two axes. The literal in apostrophes that begins the specifications for each of these subcommands provides a label for each axis. The literals following the keyword LABELED for the BASE AXIS command are used to label the divisions of the base axis (the four sets of bars). The RANGE specification to the SIDE AXIS subcommand defines a preferred range for the axis scale, and the REFERENCE specification requests that a line be drawn through the value 29.6 (previously determined to be the mean for the entire company). (See Sections 24.33 and 24.34.)
- The LEGEND TITLE and LEGEND LABELS subcommands specify annotation for the legend (see Section 24.35).
- The COLORS subcommand specifies three colors, in addition to black, to be used to draw the plot. These are whatever colors are available as the first, second, and third colors on the graphics device—red, green, and blue in the case of the plotter used for this example (see Section 24.37).
- The MISSING subcommand overrides the default missing-value treatment, which is to omit cases with missing values. Here, because value 4 for JOBGRADE has been declared missing, the MISSING subcommand is needed to include support staff in the plot (see Section 24.40).

The output from this job is the bar chart on the inside front cover of this manual.

tenure information, and so forth. Instead, if you specify

```
BARCHART  PLOT=MEAN(TENURE) WITH JOBGRADE,DIVISION/
  MISSING=PLOTWISE/
```

the two charts are produced with cases omitted if they are missing data on either of the two WITH variables or TENURE.

24.41 Multiple PLOT Subcommands

More than one PLOT subcommand can be specified in a BARCHART command. This is helpful particularly when some attributes are common to all plots and others are specific to each plot. Each new PLOT subcommand returns all attributes to their defaults. You can establish your own defaults for all subsequent plots in the BARCHART command by specifying the keyword DEFAULT before any of the attribute subcommands FORMAT, TITLE, FOOTNOTE, COMMENT, X AXIS, Y AXIS, LEGEND TITLE, LEGEND LABELS, ORDER, COLOR, FONT, XPAGE, YPAGE, and MISSING.

For example, you might want to add a PLOT command to the example shown in Section 24.40 in order to generate a bar chart of mean salaries. If you simply enter a PLOT subcommand substituting SALARY for TENURE following the last subcommand affecting the previous plot, the bar chart for the variable specified will look very much like the plot shown in Figure 24.26 because all other subcommands return to defaults. A better approach is to decide which of the subcommands for the first PLOT are also applicable to the second, and then make those the defaults. All other subcommands specific to the second plot can then be specified. For example, the following command produces both the plot shown in 24.40 and the one shown in 24.41.

```
BARCHART  PLOT=MEAN(TENURE) WITH JOBGRADE BY SHIFT/
  DEFAULT FORMAT=HORIZONTAL,FRAME,FANCY/
  TITLE='CHICAGO HOME FURNISHING'
       'Employee Tenure - Sales Department'/
  DEFAULT FOOTNOTE='As of December 1980'/
  COMMENT='G.Wong, D.P.'/
  DEFAULT BASE AXIS='Job Category' LABELED 'Salesclerks'
                    'Supervisors' 'Managers' 'Support'/
  SIDE AXIS='Mean Tenure in Months'
           RANGE 0,50 REFERENCE 29.6/
  DEFAULT LEGEND TITLE='Shift'/
  DEFAULT LEGEND LABELS='Day' 'Evening' 'Weekend'/
  DEFAULT ORDER=1,5,9/
  DEFAULT MISSING=NONE/
  PLOT=MEAN(SALARY) WITH JOBGRADE BY SHIFT/
  TITLE='CHICAGO HOME FURNISHING'
       'Employee Salaries - Sales Department'/
  SIDE AXIS='Mean Yearly Salary' REFERENCE 15300/
```

If you want the same plot quality and format for the second PLOT subcommand, the first subcommand you want to establish as the default is FORMAT. Because the date produced, the base variable, and the control variable are the same, the FOOTNOTE, BASE AXIS, LEGEND TITLE, LEGEND LABELS, and ORDER specifications apply to both plots. However, the title should change to reflect the change in content. The comment can be allowed to return to the default null string. Finally, since you want the other staff included in both bar charts, the MISSING=NONE specification should also apply to both plots.

Because you want to specify a different side axis label and a different reference line, you specify SIDE AXIS following the second PLOT subcommand. Therefore, the plot produced by the second PLOT subcommand (shown in Figure 24.41) looks very much like the first one (shown in Figure 24.40).

Figure 24.41 The plot from the second PLOT subcommand

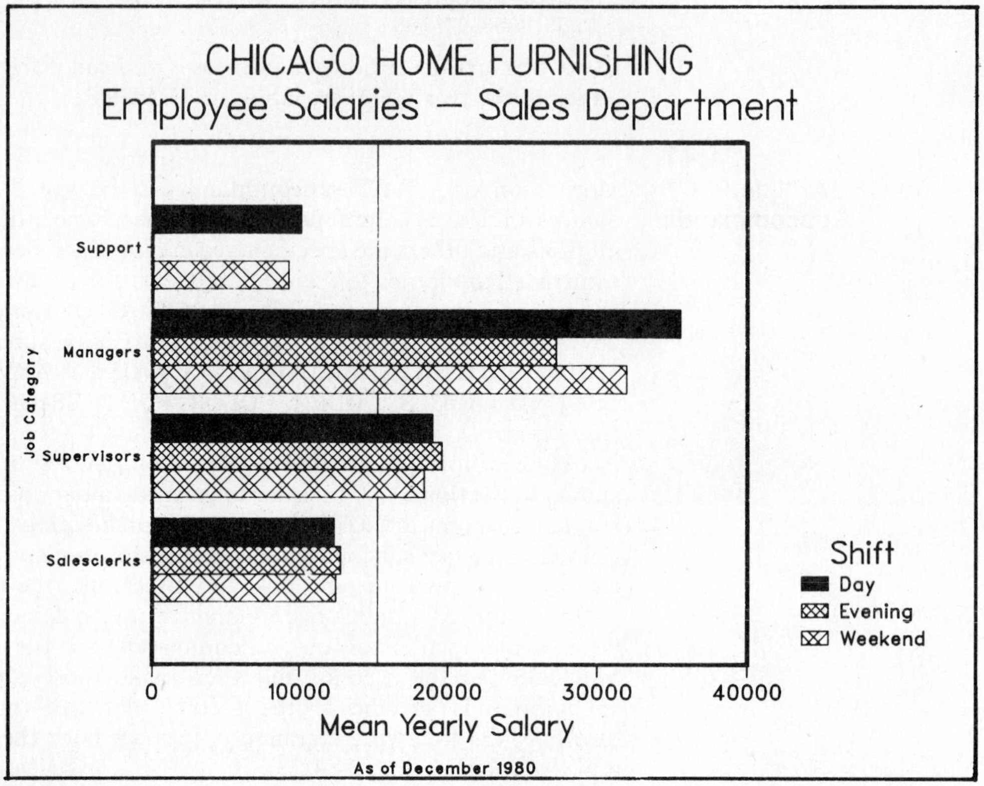

24.42 THE LINECHART PROCEDURE

The LINECHART command must include at least one PLOT subcommand to identify the function (count, percent, mean, regression, and so forth) and to name the variable or variables to be plotted. In addition, LINECHART includes the FORMAT subcommand to control plot quality and contents; TITLE, FOOTNOTE, and COMMENT to control annotation; X AXIS and Y AXIS to label and define the axes; the CURVES subcommand to define the way points are connected with or without markers; LEGEND TITLE and LEGEND LABELS to provide a title and labels for the line chart legend; COLORS and ORDER to control colors, line patterns and markers, and shade patterns; XPAGE, YPAGE, and FONT to control page dimensions and type style; MISSING for selecting the missing-value treatment. The SAVE subcommand, which allows you to save a file for input to the TELL-A-GRAF package, is documented in Section 24.65. Subcommand keywords are followed in most cases by an optional equals sign and by specifications, and are separated from other subcommands by slashes.

More than one PLOT subcommand can be specified in a LINECHART command. Unless otherwise altered, all subcommand specifications return to defaults with each new PLOT subcommand. You can establish your own defaults by prefacing the subcommand keyword with DEFAULT, thus eliminating the need for repetitive specifications. Multiple PLOT specifications are discussed in Section 24.61.

24.43 The PLOT Subcommand

The PLOT subcommand for LINECHART defines the function and names the variable or variables for which a line chart is produced. The PLOT subcommand for LINECHART is divided into three parts:

- The required *function* part names the function (and the dependent variable when appropriate) that determines the vertical or *Y axis*.
- The required *WITH* part names the variable whose values govern the horizontal or *X axis*.
- The optional *BY* part separates each curve into a set of curves according to the categories of a *control variable*.

In the example

```
LINECHART  PLOT=MEAN(ATTEND) WITH AGE BY SEX/
```

MEAN is the function plotted on the Y axis, the range of which is determined by the lowest and highest mean values of variable ATTEND (church attendance). AGE is the variable whose values are on the X axis. Therefore, the curve plotted describes the relationship between church attendance and the person's age. This curve is actually divided into two curves describing the relationship between church attendance and age for each sex because that variable is named in the BY part.

PLOT must be the first subcommand specified. None of the variables named can be alphanumeric; they must be recoded to numeric. The BY variable named need not be integer-valued, but should have a limited number of possible values. In any case, LINECHART cannot accommodate more than 15 curves on a line chart.

24.44 The Function and WITH Specifications

The first required part of the PLOT subcommand is the name of a function that establishes the Y axis. If the function is a count, percent, or proportion, no variable is named. If the function is a mean, sum, values, or regression, the name of the variable is enclosed in parentheses following the function keyword. Functions are

COUNT *Plot the frequency of each value of the X axis variable.*

CCOUNT *Plot the cumulative frequency of the X axis variable.*

PERCENT *Plot the relative frequency of each value of the X axis variable.*

CPERCENT *Plot the cumulative relative frequency of the X axis variable.*

PROPORTION *Plot the proportion of each value of the X axis variable.*

CPROPORTION *Plot the cumulative proportion of the X axis variable.*

MEAN(varname) *Plot the means of the Y axis variable for values of the X axis variable.*

SMEAN(varname) *Plot the standardized means of the Y axis variable.*

SD1(varname) *Plot the mean plus and minus one standard deviation.* Functions SD2 and SD3 request the mean plus and minus two and three standard deviations respectively.

SUM(varname) *Plot the sums of the Y axis variable for values of the X axis variable.*

CSUM(varname) *Plot the cumulative sum of the X axis variable.*

VALUES(varname) *Plot the values of the Y axis variable for values of the X axis variable.* This is a scatterplot, so the default is not to connect the points (see Section 24.56).

REG(varname) *Plot the regression of Y on X.*

M90(varname) *Plot the regression line and the 90% confidence interval for the mean.* Functions M95 and M99 request the regression line and the 95% and 99% confidence intervals for the mean.

I90(varname) *Plot the regression line and the 90% confidence interval for an individual observation.* Functions I95 and I99 request the regression line and the 95% and 99% confidence intervals for an individual observation.

The mean and standard deviation plots (SD1, SD2, SD3) and the regression line with confidence intervals (M90, I90, M95, and so forth) each generate at least three curves. If a control variable is specified, they generate three times the number of values of the control variable. The ORDER subcommand default is reset in order to make plus/minus standard deviation lines and upper/lower confidence bounds identical in pattern and color. Override this default with caution.

Note that, if the X axis variable is continuous, there is no grouping for the mean functions (MEAN, SMEAN, SD1, and so forth). Therefore the curves generated could look like a scatterplot with all points connected since each point is likely to be the mean for individual values of the X axis variable. If you want to group, use the SPSS^X RECODE command.

The function part is usually followed immediately by the keyword WITH and the name of the variable whose values determine the X axis. This completes the minimum required syntax of the PLOT subcommand in LINECHART. For example, to plot the mean salary with the length of time employees have been with the company, specify:

```
LINECHART     PLOT=MEAN(SALARY) WITH TENURE/
```

The function selected is the MEAN and the dependent variable is SALARY. The X axis (independent) variable is TENURE, which is the length of time an employee has been with the company measured in months. The plot produced by this example is developed in the next section by adding a control variable.

24.45 Keyword BY

Adding a control variable is simply a matter of specifying the keyword BY followed by the control variable. For example, if you name JOBGRADE in the BY part, the curve describing the mean salary with tenure for the whole company is broken into several curves, one for each job grade.

```
LINECHART  PLOT=MEAN(SALARY) WITH TENURE BY JOBGRADE/
```

The plot produced by this command is shown in Figure 24.4. It accepts defaults for all other LINECHART subcommands. To see this example fully developed as the discussion of altering the default specifications for the other subcommands progresses, pick up the discussion beginning with Section 24.49. To see the complete syntax possibilities for the PLOT subcommand, see the following sections on qualifying each variable named with a selector, on specifying multiple variables within each part, and on superimposing one line chart on another.

24.46 Selectors

Each variable named in the function, WITH, and BY parts of the PLOT subcommand can be followed by parentheses enclosing a selector which consists of a logical operator and a value or list of values, as in SHIFT(NE 3). Relational operators are LT, LE, EQ, NE, GE, and GT which mean respectively less than, less than or equal to, equal to, not equal to, greater than or equal to, and greater than. If you omit the logical operator, EQ is assumed. EQ and NE can be followed by a list of numbers where (EQ 1,2,3) means equal to 1, 2, or 3, and (NE 1,2,3) means not equal to 1, 2, and 3. All other operators are followed by a single value. If a case satisfies the condition, it is used in constructing the line chart specified.

For example, to produce a line chart of the mean salary with tenure for sales staff only, specify JOBGRADE(EQ 1) in the BY part. Or, since the EQ operator is the default, specify:

```
LINECHART  PLOT=MEAN(SALARY) WITH TENURE BY JOBGRADE(1)/
```

This example is developed in Section 24.47.

To limit the same line chart to those with at least one year at the company, specify:

```
LINECHART  PLOT=MEAN(SALARY) WITH TENURE(GE 12) BY JOBGRADE(1)/
```

If you want the line chart to be limited to those who have a salary of $15,000 or above, specify:

```
LINECHART  PLOT=MEAN(SALARY(GE 15000)) WITH TENURE BY JOBGRADE/
```

Because the variable named in the function part is already enclosed in parentheses, the selector for that variable must be included within those parentheses as shown in this example.

24.47 Multiple Functions

Multiple variable specifications are prohibited in the WITH and BY parts of the PLOT subcommand for LINECHART. For an alternative, see Section 24.48 on superimposing line charts.

More than one function can be specified in the PLOT subcommand and more than one variable can be specified for the same function. For instance, the specification

```
LINECHART  PLOT=MEAN(SALARY) VALUES(SALARY) WITH TENURE BY JOBGRADE(2)/
```

produces one curve for the mean salary superimposed on a scatterplot of the salary values (drawn in that order). The plot is limited to a single category of JOBGRADE. This plot is shown in Figure 24.63.

You can also name more than one variable for the same function. With either multiple functions or multiple variables for the same function, be careful that scales of the variables are comparable and that the ranges produced by the functions are similar.

The result of multiple specifications in the function part is represented in multiple curves in the same way that multiple curves are drawn for values of a control variable. Each additional variable or function specified increases the amount of information contained in a single line chart and therefore increases the detail. In any case, you cannot put more than 15 curves on one chart. Complicated line charts can become too cluttered to be readable. Consider the alternative of multiple plots discussed in Section 24.61, particularly since you have the possibility of putting them on the same page when you use the postprocessor option discussed in Section 24.67.

24.48 Superimposing Line Charts

You can repeat the set of function, WITH, and optional BY parts within a single PLOT subcommand for LINECHART in order to superimpose multiple line charts on the same plot. For example, if you have both measures of employee tenure with the company and tenure in a particular job grade (variable JTENURE), you may want to compare the two measures with salary levels on the same plot.

```
LINECHART  PLOT=MEAN(SALARY) WITH TENURE BY JOBGRADE(2)
                MEAN(SALARY) WITH JTENURE BY JOBGRADE(2)/
```

Note that the scale calculated for both the X and Y axes are based upon the results of both line charts. Therefore, the variables named in both the function and WITH parts of the two specifications must be similar. Note also that the BY variable specification affects only the function and WITH specifications immediately preceding it. That is, if the first BY specification did not appear in the example above, only the plot of mean salary with JTENURE would be limited to cases within the second job category.

24.49 The FORMAT Subcommand

Specify the display quality and format of the line charts using the FORMAT subcommand. Quality refers to the type of characters used, the density of certain lines drawn, and the first shade pattern. For line charts, format options include a frame around the chart, grid lines within the chart, and shading below the curves. If one of the following keywords is preceded by NO, the opposite effect takes place.

SIMPLE* *Produce a simple plot.* Single-stroke characters, single curves, and solid grids are drawn, and shade pattern 1 is cross-hatched instead of solid (Section 24.55). Special fonts are not available. This is equivalent to NO FANCY.

FANCY *Produce a fancy plot.* Double-stroke characters, dense curves, and dashed grid lines are drawn, pattern 1 is solid, and special fonts are available. This is equivalent to NO SIMPLE.

FRAME *Draw a frame around the chart.* The X and Y axis lines are completed around the chart. The default is NO FRAME.

XGRID *Draw grid lines perpendicular to the X axis.*

YGRID *Draw grid lines perpendicular to the Y axis.*

GRID *Draw grid lines in both directions.* The default is NO GRID.

SHADE *Stack the curves and shade between them.* This is similar to a stacked bar chart. The curves must have identical ranges. The default is NO SHADE. See the example in Section 24.64.

DUMP *Dump the data values to the file specified on the PROCEDURE OUTPUT command.* Each curve (or set of scatterplot values) is a set of data and each data set is preceded by a record containing CURVE *nn* starting in column 2, where *nn* is the number of the curve. The data set is composed of data pairs of X axis value and Y axis value written in (1X,6G13.6) format. The default is NO DUMP.

Thus, the default line chart quality is SIMPLE, NO FRAME, NO GRID, and NO SHADE as can be seen in any of the previous examples. To frame the chart started in Section 24.45 and produce it with increased quality, specify:

```
LINECHART  PLOT=MEAN(SALARY) WITH TENURE BY JOBGRADE/
  FORMAT=FRAME,FANCY/
```

The effects of these format changes are shown in Figure 24.60.

24.50 The TITLE, FOOTNOTE, and COMMENT Subcommands

The three subcommands that affect the text displayed along with your line chart are TITLE for putting lines of text above the chart, FOOTNOTE below the chart, and COMMENT vertically along the lower left edge of the plot. They are specified according to the rules described in Section 24.10.

As shown in the previous figures, the default title for a line chart is taken from the PLOT subcommand. The default footnote and comment are null. For example, if you want a different title and need a footnote, specify:

```
LINECHART  PLOT=MEAN(SALARY) WITH TENURE BY JOBGRADE/
  FORMAT=FRAME,FANCY/
  TITLE='CHICAGO HOME FURNISHING'
       'Employee Salary Analysis - Sales Department'/
  FOOTNOTE='As of December 1980'/
```

The effects of these subcommands are shown in Figure 24.60.

24.51 Controlling the Axes and the Curves

You can control how the X and Y axes are scaled and labeled with the X AXIS and Y AXIS subcommands. The CURVES subcommand is used to specify how curves are to be connected with or without markers. With the LEGEND TITLE and LEGEND LABELS subcommands, you can specify your own title and labels for the control variable or variables. Finally, you can control the patterns and markers or colors chosen to distinguish the different curves (and shading) using the ORDER and COLORS subcommands.

24.52 The X AXIS Subcommand

By default, LINECHART does not provide an X axis label, and the axis is linear with no division labels (see Figure 24.4 for an example). You can specify an axis label up to 40 characters long as the first specification in the X AXIS subcommand or following the keyword NAME documented below. To control the X axis divisions, use one of the following keywords.

LINEAR* *Divide the X axis linearly.* LINECHART computes the division marks based on the range of the X axis variable.

LOG *Divide the X axis on a logarithmic scale.* Overrides LINEAR.

RANGE min,max *Use these values for the scale.* The minimum and maximum default to the lowest and highest values of the X axis variable. These values may not be the exact scale limitations but are used to fit an appropriate scale. RANGE can be specified only with LINEAR or LOG scales.

LABELED *Label the X axis.* If no labels are provided, LINECHART labels the X axis divisions with the value labels. If a value label is not available, the division is labeled with the variable name followed by an equals sign and the value. You can specify your own labels as literals up to 16 characters long following the LABELED keyword. Overrides LINEAR.

MONTHLY *Give the X axis divisions monthly labels.* JAN corresponds to values 1, 13, 25, and so forth; FEB corresponds to 2, 14, and so forth. Overrides LINEAR.

REFERENCE value *Draw a vertical reference line through this value.* The value must be within the RANGE if RANGE is specified.

NAME 'label' *Assign this label to the X axis.* The X axis label either is the first X AXIS specification or follows the NAME keyword anywhere else in the specification field. This label can be up to 40 characters long and must be enclosed in apostrophes or quotation marks.

For example, to label the X axis and to specify a reference line at the mean value for TENURE, specify:

```
LINECHART PLOT=MEAN(SALARY) WITH TENURE BY JOBGRADE/
  FORMAT=FRAME,FANCY/
  TITLE='CHICAGO HOME FURNISHING'
        'Employee Salary Analysis - Sales Department'/
  FOOTNOTE='As of December 1980'/
  X AXIS='Employment Tenure in Months' REFERENCE 29.7/
```

The effects of adding a label and a reference line to the X axis are shown in Figure 24.60.

When you request LABELED or MONTHLY for the X axis, LINECHART may not be able to add the labels if the number of values across the axis is so great that the values would be too small. In this case, the axis is forced to LINEAR.

24.53 The Y AXIS Subcommand

The Y AXIS subcommand defines the label and scale of the Y axis. It can be specified in two ways: first, with an optional axis label up to 40 characters long; alternatively, following the NAME keyword documented below. The remainder of the Y AXIS specification defines the scale and the reference according to the following keywords:

LINEAR* *Divide the Y axis on a linear scale.*

LOG *Divide the Y axis on a logarithmic scale.* Overrides LINEAR.

RANGE min,max *Use these values for the scale.* The minimum and maximum default to the lowest and highest values resulting from the function part of the PLOT subcommand. These values may not be the exact scale limitations but are used to fit an appropriate scale. RANGE can be specified only with LINEAR or LOG axes.

REFERENCE value *Draw a line through this value perpendicular to the Y axis.* The reference value must be within RANGE if RANGE is specified.

NAME 'label' *Assign this label to the Y axis.* The Y axis label is either the first Y AXIS specification or follows the NAME keyword anywhere else in the specification field. This label can be up to 40 characters long and must be enclosed in apostrophes or quotation marks.

For example, to label the Y axis and provide a reference line at the mean salary for the whole company, specify:

```
LINECHART  PLOT=MEAN(SALARY) WITH TENURE BY JOBGRADE/
  FORMAT=FRAME,FANCY/
  TITLE='CHICAGO HOME FURNISHING'
       'Employee Salary Analysis - Sales Department'/
  FOOTNOTE='As of December 1980'/
  X AXIS='Employment Tenure in Months' REFERENCE 29.7/
  Y AXIS='Mean Salary' REFERENCE 15600/
```

See the plot in Figure 24.60 for the results of this specification.

24.54 The CURVES Subcommand

Curves are drawn on the plot in a specific order. If they are the result of a BY (control) variable, they are generated in ascending value order for that variable (JOBGRADE=1 first, JOBGRADE=2 second, and so forth). If they are the result of multiple functions or multiple variables for the same function, they are created as the functions or variables are specified left to right. If there are multiple specifications in the function part and there is a control variable, the function part rotates slowest. For example, in the specification

```
LINECHART  PLOT=MEAN(INCOME1,INCOME2) WITH EDUC BY SEX/
```

four curves are drawn: the first is the mean of INCOME1 for the first value of SEX, the second is the mean of INCOME1 for the second value of SEX, the third and fourth are the mean of INCOME2 for each value of SEX.

If the function is the mean with standard deviations or a regression line with confidence bounds, the mean or regression line is drawn first, then the plus standard deviation or the upper bound, then the minus standard deviation or the lower bound. In discussions of order, the VALUES function generates a "curve" in the normal order, even though lines are not drawn through the points.

You can follow the general rule that curves are drawn left to right as you specify functions and variables left to right in the PLOT subcommand. The same rule applies when more than one line chart is superimposed on the same plot. You must know this order not only to assign patterns or legend labels but to distinguish an individual curve or a subset of curves on the CURVES subcommand.

Use the CURVES subcommand to define how data points should be interpolated and whether individual points should be marked. You can specify each curve separately, groups of curves, or all curves at once. The first CURVES specification must be the keyword ALL or a number list indicating the curves you are specifying. The list is composed of integers from 1 to the number of curves. You can use the keyword TO to specify a range, as in 2 TO 5. Any number not mentioned leaves the corresponding curve at its default. You can then control the curves with the following keywords.

STRAIGHT* *Use a straight line to connect the data points.* This is the default for all functions except VALUES.

SPLINE *Use a spline interpolation to connect the data points.*

STEP *Draw the curve in steps centered on the data points.*

POINTS *Don't connect the data points.* This is the default for the VALUES function.

MARKERS *Place markers at every point on the curves.* The default specification is NO MARKERS for curves. Also by default, the function VALUES has markers since there is no curve. Keyword NO is used with MARKERS to turn off a user-defined default.

To define groups of curves, you can repeat the entire specification beginning with the number list. For example, if you prefer to have the first three curves connected with spline interpolated lines and the fourth connected in steps (anticipating inclusion of the fourth job grade in the final plot), specify:

```
LINECHART  PLOT=MEAN(SALARY) WITH TENURE BY JOBGRADE/
  FORMAT=FRAME,FANCY/
  TITLE='CHICAGO HOME FURNISHING'
        'Employee Salary Analysis - Sales Department'/
  FOOTNOTE='As of December 1980'/
  X AXIS='Employment Tenure in Months' REFERENCE 29.7/
  Y AXIS='Mean Salary' REFERENCE 15600/
  CURVES=1 TO 3 SPLINE, 4 STEP/
```

The curves drawn in this manner are shown in Figure 24.60.

24.55 The LEGEND TITLE and LEGEND LABELS Subcommands

Use the LEGEND LABELS subcommand to provide a title up to 20 characters long for the legend. The default title is the word "Legend." To provide your own labels for the categories of the control variable and/or to the multiple functions, use the LEGEND LABELS subcommand. These labels can also be up to 20 characters. For a single function and a BY variable, the control variable's value labels are used by default; and if there are no value labels, the variable name followed by the value is used. For multiple functions and a control variable, combinations of the function keyword, value labels, and the variable name followed by the value are used. When the PLOT specification is complicated, however, you should probably provide your own labels according to the order described in Section 24.54.

For example, to title the legend box and provide your own labels for the control variable JOBGRADE, specify:

```
LINECHART  PLOT=MEAN(SALARY) WITH TENURE BY JOBGRADE/
  FORMAT=FRAME,FANCY/
  TITLE='CHICAGO HOME FURNISHING'
        'Employee Salary Analysis - Sales Department'/
  FOOTNOTE='As of December 1980'/
  X AXIS='Employment Tenure in Months' REFERENCE 29.7/
  Y AXIS='Mean Salary' REFERENCE 15600/
  CURVES=1 TO 3 SPLINE, 4 STEP/
  LEGEND TITLE='Job Category'/
  LEGEND LABELS='Salesclerks' 'Supervisors'
               'Managers' 'Support'/
```

The fourth legend label appears in the final plot shown in Figure 24.60 as a result of including the previously missing fourth category.

24.56 The ORDER Subcommand

The ORDER subcommand controls the order in which LINECHART uses patterns and markers from those shown in Figures 24.56a and 24.56b. By default, curve or shade patterns are applied in the order curves are drawn on each plot, which is the order described in Section 24.54.

Figure 24.56a The LINECHART curve patterns and markers

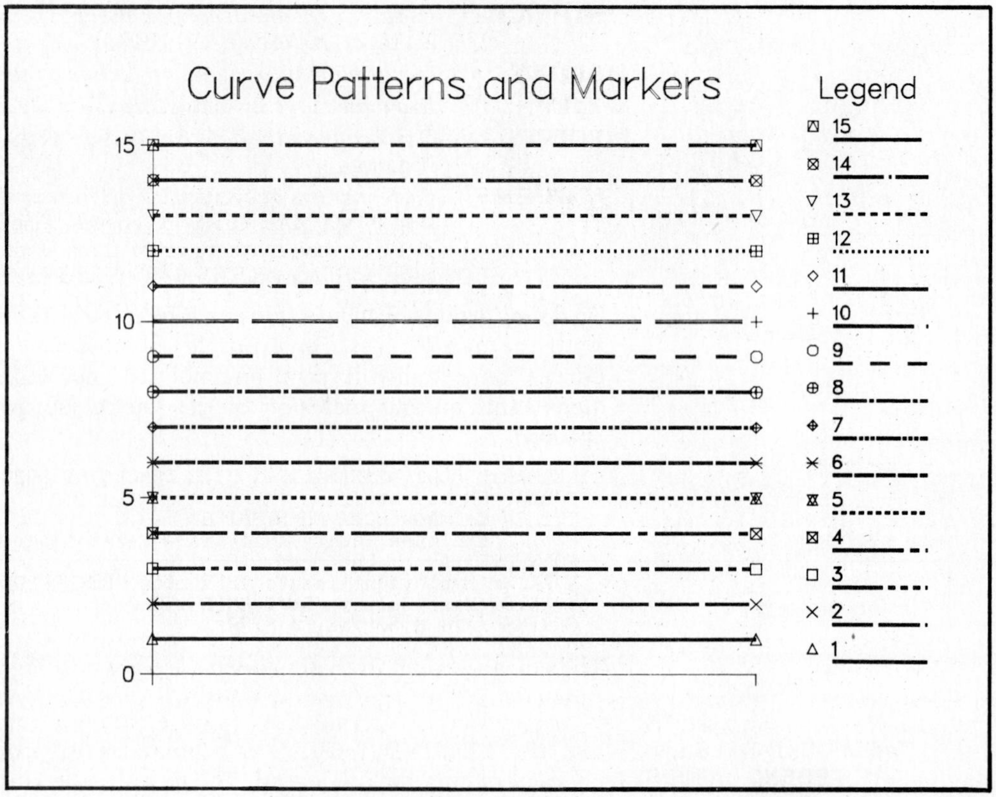

To choose your own curve patterns, use the ORDER subcommand to specify the corresponding pattern numbers in the order the curves are drawn. For example, if you want solid curve pattern 1 applied to the fourth curve representing the support staff for variable JOBGRADE and curve patterns 5, 6, and 7 applied to the first three categories, specify:

```
LINECHART  PLOT=MEAN(SALARY) WITH TENURE BY JOBGRADE/
  FORMAT=FRAME,FANCY/
  TITLE='CHICAGO HOME FURNISHING'
       'Employee Salary Analysis - Sales Department'/
  FOOTNOTE='As of December 1980'/
  X AXIS='Employment Tenure in Months' REFERENCE 29.7/
  Y AXIS='Mean Salary' REFERENCE 15600/
  CURVES=1 TO 3 SPLINE, 4 STEP/
  LEGEND TITLE='Job Category'/
  LEGEND LABELS='Salesclerks' 'Supervisors'
               'Managers' 'Support'/
  ORDER=5,6,7,1/
```

Enter pattern numbers from 1 to 15 for the curves or shading you want to alter, even if you might be respecifying the default value for a particular curve. If you specify fewer pattern numbers than there are curves, the remaining curves have the default patterns in the original sequence. If you specify more, the remainder are not used. The effect of choosing a different

Figure 24.56b The LINECHART shade patterns

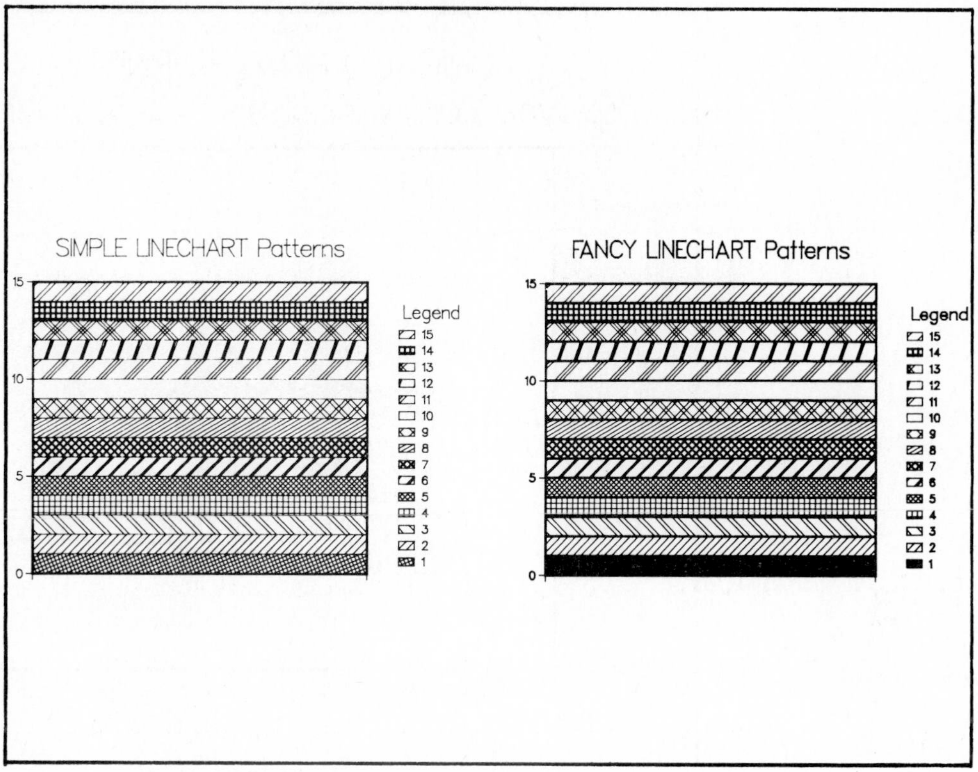

pattern is shown in Figure 24.60. You can select the same pattern for different curves in a set by repeating its order number.

Use caution in overriding the default patterns when you are using any of the mean functions with standard deviations or the regression functions with confidence limits (Section 24.44). The default patterns are set so that the standard deviation curves and the confidence limits have the same pattern. If you want to override them, they are created following the mean curve or the regression curve, with the plus standard deviation or the upper confidence limit coming next.

You should also know something about the resolution of the final device you intend to use to produce the final plots. If the device has high resolution, you can use any curve pattern you want. If it has relatively low resolution, you may want to stay with the default patterns because they are chosen to be distinguishable on these kinds of devices.

24.57 The COLORS Subcommand

To produce plots, you must know how many colors the device supports in addition to black. A black-and-white device supports zero additional colors, an eight-pen plotter supports seven additional colors. The default specification for the COLORS subcommand is 0.

If you intend to produce your line chart on a four-color device, to take advantage of the three additional colors, specify:

```
COLORS=3/
```

If you specify more than zero colors, LINECHART uses the additional colors to draw the curves and markers, using all available colors in one pattern before moving to the next pattern in the default order. To override the default color/pattern combinations, use the ORDER subcommand as documented for PIECHART (see Section 24.15).

Figure 24.60 An enhanced line chart

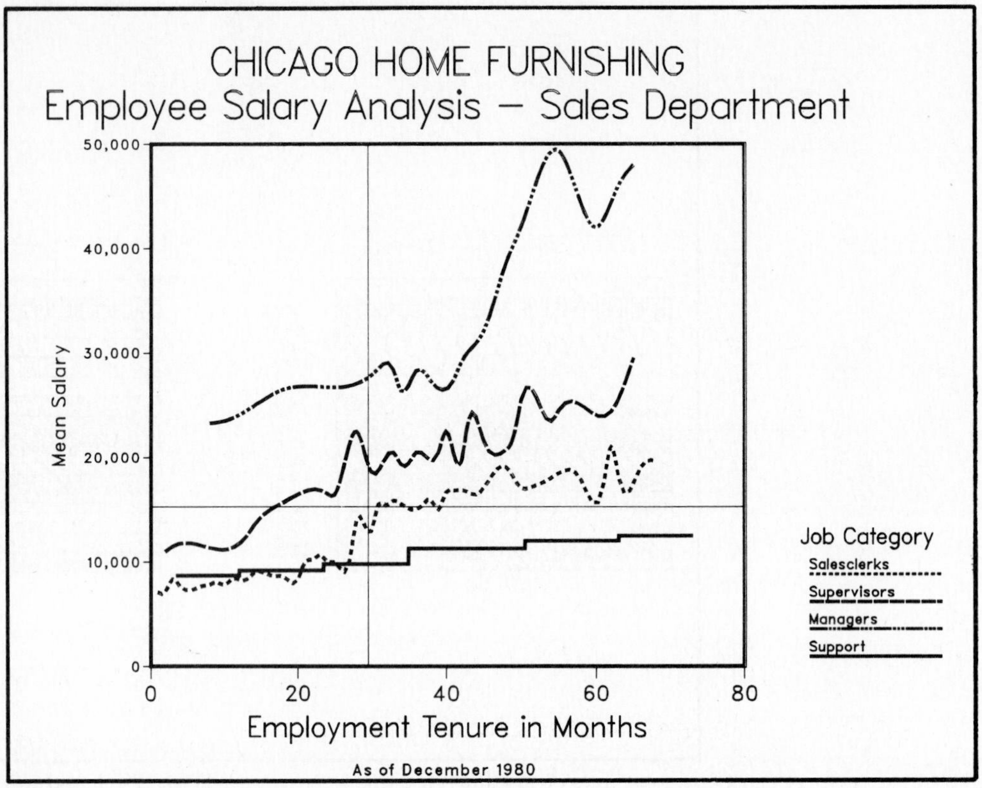

24.58 The FONT Subcommand

If you specify FORMAT=FANCY, you can choose among four fonts: DUPLEX, COMPLEX, TRIPLEX, and GOTHIC. Examples of these styles are in Figure 24.16. Your choice of font applies to all annotation in the graph except the comment line, which is always duplex when FORMAT=FANCY.

24.59 The XPAGE and YPAGE Subcommands

If the default page size, 11 inches wide by 8½ inches high, is not satisfactory, you can change it with the XPAGE and YPAGE commands documented in Section 24.17.

24.60 The MISSING Subcommand

By default, LINECHART does not include a case in calculating data points if the case has missing values on the variables involved in the particular curve. You can control missing-value treatment by using the MISSING subcommand with one of the following keyword specifications.

LINEWISE* *Omit cases with missing values on the variable used in the curve being produced.* If you specify multiple variables in the function part of the PLOT subcommand, cases are examined for missing values for each variable independently. Also, if you superimpose line charts, cases are examined for each chart separately.

PLOTWISE *Omit cases with missing values on any variable named in the PLOT subcommand.* Line charts produced from multiple-variable specifications or from superimposed line charts are based on the same cases.

NONE *Include all cases regardless of missing values.*

To tell LINECHART to ignore missing-value declarations for all variables specified in the PLOT subcommand, use keyword NONE. For example, clerical and other staff were declared missing to separate support personnel from the rest of the staff and thus were excluded by the default missing-value treatment from the chart shown in Figure 24.4. To include them in the final display, specify:

```
LINECHART  PLOT=MEAN(SALARY) WITH TENURE BY JOBGRADE/
  FORMAT=FRAME,FANCY/
  TITLE='CHICAGO HOME FURNISHING'
       'Employee Salary Analysis - Sales Department'/
  FOOTNOTE='As of December 1980'/
  X AXIS='Employment Tenure in Months' REFERENCE 29.6/
  Y AXIS='Mean Salary' REFERENCE 15300/
  CURVES=1 TO 3 SPLINE, 4 STEP/
  LEGEND TITLE='Job Category'/
  LEGEND LABELS='Salesclerks' 'Supervisors'
                'Managers' 'Support'/
  ORDER=5,6,7,1/
  MISSING=NONE/
```

The plot produced by this command is shown in Figure 24.60. Note that the additional curve, the fourth legend label, the different reference values, and the additional pattern were specified to account for the inclusion of the missing value. If these additions were not specified, the curve would have been connected with straight lines between points, the legend label would have defaulted to the value label, and the pattern would have been pattern 4 from Figure 24.56a instead of the solid pattern selected with number 1. The reference lines describing the means would not have been correct for the full set of cases in the chart.

24.61 Multiple PLOT Subcommands

More than one PLOT subcommand can be specified in a LINECHART command. This is helpful particularly when some attributes are common to all plots and others are specific to each plot. Each new PLOT subcommand returns all attributes to their defaults. You can establish your own defaults for all subsequent plots in the LINECHART command by specifying the keyword DEFAULT before any of the attribute subcommands FORMAT, TITLE, FOOTNOTE, COMMENT, X AXIS, Y AXIS, CURVES, LEGEND TITLE, LEGEND LABELS, ORDER, COLOR, FONT, XPAGE, YPAGE, and MISSING.

For example, you might want to support the plot shown in Figure 24.60 with plots that show how individual salaries are distributed about the mean within each job category. You decide to use four separate plots in order to focus on the range appropriate for each category and to avoid crowding too much information into a single plot. You can combine the plots in one LINECHART command and define your own defaults to save repeating subcommands.

```
LINECHART  PLOT=MEAN(SALARY) WITH TENURE BY JOBGRADE /
  DEFAULT FORMAT=FRAME,FANCY/
  TITLE='CHICAGO HOME FURNISHING'
       'Employee Salary Analysis - Sales Department'/
  DEFAULT FOOTNOTE='As of December 1980'/
  X AXIS='Employment Tenure in Months' REFERENCE 29.6/
  Y AXIS='Mean Salary' REFERENCE 15300/
  CURVES=1 TO 3 SPLINE, 4 STEP/
  LEGEND TITLE='Job Category'/
  LEGEND LABELS='Salesclerks' 'Supervisors'
                'Managers' 'Support'/
  ORDER=5,6,7,1/
  DEFAULT MISSING=NONE/
  PLOT=MEAN(SALARY) VALUES(SALARY) WITH TENURE BY JOBGRADE(1)/
  TITLE='Salesclerks'/
  DEFAULT X AXIS='Employment Tenure in Months'/
  DEFAULT Y AXIS='Salary'/
  DEFAULT LEGEND TITLE=' '/
  DEFAULT LEGEND LABELS='Mean' 'Individual'/
  DEFAULT ORDER=1,1/
  PLOT=MEAN(SALARY) VALUES(SALARY) WITH TENURE BY JOBGRADE(2)/
  TITLE='Sales Department Supervisors'/
  PLOT=MEAN(SALARY) VALUES(SALARY) WITH TENURE BY JOBGRADE(3)/
  TITLE='Sales Department Managers'/
  PLOT=MEAN(SALARY) VALUES(SALARY) WITH TENURE BY JOBGRADE(4)/
  TITLE='Sales Support Staff'/
```

The desired format, footnote, and missing-value treatment are consistent for all plots, so you can define them as defaults following the first PLOT subcommand and they will apply to all subsequent plots (unless you specifically override them). The X and Y axis labels and the legend title and labels are the same for the last four plots, so you define them as defaults following the second PLOT subcommand. By specifying DEFAULT ORDER =1,1 you obtain for the four plots the curve pattern and the marker for pattern 1; had you not specified an order, you would have obtained the first curve pattern and the second marker. Since you want straight-line interpolation of points, you let the CURVES specifications from the first plot revert to the defaults. And, since you need separate titles to identify the four plots, you specify them individually.

In this example, titles are chosen in anticipation of combining the plots under a common title. The example continues in the annotated session for the SPSS Graphics Postprocessor.

24.62 LINECHART Applications

LINECHART applications are probably more varied than those of either PIECHART or BARCHART because of the greater variety of relationships that line charts can show between variables. A single line chart can vary from a single curve to a scatterplot to a shaded line chart. Earlier sections have illustrated some applications of single and multiple curves. The following examples illustrate LINECHART applications involving regression lines and shaded charts.

24.63 Plotting Regression Lines

To produce a regression line and confidence intervals superimposed on a scatterplot, you must use both the VALUES function to obtain the scatter-

Figure 24.63 A regression line with confidence bounds

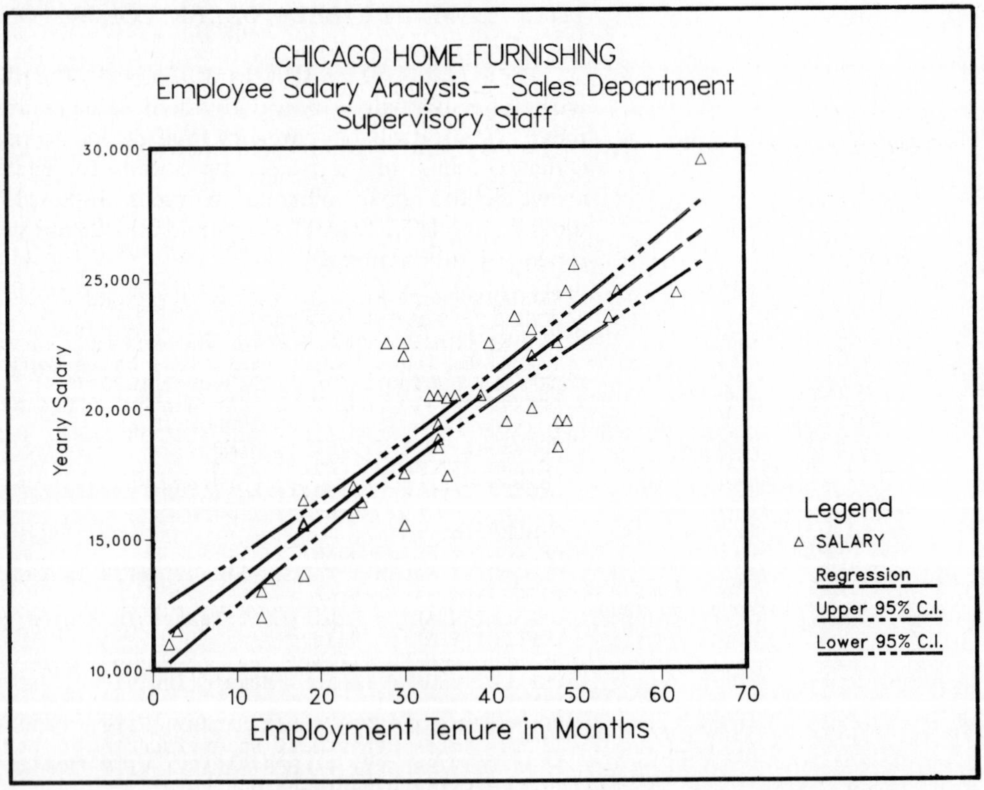

plot and one of the regression functions to draw the regression line. For example, to produce a regression line and confidence bounds for the mean salary of supervisory staff members based on their tenure with the company, superimposed on a scatterplot, specify:

```
SELECT IF   (JOBGRADE EQ 2)
LINECHART  PLOT VALUES(SALARY) M95(SALARY) WITH TENURE/
  FORMAT FRAME,FANCY/
  TITLE 'CHICAGO HOME FURNISHING'
        'Employee Salary Analysis - Sales Department'
        'Supervisory Staff'/
  X AXIS 'Employment Tenure in Months'/
  Y AXIS 'Yearly Salary'/
```

The SELECT IF command is used in this example in place of BY JOBGRADE(2) to simplify the legend box.

24.64 Shaded Line Charts

To produce a shaded line chart with two or more curves, the X axis ranges and the Y axis scales must be identical. For instance, the plot shown in Figure 24.60 cannot be shaded since the minimum and maximum values of TENURE vary for the four job categories. In addition, it would make no sense to stack the mean salary values on the Y axis.

A better example is found in another data file for the same company where sales figures are recorded for the four divisions in variables FURN, APPL, HARD, and CARP for each quarter since January, 1975. Since the hardware and carpeting divisions opened in 1976, sales values of 0 were entered for previous quarters. To produce a plot of gross receipts across quarters subdivided into the four divisions, specify:

```
LINECHART  PLOT SUM(FURN,APPL,HARD,CARP) WITH QUARTER/
  FORMAT FRAME,FANCY,SHADE/
  TITLE 'CHICAGO HOME FURNISHING'
        'Analysis of Quarterly Sales'/
  Y AXIS 'Sales in Dollars'/
  X AXIS LABELED '1975' ' ' ' ' ' ' '1976' ' ' ' ' ' '
                 '1977' ' ' ' ' ' ' '1978' ' ' ' ' ' '
                 '1979' ' ' ' ' ' ' '1980' ' ' ' ' ' '  /
  LEGEND TITLE ' ' /
  LEGEND LABELS 'Furniture' 'Appliance'
                'Hardware' 'Carpeting'/
  CURVES ALL SPLINE/
  ORDER 1,8,5,7/
```

In this example, shown in Figure 24.64a, note how the X axis yearly labels were applied, how the shading patterns were selected from Figure 24.56b, and how the legend title was suppressed. It makes good sense in this case to stack the curves since the Y axis measures total company sales by quarter. Sometimes it is also helpful to represent subpopulations as a proportion of the whole. In this example, it would be interesting to chart the contribution of each division to the total company sales across time. To do this, four new variables must be computed that measure the percentages.

```
COMPUTE  TOTAL=(CARP+FURN+APPL+HARD)
COMPUTE  PCARP=CARP*100/TOTAL
COMPUTE  PFURN=FURN*100/TOTAL
COMPUTE  PAPPL=APPL*100/TOTAL
COMPUTE  PHARD=HARD*100/TOTAL
```

Then, since all the subcommands for the previous example except Y AXIS apply to this plot, the LINECHART command that would produce both the plot shown in Figure 24.64a and the one shown in Figure 24.64b is

```
LINECHART  PLOT SUM(FURN,APPL,HARD,CARP) WITH QUARTER/
  DEFAULT FORMAT FRAME,FANCY,SHADE/
  DEFAULT TITLE 'CHICAGO HOME FURNISHING'
               'Analysis of Quarterly Sales'/
  Y AXIS 'Sales in Dollars'/
  DEFAULT X AXIS LABELED '1975' ' ' ' ' ' ' '1976' ' ' ' ' ' '
                         '1977' ' ' ' ' ' ' '1978' ' ' ' ' ' '
                         '1979' ' ' ' ' ' ' '1980' ' ' ' ' ' ' '/
  DEFAULT LEGEND TITLE ' ' /
  DEFAULT LEGEND LABELS 'Furniture' 'Appliance'
                        'Hardware' 'Carpeting'/
  DEFAULT CURVES ALL SPLINE/
  DEFAULT ORDER 1,8,5,7/
  PLOT SUM(PFURN,PAPPL,PHARD,PCARP) WITH QUARTER/
  Y AXIS 'Percent Total Sales' RANGE 0 100/
```

The RANGE specification on the Y AXIS subcommand for the second plot forces the plot boundary to stop at 100.

To produce the same plot on a four-color plotter, as illustrated in the shaded plot on the inside back cover of this manual, specify:

```
COLORS=3/
```

and select an order of patterns suitable for three additional colors. The order established for the first two plots, 1, 8, 5, 7, would use only two colors (see Table 24.15), so for the plot shown on the inside back cover, patterns are restored to system defaults, ORDER=1, 2, 3, 4.

24.65 THE TELL-A-GRAF INTERFACE

SPSS Graphics provides all of the basic elements for graphic presentation of pie, bar, and line charts. In addition, many options are provided for enhancing each plot to accommodate various modes of presentation and a number of aesthetic choices. However, this is not all there is to modification and enhancement of high-quality graphics. Each of the three SPSS Graphics procedures features the SAVE subcommand, which directs a plot to be saved into a permanent file system used by the TELL-A-GRAF graphics system. SPSS-generated plots can be further enhanced with different types and sizes of lettering, extended annotation, layout development, shading, blanking, and so forth, via the CONTINUE command in TELL-A-GRAF.

TELL-A-GRAF is a convenient, interactive proprietary software product of ISSCO, Integrated Software Systems Corporation, of San Diego, California. The documentation for and information about TELL-A-GRAF is available from them. Look especially for discussions of options and annotation in the Reference Manual.

The SPSS Graphics SAVE subcommand can be specified at any point after the PLOT subcommand that initiates the plot you want to save for TELL-A-GRAF. The specification for SAVE is the name of the plot you will specify on the DRAW or CONTINUE commands in TELL-A-GRAF. The name must begin with an alphabetic character and can be no longer than 12 letters or digits. There is no default, and SAVE cannot be prefaced by DEFAULT.

For example, to save the two pie charts generated in Section 24.19, specify:

```
PIECHART  PLOT=JOBGRADE/ DEFAULT FORMAT=FANCY,SORT/
  DEFAULT TITLE='CHICAGO HOME FURNISHING'
               'Employee Study - Sales Department'/
  DEFAULT FOOTNOTE='As of December 1980'/
  SEGMENT LABELS=(1)'Salesclerks' (2)'Supervisors'
                 (3)'Managers' (4)'Support'/
  EXPLODE=3/ ORDER=5,2,1,10/
  DEFAULT MISSING=NONE/
  SAVE=CHICAGOPIE1/
  PLOT=DIVISION/
  SEGMENT LABELS=(1)'Carpeting' (2)'Appliances'
                 (3)'Furniture' (4)'Hardware'/
  SAVE=CHICAGOPIE2/
```

Figure 24.64a A shaded line chart—sales

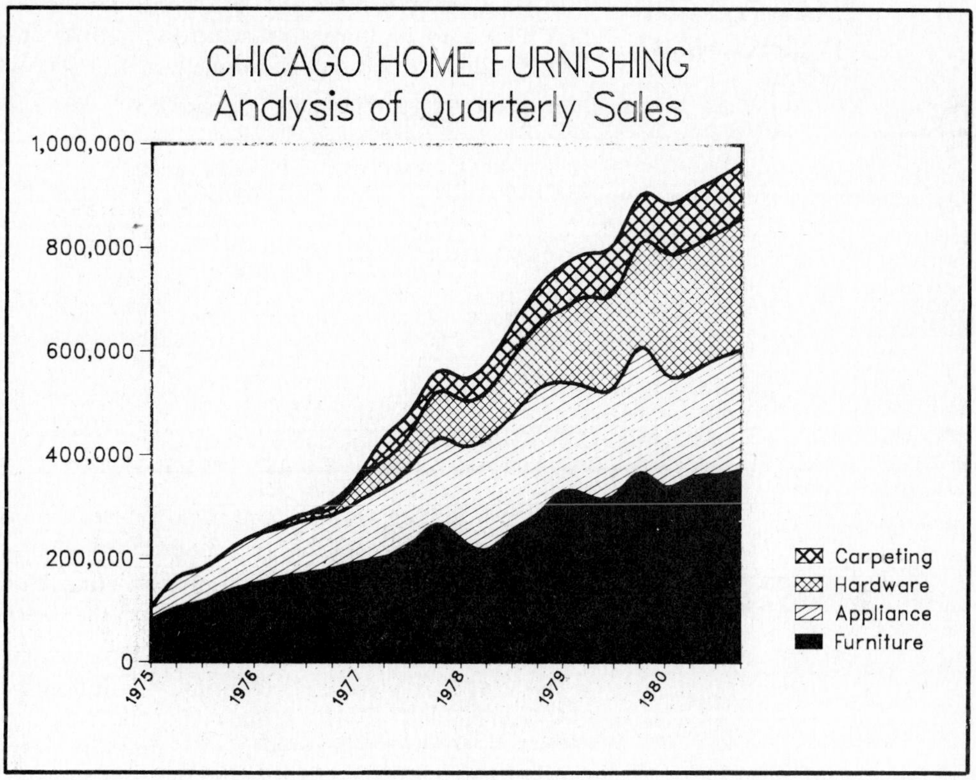

Figure 24.64b A shaded line chart—percent of sales

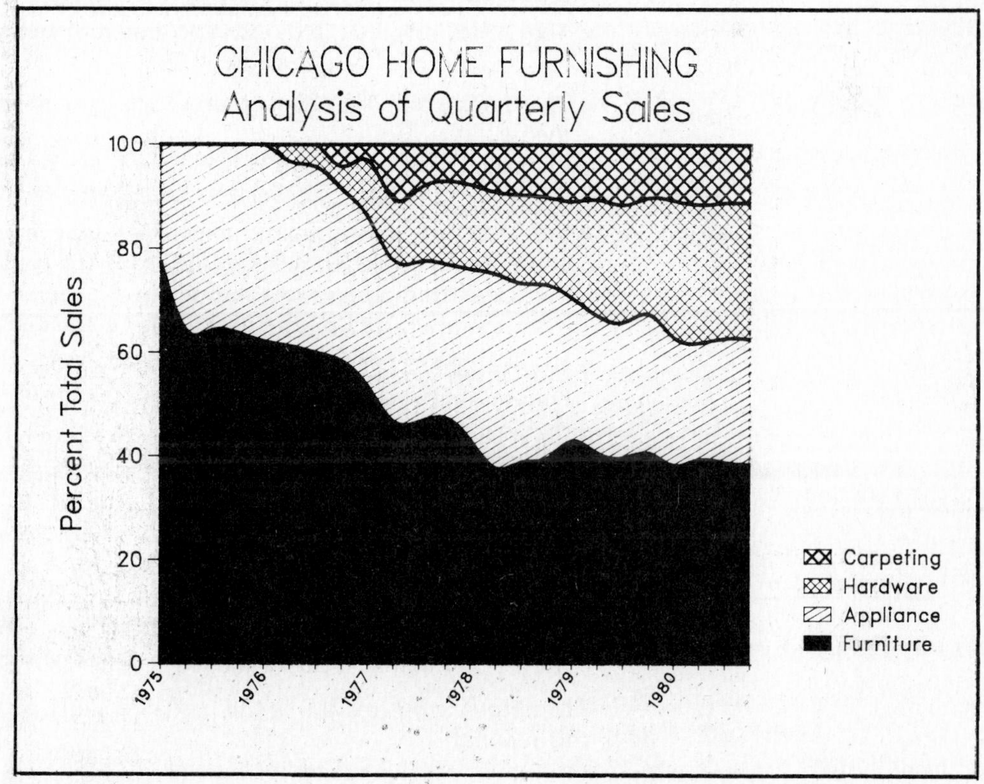

ANNOTATED EXAMPLE FOR LINECHART

The data for this example come from the same personnel file used for the PIECHART and BARCHART examples and throughout this chapter. The task here is to produce a presentation-quality chart showing the relationship of salary to job tenure for each of four job categories.

```
FILE HANDLE  EMPLOYEE/ file specifications
GET  FILE=EMPLOYEE

FILE HANDLE  EMPPLOT3/ file specifications
GRAPHICS OUTPUT  OUTFILE=EMPPLOT3

LINECHART  PLOT=MEAN(SALARY) WITH TENURE BY JOBGRADE/
  FORMAT=FRAME,FANCY/
  TITLE='CHICAGO HOME FURNISHING'
      'Employee Salary Analysis - Sales Department'/
  FOOTNOTE='As of December 1980'/
  X AXIS='Employment Tenure in Months' REFERENCE 29.6/
  Y AXIS='Mean Salary' REFERENCE 15300/
  CURVES=1 TO 3 SPLINE, 4 STEP/
  LEGEND TITLE='Job Category'/
  LEGEND LABELS='Salesclerks' 'Supervisors'
    'Managers' 'Support'/
  COLORS=3/ ORDER=1,2,3,13/  MISSING=NONE/
```

- The first FILE HANDLE command defines the system file accessed by the GET command (see Chapters 3 and 5).
- The second FILE HANDLE command defines the output file named on the GRAPHICS OUTPUT command. This is the *intermediate file* to be accessed by the Graphics Postprocessor (see Section 24.66).
- The PLOT subcommand identifies the function (MEAN) and the dependent variable (SALARY) that define the Y axis, the independent variable (TENURE) that defines the X axis, and the control variable (JOBGRADE) that divides the chart into four lines, one for each job classification (see Sections 24.43 through 24.48).
- The FORMAT subcommand requests a frame and a fancy format (see Section 24.49).
- The TITLE and FOOTNOTE subcommands define a two-line title and a one-line footnote (see Section 24.50).
- The X AXIS and Y AXIS subcommands override default specifications for the two axes. Both commands specify a label for the axis and a reference line to be drawn through values previously determined to be means for the entire company (see Sections 24.52 and 24.53).
- The CURVES subcommand specifies spline interpolation for the data points for the first three job categories (instead of the default straight lines between points) and a stepped line to emphasize the correspondence between salary and tenure for support personnel (see Section 24.54).
- The LEGEND TITLE and LEGEND LABELS subcommands specify annotation for the legend (see Section 24.55).
- The COLORS subcommand specifies three colors, in addition to black, to be used to draw the plot. (see Section 24.57).
- The ORDER subcommand selects the order in which combinations of color and pattern are applied to the curves. (see Section 24.56).
- The MISSING subcommand overrides the default missing-value treatment, which is to omit cases with missing values. Here, because value 4 for JOBGRADE has been declared missing, the MISSING subcommand is needed to include support staff in the plot (see Section 24.60).

The output from this job is the first line chart on the inside back cover of this manual.

The names CHICAGOPIE1 and CHICAGOPIE2 can then be used with the TELL-A-GRAF CONTINUE command to develop these plots further. When you execute the SPSS Graphics Postprocessor, you will be prompted for more information about the PRMFILE, which is your link to TELL-A-GRAF. If your installation has both SPSS Graphics and TELL-A-GRAF, it will have additional documentation on the interface between the two.

In BARCHART and LINECHART, each SAVE subcommand saves the single plot generated by the preceding PLOT subcommand. In PIECHART, only the last plot generated by a control (BY) variable in a PLOT subcommand is saved.

24.66 THE GRAPHICS OUTPUT COMMAND

The three Graphics procedures within SPSS^{X} write plots to an *intermediate file* that is then accessed by the Graphics Postprocessor to draw the plots on a graphics device. To identify the intermediate file, give the file handle on the GRAPHICS OUTPUT command preceding the Graphics procedures, as in:

```
GRAPHICS OUTPUT  OUTFILE=CHIGPLTS
```

Unlike the file named on a PROCEDURE OUTPUT command, which contains the output from just one procedure command (Chapter 17), the file named on the GRAPHICS OUTPUT command accepts the output from all PIECHART, BARCHART, and LINECHART commands in your job. If you enter more than one GRAPHICS OUTPUT command, plots are written to the most recently named output file.

24.67 THE SPSS GRAPHICS POSTPROCESSOR

The SPSS Graphics Postprocessor, SPSSGP, is an interactive system that allows you to preview your plots on one device and send those that you like to a second device for final production. The postprocessor also allows you to combine two or more plots on the same page before sending them to the final plotting device.

The postprocessor may also be available in batch mode at your installation, usually as a built-in second step to your SPSS Batch System job. The batch application of the postprocessor allows you to enter postprocessor commands in a batch job. If your installation makes the batch facility available, you can obtain information about it via the INFO command (see Chapter 2).

To operate the SPSS Graphics Postprocessor, sign on to your local installation's host system and access it according to local documentation. You will either name your intermediate file as part of the command(s) that access the postprocessor or be prompted for the file name once you are in the postprocessor session. When the postprocessor has found your file and identified it as an intermediate graphics file, it asks for the name of the your primary graphics device. If you plan to preview your plots on one device and send them to another for production, the primary device should be the one on which you are doing your previewing. Depending on your choice of device, the postprocessor may prompt for other information, such as model number or pen speed.

If you are uncertain of an answer, you can get brief instructions by entering HELP or just a question mark. For example, if you name a device that is not usually connected to your terminal, you are prompted for the mode of operation; and if you are unsure how to respond, you can ask for

ANNOTATED EXAMPLE FOR THE SPSS GRAPHICS POSTPROCESSOR

In Section 24.61, four line charts are produced with titles suitable for combining on one page under one general title. In the following session of the SPSS Graphics Postprocessor those plots are combined for preview on a graphics terminal and then sent to a pen plotter for a final version.

The first task is to access the postprocessor and name your intermediate graphics file. That process varies not only by computer and operating system but by individual installation. Information is available via the INFO command (see Chapter 2). In the following session, the postprocessor is accessed by the simple command SPSSGP, and it prompts for the intermediate file.

```
spssgp
SPSS GRAPHICS POSTPROCESSOR - RELEASE 2.0
TYPE HELP FOR HELP.


INTERMEDIATE FILE?
empplot4
```

The next information the postprocessor needs is the name of the primary graphics device you are using. You name the Hewlett-Packard 2648 terminal.

```
PRIMARY DEVICE?
hp2648
```

The postprocessor then offers you the choice of using hardware characters. Hardware characters are used only in simple and preview plots, and they speed drawing, so you answer yes.

```
HARDWARE CHARACTERS? (Y/N)
y
```

The postprocessor has enough information to begin processing, so it asks for your command. First you want to examine the contents of your file. You see that the plots you want to combine are there, but they are not in the order in which you want to combine them.

```
COMMAND?
contents
TABLE OF CONTENTS

PLOT
  1  LINE        "CHICAGO HOME FURNISHING""Employee Salary Analysis "
  2  LINE        "Salesclerks"
  3  LINE        "Sales Department Supervisors"
  4  LINE        "Sales Department Managers"
  5  LINE        "Sales Support Staff"
```

Because you simply want to see quickly how your plots will look, you ask for preview-quality plots.

```
COMMAND?
preview
```

You combine the plots in the order you prefer, and the postprocessor prompts for a title. Once you give the title the plots are drawn on your terminal.

```
COMMAND?
combine 4,3,2,5
TITLE?
Chicago Home Furnishing Salary Analysis
```

Since they appear to be satisfactory, you now want to plot them on your secondary device. You hit the carriage return when the plots are completed on the HP2648; and when the postprocessor prompts for a new command, you name the HP7221 pen plotter as your secondary device. It must be attached to your primary device before you can send it plots. The postprocessor asks for additional information. Being uncertain what to reply to the PEN SPEED? prompt, you enter a question mark. Since the default appears satisfactory, when the prompt returns you simply hit return.

```
COMMAND?
assign
SECONDARY DEVICE?
hp7221
MODEL TYPE?
b
PEN SPEED?
?
ENTER THE PEN SPEED YOU WANT BETWEEN 1-36.
DEFAULT 32 WILL BE USED IF YOU JUST HIT RETURN.
SLOWER PEN SPEEDS WILL RESULT IN BETTER SHADE QUALITY.
(PEN SPEEDS ARE MEASURED IN CM/SEC/SEC ACCELERATION.)

PEN SPEED?
```

You turn off the preview specification in order to produce fully formatted, color plots.

```
COMMAND?
no preview
COMMAND?
send
```

At this point the combined plots are drawn on the HP7221. When they are completed, you enter a carriage return, the postprocessor once again responds with COMMAND?, and you can either produce more plots on either device or enter QUIT, END, or STOP to end the session.

Combined plots

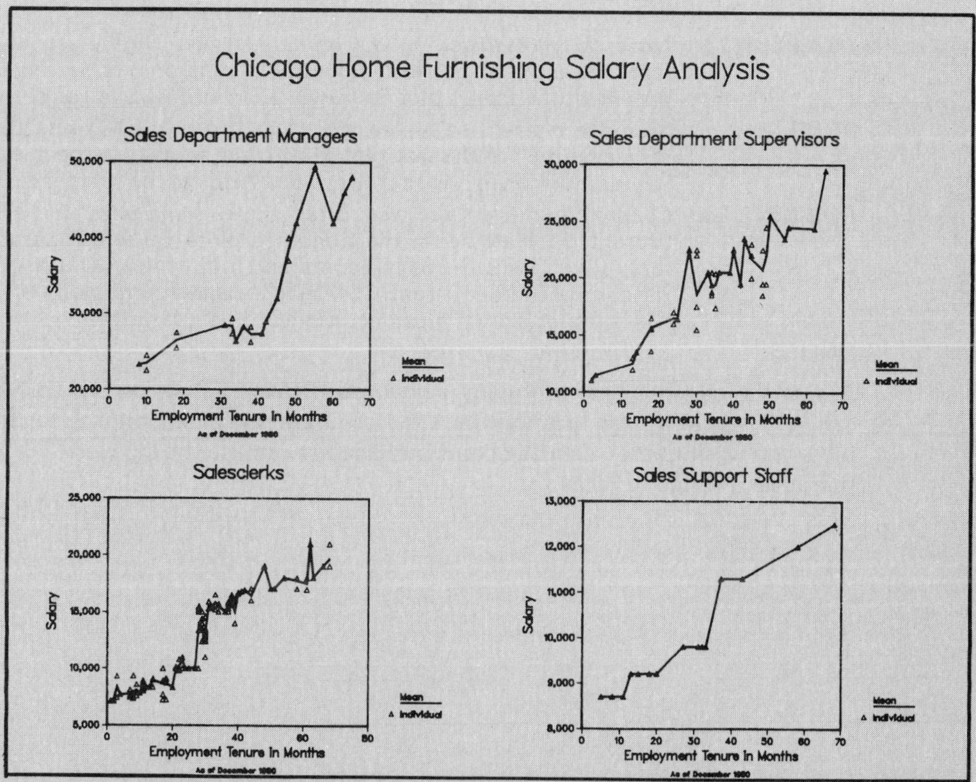

help, as in:

```
PRIMARY DEVICE?
calcomp
PLOTTER MODE?
?
HOW IS THE PLOTTER CONNECTED TO YOUR COMPUTER?
  DIRECT:  DIRECTLY ASSIGNED TO YOUR SESSION OR JOB
  INDIRECT:  ACCESSED VIA PLOT FILE, TAPE, OR SPOOL
  REMOTE:  CONNECTED TO YOUR TERMINAL
INDIRECT IS MOST COMMON. ASK YOUR SPSS COORDINATOR IF
YOU ARE UNSURE HOW YOUR PLOTTER IS CONNECTED.
```

Once the postprocessor has enough information to proceed, it prompts with COMMAND?.

You operate the postprocessor with seven commands.

HELP *Give a short explanation of the prompt.* For help regarding any of the commands, enter HELP followed by the command keyword.

PREVIEW *Display plots in simple format with no colors.* For all subsequent DRAW and SEND commands, your plots are forced to simple format and to black-and-white for preview purposes. This can be overridden at any time by respecifying the default NO PREVIEW, which means that all plots are displayed as created.

ASSIGN *Assign the secondary device.* You are prompted for details. A carriage return to the device prompt assigns the secondary device to the primary device (used to alter your assignment during the postprocessor session).

CONTENTS *Display the plot contents of the file.* The table of contents contains the plot number, plot type, and title text for each plot in the file.

DRAW list *Draw the plots listed on the primary device.* DRAW sets the target pointer to the last plot drawn plus one. If no list is provided, the target plot is drawn. Keyword ALL is valid.

SEND list *Send the plots listed to the secondary device.* SEND sets the target pointer to the last plot sent. If no number is specified, the last plot drawn is sent. Keyword ALL can be specified.

COMBINE list *Combine and draw the plots listed on the same page.* You are prompted for a title for the combined plots (up to 80 characters). If you issue the SEND command following a COMBINE, the combined page is sent. COMBINE sets the target pointer to the last plot drawn plus one. Keyword ALL is valid.

QUIT *Exit from the postprocessor.*

Any of the number lists following keywords DRAW, SEND, or COMBINE can be a single integer number or a list of numbers corresponding to the plots you want to plot, send, or combine. The list can use the keyword TO to reference a range of plots.

Independent Samples:

T-TEST GROUPS = varname ({**1, 2** | value | val1, val2})/VARIABLES = varlist

Paired Samples:

T-TEST PAIRS = varlist [WITH varlist] [/varlist . . .]

OPTIONS:
1 Include missing values.
2 Exclude missing values listwise.
3 Suppress variable labels.
4 Narrow formatting.

25

OVERVIEW, **25.1**

OPERATION, **25.2**
- Independent Samples, **25.3**
  - The GROUPS Subcommand, **25.4**
  - The VARIABLES Subcommand, **25.5**
- Paired Samples, **25.6**
- Independent and Paired Designs, **25.7**
- One-Tailed Significance Levels, **25.8**
- Missing Values, **25.9**
- Formatting Options, **25.10**

LIMITATIONS, **25.11**

Chapter 25 T-TEST

T-TEST compares sample means by calculating Student's t and tests the significance of the difference between the means. It tests either independent samples (different groups of cases) or paired samples (different variables). Other procedures that compare group means are ANOVA (Chapter 26), ONEWAY (Chapter 27), and MANOVA (Chapter 28).

25.1 OVERVIEW

T-TEST produces Student's t, degrees of freedom, and two-tailed probability for a comparison of two means. In addition, the mean, standard deviation, and standard error are displayed for each variable.

Independent-Samples Test. The GROUPS and VARIABLES subcommands divide the cases into two groups for a comparison of sample means. Both pooled- and separate-variance estimates are calculated, along with the F value used to test homogeneity of variances and its significance level. (See Section 25.3.)

Paired-Samples Test. The PAIRS subcommand compares means for variables and also reports the difference between means and the correlation coefficient. (See Section 25.6.)

Two-Tailed Significance Levels. T-TEST calculates the probability of the t value based on a two-tailed test of significance.

Missing Values. By default, T-TEST excludes cases with missing values on an analysis-by-analysis basis. Optionally, you can tell $SPSS^X$ to handle missing values as if they were valid or to delete cases with missing values listwise. (See Section 25.9.)

Formatting Options. You can suppress the printing of variable labels. You can also restrict the output to an 80-character width. (See Section 25.10.)

Statistics. There are no optional statistics for T-TEST. All statistics available are printed by default.

25.2 OPERATION

The T-TEST command operates by means of subcommands and associated OPTIONS commands. You can request tests of independent samples and one or more paired samples.

25.3 Independent Samples

An independent-samples test divides the cases into two groups and compares the group means on a single variable. This test requires the GROUPS and VARIABLES subcommands. You can specify only one independent-samples test per T-TEST command. The GROUPS subcommand must precede the VARIABLES subcommand, and the two must be separated by a slash.

ANNOTATED EXAMPLE FOR T-TEST

The example illustrating T-TEST analyzes 1979 prices and earnings in 45 cities around the world, compiled by the Union Bank of Switzerland. The variables are

- WORLD—the economic class of the country in which the city is located. The 45 cities are divided into three groups: cities in economically developed nations such as the United States and most European nations; cities in nations that are members of the Organization for Petroleum Exporting Countries (OPEC); and cities in underdeveloped countries. These groups are coded from 1 to 3 and are labeled 1ST WORLD, PETRO WORLD, and 3RD WORLD, respectively.
- NTCPRI—the city's net price level, based on more than 100 goods and services weighted by consumer habits. NTCPRI is expressed as the percentage above or below that of Zurich, where Zurich equals 100%.
- NTCSAL—the city's net salary level, calculated from average net hourly earnings in 12 occupations. NTCSAL is expressed as a percentage above or below that of Zurich, where Zurich equals 100%.
- NTCPUR—the city's net purchasing power level, calculated as the ratio of labor expended (measured in number of working hours) to the cost of more than 100 goods and services, weighted by consumer habits. NTCPUR is expressed as a percentage above or below that of Zurich, where Zurich equals 100%.
- WCLOTHES—the cost of medium-priced women's clothes, expressed as the percentage above or below that of Zurich, where Zurich equals 100%.
- MCLOTHES—the cost of medium-priced men's clothes, expressed as the percentage above or below that of Zurich, where Zurich equals 100%.

In this example we compare mean price, salary and purchasing power for cities grouped by economic class. We also compare the mean costs of women's and men's clothes. The SPSS^X commands are:

```
FILE HANDLE  CITY/ file specifications
GET  FILE=CITY/KEEP=NTCPRI, NTCSAL, NTCPUR, WCLOTHES, MCLOTHES, WORLD
VAR LABELS  WCLOTHES, MEDIUM-PRICED WOMEN'S CLOTHES/
            MCLOTHES, MEDIUM-PRICED MEN'S CLOTHES/
T-TEST  GROUPS=WORLD (1,3)/VARIABLES=NTCPRI NTCSAL NTCPUR/
   PAIRS=WCLOTHES MCLOTHES/NTCPRI WITH NTCPUR NTCSAL
FINISH
```

- The FILE HANDLE identifies the CITY data file and gives the operating-system specifications (see Chapter 3).
- The GET command defines the data to SPSS^X and selects the variables needed for analysis (see Chapter 5).
- The VAR LABELS commands assign new labels to the variables WCLOTHES and MCLOTHES (see Chapter 3).
- The T-TEST command requests an independent-samples test and a paired-samples test. For the independent-samples test, the variable WORLD specifies a grouping criterion that compares cities in first-world countries to cities in third-world countries. Cities in petro-world countries are not included.

Output from T-TEST command

T - T E S T

GROUP 1 - WORLD EQ 1.
GROUP 2 - WORLD EQ 3.

VARIABLE	NUMBER OF CASES	MEAN	STANDARD DEVIATION	STANDARD ERROR	F VALUE	2-TAIL PROB.	POOLED VARIANCE ESTIMATE T VALUE	DEGREES OF FREEDOM	2-TAIL PROB.	SEPARATE VARIANCE ESTIMATE T VALUE	DEGREES OF FREEDOM	2-TAIL PROB.
NTCPRI NET PRICE LEVEL												
GROUP 1	25	83.8400	13.309	2.662	1.23	0.637	3.50	36	0.001	3.38	22.28	0.003
GROUP 2	13	67.3077	14.773	4.097								
NTCSAL NET SALARY LEVEL												
GROUP 1	25	64.4000	19.026	3.805	2.06	0.210	6.33	35	0.000	7.18	30.07	0.000
GROUP 2	12	25.6667	13.241	3.822								
NTCPUR NET PURCHASING LEVEL												
GROUP 1	25	76.7600	21.491	4.298	1.50	0.493	6.28	35	0.000	6.74	26.26	0.000
GROUP 2	12	31.9167	17.573	5.073								

T - T E S T

VARIABLE	NUMBER OF CASES	MEAN	STANDARD DEVIATION	STANDARD ERROR	(DIFFERENCE) MEAN	STANDARD DEVIATION	STANDARD ERROR	CORR.	2-TAIL PROB.	T VALUE	DEGREES OF FREEDOM	2-TAIL PROB.
WCLOTHES MEDIUM-PRICED WOMEN'S CLOTHES		80.7111	30.195	4.501								
	45				-6.3333	17.916	2.671	0.807	0.000	-2.37	44	0.022
MCLOTHES MEDIUM-PRICED MEN'S CLOTHES		87.0444	26.192	3.905								
NTCPRI NET PRICE LEVEL		82.1591	19.773	2.981								
	44				23.4545	33.310	5.022	0.098	0.528	4.67	43	0.000
NTCPUR NET PURCHASING LEVEL		58.7045	28.806	4.343								
NTCPRI NET PRICE LEVEL		82.1591	19.773	2.981								
	44				31.8182	22.753	3.430	0.482	0.001	9.28	43	0.000
NTCSAL NET SALARY LEVEL		50.3409	24.295	3.663								

25.4 The GROUPS Subcommand

The GROUPS subcommand followed by an equals sign names the variable and the criterion for dividing the cases into two groups. You can name only one variable, which must be numeric or string. Long strings are truncated to short strings to define the categories. You can use any one of three different methods to define the two groups. In the first method, a single value in parentheses groups all cases with a code equal to or greater than the value into one group, and the remaining cases into the other group. For example, the command

```
T-TEST GROUPS=WORLD(2)/VARIABLES=NTCPUR
```

groups together all cases with the value of WORLD greater than or equal to 2. The remaining cases go into the other group. See Figure 25.4 for the output from this command.

Figure 25.4 Independent-samples T-TEST

```
- - - - - - - - - - - - - - - - - - - - - - - - - - - - - - T - T E S T - - - - - - - - - - - - - - - - - - - - - - - - - - - - - -

GROUP 1 - WORLD    GE         2.
GROUP 2 - WORLD    LT         2.
                                                                     * POOLED VARIANCE ESTIMATE * SEPARATE VARIANCE ESTIMATE
                                                     *               *                          *
VARIABLE        NUMBER                  STANDARD   STANDARD  *    F    2-TAIL *    T   DEGREES OF 2-TAIL *    T   DEGREES OF  2-TAIL
               OF CASES      MEAN      DEVIATION     ERROR   *  VALUE  PROB.  *  VALUE  FREEDOM   PROB.  *  VALUE  FREEDOM    PROB.
------------------------------------------------------------------------------------------------------------------------------------

NTCPUR    NET PURCHASING LEVEL                               *                *                          *
     GROUP 1     19      34.9474     17.831      4.091       *                *                          *
                                                             *   1.45  0.420  *  -6.87     42     0.000  *  -7.05    41.63    0.000
     GROUP 2     25      76.7600     21.491      4.298       *                *                          *
                                                             *                *                          *
------------------------------------------------------------------------------------------------------------------------------------
```

Alternatively, if you specify two values in parentheses, one group includes cases with the first value on the grouping variable, and the other includes cases with the second value, as in:

```
T-TEST  GROUPS=WORLD(1,3)/VARIABLES=NTCPUR
```

In this example, cases with values other than 1 or 3 for variable WORLD are not used.

If the grouping variable has only two values, coded 1 and 2, respectively, you do not have to specify a value list. For example, the command

```
T-TEST  GROUPS=SEX/VARIABLES=GRADES
```

groups all cases having the value 1 for SEX into one group and cases having the value 2 for SEX into the other group. All other cases are not used.

25.5 The VARIABLES Subcommand

The VARIABLES subcommand follows the GROUPS subcommand and names the variables being analyzed. You can use only numeric variables, and you can name up to 50 variables. The specifications for the variable list follow the usual SPSS^X conventions (see Chapter 2). For example,

```
T-TEST  GROUPS=WORLD(1,3)/VARIABLES=NTCPRI NTCSAL NTCPUR
```

compares the means of the two groups defined by WORLD for the variables NTCPRI, NTCSAL, and NTCPUR, while

```
T-TEST  GROUPS=WORLD(1,3)/VARIABLES=NTCPRI TO MCLOTHES
```

compares the means of the groups defined by WORLD for all variables between and including NTCPRI and MCLOTHES.

25.6 Paired Samples

A paired-samples test compares two variables with each other. A typical application of a paired-samples test is the comparison of pre- and post-course test scores for students in a class. To obtain a paired-samples *t* test, use the PAIRS subcommand.

The PAIRS subcommand names the variables being compared. You can use only numeric variables, and you can name up to 400 variables. The following command produces a comparison of two variables:

```
T-TEST  PAIRS=WCLOTHES MCLOTHES
```

Figure 25.6 shows the output produced by the PAIRS subcommand.

Figure 25.6 Paired-samples T-TEST

```
- - - - - - - - - - - - - - - - - - - - - - - - - - - - - - T - T E S T - - - - - - - - - - - - - - - - - - - - - - - - - - - - - -

VARIABLE   NUMBER                  STANDARD   STANDARD   *(DIFFERENCE) STANDARD    STANDARD   *      2-TAIL *    T     DEGREES OF 2-TAIL
           OF CASES      MEAN     DEVIATION      ERROR   *      MEAN   DEVIATION      ERROR   * CORR. PROB. * VALUE    FREEDOM   PROB.
--------------------------------------------------------------------------------------------------------------------------------------
WCLOTHES   MEDIUM-PRICED WOMEN'S CLOTHES                  *                                   *             *
                      80.7111      30.195      4.501      *                                   *             *
              45                                          *   -6.3333     17.916      2.671   * 0.807 0.000 *  -2.37       44      0.022
                      87.0444      26.192      3.905      *                                   *             *
MCLOTHES   MEDIUM-PRICED MEN'S CLOTHES                    *                                   *             *
--------------------------------------------------------------------------------------------------------------------------------------
```

If you specify a list of variables, each variable is compared with every other variable. For example, the command

```
T-TEST PAIRS=TEACHER CONSTRUC MANAGER
```

compares TEACHER with CONSTRUC, TEACHER with MANAGER, and CONSTRUC with MANAGER.

You can use the keyword WITH to request a test comparing every variable to the left of the keyword with every variable to the right of the keyword. For example,

```
T-TEST  PAIRS=TEACHER MANAGER WITH CONSTRUC ENGINEER
```

compares TEACHER with CONSTRUC, TEACHER with ENGINEER, MANAGER with CONSTRUC, and MANAGER with ENGINEER. TEACHER is not compared with MANAGER, and CONSTRUC is not compared with ENGINEER.

You can use the slash to separate analysis lists, as in

```
T-TEST  PAIRS=WCLOTHES MCLOTHES/NTCPRI WITH NTCPUR NTCSAL
```

which specifies two analysis lists.

25.7 Independent and Paired Designs

You can request both independent- and paired-samples tests on a single T-TEST command. You must specify the independent-samples test first. Thus, the GROUPS subcommand is first, followed by the VARIABLES subcommand and the PAIRS subcommand, as in:

```
T-TEST   GROUPS= WORLD(1,3)/VARIABLES=NTCPRI NTCSAL NTCPUR/
  PAIRS=WCLOTHES MCLOTHES
```

25.8 One-Tailed Significance Levels

By default, the probability is based on the two-tailed test. This is appropriate when significant differences in either direction are of interest. When theoretical considerations predict that the difference will be in a given direction (such as the Group 1 mean will be higher than the Group 2 mean), a one-tailed test is appropriate. To calculate the one-tailed probability, divide the two-tailed probability by 2.

25.9 Missing Values

By default, T-TEST deletes cases with missing values on an analysis-by-analysis basis. For independent-samples tests, cases missing on either the grouping variable or the analysis variable are excluded from the analysis of that variable. For paired-samples tests, a case missing on either of the variables in a given pair is excluded from the analysis of that pair. Two missing-value options are available:

OPTION 1 *Include missing values.* User-defined missing values are included in the analysis.

OPTION 2 *Exclude missing values listwise.* If a case is missing on any variable named, it is excluded from all analyses.

25.10 Formatting Options

Figures 25.4 and 25.6 illustrate the default output format used in T-TEST. You can modify this format in two ways by means of the OPTIONS command following T-TEST. Option 3 suppresses variable labels and Option 4 limits the output to a width of 80 characters. For example, the commands

```
T-TEST   PAIRS=WCLOTHES MCLOTHES
OPTIONS  3 4
```

produce the output in Figure 25.10. This is the same analysis shown in Figure 25.6, but with Options 3 and 4 in effect.

OPTION 3 *Suppress variable labels.*

OPTION 4 *Print with an 80-character width.*

Figure 25.10 T-TEST output with Options 3 and 4

```
- - - - - - - - - - - - - - - - - - T - T E S T- - - - - - - - - - - - - - - - - -

VARIABLE     NUMBER                 STANDARD   STANDARD
            OF CASES       MEAN    DEVIATION     ERROR
------------------------------------------------------------
WCLOTHES
                  45    80.7111       30.195      4.501

                  45    87.0444       26.192      3.905
MCLOTHES
------------------------------------------------------------

(DIFFERENCE) STANDARD    STANDARD    *        2-TAIL *     T    DEGREES OF  2-TAIL
    MEAN    DEVIATION     ERROR      * CORR.  PROB.  *   VALUE    FREEDOM    PROB.
-------------------------------------------------------------------------------------
   -6.3333     17.916      2.671     * 0.807  0.000  *   -2.37       44      0.022
-------------------------------------------------------------------------------------
```

25.11 LIMITATIONS

The following limitations apply to procedure T-TEST:

- A maximum of 1 each of GROUPS, VARIABLES, and PAIRS subcommands per T-TEST command. The PAIRS specification must appear last.
- A maximum of 1 grouping variable and 50 analysis variables for independent-samples tests.
- A maximum of 400 variables for paired-samples tests.

ANOVA varlist BY varlist (min, max) . . . varlist (min, max) [WITH varlist]
[/varlist . . .]

OPTIONS
1 Include missing values.
2 Suppress labels.
3 Delete interaction terms.
4 Delete three-way and higher interaction terms.
5 Delete four-way and higher interaction terms.
6 Delete five-way interaction terms.
7 Process covariates concurrently with main effects.
8 Process covariates after main effects.
9 Regression approach.
10 Hierarchical approach.
11 Narrow formatting.

STATISTICS
1 MCA table.
2 Unstandardized regression coefficients.
3 Cell means.

OVERVIEW, **26.1**
OPERATION, **26.2**
Specifying Full Factorial ANOVA Models, **26.3**
Cell Means, **26.4**
Suppressing Interaction Effects, **26.5**
Specifying Covariates, **26.6**
Order of Entry of Covariates, **26.7**
Regression Coefficients for the Covariates, **26.8**
Methods for Decomposing Sums of Squares, **26.9**
Summary of Analysis Methods, **26.10**
Multiple Classification Analysis, **26.11**
Missing Values, **26.12**
Formatting Options, **26.13**
LIMITATIONS, **26.14**

Chapter 26 ANOVA

Procedure ANOVA performs analysis of variance for factorial designs, with the default being the full factorial model. Although you can specify covariates, ANOVA does not permit a full analysis of covariance. You can choose among three methods for decomposing sums of squares, and you have control over the order of entry of covariates and factor main effects. You can also request a multiple classification analysis table.

ANOVA is not intended for comprehensive analyses of variance or analyses of covariance. For multiple dependent variables, repeated measures designs, factor-by-covariate interactions in the analysis of covariance, or nested or nonfactorial designs, use the MANOVA procedure (see Chapter 28).

For one-way analysis of variance, you might prefer procedure ONEWAY (see Chapter 27). ONEWAY computes contrasts and multiple comparison tests. ONEWAY also provides a test for trends across categories of an interval-level independent variable and several homogeneity-of-variance test statistics. BREAKDOWN provides summary statistics and one-way analyses of variance when all independent variables are categorical (see Chapter 22). T-TEST can be used in the two-group situation, especially when a paired comparison is mandated (see Chapter 25).

26.1 OVERVIEW

Analysis of variance tests the hypothesis that the group means of the dependent variable are equal. The dependent variable is interval level, and one or more categorical variables define the groups. These categorical variables are termed *factors*. The ANOVA procedure also allows you to include continuous explanatory variables, termed *covariates*. When there are five or fewer factors, the default model is *full factorial*, meaning that all interaction terms are included. If there are more than five factors, only interaction terms up to order five are included.

Cell Means. You can request means and counts for each dependent variable for groups defined by each factor and each combination of factors up to the fifth level. (See Section 26.4.)

Suppressing Interaction Effects. You can suppress the effects of various orders of interaction. (See Section 26.5.)

Specifying Covariates. You can introduce covariates into the model by means of the WITH keyword. (See Section 26.6.)

Order of Entry of Covariates. By default, SPSS^X processes covariates before main effects for factors. You can, however, tell SPSS^X to process covariates with or after main effects for factors. (See Section 26.7.)

Regression Coefficients for Covariates. You can request unstandardized regression coefficients for covariates. The coefficients are computed at the point where the covariates are entered into the equation. Thus, their values depend on the type of design you have specified. (See Section 26.8.)

Multiple Classification Analysis. You can request multiple classification analysis (MCA) results. In the MCA table, effects are expressed as deviations from the grand mean. The table includes a listing of unadjusted category effects for each factor, category effects adjusted for other factors, category effects adjusted for all factors and covariates, and eta and beta values. (See Section 26.11.)

Methods for Decomposing Sums of Squares. By default, the program uses what is termed the classic experimental approach. You can request either the regression approach or the hierarchical approach. (See Section 26.9.)

Missing Values. By default, cases are deleted if they have missing values on any variable in your entire ANOVA variable list. You can tell SPSS^X to ignore missing-data indicators and to include all cases in the computations. (See Section 26.12.)

Formatting Options. ANOVA prints analysis of variance results using program format defaults. However, you can suppress both variable and value labels, and you can restrict the output to an 80-character width. (See Section 26.13.)

26.2 OPERATION

The ANOVA procedure is operated by the ANOVA command and optional STATISTICS and OPTIONS commands. ANOVA performs one- to five-way analyses of variance and covariance for factorial designs. Analysis of variance is discussed in Sections 26.3 through 26.5, and analysis of covariance in Sections 26.6 through 26.8.

26.3 Specifying Full Factorial ANOVA Models

The simplest ANOVA command contains one *analysis list* with a *dependent variable list* and a *factor variable list*. In the command

```
ANOVA  PRESTIGE BY REGION(1,9)
```

PRESTIGE is the dependent variable and REGION is the factor, with minimum and maximum values of 1 and 9.

- A dependent variable list can name up to five dependent variables. If two or more variables are named, they are treated as a series of separate dependent variables, not as joint dependent variables.
- The factor variable list follows the keyword BY. Each analysis list can include only one BY keyword. Up to 10 integer-valued factors can be named, but a maximum of five interaction effects can be produced.
- Every factor variable must have a value range indicating its highest and lowest coded values. The values are separated by a comma and are enclosed in parentheses. If two or more factors have the same value range, the value range can be listed following the last factor it applies to. Thus, the value range specification can follow each factor, each subset of factors, or the entire factor list.
- The value range specification need not correspond exactly to the actual range of values of a variable or variables in a factor list. Cases outside the specified range are automatically excluded from the analysis (see Section 26.9). However, bounds larger than the actual range needlessly increase the memory required to process the ANOVA command.
- The factor variables must be integers. If a noninteger variable is used as a factor, the values are truncated.

The command

```
ANOVA  PRESTIGE BY REGION(1,9) SEX(1,2)
```

is a two-way analysis of variance with PRESTIGE as the dependent variable, and REGION and SEX as factors. By default, the model effects are the REGION and SEX main effects and the REGION by SEX interaction. The command

```
ANOVA  PRESTIGE,RINCOME BY REGION(1,9) SEX,RACE(1,2)
```

specifies two three-way analyses of variance: PRESTIGE by REGION, SEX, and RACE; and RINCOME by REGION, SEX, and RACE. Variables SEX and RACE have the same minimum and maximum values.

You can specify more than one design on the same ANOVA command by separating the analysis lists with a slash, as in

```
ANOVA  PRESTIGE BY REGION(1,9) SEX,RACE(1,2)
       /RINCOME BY SEX,RACE(1,2)
```

which specifies a three-way analysis of variance of PRESTIGE by REGION, SEX, and RACE and a two-way analysis of variance of RINCOME by SEX and RACE. The output from the three-way design is shown in Figure 26.3.

Figure 26.3 A full factorial model

```
FILE:      GENERAL SOCIAL SURVEY 1980(N=500)

              * * *  A N A L Y S I S   O F   V A R I A N C E  * * *

              PRESTIGE RESP'S OCCUPATIONAL PRESTIGE SCORE
          BY  REGION    REGION OF INTERVIEW
              SEX
              RACE
                                        SUM OF                      MEAN              SIGNIF
SOURCE OF VARIATION                    SQUARES       DF           SQUARE        F      OF F

MAIN EFFECTS                          6700.371       10          670.037    4.007    0.000
   REGION                             3569.855        8          446.232    2.669    0.007
   SEX                                   2.727        1            2.727    0.016    0.898
   RACE                               2476.838        1         2476.838   14.813    0.000

2-WAY INTERACTIONS                    4473.061       17          263.121    1.574    0.068
   REGION    SEX                      1365.014        8          170.627    1.020    0.420
   REGION    RACE                     2785.131        8          348.141    2.082    0.036
   SEX       RACE                      366.033        1          366.033    2.189    0.140

3-WAY INTERACTIONS                    1535.267        6          255.878    1.530    0.167
   REGION    SEX       RACE           1535.267        6          255.878    1.530    0.167

EXPLAINED                            12708.698       33          385.112    2.303    0.000

RESIDUAL                             70729.394      423          167.209

TOTAL                                83438.092      456          182.978
     500 CASES WERE PROCESSED.
      43 CASES (   8.6 PCT) WERE MISSING.
```

26.4 Cell Means

Statistic 3 prints the means and counts table. The means and counts of each dependent variable are printed for each cell as defined by the factors and combinations of factors. This statistic is not available with Option 9 (the regression approach, Section 26.9). The commands

```
ANOVA  PRESTIGE BY REGION(1,9) SEX,RACE(1,2)
STATISTICS 3
```

produce the cell means and counts table shown in Figure 26.4 (only the first page of the output is shown).

Figure 26.4 Part of a means and counts table

```
FILE:     GENERAL SOCIAL SURVEY 1980(N=500)
                                  * * *  C E L L   M E A N S  * * *

                 PRESTIGE   RESP'S OCCUPATIONAL PRESTIGE SCORE
              BY REGION     REGION OF INTERVIEW
                 SEX
                 RACE
TOTAL POPULATION

    39.52
 (   457)

REGION
        1           2           3           4           5           6           7           8           9

    38.13       36.72       39.35       40.26       39.57       28.77       40.72       42.58       45.15
 (    31)   (    93)   (    97)   (    39)   (    56)   (    13)   (    47)   (    33)   (    48)

SEX
        1           2

    39.81       39.24
 (   223)   (   234)

RACE
        1           2

    40.49       32.45
 (   402)   (    55)


             SEX
                        1           2
REGION
           1        38.33       38.00
                 (    12)   (    19)

           2        36.27       37.20
                 (    48)   (    45)

           3        36.74       41.71
                 (    46)   (    51)

           4        41.70       38.74
                 (    20)   (    19)

           5        41.33       38.25
                 (    24)   (    32)
```

For each dependent variable, a separate table is printed for each effect, showing the means and cell counts for each combination of values of the factors that define the effect, ignoring all other factors. If any of Options 3 through 6, which suppress higher order interactions, are specified, cell means corresponding to suppressed interaction terms are not printed. The means printed are the observed means in each cell, and they are produced only for dependent variables, not for covariates.

STATISTIC 3 *Means and counts table.* This statistic is not available with Option 9.

26.5 Suppressing Interaction Effects

Options 3 through 6 suppress the effects of various orders of interaction. The default is to examine all the interaction effects up to and including the fifth order.

Option 3 suppresses all interaction terms; only main effects and covariate effects appear in the ANOVA table, with interaction sums of squares pooled into the error (residual) sum of squares. To suppress all interaction effects, specify:

```
ANOVA  PRESTIGE BY REGION(1,9) SEX,RACE(1,2)
OPTIONS 3
```

The resulting main effects model is shown in Figure 26.5.

Figure 26.5 A main effects model

```
FILE:      GENERAL SOCIAL SURVEY 1980(N=500)

          * * *  A N A L Y S I S   O F   V A R I A N C E  * * *

               PRESTIGE RESP'S OCCUPATIONAL PRESTIGE SCORE
          BY   REGION   REGION OF INTERVIEW
               SEX
               RACE

                                       SUM OF                    MEAN            SIGNIF
SOURCE OF VARIATION                   SQUARES        DF        SQUARE        F    OF F

MAIN EFFECTS                         6700.371        10       670.037    3.894   0.000
   REGION                            3569.855         8       446.232    2.594   0.009
   SEX                                  2.727         1         2.727    0.016   0.900
   RACE                              2476.838         1      2476.838   14.395   0.000

EXPLAINED                            6700.371        10       670.037    3.894   0.000

RESIDUAL                            76737.721       446       172.058

TOTAL                               83438.092       456       182.978

    500 CASES WERE PROCESSED.
     43 CASES (  8.6 PCT) WERE MISSING.
```

OPTION 3 *Delete all interaction terms from the model.* All interaction sums of squares are pooled into the error sum of squares.

OPTION 4 *Delete three-way and higher interaction terms.* Three-way and higher terms are pooled into the error sum of squares.

OPTION 5 *Delete four-way and higher interaction terms.* Four-way and higher terms are pooled into the error sum of squares.

OPTION 6 *Delete five-way interaction terms.* The five-way term is pooled with the error sum of squares.

26.6 Specifying Covariates

The *covariate list* can name up to 10 variables as covariates. The list follows the keyword WITH, as in:

```
ANOVA  PRESTIGE BY REGION(1,9) SEX,RACE(1,2) WITH EDUC
```

This command produces the output shown in Figure 26.6.

Figure 26.6 A model with a covariate

```
FILE:      GENERAL SOCIAL SURVEY 1980(N=500)

          * * *  A N A L Y S I S   O F   V A R I A N C E  * * *

               PRESTIGE RESP'S OCCUPATIONAL PRESTIGE SCORE
          BY   REGION   REGION OF INTERVIEW
               SEX
               RACE
          WITH EDUC     HIGHEST YEAR SCHOOL  COMPLETED

                                       SUM OF                    MEAN            SIGNIF
SOURCE OF VARIATION                   SQUARES        DF        SQUARE        F    OF F

COVARIATES                          23715.522         1     23715.522  191.701   0.000
   EDUC                             23715.522         1     23715.522  191.701   0.000

MAIN EFFECTS                         2708.380        10       270.838    2.189   0.018
   REGION                            1202.574         8       150.322    1.215   0.288
   SEX                                 10.610         1        10.610    0.086   0.770
   RACE                              1425.415         1      1425.415   11.522   0.001

2-WAY INTERACTIONS                   3144.833        17       184.990    1.495   0.092
   REGION    SEX                     1349.220         8       168.653    1.363   0.211
   REGION    RACE                    1138.839         8       142.355    1.151   0.328
   SEX       RACE                     534.154         1       534.154    4.318   0.038

3-WAY INTERACTIONS                   1663.399         6       277.233    2.241   0.039
   REGION    SEX       RACE          1663.399         6       277.233    2.241   0.039

EXPLAINED                           31232.135        34       918.592    7.425   0.0

RESIDUAL                            52205.957       422       123.711

TOTAL                               83438.092       456       182.978

    500 CASES WERE PROCESSED.
     43 CASES (  8.6 PCT) WERE MISSING.
```

26.7 Order of Entry of Covariates

You can specify the order in which blocks of covariates and factor main effects are to be assessed. By default, when neither Option 7 nor 8 is specified, the covariates are assessed first. Main effects are assessed after adjusting for the covariates. When Option 7 is specified, the covariates and factors are processed concurrently. If Option 8 is specified, the block of covariates is assessed after the main effects for factors have been included. Note that order of entry is irrelevant when Option 9 is in effect (see Section 26.9).

OPTION 7 *Process covariates concurrently with main effects for factors.*

OPTION 8 *Process covariates after main effects for factors.*

26.8 Regression Coefficients for the Covariates

Statistic 2 requests the unstandardized regression coefficients for the covariates. The regression coefficients are computed at the point where the covariates are entered into the equation. Thus, their values depend on the type of design you have specified using Options 7 through 10 or their defaults (see Section 26.9 for discussion of Options 9 and 10). The coefficients are printed immediately below the ANOVA summary table in the output. If Statistic 2 were requested for the analysis shown in Figure 26.6, the regression coefficient for EDUC, which would follow the ANOVA information, would appear as shown in Figure 26.8.

Figure 26.8 The regression coefficient

```
COVARIATE   RAW REGRESSION COEFFICIENT

EDUC              2.331

     500 CASES WERE PROCESSED.
      43 CASES (  8.6 PCT) WERE MISSING.
```

STATISTIC 2 *Unstandardized regression coefficients.* Prints unstandardized regression coefficients for the covariates.

26.9 Methods for Decomposing Sums of Squares

ANOVA has three methods for decomposing sums of squares. The default method is the *classic experimental approach,* in which each type of effect is assessed separately in the following order (unless Option 7 or 8 has been specified):

- Effects of covariates.
- Main effects of factors.
- Two-way interaction effects.
- Three-way interaction effects.
- Four-way interaction effects.
- Five-way interaction effects.

The effects within each type are adjusted for all other effects in that type and also for the effects of all prior types (see Table 26.9).

Option 9 requests the *regression approach.* In the regression approach, all effects are assessed simultaneously, with each effect adjusted for all other effects in the model. Some restrictions apply to the use of Option 9:

- The lowest specified categories of all the independent variables must have a marginal frequency of at least one, since the lowest specified category is used as the reference category. If this rule is not followed, no ANOVA table is produced, and a message is printed identifying the first offending variable.

- Given an n-way crosstabulation of the independent variables, there must be no empty cells defined by the lowest specified category of any of the independent variables. If this restriction is violated, one or more levels of interaction effects are suppressed, and a warning message is issued. However, this constraint does not apply to categories defined for an independent variable which do not occur in the data. For example, given two independent variables, each with categories of 1, 2, and 4, the (1,1), (1,2), (1,4), (2,1), and (4,1) cells must not be empty. The (1,3), (2,3), (3,3), (4,3), (3,1), (3,2), and (3,4) cells are empty by definition, and the (2,2), (2,4), (4,2), and (4,4) cells may be empty, although the degrees of freedom will be reduced accordingly.

To comply with these restrictions, specify precisely the lowest nonempty category of each independent variable. Specifying a value range of (0,9) for a variable that actually has values of 1 through 9 results in an error and no ANOVA table is produced.

Option 10 requests the *hierarchical approach.* The hierarchical approach differs from the classic experimental approach only in the way it handles covariate and factor main effects. In the hierarchical approach, the factor main effects and the covariate effects are assessed hierarchically; the factor main effects are adjusted only for the factor main effects already assessed, and the covariate effects are adjusted only for the covariates already assessed. The order in which the factors are listed on the ANOVA command determines the order in which they are assessed.

The command

```
ANOVA  Y BY A,B,C(0,3)
```

specifies three factor variables: A, B, and C. Table 26.9 summarizes the three approaches with respect to this example. With the default classic experimental approach, each main effect is assessed with the two other main effects held constant, and two-way interactions are assessed with all main effects and other two-way interactions held constant. The three-way interaction is assessed with all main effects and two-way interactions held constant. Option 9 yields a regression solution, in which each factor or interaction is assessed with all other factors and interactions held constant. With Option 10, the order in which the factors and covariates are listed on the ANOVA command determines the order in which they are assessed in the hierarchical analysis.

Table 26.9 Terms adjusted for under each option

Effect	Default	Option 9	Option 10
A	B,C	ALL OTHERS	NONE
B	A,C	ALL OTHERS	A
C	A,B	ALL OTHERS	A,B
AB	A,B,C,AC,BC	ALL OTHERS	A,B,C,AC,BC
AC	A,B,C,AB,BC	ALL OTHERS	A,B,C,AB,BC
BC	A,B,C,AB,AC	ALL OTHERS	A,B,C,AB,AC
ABC	A,B,C,AB,AC,BC	ALL OTHERS	A,B,C,AB,AC,BC

OPTION 9 *Regression approach.* Option 9 overrides Options 7 and 8. All effects are assessed for their partial contribution, so order is irrelevant. Statistics 1 and 3 are not available with the regression approach.

OPTION 10 *Hierarchical approach.*

ANNOTATED EXAMPLE FOR ANOVA

The example illustrating the use of ANOVA is a three-way analysis of variance with one covariate. The data are 500 cases from the 1980 General Social Survey. The variables are

- PRESTIGE—the respondent's occupational prestige scale score. PRESTIGE is the dependent variable.
- EDUC—the respondent's education in years.
- RACE—the respondent's race, coded 1=WHITE, 2=BLACK, and 3=OTHER.
- SEX—the respondent's sex, coded 1=MALE and 2=FEMALE.
- REGION—The respondent's residence, coded as one of nine regions.

The task is twofold: determine the degree to which the American occupational structure differs across race, sex, and region; and measure the effect of the respondent's educational level, since education might prove to be a concomitant influence. The SPSS^X commands are

```
FILE HANDLE GSS80/ file specifications
GET   FILE=GSS80/KEEP PRESTIGE EDUC RACE SEX REGION
ANOVA  PRESTIGE BY REGION(1,9) SEX,RACE(1,2) WITH EDUC
STATISTICS 2
OPTIONS 10,11
```

- The FILE HANDLE identifies the GSS80 data file and gives the operating-system specifications (see Chapter 3).
- The GET command defines the data to SPSS^X and selects the variables needed for the analysis (see Chapter 5).
- The ANOVA command names PRESTIGE as the dependent variable; REGION, SEX, and RACE as the factors; and EDUC as the covariate. The minimum and maximum values for REGION are 1 and 9, and the minimum and maximum values for both SEX and RACE are 1 and 2. Since variable RACE actually has values 1, 2, and 3, cases with value 3 are eliminated from the model.
- Statistic 2 requests the regression coefficient for the covariate EDUC (see Section 26.8).
- Option 10 requests the hierarchical approach for decomposing sums of squares. The covariate EDUC is assessed first to establish statistical control. Then the effect of REGION is assessed; next, the effect of SEX adjusted for REGION; and next, the effect of RACE adjusted for REGION and SEX. Finally, each of the interaction effects is assessed (see Section 26.9).
- Option 11 tells SPSS^X to display the results within an 80-character width (see Section 26.13).

Analysis of variance output

```
             * * *  A N A L Y S I S   O F   V A R I A N C E  * * *

                PRESTIGE RESP'S OCCUPATIONAL PRESTIGE SCORE
           BY   REGION   REGION OF INTERVIEW
                SEX
                RACE
           WITH EDUC      HIGHEST YEAR SCHOOL  COMPLETED

                                       SUM OF                   MEAN             SIGNIF
SOURCE OF VARIATION                    SQUARES       DF         SQUARE      F      OF F

COVARIATES                            23715.522       1      23715.522 191.701   0.000
   EDUC                               23715.522       1      23715.522 191.701   0.000

MAIN EFFECTS                           2708.380      10        270.838   2.189   0.018
   REGION                              1260.552       8        157.569   1.274   0.255
   SEX                                   22.413       1         22.413   0.181   0.671
   RACE                                1425.415       1       1425.415  11.522   0.001

2-WAY INTERACTIONS                     3144.833      17        184.990   1.495   0.092
   REGION   SEX                        1349.220       8        168.653   1.363   0.211
   REGION   RACE                       1138.839       8        142.355   1.151   0.328
   SEX      RACE                        534.154       1        534.154   4.318   0.038

3-WAY INTERACTIONS                     1663.399       6        277.233   2.241   0.039
   REGION   SEX      RACE              1663.399       6        277.233   2.241   0.039

EXPLAINED                             31232.135      34        918.592   7.425   0.0

RESIDUAL                              52205.957     422        123.711

TOTAL                                 83438.092     456        182.978

COVARIATE    RAW REGRESSION COEFFICIENT

EDUC             2.331

    500 CASES WERE PROCESSED.
     43 CASES (  8.6 PCT) WERE MISSING.
```

The ANOVA output from this job includes the following standard items of information:

Source of Variation. All interactions are printed by default. In this example, the sources of variation are the covariate, the main effects, the three two-way interactions, the three-way interaction, plus the explained, residual, and total variation.

Sum of Squares. The sum of squares associated with each effect is in part a function of the analysis of variance method chosen. In this example, Option 10, the *hierarchical approach*, was requested. Compare this output to the sum of squares shown in Figure 26.6, where the default classical experimental approach was used to analyze the same ANOVA model. See Section 26.9 for a further discussion of analysis of variance approaches available in ANOVA.

Degrees of Freedom (DF). The degrees of freedom associated with each effect.

Mean Square. The sum of squares divided by the degrees of freedom.

F and Significance of F. The *F* statistic and the significance level of the *F* statistic for each effect.

Finally, $SPSS^X$ prints the number of cases processed as well as the number of missing cases. By default, cases with missing values on any of the variables named are excluded from the analysis. In the example job, 43 cases (8.6 percent of the data) are excluded due to missing values (Section 26.12) or values out of range (Section 26.3) for the RACE variable.

26.10 Summary of Analysis Methods

Methods for decomposing sums of squares have been discussed in Section 26.9, and the order of entry of covariates is discussed in Section 26.7. Table 26.10 summarizes what happens when various exclusive combinations of these options and their defaults are invoked.

Table 26.10 Combinations of Options 7 through 10

	Assessments between types of effects	Assessments within the same type of effect
Default	*Covariates* THEN *Factors* THEN *Interactions*	*Covariates:* adjust for all other covariates *Factors:* adjust for covariates and all other factors *Interactions:* adjust for covariates, factors, and all other interactions of the same and lower orders
Option 7	*Factors* and *Covariates* concurrently THEN *Interactions*	*Covariates:* adjust for factors and all other covariates *Factors:* adjust for covariates and all other factors *Interactions:* adjust for covariates, factors, and all other interactions of the same and lower orders
Option 8	*Factors* THEN *Covariates* THEN *Interactions*	*Factors:* adjust for all other factors *Covariates:* adjust for factors and all other covariates *Interactions:* adjust for covariates, factors, and all other interactions of the same and lower orders
Option 9	*Covariates, Factors,* and *Interactions* simultaneously	*Covariates:* adjust for factors, interactions, and all other covariates *Factors:* adjust for covariates, interactions, and all other factors *Interactions:* adjust for covariates, factors, and all other interactions
Option 10	*Covariates* THEN *Factors* THEN *Interactions*	*Covariates:* adjust for covariates, that are preceding in the list *Factors:* adjust for covariates and factors preceding in the list *Interactions:* adjust for covariates, factors, and all other interactions of the same and lower orders
Options 7 and 10	*Factors* and *Covariates* concurrently THEN *Interactions*	*Factors:* adjust only for preceding factors *Covariates:* adjust for factors and preceding covariates *Interactions:* adjust for covariates, factors, and all other interactions of the same and lower orders
Options 8 and 10	*Factors* THEN *Covariates* THEN *Interactions*	*Factors:* adjust only for preceding factors *Covariates:* adjust for factors and preceding covariates *Interactions:* adjust for covariates, factors, and all other interactions of the same and lower orders

26.11 Multiple Classification Analysis

Statistic 1 produces MCA output, which consists of the grand mean of the dependent variable and a table of category means for each factor expressed as deviations from the grand mean. The latter are sometimes termed *treatment effects*. The category means expressed as deviations convey the magnitude of the effect of each category within a factor (Andrews, 1973). The commands

```
ANOVA  PRESTIGE BY REGION(1,9) SEX,RACE(1,2) WITH EDUC
STATISTICS 1
```

produce the MCA table shown in Figure 26.11.

Figure 26.11 The MCA table

```
FILE:       GENERAL SOCIAL SURVEY 1980(N=500)

 * * *  M U L T I P L E   C L A S S I F I C A T I O N   A N A L Y S I S  * * *

           PRESTIGE RESP'S OCCUPATIONAL PRESTIGE SCORE
        BY REGION   REGION OF INTERVIEW
           SEX
           RACE
      WITH EDUC     HIGHEST YEAR SCHOOL  COMPLETED

GRAND MEAN =    39.52                                                  ADJUSTED FOR
                                                        ADJUSTED FOR   INDEPENDENTS
                                            UNADJUSTED  INDEPENDENTS   + COVARIATES
VARIABLE + CATEGORY                 N       DEV'N  ETA  DEV'N   BETA   DEV'N   BETA

REGION
   1 NEW ENGLAND                   31       -1.39                       1.73
   2 MIDDLE ATLANTIC               93       -2.80                      -2.53
   3 E. NOR. CENTRAL               97       -0.17                      -0.53
   4 W. NOR. CENTRAL               39        0.74                       0.55
   5 SOUTH ATLANTIC                56        0.05                       1.02
   6 E. SOU. CENTRAL               13      -10.75                      -2.02
   7 W. SOU. CENTRAL               47        1.20                       1.07
   8 MOUNTAIN                      33        3.06                       0.25
   9 PACIFIC                       48        5.63                       2.57
                                                   0.22                        0.12

SEX
   1 MALE                         223        0.29                       0.16
   2 FEMALE                       234       -0.28                      -0.15
                                                   0.02                        0.01

RACE
   1 WHITE                        402        0.97                       0.67
   2 BLACK                         55       -7.06                      -4.91
                                                   0.19                        0.13

MULTIPLE R SQUARED                                                      0.317
MULTIPLE R                                                              0.563
```

In an MCA table, deviation values are printed in three forms: unadjusted; adjusted for main effects of other factors; and adjusted for main effects of other factors and covariates, if applicable. The adjusted values show the effect of a certain category within a given factor after variation due to other factors, and sometimes other covariates, has been taken into account.

The results of the MCA table are affected by the form of analysis specified by Options 7 through 10 or their defaults. If covariates are present, a complete MCA table can be obtained only in conjunction with Option 8, Options 8 and 10, or Options 7 and 10. If you have specified a model in which factors are not processed first, effects adjusted only for factors do not appear in the MCA table. For example, in Figure 26.11, the middle column, "ADJUSTED FOR INDEPENDENTS," is empty because covariates were entered first. If you have specified Option 9, no MCA table is produced. Ordinarily, if the MCA table is of interest, it is desirable that interaction terms not be statistically significant.

The MCA table contains several measures of association. First, a correlation ratio, the eta statistic, is associated with the set of unadjusted category effects for each factor in the MCA table; the square of eta indicates the proportion of variance explained by a given factor (all categories considered). Beta is a statistic associated with the adjusted category effects for each factor. More specifically, beta is a standardized regression coefficient in the sense used in multiple regression. Finally, multiple R appears at the bottom of the MCA table. Just as in multiple regression, this R can be squared to indicate the variance in the dependent variable "accounted for" by all factors, covariates, and factor-by-factor interaction terms.

STATISTIC 1 *Multiple classification analysis.* The MCA table is not produced when Option 9 is in effect.

26.12 Missing Values

By default, a case that is missing for any variable named in the analysis list is deleted for all analyses specified by that list. Option 1 instructs the program to ignore missing-data indicators and to include all cases in the computations.

OPTION 1 *Include missing data.*

26.13 Formatting Options

Two options control the format of the output. Option 2 suppresses variable and value labels. By default, if variable or value labels have been defined, they are used in the table. Option 11 limits output to 80 print columns. The default is to use the full line-printer width of 132 characters (131 on some machines). The annotated example for ANOVA shows output produced with Option 11.

OPTION 2 *Suppress variable and value labels.*
OPTION 11 *Print with an 80-character width.*

26.14 LIMITATIONS

The following limitations apply to procedure ANOVA:

- A maximum of 5 ANOVA analysis lists.
- A maximum of 5 dependent variables per analysis list.
- A maximum of 10 independent variables per analysis list.
- A maximum of 10 covariates per analysis list.
- A maximum of 5 interaction levels.
- A maximum of 25 value labels per variable displayed in the MCA table.
- The combined number of categories for all factors in an analysis list plus the number of covariates must be less than the sample size.

ONEWAY varlist BY varname (min, max)

[/POLYNOMIAL = n] [/CONTRAST = coefficient list]

[/RANGES = {LSD | DUNCAN | SNK | TUKEYB | TUKEY | LSDMOD | SCHEFFE | ranges values} ({**0.05** | alpha})]

OPTIONS:
1 Include missing values.
2 Exclude missing values listwise.
3 Suppress variable labels.
4 Matrix output of frequencies, means, standard deviations.
6 Use value labels for group labels.
7 Matrix input of frequencies, means, standard deviations.
8 Matrix input of frequencies, means, pooled variance, degrees of freedom.
10 Harmonic mean for range tests.

STATISTICS:
1 Descriptive statistics.
2 Fixed- and random-effects measures.
3 Homogeneity-of-variance tests.

OVERVIEW, **27.1**

OPERATION, **27.2**
- Specifying the Design, **27.3**
- The POLYNOMIAL Subcommand, **27.4**
- The CONTRAST Subcommand, **27.5**
- The RANGES Subcommand, **27.6**
  - User-Specified Ranges, **27.7**
  - Harmonic Means, **27.8**
- Optional Statistics, **27.9**
- Missing Values, **27.10**
- Formatting Options, **27.11**
- Matrix Materials, **27.12**
  - Writing Matrices, **27.13**
  - Reading Matrices, **27.14**

LIMITATIONS, **27.15**

Chapter 27 ONEWAY

Procedure ONEWAY produces a one-way analysis of variance for an interval-level variable by one independent variable. Although procedures ANOVA (Chapter 26) and MANOVA (Chapter 28) can also produce a one-way analysis of variance, ONEWAY performs several optional tests not available in those procedures. You can test for trends across categories, specify contrasts, and use a variety of range tests.

27.1 OVERVIEW

ONEWAY can analyze several dependent variables by one independent variable with one specification of the procedure. By default, ONEWAY produces a standard analysis of variance table for each dependent variable. In addition to the analysis of variance table, you can specify optional statistical tests, formats, and methods of handling missing data. ONEWAY also reads and writes matrix materials.

Tests for Trends. The POLYNOMIAL subcommand partitions the between-groups sum of squares into linear, quadratic, cubic, and higher-order trend components. (See Section 27.4.)

A Priori Contrasts. The CONTRAST subcommand requests contrasts tested by the *t* statistic. You can specify up to ten different contrast vectors. (See Section 27.5.)

Range Tests. The RANGE subcommand requests any of seven different range tests for comparisons of all possible pairs of group means. (See Section 27.6.)

Optional Statistics. In addition to the default display, you can obtain means, standard deviations, and other descriptive information about each group. Both fixed- and random-effects measures as well as several tests for homogeneity of variance are available. (See Section 27.9.)

Missing Values. By default, ONEWAY excludes cases with missing values on an analysis-by-analysis basis. Optionally, you can request that missing values be handled as if they were valid or that cases with missing values be deleted listwise. (See Section 27.10.)

Formatting Options. You can obtain group labels derived from value labels. You can also suppress the printing of variable labels. (See Section 27.11.)

Matrix Input and Output. ONEWAY writes out category frequencies, means, and standard deviations that can be used in subsequent ONEWAY jobs. It also reads matrix materials consisting of category frequencies, means, pooled variance, and degrees of freedom for the pooled variance. (See Section 27.12.)

27.2 OPERATION

Procedure ONEWAY operates via subcommands and associated OPTIONS and STATISTICS commands. You must supply a dependent variable list and the independent variable with its range of integer values. Optional subcommands produce tests for trends, contrasts, and ranges. These subcommands appear after the analysis specification and can be entered in any order.

27.3 Specifying the Design

A ONEWAY analysis list contains a dependent variable list and one independent (grouping) variable with its minimum and maximum values. Use only one analysis list per ONEWAY command. For example, the command

```
ONEWAY  WELL BY EDUC6 (1,6)
```

specifies a one-way analysis of variance of WELL, the dependent variable, by EDUC6, the independent variable with minimum and maximum values of 1 and 6. Figure 27.3 shows the output from this command.

You can name up to 100 dependent variables but only one independent variable per analysis list. Dependent variables must be numeric. The independent variable follows the keyword BY, and you must include a value range specifying the highest and lowest values to be used in the analysis. These values are separated by a comma and enclosed in parentheses.

While you can specify any number of categories for the independent variable, contrasts and multiple comparison tests are not available for more than 50 groups. ONEWAY deletes empty groups for the analysis of variance and range tests. The independent variable must have integer values. Noninteger values encountered in the independent variable are truncated.

Figure 27.3 Analysis of variance table from ONEWAY

```
- - - - - - - - - - - - - - - - - - - - - - - - - - - O N E W A Y - - - - - - - - - - - - - - - - - - - - - - - - - -

     VARIABLE  WELL          SENSE OF WELL-BEING SCALE
  BY VARIABLE  EDUC6         EDUCATION IN 6 CATEGORIES

                                        ANALYSIS OF VARIANCE

               SOURCE            D.F.    SUM OF SQUARES    MEAN SQUARES        F RATIO    F PROB.

      BETWEEN GROUPS               5         361.3217          72.2643          11.526    0.0000

      WITHIN GROUPS              494        3097.3463           6.2699

      TOTAL                      499        3458.6680
```

27.4 The POLYNOMIAL Subcommand

The POLYNOMIAL subcommand partitions the between-groups sum of squares into linear, quadratic, cubic, or higher-order trend components. Specify this subcommand after the analysis specification, as in:

```
ONEWAY  WELL BY EDUC6 (1,6)/
  POLYNOMIAL = 2
```

The value specified in the POLYNOMIAL subcommand denotes the highest degree polynomial to be used. This value must be a positive integer less than or equal to 5 and less than the number of groups. Use only one POLYNOMIAL subcommand per ONEWAY command. If you specify more than one, SPSS^X uses only the last one named.

When you use the POLYNOMIAL subcommand with balanced designs, ONEWAY computes the sum of squares for each order polynomial from weighted polynomial contrasts, using the group code as the metric. These contrasts are orthogonal; hence the sum of squares for each order polynomial are statistically independent. If the design is unbalanced and there is equal spacing between groups, ONEWAY also computes sums of squares using the unweighted polynomial contrasts. These contrasts are not orthogonal. The deviation sums of squares are always calculated from the weighted sums of squares (Speed, 1976).

Figure 27.4 is the analysis of variance table with second-order (quadratic) polynomial contrasts specified for an unbalanced design.

Figure 27.4 Polynomial contrasts

```
- - - - - - - - - - - - - - - - - - - - - - - - - - O N E W A Y - - - - - - - - - - - - - - - - - - - - - - - - -

      VARIABLE  WELL          SENSE OF WELL-BEING SCALE
   BY VARIABLE  EDUC6         EDUCATION IN 6 CATEGORIES

                                          ANALYSIS OF VARIANCE

              SOURCE              D.F.    SUM OF SQUARES     MEAN SQUARES         F RATIO    F PROB.

      BETWEEN GROUPS                5          361.3217           72.2643          11.526    0.0000

         LINEAR TERM (UNWEIGHTED)   1          257.3422          257.3422          41.044    0.0000
         LINEAR TERM   (WEIGHTED)   1          307.2051          307.2051          48.997    0.0000
           DEVIATION FROM  LINEAR   4           54.1166           13.5291           2.158    0.0727

         QUAD. TERM (UNWEIGHTED)    1            6.6073            6.6073           1.054    0.3051
         QUAD. TERM   (WEIGHTED)    1           16.6406           16.6406           2.654    0.1039
           DEVIATION FROM   QUAD.   3           37.4759           12.4920           1.992    0.1142

      WITHIN GROUPS               494         3097.3463            6.2699

      TOTAL                       499         3458.6680
```

27.5 The CONTRAST Subcommand

The CONTRAST subcommand specifies a priori contrasts to be tested by the *t* statistic. The specification for the CONTRAST subcommand is a vector of coefficients, with each coefficient corresponding to a category of the grouping variable. For example, the command

```
ONEWAY  WELL BY EDUC6(1,6)/
   CONTRAST = -1 -1 -1 -1 2 2/
```

contrasts the combination of the first four groups with the combination of the last two groups. On the other hand, the command

```
ONEWAY  WELL BY EDUC6(1,6)/
   CONTRAST = -1 0 0 0 0 1/
```

contrasts the first group with the last group. You can also specify fractional weights, as in:

```
   CONTRAST = -1 0 0 0 .5 .5/
```

This subcommand contrasts Group 1 and the combination of Groups 5 and 6.

For most applications, the coefficients should sum to zero. Those sets that do not sum to zero are used, but a warning message is printed. In addition, you can use the repeat notation $n * c$ to specify the same coefficient for a consecutive set of means. For example,

```
   CONTRAST = 1 4*0 -1/
```

specifies a contrast coefficient of 1 for Group 1, 0 for Groups 2 through 5, and −1 for Group 6. You must specify a contrast for every group implied by the range specification in the analysis list, even if a group is empty. However, you do not have to specify trailing zeros. For example,

```
   CONTRAST = -1 2*0 1 2*0/

   CONTRAST = -1 0 0 1 0 0/

   CONTRAST = -1 2*0 1/
```

all specify the same set of contrast coefficients for a six-group analysis.

You can specify only one set of contrast coefficients per CONTRAST subcommand and no more than 50 coefficients per set. SPSS^X ignores the CONTRAST subcommand if the range of values for the group variable exceeds 50. The maximum number of CONTRAST subcommands per ONEWAY procedure is 10. For example,

```
ONEWAY  WELL BY EDUC6 (0,6)/
   CONTRAST = 2*-1, 2*1/
   CONTRAST = 2*0, 2*-1, 2*1/
   CONTRAST = 2*-1, 2*0, 2*1/
```

specifies three different contrasts for the one-way analysis of variance model. Figure 27.5 shows the output produced by these CONTRAST subcommands. Output for each contrast list includes the value of the contrast, the standard error of the contrast, the *t* statistic, the degrees of freedom for *t*, and the two-tailed probability of *t*. Both pooled- and separate-variance estimates are printed.

Figure 27.5 Contrasts

```
- - - - - - - - - - - - - - - - - - - - - - - - - - O N E W A Y - - - - - - - - - - - - - - - - - - - - - - - - - -

    VARIABLE  WELL          SENSE OF WELL-BEING SCALE
 BY VARIABLE  EDUC6         EDUCATION IN 6 CATEGORIES

  CONTRAST COEFFICIENT MATRIX

              GRP 1      GRP 3      GRP 5
                   GRP 2      GRP 4      GRP 6

 CONTRAST  1  -1.0  -1.0   1.0   1.0   0.0   0.0

 CONTRAST  2   0.0   0.0  -1.0  -1.0   1.0   1.0

 CONTRAST  3  -1.0  -1.0   0.0   0.0   1.0   1.0
```

		POOLED VARIANCE ESTIMATE				SEPARATE VARIANCE ESTIMATE			
	VALUE	S. ERROR	T VALUE	D.F.	T PROB.	S. ERROR	T VALUE	D.F.	T PROB.
CONTRAST 1	3.3207	0.5230	6.349	494.0	0.000	0.5401	6.148	252.5	0.000
CONTRAST 2	1.1517	0.6613	1.742	494.0	0.082	0.6108	1.886	123.2	0.062
CONTRAST 3	4.4724	0.6990	6.398	494.0	0.000	0.6984	6.404	172.7	0.000

27.6 The RANGES Subcommand

The RANGES subcommand specifies any of seven different tests appropriate for multiple comparisons between means. Each RANGES subcommand specifies one test. For example,

```
ONEWAY  WELL BY EDUC6 (0,6)/
   POLYNOMIAL = 2/
   CONTRAST = 2*-1,2*1/
   CONTRAST = 2*0, 2-*1, 2*1/
   CONTRAST = 2*-1,2*0,2*1/
   RANGES = SNK/
   RANGES = SCHEFFE (.01)
```

produces two different range tests. Figure 27.6a shows the output produced by this example. ONEWAY does not calculate the range tests if more than 50 groups are encountered in the data. A maximum of 10 RANGES subcommands are permitted, and they cannot be separated by CONTRAST or POLYNOMIAL subcommands.

Figure 27.6a Multiple group comparisons

```
- - - - - - - - - - - - - - - - - - - - - - - - - - - O N E W A Y - - - - - - - - - - - - - - - - - - - - - - - - - -

      VARIABLE  WELL          SENSE OF WELL-BEING SCALE
   BY VARIABLE  EDUC6         EDUCATION IN 6 CATEGORIES

MULTIPLE RANGE TEST

SCHEFFE PROCEDURE
RANGES FOR THE 0.010 LEVEL -

           5.53  5.53  5.53  5.53  5.53

THE RANGES ABOVE ARE TABLE RANGES.  THE VALUE ACTUALLY COMPARED WITH MEAN(J)-MEAN(I) IS..
       1.7706 * RANGE * DSQRT(1/N(I) + 1/N(J))

  (*) DENOTES PAIRS OF GROUPS SIGNIFICANTLY DIFFERENT AT THE 0.010 LEVEL

                            G G G G G G
                            R R R R R R
                            P P P P P P

    MEAN        GROUP       1 2 3 4 5 6

    2.6462      GRP 1
    2.7737      GRP 2
    4.1796      GRP 3       * *
    4.5610      GRP 4       * *
    4.6625      GRP 5       * *
    5.2297      GRP 6       * *
```

Figure 27.6b Homogeneous subsets

```
- - - - - - - - - - - - - - - - - - - - - - - - - - - O N E W A Y - - - - - - - - - - - - - - - - - - - - - - - - - -

      VARIABLE  WELL          SENSE OF WELL-BEING SCALE
   BY VARIABLE  EDUC6         EDUCATION IN 6 CATEGORIES

MULTIPLE RANGE TEST

STUDENT-NEWMAN-KEULS PROCEDURE
RANGES FOR THE 0.050 LEVEL -

           2.81  3.34  3.65  3.88  4.05

THE RANGES ABOVE ARE TABLE RANGES.  THE VALUE ACTUALLY COMPARED WITH MEAN(J)-MEAN(I) IS..
       1.7706 * RANGE * DSQRT(1/N(I) + 1/N(J))

  (*) DENOTES PAIRS OF GROUPS SIGNIFICANTLY DIFFERENT AT THE 0.050 LEVEL

                            G G G G G G
                            R R R R R R
                            P P P P P P

    MEAN        GROUP       1 2 3 4 5 6

    2.6462      GRP 1
    2.7737      GRP 2
    4.1796      GRP 3       * *
    4.5610      GRP 4       * *
    4.6625      GRP 5       * *
    5.2297      GRP 6       * *

  HOMOGENEOUS SUBSETS     (SUBSETS OF GROUPS, WHOSE HIGHEST AND LOWEST MEANS DO NOT DIFFER BY MORE THAN
                           THE SHORTEST SIGNIFICANT RANGE FOR A SUBSET OF THAT SIZE)

SUBSET  1                 TABLE RANGE =  2.81              COMPARISON VALUE =         0.7997
                                               MAX DIFFERENCE WITHIN SUBSET =         0.1275

GROUP        GRP 1         GRP 2
MEAN         2.6462        2.7737
- - - - - - - - - - - - - - - - -

SUBSET  2                 TABLE RANGE =  3.65              COMPARISON VALUE =         1.1671
                                               MAX DIFFERENCE WITHIN SUBSET =         1.0502

GROUP        GRP 3         GRP 4         GRP 5         GRP 6
MEAN         4.1796        4.5610        4.6625        5.2297
- - - - - - - - - - - - - - - - - - - - - - - - - - - - - - -
```

The following tests can be specified with the RANGES subcommand:

LSD *Least-significant difference.* Any alpha between 0 and 1 can be specified. The default alpha is .05.

DUNCAN *Duncan's multiple range test.* The default alpha is .05. Only .01, .05, and .10 are used. DUNCAN uses an alpha value of .01 if the alpha specified is less than .05; .05 if the alpha specified is greater than or equal to .05 but less than .10; and .10 if the alpha specified is greater than or equal to .10.

SNK *Student-Newman-Keuls.* Only .05 is available as the alpha value.

TUKEYB *Tukey's alternate procedure.* Only .05 is available as the alpha value.

TUKEY *Honestly significant difference.* Only .05 is available as the alpha value.

LSDMOD *Modified LSD.* Any alpha between 0 and 1 can be specified. The default alpha is .05.

SCHEFFE *Scheffe's test.* Any alpha between 0 and 1 can be specified. The default alpha is .05.

Range tests produce two types of output, depending on the design and the procedure used to calculate the range tests. First, range tests always produce multiple comparisons between all groups (see Figure 27.6a). In this type of output, nonempty group means are sorted in ascending order. Asterisks in the matrix indicate significantly different group means. For example, the asterisks in Figure 27.6a indicate that the means for Groups 3 through 6 are significantly different from the means for Groups 1 and 2.

In addition to this output, homogeneous subsets are calculated for balanced designs and for all designs that use either the Duncan (DUNCAN) or the Student-Newman-Keuls (SNK) procedure to calculate multiple range tests. Figure 27.6b shows this type of output. In this example, two subsets are produced. The first subset includes Groups 1 and 2, and the second includes Groups 3 through 6. The means of the groups included within a subset are *not* significantly different.

27.7 User-Specified Ranges

You can specify any other type of range by coding specific range values. You can specify up to $k - 1$ range values in ascending order, where k is the number of groups and where the range value times the standard error of the combined subset is the critical value. For example,

```
ONEWAY  WELL BY EDUC6(1,6)/
   RANGES=2.81, 3.34, 3.65, 3.88, 4.05/
```

produces the same results as in the SNK test displayed Figure 27.6b. If less than $k - 1$ values are specified, the last value specified is used for the remaining ones. You can also specify n repetitions of the same value with the form $n * r$. To use a single critical value for all subsets, specify one range value, as in:

```
ONEWAY  WELL BY EDUC6(1,6)/
   RANGES=5.53/
```

This specification produces the same results as the Scheffe test displayed in Figure 27.6a.

27.8 Harmonic Means

By default, the range tests use the harmonic mean of the sizes of the two groups being compared. To use the harmonic mean of *all* group sizes, specify Option 10 on the associated OPTIONS command. If Option 10 is used, ONEWAY calculates homogeneous subsets for SCHEFFE, TUKEY, TUKEYB, and LSDMOD tests on unbalanced designs.

OPTION 10 *Harmonic mean for range tests.* If the harmonic mean is used for unbalanced designs, ONEWAY determines homogeneous subsets for all range tests.

27.9 Optional Statistics

Three optional statistics are available via the associated STATISTICS command.

STATISTIC 1 *Group descriptive statistics.* Prints the number of cases, mean, standard deviation, standard error, minimum, maximum, and 95% confidence interval for each dependent variable for each group.

STATISTIC 2 *Fixed- and random-effects measures.* Prints the standard deviation, standard error, and 95% confidence interval for the fixed-effects model, and the standard error, 95% confidence interval, and estimate of between-component variance for the random-effects model.

STATISTIC 3 *Homogeneity-of-variance tests.* Prints Cochran's *C*, the Bartlett-Box *F*, and Hartley's *F* max.

To request all available statistics, specify:

```
ONEWAY  WELL BY EDUC6 (0,6)/
STATISTICS  ALL
```

See the display shown in Figure 27.9.

Figure 27.9 Statistics available with ONEWAY

```
                                      STANDARD      STANDARD
GROUP        COUNT          MEAN     DEVIATION        ERROR        MINIMUM        MAXIMUM         95 PCT CONF INT FOR MEAN

GRP 1           65        2.6462        2.7539       0.3416       -4.0000         8.5000         1.9638  TO         3.3285
GRP 2           95        2.7737        2.8674       0.2942       -5.0000         8.5000         2.1896  TO         3.3578
GRP 3          181        4.1796        2.4220       0.1800       -4.0000         9.0000         3.8243  TO         4.5348
GRP 4           82        4.5610        2.1450       0.2369       -0.5000         9.0000         4.0897  TO         5.0323
GRP 5           40        4.6625        2.3490       0.3714       -1.0000         8.0000         3.9113  TO         5.4137
GRP 6           37        5.2297        2.3291       0.3829       -1.5000         9.0000         4.4532  TO         6.0063

TOTAL          500        3.8920        2.6327       0.1177       -5.0000         9.0000         3.6607  TO         4.1233

           FIXED EFFECTS MODEL          2.5040       0.1120                                      3.6720  TO         4.1120

          RANDOM EFFECTS MODEL                       0.4492                                      2.7374  TO         5.0466

RANDOM EFFECTS MODEL - ESTIMATE OF BETWEEN COMPONENT VARIANCE          0.8491


TESTS FOR HOMOGENEITY OF VARIANCES

     COCHRANS C = MAX. VARIANCE/SUM(VARIANCES) =   .2209, P =  .093 (APPROX.)
     BARTLETT-BOX F =                             1.905 , P =  .090
     MAXIMUM VARIANCE / MINIMUM VARIANCE          1.787
```

27.10 Missing Values

By default, ONEWAY deletes cases with missing values on an analysis-by-analysis basis. A case missing on either the dependent variable or grouping variable for a given analysis is not used for that analysis. Also, a case outside the range specified for the grouping variable is not used. Two missing-value options are available.

OPTION 1 *Include missing values.* User-defined missing values are included in the analysis.

OPTION 2 *Exclude missing values listwise.* Cases missing on any variable named are excluded from all analyses.

27.11 Formatting Options

By default, ONEWAY prints the variable labels defined for the variables in the analysis. Use Option 3 to suppress the printing of variable labels. The default output also identifies groups as GRP1, GRP2, and so forth. With Option 6 you can obtain group labels using the first eight characters of the value labels defined for the independent variable. Figure 27.11 is the output from the following example of range tests specified along with Option 6:

```
ONEWAY  WELL BY EDUC6(1,6)/
   RANGES=TUKEY
OPTIONS  6
```

OPTION 3 *Suppress variable labels.*

OPTION 6 *Use the first eight characters from value labels for group labels.*

Figure 27.11 Output with Option 6

```
- - - - - - - - - - - - - - - - - - - - - - - - - - - - - O N E W A Y - - - - - - - - - - - - - - - - - - - - - - - - - - -

     VARIABLE  WELL          SENSE OF WELL-BEING SCALE
  BY VARIABLE  EDUC6         EDUCATION IN 6 CATEGORIES


MULTIPLE RANGE TEST


TUKEY-HSD PROCEDURE
RANGES FOR THE 0.050 LEVEL -

          4.05  4.05  4.05  4.05  4.05

THE RANGES ABOVE ARE TABLE RANGES.  THE VALUE ACTUALLY COMPARED WITH MEAN(J)-MEAN(I) IS..
        1.7706 * RANGE * DSQRT(1/N(I) + 1/N(J))

  (*) DENOTES PAIRS OF GROUPS SIGNIFICANTLY DIFFERENT AT THE 0.050 LEVEL

                             G S H S C G
                             R O I O O R
                             A M G M L A
                             D E H E L D
                             E       E
                               H S C G S
                             S I C O E C
     MEAN        GROUP       C G H L   H

     2.6462      GRADE SC
     2.7737      SOME HIG
     4.1796      HIGH SCH    * *
     4.5610      SOME COL    * *
     4.6625      COLLEGE     * *
     5.2297      GRAD SCH    * *
```

27.12 Matrix Materials

ONEWAY can both read and write matrix materials. It writes out frequencies, means, and standard deviations in a format that it can also read. In addition, it reads frequencies, means, and pooled variance.

27.13 Writing Matrices

To write matrix materials to a file, specify Option 4 on the associated OPTIONS command. For each dependent variable, ONEWAY writes out a vector of category frequencies, a vector of means, and a vector of standard deviations. These materials are written 80 characters per line, and each vector begins on a new line. The format for the frequencies vector is F10.0, and the format for the means and standard deviation vectors is F10.4. Each line has a maximum of eight values. Thus, if the dependent variable has ten categories, six lines of matrix materials are written. The first two lines contain the category frequencies; the next two, the means; and the last two, the standard deviations.

If you specify Option 4, you must also specify the file to which the materials are written using the PROCEDURE OUTPUT command (see Chapter 17). In the following example, the matrix materials are written to the file referenced by the ONEMAT file handle:

```
FILE HANDLE  GSS80/ file specifications
FILE HANDLE  ONEMAT/ file specifications
GET  FILE=GSS80
PROCEDURE OUTPUT  FILE=ONEMAT
ONEWAY  WELL BY EDUC6(1,6)
OPTIONS  4
```

OPTION 4 *Write matrix materials to a file.* Writes a vector of frequencies, a vector of means, and a vector of standard deviations.

27.14 Reading Matrices

ONEWAY reads two types of matrix materials. The first type is the materials it writes with Option 4. These materials include a vector of frequencies, a vector of means, and a vector of standard deviations. The second type consists of a vector of category frequencies, a vector of means, a record containing the pooled variance (within-groups mean square), and optionally, the degrees of freedom. If you omit the degrees of freedom, then $n - k$ is assumed, where n is the number of cases and k is the number of groups. When you use the second type of matrix materials, you cannot compute Statistics 1, 2, and 3 nor the separate variance estimate for contrasts specified by the CONTRAST subcommand. With the first type of matrix materials, you can compute all available statistics.

OPTION 7 *Matrix input.* Input includes a vector of frequencies, a vector of means, and a vector of standard deviations. Use this option to read matrix materials written by Option 4.

OPTION 8 *Matrix input.* Input includes a vector of frequencies, a vector of means, pooled variance, and degrees of freedom for the pooled variance.

For either option, each vector begins on a new line and can be entered in either fixed or freefield format.

In addition to specifying Option 7 or 8, you must use the NUMERIC command and an INPUT MATRIX command within an input program to read matrix materials from a file. The variable names on the ONEWAY command must agree with the variable names on the NUMERIC command (see Chapter 17). Unless you are reading matrix materials produced by ONEWAY, it is easier to use freefield input with the FREE subcommand on the INPUT MATRIX command. The following example uses Option 8 to replicate Figure 27.3:

```
INPUT PROGRAM
NUMERIC  WELL EDUC
INPUT MATRIX  FREE
END INPUT PROGRAM
ONEWAY  WELL BY EDUC(1,6)
OPTIONS  8
BEGIN DATA
65 95 181 82 40 37
2.6462 2.7737 4.1796 4.5610 4.6625 5.2297
6.2699 494
END DATA
```

27.15 LIMITATIONS

The following limitations apply to procedure ONEWAY.

- A maximum of 100 dependent variables and 1 independent variable.
- An unlimited number of categories for the independent variable. However, contrasts and range tests are not performed if the actual number of nonempty categories exceeds 50.
- Only 1 POLYNOMIAL subcommand.
- A maximum of 10 CONTRAST subcommands and 10 RANGES subcommands.
- Any alpha values between 0 and 1 are permitted for the LSD, LSDMOD, and SCHEFFE range tests. SNK, TUKEY, and TUKEYB use an alpha value of .05, regardless of what is specified. DUNCAN uses an alpha value of .01 if the alpha specified is less than .05; .05 if the alpha specified is greater than or equal to .05 but less than .10; .10 if the alpha specified is greater than or equal to .10; or .05 if no alpha is specified.

ANNOTATED EXAMPLE FOR ONEWAY

This example analyzes a 500-case sample from the 1980 General Social Survey. The variables are

- WELL—the respondent's score on a scale measuring sense of well-being. WELL is the dependent variable, computed from measures of happiness, health, life, helpfulness of others, trust of others, and satisfaction with city, hobbies, family life and friendships.
- EDUC—the respondent's education in six categories, where the original codes are years of education completed.

In this example we determine the degree to which sense of well-being differs across educational levels. The SPSS^X commands are

```
FILE HANDLE  GSS80/ file specifications
GET FILE GSS80/KEEP EDUC HAPPY HEALTH LIFE HELPFUL TRUST
                    SATCITY SATHOBBY SATFAM SATFRND
COUNT  X1=HAPPY HEALTH LIFE HELPFUL TRUST SATCITY SATHOBBY
            SATFAM SATFRND(1)
COUNT  X2=HAPPY HEALTH SATCITY SATHOBBY SATFAM SATFRND(2)
COUNT  X3=HEALTH HELPFUL TRUST (3)
COUNT  X4=SATCITY SATHOBBY SATFAM SATFRND(6)
COUNT  X5=HAPPY LIFE (3)
COUNT  X6=SATCITY SATHOBBY SATFAM SATFRND(7)
COMPUTE WELL=X1 + X2*.5 - X3*.5 - X4*.5 - X5 - X6
VAR LABELS  WELL 'SENSE OF WELL-BEING SCALE'
RECODE  EDUC (0 THRU 8=1)(9,10,11=2)(12=3)(13,14,15=4)
             (16=5)(17,18,19,20=6) INTO EDUC6
VAR LABELS  EDUC6 'EDUCATION IN 6 CATEGORIES'
VALUE LABELS  EDUC6 1 'GRADE SCHOOL OR LESS' 2 'SOME HIGH SCHOOL'
                    3 'HIGH SCH GRAD' 4 'SOME COLLEGE' 5 'COLLEGE GRAD'
                    6 'GRAD SCH'
ONEWAY  WELL BY EDUC6(1,6)
   POLYNOMIAL = 2/
   CONTRAST = 2*-1, 2*1/
   CONTRAST = 2*0, 2*-1, 2*1/
   CONTRAST = 2*-1, 2*0, 2*1/
   RANGES = SNK/
   RANGES = SCHEFFE (.01)
STATISTICS  ALL
FINISH
```

- The FILE HANDLE identifies the GSS80 data file and gives the operating-system specifications (see Chapter 3).
- The GET command defines the data to SPSS^X and selects the variables needed for analysis (see Chapter 5).
- The COUNT and COMPUTE commands create variable WELL by counting the number of "satisfied" responses for each variable on the scale and computing a weighted sum of these responses (see Chapter 6).
- The RECODE command creates the variable EDUC6 which contains the recoded six categories of education (see Chapter 6).
- The VAR LABELS and VALUE LABELS commands assign labels to the new variables, WELL and EDUC6 (see Chapter 3).
- The ONEWAY command names WELL as the dependent variable and EDUC6 as the independent variable. The minimum and maximum values for EDUC6 are 1 and 6 (see Figure 27.3).
- The POLYNOMIAL subcommand specifies second-order polynomial contrasts. The sum of squares using the unweighted polynomial contrasts is calculated because the analysis design is unbalanced (see Figure 27.4).
- The CONTRAST subcommands request three different contrasts (see Figure 27.5).
- The RANGES subcommands calculate multiple comparisons between means using the Student-Newman-Keuls and Scheffe tests (see Figures 27.6a and 27.6b).
- The STATISTICS command requests all the optional statistics (see Figure 27.9).

```
MANOVA  dependent varlist [BY factor list (low, high) [factor list . . . ]
            [WITH covariate list]]
 [/WSFACTORS = name (levels) name . . . ]

                                                        {DEVIATIONS (refcat)  }
                                   [ORTHONORM]          {DIFFERENCE           }
                                                        {HELMERT              }
 [/TRANSFORM [(varlist [/varlist])] = [{CONTRAST}]  [({SIMPLE (refcat)       })]]
                                       {BASIS   }       {REPEATED             }
                                                        {POLYNOMIAL [(metric)]}
                                                        {SPECIAL (matrix)     }

 [/WSDESIGN = effect effect . . . ]
 [/MEASURE = newname newname . . . ]
 [/RENAME = {newname} {newname} . . . ]
            {*      } {*      }

              {[CELLINFO ([MEANS]  [SSCP]  [COV]  [COR])]
              {[HOMOGENEITY ([BARTLETT]  [COCHRAN]  [BOXM])]
              {[FORMAT ({WIDE  })]
              {         {NARROW}
              {[DESIGN ([ONEWAY]  [OVERALL]  [DECOMP]  [BIAS]
              {         [SOLUTION])]
              {[PRINTCOMPS ([COR]  [NCOMP(n)]  [MINEIGEN(eigencut)]
              {              [COV]  [ROTATE(rottype)])]
              {[ERROR ([SSCP]  [COV]  [COR]  [STDDEV])]
              {[SIGNIF ([MULTIV]  [EIGEN]  [DIMENR]  [UNIV]
 [/ {PRINT  } = {         [HYPOTH]  [STEPDOWN]  [AVERF]  [BRIEF]              }]
    {NOPRINT}   {         [AVONLY]  [SINGLEDF])]
              {[DISCRIM ([RAW]  [STAN]  [ESTIM]  [COR]
              {          [ROTATE(rottype)]  [ALPHA(alpha)])]
              {[PARAMETERS ([ESTIM]  [ORTHO]  [COR]  [NEGSUM])]
              {                                          {factor name     }
              {[OMEANS ([VARIABLES (varlist)]  [TABLES ({factor BY factor})])]
              {                                          {CONSTANT        }
              {[PMEANS ([VARIABLES (varlist)]           {factor name     }
              {          [ERROR (erroron)]    [TABLES ({factor BY factor})])]
              {                                          {CONSTANT        }
              {[POBS [ERROR (erroron)]]  [TRANSFORM]

 [/PLOT = [CELLPLOTS]  [STEMLEAF]  [ZCORR]
          [POBS]  [NORMAL]  [BOXPLOTS]  [PMEANS]
          [SIZE ({40  } , {25   })]]
                 {nhor}   {nvert}

 [/METHOD = [MODELTYPE ({MEANS       })]
                        {OBSERVATIONS}
   [ESTIMATION ({QR       }  {NOLASTRES}  {NOBALANCED}
                {CHOLESKY}   {LASTRES  }  {BALANCED  }
                {CONSTANT  }                {SEQUENTIAL}
                {NOCONSTANT})]  [SSTYPE ({UNIQUE    })]]

 [/READ [ = SUMMARY]]  [/WRITE [ = SUMMARY]]

                                                     dependent varlist
 [/ANALYSIS [([REPEATED] {CONDITIONAL  })] = [WITH covariate varlist]
                         {UNCONDITIONAL}        [/dependent varlist . . . ]]

 [/PARTITION (factorname) [ = ({1, 1 . . .  })]]
                               {df, df . . .}

                          {DEVIATION [(refcat)]             }
                          {SIMPLE [(refcat)]                }
                          {DIFFERENCE                       }
 [/CONTRAST (factorname) = {HELMERT                          }]
                          {REPEATED                         }
                          {POLYNOMIAL [({1, 2, 3, . . . })] }
                          {             {metric          }  }
                          {SPECIAL (matrix)                 }

 [/SETCONST = [ZETA ({10^-8})]  [EPS ({10^-8})]]
                     {zeta }          {eps  }

            {WITHIN           }      {W }
 [/ERROR = {RESIDUAL         }  or  {R }]
            {WITHIN + RESIDUAL}      {WR}
            {n                }

             {[CONSTANT . . . ]
             {[effect effect . . . ]
             {[CONTIN (varlist) . . . ]
             {[effects BY effects . . . ]
             {[effects {WITHIN} effects . . . ]
             {         {W     }
 [/DESIGN = {[effect + effect . . . ]                                          }]
             {[factor (level) . . . [WITHIN factor (partition) . . . ]]
             {[CONPLUS . . . ]
             {[MWITHIN . . . ]
             {                                       {WITHIN  }
             {[{terms-to-be-tested}  {AGAINST}  {RESIDUAL}  or  {W }]
             { {term = n          }  {VS     }  {WR      }      {R }
             {                                       {n       }      {RW}
```

OPTIONS:

1 Include missing values.

OVERVIEW, **28.1**

OPERATION, **28.2**

- The MANOVA Specification, **28.3**
- The ANALYSIS Subcommand, **28.7**
- The DESIGN Subcommand, **28.8**
- The WSFACTORS Subcommand, **28.20**
- The WSDESIGN Subcommand, **28.21**
- The ANALYSIS Subcommand for Repeated Measures Designs, **28.22**
- The MEASURE Subcommand, **28.23**
- The TRANSFORM Subcommand, **28.24**
- The RENAME Subcommand, **28.29**
- The METHOD Subcommand, **28.30**
- The PARTITION Subcommand, **28.34**
- The CONTRAST Subcommand, **28.35**
- The SETCONST Subcommand, **28.36**
- The ERROR Subcommand, **28.37**
- The PRINT and NOPRINT Subcommands, **28.38**
- The PLOT Subcommand, **28.52**
- Matrix Materials, **28.53**
- The WRITE Subcommand, **28.54**
- The READ Subcommand, **28.55**
- Missing Values, **28.56**

EXAMPLES OF COMMON DESIGNS, **28.57**

- Univariate Analysis of Variance, **28.58**
- Randomized Block Designs, **28.64**
- Latin and Other Squares, **28.68**
- Nested Designs, **28.69**

MANOVA EXAMPLES, **28.70**

- Example 1: Analysis of Covariance Designs, **28.71**
- Example 2: Multivariate One-Way ANOVA, **28.72**
- Example 3: Multivariate Multiple Regression, Canonical Correlation, **28.73**
- Example 4: Repeated Measures, **28.74**
- Example 5: Repeated Measures with a Constant Covariate, **28.75**
- Example 6: Repeated Measures with a Varying Covariate, **28.76**
- Example 7: A Doubly Multivariate Repeated Measures Design, **28.77**
- Example 8: Profile Analysis, **28.78**

Chapter 28 MANOVA: General Linear Models

SPSS^{X} MANOVA is a generalized multivariate analysis of variance and covariance program. This procedure performs univariate and multivariate linear estimation and tests of hypotheses for any crossed and/or nested design with or without covariates. You have complete control of the model specification. For example, you can test for effects jointly, or you can specify single-degree-of-freedom partitions. Also, you can specify interaction effects between factors and covariates.

With MANOVA you can perform analysis of variance and analysis of covariance, and you can analyze designs such as randomized block, split-plot, nested, and repeated measures designs. You can also estimate multivariate regressions and obtain principal components, discriminant function coefficients, canonical correlations, and other statistics for a variety of general linear models. Section 28.57 gives some examples of common designs and Section 28.70 gives some extended examples with output.

28.1 OVERVIEW

MANOVA is a subcommand-driven procedure with a large number of subcommands. At a minimum, specify the variables you wish to analyze. The MANOVA specification is the only required specification (see Section 28.3). The MANOVA subcommands fall into four general categories: subcommands which specify the design, subcommands which control the format and amount of output, subcommands which control the reading and writing of matrix materials, and subcommands which specify computational options and model specifications.

Specifying the Factor and Data Structures. The WSFACTORS subcommand provides the within-subjects factors for a repeated measures design (see Section 28.20). The WSDESIGN subcommand specifies the model for the within-subjects factors (see Section 28.21). The MEASURE subcommand specifies names for pooled results in doubly multivariate repeated measures designs (see Section 28.23). The TRANSFORM subcommand requests a linear transformation of the dependent variables and covariates (see Section 28.24). The RENAME subcommand renames the transformed variables (see Section 28.29).

Optional Printed Output. The PRINT subcommand specifies optional printed output (see Section 28.38). The PLOT subcommand specifies optional line-printer plots (see Section 28.52).

Computational Options and Model Specifications. The ANALYSIS subcommand subsets and/or reorders the variables named on the MANOVA specification (see Section 28.7). The DESIGN subcommand specifies the design model to be analyzed. The DESIGN specification should be the last subcommand of a complete MANOVA specification (see Section 28.8). The METHOD subcommand provides several options for parameter estimation (see Section 28.30). The PARTITION subcommand subdivides the degrees of freedom of a factor (see Section 28.34). The CONTRAST subcommand specifies the type of contrast desired for a factor (see Section 28.35). The SETCONST subcommand sets two algorithm-tuning parameters, which are used throughout the MANOVA procedure (see Section 28.36). The ERROR subcommand specifies the error term to be used in the model (see Section 28.37). By default, cases with missing values are excluded from the analysis. Use the associated OPTIONS command to include missing values (see Section 28.56).

The following is an example of specifications for MANOVA:

```
MANOVA Y BY A(1,3) B(1,4) WITH X/
 PRINT=PMEANS/
 METHOD=SSTYPE(SEQUENTIAL)/
 DESIGN=A,B/
 METHOD=SSTYPE(UNIQUE)/
 DESIGN=A,B,A BY B/
```

The MANOVA specification specifies an analysis of covariance model with Y as the dependent variable, X as the covariate, and A and B as factor variables with three and four levels respectively. The PRINT subcommand prints predicted means. The METHOD subcommand indicates sequential sums of squares. These two options apply to the first DESIGN specification, which requests a main effects model. The second METHOD subcommand requests the regression approach for estimating the parameters in the second DESIGN specification (a full factorial model). The PRINT subcommand also applies to the second DESIGN.

Note that if the last subcommand is not a DESIGN specification, MANOVA generates a full factorial model specification for the problem.

Matrix Materials. MANOVA writes a set of matrix materials that it can read in a subsequent analysis. The WRITE subcommand writes matrices and related material (Section 28.54) and the READ subcommand reads them (Section 28.55). If you contemplate further analyses, you can save the computational time required to build intermediate matrices each time by saving these matrix materials and reusing them.

28.2 OPERATION

The MANOVA procedure is subcommand driven. You must name the variables being analyzed and indicate the dependent variables, factors, and covariates. The variables specification must come first. The DESIGN subcommand (Section 28.8) specifies the model to be fit. One model is produced for each DESIGN subcommand. All subcommands can be used more than once and, with the exception of the DESIGN subcommand, carry from model to model unless explicitly overridden.

All subcommands begin with the subcommand keyword followed by an optional equals sign and specifications. All subcommands are terminated with a slash. Subcommand keywords can be abbreviated to the first three characters.

28.3 The MANOVA Specification

The MANOVA specification lists the variables to be used in models. MANOVA uses three types of variables. *Dependent variables* are interval-level variables. *Factors* are categorical variables. *Covariates* are interval-level variables. You can specify dependent variables, dependent variables and factors, dependent variables and covariates, or all three.

28.4 Dependent Variable List

The *dependent variable list* specifies variables to be used as dependent variables in the analysis. It must be the first list. You can use the TO convention to refer to consecutive variables. For example,

```
MANOVA DRUG1 TO DRUG4/
  WSFACTORS=TRIAL(4)/
  WSDESIGN=TRIAL/
  ANALYSIS(REPEATED)
```

specifies only dependent variables and produces a repeated measures design with no between-subjects factor. By default, MANOVA treats a list of dependent variables as jointly dependent, implying a multivariate design. However, you can change the role of a variable or its inclusion status in the analysis with the ANALYSIS specification (see Section 28.7).

28.5 Factor List

The *factor list* follows the keyword BY and specifies those variables to be used as factors in the analysis. Follow each factor with an integer value range enclosed in parentheses: the first integer denotes the lowest value for a factor and the second integer denotes the highest. For example,

```
MANOVA  Y BY A(1,3)
```

specifies one factor with three levels. Cases with values outside these bounds are excluded from the analysis. If several factors have the same value range, you can specify a list of factors followed by a single value range in parentheses. For example,

```
MANOVA Y BY FACTOR1 FACTOR2 FACTOR3(3,5)
```

excludes all cases in which the values of FACTOR1, FACTOR2, or FACTOR3 lie outside the range 3 through 5 and includes cases with values 3, 4, and 5.

Since MANOVA requires integer values for factor levels, you should recode noninteger values for factors into consecutive integer values. For example, you could recode the six-value alphanumeric variable RELIGION, with values 'CATH', 'PROT', 'JEW ', 'NONE', 'OTHE', and '   ', into an integer factor, as in:

```
RECODE RELIGION('CATH'=1)('PROT'=2)('JEW '=3)('NONE'=4)
  ('OTHE'=5)('    '=99) INTO NRELIG
MISSING VALUES NRELIG(99)
```

The MISSING VALUES command defines category 99 as missing. Therefore, NRELIG is a five-category factor. You can then specify

```
MANOVA ATTIT1 BY NRELIG(1,5)
```

on the MANOVA command.

If you have a wide value range for a factor in which most categories are empty, you can decrease processing time by recoding the variable to consecutive values. For example, suppose that factor F has three nonempty categories, represented by the numeric codes 1, 3, and 20. To recode F to have consecutive values 1, 2, and 3, specify:

```
RECODE F(1=1)(3=2)(20=3)
MANOVA Y BY F(1,3)/
```

Certain "one-cell" designs, such as univariate and multivariate regression analysis, canonical correlation, and one-sample Hotelling's T^2, do not require a factor specification. To perform these analyses, omit the keyword BY and the factor list.

28.6 Covariate List

The *covariate list* following the keyword WITH specifies the continuous variables to be used as covariates in the analysis. For example,

```
MANOVA  Y BY A(1,3) WITH X
```

specifies one dependent variable, Y; one factor with three levels, A; and one covariate, X. Omit the keyword WITH and the covariate list if there are no covariates in the model.

28.7 The ANALYSIS Subcommand

The ANALYSIS subcommand subsets and reorders the dependent variables and covariates. You can specify only one ANALYSIS subcommand per DESIGN subcommand. You can drop variables from an analysis, change dependent variables to covariates, or change covariates to dependent variables. A special form of the ANALYSIS subcommand signals repeated measures analysis (see Section 28.22). The ANALYSIS specification completely overrides the dependent variables list and covariates list in the MANOVA command specification. However, the ANALYSIS specification does not affect factors. Variables not included in the ANALYSIS subcommand may be incorporated into the analysis via the DESIGN subcommand (see Section 28.8). You can name only those variables in the original variable list of the MANOVA command.

You can use the ANALYSIS subcommand with the keyword WITH to redefine dependent variables and covariates. For example,

```
MANOVA A,B,C BY FAC(1,4)/
          ANALYSIS=A,B WITH C/
```

changes C from a dependent variable to a covariate, while

```
MANOVA A,B,C BY FAC(1,4) WITH D,E/
          ANALYSIS=A,B,C,D WITH E/
```

changes covariate D to a dependent variable.

You can delete dependent or covariate variables from the analysis, as in

```
MANOVA A,B,C BY FAC(1,4) WITH D,E/
          ANALYSIS=A/
```

which deletes variables B, C, D, and E from the analysis.

You can use the ANALYSIS subcommand to request separate analyses. The lists must not overlap; that is, they must not name the same variables. For example,

```
MANOVA A,B,C BY FAC(1,4) WITH D,E/
          ANALYSIS = (A,B/ C/ D WITH E)/
```

specifies three analyses: the first with A and B as dependent variables, the second with C dependent, and the third with D dependent and E a covariate. You can specify the same analysis using three separate ANALYSIS subcommands; however, separate ANALYSIS subcommands require complete re-estimation for all subsequent designs. The single subcommand above is much cheaper to use because it requires reordering only already-computed estimates.

To request three separate analyses and variable F as a global covariate, specify

```
MANOVA A, B, C, D, E, F BY FAC(1,4)/
          ANALYSIS = ( A, B/ C/ D WITH E ) WITH F /
```

which is equivalent to

```
MANOVA A, B, C, D, E, F BY FAC(1,4)/
  ANALYSIS = A B WITH F/
  DESIGN/
  ANALYSIS = C WITH F/
  DESIGN/
  ANALYSIS = D WITH E F/
```

You can use special keywords CONDITIONAL and UNCONDITIONAL when specifying multiple analyses. UNCONDITIONAL specifies that each list be used "as is," independent of the others. UNCONDITIONAL is the default. CONDITIONAL requests that subsequent lists include as covariates all previous dependent variables on that ANALYSIS subcommand. For example,

```
MANOVA A, B, C, D, E, F BY FAC(1,4)/
       ANALYSIS(CONDITIONAL) = (A B C / D E ) WITH F/
```

is equivalent to

```
MANOVA A, B, C, D, E, F BY FAC(1,4)/
       ANALYSIS = A B C WITH F/
       DESIGN/
       ANALYSIS = D E WITH A B C F/
```

when applied to the same design. You can specify a final covariate list outside the parentheses. These covariates apply to every list within the parentheses, regardless of whether you specify CONDITIONAL or UNCONDITIONAL. The variables in this global covariate list must not be specified in the individual lists.

28.8 The DESIGN Subcommand

The DESIGN subcommand specifies the between-subjects model for the analysis. You can use multiple DESIGN subcommands. The DESIGN subcommand should be the last subcommand for a given model. All the other optional subcommands apply to a subsequent DESIGN subcommand. The default model is a full factorial model. Use the DESIGN subcommand to specify a list of effects for the model. Separate effects by blanks or commas.

The following sections describe design specifications.

28.9 Simple Main Effects

To specify a model that includes only the main effect terms, list the factors on the DESIGN subcommand, as in:

```
MANOVA Y BY CAT(1,2) DRUG(1,3)/
   DESIGN= CAT,DRUG/
```

28.10 Interaction Terms

The keyword BY indicates an interaction term. To specify a model containing main effects A, B, and C and the A by B and B by C interactions, specify:

```
MANOVA Y BY A B C (1,3)/
   DESIGN= A, B, C, A BY B, B BY C/
```

The three-way interaction of A, B, and C is written as A BY B BY C.

28.11 Single-Degree-of-Freedom Effects

Use the PARTITION subcommand (Section 28.34) prior to specifying single-degree-of-freedom effects, as in:

```
MANOVA Y BY TREATMNT(1,4)/
   CONTRAST(TREATMNT)=SPECIAL(1 1 1 1, 1 -1 0 0, 4 4 -8 0,
                              4 4 1 -9)/
   PARTITION(TREATMNT)/
   DESIGN=TREATMNT(1),TREATMNT(2),TREATMNT(3)
```

To refer to a given subdivision of a factor on the DESIGN subcommand, follow the factor name by the number, in parentheses, of the subdivision. Thus, if AGE has 12 levels and appears in a partition subcommand, as in

```
PARTITION(AGE) = (6,3,2)/
DESIGN = AGE(2) BY TREATMNT
```

AGE(2) refers to the second partition containing three degrees of freedom. However, in the subcommand

```
DESIGN = TREATMNT WITHIN AGE(2)
```

factor TREATMNT is nested within the second *level* of factor AGE, not the second partition. Subscripts on factors appearing after a WITHIN (or W) refer to levels of the factor. Otherwise, subscripts refer to partitions.

28.12 Keyword CONTIN

The keyword CONTIN incorporates interval variables into a single effect. Interval variables included in the design cannot be specified in the previous ANALYSIS subcommand as either dependent variables or covariates. The order of variables excluded from an analysis is the same relative order as defined by the original MANOVA variable list. For example, in

```
MANOVA A, B, C BY F(1,2) WITH D, E/
 ANALYSIS = B WITH D /
```

the order of the interval variables excluded from the analysis is A, C, and E. To incorporate all interval variables from A to E into a single effect with as many degrees of freedom as variables in the list, specify:

```
DESIGN = CONTIN(A TO E)/
```

The following specifications are also valid:

```
DESIGN = CONTIN(A,B,C TO E,F)/
DESIGN = CONTIN(A)/
DESIGN = A, CONTIN(B), CONTIN(C TO E)/
```

B and CONTIN(B) are identical. You cannot use the TO convention outside of parentheses.

The CONTIN keyword allows for unusual covariate analyses. For example,

```
MANOVA A,B,C,D BY F1,F2 (1,2)/
 ANALYSIS = A /
 DESIGN = CONTIN(B, C), F1, D, F2 /
```

eliminates covariates B and C from both factors F1 and F2 but eliminates covariate D from only factor F2.

If the DESIGN specification above did not include parentheses, it would generate covariate analysis with covariates B and C not lumped together, with covariate B unadjusted, and with covariate C adjusted for B. The rest of the covariate analysis is the same as the previous one. This example assumes that hierarchical sums of squares—the default—are being used.

28.13 Interactions Between Factors and Interval Variables

You can specify interactions between factors and interval variables which have been excluded via an ANALYSIS subcommand. However, you cannot specify interactions between or among interval variables. For example, suppose FAC1 is a factor and COV1 and COV2 are interval variables. The following are some of the valid interactions you can specify:

```
COV1 BY FAC1
CONTIN(COV1, COV2) BY FAC1
FAC1 BY COV2
```

You *cannot* specify covariate-by-covariate interaction terms. Use COMPUTE commands to create interactions between or among interval variables. For example,

```
COMPUTE XX = X * X
COMPUTE XY = X * Y
MANOVA X, Y, XX, XY BY FAC(1,4)/
 ANALYSIS = Y/
 DESIGN = X, XX, XY, FAC/
```

computes two interaction terms, XX and XY, to use in the design.

An important use of factor-by-variable interactions is to produce an effect which tests the homogeneity-of-regression hypothesis fundamental to the analysis of covariance. For example, assume an analysis with one dependent variable Y and two covariates, Z1 and Z2, with two factors AGE and TREATMNT. To test the hypothesis of parallel (homogeneous) regressions, use:

```
MANOVA Y, Z1,Z2 BY AGE(1,5),TREATMNT(1,3) /
 ANALYSIS = Y /
 DESIGN = CONTIN( Z1 Z2 ),AGE,TREATMNT, AGE BY TREATMNT,
          CONTIN(Z1,Z2) BY AGE +
          CONTIN(Z1,Z2) BY TREATMNT +
          CONTIN(Z1,Z2) BY AGE BY TREATMNT/
```

The last effect, a lumped covariate-by-factor effect, tests the parallelism hypothesis. It is important that the effects of the common regression CONTIN(Z1,Z2) and group mean differences (AGE, TREATMNT, and AGE BY TREATMNT) be removed before testing the effect of separate regressions provided by CONTIN(Z1,Z2) BY AGE + CONTIN(Z1,Z2) BY TREATMNT + CONTIN(Z1,Z2) BY AGE BY TREATMNT.

28.14 Nested Designs

WITHIN, or W, indicates nesting, as in:

```
DESIGN = AGE WITHIN TREATMNT /
DESIGN = TREATMNT, COV1 WITHIN TREATMNT /
```

The second design calculates the regression coefficients of the continuous variable COV1 within each cell of the factor TREATMNT. The term to the left of WITHIN is nested in the term to the right of WITHIN, up to the end of the term or a plus sign, as in:

```
DESIGN = A WITHIN B BY C BY D /
```

This design states that factor A is nested within B by C by D.

28.15 Lumped Effects

A plus sign (+) lumps effects together. For example,

```
DESIGN=AGE + AGE BY TREATMNT
```

combines the terms AGE and AGE by TREATMNT into a single term. Note that keyword BY is evaluated before the plus sign.

28.16 Keyword CONSPLUS

Use CONSPLUS to obtain estimates which consist of the sums of the parameter values and the grand means of the dependent variables. For example,

```
DESIGN = CONSPLUS AGE /
```

adds the means for each dependent variable to the parameters for each level of AGE. This process produces weighted marginals for each of the dependent variables by AGE. Since these means are adjusted for any covariates present, they are also the customary *adjusted means* when covariates are used.

You can obtain unweighted means by specifying the full factorial model, excluding those terms "contained" by an effect, and prefixing the effect whose means are to be found by CONSPLUS. For example, to find the unweighted marginal means for AGE in a two-factor design, specify:

```
DESIGN = CONSPLUS AGE, TREATMNT, AGE BY TREATMNT/
```

You can use the keywords OMEANS and PMEANS on the PRINT subcommand (Section 28.38) to display marginal and adjusted means. However, only by using the CONSPLUS approach can you obtain the standard errors of the marginal means. Specify only one CONSPLUS keyword on a given DESIGN subcommand.

28.17 Error Terms

Three of the most frequently used error terms are (1) within-cells, (2) residual, and (3) combined within-cells and residual. These error terms are represented by the following keywords on the DESIGN subcommand:

- WITHIN or W—within-cells error terms.
- RESIDUAL or R—residual error term.
- WR or RW—combined within-cells and residual error terms.

To test a term against one of these error terms, name the term followed by keywords VS or AGAINST and the error term keyword. For example, to test the term AGE by SEX against the residual error term, specify:

```
DESIGN=AGE BY SEX AGAINST RESIDUAL
```

For many designs, such as components of variance models, the common error terms are not sufficient. You can create up to 10 user-defined error terms by declaring any term in the design to be an error term. To create an error term, specify

term = *n*

where *n* is an integer from 1 to 10. For example,

```
DESIGN=AGE BY TREATMNT = 1
```

designates the term AGE by TREATMNT as error term 1.

To use a special error term in a test of significance, specify:

```
term    (VS)      n
      (AGAINST)
```

For example, to define AGE by TREATMNT as special error term 2 and test it against the residual error term, specify:

```
DESIGN=AGE BY TREATMNT = 2 VS RESIDUAL
```

You can specify a complete nested design, as in:

```
DESIGN=A VS 1,B WITHIN A=1 VS 2,
     C WITHIN B WITHIN A=2 VS WITHIN
```

This design specifies that A be tested against error term 1, which is the effect of B nested within A, and that B be tested against error term 2. Error term 2 is defined as C nested within B nested within A and is tested against the within-cells error term.

Any term present in the design but not given in the DESIGN specification is lumped into the residual error term.

28.18 Keyword CONSTANT

Use the keyword CONSTANT to include the constant term in a model. Generally, MANOVA automatically includes the constant (correction to mean) term in the model. However, if you specify NOCONSTANT in the

METHOD subcommand (Section 28.30), MANOVA does not include the constant unless you specifically include it in the DESIGN by using the keyword CONSTANT, as in:

```
DESIGN = CONSTANT, AGE /
```

You can specify an error term for the constant, as in:

```
DESIGN = CONSTANT VS 1 /
```

If you use the keyword CONSTANT you cannot use CONSTANT as a variable name.

28.19 Keyword MWITHIN

Use the MWITHIN keyword on the DESIGN or WSDESIGN subcommand to suppress the reparameterization of factors. MWITHIN turns on nesting for a term. Several MWITHIN keywords can appear on a single DESIGN subcommand to ease the testing of simple effects in repeated measures designs. Consider the following:

```
MANOVA  Y1 Y2 Y3 BY GROUP(1,2)/
  WSFACTOR=TIME(3)/
  WSDESIGN=MWITHIN TIME(1) MWITHIN TIME(2) MWITHIN TIME(3)/
  ANALYSIS(REPEATED)/
  DESIGN=GROUP/
```

TIME(1) refers to the first level of TIME, not the first partition. The WSDESIGN specification generates an identity matrix to transform Y1, Y2, and Y3; that is, no transformation is performed. The *F* statistic corresponding to GROUP by MWITHIN TIME(1) can be used to test the difference in means between Group 1 and Group 2 under the first level of TIME. Similarly, the *F* value of GROUP by MWITHIN TIME(2) tests the difference between Group 1 and Group 2 for the second level of TIME. To test the simple effects of TIME within each group of subjects, specify:

```
MANOVA  Y1 Y2 Y3 BY GROUP(1,2)/
   WSFACTORS=TIME(3)/
   WSDESIGN=TIME/
   ANALYSIS(REPEATED)/
   DESIGN=MWITHIN GROUP(1) MWITHIN GROUP(2)/
```

28.20 The WSFACTORS Subcommand

SPSS^X MANOVA has a number of subcommands which facilitate repeated measures analysis. The first of these is the WSFACTORS subcommand, which provides the names and number of levels for within-subjects factors when you use the multivariate data setup. For examples of the use of the WSFACTORS subcommand, see Sections 28.74 through 28.77.

To supply a within-subjects factor name for DRUG1 to DRUG4, specify:

```
MANOVA  DRUG1 TO DRUG4/
  WSFACTORS=TRIAL(4)
```

Each name follows the naming conventions of SPSS^X, and each name must be unique. That is, a within-subjects factor name cannot be the same as that of any dependent variable, between-subjects factor, or covariate in the MANOVA job. The within-subjects factors exist only during the MANOVA analysis.

Specify WSFACTORS once in a given MANOVA command. WSFACTORS must be the first subcommand after the MANOVA specification. Specify no more than 20 within-subjects and grouping factors altogether. To specify a single within-subjects factor with four levels, use:

```
MANOVA  DRUG1 TO DRUG4/
   WSFACTORS = TRIAL(4)/
```

To specify two within-subjects factors, the first with two levels and the second with three levels, use:

```
MANOVA  Y1 TO Y6 BY GROUP(1,2)/
  WSFACTORS = DRUG(2),DOSE(3)/
```

The order in which you name dependent variables on the MANOVA specification *must* correspond to the order and levels of named within-subjects factors. Because of this, the number of dependent variables on the MANOVA specification is necessarily an integral multiple of the product of the number of levels of the within-subjects factors.

For example, suppose you measure temperature and weight at two different times (AM and PM) on three successive days in four groups of animals. In this case, you have a repeated measures design with one between-subjects factor (GROUP) and two within-subjects factors (AMPM and DAY). Use the following MANOVA specifications to indicate the experimental structure:

```
MANOVA TEMP1 TO TEMP6,WEIGHT1 TO WEIGHT6 BY GROUP(1,4)/
  WSFACTORS = AMPM(2), DAY(3)/
```

The dependent variables, temperature and weight, each have six values across occasions, represented by six variables. The order in which you list variables is *crucial*: it must correspond to the matching levels of the within-subjects factors. For the above example, the correspondence between dependent variables and within-subjects effects is as follows:

Variable	AMPM	DAY
TEMP1, WEIGHT1	1	1
TEMP2, WEIGHT2	1	2
TEMP3, WEIGHT3	1	3
TEMP4, WEIGHT4	2	1
TEMP5, WEIGHT5	2	2
TEMP6, WEIGHT6	2	3

The index value of the rightmost within-subjects factor in the WSFACTORS list increments most rapidly.

Note that the above example is incomplete. Generally, the analysis of a design incorporating within-subjects factors requires either the use of the TRANSFORM subcommand to transform the dependent variables prior to the ANALYSIS and DESIGN specifications, or the use of other MANOVA subcommands, such as WSDESIGN, and ANALYSIS(REPEATED). See the relevant syntactical discussions in the following sections, as well as examples in Sections 28.71 through 28.78.

28.21 The WSDESIGN Subcommand

The WSDESIGN subcommand specifies a within-subjects model and creates a within-subjects transformation matrix based upon the current ordering of the interval variables and the product of the levels of the within-subjects factors. MANOVA generates the transformation matrix from the basis matrices corresponding to the contrast matrices specified in any preceding CONTRAST subcommands for the within-subjects factors. You can specify the same specifications as on the DESIGN subcommand (Section 28.8), except for any of the following:

- Error term references and definitions.
- The CONSPLUS keyword.
- The CONSTANT keyword.
- Interval-level variables.
- Between-subjects factors.

The first row of the transformation matrix generated from this design is always a row of ones corresponding to the constant term. MANOVA generates successive rows of the transformation matrix in left-to-right order, based on the indicated effects.

Consider the example discussed in Section 28.20. Recall that weight and temperature are measured at two different times (AM and PM) on three successive days in four groups of animals. Assume we want a comparison of the two levels of the AMPM factor and comparisons of the three days in the DAY factor. The following transformation specifies a design of interest:

```
MANOVA TEMP1 TO TEMP6,WEIGHT1 TO WEIGHT6 BY GROUP(1,4)/
   WSFACTORS = AMPM(2), DAYS(3)/
   WSDESIGN = AMPM, DAYS, AMPM BY DAYS/
```

28.22 The ANALYSIS Subcommand for Repeated Measures Designs

The ANALYSIS subcommand with special keyword REPEATED requests an automatic cycling through the within-subjects effects defined by previous WSDESIGN and WSFACTORS subcommands. In the absence of either of these subcommands, MANOVA issues an error message. Otherwise, the effect is as if you had entered an ANALYSIS subcommand with variable lists defined by the within-subjects factors. If you use ANALYSIS(REPEATED), the effects are nicely labeled. As with other ANALYSIS subcommands, you can choose either CONDITIONAL or UNCONDITIONAL analysis.

To use the ANALYSIS(REPEATED) subcommand, your data should be organized in the *multivariate setup*. That is, all scores for the same subject should reside on the same case.

Consider the MANOVA command discussed in Sections 28.20 and 28.21:

```
MANOVA TEMP1 TO TEMP6 BY GROUP(1,4)
 WITH WEIGHT1 TO WEIGHT6/
 WSFACTORS = AMPM(2), DAY(3) /
 WSDESIGN  = AMPM, DAY, AMPM BY DAY /
 ANALYSIS(REPEATED)/
```

In this example ANALYSIS(REPEATED) produces the same results as specifying:

```
   ANALYSIS = ( TEMP1 WITH WEIGHT1 /
                TEMP2 WITH WEIGHT2 /
                TEMP3, TEMP4 WITH WEIGHT3, WEIGHT4/
                TEMP5, TEMP6 WITH WEIGHT5, WEIGHT6 ) /
```

You can specify variables on the ANALYSIS(REPEATED) subcommand. This allows you to examine many models in the same MANOVA invocation. Named variables can be either dependent variables or covariates, but you must first name them in the initial MANOVA specification.

For example, in the following MANOVA job, Y1 to Y3 and Z1 to Z3 are doubly multivariate repeated measures, A is a between-subjects factor, X1 to X3 are varying covariates, and W1 to W3 are a duplicated constant covariate.

```
TITLE REPEATED MEASURES MULTIVARIATE ANCOVA
DATA LIST NOTABLE / A 1 W 3 X1 5 X2 7 X3 9 Y1 Y2 Y3 Z1 Z2 Z3 11-28
COMPUTE W1 = W
COMPUTE W2 = W
COMPUTE W3 = W
MANOVA Y1 Y2 Y3 Z1 Z2 Z3 BY A(1,2) WITH X1 X2 X3 W1 W2 W3/
 WSFACTORS = TIME( 3 )/
 WSDESIGN/
 MEASURES = Y Z X W/
 ANALYSIS(REPEATED) = Y1 Y2 Y3 WITH X1 X2 X3 W1 W2 W3/
 DESIGN/
 ANALYSIS(REPEATED) = Y1 Y2 Y3 Z1 Z2 Z3/
 DESIGN/
BEGIN DATA
data lines
END DATA
```

The first ANALYSIS subcommand names the Y variables as dependent variables, making the design singly multivariate; the second ANALYSIS subcommand names both the Y variables and the Z variables as dependent while omitting the covariates.

28.23 The MEASURE Subcommand

You can use SPSS^X MANOVA to analyze *doubly multivariate* repeated measures designs in which subjects are measured on two or more responses on two or more occasions. When the data are entered using the multivariate setup, you can use the MEASURE subcommand to name the multivariate pooled results, as in:

```
MANOVA  TEMP1 TO TEMP6, WEIGHT1 TO WEIGHT6 BY GROUP(1,4)/
        WSFACTOR=AMPM(2), DAYS(3)/
        MEASURE=TEMP WEIGHT/
        WSDESIGN=AMPM DAYS, AMPM BY DAYS
```

If you request SIGNIF(AVERF) on the PRINT subcommand, SPSS^X prints the pooled or "averaged" results as well as the multivariate results. If you specify names on the MEASURE subcommand, SPSS^X uses the indicated names. If you omit the MEASURE subcommand but ask for averaged results, MANOVA prints the results but uses its own labeling. Thus, the MEASURE subcommand is optional. For an example of the use of the MEASURE subcommand, see Section 28.77.

28.24 The TRANSFORM Subcommand

The TRANSFORM subcommand specifies linear transformations of the dependent variables and covariates. Specify variable lists in parentheses separated by slashes. Each list must contain the same number of variables. MANOVA applies the indicated transformation to each list. By default, MANOVA transforms all dependent variables and covariates. Variables not included in one of the lists are left untouched. For example,

```
MANOVA  Y1 Y2 Y3 BY A B(1,3) WITH X1 X2 X3/
        TRANSFORM(Y1 Y2 Y3)=REPEATED/
```

transforms Y1, Y2, and Y3. Specify any number of TRANSFORM subcommands in a MANOVA job. A TRANSFORM subcommand is in effect until MANOVA encounters another one.

Seven types of transformations are available. You can specify keywords CONTRAST, BASIS, or ORTHONORM prior to the type of transformation.

CONTRAST *Generate the transformation matrix directly from the contrast matrix of the given type.* CONTRAST is the default.

BASIS *Generate the transformation matrix from the one-way basis corresponding to the specified CONTRAST.*

ORTHONORM *Orthonormalize the transformation matrix by rows before use.* MANOVA zeroes out redundant rows. By default, MANOVA does not orthonormalize rows.

Use any of the following transformation keywords after the CONTRAST or BASIS keyword (if specified).

DEVIATIONS(refcat) *Compare a dependent variable with the mean of the dependent variables in the list.* By default, MANOVA omits the comparison of the last variable to the list of variables. However, you can omit a variable other than the last by specifying the number of the omitted variable in parentheses.

DIFFERENCE *Compare a dependent variable with the mean of the previous dependent variables in the list.* Also known as reverse Helmert.

HELMERT	*Compare a dependent variable with the mean of the subsequent dependent variables in the list.*
SIMPLE(refcat)	*Compare each dependent variable with the last.* However, you can specify a variable other than the last as a reference variable by giving the number of the variable in parentheses.
REPEATED	*Compare contiguous variable pairs, thereby producing difference scores.* (See Section 28.25.)
POLYNOMIAL(metric)	*Fit orthogonal polynomials to the variables in the transformation list.* The default metric is equal spacing; you can specify your own metric. (See Section 28.26.)
SPECIAL(matrix)	*Your own transformation matrix reflecting combinations of interest.* The matrix must be square with the number of rows and columns equal to the number of variables being transformed. (See Section 28.27.)

Some examples of the use of TRANSFORM follow in Sections 28.25, 28.26, and 28.27.

28.25 Keyword REPEATED

Schematically, the REPEATED keyword produces the following transformation:

```
(VAR1)              (1/p  1/p  1/p  . . .  1/p  1/p)  (VAR1)
(VAR2)              ( 1   -1    0   . . .   0    0 )  (VAR2)
(VAR3)              ( 0    1   -1   . . .   0    0 )  (VAR3)
  .        =        (               . . .          )    .
  .                 (               . . .          )    .
  .                 (               . . .          )    .
(VARp)              ( 0    0    0   . . .   1   -1 )  (VARp)
(new variables)     (p ×p transformation matrix)      (old variables)
```

where p is the number of variables being transformed. For example, the specification TRANSFORM(A,B,C)=REPEATED results in the following for each case:

- A is replaced by (A+B+C)/3
- B is replaced by (A−B)
- C is replaced by (B−C)

This transformation is useful in profile analysis and repeated measures designs where difference scores are used.

28.26 Keyword POLYNOMIAL

MANOVA fits orthogonal polynomials to the variables in the transformation list. The mean of the variables replaces the first variable, the linear component replaces the second variable, the quadratic component replaces the third variable, and so on.

Supply the metric for the polynomial transformation in parentheses following the POLYNOMIAL keyword. The metric indicates the spacing between the points represented by the values of the variables. For equal spacing, specify a metric consisting of the integers 1 to *p*, where *p* is the number of variables transformed, as in:

```
TRANSFORM(A,B,C,D) = POLYNOMIAL(1,2,3,4)/
```

Since equal spacing is the default, you can specify POLYNOMIAL without indicating the metric. You can also indicate unequal spacing. For example, consider fitting a set of five variables representing five successive measurements of body weight. To explore the significance of any curvilinear trend in the change in body weight with respect to time, you must extract the various polynomial components.

Assume the following scheme:

Variable	Contents
WT1	Body weight on 1st day
WT2	Body weight on 3rd day
WT3	Body weight on 7th day
WT4	Body weight on 12th day
WT5	Body weight on 20th day

The following TRANSFORM subcommand builds the desired polynomial components:

```
TRANSFORM(WT1,WT2,WT3,WT4,WT5)=POLYNOMIAL(1,3,7,12,20)/
```

The transformation in matrix terms is

(WT1)	mean		(	)	(WT1)
(WT2)	linear comp.		(orthogonal polynomial	)	(WT2)
(WT3)	quadratic comp.	=	(coefficients generated	)	(WT3)
(WT4)	cubic comp.		(from metric	)	(WT4)
(WT5)	quartic comp.		(	)	(WT5)
(new variables)			(transformation matrix	)	(old variables)

The results of the transformation are

New variable	Original contents for each case replaced by
WT1	(WT1+WT2+WT3+WT4+WT5) / 5
WT2	linear component of polynomial
WT3	quadratic component of polynomial
WT4	cubic component of polynomial
WT5	quartic component of polynomial

28.27 Keyword SPECIAL

The arbitrary transformation matrix is entered rowwise in parentheses following the SPECIAL keyword. The matrix must be square with the number of rows and columns equal to the number of variables being transformed. For example, the transformation

$$\begin{pmatrix} 1 & 1 & -1 \\ 2 & 0 & 1 \\ 1 & 0 & -1 \end{pmatrix}$$

appears as

```
TRANSFORM(VAR1,VAR2,VAR3)=SPECIAL( 1  1  -1,
                                   2  0   1,
                                   1  0  -1 )/
```

28.28 Multiple Variable Lists

You can apply the same transformation to subsets of dependent variables. For example, you might want to apply a special transformation to VAR1 to VAR3 and VAR4 to VAR6. In matrix terms, we represent the transformation as follows:

(VAR1)		(1	1	−1	0	0	0)	(VAR1)
(VAR2)		(2	0	1	0	0	0)	(VAR2)
(VAR3)	=	(1	0	−1	0	0	0)	(VAR3)
(VAR4)		(0	0	0	1	1	−1)	(VAR4)
(VAR5)		(0	0	0	2	0	1)	(VAR5)
(VAR6)		(0	0	0	1	0	−1)	(VAR6)

The TRANSFORM specification is as follows:

```
TRANSFORM(VAR1 TO VAR3, VAR4 TO VAR6) =
 SPECIAL(1  1  -1  0  0  0,
         2  0   1  0  0  0,
         1  0  -1  0  0  0,
         0  0   0  1  1 -1,
         0  0   0  2  0  1,
         0  0   0  1  0 -1 ) /
```

You can abbreviate this specification using multiple variable lists:

```
TRANSFORM(VAR1 TO VAR3/VAR4 TO VAR6) =
 SPECIAL(  1   1  -1
           2   0   1
           1   0  -1 ) /
```

You can use the RENAME subcommand to give the transformed variables new names which reflect the transformation employed (see Section 28.24). If you use RENAME, MANOVA uses the new names for the duration of the analysis. This is useful because it shows that transformed variables, not the original variables, are in the analysis. If you do not use RENAME, MANOVA uses the original names.

If you specify the TRANSFORM keyword on the PRINT subcommand when you use the TRANSFORM subcommand, MANOVA prints the transformation matrix (see Section 28.38).

28.29 The RENAME Subcommand

Use the RENAME subcommand to rename dependent variables and covariates when you have transformed them using either the TRANSFORM or WSDESIGN subcommand. All dependent variables and covariates must be accounted for in the RENAME specification. In doing so, you can "rename" a variable to itself or you can use an asterisk (*) to retain the original name, as in:

```
MANOVA A,B,C,V4,V5 BY TREATMNT(1,3)/
 TRANSFORM(A,B,C)=REPEATED/
 RENAME = MEANABC, AMINUSB, BMINUSC, *, */
```

The results of the TRANSFORM subcommand are

Variable	New meaning
A	(A+B+C)/3
B	A−B
C	B−C
V4	V4 (unchanged)
V5	V5 (unchanged)

The RENAME subcommand supplies new names to clarify the transformation. Successive output from this MANOVA job prints MEANABC instead of the variable name A, AMINUSB instead of B, and BMINUSC instead of C. V4 and V5 are unchanged. The following example uses renaming after a polynomial transformation.

```
MANOVA WT1,WT2,WT3,WT4,WT5 BY TREATMNT(1,3)/
 TRANSFORM = POLYNOMIAL (1,2,3,4,5)/
 RENAME = MEAN,LINEAR,QUAD,CUBIC,QUARTIC/
```

Successive output from this MANOVA run prints the five polynomial component names instead of the variable names WT1 to WT5.

References to the dependent variables or covariates in specifications following the RENAME subcommand *must* use the new names. MANOVA does not retain the old names.

28.30 The METHOD Subcommand

Use the METHOD subcommand to control computational aspects of your MANOVA analysis. Three keywords are available:

MODELTYPE *The model for parameter estimation.*
ESTIMATION *How parameters are to be estimated.*
SSTYPE *The method of partitioning sums of squares.*

Each keyword has several options available. Specify these options in parentheses following the keyword.

28.31 Keyword MODELTYPE

The MODELTYPE keyword specifies the model for parameter estimation. MEANS requests that MANOVA use the cell means model in parameter estimation; this is the default. OBSERVATIONS requests that MANOVA use the observations model in parameter estimation. When you specify interval variables in the DESIGN subcommand, MANOVA automatically uses the observations model. Computing parameter estimates using the observations model is much costlier than obtaining the same estimates using the means model. Thus, you should use the observations model only when appropriate.

28.32 Keyword ESTIMATION

The ESTIMATION keyword specifies how MANOVA is to estimate parameters. This task is the fundamental numerical process in MANOVA. The ESTIMATION keyword presents four binary choices.

QR or CHOLESKY. QR, the default, estimates parameters using Householder transformations to effect a QR (orthogonal) decomposition of the design matrix. This method bypasses the normal equations and the inaccuracies that can result from creating the cross-product matrix, and it generally results in extremely accurate estimates of the parameters. A less expensive—and sometimes less accurate procedure—is to solve the normal equations using the Cholesky method. Select this method by specifying the CHOLESKY keyword.

NOBALANCED or BALANCED. By default, MANOVA assumes that you are analyzing an unbalanced design. However, if your design is balanced and orthogonal, you can request balanced processing by specifying the BALANCED keyword. Balanced processing can result in substantial savings in processing time. Use the BALANCED keyword if your design meets the following requirements:

- All cells are filled.
- The cell-means model applies.
- The cell sizes for all cells are equal.
- The contrast type for each factor is orthogonal.

MANOVA cannot detect a balanced design; you must tell MANOVA to use it. If you request balanced processing but the design does not conform to the above requirements, then MANOVA reverts to the general unbalanced processing using either QR or Cholesky estimation, whichever you specify.

NOLASTRES or LASTRES. Factorial designs involving many factors frequently include a highest order interaction term corresponding to a large number of columns in the reduced model matrix and thus include a large number of estimated parameters. If you do not need parameter estimates for the highest order interaction, you can suppress their estimation. This can result in substantial savings in processing time. When you suppress parameter estimation, you can still obtain the significance test for the interaction because MANOVA can calculate the sum of squares attributable to this effect by subtraction if you specify this interaction last in the model.

The LASTRES keyword causes MANOVA to compute the last effect in the design by subtracting the among-groups sum of squares and cross-products from the total sum of squares and cross-products. LASTRES can also be valuable in analyses involving missing cells—the labor of determining the confounded effects is saved. NOLASTRES reverses the effect of LASTRES. Note that the last effect with LASTRES specified *must not* contain any interval variables. Also, do not use LASTRES if you have specified UNIQUE sum of squares decomposition. This is because the sum of squares will not add up to the total sum of squares, except for balanced designs. Thus, the sum of squares for the last effect cannot be computed by subtraction.

CONSTANT or NOCONSTANT. CONSTANT requests that the model include a constant (intercept) term, even if you do not explicitly specify one in the DESIGN subcommand. CONSTANT is the default. NOCONSTANT suppresses the constant term from the model. MANOVA does not fit the constant unless you explicitly specify it in the DESIGN subcommand.

28.33 Keyword SSTYPE

By default, SPSS^X MANOVA partitions the sums of squares attributable to terms in the model in a hierarchical fashion. MANOVA adjusts a term for all terms to its left in a given DESIGN specification. Thus, a term is confounded with all terms to its right. Sequential decomposition results in an orthogonal decomposition of the sums of squares—the sums of squares for model terms do not overlap. These sums of squares are also produced when the keyword SEQUENTIAL appears.

For unbalanced designs, however, the sums of squares for any one ordering of effects might not be sufficient. Further, the hypotheses corresponding to those sums of squares for any but the last term in the ordering can be difficult to interpret since, in parametric terms, they represent combinations of means weighted by the observed cell frequencies. An alternative set of sums of squares which can be of greater interest results from ordering each term last in the design—thereby correcting each term for every other term in the model. Such sums of squares correspond to unweighted combinations of means. To obtain these sums of squares, specify UNIQUE. This approach to decomposing sums of squares is often termed the *regression approach* because, as in regression, each effect is assessed with respect to every effect in the model.

SEQUENTIAL is also termed the method of fitting constants. In designs with no empty cells, UNIQUE is the method of weighted squares of means.

Note that the sums of squares produced by UNIQUE are not orthogonal except for balanced designs. Thus, they will not add up to the total sum of squares for the model.

28.34 The PARTITION Subcommand

The PARTITION subcommand subdivides the degrees of freedom associated with a factor. Specify the factor name in parentheses following the subcommand name. Following an equals sign, specify a parenthetical list of integers to indicate the degrees of freedom for each partition. The number of degrees of freedom associated with a factor is one less than the number of levels for the factor. Each value in the partition list must be greater than zero and less than or equal to the total number of degrees of freedom for the factor. Further, the sum of the partition degrees of freedom must be less than or equal to the total number of degrees of freedom for the factor. The maximum number of partitions allowed for a factor (achieved by specifying all individual degrees of freedom equal to one) is likewise the total number of degrees of freedom for the factor. If the total sum of the degrees of freedom is less than the degrees of freedom for the factor, then MANOVA builds a final partition category containing the remaining degrees of freedom.

For example, consider the factor TREATMNT, which has 12 levels, or 11 degrees of freedom. To partition TREATMNT into single degrees of freedom, specify

```
PARTITION(TREATMNT) = (1,1,1,1,1,1,1,1,1,1,1)/
```

or use a repeat factor by specifying an asterisk, as in:

```
PARTITION(TREATMNT) = (11*1)/
```

A third way to request a single-degree-of-freedom partition is as follows:

```
PARTITION(TREATMNT)/
```

The default degrees-of-freedom vector consists of all ones. This is also the initial partition ascribed to any factor.

To partition TREATMNT into three subdivisions, the first containing three degrees of freedom, the second two degrees of freedom, and the third six degrees of freedom, specify:

```
PARTITION(TREATMNT) = (3,2,6)/
```

You can also effect the same partition by specifying:

```
PARTITION(TREATMNT) = (3,2)/
```

MANOVA automatically generates a third partition with 6 (11−3−2) degrees of freedom in this case.

28.35 The CONTRAST Subcommand

Use the CONTRAST subcommand to specify the contrast desired for a factor:

```
                         DEVIATION (refcat)
                         DIFFERENCE
                         HELMERT
CONTRAST(factorname) =   SIMPLE (refcat)    /
                         REPEATED
                         POLYNOMIAL (metric)
                         SPECIAL (matrix)
```

where *factorname* is the factor whose contrast is being selected.

DEVIATION *The deviations from the grand means.*

In matrix terms, these contrasts have the form

mean	(1/k	1/k	. . .	1/k	1/k)
df(1)	(1 − 1/k	−1/k	. . .	−1/k	−1/k)
df(2)	(−1/k	1 − 1/k	. . .	−1/k	−1/k)
.			.		
.			.		
.			.		

where *k* is the number of levels for the factor. For example, the deviation contrasts for a factor with three levels are as follows:

```
( 1/3    1/3    1/3)
( 2/3   -1/3   -1/3)
(-1/3    2/3   -1/3)
```

MANOVA omits the deviation for the last category. However, the deviation effect for this reference category equals the negative sum of the deviations for the other categories since the deviations must sum to zero.

To omit a category other than the last, specify the number of the omitted category in parentheses after the DEVIATION keyword. For example, the subcommand

```
CONTRAST(FACTOR) = DEVIATION(2) /
```

where FACTOR has three levels, results in a contrast matrix of the form

```
( 1/3    1/3    1/3)
( 2/3   -1/3   -1/3)
(-1/3   -1/3    2/3)
```

which obtains the deviations for the first and third categories and omits the second.

DIFFERENCE *Difference or reverse Helmert contrasts.* Compare levels of a factor with the mean of the previous levels of the factor.

The general matrix form is

mean	(1/k	1/k	1/k	. . .	1/k)
df(1)	(−1	1	0	. . .	0)
df(2)	(−1/2	−1/2	1	. . .	0)
.		.			
.		.			
.		.			
df(k−1)	(−1/(k−1)	−1/(k−1)	−1/(k−1)	. . .	1)

where *k* is the number of levels of the factor. For example, a factor with four levels has a difference contrast matrix of the following form:

```
( 1/4    1/4    1/4    1/4)
( -1      1      0      0 )
(-1/2   -1/2     1      0 )
(-1/3   -1/3   -1/3     1 )
```

SIMPLE *Simple contrasts.* Compare each level of a factor to the last.

The general matrix form is

mean	(1/k	1/k	. . .	1/k	1/k)
df(1)	(1	0	. . .	0	−1)
df(2)	(0	1	. . .	0	−1)
.			.		
.			.		
.			.		
df(k-1)	(0	0	. . .	1	−1)

where *k* is the number of levels of the factor.

For example, a factor with four levels has a simple contrast matrix of the following form:

(1/4	1/4	1/4	1/4)
(1	0	0	−1)
(0	1	0	−1)
(0	0	1	−1)

To use another category besides the last as a reference category, specify the level of the reference category in parentheses after the SIMPLE keyword. For example, the request

```
CONTRAST(FACTOR) = SIMPLE(2)/
```

where FACTOR has four levels produces a contrast matrix of the form

(1/4	1/4	1/4	1/4)
(1	−1	0	0)
(0	−1	1	0)
(0	−1	0	1)

HELMERT *Helmert contrasts.* Compare levels of a factor with the mean of the subsequent levels of the factor.

The general matrix form is

mean	(1/k	1/k	. . .	1/k	1/k)
df(1)	(1	−1/(k−1)	. . .	−1/(k−1)	−1/(k−1))
df(2)	(0	1	. . .	−1/(k−2)	−1/(k−2))
.	(	.		.	)
.	(	.		.	)
.	(	.		.	)
df(k−2)	(0	0	1	−1/2	−1/2)
df(k−1)	(0	0	. . .	1	−1)

where k is the number of levels of the factor. For example, a factor with four levels has a Helmert contrast matrix of the following form:

(1/4	1/4	1/4	1/4)
(1	−1/3	−1/3	−1/3)
(0	1	−1/2	−1/2)
(0	0	1	−1)

POLYNOMIAL *Orthogonal polynomial contrasts.*

You can specify the spacing between levels of the treatment measured by the given factor. You can signify equal spacing by specifying consecutive integers from 1 to k, where k is the number of levels of the factor. Equal spacing is the default if you omit a metric. For example,

```
CONTRAST(DRUG) = POLYNOMIAL/
```

is the same as

```
CONTRAST(DRUG) = POLYNOMIAL (1,2,3)/
```

Equal spacing is not always necessary, however. For example, suppose factor DRUG represents different dosages of a drug given to three groups. If the dosage administered to the second group is twice that of the first group, and that of the third group is three times that of the first group, then the treatment levels are equally spaced and an appropriate metric for this situation consists of consecutive integers:

```
CONTRAST(DRUG)=POLYNOMIAL(1,2,3)/
```

If, however, the dosage administered to the second group is four times the dosage level given the first group, and the dosage given the third group is seven times that of the first, then an appropriate metric is:

```
CONTRAST(DRUG)=POLYNOMIAL (1,4,7)/
```

In either case, the result of the contrast specification is that the first degree of freedom for DRUG contains the linear effect of the dosage levels and the second degree of freedom contains the quadratic effect. In general, the first degree of freedom receives the linear effect, the second degree of freedom the quadratic effect, the third degree of freedom the cubic, and so on for the higher order effects. Polynomial contrasts are especially useful in tests of trends and for investigating the nature of response surfaces. You can also use polynomial contrasts to perform nonlinear curve-fitting, such as curvilinear regression.

REPEATED *Compare adjacent levels of a factor.*

The general matrix form is

mean	(1/k	1/k	1/k	. . .	1/k	1/k)
df(1)	(1	−1	0	. . .	0	0)
df(2)	(0	1	−1	. . .	0	0)
.	(	.			.	)
.	(	.			.	)
.	(	.			.	)
df(k − 1)	(0	0	0	. . .	1	−1)

where k is the number of levels for the factors.

For example, the repeated contrasts for a factor with four levels areas follows:

(1/4	1/4	1/4	1/4)
(1	−1	0	0)
(0	1	−1	0)
(0	0	1	−1)

These contrasts are useful in profile analysis and wherever difference scores are needed.

SPECIAL *A user-defined contrast.*

SPECIAL allows entry of special contrasts in the form of square matrices with as many rows and columns as there are levels of the factor. The first row entered is always the mean, or constant, effect, and represents the set of weights indicating how MANOVA is to average other factors, if any, over the given factor. Generally, this contrast is a vector of ones.

The remaining rows of the matrix contain the special contrasts indicating the desired comparisons between levels of the factor. Usually, orthogonal contrasts are the most useful. Orthogonal contrasts are statistically independent and nonredundant. Contrasts are *orthogonal* if (1) for each row, contrast coefficients sum to zero, and (2) the products of corresponding coefficients for all pairs of disjoint rows also sum to zero.

For example, suppose TREATMNT has four levels and you want to compare the various levels of treatment with each other. An appropriate special contrast is

(1	1	1	1)	weights for mean calculation
(3	−1	−1	−1)	compare 1st with 2nd through 4th
(0	2	−1	−1)	compare 2nd with 3rd and 4th
(0	0	1	−1)	compare 3rd with 4th

which you specify by means of the following CONTRAST subcommand:

```
CONTRAST(TREATMNT) = SPECIAL( 1  1  1  1
                              3 -1 -1 -1
                              0  2 -1 -1
                              0  0  1 -1 )/
```

Each row except the means row sums to zero:

Row 2	$3 + (-1) + (-1) + (-1)$	$= 3 - 3 = 0$
Row 3	$2 + (-1) + (-1)$	$= 2 - 2 = 0$
Row 4	$1 + (-1)$	$= 1 - 1 = 0$

Products of each pair of disjoint rows sum to zero:

Rows 2 and 3	$3(0)$	$+ (-1)(2)$	$+ (-1)(-1)$	$+ (-1)(-1)$	$= 0$
Rows 2 and 4	$3(0)$	$+ (-1)(0)$	$+ (-1)(1)$	$+ (-1)(-1)$	$= 0$
Rows 3 and 4	$0(0)$	$+ 2(0)$	$+ (-1)1$	$+ (-1)(-1)$	$= 0$

The special contrasts need not be orthogonal. However, they must not be linear combinations of each other. If they are, MANOVA reports the linear dependency and ceases processing. Difference, Helmert, and polynomial contrasts are orthogonal contrasts.

28.36 The SETCONST Subcommand

The SETCONST subcommand sets important constants used throughout the MANOVA procedure.

ZETA(zeta) *Set the absolute value of zero used for printing purposes and when constructing basis matrices for estimation.* The default value of ZETA is 10^{-8}.

EPS(eps) *Set the relative value of zero used in checking the diagonal elements of matrices when performing the QR reduction or Cholesky decompositions.* The default value of EPS is 10^{-8}.

28.37 The ERROR Subcommand

The ERROR subcommand specifies the default error term for each between-subjects effect in subsequent designs.

WITHIN *Within-cells error term.* Can be abbreviated to W.

RESIDUAL *Residual error term.* Can be abbreviated to R.

WITHIN+RESIDUAL *Pooled within-cells and residual error terms.* Can be abbreviated to WR or RW.

n *Model term.*

MANOVA chooses an error term based on the following criteria:

- MANOVA uses the within-cells error term if it exists.
- If there is no within-cells error, MANOVA uses the residual error.
- For designs processed using the observations model, the pooled within-cells and residual error term is the default.

If you request both the pooled within-cells and residual errors and one of these does not exist, then MANOVA uses the other error term alone.

You can designate a model term as the default error by giving its error term number. You must explicitly define the error term numbers in the DESIGN subcommand. If the specified error term number is not defined for a particular design, then MANOVA does not carry out the significance tests using that error term, although MANOVA presents the parameter estimates and hypothesis sums of squares.

For example, in the command

```
MANOVA DEP BY A(1,2), B(1,4)/
 ERROR = 1/
 DESIGN = A, B, A BY B = 1/
 DESIGN = A, B/
```

the default error term, error term 1, applies to the first design since the A by B term is present in the model and is defined as error term 1. However, the A by B term is not present in the second design, and no other term has been defined as error 1 instead. Thus, no significance tests for A and B are printed, although the hypothesis sums of squares are reported.

28.38 The PRINT and NOPRINT Subcommands

The PRINT and NOPRINT subcommands control the amount of printed output produced by MANOVA. The syntax for both subcommands is identical. PRINT requests that specified output be produced while NOPRINT suppresses output. PRINT and NOPRINT control several classes of information. Each general specification has several subspecifications. For example,

```
MANOVA  Y BY A(1,3) WITH X/
        PRINT=CELLINFO(MEANS)
```

prints cell means. The following general specifications are available:

CELLINFO *Cells information.*
HOMOGENEITY *Homogeneity-of-variance tests.*
DESIGN *Design information.*
PRINCOMPS *Principal components statistics.*
ERROR *Error matrices.*
SIGNIF *Significance tests.*
DISCRIM *Discriminant analysis.*
PARAMETERS *Estimated parameters.*
OMEANS *Observed means.*
PMEANS *Predicted and adjusted means.*
POBS *Predicted values and residuals.*
TRANSFORM *Transformation matrix.*
FORMAT *Format display.*

28.39 Keyword CELLINFO

Use CELLINFO to request the following statistics:

MEANS *Cell means, standard deviations, and counts.*
SSCP *Cell sums of squares and cross-products matrices.*
COV *Cell variance-covariance matrices.*
COR *Cell correlation matrices.*

For example,

```
MANOVA  Y BY A(1,3)/
  PRINT=CELLINFO(MEANS)
```

prints the means of Y for each category of A.

28.40 Keyword HOMOGENEITY

Use HOMOGENEITY to request a test for homogeneity of variance:

BARTLETT *Bartlett-Box* F *test.*
COCHRAN *Cochran's* C.
BOXM *Box's* M *(multivariate case only).*

Box's M is especially useful in the analysis of repeated measures designs when you have used the multivariate setup. See Section 28.74 for an example of this use of Box's *M*. Note that computation of Box's *M* requires the variance-covariance matrices for each cell and thus can be an expensive statistic in terms of computer time and memory.

28.41 Keyword DESIGN

Use DESIGN to request the following:

ONEWAY *The one-way basis for each factor.*
OVERALL *The overall reduced-model basis (design matrix).*
DECOMP *The QR/CHOLESKY decomposition of the design.*
BIAS *Contamination coefficients displaying the bias present in the design.*
SOLUTION *Coefficients of the linear combinations of the cell means being tested.*

The decomposition of the design (DECOMP) and the bias (BIAS) computed from the decomposition can provide valuable information on the confounding of the effects and the estimability of the chosen contrasts. This is particularly useful in designs with unpatterned empty cells. Likewise, the solution matrix shows the exact linear combinations of cell means used to test effects and can be useful when you are interpreting effects.

28.42 Keyword PRINCOMPS

Use PRINCOMPS to request the following statistics:

COR *Principal components analysis of the error correlation matrix.*

COV *Principal components analysis of the error variance-covariance matrix.*

ROTATE(rottype) *Rotation of the principal component loadings.* For rottype, substitute VARIMAX, EQUAMAX, QUARTIMAX, or NOROTATE.

NCOMP(n) *The number of principal components to be rotated.* Specify *n*, or let *n* default to all components extracted.

MINEIGEN(eigcut) *The eigenvalue cutoff value for principal component extraction.*

PRINCOMPS requests a principal components analysis of each error SSCP in a multivariate design. COR prints principal components of the error correlation matrix; COV prints principal components of the error variance-covariance matrix. Factors extracted from these matrices are corrected for group differences and covariates. Such factors tend to be more useful than factors extracted from an uncorrected matrix when significant group differences are present or when a significant amount of error variance is accounted for by the covariates.

The ROTATE(rottyp) keyword specifies a rotation technique for the principal component loadings. Rotation can aid interpretation of the principal components. You can choose from three rotation algorithms—VARIMAX, EQUAMAX, and QUARTIMAX. Use NOROTATE to inhibit rotation. If you do not specify ROTATE, no rotation is done.

By default, MANOVA rotates all components. To rotate fewer components, specify the number in parentheses after the NCOMP keyword or specify the cutoff value for eigenvalues on the MINEIGEN keyword. For example,

```
PRINT = PRINCOMPS(COR ROTATE(VARIMAX) NCOMP(3) )/
```

rotates the first three components, while

```
PRINT = PRINCOMPS(COR ROTATE(VARIMAX) MINEIGEN(1.5) )/
```

rotates those components with eigenvalues greater than 1.5.

If you specify an *n* greater than the number of components, MANOVA simply rotates all components. If you specify an *n* less than two, MANOVA rotates at least two components. However, if fewer than two eigenvalues are greater than *eigcut*, no rotation is performed.

A principal components analysis requires the extraction of eigenvalues and eigenvectors. This is an expensive process if there is a large dependent variable list.

28.43 Keyword ERROR

ERROR prints the following statistics:

SSCP *Error sums of squares and cross-products matrix.*
COV *Error variance-covariance matrix.*
COR *Error correlation matrix and standard deviations.*
STDV *Error standard deviations (univariate case).*

When you specify ERROR(COR) in the multivariate case, MANOVA routinely prints the determinant and Bartlett's test of sphericity, which is a test of whether the error correlation matrix is the identity matrix. The test of sphericity is especially useful when the dependent variables are transformed variables in a repeated measures analysis. See the examples in Sections 28.70 through 28.78.

28.44 Keyword SIGNIF

SIGNIF prints the following statistics:

MULTIV *Multivariate* F *tests for group differences* (default display).
EIGEN *Eigenvalues of* $S_h S_e^{-1}$ *(default display).*
DIMENR *A dimension-reduction analysis* (default display).
UNIV *Univariate* F *tests* (default display).
HYPOTH *The hypothesis SSCP matrix*
STEPDOWN *Roy-Bargmann step-down* F *tests.*
AVERF *An averaged* F *test, for repeated measures.*
BRIEF *A shortened multivariate output.* BRIEF overrides all the above.
AVONLY *Averaged results only.* Use with repeated measures.
SINGLEDF *Single-degree-of-freedom listings of effects.*

The output with BRIEF specified consists of a table similar in appearance to a univariate ANOVA table but with the generalized *F* and Wilks' lambda replacing the univariate *F*.

28.45 Keyword DISCRIM

DISCRIM requests a canonical analysis of dependent and independent variable sets in multivariate analyses. If the predictor set of variables is continuous, MANOVA prints a canonical correlation analysis. If the predictor set of variables is categorical, MANOVA prints a canonical discriminant analysis. See Section 28.73 for an example of both canonical discriminant and canonical correlation analyses in MANOVA.

DISCRIM prints the following statistics:

RAW *Raw discriminant function coefficients.*
STAN *Standardized discriminant function coefficients.*
ESTIM *Effect estimates in discriminant function space.*
COR *Correlations between the dependent and canonical variables defined by the discriminant functions.*
ROTATE(rottyp) *Rotation of the matrix of correlations between dependent and canonical variates.* Specify VARIMAX, EQUAMAX, or QUARTIMAX.
ALPHA(alpha) *The significance level of the canonical variate.* The default is .15.

The ROTATE keyword provides rotation of the correlations between the dependent and canonical variates obtained for each effect. MANOVA does this in the case of canonical discriminant analysis but not in the case of multivariate regression.

MANOVA does not perform rotation unless there are at least two significant canonical variates. The number of significant canonical variates depends on the rank of $S_hS_e^{-1}$ for a given effect and also on the significance level chosen. This significance level is .15 by default, but you can change the test significance level by using the ALPHA(alpha) keyword. The alpha value specified with ALPHA indicates the cutoff value for the significance of the discriminant functions in multivariate analysis; alpha must be a decimal number from 0 to 1. MANOVA reports discriminant analysis results only for those functions with a significance level less than alpha. The default value of alpha is .15. Setting alpha=1.0 results in the printing of all discriminant functions. Specifying alpha to be negative or greater than 1 results in alpha being set to the default of .15.

`PRINT = DISCRIM(RAW ALPHA(0.0)) /`	reports no functions
`PRINT = DISCRIM(RAW ALPHA(1.0)) /`	reports all functions
`PRINT = DISCRIM(RAW ALPHA(.05)) /`	reports functions significant at .05 level or better

28.46 Keyword PARAMETERS

PARAMETERS prints output relating to the estimated parameters.

ESTIM *The estimates themselves, along with their standard errors,* t *tests, and confidence intervals*. This is the default display.

ORTHO *The orthogonal estimates of parameters used to produce the sums of squares.*

COR *Correlations among the parameters.*

NEGSUM *For main effects, the negative sum of the other parameters* (representing the parameter for the omitted category).

28.47 Keyword OMEANS

The OMEANS specification prints tables of combined observed means. Specify the keyword VARIABLES in parentheses followed by the names of dependent variables and covariates in parentheses, as in:

```
MANOVA  Y BY A(1,4) B(1,2) WITH X/
        PRINT=OMEANS(VARIABLES(Y))/
```

If you omit the variable list, MANOVA prints combined means for all variables. Moreover, MANOVA prints both weighted and unweighted means. Consider, for example, a two-way analysis of covariance for the data displayed in Table 28.47, with Y as the response variable and X as the covariate.

Table 28.47

	A: 1		2		3		4	
B	Y	X	Y	X	Y	X	Y	X
1	8	2	8	7	10	5	6	3
	7	5	9	9			4	5
2	6	4	8	3	6	2	9	3
	7	5	6	2	8	5		

The weighted mean for a particular treatment is obtained by summing the scores of all subjects receiving that treatment and dividing by the total number of subjects included in the sum. For example, the weighted mean of Y for the first level of factor B (B_1) is

(8+7+8+9+10+6+4)/7 = 7.429

The unweighted treatment mean is obtained by averaging the cell means receiving that treatment. Thus the unweighted mean of Y for B_1 is

(7.5+8.5+10+5)/4 = 7.75

You can print tables of observed means with the keyword TABLE. For the above example,

```
PRINT=OMEANS(TABLES(A B, A BY B))
```

prints the treatment means (weighted and unweighted) of Y and X for factors A, B, and A by B in the following tables:

A	(collapsing over B)
B	(collapsing over A)
A BY B	(the observed cell means themselves)

For example,

```
PRINT=OMEANS(VARIABLE(Y),TABLES(A,B))/
```

requests the treatment means of Y for factors A and B. The combined observed means are given in Figure 28.47.

Figure 28.47 Observed means of Y for factors A and B

```
COMBINED OBSERVED MEANS FOR A
VARIABLE .. Y

         A

         1          WGT.      7.00000
                  UNWGT.      7.00000

         2          WGT.      7.75000
                  UNWGT.      7.75000

         3          WGT.      8.00000
                  UNWGT.      8.50000

         4          WGT.      6.33333
                  UNWGT.      7.00000

- - - - - - - - - - - - - - - - - - - - - - - - - - - - - - - - - - -

COMBINED OBSERVED MEANS FOR B
VARIABLE .. Y

         B

         1          WGT.      7.42857
                  UNWGT.      7.75000

         2          WGT.      7.14286
                  UNWGT.      7.37500
```

Use the keyword CONSTANT to obtain grand means. For example,

```
PRINT = OMEANS(VARIABLES(Y) TABLES(CONSTANT))/
```

prints only the grand mean for variable Y.

28.48 Keyword PMEANS

PMEANS requests computation of predicted and adjusted (for covariates) means. MANOVA prints these for each error term in each design. Note that this is an expensive set of statistics to produce. You can obtain predicted and adjusted means combined across subclasses using the VARIABLES, TABLES, and ERROR specifications. The format of the variable list and the table requests is the same as for OMEANS. For example,

```
MANOVA  Y WITH A(1,4) B(1,2) WITH X/
        PRINT=PMEANS(TABLES(A))
```

prints the predicted means for variable Y for the A table. If no covariates are present in the model, the adjusted mean (labeled ADJ. MEAN in the output) and the predicted mean (labeled EST. MEAN in the output) are the same and are equal to the predicted cell mean (Finn, 1974, p. 376).

To obtain tables of combined (adjusted) predicted means, specify

```
PRINT=PMEANS(TABLES(A,B))/
```

which produces a table of the adjusted and predicted means of Y for each cell and the marginal predicted means for factors A and B (see Figures 28.48a and 28.48b). Note that if the variable and factor lists are not both given in the PMEANS subcommand, only the output shown in Figure 28.48b is printed.

Figure 28.48a Predicted means of Y for factors A and B

```
COMBINED ESTIMATED MEANS FOR A
VARIABLE .. Y

          A

          1      UNWGT.      7.01630

          2      UNWGT.      7.65761

          3      UNWGT.      8.51630

          4      UNWGT.      7.05978

- - - - - - - - - - - - - - - - - - - - - - - - - - - - - - - - - - - - -

COMBINED ESTIMATED MEANS FOR B
VARIABLE .. Y

          B

          1      UNWGT.      7.66848

          2      UNWGT.      7.45652
```

Figure 28.48b Adjusted and estimated means

```
ADJUSTED AND ESTIMATED MEANS

VARIABLE .. Y
       FACTOR          CODE              OBS. MEAN    ADJ. MEAN    EST. MEAN    RAW RESID.   STD. RESID.

 A                      1
  B                      1                 7.50000      7.60714      7.49490       .00510       .00425
  B                      2                 6.50000      6.46429      6.49490       .00510       .00425

 A                      2
  B                      1                 8.50000      7.96429      8.49490       .00510       .00425
  B                      2                 7.00000      7.25000      6.99490       .00510       .00425

 A                      3
  B                      1                10.00000      9.89286      9.99490       .00510       .00425
  B                      2                 7.00000      7.10714      6.99490       .00510       .00425

 A                      4
  B                      1                 5.00000      5.03571      4.99490       .00510       .00425
  B                      2                 9.00000      9.17857      8.99490       .00510       .00425
```

In designs with covariates and multiple error terms, use the ERROR(error) specification to designate which error term's regression coefficients are to be used in calculating the predicted means. The format for specifying an error term with ERROR follows that of the ERROR subcommand. If no error term is supplied when it is needed, MANOVA will not calculate predicted means. Predicted means are also suppressed if the last term is being calculated by subtraction (METHOD = ESTIM(LASTRES)) or the design contains the CONSPLUS keyword (see Section 28.8).

If you use the WSFACTORS and WSDESIGN subcommands to do a repeated measures design, PMEANS prints the means of the orthonormalized variables. If you place the PRINT subcommand following the TRANSFORM subcommand, PMEANS uses the scale of the transformed variables.

28.49 Keyword POBS

POBS prints predicted values and residuals for each case used in the analysis. The output includes

- The observed value of each dependent variable.
- The predicted value of each dependent variable.
- The residual (observed − predicted).
- The standardized residual (residual divided by the error standard deviation).

For example, consider the following MANOVA specification:

```
MANOVA   SYNTH EVAL WITH ZINTEL ZCONOBV ZCONRMT ZJOB CI1 CI2 CI3/
         PRINT=POBS(VARIABLES(SYNTH EVAL)ERROR(WITHIN))
```

There are two dependent variables and seven covariates, making this a multivariate multiple regression. The POBS keyword requests regression-related casewise output for both dependent variables. The ERROR keyword specifies the within-cells error as the error term for the analysis. As with PMEANS, use the ERROR specification for designs with covariates and multiple error terms. No output results if the error term is not specified when needed. Predicted observations are also suppressed if the last term is being calculated by subtraction (METHOD = ESTIM(LASTRES)) or the DESIGN subcommand contains the CONSPLUS keyword.

If the designated error term does not exist for a given design, no predicted values or residuals are calculated. This is an expensive set of statistics to compute.

28.50 Keyword TRANSFORM

Specify TRANSFORM to print the transformation matrix, which shows how MANOVA is transforming the variables in the analysis when you use the multivariate setup in repeated measures and specify a WSFACTORS command. In SPSS^X MANOVA, the program does not automatically print this matrix. To display this matrix, specify:

```
PRINT = TRANSFORM/
```

To override this, specify the following subcommand later on the MANOVA command:

```
NOPRINT = TRANSFORM/
```

28.51 Keyword FORMAT

By default, MANOVA formats all displays for a page width of 132 columns. Use the FORMAT keyword to override the default. Specify NARROW to restrict displays to 72 columns. The default is WIDE.

28.52 The PLOT Subcommand

The PLOT subcommand requests line-printer plots. The following plots are available.

CELLPLOTS *Plot cell statistics, including a plot of cell means vs. cell variances, a plot of cell means vs. cell standard deviations, and a histogram of cell means, for each interval variable (response variables and covariates) defined in the MANOVA specification.* The first two plots aid in detecting heteroscedasticity (nonhomogeneous variances) and in determining an appropriate transformation of the data (if one is needed). The third plot gives distributional information for the cell means.

Figure 28.52a Cell plots

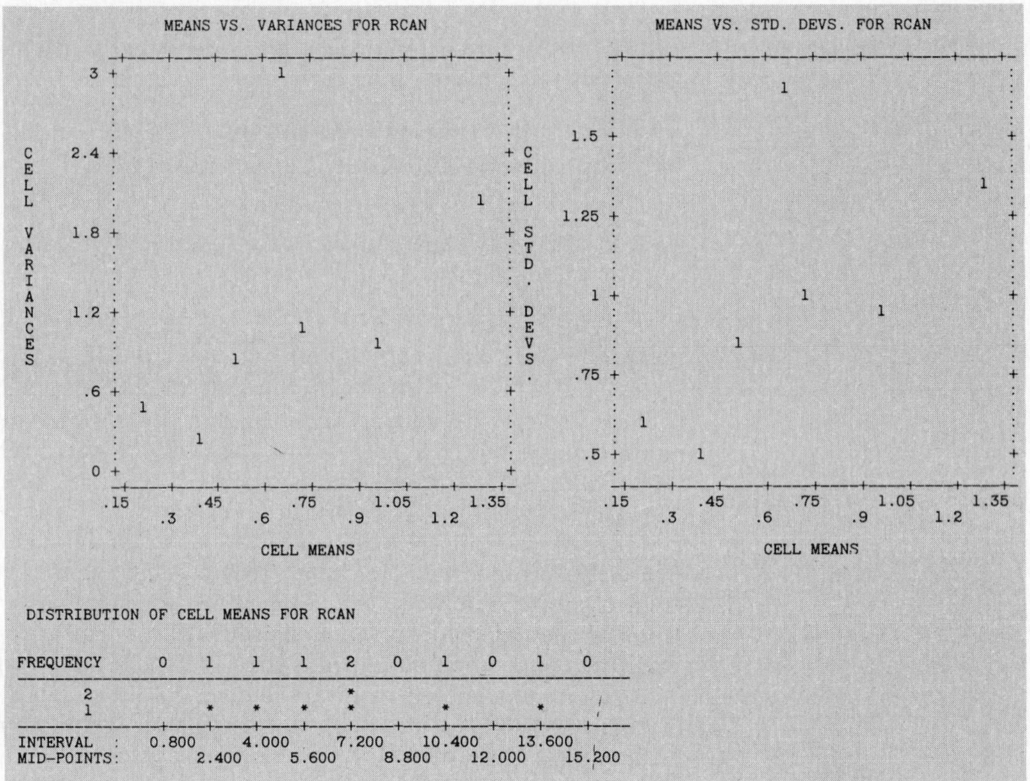

BOXPLOTS *Plot a boxplot for each interval variable (Tukey, 1977).* Boxplots provide a simple graphic means of comparing the cells in terms of mean location and spread. Note that the data must be stored in memory for these plots as well. Again, if there is not enough memory, boxplots are not produced.

Figure 28.52b Boxplots

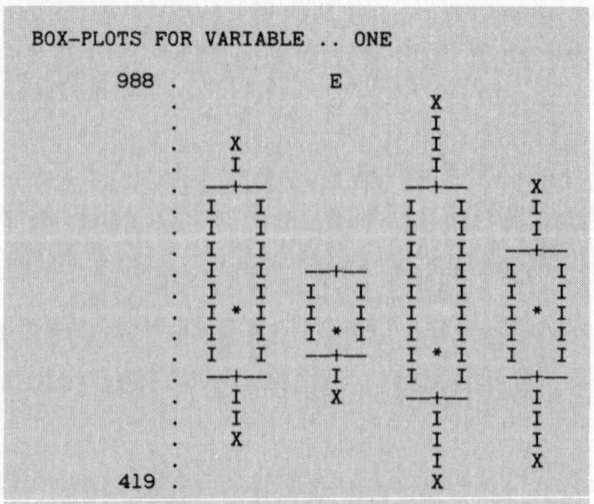

NORMAL *Plot a normal plot and a detrended normal plot for each interval variable.* MANOVA ranks the scores on each variable and plots the ranks against the expected normal deviate or detrended expected normal deviate for that rank. These plots aid in detecting non-normality and outlying observations. Note that these plots are expensive in terms of memory, because all data must be stored in order to compute ranks. Should there not be enough memory to store the data, SPSSˣ MANOVA prints a warning and skips these plots.

Figure 28.52c Normal plots

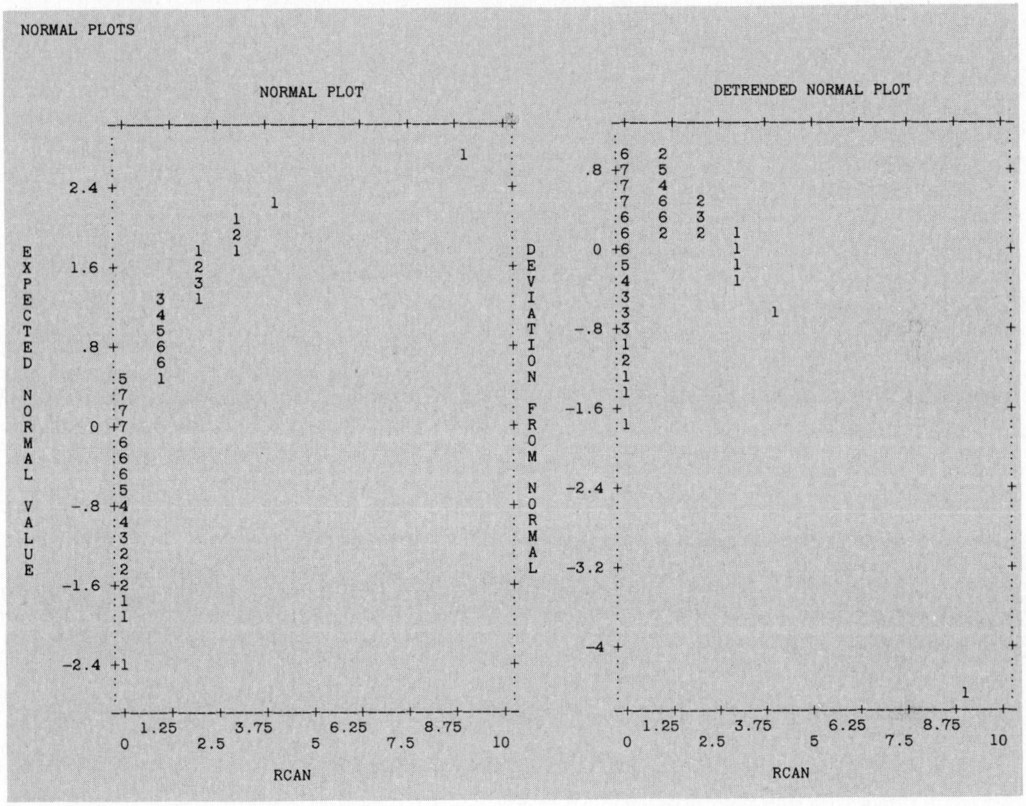

STEMLEAF *Plot a stem-and-leaf display for each interval variable (Tukey, 1977).* This display is a histogram which preserves the data scores. Again, these plots require storage of all data in memory and are not produced if the data do not fit.

Figure 28.52d Stem-and-leaf plot

```
STEM-AND-LEAF DISPLAY FOR VARIABLE .. ONE

   4 . 257
   5 . 02345667889999
   6 . 01445567
   7 . 0011568
   8 . 4555
   9 . 1359
```

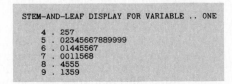

ZCORR *Plot a half-normal plot of the partial correlations among the dependent variables in a multivariate analysis.* MANOVA first transforms the correlations using Fisher's Z transformation. A straight line indicates that no significant correlations exist among the dependent variables.

Figure 28.52e Half-normal plot of partial correlations

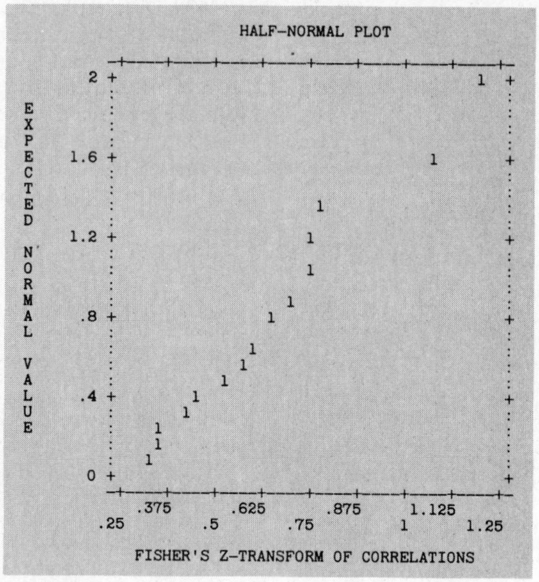

PMEANS *Plot a group-order plot of the estimated, adjusted, and observed means for each dependent variable and a group-order plot of the mean residuals for each dependent variable.* When there is more than one factor in the analysis, MANOVA varies the rightmost factor most quickly. You must also specify PRINT=PMEANS in order to obtain this plot.

Figure 28.52f Predicted means plot

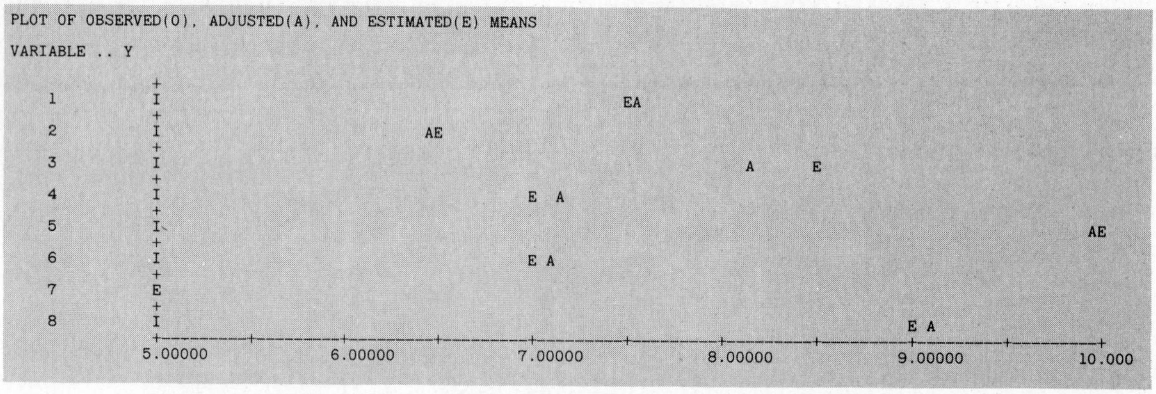

POBS *Print a plot of observed values vs. standardized residuals, a plot of predicted values vs. standardized residuals, a plot of case number vs. standardized residuals, and a normal probability plot and a detrended normal probability plot for the standardized residuals.* You must also specify PRINT=POBS or this plot is not produced.

SIZE *Change the dimensions of MANOVA plots.* By default, MANOVA prints all plots in an area 40 horizontal spaces by 25 vertical spaces. This space accomodates two plots side-by-side and four plots on a printer page in standard batch-size output. The specification SIZE(80, 40) changes the dimensions to 80 horizontal spaces and 40 vertical spaces. If the specified plot sizes fall outside the range of the device on which the plot is to be printed, plot sizes will be adjusted by MANOVA.

28.53 Matrix Materials

Procedure MANOVA writes a set of matrix materials that it can read in a subsequent job. The WRITE subcommand writes these materials and the READ subcommand reads them.

28.54 The WRITE Subcommand

The WRITE subcommand has the format

```
WRITE=SUMMARY/
```

which you can abbreviate as

```
WRITE/
```

The WRITE subcommand sends results to an external file named on the PROCEDURE OUTPUT command (see Chapter 17). MANOVA writes 6 types of records to the external file. Record type 1 contains design information (see Figure 28.54a). MANOVA next prints out pairs of record types 2 and 3 containing cell identifiers and cell means (see Figure 28.54b). Following the pairs of record types 2 and 3, MANOVA writes out out the cell counts on record type 4 (see Figure 28.54c). MANOVA writes the within-cell error correlation matrix in lower triangular form with 1s on the diagonal on record type 5. The correlations are written in F10.6 format. Finally, MANOVA writes out the within-cell standard deviations on record type 6 (see Figure 28.54d).

Figure 28.54a Record type 1

```
01 - 10   Number of nonempty cells
11 - 20   Total number of observations
21 - 30   Number of factors
31 - 40   Number of interval variables--dependent and covariate
```

Figure 28.54b Record types 2 and 3

```
01 - 08   Cell code for first factor
09 - 16   Cell code for second factor
17 - 24   Cell code for third factor
...and so forth

01 - 16   Cell mean for first interval variable
17 - 32   Cell mean for second interval variable
33 - 48   Cell mean for third interval variable
...and so forth
```

Figure 28.54c Record type 4

```
01 - 10   Count for first cell
11 - 20   Count for second cell
21 - 30   Count for third cell
...and so forth
```

Figure 28.54d Record type 6

```
01 - 16   Within-cell standard deviations for first interval var
17 - 32   Within-cell standard deviations for second interval var
33 - 48   Within-cell standard deviations for third interval var
...and so forth
```

MANOVA writes records with an 80-column format. If MANOVA is writing a lot of information, it wraps the information into subsequent records, as many as needed. Note that MANOVA writes the records out back to back with no identifiers. MANOVA can read the written file in another job, or you can use the information in another program.

Figure 28.54e shows part of an SPSS^X command file containing a multivariate analysis of variance. The example uses Finn's dental calculus data (1974). The FILE HANDLE command defines the file to which the matrix materials are being written (see Chapter 3). The PROCEDURE OUTPUT command specifies that the materials are being written to file handle MANOUT. For more information on writing matrix materials see Chapter 17. The WRITE subcommand invokes the writing of materials to the external file. Figure 28.54f shows the output file produced by these commands.

Figure 28.54e SPSS^X command file with WRITE subcommand

```
TITLE MULTIVARIATE EXAMPLE WITH WRITE.
FILE HANDLE  MANOUT/ file specifications
DATA LIST NOTABLE / YEAR TR 1-2 RCAN RLI RCI LCI LLI LCAN 3-14
PROCEDURE OUTPUT OUTFILE=MANOUT
MANOVA RCAN RLI RCI LCI LLI LCAN BY YEAR(1,2) TR(1,5)/
 WRITE/
 DESIGN/
BEGIN DATA
 ...and so forth
```

Figure 28.54f Contents of the written file

```
        7        107          2          6
     1       1
7.500000000E-01 2.250000000E+00 3.750000000E+00 4.125000000E+00 2.250000000E+00
8.750000000E-01
     1       2
1.333333333E+00 1.777777778E+00 3.111111111E+00 3.333333333E+00 2.555555556E+00
1.555555556E+00
     1       3
4.285714286E-01 8.571428571E-01 1.285714286E+00 1.571428571E+00 1.000000000E+00
4.285714286E-01
     1       4
1.000000000E+00 8.000000000E-01 2.000000000E+00 1.200000000E+00 6.000000000E-01
0.000000000E+00
     2       1
6.785714286E-01 1.571428571E+00 2.714285714E+00 2.750000000E+00 1.571428571E+00
7.142857143E-01
     2       3
5.416666667E-01 7.916666667E-01 2.083333333E+00 1.708333333E+00 9.583333333E-01
6.666666667E-01
     2       5
2.307692308E-01 4.230769231E-01 7.692307692E-01 1.307692308E+00 6.538461538E-01
1.923076923E-01
        8          9          7          5         28         24         26
   1.00000
    .53627    1.00000
    .33516     .65284    1.00000
    .36699     .64656     .84162    1.00000
    .35675     .58626     .67045     .79831    1.00000
    .61946     .49462     .43238     .41537     .55013    1.00000
1.174287642E+00 1.618253158E+00 2.059078590E+00 2.488244523E+00 1.756764964E+00
1.256573072E+00
```

28.55 The READ Subcommand

The READ subcommand reads the materials written by the WRITE subcommand. The READ subcommand has the form

```
READ=SUMMARY/
```

which you can abbreviate as

```
READ/
```

Use READ in conjunction with an SPSS^X input program.

Figure 28.55 shows an SPSS^X job which reads the output file produced in Section 28.54. NUMERIC establishes an active file, and INPUT MATRIX reads the contents of the external file. You must enclose the NUMERIC command within an INPUT PROGRAM. The FILE HANDLE command defines the file containing the matrix materials (see Chapter 3). For more information on reading matrices, see Chapter 17. The MANOVA command invokes the analysis, and specifies READ.

Figure 28.55 SPSS^X commands to read output file

```
FILE HANDLE  MANOUT/ file specifications
INPUT PROGRAM
NUMERIC RCAN RLI RCI LCI LLI LCAN YEAR TR
INPUT MATRIX FILE=MANOUT
END INPUT PROGRAM
MANOVA RCAN RLI RCI LCI LLI LCAN BY YEAR(1,2) TR(1,5)/
 READ/
 DESIGN/
```

28.56 Missing Values

By default, cases with missing values on any of the variables named in the MANOVA specification are included. To treat missing values as if they were not missing, use Option 1 on the associated OPTIONS commmand.

OPTION 1 *Include missing values.*

You must also include the missing values within the range for categorical variables to enter the cases into the analysis.

28.57 EXAMPLES OF COMMON DESIGNS

Sections 28.58 through 28.69 describe some of the more commonly used designs which can be analyzed with MANOVA. These sections include sample MANOVA command setups to produce these designs. Sections 28.70 through 28.78 also provide examples with annotated output.

28.58 Univariate Analysis of Variance

The basic features of MANOVA useful for univariate analysis of variance are illustrated in the following example taken from Winer (1971, p. 436). An experiment was conducted to evaluate the relative effectiveness of three drugs (factor DRUG) in bringing about behavioral changes in two categories of patients (factor CAT). Three patients in each category were assigned at random to one of three drugs, and criterion ratings (Y) were made for each patient.

The MANOVA specification defines Y as the dependent variable and CAT and DRUG as the factor variables with two and three levels, respectively. Since only one dependent variable (Y) is indicated, a univariate analysis of variance is requested.

```
MANOVA  Y BY CAT(1,2) DRUG(1,3)
```

The default model generated from the MANOVA specification is a full factorial model.

Additional printed output can be obtained by using the PRINT subcommand. For instance, tests of homogeneity of within-cells variance are produced by specifying:

```
MANOVA Y BY CAT(1,2) DRUG(1,3)/
   PRINT=HOMOGENEITY(BARTLETT,COCHRAN)/
```

The cell statistics, including the mean, standard deviation, number of observations, and the 95% confidence intervals for the population means can be obtained using:

```
MANOVA Y BY CAT(1,2) DRUG(1,3)/
   PRINT=CELLINFO(MEANS)/
```

28.59 Specifying a Model with the DESIGN Subcommand

If the desired model is not full factorial, the model must be specified using the DESIGN subcommand. To specify a model that includes only the main effect terms, use:

```
MANOVA Y BY CAT(1,2) DRUG(1,3)/
   DESIGN= CAT,DRUG/
```

28.60 Specifying the ERROR Term

Unless otherwise requested, the within-cells mean square is used as the denominator for all the *F* values. If there is no within-cells error, the residual error is used. The residual mean square is the mean square for all terms not specified in the DESIGN subcommand. For example, if the model containing only main effects for DRUG and CAT is requested using

```
DESIGN= CAT,DRUG/
```

the residual error term is the mean square for the CAT by DRUG interaction. See Section 28.37 for rules governing the use of the ERROR subcommand. Use the DESIGN subcommand to indicate whether different error terms are to be used for the various terms in the design specification. See Section 28.8 for further details.

28.61 Using DESIGN and ERROR

The following specification requests a main effects model. The pooled interaction term (denoted as *R* for residual) and the within-cells error (denoted as *W*) are used as the error.

```
MANOVA  Y BY CAT(1,2) DRUG(1,3)/
        ERROR=W+R/
        DESIGN=CAT,DRUG
```

The ERROR subcommand must precede the design specification to which it applies.

The following produces the same results:

```
MANOVA Y BY CAT(1,2) DRUG(1,3)/
   DESIGN = CAT VS W+R, DRUG VS W+R/
```

28.62 Partitioning the Sum of Squares

Often it is desirable to partition the sum of squares associated with the various effects into a number of components that are more relevant to the individual questions of interest (see Cochran & Cox, 1957). In MANOVA, partitions are controlled by the keyword PARTITION followed by the name of the factor and the degrees of freedom associated with each component. To partition the sum of squares for factor DRUG into two components with one degree of freedom each, specify:

```
MANOVA  Y BY CAT(1,2) DRUG(1,3)/
   PARTITION(DRUG)=(1,1)/
   DESIGN=CAT,DRUG(1),DRUG(2),CAT BY DRUG/
```

The first component is denoted by DRUG(1), and the second by DRUG(2).

The default contrasts used for partitioning are deviation contrasts (see Section 28.35). In this example, the deviation contrasts are not orthogonal, so the two contrasts for DRUG(1) and DRUG(2) are not independent.

28.63 Contrasts

MANOVA allows specification of six different contrast types: deviation, difference, Helmert, simple, repeated, and polynomial. You can also specify any other contrast matrix via the SPECIAL keyword.

For example, to specify user-supplied orthogonal contrasts for the DRUG factor, use the following:

```
MANOVA  Y BY CAT(1,2) DRUG(1,3)/
   CONTRAST(DRUG)=SPECIAL(1 1 1 -1 2 -1 1 0 -1)/
   PARTITION(DRUG)=(1,1)/
   DESIGN=CAT,DRUG(1),DRUG(2),CAT BY DRUG(1),CAT BY DRUG(2)
```

The first set of coefficients (1 1 1) is always the weights for obtaining the constant term. Following the weights vector are the contrasts. The number of contrasts should be equal to the degrees of freedom for the factor. The first contrast (−1 2 −1) defines a contrast between level 2 and the combination of levels 1 and 3 for factor DRUG. The second contrast (1 0 −1) requests a comparison between levels 1 and 3 of DRUG. For most applications, you should be sure that each set of contrast coefficients sum to zero.

Since the inner product of the two contrasts is 0 and the sample sizes in all cells are equal, i.e., $(-1)(1) + 2(0) + (-1)(-1) = 0$, the two contrasts are independent. In this example, the DRUG(1) partition can be used to test the hypothesis $\beta_2 = (\beta_1 + \beta_3)/2$ while the second contrast tests $\beta_1 = \beta_3$.

28.64 Randomized Block Designs

In randomized block designs, the experimental unit is divided into groups (blocks). The main object is to keep the experimental errors within each group as small as possible. The accuracy of the experiment is increased by making comparisons within the resulting relatively homogeneous experimental units.

28.65 Complete Randomized Block Designs

A randomized block design is called complete if each block contains every level of the treatment. Table 28.65 is an example of a complete randomized block design with four treatments, A, B, C, and D, and three blocks.

Table 28.65 Complete randomized block design

Block 1	Block 2	Block 3
A	D	A
B	B	C
C	A	B
D	C	D

Let Y, TRT, and BLK be the response, treatment, and block variables, respectively. The MANOVA specifications needed to perform the analysis of this design are as follows:

```
MANOVA   Y BY BLK(1,3) TRT(1,4)/
   DESIGN=BLK,TRT/
```

In most applications the significance of the block differences is assumed, and treatment effects are corrected for the block effects. Although it does not make any difference here since the design is balanced and complete, in general the treatment effects should be adjusted.

28.66 Balanced Incomplete (Randomized) Block Designs (BIB)

In some randomized block designs it may not be possible to apply all treatments in every block. If the block size is less than the number of treatments, the design is called incomplete. An incomplete block design is called balanced if

- Each block contains exactly k treatments.
- Each treatment appears in r blocks.
- Any pair of treatments appears together l times.

Thus a BIB can be described in terms of the parameters t (number of treatments), b (number of blocks), k, r, and l.

The following example is taken from Cochran and Cox (1957, p. 443). It is a BIB design with t=6, b=15, k=2, r=5, and l=1. The blocks are grouped into 5 replications.

The MANOVA specification for this analysis is as follows:

```
MANOVA  DEP BY REPLICS(1,5) TREATMNT(1,6) BLOCKS(1,3)/
        DESIGN=REPLICS TREATMNT BLOCKS W REPLICS/
        DESIGN=REPLICS BLOCKS W REPLICS TREATMNT
```

The first design specification requests the blocks within replications adjusted for treatment effects. The second specification asks for the treatment effects adjusted for the blocks.

28.67 Partially Balanced Incomplete Block Designs (PBIB)

Because balanced incomplete block designs often require a large number of blocks, it may not be possible to find a design that fits the size of the experiment. A general class of BIB designs that do not have the uniform variances for treatment contrasts but still permit the estimation of treatment differences are the partially balanced incomplete block designs.

PBIB designs represent a large class of designs, many of which can be found in Cochran and Cox (1957). An example with $t=15$, $b=15$, $k=4$, and $r=4$ is given on page 456 of that text. The MANOVA specifications are as follows:

```
MANOVA  DEP BY BLOCKS(1,5) TREATMNT(1,15)/
   DESIGN=BLOCKS TREATMNT
```

28.68 Latin and Other Squares

A Latin square is a design in which each treatment appears exactly once in each row and column. The main interest is still on the estimation of treatment differences, but there are two restrictions on the randomization of the treatment assignment.

The following MANOVA specifications can be used to analyze a 4 × 4 Latin square:

```
MANOVA Y BY ROW(1,4),COL(1,4),TRT(1,4)/
   DESIGN=ROW,COL,TRT/
```

If another restriction on the randomization is placed on a Latin square, a Graeco-Latin square results. The analysis of variance for a Graeco-Latin square is very similar to that for a Latin square. Use GREEK to denote the third restriction factor on a 4 × 4 Graeco-Latin square. The MANOVA specification would be as follows:

```
MANOVA Y BY ROW(1,4), COL(1,4), GREEK(1,4), TRT(1,4)/
   DESIGN=ROW,COL,GREEK,TRT/
```

Note that a small Graeco-Latin square design may not be very practical, since very few degrees of freedom are left for the residual.

28.69 Nested Designs

A nested design arranges the experimental units hierarchically. For example, consider an experiment to compare the yield of wheat per acre for different areas in a given state. Five counties are selected at random, and then three townships are randomly selected from each county. From each township two farms are selected and the yield of wheat per acre is obtained. The resulting experiment produces 30 (5 × 3 × 2) experimental units. The factors in this experiment are county and township, and the township effects are *nested* under the county factor, since a given township appears only under one of the five counties. In other words, the county factor is not *crossed* with township factor and so the interaction between county and township is not estimable.

The model for this two-factor nested design is

$$Y_{ijk} = \mu + \alpha_i + \beta_{j(i)} + \epsilon_{ijk}$$

where α_i is the county effect and $\beta_{j(i)}$ is the township effect nested under the county effect.

Since α_i should be tested against variation within α_i, i.e., $\beta_{j(i)}$, the following MANOVA specfications can be used:

```
MANOVA Y BY COUNTY(1,5),TOWN(1,3)/
   DESIGN=COUNTY VS 1, TOWN WITHIN COUNTY=1 VS WITHIN/
```

The first keyword WITHIN (or just W) indicates nesting. The DESIGN specification requests that COUNTY be tested against error term 1 which is the effect of TOWN(nested within COUNTY), and that the within-cells error term (the second WITHIN) be used for testing the TOWN effect.

When crossing and nesting are both used in the design, attention must be paid to the choice of appropriate error terms for testing the various effects. Consider a three-factor example, with factors A, B, and C. If C is nested within B and B is nested within A, the DESIGN specification is

```
   DESIGN=A VS 1, B W A=1 VS 2, C W B W A=2 VS WITHIN/
```

If C is nested within B and B is crossed with A, the DESIGN specification is

```
   DESIGN=A VS 2, B VS 1, C W B=1 VS WITHIN,
          A BY B VS 2, A BY C W B=2 VS WITHIN/
```

An experiment was conducted to compare a new gun-loading method with the existing one (Hicks, 1973, p. 195). Three teams were chosen randomly from each of three groups. Each team used the two methods of gun loading in random order. The MANOVA specifications are as follows:

```
MANOVA RESP BY METHOD(1,2) GROUP TEAM(1,3)/
   DESIGN=METHOD VS 1, GROUP VS 2,
   METHOD BY GROUP VS 1, TEAM W GROUP=2,
   METHOD BY TEAM W GROUP=1
```

ANNOTATED EXAMPLE FOR MANOVA

MANOVA provides extensive facilities for repeated measures analysis. This example is, to a great degree, a simple generalization of the paired *t* test situation. Instead of measurements on two occasions, however, there are measurements on four occasions. The same subjects are measured on each occasion, so a simple one-way analysis of variance is inappropriate. This analysis takes advantage of the *multivariate setup*, in which all of a subject's scores across occasions reside in the same SPSS^X case. That is, the data have the following structure:

Case	Subject	Score 1	Score 2	Score 3	Score 4
1	1	30	28	16	34
2	2	14	18	10	22

This is in contrast to the *univariate setup*, in which a subject's scores across occasions spill down the cases, as in:

Case	Subject	Score
1	1	30
2	1	28
3	1	16
4	1	34
5	2	14
6	2	18
7	2	10
8	2	22

On balance, we recommend the multivariate setup because the univariate setup has certain drawbacks. First, the univariate setup forces you to spread your data over many more cases, and you pay for processing time by the case. Second, analysis of the univariate setup implies that you are using a mixed-model analysis of variance approach to the data. That is, *subject* is a random effect nested under between-subjects factors, when the latter are present. In this approach, certain *symmetry conditions* must be met (Huynh & Mandevill,1979), and in practice these conditions are quite restrictive. Third, specification of the DESIGN subcommand in the univariate mixed model can be very complicated. Fourth, the univariate setup is computationally inefficient, in the sense that it can take much more memory and processing time than the equivalent multivariate setup. Fifth, in most cases, the univariate results are fully retrievable from a MANOVA job that uses the multivariate setup.

You should note that while all repeated measures examples shown in this document use the multivariate setup for the data, you will see references to statistics produced using the multivariate approach and statistics produced using the univariate approach. The latter set of statistics are produced using a multivariate setup, but they are the same statistics that MANOVA would produce if the univariate setup had been used. You can obtain univariate statistics by specifying PRINT=SIGNIF (AVERF).

There are a few situations where you might turn to the univariate setup. When assumptions are met, the univariate approach has greater power. Under certain data configurations, the univariate mixed model makes fuller use of the data, such as in the following situations: too small a number of subjects in the model, too many empty cells in the repeated measures model, or the imposition of certain designs on the repeated measures, such as latin square order.

The data used for this example is an experiment which studies the effects of four drugs upon reaction time to a series of tasks (Winer, 1971). The subjects are trained in the tasks prior to the experiment, so that the learning of the tasks does not confound the analysis. There are five subjects in the analysis. The experimenter observes each subject under each drug, and the order of administration of drugs is randomized. The SPSS^{X} commands are

```
TITLE A BASIC REPEATED MEASURES EXAMPLE
COMMENT THE DATA REPRESENT 4 MEASURES ON 5 INDIVIDUALS.
 THIS IS A SIMPLE REPEATED MEASURES DESIGN.
 THE DATA COME FROM WINER, PAGE 268.
DATA LIST / DRUG1 DRUG2 DRUG3 DRUG4 (4F3.0)
MANOVA DRUG1 TO DRUG4/
 WSFACTORS=TRIAL(4)/
 CONTRAST(TRIAL)=SPECIAL(4*1, 1,-1,0,0,
                          1,1,0,-2, 1,1,-3,1)/
 WSDESIGN=TRIAL/
 PRINT=CELLINFO(MEANS)
  TRANSFORM
  ERROR(COR)
  SIGNIF(AVERF)/
 ANALYSIS(REPEATED)/
 DESIGN/
BEGIN DATA
 30 28 16 34
 14 18 10 22
 24 20 18 30
 38 34 20 44
 26 28 14 30
END DATA
```

- The TITLE command prints a title at the top of each page of display output, and the COMMENT command inserts comments that print back with the commands on the display (see Chapter 4).
- The DATA LIST command defines four variables from the data in the command file (see Chapter 3).
- The MANOVA specification names DRUG1 to DRUG4 as four joint dependent variables. There are no between-subjects factors or covariates in the analysis.
- The WSFACTORS subcommand defines TRIAL as a within-subjects factor. A *4* is placed in parentheses after the factor name since there are four drugs (see Section 28.20).
- The CONTRAST subcommand specifies a special set of contrasts for comparisons of the means across scores. The within-subjects factor requires *orthogonal* contrasts, so you could specify difference, helmert, or polynomial contrasts. The example uses SPECIAL, supplying contrasts among the means. If you do not specify orthogonal contrasts for the within-subjects factor, MANOVA takes your specified contrasts and orthonormalizes them. The first row of the special matrix is always the contrast for the overall mean and is typically a set of 1s. The remaining rows of the matrix contain the special contrasts signifying the desired comparisons between levels of the factor. From an inspection of the four means, we decide on the following comparisons: (1) the mean of DRUG1 versus the mean of DRUG2; (2) the means of DRUG1 and DRUG2 versus the mean of DRUG4; and (3) the means of DRUG1, DRUG2, and DRUG4 versus DRUG3 (see Section 28.35).
- The WSDESIGN subcommand specifies TRIAL, the one within-subjects factor (see Section 28.21).
- The PRINT subcommand has four specifications. CELLINFO prints the means (see Figure A). TRANSFORM prints the orthonormalized transformation matrix, which directly reflects the contrasts on the within-subjects factor (see Figure B). ERROR(COR) prints the error correlation matrix along with some ancillary statistics. Assessment of the statistics tells whether or not it is appropriate to work with the univariate approach statistics (see Figure F). SIGNIF(AVERF) prints the univariate approach statistics. Provided that certain assumptions are met, you can turn to these statistics for a test of significance (see Figure H).
- The ANALYSIS subcommand specifies a repeated measures analysis. MANOVA builds the indicated orthonormal transformation matrix and uses this matrix to transform the original response variables. MANOVA then cycles through the within-subjects effects defined by the WSDESIGN subcommand and represented by sets of the transformed variables (see Section 28.22).
- Finally, the DESIGN subcommand specifies the model for the between-subjects factor. Since there is no between-subjects factor in this model, the DESIGN subcommand simply triggers the analysis (see Section 28.8).

Portions of the display output are shown in Figures A through H.

- Figure A shows the cell means and standard deviations. Inspection of the cell means provides a rationale for the special contrast used in the analysis. Notice that the means for DRUG1 and DRUG2 have the smallest difference. Then, the mean for DRUG4 has a smaller difference from these two than does the mean for DRUG3. Finally, the mean for DRUG3 is most different from the others.

Annotated Example for MANOVA *continued*

A Cell means and standard deviations

```
CELL MEANS AND STANDARD DEVIATIONS
VARIABLE .. DRUG1
                                           MEAN      STD. DEV.         N   95 PERCENT CONF. INTERVAL

FOR ENTIRE SAMPLE                      26.40000        8.76356         5      15.51878      37.28122
- - - - - - - - - - - - - - - - - - - - - - - - - - - - - - - - - - - - - - - - - - - - - - - - - -
VARIABLE .. DRUG2
                                           MEAN      STD. DEV.         N   95 PERCENT CONF. INTERVAL

FOR ENTIRE SAMPLE                      25.60000        6.54217         5      17.47695      33.72305
- - - - - - - - - - - - - - - - - - - - - - - - - - - - - - - - - - - - - - - - - - - - - - - - - -
VARIABLE .. DRUG3
                                           MEAN      STD. DEV.         N   95 PERCENT CONF. INTERVAL

FOR ENTIRE SAMPLE                      15.60000        3.84708         5      10.82330      20.37670
- - - - - - - - - - - - - - - - - - - - - - - - - - - - - - - - - - - - - - - - - - - - - - - - - -
VARIABLE .. DRUG4
                                           MEAN      STD. DEV.         N   95 PERCENT CONF. INTERVAL

FOR ENTIRE SAMPLE                      32.00000        8.00000         5      22.06685      41.93315
```

- Figure B shows the within-subjects design. The orthonormalized transformation matrix shows the contrasts on the means. The original contrasts on the CONTRAST subcommand are orthogonal. MANOVA normalizes the contrasts so that the sum of squares of any column of the matrix is 1.

B Within-subjects design

```
CORRESPONDENCE BETWEEN EFFECTS AND COLUMNS OF WITHIN-SUBJECTS DESIGN 1

 STARTING  ENDING
  COLUMN   COLUMN    EFFECT NAME

     1        1      CONSTANT
     2        4      TRIAL
- - - - - - - - - - - - - - - - - - - - - - - - - - - - - - - - - - - - - - - - - - - - - - - - - -

ORTHONORMALIZED TRANSFORMATION MATRIX (TRANSPOSED)

                             1               2               3               4

         1             .50000          .70711          .40825          .28868
         2             .50000         -.70711          .40825          .28868
         3             .50000         0.0             0.0             -.86603
         4             .50000         0.0             -.81650          .28868
```

- Figure C shows the beginning of the default display of the multivariate repeated measures analysis. MANOVA tells you that it is using transformed variables in the analysis; this is signified by an asterisk (*) and a message.

C CONSTANT within-subjects effect

```
ORDER OF VARIABLES FOR ANALYSIS

  VARIATES     COVARIATES     NOT USED

  *DRUG1                      DRUG2
                              DRUG3
                              DRUG4

   1 DEPENDENT VARIABLE
   0 COVARIATES
   3 VARIABLES NOT USED
- - - - - - - - - - - - - - - - - - - - - - - - - - - - - - - - - - - - - - - - - - - - - - - -

      NOTE..  "*" MARKS TRANSFORMED VARIABLES.

              THESE TRANSFORMED VARIABLES CORRESPOND TO THE
              'CONSTANT' WITHIN-SUBJECT EFFECT.
```

- Figure D shows the test of significance for the between-subjects effect, which in this example is just the overall constant.

D Analysis of variance for CONSTANT

TESTS OF SIGNIFICANCE FOR DRUG1 USING SEQUENTIAL SUMS OF SQUARES

SOURCE OF VARIATION	SUM OF SQUARES	DF	MEAN SQUARE	F	SIG. OF F
WITHIN CELLS	680.80000	4	170.20000		
CONSTANT	12400.20000	1	12400.20000	72.85664	.001

- Figure E shows the next cycle of the analysis, which is the test for the TRIAL within-subjects effect. MANOVA jointly tests the three transformed variables, making this a multivariate test.

E TRIAL within-subjects effect

```
ORDER OF VARIABLES FOR ANALYSIS

  VARIATES     COVARIATES     NOT USED

  *DRUG2                      DRUG1
  *DRUG3
  *DRUG4

   3 DEPENDENT VARIABLES
   0 COVARIATES
   1 VARIABLE NOT USED
- - - - - - - - - - - - - - - - - - - - - - - - - - - - - - - - - - - - - - - - - - - - - - - -

      NOTE..  "*" MARKS TRANSFORMED VARIABLES.

              THESE TRANSFORMED VARIABLES CORRESPOND TO THE
              'TRIAL' WITHIN-SUBJECT EFFECT.
```

- Figure F shows the results from specifying ERROR(COR). Bartlett's test of sphericity tests whether the correlation matrix of the transformed variables is the identity matrix, in which case the transformed variables are uncorrelated. The observed significance level of the test, .598, does not reject the null hypothesis of sphericity. The F_{max} statistic is not significant at the .05 level, so we assume that the variances of the transformed variables are equal. Given that there is no between-subjects factor, these data satisfy the *symmetry conditions* that must be met if you wish to apply the univariate-approach statistical results. For more on the symmetry conditions, see Example 4 in Section 28.74.

F Error correlation statistics

WITHIN CELLS CORRELATIONS WITH STD. DEVS. ON DIAGONAL

	DRUG2	DRUG3	DRUG4
DRUG2	2.56905		
DRUG3	-.64875	1.73205	
DRUG4	.29109	.14199	4.31277

STATISTICS FOR WITHIN CELLS CORRELATIONS

DETERMINANT =	.42060
BARTLETT TEST OF SPHERICITY =	1.87647 WITH 3 D. F.
SIGNIFICANCE =	.598
F(MAX) CRITERION =	6.20000 WITH (3,4) D. F.

- Figure G shows the multivariate tests of significance of the trial within-subjects effect. The multivariate tests are significant at the .05 level. The univariate *F* tests reveal more detailed aspects of the pattern. Recall that the DRUG2 effect after transformation is the first contrast of interest: the contrast between the mean of DRUG1 and the mean of DRUG2. The *F* statistic for this effect is not significant, which leads to the conclusion that these two drugs produced no difference in reaction time. On the other hand, the transformed DRUG3 and DRUG4 effects are significant at the .01 level.

G Multivariate tests of significance

EFFECT .. TRIAL

MULTIVARIATE TESTS OF SIGNIFICANCE (S = 1, M = 1/2, N = 0)

TEST NAME	VALUE	APPROX. F	HYPOTH. DF	ERROR DF	SIG. OF F
PILLAIS	.97707	28.41231	3.00	2.00	.034
HOTELLINGS	42.61846	28.41231	3.00	2.00	.034
WILKS	.02293	28.41231	3.00	2.00	.034
ROYS	.97707				

UNIVARIATE F-TESTS WITH (1,4) D. F.

VARIABLE	HYPOTH. SS	ERROR SS	HYPOTH. MS	ERROR MS	F	SIG. OF F
DRUG2	1.60000	26.40000	1.60000	6.60000	.24242	.648
DRUG3	120.00000	12.00000	120.00000	3.00000	40.00000	.003
DRUG4	576.60000	74.40000	576.60000	18.60000	31.00000	.005

- Finally, Figure H shows the averaged test of significance for the drug effect; these are the *univariate approach* statistics. There are 12 error degrees of freedom for this test, while there are two error degrees of freedom for the multivariate tests. Given the error correlation results above, the averaged test is appropriate. The observed level of significance of this test is less than .0005, so the averaged *F* test corroborates the multivariate test results.

H Averaged test of significance

AVERAGED TESTS OF SIGNIFICANCE FOR DRUG USING SEQUENTIAL SUMS OF SQUARES

SOURCE OF VARIATION	SUM OF SQUARES	DF	MEAN SQUARE	F	SIG. OF F
WITHIN CELLS	112.80000	12	9.40000		
TRIAL	698.20000	3	232.73333	24.75887	.000

28.70 MANOVA EXAMPLES

MANOVA can be used to analyze many different types of designs. The following examples, although not exhaustive, demonstrate some of the more commonly used models. Most of these examples have been obtained from books and articles.

28.71 Example 1: Analysis of Covariance Designs

This example demonstrates using MANOVA for analysis of variance and analysis of covariance designs. The data are from Winer (1971). There is one factor, A, which represents three methods of training and one covariate, X, which is an aptitude test score. The dependent variable Y is the score on an achievement test administered after the training program. The SPSS^X commands are

```
COMMENT THE DATA COME FROM WINER'S STATISTICAL PRINCIPLES
 IN EXPERIMENTAL DESIGN, PAGE 776.
 Y IS A DEPENDENT VARIABLE.
 X IS A COVARIATE.
 A IS A FACTOR.
DATA LIST / A 1 X Y 2-5
COMMENT I.  THIS FIRST MANOVA COMMAND DOES ONEWAY ANALYSIS OF VARIANCE.
MANOVA Y BY A(1,3)/
 DESIGN/
BEGIN DATA
data lines
END DATA
COMMENT II.  THE SECOND MANOVA DOES A DEFAULT ANALYSIS OF COVARIANCE.
 NOTE:  THE DEFAULT ASSUMES HOMOGENEOUS SLOPES.
MANOVA Y BY A(1,3) WITH X/
 PRINT=PMEANS/
 DESIGN/
 /* III.  THE THIRD DESIGN TESTS THE FACTOR BY COVARIATE
 /* INTERACTION TERM.  THIS TESTS WHETHER THE PARALLEL SLOPES
 /* ASSUMPTION IS WARRANTED.
 ANALYSIS=Y/
 DESIGN= X, A, A BY X/
 /* IV.  THE FOURTH DESIGN SHOWS HOW TO FIT SEPARATE
 /* SLOPES.  YOU WOULD DO THIS IF THE FACTOR BY COVARIATE
 /* INTERACTION TERM IS SIGNIFICANT.
 DESIGN= X WITHIN A, A
```

- The DATA LIST command reads the three variables, A, X, and Y, from the data included in the command file (see Chapter 3).
- The first MANOVA command specifies a one-way analysis of variance using the default DESIGN subcommand (see Section 28.8).
- The second MANOVA command specifies the second through fourth models. The second model is a default analysis of covariance using the default DESIGN subcommand. The default analysis fits covariates, factors, and factor-by-factor interactions if you specify more than one factor, and assumes homogeneous slopes.
- The PRINT subcommand prints predicted means for the second through fourth models (see Section 28.38).
- The third analysis shows how to test the assumption of homogeneous slopes. The ANALYSIS subcommand indicates the dependent variable (see Section 28.7). The DESIGN subcommand indicates effects, including the factor-by-covariate interaction.
- The fourth analysis shows how to fit separate regression coefficients in each of the three groups of the factor. As in the third analysis, the ANALYSIS subcommand indicates the dependent variable for the analysis. The WITHIN keyword on the DESIGN subcommand fits separate regression models within each of the three groups of factor A.

Portions of the display output are shown in Figures 28.71a through 28.71e.

- Figure 28.71a shows the default display for the first analysis. The display includes the analysis of variance table and the estimated parameters under the model.

Figure 28.71a Example 1: Results for first analysis

```
TESTS OF SIGNIFICANCE FOR Y USING SEQUENTIAL SUMS OF SQUARES
SOURCE OF VARIATION                         SUM OF SQUARES      DF   MEAN SQUARE           F    SIG. OF F

WITHIN CELLS                                      26.85714      18       1.49206
CONSTANT                                         817.19048       1     817.19048   547.69149          0.0
A                                                 36.95238       2      18.47619    12.38298         .000
- - - - - - - - - - - - - - - - - - - - - - - - - - - - - - - - - - - - - - - - - - - - - - - - - - - - -

ESTIMATES FOR Y
CONSTANT
 PARAMETER         COEFF.       STD. ERR.        T-VALUE     SIG. OF T    LOWER .95 CL   UPPER .95 CL

      1     6.2380952381          .26655       23.40281          0.0          5.67809        6.79810
A
 PARAMETER         COEFF.       STD. ERR.        T-VALUE     SIG. OF T    LOWER .95 CL   UPPER .95 CL

      2    -1.8095238095          .37696       -4.80027         .000         -2.60149       -1.01755
      3     1.3333333333          .37696        3.53704         .002           .54136        2.12530
```

- Figure 28.71b shows the default display for the second analysis, which includes the covariate X. MANOVA prints the analysis of variance table, the parameter estimates adjusted for X, and regression statistics associated with X.

Figure 28.71b Example 1: Results for second analysis

```
TESTS OF SIGNIFICANCE FOR Y USING SEQUENTIAL SUMS OF SQUARES
SOURCE OF VARIATION                         SUM OF SQUARES      DF   MEAN SQUARE           F    SIG. OF F

WITHIN CELLS                                      10.30204      17        .60600
REGRESSION                                        16.55510       1      16.55510    27.31854         .000
CONSTANT                                          58.05399       1      58.05399    95.79829          0.0
A                                                 16.93200       2       8.46600    13.97024         .000
- - - - - - - - - - - - - - - - - - - - - - - - - - - - - - - - - - - - - - - - - - - - - - - - - - - - -

ESTIMATES FOR Y ADJUSTED FOR 1 COVARIATE
CONSTANT
 PARAMETER         COEFF.       STD. ERR.        T-VALUE     SIG. OF T    LOWER .95 CL   UPPER .95 CL

      1     4.1863945578          .42772        9.78766         .000          3.28398        5.08881
A
 PARAMETER         COEFF.       STD. ERR.        T-VALUE     SIG. OF T    LOWER .95 CL   UPPER .95 CL

      2    -1.3496598639          .25584       -5.27535         .000         -1.88944        -.80988
      3      .8380952381          .25825        3.24530         .005           .29324        1.38295
- - - - - - - - - - - - - - - - - - - - - - - - - - - - - - - - - - - - - - - - - - - - - - - - - - - - -

REGRESSION ANALYSIS FOR WITHIN CELLS ERROR TERM
DEPENDENT VARIABLE .. Y
COVARIATE            B          BETA      STD. ERR.       T-VALUE     SIG. OF T  LOWER .95 CL  UPPER .95 CL

X           .7428571429   .7851199742       .14213       5.22671          .000        .44300       1.04272
```

- Figure 28.71c shows the table of predicted means for the second analysis requested with the keyword PMEANS on the PRINT subcommand. MANOVA prints the observed means, the adjusted means, which are adjusted for the covariate, and the estimated means, which are the cell means estimated with knowledge of A.

Figure 28.71c Example 1: Adjusted means for second analysis

ADJUSTED AND ESTIMATED MEANS

VARIABLE .. Y

FACTOR	CODE	OBS. MEAN	ADJ. MEAN	EST. MEAN	RAW RESID.	STD. RESID.
A	1	4.42857	4.88844	4.42857	0.0	0.0
A	2	7.57143	7.07619	7.57143	0.0	0.0
A	3	6.71429	6.74966	6.71429	0.0	0.0

- Figure 28.71d shows the analysis of variance table for the third analysis. Since the A by X interaction is not significant, we do not reject the hypothesis of parallel slopes. That is, we can assume that the effect of change in X on Y is the same across levels of A.

Figure 28.71d Example 1: Analysis of variance table for third analysis

TESTS OF SIGNIFICANCE FOR Y USING SEQUENTIAL SUMS OF SQUARES

SOURCE OF VARIATION	SUM OF SQUARES	DF	MEAN SQUARE	F	SIG. OF F
WITHIN+RESIDUAL	9.63490	15	.64233		
CONSTANT	817.19048	1	817.19048	1272.23505	0.0
X	36.57548	1	36.57548	56.94218	0.0
A	16.93200	2	8.46600	13.18021	.000
A BY X	.66714	2	.33357	.51932	.605

- Finally, Figure 28.71e shows the analysis of variance table for the fourth analysis. The X WITHIN A effect is the joint effect of the separate regressions. Since the third analysis shows the factor-by-covariate interaction to be nonsignificant, the second analysis is the preferred solution.

Figure 28.71e Example 1: Analysis of variance table for fourth analysis

TESTS OF SIGNIFICANCE FOR Y USING SEQUENTIAL SUMS OF SQUARES

SOURCE OF VARIATION	SUM OF SQUARES	DF	MEAN SQUARE	F	SIG. OF F
WITHIN+RESIDUAL	9.63490	15	.64233		
CONSTANT	817.19048	1	817.19048	1272.23505	0.0
X WITHIN A	47.48204	3	15.82735	24.64065	0.0
A	6.69258	2	3.34629	5.20964	.019

28.72 Example 2: Multivariate One-Way ANOVA

This example does multivariate one-way analysis of variance with one three-level factor and four dependent variables that are jointly analyzed. In addition to the standard test for the difference in means, you can obtain a canonical discriminant analysis. When analyzing data structures of this type, you can consider turning the problem around and using the DISCRIMINANT procedure (see Chapter 34).

The data are the iris data from Fisher (1936). Fisher collected four measures on each of three species of irises. The four measures are the four dependent variables and the species is the factor variable. There are 50 observations in each species group. The SPSS^X commands are

```
TITLE IRISDATA - TO DO ANYTHING WITH FISHER'S IRIS DATA
COMMENT FISHER'S IRIS DATA IS THE CLASSICAL DISCRIMINANT
 ANALYSIS EXAMPLE.  WE WILL USE IT TO ILLUSTRATE
 MULTIVARIATE ONEWAY ANALYSIS OF VARIANCE.

DATA LIST / SEPALLEN 1-2 SEPALWID PETALLEN PETALWID 3-11 TYPE 12-13
VARIABLE LABELS SEPALLEN 'SEPAL LENGTH'
   SEPALWID 'SEPAL WIDTH'
   PETALLEN 'PETAL LENGTH'
   PETALWID 'PETAL WIDTH'
   TYPE 'TYPE OF IRIS'
VALUE LABELS TYPE 1 'SETOSA' 2 'VERSICOLOR' 3 'VIRGINICA'

MANOVA SEPALLEN SEPALWID PETALLEN PETALWID BY TYPE(1,3)/
 PRINT=CELLINFO(MEANS)
       HOMOGENEITY(BOXM)
       ERROR(COR)
       DISCRIM(RAW STAN ESTIM COR)/
 DESIGN/
BEGIN DATA
data lines
END DATA
```

- The TITLE command prints a title on each page of the display output, and the COMMENT command inserts comments that print back with the commands on the display (see Chapter 4).
- The DATA LIST command reads five variables—SEPALLEN, SEPALWID, PETALLEN, PETALWID, and TYPE—from the data in the command file (see Chapter 3).
- The VARIABLE LABELS and VALUE LABELS commands assign labels that are printed on the display output (see Chapter 3).
- The MANOVA specification lists four dependent variables and one factor.
- The PRINT subcommand requests several types of displays (see Section 28.38). CELLINFO(MEANS) prints the group means for each of the dependent variables (see Figure 28.72a).
- HOMOGENEITY(BOXM) prints Box's *M* statistic, which is a multivariate test for homogeneity of variance (see Figure 28.72b).
- ERROR(COR) prints the error correlation matrix, the standard deviations of the dependent variables, and Bartlett's test of sphericity (see Figure 28.72c).
- DISCRIM(RAW STAN ESTIM COR) requests a canonical discriminant analysis relating the four dependent variables to the TYPE factor. RAW prints discriminant function coefficients, STAN prints standardized discriminant function coefficients, ESTIM prints effect estimates in discriminant function space, and COR prints correlations between the dependent variables and the canonical variables defined by the discriminant functions (see Figure 28.72e).

Figures 28.72a through 28.72e show portions of the display.

- Figure 28.72a shows the cell means and standard deviations displayed with CELLINFO(MEANS). There are large differences in both means and standard deviations for the four dependent variables by the type of iris.

Figure 28.72a Example 2: Cell statistics

CELL MEANS AND STANDARD DEVIATIONS

VARIABLE .. SEPALLEN SEPAL LENGTH

FACTOR	CODE	MEAN	STD. DEV.	N	95 PERCENT CONF.	INTERVAL
TYPE	SETOSA	50.06000	3.52490	50	49.05824	51.06176
TYPE	VERSICOL	59.36000	5.16171	50	57.89306	60.82694
TYPE	VIRGINIC	65.88000	6.35880	50	64.07285	67.68715
FOR ENTIRE SAMPLE		58.43333	8.28066	150	57.09732	59.76934

VARIABLE .. SEPALWID SEPAL WIDTH

FACTOR	CODE	MEAN	STD. DEV.	N	95 PERCENT CONF.	INTERVAL
TYPE	SETOSA	34.28000	3.79064	50	33.20271	35.35729
TYPE	VERSICOL	27.70000	3.13798	50	26.80820	28.59180
TYPE	VIRGINIC	29.74000	3.22497	50	28.82347	30.65653
FOR ENTIRE SAMPLE		30.57333	4.35866	150	29.87010	31.27656

VARIABLE .. PETALLEN PETAL LENGTH

FACTOR	CODE	MEAN	STD. DEV.	N	95 PERCENT CONF.	INTERVAL
TYPE	SETOSA	14.62000	1.73664	50	14.12645	15.11355
TYPE	VERSICOL	42.60000	4.69911	50	41.26453	43.93547
TYPE	VIRGINIC	55.52000	5.51895	50	53.95153	57.08847
FOR ENTIRE SAMPLE		37.58000	17.65298	150	34.73185	40.42815

VARIABLE .. PETALWID PETAL WIDTH

FACTOR	CODE	MEAN	STD. DEV.	N	95 PERCENT CONF.	INTERVAL
TYPE	SETOSA	2.46000	1.05386	50	2.16050	2.75950
TYPE	VERSICOL	13.26000	1.97753	50	12.69799	13.82201
TYPE	VIRGINIC	20.26000	2.74650	50	19.47945	21.04055
FOR ENTIRE SAMPLE		11.99333	7.62238	150	10.76353	13.22313

- Figure 28.72b shows the tests for homogeneity-of-dispersion matrices displayed with HOMOGENEITY(BOXM). Both the *F* approximation and the chi-square approximation indicate rejection of the hypothesis of homogeneity.

Figure 28.72b Example 2: Tests for homogeneity-of-dispersion matrices

```
CELL NUMBER .. 1

DETERMINANT OF VARIANCE-COVARIANCE MATRIX =        211.30877
LOG(DETERMINANT) =                                   5.35332

- - - - - - - - - -

CELL NUMBER .. 2

DETERMINANT OF VARIANCE-COVARIANCE MATRIX =       1893.82847
LOG(DETERMINANT) =                                   7.54636

- - - - - - - - - -

CELL NUMBER .. 3

DETERMINANT OF VARIANCE-COVARIANCE MATRIX =      13274.79317
LOG(DETERMINANT) =                                   9.49362

- - - - - - - - - -

DETERMINANT OF POOLED VARIANCE-COVARIANCE MATRIX      4732.18336
LOG(DETERMINANT) =                                       8.46214

MULTIVARIATE TEST FOR HOMOGENEITY OF DISPERSION MATRICES

BOXS M =                        146.66325
F WITH (20,77566) DF =            7.04526, P =   .000 (APPROX.)
CHI-SQUARE WITH 20 DF =         140.94305, P =   .000 (APPROX.)
```

- Figure 28.72c shows the results of specifying ERROR(COR). The within-cells correlations are the pooled within-groups correlations between the four dependent variables; that is, differences in TYPE are taken into account. MANOVA displays the standard deviations of the four variables on the diagonal. The Bartlett test of sphericity tests whether the within-cells correlation matrix is the identity matrix. Given the low significance level, this assumption is rejected. The F_{max} statistic tests whether the four within-cells variances are equal. A table for the F_{max} distribution is found in Winer (1971).

Figure 28.72c Example 2: Within-cells correlations results

WITHIN CELLS CORRELATIONS WITH STD. DEVS. ON DIAGONAL

	SEPALLEN	SEPALWID	PETALLEN	PETALWID
SEPALLEN	5.14789			
SEPALWID	.53024	3.39688		
PETALLEN	.75616	.37792	4.30334	
PETALWID	.36451	.47053	.48446	2.04650

STATISTICS FOR WITHIN CELLS CORRELATIONS

DETERMINANT = .19953
BARTLETT TEST OF SPHERICITY = 233.44151 WITH 6 D. F.
SIGNIFICANCE = 0.0

F(MAX) CRITERION = 6.32755 WITH (4,147) D. F.

- Figure 28.72d shows the default display of multivariate and univariate tests of significance for the hypothesis that all group means are equal. All test statistics indicate rejection of the hypothesis. The canonical discriminant analysis has two dimensions. This follows the standard criterion, which takes the lesser of the number of dependent variables and number of groups minus one as the maximum dimensionality of a problem. The dimension reduction analysis shows that both dimensions are significant, while the eigenvalues and canonical correlations show that the first of the two functions is overwhelmingly predominant.

Figure 28.72d Example 2: Test results

EFFECT .. TYPE

MULTIVARIATE TESTS OF SIGNIFICANCE (S = 2, M = 1/2, N = 71)

TEST NAME	VALUE	APPROX. F	HYPOTH. DF	ERROR DF	SIG. OF F
PILLAIS	1.19190	53.46649	8.00	290.00	0.0
HOTELLINGS	32.47732	580.53210	8.00	286.00	0.0
WILKS	.02344	199.14534	8.00	288.00	0.0
ROYS	.96987				

EIGENVALUES AND CANONICAL CORRELATIONS

ROOT NO.	EIGENVALUE	PCT.	CUM. PCT.	CANON. COR.
1	32.19193	99.12126	99.12126	.98482
2	.28539	.87874	100.00000	.47120

DIMENSION REDUCTION ANALYSIS

ROOTS	WILKS LAMBDA	F	HYPOTH. DF	ERROR DF	SIG. OF F
1 TO 2	.02344	199.14534	8.00	288.00	0.0
2 TO 2	.77797	13.74634	3.00	144.50	.000

UNIVARIATE F-TESTS WITH (2,147) D. F.

VARIABLE	HYPOTH. SS	ERROR SS	HYPOTH. MS	ERROR MS	F	SIG. OF F
SEPALLEN	6321.21333	3895.62000	3160.60667	26.50082	119.26450	0.0
SEPALWID	1134.49333	1696.20000	567.24667	11.53878	49.16004	.000
PETALLEN	43710.28000	2722.26000	21855.14000	18.51878	1180.16118	0.0
PETALWID	8041.33333	615.66000	4020.66667	4.18816	960.00715	0.0

- Figure 28.72e shows the results of specifying DISCRIM on the PRINT subcommand. The correlations between dependent and canonical variables show that the first function is primarily the petal measures, while the second function is primarily the width measures.

Figure 28.72e Example 2: Canonical discriminant results

```
EFFECT .. TYPE

RAW DISCRIMINANT FUNCTION COEFFICIENTS

          FUNCTION NO.

VARIABLE                1                2

SEPALLEN           .08294          -.00241
SEPALWID           .15345          -.21645
PETALLEN          -.22012           .09319
PETALWID          -.28105          -.28392

- - - - - - - - - - - - - - - - - - - - - - - - - - - - - - - - - - - - - - - -

STANDARDIZED DISCRIMINANT FUNCTION COEFFICIENTS

          FUNCTION NO.

VARIABLE                1                2

SEPALLEN           .42695          -.01241
SEPALWID           .52124          -.73526
PETALLEN          -.94726           .40104
PETALWID          -.57516          -.58104

- - - - - - - - - - - - - - - - - - - - - - - - - - - - - - - - - - - - - - - -

ESTIMATES OF EFFECTS FOR CANONICAL VARIABLES

          CANONICAL VARIABLE

 PARAMETER              1                2

        2         7.60760          -.21513
        3        -1.82505           .72790

- - - - - - - - - - - - - - - - - - - - - - - - - - - - - - - - - - - - - - - -

CORRELATIONS BETWEEN DEPENDENT AND CANONICAL VARIABLES

          CANONICAL VARIABLE

VARIABLE                1                2

SEPALLEN          -.22260          -.31081
SEPALWID           .11901          -.86368
PETALLEN          -.70607          -.16770
PETALWID          -.63318          -.73724
```

28.73 Example 3: Multivariate Multiple Regression, Canonical Correlation

Example 3 uses MANOVA to do multivariate multiple regression and canonical correlation analysis. MANOVA produces multivariate results, individual regression results, and analysis of residuals, although residual analysis is not as extensive in MANOVA as in REGRESSION. Since there is no canonical correlation procedure in SPSS^X, use MANOVA to do canonical correlation analysis.

The data for this example come from Finn (1974). The data were obtained from tests administered to 60 eleventh-grade students in a western New York metropolitan school. There are two dependent variables —synthesis and evaluation—which measure achievement. The independent variables are of three types. First, there is *general intelligence*, as measured by a standard test. Second, there are three measures of creativity. *Consequences obvious* "involves the ability of the subject to list direct consequences of a given hypothetical event." *Consequences remote* "involves identifying more remote or original consequences of similar situations." *Possible jobs* "involves the ability to list a quantity of occupations that might be represented by a given emblem or symbol" (p. 11). Third, in his analysis, Finn uses multiplicative interactions of the three creativity measures with intelligence to assess whether creativity has a greater effect on the achievement of individuals having high intelligence than on individuals of low intelligence. Finn uses standard scores for the independent variables. The SPSS^X commands are

```
TITLE FINN'S MULTIVARIATE MULTIPLE REGRESSION
DATA LIST  / SYNTH 1 EVAL 3 CONOBV 5-8(1) CONRMT 9-12(1)
 JOB 14-17(1) INTEL 19-23(1)
MISSING VALUES SYNTH TO INTEL(9.9)
CONDESCRIPTIVE INTEL CONOBV CONRMT JOB
OPTIONS 3 5
BEGIN DATA
data lines
END DATA
COMMENT USE COMPUTE TO CREATE INTERACTION TERMS.
COMPUTE CI1=ZCONOBV*ZINTEL
COMPUTE CI2=ZCONRMT*ZINTEL
COMPUTE CI3=ZJOB*ZINTEL
MANOVA  SYNTH EVAL WITH ZINTEL ZCONOBV ZCONRMT ZJOB CI1 CI2 CI3/
 PRINT=
 ERROR(SSCP COV COR)
 SIGNIF(HYPOTH STEPDOWN)
 DISCRIM(RAW,STAN,ESTIM,COR,ALPHA(1.0))
 POBS(ERROR(WITHIN))/
 PLOT=POBS/
 DESIGN/
```

- The TITLE command prints a title at the top of each page of the display output (see Chapter 4).
- The DATA LIST command defines six variables. SYNTH and EVAL are the dependent variables, and CONOBV, CONRMT, JOB, and INTEL are the independent variables (see Chapter 3).
- Option 3 on the CONDESCRIPTIVE procedure computes standardized scores for the intelligence and creativity measures. The new variables—ZINTEL, ZCONOBV, ZCONRMT, and ZJOB—are automatically added to the active file. Option 5 of CONDESCRIPTIVE specifies listwise deletion of missing values for the calculation (see Chapter 19).
- The COMPUTE commands compute three interaction variables—CI1, CI2, and CI3—from the standardized variables created with CONDESCRIPTIVE (see Chapter 6).
- The MANOVA specification names SYNTH and EVAL as joint dependent variables and specifies seven covariates—ZINTEL, ZCONOBV, ZCONRMT, ZJOB, CI1, CI2, and CI3.
- The PRINT subcommand requests several displays (see Section 28.38). The ERROR keyword prints the error sums-of-squares and cross-products matrix, the error variance-covariance matrix, and the error correlation matrix with standard deviations on the diagonal (see Figure 28.73a).
- The SIGNIF keyword has two specifications. HYPOTH prints the hypothesis sums-of-squares and cross-products matrices (see Figure 28.73a). STEPDOWN prints the Roy-Bargmann step-down *F* tests for the dependent variables (see Figure 28.73b).
- The DISCRIM keyword requests a canonical analysis. The results correspond to canonical correlation analysis since a set of continuous dependent variables are related to a set of continuous independent variables. The RAW keyword prints canonical function coefficients; the STAN keyword prints standardized canonical function coefficients; the ESTIM function produces effect estimates in canonical function space; the COR keyword prints correlations between the original variables and the canonical variables defined by the canonical functions; the ALPHA keyword sets a generous cutoff value for the significance of the canonical functions in the analysis, thereby ensuring that MANOVA calculates all

possible canonical functions. Two is the maximum possible in this analysis (see Figures 28.73c and 28.73d).

- The POBS keyword prints four casewise results for each dependent variable: the observed value of the dependent variable, the predicted value of the dependent variable, the residual value, and the standardized residual where standardization consists of dividing the residual by the error standard deviation (see Figure 28.73f).
- The PLOT subcommand produces plots of the observed and predicted values and case number against standardized residuals and normal and detrended normal probability plots for the standardized residuals (see Figures 28.73g through 28.73i).

Portions of the output are shown in Figures 28.73a through 28.73i.

- Figure 28.73a shows within-cells statistical results. The correlation of .37978 is the partial correlation of SYNTH and EVAL, taking into account the independent variable set. The two standard deviations are adjusted. The Bartlett test of sphericity leads to rejection of the hypothesis that the partial correlation between SYNTH and EVAL is zero. Figure 28.73a also shows the adjusted variance-covariance matrix, the error SSCP matrix, and the hypothesis SSCP matrix for the regression effect.

Figure 28.73a Example 3: Within-cells results and hypothesis SSCP

```
ADJUSTED WITHIN CELLS CORRELATIONS WITH STD. DEVS. ON DIAGONAL

                     SYNTH            EVAL

SYNTH              1.37049
EVAL                .37978         1.51256

- - - - - - - - - - - - - - - - - - - - - - - - - - - - - - - - - - - - - - - -

STATISTICS FOR ADJUSTED WITHIN CELLS CORRELATIONS

DETERMINANT =                       .85577
BARTLETT TEST OF SPHERICITY =      7.86555 WITH 1 D. F.
SIGNIFICANCE =                        .005

F(MAX) CRITERION =                 1.21806 WITH (2,52) D. F.

ADJUSTED WITHIN CELLS VARIANCES AND COVARIANCES

                     SYNTH            EVAL

SYNTH              1.87825
EVAL                .78726         2.28783
- - - - - - - - - - - - - - - - - - - - - - - - - - - - - - - - - - - - - - - -

ADJUSTED WITHIN CELLS SUM-OF-SQUARES AND CROSS-PRODUCTS

                     SYNTH            EVAL

SYNTH             97.66914
EVAL              40.93737       118.96727

- - - - - - - - - - - - - - - - - - - - - - - - - - - - - - - - - - - - - - - -

ADJUSTED HYPOTHESIS SUM-OF-SQUARES AND CROSS-PRODUCTS

                     SYNTH            EVAL

SYNTH             81.18086
EVAL              69.41263        67.21606
```

- Figure 28.73b shows the default display and the step-down display. Both the multivariate and univariate test results indicate that the predictor set has statistically significant impact on the dependent variables. While two dimensions are fit, it appears that one dimension will suffice. Of the two eigenvalues, the first eigenvalue has most of the variance associated with it, while the second eigenvalue has relatively little variability associated with it. Likewise, the first canonical correlation is moderately sized, while the second canonical correlation is negligible in magnitude. Provided that you accept the ordering of the criterion variables—SYNTH, then EVAL—the step-down *F* tests show that after taking SYNTH into account EVAL does not contribute to the association with the predictors.

Figure 28.73b Example 3: Test results and dimensionality statistics

```
EFFECT .. WITHIN CELLS REGRESSION
MULTIVARIATE TESTS OF SIGNIFICANCE (S = 2, M = 2 , N = 24 1/2)

TEST NAME           VALUE      APPROX. F     HYPOTH. DF        ERROR DF       SIG. OF F

PILLAIS            .55946       2.88501          14.00          104.00           .001
HOTELLINGS        1.05995       3.78553          14.00          100.00           .000
WILKS              .47077       3.33286          14.00          102.00           .000
ROYS               .49886
- - - - - - - - - - - - - - - - - - - - - - - - - - - - - - - - - - - - - - - - - - - -

EIGENVALUES AND CANONICAL CORRELATIONS

ROOT NO.     EIGENVALUE          PCT.     CUM. PCT.    CANON. COR.  SQUARED COR.

    1          .99544        93.91374     93.91374        .70630       .49886
    2          .06451         6.08626    100.00000        .24617       .06060
- - - - - - - - - - - - - - - - - - - - - - - - - - - - - - - - - - - - - - - - - - - -

DIMENSION REDUCTION ANALYSIS

ROOTS          WILKS LAMBDA              F       HYPOTH. DF        ERROR DF        SIG. OF F

1 TO 2             .47077          3.33286            14.00          102.00            .000
2 TO 2             .93940           .55565             6.00          105.00            .765
- - - - - - - - - - - - - - - - - - - - - - - - - - - - - - - - - - - - - - - - - - - -

UNIVARIATE F-TESTS WITH (7,52) D. F.

VARIABLE     SQ. MUL. R        MUL. R    ADJ. R-SQ.      HYPOTH MS       ERROR MS              F       SIG. OF F

SYNTH            .45390        .67372        .38039       11.59727        1.87825        6.17450            .000
EVAL             .36102        .60085        .27500        9.60229        2.28783        4.19712            .001
- - - - - - - - - - - - - - - - - - - - - - - - - - - - - - - - - - - - - - - - - - - -

ROY-BARGMAN STEPDOWN F - TESTS

VARIABLE        HYPOTH. MS        ERROR MS     STEP-DOWN F        HYPOTH. DF         ERROR DF       SIG. OF F

SYNTH             11.59727         1.87825         6.17450                 7               52            .000
EVAL               2.32700         1.99625         1.16569                 7               51            .339
```

- Figure 28.73c shows canonical results for the two dependent variables. Recall that only the first canonical function is statistically significant. Correlations between the dependent variables and the first canonical variable are of similar magnitude. The part of the figure labeled "VARIANCE EXPLAINED BY CANONICAL VARIABLES OF DEPENDENT VARIABLES" provides a *redundancy analysis* (Cooley & Lohnes, 1971).

Figure 28.73c Example 3: Canonical results for dependent variables

```
RAW CANONICAL COEFFICIENTS FOR DEPENDENT VARIABLES
            FUNCTION NO.

VARIABLE                 1              2

SYNTH               .40444         -.59708
EVAL                .22637          .66958
- - - - - - - - - - - - - - - - - - - - - - - - - - - - - - - - - - - - - - - - - - - -

STANDARDIZED CANONICAL COEFFICIENTS FOR DEPENDENT VARIABLES
            FUNCTION NO.

VARIABLE                 1              2

SYNTH               .70415        -1.03956
EVAL                .40212         1.18946
- - - - - - - - - - - - - - - - - - - - - - - - - - - - - - - - - - - - - - - - - - - -
```

```
CORRELATIONS BETWEEN DEPENDENT AND CANONICAL VARIABLES
          FUNCTION NO.
VARIABLE                 1                2

SYNTH               .94733          -.32027
EVAL                .82794           .56081
- - - - - - - - - - - - - - - - - - - - - - - - - - - - - - - - - - - - - - - -

VARIANCE EXPLAINED BY CANONICAL VARIABLES OF DEPENDENT VARIABLES

CAN. VAR.      PCT VAR DEP     CUM PCT DEP     PCT VAR COV     CUM PCT COV

        1         79.14597        79.14597        39.48249        39.48249
        2         20.85403       100.00000         1.26379        40.74628
```

• Figure 28.73d shows the analogous canonical results for the covariates. The correlations between covariates and the first canonical variable load most heavily on intelligence.

Figure 28.73d Example 3: Canonical results for the covariates

```
RAW CANONICAL COEFFICIENTS FOR COVARIATES
          FUNCTION NO.
COVARIATE                1                2

ZINTEL              .84825          -.10334
ZCONOBV             .26535           .22951
ZCONRMT             .19301           .47229
ZJOB               -.06403          -.27927
CI1                -.01367          1.03503
CI2                -.07571          -.32373
CI3                 .20707          -.04665
- - - - - - - - - - - - - - - - - - - - - - - - - - - - - - - - - - - - - - - -

STANDARDIZED CANONICAL COEFFICIENTS FOR COVARIATES
          CAN. VAR.
COVARIATE                1                2

ZINTEL              .84825          -.10334
ZCONOBV             .26535           .22951
ZCONRMT             .19301           .47229
ZJOB               -.06403          -.27927
CI1                -.01172           .88718
CI2                -.10086          -.43125

STANDARDIZED CANONICAL COEFFICIENTS FOR COVARIATES (CONT.)
          CAN. VAR.
COVARIATE                1                2

CI3                 .21699          -.04889
- - - - - - - - - - - - - - - - - - - - - - - - - - - - - - - - - - - - - - - -

CORRELATIONS BETWEEN COVARIATES AND CANONICAL VARIABLES
          CAN. VAR.
COVARIATE                1                2

ZINTEL              .94646          -.09081
ZCONOBV             .30260          -.06104
ZCONRMT             .56188           .41804
ZJOB                .57787          -.12674
CI1                 .17980           .86843
CI2                 .49440          -.01020
CI3                 .44879           .06254
- - - - - - - - - - - - - - - - - - - - - - - - - - - - - - - - - - - - - - - -

VARIANCE EXPLAINED BY CANONICAL VARIABLES OF THE COVARIATES

CAN. VAR.      PCT VAR DEP     CUM PCT DEP     PCT VAR COV     CUM PCT COV

        1         15.07395        15.07395        30.21700        30.21700
        2           .83195        15.90590        13.72818        43.94518
```

• Figure 28.73e shows the default display of the regression results for the two dependent variables.

Figure 28.73e Example 3: Regression results

REGRESSION ANALYSIS FOR WITHIN CELLS ERROR TERM

DEPENDENT VARIABLE .. SYNTH

COVARIATE	B	BETA	STD. ERR.	T-VALUE	SIG. OF T	LOWER .95 CL	UPPER .95 CL
ZINTEL	1.0023515611	.5757069725	.21712	4.61656	.000	.56667	1.43804
ZCONOBV	.2776147955	.1594498336	.23559	1.17836	.244	-.19514	.75037
ZCONRMT	.1600206340	.0919088708	.23801	.67232	.504	-.31759	.63763
ZJOB	-.0362512720	-.0208211489	.26665	-.13595	.892	-.57132	.49882
CI1	-.1579990497	-.0777852525	.23587	-.66986	.506	-.63130	.31530
CI2	-.0437613801	-.0334827062	.21472	-.20380	.839	-.47463	.38711
CI3	.2476316205	.1490442471	.25225	.98169	.331	-.25855	.75381

DEPENDENT VARIABLE .. EVAL

COVARIATE	B	BETA	STD. ERR.	T-VALUE	SIG. OF T	LOWER .95 CL	UPPER .95 CL
ZINTEL	.8558203945	.4817681902	.23963	3.57146	.001	.37497	1.33667
ZCONOBV	.3319337251	.1868559423	.26002	1.27659	.207	-.18982	.85369
ZCONRMT	.3163314691	.1780729336	.26269	1.20422	.234	-.21079	.84345
ZJOB	-.1350002290	-.0759958746	.29429	-.45873	.648	-.72554	.45554
CI1	.2396403477	.1156316715	.26032	.92057	.362	-.28273	.76201
CI2	-.1580419455	-.1185157260	.23698	-.66690	.508	-.63358	.31749
CI3	.2036655452	.1201436311	.27840	.73156	.468	-.35498	.76231

- Figure 28.73f shows a portion of the casewise results for the synthesis variable produced by PRINT=POBS.

Figure 28.73f Example 3: Casewise output

OBSERVED AND PREDICTED VALUES FOR EACH CASE

DEPENDENT VARIABLE.. SYNTH

CASE NO.	OBSERVED	PREDICTED	RAW RESID.	STD RESID.
1	5.00000	2.82408	2.17592	1.58769
2	0.0	1.90538	-1.90538	-1.39029
4	4.00000	3.64830	.35170	.25662
5	1.00000	2.03041	-1.03041	-.75185
6	7.00000	4.20982	2.79018	2.03590
7	1.00000	1.95046	-.95046	-.69351
8	2.00000	2.03649	-.03649	-.02662
9	1.00000	1.76344	-.76344	-.55705
10	4.00000	3.86086	.13914	.10153

- Figure 28.73g shows two plots. The plot of the observed versus predicted values for SYNTH reflects the multiple *R* for the model. The plot of the observed values versus the residuals shows the way in which residuals vary in sign and magnitude across values of the dependent variable.

Figure 28.73g Example 3: Observed values vs. predicted values and residuals

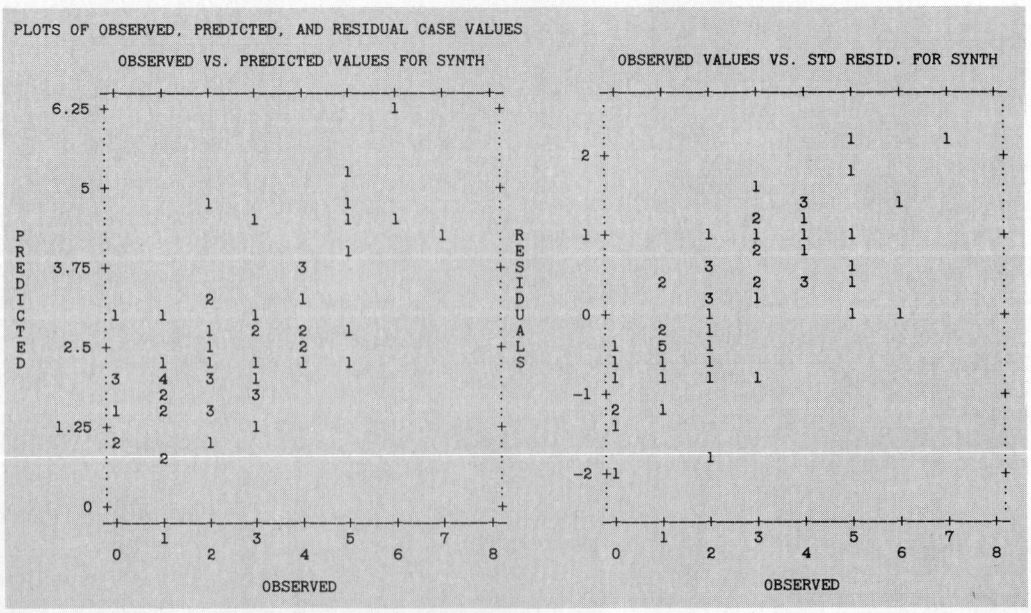

- Figure 28.73h shows two plots: the plot of the residuals versus the predicted values and the plot of case number versus residuals. The latter plot is useful when there is some meaning to the order of cases in your file.

Figure 28.73h Example 3: Residuals vs. predicted values and order

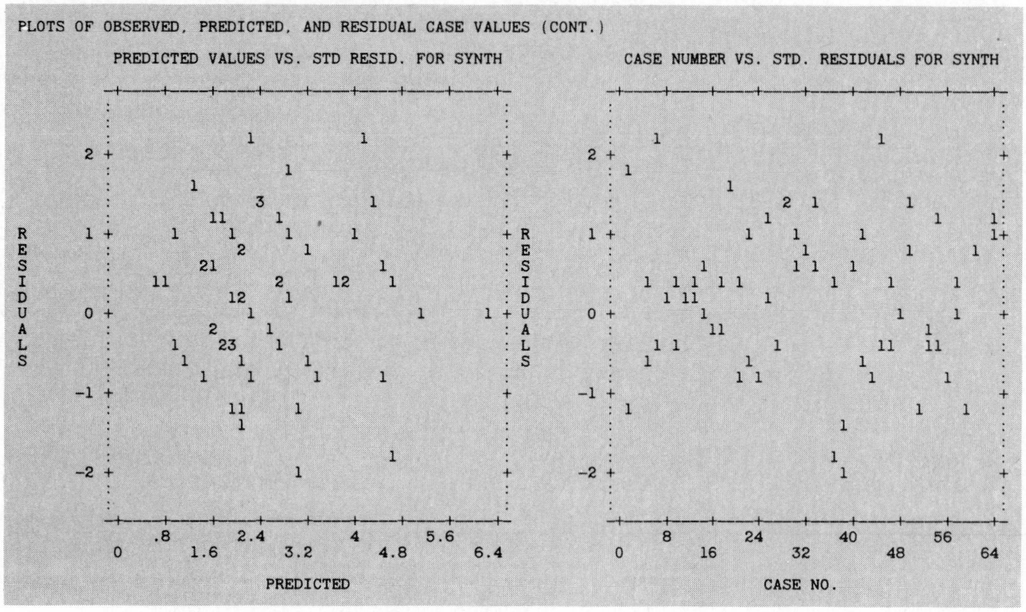

- Finally, Figure 28.73i shows the normal plot of the residuals and the detrended normal plot of the residuals.

Figure 28.73i Example 3: Normal plot and detrended normal plot

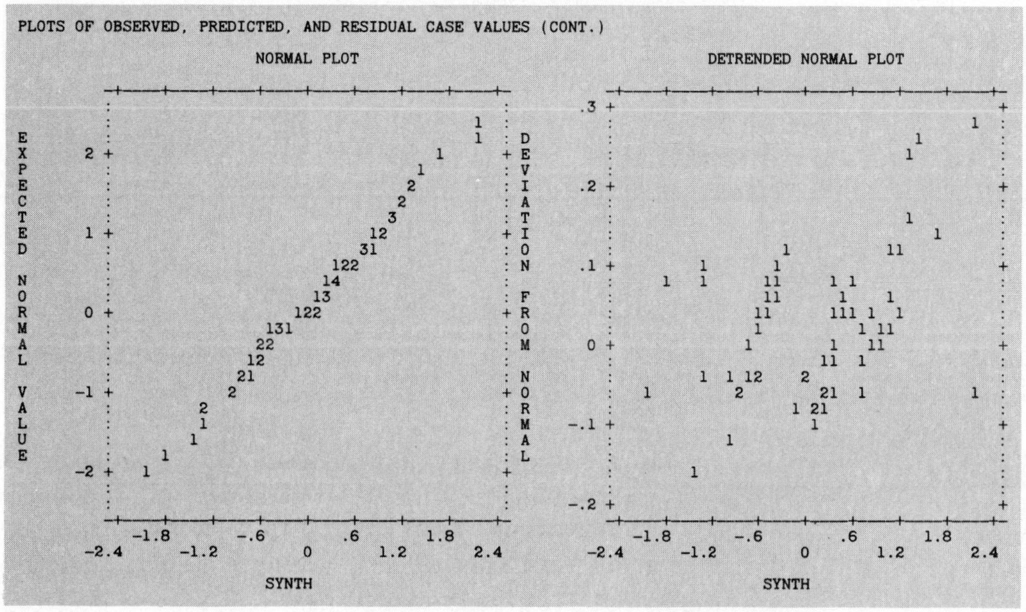

28.74 Example 4: Repeated Measures

The data for this example appear in Elashoff (1981). An introductory discussion is found in the annotated example for MANOVA. There is one between-subjects factor, GROUP, with two levels. There are two within-subjects factors: two types of drugs are administered at each of three doses. This study aims to estimate the relative potency of the two drugs in inhibiting a response to a stimulus. Subjects in Group 1 received the three doses of Drug 1 first and the three doses of Drug 2 second. Subjects in Group 2 received Drug 2 first and then Drug 1. Every subject has six response scores. The multivariate setup supplies all relevant statistics. This example also shows a test of the symmetry assumption.

The univariate results of the analysis of repeated measures designs are by-products of the multivariate computations. To use the univariate results, which have greater statistical power, the following two conditions must be met:

- The covariance matrices for the associated set of orthonormal variables are identical across all levels of the between-subjects factors. This is the usual homogeneity-of-variance assumption.
- The common covariance matrix has a sphericity pattern, that is, equal variances on the diagonal and zero covariances off the diagonal.

These two conditions are termed the *symmetry conditions*, and they are necessary and sufficient conditions. Note that both conditions are based on the orthonormal transformed variables and not on the original repeated measures variables. The SPSS^X commands are

```
TITLE A REPEATED MEASURES DESIGN EXAMPLE
COMMENT THIS EXAMPLE HAS 2 WITHIN-SUBJECTS FACTORS
 AND 1 BETWEEN SUBJECT FACTOR
DATA LIST / Y1 Y2 Y3 Y4 Y5 Y6 1-18 GROUP 20
MANOVA Y1 TO Y6 BY GROUP(1,2)/
 WSFACTOR=DRUG(2) DOSE(3)/
 CONTRAST(DOSE)=POLYNOMIAL(1,2,6)/
 WSDESIGN=DRUG, DOSE,DRUG BY DOSE/
 PRINT=TRANSFORM
  HOMOGENEITY(BOXM)
  ERROR(COR)
  SIGNIF(AVERF)/
 ANALYSIS(REPEATED)/
 DESIGN/
BEGIN DATA
 19 22 28 16 26 22 1
 11 19 30 12 18 28 1
 20 24 24 24 22 29 1
 21 25 25 15 10 26 1
 18 24 29 19 26 28 1
 17 23 28 15 23 22 1
 20 23 23 26 21 28 1
 14 20 29 25 29 29 1
 16 20 24 30 34 36 2
 26 26 26 24 30 32 2
 22 27 23 33 36 45 2
 16 18 29 27 26 34 2
 19 21 20 22 22 21 2
 20 25 25 29 29 33 2
 21 22 23 27 26 35 2
 17 20 22 23 26 28 2
END DATA
```

- The TITLE command prints a title at the top of each page of display output, and the COMMENT command inserts comments that print back with the commands on the display (see Chapter 4).
- The DATA LIST command defines seven variables from the data in the command file (see Chapter 3).
- The MANOVA specification names six joint dependent variables—Y1 to Y6—and one between-subjects factor—GROUP.

- The WSFACTORS subcommand defines the within-subjects factors, DRUG with 2 levels and DOSE with 3 levels. The order in which you specify the factors is crucial; you *must* specify them in the order corresponding to the dependent variable list. Conversely, name your dependent variables in a known and intended order. Note that the index value of the rightmost within-subjects factor increments most rapidly (see Section 28.20).
- The CONTRAST subcommand specifies a polynomial contrast for DOSE. The spacing 1,2,6 reflects the levels of administered doses in the experiment (see Section 28.35).
- The WSDESIGN subcommand specifies the full factorial model for the within-subjects factors (see Section 28.21).
- The PRINT subcommand specifies several useful statistics. TRANSFORM prints the orthonormalized transformation matrix, which shows how MANOVA transforms the dependent variables to build the within-subjects effects (see Figure 28.74b). HOMOGENEITY(BOXM) prints a multivariate test for the homogeneity-of-dispersion matrices. Data for which the homogeneity assumption is not rejected meet the first condition for symmetry indicated above (see Figure 28.74a). ERROR(COR) prints within-cells correlations and associated statistics when more than one transformed variable corresponds to a within-subjects effect (see Figures 28.74e and 28.74i). SIGNIF(AVERF) prints the average *F*, which is a univariate approach statistic (see Figure 28.74h).
- ANALYSIS(REPEATED) invokes a repeated measures analysis using the orthonormal transformations to build within-subjects effects (see Section 28.22).
- The DESIGN subcommand specifies the between-subjects design. By default, MANOVA enters the one between-subjects factor (see Section 28.8).

Portions of the display output are shown in Figures 28.74a through 28.74k.

- Figure 28.74a shows the multivariate test for homogeneity-of-dispersion matrices. Given the large significance levels, the test does not reject the hypothesis of homogeneity. The data do not appear to violate the first symmetry condition.

Figure 28.74a Example 4: Symmetry condition 1

```
CELL NUMBER .. 1

DETERMINANT OF VARIANCE-COVARIANCE MATRIX =        4138.01612
LOG(DETERMINANT) =                                    8.32797

- - - - - - - - - -

CELL NUMBER .. 2

DETERMINANT OF VARIANCE-COVARIANCE MATRIX =       23150.55748
LOG(DETERMINANT) =                                   10.04977

- - - - - - - - - -

DETERMINANT OF POOLED VARIANCE-COVARIANCE MATRIX    329610.63417
LOG(DETERMINANT) =                                      12.70567

- - - - - - - - - - - - - - - - - - - - - - - - - - - - - - - - - - - - - - - - - - - - - -

MULTIVARIATE TEST FOR HOMOGENEITY OF DISPERSION MATRICES

BOXS M =                           49.23512
F WITH (21,720) DF =                1.21162, P =   .233 (APPROX.)
CHI-SQUARE WITH 21 DF =            26.87836, P =   .175 (APPROX.)
```

- Figure 28.74b shows the correspondence between within-subjects effects and columns of the orthonormalized transformation matrix. Column 1 is the constant effect; column 2 is the drug effect; column 3 is the dose-linear effect; column 4 is the dose-quadratic effect; column 5 is the drug-by-dose-linear interaction; and column 6 is the drug-by-dose-quadratic interaction.

Figure 28.74b Example 4: Within-subjects design

CORRESPONDENCE BETWEEN EFFECTS AND COLUMNS OF WITHIN-SUBJECTS DESIGN 1

STARTING COLUMN	ENDING COLUMN	EFFECT NAME
1	1	CONSTANT
2	2	DRUG
3	4	DOSE
5	6	DRUG BY DOSE

ORTHONORMALIZED TRANSFORMATION MATRIX (TRANSPOSED)

	1	2	3	4	5	6
1	.40825	.40825	-.37796	.43644	-.37796	.43644
2	.40825	.40825	-.18898	-.54554	-.18898	-.54554
3	.40825	.40825	.56695	.10911	.56695	.10911
4	.40825	-.40825	-.37796	.43644	.37796	-.43644
5	.40825	-.40825	-.18898	-.54554	.18898	.54554
6	.40825	-.40825	.56695	.10911	-.56695	-.10911

- Figure 28.74c shows the default display of tests of significance for transformed-Y1, which is the constant within-subjects effect. The constant within-subjects effect tests the between-subjects factor.

Figure 28.74c Example 4: Constant within-subjects effect

TESTS OF SIGNIFICANCE FOR Y1 USING SEQUENTIAL SUMS OF SQUARES

SOURCE OF VARIATION	SUM OF SQUARES	DF	MEAN SQUARE	F	SIG. OF F
WITHIN CELLS	532.97917	14	38.06994		
CONSTANT	55632.51042	1	55632.51042	1461.32381	0.0
GROUP	270.01042	1	270.01042	7.09248	.019

- Figure 28.74d shows the default display of tests of significance for transformed-Y2, which is the drug within-subjects effect. This effect tests drug and group by drug.

Figure 28.74d Example 4: DRUG within-subjects effect

TESTS OF SIGNIFICANCE FOR Y2 USING SEQUENTIAL SUMS OF SQUARES

SOURCE OF VARIATION	SUM OF SQUARES	DF	MEAN SQUARE	F	SIG. OF F
WITHIN CELLS	375.64583	14	26.83185		
DRUG	348.84375	1	348.84375	13.00111	.003
GROUP AND DRUG	326.34375	1	326.34375	12.16255	.004

- Figure 28.74e shows the within-cells correlations and related statistics for transformed-Y3 and transformed-Y4, which jointly correspond to the dose within-subjects effect. Bartlett's test of sphericity is nonsignificant, as is the F_{max} statistic, so the data do not appear to violate the second symmetry condition for the dose within-subjects effect. Therefore, you can use *univariate* test results in assessing the dose-related effects.

Figure 28.74e Example 4: Symmetry condition 2 for DOSE effect

```
ORDER OF VARIABLES FOR ANALYSIS

  VARIATES     COVARIATES     NOT USED

  *Y3                         Y1
  *Y4                         Y2
                              Y5
                              Y6

   2 DEPENDENT VARIABLES
   0 COVARIATES
   4 VARIABLES NOT USED
- - - - - - - - - - - - - - - - - - - - - - - - - - - - - - - - - - - - - - - -

     NOTE..  "*" MARKS TRANSFORMED VARIABLES.

             THESE TRANSFORMED VARIABLES CORRESPOND TO THE
             'DOSE' WITHIN-SUBJECT EFFECT.
- - - - - - - - - - - - - - - - - - - - - - - - - - - - - - - - - - - - - - - -

WITHIN CELLS CORRELATIONS WITH STD. DEVS. ON DIAGONAL

                       Y3              Y4

Y3                3.75557
Y4                -.10921         2.58427
- - - - - - - - - - - - - - - - - - - - - - - - - - - - - - - - - - - - - - - -

STATISTICS FOR WITHIN CELLS CORRELATIONS

DETERMINANT =                     .98807
BARTLETT TEST OF SPHERICITY =     .14997 WITH 1 D. F.
SIGNIFICANCE =                     .699

F(MAX) CRITERION =               2.11190 WITH (2,14) D. F.
```

- Figures 28.74f and 28.74g show the default display of multivariate test results for dose-related effects. In Figure 28.74g, the univariate *F* test for variable Y3 is the linear effect of DOSE, and Y4 is the quadratic effect of DOSE. Figure 28.74h shows the univariate test results for the dose-related effects.

Figure 28.74f Example 4: GROUP by DOSE multivariate tests

```
EFFECT .. GROUP AND DOSE

MULTIVARIATE TESTS OF SIGNIFICANCE (S = 1, M = 0, N = 5 1/2)

TEST NAME          VALUE     APPROX. F     HYPOTH. DF       ERROR DF      SIG. OF F

PILLAIS           .18262       1.45223           2.00          13.00          .270
HOTELLINGS        .22342       1.45223           2.00          13.00          .270
WILKS             .81738       1.45223           2.00          13.00          .270
ROYS              .18262
- - - - - - - - - - - - - - - - - - - - - - - - - - - - - - - - - - - - - - - -

UNIVARIATE F-TESTS WITH (1,14) D. F.

VARIABLE        HYPOTH. SS      ERROR SS     HYPOTH. MS       ERROR MS            F      SIG. OF F

Y3                37.14509     197.45982       37.14509       14.10427      2.63361           .127
Y4                 5.12574      93.49851        5.12574        6.67847       .76750           .396
```

Figure 28.74g Example 4: DOSE multivariate test results

```
EFFECT .. DOSE

MULTIVARIATE TESTS OF SIGNIFICANCE (S = 1, M = 0, N = 5 1/2)

TEST NAME          VALUE     APPROX. F     HYPOTH. DF       ERROR DF      SIG. OF F

PILLAIS           .79534      25.26075           2.00          13.00          .000
HOTELLINGS       3.88627      25.26075           2.00          13.00          .000
WILKS             .20466      25.26075           2.00          13.00          .000
ROYS              .79534
- - - - - - - - - - - - - - - - - - - - - - - - - - - - - - - - - - - - - - - -

UNIVARIATE F-TESTS WITH (1,14) D. F.

VARIABLE        HYPOTH. SS      ERROR SS     HYPOTH. MS       ERROR MS            F      SIG. OF F

Y3               702.50223     197.45982      702.50223       14.10427     49.80776           .000
Y4                56.26860      93.49851       56.26860        6.67847      8.42538           .012
```

Figure 28.74h Example 4: DOSE and GROUP by DOSE univariate results

AVERAGED TESTS OF SIGNIFICANCE FOR Y USING SEQUENTIAL SUMS OF SQUARES

SOURCE OF VARIATION	SUM OF SQUARES	DF	MEAN SQUARE	F	SIG. OF F
WITHIN CELLS	290.95833	28	10.39137		
DOSE	758.77083	2	379.38542	36.50967	0.0
GROUP AND DOSE	42.27083	2	21.13542	2.03394	.150

- Figure 28.74i shows the within-cells correlations and related statistics for transformed-Y5 and transformed-Y6, which jointly correspond to the drug-by-dose interactions. This time, test statistics lead to rejection of the second symmetry condition. Therefore, you should use the *multivariate* test results in assessing effects.

Figure 28.74i Example 4: Symmetry condition 2 for DRUG by DOSE effect

```
ORDER OF VARIABLES FOR ANALYSIS

  VARIATES     COVARIATES     NOT USED

  *Y5                         Y1
  *Y6                         Y2
                              Y3
                              Y4

  2 DEPENDENT VARIABLES
  0 COVARIATES
  4 VARIABLES NOT USED
- - - - - - - - - - - - - - - - - - - - - - - - - - - - - - - - - - - - - - -

     NOTE..  "*" MARKS TRANSFORMED VARIABLES.

             THESE TRANSFORMED VARIABLES CORRESPOND TO THE
             'DRUG BY DOSE' WITHIN-SUBJECT EFFECT.
- - - - - - - - - - - - - - - - - - - - - - - - - - - - - - - - - - - - - - -

WITHIN CELLS CORRELATIONS WITH STD. DEVS. ON DIAGONAL

                      Y5             Y6

Y5               3.31754
Y6                .57501        2.58715
- - - - - - - - - - - - - - - - - - - - - - - - - - - - - - - - - - - - - - -

STATISTICS FOR WITHIN CELLS CORRELATIONS

DETERMINANT =                    .66937
BARTLETT TEST OF SPHERICITY =   5.01781 WITH 1 D. F.
SIGNIFICANCE =                     .025

F(MAX) CRITERION =              1.64433 WITH (2,14) D. F.
```

- Figures 28.74j and 28.74k show the default display of multivariate test results for the drug-by-dose effects. Given the observed levels of significance, no effects are statistically significant.

Figure 28.74j Example 4: GROUP by DRUG by DOSE results

EFFECT .. GROUP AND DRUG BY DOSE

MULTIVARIATE TESTS OF SIGNIFICANCE (S = 1, M = 0, N = 5 1/2)

TEST NAME	VALUE	APPROX. F	HYPOTH. DF	ERROR DF	SIG. OF F
PILLAIS	.14314	1.08583	2.00	13.00	.366
HOTELLINGS	.16705	1.08583	2.00	13.00	.366
WILKS	.85686	1.08583	2.00	13.00	.366
ROYS	.14314				

UNIVARIATE F-TESTS WITH (1,14) D. F.

VARIABLE	HYPOTH. SS	ERROR SS	HYPOTH. MS	ERROR MS	F	SIG. OF F
Y5	14.64509	154.08482	14.64509	11.00606	1.33064	.268
Y6	.16741	93.70685	.16741	6.69335	.02501	.877

Figure 28.74k Example 4: DRUG by DOSE results

```
EFFECT .. DRUG BY DOSE

MULTIVARIATE TESTS OF SIGNIFICANCE (S = 1, M = 0, N = 5 1/2)

TEST NAME            VALUE      APPROX. F      HYPOTH. DF       ERROR DF       SIG. OF F

PILLAIS             .12604        .93739           2.00           13.00           .417
HOTELLINGS          .14421        .93739           2.00           13.00           .417
WILKS               .87396        .93739           2.00           13.00           .417
ROYS                .12604

- - - - - - - - - - - - - - - - - - - - - - - - - - - - - - - - - - - - - - - - - - - - -

UNIVARIATE F-TESTS WITH (1,14) D. F.

VARIABLE        HYPOTH. SS       ERROR SS      HYPOTH. MS       ERROR MS            F      SIG. OF F

Y5                  .80580      154.08482          .80580       11.00606       .07321           .791
Y6                11.25670       93.70685        11.25670        6.69335      1.68177           .216
```

28.75 Example 5: Repeated Measures with a Constant Covariate

This example shows repeated measures analysis with a constant covariate. You must specify as many covariates as dependent variables. If the covariate is constant across the repeated measures factor, use COMPUTE to create as many replicates of the covariate as you need.

The data are obtained from a 2 × 2 factorial experiment with repeated measures on factor B (Winer, 1971). Variables Y1 and Y2 are scores for the two occasions. Factor A is the between-subjects factor. There are four subjects under each level of factor A. The covariate measure X is obtained before the administration of any of the treatments, and it is therefore constant for both levels of the within-subjects factor B. The SPSS^X commands are

```
TITLE COVARIATE CONSTANT OVER TRIALS:  WINER, PAGE 803
DATA LIST / A, X, Y1, Y2 (4F3.0)
COMPUTE X2 = X
MANOVA Y1, Y2 BY A(1,2) WITH X, X2/
 WSFACTORS = B( 2 )/
 WSDESIGN = B/
 ANALYSIS(REPEATED)/
 PRINT= TRANSFORM/
 DESIGN = A/
BEGIN DATA
data lines
END DATA
```

- The TITLE command prints a title at the top of each page of display output (see Chapter 4).
- The DATA LIST command defines four variables from the data in the command file (see Chapter 3).
- The COMPUTE command computes X2, which is a copy of the covariate X (see Chapter 6).
- The MANOVA specification specifies Y1 and Y2 as joint dependent variables, A as the between-subjects factor, and X and X2 as covariates. In the general case, the number of covariates *must* be an integer multiple of the number of dependent variables. In this case, the number of variables in the two sets is equal.
- The WSFACTORS subcommand specifies B as the within-subjects factor (see Section 28.20).
- The WSDESIGN subcommand specifies the within-subjects design, which here simply names B (see Section 28.21).
- ANALYSIS(REPEATED) invokes a repeated measures analysis (see Section 28.22).
- The PRINT subcommand specifies printing of the orthonormalized transformation matrix (see Sections 28.38 and 28.50 and Figure 28.75a).

- The DESIGN subcommand specifies the between-subjects design (see Section 28.8).

Portions of the display output are shown in Figures 28.75a through 28.75c.

- Figure 28.75a shows the correspondence between within-subjects effects and columns of the design matrix, as well as the orthonormalized transformation matrix. Note the block diagonal structure of the transformation matrix. MANOVA uses the same transformations on dependent variable–covariate pairs. Column 1 is the transformation producing new Y1; column 2 is the transformation producing new Y2; column 3 is the transformation producing new X; and column 4 is the transformation producing new X2.

Figure 28.75a Example 5: Within-subjects design

```
CORRESPONDENCE BETWEEN EFFECTS AND COLUMNS OF WITHIN-SUBJECTS DESIGN 1

 STARTING  ENDING
  COLUMN   COLUMN    EFFECT NAME

     1        1      CONSTANT
     2        2      B

- - - - - - - - - - - - - - - - - - - - - - - - - - - - - - - - - - - - - - - -

ORTHONORMALIZED TRANSFORMATION MATRIX (TRANSPOSED)

                         1               2               3               4

     1              .70711          .70711         0.0             0.0
     2              .70711         -.70711         0.0             0.0
     3             0.0             0.0              .70711          .70711
     4             0.0             0.0              .70711         -.70711
```

- Figure 28.75b shows the default display of the test for the between-subjects effect. MANOVA uses transformed-Y1 and transformed-X in the analysis. The analysis of variance table shows a test of significance for the between-subjects factor, A, adjusted for covariate X. Differences in means on the between-subjects factor are not statistically significant. The regression coefficient for X is 1.022.

Figure 28.75b Example 5: Constant within-subjects effect

```
ORDER OF VARIABLES FOR ANALYSIS

  VARIATES     COVARIATES     NOT USED

  *Y1             *X          Y2
                              X2

  1 DEPENDENT VARIABLE
  1 COVARIATE
  2 VARIABLES NOT USED

- - - - - - - - - - - - - - - - - - - - - - - - - - - - - - - - - - - - - - - -

     NOTE..  "*" MARKS TRANSFORMED VARIABLES.

             THESE TRANSFORMED VARIABLES CORRESPOND TO THE
             'CONSTANT' WITHIN-SUBJECT EFFECT.

- - - - - - - - - - - - - - - - - - - - - - - - - - - - - - - - - - - - - - - -

TESTS OF SIGNIFICANCE FOR Y1 USING SEQUENTIAL SUMS OF SQUARES

SOURCE OF VARIATION                    SUM OF SQUARES       DF   MEAN SQUARE             F    SIG. OF F

WITHIN CELLS                                 61.29820        5      12.25964
REGRESSION                                  166.57680        1     166.57680      13.58741         .014
CONSTANT                                    400.66845        1     400.66845      32.68191         .002
A                                            44.49160        1      44.49160       3.62911         .115

- - - - - - - - - - - - - - - - - - - - - - - - - - - - - - - - - - - - - - - -
REGRESSION ANALYSIS FOR WITHIN CELLS ERROR TERM

DEPENDENT VARIABLE .. Y1

COVARIATE              B          BETA     STD. ERR.       T-VALUE     SIG. OF T  LOWER .95 CL  UPPER .95 CL

X           1.0219435737   .8549858355        .27724       3.68611          .014        .30928       1.73461
```

- Figure 28.75c shows the default display of the test for the B within-subjects effect. Since the values for X2 are 0 after transformation, no adjustment is done, and MANOVA returns one degree of freedom to the within-cells term. The analysis of variance table contains tests of significance for B and the A by B interaction.

Figure 28.75c Example 5: B within-subjects effect

```
ORDER OF VARIABLES FOR ANALYSIS

  VARIATES     COVARIATES     NOT USED

  *Y2          *X2            Y1
                              X

   1 DEPENDENT VARIABLE
   1 COVARIATE
   2 VARIABLES NOT USED

- - - - - - - - - - - - - - - - - - - - - - - - - - - - - - - - - - - - - - - - - - - - - - - - -

     NOTE..  "*" MARKS TRANSFORMED VARIABLES.

             THESE TRANSFORMED VARIABLES CORRESPOND TO THE
             'B' WITHIN-SUBJECT EFFECT.

- - - - - - - - - - - - - - - - - - - - - - - - - - - - - - - - - - - - - - - - - - - - - - - - - -

* * * * * * * * * * * * * * * * * * * * * * * * * * * * * * * * * * * * *
*                  *                                                     *
*   W A R N I N G  * FOR WITHIN CELLS ERROR MATRIX, THESE COVARIATES     *
*                  * APPEAR LINEARLY DEPENDENT ON PRECEDING              *
*                  * VARIABLES ...                                       *
*                  *   X2                                                *
*                  * 1 D.F. WILL BE RETURNED TO THIS ERROR TERM.         *
*                  *                                                     *
* * * * * * * * * * * * * * * * * * * * * * * * * * * * * * * * * * * * *

- - - - - - - - - - - - - - - - - - - - - - - - - - - - - - - - - - - - - - - - - - - - - - - - - -

TESTS OF SIGNIFICANCE FOR Y2 USING SEQUENTIAL SUMS OF SQUARES

SOURCE OF VARIATION                 SUM OF SQUARES      DF   MEAN SQUARE          F    SIG. OF F

WITHIN CELLS                               6.37500       6       1.06250
B                                         85.56250       1      85.56250    80.52941        .000
A AND B                                     .56250       1        .56250      .52941        .494
```

28.76 Example 6: Repeated Measures with a Varying Covariate

You can use MANOVA to perform repeated measures analysis with a varying covariate. The model is a 3 × 2 factorial experiment with repeated measures on factor B (Winer, 1971). There are three subjects in each group. You can obtain regression coefficients for both the between-subjects effect and the within-subjects effect. See Winer for a discussion of a statistic which tests the equality of these two regression coefficients. In this analysis, since there are only two levels of the within-subjects factor, the univariate and multivariate approaches are identical. However, for a model which has more than two levels on any of the within-subjects factors with covariates varying over the repeated measures trials, interpret the multivariate results with caution. In certain models, there may be some question concerning the propriety of controlling for all covariates. On the other hand, the univariate results obtained from the multivariate setup are usable. The SPSS^X commands are

```
TITLE COVARIATE VARYING OVER TRIALS:  WINER, PAGE 806.
DATA LIST / GROUP, B1X, B1Y, B2X, B2Y (5F3.0)
VALUE LABELS GROUP 1 'A1' 2 'A2' 3 'A3'
MANOVA B1Y, B2Y BY GROUP(1,3) WITH B1X, B2X/
 WSFACTOR = B( 2 )/
 WSDESIGN /
 PRINT = TRANSFORM/
 ANALYSIS(REPEATED)/
 DESIGN/
BEGIN DATA
  1  3  8  4 14
  1  5 11  9 18
  1 11 16 14 22
  2  2  6  1  8
  2  8 12  9 14
  2 10  9  9 10
  3  7 10  4 10
  3  8 14 10 18
  3  9 15 12 22
END DATA
```

- The TITLE command prints a title at the top of each page of display output (see Chapter 4).
- The DATA LIST command defines five variables from the data in the command file, and the VALUE LABELS command assigns labels to the values for variable GROUP (see Chapter 3).
- The MANOVA command specifies B1Y and B2Y as joint dependent variables, GROUP as a three-level between-subjects factor, and B1X and B2X as covariates. The two dependent variables and two covariates contain pairs of scores obtained on two occasions.
- The WSFACTORS subcommand specifies B as the two-level within-subjects factor (see Section 28.20).
- The WSDESIGN subcommand specifies the single within-subjects factor (see Section 28.21).
- The PRINT subcommand prints the orthonormalized transformation matrix (see Sections 28.38, 28.50, and Figure 28.76a).
- ANALYSIS specifies a repeated measures analysis. DESIGN specifies the between-subjects design (see Sections 28.8 and 28.22).

Portions of the display output are shown in Figures 28.76a through 28.76c.

- Figure 28.76a shows the orthonormalized transformation matrix, which is block diagonal. Columns 1 and 2 correspond to transformations of the dependent variables, while columns 3 and 4 correspond to transformations of the covariates.

Figure 28.76a Example 6: Within-subjects design

```
CORRESPONDENCE BETWEEN EFFECTS AND COLUMNS OF WITHIN-SUBJECTS DESIGN 1

 STARTING  ENDING
  COLUMN   COLUMN    EFFECT NAME

    1        1       CONSTANT
    2        2       B

- - - - - - - - - - - - - - - - - - - - - - - - - - - - - - - - - - - - - - - -

ORTHONORMALIZED TRANSFORMATION MATRIX (TRANSPOSED)

                       1              2              3              4

      1             .70711         .70711        0.0            0.0
      2             .70711        -.70711        0.0            0.0
      3            0.0            0.0             .70711         .70711
      4            0.0            0.0             .70711        -.70711
```

- Figure 28.76b shows the tests of significance for the GROUP effect, which is not significant.

Figure 28.76b Example 6: Constant within-subjects effect

```
ORDER OF VARIABLES FOR ANALYSIS

  VARIATES      COVARIATES      NOT USED

  *B1Y          *B1X            B2Y
                                B2X

   1 DEPENDENT VARIABLE
   1 COVARIATE
   2 VARIABLES NOT USED
- - - - - - - - - - - - - - - - - - - - - - - - - - - - - - - - - - - - - - - - - - - - - - - - - - - -

     NOTE..  "*" MARKS TRANSFORMED VARIABLES.

             THESE TRANSFORMED VARIABLES CORRESPOND TO THE
             'CONSTANT' WITHIN-SUBJECT EFFECT.
- - - - - - - - - - - - - - - - - - - - - - - - - - - - - - - - - - - - - - - - - - - - - - - - - - - -

TESTS OF SIGNIFICANCE FOR B1Y USING SEQUENTIAL SUMS OF SQUARES

SOURCE OF VARIATION                       SUM OF SQUARES        DF   MEAN SQUARE            F    SIG. OF F

WITHIN CELLS                                    44.37049         5      8.87410
REGRESSION                                     132.62951         1    132.62951      14.94569         .012
CONSTANT                                       128.78926         1    128.78926      14.51294         .013
GROUP                                           54.25900         2     27.12950       3.05716         .136

REGRESSION ANALYSIS FOR WITHIN CELLS ERROR TERM

DEPENDENT VARIABLE .. B1Y

COVARIATE             B          BETA     STD. ERR.      T-VALUE    SIG. OF T  LOWER .95 CL  UPPER .95 CL

B1X         .8474729242   .8656323009        .21921      3.86597         .012        .28397       1.41097
```

- Figure 28.76c shows the tests of significance for the B within-subjects effect.

Figure 28.76c Example 6: Within-subjects effect

```
  VARIATES      COVARIATES      NOT USED

  *B2Y          *B2X            B1Y
                                B1X

   1 DEPENDENT VARIABLE
   1 COVARIATE
   2 VARIABLES NOT USED
- - - - - - - - - - - - - - - - - - - - - - - - - - - - - - - - - - - - - - - - - - - - - - - - - - - -

     NOTE..  "*" MARKS TRANSFORMED VARIABLES.

             THESE TRANSFORMED VARIABLES CORRESPOND TO THE
             'B' WITHIN-SUBJECT EFFECT.
- - - - - - - - - - - - - - - - - - - - - - - - - - - - - - - - - - - - - - - - - - - - - - - - - - - -

TESTS OF SIGNIFICANCE FOR B2Y USING SEQUENTIAL SUMS OF SQUARES

SOURCE OF VARIATION                       SUM OF SQUARES        DF   MEAN SQUARE            F    SIG. OF F

WITHIN CELLS                                     2.99802         5       .59960
REGRESSION                                      10.00198         1     10.00198      16.68101         .010
B                                               31.54703         1     31.54703      52.61318         .001
GROUP AND B                                      2.33929         2      1.16964       1.95069         .236

REGRESSION ANALYSIS FOR WITHIN CELLS ERROR TERM

DEPENDENT VARIABLE .. B2Y

COVARIATE             B          BETA     STD. ERR.      T-VALUE    SIG. OF T  LOWER .95 CL  UPPER .95 CL

B2X         .8452380952   .8771450247        .20695      4.08424         .010        .31326       1.37721
```

28.77 Example 7: A Doubly Multivariate Repeated Measures Design

This example illustrates how to analyze a doubly multivariate repeated measures design using the multivariate setup. The data consist of 53 subjects with 15 response variables recorded for each subject. Each of five types of tests are administered on three occasions to the subjects. Therefore, time is a within-subjects factor. There are two between-subjects factors: a two-level sex variable and a three-level group variable.

The model is multivariate in two senses. First, when a subject is measured across occasions with respect to a given item, the multivariate setup specifies each of the scores on the same SPSS^X case. Second, each subject is measured with respect to more than one item at each occasion, thereby inducing multivariate considerations. This example illustrates the use of the MEASURE subcommand to label the results of the univariate approach.

Use the following rules when performing this type of analysis with MANOVA:

- Specify variables measuring a given attribute across occasions consecutively and in order.
- The number of dependent variables in the MANOVA specification must be an integer multiple of the number of within-subjects levels.

The SPSS^X commands are

```
TITLE  A MULTIVARIATE REPEATED MEASURES DESIGN.
COMMENT THIS A DOUBLY MULTIVARIATE REPEATED MEASURES DESIGN WITH
 THE DATA AS FOLLOWS:
                                          TIME

                                 1                2              3

                              PREDIS          POSTDIS        FOLODIS
                              PREPROB         POSTPROB       FOLOPROB
                              PRESELF         POSTSELF       FOLOSELF
                              PRENEG          POSTNEG        FOLONEG
                              PRETHER         POSTTHER       FOLOTHER

DATA LIST / GROUP, SEX, PREDIS, PREPROB, PRESELF, PRENEG,
 PRETHER, POSTDIS, POSTPROB, POSTSELF, POSTNEG, POSTTHER,
 FOLODIS, FOLOPROB, FOLOSELF, FOLONEG, FOLOTHER
 (2F1.0,4X,2F6.3,3F3.0,2F6.3,3F3.0,2F6.3,3F3.0)
MANOVA PREDIS POSTDIS FOLODIS PREPROB POSTPROB FOLOPROB
 PRESELF POSTSELF FOLOSELF PRENEG POSTNEG FOLONEG
 PRETHER POSTTHER FOLOTHER BY SEX(1,2), GROUP(1,3)/
 WSFACTOR = TIME( 3 )/
 MEASURE = DIS PROB SELF NEG THER/
 CONTRAST(TIME) = POLYNOMIAL(1 2 3)/
 WSDESIGN = TIME /
 PRINT = SIGNIF(HYPOTH AVERF)/
 ANALYSIS(REPEATED) /
 DESIGN/
BEGIN DATA
data lines
END DATA
```

- The TITLE command prints a title at the top of each page of display output, and the COMMENT command inserts comments that print back with the commands on the display (see Chapter 4).
- The DATA LIST command defines 17 variables from the data in the command file (see Chapter 3).

- The MANOVA command specifies the 15 dependent variables and the two between-subjects factors. The prefixes PRE, POST, and FOLO indicate the three occasions. The root names DIS, PROB, SELF, NEG, and THER indicate the five types of measures. Notice the order of the variables. All DIS variables appear first, then all PROB variables, and so on. Within each group of three variables, the order of time is the same.
- The WSFACTORS subcommand specifies TIME as a within-subjects factor. The number of dependent variables in the MANOVA specification is an integer multiple of the number of levels of the within-subjects factor (see Section 28.20).
- The MEASURE subcommand lists five names, which MANOVA uses for labeling univariate results (see Section 28.23).
- The CONTRAST subcommand specifies a polynomial contrast for TIME (see Section 28.35).
- The WSDESIGN subcommand specifies the within-subjects factor, TIME (see Section 28.21).
- The PRINT subcommand prints the hypothesis SSCP matrices (Figure 28.77d) and the averaged statistics corresponding to the univariate approach (Figure 28.77f).
- ANALYSIS(REPEATED) and DESIGN specify repeated measures analysis and the between-subjects design (see Sections 28.8 and 28.22).

Portions of the display output are shown in Figures 28.77a through 28.77g.

- Figure 28.77a shows the tests of significance of the SEX by GROUP interaction; Figure 28.77b shows the tests of significance of the GROUP effect; and Figure 28.77c shows the tests of significance of the SEX effect.

Figure 28.77a Example 7: SEX by GROUP effect

```
EFFECT .. SEX BY GROUP

MULTIVARIATE TESTS OF SIGNIFICANCE (S = 2, M = 1 , N = 20 1/2)

TEST NAME          VALUE       APPROX. F     HYPOTH. DF          ERROR DF          SIG. OF F

PILLAIS            .14819        .70421          10.00              88.00              .718
HOTELLINGS         .16349        .68665          10.00              84.00              .734
WILKS              .85594        .69560          10.00              86.00              .726
ROYS               .11102
```

Figure 28.77b Example 7: GROUP effect

```
EFFECT .. GROUP

MULTIVARIATE TESTS OF SIGNIFICANCE (S = 2, M = 1 , N = 20 1/2)

TEST NAME          VALUE       APPROX. F     HYPOTH. DF          ERROR DF          SIG. OF F

PILLAIS            .22307       1.10473          10.00              88.00              .368
HOTELLINGS         .26407       1.10911          10.00              84.00              .365
WILKS              .78484       1.10753          10.00              86.00              .366
ROYS               .17886
```

Figure 28.77c Example 7: SEX effect

```
EFFECT .. SEX

MULTIVARIATE TESTS OF SIGNIFICANCE (S = 1, M = 1 1/2, N = 20 1/2)

TEST NAME          VALUE       APPROX. F     HYPOTH. DF          ERROR DF          SIG. OF F

PILLAIS            .19749       2.11642           5.00              43.00              .082
HOTELLINGS         .24610       2.11642           5.00              43.00              .082
WILKS              .80251       2.11642           5.00              43.00              .082
ROYS               .19749
```

- Figure 28.77d shows the adjusted hypothesis SSCP matrix for the SEX by GROUP by TIME effect, and Figure 28.77e shows the default multivariate-approach test statistics for the SEX by GROUP by TIME effect.

Figure 28.77d Example 7: Hypothesis SSCP matrix for SEX by GROUP by TIME effect

EFFECT .. SEX BY GROUP BY TIME

ADJUSTED HYPOTHESIS SUM-OF-SQUARES AND CROSS-PRODUCTS

	POSTDIS	FOLODIS	POSTPROB	FOLOPROB	POSTSELF	FOLOSELF	POSTNEG
POSTDIS	.16123						
FOLODIS	-.19762	.33300					
POSTPROB	.14595	-.04226	.33777				
FOLOPROB	-.13805	.13589	-.17512	.13043			
POSTSELF	.15726	-.92824	-.96459	.13527	6.11199		
FOLOSELF	-.28690	.89645	.56024	.04571	-4.69360	3.77997	
POSTNEG	3.86160	-6.37782	1.02034	-2.70282	17.09124	-16.74162	122.28503
FOLONEG	-1.13667	1.42390	-.98279	.96199	-1.35733	2.20682	-27.78012
POSTTHER	3.35852	-7.96836	-2.75699	-1.46203	34.48205	-29.09195	150.22274
FOLOTHER	1.97604	-.26219	5.03949	-2.48460	-15.57064	9.44523	8.19825

	FOLONEG	POSTTHER	FOLOTHER
FOLONEG	8.02386		
POSTTHER	-24.97956	233.39190	
FOLOTHER	-13.20086	-50.47842	75.60308

Figure 28.77e Example 7: Multivariate approach for SEX by GROUP by TIME effect

EFFECT .. SEX BY GROUP BY TIME

MULTIVARIATE TESTS OF SIGNIFICANCE (S = 2, M = 3 1/2, N = 18)

TEST NAME	VALUE	APPROX. F	HYPOTH. DF	ERROR DF	SIG. OF F
PILLAIS	.47001	1.19806	20.00	78.00	.279
HOTELLINGS	.63755	1.17947	20.00	74.00	.296
WILKS	.58008	1.18930	20.00	76.00	.287
ROYS	.30669				

- Figure 28.77f shows the "averaged" adjusted hypothesis SSCP matrix for the SEX by GROUP by TIME effect. This matrix results from the univariate approach to the data. MANOVA uses the names supplied on the MEASURES subcommand to label the pooled effects. Compare this matrix with the one in Figure 28.77d. In the averaged hypothesis SSCP matrix, for example, the DIS sum of squares is .49423. This number is the trace of the submatrix in Figure 28.77d formed by all DIS effects, that is, POSTDIS and FOLODIS. In other words, .49423 is the sum of .16123 and .33300. MANOVA similarly combines submatrix trace elements of the multivariate-approach adjusted hypothesis SSCP matrix to compute the rest of the elements of the univariate-approach adjusted hypothesis SSCP matrix. Although not shown, the averaged error SSCP matrix is similarly computed.

Figure 28.77f Example 7: Averaged hypothesis SSCP matrix

EFFECT .. SEX BY GROUP BY TIME

ADJUSTED HYPOTHESIS SUM-OF-SQUARES AND CROSS-PRODUCTS

	DIS	PROB	SELF	NEG	THER
DIS	.49423				
PROB	.28185	.46820			
SELF	1.05372	-.91888	9.89196		
NEG	5.28550	1.98233	19.29806	130.30889	
THER	3.09633	-5.24159	43.92728	137.02188	308.99498

- Finally, Figure 28.77g shows the univariate-approach test statistics for the SEX by GROUP by TIME effect. Compare this with Figure 28.77e.

Figure 28.77g Example 7: Univariate approach for SEX by GROUP by TIME effect

EFFECT .. SEX BY GROUP BY TIME

MULTIVARIATE TESTS OF SIGNIFICANCE (S = 4, M = 0, N = 44)

TEST NAME	VALUE	APPROX. F	HYPOTH. DF	ERROR DF	SIG. OF F
PILLAIS	.23198	1.14512	20.00	372.00	.301
HOTELLINGS	.25801	1.14172	20.00	354.00	.305
WILKS	.78311	1.14534	20.00	299.45	.302
ROYS	.12791				

28.78 Example 8: Profile Analysis

In the previous repeated measures examples, we imposed a design on the dependent variables using ANALYSIS(REPEATED) and its implicit orthornormal transformation of the dependent variables. The distinct dependent variables were really measures of the same items across occasions. However, not all analyses require a formal treatment structure on the dependent variables; instead, you may simply be interested in making specific kinds of comparisons among nonrepeated dependent variables. Such analyses are termed *profile analyses*.

Data in profile analysis consist of *p* commensurable responses that have been collected from independent sampling units grouped according to *k* treatments or experimental conditions. In profile analysis, there are three questions of interest:

- *Parallelism of profiles.* Are the population-mean profiles similar, in the sense that the line segments of adjacent tests are parallel?
- *Equal treatment levels.* Assuming parallelism, are the treatment levels equal?
- *Equal response means.* Assuming parallelism, are the response means equal?

The analysis proceeds very much along the same lines as that for repeated measures data. That is, you transform the data to new variables which incorporate the effects of interest. The difference from repeated measures analysis lies in the nature of the data themselves: profile analysis does not assume any correspondence between treatment interventions and dependent variables. Also, the pooled results are generally not of interest. You should *not* request orthonormalization of the new variables in profile analysis. This example appears in Morrison (1976, p. 210). Three scales—A, B, and C—measuring certain maternal attitudes are administered to 21 mothers participating in a study of child development. As part of the study, each mother has been assigned to one of four socioeconomic status (SES) groups. Thus, there are three responses, four treatment levels, and 21 subjects. The three hypotheses to be tested are

- Are the scale profiles in the four SES groups parallel?
- Given 1, are class effects equal over all responses?
- Given 1, are response means equal?

To conduct the tests, first transform the observations to the differences of scales A and B and scales B and C. The SPSS^{X} commands are

```
TITLE PROFILE ANALYSIS
COMMENT THIS EXAMPLE IS FROM MORRISON, P.209.
DATA LIST / SOCLASS 1 A 3-4 B 6-7 C 9-10
REPORT VARS=A B C/
 BREAK=SOCLASS/
 SUM=MEAN/
BEGIN DATA
1 19 20 18
1 20 21 19
1 19 22 22
1 18 19 21
1 16 18 20
1 17 22 19
1 20 19 20
1 15 19 19
2 12 14 12
2 15 15 17
2 15 17 15
2 13 14 14
2 14 16 13
3 15 14 17
3 13 14 15
3 12 15 15
3 12 13 13
4  8  9 10
4 10 10 12
4 11 10 10
4 11  7 12
END DATA
MANOVA A,B,C BY SOCLASS(1,4)/
 TRANSFORM= REPEATED/
 RENAME= AVERAGE,AMINUSB,BMINUSC /
 PRINT=TRANSFORM/
 ANALYSIS =(AMINUSB, BMINUSC/AVERAGE)/
 DESIGN/
```

- The TITLE command prints a title at the top of each page of display output, and the COMMENT command inserts comments that print back with the commands on the display (see Chapter 4).
- The DATA LIST command defines four variables from the data in the command file (see Chapter 3).
- REPORT displays the means on the three response variables within each of the four SES groups (see Figure 28.78a and Chapter 23).
- The MANOVA command names A, B, and C as three response variables and SOCLASS as a four-level factor.
- TRANSFORM creates three transformed variables: an average effect and two adjacent differences, A-B and B-C (see Section 28.24).
- The RENAME subcommand names the transformed variables for use on the display output (see Section 28.29).
- The PRINT subcommand prints the transformation matrix (see Figure 28.78b).
- The ANALYSIS subcommand specifies two analyses. In the first analysis, AMINUSB and BMINUSC are joint dependent variables, and in the second analysis, AVERAGE is the dependent variable. The first analysis tests Hypotheses 1 and 3 stated above; the second analysis tests Hypothesis 2 (see Section 28.7).
- The DESIGN subcommand indicates the default design, which enters the SOCLASS effect (see Section 28.8).

Portions of the display output are shown in Figures 28.78a through 28.78f.

- Figure 28.78a shows the output from REPORT. The rows of means are the four "profiles" corresponding to the four levels of SES.

Figure 28.78a Example 8: REPORT output showing mean profiles

```
PROFILE ANALYSIS                                                          PAGE    1
 SOCLASS           A             B             C

        1

     MEAN      18.00         20.00         19.75
        2

     MEAN      13.80         15.20         14.20
        3

     MEAN      13.00         14.00         15.00
        4

     MEAN      10.00          9.00         11.00
```

- Figure 28.78b shows the transformation matrix. Column 1 is the average effect; column 2 is the A-B difference; and column 3 is the B-C difference.

Figure 28.78b Example 8: Transformation matrix

```
TRANSFORMATION MATRIX (TRANSPOSED)
                        1              2              3

        1          .33333        1.00000         0.0
        2          .33333       -1.00000         1.00000
        3          .33333        0.0            -1.00000
```

- Figure 28.78c shows the variables used for the first analysis. Transformed and renamed variables AMINUSB and BMINUSC are joint dependent variables in the first analysis.

Figure 28.78c Example 8: Model 1 variables

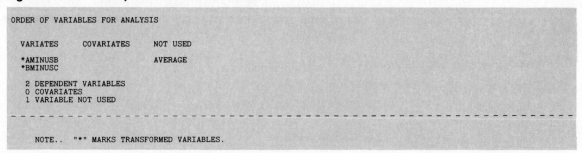

```
ORDER OF VARIABLES FOR ANALYSIS

  VARIATES     COVARIATES     NOT USED

  *AMINUSB                    AVERAGE
  *BMINUSC

   2 DEPENDENT VARIABLES
   0 COVARIATES
   1 VARIABLE NOT USED
- - - - - - - - - - - - - - - - - - - - - - - - - - - - - - - - - - - - - - - - - -

      NOTE..  "*" MARKS TRANSFORMED VARIABLES.
```

- Figure 28.78d shows the tests of significance of the SOCLASS effect on the joint dependent variables. This portion of the output shows a test for Hypothesis 1—the test of parallelism. Nonsignificant test statistics indicate that AMINUSB and BMINUSC are the same across SES levels, in which case you can assume that the profiles are parallel. In the output, the significance levels of the test statistics are indeed large enough to assume parallelism.

Figure 28.78d Example 8: Test of parallelism

```
EFFECT .. SOCLASS
MULTIVARIATE TESTS OF SIGNIFICANCE (S = 2, M = 0, N = 7 )

TEST NAME            VALUE       APPROX. F      HYPOTH. DF          ERROR DF         SIG. OF F

PILLAIS             .48726        1.82526             6.00             34.00              .123
HOTELLINGS          .68534        1.71336             6.00             30.00              .152
WILKS               .56333        1.77253             6.00             32.00              .136
ROYS                .33724

- - - - - - - - - - - - - - - - - - - - - - - - - - - - - - - - - - - - - - - - - - - - - - - -

EIGENVALUES AND CANONICAL CORRELATIONS

ROOT NO.      EIGENVALUE          PCT.      CUM. PCT.    CANON. COR.

      1          .50885      74.24730        74.24730         .58073
      2          .17649      25.75270       100.00000         .38732

- - - - - - - - - - - - - - - - - - - - - - - - - - - - - - - - - - - - - - - - - - - - - - - -

DIMENSION REDUCTION ANALYSIS

ROOTS         WILKS LAMBDA               F       HYPOTH. DF          ERROR DF        SIG. OF F

1 TO 2              .56333         1.77253             6.00             32.00             .136
2 TO 2              .84998         1.39694             2.00             33.00             .262

- - - - - - - - - - - - - - - - - - - - - - - - - - - - - - - - - - - - - - - - - - - - - - - -

UNIVARIATE F-TESTS WITH (3,17) D. F.

VARIABLE        HYPOTH. SS        ERROR SS       HYPOTH. MS          ERROR MS                F        SIG. OF F

AMINUSB           24.60952        51.20000          8.20317           3.01176          2.72371             .077
BMINUSC           24.30952        61.50000          8.10317           3.61765          2.23990             .121
```

- Figure 28.78e shows the tests of significance of the "constant" effect in the same model. This portion of the output is a test of Hypothesis 3—the test of equal response means. The observed level of significance is .004, which leads to rejection of the hypothesis of equal mean responses. The univariate *F* statistics for AMINUSB and BMINUSC shows an AMINUSB effect which is significant at the .01 level. From this we conclude that the principal difference among scale profiles occurs for scales A and B. On the other hand, scales B and C do not significantly differ.

Figure 28.78e Example 8: Test of equality of scale means

```
EFFECT .. CONSTANT
MULTIVARIATE TESTS OF SIGNIFICANCE (S = 1, M = 0, N = 7 )

TEST NAME            VALUE       APPROX. F      HYPOTH. DF          ERROR DF         SIG. OF F

PILLAIS             .49871        7.95884             2.00             16.00              .004
HOTELLINGS          .99486        7.95884             2.00             16.00              .004
WILKS               .50129        7.95884             2.00             16.00              .004
ROYS                .49871

- - - - - - - - - - - - - - - - - - - - - - - - - - - - - - - - - - - - - - - - - - - - - - - -

EIGENVALUES AND CANONICAL CORRELATIONS

ROOT NO.      EIGENVALUE          PCT.      CUM. PCT.    CANON. COR.

      1          .99486     100.00000       100.00000         .70619

- - - - - - - - - - - - - - - - - - - - - - - - - - - - - - - - - - - - - - - - - - - - - - - -

DIMENSION REDUCTION ANALYSIS

ROOTS         WILKS LAMBDA               F       HYPOTH. DF          ERROR DF        SIG. OF F

1 TO 1              .50129         7.95884             2.00             16.00             .004

- - - - - - - - - - - - - - - - - - - - - - - - - - - - - - - - - - - - - - - - - - - - - - - -

UNIVARIATE F-TESTS WITH (1,17) D. F.

VARIABLE        HYPOTH. SS        ERROR SS       HYPOTH. MS          ERROR MS                F        SIG. OF F

AMINUSB           25.19048        51.20000         25.19048           3.01176          8.36403             .010
BMINUSC            1.19048        61.50000          1.19048           3.61765           .32907             .574
```

- Figure 28.78f shows the results for the second analysis specified on the ANALYSIS subcommand. The dependent variable is AVERAGE. If there are no significant differences in the means of AVERAGE across the four levels of SOCLASS, then we do not reject Hypothesis 2—the test of equal class effects. However, the highly significant *F* statistic for SOCLASS leads to rejection of the hypothesis of equal means. The SOCLASS parameter estimates, while not exhausting the comparisons that can be made, show that the mean of level 1 differs significantly from the means of the other levels.

Figure 28.78f Example 8: Test of equality of class effects

```
ORDER OF VARIABLES FOR ANALYSIS

  VARIATES     COVARIATES     NOT USED

  *AVERAGE                    AMINUSB
                              BMINUSC

   1 DEPENDENT VARIABLE
   0 COVARIATES
   2 VARIABLES NOT USED

- - - - - - - - - - - - - - - - - - - - - - - - - - - - - - - - - - - - - - - - - - - - - - - - - - - -

     NOTE..  "*" MARKS TRANSFORMED VARIABLES.

TESTS OF SIGNIFICANCE FOR AVERAGE USING SEQUENTIAL SUMS OF SQUARES

SOURCE OF VARIATION                       SUM OF SQUARES         DF   MEAN SQUARE           F      SIG. OF F

WITHIN CELLS                                  19.81111           17       1.16536
CONSTANT                                    4937.33333            1    4937.33333   4236.74706         0.0
SOCLASS                                      247.96667            3      82.65556     70.92709         0.0

- - - - - - - - - - - - - - - - - - - - - - - - - - - - - - - - - - - - - - - - - - - - - - - - - - - -

ESTIMATES FOR AVERAGE

CONSTANT

 PARAMETER          COEFF.         STD. ERR.         T-VALUE       SIG. OF T    LOWER .95 CL    UPPER .95 CL

         1   14.4125000000            .24513        58.79527             0.0        13.89532        14.92968

SOCLASS

 PARAMETER          COEFF.         STD. ERR.         T-VALUE       SIG. OF T    LOWER .95 CL    UPPER .95 CL

         2    4.8375000000            .36459        13.26843             0.0         4.06829         5.60671
         3    -.0125000000            .42027         -.02974            .977         -.89919          .87419
         4    -.4125000000            .45361         -.90938            .376        -1.36953          .54453
```

29

```
LOGLINEAR varlist (low, high) . . . [BY] varlist (low, high)
  [WITH covariate varlist]

  [/WIDTH = {132}]
            {72 }

  [/CWEIGHT = {varname }]  [/CWEIGHT = (matrix) . . . ]
              {(matrix)}

  [/GRESID = {varlist }]  [/GRESID = . . . ]
             {(matrix)}

             {DEFAULT}                {ESTIM  }
             {FREQ   }                {COR    }
             {RESID  }                {DESIGN }
  [/PRINT = {DESIGN }]  [/NOPRINT = {RESID  }]
             {ESTIM  }                {FREQ   }
             {COR    }                {DEFAULT}
             {ALL    }                {ALL    }

            {DEFAULT  }
            {RESID    }
  [/PLOT = {NORMPROB }]
            {NONE**   }

                          {SIMPLE [(refcat)]                     }
                          {DIFFERENCE                            }
                          {HELMERT                               }
                          {DEVIATION [(refcat)]                  }
  [/CONTRAST (varname) = {REPEATED                              }] . . . [/CONTRAST . . . ]
                          {POLYNOMIAL [({1, 2, 3, . . .})]       }
                          {             {metric        }         }
                          {SPECIAL (matrix)                      }

  [/CRITERIA = [CONVERGE ({0.001})]  [ITERATE ({20})]  [DELTA ({0.5})]
                          {eps  }              {n }            {d  }
               [DEFAULT]]

  [/DESIGN = effect effect . . . effect BY effect . . . ]  [/DESIGN . . . ]
```

***Default if the subcommand is omitted.*

OPTIONS:
1 Include missing values.

OVERVIEW, **29.1**

OPERATION, **29.2**
- The LOGLINEAR Specification, **29.3**
  - The Logit Model, **29.4**
  - Specifying Covariates, **29.5**
- The DESIGN Subcommand, **29.6**
  - Specifying Main Effects Models, **29.7**
  - Specifying Interactions: Keyword BY, **29.8**
  - Specifying Covariates, **29.9**
  - Single-Degree-of-Freedom Partitions, **29.10**
- The CWEIGHT Subcommand, **29.11**
- The GRESID Subcommand, **29.12**
- The PRINT and NOPRINT Subcommands, **29.13**
- The PLOT Subcommand, **29.14**
- The CONTRAST Subcommand, **29.15**
  - Contrasts for a Multinomial Logit Model, **29.16**
  - Contrasts for a Linear Logit Model, **29.17**
  - Contrasts for a Logistic Regression Model, **29.18**
- The CRITERIA Subcommand, **29.19**
- The WIDTH Subcommand, **29.20**
- Missing Values, **29.21**

LOGLINEAR EXAMPLES, **29.22**
- Example 1: A General Log-linear Model, **29.23**
- Example 2: A Multinomial Logit Model, **29.24**
- Example 3: Frequency Table Models, **29.25**
- Example 4: A Linear Logit Model, **29.26**
- Example 5: Logistic Regression Model, **29.27**
- Example 6: Multinomial Response Models, **29.28**
- Example 7: A Distance Model, **29.29**

Chapter 29 LOGLINEAR

The LOGLINEAR procedure is a general procedure which does model fitting, hypothesis testing, and parameter estimation for any model that has categorical variables as its major components. As such, LOGLINEAR subsumes a variety of related techniques, including general models of multi-way contingency tables, logit models, logistic regression, quasi-independence models, and so on.

29.1 OVERVIEW

LOGLINEAR models cell frequencies using the multinomial response model and produces maximum likelihood estimates of parameters by means of the Newton-Raphson algorithm. Output includes observed and expected cell frequencies and percentages; residuals, standardized residuals, and adjusted residuals; and the Pearson chi-square statistic and the likelihood ratio chi-square. For models with dependent variables, LOGLINEAR prints an analysis of dispersion, along with two measures of association. You can request printing of the design matrix; parameter estimates, standard errors, standardized values, and confidence intervals; and the correlation matrix of parameter estimates. You can produce plots of the adjusted residuals against observed and expected counts, as well as normal and detrended normal plots of the adjusted residuals. Examples of models that can be tested with LOGLINEAR and the display produced begin with Section 29.22.

LOGLINEAR is a subcommand-driven procedure. At a minimum, specify the variables you wish to analyze (see Sections 29.3 through 29.5). Optionally, specify subcommands in the following contexts.

Specifying the Model. Use the DESIGN subcommand to specify the model or models to be fit (see Section 29.6).

Cell Weights. Use the CWEIGHT subcommand to specify cell weights for the model (see Section 29.11).

Optional Printed Output. Use the PRINT and NOPRINT subcommands to control the types of display output (see Section 29.13).

Optional Plots. Use the PLOT subcommand to produce optional plots of adjusted residuals against observed and expected counts, and normal and detrended normal plots (see Section 29.14).

Linear Combinations. Use the GRESID subcommand to calculate linear combinations of observed cell frequencies, expected cell frequencies, and adjusted residuals (see Section 29.12).

Contrasts. Use the CONTRAST subcommand to indicate the type of contrast desired for a factor (see Section 29.15).

Criteria for Algorithm. Use the CRITERIA subcommand to control the values of algorithm tuning parameters (see Section 29.19).

Formatting Options. Use the WIDTH subcommand to control the width of the display output (see Section 29.20).

Missing Values. Use Option 1 on the associated OPTIONS command to include cases with missing values in the analysis (see Section 29.21).

29.2 OPERATION

The LOGLINEAR procedure is subcommand driven. You must name the variables being analyzed and indicate the dependent variable and any covariates. The variables specification must come first. The DESIGN subcommand specifies the model to be fit (see Section 29.6). One model is produced for each DESIGN subcommand. All subcommands can be used more than once and, with the exception of the DESIGN subcommand, are carried from model to model unless explicitly overridden. The subcommands that affect a DESIGN subcommand should be placed before the DESIGN subcommand. If subcommands are placed after the last DESIGN subcommand, LOGLINEAR generates the saturated model.

All subcommands begin with the subcommand keyword followed by an optional equals sign and specifications. All subcommands are terminated with a slash. Subcommand keywords can be abbreviated to the first three characters.

29.3 The LOGLINEAR Specification

The only required specification for LOGLINEAR is the set of variables used in the models. LOGLINEAR analyzes two classes of variables: categorical and continuous. *Categorical variables* must be numeric and integer. Specify a range in parentheses indicating the minimum and maximum values. For example,

```
LOGLINEAR  DPREF(2,3) RACE(1,2)
```

builds a 2 × 2 frequency table for analysis. Cases with values outside the range are excluded from the analysis and noninteger values within the range are truncated for purposes of building the table. In general, the value range specified should match the values in the data. That is, if the range specified for a variable is 1 and 4, there should be cases for values 1, 2, 3, and 4. Empty categories waste workspace and can cause computational problems.

If several variables have the same range, you can specify the range following the last variable in the list, as in:

```
LOGLINEAR  DPREF(2,3) RACE CAMP(1,2)
```

This is a general log-linear model since no BY keyword appears. The design defaults to a saturated model in which all main effects and interaction effects are fitted. Figure 29.3 shows the default display output for this LOGLINEAR command.

Figure 29.3 contains three major sets of information. The first set of information consists of the observed frequencies, the expected frequencies, and three types of residuals. The column labeled CODE contains value labels identifying the cells. If none are defined, it uses the observed value. Note that the table prints only the first eight characters of the value label. Since this is a saturated model, all residuals are zero with the exception of rounding error. Similarly, the goodness-of-fit statistics, which constitute the second set of information, are also zero. The third set of information concerns the parameter estimates; it is comprised of the value of the coefficient, the standard error of the coefficient, the standardized value (labeled Z-VALUE) of the coefficient, and the 95% confidence interval for the coefficient. The standardized value is distributed approximately as a standard normal variate. Thus, only the main effect for RACE and the interaction effect for DPREF by RACE by CAMP are not significant at the .05 level.

Figure 29.3 Default LOGLINEAR display

```
* * * * * * * * * * * * * * * * * * * * * * * L O G   L I N E A R   A N A L Y S I S * * * * * * * * * * * * * * * * * * * * * * *

CORRESPONDENCE BETWEEN EFFECTS AND COLUMNS OF DESIGN/MODEL 1

 STARTING  ENDING
  COLUMN   COLUMN    EFFECT NAME

     1        1      DPREF
     2        2      RACE
     3        3      CAMP
     4        4      DPREF BY RACE
     5        5      DPREF BY CAMP
     6        6      RACE BY CAMP
     7        7      DPREF BY RACE BY CAMP

- - - - - - - - - - - - - - - - - - - - - - - - - - - - - - - - - - - - - - - - - - - - - - - - - - - - - - - - - - - - - - - -

*** ML CONVERGED AT ITERATION  3. THE CONVERGE CRITERION =    .00091

- - - - - - - - - - - - - - - - - - - - - - - - - - - - - - - - - - - - - - - - - - - - - - - - - - - - - - - - - - - - - - - -

 OBSERVED, EXPECTED FREQUENCIES AND RESIDUALS

      FACTOR           CODE                OBS. COUNT & PCT.   EXP. COUNT & PCT.      RESIDUAL   STD. RESID.   ADJ. RESID.


 DPREF              NORTH
  RACE               BLACK
   CAMP               NORTH                  770.00 (  9.58)     770.00 (  9.58)        .00003       .00000        0.0
   CAMP               SOUTH                 1257.00 ( 15.64)    1257.00 ( 15.64)        .00006       .00000        0.0
  RACE               WHITE
   CAMP               NORTH                 1059.00 ( 13.18)    1059.00 ( 13.18)        .00006       .00000        0.0
   CAMP               SOUTH                  965.00 ( 12.01)     965.00 ( 12.01)        .00005       .00000        0.0

 DPREF              SOUTH
  RACE               BLACK
   CAMP               NORTH                  306.00 (  3.81)     306.00 (  3.81)       -.00018      -.00001        0.0
   CAMP               SOUTH                 1962.00 ( 24.41)    1962.00 ( 24.41)        .00005       .00000        0.0
  RACE               WHITE
   CAMP               NORTH                  338.00 (  4.21)     338.00 (  4.21)       -.00014      -.00001        0.0
   CAMP               SOUTH                 1380.00 ( 17.17)    1380.00 ( 17.17)        .00006       .00000        0.0
* * * * * * * * * * * * * * * * * * * * * * * L O G   L I N E A R   A N A L Y S I S * * * * * * * * * * * * * * * * * * * * * * *

GOODNESS-OF-FIT TEST STATISTICS

   LIKELIHOOD RATIO CHI SQUARE =     0.0           DF = 0  P =  1.000
            PEARSON CHI SQUARE =     0.0           DF = 0  P =  1.000

- - - - - - - - - - - - - - - - - - - - - - - - - - - - - - - - - - - - - - - - - - - - - - - - - - - - - - - - - - - - - - - -

ESTIMATES FOR PARAMETERS

DPREF

 PARAMETER          COEFF.          STD. ERR.          Z-VALUE     LOWER 95 CI       UPPER 95 CI

        1      .1577364511           .01343          11.74899           .13142            .18405

RACE

 PARAMETER          COEFF.          STD. ERR.          Z-VALUE     LOWER 95 CI       UPPER 95 CI

        2      .0247606931           .01343           1.84430          -.00155            .05107

CAMP

 PARAMETER          COEFF.          STD. ERR.          Z-VALUE     LOWER 95 CI       UPPER 95 CI

        3     -.4577583472           .01343         -34.09610          -.48407           -.43144

DPREF BY RACE

 PARAMETER          COEFF.          STD. ERR.          Z-VALUE     LOWER 95 CI       UPPER 95 CI

        4     -.0383443700           .01343          -2.85608          -.06466           -.01203

DPREF BY CAMP

 PARAMETER          COEFF.          STD. ERR.          Z-VALUE     LOWER 95 CI       UPPER 95 CI

        5      .3584732365           .01343          26.70086           .33216            .38479

RACE BY CAMP

 PARAMETER          COEFF.          STD. ERR.          Z-VALUE     LOWER 95 CI       UPPER 95 CI

        6     -.1292983055           .01343          -9.63078          -.15561           -.10298

DPREF BY RACE BY CAMP

 PARAMETER          COEFF.          STD. ERR.          Z-VALUE     LOWER 95 CI       UPPER 95 CI

        7     -.0164629274           .01343          -1.22624          -.04278            .00985
```

29.4 The Logit Model

Use the BY keyword to segregate the independent variables from the dependent variables in a logit model, as in:

```
LOGLINEAR DPREF(2,3) BY RACE CAMP(1,2)
```

Categorical variables preceding the keyword BY are the dependent variables; categorical variables following the keyword BY are the independent variables. Usually you also specify a DESIGN subcommand to request the desired logit model (see Section 29.6 and the annotated example).

LOGLINEAR prints an analysis of dispersion and two measures of association: entropy and concentration. These measures are discussed in Haberman (1982) and can be used to quantify the magnitude of association among the variables. Both are proportional reduction in error measures. The entropy statistic is analogous to Theil's entropy measure (1970) while the concentration statistic is analogous to Goodman and Kruskal's tau-*b*. Both statistics measure the strength of association between the dependent variable and the predictor variable set. Figure 29.4 is the display of these measures produced by the above LOGLINEAR command.

Figure 29.4 Measures of association for the logit model

```
ANALYSIS OF DISPERSION

                              DISPERSION
  SOURCE OF VARIATION     ENTROPY  CONCENTRATION      DF

     DUE TO MODEL         413.233        399.761
     DUE TO RESIDUAL     5157.328       3618.476
     TOTAL               5570.561       4018.237     8036
- - - - - - - - - - - - - - - - - - - - - - - - - - - - - - - - - - - - - - - -

MEASURES OF ASSOCIATION

         ENTROPY =    .074182
   CONCENTRATION =    .099487
```

29.5 Specifying Covariates

Your model can include covariates. Covariates are continuous variables and do not need a value range specification. You cannot name a variable as both a categorical variable and covariate. Specify covariates at the end of the variables specification following the keyword WITH, as in:

```
LOGLINEAR DPREF(2,3) RACE CAMP(1,2) WITH CONSTANT
```

To enter covariates into the model you must specify them on the DESIGN subcommand (see Section 29.6).

29.6 The DESIGN Subcommand

The DESIGN subcommand specifies the model or models to be fit. The default model, requiring no specification, is the saturated model. All main effects and all interaction effects are fit in the saturated model. If you are using the keyword BY to define a logit model, the completely saturated model contains redundant effects. These are ignored for the analysis.

You can use one or more DESIGN subcommands on a LOGLINEAR command. Each DESIGN subcommand specifies one model. Specify simple effects by naming variables listed on the variables specification. Specify interactions using the keyword BY. Specify single-degree-of-freedom partitions in parentheses following the variable name.

29.7 Specifying Main Effects Models

To fit the A main effect only on a simple crosstabulation between A and B, specify:

```
LOGLINEAR A(1,4) B(1,5)/
  DESIGN=A/
```

This is known as a model for the homogeneity of B-category probabilities; it fits the marginal frequencies on A, but assumes that membership in any of the categories of B is equiprobable.

To fit the A and B main effects, specify:

```
LOGLINEAR A(1,4) B(1,5)/
  DESIGN=A,B/
```

This is known as a model testing the independence of A and B. This model fits the marginals on both A and B, and it is formally identical to the standard chi-square test of independence in contingency tables.

29.8 Specifying Interactions: Keyword BY

Use the BY keyword to specify interaction terms. To fit the saturated model, which consists of the A main effect, the B main effect, and the interaction of A and B, specify:

```
LOGLINEAR A(1,4)B(1,5)/
  DESIGN=A,B,A BY B/
```

For the general log-linear model, this DESIGN specification is the same as the default model. That is, the following specification is equivalent to the above:

```
LOGLINEAR A(1,4)B(1,5)/
   DESIGN/
```

29.9 Specifying Covariates

You can include covariates in the model as follows:

```
LOGLINEAR HUSED WIFED(1,4) WITH DISTANCE/
   DESIGN=HUSED WIFED DISTANCE/
```

First, specify the covariate following the keyword WITH in the variables specification; then, name the covariate on the DESIGN subcommand. You can specify an interaction of a covariate and an independent variable. However, a covariate-by-covariate interaction is not allowed. Instead, use COMPUTE to create interaction variables. Example 7 (see Section 29.29) uses a covariate to specify a distance function.

To specify an *equiprobability model,* use a covariate which is actually a constant of 1 on the DESIGN subcommand, as in:

```
COMPUTE  X=1
LOGLINEAR  MONTH(1,18) WITH X/
  DESIGN=X
```

This model tests whether the frequencies in the 18-cell table are equal. Example 3 (Section 29.25) uses a covariate to obtain the equiprobability model.

29.10 Single-Degree-of-Freedom Partitions

A factor name followed by an integer in parentheses refers to a single-degree-of-freedom partition of a specified contrast. For example, you can specify a simultaneous linear logit model, as in:

```
LOGLINEAR A(1,4) BY B(1,5)/
  CONTRAST(B)=POLYNOMIAL/
  DESIGN=A,A BY B(1)/
```

B(1) refers to the first partition of B, which is the linear effect of B; this follows from the contrast specified. Examples 4 (Section 29.26) and 5 (Section 29.27) use single-degree-of-freedom partitions.

29.11 The CWEIGHT Subcommand

Use the CWEIGHT subcommand to specify cell weights for the model. By default, cell weights are equal to 1.

You can specify a numeric variable on the CWEIGHT subcommand, as in:

```
LOGLINEAR  HUSED WIFED(1,4) WITH DISTANCE/
  CWEIGHT=CWT/
```

Name only one SPSSˣ variable as a weight variable on a LOGLINEAR command.

An alternative is to specify a matrix of weights enclosed in parentheses on the CWEIGHT subcommand. The matrix must contain the same number of elements as the product of the levels of the categorical variables. If you specify weights for a multiple-factor model, the index value of the rightmost factor increments most rapidly. For example, the CWEIGHT subcommand

```
LOGLINEAR A(1,2) BY B(1,3) C(1,2)/
  CWEIGHT=(0 1 1 1 0 1 1 1 0 1 1 1)/
```

assigns cell weights as follows:

```
A B C WEIGHT
1 1 1   0
1 1 2   1
1 2 1   1
1 2 2   1
1 3 1   0
1 3 2   1
2 1 1   1
2 1 2   1
2 2 1   0
2 2 2   1
2 3 1   1
2 3 2   1
```

You can use an asterisk to signify repetitions of the same value, as in

```
LOGLINEAR A(1,2) BY B(1,3) C(1,2)/
   CWEIGHT=(0 3*1 0 3*1 0 3*1)/
```

which specifies the same matrix of weights as above. If you use a matrix of weights on the CWEIGHT subcommand, you can specify more than one CWEIGHT subcommand, as in:

```
LOGLINEAR  A B (1,4)/
  CWEIGHT=(0,4*1,0,4*1,0,4*1,0)/
  DESIGN=A,B/
  CWEIGHT=(16*1)/
  DESIGN=A,B
```

The CWEIGHT specification remains in effect until explicitly overridden with another CWEIGHT subcommand. The previous example uses a second CWEIGHT subcommand to return to the default cell weights.

You can use the CWEIGHT subcommand to impose structural, or *a priori*, zeros on the model. This feature is useful in the analysis of symmetric tables. For example, to impose structural zeros on the diagonal of a symmetric crosstabulation table, specify:

```
COMPUTE  CWT=1
IF (HUSED EQ WIFED) CWT=0
LOGLINEAR  HUSED WIFED(1,4) WITH DISTANCE/
  CWEIGHT=CWT/
```

CWT equals 0 when HUSED equals WIFED. Alternatively, you can specify the CWEIGHT matrix, as in:

```
   CWEIGHT = (0, 4*1, 0, 4*1, 0, 4*1, 0)/
```

Example 7 (see Section 29.29) uses the CWEIGHT subcommand.

29.12 The GRESID Subcommand

The GRESID subcommand calculates linear combinations of observed cell frequencies, expected cell frequencies, and adjusted residuals. Specify a variable or variables, or a matrix whose contents are coefficients of the desired linear combinations. The rules of the matrix specification are identical to the rules for CWEIGHT (see Section 29.11). You can specify multiple GRESID subcommands, but only one GRESID subcommand can invoke an SPSSˣ variable. If you use a matrix, it must contain as many elements as the number of cells implied by the variables specification, as in:

```
LOGLINEAR  MONTH(1,18) WITH Z/
  GRESID=(6*1,12*0)/
  GRESID=(6*0,6*1,6*0)/
  GRESID=(12*0,6*1)/
  DESIGN=Z
```

The first GRESID subcommand combines the first six months into an "early" effect, the second GRESID subcommand combines the second six months into a "middle" effect, and the third GRESID subcommand combines the last six observations into a "late" effect. For each effect, LOGLINEAR prints out the observed and expected count, the residual, the standardized residual, and the adjusted residual. Example 3 (see Section 29.25) shows the display output for this analysis of a frequency table containing data on 18 consecutive months.

29.13 The PRINT and NOPRINT Subcommands

Use the PRINT subcommand to request statistics and display not produced by default. Or use the NOPRINT subcommand to suppress the printing of results. You can use the following keywords on both the PRINT and NOPRINT subcommands.

FREQ *Observed and expected cell frequencies and percentages.* This is displayed by default.

RESID *Raw, standardized, and adjusted residuals.* This is displayed by default.

DESIGN *The design matrix of the model, showing the contrasts used.*

ESTIM *The parameter estimates of the model.* If you do not specify a design on the DESIGN subcommand, LOGLINEAR generates a saturated model and prints the parameter estimates for the saturated model by default.

COR *The correlation matrix of the parameter estimates.*

ALL *All available output.*

DEFAULT *FREQ and RESID.* ESTIM is also printed by default if the DESIGN subcommand is not used.

By default, LOGLINEAR prints the frequency table and residuals. You can use the PRINT subcommand to request additional items and you can use the NOPRINT subcommand to turn off defaults. You can specify multiple PRINT and NOPRINT subcommands. The specifications are cumulative, as in:

```
LOGLINEAR A(1,2) B(1,2)/
  PRINT=ESTIM/
  NOPRINT=DEFAULT/
  DESIGN=A,B,A BY B/
  PRINT=ALL/
  DESIGN=A,B/
```

This LOGLINEAR command specifies two designs. The first design is the saturated model. Since it fits the data exactly, you do not want to see the frequencies and residuals. Rather, you want to see parameter estimates. To print the parameter estimates, specify PRINT=ESTIM, and to suppress the frequencies and residuals output, specify NOPRINT=DEFAULT. The second design is the main effects model, which implicitly tests the hypothesis of no association. The PRINT subcommand prints all available display output for this model.

29.14 The PLOT Subcommand

The PLOT subcommand produces optional plots. None are printed by default. The following keywords are available:

RESID *Plots of adjusted residuals against observed and expected counts.*

NORMPROB *Normal and detrended normal plots of the adjusted residuals.*

NONE *No plots.*
DEFAULT *RESID and NORMPROB.*

If you specify a PLOT subcommand with no keywords, no plots are printed. You can use multiple PLOT subcommands on one LOGLINEAR command. The specifications are cumulative. For example,

```
LOGLINEAR  RESPONSE(1,2) BY TIME(1,4)/
  CONTRAST(TIME) = SPECIAL(4*1, 7 14 27 51, 8*1)/
  PLOT=DEFAULT/
  DESIGN=RESPONSE TIME(1) BY RESPONSE/
  PLOT=NONE/
  DESIGN/
```

prints RESID and NORMPROB plots for the first design. No plots are printed for the second design. Figure 29.27d is an example of the plots produced by LOGLINEAR.

29.15 The CONTRAST Subcommand

The CONTRAST subcommand indicates the type of contrast desired for a *factor.* A factor is a categorical dependent or independent variable. Specify the variable name in parentheses and the contrast chosen, as in

```
LOGLINEAR  MENTHLTH(1,4) BY PARENTSE(1,6)/
   CONTRAST(MENTHLTH)=POLYNOMIAL/
```

which applies a polynomial contrast to MENTHLTH.

Contrasts in LOGLINEAR are more general than contrasts in MANOVA. In LOGLINEAR, contrasts do not have to sum to 0 or be orthogonal. The following contrasts are available:

DEVIATION(refcat) *Deviations from the overall effect.* By default, LOGLINEAR uses the last category of the factor variable as the reference category. Optionally, you can specify the value that you want used as the reference category enclosed in parentheses after the keyword DEVIATIONS.

DIFFERENCE *Levels of a factor with the average effect of previous levels of a factor.* Also known as *reverse Helmert* contrasts.

HELMERT *Levels of a factor with the average effect of subsequent levels of a factor.*

SIMPLE(refcat) *Each level of a factor to the last level.* This is the default if you do not use the CONTRAST subcommand. By default, LOGLINEAR uses the last category of the factor variable as the reference category. Optionally, you can specify the value that you want used as the reference category enclosed in parentheses after the keyword SIMPLE.

REPEATED *Adjacent comparisons across levels of a factor.*

POLYNOMIAL(metric) *Orthogonal polynomial contrasts.* The default is equal spacing. Optionally, you can specify the coefficients of the linear polynomial in parentheses, indicating the spacing between levels of the treatment measured by the given factor.

SPECIAL(matrix) *User-defined contrast.* You must specify as many elements as the number of categories squared.

Only one contrast is in effect for each factor for a DESIGN subcommand. If you do not use the CONTRAST subcommand, the contrast defaults to SIMPLE for each factor. Use separate CONTRAST subcommands for each factor for which you specify contrasts. A contrast specification remains in effect for subsequent designs until explicitly overridden with another CONTRAST subcommand, as in:

```
LOGLINEAR  A(1,4) BY B(1,4)/
  CONTRAST(B)=POLYNOMIAL/
  DESIGN=A A BY B(1)/
  CONTRAST(B)=SIMPLE/
  DESIGN=A A BY B(1)/
```

The first CONTRAST subcommand requests polynomial contrasts of B for the first design. The second CONTRAST subcommand requests the default contrast of B, with the last category (value 4) used as the reference category for the second DESIGN subcommand.

You can print the design matrix used for the contrasts by specifying the DESIGN keyword on the PRINT subcommand (see Section 29.13).

29.16 Contrasts for a Multinomial Logit Model

Contrasts are frequently used for a multinomial logit model, in which the dependent variable has more than two categories. The following example builds special contrasts among the five categories of the dependent variable. The variable PREF measures preference for training camps among Army recruits. For PREF, 1=stay, 2=move to north, 3=move to south, 4=move to unnamed camp, and 5=undecided.

```
LOGLINEAR  PREF(1,5) BY RACE ORIGIN CAMP(1,2)/
  CONTRAST(PREF)=SPECIAL(5*1,  1 1 1 1 -4,  3 -1 -1 -1 0,  0 1 1 -2 0,
    0 1 -1 0 0)/
```

The four contrasts are (1) move or stay vs. undecided; (2) stay vs. move; (3) named camp vs. unnamed; and (4) northern vs. southern camp.

29.17 Contrasts for a Linear Logit Model

One use of the CONTRAST subcommand is for fitting linear logit models. Example 4 (see Section 29.26) uses education to predict response on an attitude item. The form of the CONTRAST subcommand in Example 4 is as follows:

```
LOGLINEAR RESPONSE(1,2) BY YEAR(0,20)/
  PRINT=DEFAULT ESTIM/
  CONTRAST(YEAR)=SPECIAL(21*1,  -10,  -9,  -8,  -7,  -6,  -5,  -4,
                                -3,  -2,  -1,  0,  1,  2,  3,  4,  5,  6,  7,
                                8,  9,  10,  399*1)/
  DESIGN=RESPONSE RESPONSE BY YEAR(1)/
```

YEAR measures years of education and ranges from 0 to 20. Therefore, allowing for the constant effect, YEAR has 20 estimable parameters associated with it. The SPECIAL contrast specifies the constant—that is, 21*1—and the linear effect of YEAR—that is, −10 to 10. The other 399 1s fill out the 21*21 matrix.

29.18 Contrasts for a Logistic Regression Model

In Example 5 (Section 29.27), the following CONTRAST is used to transform the independent variable into a metric variable.

```
LOGLINEAR RESPONSE(1,2) BY TIME(1,4)/
  CONTRAST(TIME) = SPECIAL(4*1,  7 14 27 51,  8*1)/
  PRINT=ALL/PLOT=DEFAULT/
  DESIGN=RESPONSE, TIME(1) BY RESPONSE/
```

TIME represents elapsed time in days. Therefore, the weights in the contrast represent the metric of the passage of time.

ANNOTATED EXAMPLE OF A LOGIT MODEL

The logit model is a special case of the general log-linear model in which one or more variables are treated as dependent, and the rest are used as independent variables. Typically, logit models use dichotomous variables but can be used for polytomous variables. This example uses dichotomous variables to analyze data from *The American Soldier* by Stouffer et al. (1948). The researchers interviewed soldiers in training camps. The variables used in this example are

- PREF—preference for training camps, where 1=stay in the same camp, 2=move to a northern camp, 3=move to a southern camp, 4=move—but undecided about location, and 5=undecided.
- RACE—race of soldier, where 1=black and 2=white.
- ORIGIN, CAMP—geographic origin and geographic location of camp, where 1=north and 2=south.
- FREQ—actual cell count obtained from the published table.

In this example, we transform the preference variable into the dichotomy north vs. south. Typically, the first step in fitting a logit model is to use a saturated model and remove nonsignificant effects. This example fits only the significant effects in the interest of parsimony. The SPSS^X commands are

```
TITLE 'Stouffer''s American Soldier'
DATA LIST LIST / RACE  ORIGIN  CAMP  PREF  FREQ
WEIGHT BY FREQ
VARIABLE LABELS RACE 'RACE OF RESPONDENT'
 ORIGIN 'GEOGRAPHICAL ORIGIN'
 CAMP 'PRESENT CAMP'
 PREF 'PREFENCE FOR LOCATION'
VALUE LABELS RACE 1 'BLACK' 2 'WHITE'/
 ORIGIN 1 'NORTH' 2 'SOUTH'/
 CAMP 1 'NORTH' 2 'SOUTH'/
 PREF 1 'STAY' 2 'GO NORTH' 3 'GO SOUTH'
  4 'MOVE UNDECIDED' 5 'UNDECIDED'

COMMENT COLLAPSE CATEGORIES INTO A DICHOTOMY
DO IF (CAMP EQ 1)
+  RECODE PREF(1=2)(3=3)(ELSE=0) INTO DPREF
+  ELSE
+  RECODE PREF(1=3)(2=2)(ELSE=0) INTO DPREF
END IF

VARIABLE LABELS DPREF 'PREFERENCE FOR LOCATION'
VALUE LABELS DPREF 2 'NORTH' 3 'SOUTH'

LOGLINEAR DPREF(2,3) BY RACE ORIGIN CAMP(1,2)/
  PRINT=DEFAULT ESTIM/
  DESIGN=DPREF, DPREF BY RACE, DPREF BY ORIGIN, DPREF BY CAMP,
    DPREF BY ORIGIN BY CAMP
BEGIN DATA
1 1 1 1 196
1 1 1 2 191
1 1 1 3  36
1 1 1 4  41
1 1 1 5  52
2 2 2 1 481
     .
     .
     .
2 2 2 2  91
2 2 2 3 389
2 2 2 4  91
2 2 2 5  91
END DATA
```

- The DATA LIST command reads the data with a LIST format. The LIST format is a freefield format with each case beginning on a new record (see Chapter 3).
- Variable FREQ is the actual cell count obtained from the published table. The WEIGHT command weights each case (which is actually a cell) back to the sample size (see Chapter 10).

- The transformations inside the DO IF—END IF structure transform the five category preference variable into a dichotomy (see Chapters 6 and 8).
- The LOGLINEAR command specifies one design. The DESIGN subcommand specifies the dependent variable, as well as interactions involving the dependent variable. Note that this design is not the saturated model. When you specify a logit model with the keyword BY and do not use a DESIGN subcommand, LOGLINEAR implicitly includes all the effects and interactions of independent factors (see Section 29.6). See Haberman (1979) for more details.
- The PRINT subcommand prints the frequencies and residuals table as well as the estimates for the parameters (see Section 29.13).

Figures A and B contain portions of the display for this job. Figure A shows the final model fit. The chi-square statistics show a good fit, and all of the adjusted residuals are less than 1.

Figure B shows the parameter estimates for the final model. To obtain regression-like coefficients multiply the estimates by 2 (see Haberman, 1978, p. 294). Use these coefficients to obtain log-odds coefficients; use their anti-log to translate the model into odds rather than log odds. Table A shows the model coefficients.

Table A Model coefficients

Effect	Coefficient	Coefficient*2	Antilog
DPREF	0.135	0.270	1.311
DPREF BY RACE	.186	.371	1.450
DPREF BY ORIGIN	.620	1.239	3.452
DPREF BY CAMP	.379	.759	2.136
DPREF BY ORIGIN BY CAMP	-.074	-.149	.862

The regression-like model implied by the coefficients is

$$\ln(F_{ijk1}/F_{ijk2}) = B + B(A)_i + B(B)_j + B(C)_k + B(BC)_{jk}$$

where F is an expected frequency, and

B equals	0.270	
$B(A)_i$ equals	0.371	for $i=1$
	−0.371	for $i=2$
$B(B)_j$ equals	1.239	for $j=1$
	−1.239	for $j=2$
$B(C)_k$ equals	0.759	for $k=1$
	−0.759	for $k=2$
$B(BC)_{jk}$ equals	−0.149	for $j=k$
	0.149	for j ne k

To evaluate the model in terms of odds rather than log odds, use an analogous multiplicative model, with the antilogs shown in Table A as coefficients. That is,

$$(F_{ijk}1/F_{ijk2}) = T * T(A)_i * T(B)_j * T(C)_k * T(BC)_{jk}$$

where

T equals	1.311	
$T(A)_i$ equals	1.450	for $i=1$
	1/1.450	for $i=2$
$T(B)_j$ equals	3.452	for $j=1$
	1/3.452	for $j=2$
$T(C)_k$ equals	2.136	for $k=1$
	1/2.136	for $k=2$
$T(BC)_{jk}$ equals	0.862	for $j=k$
	1/0.862	for j ne k

For example, consider someone whose race is black, who is originally from the north, and who is presently located in a northern camp. For this individual, i=j=k=1 because of the coding of the variable indicated at the beginning of this example. This person's observed odds of preferring northern versus southern camp location is 10.75 (91.49/8.51) from Figure A. The expected odds given the model is 12.072 (92.35/7.65) from Figure A. The model decomposes these expected odds into components

$$12.072=(1.311)(1.450)(3.452)(2.136)(0.862)$$

where the effects are interpretable.

- 1.311 is the mean or overall effect.
- 1.450 is the race effect indicating the net effect of being black versus white on preference of camp location. Other things equal, blacks prefer northern camp locations by 1.450 to 1.
- 3.452 is the net effect of region of origin on present preference. Other things equal, someone originally from the north prefers a northern camp location by 3.452 to 1.
- 2.136 is the net effect of present location on camp preference. Other things equal, someone presently located in the north states a northern preference over twice as often as they state a southern preference.
- 0.862 is the interaction effect between region of origin and present camp location. The effect is negative; this means that the effect of being a northerner in a northern camp is less positive than is indicated by combining the main effect of being a northerner with the main effect of being in a northern camp.

A Model fit

OBSERVED, EXPECTED FREQUENCIES AND RESIDUALS

FACTOR	CODE	OBS. COUNT & PCT.	EXP. COUNT & PCT.	RESIDUAL	STD. RESID.	ADJ. RESID.
DPREF	NORTH					
RACE	BLACK					
ORIGIN	NORTH					
CAMP	NORTH	387.00 (91.49)	390.64 (92.35)	-3.64309	-.18432	-.77144
CAMP	SOUTH	876.00 (77.80)	879.35 (78.09)	-3.34785	-.11290	-.41778
ORIGIN	SOUTH					
CAMP	NORTH	383.00 (58.65)	376.80 (57.70)	6.20005	.31940	.99936
CAMP	SOUTH	381.00 (18.20)	380.21 (18.17)	.79089	.04056	.11312
RACE	WHITE					
ORIGIN	NORTH					
CAMP	NORTH	955.00 (85.50)	951.36 (85.17)	3.64309	.11811	.77144
CAMP	SOUTH	874.00 (63.15)	870.65 (62.91)	3.34785	.11346	.41778
ORIGIN	SOUTH					
CAMP	NORTH	104.00 (37.14)	110.20 (39.36)	-6.20005	-.59061	-.99936
CAMP	SOUTH	91.00 (9.47)	91.79 (9.55)	-.79089	-.08255	-.11312
DPREF	SOUTH					
RACE	BLACK					
ORIGIN	NORTH					
CAMP	NORTH	36.00 (8.51)	32.36 (7.65)	3.64309	.64045	.77144
CAMP	SOUTH	250.00 (22.20)	246.65 (21.91)	3.34785	.21317	.41778
ORIGIN	SOUTH					
CAMP	NORTH	270.00 (41.35)	276.20 (42.30)	-6.20005	-.37306	-.99936
CAMP	SOUTH	1712.00 (81.80)	1712.79 (81.83)	-.79089	-.01911	-.11312
RACE	WHITE					
ORIGIN	NORTH					
CAMP	NORTH	162.00 (14.50)	165.64 (14.83)	-3.64309	-.28306	-.77144
CAMP	SOUTH	510.00 (36.85)	513.35 (37.09)	-3.34785	-.14776	-.41778
ORIGIN	SOUTH					
CAMP	NORTH	176.00 (62.86)	169.80 (60.64)	6.20005	.47580	.99936
CAMP	SOUTH	870.00 (90.53)	869.21 (90.45)	.79089	.02683	.11312

GOODNESS-OF-FIT TEST STATISTICS

LIKELIHOOD RATIO CHI SQUARE =	1.44756	DF = 3	P = .694
PEARSON CHI SQUARE =	1.45707	DF = 3	P = .692

B Parameter estimates

ESTIMATES FOR PARAMETERS

DPREF

PARAMETER	COEFF.	STD. ERR.	Z-VALUE	LOWER 95 CI	UPPER 95 CI
1	.1352217166	.01518	8.90608	.10546	.16498

DPREF BY RACE

PARAMETER	COEFF.	STD. ERR.	Z-VALUE	LOWER 95 CI	UPPER 95 CI
2	.1857281674	.01557	11.93145	.15522	.21624

DPREF BY ORIGIN

PARAMETER	COEFF.	STD. ERR.	Z-VALUE	LOWER 95 CI	UPPER 95 CI
3	.6195921388	.01687	36.72886	.58653	.65266

DPREF BY CAMP

PARAMETER	COEFF.	STD. ERR.	Z-VALUE	LOWER 95 CI	UPPER 95 CI
4	.3794390119	.01534	24.73658	.34937	.40950

DPREF BY ORIGIN BY CAMP

PARAMETER	COEFF.	STD. ERR.	Z-VALUE	LOWER 95 CI	UPPER 95 CI
5	-.0744977447	.01521	-4.89942	-.10430	-.04470

29.19 The CRITERIA Subcommand

The CRITERIA subcommand specifies the values of some constants in the Newton-Raphson algorithm, the estimation algorithm in LOGLINEAR. The following keywords are available:

CONVERGE(eps) *Convergence criterion.* Specify a value for the convergence criterion. The default is .001.

ITERATION(n) *Maximum number of iterations.* Specify the maximum number of iterations for the algorithm. The default number is 20.

DELTA(d) *Cell delta value.* The value of delta is added to each cell frequency before analysis. The default value is .5.

DEFAULT *Default values are used.* You can use DEFAULT to reset the parameters to the default.

For example, to increase the maximum number of iterations to 50, specify:

```
LOGLINEAR  DPREF(2,3) BY RACE ORIGIN CAMP(1,2)/
  CRITERIA=ITERATION(50)
```

Defaults or specifications remain in effect until overriden with another CRITERIA subcommand.

29.20 The WIDTH Subcommand

The default width for the display is 132. You can use the WIDTH subcommand to specify a width of 72 to avoid wrap on short-carriage terminals. Only one width can be in effect at a time and it controls all display. The WIDTH subcommand can be placed anywhere after the variables specification. Figure 29.20 is an example of the frequencies and residuals display with WIDTH=72 in effect. This figure uses the same data as Figure 29.3.

```
LOGLINEAR  DPREF(2,3) RACE CAMP(1,2)/
  WIDTH=72
```

Figure 29.20 Narrow display

OBSERVED, EXPECTED FREQUENCIES AND RESIDUALS

CELL	OBS COUNT	EXP COUNT	RESIDUAL	STD RESID.	ADJ. RESID.
1	770.000	770.000	.000	.000	0.0
2	1257.000	1257.000	.000	.000	0.0
3	1059.000	1059.000	.000	.000	0.0
4	965.000	965.000	.000	.000	0.0
5	306.000	306.000	-.000	-.000	0.0
6	1962.000	1962.000	.000	.000	0.0
7	338.000	338.000	-.000	-.000	0.0
8	1380.000	1380.000	.000	.000	0.0

Note, however, that the narrow format for the frequencies table suppresses the printing of variable names and values. Cell 1 corresponds to DPREF=1, RACE=1, and CAMP=1, cell 2 corresponds to DPREF=1, RACE=1, and CAMP=2, and so forth.

29.21 Missing Values

By default, LOGLINEAR deletes cases with missing values on any variable listed on the variables specification. To include cases with user-defined missing values, specify Option 1 on the associated OPTIONS command. Cases with system-missing values are always deleted from the analysis. If you specify Option 1, you must also include the missing values in the value range specification on the LOGLINEAR command.

OPTION 1 *Include missing values.*

29.22 LOGLINEAR EXAMPLES

You can use LOGLINEAR to analyze many types of designs for categorical variables. Combinations of variables specifications, CWEIGHT, CONTRAST, GRESID, and DESIGN subcommands can produce general log-linear models, logit models, quasi-independence models, logistic regressions, and others. The following examples and the annotated example, although not exhaustive, demonstrate many of the types of models you can analyze. Most of these examples have been obtained from books and articles on the analysis of categorical data. The examples use the WEIGHT command (Chapter 10) to replicate the published tables.

29.23 Example 1: A General Log-linear Model

The general log-linear model has all dependent variables. This example uses the same data analyzed as a logit model in the annotated example. The general log-linear model treats all variables as jointly dependent. The following LOGLINEAR command is used to request this model:

```
LOGLINEAR DPREF(2,3) RACE ORIGIN CAMP(1,2)/
  PRINT=DEFAULT ESTIM/
  DESIGN=DPREF, RACE, ORIGIN, CAMP,
    DPREF BY RACE, DPREF BY ORIGIN, DPREF BY CAMP,
    RACE BY CAMP, RACE BY ORIGIN, ORIGIN BY CAMP,
    RACE BY ORIGIN BY CAMP,
    DPREF BY ORIGIN BY CAMP
```

The LOGLINEAR command for the general log-linear model does not use the keyword BY. The DESIGN subcommand uses all the variables as main effects or as part of an interaction term. Compare this with the logit model shown in Section 29.30, which uses the dependent variable and interactions involving the dependent variable.

Figures 29.23a and 29.23b are the display produced by this example. Figure 29.23a shows that expected frequencies are identical to the logit model in the annotated example (Figure A). However, observed and expected cell percentages differ. In the logit model, cell percentages sum to

Figure 29.23a Log-linear model fit for Example 1

```
OBSERVED, EXPECTED FREQUENCIES AND RESIDUALS

    FACTOR          CODE              OBS. COUNT & PCT.   EXP. COUNT & PCT.     RESIDUAL   STD. RESID.   ADJ. RESID.

DPREF             NORTH
 RACE              BLACK
  ORIGIN            NORTH
   CAMP              NORTH              387.00 (  4.82)     390.64 (  4.86)     -3.64309      -.18432       -.77144
   CAMP              SOUTH              876.00 ( 10.90)     879.35 ( 10.94)     -3.34785      -.11290       -.41778
  ORIGIN            SOUTH
   CAMP              NORTH              383.00 (  4.77)     376.80 (  4.69)      6.20005       .31940        .99936
   CAMP              SOUTH              381.00 (  4.74)     380.21 (  4.73)       .79089       .04056        .11312
 RACE              WHITE
  ORIGIN            NORTH
   CAMP              NORTH              955.00 ( 11.88)     951.36 ( 11.84)      3.64309       .11811        .77144
   CAMP              SOUTH              874.00 ( 10.87)     870.65 ( 10.83)      3.34785       .11346        .41778
  ORIGIN            SOUTH
   CAMP              NORTH              104.00 (  1.29)     110.20 (  1.37)     -6.20005      -.59061       -.99936
   CAMP              SOUTH               91.00 (  1.13)      91.79 (  1.14)      -.79089      -.08255       -.11312

DPREF             SOUTH
 RACE              BLACK
  ORIGIN            NORTH
   CAMP              NORTH               36.00 (   .45)      32.36 (   .40)      3.64309       .64045        .77144
   CAMP              SOUTH              250.00 (  3.11)     246.65 (  3.07)      3.34785       .21317        .41778
  ORIGIN            SOUTH
   CAMP              NORTH              270.00 (  3.36)     276.20 (  3.44)     -6.20005      -.37306       -.99936
   CAMP              SOUTH             1712.00 ( 21.30)    1712.79 ( 21.31)      -.79089      -.01911       -.11312
 RACE              WHITE
  ORIGIN            NORTH
   CAMP              NORTH              162.00 (  2.02)     165.64 (  2.06)     -3.64309      -.28306       -.77144
   CAMP              SOUTH              510.00 (  6.35)     513.35 (  6.39)     -3.34785      -.14776       -.41778
  ORIGIN            SOUTH
   CAMP              NORTH              176.00 (  2.19)     169.80 (  2.11)      6.20005       .47580        .99936
   CAMP              SOUTH              870.00 ( 10.82)     869.21 ( 10.82)       .79089       .02683        .11312
- - - - - - - - - - - - - - - - - - - - - - - - - - - - - - - - - - - - - - - - - - - - - - - - - - - - - - - -

GOODNESS-OF-FIT TEST STATISTICS

  LIKELIHOOD RATIO CHI SQUARE =     1.44756    DF = 3  P =   .694
            PEARSON CHI SQUARE =     1.45707    DF = 3  P =   .692
```

Figure 29.23b Parameter estimates for Example 1

ESTIMATES FOR PARAMETERS

PARAMETER	COEFF.	STD. ERR.	Z-VALUE	LOWER 95 CI	UPPER 95 CI
DPREF					
1	.1352217166	.01518	8.90608	.10546	.16498
RACE					
2	.0355803941	.01363	2.61113	.00887	.06229
ORIGIN					
3	.0403904261	.01614	2.50201	.00875	.07203
CAMP					
4	-.4480592813	.01614	-27.76919	-.47968	-.41643
DPREF BY RACE					
5	.1857281674	.01557	11.93145	.15522	.21624
DPREF BY ORIGIN					
6	.6195921388	.01687	36.72886	.58653	.65266
DPREF BY CAMP					
7	.3794390119	.01534	24.73658	.34937	.40950
RACE BY CAMP					
8	-.1364780340	.01413	-9.65595	-.16418	-.10878
RACE BY ORIGIN					
9	-.4413477997	.01591	-27.73754	-.47253	-.41016
ORIGIN BY CAMP					
10	-.0375668525	.01632	-2.30190	-.06955	-.00558
RACE BY ORIGIN BY CAMP					
11	-.0885302170	.01359	-6.51497	-.11516	-.06190
DPREF BY ORIGIN BY CAMP					
12	-.0744977447	.01521	-4.89942	-.10430	-.04470

100 across categories of the dependent variable within each combination of independent variable values. In other words, cell percentages in the logit model are comparable to row or column percentages in crosstabulation. In the general model, they sum to 100 across all categories and are comparable to total percentages in a crosstabulation.

Compare Figure 29.23b with Figure B in the annotated example. Note that identical results are produced for effects in common in the two models.

29.24 Example 2: A Multinomial Logit Model

The annotated example and Example 1 (see Section 29.23) analyze Stouffer's data with "preference for location" transformed into a dichotomy. Example 2 uses the original five-category preference variable to demonstrate the multinomial logit model. This example uses a special contrast to make desired comparisons among the categories of the dependent variable. The LOGLINEAR command is as follows:

```
LOGLINEAR PREF(1,5) BY RACE ORIGIN CAMP(1,2)/
  PRINT=DEFAULT ESTIM/
  CONTRAST(PREF)=SPECIAL(5*1,1 1 1 1 -4,3 -1 -1 -1 0,
    0 1 1 -2 0,0 1 -1 0 0)/
  DESIGN=PREF, PREF BY RACE, PREF BY ORIGIN, PREF BY CAMP,
    PREF BY RACE BY ORIGIN, PREF BY RACE BY CAMP,
    PREF BY ORIGIN BY CAMP, PREF BY RACE BY ORIGIN BY CAMP
```

Figure 29.24 is the display of the parameter estimates for Example 2. This example fits the saturated model. If no DESIGN subcommand had been specified, the saturated model would have also included effects that are redundant when a logit model is specified. Parameter estimates for a multinomial model can be more interpretable when you specify special contrasts as in this example. The CONTRAST subcommand contrasts the movers and stayers vs. the undecided, the movers vs. the stayers, the decided vs. the undecided, and northern vs. southern camps.

Figure 29.24 Parameter estimates for Example 2

ESTIMATES FOR PARAMETERS

PREF

PARAMETER	COEFF.	STD. ERR.	Z-VALUE	LOWER 95 CI	UPPER 95 CI
1	.1238334136	.00810	15.28061	.10795	.13972
2	.0727402118	.00828	8.78197	.05651	.08897
3	.2049876788	.01413	14.50302	.17728	.23269
4	.1285119295	.02076	6.19138	.08783	.16919

PREF BY RACE

PARAMETER	COEFF.	STD. ERR.	Z-VALUE	LOWER 95 CI	UPPER 95 CI
5	-.0052109010	.00810	-.64301	-.02109	.01067
6	-.0063067819	.00828	-.76142	-.02254	.00993
7	.0061856967	.01413	.43764	-.02152	.03389
8	.0971164628	.02076	4.67883	.05643	.13780

PREF BY ORIGIN

PARAMETER	COEFF.	STD. ERR.	Z-VALUE	LOWER 95 CI	UPPER 95 CI
9	-.0022335795	.00810	-.27562	-.01812	.01365
10	-.0586966680	.00828	-7.08648	-.07493	-.04246
11	-.0026996815	.01413	-.19100	-.03040	.02500
12	.6575469865	.02076	31.67897	.61686	.69823

PREF BY CAMP

PARAMETER	COEFF.	STD. ERR.	Z-VALUE	LOWER 95 CI	UPPER 95 CI
13	-.0191154142	.00810	-2.35877	-.03500	-.00323
14	.0323382145	.00828	3.90421	.01610	.04857
15	.0042139929	.01413	.29814	-.02349	.03192
16	-.0153840298	.02076	-.74116	-.05607	.02530

PREF BY RACE BY ORIGIN

PARAMETER	COEFF.	STD. ERR.	Z-VALUE	LOWER 95 CI	UPPER 95 CI
17	-.0032133869	.00810	-.39652	-.01910	.01267
18	-.0236657809	.00828	-2.85718	-.03990	-.00743
19	.0616206639	.01413	4.35971	.03392	.08932
20	-.0516436869	.02076	-2.48806	-.09233	-.01096

PREF BY RACE BY CAMP

PARAMETER	COEFF.	STD. ERR.	Z-VALUE	LOWER 95 CI	UPPER 95 CI
21	.0030182528	.00810	.37244	-.01287	.01890
22	.1032579366	.00828	12.46639	.08702	.11949
23	-.0190277350	.01413	-1.34623	-.04673	.00868
24	.0083440312	.02076	.40199	-.03234	.04903

PREF BY ORIGIN BY CAMP

PARAMETER	COEFF.	STD. ERR.	Z-VALUE	LOWER 95 CI	UPPER 95 CI
25	.0048675160	.00810	.60063	-.01102	.02075
26	.1321377574	.00828	15.95307	.11590	.14837
27	-.0091332684	.01413	-.64619	-.03684	.01857
28	-.0312036108	.02076	-1.50331	-.07189	.00948

PREF BY RACE BY ORIGIN BY CAMP

PARAMETER	COEFF.	STD. ERR.	Z-VALUE	LOWER 95 CI	UPPER 95 CI
29	-.0008206899	.00810	-.10127	-.01670	.01506
30	.0219434059	.00828	2.64924	.00571	.03818
31	-.0113726417	.01413	-.80462	-.03908	.01633
32	.0410891620	.02076	1.97957	.00041	.08177

29.25 Example 3: Frequency Table Models

You can use LOGLINEAR to analyze one-dimensional frequency tables by means of chi-square-based analysis. Example 3 uses data on the recall of stressful events over time (Haberman, 1978). Each case in the published table is one recall of a stressful event, and the measure is the length of time since the event occurred in months. The example tests two separate models: the equiprobability model and the log-linear time-trend model. The following SPSSX commands are used:

```
DATA LIST LIST / MONTH  WT
COMPUTE X=1
COMPUTE Z=MONTH
WEIGHT BY WT

LOGLINEAR MONTH(1,18) WITH X Z/
 PRINT = ALL/
 /*USE GRESID TO TEST COMBINATIONS OF THE OBSERVED FREQUENCIES
 /*NOTE:  THE THREE EFFECTS ARE EARLY, MIDDLE, AND LATE
 GRESID =(6*1,12*0)/
 GRESID=(6*0,6*1,6*0)/
 GRESID=(12*0,6*1)/
 /*MODEL 1:  THE EQUIPROBABILITY MODEL
 DESIGN = X/
 /*MODEL 2:  THE LOG-LINEAR TIME-TREND MODEL
 DESIGN = Z/
BEGIN DATA
 1 15 1 0
 2 11 1 0
 3 14 1 0
       .
       .
       .
16  1 0 1
17  1 0 1
18  4 0 1
END DATA
```

- The DATA LIST command reads two variables: MONTH, scaled from 1 to 18; and WT, which contains the frequencies. It uses the LIST format.
- COMPUTE X=1 computes a vector of 1s.
- The second COMPUTE computes an index vector ranging from 1 to 18.
- The WEIGHT command is used to replicate the original file.
- The LOGLINEAR command names MONTH as the dependent variable and the two index variables as covariates.
- The GRESID subcommands request three linear combinations of the data: the first six, the middle six, and the last six observations, respectively, are combined. Generalized residual contrasts produce some of the statistics already seen: the observed count, the expected count, the residual, the standardized residual, and the adjusted residual.
- DESIGN=X tests the equiprobability model. This model assumes that the probability of dating an event in a particular past month is constant for all months. The covariate is a constant for this type of model.
- DESIGN=Z fits a log-linear time-trend model. The log of the cell probabilities is a linear function of the time before the interview. The index variable reflects the time period being studied for this type of model.

Figure 29.25a shows the frequencies and residuals for the equiprobability model. The expected counts and expected percentages are constant across all cells in the equiprobability model.

Figure 29.25a The equiprobability model fit for Example 3

OBSERVED, EXPECTED FREQUENCIES AND RESIDUALS

FACTOR	CODE	OBS. COUNT & PCT.	EXP. COUNT & PCT.	RESIDUAL	STD. RESID.	ADJ. RESID.
MONTH	1	15.00 (10.20)	8.17 (5.56)	6.83333	2.39117	2.46049
MONTH	2	11.00 (7.48)	8.17 (5.56)	2.83333	.99146	1.02020
MONTH	3	14.00 (9.52)	8.17 (5.56)	5.83333	2.04124	2.10042
MONTH	4	17.00 (11.56)	8.17 (5.56)	8.83333	3.09102	3.18064
MONTH	5	5.00 (3.40)	8.17 (5.56)	-3.16667	-1.10810	-1.14023
MONTH	6	11.00 (7.48)	8.17 (5.56)	2.83333	.99146	1.02020
MONTH	7	10.00 (6.80)	8.17 (5.56)	1.83333	.64153	.66013
MONTH	8	4.00 (2.72)	8.17 (5.56)	-4.16667	-1.45803	-1.50030
MONTH	9	8.00 (5.44)	8.17 (5.56)	-.16667	-.05832	-.06001
MONTH	10	10.00 (6.80)	8.17 (5.56)	1.83333	.64153	.66013
MONTH	11	7.00 (4.76)	8.17 (5.56)	-1.16667	-.40825	-.42008
MONTH	12	9.00 (6.12)	8.17 (5.56)	.83333	.29161	.30006
MONTH	13	11.00 (7.48)	8.17 (5.56)	2.83333	.99146	1.02020
MONTH	14	3.00 (2.04)	8.17 (5.56)	-5.16667	-1.80796	-1.86037
MONTH	15	6.00 (4.08)	8.17 (5.56)	-2.16667	-.75818	-.78016
MONTH	16	1.00 (.68)	8.17 (5.56)	-7.16667	-2.50781	-2.58052
MONTH	17	1.00 (.68)	8.17 (5.56)	-7.16667	-2.50781	-2.58052
MONTH	18	4.00 (2.72)	8.17 (5.56)	-4.16667	-1.45803	-1.50030

GOODNESS-OF-FIT TEST STATISTICS

LIKELIHOOD RATIO CHI SQUARE =	50.84270	DF = 17	P = .000
PEARSON CHI SQUARE =	45.36735	DF = 17	P = .000

Figure 29.25b is the display produced by the GRESID subcommands for the equiprobability model. The model systematically underpredicts the early scores and overpredicts the late scores in a way which cannot be ignored: the adjusted residuals are greater than 4 in magnitude in these two instances.

Figure 29.25b Generalized residuals for the equiprobability model for Example 3

GENERALIZED RESIDUAL

CONTRAST	OBS. COUNT	EXP. COUNT	RESIDUAL	STD. RESID.	ADJ. RESID.
1	73.00000	49.00000	24.00000	3.42857	4.19913
2	48.00000	49.00000	-1.00000	-.14286	-.17496
3	26.00000	49.00000	-23.00000	-3.28571	-4.02416

Figure 29.25c shows the fit under the time-trend model. The expected counts come much closer to the observed counts using this model. With the exception of Month 13, the adjusted residuals are all under 2 in magnitude.

Figure 29.25c The time-trend model fit for Example 3

OBSERVED, EXPECTED FREQUENCIES AND RESIDUALS

FACTOR	CODE	OBS. COUNT & PCT.	EXP. COUNT & PCT.	RESIDUAL	STD. RESID.	ADJ. RESID.
MONTH	1	15.00 (10.20)	15.17 (10.32)	-.17107	-.04392	-.05157
MONTH	2	11.00 (7.48)	13.95 (9.49)	-2.95197	-.79030	-.88727
MONTH	3	14.00 (9.52)	12.83 (8.73)	1.16916	.32640	.35509
MONTH	4	17.00 (11.56)	11.80 (8.03)	5.20020	1.51385	1.61114
MONTH	5	5.00 (3.40)	10.85 (7.38)	-5.85161	-1.77635	-1.86253
MONTH	6	11.00 (7.48)	9.98 (6.79)	1.02038	.32300	.33545
MONTH	7	10.00 (6.80)	9.18 (6.24)	.82231	.27144	.28037
MONTH	8	4.00 (2.72)	8.44 (5.74)	-4.44020	-1.52836	-1.57513
MONTH	9	8.00 (5.44)	7.76 (5.28)	.23802	.08543	.08807
MONTH	10	10.00 (6.80)	7.14 (4.86)	2.86174	1.07111	1.10651
MONTH	11	7.00 (4.76)	6.56 (4.47)	.43535	.16991	.17616
MONTH	12	9.00 (6.12)	6.04 (4.11)	2.96286	1.20586	1.25602
MONTH	13	11.00 (7.48)	5.55 (3.78)	5.44798	2.31212	2.42137
MONTH	14	3.00 (2.04)	5.11 (3.47)	-2.10588	-.93196	-.98178
MONTH	15	6.00 (4.08)	4.70 (3.19)	1.30441	.60196	.63807
MONTH	16	1.00 (.68)	4.32 (2.94)	-3.31827	-1.59682	-1.70324
MONTH	17	1.00 (.68)	3.97 (2.70)	-2.97127	-1.49100	-1.60026
MONTH	18	4.00 (2.72)	3.65 (2.48)	.34785	.18202	.19654

GOODNESS-OF-FIT TEST STATISTICS

LIKELIHOOD RATIO CHI SQUARE =	24.57038	DF = 16	P = .078
PEARSON CHI SQUARE =	22.71450	DF = 16	P = .122

Figure 29.25d shows the output from the GRESID specifications for the time-trend model. In this model, the early, middle, and late contrasts now conform more closely to the observed frequencies than in the equiprobability model.

Figure 29.25d Generalized residuals for the time-trend model for Example 3

GENERALIZED RESIDUAL

CONTRAST	OBS. COUNT	EXP. COUNT	RESIDUAL	STD. RESID.	ADJ. RESID.
1	73.00000	74.58491	-1.58491	-.18352	-.48367
2	48.00000	45.11992	2.88008	.42877	.53362
3	26.00000	27.29516	-1.29516	-.24790	-.43163

29.26 Example 4: A Linear Logit Model

Example 4 is a linear logit model with one predictor. The level of education in years is used to predict the attitude of men toward women staying at home rather than working (Haberman, 1982). This variable is dichotomous. The SPSS^X commands are as follows:

```
DATA LIST LIST/YEAR RESPONSE WT
WEIGHT BY WT
VALUE LABELS RESPONSE 1 'AGREE' 2 'DISAGREE'
LOGLINEAR RESPONSE(1,2) BY YEAR(0,20)/
 PRINT=DEFAULT ESTIM/
 CONTRAST(YEAR)=SPECIAL(21*1, -10, -9, -8, -7, -6, -5, -4,
                        -3, -2, -1, 0, 1, 2, 3, 4, 5, 6, 7,
                         8, 9, 10, 399*1 )/
 DESIGN=RESPONSE RESPONSE BY YEAR(1)/
BEGIN DATA
 0 1  4
 0 2  2
   .
   .
   .
20 1  3
20 2 20
END DATA
```

- The DATA LIST command reads YEAR, RESPONSE, and WT, which is the frequency for each cell.
- The WEIGHT command weights the table to the original sample size.
- The variables specification on the LOGLINEAR command uses the keyword BY to define a logit model.
- The CONTRAST subcommand specifies a special contrast. The full design matrix is a 21*21 matrix. The first effect fit is the constant effect, so the special contrast begins with 21 1s. The second effect is the linear effect, parameterized as years of education minus 10. Higher order effects are not of interest, so 1s are used to fill out the matrix.
- The DESIGN subcommand fits the RESPONSE effect and the RESPONSE by linear-YEAR effect.

Figure 29.26a shows the linear logit fit. The chi-square statistics are all nonsignificant, and the largest adjusted residual is 1.99. Figure 29.26b shows the analysis of dispersion and the two measures of association. The two statistics indicate that there is about a 10% reduction in errors of classification on the response variable with knowledge of years of education. Figure 29.26c is the parameter estimates for the model.

You could get the same results by first calculating a variable equal to YEAR−10 and then specifying this new variable as a covariate on the LOGLINEAR command, as in:

```
COMPUTE X=YEAR-10
LOGLINEAR RESPONSE(1,2) BY YEAR (0,20) WITH X/
  PRINT=DEFAULT ESTIM/
  DESIGN=RESPONSE RESPONSE BY X/
```

Using this approach, you do not need to specify the CONTRAST subcommand on the LOGLINEAR command.

Figure 29.26a Linear logit model fit for Example 4

OBSERVED, EXPECTED FREQUENCIES AND RESIDUALS

FACTOR	CODE	OBS. COUNT & PCT.	EXP. COUNT & PCT.	RESIDUAL	STD. RESID.	ADJ. RESID.
RESPONSE	AGREE					
YEAR	0	4.00 (66.67)	5.34 (89.07)	-1.34437	-.58153	-1.78840
YEAR	1	2.00 (100.00)	1.73 (86.58)	.26844	.20400	.55987
YEAR	2	4.00 (100.00)	3.34 (83.62)	.65524	.35828	.89476
YEAR	3	6.00 (66.67)	7.21 (80.16)	-1.21410	-.45203	-1.03850
YEAR	4	5.00 (50.00)	7.62 (76.17)	-2.61712	-.94826	-1.98872
YEAR	5	13.00 (65.00)	14.33 (71.67)	-1.33363	-.35226	-.69006
YEAR	6	25.00 (73.53)	22.67 (66.69)	2.32664	.48862	.89930
YEAR	7	27.00 (64.29)	25.75 (61.30)	1.25335	.24701	.42125
YEAR	8	75.00 (60.48)	68.98 (55.63)	6.02431	.72537	1.25636
YEAR	9	29.00 (50.00)	28.88 (49.80)	.11670	.02171	.03204
YEAR	10	32.00 (41.56)	33.86 (43.98)	-1.86267	-.32009	-.44692
YEAR	11	36.00 (37.89)	36.40 (38.32)	-.40143	-.06653	-.08861
YEAR	12	115.00 (31.94)	118.65 (32.96)	-3.64528	-.33466	-.49574
YEAR	13	31.00 (30.69)	28.29 (28.01)	2.71379	.51026	.63482
YEAR	14	28.00 (26.17)	25.19 (23.54)	2.81445	.56081	.68848
YEAR	15	9.00 (28.13)	6.27 (19.59)	2.73166	1.09106	1.24697
YEAR	16	15.00 (12.00)	20.20 (16.16)	-5.20226	-1.15742	-1.43092
YEAR	17	3.00 (9.38)	4.24 (13.24)	-1.23547	-.60032	-.66592
YEAR	18	1.00 (3.45)	3.12 (10.77)	-2.12375	-1.20161	-1.31361
YEAR	19	2.00 (13.33)	1.31 (8.72)	.69201	.60507	.64427
YEAR	20	3.00 (13.04)	1.62 (7.03)	1.38348	1.08814	1.15938
RESPONSE	DISAGREE					
YEAR	0	2.00 (33.33)	.66 (10.93)	1.34437	1.66030	1.78840
YEAR	1	0.0 (0.0)	.27 (13.42)	-.26844	-.51811	-.55987
YEAR	2	0.0 (0.0)	.66 (16.38)	-.65524	-.80947	-.89476
YEAR	3	3.00 (33.33)	1.79 (19.84)	1.21410	.90850	1.03850
YEAR	4	5.00 (50.00)	2.38 (23.83)	2.61712	1.69540	1.98872
YEAR	5	7.00 (35.00)	5.67 (28.33)	1.33363	.56025	.69006
YEAR	6	9.00 (26.47)	11.33 (33.31)	-2.32664	-.69132	-.89930
YEAR	7	15.00 (35.71)	16.25 (38.70)	-1.25335	-.31088	-.42125
YEAR	8	49.00 (39.52)	55.02 (44.37)	-6.02431	-.81214	-1.25636
YEAR	9	29.00 (50.00)	29.12 (50.20)	-.11670	-.02163	-.03204
YEAR	10	45.00 (58.44)	43.14 (56.02)	1.86267	.28360	.44692
YEAR	11	59.00 (62.11)	58.60 (61.68)	.40143	.05244	.08861
YEAR	12	245.00 (68.06)	241.35 (67.04)	3.64528	.23464	.49574
YEAR	13	70.00 (69.31)	72.71 (71.99)	-2.71379	-.31825	-.63482
YEAR	14	79.00 (73.83)	81.81 (76.46)	-2.81445	-.31116	-.68848
YEAR	15	23.00 (71.88)	25.73 (80.41)	-2.73166	-.53851	-1.24697
YEAR	16	110.00 (88.00)	104.80 (83.84)	5.20226	.50818	1.43092
YEAR	17	29.00 (90.63)	27.76 (86.76)	1.23547	.23447	.66592
YEAR	18	28.00 (96.55)	25.88 (89.23)	2.12375	.41750	1.31361
YEAR	19	13.00 (86.67)	13.69 (91.28)	-.69201	-.18702	-.64427
YEAR	20	20.00 (86.96)	21.38 (92.97)	-1.38348	-.29918	-1.15938

GOODNESS-OF-FIT TEST STATISTICS

LIKELIHOOD RATIO CHI SQUARE =	18.94502	DF = 19	P = .460
PEARSON CHI SQUARE =	19.40725	DF = 19	P = .431

Figure 29.26b Linear logit model analysis of dispersion for Example 4

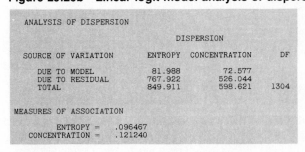

ANALYSIS OF DISPERSION

	DISPERSION		
SOURCE OF VARIATION	ENTROPY	CONCENTRATION	DF
DUE TO MODEL	81.988	72.577	
DUE TO RESIDUAL	767.922	526.044	
TOTAL	849.911	598.621	1304

MEASURES OF ASSOCIATION

ENTROPY = .096467
CONCENTRATION = .121240

Figure 29.26c Linear logit model parameter estimates for Example 4

ESTIMATES FOR PARAMETERS

RESPONSE

PARAMETER	COEFF.	STD. ERR.	Z-VALUE	LOWER 95 CI	UPPER 95 CI
1	-.1210376490	.03334	-3.63002	-.18639	-.05568

RESPONSE BY YEAR(1)

PARAMETER	COEFF.	STD. ERR.	Z-VALUE	LOWER 95 CI	UPPER 95 CI
2	-.1170135446	.01009	-11.59226	-.13680	-.09723

29.27 Example 5: Logistic Regression Model

In the logistic regression model, a dichotomous dependent variable is predicted by one or more independent variables. The independent variables can be categorical, although one must be measured at the interval level of measurement.

Example 5 is a logistic regression in which a contrast is used to transform the independent variable into a metric variable. The data for this example is taken from Dixon (1979). At a specified time, measured in number of days, a number of objects are tested and the number of failures are recorded. In this example, time is a metric variable, not merely an evenly spaced ordinal variable. RESPONSE is the dependent variable, and TIME is the independent variable. The following SPSS^{X} commands are used:

```
TITLE A LOGISTIC REGRESSION EXAMPLE FROM BMDP(1979) P.517.1
DATA LIST LIST/ RESPONSE TIME WT *
VALUE LABELS RESPONSE 1 'SUCCESS' 2 'FAILURE'
WEIGHT BY WT

LOGLINEAR RESPONSE(1,2) BY TIME(1,4)/
          CONTRAST(TIME) = SPECIAL(4*1, 7 14 27 51, 8*1)/
          PRINT = ALL/PLOT = DEFAULT/
          DESIGN = RESPONSE, TIME(1) BY RESPONSE/
BEGIN DATA
1 1  55
2 1   0
1 2 155
2 2   2
1 3 152
2 3   7
1 4  13
2 4   3
END DATA
```

- The BY keyword in the variables specification indicates a logit model.
- The PRINT subcommand requests all printed materials, and the PLOT subcommand requests the default plots.
- The SPECIAL contrast on the CONTRAST subcommand specifies the metric of time. The constant effect is specified first, followed by the linear effect in the metric of time: 7, 14, 27, 51. Since no higher order effect is of interest, the matrix is filled out with 1s.
- The DESIGN subcommand fits RESPONSE and RESPONSE by linear-TIME.

Figure 29.27a Model design for Example 5

```
CORRESPONDENCE BETWEEN EFFECTS AND COLUMNS OF DESIGN/MODEL 1

 STARTING  ENDING
  COLUMN   COLUMN    EFFECT NAME

     1        1      RESPONSE
     2        2      TIME(1) BY RESPONSE

- - - - - - - - - - - - - - - - - - - - - - - - - - - - - - - - - - - - - - - -

 DESIGN MATRIX

 1-RESPONSE  2-TIME

FACTOR                                      PARAMETER

   1  2             1          2

   1  1        1.00000    7.00000
   1  2        1.00000   14.00000
   1  3        1.00000   27.00000
   1  4        1.00000   51.00000
   2  1       -1.00000   -7.00000
   2  2       -1.00000  -14.00000
   2  3       -1.00000  -27.00000
   2  4       -1.00000  -51.00000
```

Figure 29.27a shows the design matrix for the model. Figure 29.27b shows the logistic regression fit. Overall, the fit is good. Both chi-square statistics are nonsignificant, and all adjusted residuals are well under 2 in magnitude. Figure 29.27c shows the estimated parameters and the correlation matrix of parameter estimates. As in logit models, you can multiply the two parameter values by 2 to obtain the constant and the regression coefficient for the logistic model. Finally, Figure 29.27d shows the normal and detrended normal plots of the residuals against their expected values produced by the NORMPROB default keyword. The plots show the characteristic S-curve shape associated with logistic regression.

If the metric of the time measure is recorded on your data, you can specify the metric variable as a covariate and not specify the CONTRAST subcommand, as in:

```
DATA LIST LIST/RESPONSE TIME X WT
WEIGHT BY WT
LOGLINEAR RESPONSE (1,2) BY TIME(1,4) WITH X/
  PRINT=ALL/PLOT=DEFAULT/
  DESIGN=RESPONSE, X BY RESPONSE/
BEGIN DATA
1 1 7 55
2 1 7 0
1 2 14 155
2 2 14 2
1 3 27 152
2 3 27 7
1 4 51 13
2 4 51 3
END DATA
```

This approach can easily be extended to two or more independent variables with the metric values of the independent variables recorded in separate variables and specified as covariates on the LOGLINEAR variables specification and DESIGN subcommand.

Figure 29.27b Model fit for Example 5

```
OBSERVED, EXPECTED FREQUENCIES AND RESIDUALS

    FACTOR          CODE           OBS. COUNT & PCT.   EXP. COUNT & PCT.     RESIDUAL  STD. RESID.  ADJ. RESID.

RESPONSE        SUCCESS
 TIME                  1           55.00 (100.00)      54.57 ( 99.22)         .42709      .05781       .71030
 TIME                  2          155.00 ( 98.73)     154.87 ( 98.64)         .13217      .01062       .12261
 TIME                  3          152.00 ( 95.60)     152.99 ( 96.22)       -.98675     -.07978      -.60851
 TIME                  4           13.00 ( 81.25)      12.57 ( 78.58)         .42750      .12056       .69641

RESPONSE        FAILURE
 TIME                  1             0.0 (   0.0 )       .43 (   .78)       -.42709     -.65352      -.71030
 TIME                  2            2.00 (  1.27)       2.13 (  1.36)       -.13217     -.09051      -.12261
 TIME                  3            7.00 (  4.40)       6.01 (  3.78)         .98675      .40239       .60851
 TIME                  4            3.00 ( 18.75)       3.43 ( 21.42)       -.42750     -.23091      -.69641
- - - - - - - - - - - - - - - - - - - - - - - - - - - - - - - - - - - - - - - - - - - - - - - - - - - - -

GOODNESS-OF-FIT TEST STATISTICS

  LIKELIHOOD RATIO CHI SQUARE =    1.09615    DF = 2  P =   .578
           PEARSON CHI SQUARE =     .67488    DF = 2  P =   .714
```

Figure 29.27c Estimated parameters for Example 5

```
ESTIMATES FOR PARAMETERS

RESPONSE

 PARAMETER           COEFF.          STD. ERR.          Z-VALUE     LOWER 95 CI      UPPER 95 CI

      1       2.7075886119             .36377          7.44312         1.99460          3.42058

TIME(1) BY RESPONSE

 PARAMETER           COEFF.          STD. ERR.          Z-VALUE     LOWER 95 CI      UPPER 95 CI

      2       -.0403479895             .01118         -3.60955         -.06226          -.01844
- - - - - - - - - - - - - - - - - - - - - - - - - - - - - - - - - - - - - - - - - - - - - - - - - - - - -

CORRELATION MATRIX OF PARAMETER ESTIMATES

PARAMETER                                         PARAMETER

                   1          2

  1          1.00000
  2          -.91014    1.00000
```

Figure 29.27d Plot of adjusted residuals for Example 5

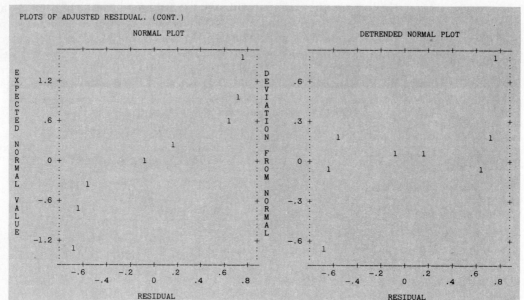

```
PLOTS OF ADJUSTED RESIDUAL. (CONT.)
                         NORMAL PLOT                                          DETRENDED NORMAL PLOT

         +----+----+----+----+----+----+----+----+--              +----+----+----+----+----+----+----+----+---
         :                                      1 :               :                                       1 :
         :                                        :               :                                         :
E        :                                        : D             :                                         :
X    1.2 +                                        + E       .6 +                                         +
P        :                                        : V             :                                         :
E        :                                      1 : I             :                                         :
C        :                                        : A             :                                         :
T        :                                        : T             :                                         :
E     .6 +                                    1   + I       .3 +                                         +
D        :                                        : O             :                                         :
         :                                        : N             :     1                                1  :
N        :                        1               :               :                                         :
O        :                                        : F             :                 1     1                 :
R      0 +                  1                     + R        0 +                                         +
M        :                                        : O             :   1                                1    :
A        :                                        : M             :                                         :
L        :      1                                 :               :                                         :
         :                                        : N             :                                         :
V    -.6 +                                        + O      -.3 +                                         +
A        :   1                                    : R             :                                         :
L        :                                        : M             :                                         :
U        :                                        : A             :                                         :
E        :                                        : L             :                                         :
    -1.2 +                                        +        -.6 +                                         +
         :  1                                     :               :  1                                      :
         :                                        :               :                                         :
         +----+----+----+----+----+----+----+----+--              +----+----+----+----+----+----+----+----+---
             -.6       -.2        .2        .6                        -.6       -.2        .2        .6
                  -.4        0         .4        .8                        -.4        0         .4        .8

                         RESIDUAL                                               RESIDUAL
```

29.28 Example 6: Multinomial Response Models

Example 6 illustrates the use of the CONTRAST subcommand and single-degree-of-freedom partitions to analyze a 4 × 6 crosstabulation table. The multinomial response models fit are generalizations of the logit model in the annotated example.

This example models the relationship between two variables— mental health status (MENTHLTH) by parental socioeconomic status (SES) (Haberman, 1979). MENTHLTH is scaled from 1 to 4 corresponding to Well and Impaired poles. SES is scaled from 1 to 6 corresponding to High and Low poles. The SPSS^X commands are

```
DATA LIST LIST/ MENTHLTH SES WT *
VARIABLE LABELS MENTHLTH 'MENTAL HEALTH CATEGORY'
           SES 'PARENTAL SE STATUS'
VALUE LABELS MENTHLTH 1 'WELL'  2 'MILD'  3 'MODERATE' 4 'IMPAIRED'/
 SES 1 'A--HIGH' 2 'B' 3 'C' 4 'D' 5 'E' 6 'F--LOW'
WEIGHT BY WT

LOGLINEAR MENTHLTH(1,4) BY SES(1,6)/
 CONTRAST(MENTHLTH) = POLYNOMIAL/
 CONTRAST(SES) = POLYNOMIAL/
 PRINT = DEFAULT ESTIM/
 /*MODEL 1:  THE MODEL OF COLUMN HOMOGENEITY
 DESIGN=MENTHLTH/
 /*MODEL 2:  THE SIMULTANEOUS LINEAR LOGIT MODEL
 DESIGN = MENTHLTH, MENTHLTH BY SES(1)/
 /*MODEL 3:  THE MODEL OF LINEAR BY LINEAR INTERACTION
 DESIGN = MENTHLTH, MENTHLTH(1) BY SES(1)/
 /*MODEL 4:  A MODEL FOR KNOWN ROW SCORES AND UNKNOWN COLUMN SCORES
 DESIGN = MENTHLTH, MENTHLTH(1) BY SES/
BEGIN DATA
1 1  64 7
1 2  57 4
1 3  57 3
1 4  72 8
1 5  36 9
1 6  21 5
    .
    .
    .
4 1  46 7
4 2  40 5
4 3  60 6
4 4  94 8
4 5  78 9
4 6  71 9
END DATA
```

- The BY keyword in the variables specification indicates a logit model.
- The CONTRAST subcommands specify polynomial contrasts for MENTHLTH and SES. The polynomial contrast is often useful in the analysis of polytomous variables.
- The PRINT subcommand requests the DEFAULT (keywords FREQ and RESID) and ESTIM display output for all models.
- In Model 1, only the dependent variable appears on the DESIGN subcommand. This model is termed the model for column homogeneity because it fits the same expected cell percentage to all frequencies of a given column. Model 1 fits three parameters associated with the MENTHLTH effect and assumes no association between MENTHLTH and SES.
- Model 2 is termed the simultaneous linear logit model. It fits three parameters for the MENTHLTH effect, plus three parameters for the MENTHLTH by linear-SES interaction. That is, each dependent-variable logit is a linear function of the parents' socioeconomic score.
- Model 3 is the model of the linear-by-linear interaction. It fits four parameters—three for MENTHLTH and one for the linear-by-linear interaction of MENTHLTH and SES. Model 3 is the most parsimonious model accounting for association between MENTHLTH and SES.
- Model 4 is a model for known row scores and unknown column scores. Scores are given for the independent variable categories, but scores for the categories of the dependent variable are unknown. "Unknown" means that no scale for the dependent variable is assumed. The model fits three parameters for the MENTHLTH effect and five for the MENTHLTH-linear by SES interaction. Model 4 stands somewhat apart from Models 2 and 3 but appears here for the sake of completeness.

Figure 29.28a shows the Model 1 fit. The goodness-of-fit statistics show lack of fit of this model.

Figure 29.28a Model 1 fit for Example 6

OBSERVED, EXPECTED FREQUENCIES AND RESIDUALS

FACTOR	CODE	OBS. COUNT & PCT.	EXP. COUNT & PCT.	RESIDUAL	STD. RESID.	ADJ. RESID.
MENTHLTH	WELL					
SES	A--HIGH	64.00 (24.43)	48.45 (18.49)	15.54578	2.23330	2.69558
SES	B	57.00 (23.27)	45.31 (18.49)	11.68976	1.73663	2.08348
SES	C	57.00 (19.86)	53.08 (18.49)	3.92229	.53837	.65570
SES	D	72.00 (18.75)	71.02 (18.49)	.98313	.11666	.14739
SES	E	36.00 (13.58)	49.01 (18.49)	-13.00904	-1.85826	-2.24532
SES	F--LOW	21.00 (9.68)	40.13 (18.49)	-19.13193	-3.02005	-3.58790
MENTHLTH	MILD					
SES	A--HIGH	94.00 (35.88)	95.01 (36.27)	-1.01446	-.10407	-.14205
SES	B	94.00 (38.37)	88.85 (36.27)	5.15060	.54643	.74134
SES	C	105.00 (36.59)	104.08 (36.27)	.91928	.09011	.12411
SES	D	141.00 (36.72)	139.26 (36.27)	1.74217	.14763	.21092
SES	E	97.00 (36.60)	96.10 (36.27)	.89759	.09156	.12511
SES	F--LOW	71.00 (32.72)	78.70 (36.27)	-7.69518	-.86745	-1.16540
MENTHLTH	MODERATE					
SES	A--HIGH	58.00 (22.14)	57.13 (21.81)	.86506	.11444	.14103
SES	B	54.00 (22.04)	53.43 (21.81)	.57229	.07829	.09590
SES	C	65.00 (22.65)	62.59 (21.81)	2.41325	.30504	.37931
SES	D	77.00 (20.05)	83.74 (21.81)	-6.73976	-.73651	-.95000
SES	E	54.00 (20.38)	57.79 (21.81)	-3.78916	-.49845	-.61490
SES	F--LOW	54.00 (24.88)	47.32 (21.81)	6.67831	.97082	1.17754
MENTHLTH	IMPAIRED					
SES	A--HIGH	46.00 (17.56)	61.40 (23.43)	-15.39639	-1.96493	-2.44697
SES	B	40.00 (16.33)	57.41 (23.43)	-17.41265	-2.29806	-2.84458
SES	C	60.00 (20.91)	67.25 (23.43)	-7.25482	-.88464	-1.11164
SES	D	94.00 (24.48)	89.99 (23.43)	4.01446	.42320	.55163
SES	E	78.00 (29.43)	62.10 (23.43)	15.90060	2.01776	2.51546
SES	F--LOW	71.00 (32.72)	50.85 (23.43)	20.14880	2.82552	3.46338

GOODNESS-OF-FIT TEST STATISTICS

LIKELIHOOD RATIO CHI SQUARE =	47.41785	DF = 15	P = .000
PEARSON CHI SQUARE =	45.98526	DF = 15	P = .000

Figure 29.28b shows the Model 2 fit. The goodness-of-fit statistics indicate good fit, and the adjusted residuals are all less than 2 in magnitude.

Figure 29.28b Model 2 fit for Example 6

OBSERVED, EXPECTED FREQUENCIES AND RESIDUALS

FACTOR	CODE	OBS. COUNT & PCT.	EXP. COUNT & PCT.	RESIDUAL	STD. RESID.	ADJ. RESID.
MENTHLTH	WELL					
SES	A--HIGH	64.00 (24.43)	68.57 (26.17)	-4.56586	-.55140	-.99816
SES	B	57.00 (23.27)	55.68 (22.73)	1.31605	.17636	.23453
SES	C	57.00 (19.86)	56.11 (19.55)	.89427	.11939	.14748
SES	D	72.00 (18.75)	63.94 (16.65)	8.05505	1.00731	1.29701
SES	E	36.00 (13.58)	37.23 (14.05)	-1.22781	-.20123	-.25999
SES	F--LOW	21.00 (9.68)	25.47 (11.74)	-4.47170	-.88602	-1.20006
MENTHLTH	MILD					
SES	A--HIGH	94.00 (35.88)	96.92 (36.99)	-2.91924	-.29653	-.54890
SES	B	94.00 (38.37)	91.00 (37.14)	2.99961	.31444	.46509
SES	C	105.00 (36.59)	106.01 (36.94)	-1.00626	-.09773	-.13682
SES	D	141.00 (36.72)	139.68 (36.38)	1.31761	.11148	.16248
SES	E	97.00 (36.60)	94.02 (35.48)	2.98135	.30747	.45845
SES	F--LOW	71.00 (32.72)	74.37 (34.27)	-3.37306	-.39113	-.65008
MENTHLTH	MODERATE					
SES	A--HIGH	58.00 (22.14)	55.70 (21.26)	2.29665	.30772	.50532
SES	B	54.00 (22.04)	53.27 (21.74)	.73020	.10005	.13271
SES	C	65.00 (22.65)	63.20 (22.02)	1.79726	.22607	.28466
SES	D	77.00 (20.05)	84.82 (22.09)	-7.82279	-.84939	-1.11765
SES	E	54.00 (20.38)	58.15 (21.94)	-4.15023	-.54425	-.73793
SES	F--LOW	54.00 (24.88)	46.85 (21.59)	7.14892	1.04443	1.59126
MENTHLTH	IMPAIRED					
SES	A--HIGH	46.00 (17.56)	40.81 (15.58)	5.18845	.81217	1.21727
SES	B	40.00 (16.33)	45.05 (18.39)	-5.04585	-.75181	-.97936
SES	C	60.00 (20.91)	61.69 (21.49)	-1.68527	-.21458	-.27109
SES	D	94.00 (24.48)	95.55 (24.88)	-1.54986	-.15855	-.21154
SES	E	78.00 (29.43)	75.60 (28.53)	2.39668	.27564	.39026
SES	F--LOW	71.00 (32.72)	70.30 (32.40)	.69585	.08299	.14211

GOODNESS-OF-FIT TEST STATISTICS

LIKELIHOOD RATIO CHI SQUARE =	6.28076	DF = 12	P = .901
PEARSON CHI SQUARE =	6.28911	DF = 12	P = .901

Figure 29.28c shows the Model 3 fit. Model 3 fits the data, and since Model 3 is simpler it is preferable to Model 2. Figure 29.28d shows the parameter estimates for Model 3.

Figure 29.28c Model 3 fit for Example 6

OBSERVED, EXPECTED FREQUENCIES AND RESIDUALS

FACTOR	CODE	OBS. COUNT & PCT.	EXP. COUNT & PCT.	RESIDUAL	STD. RESID.	ADJ. RESID.
MENTHLTH	WELL					
SES	A--HIGH	64.00 (24.43)	65.29 (24.92)	-1.29084	-.15975	-.23041
SES	B	57.00 (23.27)	54.21 (22.13)	2.78650	.37845	.48502
SES	C	57.00 (19.86)	55.91 (19.48)	1.09170	.14600	.18020
SES	D	72.00 (18.75)	65.28 (17.00)	6.72340	.83217	1.04731
SES	E	36.00 (13.58)	38.96 (14.70)	-2.96162	-.47447	-.57930
SES	F--LOW	21.00 (9.68)	27.35 (12.60)	-6.34913	-1.21407	-1.49986
MENTHLTH	MILD					
SES	A--HIGH	94.00 (35.88)	104.42 (39.86)	-10.42337	-1.02002	-1.46728
SES	B	94.00 (38.37)	94.94 (38.75)	-.93747	-.09621	-.13504
SES	C	105.00 (36.59)	107.20 (37.35)	-2.19911	-.21240	-.29671
SES	D	141.00 (36.72)	137.04 (35.69)	3.95692	.33801	.48072
SES	E	97.00 (36.60)	89.56 (33.80)	7.43852	.78601	1.06403
SES	F--LOW	71.00 (32.72)	68.84 (31.72)	2.16450	.26089	.35085
MENTHLTH	MODERATE					
SES	A--HIGH	58.00 (22.14)	50.15 (19.14)	7.85456	1.10919	1.36468
SES	B	54.00 (22.04)	49.92 (20.37)	4.08213	.57778	.70218
SES	C	65.00 (22.65)	61.72 (21.50)	3.28450	.41809	.51849
SES	D	77.00 (20.05)	86.39 (22.50)	-9.38630	-1.00989	-1.31712
SES	E	54.00 (20.38)	61.81 (23.33)	-7.81498	-.99399	-1.25212
SES	F--LOW	54.00 (24.88)	52.02 (23.97)	1.98009	.27454	.34207
MENTHLTH	IMPAIRED					
SES	A--HIGH	46.00 (17.56)	42.14 (16.08)	3.85965	.59456	.81007
SES	B	40.00 (16.33)	45.93 (18.75)	-5.93116	-.87516	-1.09956
SES	C	60.00 (20.91)	62.18 (21.66)	-2.17708	-.27610	-.34538
SES	D	94.00 (24.48)	95.29 (24.82)	-1.29402	-.13256	-.17662
SES	E	78.00 (29.43)	74.66 (28.17)	3.33807	.38632	.52919
SES	F--LOW	71.00 (32.72)	68.80 (31.70)	2.20454	.26579	.39945

GOODNESS-OF-FIT TEST STATISTICS

LIKELIHOOD RATIO CHI SQUARE =	9.89512	DF = 14	P = .770
PEARSON CHI SQUARE =	9.73185	DF = 14	P = .782

Figure 29.28d Model 3 parameter estimates for Example 6

ESTIMATES FOR PARAMETERS

MENTHLTH

PARAMETER	COEFF.	STD. ERR.	Z-VALUE	LOWER 95 CI	UPPER 95 CI
1	.0492160727	.05392	.91272	-.05647	.15490
2	-.3217618318	.05109	-6.29802	-.42190	-.22163
3	.3941588489	.04777	8.25112	.30053	.48779

MENTHLTH(1) BY SES(1)

PARAMETER	COEFF.	STD. ERR.	Z-VALUE	LOWER 95 CI	UPPER 95 CI
4	.8482955490	.14037	6.04331	.57317	1.12342

Finally, Figure 29.28e shows the Model 4 fit.

Figure 29.28e Model 4 fit for Example 6

OBSERVED, EXPECTED FREQUENCIES AND RESIDUALS

FACTOR	CODE	OBS. COUNT & PCT.	EXP. COUNT & PCT.	RESIDUAL	STD. RESID.	ADJ. RESID.
MENTHLTH	WELL					
SES	A--HIGH	64.00 (24.43)	60.15 (22.96)	3.84884	.49626	.88672
SES	B	57.00 (23.27)	57.26 (23.37)	-.25959	-.03431	-.06129
SES	C	57.00 (19.86)	56.43 (19.66)	.56502	.07521	.12846
SES	D	72.00 (18.75)	69.86 (18.19)	2.13895	.25591	.44229
SES	E	36.00 (13.58)	38.52 (14.53)	-2.51590	-.40539	-.62810
SES	F--LOW	21.00 (9.68)	24.78 (11.42)	-3.77731	-.75885	-1.09531
MENTHLTH	MILD					
SES	A--HIGH	94.00 (35.88)	102.54 (39.14)	-8.54310	-.84365	-1.23351
SES	B	94.00 (38.37)	96.31 (39.31)	-2.30594	-.23497	-.34102
SES	C	105.00 (36.59)	107.58 (37.48)	-2.57757	-.24851	-.36841
SES	D	141.00 (36.72)	140.38 (36.56)	.61849	.05220	.08046
SES	E	97.00 (36.60)	89.22 (33.67)	7.78288	.82398	1.22335
SES	F--LOW	71.00 (32.72)	65.97 (30.40)	5.02524	.61868	.91490
MENTHLTH	MODERATE					
SES	A--HIGH	58.00 (22.14)	52.46 (20.02)	5.53970	.76484	.97813
SES	B	54.00 (22.04)	48.61 (19.84)	5.39065	.77318	.98371
SES	C	65.00 (22.65)	61.54 (21.44)	3.46007	.44107	.56865
SES	D	77.00 (20.05)	84.65 (22.05)	-7.65382	-.83187	-1.11332
SES	E	54.00 (20.38)	62.02 (23.40)	-8.01806	-1.01815	-1.30212
SES	F--LOW	54.00 (24.88)	52.72 (24.29)	1.28146	.17649	.22126
MENTHLTH	IMPAIRED					
SES	A--HIGH	46.00 (17.56)	46.85 (17.88)	-.84543	-.12352	-.22973
SES	B	40.00 (16.33)	42.83 (17.48)	-2.82512	-.43171	-.79247
SES	C	60.00 (20.91)	61.45 (21.41)	-1.44752	-.18466	-.36922
SES	D	94.00 (24.48)	89.10 (23.20)	4.89638	.51871	1.11040
SES	E	78.00 (29.43)	75.25 (28.40)	2.75108	.31714	.70582
SES	F--LOW	71.00 (32.72)	73.53 (33.88)	-2.52939	-.29497	-.70107

GOODNESS-OF-FIT TEST STATISTICS

LIKELIHOOD RATIO CHI SQUARE =	6.82933	DF = 10	P =	.741
PEARSON CHI SQUARE =	6.78143	DF = 10	P =	.746

29.29 Example 7: A Distance Model

Example 7 demonstrates the use of the CWEIGHT subcommand to impose zeros on the diagonal of a symmetric table and the use of a covariate to fit a model with a distance function. Distance models are used for ordered symmetric tables. Example 7 models the relationship between husband's education level (HUSED) and wife's education level (WIFED) (Haberman, 1979). HUSED and WIFED are ordinal variables with four levels. The original table has one empty cell. There is no woman with a graduate degree whose husband has less than a high-school education. To avoid degree-of-freedom problems, this cell is set to a small number in the table.

The SPSS^X commands are

```
TITLE 'HABERMAN''S DISTANCE MODEL, PAGE 500'
DATA LIST  LIST/ HUSED WIFED WT *
VARIABLE LABELS  HUSED 'HUSBAND''S EDUCATION'
                 WIFED 'WIFE''S EDUCATION'
VALUE LABELS  HUSED WIFED 1 '< HS' 2 'HS OR JC'
  3 'COLLEGE' 4 'GRAD DEG'
WEIGHT  BY WT
COMPUTE  DISTANCE=ABS(HUSED - WIFED)
COMPUTE  CWT=1
IF (HUSED EQ WIFED) CWT=0

LOGLINEAR  HUSED WIFED(1,4) WITH DISTANCE/
  CWEIGHT=CWT/PRINT DEF ESTIM/
  DESIGN=HUSED WIFED DISTANCE
BEGIN DATA
1 1 259
1 2 123
1 3   2
1 4   0.1
2 1  82
2 2 370
2 3  30
2 4   7
3 1   5
3 2  59
3 3  34
3 4   4
4 1   2
4 2  41
4 3  29
4 4   8
END DATA
FINISH
```

- The DATA LIST command defines HUSED, WIFED, and WT, which is the frequency count for each cell.
- The WEIGHT command weights the table to the original sample size.
- The first COMPUTE command computes the distance function, which is the absolute distance between husband's and wife's education.
- The second COMPUTE and the IF command create the variable CWT. CWT is set to 0 for the cases in the diagonal cells of the table and to 1 for all other cases.
- The variables specification on the LOGLINEAR command defines a general log-linear model with the distance function as a covariate.
- The CWEIGHT subcommand specifies the variable CWT, which imposes zeros on the diagonal.
- The DESIGN subcommand names the main effects and the covariate. Note that it is not a saturated model.

Figure 29.29 contains the fit and parameter estimates for the model.

Figure 29.29 Display for Example 7

```
OBSERVED, EXPECTED FREQUENCIES AND RESIDUALS

     FACTOR          CODE              OBS. COUNT & PCT.   EXP. COUNT & PCT.      RESIDUAL   STD. RESID.   ADJ. RESID.

HUSED               < HS
 WIFED              < HS                  0.0  (  0.0 )       0.0  (  0.0 )     0.0          0.0           0.0
 WIFED              HS OR JC            123.00 ( 32.02)     121.97 ( 31.76)     1.02551       .09286        .75726
 WIFED              COLLEGE               2.00 (   .52)       2.71 (   .70)     -.70541      -.42887       -.53750
 WIFED              GRAD DEG               .10 (   .03)        .42 (   .11)     -.32010      -.49387       -.51832

HUSED               HS OR JC
 WIFED              < HS                 82.00 ( 21.35)      83.03 ( 21.62)    -1.02551      -.11255       -.75726
 WIFED              HS OR JC              0.0  (  0.0 )       0.0  (  0.0 )     0.0          0.0           0.0
 WIFED              COLLEGE              30.00 (  7.81)      31.14 (  8.11)    -1.13912      -.20413       -.60675
 WIFED              GRAD DEG              7.00 (  1.82)       4.84 (  1.26)     2.16464       .98440       1.46483

HUSED               COLLEGE
 WIFED              < HS                  5.00 (  1.30)       3.47 (   .90)     1.52947       .82100       1.08181
 WIFED              HS OR JC             59.00 ( 15.36)      58.68 ( 15.28)      .31507       .04113        .15945
 WIFED              COLLEGE               0.0  (  0.0 )       0.0  (  0.0 )     0.0          0.0           0.0
 WIFED              GRAD DEG              4.00 (  1.04)       5.84 (  1.52)    -1.84453      -.76298      -1.25934

HUSED               GRAD DEG
 WIFED              < HS                  2.00 (   .52)       2.50 (   .65)     -.50395      -.31848       -.38627
 WIFED              HS OR JC             41.00 ( 10.67)      42.34 ( 11.02)    -1.34058      -.20602       -.70578
 WIFED              COLLEGE              29.00 (  7.55)      27.16 (  7.07)     1.84453       .35396       1.25934
 WIFED              GRAD DEG              0.0  (  0.0 )       0.0  (  0.0 )     0.0          0.0           0.0
- - - - - - - - - - - - - - - - - - - - - - - - - - - - - - - - - - - - - - - - - - - - - - - - - - - - - - - - - -

GOODNESS-OF-FIT TEST STATISTICS

   LIKELIHOOD RATIO CHI SQUARE =     2.99300    DF = 4  P =   .559
             PEARSON CHI SQUARE =    2.98686    DF = 4  P =   .560

- - - - - - - - - - - - - - - - - - - - - - - - - - - - - - - - - - - - - - - - - - - - - - - - - - - - - - - - - -

ESTIMATES FOR PARAMETERS

HUSED

 PARAMETER          COEFF.          STD. ERR.        Z-VALUE      LOWER 95 CI      UPPER 95 CI

         1     -.1633790844           .12325        -1.32561          -.40495           .07819
         2      .5976368139           .16018         3.73106           .28369           .91159
         3     -.8950079354           .12962        -6.90487         -1.14906          -.64095

WIFED

 PARAMETER          COEFF.          STD. ERR.        Z-VALUE      LOWER 95 CI      UPPER 95 CI

         4      .2489999000           .15437         1.61301          -.05356           .55156
         5     1.3946797275           .14979         9.31103          1.10110          1.68826
         6     -.7316830779           .15862        -4.61287         -1.04257          -.42079

DISTANCE

 PARAMETER          COEFF.          STD. ERR.        Z-VALUE      LOWER 95 CI      UPPER 95 CI

         7    -1.6821952195           .20332        -8.27375         -2.08070         -1.28369
```

30

SCATTERGRAM varname [($\left\{\begin{matrix}\text{LOWEST, HIGHEST}\\ \text{min, max}\end{matrix}\right\}$)] [varname . . .]

[varlist] [WITH varlist . . .] [/varlist . . .]

OPTIONS:
1 Include missing values.
2 Exclude missing values listwise.
3 Suppress variable labels.
4 Suppress grid lines.
5 Diagonal grid lines.
6 Two-tailed test of significance.
7 Automatic integer scaling.
8 Random sampling.

STATISTICS:
1 Pearson's *r*.
2 r^2.
3 Significance of *r*.
4 Standard error of the estimate.
5 Y intercept.
6 Slope.

OVERVIEW, **30.1**
OPERATION, **30.2**
Specifying the Design, **30.3**
Default Scatterplot, **30.4**
Scaling, **30.5**
Setting Bounds, **30.6**
Integer Scaling, **30.7**
Optional Statistics, **30.8**
Missing Values, **30.9**
Formatting Options, **30.10**
Random Sampling, **30.11**
LIMITATIONS, **30.12**

Chapter 30 SCATTERGRAM

SCATTERGRAM prints bivariate plots in which one variable defines the vertical axis and the other defines the horizontal axis, and each point represents the values for one case on the two variables. Optionally, the procedure prints statistics associated with the simple regression of one variable upon the other. The scatterplots produced by SCATTERGRAM are printer plots, while the LINECHART procedure produces scatterplots for graphics devices (see Chapter 24).

30.1 OVERVIEW

SCATTERGRAM produces one scatterplot for each pair of variables specified on one or more variable lists. Only a variable list is required, but you can also control scaling of the axes, obtain regression statistics, alter the handling of missing values and the printing of grid lines, and take a random sample when your file contains too many cases for a plot.

Scaling. By default, SCATTERGRAM uses the minimum and maximum observed values for the variables to scale the scatterplot. It then divides the ranges into regular intervals to print labels along the axes. You can specify upper and lower bounds for the variables being plotted or you can specify integer scaling. (See Section 30.5.)

Regression Statistics. Statistics for simple linear regression are available via the STATISTICS command. These statistics include Pearson's r, r^2, significance of r, standard error of estimate, Y intercept, and the slope of the regression line. A two-tailed test of significance is also available. (See Section 30.8.)

Missing Values. By default, SCATTERGRAM deletes cases with missing values on a plot-by-plot basis. You can request that missing values be included or that cases with missing values be deleted listwise. (See Section 30.9.)

Formatting Options. By default, SCATTERGRAM overlays vertical and horizontal grid lines on the scatterplot. You can suppress the grid lines or use diagonal grid lines. (See Section 30.10.)

Random Sampling. To build scatterplots, SCATTERGRAM must store cases in memory. You can request a random sample of cases when there is not enough space to store all the cases. (See Section 30.11.)

30.2 OPERATION

The SCATTERGRAM procedure operates via the SCATTERGRAM command and optional STATISTICS and OPTIONS commands. The SCATTERGRAM procedure has no subcommands.

30.3 Specifying the Design

To obtain one scatterplot for each variable with every other variable in the list, specify a simple variable list, as in:

```
SCATTERGRAM NTCPRI NTCSAL
```

This example produces the scatterplot shown in Figure 30.3. The first variable in a pair is always on the Y axis, and the second variable is always on the X axis. You can name up to 100 variables on a SCATTERGRAM command. One scatterplot is produced for each pair of variables implied by the list. The scatterplots are produced in the following order: the first variable named is plotted against the remaining variables; then the second variable named is plotted against the remaining variables, and so on. For example

```
SCATTERGRAM NTCPRI NTCSAL TEACHER MANAGER
```

plots NTCPRI with NTCSAL, NTCPRI with TEACHER, NTCPRI with MANAGER, NTCSAL with TEACHER, NTCSAL with MANAGER, and TEACHER with MANAGER, in that order.

Figure 30.3 A default scatterplot

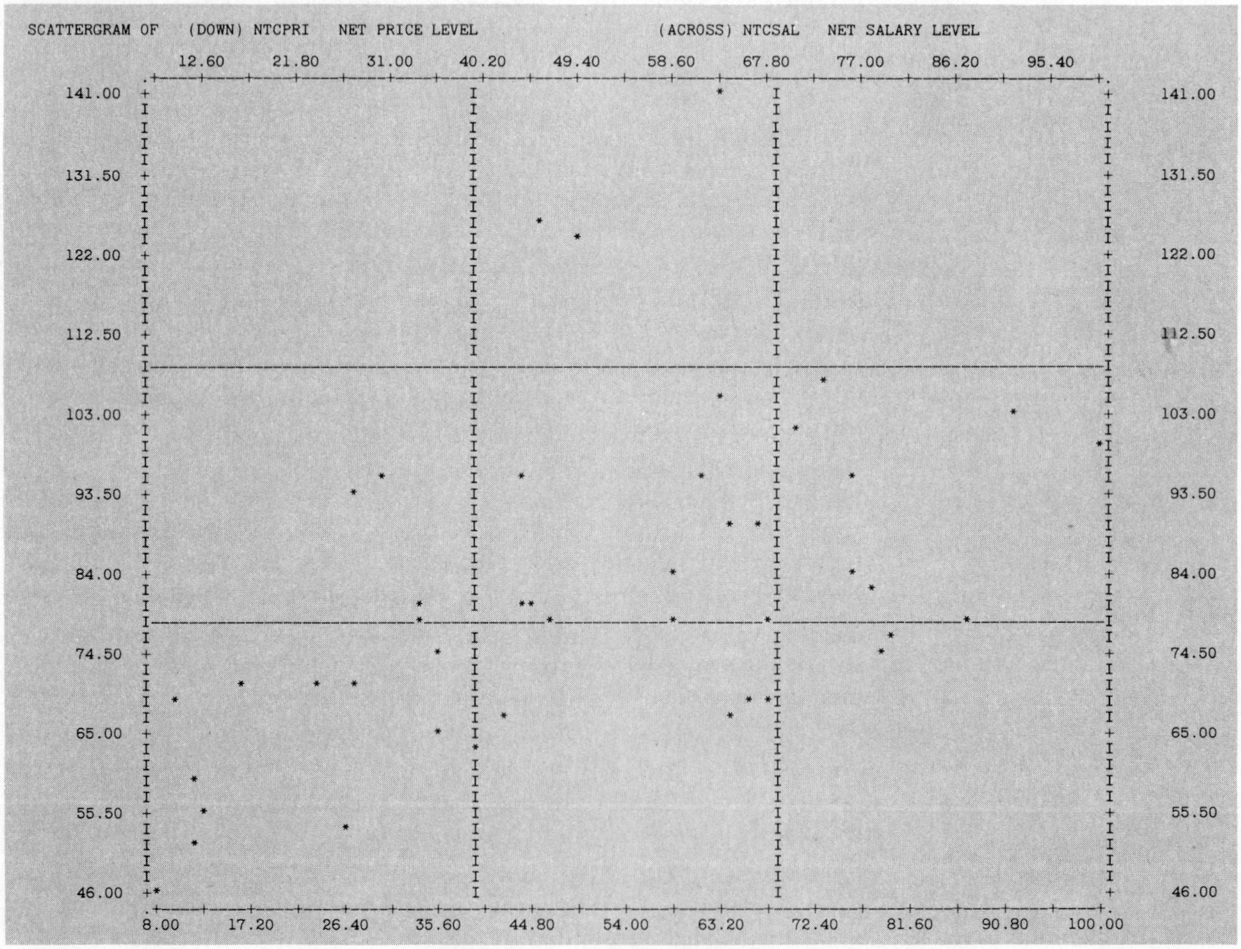

The specifications for the variable lists follow the usual SPSS^X conventions (see Chapter 2). You can use the keyword TO to name a set of adjacent variables in the file, as in:

```
SCATTERGRAM NTCPRI NTCSAL MANAGER TO FTEX
```

This list names the variables NTCPRI, NTCSAL, and all the variables between and including MANAGER and FTEX.

Use the keyword WITH to request scatterplots of one set of variables with another set. All variables to the left of the keyword are plotted with all variables to the right of the keyword. For example,

```
SCATTERGRAM  NTCPRI NTCSAL WITH MANAGER ENGINEER
```

plots NTCPRI with MANAGER and ENGINEER, and NTCSAL with MANAGER and ENGINEER. NTCPRI is not plotted with NTCSAL and MANAGER is not plotted with ENGINEER.

Use a slash to separate variable lists on one SCATTERGRAM command. For example,

```
SCATTERGRAM  NTCPRI WITH NTCSAL/FOOD TO RENT
```

contains two variable lists. You can request up to 25 sets of scatterplots (24 slashes) in one SCATTERGRAM command. Regardless of the number of lists, the total number of variables cannot exceed 100.

30.4 Default Scatterplot

The scatterplot has 51 vertical units and 101 horizontal units. Each scatterplot prints on one page, requires 55 lines per page, and is unaffected by the PAGESIZE subcommand on the SET command (see Chapter 4). Values along the axes are scaled to the minimum and maximum observed values for each variable unless you specify the upper and lower bounds or use integer scaling (see Sections 30.6 and 30.7). Along the vertical axis, hash marks and their corresponding numerical values occur at units 1, 6, 11, 16, . . . 46, and 51. These are printed both on the left and right sides of the graph. Along the horizontal axis, hash marks are placed at every fifth location. Units 1, 11, 21, . . . 91, and 101 have numeric labels along the bottom edge of the graph, and units 6, 16, 26, . . . 86, and 96 have labels along the top. Decimal places for these values are controlled by the print formats for the variables being plotted.

Two vertical and two horizontal lines divide each axis into three sections, dividing the graph into nine nearly equal rectangles. These lines are drawn through the 35th and 67th horizontal units and through the 18th and 34th vertical units.

An asterisk represents the data point when a single case falls into a printing position. If two through eight cases fall into the same position, the actual number of cases is printed. Nine or more cases are represented by the number 9. Since each printing position represents a small rectangle of territory, points that are not identical but very similar may be included in the same position.

30.5 Scaling

Three scaling methods are available. By default, SCATTERGRAM uses the observed minimum and maximum values for each variable to set the upper and lower endpoints of the scale. You can set the scale by specifying the upper and lower bounds for each variable to be plotted. If you specify integer scaling, SCATTERGRAM automatically chooses upper and lower bounds equal to or more generous than the observed minimum and maximum values.

30.6 Setting Bounds

To set upper and lower bounds of a scale, specify first the lowest value and then the highest value in parentheses following the variable name. Cases are excluded from the scatterplot if they fall outside the specified range. If

ANNOTATED EXAMPLE FOR SCATTERGRAM

The example illustrating SCATTERGRAM produces a scatterplot using a 500-case sample from the 1980 General Social Survey. The variables are

- PRESTIGE—the respondent's occupational prestige scale score.
- SPPRES—the spouse's occupational prestige scale score.

In this example we plot the data points for the respondent's occupational prestige scale score with the spouse's occupational prestige scale score. The $SPSS^X$ commands are

```
FILE HANDLE  GSS80/ file specifications
GET  FILE=GSS80/KEEP PRESTIGE SPPRES
SCATTERGRAM  PRESTIGE SPPRES
OPTIONS  4 7
STATISTICS  ALL
```

- The FILE HANDLE identifies the GSS80 data file and gives the operating-system specifications (see Chapter 3).
- The GET command defines the data to $SPSS^X$ and selects the variables needed for the analysis (see Chapter 5).
- The SCATTERGRAM command requests a scatterplot with PRESTIGE plotted on the vertical axis and SPPRES plotted on the horizontal axis. Since no missing-value options are requested, cases with missing values on either variable are not used.
- The STATISTICS command requests all the optional statistics (see Section 30.8).
- Option 4 suppresses grid lines on the scatterplot (see Section 30.10).
- Option 7 produces integer scaling (see Section 30.7). Note the integer labels on the X and Y axes.

A plot with integer scaling

SCATTERGRAM OF (DOWN) PRESTIGE RESP'S OCCUPATIONAL PRESTIGE SCO (ACROSS) SPPRES SPOUSE'S OCCUPATIONAL PRESTIGE S

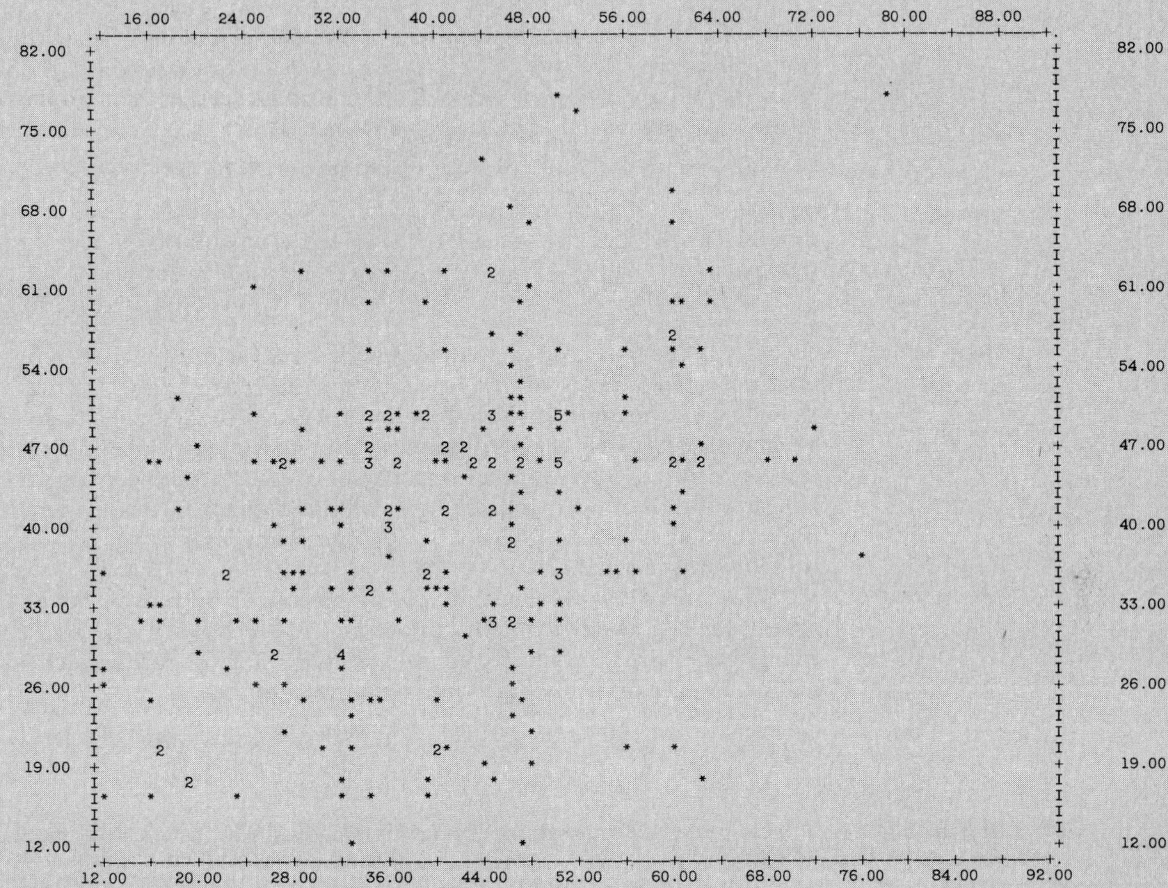

STATISTICS..

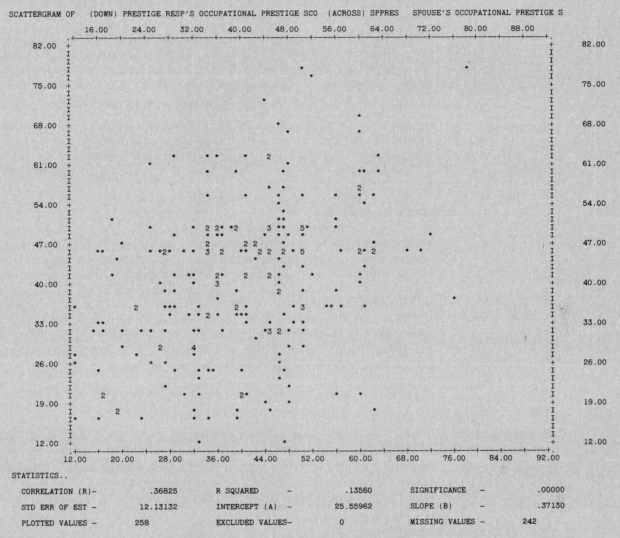

CORRELATION (R)-	.36825	R SQUARED -	.13560	SIGNIFICANCE -	.00000
STD ERR OF EST -	12.13132	INTERCEPT (A) -	25.55962	SLOPE (B) -	.37130
PLOTTED VALUES -	258	EXCLUDED VALUES-	0	MISSING VALUES -	242

'********' IS PRINTED IF A COEFFICIENT CANNOT BE COMPUTED.

the range is more generous than the observed values, some areas on the perimeter of the scatterplot will be empty. For example,

```
SCATTERGRAM  NTCPRI(50,150) WITH NTCSAL
```

plots only those cases whose values for variable NTCPRI fall within the range 50 through 150. Use the keywords LOWEST (or LO) and HIGHEST (or HI) to bound a variable on one end only. A range specification applies only to the *preceding* variable in the variable list. Thus,

```
SCATTERGRAM    PRESTIGE SPPRES (25,HIGHEST) WITH PAPRES16
```

bounds only SPPRES and not PRESTIGE. Cases excluded from a scatterplot by a range specification are not used in the calculation of any statistics requested.

30.7 Integer Scaling

By default, the observed or bounded range for a variable is divided by 10 to obtain vertical labels or by 20 to obtain horizontal labels. Thus, even though your variables may have only integer values, if the range is not evenly divisible the scatterplot may have noninteger labels. To ensure integer labels, specify Option 7 on an associated OPTIONS command. If the lowest value is not an integer, it is rounded down to an integer. If the highest value is not an integer that produces integer scaling, it is rounded up to an integer that does.

You cannot use Option 7 if you set the upper and lower bounds of a scale. However, you can name upper and lower bounds and also obtain integer labeling if you specify an integer divisible by 10 for the vertical axis and an integer divisible by 20 for the horizontal axis.

OPTION 7 *Automatic integer scaling.* Produces integer scatterplot labels.

30.8 Optional Statistics

You can request some simple linear regression statistics with the associated STATISTICS command. Statistics are calculated on cases plotted within the scatterplot. If you specify a range that excludes cases, the excluded cases are *not* used in the calculation of the regression statistics. The following statistics are available for SCATTERGRAM:

STATISTIC 1 *Pearson's r.*
STATISTIC 2 r^2.
STATISTIC 3 *Significance of r.*
STATISTIC 4 *Standard error of the estimate.*
STATISTIC 5 *Intercept with the vertical axis.*
STATISTIC 6 *Slope.*

To request all available statistics, specify:

```
SCATTERGRAM  NTCPRI NTCSAL
STATISTICS  ALL
```

Figure 30.8 shows these statistics, which are associated with the scatterplot in Figure 30.3.

Figure 30.8 Statistics available with SCATTERGRAM

```
STATISTICS..
  CORRELATION (R)-        .48245      R SQUARED        -        .23276      SIGNIFICANCE    -        .00046
  STD ERR OF EST -      17.52468      INTERCEPT (A)    -      62.39233      SLOPE (B)       -        .39266
  PLOTTED VALUES -      44            EXCLUDED VALUES-         0            MISSING VALUES  -       1

            '********' IS PRINTED IF A COEFFICIENT CANNOT BE COMPUTED.
```

By default, the test of the significance of *r* is a one-tailed test. To obtain the two-tailed test, specify Option 6 on the associated OPTIONS command.

OPTION 6 *Two-tailed test of significance for Statistic 3.*

30.9 Missing Values

By default SCATTERGRAM deletes cases with missing values on a plot-by-plot basis. If a case is missing on either variable for a given scatterplot, it is not used. Two optional ways of handling missing values are available via the associated OPTIONS command.

OPTION 1 *Include missing values.* User-defined missing values are included in both the scatterplot and statistics.

OPTION 2 *Exclude missing values listwise.* If a case is missing on any variable named within one variable list, it is excluded from all the scatterplots implied by that list. If you use the slash to specify multiple lists, a case missing for one list may be nonmissing in another.

30.10 Formatting Options

By default, SCATTERGRAM prints variable labels on the banner above the scatterplot and prints a grid that divides the scatterplot into nine rectangles. Use Option 3 to suppress the printing of variable labels. To suppress grid lines, use Option 4. You can produce diagonal grid lines with Option 5. There will be two diagonal lines that divide the scatterplot into four equal-sized triangles. If you specify both Option 4 and 5, diagonal grid lines are used.

OPTION 3 *Suppress variable labels.*

OPTION 4 *Suppress grid lines.*

OPTION 5 *Use diagonal grid lines.*

30.11 Random Sampling

SCATTERGRAM must store cases in memory to build scatterplots. You may not have sufficient computer resources to store all the cases required to produce the scatterplots requested. Option 8 selects a random sample of cases when there is not enough space to store all the cases. It samples the maximum number of cases that can be stored within the available space.

OPTION 8 *Random sampling.* Randomly sample cases, maximizing the sample for the available space.

30.12 LIMITATIONS

The following limitations apply to SCATTERGRAM:

- A maximum of 100 variables total per SCATTERGRAM command.
- A maximum of 25 different variable lists.

PEARSON CORR varlist [WITH varlist] [/varlist . . .]

OPTIONS:
1 Include missing values.
2 Exclude missing values listwise.
3 Two-tailed test of significance.
4 Write matrix materials to a file.
5 Suppress printing of *n* and significance level.
6 Print only nonredundant coefficients in serial string format.

STATISTICS:
1 Univariate mean, standard deviation, and *n*.
2 Cross-product deviations and covariance.

OVERVIEW, **31.1**
OPERATION, **31.2**
Specifying the Design, **31.3**
Two-Tailed Significance Levels, **31.4**
Optional Statistics, **31.5**
Missing Values, **31.6**
Formatting Options, **31.7**
Writing Matrix Materials, **31.8**
LIMITATIONS, **31.9**

Chapter 31 PEARSON CORR

Procedure PEARSON CORR produces Pearson product-moment correlations with significance levels and, optionally, univariate statistics, covariances and cross-product deviations. Other procedures that also produce correlation matrices are PARTIAL CORR (Chapter 32), REGRESSION (Chapter 33), DISCRIMINANT (Chapter 34), and FACTOR (Chapter 35).

31.1 OVERVIEW

PEARSON CORR produces one or more matrices of correlation coefficients. For each coefficient, PEARSON CORR prints the number of cases used and the significance level. In addition to the correlation matrix, you can specify optional statistics, formats, and methods of handling missing data. PEARSON CORR also writes matrix materials which can be used by other procedures.

Types of Matrices. You can specify one or more correlation matrices with one PEARSON CORR command. A simple variable list produces a square matrix. You can also request a rectangular matrix of correlations between specific pairs of variables or between lists of variables. (See Section 31.3.)

Significance Levels. By default, the significance level for each coefficient is based on a one-tailed test. Optionally you can request that the significance level be calculated using a two-tailed test. (See Section 31.4.)

Optional Statistics. In addition to the correlation coefficient, number of cases, and significance level, you can obtain the mean, standard deviation, and number of nonmissing cases for each variable and the cross-product deviations and covariance for each pair of variables. (See Section 31.5.)

Missing Values. By default, PEARSON CORR excludes cases with missing values on an analysis-by-analysis basis. Optionally, you can request that missing values be handled as if they were valid or that cases with missing values be deleted listwise. (See Section 31.6.)

Formatting Options. You can print more rows and columns of coefficients than the default format allows and suppress the number of cases and significance level for each coefficient. You can also print only the nonredundant coefficients. (See Section 31.7.)

Matrix Output. PEARSON CORR writes out a square matrix of correlation coefficients and the number of cases used to compute each coefficient. These materials can be read by other SPSS^X procedures. (See Section 31.8.)

31.2 OPERATION

PEARSON CORR operates via a list of variables and associated OPTIONS and STATISTICS commands. You can specify several lists of variables separated by slashes and you can use the keyword WITH to obtain the correlations of one set of variables with another set.

31.3 Specifying the Design

PEARSON CORR prints either a square (symmetric) or rectangular (asymmetric) matrix, depending on how you specify the variable list. Both forms of the specification permit the use of the keyword TO to reference consecutive variables. If you provide a simple list of variables, PEARSON CORR prints the correlations of each variable with every other variable in the list in a square or lower-triangular matrix. For example, the command

```
PEARSON CORR FOOD RENT PUBTRANS TEACHER COOK ENGINEER
```

produces the square matrix in Figure 31.3a. The correlation of a variable with itself is always 1.0000 and can be found on the diagonal of the matrix. Each pair of variables appears twice in the matrix (e.g., FOOD with RENT and RENT with FOOD). Since the correlation coefficient is a symmetrical measure, these two values are identical, and the upper and lower triangles of the matrix are mirror images of each other. Use this form of the PEARSON CORR specification when you want to write the correlation matrix for use with another procedure or program (see Section 31.8).

Figure 31.3a Default matrix from a simple variable list

```
- - - - - - - - - - - - P E A R S O N   C O R R E L A T I O N   C O E F F I C I E N T S - - - - - - - - - - - -

             FOOD         RENT         PUBTRANS     TEACHER      COOK         ENGINEER

FOOD         1.0000       0.2598       0.5798       0.5469       0.3945       0.4823
            (    0)      (   45)      (   45)      (   44)      (   44)      (   44)
            P=*****      P=0.042      P=0.000      P=0.000      P=0.004      P=0.000

RENT         0.2598       1.0000      -0.0111      -0.0249       0.1440       0.2528
            (   45)      (    0)      (   45)      (   44)      (   44)      (   44)
            P=0.042      P=*****      P=0.471      P=0.436      P=0.175      P=0.049

PUBTRANS     0.5798      -0.0111       1.0000       0.6858       0.6058       0.6358
            (   45)      (   45)      (    0)      (   44)      (   44)      (   44)
            P=0.000      P=0.471      P=*****      P=0.000      P=0.000      P=0.000

TEACHER      0.5469      -0.0249       0.6858       1.0000       0.6215       0.6573
            (   44)      (   44)      (   44)      (    0)      (   43)      (   43)
            P=0.000      P=0.436      P=0.000      P=*****      P=0.000      P=0.000

COOK         0.3945       0.1440       0.6058       0.6215       1.0000       0.7502
            (   44)      (   44)      (   44)      (   43)      (    0)      (   44)
            P=0.004      P=0.175      P=0.000      P=0.000      P=*****      P=0.000

ENGINEER     0.4823       0.2528       0.6358       0.6573       0.7502       1.0000
            (   44)      (   44)      (   44)      (   43)      (   44)      (    0)
            P=0.000      P=0.049      P=0.000      P=0.000      P=0.000      P=*****

(COEFFICIENT / (CASES) / SIGNIFICANCE)      (A VALUE OF 99.0000 IS PRINTED IF A COEFFICIENT CANNOT BE COMPUTED)
```

To obtain the rectangular matrix, specify two variable lists separated by the keyword WITH. SPSS^X then prints a rectangular matrix of variables in the first list correlated with variables in the second list. For example,

```
PEARSON CORR MECHANIC BUS WITH PUBTRANS
```

produces two correlations, MECHANIC with PUBTRANS and BUS with PUBTRANS, while

```
PEARSON CORR FOOD RENT WITH COOK TEACHER MANAGER ENGINEER
```

produces the eight correlations shown in Figure 31.3b. The variables listed before the keyword WITH define the rows of the matrix and those listed after the keyword WITH define the columns. Unless a variable is in both lists, there are no identity coefficients or redundant coefficients in the matrix. If you want to write the correlation matrix for use with another procedure or program, do not use the keyword WITH (see Section 31.8).

Figure 31.3b Default matrix from a variable list using WITH

```
- - - - - - - - - - - - P E A R S O N   C O R R E L A T I O N   C O E F F I C I E N T S - - - - - - - - - - - -

              COOK       TEACHER     MANAGER     ENGINEER

FOOD          0.3945      0.5469      0.5304      0.4823
             (   44)     (   44)     (   44)     (   44)
             P=0.004     P=0.000     P=0.000     P=0.000

RENT          0.1440     -0.0249      0.2069      0.2528
             (   44)     (   44)     (   44)     (   44)
             P=0.175     P=0.436     P=0.089     P=0.049

(COEFFICIENT / (CASES) / SIGNIFICANCE)      (A VALUE OF 99.0000 IS PRINTED IF A COEFFICIENT CANNOT BE COMPUTED)
```

You can request more than one matrix on a PEARSON CORR command. Use a slash (/) to separate the specifications for each of the requested matrices. For example,

```
PEARSON CORR  FOOD RENT WITH COOK TEACHER MANAGER ENGINEER/
   FOOD TO ENGINEER/ PUBTRANS WITH MECHANIC
```

produces three separate correlation matrices. The first matrix contains eight nonredundant coefficients, the second matrix is a square matrix of all the variables from FOOD to ENGINEER, and the third matrix consists of one coefficient for PUBTRANS and MECHANIC.

You can specify up to 40 variable lists with one PEARSON CORR command and can name or imply up to 500 variables total. A maximum of 250 individual elements may appear. Each unique occurrence of a variable name, keyword, or special delimiter counts as 1 toward this total. Variables implied by the TO convention do not count toward this total.

A key below each matrix indicates what information is contained in the matrix. The following line

```
COEFFICIENT / (CASES) / SIGNIFICANCE
```

appears in the default matrix formats in Figures 31.3a and 31.3b and indicates that each entry in the matrix contains these three pieces of information in the order indicated and that the number of cases is enclosed in parentheses. When other formats are chosen the key is adjusted accordingly (see Section 31.7).

If all cases have a missing value for a given pair of variables or if they all have the same value for a variable, the coefficient cannot be computed. Since Pearson correlations always have a value in the range −1.00 to 1.00, the value 99.0000 calls attention to those that cannot be calculated.

31.4 Two-Tailed Significance Levels

By default, the significance level printed below the correlation coefficient is based on a one-tailed test. This test is appropriate when the direction of the relationship between a pair of variables can be specified in advance of the analysis. When the direction of the relationship cannot be determined in advance, as is often the case in exploratory data analysis, a two-tailed test is appropriate. To override the default and request that the significance level be calculated using the two-tailed test, use Option 3.

OPTION 3 *Two-tailed test of significance.*

31.5 Optional Statistics

The correlation coefficient, number of cases, and significance level are automatically printed for every combination of variable pairs in the variable list. You can obtain additional statistics with the associated STATISTICS command, as in:

```
PEARSON CORR  FOOD RENT PUBTRANS TEACHER COOK ENGINEER
STATISTICS  1, 2
```

ANNOTATED EXAMPLE FOR PEARSON CORR

This example analyzes 1979 prices and earnings in 45 cities around the world, compiled by the Union Bank of Switzerland. The variables are

- FOOD—the average net cost of 39 different food and beverage items in the city, expressed as a percentage above or below that of Zurich, where Zurich equals 100%.
- RENT—the average gross monthly rent in the city, expressed as a percentage above or below that of Zurich, where Zurich equals 100%.
- SERVICE—the average cost of 28 different goods and services in the city, expressed as a percentage above or below that of Zurich, where Zurich equals 100%.
- PUBTRANS—the average cost of a three-mile taxi ride within city limits, expressed as a percentage above or below that of Zurich, where Zurich equals 100%.
- TEACHER, COOK, ENGINEER, MECHANIC, BUS—the average gross annual earnings of primary-grade teachers in public schools, cooks, electrical engineers, automobile mechanics, and municipal bus drivers, working from 5 to 10 years in their respective occupations. Each of these variables is expressed as a percentage above or below those of Zurich, where Zurich equals 100%.

In this example, we determine the degree to which variation in the costs of goods and services in a city is related to variation in earnings in several occupations. We use PEARSON CORR to compute correlations between the average costs of various goods and services and the average gross earnings in five different occupations. The SPSS^X commands are

```
FILE HANDLE  CITY/ file specifications
GET  FILE=CITY
PEARSON CORR  FOOD RENT PUBTRANS TEACHER COOK ENGINEER/
   SERVICE PUBTRANS WITH MECHANIC BUS
STATISTICS  1, 2
OPTIONS  6
FINISH
```

- The FILE HANDLE identifies the CITY data file and gives the operating-system specifications (see Chapter 3).
- The GET command defines the data to SPSS^X and selects the variables needed for analysis (see Chapter 5).
- The PEARSON CORR command requests two correlation matrices. The first variable list produces correlation coefficients for each variable with every other variable. However, the redundant coefficients will be suppressed with Option 6. The second variable list produces four coefficients, pairing SERVICE with MECHANIC and BUS, and PUBTRANS with MECHANIC and BUS (see Section 31.3 and Figure B).
- The STATISTICS command requests the mean, standard deviation, and number of nonmissing cases for each variable, and the cross-product deviations and covariance for each pair of variables. The statistics for all the variable lists preceed all the correlation matrices (see Section 31.5 and Figure A).
- Option 6 suppresses redundant coefficients in both correlation matrices (see Section 31.7).

A Pearson correlation statistics

VARIABLE	CASES	MEAN	STD DEV
FOOD	45	70.4667	18.7442
RENT	45	120.0889	94.2250
PUBTRANS	45	48.1111	24.8141
TEACHER	44	38.3182	25.1819
COOK	44	64.6591	30.2785
ENGINEER	44	60.0455	26.1747
SERVICE	45	73.0889	19.0070
MECHANIC	44	50.7045	30.7462
BUS	43	42.9535	27.3652

VARIABLES		CASES	CROSS-PROD DEV	VARIANCE-COVAR	VARIABLES		CASES	CROSS-PROD DEV	VARIANCE-COVAR
FOOD	RENT	45	20191.1333	458.8894	FOOD	PUBTRANS	45	11865.6667	269.6742
FOOD	TEACHER	44	11227.9545	261.1152	FOOD	COOK	44	9561.0000	222.3488
FOOD	ENGINEER	44	10103.0000	234.9535	RENT	PUBTRANS	45	-1139.4444	-25.8965
RENT	TEACHER	44	-2566.6364	-59.6892	RENT	COOK	44	17747.2500	412.7267
RENT	ENGINEER	44	26927.5000	626.2209	PUBTRANS	TEACHER	44	18637.7727	433.4366
PUBTRANS	COOK	44	19434.2727	451.9598	PUBTRANS	ENGINEER	44	17630.3636	410.0085
TEACHER	COOK	43	20326.3023	483.9596	TEACHER	ENGINEER	43	18627.4884	443.5116
COOK	ENGINEER	44	25566.6818	594.5740					

VARIABLES		CASES	CROSS-PROD DEV	VARIANCE-COVAR	VARIABLES		CASES	CROSS-PROD DEV	VARIANCE-COVAR
SERVICE	MECHANIC	44	12034.8636	279.8805	SERVICE	BUS	43	12806.0233	304.9053
PUBTRANS	MECHANIC	44	23897.6364	555.7590	PUBTRANS	BUS	43	21561.6744	513.3732

B Pearson correlation matrices

```
- - - - - - - - - - - - - - P E A R S O N   C O R R E L A T I O N   C O E F F I C I E N T S - - - - - - - - - - - - - -
VARIABLE           VARIABLE           VARIABLE           VARIABLE           VARIABLE           VARIABLE
PAIR               PAIR               PAIR               PAIR               PAIR               PAIR
--------           --------           --------           --------           --------           --------

FOOD      .2598    FOOD      .5798    FOOD      .5469    FOOD      .3945    FOOD      .4823    RENT     -.0111
WITH    N(  45)    WITH    N(  45)    WITH    N(  44)    WITH    N(  44)    WITH    N(  44)    WITH    N(  45)
RENT    SIG .042   PUBTRANS SIG .000  TEACHER  SIG .000  COOK     SIG .004  ENGINEER SIG .000  PUBTRANS SIG .471

RENT     -.0249    RENT      .1440    RENT      .2528    PUBTRANS  .6858    PUBTRANS  .6058    PUBTRANS  .6358
WITH    N(  44)    WITH    N(  44)    WITH    N(  44)    WITH    N(  44)    WITH    N(  44)    WITH    N(  44)
TEACHER SIG .436   COOK    SIG .175   ENGINEER SIG .049  TEACHER  SIG .000  COOK     SIG .000  ENGINEER SIG .000

TEACHER   .6215    TEACHER   .6573    COOK      .7502
WITH    N(  43)    WITH    N(  43)    WITH    N(  44)
COOK    SIG .000   ENGINEER SIG .000  ENGINEER SIG .000

          A VALUE OF 99.0000 IS PRINTED IF A COEFFICIENT CANNOT BE COMPUTED.
```

```
- - - - - - - - - - - - - - P E A R S O N   C O R R E L A T I O N   C O E F F I C I E N T S - - - - - - - - - - - - - -
VARIABLE           VARIABLE           VARIABLE           VARIABLE           VARIABLE           VARIABLE
PAIR               PAIR               PAIR               PAIR               PAIR               PAIR
--------           --------           --------           --------           --------           --------

SERVICE   .4842    SERVICE   .5868    PUBTRANS  .7336    PUBTRANS  .7802
WITH    N(  44)    WITH    N(  43)    WITH    N(  44)    WITH    N(  43)
MECHANIC SIG .000  BUS     SIG .000   MECHANIC SIG .000  BUS      SIG .000

          A VALUE OF 99.0000 IS PRINTED IF A COEFFICIENT CANNOT BE COMPUTED.
```

Figure 31.5 displays these statistics.

STATISTIC 1 *Mean, standard deviation, and number of nonmissing cases for each variable.* Missing values are handled on a variable-by-variable basis regardless of the missing-value option in effect for the correlations.

STATISTIC 2 *Cross-product deviations and covariance for each pair of variables.*

Figure 31.5 Statistics available with PEARSON CORR

VARIABLE	CASES	MEAN	STD DEV
FOOD	45	70.4667	18.7442
RENT	45	120.0889	94.2250
PUBTRANS	45	48.1111	24.8141
TEACHER	44	38.3182	25.1819
COOK	44	64.6591	30.2785
ENGINEER	44	60.0455	26.1747

VARIABLES		CASES	CROSS-PROD DEV	VARIANCE-COVAR	VARIABLES		CASES	CROSS-PROD DEV	VARIANCE-COVAR
FOOD	RENT	45	20191.1333	458.8894	FOOD	PUBTRANS	45	11865.6667	269.6742
FOOD	TEACHER	44	11227.9545	261.1152	FOOD	COOK	44	9561.0000	222.3488
FOOD	ENGINEER	44	10103.0000	234.9535	RENT	PUBTRANS	45	-1139.4444	-25.8965
RENT	TEACHER	44	-2566.6364	-59.6892	RENT	COOK	44	17747.2500	412.7267
RENT	ENGINEER	44	26927.5000	626.2209	PUBTRANS	TEACHER	44	18637.7727	433.4366
PUBTRANS	COOK	44	19434.2727	451.9598	PUBTRANS	ENGINEER	44	17630.3636	410.0085
TEACHER	COOK	43	20326.3023	483.9596	TEACHER	ENGINEER	43	18627.4884	443.5116
COOK	ENGINEER	44	25566.6818	594.5740					

31.6 Missing Values

By default, PEARSON CORR deletes cases with missing values on an analysis-by-analysis basis. A case missing for one or both of the pair of variables for a specific correlation coefficient is not used for that analysis. Since each coefficient is based on all cases that have valid codes on that particular pair of variables, the maximum information available is used in every calculation. This also results in a set of coefficients based on a varying number of cases. Two missing-value options are available.

OPTION 1 *Include missing values.* User-defined missing values are included in the analysis.

OPTION 2 *Exclude missing values listwise.* Each variable list on a command is evaluated separately. Cases missing on any variable named in a list are excluded from all analyses.

31.7 Formatting Options

For the default page length of 59 lines, PEARSON CORR prints correlation coefficients in 11 rows and 10 columns and displays the number of cases and the significance level. Use Option 5 to print 43 rows and 11 columns of coefficients and to suppress the number of cases and the significance level. A single star (*) following a coefficient indicates significance at the .01 level or less. Two stars (**) following a coefficient indicate significance at the .001 level or less. The commands

```
PEARSON CORR  FOOD RENT PUBTRANS TEACHER COOK ENGINEER
OPTIONS  5
```

produce a square matrix with Option 5 in effect. See Figure 31.7a. If you use the keyword WITH in a variable list, the display will be a rectangular matrix similar to Figure 31.3b, with the number of cases suppressed and stars indicating significance levels.

Figure 31.7a Modifying the default output format with Option 5

```
------------P E A R S O N   C O R R E L A T I O N   C O E F F I C I E N T S------------

            FOOD        RENT        PUBTRANS    TEACHER     COOK        ENGINEER

FOOD        1.0000       .2598       .5798**     .5469**     .3945*      .4823**
RENT         .2598      1.0000      -.0111      -.0249       .1440       .2528
PUBTRANS     .5798**    -.0111      1.0000       .6858**     .6058**     .6358**
TEACHER      .5469**    -.0249       .6858**    1.0000       .6215**     .6573**
COOK         .3945*      .1440       .6058**     .6215**    1.0000       .7502**
ENGINEER     .4823**     .2528       .6358**     .6573**     .7502**    1.0000

* - SIGNIF. LE .01      ** - SIGNIF. LE .001        (99.0000 IS PRINTED IF A COEFFICIENT CANNOT BE COMPUTED)
```

The default output also prints redundant coefficients. Use Option 6 to print only the nonredundant coefficients. They are displayed in serial string format with the coefficients from the first row of the matrix printed first, followed by all the unique (i.e., those not already printed) coefficients from the second row and so on for all of the rows in the matrix. Six coefficients are printed across the page and each is identified with the names of the variables for which it was calculated. The number of cases and significance level are printed below the correlation just as they are in the matrix form of the output. Figure 31.7b is the output from the following example with Option 6 in effect.

```
PEARSON CORR  FOOD RENT PUBTRANS TEACHER COOK ENGINEER
OPTIONS  6
```

If you specify both Option 5 and Option 6, only Option 6 will be in effect.

OPTION 5 *Suppress the printing of the number of cases and significance level.*

OPTION 6 *Print only the nonredundant coefficients in serial string format.*

Figure 31.7b Modifying the default output format with Option 6

```
--------------P E A R S O N   C O R R E L A T I O N   C O E F F I C I E N T S-------------

VARIABLE            VARIABLE            VARIABLE            VARIABLE            VARIABLE            VARIABLE
PAIR                PAIR                PAIR                PAIR                PAIR                PAIR
--------            --------            --------            --------            --------            --------

FOOD         .2598  FOOD         .5798  FOOD         .5469  FOOD         .3945  FOOD         .4823  RENT        -.0111
WITH      N(   45)  WITH      N(   45)  WITH      N(   44)  WITH      N(   44)  WITH      N(   44)  WITH      N(   45)
RENT      SIG .042  PUBTRANS  SIG .000  TEACHER   SIG .000  COOK      SIG .004  ENGINEER  SIG .000  PUBTRANS  SIG .471

RENT        -.0249  RENT         .1440  RENT         .2528  PUBTRANS     .6858  PUBTRANS     .6058  PUBTRANS     .6358
WITH      N(   44)  WITH      N(   44)  WITH      N(   44)  WITH      N(   44)  WITH      N(   44)  WITH      N(   44)
TEACHER   SIG .436  COOK      SIG .175  ENGINEER  SIG .049  TEACHER   SIG .000  COOK      SIG .000  ENGINEER  SIG .000

TEACHER      .6215  TEACHER      .6573  COOK         .7502
WITH      N(   43)  WITH      N(   43)  WITH      N(   44)
COOK      SIG .000  ENGINEER  SIG .000  ENGINEER  SIG .000

          A VALUE OF 99.0000 IS PRINTED IF A COEFFICIENT CANNOT BE COMPUTED.
```

31.8 Writing Matrix Materials

You can use PEARSON CORR to write out a square matrix of correlation coefficients and the number of cases used to compute each coefficient. Other SPSS^X procedures that can read the matrix materials produced by PEARSON CORR are PARTIAL CORR (Chapter 32), REGRESSION (Chapter 33), and FACTOR (Chapter 35). To write matrix materials to a file, specify Option 4 on the associated OPTIONS command. Matrix materials will be written for each simple variable list but will not be written for variable lists containing the keyword WITH. If you do not specify any missing-value options, each correlation matrix precedes a matrix of the *n*'s used to compute the coefficients. If you include missing values with Option 1 or exclude missing values listwise with Option 2, the correlation matrix precedes a record containing the *n* used to compute all the coefficients in the matrix. If you are processing split files (Chapter 13), a set of matrix materials is written for each split file processed. Correlation matrices are written with a format of F10.7, and each record has a maximum of eight values. Each row of the matrix begins on a new record. Matrices of *n*'s are written in the same way but with a format of F10.0.

If you specify Option 4, you must also specify the file to which the materials are written using the PROCEDURE OUTPUT command (see Chapter 17). In the following example one matrix of correlations, followed by a matrix of *n*'s, is written to the file defined by the CORRMAT file handle.

```
FILE HANDLE  CITY/ file specifications
GET FILE  CITY/KEEP FOOD RENT PUBTRANS TEACHER COOK ENGINEER
FILE HANDLE  CORRMAT/ file specifications
PROCEDURE OUTPUT  OUTFILE=CORRMAT
PEARSON CORR  FOOD TO ENGINEER
OPTIONS  4
FINISH
```

OPTION 4 *Write matrix materials to a file.* Writes the correlation matrix and the number of cases used to compute each coefficient for each simple variable list.

31.9 LIMITATIONS

The following limitations apply to PEARSON CORR:

- A maximum of 40 variable lists.
- A maximum of 500 variables total per PEARSON CORR command.
- A maximum of 250 individual elements. Each unique occurrence of a variable name, keyword, or special delimiter counts as 1 toward this total. Variables implied by the TO convention do not count toward this total.

PARTIAL CORR varlist [WITH varlist] BY control list
(order values) [/ . . .]

OPTIONS:
1 Include missing values.
2 Exclude missing values on an analysis-by-analysis basis.
3 Two-tailed test of significance.
4 Read matrix materials from a file.
5 Write matrix materials to a file.
6 Index matrix input to order of variables on active file.
7 Suppress printing of degrees of freedom and significance level.
8 Print only nonredundant coefficients in serial string format.

STATISTICS:
1 Zero-order correlations.
2 Means, standard deviations, and *n*'s.
3 Zero-order correlations if and only if any are noncomputable.

OVERVIEW, **32.1**

OPERATION, **32.2**
- Specifying the Design, **32.3**
  - Correlation List, **32.4**
  - Control List and Order Values, **32.5**
  - Specifying Multiple Analyses, **32.6**
- Two-Tailed Significance Levels, **32.7**
- Optional Statistics, **32.8**
- Missing Values, **32.9**
- Formatting Options, **32.10**
- Matrix Materials, **32.11**
  - Reading Matrices, **32.12**
  - Indexing Matrices, **32.13**
  - Writing Matrices, **32.14**

LIMITATIONS, **32.15**

Chapter 32 PARTIAL CORR

Procedure PARTIAL CORR produces partial correlation coefficients that describe the relationship between two variables while adjusting for the effects of one or more additional variables. PARTIAL CORR first calculates a matrix of Pearson product-moment correlations. Alternatively, it can read the zero-order correlation matrix as input. Other procedures that produce zero-order correlation matrices that can be read by PARTIAL CORR include PEARSON CORR (Chapter 31), REGRESSION (Chapter 33), DISCRIMINANT (Chapter 34), and FACTOR (Chapter 35).

32.1 OVERVIEW

PARTIAL CORR produces a matrix of partial correlation coefficients for up to five order values. For each coefficient, PARTIAL CORR prints the degrees of freedom and the significance level. You can specify optional statistics, formats, and methods of handling missing data. PARTIAL CORR also reads and writes matrix materials which can be used by other procedures.

Significance Levels. By default, the significance level for each partial correlation coefficient is based on a one-tailed test. Optionally, you can request that the significance level be calculated using a two-tailed test. (See Section 32.7.)

Optional Statistics. In addition to the partial correlation coefficient, degrees of freedom, and significance level, you can obtain the mean, standard deviation, and number of nonmissing cases for each variable, and zero-order correlation coefficients for each pair of variables. (See Section 32.8.)

Missing Values. By default, PARTIAL CORR excludes cases with missing values on a listwise basis. Optionally, you can request that missing values be handled as if they were valid or that cases with missing values be deleted on an analysis-by-analysis basis. (See Section 32.9.)

Formatting Options. You can print more rows and columns of coefficients than the default allows and suppress the degrees of freedom and significance level for each coefficient. You can also print only the nonredundant coefficients. (See Section 32.10.)

Matrix Input and Output. PARTIAL CORR can read and write zero-order correlation matrices. (See Section 32.11.)

32.2 OPERATION

To use PARTIAL CORR, you must supply a set of variables to be correlated, one or more control variables following the keyword BY, and a list of order values in parentheses which define the level of control. There are also associated OPTIONS and STATISTICS commands.

32.3 Specifying the Design

The PARTIAL CORR command requires three types of information:

- A correlation list of one or more pairs of variables for which partial correlations are desired. This list does *not* include the control variables.
- A control list of one or more variables which will be used as controls for the variables in the correlation list.
- One or more order values indicating the order of partials desired from the correlation and control list.

For example, the command

```
PARTIAL CORR  PUBTRANS MECHANIC BUSDRVER BY NETPURSE (1)
```

produces a square matrix containing three unique first-order partial correlations: PUBTRANS correlated with MECHANIC, controlling for NETPURSE; PUBTRANS with BUSDRVER, controlling for NETPURSE; and MECHANIC with BUSDRVER, controlling for NETPURSE. The *1* in parentheses indicates a first-order partial correlation. Figure 32.3 shows this partial correlation matrix.

Figure 32.3 First-order partial correlations

```
- - - - - - - - - - - - - - P A R T I A L   C O R R E L A T I O N   C O E F F I C I E N T S - - - - - - - - - - - - - -

CONTROLLING FOR..    NETPURSE


              PUBTRANS   MECHANIC   BUSDRVER

PUBTRANS       1.0000      .4545      .5430
              (    0)    (   40)    (   40)
              P= .       P= .001    P= .000

MECHANIC        .4545     1.0000      .6122
              (   40)    (    0)    (   40)
              P= .001    P= .       P= .000

BUSDRVER        .5430      .6122     1.0000
              (   40)    (   40)    (    0)
              P= .000    P= .000    P= .


 (COEFFICIENT / (D.F.) / SIGNIFICANCE)        (" . " IS PRINTED IF A COEFFICIENT CANNOT BE COMPUTED)
```

32.4 Correlation List

The correlation list specifies pairs of variables to be correlated while controlling for the variable(s) in the control list. The correlation list can take one of two forms. Both forms of the specification permit the use of the keyword TO to reference consecutive variables. If you provide a simple list of variables, PARTIAL CORR computes the partial correlation of each variable with every other variable in the list, producing a square or lower-triangular matrix (see the example above and Figure 32.3). The partial correlation of a variable with itself is always 1.0000 and appears on the diagonal of the matrix. Each pair of variables appears twice in the matrix (e.g., PUBTRANS with MECHANIC, and MECHANIC with PUBTRANS). Since the partial correlation coefficient is a symmetrical measure, these two values are identical, and the upper and lower triangles of the matrix are mirror images of each other.

Alternatively, you can request specific variable pairs by using the keyword WITH. One variable list followed by the keyword WITH and a second variable list produces a rectangular matrix of partial correlation coefficients. The first variable list defines the rows of the matrix and the second list defines the columns. For example,

```
PARTIAL CORR   RENT FOOD PUBTRANS WITH TEACHER MANAGER BY NETSALRY(1)
```

produces the matrix in Figure 32.4.

Figure 32.4 A matrix using the keyword WITH

```
- - - - - - - - - - - - - -P A R T I A L   C O R R E L A T I O N   C O E F F I C I E N T S- - - - - - - - - - - - - -

CONTROLLING FOR..     NETSALRY

               TEACHER      MANAGER

RENT           -.3577        .1479
               (   40)      (   40)
               P= .010      P= .175

FOOD            .1104        .0724
               (   40)      (   40)
               P= .243      P= .324

PUBTRANS        .1721       -.1475
               (   40)      (   40)
               P= .138      P= .176

 (COEFFICIENT / (D.F.) / SIGNIFICANCE)        (" . " IS PRINTED IF A COEFFICIENT CANNOT BE COMPUTED)
```

32.5 Control List and Order Values

The control list names the variables to be used as controls for each pair of variables specified by the correlation list. You can specify up to 100 control variables. The control list precedes the order values that specify the exact partials to be computed. You can specify up to 5 order values. The order values must be integers between 1 and the number of control variables.

The correlation between a pair of variables is referred to as a zero-order correlation; controlling for one variable produces a first-order partial correlation, controlling for two variables produces a second-order partial, and so on. The number of control variables determines the orders that can be requested, while the order value or values indicate the partial correlation matrix or matrices to be printed.

One partial will be produced for every unique combination of control variables which add up to the order value. For example,

```
PARTIAL CORR  RENT WITH TEACHER BY NETSALRY, NETPRICE (1)
```

produces two first-order partials: RENT with TEACHER, controlling for NETSALRY; and RENT with TEACHER, controlling for NETPRICE. The command

```
PARTIAL CORR  RENT WITH TEACHER BY NETSALRY, NETPRICE (2)
```

produces one second-order partial of RENT with TEACHER, controlling simultaneously for NETSALRY and NETPRICE. You can specify both sets of partials with one PARTIAL CORR command, as in:

```
PARTIAL CORR  RENT WITH TEACHER BY NETSALRY, NETPRICE (1,2)
```

You must use the order value even if you specify only one control variable. The following command produces both first-order and third-order partial correlations:

```
PARTIAL CORR   RENT FOOD PUBTRANS BY NETSALRY NETPURSE NETPRICE (1,3)
```

Figure 32.5 displays the four matrices produced by this command.

Figure 32.5 Multiple order values

```
- - - - - - - - - - - - - - P A R T I A L   C O R R E L A T I O N   C O E F F I C I E N T S - - - - - - - - - - - - - -
CONTROLLING FOR..    NETSALRY

                    RENT        FOOD   PUBTRANS

RENT              1.0000       .1921     -.2136
                 (    0)    (   41)    (   41)
                 P= .       P= .109    P= .084

FOOD               .1921      1.0000      .2558
                 (   41)    (    0)    (   41)
                 P= .109    P= .       P= .049

PUBTRANS          -.2136       .2558     1.0000
                 (   41)    (   41)    (    0)
                 P= .084    P= .049    P= .

 (COEFFICIENT / (D.F.) / SIGNIFICANCE)        (" . " IS PRINTED IF A COEFFICIENT CANNOT BE COMPUTED)

- - - - - - - - - - - - - - P A R T I A L   C O R R E L A T I O N   C O E F F I C I E N T S - - - - - - - - - - - - - -
CONTROLLING FOR..    NETPURSE

                    RENT        FOOD   PUBTRANS

RENT              1.0000       .2970      .0590
                 (    0)    (   41)    (   41)
                 P= .       P= .027    P= .354

FOOD               .2970      1.0000      .5085
                 (   41)    (    0)    (   41)
                 P= .027    P= .       P= .000

PUBTRANS           .0590       .5085     1.0000
                 (   41)    (   41)    (    0)
                 P= .354    P= .000    P= .

 (COEFFICIENT / (D.F.) / SIGNIFICANCE)        (" . " IS PRINTED IF A COEFFICIENT CANNOT BE COMPUTED)

- - - - - - - - - - - - - - P A R T I A L   C O R R E L A T I O N   C O E F F I C I E N T S - - - - - - - - - - - - - -
CONTROLLING FOR..    NETPRICE

                    RENT        FOOD   PUBTRANS

RENT              1.0000      -.6933     -.5690
                 (    0)    (   41)    (   41)
                 P= .       P= .000    P= .000

FOOD              -.6933      1.0000      .4382
                 (   41)    (    0)    (   41)
                 P= .000    P= .       P= .002

PUBTRANS          -.5690       .4382     1.0000
                 (   41)    (   41)    (    0)
                 P= .000    P= .002    P= .

 (COEFFICIENT / (D.F.) / SIGNIFICANCE)        (" . " IS PRINTED IF A COEFFICIENT CANNOT BE COMPUTED)

- - - - - - - - - - - - - - P A R T I A L   C O R R E L A T I O N   C O E F F I C I E N T S - - - - - - - - - - - - - -
CONTROLLING FOR..    NETSALRY  NETPURSE  NETPRICE

                    RENT        FOOD   PUBTRANS

RENT              1.0000      -.6104     -.4580
                 (    0)    (   39)    (   39)
                 P= .       P= .000    P= .001

FOOD              -.6104      1.0000      .2583
                 (   39)    (    0)    (   39)
                 P= .000    P= .       P= .052

PUBTRANS          -.4580       .2583     1.0000
                 (   39)    (   39)    (    0)
                 P= .001    P= .052    P= .

 (COEFFICIENT / (D.F.) / SIGNIFICANCE)        (" . " IS PRINTED IF A COEFFICIENT CANNOT BE COMPUTED)
```

32.6 Specifying Multiple Analyses

You can specify up to 25 partial correlation analyses on one PARTIAL CORR command, and you can name or imply up to 400 variables total. Use a slash (/) to separate each set of specifications. For example,

```
PARTIAL CORR   RENT FOOD WITH TEACHER BY NETSALRY NETPRICE (1,2)/
    WCLOTHES MCLOTHES BY NETPRICE (1)
```

produces three matrices for the first correlation list, control list, and order values. The second correlation list, control list, and order value produce one matrix.

PARTIAL CORR computes the zero-order correlation matrix for each analysis list separately. Depending upon the distribution of missing values in the variables, different sets of cases may be used for different analysis lists despite variables common to them (see Section 32.9).

32.7 Two-Tailed Significance Levels

By default, the significance level printed below the partial correlation coefficient is based on a one-tailed test. This is appropriate when the direction of the relationship between a pair of variables can be specified in advance of the analysis. When the direction of the relationship cannot be determined in advance, a two-tailed test is appropriate. Use Option 3 to request a two-tailed test.

OPTION 3 *Two-tailed test of significance.*

32.8 Optional Statistics

The partial correlation coefficient, degrees of freedom, and significance level are automatically printed. You can obtain additional statistics with the associated STATISTICS command.

STATISTIC 1 *Zero-order correlations with degrees of freedom and significance level.*

STATISTIC 2 *Mean, standard deviation, and number of nonmissing cases.*

STATISTIC 3 *Zero-order correlation coefficients if and only if any of the zero-order correlations are noncomputable.* Noncomputable coefficients are printed as a period (.).

If both Statistic 1 and Statistic 3 are requested, Statistic 1 takes precedence over Statistic 3 and the zero-order correlations are printed. The commands

```
PARTIAL CORR  BUS WCLOTHES RENT FOOD BY NTCPRI, NTCPUR (1)
STATISTICS  1, 2
OPTIONS  2
```

produce the display in Figure 32.8.

Figure 32.8 Statistics available with PARTIAL CORR

VARIABLE	MEAN	STANDARD DEV	CASES
BUS	42.9535	27.3652	43
WCLOTHES	80.7111	30.1945	45
RENT	120.0889	94.2250	45
FOOD	70.4667	18.7442	45
NTCPRI	81.3778	20.2376	45
NTCPUR	58.7045	28.8062	44

- - - - - - - - - - - - - - P A R T I A L   C O R R E L A T I O N   C O E F F I C I E N T S - - - - - - - - - - - - - -

ZERO ORDER PARTIALS

	BUS	WCLOTHES	RENT	FOOD	NTCPRI	NTCPUR
BUS	1.0000	.4547	-.0466	.5612	.3973	.8759
	(0)	(41)	(41)	(41)	(41)	(41)
	P= .	P= .001	P= .383	P= .000	P= .004	P= .000
WCLOTHES	.4547	1.0000	.5461	.4082	.7040	.3058
	(41)	(0)	(43)	(43)	(43)	(42)
	P= .001	P= .	P= .000	P= .003	P= .000	P= .022
RENT	-.0466	.5461	1.0000	.2598	.7640	-.1288
	(41)	(43)	(0)	(43)	(43)	(42)
	P= .383	P= .000	P= .	P= .042	P= .000	P= .202
FOOD	.5612	.4082	.2598	1.0000	.7344	.2952
	(41)	(43)	(43)	(0)	(43)	(42)
	P= .000	P= .003	P= .042	P= .	P= .000	P= .026
NTCPRI	.3973	.7040	.7640	.7344	1.0000	.0976
	(41)	(43)	(43)	(43)	(0)	(42)
	P= .004	P= .000	P= .000	P= .000	P= .	P= .264
NTCPUR	.8759	.3058	-.1288	.2952	.0976	1.0000
	(41)	(42)	(42)	(42)	(42)	(0)
	P= .000	P= .022	P= .202	P= .026	P= .264	P= .

(COEFFICIENT / (D.F.) / SIGNIFICANCE)   (" . " IS PRINTED IF A COEFFICIENT CANNOT BE COMPUTED)

32.9 Missing Values

By default, PARTIAL CORR deletes cases with missing values on a listwise basis. A case missing on any of the variables listed, including the set of control variables, is not used. Listwise deletion ensures that the partial correlations are computed from the same population. When you specify multiple analysis lists, missing values are handled separately for each analysis list.

Two missing-value options are available. Option 1 handles user-defined missing values as if they were not missing. Option 2 deletes missing values on an analysis-by-analysis (pairwise) basis when the zero-order correlation matrix is calculated. A case missing on one or both of a pair of variables is not used. Pairwise deletion has the advantage of using as much of the data as possible. However, the coefficients are based on a varying number of cases and can produce misleading results, depending on the number and distribution of missing values. When pairwise deletion is in effect, the degrees of freedom for a particular partial coefficient is based on the smallest number of cases used in the calculation of any of the simple correlations.

OPTION 1 *Include missing values.* User-defined missing values are included in the analysis.

OPTION 2 *Exclude missing values on an analysis-by-analysis basis.* Cases missing on one or both of a pair of variables are not used in the calculation of zero-order correlation coefficients.

32.10 Formatting Options

For the default page length of 59 lines, PARTIAL CORR prints partial correlation coefficients in 11 rows and 10 columns and displays the degrees of freedom and the significance level. Use Option 7 to print 43 rows and 11 columns of coefficients and to suppress the degrees of freedom and significance. A single star (*) following a coefficient indicates significance at the

.01 level or less. Two stars (**) following a coefficient indicate significance at the .001 level or less. The commands

```
PARTIAL CORR  BUS WCLOTHES RENT FOOD BY NTCPRI (1)
OPTIONS  7
```

produce the matrix in Figure 32.10a.

Figure 32.10a Modifying the default output with Option 7

```
- - - - - - - - - - - - - - P A R T I A L   C O R R E L A T I O N   C O E F F I C I E N T S - - - - - - - - - - - - - -
CONTROLLING FOR..    NTCPRI

               BUS   WCLOTHES       RENT        FOOD

BUS         1.0000      .2889    -.4875**     .4337*
WCLOTHES     .2889     1.0000    -.0668      -.1637
RENT       -.4875**    -.0668    1.0000      -.6628**
FOOD         .4337*    -.1637    -.6628**    1.0000

 * - SIGNIF. LE .01       ** - SIGNIF. LE .001              (" . " IS PRINTED IF A COEFFICIENT CANNOT BE COMPUTED)
```

The default output also prints redundant coefficients. Use Option 8 to print only the nonredundant coefficients. They are displayed in serial string format with the coefficients from the first row of the matrix printed first, followed by all the unique coefficients from the second row and so on for all the rows of the matrix. Six coefficients are printed across the page and each is identified with the names of the variables for which it was calculated. The degrees of freedom and significance level are printed below the partial just as they are in the matrix form of the output. Figure 32.10b is the output from the following example with Option 8 in effect.

```
PARTIAL CORR  BUSDRVER MECHANIC ENGINEER TEACHER COOK BY NETSALRY (1)
OPTIONS  8
```

Figure 32.10b Modifying the default output with Option 8

```
- - - - - - - - - - - - - - P A R T I A L   C O R R E L A T I O N   C O E F F I C I E N T S - - - - - - - - - - - - - -
CONTROLLING FOR..    NETSALRY

VARIABLE                 VARIABLE                 VARIABLE                 VARIABLE                 VARIABLE                 VARIABLE
PAIR                     PAIR                     PAIR                     PAIR                     PAIR                     PAIR
--------                 --------                 --------                 --------                 --------                 --------

BUSDRVER     .3713       BUSDRVER    -.1947       BUSDRVER     .4669       BUSDRVER    -.1246       MECHANIC    -.1480       MECHANIC     .4075
WITH      DF =   39      WITH      DF =   39      WITH      DF =   39      WITH      DF =   39      WITH      DF =   39      WITH      DF =   39
MECHANIC SIG .008        ENGINEER SIG .111        TEACHER   SIG .001       COOK      SIG .219        ENGINEER SIG .178        TEACHER   SIG .004

MECHANIC     .2598       ENGINEER    -.5198       ENGINEER     .3208       TEACHER     -.1422
WITH      DF =   39      WITH      DF =   39      WITH      DF =   39      WITH      DF =   39
COOK      SIG .050       TEACHER   SIG .000       COOK      SIG .020       COOK      SIG .188

 " . " IS PRINTED IF A COEFFICIENT CANNOT BE COMPUTED.
```

If you specify both Option 7 and Option 8, only Option 8 will be in effect.

OPTION 7 *Suppress the printing of the degrees of freedom and significance level.*

OPTION 8 *Print only the nonredundant coefficients in serial string format.*

32.11 Matrix Materials

PARTIAL CORR can read matrix input instead of cases. It also writes zero-order correlation matrices to a file which can subsequently be used by other correlational-based procedures such as REGRESSION and FACTOR. The following options apply to the use of matrices with PARTIAL CORR:

OPTION 4 *Read matrix materials.*

OPTION 5 *Write matrix materials.*

OPTION 6 *Index matrix materials to the order of variables on the active file.*

32.12 Reading Matrices

To use matrix input instead of cases, specify Option 4. You must use a NUMERIC command to define the variables (Chapter 6) and FILE HANDLE and INPUT MATRIX commands to define the output file (Chapters 3 and 17). These commands must be placed between an INPUT PROGRAM command and an END INPUT PROGRAM command (Chapter 12). PARTIAL CORR can read the matrices it writes as well as those produced by PEARSON CORR (Chapter 31), REGRESSION (Chapter 33), DISCRIMINANT (Chapter 34), and FACTOR (Chapter 35). Statistic 2 is not available with matrix input.

PARTIAL CORR can read a fixed- or freefield-format matrix of zero-order correlations. The matrix must be a square matrix and must include all the variables named in the correlation list and the control list on the PARTIAL CORR command. A fixed-format matrix must have a format of F10.7 with a maximum of eight values. Each row of the matrix must begin a new record. If you exclude missing values listwise (the default) or include missing values with Option 1, a record containing the number of cases used to compute all the coefficients in the matrix follows the correlation matrix. If you exclude missing values on an analysis-by-analysis basis with Option 2, a matrix of the *n*'s used to compute the coefficients follows the correlation matrix. The matrix of *n*'s must have an arrangement similar to that of the correlation matrix, but the format can be F10.0. The following commands demonstrate the use of matrix input in fixed format from an external file:

```
FILE HANDLE  PARTM3/ file specifications
INPUT PROGRAM
NUMERIC  PUBTRANS, MECHANIC, BUSDRVER, NETPURSE
INPUT MATRIX  FILE=PARTM3
END INPUT PROGRAM
PARTIAL CORR  PUBTRANS MECHANIC BUSDRVER BY NETPURSE(1)
OPTIONS  4
```

Optionally, if you use listwise deletion of missing data, you can supply the number of cases on the N OF CASES command (Chapter 10), as in:

```
FILE HANDLE  PARTM7/ file specifications
INPUT PROGRAM
NUMERIC  PUBTRANS, MECHANIC, BUSDRVER, NETPURSE
N OF CASES  43
INPUT MATRIX  FILE=PARTM7
END INPUT PROGRAM
PARTIAL CORR  PUBTRANS MECHANIC BUSDRVER BY NETPURSE(1)
OPTIONS  4
```

If you use a matrix with freefield format, at least one blank must separate each coefficient, and each row of the matrix must begin on a new record. To signal freefield input, use the keyword FREE on the INPUT MATRIX command, as in:

```
FILE HANDLE  PARTM6/ file specifications
INPUT PROGRAM
NUMERIC  PUBTRANS, MECHANIC, BUSDRVER, NETPURSE
INPUT MATRIX  FILE=PARTM6/ FREE
END INPUT PROGRAM
PARTIAL CORR  PUBTRANS MECHANIC BUSDRVER BY NETPURSE(1)
OPTIONS 4
```

If you specify multiple analyses (with the use of slashes) on the PARTIAL CORR command, the matrix materials must contain multiple sets of correlations and *n*'s. For example,

```
INPUT PROGRAM
NUMERIC  X1 TO X5 Y1 TO Y5 CONTROL
INPUT MATRIX  FREE
END INPUT PROGRAM
PARTIAL CORR  X1 TO X5 BY CONTROL(1)/
              Y1 TO Y5 BY CONTROL(1)
OPTIONS  4
BEGIN DATA
correlation matrix of X1 to X5 and CONTROL
n of cases
correlation matrix of Y1 TO Y5 and CONTROL
n of cases
END DATA
```

performs two analyses. If the matrix materials have a fixed format, the INPUT MATRIX command is not required.

32.13 Indexing Matrices

If your matrix materials have been computed on more variables than are used in PARTIAL CORR, use Option 6 to index the matrix. Define all the variables on the NUMERIC command, name the variables you are analyzing on the PARTIAL CORR command, and specify Option 6, as in:

```
FILE HANDLE  BIGMAT/ file specifications
INPUT PROGRAM
NUMERIC V1 TO V14 CONTROL
INPUT MATRIX FILE=BIGMAT
END INPUT PROGRAM
PARTIAL CORR V1 V3 V5 V10 TO V14 BY CONTROL(1)
OPTIONS  4 6
FINISH
```

32.14 Writing Matrices

To write matrix materials to a file, specify Option 5 on the associated OPTIONS command. Matrix materials include a square matrix of zero-order correlation coefficients for all variables named on the analysis list and the number of cases used to compute each coefficient. If you exclude missing values listwise or include missing values with Option 1, one record containing the number of cases follows the correlation matrix. If you exclude missing values on an analysis-by-analysis basis with Option 2, a matrix of *n*'s follows the correlation matrix. When you write matrix materials, you must supply a FILE HANDLE command and a PROCEDURE OUTPUT command to define the output file for the matrix materials (see Chapter 17). For example,

```
FILE HANDLE  CITY/ file specifications
GET FILE  CITY
FILE HANDLE  CORRMAT/ file specifications
PROCEDURE OUTPUT  OUTFILE=CORRMAT
PARTIAL CORR  PUBTRANS MECHANIC WITH BUS BY NETPURSE(1)
OPTIONS  5
FINISH
```

writes one set of matrix materials for the variables PUBTRANS, MECHANIC, BUS, and NETPURSE to the file CORRMAT. If you specify more than one analysis list, PARTIAL CORR writes one set of matrix materials for each list.

32.15 LIMITATIONS

The limitations in effect for PARTIAL CORR are

- A maximum of 25 requests on a single PARTIAL CORR command. Each request must contain a correlation list, a control list and order values.
- A maximum of 400 variables total can be named or implied per PARTIAL CORR command.
- A maximum of 100 control variables.
- A maximum of 5 different order values per single list. The largest order value that can appear is 100.

ANNOTATED EXAMPLE FOR PARTIAL CORR

This example analyzes 1979 prices and earnings in 45 cities around the world, compiled by the Union Bank of Switzerland. The variables are

- RENT—the average gross monthly rent in the city, expressed as a percentage above or below that of Zurich, where Zurich equals 100%.
- FOOD—the average net cost of 39 different food and beverage items in the city, expressed as a percentage above or below that of Zurich, where Zurich equals 100%.
- PUBTRANS—the average cost of a three-mile taxi ride within city limits, expressed as a percentage above or below that of Zurich, where Zurich equals 100%.
- NETPRICE—the city's net price level, based on more than 100 goods and services weighted by consumer habits. NETPRICE is expressed as a percentage above or below that of Zurich, where Zurich equals 100%.
- NETPURSE—the city's net purchasing power level, calculated as the ratio of labor expended (measured in number of working hours) to the cost of more than 100 goods and services weighted by consumer habits. NETPURSE is expressed as a percentage above or below that of Zurich, where Zurich equals 100%.
- NETSALRY—the city's net salary level, calculated from net average hourly earnings in 12 occupations. NETSALRY is expressed as a percentage above or below that of Zurich, where Zurich equals 100%.

In this example we determine the degree to which the costs of rent, food, and public transportation are related to each other, while adjusting for the effects of prices, purchasing power, and salary levels. We use PARTIAL CORR to first compute the zero-order correlations between all six variables and then compute three matrices of first-order partials that remove the effects of NETPRICE, NETPURSE, and NETSALRY, respectively. The SPSS^X commands are

```
FILE HANDLE  CITY/ file specifications
GET  FILE=CITY/
     RENAME (NTCPRI NTCPUR NTCSAL = NETPRICE NETPURSE NETSALRY)/
     KEEP RENT FOOD PUBTRANS NETPRICE NETPURSE NETSALRY
PARTIAL CORR  RENT TO PUBTRANS BY NETPRICE TO NETSALRY(1)
STATISTICS  1 2
OPTIONS  7
FINISH
```

- The FILE HANDLE identifies the CITY data file and gives the operating-system specifications (see Chapter 3).
- The GET command defines the data to SPSS^X, renames three variables, and selects the variables needed for analysis (see Chapter 5).
- The PARTIAL CORR command requests three sets of first-order partial correlations for all pairs of variables implied by RENT, FOOD, and PUBTRANS. The first set of partials controls for NETPRICE, the second set controls for NETPURSE, and the third set controls for NETSALRY (see Section 32.2).
- The STATISTICS command requests the mean, standard deviation, and number of nonmissing cases for each variable and the zero-order correlation coefficients for each pair of variables implied by the correlation list and the control list (see Section 32.8).
- Option 7 suppresses the printing of the degrees of freedom and significance levels in the zero-order correlation matrix and the first-order partial correlation matrices (see Section 32.10).
- Since no missing-value option is specified, listwise deletion of missing cases is in effect (see Section 32.9).

Output from PARTIAL CORR

VARIABLE	MEAN	STANDARD DEV	CASES
RENT	121.7500	94.6455	44
FOOD	71.0000	18.6123	44
PUBTRANS	48.8182	24.6381	44
NETPRICE	82.1591	19.7731	44
NETPURSE	58.7045	28.8062	44
NETSALRY	50.3409	24.2946	44

- - - - - - - - - - - - - - P A R T I A L   C O R R E L A T I O N   C O E F F I C I E N T S - - - - - - - - - - - - - -

ZERO ORDER PARTIALS

	RENT	FOOD	PUBTRANS	NETPRICE	NETPURSE	NETSALRY
RENT	1.0000	.2434	-.0346	.7646**	-.1288	.1531
FOOD	.2434	1.0000	.5639**	.7224**	.2952	.5800**
PUBTRANS	-.0346	.5639**	1.0000	.3953*	.6234**	.7247**
NETPRICE	.7646**	.7224**	.3953*	1.0000	.0976	.4824**
NETPURSE	-.1288	.2952	.6234**	.0976	1.0000	.9012**
NETSALRY	.1531	.5800**	.7247**	.4824**	.9012**	1.0000

* - SIGNIF. LE .01   ** - SIGNIF. LE .001   (" . " IS PRINTED IF A COEFFICIENT CANNOT BE COMPUTED)

- - - - - - - - - - - - - - P A R T I A L   C O R R E L A T I O N   C O E F F I C I E N T S - - - - - - - - - - - - - -

CONTROLLING FOR..   NETPRICE

	RENT	FOOD	PUBTRANS
RENT	1.0000	-.6933**	-.5690**
FOOD	-.6933**	1.0000	.4382*
PUBTRANS	-.5690**	.4382*	1.0000

* - SIGNIF. LE .01   ** - SIGNIF. LE .001   (" . " IS PRINTED IF A COEFFICIENT CANNOT BE COMPUTED)

- - - - - - - - - - - - - - P A R T I A L   C O R R E L A T I O N   C O E F F I C I E N T S - - - - - - - - - - - - - -

CONTROLLING FOR..   NETPURSE

	RENT	FOOD	PUBTRANS
RENT	1.0000	.2970	.0590
FOOD	.2970	1.0000	.5085**
PUBTRANS	.0590	.5085**	1.0000

* - SIGNIF. LE .01   ** - SIGNIF. LE .001   (" . " IS PRINTED IF A COEFFICIENT CANNOT BE COMPUTED)

- - - - - - - - - - - - - - P A R T I A L   C O R R E L A T I O N   C O E F F I C I E N T S - - - - - - - - - - - - - -

CONTROLLING FOR..   NETSALRY

	RENT	FOOD	PUBTRANS
RENT	1.0000	.1921	-.2136
FOOD	.1921	1.0000	.2558
PUBTRANS	-.2136	.2558	1.0000

* - SIGNIF. LE .01   ** - SIGNIF. LE .001   (" . " IS PRINTED IF A COEFFICIENT CANNOT BE COMPUTED)

```
REGRESSION [READ = [DEFAULTS] [MEAN] [STDDEV] [CORR]
                   [VARIANCE] [COV] [N] [INDEX]]

  [/WIDTH = {132}]
            {n  }

  [/SELECT = {(ALL)                    }]
             {varname relation value   }

             {LISTWISE**        }
  [/MISSING = {PAIRWISE          }]
             {MEANSUBSTITUTION  }
             {INCLUDE           }

  [/DESCRIPTIVE = [DEFAULTS] [MEAN] [STDDEV] [CORR]
                  [VARIANCE] [XPROD] [SIG] [N] [BADCORR]
                  [COV] [NONE]]

  [/WRITE = [DEFAULTS] [MEAN] [STDDEV] [CORR]
            [VARIANCE] [COV] [N] [NONE]]

               {varlist   }
  /VARIABLES = {(COLLECT) }
               {(PREVIOUS)}

  [/CRITERIA = [DEFAULTS**] [PIN ({0.05 })] [POUT ({0.1  })]
                                 {value}           {value}

    [TOLERANCE ({0.01 })]
                {value}

    [MAXSTEPS ({2v})] [FIN ({3.84 })] [FOUT ({2.71 })]]
               {n }         {value}          {value}

  [/STATISTICS = [DEFAULTS**] [R] [COEFF] [ANOVA] [ZPP] [OUTS]
                 [LABEL] [CHA] [CI] [F] [BCOV] [SES] [LINE]
                 [HISTORY] [XTX] [COND] [END] [ALL] [TOL]]

  [/ {NOORIGIN}]
     {ORIGIN  }

  /DEPENDENT = varlist

    {STEPWISE [= varlist]}
    {FORWARD [= varlist] }
  / {BACKWARD [= varlist]} [...] [/...]
    {ENTER [= varlist]   }
    {REMOVE = varlist    }

  [/TEST = (design) (design) ... ]

  [/RESIDUALS = [DEFAULTS] [DURBIN] [ID (varname)]

    [HISTOGRAM ({ZRESID })] [OUTLIERS ({ZRESID })] [POOLED]
                {tempvar}              {tempvar}

  [NORMPROB ({ZRESID })] [SIZE ({LARGE})]]
             {tempvar}          {SMALL}

  [/CASEWISE = [DEFAULTS] [OUTLIERS ({3    })] [PLOT ({ZRESID })]
                                     {value}          {tempvar}

    [DEPENDENT] [PRED] [RESID] [tempvarlist] [ALL]]

  [/SCATTERPLOT = [SIZE ({SMALL})] (varname, varname) ... ]
                         {LARGE}

  [/PARTIALPLOT = [{ALL                     }] [SIZE ({SMALL})]]
                   {varname, varname, ...   }         {LARGE}

  [/SAVE = tempvar (newname) tempvar (newname) ... ]
```

***Default if the subcommand is omitted.*

Temporary residual variables are:
PRED ADJPRED ZPRED SEPRED RESID ZRESID DRESID
SRESID SDRESID MAHAL COOK LEVER

OVERVIEW, **33.1**

OPERATION, **33.2**

- Minimum Required Syntax, **33.3**
  - The VARIABLES Subcommand, **33.4**
  - The DEPENDENT Subcommand, **33.5**
  - The Method Subcommands, **33.6**
- VARIABLES Subcommand Modifiers, **33.7**
  - The MISSING Subcommand, **33.8**
  - The DESCRIPTIVES Subcommand, **33.9**
  - The SELECT Subcommand, **33.10**
- Equation Control Modifiers, **33.11**
  - The CRITERIA Subcommand, **33.12**
  - The STATISTICS Subcommand, **33.13**
  - Regression through the Origin, **33.14**
- Analysis of Residuals, **33.15**
  - Temporary Variables, **33.16**
  - The RESIDUALS Subcommand, **33.17**
  - The CASEWISE Subcommand, **33.18**
  - The SCATTERPLOT Subcommand, **33.19**
  - The PARTIALPLOT Subcommand, **33.20**
  - The SAVE Subcommand, **33.21**
- Matrix Materials, **33.22**
  - The READ Subcommand, **33.23**
  - The WRITE Subcommand, **33.24**
- The WIDTH Subcommand, **33.25**

Chapter 33 REGRESSION

Procedure REGRESSION calculates a multiple regression equation and associated statistics and plots. Several methods for variable selection as well as statistics for analysis of residuals and influential observations are available. Several types of plots, including partial residual plots, can be displayed.

33.1 OVERVIEW

Procedure REGRESSION is driven by a series of subcommand sets. Each subcommand set groups together logically related operations or definitions and is relatively independent of the specifications used on another subcommand. One set of subcommands is related to the variables and the cases being analyzed. These subcommands specify descriptive statistics to be displayed, variables to be used, missing-value treatment to be used, whether matrix input is to be used in place of or in addition to cases, whether matrix output is to be written to an external file, whether a subset of cases is to be selected for computing regression statistics, and what printing width will be used in displays. A second set of subcommands controls the regression model. These subcommands specify the dependent variable, statistical criteria to be used in developing the model, methods of entering and removing variables from the model, whether the constant is to be suppressed, and the display of statistics for the model. The final set of subcommands controls residuals processing, including plotting and saving several different types of residuals.

Minimum Required Syntax. You must specify three things: the variables to be used, the dependent variable or variables in the analysis, and one or more variable selection methods. You can indicate variables to be analyzed in three different ways (see Section 33.4). You can specify one or more dependent variables on the DEPENDENT subcommand; you can also specify more than one DEPENDENT subcommand in one REGRESSION command (see Section 33.5). Finally, six variable selection methods are available. You can specify one or more methods and you can control the order of entry of variables (see Section 33.6).

VARIABLES Subcommand Modifiers. VARIABLES subcommand modifiers must be specified prior to the VARIABLES subcommand. They are in effect until modified. The MISSING subcommand controls missing-value treatment (see Section 33.8). The DESCRIPTIVES subcommand requests univariate statistics, such as the mean and standard deviation, and bivariate statistics, such as the correlation coefficient (see Section 33.9). The SELECT subcommand is used to select a subset of your data. The regression equation is calculated for this set of cases, but the model is assessed both for those cases for which it is calculated and for cases set aside by means of the SELECT subcommand (see Section 33.10). You can read matrix input by means of the READ subcommand (see Section 33.23). The WRITE subcommand directs output to an external file (see Section 33.24). The WIDTH subcommand controls the width of printed output (see Section 33.25).

Equation Control Modifiers. Equation control modifiers must be specified prior to the DEPENDENT subcommand. They are in effect for subsequent equations until modified. The CRITERIA subcommand alters criteria for variable inclusion and exclusion as well as values of certain program tuning parameters (see Section 33.12). The STATISTICS subcommand controls both the volume of output and the display of statistics (see Section 33.13). You can request regression through the origin (see Section 33.14).

Residual Analysis. REGRESSION computes 12 temporary variables which you can analyze and save (see Section 33.16). The RESIDUALS subcommand controls the display of summary statistics associated with residual analysis (see Section 33.17). The CASEWISE subcommand controls the display of residuals for the cases and related statistics (see Section 33.18). The SCATTERPLOT subcommand requests standardized scatterplots of designated variables (see Section 33.19). The PARTIALPLOT subcommand requests partial residual plots (see Section 33.20). The SAVE subcommand names and saves residual variables on the active file (see Section 33.21).

33.2 OPERATION

The REGRESSION procedure in SPSS^X is operated by using the REGRESSION command and its subcommands. There are no associated STATISTICS and OPTIONS commands.

33.3 Minimum Required Syntax

Only three subcommands are required. The VARIABLES subcommand lists the variables to be used in the analyses. The DEPENDENT subcommand lists the dependent variable(s). The method subcommand keywords specify the method to be used for variable selection. All other subcommands either have default values or are optional.

A Note on Defaults. There are two types of defaults. *Passive defaults* occur with no explicit effort on your part. You do not need to specify the subcommand keyword for a passive default. *Active defaults* result when you specify subcommand keywords. For example, the following three specifications are equivalent:

```
DESCRIPTIVES/

DESCRIPTIVES=DEFAULTS/

DESCRIPTIVES=MEAN STDDEV CORR/
```

The default descriptive statistics can be produced by specifying only the DESCRIPTIVES subcommand keyword, by specifying the DEFAULTS keyword on the DESCRIPTIVES subcommand, or by explicitly stating the three default statistics (the means, standard deviations, and the correlation matrix). In this chapter, two asterisks (**) following a keyword signify a passive default and one asterisk (*) signifies an active default.

33.4 The VARIABLES Subcommand

The VARIABLES subcommand lists the variables to be used in the analyses. It is a required subcommand and must be specified before the DEPENDENT subcommand and the method subcommand. This list contains all variables that are referenced in subsequent specifications.

Indicate the variables to be analyzed in three ways. First, you can specify the variables in a *variable list*, as in:

```
REGRESSION VARIABLES=SAVINGS POP15 POP75 INCOME GROWTH/
```

Second, you can use the keyword COLLECT in parentheses, which indicates that the program should assemble the list of variables from the DEPENDENT subcommands and from each of the regression method subcommands. For example,

```
REGRESSION      VARIABLES=(COLLECT)/
                DEPENDENT=SAVINGS/
                ENTER POP15 POP75 INCOME GROWTH/
```

names five variables to be used in the analysis. Third, specify PREVIOUS in parentheses to point to the variable list named in the previous VARIABLES subcommand. This is useful when you are analyzing the same set of variables in a variety of ways, for example, analyzing different subsets of cases or using different missing-value treatments.

You can use more than one VARIABLES subcommand. The following command uses three VARIABLES subcommands to specify three analyses:

```
REGRESSION VARS=IQ TO ACHIEVE/
            DEP=ACHIEVE/STEP/
           VARS=(COLLECT)/
            DEP=ATHLETIC/
             BACKWARD=AGE HEIGHT WEIGHT MUSCLES COACH
                      EQUIPMENT/
           SELECT VITAMINC GT 250/
           VARS=(PREVIOUS)/
            DEP=ATHLETIC/
            BACKWARD
```

The first set of subcommands specifies a stepwise regression with variable ACHIEVE as the dependent variable. The second analysis uses a completely different set of variables. Here the (COLLECT) keyword causes SPSS^X to use the variables mentioned on the DEPENDENT and BACKWARD method subcommands as variables for this analysis. The third analysis uses the same variables as the second but a different set of cases. The SELECT subcommand selects cases with values greater than 250 for variable VITAMINC for calculating regression statistics. The keyword (PREVIOUS) on the VARIABLES subcommand indicates that the variables used in the second analysis will also be used in this analysis. Each VARIABLES subcommand causes SPSS^X to calculate a new correlation matrix.

33.5 The DEPENDENT Subcommand

Name the dependent variable or variables with the DEPENDENT subcommand. The dependent variable or variables must be named in the VARIABLES subcommand unless you specify the (COLLECT) keyword. If you name more than one dependent variable, REGRESSION uses the same independent variables and methods for each dependent variable named. All methods are executed for the first dependent variable, then the second, and so on. None of the variables named on the DEPENDENT subcommand is treated as an independent variable in any model associated with that DEPENDENT subcommand. Each DEPENDENT subcommand initiates a new regression model, and you can specify more than one DEPENDENT subcommand for the same VARIABLES subcommand.

There are two ways to specify multiple dependent variables in the same REGRESSION command. First, you can name more than one variable on a DEPENDENT subcommand:

```
REGRESSION      VARIABLES=IQ TO ACHIEVE/
                DEPENDENT=ACHIEVE IQREPORT/STEPWISE
```

In this example, REGRESSION first uses ACHIEVE as the dependent variable, then IQREPORT as the dependent variable in a new regression model. IQREPORT is not used as an independent variable when ACHIEVE is the dependent variable, and ACHIEVE is not used as an independent variable when IQREPORT is the dependent variable.

The second way to specify multiple dependent variables in the same REGRESSION command is to use multiple DEPENDENT subcommands:

```
REGRESSION      VARIABLES=IQ TO ACHIEVE/
                 DEPENDENT=ACHIEVE/STEPWISE/
                 DEPENDENT=IQREPORT/ENTER ACHIEVE,SES,IQ/
```

In this example, IQREPORT is an independent variable in the first model, and ACHIEVE is an independent variable in the second model. Multiple dependent subcommands are useful when you wish to specify different criteria or statistics associated with the regression model through the use of optional subcommands and keywords described as equation control modifiers in Section 33.11.

33.6 The Method Subcommands

To specify the method or combination of methods that you want to use to build a multiple regression equation, use one or more method subcommands. A variable list must follow the method subcommand if you specify REMOVE as the method for building the regression equation or if you have specified VARIABLES=(COLLECT). Otherwise, the variable list following the method subcommand is optional. All variables which pass the tolerance criterion are candidates for entry (see Section 33.12).

Six equation-building methods are available in REGRESSION.

FORWARD *Forward entry.* With the forward method, variables are entered into the equation one at a time. At each step, the independent variables not yet in the equation are examined for entry. The variable with the smallest probability-of-F value is entered, provided that this value is smaller than the entry criterion PIN (see Section 33.12) and the variable passes the tolerance tests.

BACKWARD *Backward elimination.* At each step, the independent variables already in the equation are examined for removal. Variables are removed from the equation one at a time. The variable with the largest probability-of-F value is removed, provided that this value is larger than the removal criterion POUT (see Section 33.12). If no variables are in the equation prior to the BACKWARD specification, REGRESSION first enters all independent variables passing the tolerance criterion, and then removes them one at a time according to the removal criterion.

STEPWISE *Stepwise selection.* If there are independent variables already in the equation, the variable with the largest probability of F is examined for removal. If the probability of F is larger than the removal criterion POUT, the variable is removed. The equation is then recomputed without the removed variable, and the rest of the variables are examined for removal. Once no more independent variables need to be removed, all independent variables not in the equation are examined for entry. The variable with the smallest probability of F is entered if this value is smaller than the entry criterion PIN and the variable passes the tolerance tests. Once a variable has been entered, all variables in the equation are again examined for removal. This process continues until no variables in the equation need to be removed and no variables not in the equation are eligible for entry, or until the maximum number of steps has been reached (see Section 33.12).

ENTER *Forced entry.* The ENTER keyword enters all variables that satisfy the tolerance criterion. Variables are entered one at a time in order of decreasing tolerance but are treated as a single block for statistics computed for changes in the equation. If the ENTER keyword is accompanied by a list of variables, those variables are candidates for entry. Specification of ENTER without a variable list enters *all* independent variables which pass the tolerance criterion. If the order of entry of independent variables is of interest, then you must either control the order of entry by means of as many ENTER subcommands as there are independent variables or specify one of the three equation methods already discussed.

REMOVE *Forced removal.* The REMOVE keyword removes all named variables from the equation as a single block. The REMOVE keyword *must* have an accompanying variable list.

TEST *Test indicated subsets of independent variables.* The TEST method is different from the methods previously listed. TEST offers an easy way to test a variety of models using R^2 change and its test of significance as the criterion for the "best" model. TEST produces considerably less output than the other methods.

The TEST method first builds a full model and then removes different subsets of variables from the full model. Test subsets are specified in parentheses. A variable can be used in more than one subset and any number of variables can be used in a subset. All variables used in the subsets must have been previously named in the VARIABLES subcommand.

The following REGRESSION command illustrates the use of the TEST method subcommand:

```
REGRESSION     VARIABLES=SAVINGS TO GROWTH/DEPENDENT=SAVINGS/
  TEST(POP15,POP75)(POP15,INCOME)(POP15,GROWTH)(POP75,INCOME)
  (POP75,GROWTH)(INCOME,GROWTH)
```

Figure 33.6 shows the output from this command.

Figure 33.6 TEST method output

```
               * * * *   M U L T I P L E   R E G R E S S I O N   * * * *

VARIABLE LIST NUMBER 1   LISTWISE DELETION OF MISSING DATA

EQUATION NUMBER 1   DEPENDENT VARIABLE..  SAVINGS     AVG AGG PERSONAL SAVINGS RATE

BEGINNING BLOCK NUMBER  1.  METHOD: TEST       POP15     POP75     INCOME    GROWTH

VARIABLE(S) ENTERED ON STEP NUMBER  1..    GROWTH   AVG % GROWTH RATE OF DISPOSABLE INC
                                    2..    POP75    AVG % POP OVER 75 YEARS OLD
                                    3..    INCOME   AVG LEVEL REAL PER-CAP DISPOSABLE INC
                                    4..    POP15    AVG % POP UNDER 15 YEARS OLD

HYPOTHESIS TESTS

              SUM OF
   DF        SQUARES   RSQ CHG          F    SIG F       SOURCE

    2      174.01812    .17691    6.01712    .0048       POP15      POP75
    2      147.68433    .15014    5.10656    .0100       POP15      INCOME
    2      232.23474    .23610    8.03011    .0010       POP15      GROWTH
    2       49.84088    .05067    1.72338    .1900       POP75      INCOME
    2       93.40722    .09496    3.22979    .0489       POP75      GROWTH
    2       75.45698    .07671    2.60912    .0847       INCOME     GROWTH

    4      332.91725              5.75573    .0008       REGRESSION
   45      650.71100                                     RESIDUAL
   49      983.62825                                     TOTAL
```

REGRESSION first enters the variables into the equation. Then the specified subsets of variables are tested upon removal. The TEST display shows the hypothesis sum of squares, degrees of freedom, R^2 change, F statistic, significance level of F, and the source variables being tested.

You can specify multiple method subcommands within the same equation, as in:

```
REGRESSION     VARIABLES=IQ TO ACHIEVE/
               DEPENDENT=ACHIEVE/STEPWISE/ENTER
```

For example, you might wish to see how the independent variables would enter in stepwise fashion, but ultimately want all the variables in the equation.

33.7 VARIABLES Subcommand Modifiers

There are three subcommands that can precede the VARIABLES subcommand: MISSING, DESCRIPTIVES, and SELECT. These subcommands are in effect for subsequent VARIABLES subcommands unless overridden.

33.8 The MISSING Subcommand

Use the MISSING subcommand and one of the following keywords to specify alternative missing-value treatments.

LISTWISE** *Delete cases with missing values listwise.* If you specify no MISSING subcommand, by default analyses are performed using only cases with nonmissing values on all variables named on the VARIABLES subcommand.

PAIRWISE *Delete cases with missing values pairwise.* Each correlation coefficient is computed using cases with complete data for the pair of variables correlated, regardless of whether the cases have missing values for any other variables named on the VARIABLES subcommand.

MEANSUBSTITUTION *Replace missing values with the variable mean.* All cases are used in the analyses with the substitutions treated as valid observations.

INCLUDE *Include cases with missing values.* All user-missing values are treated as if they are valid values. System-missing values are not used.

Specify the missing-value treatment before the VARIABLES subcommand to which it applies. When listwise deletion of missing values is in effect, only the variables from the current VARIABLES subcommand are examined. Variables specified on previous VARIABLES subcommands are not examined unless they are also included on the current VARIABLES subcommand.

You can specify more than one MISSING subcommand on one REGRESSION command. For example, you can apply several missing-value treatments to the same model, as in:

```
REGRESSION      VARS=PAEDUC TO RINCOME/
                  DEP=RINCOME/STEP/
                MISSING=MEANS/
                VARS=(PREVIOUS)/
                  DEP=RINCOME/STEP
```

The first model uses listwise deletion of missing values (the default). The second model uses the same variables, but uses mean substitution to replace missing values.

33.9 The DESCRIPTIVES Subcommand

A DESCRIPTIVES subcommand precedes the VARIABLES subcommand to which it applies, and it remains in effect until overridden by a new list of descriptive statistics or by specifying DESCRIPTIVES=NONE. Descriptive statistics are displayed only once for each variable list, regardless of the number of models you develop from that variable list. If you use DESCRIPTIVES more than once, each must be accompanied by a new VARIABLES subcommand.

You can use the following keyword specifications for the DESCRIPTIVES subcommand to display statistics for all variables on the VARIABLES subcommand:

NONE** *Turn off all descriptive statistics.* If you do not specify the DESCRIPTIVES subcommand, no descriptive statistics are displayed. If you have requested them for a variable list, use the keyword NONE to turn them off for subsequent variable lists.

DEFAULTS* *MEAN, STDDEV, and CORR.* If you specify DESCRIPTIVES with no specifications, these are the defaults.

MEAN *Variable means.*

STDDEV *Variable standard deviations.*

VARIANCE *Variable variances.*

CORR *Correlation matrix.*

SIG *One-tailed significance levels of the correlation coefficients.*

BADCORR *Display the correlation matrix only if some coefficients cannot be computed.*

COV *Covariance matrix.*

XPROD *Cross-product deviations from the mean.*

N *Numbers of cases used to compute correlation coefficients.* Used with pairwise or mean substitution missing-value treatments.

The following example produces the output displayed in Figure 33.9:

```
REGRESSION DESCRIPTIVES=DEFAULTS VARIANCE SIG COV XPROD/
    VARS=SAVINGS TO GROWTH/
    DEP=SAVINGS/ENTER
```

Figure 33.9 DESCRIPTIVES subcommand output

```
                * * * *   M U L T I P L E   R E G R E S S I O N   * * * *
VARIABLE LIST NUMBER 1   LISTWISE DELETION OF MISSING DATA

              MEAN   STD DEV     VARIANCE  LABEL

SAVINGS      9.671     4.480       20.074  AVG AGG PERSONAL SAVINGS RATE
POP15       35.090     9.152       83.754  AVG % POP UNDER 15 YEARS OLD
POP75        2.293     1.291        1.666  AVG % POP OVER 75 YEARS OLD
INCOME    1106.778   990.851   981785.907  AVG LEVEL REAL PER-CAP DISPOSABLE INC
GROWTH       3.758     2.870        8.236  AVG % GROWTH RATE OF DISPOSABLE INC

N OF CASES =      50

CORRELATION, COVARIANCE, SIGNIFICANCE, CROSS-PRODUCT:

                 SAVINGS          POP15           POP75          INCOME          GROWTH

SAVINGS            1.000          -.456            .317            .220            .305
                  20.074        -18.679           1.830         978.181           3.919
                    .999           .001            .025            .124            .031
                 983.628       -915.253          89.694       47930.881         192.032

POP15              -.456          1.000           -.908           -.756           -.048
                 -18.679         83.754         -10.732       -6856.989          -1.256
                    .001           .999            .000            .000            .742
                -915.253       4103.951        -525.852     -335992.453         -61.549

POP75               .317          -.908           1.000            .787            .025
                   1.830        -10.732           1.666        1006.527            .094
                    .025           .000            .999            .000            .861
                  89.694       -525.852          81.638       49319.844           4.596

INCOME              .220          -.756            .787           1.000           -.129
                 978.181      -6856.989        1006.527      981785.907        -368.187
                    .124           .000            .000            .999            .370
               47930.881    -335992.453       49319.844    48107509.444      -18041.139

GROWTH              .305          -.048            .025           -.129           1.000
                   3.919         -1.256            .094        -368.187           8.236
                    .031           .742            .861            .370            .999
                 192.032        -61.549           4.596      -18041.139         403.572
```

REGRESSION first displays the requested univariate statistics—in this example, the variable means, standard deviations, and variances. Next, bivariate statistics are displayed in square format with a title indicating the order of display. In this example, first the correlation coefficient is printed; then the sample covariance; then the significance level of the correlation coefficient; and finally, the cross-product deviations from the mean.

33.10 The SELECT Subcommand

Use the SELECT subcommand to select a subset of your cases for computing the regression equation. Only selected cases contribute to the correlation coefficients and to the regression equation. Residuals and predicted values are calculated and reported for both selected and unselected cases (see Section 33.15).

The general form of the SELECT subcommand is as follows:

SELECT= varname relation value/

The *relation* can be EQ, NE, LT, LE, GT, or GE.

A SELECT subcommand must appear before the VARIABLES subcommand to which it applies. Once specified, selection remains in effect until overridden. Selection is cancelled by specifying SELECT=(ALL). For example, the command

```
REGRESSION     SELECT SEX EQ 'BOYS'/
               VARS=IQ TO ACHIEVE/
                 DEP=ACHIEVE/STEP/
               SELECT SEX EQ 'GIRLS'/
               VARS=IQ TO ACHIEVE/
                 DEP=ACHIEVE/STEP/
               SELECT (ALL)/
               VARS=IQ TO ACHIEVE/
                 DEP=ACHIEVE/STEP/
```

produces three analyses—one using only boys' data, one using only girls' data, and one using the combined data. All three VARIABLES subcommands are necessary. The correlation coefficients must be recalculated for each analysis that uses different data selection criteria.

Do not use a variable from a temporary transformation as a selection variable. If the selection variable is the result of a temporary recode specification the value of the variable will change when the file is read again. The file will be read more than once if you request residuals processing or if SPSS^X has to build another correlation matrix. If you use a variable created from temporary transformations (with IF and COMPUTE statements) the variable will disappear when the data are read again.

The SELECT subcommand *does not* override SELECT IF and SAMPLE commands placed before the REGRESSION command in your SPSS^X job. No residuals or predictors are generated for cases deleted from the active file with SELECT IF or SAMPLE commands.

33.11 Equation Control Modifiers

Three optional subcommands can be placed between the VARIABLES subcommand and the DEPENDENT subcommand that initiates the analysis. Use the CRITERIA subcommand to change the entry and removal criteria SPSS^X uses in developing the equation. Use the STATISTICS subcommand to control the statistics displayed. Use the ORIGIN subcommand to request regression through the origin. All equation control modifiers are in effect for subsequent equations unless overridden by appropriate subcommands.

33.12 The CRITERIA Subcommand

All variables are tested for *tolerance* prior to entry into an equation. The tolerance of a variable is the proportion of its variance not accounted for by other independent variables in the equation. The *minimum tolerance* of a variable is the smallest tolerance any variable already in the analysis would have if that variable were included in the analysis. A variable must pass both tolerance and minimum tolerance tests in order to enter a regression equation.

If a variable passes the tolerance criterion, it is further tested depending on the equation method specified (see Section 33.6). For method REMOVE, variables named on the subcommand are considered for removal. For method FORWARD, REGRESSION selects variables according to the probability of *F*-to-enter (keyword PIN), depending on your specification. You can override these default criteria and specify that *F*-to-enter (keyword FIN) be used instead to control entry. For method BACKWARD,

REGRESSION selects variables according to the probability of *F*-to-remove (keyword POUT). Alternatively, you can specify that *F*-to-remove (keyword FOUT) be used to control removal.

For method STEPWISE, both PIN and POUT are criteria for the equation. If the criterion for entry (PIN or FIN) is less stringent than the criterion for removal (POUT or FOUT), the STEPWISE method can cause the same variable to cycle in and out, over and over, until the maximum number of steps is reached. If you specify a PIN value that is larger than POUT, or a FIN value that is smaller than FOUT, REGRESSION issues a warning message and adjusts the POUT or FOUT values.

The criteria keywords are

DEFAULTS** *PIN(0.05), POUT(0.1), and TOLERANCE(0.01).* If you do not specify a CRITERIA subcommand, these are the defaults. If you have changed the criteria for an equation, use the keyword DEFAULTS to restore these defaults.

PIN(value) *Probability of* F*-to-enter.* The default value is 0.05.

POUT(value) *Probability of* F*-to-remove.* The default value is 0.10.

FIN(value) F*-to-enter.* If no value is specified, the default is 3.84.

FOUT(value) F*-to-remove.* If no value is specified, the default is 2.71.

TOLERANCE(value) *Tolerance.* The default value is 0.01.

MAXSTEPS(n) *Maximum number of steps.* For the STEPWISE method, the default is twice the number of independent variables. For the FORWARD and BACKWARD methods, the default maximum is the number of variables meeting the PIN and POUT or FIN and FOUT criteria. The MAXSTEPS value applies to the total model. The default value for the total model is the sum of the maximum number of steps over each method in the model.

A CRITERIA subcommand must appear before the DEPENDENT subcommand that initiates the equation and after the VARIABLES subcommand. The criteria remain in effect for all subsequent regression analyses until modified. For example,

```
REGRESSION      VARS=SALARY TO VERBAL/
                 CRITERIA=PIN(.1) POUT(.15) TOL(.0001)/
                  DEP=VERBAL/FORWARD/
                 CRITERIA=DEFAULTS/
                  DEP=VERBAL/STEPWISE
```

the first CRITERIA subcommand relaxes the default criteria for entry and removal, while the second CRITERIA subcommand reestablishes the defaults.

SPSS^X uses the last criterion that it encounters in the subcommand. For example,

```
   CRITERIA=PIN(.03) FIN(2.0)/
```

first sets the criterion to a probability of *F*-to-enter of 0.03. This criterion is replaced by the FIN specification which sets the criterion to an *F* value of 2.0.

33.13 The STATISTICS Subcommand

Use the STATISTICS subcommand to display a number of statistics for the regression equation. There are three types of STATISTICS keywords: (1) controls for the volume of output; (2) summary statistics for the equation;

and (3) statistics for the independent variables.

Volume of Output. The keywords are

DEFAULTS**	*R, ANOVA, COEFF, and OUTS*. In the absence of any STATISTICS subcommand, these are the default statistics displayed.
LINE	*Print a single summary line of output for each step performed. Full output is produced at the end of each method block.*
HISTORY	*Print a final summary report*. Contents are summary statistics computed at each step.
END	*Print one line per step (STEPWISE, FORWARD, or BACKWARD) or one line per block (ENTER, REMOVE) and full output only at the end of the model.*
ALL	*Print all summary statistics except LABEL,* F, *LINE, and END.*

Summary Statistics for the Equation. The keywords are

R**	*Multiple* R. Print the multiple R, R^2, adjusted R^2, and standard error of the estimate.
ANOVA**	*Analysis of variance table*. Print the analysis of variance table for the model, F value for multiple R, and significance level of F.
CHA	*Change in* R^2. Print the change in R^2 between steps, F value for change in R^2, and significance level of F.
BCOV	*Variance-covariance matrix for unstandardized regression coefficients*. Print a matrix with the following elements: variances of the regression estimates on the diagonal, the covariances of the regression estimates below the diagonal, and correlations of the regression estimates above the diagonal.
XTX	*Sweep matrix*. Print the current status of the sweep matrix.
COND	*Condition number bounds*. Print the lower and upper bounds for the condition number of the submatrix of the sweep matrix which contains independent variables already entered. (See Berk, 1977.)

Statistics for the Independent Variables. The keywords are

COEFF**	*Regression coefficients*. Print the unstandardized regression coefficient (B), the standard error of B, standardized regression coefficient (beta), t value for B, and two-tailed significance level of t for each variable in the equation.
OUTS**	*Coefficients and statistics for variables not yet in the equation*. Print the standardized regression coefficient (beta) if the variable were to enter the equation at the next step, t value for B, significance level of t, partial correlation with the dependent variable controlling for all variables in the equation, and minimum tolerance.
ZPP	*Correlation, part, and partial correlation*. Print the zero-order correlation of each independent variable in the equation with the dependent variable, the part correlation for each independent variable, and the partial correlation with the dependent variable controlling for the other independent variables in the equation.
CI	*95% confidence interval for the unstandardized regression coefficient.*
SES	*Approximate standard error of beta*. (See Meyer & Younger, 1976.)
TOL	*Tolerance and minimum tolerance.*
LABEL	*Variable labels.*
F	F *value for* B *and its significance level.* Displayed instead of the t value. Significance of t is the same as the significance of F in this case.

The STATISTICS subcommand must appear before the DEPENDENT subcommand. It remains in effect for all new equations until overridden by another STATISTICS subcommand.

Figure 33.13 shows a display produced by specifying ALL on the STATISTICS subcommand.

Figure 33.13 STATISTICS=ALL display

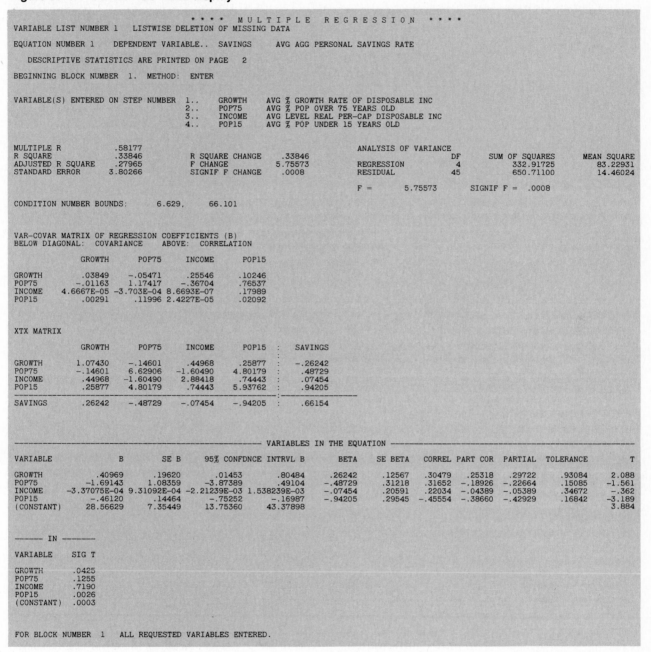

```
                                  * * * *   M U L T I P L E   R E G R E S S I O N   * * * *
VARIABLE LIST NUMBER 1   LISTWISE DELETION OF MISSING DATA

EQUATION NUMBER 1   DEPENDENT VARIABLE..  SAVINGS      AVG AGG PERSONAL SAVINGS RATE

   DESCRIPTIVE STATISTICS ARE PRINTED ON PAGE   2

BEGINNING BLOCK NUMBER  1.  METHOD:  ENTER

VARIABLE(S) ENTERED ON STEP NUMBER  1..     GROWTH    AVG % GROWTH RATE OF DISPOSABLE INC
                                    2..     POP75     AVG % POP OVER 75 YEARS OLD
                                    3..     INCOME    AVG LEVEL REAL PER-CAP DISPOSABLE INC
                                    4..     POP15     AVG % POP UNDER 15 YEARS OLD

MULTIPLE R           .58177                                             ANALYSIS OF VARIANCE
R SQUARE             .33846         R SQUARE CHANGE    .33846                                DF      SUM OF SQUARES        MEAN SQUARE
ADJUSTED R SQUARE    .27965         F CHANGE          5.75573           REGRESSION            4           332.91725           83.22931
STANDARD ERROR      3.80266         SIGNIF F CHANGE    .0008            RESIDUAL             45           650.71100           14.46024

                                                                        F =        5.75573        SIGNIF F =  .0008

CONDITION NUMBER BOUNDS:        6.629,       66.101


VAR-COVAR MATRIX OF REGRESSION COEFFICIENTS (B)
BELOW DIAGONAL:  COVARIANCE     ABOVE:  CORRELATION

                 GROWTH       POP75      INCOME       POP15

GROWTH           .03849     -.05471      .25546      .10246
POP75           -.01163     1.17417     -.36704      .76537
INCOME      4.6667E-05 -3.703E-04 8.6693E-07      .17989
POP15            .00291      .11996 2.4227E-05      .02092


XTX MATRIX

                 GROWTH       POP75      INCOME       POP15  :     SAVINGS
                                                              :
GROWTH          1.07430     -.14601      .44968      .25877  :     -.26242
POP75           -.14601     6.62906    -1.60490     4.80179  :      .48729
INCOME           .44968    -1.60490     2.88418      .74443  :      .07454
POP15            .25877     4.80179      .74443     5.93762  :      .94205
--------------------------------------------------------------:----------------
SAVINGS          .26242     -.48729     -.07454     -.94205  :      .66154


------------------------------------------------------ VARIABLES IN THE EQUATION -------------------------------------------------------

VARIABLE                B          SE B    95% CONFDNCE INTRVL B        BETA     SE BETA    CORREL PART COR  PARTIAL  TOLERANCE          T

GROWTH             .40969        .19620        .01453        .80484      .26242      .12567    .30479   .25318   .29722     .93084      2.088
POP75            -1.69143       1.08359      -3.87389        .49104     -.48729      .31218    .31652  -.18926  -.22664     .15085     -1.561
INCOME       -3.37075E-04 9.31092E-04 -2.21239E-03 1.538239E-03     -.07454      .20591    .22034  -.04389  -.05389     .34672      -.362
POP15             -.46120        .14464       -.75252       -.16987     -.94205      .29545   -.45554  -.38660  -.42929     .16842     -3.189
(CONSTANT)       28.56629       7.35449      13.75360      43.37898                                                                    3.884


------ IN -------

VARIABLE     SIG T

GROWTH       .0425
POP75        .1255
INCOME       .7190
POP15        .0026
(CONSTANT)   .0003


FOR BLOCK NUMBER  1   ALL REQUESTED VARIABLES ENTERED.
```

33.14 Regression through the Origin

Use the ORIGIN subcommand keyword to specify regression through the origin. Place the ORIGIN subcommand between the VARIABLES subcommand and the DEPENDENT subcommand. ORIGIN is in effect for all subsequent analyses unless you specify the keyword NOORIGIN.

For example,

```
REGRESSION      VARIABLES=GNP TO M1/
                ORIGIN/
                DEPENDENT=GNP/FORWARD
```

requests a regression analysis through the origin using GNP as the dependent variable and selecting variables for the model using the forward-entry method.

33.15 Analysis of Residuals

Use the following subcommands for analysis of residuals: RESIDUALS, CASEWISE, SCATTERPLOT, PARTIALPLOT, and SAVE. Any or all of these keywords can be specified in any order to obtain an analysis of residuals. For each analysis, REGRESSION can calculate 12 temporary variables containing several types of residuals, predicted values, and related measures. Optionally, these variables can be added to the active file for analysis using other SPSSX procedures.

33.16 Temporary Variables

The following temporary variables are available for the analysis of residuals.

PRED *Unstandardized predicted values.*
RESID *Unstandardized residuals.*
DRESID *Deleted residuals.*
ADJPRED *Adjusted predicted values.*
ZPRED *Standardized predicted values.*
ZRESID *Standardized residuals.*
SRESID *Studentized residuals.*
SDRESID *Studentized deleted residuals.* (See Hoaglin & Welsch, 1978.)
SEPRED *Standard errors of the predicted values.*
MAHAL *Mahalanobis' distances.*
COOK *Cook's distances.* (See Cook, 1977.)
LEVER *Leverage values.* (See Velleman & Welsch, 1981.)

33.17 The RESIDUALS Subcommand

Several measures and plots based on the residuals and predicted values for the regression equation can be displayed. Specifications for the RESIDUALS subcommand are

DEFAULTS* *SIZE(LARGE), DURBIN, NORMPROB(ZRESID), HISTOGRAM(ZRESID), and OUTLIERS(ZRESID).*

SIZE(plotsize) *Plot sizes.* The default is LARGE if the display width is at least 120 (see Section 33.25) and the page length is at least 55.

HISTOGRAM(varlist) *A histogram of the temporary variable or variables named.* The default variable is ZRESID. Other variables that can be plotted include PRED, RESID, ZPRED, DRESID, ADJPRED, SRESID, and SDRESID.

NORMPROB(varlist) *A normal probability* (P-P) *plot of standardized values.* The default variable is ZRESID. Other variables that can be plotted are PRED, RESID, ZPRED, DRESID, ADJPRED, SRESID, and SDRESID.

OUTLIERS(varlist) *The 10 worst outliers based on values of the variables specified.* The default variable is ZRESID. Other variables that can be used include RESID, SRESID, SDRESID, DRESID, MAHAL, and COOK.

DURBIN *Durbin-Watson test statistic.*

ID(varname) *Use the values from this variable to label casewise or outlier plots.* Any variable in your file can be named. If ID(varname) is not specified, cases are identified by case number. ID also labels the list of cases obtained from the CASEWISE subcommand (see Section 33.18).

POOLED *Display pooled plots and statistics for selected and nonselected cases.* The default is SEPARATE, so that if SELECT is in effect, separate copies of the summary statistics and all plots are produced for selected and nonselected cases.

The RESIDUALS subcommand must follow the last method keyword. All calculations and plots requested on the RESIDUALS subcommand are based on the regression equation produced as a result of the last method specified.

For example,

```
RESID=DEFAULT SIZE(SMALL) ID(COUNTRY)/
```

requests residual statistics and plots. DEFAULT implies a normal probability plot of standardized residuals, a histogram of standardized residuals, a table showing the 10 worst outliers based on the values of the standardized residual, the Durbin-Watson statistic, and large plot sizes. SIZE(SMALL) overrides the large plot sizes. ID(COUNTRY) names COUNTRY as a variable to identify the cases on outlier plots.

33.18 The CASEWISE Subcommand

You can display a casewise plot of any of the temporary residuals variables accompanied by a listing of the values of the dependent variable and the values of as many of the other temporary variables as can be displayed in the available page width (see Section 33.25). Candidate variables for display include the 12 temporary residual variables, the dependent variable, and the ID variable (see Section 33.17). The widest page allows a maximum of eight of these to be displayed. There is no way to display all candidate variables in one analysis.

For example,

```
CASEWISE=DEFAULT ALL SRE MAH COOK SDR/
```

displays the dependent variable SAVINGS and the six temporary variables PRED, RESID, SRESID, SDRESID, MAHAL, and COOK D for all cases, and plots the standardized residuals in the casewise plot. The display from this subcommand is shown in Figure 33.18.

The CASEWISE subcommand has the following specifications:

DEFAULTS* *OUTLIERS(3), PLOT(ZRESID), DEPENDENT, PRED, and RESID.*

OUTLIERS(value) *Limit plot to outliers defined by this value.* The plot contains those cases whose absolute value is at least as large as the value you specify. The default value is 3 for standardized residuals (ZRESID). The keyword ALL can be specified, in which case all cases are displayed. This is not recommended for large files because it results in a line being printed for each case.

PLOT(varname) *Plot the values of this temporary variable in the casewise plot.* The default variable is ZRESID. You can also specify RESID and DRESID, both of which will be standardized for the plot, or the already standardized SRESID and SDRESID.

varlist *Display the values of these variables.* Some combination of the 12 temporary variables can be specified, although not all 12 can be displayed. The defaults are DEPENDENT (for the dependent variable), PRED, and RESID.

33.19 The SCATTERPLOT Subcommand

Use the SCATTERPLOT subcommand to display a series of scatterplots of the temporary variables and the variables in the regression equation. Whenever you specify a temporary variable in a scatterplot, you must precede the keyword with an asterisk (*) to distinguish the temporary variable keyword from a standard variable name. Specifications are

SIZE(plotsize) *Plot sizes.* The default is SMALL for scatterplots. Keyword LARGE requires substantially more computer memory and should be used only when detail is required.

(varname,varname) *Plot the variables specified.* If the variable is one of the temporary variables, precede the keyword with an asterisk. Temporary variables that can be plotted include PRED, RESID, ZPRED, ZRESID, DRESID, ADJPRED, SRESID, and SDRESID. Moreover, these variables, as well as MAHAL, COOK, MAHAL, and SEPRED, can be saved on the active file and plotted later using the SCATTERGRAM procedure. Otherwise, the name can be any variable specified on the VARIABLES subcommand. Specify as many pairs in parentheses as you want plots.

The first variable named in each set of parentheses is plotted along the vertical axis. The second variable is plotted along the horizontal axis. Plotting symbols are used to represent multiple points occurring at the same print position.

All scatterplots are standardized. That is, specifying *RESID is the same as specifying *ZRESID, and *PRED is the same as *ZPRED. To obtain unstandardized scatterplots, save residuals variables on the active file for subsequent processing with procedure SCATTERGRAM.

For example,

```
SCATTERPLOT (*RES,*PRE)(*RES,SAVINGS)/
```

specifies two scatterplots—the plot of the residuals against the predicted values and the plot of the residuals against the values of the dependent variable.

Figure 33.18 Casewise plot for 50 nations

```
EQUATION NUMBER 1    DEPENDENT VARIABLE.. SAVINGS     AVG AGG PERSONAL SAVINGS RATE

CASEWISE PLOT OF STANDARDIZED RESIDUAL

*: SELECTED    M: MISSING

                 -3.0      0.0       3.0
CASE # COUNTRY    0:........:........:0   SAVINGS      *PRED     *RESID    *SRESID   *SDRESID      *MAHAL    *COOK D
     1 Australi   .         .*        .     11.43    10.5663      .8637      .2352      .2328     2.3379      .0008
     2 Austria    .         *         .     12.07    11.4538      .6162      .1728      .1709     4.9187      .0008
     3 Belgium    .         . *       .     13.17    10.9511     2.2189      .6108      .6065     3.3066      .0072
     4 Bolivia    .        *.         .      5.75     6.4484     -.6984     -.1925     -.1904     3.4041      .0007
     5 Brazil     .         .  *      .     12.88     9.3271     3.5529      .9686      .9679     2.4283      .0140
     6 Canada     .         *         .      8.79     9.1066     -.3166     -.0908     -.0898     6.7815      .0003
     7 Chile      .  *      .         .       .60     8.8422    -8.2422    -2.2091    -2.3134      .8476      .0378
     8 Colombia   .        *.         .      4.98     6.4317    -1.4517     -.3932     -.3895     1.8278      .0019
     9 Costa Ri   .         .   *     .     10.78     5.6549     5.1251     1.4017     1.4173     2.7179      .0321
    10 Denmark    .         .   *     .     16.85    11.4497     5.4003     1.4669     1.4865     2.0932      .0288
    11 Ecuador    .       * .         .      3.59     5.9957    -2.4057     -.6538     -.6496     2.1426      .0058
    12 Finland    .        *.         .     11.24    12.9210    -1.6810     -.4639     -.4598     3.5301      .0044
    13 France     .         . *       .     12.64    10.1646     2.4754      .7004      .6964     5.6940      .0155
    14 Germany    .         *         .     12.55    12.7306     -.1806     -.0497     -.0492     3.3005      .0000
    15 Greece     .       * .         .     10.67    13.7863    -3.1163     -.8622     -.8597     3.7544      .0159
    16 Guatemal   .      *  .         .      3.01     6.3653    -3.3553     -.9103     -.9086     1.9841      .0107
    17 Honduras   .         .*        .      7.70     6.9900      .7100      .1926      .1905     1.9639      .0005
    18 Iceland    .    *    .         .      1.27     7.4805    -6.2105    -1.6940    -1.7312     2.4743      .0435
    19 India      .         *         .      9.00     8.4914      .5086      .1388      .1373     2.5212      .0003
    20 Ireland    .         .  *      .     11.34     7.9490     3.3910     1.0047     1.0048     9.4195      .0544
    21 Italy      .         . *       .     14.28    12.3533     1.9267      .5244      .5201     2.2790      .0039
    22 Jamaica    .       * .         .      7.72    10.7385    -3.0185     -.8564     -.8538     5.9172      .0240
    23 Japan      .         .   *     .     21.10    15.8185     5.2815     1.5760     1.6032     9.9621      .1428
    24 Korea      .    *    .         .      3.98    10.0870    -6.1070    -1.6571    -1.6910     1.9992      .0356
    25 Libya      .       * .         .      8.89    11.7195    -2.8295    -1.0871    -1.0893    25.0614      .2681
    26 Luxembou   .        *.         .     10.35    12.0208    -1.6708     -.4597     -.4556     3.2511      .0040
    27 Malaysia   .       * .         .      4.71     7.6805    -2.9705     -.8080     -.8048     2.2178      .0091
    28 Malta      .         . *       .     15.48    12.5052     2.9748      .8153      .8123     2.9108      .0115
    29 Netherla   .         *         .     14.65    14.2244      .4256      .1174      .1161     3.4601      .0003
    30 New Zeal   .         . *       .     10.67     8.3845     2.2855      .6180      .6137     1.6767      .0044
    31 Nicaragu   .         .*        .      7.30     6.6536      .6464      .1744      .1725     1.4872      .0003
    32 Norway     .        *.         .     10.25    11.1217     -.8717     -.2349     -.2325     1.3687      .0006
    33 Panama     .      *  .         .      4.44     7.7342    -3.2942     -.8837     -.8815      .9297      .0063
    34 Paraguay   .    *    .         .      2.02     8.1458    -6.1258    -1.6699    -1.7049     2.4193      .0416
    35 Peru       .         .    *    .     12.70     6.1606     6.5394     1.7785     1.8239     2.2074      .0440
    36 Philippi   .         .    *    .     12.78     6.1050     6.6750     1.8146     1.8638     2.1685      .0452
    37 Portugal   .        *.         .     12.49    13.2586     -.7686     -.2127     -.2104     3.7803      .0010
    38 South Af   .         *         .     11.14    10.6569      .4831      .1314      .1299     2.2101      .0002
    39 South Rh   .         .*        .     13.30    12.0087     1.2913      .3707      .3671     6.8996      .0053
    40 Spain      .        *.         .     11.77    12.4413     -.6713     -.1838     -.1818     2.8091      .0006
    41 Sweden     .      *  .         .      6.86    11.1201    -4.2601    -1.1970    -1.2029     5.0955      .0406
    42 Switzerl   .         . *       .     14.13    11.6431     2.4869      .6795      .6754     2.6262      .0073
    43 Taiwan     .         . *       .     11.90     9.3639     2.5361      .6945      .6905     2.8399      .0082
    44 Tunisia    .       * .         .      2.81     5.6280    -2.8180     -.7703     -.7668     2.6738      .0096
    45 Turkey     .       * .         .      5.13     7.7957    -2.6657     -.7153     -.7114      .9625      .0042
    46 U.K.       .       * .         .      7.81    10.5025    -2.6925     -.7533     -.7496     4.7290      .0150
    47 U.S.       .        *.         .      7.56     8.6712    -1.1112     -.3580     -.3545    15.3703      .0128
    48 Uruguay    .       * .         .      9.24    11.5040    -2.2640     -.6269     -.6226     3.8193      .0085
    49 Venezuel   .         .  *      .      9.22     5.5874     3.6326      .9994      .9993     3.2478      .0189
    50 Zambia     .         .       * .     18.56     8.8091     9.7509     2.6509     2.8536     2.1722      .0966
CASE # COUNTRY    0:........:........:0   SAVINGS      *PRED     *RESID    *SRESID   *SDRESID      *MAHAL    *COOK D
                 -3.0      0.0       3.0
```

33.20 The PARTIALPLOT Subcommand

The PARTIALPLOT subcommand produces partial residual plots. Partial residual plots are scatterplots of the residuals of the dependent and an independent variable when you regress both of these variables on the rest of the independent variables. The default specification

```
PARTIALPLOT/
```

produces as many partial residual plots as there are independent variables in the model. Small plots, SIZE(SMALL), are printed by default. These plots are standardized. They have the same format as the plots produced by the SCATTERPLOT subcommand.

If you want to see only plots for some of the independent variables, name the independent variables after the subcommand keyword, as in:

```
PARTIALPLOT POP15 POP75/
```

If you prefer large plots, specify:

```
PARTIALPLOT SIZE(LARGE)
```

The plots are displayed in descending order of the standard error of *B*.

Figure 33.20 displays the partial residual plots produced by the following command:

```
REGRESSION VARIABLES=SAVINGS TO GROWTH/
  DEP=SAVINGS/ENTER/
 RESIDUALS=DEFAULTS/PARTIALPLOT
```

Figure 33.20 Partial residual plots

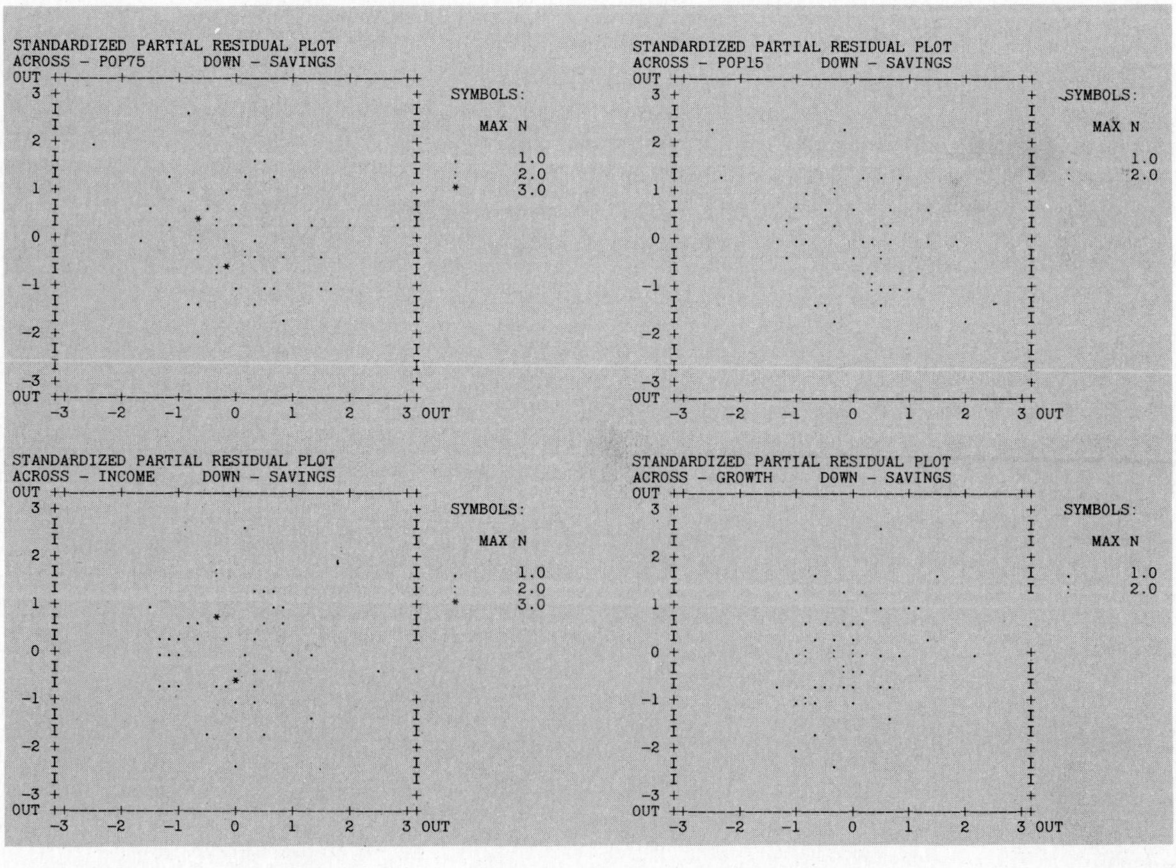

ANNOTATED EXAMPLE FOR REGRESSION

The task is to predict the average aggregate personal savings rate of a country as a function of the age distribution of the population, the average level of real per capita disposable income, and the average percentage growth rate of real per capita disposable income of a country. The data are 50 cases taken from an example in Belsley, Kuh, and Welsch (1980).

The variables are

- SAVINGS—the average aggregate personal savings rate in a country over the period 1960–1970.
- POP15—the average percentage of the population under 15 years of age over the period 1960–1970.
- POP75—the average percentage of the population over 75 years of age over the period 1960–1970.
- INCOME—the average level of real per capita disposable income in a country over the period 1960–1970, measured in United States dollars.
- GROWTH—the average percentage growth rate of INCOME over the period 1960–1970.

The SPSS^X commands are

```
FILE HANDLE COUNTRY / file specifications
DATA LIST FILE COUNTRY / COUNTRY 1-8(A) SAVINGS POP15 POP75
  INCOME GROWTH 11-60
VAR LABELS
  SAVINGS 'AVG AGG PERSONAL SAVINGS RATE'
  POP15 'AVG % POP UNDER 15 YEARS OLD'
  POP75 'AVG % POP OVER 75 YEARS OLD'
  INCOME 'AVG LEVEL REAL PER-CAP DISPOSABLE INC'
  GROWTH 'AVG % GROWTH RATE OF DPI'
REGRESSION  VARS=SAVINGS TO GROWTH/DEP=SAVINGS/ENTER/
   RESID=DEFAULT SIZE(SMALL) ID(COUNTRY)/
   SCATTERPLOT (*RES,*PRE)/PARTIALPLOT/
```

- The FILE HANDLE command assigns file handle COUNTRY to the file containing the data.
- The DATA LIST command defines the variables in file handle COUNTRY. The VAR LABELS command assigns labels to the variables.
- The REGRESSION command requests a direct-entry regression analysis with variable SAVINGS as the dependent variable.
- The RESIDUALS subcommand requests the default residual results. In addition, the SIZE(SMALL) keyword overrides the default plot sizes so that small plots are displayed. The ID(COUNTRY) keyword specifies that the values for variable COUNTRY are to be used to label outlier plots. Figure A shows the residual statistics and outlier plots. Figure B displays the histogram of the standardized residual and the normal probability plot.
- The SCATTERPLOT subcommand requests a plot of the residuals against the predicted values. Since *RES is specified first, it is plotted along the vertical axis. (See Figure C.)

A Residual statistics and outliers

```
* * * * * * * * * * * * * * * * * * * * * * * * * * * * * *
```

RESIDUALS STATISTICS:

	MIN	MAX	MEAN	STD DEV	N
*PRED	5.5874	15.8185	9.6710	2.6066	50
*ZPRED	-1.5666	2.3584	-.0000	1.0000	50
*SEPRED	.7344	2.7722	1.1481	.3612	50
*ADJPRED	5.2366	14.9290	9.7052	2.6865	50
*MAHAL	.8476	25.0613	3.9200	3.9842	50
*COOK D	.0000	.2681	.0229	.0440	50

	MIN	MAX	MEAN	STD DEV	N
*RESID	-8.2422	9.7509	.0000	3.6441	50
*ZRESID	-2.1675	2.5642	.0000	.9583	50
*SRESID	-2.2091	2.6509	-.0031	1.0053	50
*DRESID	-8.5616	10.4213	-.0342	4.0378	50
*SDRESID	-2.3134	2.8536	-.0000	1.0293	50
*LEVER	.0173	.5115	.0800	.0813	50

TOTAL CASES = 50

DURBIN-WATSON TEST = 1.68579

OUTLIERS - STANDARDIZED RESIDUAL

CASE #	COUNTRY	*ZRESID
50	Zambia	2.56423
7	Chile	-2.16749
36	Philippi	1.75534
35	Peru	1.71969
18	Iceland	-1.63321
34	Paraguay	-1.61093
24	Korea	-1.60598
10	Denmark	1.42014
23	Japan	1.38890
9	Costa Ri	1.34776

B Histograms and normal probability plots

```
* * * * * * * * * * * * * * * * * * * * * * * * * * * * * *

HISTOGRAM
STANDARDIZED RESIDUAL
NEXP N      (* = 1 CASES,    . : = NORMAL CURVE)
0  .04   OUT
0  .08  3.00
1  .20  2.67 *
0  .45  2.33
0  .91  2.00 .
2 1.67  1.67 *:
3 2.74  1.33 **:
3 4.03  1.00 ***.
7 5.31   .67 ****:**
4 6.26   .33 ****  .
6 6.62  0.0  ******.
8 6.26  -.33 *****:**
9 5.31  -.67 ****:****
3 4.03 -1.00 ***.
0 2.74 -1.33    .
3 1.67 -1.67 *:*
0  .91 -2.00 .
1  .45 -2.33 *
0  .20 -2.67
0  .08 -3.00
0  .04   OUT
```

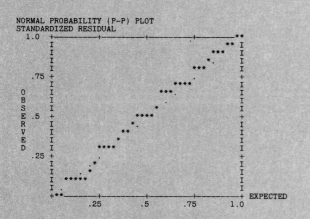

```
NORMAL PROBABILITY (P-P) PLOT
STANDARDIZED RESIDUAL
   1.0 +---------+---------+--------.+--------**
       I                                    ** I
       I                                 ***   I
       I                                *.     I
       I                             ***       I
   .75 +                             .         +
       I                         ****          I
 O     I                      ***.             I
 B     I                       .               I
 S     I                     *                 I
 E .5  +                 ****                  +
 R     I                *.                     I
 V     I              **                       I
 E     I             *                         I
 D     I         ****                          I
   .25 +         .                             +
       I       .*                              I
       I     . *                               I
       I  *****                                I
       I .                                     I
       +**-------+---------+---------+---------+ EXPECTED
                .25        .5       .75       1.0
```

C Fit against residual plots

```
* * * * * * * * * * * * * * * * * * * * * * * * * * * * * *

STANDARDIZED SCATTERPLOT
ACROSS - *PRED      DOWN - *RESID
OUT ++-----+-----+-----+-----+-----+-----++
  3 +                                     +   SYMBOLS:
    I                .                    I
    I                                     I      MAX N
  2 +                                     +
    I          :                          I   .     1.0
    I         .            .         .    I   :     2.0
  1 +         .    .  .                   +
    I               . . . . ...           I
    I           ..       .  .             I
  0 +               . . .  .  .  .        +
    I           :    .    . ....          I
    I         ..  ..     : ..   .         I
 -1 +          .   .      .               +
    I                                     I
    I             ..    .                 I
 -2 +                                     +
    I                .                    I
    I                                     I
 -3 +                                     +
OUT ++-----+-----+-----+-----+-----+-----++
     -3    -2    -1     0     1     2     3 OUT
```

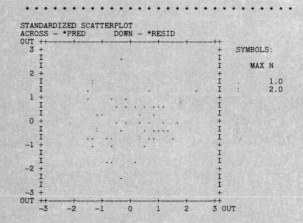

33.21 The SAVE Subcommand

Use the SAVE subcommand to save any or all of the 12 temporary variables. The general form of the SAVE subcommand is as follows:

SAVE tempvar(newname), tempvar(newname),.../

Tempvar is a temporary residual variable and *newname* is a unique variable name conforming to all SPSS^X conventions for naming variables.

For example,

```
REGRESSION     VARIABLES=SAVINGS TO GROWTH/
     DEPENDENT=SAVINGS/ENTER/
     SAVE PRED(PREDSR)/
SCATTERGRAM PREDSR WITH SAVINGS
```

saves the predicted values with variable name PREDSR. Then the SCATTERGRAM procedure can be used to plot the predicted values against the values of the dependent variable SAVINGS. Figure 33.21 shows a portion of the output from these commands.

Figure 33.21 Saving temporary variables

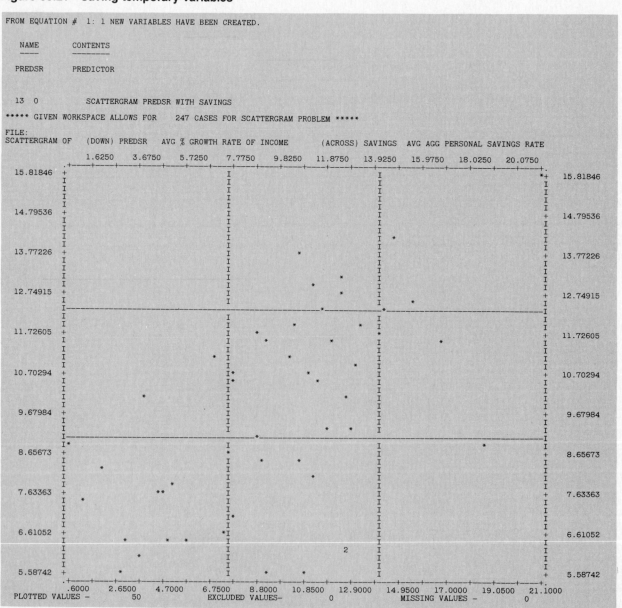

```
FROM EQUATION # 1: 1 NEW VARIABLES HAVE BEEN CREATED.

  NAME        CONTENTS
  ----        --------
 PREDSR       PREDICTOR

 13  0          SCATTERGRAM PREDSR WITH SAVINGS

***** GIVEN WORKSPACE ALLOWS FOR    247 CASES FOR SCATTERGRAM PROBLEM *****

FILE:
SCATTERGRAM OF   (DOWN) PREDSR   AVG % GROWTH RATE OF INCOME       (ACROSS) SAVINGS  AVG AGG PERSONAL SAVINGS RATE
```

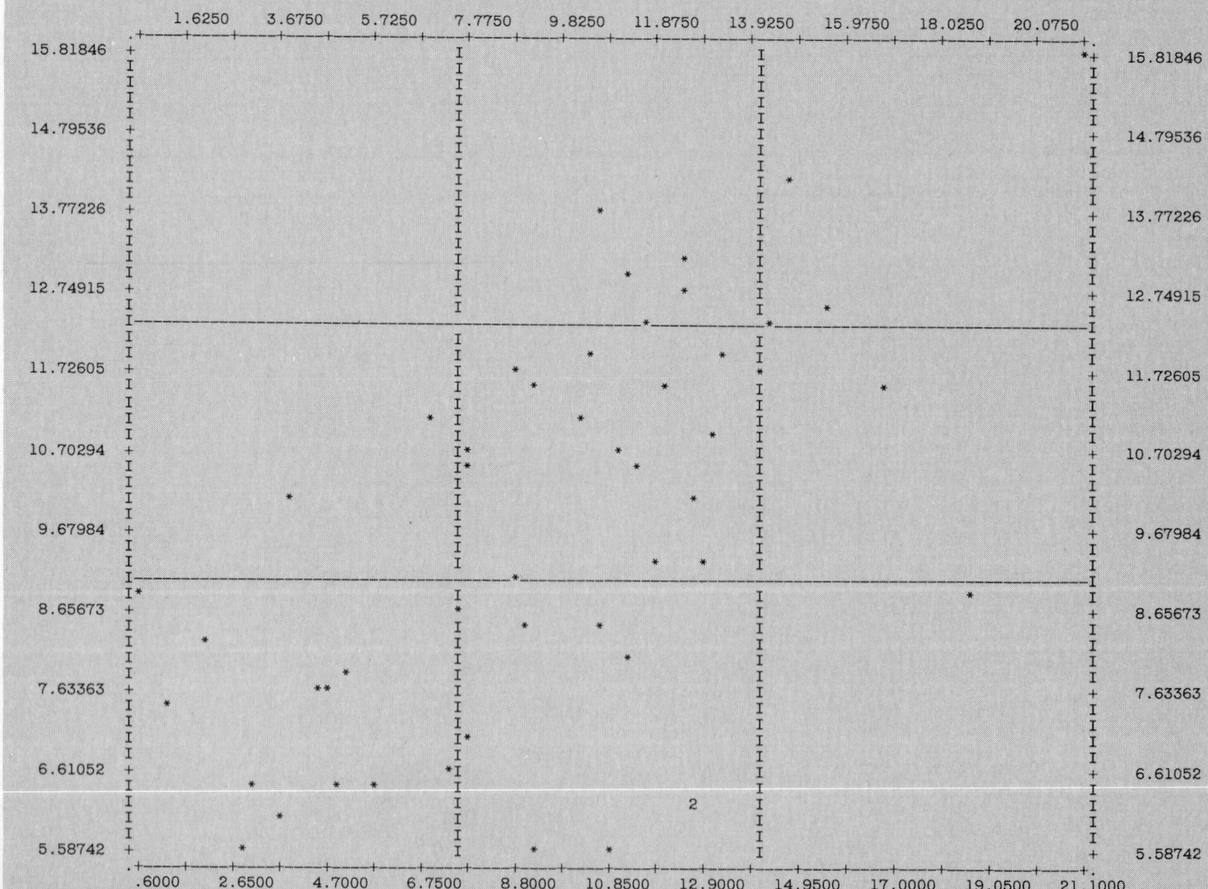


```
PLOTTED VALUES -        50         EXCLUDED VALUES-          0            MISSING VALUES -          0
```

33.22 Matrix Materials

REGRESSION can read and write matrix materials. Use the READ subcommand to read matrix materials (see Section 33.23). Use the WRITE subcommand to write matrix materials to an external file (see Section 33.24).

33.23 The READ Subcommand

If you have one or more correlation or covariance matrices to read in place of raw data, use the READ subcommand. READ must be the first subcommand specified. Only one READ subcommand can be specified in a REGRESSION command. You must employ the SPSS^X command INPUT MATRIX along with an associated FILE HANDLE command (see Chapter 17). The following keyword specifications can be used.

DEFAULTS* *MEAN, STDDEV, CORR, and N.* If you specify subcommand READ with no specifications, these are the defaults.

MEAN *The matrix is preceded by variable means.*

STDDEV *The matrix is preceded by variable standard deviations.*

VARIANCE *The matrix is preceded by variable variances.*

CORR *Correlation matrix.* Alternative to keyword COV.

COV *Covariance matrix.* Alternative to keyword CORR. You cannot read a covariance matrix if you specify pairwise deletion of missing values.

N *The number of cases used to compute correlation coefficients.* Overrides an N OF CASES command.

INDEX *Index the matrix by the number and order of variables on the DATA LIST command.* Only a single matrix is read.

Either CORR or COV can be specified. The matrix materials must be arranged in the input file in the order given above. Keyword DEFAULTS can also be used in conjunction with other keywords to reduce the length of the command, as in:

```
READ = DEFAULTS INDEX/
```

The keyword INDEX indexes the matrix by the order of variables in the dictionary. Use this keyword to read in a single matrix for several sets of model specifications.

If you read in more than one matrix, the first matrix is automatically indexed by the number and order of variables in the first VARIABLES subcommand, the second matrix by the second VARIABLES list, and so on. A separate set of data—that is, means, standard deviations, matrix, and so on—must be read in for every VARIABLES subcommand. You cannot use the (COLLECT) keyword in the VARIABLES subcommand if the READ subcommand is used.

Keyword N following either CORR or COV indicates that the number or numbers of cases on which the correlation coefficients are based follow the matrix. When either pairwise missing-value treatment (allowed only for keyword CORR) or mean substitution is used (see Section 33.8), an entire symmetric matrix of n's should accompany the matrix. If SPSS^X does not find this matrix, you are warned. If you use missing-value inclusion or listwise missing-value treatment, the n is the same for each coefficient. In this case, supply a single value in the first 10 columns of the data record following the matrix. Alternatively, you can specify the number of cases with an N OF CASES command.

If you are using matrix materials which have not been produced by SPSS^X, you can format them in either free or fixed format. REGRESSION reads free-format materials if you specify FREE on the INPUT MATRIX command. When preparing matrix materials in freefield format, begin each set of materials on a new record. If you read matrix materials in fixed format, SPSS^X expects the records to contain eight fields, each 10 columns wide. The items should contain physical decimal points. For further discussion, see Chapter 17.

You can use matrix materials with REGRESSION in two ways. One is to use matrix materials in place of a file of cases. When you do this you can obtain all results except residuals processing. That is, subcommands RESIDUALS, CASEWISE, SCATTERPLOT, PARTIALPLOT, and SAVE cannot be specified. To use matrix materials by themselves, define variables with the NUMERIC command (Chapter 6) to establish a dictionary. Use the INPUT MATRIX command (Chapter 17) to refer to the file containing the matrix materials. For example, assume that you saved the default matrix materials from REGRESSION on a file in a prior run. To read matrix materials, specify:

```
FILE HANDLE REGMAT / file specifications
INPUT PROGRAM
NUMERIC  Y X1 TO X10
INPUT MATRIX  FILE=REGMAT
END INPUT PROGRAM
REGRESSION  READ/
            VARIABLES=Y X1 TO X10/
            DEPENDENT=Y/
            STEPWISE
```

You can also use matrix input along with a file to calculate residuals and predictors based on a regression analysis from a different sample of cases. When you do this you can specify the RESIDUALS, CASEWISE, SCATTERPLOT, PARTIALPLOT, and SAVE subcommands.

REGRESSION also reads matrix materials written by other SPSS^X procedures if you use the appropriate READ subcommand specifications.

33.24 The WRITE Subcommand

The univariate descriptive statistics, correlation and covariance matrices, and *n*'s can be written to an external file using the following keyword specifications for the WRITE subcommand. You must also use the PROCEDURE OUTPUT command and an associated FILE HANDLE command (see Chapter 17).

DEFAULTS* *MEAN, STDDEV, CORR, and N.*

MEAN *Variable means.*

STDDEV *Variable standard deviation.*

VARIANCE *Variable variances.*

CORR *Correlation matrix.*

COV *Covariance matrix.*

N *The number or numbers of cases used to compute correlation coefficients.* Used with pairwise missing-value treatment or mean substitution (see Section 33.8).

NONE *Turn off previous WRITE specifications.*

A WRITE subcommand must precede the first VARIABLES subcommand to which it applies and remains in effect for all subsequent VARIABLES subcommands until overridden by a new WRITE specification or turned off by specifying WRITE=NONE.

Keyword DEFAULTS can be used in conjunction with other keywords to reduce the length of the command, as in:

```
WRITE DEFAULTS COV/
```

This command writes means, standard deviations, the covariances, and the number of cases.

When you use the WRITE subcommand, you must also use the PROCEDURE OUTPUT command (Chapter 17) to provide a file handle for the output file:

```
FILE HANDLE REGMAT / file specifications
PROCEDURE OUTPUT  OUTFILE=REGMAT
REGRESSION  DESCRIPTIVES/
            WRITE/
            VARS=SAVINGS TO GROWTH/
            DEPENDENT=SAVINGS/
            ENTER
```

writes the means, standard deviations, correlations, and number of cases in that order on file handle REGMAT. Each set of materials begins on a new record with eight items on each record. Since the default missing-value treatment is listwise, the number of cases is written as one item on the last record.

When you write an external file, REGRESSION displays a format table describing it.

33.25 The WIDTH Subcommand

You can control the width of output from REGRESSION. The default width is 132 characters, but you can specify any width from 60 to 132, as in:

```
REGRESSION      WIDTH=120/
                VARIABLES=Y TO X10/
                DEPENDENT=Y/
                ENTER
```

The width you choose affects the volume of regression statistics displayed and the amount of information displayed in a casewise residuals plot. This is especially the case when the width is quite narrow. The WIDTH subcommand can appear anywhere. If you specify more than one WIDTH subcommand, SPSS^X uses the width from the last WIDTH subcommand specified.

```
DISCRIMINANT GROUPS = varname (min, max) /VARIABLES = varlist
  [/SELECT = varname (value)]
  [/ANALYSIS = varlist (level)  [varlist . . . ]]

               DIRECT
               WILKS
  [/METHOD =   MAHAL      ]  [/TOLERANCE = {.001}]
               MAXMINF                     {t   }
               MINRESID
               RAO

  [/MAXSTEPS = {2v}]
               {m }

  [/FIN = {1.0}]  [/FOUT = {1.0}]  [/PIN = {1.0}]
          {fi }            {fo }           {pi }

  [/POUT = {1.0}]  [/VIN = {0 }]
           {po }           {vi}

                                                 EQUAL
  [/FUNCTIONS = {g − 1, 100.0, 1.0}]  [/PRIORS = SIZE       ]
                {nf, cp, sig      }              value list

  [/SAVE = [CLASS = varname]  [PROBS = rootname]
  [SCORES = rootname]]
  [/ANALYSIS = . . . ]
```

OPTIONS:
1 Include missing values.
2 Write matrix materials.
3 Read matrix materials.
4 Suppress step output.
5 Suppress summary table.
6 Varimax rotation of function matrix.
7 Varimax rotation of structure matrix.
8 Include cases with missing values during classification.
9 Classify only unselected cases.
10 Classify only unclassified cases.
11 Individual covariance matrices used for classification.

STATISTICS:
1 Group means.
2 Group standard deviations.
3 Pooled within-groups covariance matrix.
4 Pooled within-groups correlation matrix.
5 Matrix of pairwise F ratios.
6 Univariate F ratios.
7 Box's M.
8 Group covariance matrices.
9 Total covariance matrix.
10 Territorial map.
11 Unstandardized function coefficients.
12 Classification function coefficients.
13 Classification results table.
14 Casewise materials.
15 Combined plot.
16 Separate plot.

34

OVERVIEW, **34.1**

OPERATION, **34.2**
- The GROUPS Subcommand, **34.3**
- The VARIABLES Subcommand, **34.4**
- The ANALYSIS Subcommand, **34.5**
- Variable Selection, **34.6**
  - The METHOD Subcommand, **34.7**
  - Inclusion Levels, **34.8**
  - The MAXSTEPS Subcommand, **34.9**
  - Statistical Controls, **34.10**
- The FUNCTIONS Subcommand, **34.11**
- Optional Statistics for the Analysis Phase, **34.12**
- The SELECT Subcommand, **34.13**
- Rotation Options, **34.14**
- Display Options, **34.15**
- Classifying Cases, **34.16**
  - The PRIORS Subcommand, **34.17**
  - The Classification Results Table, **34.18**
  - Classification Plots, **34.19**
  - Printed Discriminant Scores, **34.20**
  - Classification Options, **34.21**
  - Using Classification Coefficients, **34.22**
- Missing Values, **34.23**
- The SAVE Subcommand, **34.24**
- Matrix Materials, **34.25**
  - Writing Matrices, **34.26**
  - Reading Matrices, **34.27**
- Summary of Syntax Rules, **34.28**

LIMITATIONS, **34.29**

Chapter 34 DISCRIMINANT

Discriminant analysis is a statistical technique in which linear combinations of variables are used to distinguish between two or more categories of cases. The variables "discriminate" between groups of cases and predict into which category or group a case falls, based upon the values of these variables.

The first task of discriminant analysis is to find the linear combination of variables that best discriminates between, or separates, groups. As in regression analysis, there are two approaches to variable selection. The direct-entry method forces a set of variables into the analysis. Alternatively, you can use stepwise methods to find a set of variables that maximizes discriminating power as defined by various criteria. After the discriminant functions have been computed, you can use coefficients to predict group membership.

Frequently, discriminant analysis is used to classify a sample in which actual group membership is unknown. You can do this in two ways with procedure DISCRIMINANT. You can combine two samples, one in which group membership is known and one in which group membership is unknown, into one sample. The cases for which group membership is known are used to compute the discriminant functions. Then, discriminant functions are used to classify all cases or only those cases for which group membership is unknown. Alternatively, you can use DISCRIMINANT to produce the matrix materials required for classification based upon one sample and then use these materials to classify the second sample.

34.1 OVERVIEW

To operate DISCRIMINANT, you must specify a grouping variable, which identifies the group into which each case falls, and a set of discriminating variables. These are the minimum requirements. The GROUPS subcommand described in Section 34.3 defines the grouping variable. Since DISCRIMINANT is capable of performing multiple analyses in which different sets of discriminating variables are used or in which different criteria are used for the entry or removal of variables, two separate subcommands are used to define the variables used in the analysis. The VARIABLES subcommand names the variables to be used in all analyses and is described in Section 34.4. The ANALYSIS subcommand names the variables to be used in the current analysis and is described in Sections 34.5 and 34.8.

In addition to the direct-entry method, DISCRIMINANT provides five methods of stepwise variable selection via the METHOD subcommand (see Section 34.7). You can also use other optional subcommands to set statistical controls for entry or removal.

Analysis Features. Two basic sets of information related to the analysis phase are always printed: statistics for the functions and coefficients for variables used in the functions. In addition, you can obtain classification function coefficients, unstandardized discriminant function coefficients, the structure matrix, univariate *F* ratios, the matrix of pairwise *F* ratios after each step, Box's *M* test, means, standard deviations, and various covariance matrices (see Section 34.12). You can use one sample to calculate the statistics required to classify another sample via the SELECT subcommand (see Section 34.13).

Classification Features. Discriminant functions calculated by DISCRIMINANT can be used to classify cases. You can specify prior probabilities for classification purposes via the PRIORS subcommand (see Section 34.17). The classification phase produces plots of classified cases, a classification results table, and other statistics to evaluate the classification (see Sections 34.18 through 34.20). By default, DISCRIMINANT uses the pooled within-groups covariance matrix to classify cases. Optionally, it uses separate-group covariance matrices. See Section 34.21 for this and other classification options.

Saving Results. Optionally, DISCRIMINANT saves two types of results for use with other SPSS^X procedures or other programs. Casewise materials, including actual group, predicted group, posterior probabilities, and discriminant scores, are automatically added to the active file. Matrix materials, including counts, standard deviations, and covariance matrices, are written to an external file. You can use these materials with SPSS^X to classify an entirely different sample. (See Sections 34.24 and 34.25.)

Missing Values. By default, cases are excluded from the computation of functions if they have missing values for any of the variables named on the VARIABLES subcommand. Optionally, you can classify these missing cases using mean substitution. (See Section 34.23.)

34.2 OPERATION

The DISCRIMINANT procedure is operated by the DISCRIMINANT command and a combination of subcommands and associated OPTIONS and STATISTICS commands. All subcommands begin with a subcommand keyword followed by an optional equals sign. Use a slash to separate subcommands. Only two subcommands are required: the GROUPS subcommand, which specifies the variable used to group cases; and the VARIABLES subcommand, which specifies the discriminating variables. All other subcommands are optional.

34.3 The GROUPS Subcommand

The GROUPS subcommand defines the groups. Each case used in the computation of discriminant functions is assigned to a group based on its value on a grouping variable. For example,

```
DISCRIMINANT  GROUPS=WORLD(1,3)/
              VARIABLES=APPL TO FSALES
```

assigns each case to one of three groups defined by the variable WORLD. You can specify only one grouping variable, and its values must be integers. The minimum and maximum specifications define the range of values for the group. For example,

```
DISCRIMINANT  GROUPS=TYPE(1,5)/VARIABLES=SYMP1 TO SYMP8
```

specifies a maximum of five groups. Empty groups are ignored and do not affect computations. For example, if no cases have the value 3 for TYPE, then only four groups are present. Cases with values that lie outside the value range are not used during the analysis phase, but they are classified during the classification phase.

34.4 The VARIABLES Subcommand

The VARIABLES subcommand names the variables to be used as predictor, or discriminating, variables during the analysis phase. The variable list on the VARIABLES subcommand follows the usual SPSS^{X} conventions for variable lists. Only numeric variables can be used. For example,

```
DISCRIMINANT  GROUPS=WORLD(1,3)/
  VARIABLES=FOOD SERVICE BUS MECHANIC CONSTRUC COOK MANAGER FSALES/
```

specifies that variables FOOD through FSALES are to be used during the analysis phase. These commands produce the default DISCRIMINANT output shown in Figures 34.4a, 34.4b, and 34.4c.

Figure 34.4a Information about the sample

```
- - - - - - - - - - - - - - - - - - - - - -   D I S C R I M I N A N T   A N A L Y S I S   - - - - - - - - - - - - - - - - - - - -

ON GROUPS DEFINED BY WORLD      ECON CLASS FOR COUNTRY


            45 (UNWEIGHTED) CASES WERE PROCESSED.
             2 OF THESE WERE EXCLUDED FROM THE ANALYSIS.
               0 HAD MISSING OR OUT-OF-RANGE GROUP CODES.
               2 HAD AT LEAST ONE MISSING DISCRIMINATING VARIABLE.
               0 HAD BOTH.
            43 (UNWEIGHTED) CASES WILL BE USED IN THE ANALYSIS.


NUMBER OF CASES BY GROUP

                 NUMBER OF CASES
  WORLD      UNWEIGHTED     WEIGHTED  LABEL

        1            25         25.0  1ST WORLD
        2             6          6.0  PETRO WORLD
        3            12         12.0  3RD WORLD

     TOTAL           43         43.0
```

Figure 34.4b Method specifications

```
- - - - - - - - - - - - - - - - - - - - - -   D I S C R I M I N A N T   A N A L Y S I S   - - - - - - - - - - - - - - - - - - - -

ON GROUPS DEFINED BY WORLD      ECON CLASS FOR COUNTRY

ANALYSIS NUMBER        1

DIRECT METHOD:  ALL VARIABLES PASSING THE TOLERANCE TEST ARE ENTERED.

     MINIMUM TOLERANCE LEVEL.................. 0.00100

CANONICAL DISCRIMINANT FUNCTIONS

     MAXIMUM NUMBER OF FUNCTIONS.............         2
     MINIMUM CUMULATIVE PERCENT OF VARIANCE...   100.00
     MAXIMUM SIGNIFICANCE OF WILKS' LAMBDA....   1.0000


PRIOR PROBABILITY FOR EACH GROUP IS 0.33333
```

The default output includes three sets of information. Figure 34.4a shows the preliminary information, describing the number of cases in each group used in the analysis. DISCRIMINANT excludes cases with missing values for any of the variables named on the VARIABLES or GROUPS subcommands during the analysis phase. See Section 34.23 for alternative missing-value treatments. Figure 34.4b shows the method used to select variables for the analysis and the various statistical criteria in effect. See Sections 34.7 through 34.10 for ways to override the default controls. Prior probabilities are printed but are used only for the classification phase. See Section 34.17 for overriding prior probabilities.

Figure 34.4c shows the actual results of the analysis. In this example, two functions are extracted. By default, standardized canonical discriminant function coefficients are printed. To obtain unstandardized canonical discriminant functions and classification function coefficients, you must use the associated STATISTICS command (see Section 34.12). Next, the structure matrix for the analysis is printed. This matrix displays the pooled within-groups correlations between the discriminant functions and the discriminating variables. To facilitate interpretation, the matrix is ordered. Variables are grouped according to the function with which they are most highly correlated. Within each such group, variables are sorted in descending order by the absolute value of the correlation coefficient. If there is more than one function, the largest correlation for each variable is flagged with an asterisk. In addition, you can rotate the structure matrix and the pattern matrix of standardized canonical discriminant functions and variables to facilitate interpretation. Sections 34.14 and 34.15 describe options related to the analysis phase. Finally, the group centroids are reported by default. Centroids are the mean discriminant scores on the functions for each group.

Figure 34.4c Function statistics

```
                                        CANONICAL DISCRIMINANT FUNCTIONS

                           PERCENT OF  CUMULATIVE    CANONICAL   :   AFTER
FUNCTION  EIGENVALUE   VARIANCE     PERCENT     CORRELATION : FUNCTION  WILKS' LAMBDA  CHI-SQUARED   D.F.  SIGNIFICANCE

                                                              :     0      0.2006551      58.625        16      0.0000
    1*       2.25481     80.93        80.93      0.8323237   :     1      0.6530949      15.550         7      0.0296
    2*       0.53117     19.07       100.00      0.5889865   :

   * MARKS THE   2 CANONICAL DISCRIMINANT FUNCTION(S) TO BE USED IN THE REMAINING ANALYSIS.


STANDARDIZED CANONICAL DISCRIMINANT FUNCTION COEFFICIENTS

             FUNC  1      FUNC  2

FOOD        -0.11919      1.03495
SERVICE      0.14114     -0.89385
BUS          0.91978     -0.35004
MECHANIC     0.61734      0.29191
CONSTRUC    -0.31667     -0.56073
COOK        -0.46470      0.70515
MANAGER     -0.56156     -0.47097
FSALES       0.32233      0.29270


POOLED WITHIN-GROUPS CORRELATIONS BETWEEN CANONICAL DISCRIMINANT FUNCTIONS AND DISCRIMINATING VARIABLES
VARIABLES ARE ORDERED BY THE FUNCTION WITH LARGEST CORRELATION AND THE MAGNITUDE OF THAT CORRELATION.

             FUNC  1      FUNC  2

BUS          0.83191*     0.11195
MECHANIC     0.69362*     0.12815
FSALES       0.66971*     0.13326
MANAGER      0.41159*     0.09707
SERVICE      0.39078*    -0.19472

FOOD         0.29384      0.46681*
COOK         0.31593      0.33120*
CONSTRUC     0.16236     -0.21002*


CANONICAL DISCRIMINANT FUNCTIONS EVALUATED AT GROUP MEANS (GROUP CENTROIDS)

   GROUP       FUNC   1      FUNC   2

       1       1.22889     -0.00274
       2      -1.69224      1.54027
       3      -1.71407     -0.76442
```

34.5 The ANALYSIS Subcommand

You can do several discriminant analyses with one DISCRIMINANT command if the grouping variable is the same across analyses. To perform multiple analyses, name all the variables to be used in the various analyses on the VARIABLES subcommand and then use the ANALYSIS subcommand to specify subsets of variables for individual analyses. The variable list follows the usual SPSS^{X} conventions for variable lists, except that the sequence of variables implied by the TO keyword refers to their order on the

VARIABLES subcommand. For analyses using the direct-entry method, specify:

```
DISCRIMINANT  GROUPS=WORLD(1,3)/
  VARIABLES=FOOD TO FSALES/
  ANALYSIS=FOOD RENT APPL SERVICE WCLOTHES/
  ANALYSIS=FOOD SERVICE BUS MECHANIC CONSTRUC COOK MANAGER FSALES/
```

Optionally, you can specify an inclusion level to control the order in which variables are entered or removed in a stepwise analysis (see Section 34.8).

34.6 Variable Selection

Several related subcommands control the selection of variables during the analysis phase. The METHOD subcommand specifies the selection criterion. The MAXSTEPS subcommand controls the number of steps in a stepwise analysis. The TOLERANCE, FIN, FOUT, PIN, POUT, and VIN subcommands override default statistical criteria for entering and removing variables. The FUNCTIONS subcommand controls the number of functions extracted. All of these subcommands are optional and are used only to override defaults. These subcommands apply only to the previous ANALYSIS specification and do not reset defaults in subsequent analyses.

34.7 The METHOD Subcommand

By default, DISCRIMINANT enters all variables specified on the analysis list (provided that no collinearity problems appear). This method is termed the *direct-entry method.* Optionally, you can specify any one of five different stepwise methods on the METHOD subcommand. These methods enter and remove variables one at time, selecting them on the basis of specific criteria. Different criteria are used for different stepwise methods. In addition, you can control the order in which variables are considered for entry or removal by a given stepwise method (see Section 34.8).

The METHOD subcommand follows the ANALYSIS subcommand and has one of the following specifications:

DIRECT *All variables are entered simultaneously, provided they satisfy the tolerance criterion.* For a discussion of controlling the tolerance criterion, see Section 34.10. DIRECT is the default method.

WILKS *The variable that minimizes the overall Wilks' lambda is selected.*

MAHAL *The variable that maximizes the Mahalanobis' distance between the two closest groups is selected.*

MAXMINF *The variable that maximizes the smallest* F *ratio between pairs of groups is selected.*

MINRESID *The variable that minimizes the sum of unexplained variation between groups is selected.*

RAO *The variable that produces the largest increase in Rao's* V *is selected.* Rao's *V* is a generalized measure of the overall separation between groups.

With all methods, all variables must satisfy the tolerance criterion before they can be entered. With the stepwise methods, all variables must also satisfy the partial *F* ratio criterion before they can be entered. Section 34.10 discusses setting the partial *F* criterion.

When any of the stepwise methods are used, variables may be removed from the equation as additional variables are entered. Variables in the equation are tested for removal on the basis of their partial *F* values, which must be smaller than a given value for removal to occur. Section 34.10 also discusses setting the partial *F* for removal. Variables are never removed when the DIRECT method (the default) is used.

34.8 Inclusion Levels

When you specify a stepwise method, you can use the ANALYSIS subcommand to control the order in which variables are considered for entry. By default, variables are examined for entry or removal on the basis of their partial *F* values. To control the order in which sets of variables are examined, specify an inclusion level in parentheses following the sets of variables. The inclusion level can be any integer between 0 and 99. For example,

```
DISCRIMINANT  GROUPS=TYPE(1,5)/VARIABLES=A TO H/
              ANALYSIS=A B C D(4) E F G H(3)/
```

sets the inclusion level to 4 for variables A, B, C, and D, and to 3 for variables E, F, G, and H.

The inclusion level controls the order in which variables are entered, the way in which they are entered, and whether or not they should be considered for removal according to the rules outlined below. All variables must still pass the tolerance criterion to be entered.

- Variables with higher inclusion levels are considered for entry before variables with lower levels. Variables do not have to be ordered by their inclusion level on the subcommand itself.
- Variables with even inclusion levels are entered together.
- Variables with odd inclusion levels are entered one variable at a time according to the stepwise method specified on the METHOD subcommand.
- Only variables with an inclusion level of 1 may be considered for removal. To make a variable with a higher inclusion level eligible for removal, name it twice on the ANALYSIS subcommand, first specifying the desired inclusion level and then an inclusion level of 1.
- An inclusion level of 0 prevents a variable from being entered, although an entry criterion is computed and printed.
- The default inclusion level is 1.

In the analysis

```
DISCRIMINANT  GROUPS=WORLD(1,3)/
  VARIABLES=FOOD SERVICE BUS MECHANIC CONSTRUC COOK MANAGER FSALES/
  ANALYSIS=FOOD TO FSALES (2)  FOOD TO FSALES(1)/
  METHOD=WILKS/
```

all variables are known to meet the minimum tolerance criterion. The stepping results are shown in Figure 34.8a. DISCRIMINANT forces all the variables in first, then removes FSALES, maximizing the overall partial *F* ratio. The summary table for the process is shown in Figure 34.8b.

34.9 The MAXSTEPS Subcommand

By default, the maximum number of steps is the number of variables with inclusion levels greater than 1 plus twice the number of variables with an inclusion level of 1. This is the maximum number of steps possible without inclusion loops, in which a variable is repeatedly cycled in and out. Use the MAXSTEPS subcommand to decrease the maximum number of steps.

MAXSTEPS=n *Controls the number of steps in a stepwise analysis.*

Figure 34.8a Stepwise output

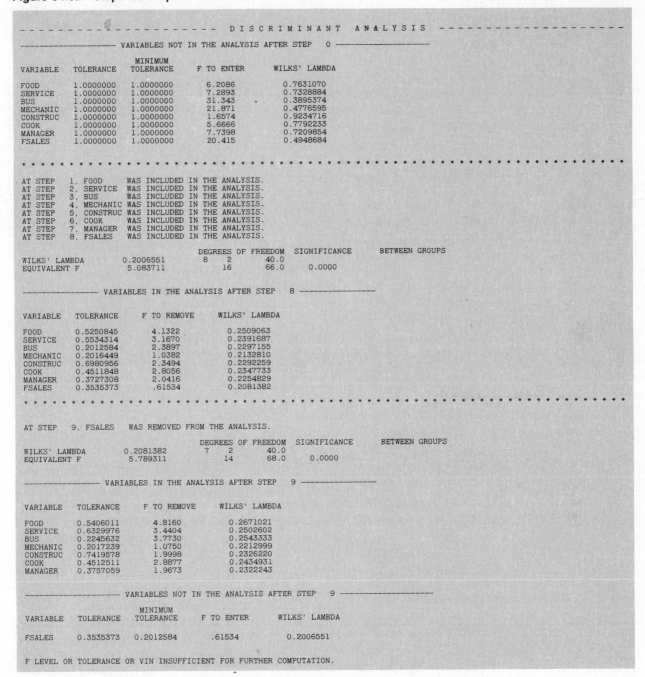

```
- - - - - - - - - - - - - - - - - - - - -  D I S C R I M I N A N T   A N A L Y S I S  - - - - - - - - - - - - - - - - - - -

-------------------- VARIABLES NOT IN THE ANALYSIS AFTER STEP   0 ------------------

                             MINIMUM
VARIABLE   TOLERANCE    TOLERANCE      F TO ENTER      WILKS' LAMBDA

FOOD       1.0000000    1.0000000       6.2086          0.7631070
SERVICE    1.0000000    1.0000000       7.2893          0.7328884
BUS        1.0000000    1.0000000       31.343          0.3895374
MECHANIC   1.0000000    1.0000000       21.871          0.4776595
CONSTRUC   1.0000000    1.0000000       1.6574          0.9234716
COOK       1.0000000    1.0000000       5.6666          0.7792233
MANAGER    1.0000000    1.0000000       7.7398          0.7209854
FSALES     1.0000000    1.0000000       20.415          0.4948684

* * * * * * * * * * * * * * * * * * * * * * * * * * * * * * * * * * * * * * * * * * * * * * * * * * * * * * * * * * * * * * *

AT STEP   1, FOOD      WAS INCLUDED IN THE ANALYSIS.
AT STEP   2, SERVICE   WAS INCLUDED IN THE ANALYSIS.
AT STEP   3, BUS       WAS INCLUDED IN THE ANALYSIS.
AT STEP   4, MECHANIC  WAS INCLUDED IN THE ANALYSIS.
AT STEP   5, CONSTRUC  WAS INCLUDED IN THE ANALYSIS.
AT STEP   6, COOK      WAS INCLUDED IN THE ANALYSIS.
AT STEP   7, MANAGER   WAS INCLUDED IN THE ANALYSIS.
AT STEP   8, FSALES    WAS INCLUDED IN THE ANALYSIS.

                                           DEGREES OF FREEDOM  SIGNIFICANCE       BETWEEN GROUPS
WILKS' LAMBDA          0.2006551              8    2      40.0
EQUIVALENT F           5.083711                  16       66.0       0.0000

---------------- VARIABLES IN THE ANALYSIS AFTER STEP   8 ----------------

VARIABLE   TOLERANCE     F TO REMOVE     WILKS' LAMBDA

FOOD       0.5250845       4.1322          0.2509063
SERVICE    0.5534314       3.1670          0.2391687
BUS        0.2012584       2.3897          0.2297155
MECHANIC   0.2016449       1.0382          0.2132810
CONSTRUC   0.6980956       2.3494          0.2292259
COOK       0.4511848       2.8056          0.2347733
MANAGER    0.3727308       2.0416          0.2254829
FSALES     0.3535373       .61534          0.2081382
* * * * * * * * * * * * * * * * * * * * * * * * * * * * * * * * * * * * * * * * * * * * * * * * * * * * * * * * * * * * * * *

AT STEP   9, FSALES   WAS REMOVED FROM THE ANALYSIS.
                                           DEGREES OF FREEDOM  SIGNIFICANCE       BETWEEN GROUPS
WILKS' LAMBDA          0.2081382              7    2      40.0
EQUIVALENT F           5.789311                  14       68.0       0.0000

---------------- VARIABLES IN THE ANALYSIS AFTER STEP   9 ----------------

VARIABLE   TOLERANCE     F TO REMOVE     WILKS' LAMBDA

FOOD       0.5406011       4.8160          0.2671021
SERVICE    0.6329976       3.4404          0.2502602
BUS        0.2245632       3.7730          0.2543333
MECHANIC   0.2017239       1.0750          0.2212999
CONSTRUC   0.7419578       1.9998          0.2326220
COOK       0.4512511       2.8877          0.2434931
MANAGER    0.3757059       1.9673          0.2322243

-------------------- VARIABLES NOT IN THE ANALYSIS AFTER STEP   9 --------------------

                             MINIMUM
VARIABLE   TOLERANCE    TOLERANCE      F TO ENTER      WILKS' LAMBDA

FSALES     0.3535373    0.2012584       .61534          0.2006551

F LEVEL OR TOLERANCE OR VIN INSUFFICIENT FOR FURTHER COMPUTATION.
```

Figure 34.8b Summary table for stepwise analysis

```
                               SUMMARY TABLE

        ACTION          VARS   WILKS'
STEP ENTERED REMOVED     IN    LAMBDA    SIG.    LABEL

  1  FOOD                 1   0.763107 0.0045   AVG FOOD PRICES
  2  SERVICE              2   0.576196 0.0002   PRICE FOR SERVICES
  3  BUS                  3   0.299505 0.0000   NET BUS DRIVER'S SALARY
  4  MECHANIC             4   0.294726 0.0000   NET MECHANIC'S SALARY
  5  CONSTRUC             5   0.273900 0.0000   NET CONSTRUCTION WORKER'S SALARY
  6  COOK                 6   0.232224 0.0000   NET COOK'S SALARY
  7  MANAGER              7   0.208138 0.0000   NET MANAGER'S SALARY
  8  FSALES               8   0.200655 0.0000   NET FEMALE SALESWORKER'S SALARY
  9          FSALES       7   0.208138 0.0000   NET FEMALE SALESWORKER'S SALARY
```

ANNOTATED EXAMPLE FOR DISCRIMINANT

This example analyzes 1979 prices and earnings in 45 cities around the world, compiled by the Union Bank of Switzerland. The variables are

- FOOD—the average net cost of 39 different food and beverage items in the city, expressed as a percentage above or below that of Zurich, where Zurich equals 100%.
- SERVICE—the average cost of 28 different goods and services in the city, expressed as a percentage above or below that of Zurich, where Zurich equals 100%.
- BUS, MECHANIC, CONSTRUC, COOK, MANAGER, FSALES—the average gross annual earnings of municipal bus drivers, automobile mechanics, construction workers, cooks, managers, and female sales workers, working from five to ten years in their respective occupations. Each of these variables is expressed as a percentage above or below those of Zurich, where Zurich equals 100%.
- WORLD—economic development status of the country in which the city is located, divided into three groups: economically advanced nations, such as the United States and most European nations; nations that are members of the Organization for Petroleum Exporting Countries (OPEC); and nations that are economically underdeveloped. The groups are labeled 1ST WORLD, PETRO WORLD, and 3RD WORLD, respectively.

There are two objectives to this analysis. First, we discriminate between cities in different categories by examining their wage and price structures. Secondly, we predict a city's economic class category from coefficients calculated using wages and prices as predictors. The SPSS^X commands are

```
FILE HANDLE UNIONBK / file specifications
FILE HANDLE NEWUNION / file specifications
GET FILE UNIONBK
DISCRIMINANT GROUPS=WORLD(1,3)/
  VARIABLES=FOOD SERVICE BUS MECHANIC CONSTRUC COOK MANAGER FSALES/
  PRIORS=SIZE/SAVE = CLASS=PRDCLAS SCORES=DISCSCR/
STATISTICS 11 13
SAVE OUTFILE NEWUNION
```

- The FILE HANDLE commands identify the old and new system files and give the operating-system specifications (see Chapter 3).
- The GET command defines the data to SPSS^X from the system file UNIONBK (see Chapter 5).
- The DISCRIMINANT command requests a three-group discriminant analysis. The variables FOOD, SERVICE, BUS, MECHANIC, CONSTRUC, COOK, MANAGER, and FSALES are used as discriminating variables during the analysis phase (see Section 34.4). During the classification phase, prior probabilities are equal to the size of the known groups (see Section 34.17 and Figure A). Three variables are saved on the active file: the predicted group for each of the classified cases (variable PRDCLAS) and the two discriminant scores (variables DISCSCR1 and DISCSCR2). The saved variables are shown in Figure B (see Section 34.24).
- The STATISTICS command requests printing of the unstandardized discriminant functions and the classification results table (see Sections 34.12 and 34.18 and Figure C).
- The SAVE command saves the file with the three variables PRDCLAS, DISCSCR1, and DISCSCR2 as an SPSS^X system file with the file handle NEWUNION (see Chapter 5).

A Prior probabilities

```
PRIOR PROBABILITIES

   GROUP     PRIOR      LABEL

       1   0.58140      1ST WORLD
       2   0.13953      PETRO WORLD
       3   0.27907      3RD WORLD

   TOTAL   1.00000
```

B The saved variables

```
FOLLOWING VARIABLES HAVE BEEN CREATED:

  NAME          LABEL

--------     ----------------------------------------

PRDCLAS  --- PREDICTED GROUP FOR ANALYSIS     1

DISCSCR1 --- FUNCTION    1 FOR ANALYSIS       1

DISCSCR2 --- FUNCTION    2 FOR ANALYSIS       1
```

C Discriminant coefficients and classification results

```
UNSTANDARDIZED CANONICAL DISCRIMINANT FUNCTION COEFFICIENTS

              FUNC  1         FUNC  2

FOOD        -.7133619D-02   .6194062D-01
SERVICE      .8472984D-02  -.5365943D-01
BUS          .5255502D-01  -.2000084D-01
MECHANIC     .2805062D-01   .1326366D-01
CONSTRUC    -.4256104D-02  -.7536312D-02
COOK        -.1677760D-01   .2545888D-01
MANAGER     -.2570614D-01  -.2155895D-01
FSALES       .1637516D-01   .1486991D-01
(CONSTANT)  -1.852548      -.9620797


CLASSIFICATION RESULTS -

                          NO. OF    PREDICTED  GROUP  MEMBERSHIP
   ACTUAL GROUP           CASES          1           2           3
--------------------     ------   --------    --------    --------

GROUP        1              25         24           1           0
1ST WORLD                            96.0%        4.0%        0.0%

GROUP        2               6          0           5           1
PETRO WORLD                           0.0%       83.3%       16.7%

GROUP        3              12          1           0          11
3RD WORLD                             8.3%        0.0%       91.7%

PERCENT OF "GROUPED" CASES CORRECTLY CLASSIFIED:  93.02%

CLASSIFICATION PROCESSING SUMMARY

        45 CASES WERE PROCESSED.
         0 CASES WERE EXCLUDED FOR MISSING OR OUT-OF-RANGE GROUP CODES.
         2 CASES HAD AT LEAST ONE MISSING DISCRIMINATING VARIABLE.
        43 CASES WERE USED FOR PRINTED OUTPUT.
```

34.10 Statistical Controls

You can use several subcommands to override default controls on stepping, such as the tolerance level and *F*-to-enter or *F*-to-remove. These subcommands follow the METHOD subcommand in any order.

TOLERANCE=n *Tolerance level.* The default tolerance level is .001. You can set it to any decimal number between 0 and 1. All variables are tested against this level prior to inclusion for all methods. The tolerance of a variable in the analysis at any given step is the proportion of its within-groups variance not accounted for by other variables in the analysis. The tolerance level also applies to the minimum tolerance level of a variable reported in stepwise methods. The *minimum tolerance* of a variable is the smallest tolerance any variable in the analysis would have if the variable in question were included.

FIN=n F*-to-enter*. The default *F*-to-enter is 1.0. This corresponds to a significance level of about .5 for large sample sizes. You may set it to any number including 0. If you specify DIRECT on the METHOD subcommand no check is made for *F*-to-enter.

FOUT=n F*-to-remove*. The default *F*-to-remove is 1.0. As additional variables are entered into the equation, the partial *F* value for variables already in the equation changes. If it falls below the *F*-to-remove *and* the variable has an inclusion level of 1, the variable is removed. Variables are not removed with the direct-entry method.

PIN=n *Probability of* F*-to-enter*. There is no default. The *F*-to-enter is used in lieu of the probability of *F*-to-enter in the absence of the PIN subcommand. Since the probability of *F* depends upon the degrees of freedom, this value can change at each step as variables are entered or removed. Use the PIN subcommand to keep the minimum *F*'s at a fixed significance level. PIN overrides FIN if both are used.

POUT=n *Probability of* F*-to-remove*. By default, a variable with an inclusion level of 1 is removed from the equation for the stepwise methods if its *F*-to-remove falls below the FIN specification. The POUT specification is directly analogous to the PIN specification. POUT overrides FOUT if both are used.

VIN=n *Rao's* V*-to-enter*. The default value is 0. If you use the RAO method, variables satisfying the criteria for entry, such as *F*-to-enter, may actually cause a decrease in Rao's *V* for the equation. The default VIN prevents this but does not prevent variables that do not provide any additional separation between groups from being added. The test for VIN applies only when you specify RAO on the METHOD subcommand.

34.11 The FUNCTIONS Subcommand

By default, DISCRIMINANT computes the maximum number of functions that are mathematically possible. The maximum number of functions that can be derived for a given analysis is the number of groups minus one or the number of discriminating variables, whichever is less. Use the FUNCTIONS subcommand to set more restrictive criteria for the extraction of functions. The FUNCTIONS subcommand has three parameters:

nf *Maximum number of functions*. The default is the number of groups minus one or the number of discriminating variables, whichever is less.

cp *Cumulative percentage of eigenvalues*. The default is 100%.

sig *Significance level of function*. The default is 1.0.

Although you can restrict the number of functions with only one parameter at a time, all three must be specified in the following order: *nf, cp, sig*. For example, to specify a minimum cumulative percentage, *cp*, you must specify *nf*. Or, to specify a minimum significance level, *sig*, for a five-group analysis, you must also specify *nf* and *cp*, as in:

```
DISCRIMINANT  GROUPS=CLASS(1,5)/
  VARIABLES = SCORE1 TO SCORE20/
  FUNCTIONS=4,100,.80/
```

Four functions and a cumulative percentage of eigenvalues of 100 do not restrict the number of functions extracted since they are the default parameters. The number of functions is restricted by the requirement that each function must have a significance level of .80 or less. If more than one nondefault restriction is specified on the FUNCTIONS subcommand, SPSS^X uses the first one encountered.

34.12 Optional Statistics for the Analysis Phase

The default statistics produced by the analysis phase include

Summary Statistics. Eigenvalues, percent of variance, cumulative percent of variance, canonical correlations, Wilks' lambda, chi-square, degrees of freedom, and significance of chi-square are reported for the functions.

Step Statistics. Wilks' lambda, equivalent *F*, degrees of freedom, and significance of *F* are reported for each step. Tolerance, *F*-to-remove, and the stepping criterion value are reported for each variable in the equation. Tolerance, minimum tolerance, *F*-to-enter, and the stepping criterion value are reported for each variable not in the equation.

Final Statistics. Standardized canonical discriminant function coefficients, the structure matrix of discriminant functions and all variables named in the analysis (whether they entered the equation or not), and functions evaluated at group means, are reported following the last step.

In addition, you can specify the following optional statistics on the associated STATISTICS command:

STATISTIC 1 *Means.* Prints total and group means for all variables named on the ANALYSIS subcommand.

STATISTIC 2 *Standard deviations.* Prints total and group standard deviations for all variables named on the ANALYSIS subcommand.

STATISTIC 3 *Pooled within-groups covariance matrix.*

STATISTIC 4 *Pooled within-groups correlation matrix.*

STATISTIC 5 *Matrix of pairwise* F *ratios.* Prints the *F* ratio for each pair of groups. This *F* is the significance test for the Mahalanobis' distance between groups. This statistic is available only with the stepwise methods.

STATISTIC 6 *Univariate* F *ratios.* Prints *F* for each variable. This is a one-way analysis of variance test for equality of group means on a single discriminating variable.

STATISTIC 7 *Box's* M *test.* This is a test for equality of group covariance matrices.

STATISTIC 8 *Group covariance matrices.*

STATISTIC 9 *Total covariance matrix.*

STATISTIC 11 *Unstandardized canonical discriminant functions.*

STATISTIC 12 *Classification function coefficients.* Although DISCRIMINANT does not directly use these coefficients to classify cases, you can use them to classify other samples (see Section 34.22).

34.13 The SELECT Subcommand

Use the SELECT subcommand to select a subset of cases for computing basic statistics and coefficients. You can then use these coefficients to classify either all the cases or only the unselected cases.

The specification for the SELECT subcommand is a variable name followed by a value in parentheses. Only cases with the specified value on the selection variable are used during the analysis phase. The value must be an integer, as in

```
DISCRIMINANT  GROUPS=TYPE(1,5)/VARIABLES=A TO H/
              SELECT=LASTYEAR(81)
```

which limits the analysis phase to cases containing the value 81 for variable LASTYEAR. The SELECT subcommand must precede the first ANALYSIS subcommand and remains in effect for all analyses.

The following example demonstrates the use of the SELECT subcommand to compute coefficients on a 40% random sample of the cases:

```
COMPUTE      SET=UNIFORM(1) > .4
DISCRIMINANT  GROUPS=WORLD(1,3)/
  VARIABLES=FOOD APPL SERVICE RENT/
  SELECT=SET(0)/
  METHOD=WILKS
```

When you use the SELECT subcommand, DISCRIMINANT by default reports classification statistics separately for selected and unselected cases. To limit classification to unselected cases, use the options described in Section 34.21.

34.14 Rotation Options

The pattern and structure matrices printed during the analysis phase may be rotated to facilitate interpretation of results. To obtain a VARIMAX rotation, specify either Option 6 or 7 on the associated OPTIONS command.

OPTION 6 *Rotate pattern matrix.*

OPTION 7 *Rotate structure matrix.*

Neither Option 6 nor Option 7 affects the classification of cases since the rotation is orthogonal.

34.15 Display Options

Two options are available to reduce the amount of output produced during stepwise analysis.

OPTION 4 *Suppress printing of step-by-step output.*

OPTION 5 *Suppress printing of the summary table.*

These two options only affect printing, not the computation of intermediate results.

34.16 Classifying Cases

Once DISCRIMINANT has completed the analysis phase, you can use the results to classify your cases. DISCRIMINANT provides a variety of statistics for evaluating the ability of a particular model to classify cases, along with several subcommands and options to control the classification phase. You can use the SELECT subcommand during the analysis phase to compute the statistics and coefficients used to classify cases on the basis of a subset of cases (see Section 34.13). You can use the PRIORS subcommand to control prior probabilities for classification (see Section 34.17). Sections 34.18 through 34.20 describe the various statistics and plots available for the classification phase. Section 34.21 describes the options applying to the classification phase, and Section 34.22 describes the use of classification coefficients.

34.17 The PRIORS Subcommand

By default, DISCRIMINANT assumes equal probabilities for group membership when classifying cases. If your model consists of four groups, the prior probability of a case falling into any one group is .25. You can provide different prior probabilities with the PRIORS subcommand. Prior probabilities are not used during the analysis stage. If you do provide unequal prior probabilities, DISCRIMINANT adjusts the classification coefficients to reflect this prior knowledge. Specify one of the following on the PRIORS subcommand:

EQUAL *Equal prior probabilities.* This is the default specification.

SIZE *Proportion of cases actually falling into each group.* If 50% of the cases included in the analysis fall into the first group, 25% in the second, and 25% in the third, the prior probabilities are .5, .25, and .25, respectively. Group size is determined after cases with missing values for the discriminating variables are deleted.

Value list *User-specified prior probabilities.* A list of probabilities summing to 1.0 is specified.

Specifying a list of prior probabilities is often used to produce classification coefficients for samples with known group membership. For example, if you have five groups, the value list might look like the following:

```
DISCRIMINANT  GROUPS=TYPE(1,5)/VARIABLES=A TO H/
              PRIORS = .25 .2 .3 .1 .15/
```

If adjacent groups have the same prior probability, you can use a replication factor instead of listing each prior probability individually. For example,

```
DISCRIMINANT  GROUPS=TYPE(1,5)/VARIABLES=A TO H/
              PRIORS = 4*.15,.4/
```

establishes prior probabilities of .15 for the first four groups and .4 for the last group in a five-group model. The value list must name or imply as many prior probabilities as groups. You can specify a prior probability of 0. However, no cases falling into a group assigned a prior probability of 0 are classified into that group. If the sum of the prior probabilities is not 1, SPSS^X rescales the probabilities to sum to 1 and issues a warning.

34.18 The Classification Results Table

The classification results table tells you what proportion of cases are classified correctly and if there is evidence of systematic misclassification of particular cases. To obtain the classification results table, specify Statistic 13 on the associated STATISTICS command, as in:

```
DISCRIMINANT  GROUPS=WORLD(1,3)/
  VARIABLES=FOOD SERVICE BUS MECHANIC CONSTRUC COOK MANAGER FSALES/
  METHOD=WILKS/
  PRIORS=SIZE/
STATISTICS  10 12 13 14 15
```

As shown in Figure 34.18, the overall classification rate is nearly 91%. (Note: All figures in Sections 34.18 through 34.20 were produced by the above commands.)

STATISTIC 13 *Classification results table.* If you include a SELECT subcommand in your specifications, two tables are produced, one for selected cases and one for unselected cases.

The analysis is most successful in classifying cities from Group 1, and least successful in classifying cities from Group 2. These results suggest a greater diversity among cities in Group 2 in terms of the discriminating variables, and that two of these cases resemble Group 3 cases more closely than other Group 2 cases.

Figure 34.18 Classification results table

```
CLASSIFICATION RESULTS -

                          NO. OF    PREDICTED GROUP MEMBERSHIP
   ACTUAL GROUP           CASES          1          2          3
--------------------     ------     --------   --------   --------

GROUP         1              25         24          1          0
1ST WORLD                             96.0%       4.0%       0.0%

GROUP         2               6          0          4          2
PETRO WORLD                            0.0%      66.7%      33.3%

GROUP         3              12          1          0         11
3RD WORLD                              8.3%       0.0%      91.7%

PERCENT OF "GROUPED" CASES CORRECTLY CLASSIFIED:  90.70%

CLASSIFICATION PROCESSING SUMMARY

        45 CASES WERE PROCESSED.
         0 CASES WERE EXCLUDED FOR MISSING OR OUT-OF-RANGE GROUP CODES.
         2 CASES HAD AT LEAST ONE MISSING DISCRIMINATING VARIABLE.
        43 CASES WERE USED FOR PRINTED OUTPUT.
```

34.19 Classification Plots

Classification plots are useful for examining the relationship of groups to each other and graphically depicting misclassification. These plots have two forms, depending on the number of functions produced by your analysis. If your analysis produces more than one discriminant function, two types of scatterplots and a territorial map are available. The separate-groups scatterplot produces a scatterplot for each group. The all-groups scatterplot plots all groups on one scatterplot using different symbols to represent each group. The axes of the scatterplots are the discriminant scores calculated from the first two discriminant functions extracted during analysis. The territorial map can be used with either of these scatterplots. It outlines the general territory for each group and contains registration marks so that if you make a transparency of the scatterplot it can be placed upon the map to identify misclassified cases.

If your analysis produces only one function (you have only two groups or you restrict the number of functions to one), scatterplots are not possible since only one dimension exists in which to plot a case. Instead, DISCRIMINANT produces all-groups and separate-groups histograms of the discriminant scores.

Classification plots are requested via the associated STATISTICS command.

STATISTIC 10 *Territorial map.* This statistic is ignored for analyses producing only one function.

STATISTIC 15 *All-groups plot.* The first two functions define the axes. This statistic produces histograms for one-function analyses.

STATISTIC 16 *Separate-groups plots.* These are the same types of plots produced by Statistic 15. However, each plot contains cases for one group only. If your model has three groups, three scatterplots are produced, unless you restrict the analysis to compute only one function. For one-function analyses, histograms are produced.

Figure 34.19a shows the territorial map and Figure 34.19b shows the all-groups scatterplot. If you compare the territorial map with the all-groups plot, you can identify the misclassified cases. These are the cases not falling within the outline boundaries on the territorial map.

Figure 34.19c is the all-groups histogram produced when you use the FUNCTIONS subcommand to restrict the number of functions to one. This histogram is produced by specifying FUNCTIONS=1 in addition to the specifications in Section 34.18. The horizontal axis is the one discriminant function extracted during the analysis phase. The groups into which cases are classified given their discriminant scores are indicated by the labeling of the horizontal axis. Since no cases are classified into Group 2, the value 2 does not appear on the horizontal axis. No cases are classified into Group 2 because its centroid is extremely close to Group 3 and the cutoff points are very narrow (because of the relatively small prior probability for Group 2).

The histogram is a *stacked* histogram. In a given interval, Group 1 cases are printed first, then the Group 2 cases for that interval, and finally the Group 3 cases. For example, the seventh bar from the left shows four cases in this interval (two symbols represent one case in this histogram). Three cases are from Group 2 and one case is from Group 3.

Figure 34.19a Territorial map

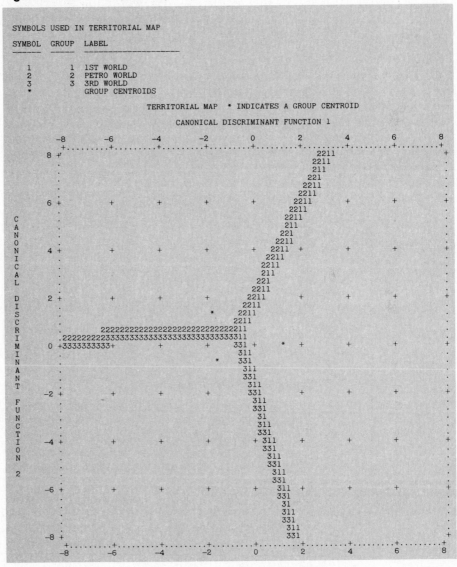

```
SYMBOLS USED IN TERRITORIAL MAP

SYMBOL  GROUP  LABEL
------  -----  --------------------

   1       1   1ST WORLD
   2       2   PETRO WORLD
   3       3   3RD WORLD
   *           GROUP CENTROIDS

                    TERRITORIAL MAP  * INDICATES A GROUP CENTROID

                          CANONICAL DISCRIMINANT FUNCTION 1

        -8        -6        -4        -2         0         2         4         6         8
         +.........+.........+.........+.........+.........+.........+.........+.........+
       8 +                                                    2211                       +
         .                                                   2211                        .
         .                                                   211                         .
         .                                                  221                          .
         .                                                 2211                          .
         .                                                2211                           .
       6 +         +         +         +         +       2211        +         +         +
         .                                              2211                             .
C        .                                             2211                              .
A        .                                             211                               .
N        .                                            221                                .
O        .                                           2211                                .
N      4 +         +         +         +         +  2211   +         +         +         +
I        .                                         2211                                  .
C        .                                        2211                                   .
A        .                                        211                                    .
L        .                                       221                                     .
         .                                      2211                                     .
D      2 +         +         +         +       2211        +         +         +         +
I        .                                    2211                                       .
S        .                              *    2211                                        .
C        .                                  2211                                         .
R        .       22222222222222222222222222222211                                         .
I        .22222222233333333333333333333333333311                                         .
M      0 +3333333333+        +         +     331 +     *   +         +         +         +
I        .                                    311                                        .
N        .                               *    331                                        .
A        .                                     311                                       .
N        .                                     331                                       .
T        .                                      311                                      .
      -2 +         +         +         +        331        +         +         +         +
F        .                                       311                                     .
U        .                                       331                                     .
N        .                                        31                                     .
C        .                                        311                                    .
T        .                                        331                                    .
I     -4 +         +         +         +         + 311     +         +         +         +
O        .                                         331                                   .
N        .                                          311                                  .
         .                                          331                                  .
2        .                                           311                                 .
         .                                           331                                 .
      -6 +         +         +         +         +    311  +         +         +         +
         .                                            331                                .
         .                                             31                                .
         .                                             311                               .
         .                                             331                               .
         .                                              311                              .
      -8 +                                              331                              +
         +.........+.........+.........+.........+.........+.........+.........+.........+
        -8        -6        -4        -2         0         2         4         6         8
```

Figure 34.19b All-groups scatterplot

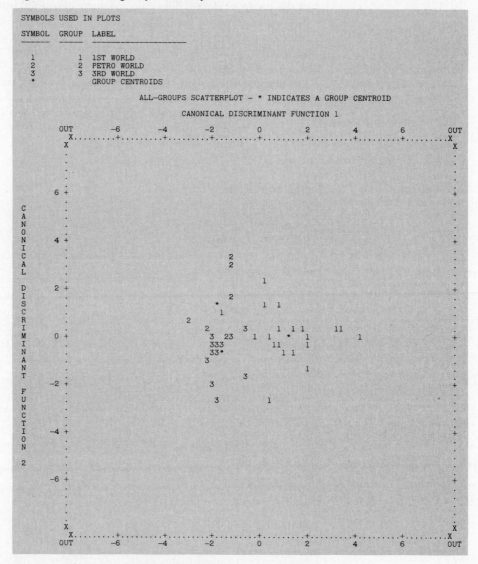

```
SYMBOLS USED IN PLOTS

SYMBOL  GROUP  LABEL
------  -----  --------------------

  1        1  1ST WORLD
  2        2  PETRO WORLD
  3        3  3RD WORLD
  *           GROUP CENTROIDS

                         ALL-GROUPS SCATTERPLOT - * INDICATES A GROUP CENTROID

                                  CANONICAL DISCRIMINANT FUNCTION 1

        OUT        -6        -4        -2         0         2         4         6         OUT
          X.........+.........+.........+.........+.........+.........+.........+.........X
         X                                                                                 X
         .                                                                                 .
         .                                                                                 .
         .                                                                                 .
         .                                                                                 .
         .                                                                                 .
       6 +                                                                                 +
         .                                                                                 .
C        .                                                                                 .
A        .                                                                                 .
N        .                                                                                 .
O        .                                                                                 .
N      4 +                                                                                 +
I        .                                                                                 .
C        .                                  2                                              .
A        .                                  2                                              .
L        .                                                                                 .
         .                                         1                                       .
D      2 +                                                                                 +
I        .                                  2                                              .
S        .                               *         1  1                                    .
C        .                                1                                                .
R        .                         2                                                       .
I        .                             2       3      1  1 1      11                       .
M      0 +                              3  23    1  1   *   1          1                   +
I        .                              333          11     1                              .
N        .                              33*            1 1                                 .
A        .                             3                                                   .
N        .                                                  1                              .
T        .                                     3                                           .
      -2 +                              3                                                  +
F        .                                                                                 .
U        .                               3          1                                      .
N        .                                                                                 .
C        .                                                                                 .
T        .                                                                                 .
I     -4 +                                                                                 +
O        .                                                                                 .
N        .                                                                                 .
         .                                                                                 .
2        .                                                                                 .
         .                                                                                 .
      -6 +                                                                                 +
         .                                                                                 .
         .                                                                                 .
         .                                                                                 .
         .                                                                                 .
         .                                                                                 .
         X                                                                                 X
          X.........+.........+.........+.........+.........+.........+.........+.........X
        OUT        -6        -4        -2         0         2         4         6         OUT
```

Figure 34.19c All-groups histogram

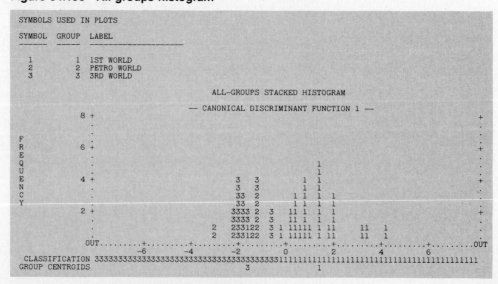

```
SYMBOLS USED IN PLOTS

SYMBOL  GROUP  LABEL
------  -----  --------------------

  1        1  1ST WORLD
  2        2  PETRO WORLD
  3        3  3RD WORLD

                                         ALL-GROUPS STACKED HISTOGRAM

                                    -- CANONICAL DISCRIMINANT FUNCTION 1 --
             8 +                                                                                 +
               .                                                                                 .
               .                                                                                 .
F              .                                                                                 .
R            6 +                                                                                 +
E              .                                                                                 .
Q              .                                               1                                 .
U              .                                               1                                 .
E            4 +                              3   3         1  1                                 +
N              .                              3   3         1  1                                 .
C              .                              33  2       1 1  1  1                              .
Y              .                              33  2       1 1  1  1                              .
             2 +                             3333 2  3   11 1  1  1                              +
               .                             3333 2  3   11 1  1  1                              .
               .                         2   233122  3 1 11111 1 11     11   1                   .
               .                         2   233122  3 1 11111 1 11     11   1                   .
              OUT.........+.........+.........+.........+.........+.........+.........+.........OUT
                         -6        -4        -2         0         2         4         6
 CLASSIFICATION 333333333333333333333333333333333333333111111111111111111111111111111111111111111
GROUP CENTROIDS                                 3              1
```

34.20 Printed Discriminant Scores

In addition to the tables, plots, and histograms described in the previous sections, you can also obtain casewise information, including observed group, classified group, and group membership probabilities. Casewise classification results are useful for examining particular cases. Casewise information is available via Statistic 14 on the associated STATISTICS command.

STATISTIC 14 *Discriminant scores and classification information.* Prints the following information for each case classified: case sequence number; number of missing values in the case; value on SELECT variable; actual group; highest group classification (G); the probability of a case in group G being that far from the centroid (P(D/G)); the probability of the case being in group G and having a score of D (P(G/D)); second-highest group classification and its P(G/D); and the discriminant scores.

Figure 34.20 shows the printed casewise classification information. Misclassified cases are identified with three asterisks. For example, the 16th case, which is in Group 1, is classified into Group 2.

Figure 34.20 Casewise discriminant scores

CASE SEQNUM	MIS VAL	SEL	ACTUAL GROUP		HIGHEST PROBABILITY GROUP	P(D/G)	P(G/D)	2ND HIGHEST GROUP	P(G/D)	DISCRIMINANT SCORES	
1			2		2	0.2237	0.9904	1	0.0060	-1.2634	3.1642
2			1		1	0.7669	0.9952	3	0.0046	1.4846	-0.6631
3			3		3	0.4221	0.7918	1	0.2039	-0.6226	-1.5905
4			2		2	0.3824	0.6049	3	0.3942	-2.9357	0.8136
5			3		3	0.6836	0.7885	2	0.1955	-1.9595	0.0447
6			3		3	0.9738	0.9438	2	0.0424	-1.8694	-0.7051
7			1		1	0.7674	0.9941	3	0.0057	1.4138	-0.6872
8			3		3	0.8412	0.8847	2	0.1026	-1.9899	-0.2915
9			2		2	0.8862	0.8226	3	0.1175	-1.2401	1.5438
10			1		1	0.1033	1.0000	3	0.0000	3.3124	0.3338
11			1		1	0.8410	0.9986	3	0.0011	1.7374	0.2637
12			3		3	0.1722	0.9959	1	0.0036	-1.8354	-2.6363
13			1		1	0.3779	0.9980	3	0.0020	1.9237	-1.1861
14			1		1	0.0129	1.0000	3	0.0000	4.1539	0.1168
15			1		1	0.7484	0.9412	3	0.0491	0.4450	0.0276
16			1	***	2	0.8796	0.6574	3	0.3036	-1.5780	1.0140
17			3		3	0.6765	0.7249	2	0.1461	-1.1817	-0.0190
18			2	***	3	0.7685	0.7910	2	0.1411	-1.4202	-0.0811
20			1		1	0.3590	0.6891	3	0.2738	-0.2152	-0.1588
22			1		1	0.9019	0.9786	3	0.0196	0.8682	-0.2934
23			1		1	0.7512	0.9992	3	0.0007	1.9619	-0.0198
24			1		1	0.7530	0.9989	3	0.0010	1.9151	-0.2442
25			3	***	1	0.2157	0.5147	3	0.3541	-0.5256	0.2731
26			3		3	0.8819	0.9257	2	0.0656	-2.0777	-0.5117
27			2	***	3	0.4244	0.6462	2	0.3471	-2.2848	0.3740
28			1		1	0.7321	0.9377	3	0.0513	0.4183	0.0657
29			1		1	0.7437	0.9846	3	0.0149	1.0907	-0.7506
30			1		1	0.2604	0.8708	2	0.1042	0.2875	1.3693
31			1		1	0.9329	0.9968	3	0.0024	1.4481	0.2938
32			3		3	0.9169	0.8957	2	0.0835	-1.7965	-0.3808
33			1		1	0.9063	0.9765	3	0.0211	0.8175	-0.2038
34			3		3	0.8551	0.9723	2	0.0228	-2.1569	-1.0031
35			1		1	0.4503	0.9745	2	0.0188	0.8308	1.2164
36			3		3	0.4472	0.9944	1	0.0029	-2.0865	-1.9606
37			3		3	0.9525	0.9025	2	0.0697	-1.6762	-0.4594
38			1		1	0.8268	0.9806	3	0.0127	0.8099	0.4829
39			1		1	0.7213	0.9417	3	0.0546	0.5361	-0.4418
40			2		2	0.2182	0.9899	1	0.0066	-1.2320	3.1699
41			1		1	0.0256	0.6523	3	0.3475	0.3369	-2.5546
42			1		1	0.0279	0.5611	2	0.4310	0.2267	2.4998
43			1		1	0.9740	0.9958	3	0.0033	1.3690	0.1718
44			1		1	0.7380	0.9916	3	0.0082	1.3082	-0.7626
45			1		1	0.1159	1.0000	3	0.0000	3.2514	0.3658

34.21 Classification Options

Three options related to the classification phase are available via the associated OPTIONS command. Two options control case selection, and the third specifies how the cases are classified.

OPTION 9 *Classify only unselected cases.* If you use the SELECT subcommand, by default DISCRIMINANT classifies all nonmissing cases. Two sets of classification results are produced, one for the selected cases and one for the nonselected cases. Option 9 suppresses the classification phase for cases selected via the SELECT subcommand.

OPTION 10 *Classify only unclassified cases.* Cases whose values on the grouping variable fall outside the range specified on the GROUPS subcommand are considered initially unclassified. During classification, these ungrouped cases are classified as a separate entry in the classification results table. Option 10 suppresses classification of cases that fall into the range specified on the GROUPS subcommand and classifies only cases falling outside the range.

OPTION 11 *Use separate-group covariance matrices of the discriminant functions for classification.* By default, DISCRIMINANT uses the pooled within-groups covariance matrix to classify cases. Option 11 uses the separate-group covariance matrices for classification. However, since classification is based on the discriminant functions and not the original variables, this option is not equivalent to quadratic discrimination (Tatsuoka, 1971).

34.22 Using Classification Coefficients

DISCRIMINANT classifies your cases when you specify any of Statistics 10, 13, 14, 15, or 16, or the SAVE subcommand (see Section 34.24). However, DISCRIMINANT is often used on a sample to obtain the materials necessary for classifying a large target sample. Sections 34.26 and 34.27 discuss using matrix materials to classify one sample based on the analysis of another sample. This section describes how to classify a target sample using the classification coefficients produced by Statistic 12.

Statistic 12 produces one set of classification coefficients for each group. The equation for one group is

$$C_i = c_{i1}V_1 + c_{i2}V_2 + \ldots + c_{ij}V_j + \ldots + c_{ip}V_p + c_{i0}$$

where C_i is the classification score for group i, the c_{ij}'s are the classification coefficients, c_{i0} is the constant, and the V's are the discriminating variables. A case is classified into the group that produces the highest classification score. If you have three groups, you must compute three linear combinations for each case in the target sample.

For example, assume you have a sample that you want to classify from the classification coefficients produced using the commands in Section 34.18. Figure 34.22 shows the classification coefficients.

Figure 34.22 Classification coefficients

CLASSIFICATION FUNCTION COEFFICIENTS
(FISHER'S LINEAR DISCRIMINANT FUNCTIONS)

WORLD =	1 FIRST WORLD	2 PETRO WORLD	3 THIRD WORLD
FOOD	.1833804	.2957176	.1474484
SERVICE	.1959324	.8005063D-01	.1919391
BUS	-.7968080D-01	-.2760144	-.2476949
MECHANIC	.1843633	.1234733	.9310405D-01
CONSTRUC	-.1206325D-01	-.1239856D-01	.3478106D-02
COOK	-.1488994D-01	.7321305D-01	.1464037D-01
MANAGER	-.2942906D-01	.1045250D-01	.5799628D-01
(CONSTANT)	-17.53128	-16.53582	-12.08814

To classify the cases in the target sample, use the following transformations:

```
COMPUTE  GRP1 = .1833804*FOOD + .1959324*SERVICE -.07968080*BUS +
         .1843633*MECHANIC  - .01206325*CONSTUC - .01488994*COOK -
         .02942906*MANAGER - 17.53128
COMPUTE  GRP2 = .2957176*FOOD + .08005063*SERVICE - .2760144*BUS +
         .1234733*MECHANIC - .01239856*CONSTRUC + .07321305*COOK +
         .1045250*MANAGER - 16.53582
COMPUTE  GRP3 = .1474484*FOOD + .1919391*SERVICE -.2476949*BUS +
         .09310405*MECHANIC + .003478106*CONSTRUC + .01464037*COOK +
         .05799628*MANAGER - 12.08814
IF  (GRP1 > MAX(GRP2,GRP3)) CLASS = 1
IF  (GRP2 > MAX(GRP1,GRP3)) CLASS = 2
IF  (GRP3 > MAX(GRP1,GRP2)) CLASS = 3
```

34.23 Missing Values

By default, cases missing on any of the variables named on the VARIABLES subcommand and cases out of range or missing on the GROUPS subcommand are not used during the analysis phase. Cases missing or out of range on the GROUPS variable are used during the classification phase. Two missing-data options for variables named on the VARIABLES subcommand are available.

OPTION 1 *Include missing values.* User-missing values are treated as valid values. Only the system-missing value is treated as missing.

OPTION 8 *Substitute means for missing values during classification.* Cases with missing values are not used during analysis. During classification, means are substituted for missing values and cases containing missing values are classified.

34.24 The SAVE Subcommand

Much of the casewise information produced by Statistic 14 can be added to the active file. The SAVE subcommand specifies the type of information to be saved and the variable names assigned to each piece of information. Three different types of variables can be saved using the following keywords:

CLASS *Save a variable containing the predicted group value.*

PROBS *Save the probabilities of group membership for each case.* For example, if you have three groups, the first probability is the probability of the case being in Group 1 given its discriminant scores, the second probability is its probability of being in Group 2, and the third probability is its probability of being in Group 3. Since DISCRIMINANT produces more than one probability, a *rootname* is used to create a set of variables of the form alpha1 to alphan. The rootname cannot exceed seven characters.

SCORES *Save the discriminant scores.* The number of scores equals the number of functions derived. As with the PROBS parameter, the rootname is used to create a set of variables.

Consider the following example:

```
DISCRIMINANT  GROUPS=WORLD(1,3)/
  VARIABLES=FOOD TO FSALES/
  SAVE = CLASS=PRDCLAS  SCORES=SCORE  PROBS=PRB
```

Since the number of groups is 3, DISCRIMINANT writes out 6 variables.

Table 34.24 Saved casewise results

Name	Description
PRDCLAS	Predicted Group
SCORE1	Discriminant score for Function 1
SCORE2	Discriminant score for Function 2
PRB1	Probability of being in Group 1
PRB2	Probability of being in Group 2
PRB3	Probability of being in Group 3

You do not have to request all three types of variables on the SAVE subcommand. Only those specified are saved. You can specify the keywords in any order, but the order in which the variables are added to the file is fixed. The group variable (CLASS) is always written first, followed by discriminant scores (SCORES), and probabilities (PROBS). Variable labels are provided automatically for the newly saved variables. Any value labels defined for the group variable are also saved for the classified-group variable.

The SAVE subcommand applies only to the previous ANALYSIS subcommand. If there are multiple analyses and you want to save casewise materials from each, you must use multiple SAVE subcommands, as in:

```
DISCRIMINANT  GROUPS = WORLD(1,3)/
  VARIABLES = FOOD TO FSALES/
  ANALYSIS = FOOD SERVICE/
  SAVE = CLASS=PRDCLAS SCORES=COSTSCR/
  ANALYSIS = BUS TO FSALES
  SAVE = CLASS=SALCLAS SCORES=SALSCR/
```

34.25 Matrix Materials

DISCRIMINANT reads and writes matrix materials so that an analysis performed on one file can be used to classify another file. Assume you have two files: the first file contains group codes and variables used to classify groups, and the second file contains only the variables used to classify groups. You can use the first file to produce matrix materials that can then be used along with the variables in the second file to classify the cases in the second file. Use the following options to specify matrix input and output.

OPTION 2 *Write matrix materials.*

OPTION 3 *Read matrix materials.*

34.26 Writing Matrices

Option 2 produces matrix materials in the form of 80 column records for each group specified on the GROUPS subcommand. Although their format is designed explicitly for use with SPSS^X DISCRIMINANT, these materials can be used with other programs as well. For each group, a record containing the group code, the unweighted and weighted counts, and the value label defined for the group code is written. The next set of records contains the group means for each of the variables named on the VARIABLES subcommand. The final set of records contains either group covariance matrices or pooled within-groups covariance matrices, depending upon whether Statistic 7 or 8 or Option 11 is in effect.

If Statistic 7 or 8 or Option 11 is in effect, separate-group covariance matrices are required by DISCRIMINANT and therefore are written out with the other matrix materials. If neither Statistic 7 nor 8 nor Option 11 is in effect, only the pooled within-groups covariance matrix is written. Separate-group covariance matrices are written along with the other materials for each group following the means for that group. The pooled within-groups covariance matrix follows all other matrix materials. Table 34.26a shows the order of matrix materials when Statistic 7 or 8 or Option 11 is in effect. Table 34.26b shows the order of matrix materials when neither Statistic 7 nor 8 nor Option 11 is in effect.

Table 34.26a Matrix materials with separate-group covariance matrices

Group 1	code, counts, labels
	means
	group covariance matrix
Group 2	code, counts, labels
	means
	group covariance matrix
	.
	.
	.

Table 34.26b Matrix materials with the pooled within-groups covariance matrix

Group 1	code, counts, labels means
Group 2	code, counts, labels means
	.
	.
	.
	pooled within-groups covariance matrix

When a group specified on the GROUPS subcommand is empty, the set of means is not written. Separate-group covariance matrices are not written for empty groups, groups that contain only one case, or groups where the sum of the weights is not greater than one. Similarly, pooled within-groups covariance matrices are not written if the total sum of case weights or the total number of cases is less than or equal to the number of groups. DISCRIMINANT can read matrix materials with missing information. It verifies group counts from the first record for each group and does not expect complete sets of materials for empty groups.

The records have the following format:

- The code, counts, and labels record produced for each group contains the group code in columns 1–10 (F10.0), the unweighted count in columns 11–20 (F10.0), the weighted count in columns 21–33 (F13.2), and the value label in columns 35–54 (A20).
- Five means are written per record, using 16 columns per variable. Nine significant digits are always written.
- Covariance matrices are written in lower-triangular form using 16 columns per variable. Only the first element of the first row, the first two elements of the second row, the first three elements of third row, and so on, are written. Each row starts on a new record.

To save the matrix materials on a file, specify Option 2 on the associated OPTIONS command and use a PROCEDURE OUTPUT command before the DISCRIMINANT command to name the file handle for the file being written (see Chapter 17). For example,

```
FILE HANDLE CITY / file specifications
FILE HANDLE MATOUT / file specifications
GET FILE=CITY
  .
  .
  .
PROCEDURE OUTPUT  OUTFILE=MATOUT
DISCRIMINANT  GROUPS=WORLD (1,3)/
              VARIABLES=FOOD APPL SERVICE RENT/
              METHOD=WILKS
OPTIONS  2
```

saves the matrix materials on the file referred to by MATOUT.

34.27 Reading Matrices

You can use the matrix materials created by DISCRIMINANT in two ways. First, you can use matrix input for the analysis phase only. For example, you might be interested in testing several different methods of variable selection. In this case, DISCRIMINANT uses only the matrix materials and does not perform any classifications. Second, you can use the matrix materials computed from one sample to classify cases in another sample. In this case, both matrix materials and cases are used for the classification phase.

To use matrix materials by themselves, you must use an INPUT MATRIX command prior to the DISCRIMINANT command and specify Option 3 on the associated OPTIONS command. Since you are not reading in any cases, you must define variables corresponding to the matrix materials with the NUMERIC command (see Chapter 6). Both the NUMERIC and INPUT MATRIX commands must be part of an input program (see Chapter 17), as in:

```
FILE HANDLE DISCMAT / file specifications
INPUT PROGRAM
NUMERIC  CLASS X1 X2 X3 X4 X5
INPUT MATRIX  FILE=DISCMAT
END INPUT PROGRAM
DISCRIMINANT  GROUPS=CLASS(1,4)/
              VARIABLES=X1 TO X5/
              METHOD=WILKS/
              METHOD=MAHAL
OPTIONS  3 6
STATISTICS  5 11 12
```

To use matrix materials calculated from one file to classify cases in the active file, you need to use only the INPUT MATRIX command to refer to the file with the matrix materials (along with the associated FILE HANDLE command). In the following example, matrix materials are calculated from file handle SAMPLE and are then used to classify cases from file handle PREDICT:

```
FILE HANDLE SAMPLE / file specifications
FILE HANDLE PREDICT / file specifications
FILE HANDLE DISCMAT / file specifiacations
GET FILE=SAMPLE
PROCEDURE OUTPUT  OUTFILE=DISCMAT
DISCRIMINANT  GROUPS=CLASS(1,4)/
              VARIABLES=X1 TO X5/
              METHOD=WILKS
OPTIONS       2
GET FILE=PREDICT
INPUT MATRIX FILE=DISCMAT
DISCRIMINANT  GROUPS=CLASS(1,4)/
              VARIABLES=X1 TO X5/
              METHOD=WILKS/
OPTIONS       3 4 5
STATISTICS 10 13 14 15
```

34.28 Summary of Syntax Rules

The following rules apply to the operation of the DISCRIMINANT procedure:

- The only required subcommands are GROUPS and VARIABLES. All other subcommands are optional.
- The ANALYSIS subcommand specifies one analysis.
- GROUPS, VARIABLES, and SELECT can be specified in any order, followed by ANALYSIS. All other subcommands (METHOD, MAXSTEPS, TOLERANCE, FIN, FOUT, PIN, POUT, VIN, FUNCTIONS, PRIORS, and SAVE) may be entered in any order following the ANALYSIS subcommand.
- METHOD, MAXSTEPS, TOLERANCE, FIN, FOUT, PIN, POUT, VIN, FUNCTIONS, PRIORS, and SAVE apply only to the previous ANALYSIS subcommand.
- If METHOD, MAXSTEPS, TOLERANCE, FIN, FOUT, PIN, POUT, VIN, FUNCTIONS, PRIORS, and SAVE are used more than once for a given ANALYSIS subcommand, the first specification named is in effect for that command.

The following example illustrates these rules:

```
DISCRIMINANT  GROUPS=WORLD(1,3)/
  VARIABLES=FOOD TO FSALES/
  SAVE=CLASS DIRECT SCORES=SCORE/
  ANALYSIS=FOOD TO FSALES/
  PRIORS=SIZE/
  SAVE=CLASS CLASSA/
  ANALYSIS=FOOD TO FSALES/
  METHOD=WILKS/
  PIN=.01/
  SAVE=CLASS WILKS/
  ANALYSIS=FOOD TO FSALES/
  METHOD=WILKS/PIN=.01/PRIORS=SIZE
  SAVE=CLASS WILKSA
```

This command produces four analyses:

- The first analysis uses the direct-entry method, taking all defaults, and saves the predicted group as variable DIRECT and discriminant scores as SCORE1 and SCORE2.
- The second analysis makes a priors adjustment and saves the predicted group as CLASSA.
- The third analyis is a stepwise analysis using the WILKS method. It sets the probability of *F*-to-enter to .01 and saves the predicted group as WILKS.
- The fourth analysis is the same as the third analysis except that it adjusts for prior probabilities and saves the predicted group as WILKSA.

34.29 LIMITATIONS

The following limitations apply to procedure DISCRIMINANT:

- Only 1 GROUPS, one SELECT, and one VARIABLES subcommand may be used per DISCRIMINANT command.
- Pairwise deletion of missing data is not available.

```
FACTOR VARIABLES = varlist [/MISSING = {LISTWISE**
                                        PAIRWISE
                                        MEANSUB
                                        INCLUDE
                                        DEFAULT    }]

 [/READ = {CORRELATION [TRIANGLE]}]  [/WRITE = {CORRELATION}]
          {FACTOR(n)             }             {FACTOR     }
          {DEFAULT               }             {DEFAULT    }

 [/WIDTH = {132}]  [/ANALYSIS = varlist . . . ]  [/ANALYSIS . . . ]
           {n  }

 [/PRINT = [DEFAULT**]  [INITIAL]  [EXTRACTION]  [ROTATION]
           [UNIVARIATE]  [CORRELATION]  [DET]  [INV]  [REPR]  [AIC]
           [KMO]  [FSCORE]  [SIG]  [ALL]]

 [/FORMAT = [SORT]  [BLANK(n)]  [DEFAULT**]]

 [/CRITERIA = [FACTORS(n)]  [MINEIGEN ({1.0})]  [ITERATE ({25})]
                                       {eig}               {ni}

   [RCONVERGE ({0.0001})]  [DELTA ({0})]  [{KAISER  }]
               {r1    }             {d}     {NOKAISER}

   [ECONVERGE ({0.001})]]
               {e1   }

 [/EXTRACTION = {PC**   }]  [/ROTATION = {VARIMAX** }]
                {PAF    }                {EQUAMAX   }
                {ALPHA  }                {QUARTIMAX }
                {IMAGE  }                {OBLIMIN   }
                {ULS    }                {NOROTATE  }
                {GLS    }                {DEFAULT   }
                {ML     }
                {PA1    }
                {PA2    }
                {DEFAULT}

   [/EXTRACTION . . . ]  [/ROTATION . . . ]

 [/DIAGONAL = value list]  [/PLOT = [EIGEN]  [ROTATION (n1, n2)]]

 [/SAVE = [{REG    } ({ALL} rootname)]]  [/SAVE . . . ]
           {BART   }   {n  }
           {AR     }
           {DEFAULT}
```

***Default if the subcommand is omitted.*

OVERVIEW, **35.1**

OPERATION, **35.2**

- The Variable Selection Block, **35.3**
  - The VARIABLES Subcommand, **35.4**
  - The MISSING Subcommand, **35.5**
  - The WIDTH Subcommand, **35.6**
- The Extraction Block, **35.7**
  - The ANALYSIS Subcommand, **35.8**
  - The EXTRACTION Subcommand, **35.9**
  - The PRINT Subcommand, **35.10**
  - The FORMAT Subcommand, **35.11**
  - The PLOT Subcommand, **35.12**
  - The CRITERIA Subcommand, **35.13**
  - The DIAGONAL Subcommand, **35.14**
- The ROTATION Subcommand, **35.15**
- The SAVE Subcommand, **35.16**
- Matrix Materials, **35.17**
  - The READ Subcommand, **35.18**
  - The WRITE Subcommand, **35.19**

LIMITATIONS AND SUMMARY OF SYNTAX, **35.20**

Chapter 35 FACTOR

Procedure FACTOR produces principal components analysis results and factor analysis results. There are no limitations to the number of analyses, the number of variables, the number of extractions, or the number of rotations. You can choose from among six extraction techniques. FACTOR accepts matrix input in the form of correlation matrices or factor loading matrices and also writes these materials to an external file. You can control the number of factors extracted, the number of iterations for extraction and rotation, and other rotation parameters. You can calculate factor scores and save them on the active file.

35.1 OVERVIEW

Factor analysis is logically a four-step process:

- Decide on the variables you wish to analyze. Factor analysis and principal components analysis make no distinction between dependent and independent variables, but instead treat all variables as a dependent set. The basis of the analysis is a correlation matrix built from the variables you name.
- Decide on an extraction technique. In particular, you must decide whether you wish to perform principal components analysis or factor analysis. If the latter, then you must choose from among the extraction techniques available.
- Decide on a rotation technique to aid in interpretation. FACTOR provides several orthogonal and oblique rotations.
- Decide whether you want to save factor scores from the analysis. FACTOR calculates factor scores (also called factor scales) and adds them to your active file. Three methods of calculating factor scores are available.

FACTOR has four *blocks* of subcommands corresponding to the four steps of factor analysis.

Variable Selection Block. The variable selection block consists of some combination of the VARIABLES (Section 35.4), MISSING (Section 35.5), WIDTH (Section 35.6), and READ (Section 35.18) subcommands. VARIABLES is the only required subcommand. These subcommands can be specified in any order.

Extraction Block. The extraction block consists of some combination of the ANALYSIS (Section 35.8), PRINT (Section 35.10), FORMAT (Section 35.11), CRITERIA (Section 35.13), WRITE (Section 35.19), DIAGONAL (Section 35.14), PLOT (Section 35.12), and EXTRACTION (Section 35.9) subcommands. With the exception of the ANALYSIS subcommand which must come first, these subcommands can be specified in any order. If you omit the EXTRACTION subcommand, FACTOR gives you principal components with defaults in effect. Specify any or all of the subcommands to override defaults. You can specify more than one extraction block for an ANALYSIS subcommand. For example, you can test various extraction methods for the same set of variables.

Rotation Block. The rotation block consists of the ROTATION subcommand (Section 35.15). You can specify more than one rotation method for an extraction.

Save Block. The save block consists of the SAVE subcommand (Section 35.16). FACTOR calculates factor scores and adds them to the active file. If you omit the SAVE subcommand, FACTOR does not calculate factor scores. There are three different methods available for calculating factor scores, and you can use more than one for each extraction and rotation.

Within one invocation of FACTOR you can perform several different analyses. You can specify multiple ANALYSIS subcommands, multiple EXTRACTION subcommands for each ANALYSIS subcommand, multiple ROTATION subcommands for each EXTRACTION subcommand, and multiple methods of calculating factor scores for each ROTATION subcommand.

35.2 OPERATION

The FACTOR procedure in SPSS^X is subcommand driven. Each subcommand begins with a subcommand keyword followed by an optional equals sign and subcommand specifications and is terminated by a slash. All keywords can be abbreviated to the first three characters.

A Note on Defaults. FACTOR is an extensive, keyword-driven procedure in which there are many defaults. There are two types of defaults. *Passive defaults* result with no explicit effort on your part. Listwise missing-value deletion is an example of this (see Section 35.5). *Active defaults* result when subcommands are specified that invoke features of the program not supplied unless you request them. In the following documentation, two asterisks (**) signify a passive default and one asterisk (*) signifies an active default.

35.3 The Variable Selection Block

The following rules apply to variable selection block subcommands:

- The VARIABLES, MISSING, and WIDTH subcommands can be entered in any order.
- If more than one MISSING or WIDTH subcommand is used, the last specified is in effect.

35.4 The VARIABLES Subcommand

The VARIABLES subcommand is the only required subcommand in FACTOR. Use VARIABLES to establish the master list of variables for analysis. For example,

```
FACTOR  VARIABLES=ABDEFECT TO ABSINGLE/
```

produces the default principle components analysis of six abortion scale items. The variable list follows the usual SPSS^X conventions. The keyword TO can be used to reference a consecutive set of variables on the active file and the keyword ALL can be used to reference all variables on the active file. Variables must be numeric. Only variables named on the VARIABLES subcommand can be referred to in subsequent subcommands. Only one VARIABLES subcommand is permitted.

35.5 The MISSING Subcommand

FACTOR builds a correlation matrix of variables named on the VARIABLES subcommand before it produces any factor results. To select the missing-value treatment, specify *one* of the following keywords on the MISSING subcommand:

LISTWISE** *Delete missing values listwise.* If you do not specify a MISSING subcommand, by default, analyses are performed using only cases with nonmissing values on all variables in the VARIABLES subcommand.

PAIRWISE *Delete missing values pairwise.* Each correlation coefficient is computed using cases with complete data on the pair of variables correlated, regardless of whether the cases have missing values on any other variables in the VARIABLES list.

MEANSUB *Replace missing values with the variable mean.* All cases are used in the analyses with the substitutions treated as valid observations.

INCLUDE *Include missing values.* All user-missing values are treated as if they are valid values. System-missing values are always missing.

DEFAULT** *Delete missing values listwise.* Keywords DEFAULT and LISTWISE have the same effect.

For example,

```
FACTOR  VARIABLES=ABDEFECT TO ABSINGLE/
  MISSING=MEANSUB/
```

uses mean substitution for missing values. Only one missing-value treatment is in effect for an invocation of FACTOR. If you specify MISSING more than once, the last specified is used.

35.6 The WIDTH Subcommand

You can control the width of the output from FACTOR. The default width is 132 characters, but you can specify any width from 72 to 132, as in:

```
FACTOR  VARIABLES=ABDEFECT TO ABSINGLE/
  MISSING=MEANSUB/
  WIDTH=100/
```

Specify WIDTH once as part of the variable selection block.

n *Maximum width in characters of display.*

DEFAULT** *The default width is 132.*

You can make system width declarations for your SPSS^X run by using the SET command (see Chapter 4). The following points should be considered in controlling the width of your output.

- A WIDTH subcommmand in FACTOR overrides any system width declarations made using the SET command.
- If you use WIDTH more than once, the last specified is in effect for the procedure.
- If system width is declared but FACTOR width is not declared, FACTOR uses the minimum of the system width declaration and 132.
- Finally, if neither width is declared, FACTOR uses the default width of 132.

35.7 The Extraction Block

The following rules apply to extraction block subcommands.

- Multiple extractions can be specified for each ANALYSIS subcommand.
- Only one set of FORMAT, PRINT, and PLOT subcommands are in effect for all the extractions specified within the block.
- Multiple CRITERIA subcommands can be specified for each extraction. Previously specified criteria remain in effect for all analyses until explicitly overriden with another CRITERIA subcommand.

Note that some of these subcommands also print the rotation results.

35.8 The ANALYSIS Subcommand

The ANALYSIS subcommand is used to specify a subset of the variables named on the VARIABLES subcommand. For example,

```
FACTOR  VARIABLES=X1 TO X10/
  MISSING=MEANSUB/
  WIDTH=120/
  ANALYSIS=X1 TO X8/
```

restricts the analysis to variables X1 to X8. If you omit the ANALYSIS subcommand, FACTOR uses all variables named on the VARIABLES subcommand. The keyword TO refers to the positional ordering of variables as named on the VARIABLES subcommand, and not to their order on the active file. The keyword ALL refers to all variables named on the VARIABLES command.

Use the ANALYSIS subcommand in two contexts: to subset variables for analysis, as in the above, or to perform different analyses on the same set of variables. You can use more than one ANALYSIS subcommand. For example,

```
FACTOR  VARIABLES=ABDEFECT TO ABSINGLE FEBEAR FEPOL/
  ANALYSIS=ABDEFECT TO FEPOL/
  ANALYSIS=ABDEFECT TO ABSINGLE
```

specifies two complete analyses.

35.9 The EXTRACTION Subcommand

Use one of the following keywords to specify the factor extraction technique to be used.

PC** *Principal components analysis* (Harman, 1976).

PA1** *Principal components analysis*. Equivalent to PC.

PAF *Principal axis factoring* (Harman, 1976).

PA2 *Principal axis factoring*. Equivalent to PAF.

ALPHA *Alpha factoring* (Kaiser, 1963).

IMAGE *Image factoring* (Kaiser and Caffry, 1963).

ULS *Unweighted least squares* (Harman and Jones, 1966).

GLS *Generalized least squares*.

ML *Maximum likelihood* (Jöreskog and Lawley, 1968).

DEFAULT** *The default is principal components analysis*.

For example,

```
FACTOR  VARIABLES=ABDEFECT TO ABSINGLE/
  MISSING=MEANSUB/
  WIDTH=100/
  EXTRACTION=ULS/
```

specifies unweighted least squares extraction. You can specify more than one extraction method for a given ANALYSIS subcommand. The following example specifies two different extractions:

```
FACTOR  VARIABLES=ABDEFECT TO ABSINGLE/
  MISSING=MEANSUB/
  WIDTH=100/
  EXTRACTION=ULS/
  EXTRACTION=ML
```

35.10 The PRINT Subcommand

Use the PRINT subcommand and any of the following keyword specifications to print results, many of which are not printed by default.

UNIVARIATE *Valid n's, means, and standard deviations*. (Not available with matrix input.)

INITIAL** *Initial communalities, eigenvalues of the correlation matrix, and percent of variance explained*.

CORRELATION *Correlation matrix*.

SIG *Significance levels of correlations.*

DET *The determinant of the correlation matrix.*

INV *The inverse of the correlation matrix.*

AIC *The anti-image covariance and correlation matrices* (Kaiser, 1970). The measure of sampling adequacy for the individual variable is printed on the diagonal of the anti-image correlation matrix.

KMO *The Kaiser-Meyer-Olkin measure of sampling adequacy and Bartletts's test of sphericity.* Tests of significance are not computed with matrix input if an N OF CASES command is not used.

EXTRACTION** *Communalities, eigenvalues, and unrotated factor loadings.*

REPR *Reproduced correlations and residual correlations.*

ROTATION** *Rotated factor pattern and structure matrices, the factor transformation matrix, and the factor correlation matrix.*

FSCORE *The factor score coefficient matrix.*

ALL *All available statistics.*

DEFAULT** *Specifies INITIAL, EXTRACTION, and ROTATION.*

For example,

```
FACTOR  VARIABLES=ABDEFECT TO ABSINGLE/
  MISSING=MEANSUB/
  WIDTH=100/
  PRINT=AIC KMO REPR/
  EXTRACTION=ULS/
  ROTATION=VARIMAX
```

requests the anti-image correlation and covariance matrices, the Kaiser-Meyer-Olkin measure of sampling adequacy, and the reproduced correlation matrix. Note that all symmetric matrices are printed in lower-triangular form. Figure 35.10 is the display produced by this PRINT subcommand.

Figure 35.10 Nondefault display from PRINT subcommand

```
---------------- F A C T O R   A N A L Y S I S ----------------

ANALYSIS NUMBER  1  REPLACEMENT OF MISSING VALUES WITH THE MEAN

KAISER-MEYER-OLKIN MEASURE OF SAMPLING ADEQUACY =  .81562

BARTLETT TEST OF SPHERICITY = 1346.8207, SIGNIFICANCE =    0.0

THERE ARE   12 (40.0%) OFF-DIAGONAL ELEMENTS OF AIC MATRIX > 0.09

ANTI-IMAGE COVARIANCE MATRIX:

              ABDEFECT     ABNOMORE      ABHLTH       ABPOOR      ABRAPE      ABSINGLE

ABDEFECT       .55012
ABNOMORE      -.02219       .33253
ABHLTH        -.22676       .00421       .64445
ABPOOR        -.02235      -.17065       .00034      .33400
ABRAPE        -.19466      -.01936      -.13492     -.03626      .60240
ABSINGLE      -.01953      -.13193      -.02753     -.12332     -.03027      .39606

ANTI-IMAGE CORRELATION MATRIX:

           ABDEFECT  ABNOMORE    ABHLTH    ABPOOR    ABRAPE  ABSINGLE

ABDEFECT    .80138
ABNOMORE   -.05189    .79197
ABHLTH     -.38085    .00910    .80429
ABPOOR     -.05213   -.51206    .00073    .79898
ABRAPE     -.33815   -.04325   -.21654   -.08083    .85544
ABSINGLE   -.04184   -.36354   -.05449   -.33907   -.06196    .85066

MEASURES OF SAMPLING ADEQUACY (MSA) ARE PRINTED ON THE DIAGONAL.

REPRODUCED CORRELATION MATRIX:

              ABDEFECT     ABNOMORE      ABHLTH       ABPOOR      ABRAPE      ABSINGLE

ABDEFECT       .65233*      .00440       .00004       .00070      .00053     -.00580
ABNOMORE       .37662       .78502*     -.00230      -.00054     -.00301      .00083
ABHLTH         .56003       .28454       .48344*     -.00413     -.00064      .00723
ABPOOR         .38828       .77994       .29536       .77532*     .00381     -.00024
ABRAPE         .56422       .39551       .47961       .40415      .49658*    -.00087
ABSINGLE       .38839       .72900       .29894       .72544      .39798      .68014*

THE LOWER LEFT TRIANGLE CONTAINS THE REPRODUCED CORRELATION MATRIX;
THE DIAGONAL, COMMUNALITIES; AND THE UPPER RIGHT TRIANGLE, RESIDUALS
BETWEEN THE OBSERVED CORRELATIONS AND THE REPRODUCED CORRELATIONS.

THERE ARE    0 ( 0.0%) RESIDUALS (ABOVE DIAGONAL) THAT ARE > 0.05
```

If you omit the PRINT subcommand, you obtain the defaults. To obtain the defaults plus nondefaults, you must specify them with the DEFAULT keyword or INITIAL, EXTRACTION, and ROTATION.

35.11 The FORMAT Subcommand

The FORMAT subcommand reformats the factor loading and structure matrices to ease interpretability.

SORT *Order the factor loadings by magnitude.* Aids in identifying clusters of variables.

BLANK(n) *Suppress coefficients lower in absolute value than threshold* n.

DEFAULT** *Deactivate blanking and sorting.* Variables appear in the order in which they are named, and all loadings are shown.

For example,

```
FACTOR  VARIABLES=ABDEFECT TO ABSINGLE/
  MISSING=MEANSUB/
  WIDTH=100/
  ANALYSIS=ABDEFECT TO ABSINGLE/
  FORMAT=SORT BLANK(.3)/
  EXTRACTION=ULS/
```

specifies that loadings be ordered by magnitude and that loadings smaller in magnitude than 0.3 not be printed. Figure 35.11a is a sorted factor loading matrix with BLANK(.3). Compare it to Figure 35.11b, which is the same matrix unsorted with all loadings printed.

Figure 35.11a A sorted and blanked factor loading matrix

ROTATED FACTOR MATRIX:

	FACTOR 1	FACTOR 2
ABNOMORE	.85518	
ABPOOR	.84428	
ABSINGLE	.77944	
ABDEFECT		.77403
ABHLTH		.67921
ABRAPE		.64302

Figure 35.11b A default factor loading matrix

ROTATED FACTOR MATRIX:

	FACTOR 1	FACTOR 2
ABDEFECT	.23069	.77403
ABNOMORE	.85518	.23170
ABHLTH	.14870	.67921
ABPOOR	.84428	.25002
ABRAPE	.28827	.64302
ABSINGLE	.77944	.26948

35.12 The PLOT Subcommand

Use the PLOT subcommand to obtain a scree plot or a plot of the variables in rotated factor space. The scree plot aids in identifying the number of factors needed (Cattell, 1966). It is named for its resemblance to scree, the geological term for an accumulation of stones or rocky debris lying on a slope or at the base of a hill or cliff.

The plot of variables in factor space is a graphic representation of the rotated factor loadings which aids in substantive identification of factors. It is not printed if the ROTATION command is not implicitly or explicitly specified (see Section 35.15).

EIGEN *The scree plot.* Plots the eigenvalues in descending order.

ROTATION(n1 n2) *Plot the variables in factor space.* Specify *n1* and *n2*, which are the numbers to be plotted.

The following FACTOR command requests a scree plot.

```
FACTOR  VARIABLES=ABDEFECT TO ABSINGLE/
  MISSING=MEANSUB/
  WIDTH=100/
  ANALYSIS=ABDEFECT TO ABSINGLE/
  FORMAT=SORT BLANK(.3)/
  CRITERIA=ITERATE(10)/
  PLOT=EIGEN/
  EXTRACTION=ULS/
  ROTATION=VARIMAX
```

Figure 35.12 is the scree plot produced by this example.

Figure 35.12 Scree plot

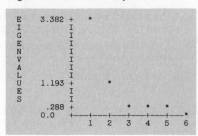

```
E    3.382 +    *
I          I
G          I
E          I
N          I
V          I
A          I
L          I
U    1.193 +         *
E          I
S          I
      .288 +              *    *    *
     0.0   +----+----+----+----+----+----*
                1    2    3    4    5    6
```

35.13 The CRITERIA Subcommand

Use the CRITERIA subcommand to override extraction and rotation defaults. You can specify one CRITERIA subcommand for each extraction and each rotation within each extraction.

FACTORS(nf) *The number of factors extracted.* The default is the number of eigenvalues greater than MINEIGEN.

MINEIGEN(eg) *Minimum eigenvalue used to control the number of factors.* The default MINEIGEN is 1.

ITERATE(ni) *The number of iterations for the factor solution.* The default ITERATE is 25.

ECONVERGE(e1) *The convergence criterion for extraction.* The default ECONVERGE is 0.001.

RCONVERGE(e2) *The convergence criterion for rotation.* The default RCONVERGE is 0.0001.

KAISER** *Kaiser normalization.* The default.

NOKAISER *No Kaiser normalization.*

DELTA(d) *The value of delta for direct oblimin rotation.* The default DELTA is 0.

DEFAULT** *Use default values.* Default values are shown with each CRITERIA keyword.

For example, to specify the maximum number of iterations for extraction, use the ITERATE keyword, as in:

```
FACTOR  VARIABLES=ABDEFECT TO ABSINGLE/
  MISSING=MEANSUB/
  WIDTH=100/
  ANALYSIS=ABDEFECT TO ABSINGLE/
  PRINT=CORRELATION DET REPR/
  FORMAT=SORT BLANK(.3)/
  CRITERIA=ITERATE(10)/
  EXTRACTION=ULS/
```

The above FACTOR command limits the number of iterations during extraction to 10.

If you use the CRITERIA subcommand to override defaults, they remain in effect for subsequent analyses until explicitly overriden. You can use the keyword DEFAULT to return to FACTOR's defaults for CRITERIA.

For example,

```
FACTOR  VARIABLES=ABDEFECT TO ABSINGLE/
  CRITERIA=FACTORS(6)/
  EXTRACTION=PC/
  ANALYSIS=ABDEFECT TO ABSINGLE/
  CRITERIA=DEFAULT/
  EXTRACTION=ML/
  ROTATION=VARIMAX
```

turns off the FACTORS specification for the second analyses.

35.14 The DIAGONAL Subcommand

Use the DIAGONAL subcommand to specify initial diagonal values in conjunction with principal axis factoring. Specify one of the following:

valuelist *Diagonal values.* User-supplied diagonal values are only used for principal axis factoring (EXTRACTION=PAF).

DEFAULT** *1's on the diagonal for principal components or initial communality estimates on the diagonal for factor methods.*

The following example demonstrates the use of the DIAGONAL subcommand:

```
FACTOR  VARIABLES=ABDEFECT TO ABSINGLE/
  DIAGONAL=.55 .45 .35 .40 .60 .70/
  EXTRACTION=PAF/
  ROTATION=VARIMAX
```

You can use the asterisk operator to indicate replications of the same diagonal value, as in:

```
FACTOR  VARIABLES=ABDEFECT TO ABSINGLE/
  DIAGONAL=.55 .45 3*.40 .70/
  EXTRACTION=PAF/
  ROTATION=VARIMAX
```

35.15 The ROTATION Subcommand

If you do not use the EXTRACTION subcommand, the default factor rotation method is VARIMAX. If you use the EXTRACTION subcommand but do not use the ROTATION subcommand, the factor loadings are not rotated. If you want the plot of variables in unrotated factor space produced by the PLOT subcommand (Section 35.12), use the ROTATE subcommand with keyword NOROTATE.

VARIMAX** *Varimax rotation.*

EQUAMAX *Equamax rotation.*

QUARTIMAX *Quartimax rotation.*

OBLIMIN *Direct oblimin rotation.*

NOROTATE *No rotation.*

DEFAULT** *The default is varimax rotation.*

For example, the command

```
FACTOR  VARIABLES=ABDEFECT TO ABSINGLE/
  MISSING=MEANSUB/
  WIDTH=100/
  ANALYSIS=ABDEFECT TO ABSINGLE/
  PRINT=CORRELATION DET REPR/
  FORMAT=SORT BLANK(.3)/
  CRITERIA=ITERATE(10)/
  PLOT=EIGEN ROTATION(1 2)/
  EXTRACTION=ULS/
  ROTATION/
```

specifies varimax rotation.

You can specify more than one rotation for a given extraction. For example,

```
FACTOR  VARIABLES=ABDEFECT TO ABSINGLE/
  EXTRACTION=ML/
  ROTATION=VARIMAX/
  ROTATION=QUARTIMAX/
  ROTATION=OBLIQUE
```

specifies three different rotations for maximum likelihood extraction.

35.16 The SAVE Subcommand

Use the SAVE subcommand to compute and save factor scores on the active file. Indicate the method to be used in calculating factor scores, how many factor scores to calculate, and a *rootname* to be used in naming the factor scores.

First, choose one of the following method keywords:

REG* *The regression method.*

BART *The Bartlett method.*

AR *The Anderson-Rubin method.*

DEFAULT* *The default is the regression method.*

Second, specify the number of desired factor scores. The maximum number you may specify is equal to the order of the factor solution. You can use the keyword ALL to calculate all possible factor scores.

Third, specify a seven-character-maximum rootname to be used in naming the factor scores. FACTOR names the factor scores sequentially. If you are calculating factor scores for a many-factor solution, make sure that the rootname is short enough to accommodate the number of the highest-order factor score variable. When FACTOR saves the variables on the active file it automatically supplies a variable label with the method used to calculate it, its positional order, and the analysis number (see Figure E in the annotated example).

For example, the following FACTOR command saves factor scores for the abortion items. Note that the parentheses *are* required.

```
FACTOR  VARIABLES=ABDEFECT TO ABSINGLE/
  MISSING=MEANSUB/
  WIDTH=100/
  ANALYSIS=ABDEFECT TO ABSINGLE/
  PRINT=CORRELATION DET REPR/
  FORMAT=SORT BLANK(.3)/
  CRITERIA=FACTORS(2)/
  PLOT=EIGEN ROTATION(1 2)/
  EXTRACTION=ULS/
  ROTATION=VARIMAX/
  SAVE AR (ALL FSULS)/
```

FACTOR calculates two factor scores named FSULS1 and FSULS2 using the Anderson-Rubin method and saves them on the active file.

You can use multiple SAVE subcommands for an extraction. For example,

```
FACTOR  VARIABLES=ABDEFECT TO ABSINGLE/
  MISSING=MEANSUB/
  WIDTH=100/
  ANALYSIS=ABDEFECT TO ABSINGLE/
  PRINT=CORRELATION DET REPR/
  FORMAT=SORT BLANK(.3)/
  CRITERIA=FACTORS(2)/
  PLOT=EIGEN ROTATION(1 2)/
  EXTRACTION=ULS/
  ROTATION=VARIMAX/
  SAVE AR (ALL FSULS)/
  SAVE BART (ALL BFAC)
```

saves two sets of factor scores. The first set is computed using the Anderson-Rubin method and the second is computed using the Bartlett method.

ANNOTATED EXAMPLE FOR FACTOR

For example, six abortion items are used from a 500-case sample of the 1980 General Social Survey. Respondents indicate whether they favor or oppose abortion in the following contexts:

- ABHLTH—if the woman's health is seriously endangered.
- ABRAPE—if the woman is pregnant as a result of rape.
- ABDEFECT—if there is a strong chance of a serious defect in the child.
- ABPOOR—if the woman has a low income and cannot afford more children.
- ABSINGLE—if the woman is not married and doesn't want the child.
- ABNOMORE—if the woman is married and wants no more children.

The SPSS^{X} commands are

```
TITLE  FACTOR ANALYSIS OF ABORTION ITEMS
FILE HANDLE GSS80/ file specifications
GET  FILE GSS80/KEEP ABDEFECT TO ABSINGLE
COMMENT  RECODE THE ITEMS SO THAT 1 IS FAVOR AND 0 IS OPPOSE
RECODE  ABDEFECT TO ABSINGLE(1=1)(2=0)
MISSING VALUES  ABDEFECT TO ABSINGLE(7 THRU 9)
VALUE LABELS  ABDEFECT TO ABSINGLE
  0 'NO' 1 'YES' 7 'NAP' 8 'DK' 9 'NA'/
FACTOR  VARIABLES=ABDEFECT TO ABSINGLE/
 MISSING=MEANSUB/
 WIDTH=100/
 FORMAT=SORT BLANK(.3)/
 PLOT=ROTATION(1 2)/
 EXTRACTION=ULS/
 ROTATION=OBLIQUE/
 SAVE REG (ALL FSULS)/
```

- The FILE HANDLE command identifies the GSS80 system file and gives the operating-system specifications.
- The TITLE command puts the title, FACTOR ANALYSIS OF ABORTION ITEMS, at the top of each page of output for this job (see Chapter 4).
- The GET command accesses the data file and keeps only those variables that will be used in this job (see Chapter 5).
- The RECODE, MISSING VALUES, and VALUE LABELS commands redefine the abortion items and label the redefined responses for this job (see Chapters 3 and 6).
- The FACTOR command invokes the FACTOR procedure. The VARIABLES subcommand names all the variables that are used in this FACTOR job (see Section 35.4).
- The MISSING subcommand forces mean substitution for missing data (see Section 35.5).
- The WIDTH subcommand limits the width of the output to 100 columns (see Section 35.6).
- The FORMAT subcommand displays the factor loadings in descending order of magnitude and suppresses the printing of factor loadings less than 0.3 (see Section 35.11 and Figures C and D).
- The EXTRACTION subcommand specifies unweighted least squares as the method of extraction (see Section 35.9).
- The ROTATION subcommand specifies an oblique rotation (see Section 35.15).
- The SAVE subcommand computes all possible factor scores using the regression method (see Section 35.16).

Portions of the output produced by this set of commands appear in Figures A through E.

Initial Statistics. Figure A contains the initial statistics which are produced by default. Initial statistics are the initial communalities, eigenvalues of the correlation matrix, and percentage of variance explained.

A Initial statistics

```
---------------- F A C T O R   A N A L Y S I S ----------------

ANALYSIS NUMBER  1  REPLACEMENT OF MISSING VALUES WITH THE MEAN


EXTRACTION  1  FOR ANALYSIS  1, UNWEIGHTED LEAST SQUARES (ULS)


INITIAL STATISTICS:

VARIABLE     COMMUNALITY      FACTOR   EIGENVALUE   PCT OF VAR   CUM PCT

ABDEFECT          .44988         1      3.38153        56.4        56.4
ABNOMORE          .66747         2      1.19287        19.9        76.2
ABHLTH            .35555         3       .50823         8.5        84.7
ABPOOR            .66600         4       .40867         6.8        91.5
ABRAPE            .39760         5       .28847         4.8        96.3
ABSINGLE          .60394         6       .22024         3.7       100.0
```

Extraction Statistics. Figure B contains the extraction statistics which are produced by default. Extraction statistics are the communalities, eigenvalues, and unrotated factor loadings. Note the effect of sorting and blanking produced by the FORMAT subcommand.

B Extraction statistics

```
  ULS EXTRACTED   2 FACTORS. 5 ITERATIONS REQUIRED.

FACTOR MATRIX:

             FACTOR  1     FACTOR  2

ABPOOR        .81970       -.32158
ABNOMORE      .81704       -.34273
ABSINGLE      .78051
ABDEFECT      .65764        .46888
ABRAPE        .62257        .33014
ABHLTH        .53469        .44445


FINAL STATISTICS:

VARIABLE     COMMUNALITY      FACTOR   EIGENVALUE   PCT OF VAR   CUM PCT

ABDEFECT          .65233         1      3.05462        50.9        50.9
ABNOMORE          .78502         2       .81821        13.6        64.5
ABHLTH            .48344
ABPOOR            .77532
ABRAPE            .49658
ABSINGLE          .68014
```

Rotation Statistics. Figure C contains the rotation statistics which are produced by default if the model is rotated. They are the rotated factor pattern and structure matrices (since this is an oblique rotation), the factor transformation matrix, and the factor correlation matrix.

C Rotation statistics

```
---------------- F A C T O R   A N A L Y S I S ----------------


OBLIMIN   ROTATION  1  FOR EXTRACTION  1  IN ANALYSIS  1 - KAISER NORMALIZATION.

  OBLIMIN CONVERGED IN    4 ITERATIONS.

PATTERN MATRIX:

              FACTOR  1     FACTOR  2

ABNOMORE       .90007
ABPOOR         .88136
ABSINGLE       .80050

ABDEFECT                     .80734
ABHLTH                       .72675
ABRAPE                       .63777


STRUCTURE MATRIX:

              FACTOR  1     FACTOR  2

ABNOMORE       .88574        .46583
ABPOOR         .88052        .48028
ABSINGLE       .82393        .48046

ABDEFECT       .44195        .80767
ABRAPE         .45976        .69852
ABHLTH         .33632        .69342


FACTOR CORRELATION MATRIX:

              FACTOR  1    FACTOR  2

FACTOR  1     1.00000
FACTOR  2      .54667      1.00000
```

Factor Plot. Figure D contains the plot of variables in the rotated factor space. Although the rotation is oblique, the plot axes are orthogonal. Since factor 1 overlaps with factor 3 and factor 2 overlaps with factor 4, they do not appear on the plot.

D Factor plot

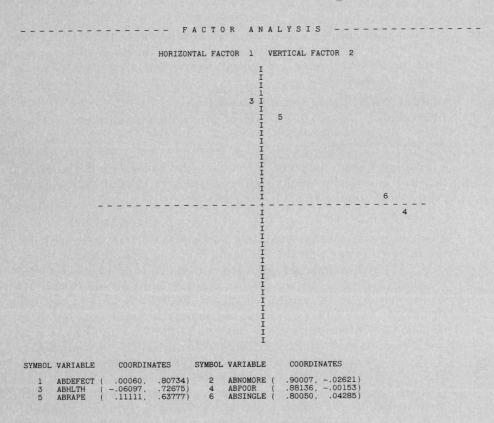

```
- - - - - - - - - - - - - - - -   F A C T O R   A N A L Y S I S   - - - - - - - - - - - - - - - -

                          HORIZONTAL FACTOR  1   VERTICAL FACTOR  2

                                           I
                                           I
                                           I
                                           I
                                         3 I
                                           I
                                           I   5
                                           I
                                           I
                                           I
                                           I
                                           I
                                           I
                                           I
                                           I
                                           I
                                           I                          6
          - - - - - - - - - - - - - - - - -+- - - - - - - - - - - - - - - - - -
                                           I                              4
                                           I
                                           I
                                           I
                                           I
                                           I
                                           I
                                           I
                                           I
                                           I
                                           I
                                           I
                                           I
                                           I
                                           I
                                           I
                                           I

SYMBOL VARIABLE      COORDINATES       SYMBOL VARIABLE       COORDINATES

   1   ABDEFECT (  .00060,  .80734)      2   ABNOMORE (  .90007, -.02621)
   3   ABHLTH   ( -.06097,  .72675)      4   ABPOOR   (  .88136, -.00153)
   5   ABRAPE   (  .11111,  .63777)      6   ABSINGLE (  .80050,  .04285)
```

Saved Factor Scores. Figure E contains the information for the factor scores which are saved as new variables on the active file as a result of the SAVE subcommand.

E Saved factor scores

```
- - - - - - - - - - - - - - - -   F A C T O R   A N A L Y S I S   - - - - - - - - - - - - - - - -

  2 REGRESSION FACTOR SCORES WILL BE SAVED WITH ROOTNAME: FSULS

FOLLOWING FACTOR SCORES WILL BE ADDED TO THE ACTIVE FILE:

  NAME        LABEL

FSULS1      REGR FACTOR SCORE   1 FOR ANALYSIS    1
FSULS2      REGR FACTOR SCORE   2 FOR ANALYSIS    1
```

35.17 Matrix Materials

FACTOR accepts matrix materials in the form of a correlation matrix or a factor loading matrix in lieu of a case file. It also writes one of these materials to an external file for use in a subsequent job. If you use matrix input you cannot obtain factor scores. Section 35.18 discusses the reading of matrices and Section 35.19 discusses the writing of matrices.

35.18 The READ Subcommand

You can read either the correlation matrix or the factor loadings into FACTOR. Specify *one* of the following keywords on the READ subcommand. Place the READ subcommand among the subcommands constituting the variable selection block.

CORRELATION* *Read the correlation matrix.*

FACTOR(nf) *Read the factor matrix. nf* indicates the number of factors in the analysis.

DEFAULT* *Read the correlation matrix.*

You can enter a correlation matrix in lower-triangular form if it contains a diagonal of ones by specifying the keyword TRIANGLE following the keyword COR on the READ subcommand:

```
READ=COR TRIANGLE/
```

To use a correlation or factor loading matrix with FACTOR, you must define variables with the NUMERIC command inside an input program, use the INPUT MATRIX command to signal matrix input and define a file handle if the matrix resides on an external file, and use the READ subcommand. If you supply an N OF CASES command, FACTOR is able to calculate significance levels for the extraction techniques that use chi-square as a test statistic for the adequacy of the model and Bartlett's test of sphericity which is available with the KMO keyword on the PRINT subcommand.

If you use correlation matrices written by other procedures such as PEARSON CORR, FACTOR skips the record or matrix of *n*'s but prints a warning message. Note that you cannot use multiple sets of matrix materials produced by other procedures in FACTOR. Typically, PEARSON CORR, PARTIAL CORR, and other procedures produce multiple sets of materials for multiple variable lists or when run with split file processing. For details on using matrix materials, see Chapter 17.

The following SPSS^X commands read a correlation matrix from an external file:

```
FILE HANDLE  MAT/file specifications
INPUT PROGRAM
NUMERIC  X1 TO X10
END INPUT PROGRAM
INPUT MATRIX  FILE=MAT
FACTOR  READ/VARIABLES=X1 TO X10/
```

35.19 The WRITE Subcommand

Use the WRITE subcommand to write the correlation matrix or the factor loadings to a specified file. Specify any of the following keywords.

CORRELATION* *Write the correlation matrix.*

FACTOR *Write the factor matrix.*

DEFAULT* *Write the correlation matrix.*

To write matrix materials, you must use a FILE HANDLE command to define a handle for the file containing matrix materials, a PROCEDURE OUTPUT command to signal matrix output, and the WRITE subcommand.

For more on writing out matrix materials, see Chapter 17. For example,

```
FILE HANDLE  GSS80/file specifications
FILE HANDLE  MATOUT/file specifications
GET FILE=GSS80
PROCEDURE OUTPUT  OUTFILE=MATOUT
FACTOR  VARIABLES=CONBUS TO CONARMY/
  WRITE CORRELATION
```

writes the correlation matrix to the file referenced by MATOUT.

If you plan to read the matrix materials written by FACTOR with FACTOR in a subsequent job, do not write out more than one type of matrix since FACTOR will not be able to read it.

35.20 LIMITATIONS AND SUMMARY OF SYNTAX

The following rules apply to FACTOR subcommands:

- The only required subcommand is VARIABLES.
- Only 1 MISSING, WIDTH, READ, and WRITE subcommand can be in effect for the FACTOR procedure. If any of these is specified more than once, the last specified is in effect for the entire procedure.
- If the EXTRACTION command is omitted, ROTATION defaults to VARIMAX; otherwise it defaults to NOROTATE.
- Only 1 PRINT, PLOT, and DIAGONAL subcommand can be in effect for each ANALYSIS subcommand. If any of these is specified more than once in a given extraction block, the last one specified for that extraction block is in effect.
- Specifications on the CRITERIA subcommand carry over from analysis to analysis until explicitly overridden with a subsequent CRITERIA subcommand.

NONPAR CORR varlist [WITH varlist] [/varlist . . .]

OPTIONS:
1 Include missing values.
2 Exclude missing values listwise.
3 Two-tailed test of significance.
4 Write matrix materials to a file.
5 Kendall's tau-*b*.
6 Kendall's tau-*b* and Spearman's rho.
7 Random sampling.
8 Suppress printing of *n* and significance level.
9 Serial string formatting.

OVERVIEW, **36.1**
OPERATION, **36.2**
- Specifying the Design, **36.3**
- Types of Coefficients, **36.4**
- Two-Tailed Significance Tests, **36.5**
- Missing Values, **36.6**
- Formatting Options, **36.7**
- Random Sampling, **36.8**
- Writing Matrix Materials, **36.9**

LIMITATIONS, **36.10**

Chapter 36 NONPAR CORR

NONPAR CORR computes two rank-order correlation coefficients, Spearman's rho and Kendall's tau-*b*, with their significance levels. You can obtain either or both coefficients. When you use NONPAR CORR, $SPSS^X$ automatically computes the ranks and stores the cases in memory. Therefore, memory required is directly proportional to the number of cases being analyzed.

36.1 OVERVIEW

NONPAR CORR produces one or more matrices of correlation coefficients. For each coefficient, NONPAR CORR prints the number of cases used and the significance level. You can specify optional formats, methods of handling missing data, and random sampling of cases. NONPAR CORR also writes matrix materials which can be used by other procedures.

Selecting Coefficients. By default, NONPAR CORR computes Spearman coefficients. You may also specify only Kendall coefficients or both coefficients. (See Section 36.4.)

Significance Levels. By default, the significance level for each coefficient is based on a one-tailed test. Optionally, you can request that the significance level be calculated using a two-tailed test. (See Section 36.5.)

Missing Values. By default, NONPAR CORR excludes cases with missing values on an analysis-by-analysis basis. Optionally, you can request that missing values be handled as if they were valid or that cases with missing values be deleted listwise. (See Section 36.6.)

Formatting Options. You can print more rows and columns of coefficients than the default format allows and suppress the number of cases and significance level for each coefficient. You can also print coefficients in serial format. (See Section 36.7.)

Random Sampling. NONPAR CORR must store cases in memory for ranking. You can request a random sample of cases when there is not enough space to store all the cases. (See Section 36.8.)

Matrix Output. NONPAR CORR writes out a square matrix of correlation coefficients and the number of cases used to compute each coefficient. These materials can be read by other $SPSS^X$ procedures. (See Section 36.9.)

Statistics. There are no optional statistics for NONPAR CORR. All statistics available for the requested coefficients are printed by default.

36.2 OPERATION

NONPAR CORR operates via a list of variables, as in procedure PEARSON CORR (Chapter 31), and uses the associated OPTIONS command. You can specify several lists of variables separated by slashes and you can use the keyword WITH to obtain the correlations of one set of variables with another set.

36.3 Specifying the Design

NONPAR CORR prints either a lower-triangular or a rectangular matrix depending on how you specify the variable list. Both forms of the specification permit the use of the keyword TO to reference contiguous variables. The variables must be numeric. If you provide a simple list of variables, NONPAR CORR prints the correlations of each variable with every other variable in the list in a lower-triangular matrix. For example, the command

```
NONPAR CORR  PRESTIGE SPPRES PAPRES16 DEGREE PADEG MADEG
```

produces the triangular matrix in Figure 36.3a. The correlation of a variable with itself (the diagonal) and redundant coefficients are not printed. Use this form of the NONPAR CORR specification when you want to write the correlation matrix for use with another procedure or program (see Section 36.9). As indicated in the banner in Figure 36.3a, the default coefficients produced by NONPAR CORR are Spearman correlations. The number of cases upon which the correlations are based and the one-tailed significance level are printed for each correlation. To obtain Kendall coefficients, you must use the OPTIONS command (see Section 36.4).

Figure 36.3a A lower-triangular default matrix

```
- - - - - - - - - - - - -  S P E A R M A N   C O R R E L A T I O N   C O E F F I C I E N T S  - - - - - - - - - - - - -

SPPRES          .3608
             N(  258)
             SIG .000

PAPRES16        .2934         .2021
             N(  382)      N(  235)
             SIG .000      SIG .001

DEGREE          .5262         .3864         .3438
             N(  461)      N(  277)      N(  412)
             SIG .000      SIG .000      SIG .000

PADEG           .2397         .1306         .3908         .3820
             N(  352)      N(  219)      N(  376)      N(  377)
             SIG .000      SIG .027      SIG .000      SIG .000

MADEG           .1781         .1323         .2593         .3829         .5965
             N(  406)      N(  244)      N(  372)      N(  442)      N(  356)
             SIG .000      SIG .019      SIG .000      SIG .000      SIG .000

             PRESTIGE       SPPRES     PAPRES16       DEGREE         PADEG

" . " IS PRINTED IF A COEFFICIENT CANNOT BE COMPUTED.
```

To obtain the rectangular matrix, specify two variable lists separated by the keyword WITH. NONPAR CORR then prints a rectangular matrix of variables in the first list correlated with variables in the second list. For example,

```
NONPAR CORR  PRESTIGE SPPRES PAPRES16 WITH DEGREE PADEG MADEG
```

produces the nine correlations shown in Figure 36.3b. The variables listed before the keyword WITH define the rows of the matrix, and those listed after the keyword WITH define the columns. Unless a variable is in both lists, there are no identity coefficients in the matrix. If you want to write the correlation matrix for use with another procedure or program, do not use the keyword WITH (see Section 36.9).

You can request more than one matrix on a NONPAR CORR command. Use a slash to separate the specifications for each of the requested matrices. For example,

```
NONPAR CORR  SPPRES PAPRES16 PRESTIGE/SATCITY WITH SATHOBBY SATFAM
```

produces two separate correlation matrices. The first matrix contains three coefficients in triangular form. The second matrix is rectangular and

Figure 36.3b A matrix from a variable list using WITH

```
- - - - - - - - - - - -  S P E A R M A N   C O R R E L A T I O N   C O E F F I C I E N T S  - - - - - - - - - - - -

              DEGREE       PADEG        MADEG

PRESTIGE        .5262        .2397        .1781
             N(  461)     N(  352)     N(  406)
             SIG .000     SIG .000     SIG .000

SPPRES          .3864        .1306        .1323
             N(  277)     N(  219)     N(  244)
             SIG .000     SIG .027     SIG .019

PAPRES16        .3438        .3908        .2593
             N(  412)     N(  376)     N(  372)
             SIG .000     SIG .000     SIG .000

 " . " IS PRINTED IF A COEFFICIENT CANNOT BE COMPUTED.
```

contains two coefficients. You can specify up to 25 variable lists with one NONPAR CORR command and name or imply up to 100 variables on all lists.

If all cases have a missing value for a given pair of variables, or they all have the same value for a variable, the coefficient cannot be computed. Because Spearman's rho and Kendall's tau-*b* coefficients always have a value in the range −1.00 to 1.00, NONPAR CORR prints a decimal point if a correlation cannot be computed.

36.4 Types of Coefficients

NONPAR CORR computes two different correlations: Spearman's rho and Kendall's tau-*b*. Both are based on ranks. By default, NONPAR CORR computes Spearman correlations. To obtain only Kendall's tau-*b*, specify Option 5. To obtain both coefficients, specify Option 6.

OPTION 5 *Kendall's tau-*b. Only Kendall coefficients are displayed.

OPTION 6 *Kendall and Spearman coefficients.* Both coefficients are displayed.

36.5 Two-Tailed Significance Tests

By default, the significance level printed below the coefficient is based on a one-tailed test. This test is appropriate when the direction of the relationship between a pair of variables can be specified in advance of the analysis. When the direction of the relationship cannot be determined in advance, a two-tailed test is appropriate. To override the default and request that the significance level be calculated using the two-tailed test, use Option 3.

OPTION 3 *Two-tailed test of significance.*

36.6 Missing Values

By default, NONPAR CORR deletes cases with missing values on an analysis-by-analysis basis. A case missing for one or both of the pair of variables for a specific correlation coefficient is not used for that analysis. Because each coefficient is based on all cases that have valid codes on that particular pair of variables, the maximum information available is used in every calculation. This also results in a set of coefficients based on a varying number of cases. Two missing-value options are available:

OPTION 1 *Include missing values.* User-defined missing values are treated as if they are not missing.

OPTION 2 *Exclude missing values listwise.* Each variable list on a command is evaluated separately. Cases missing on any variable named in a list are excluded from all analyses. If you use the slash to specify multiple matrices, a case missing for one matrix may be used in another matrix. This option decreases the amount of memory required and significantly decreases computational time.

ANNOTATED EXAMPLE FOR NONPAR CORR

The example illustrating NONPAR CORR analyzes a 500-case sample from the 1980 General Social Survey. The variables are

- PRESTIGE—the respondent's occupational prestige scale score.
- SPPRES—the spouse's occupational prestige scale score.
- PAPRES16—the father's occupational prestige scale score when the respondent was growing up.
- DEGREE, PADEG, MADEG—the highest educational degree earned by the respondent, the father, and the mother, respectively. Each of these variables has four categories to code high school, junior college, college, and graduate degrees.

This example determines the degree to which variation in three measures of occupational prestige and three measures of educational attainment are related. NONPAR CORR computes nonparametric correlation coefficients for the ranked data. The SPSS^X commands are

```
FILE HANDLE  GSS80/ file specifications
GET  FILE GSS80/KEEP PRESTIGE SPPRES PAPRES16 DEGREE PADEG MADEG
NONPAR CORR  PRESTIGE TO MADEG
OPTIONS  2 6 9
FINISH
```

- The FILE HANDLE identifies the GSS80 data file and gives the operating-system specifications (see Chapter 3).
- The GET command defines the data to SPSS^X and selects the variables needed for the analysis (see Chapter 5).
- The NONPAR CORR command requests correlation coefficients for one simple variable list. This form of the NONPAR CORR command produces a lower-triangular matrix (see Section 36.3).
- Option 2 excludes missing values listwise. Cases missing on any of the six variables are not used in the calculation of any coefficients (see Section 36.6).
- Option 6 requests both Kendall and Spearman correlation matrices (see Section 36.4).
- Option 9 prints each lower-triangular matrix in serial format (see Section 36.7).

Output from the NONPAR CORR command

```
- - - - - - - - - - - - - -  K E N D A L L   C O R R E L A T I O N   C O E F F I C I E N T S - - - - - - - - - - - - -
VARIABLE                VARIABLE                VARIABLE                VARIABLE                VARIABLE                VARIABLE
PAIR                    PAIR                    PAIR                    PAIR                    PAIR                    PAIR
--------                --------                --------                --------                --------                --------


PRESTIGE      .2354     PRESTIGE      .1970     PRESTIGE      .4564     PRESTIGE      .1618     PRESTIGE      .1987     SPPRES        .1386
WITH       N(  192)     WITH       N(  192)     WITH       N(  192)     WITH       N(  192)     WITH       N(  192)     WITH       N(  192)
SPPRES     SIG .000     PAPRES16   SIG .000     DEGREE     SIG .000     PADEG      SIG .003     MADEG      SIG .000     PAPRES16   SIG .003


SPPRES        .2875     SPPRES        .0975     SPPRES        .0707     PAPRES16      .2642     PAPRES16      .2875     PAPRES16      .1949
WITH       N(  192)     WITH       N(  192)     WITH       N(  192)     WITH       N(  192)     WITH       N(  192)     WITH       N(  192)
DEGREE     SIG .000     PADEG      SIG .047     MADEG      SIG .116     DEGREE     SIG .000     PADEG      SIG .000     MADEG      SIG .001


DEGREE        .3434     DEGREE        .3141     PADEG         .5545
WITH       N(  192)     WITH       N(  192)     WITH       N(  192)
PADEG      SIG .000     MADEG      SIG .000     MADEG      SIG .000

  " . " IS PRINTED IF A COEFFICIENT CANNOT BE COMPUTED.


- - - - - - - - - - - - -  S P E A R M A N   C O R R E L A T I O N   C O E F F I C I E N T S - - - - - - - - - - - - -

VARIABLE                VARIABLE                VARIABLE                VARIABLE                VARIABLE                VARIABLE
PAIR                    PAIR                    PAIR                    PAIR                    PAIR                    PAIR
--------                --------                --------                --------                --------                --------


PRESTIGE      .3374     PRESTIGE      .2694     PRESTIGE      .5547     PRESTIGE      .1996     PRESTIGE      .2435     SPPRES        .1971
WITH       N(  192)     WITH       N(  192)     WITH       N(  192)     WITH       N(  192)     WITH       N(  192)     WITH       N(  192)
SPPRES     SIG .000     PAPRES16   SIG .000     DEGREE     SIG .000     PADEG      SIG .003     MADEG      SIG .000     PAPRES16   SIG .003


SPPRES        .3613     SPPRES        .1175     SPPRES        .0851     PAPRES16      .3332     PAPRES16      .3440     PAPRES16      .2368
WITH       N(  192)     WITH       N(  192)     WITH       N(  192)     WITH       N(  192)     WITH       N(  192)     WITH       N(  192)
DEGREE     SIG .000     PADEG      SIG .052     MADEG      SIG .120     DEGREE     SIG .000     PADEG      SIG .000     MADEG      SIG .000


DEGREE        .3710     DEGREE        .3387     PADEG         .5774
WITH       N(  192)     WITH       N(  192)     WITH       N(  192)
PADEG      SIG .000     MADEG      SIG .000     MADEG      SIG .000

  " . " IS PRINTED IF A COEFFICIENT CANNOT BE COMPUTED.
       END OF JOB.
```

36.7 Formatting Options

For the default page length of 59 lines, NONPAR CORR prints correlation coefficients in 9 rows and 10 columns and displays the number of cases and the significance level. Use Option 8 to print 45 rows and 10 columns of coefficients and suppress the number of cases and the significance level. An asterisk (*) following a coefficient indicates significance at the .01 level or less. Two asterisks (**) following a coefficient indicate significance at the .001 level or less. The commands

```
NONPAR CORR  PRESTIGE SPPRES PAPRES16 DEGREE PADEG MADEG
OPTIONS  8
```

produce the triangular matrix in Figure 36.7a. If you use the keyword WITH in a variable list, the display will be a rectangular matrix similar to Figure 36.3b, with the number of cases suppressed and stars indicating significance levels.

Figure 36.7a Modifying the default output format with Option 8

```
- - - - - - - - - - - - -  S P E A R M A N   C O R R E L A T I O N   C O E F F I C I E N T S  - - - - - - - - - - - - -

SPPRES          .3608**
PAPRES16        .2934**     .2021**
DEGREE          .5262**     .3864**     .3438**
PADEG           .2397**     .1306       .3908**     .3820**
MADEG           .1781**     .1323       .2593**     .3829**     .5965**

            PRESTIGE      SPPRES    PAPRES16      DEGREE       PADEG

* - SIGNIF. LE .01        ** - SIGNIF. LE .001           " . " IS PRINTED IF A COEFFICIENT CANNOT BE COMPUTED.
```

Use Option 9 to print coefficients in serial string format with the coefficients from the first row of the matrix printed first, followed by the coefficients from the second row, and so on for all of the rows in the matrix. Six coefficients are printed across the page, and each is identified with the names of the variables for which it was calculated. The number of cases and significance level are printed below the correlation just as they are in the default matrix form of the output. Figure 36.7b is the output from the following example with Option 9 in effect:

```
NONPAR CORR  PRESTIGE SPPRES PAPRES16 WITH DEGREE PADEG MADEG
OPTIONS  9
```

If you specify both Option 8 and Option 9, only Option 9 will be in effect.

OPTION 8 *Suppress the printing of the number of cases and significance level.*
OPTION 9 *Serial formatting.*

Figure 36.7b Modifying the default output format with Option 9

```
- - - - - - - - - - - - -  S P E A R M A N   C O R R E L A T I O N   C O E F F I C I E N T S  - - - - - - - - - - - - -
VARIABLE                VARIABLE                VARIABLE                VARIABLE                VARIABLE                VARIABLE
PAIR                    PAIR                    PAIR                    PAIR                    PAIR                    PAIR
--------                --------                --------                --------                --------                --------
PRESTIGE     .5262      PRESTIGE     .2397      PRESTIGE     .1781      SPPRES       .3864      SPPRES       .1306      SPPRES       .1323
WITH      N( 461)       WITH      N( 352)       WITH      N( 406)       WITH      N( 277)       WITH      N( 219)       WITH      N( 244)
DEGREE    SIG .000      PADEG     SIG .000      MADEG     SIG .000      DEGREE    SIG .000      PADEG     SIG .027      MADEG     SIG .019

PAPRES16     .3438      PAPRES16     .3908      PAPRES16     .2593
WITH      N( 412)       WITH      N( 376)       WITH      N( 372)
DEGREE    SIG .000      PADEG     SIG .000      MADEG     SIG .000

 " . " IS PRINTED IF A COEFFICIENT CANNOT BE COMPUTED.
```

36.8 Random Sampling

NONPAR CORR must store cases in memory to build matrices. You may not have sufficient computer resources to store all the cases to produce the coefficients requested. Option 7 selects a random sample of cases when there is not enough space to store all the cases.

OPTION 7 *Random sampling.* If NONPAR CORR runs out of space when storing the cases, it randomly samples cases.

36.9 Writing Matrix Materials

You can use NONPAR CORR to write out a square matrix of correlation coefficients and the number of cases used to compute each coefficient. To write matrix materials to a file, specify Option 4 on the associated OPTIONS command. Matrix materials will be written for each simple variable list but will not be written for variable lists containing the keyword WITH. If you do not specify any missing-value options, each correlation matrix precedes a matrix of the *n*'s used to compute the coefficients. If you include missing values with Option 1 or exclude missing values listwise with Option 2, the correlation matrix precedes a record containing the *n* used to compute all the coefficients in the matrix. If you are processing split files (Chapter 13), a set of matrix materials is written for each split file processed. Correlation matrices are written with a format of F10.7, and each record has a maximum of eight values. Each row of the matrix begins on a new record. Matrices of *n*'s are written in the same way but with a format of F10.0.

If you specify both Kendall and Spearman coefficients with Option 6, NONPAR CORR writes matrix materials to the output file in the same order they are printed in the display. All the Kendall correlation matrices and their associated *n*'s are written first, followed by the Spearman correlation matrices and their associated *n*'s.

OPTION 4 *Write matrix materials to a file.* Writes Kendall or Spearman or both correlation matrices and the number of cases used to compute each coefficient for each simple variable list.

If you specify Option 4, you must also specify the file to which the materials are written using the FILE HANDLE and PROCEDURE OUTPUT commands (see Chapters 3 and 17). In the following example, four correlation matrices, each followed by a matrix of *n*'s, are written to the file defined by the GSS80MAT file handle.

```
FILE HANDLE GSS80/ file specifications
GET FILE  GSS80/KEEP PRESTIGE SPPRES PAPRES16 DEGREE PADEG MADEG
   NATHEAL TO NATARMS
FILE HANDLE GSS80MAT/ file specifications
PROCEDURE OUTPUT  FILE=GSS80MAT
NONPAR CORR  PRESTIGE TO MADEG/ NATHEAL TO NATARMS
OPTIONS  4 6
```

Since Option 6 is specified, the GSS80MAT output file contains the Kendall coefficients for the first variable list (PRESTIGE TO MADEG), the KENDALL coefficients for the second variable list (NATHEAL TO NATARMS), the Spearman coefficients for the first variable list, and the Spearman coefficients for the second variable list.

36.10 LIMITATIONS

The following limitations apply to NONPAR CORR:

- A maximum of 25 variable lists.
- A maximum of 100 variables total per NONPAR CORR command.

```
NPAR TESTS  [CHISQUARE = varlist [(lo, hi)]]  [/EXPECTED = {EQUAL      }]
                                                           {f1, f2,... fn}

       {UNIFORM [, lo, hi]}
 [/K-S ({NORMAL [, m, sd] }) = varlist]
       {POISSON [, m]     }

        {MEAN  }
 [/RUNS ({MEDIAN}) = varlist]
        {MODE  }
        {value }

 [/BINOMIAL [(p)] = varlist ({value 1, value 2})]
                             {value           }
 [/MCNEMAR = varlist]
 [/SIGN = varlist]
 [/WILCOXON = varlist]
 [/COCHRAN = varlist]
 [/FRIEDMAN = varlist]
 [/KENDALL = varlist]
 [/MEDIAN [(value)] = varlist BY var (value 1, value 2)]
 [/M-W = varlist BY var (value 1, value 2)]
 [/K-S = varlist BY var (value 1, value 2)]
 [/W-W = varlist BY var (value 1, value 2)]
 [/MOSES [(n)] = varlist BY var (value 1, value 2)]
 [/K-W = varlist BY var (value 1, value 2)]
```

OPTIONS:

1 Include missing values.
2 Exclude missing values listwise.
3 Sequential pairing of variables for two related samples.
4 Random sampling.

STATISTICS:

1 Mean, maximum, minimum, standard deviation, and *n* of cases.
2 Quartiles and *n* of cases.

INTRODUCTION TO NONPARAMETRIC TESTS, **37.1**

OVERVIEW, **37.2**

OPERATION, **37.3**

- One-Sample Tests, **37.4**
  - One-Sample Chi-Square Test, **37.5**
  - Kolmogorov-Smirnov One-Sample Test, **37.6**
  - Runs Test, **37.7**
  - Binomial Test, **37.8**
- Tests for Two Related Samples, **37.9**
  - McNemar Test, **37.10**
  - Sign Test, **37.11**
  - Wilcoxon Matched-Pairs Signed-Ranks Test, **37.12**
- Tests for *k* Related Samples, **37.13**
  - Cochran *Q* Test, **37.14**
  - Friedman Test, **37.15**
  - Kendall Coefficient of Concordance, **37.16**
- Tests for Two Independent Samples, **37.17**
  - Two-Sample Median Test, **37.18**
  - Mann-Whitney *U* Test, **37.19**
  - Kolmogorov-Smirnov Two-Sample Test, **37.20**
  - Wald-Wolfowitz Runs Test, **37.21**
  - Moses Test of Extreme Reactions, **37.22**
- Tests for *k* Independent Samples, **37.23**
  - *k*-Sample Median Test, **37.24**
  - Kruskal-Wallis One-Way Analysis of Variance, **37.25**
- Optional Statistics, **37.26**
- Missing Values, **37.27**
- Random Sampling, **37.28**
- Aliases for Subcommand Names, **37.29**

LIMITATIONS, **37.30**

Chapter 37 NPAR TESTS

Procedure NPAR TESTS is a collection of nonparametric tests which make minimal assumptions about the underlying distributions of data. Many of these tests are based upon ranks, so this procedure must store cases in memory. The amount of memory required is directly proportional to the number of cases being analyzed. In addition to the nonparametric tests performed by NPAR TESTS, CROSSTABS is available for the *k*-sample chi-square and Fisher's exact test (see Chapter 20).

37.1 INTRODUCTION TO NONPARAMETRIC TESTS

A wide variety of nonparametric tests are available in NPAR TESTS. Table 37.1 summarizes the tests available. All of these tests are described in Siegel (1956). The tests differ in their assumptions about the level of measurement, the hypotheses being tested, and the organization of data. One-sample tests analyze one variable, tests for two related samples compare one variable with another, tests for *k* related samples compare several variables, and independent-sample tests analyze one variable grouped by categories of another variable.

Table 37.1 Nonparametric tests available in NPAR TESTS

Data organization	Nominal scale	Ordinal scale
1 sample	Chi-square Runs Binomial	Kolmogorov-Smirnov
2 related samples	McNemar	Sign Wilcoxon Kendall coefficient of concordance
k related samples	Cochran Q	Friedman two-way Anova Kendall coefficient of concordance
2 independent samples		Median Mann-Whitney Kolmogorov-Smirnov Wald-Wolfowitz Moses
k independent samples		Median Kruskal-Wallis

37.2 OVERVIEW

NPAR TESTS produces one or more nonparametric tests. In addition to the test statistics, you can specify optional statistics, methods of handling missing data, and random sampling. You can also request special pairing with tests for two related samples. Most of the examples used in this chapter are taken from Siegel (1956). You should consult Siegel and the other references listed at the end of this chapter for interpretations of the results.

Selecting Nonparametric Tests. The nonparametric tests available with NPAR TESTS require specific types of data organization. NPAR TESTS include one-sample tests (Sections 37.5 through 37.8), tests for two related samples (Sections 37.10 through 37.12), tests for *k* related samples (Sections 37.14 through 37.16), tests for two independent samples (Sections 37.18 through 37.22), and tests for *k* independent samples (Sections 37.24 and 37.25).

Special Pairing for Two Related Samples. If you specify tests for two related samples, a simple variable list produces all possible pairs of variables. Two variable lists separated by the keyword WITH pair all variables in the first list with all variables in the second list. Optionally, you can request sequential pairing (see Section 37.9).

Optional Statistics. In addition to the statistics associated with each test, you can obtain the mean, minimum, maximum, and standard deviation for each variable named on all the subcommands, as well as medians and quartiles (see Section 37.26).

Missing Values. By default, NPAR TESTS excludes cases with missing values on a test-by-test basis. Optionally, you can request that missing values be handled as if they were valid or that cases with missing values be deleted listwise (see Section 37.27).

Random Sampling. NPAR TESTS must store cases in memory for tests that use ranks. You can request a random sample of cases when there is not enough space to store all the cases (see Section 37.28).

37.3 OPERATION

NPAR TESTS operates via subcommands and associated OPTIONS and STATISTICS commands. The general form of the NPAR TESTS command is:

NPAR TESTS *testname* [(*parameters*)] = *varlist*/

Each subcommand names a specific test followed by a variable list and terminates with a slash. You can use the keyword TO to reference contiguous variables in the active file. The form of the variable list differs with the data organization required for the test. You can request any or all of the tests available on one NPAR TESTS command. Some tests require additional parameters and the CHISQUARE test has an optional subcommand. The equals sign is optional in all subcommands.

37.4 One-Sample Tests

A one-sample test uses the entire set of observations for the variable being tested. One-sample tests have the following general form:

NPAR TESTS *testname* [(*parameters*)] = *varlist*/

You must specify the name of the test and one or more variables to be tested. Each variable in the list produces one test. For example, the command

```
NPAR TESTS  CHISQUARE = GRADE EVAL1 TO EVAL5/
```

specifies one-sample chi-square tests for GRADE and all the variables between and including EVAL1 and EVAL5.

The following one-sample tests are available:

CHISQUARE *Chi-square one-sample test.* This is a goodness-of-fit test. For data that fall into categories, it tests whether a significant difference exists between the observed number of cases in each category and the expected number specified (see Section 37.5).

K-S *Kolmogorov-Smirnov one-sample test.* This is a goodness-of-fit test. For interval-level data, K-S tests whether the observations could reasonably have come from a particular distribution where you specify uniform, normal, or Poisson distributions (see Section 37.6).

RUNS *Runs test.* This is a test of randomness for dichotomous variables to determine whether the order or sequence in which observations are obtained is random (see Section 37.7).

BINOMIAL *Binomial test.* This is a test for goodness of fit for dichotomous variables. It tests whether or not a significant difference exists between the observed number in each category and the expected number under a specified binomial distribution (see Section 37.8).

37.5 One-Sample Chi-Square Test

Subcommand CHISQUARE performs the one-sample chi-square test. CHISQUARE tabulates a variable into categories and computes a chi-square statistic based on the differences between observed and expected frequencies. By default, the CHISQUARE test assumes equal expected frequencies. To specify expected frequencies, use the associated EXPECTED subcommand.

The two subcommands have the following general form:

NPAR TESTS CHISQUARE = *varlist* [(lo,hi)] /
EXPECTED = *f1, f2, ... fn*/

The range following the variable list is optional. If you do not specify a range, each distinct value encountered is defined as a category. For example, the command

```
NPAR TESTS  CHISQUARE = RANK
```

computes a chi-square test using every value encountered for the variable RANK. If you do specify a range, integer-valued categories are established for each value within the inclusive range. Noninteger values are truncated, and cases with values outside the bounds are excluded. For example,

```
NPAR TESTS  CHISQUARE = RANK (1,4)/
```

uses only the values 1 through 4 for the chi-square test of the variable RANK.

To specify expected frequencies, percentages, or proportions, use a value list on the EXPECTED subcommand. You must specify a value greater than zero for each observed category of the data. The values listed after the EXPECTED subcommand are summed. Each value is then divided by this sum to calculate the proportion of cases expected in the corresponding category. For example,

```
NPAR TESTS  CHISQUARE = RANK (1,4)/EXPECTED = 3 4 5 4
```

specifies values for four categories of variable RANK. The value list is interpreted as proportions, not absolute values. The command above specifies that the expected proportions are 3/16, 4/16, 5/16, and 4/16 for categories 1, 2, 3, and 4, respectively. You can specify the same expected proportion for two or more consecutive categories with an asterisk (*), as in:

```
NPAR TESTS  CHISQUARE = A (1,5)/ EXPECTED = 12, 3*16, 18/
```

This command tests the observed frequencies for variable A against the hypothetical distribution of 12/78 occurrences of category 1; 16/78 occurrences each of categories 2, 3, and 4; and 18/78 occurrences of category 5.

You can use the keyword EQUAL to specify equal expected proportions, as in:

```
NPAR TESTS  CHISQUARE = RANK/ EXPECTED = EQUAL
```

This command produces the same results as the CHISQUARE subcommand alone.

The EXPECTED subcommand applies to all variables named on the preceding CHISQUARE subcommand. If you want to specify different expected proportions for each variable, use multiple combinations of the CHISQUARE and EXPECTED subcommands. If you want to test the same variable against different proportions, you can also use multiple combinations.

The following example requests two chi-square tests. First, the frequencies for all categories of POSTPOS are compared against equal expected frequencies. The second CHISQUARE subcommand specifies eight expected proportions.

```
TITLE  NPAR TESTS
SUBTITLE  'CHISQUARE TEST, SIEGEL, P. 45'
DATA LIST  /POSTPOS 1-2 NWINS 4-5
VAR LABELS  POSTPOS 'POST POSITION'/
WEIGHT  BY NWINS
NPAR TESTS  CHISQUARE = POSTPOS/
   CHISQUARE = POSTPOS/EXPECTED=22,20,4*18,16,14
BEGIN DATA
 2 19
 7 15
 4 25
 5 17
 8 11
 3 18
 6 10
 1 29
END DATA
```

This example produces the output in Figure 37.5. For each test, the display shows the number of observed cases and expected cases in each category; the residual (observed minus expected) for each category; and the chi-square statistic, degrees of freedom, and significance of the chi-square.

37.6 Kolmogorov-Smirnov One-Sample Test

Subcommand K-S performs a Kolmogorov-Smirnov one-sample test. K-S compares the cumulative distribution function for a variable with a specified distribution, which may be uniform, normal, or Poisson. The Kolmogorov-Smirnov *Z* is computed from the largest difference (in absolute value) between the observed and theoretical distribution functions.

The K-S subcommand has the following general form:

NPAR TESTS K-S (*dis* [*parameters*]) = *varlist*/

where *dis* is one of the three distributions: UNIFORM, NORMAL, or

Figure 37.5 One-sample chi-square test

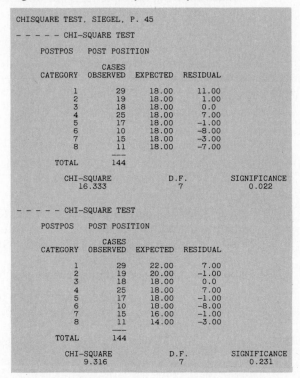

```
CHISQUARE TEST, SIEGEL, P. 45

- - - - -  CHI-SQUARE TEST

     POSTPOS   POST POSITION

                  CASES
     CATEGORY  OBSERVED  EXPECTED  RESIDUAL

            1        29     18.00     11.00
            2        19     18.00      1.00
            3        18     18.00      0.0
            4        25     18.00      7.00
            5        17     18.00     -1.00
            6        10     18.00     -8.00
            7        15     18.00     -3.00
            8        11     18.00     -7.00
                    ---
        TOTAL       144

         CHI-SQUARE             D.F.           SIGNIFICANCE
            16.333                 7                 0.022

- - - - -  CHI-SQUARE TEST

     POSTPOS   POST POSITION

                  CASES
     CATEGORY  OBSERVED  EXPECTED  RESIDUAL

            1        29     22.00      7.00
            2        19     20.00     -1.00
            3        18     18.00      0.0
            4        25     18.00      7.00
            5        17     18.00     -1.00
            6        10     18.00     -8.00
            7        15     16.00     -1.00
            8        11     14.00     -3.00
                    ---
        TOTAL       144

         CHI-SQUARE             D.F.           SIGNIFICANCE
             9.316                 7                 0.231
```

POISSON. Each of these distributions has optional parameters:

UNIFORM *Uniform distribution.* The optional parameters are the minimum and maximum values (in that order). If you do not specify them, K-S uses the observed minimum and maximum values.

NORMAL *Normal distribution.* The optional parameters are the mean and standard deviation (in that order). If you do not specify them, K-S uses the observed mean and standard deviation.

POISSON *Poisson distribution.* The one optional parameter is the mean. If you do not specify it, K-S uses the observed mean. A word of caution about testing against a Poisson distribution: if the mean of the test distribution is large, evaluating the probabilities is a very time-consuming process. If a mean of 100,000 or larger is used, K-S uses a normal approximation to the Poisson distribution.

For example, the command

```
NPAR TESTS  K-S (UNIFORM) = A/
```

compares the distribution for variable A with a uniform distribution which has the same range as variable A, while the command

```
NPAR TESTS  K-S (NORMAL,0,1) = B
```

compares the distribution for variable B with a normal distribution which has a mean of 0 and standard deviation of 1.

K-S assumes that the test distribution is entirely specified in advance. When parameters of the test distribution are estimated from the sample, the distribution of the test statistic changes. NPAR TESTS does not provide any correction for this.

The following example tests variable X against a uniform distribution with a range of 0 through 1.

```
TITLE  NPAR TESTS
SUBTITLE  'KOLMOGOROV-SMIRNOV TEST, CONOVER, P. 296'
DATA LIST  /X 1-3 (3)
NPAR TESTS  K-S (UNIFORM,0,1) = X
BEGIN DATA
621
503
203
477
710
581
329
480
554
382
END DATA
```

Figure 37.6 is the output produced by the K-S subcommand. It prints the distribution selected for the test; the most extreme positive, negative, and absolute differences; and the Kolmogorov-Smirnov *Z* and its significance.

Figure 37.6 Kolmogorov-Smirnov test

```
KOLMOGOROV-SMIRNOV TEST, CONOVER, P. 296

- - - - - KOLMOGOROV - SMIRNOV GOODNESS OF FIT TEST

    X


    TEST DISTRIBUTION  -  UNIFORM        RANGE:  0.0    TO 1.000

              CASES:  10

              MOST EXTREME DIFFERENCES
        ABSOLUTE          POSITIVE          NEGATIVE              K-S Z          2-TAILED P
         0.29000           0.29000          -0.22900              0.917               0.370
```

37.7 Runs Test

Subcommand RUNS performs the runs test to determine the randomness of observations for dichotomous variables. A run is defined as a sequence of one of the values which is preceded and followed by the other data value (or the end of the series). For example, the following sequence

| 1 1 | 0 0 0 | 1 | 0 0 0 0 | 1 | 0 | 1 |

contains seven runs (vertical bars are used to separate the runs).

The RUNS subcommand has the following general form:

NPAR TESTS RUNS (*cutpoint*) = *varlist*/

You must specify a cutting point to dichotomize the variable. You may use either the observed mean, median, or mode or a specified value as a cutting point. Specify one of the following for *cutpoint*:

MEAN *Mean.* All values below the observed mean are one category. All values equal to or greater than the mean are the other category.

MEDIAN *Median.* All values below the observed median are one category; values equal to or greater than the median are the other category.

MODE *Mode.* All values below the observed mode are one category; values equal to or greater than the mode are the other category.

value *Specified value.* All values below the specified value are one category; values equal to or above the specified value are the other category.

Even though the variable may be dichotomized already, you still must specify a cutting point. For example, if the variable has values 0 and 1, you can use 1 as the cutting point.

The following example of the RUNS subcommand also illustrates the use of SPSS^X to analyze several files in one execution. The variable SCORE is defined on the first active file and two runs tests are performed, one with the sample median as the cutting point and the other with the value 24.5 as the cutting point. Then the DATA LIST command defines a new active file containing the variable SEX, for which another runs test is performed.

```
TITLE  NPAR TESTS
SUBTITLE   'RUNS TEST, SIEGEL, P. 55'
DATA LIST   /SCORE 1-2
VAR LABELS   SCORE 'AGGRESSION SCORE'
NPAR TESTS   RUNS(MEDIAN) = SCORE/
    RUNS(24.5) = SCORE/
BEGIN DATA
31
23
36
  ...
 7
 6
 8
END DATA
SUBTITLE   'RUNS TEST, SIEGEL, P. 57'
DATA LIST   /SEX 1
NPAR TESTS   RUNS (1)=SEX/
BEGIN DATA
1
0
1
  ...
0
1
1
END DATA
```

Figure 37.7 is the output produced by the RUNS subcommand. For each test, the display shows the test value (cutting point), number of runs, number of cases below the cutting point, number of cases equal to or greater than the cutting point, and test statistic *Z* with its significance level.

Figure 37.7 Runs test

```
RUNS TEST, SIEGEL, P. 55

- - - - - RUNS TEST

     SCORE      AGGRESSION SCORE


            RUNS:    10                       TEST VALUE = 25.0 (MEDIAN)

            CASES:   12    LT MEDIAN
                     12    GE MEDIAN                     Z = -1.0436
                     --
                     24    TOTAL             1-TAILED P =    .2967

- - - - - RUNS TEST

     SCORE      AGGRESSION SCORE


            RUNS:    10                          TEST VALUE = 24.5000

            CASES:   12    LT 24.5000
                     12    GE 24.5000                    Z = -1.0436
                     --
                     24    TOTAL                1-TAILED P =    .2967

RUNS TEST, SIEGEL, P. 57

- - - - - RUNS TEST

     SEX


            RUNS:    35                 TEST VALUE = 1

            CASES:   20    LT 1

                     30    GE 1                     Z =  2.9794
                     --
                     50    TOTAL       1-TAILED P =    .0029
```

37.8 Binomial Test

Subcommand BINOMIAL performs the binomial test. It compares the observed frequency in each category of a dichotomous variable with expected frequencies under a binomial distribution. BINOMIAL tabulates a variable into two categories based on the way you specify a cutting point.

The BINOMIAL subcommand has the following general form:

NPAR TESTS BINOMIAL[(*p*)] = *varlist*(*value* or *value1*,*value2*)

where *p* is the proportion of cases expected in the *first* category. The proportion is compared to the test proportion and the significance test is performed. The default test proportion is .5, but you can specify any other proportion. If the proportion is .5, BINOMIAL computes a two-tailed probability. If it is anything else, BINOMIAL computes a one-tailed probability.

If you name one value in parentheses following the variable list, it is used as a cutting point. All cases equal to or less than the cutting point form the first category; all remaining cases form the second category. If you specify two values in parentheses following the variable list, all cases with *value1* are in the first category and all cases with *value2* are in the second category. The frequencies in these categories are compared to the proportion you specify for *p*, or to .5 if you do not specify *p*.

The following example tests the distribution of the variable METHOD against the default proportion of .5. METHOD is a dichotomous variable with two values, 1 and 2.

```
TITLE  NPAR TESTS
SUBTITLE  'BINOMIAL TEST, SIEGEL, P. 40'
DATA LIST  /METHOD 1
NPAR TESTS  BINOMIAL=METHOD(1,2)/
BEGIN DATA
1
1
1
  ...
1
2
2
END DATA
```

Figure 37.8 is the output produced by the BINOMIAL subcommand. It displays the test proportion of cases, number of cases in each category, and significance level.

Figure 37.8 Binomial test

```
BINOMIAL TEST, SIEGEL, P. 40

- - - - - BINOMIAL TEST

    METHOD

     CASES

        16    = 1              TEST PROB. =    .5000
         2    = 2
        --                     2-TAILED P =    .0007
        18   TOTAL
```

37.9 Tests for Two Related Samples

Tests for two related samples compare pairs of variables and have the following general form:

NPAR TESTS *testname* = *varlist* WITH *varlist* /

You must specify the name of the test and two or more variables to be tested. The following tests are available for two related samples:

MCNEMAR *McNemar test.* This is a test of difference in changes of proportions for dichotomous variables. It is most useful in "before and after" experimental designs to detect any significant changes in proportions of subjects from one category to another (see Section 37.10).

SIGN *Sign test.* This test compares the signs of the differences between pairs of variables for each observation (see Section 37.11).

WILCOXON *Wilcoxon matched-pairs signed-ranks test.* This test analyzes the differences between the paired observations, also taking into account the magnitude of the differences (see Section 37.12).

If you specify a simple variable list, a test is performed for each variable paired with every other variable on the list. For example, the command

```
NPAR TESTS  MCNEMAR = A B C/
```

produces McNemar tests for each possible pair of variables: A with B, A with C, and B with C. To obtain tests for specific pairs of variables, use two variables lists separated by the keyword WITH. Each variable in the first list will be tested with each variable in the second list. For example,

```
NPAR TESTS  SIGN = A WITH B C
```

produces sign tests for A with B and A with C. No test is performed for B with C.

In tests for two related samples, you can pair variables sequentially when you supply a simple variable list. Use Option 3 to pair the first variable in the list with the second, the second variable with the third, and so on. For example,

```
NPAR TESTS  MCNEMAR = A B C D E
OPTIONS  3
```

pairs A with B, B with C, C with D, and D with E. If you use Option 3 when you specify the keyword WITH, the first variable in the first list is paired with the first variable in the second list, the second variable in the first list is paired with the second variable in the second list, and so on. You must name or imply the same number of variables in both lists. For example,

```
NPAR TESTS  MCNEMAR = A B WITH C D
OPTIONS  3
```

pairs A with C and B with D.

OPTION 3 *Special pairing option for tests for two related samples.* If you specify a simple variable list, sequential pairs are tested. If you use the keyword WITH in the variable list, the first variable in the first list is tested with the first variable in the second list, and so on. The lists must be of equal length.

37.10 McNemar Test

Subcommand MCNEMAR performs the McNemar test. It tabulates a 2×2 table for each pair of dichotomous variables. If your data are not dichotomous, you must recode them. The test is not performed for variables with more than two values and a chi-square statistic is computed for cases having different values for the two variables. If fewer than 10 cases change values from the first variable to the second variable, the binomial distribution is used to compute the significance level.

The MCNEMAR subcommand has the following general form:

NPAR TESTS MCNEMAR = *varlist/*

The following example performs the McNemar test for variables CONTACT1 with CONTACT2.

```
TITLE  NPAR TESTS
SUBTITLE  'MCNEMAR TEST, SIEGEL, P. 65'
DATA LIST  /CONTACT1 CONTACT2 NUMBER 1-6
WEIGHT  BY NUMBER
NPAR TESTS  MCNEMAR = CONTACT1 CONTACT2
BEGIN DATA
 1-114
 1 1 4
-1-1 3
-1 1 4
END DATA
```

Figure 37.10 is the output produced by the MCNEMAR subcommand. It prints the 2 × 2 table, the chi-square statistic, and its significance level.

Figure 37.10 McNemar test

```
MCNEMAR TEST, SIEGEL, P. 65

- - - - - MCNEMAR TEST

    CONTACT1
WITH CONTACT2


                               CONTACT2
                                1         -1                 CASES          25
                     I----------I----------I
                  -1 I        4 I        3 I
 CONTACT1            I----------I----------I           (BINOMIAL)
                   1 I        4 I       14 I           2-TAILED P        .0309
                     I----------I----------I
```

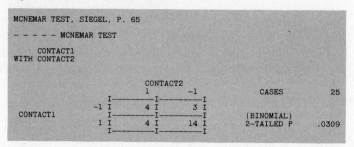

37.11 Sign Test

The SIGN subcommand performs the sign test. It counts the positive and negative differences between the pair of variables and ignores zero differences. Under the null hypothesis for large sample sizes, the test statistic Z is approximately normally distributed with mean 0 and variance 1. The binomial distribution is used to compute an exact significance level if 25 or fewer differences are observed.

The SIGN subcommand has the following general form:

NPAR TESTS SIGN = *varlist/*

In the following example, the SIGN subcommand is used first to test MOTHER with FATHER, and then to test BEFORE with AFTER.

```
TITLE  NPAR TESTS
SUBTITLE  'SIGN TEST, SIEGEL, P. 70'
DATA LIST  /MOTHER FATHER 1-2
VAR LABELS  MOTHER 'MOTHER''S INSIGHT RATED'/
            FATHER 'FATHER''S INSIGHT RATED'
NPAR TESTS  SIGN = FATHER WITH MOTHER
BEGIN DATA
42
43
53
  ...
55
53
51
END DATA
SUBTITLE  'SIGN TEST, SIEGEL, P. 73'
DATA LIST  /BEFORE AFTER 1-2 COUNT 3-4
WEIGHT  BY COUNT
RECODE  BEFORE AFTER (0 = -1)
NPAR TESTS  SIGN = BEFORE WITH AFTER
BEGIN DATA
1059
11 7
00 8
0126
END DATA
```

This example produces the output in Figure 37.11. For each test, the display shows the number of positive and negative differences. The first sign test uses the significance level from the binomial distribution because only 17 differences are observed. The second sign test uses the significance level from the *Z* statistic because more than 25 differences are observed.

Figure 37.11 Sign test

```
SIGN TEST, SIEGEL, P. 70

- - - - - SIGN TEST

     FATHER     FATHER'S INSIGHT RATED
WITH MOTHER     MOTHER'S INSIGHT RATED


              CASES

                 3   - DIFFS (MOTHER LT FATHER)
                11   + DIFFS (MOTHER GT FATHER)        (BINOMIAL)
                 3     TIES                            2-TAILED P =        .0574
                --
                17     TOTAL

SIGN TEST, SIEGEL, P. 73

- - - - - SIGN TEST

     BEFORE
WITH AFTER


              CASES

                59   - DIFFS (AFTER LT BEFORE)                   Z =      3.4709
                26   + DIFFS (AFTER GT BEFORE)
                15     TIES                            2-TAILED P =        .0005
               ---
               100     TOTAL
```

37.12 Wilcoxon Matched-Pairs Signed-Ranks Test

The WILCOXON subcommand performs the Wilcoxon test. WILCOXON computes the differences between the pair of variables, ranks the absolute differences, sums the positive and negative ranks, and computes the test statistic *Z* from the positive and negative rank sums. Under the null hypothesis, *Z* is approximately normally distributed with mean 0 and variance 1 for large sample sizes.

The WILCOXON subcommand has the following general form:

NPAR TESTS WILCOXON = *varlist*/

The following example performs two Wilcoxon tests. The first example matches SCHOOL with HOME. The second example computes DUM as a constant with value 0 and matches it with D.

```
TITLE  NPAR TESTS
SUBTITLE  'WILCOXON MATCHED PAIRS TEST, SIEGEL, P. 79'
DATA LIST  /SCHOOL HOME 1-4
VAR LABELS  SCHOOL 'SOCIAL PERCEPTIVENESS OF SCHOOL TWIN'/
            HOME 'SOCIAL PERCEPTIVENESS OF HOME TWIN'
NPAR TESTS  WILCOXON = ALL
BEGIN DATA
8263
6942
7374
4337
5851
5643
7680
8582
END DATA
SUBTITLE 'WILCOXON MATCHED PAIRS, SIEGEL, P. 82'
DATA LIST /D 1-2
COMPUTE  DUM=0
VAR LABELS  D 'DECISION LATENCY TIME'/
NPAR TESTS  WILCOXON = D WITH DUM
BEGIN DATA
-2
0
0
  ...
2
3
-1
END DATA
```

Figure 37.12 is the output produced by these two WILCOXON tests. For each test, the display shows the mean rank for each variable; the number of positive, negative, and tied ranks; and the test statistic *Z* and its significance level.

Figure 37.12 Wilcoxon matched-pairs signed-ranks test

```
WILCOXON MATCHED PAIRS TEST, SIEGEL, P. 79

- - - - - WILCOXON MATCHED-PAIRS SIGNED-RANKS TEST

    SCHOOL      SOCIAL PERCEPTIVENESS OF SCHOOL TWIN
WITH HOME       SOCIAL PERCEPTIVENESS OF HOME TWIN

    MEAN RANK     CASES

        5.33           6  - RANKS (HOME LT SCHOOL)
        2.00           2  + RANKS (HOME GT SCHOOL)
                       0    TIES
                       -
                       8    TOTAL

         Z =    -1.9604                2-TAILED P =   .0500

WILCOXON MATCHED PAIRS, SIEGEL, P. 82

- - - - - WILCOXON MATCHED-PAIRS SIGNED-RANKS TEST

     D          DECISION LATENCY TIME
WITH DUM

     MEAN RANK     CASES

         14.90        20  - RANKS (DUM LT D)
          8.83         6  + RANKS (DUM GT D)
                       4    TIES
                      --
                      30    TOTAL

          Z =    -3.1113               2-TAILED P =   .0019
```

37.13 Tests for *k* Related Samples

Tests for *k* related samples compare sets of variables and have the following general form:

NPAR TESTS *testname* = *varlist*/

You must specify the name of the test and two or more variables to be tested. The *k* variables in the list produce one test for *k* related samples. The following tests for *k* related samples are available:

COCHRAN *Cochran's* Q *test.* This is a test of difference of proportions. It tests whether the proportions in the categories are the same over all variables (see Section 37.14).

FRIEDMAN *Friedman test.* FRIEDMAN tests the null hypothesis that the *k* samples have been drawn from the same population (see Section 37.15).

KENDALL *Kendall's* W *coefficient of concordance.* Kendall's *W* is a measure of agreement among raters or judges. Each case is one judge's rating of several entities (variables) (see Section 37.16).

37.14 Cochran *Q* Test

Subcommand COCHRAN performs the Cochran *Q* test. It tabulates a $2 \times k$ contingency table (category vs. variable) for dichotomous variables and computes the proportions for each variable. If your data are not dichotomous, you must recode them. Cochran's *Q* statistic has approximately a chi-square distribution.

The COCHRAN subcommand has the following general form:

NPAR TESTS COCHRAN = *varlist*/

The following example tests variables R1, R2, and R3; each variable has a value of 0 or 1.

```
TITLE  NPAR TESTS
SUBTITLE  'COCHRAN Q TEST, SIEGEL, P. 164'
DATA LIST  /R1 TO R3 1-3
VAR LABELS  R1 'RESPONSE TO NICE INTERVIEW'/
            R2 'RESPONSE TO RESERVED INTERVIEW'/
            R3 'RESPONSE TO HARSH INTERVIEW'
NPAR TESTS  COCHRAN = R1 TO R3
BEGIN DATA
111
111
110
  ...
010
100
000
END DATA
```

Figure 37.14 is the output produced by the COCHRAN subcommand. It displays the number of cases in each category for each variable, Cochran's Q with its degrees of freedom, and the significance level for Q.

Figure 37.14 Cochran *Q* test

```
COCHRAN Q TEST, SIEGEL, P. 164

- - - - - COCHRAN Q TEST

  CASES

  = 1  = 0   VARIABLE

   13    5   R1            RESPONSE TO NICE INTERVIEW
   13    5   R2            RESPONSE TO RESERVED INTERVIEW
    3   15   R3            RESPONSE TO HARSH INTERVIEW

         CASES          COCHRAN Q           D.F.   SIGNIFICANCE
           18            16.6667              2          .0002
```

37.15 Friedman Test

Subcommand FRIEDMAN peforms the Friedman test. It ranks the k variables from 1 to k for each case, calculates the mean rank for each variable over all the cases, and then calculates a test statistic with approximately a chi-square distribution.

The FRIEDMAN subcommand has the following general form:

NPAR TESTS FRIEDMAN = *varlist/*

The following example analyzes variables RR, RU, and UR.

```
TITLE  NPAR TESTS
SUBTITLE  'FRIEDMAN TWO-WAY TEST, SIEGEL, P. 171'
DATA LIST  /RR RU UR 1-3
VAR LABELS  RR 'TOTAL REINFORCEMENT'/
            RU 'PARTIAL WITH REINFORCED TRIAL'/
            UR 'PARTIAL WITH UNREINFORCED TRIAL'
NPAR TESTS  FRIEDMAN = RR RU UR
BEGIN DATA
264
462
396
  ...
321
642
231
END DATA
```

Figure 37.15 is the output produced by the FRIEDMAN subcommand. It displays the mean rank for each variable, the chi-square statistic with its degrees of freedom, and the significance level for the chi-square.

Figure 37.15 Friedman test

```
FRIEDMAN TWO-WAY TEST, SIEGEL, P. 171

- - - - - FRIEDMAN TWO-WAY ANOVA

     MEAN RANK   VARIABLE

        2.19     RR          TOTAL REINFORCEMENT
        2.36     RU          PARTIAL WITH REINFORCED TRIAL
        1.44     UR          PARTIAL WITH UNREINFORCED TRIAL

        CASES          CHI-SQUARE          D.F.    SIGNIFICANCE
          18             8.5833              2          .0137
```

37.16 Kendall Coefficient of Concordance

Subcommand KENDALL calculates Kendall's *W*. It ranks the *k* variables from 1 to *k* for each case, calculates the mean rank for each variable over all the cases, and then calculates Kendall's *W* and a corresponding chi-square statistic, correcting for ties. *W* ranges between 0 and 1, with 0 signifying no agreement and 1 signifying complete agreement.

The KENDALL subcommand has the following general form:

NPAR TESTS KENDALL = *varlist*/

This test assumes that each case is a judge or rater. If you want to perform this test with variables as judges and cases as entities, you must first transpose your data matrix.

The following example uses three judges and 10 entities:

```
TITLE  NPAR TESTS
SUBTITLE  'KENDALL W, SIEGEL, P. 234'
DATA LIST   /A B C D E F G H I J 1-40(1)
NPAR TESTS  KENDALL = ALL
BEGIN DATA
 1.0 4.5 2.0 4.5 3.0 7.5 6.0 9.0 7.5 10.
 2.5 1.0 2.5 4.5 4.5 8.0 9.0 6.5 10. 6.5
 2.0 1.0 4.5 4.5 4.5 4.5 8.0 8.0 8.0 10.
END DATA
```

Figure 37.16 is the output produced by the KENDALL subcommand. It displays the number of cases, Kendall's *W*, the chi-square statistic with its degrees of freedom, and the test of significance for the chi-square. A small probability indicates a high degree of concordance.

Figure 37.16 Kendall coefficient of concordance

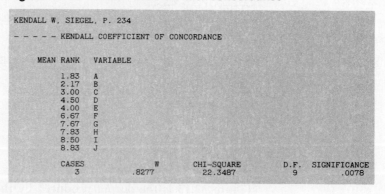

```
KENDALL W, SIEGEL, P. 234

- - - - - KENDALL COEFFICIENT OF CONCORDANCE

     MEAN RANK   VARIABLE

        1.83     A
        2.17     B
        3.00     C
        4.50     D
        4.00     E
        6.67     F
        7.67     G
        7.83     H
        8.50     I
        8.83     J

        CASES               W          CHI-SQUARE          D.F.   SIGNIFICANCE
          3             .8277            22.3487             9          .0078
```

37.17 Tests for Two Independent Samples

Tests for two independent samples compare two groups of cases on one variable. These test have the following general form:

NPAR TESTS *testname* = *varlist* BY *var*(*value1*,*value2*)/

You must specify the name of the test and one or more variables to be tested. Each variable in the list produces one test. The variable following the keyword BY splits the file into two groups or samples. All cases with *value1* are in the first group, and all cases with *value2* are in the second group. The following tests are available for two independent samples:

MEDIAN *Two-sample median test.* This test determines whether the two groups are drawn from populations with the same median (see Section 37.18).

M-W *Mann-Whitney* U *test.* Like the median test, M-W tests whether the two groups are drawn from the same population. It is more powerful than the median test because it uses the rank of each case, not just its location relative to the median (see Section 37.19).

K-S *Kolmogorov-Smirnov two-sample test.* This is a test of homogeneity of distribution. It is sensitive to any difference between the two distributions, including the median, dispersion, skewness, and so on (see Section 37.20).

W-W *Wald-Wolfowitz runs test.* This is also a test of homogeneity of distributions (see Section 37.21).

MOSES *Moses test of extreme reactions.* This is a test of difference in range. It treats the first group as the control group and the second as the experimental group (see Section 37.22).

37.18 Two-Sample Median Test

Subcommand MEDIAN performs the two-sample median test. MEDIAN tabulates a 2 × 2 contingency table with counts of the number of cases greater than the median and less than or equal to the median for the two groups. You can specify a value as a cutting point or use the calculated median from the data. If the total number of cases is greater than 30, a chi-square statistic is computed. Fisher's exact procedure (one-tailed) is used to compute the significance level for 30 or fewer cases.

The MEDIAN subcommand has the following general form:

NPAR TESTS MEDIAN [(*value*)] = *varlist* BY *var*(*value1*,*value2*)

The value in parentheses following the keyword MEDIAN is the test median. If omitted, the calculated median is used. The MEDIAN subcommand performs either a two-sample or a *k*-sample test (see Section 37.24). When you use it for the two-sample test, you must use one of two methods to specify the cutting point for the variable that groups the cases. With the first method, *value2* must equal *value1* + 1. With the second method, *value1* must be larger than *value2*. If you use a variable that has more than two values and *value1* is smaller than *value2*, a *k*-sample median test is performed.

The following example performs two tests on the variable ANXIETY grouped by the variable EXPLAIN. The first test specifies a median of 10.5; the second test uses the sample median.

```
TITLE  NPAR TESTS
SUBTITLE  'MEDIAN TEST, SIGEL P. 114'
DATA LIST  /EXPLAIN 1 ANXIETY 3-4
VAR LABELS  EXPLAIN 'ORAL EXPLANATION OF ILLNESS CODE'/
            ANXIETY 'ORAL SOCIALIZATION ANXIETY'/
VALUE LABELS  EXPLAIN 1 'ABSENT' 2 'PRESENT'/
NPAR TESTS  MEDIAN (10.5) = ANXIETY BY EXPLAIN (1,2)/
   MEDIAN = ANXIETY BY EXPLAIN (1,2)
BEGIN DATA
2 10
2 10
2 10
  ...
1 7
1 7
1 6
END DATA
```

Figure 37.18 is the output produced by the MEDIAN subcommand. For each test, the display shows the 2 × 2 table of cases above the median and cases equal to or below the median, the chi-square statistic, and its significance level.

Figure 37.18 Two-sample median test

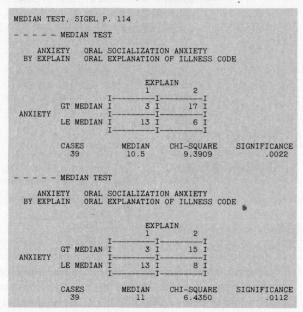

```
MEDIAN TEST, SIGEL P. 114

- - - - - MEDIAN TEST

    ANXIETY    ORAL SOCIALIZATION ANXIETY
 BY EXPLAIN    ORAL EXPLANATION OF ILLNESS CODE

                                EXPLAIN
                                 1          2
                     I----------I----------I
           GT MEDIAN I        3 I       17 I
 ANXIETY             I----------I----------I
           LE MEDIAN I       13 I        6 I
                     I----------I----------I

       CASES           MEDIAN      CHI-SQUARE     SIGNIFICANCE
        39              10.5          9.3909          .0022

- - - - - MEDIAN TEST

    ANXIETY    ORAL SOCIALIZATION ANXIETY
 BY EXPLAIN    ORAL EXPLANATION OF ILLNESS CODE

                                EXPLAIN
                                 1          2
                     I----------I----------I
           GT MEDIAN I        3 I       15 I
 ANXIETY             I----------I----------I
           LE MEDIAN I       13 I        8 I
                     I----------I----------I

       CASES           MEDIAN      CHI-SQUARE     SIGNIFICANCE
        39               11           6.4350          .0112
```

37.19 Mann-Whitney *U* Test

Subcommand M-W performs the Mann-Whitney *U* test. It ranks all the cases in order of increasing size and computes the test statistic *U*, the number of times a score from Group 1 precedes a score from Group 2. If the samples are from the same population, the distribution of scores from the two groups in the ranked list should be random; an extreme value of *U* indicates a nonrandom pattern. For samples of less than 30 cases, the exact significance level for *U* is computed using the algorithm of Dineen and Blakesly (1973). For larger samples, *U* is transformed into a normally distributed *Z* statistic.

The M-W subcommand has the following general form:

NPAR TESTS M-W = *varlist* BY *var*(*value1*,*value2*)/

The following example tests TRIALS by GROUP:

```
TITLE  NPAR TESTS
SUBTITLE  'MANN-WHITNEY TEST, SIEGEL, P. 119'
DATA LIST  /GROUP 1 TRIALS 3-5
NPAR TESTS  M-W = TRIALS BY GROUP (0,1)
BEGIN DATA
0 78
0 64
0 75
0 45
0 82
1 110
1 70
1 53
1 51
END DATA
```

Figure 37.19 is the output produced by the M-W subcommand. It prints the mean rank for each group, the Mann-Whitney *U* statistics, the Wilcoxon *W* (the rank sum of the smaller group), the exact significance level of *U* (or *W*), and the *Z* statistic and its probability level corrected for ties.

Figure 37.19 Mann-Whitney *U* test

```
MANN-WHITNEY TEST, SIEGEL, P. 119

- - - - - MANN-WHITNEY U - WILCOXON RANK SUM W TEST

    TRIALS
  BY GROUP

   MEAN RANK     CASES

        5.20         5  GROUP = 0
        4.75         4  GROUP = 1
                     -
                     9  TOTAL

                                      EXACT                 CORRECTED FOR TIES
          U                W       2-TAILED P              Z       2-TAILED P
         9.0             19.0        0.9048           -0.2449        0.8065
```

37.20 Kolmogorov-Smirnov Two-Sample Test

Subcommand K-S performs the Kolmogorov-Smirnov two-sample test. K-S computes the observed cumulative distributions for both groups and the maximum positive, negative, and absolute differences. The Kolmogorov-Smirnov *Z* is then computed along with the two-tailed probability level based on the Smirnov (1948) formula. The one-tailed test can be used to determine whether the values of one group are generally larger than the values of the other group.

The K-S two-sample subcommand has the following general form:

NPAR TESTS K-S = *varlist* BY *var(value1,value2)*/

The following example performs two separate K-S tests. First PCTERR by GRADE is analyzed, and then IDENTED by GROUP is analyzed.

```
TITLE  NPAR TESTS
SUBTITLE   'K-S TWO-SAMPLE TEST, SIEGEL, P. 130'
DATA LIST   /PCTERR 1-4(1) GRADE 6-7
VAR LABELS  PCTERR 'PERCENTAGE OF ERRORS'/
            GRADE 'GRADE IN SCHOOL'
NPAR TESTS  K-S = PCTERR BY GRADE (7,11)
BEGIN DATA
39.1 7
41.2 7
45.2 7
  ...
24.3 11
32.4 11
32.6 11
END DATA
SUBTITLE   'K-S TWO-SAMPLE TEST, SIEGEL, P. 133'
DATA LIST   /IDENTED 1-2  GROUP 4 NUMBER 6-7
VAR LABELS  IDENTED 'PHOTOS ''IDENTIFIED'''/
WEIGHT  BY NUMBER
NPAR TESTS  K-S = IDENTED BY GROUP (1,2)
BEGIN DATA
 1 1 11
 1 2  1
 4 1  7
  ...
19 1  5
19 2  6
END DATA
```

Figure 37.20 is the output produced by the K-S subcommand. For each test, the display shows the number of cases in each group; the most extreme positive, negative, and absolute differences; and the Kolmogorov-Smirnov Z and its significance.

Figure 37.20 Kolmogorov-Smirnov two-sample test

```
K-S TWO-SAMPLE TEST, SIEGEL, P. 130

- - - - - KOLMOGOROV - SMIRNOV 2-SAMPLE TEST

    PCTERR     PERCENTAGE OF ERRORS
 BY GRADE      GRADE IN SCHOOL


          CASES

              10  GRADE =  7
              10  GRADE = 11
              ---
              20  TOTAL

WARNING - DUE TO SMALL SAMPLE SIZE, PROBABILITY TABLES SHOULD BE CONSULTED.

              MOST EXTREME DIFFERENCES
       ABSOLUTE        POSITIVE          NEGATIVE           K-S Z       2-TAILED P
        0.70000         0.0              -0.70000           1.565           0.015

K-S TWO-SAMPLE TEST, SIEGEL, P. 133

- - - - - KOLMOGOROV - SMIRNOV 2-SAMPLE TEST

    IDENTED    PHOTOS 'IDENTIFIED'
 BY GROUP


          CASES

              44  GROUP = 1
              54  GROUP = 2
              ---
              98  TOTAL

WARNING - DUE TO SMALL SAMPLE SIZE, PROBABILITY TABLES SHOULD BE CONSULTED.

              MOST EXTREME DIFFERENCES
       ABSOLUTE        POSITIVE          NEGATIVE           K-S Z       2-TAILED P
        0.40572         0.00253          -0.40572           1.998           0.001
```

37.21 Wald-Wolfowitz Runs Test

Subcommand W-W performs the Wald-Wolfowitz runs test. W-W combines observations from both groups and ranks them from lowest to highest. If the samples are from the same population, the two groups should be randomly scattered throughout the ranking. A runs test is performed using group membership as the criterion. If there are ties involving observations from both groups, both the minimum and maximum number of runs possible are calculated. If the total sample size is 30 or less, the exact one-tailed significance level is calculated. Otherwise, the normal approximation is used.

The W-W subcommand has the following general form:

NPAR TESTS W-W = *varlist* BY *var*(*value1*,*value2*)/

The following example performs two tests. The test is first performed on SCORE by SEX, then on TRIALS by TYPE.

```
TITLE  NPAR TESTS
SUBTITLE  'WALD-WOLFOWITZ TEST, SIEGEL, P. 139'
DATA LIST  /SEX 1 SCORE 3-5
VAR LABELS  SCORE 'AGGRESSION SCORE'
NPAR TESTS  W-W = SCORE BY SEX (1,2)
BEGIN DATA
1  86
1  69
1  72
  ...
2  36
2  20
2  15
END DATA
SUBTITLE  'WALD-WOLFOWITZ, SIEGEL, P. 142'
DATA LIST  /TYPE 1 TRIALS 3-4
VAR LABELS  TRIALS 'RELEARNING TRIALS REQUIRED'
NPAR TESTS  W-W = TRIALS BY TYPE (0,1)
BEGIN DATA
0 20
0 55
0 29
  ...
1 22
1 15
1 14
END DATA
```

Figure 37.21 is the output produced by the W-W subcommand. The display shows the number of cases in each group, the exact number of runs for the first example (since there are no ties), and the test statistic *Z* with its significance level. The second example contains ties so both the maximum and minimum possible number of runs are displayed along with their test statistic and significance level.

Figure 37.21 Wald-Wolfowitz runs test

```
WALD-WOLFOWITZ TEST, SIEGEL, P. 139

- - - - - WALD-WOLFOWITZ RUNS TEST

    SCORE      AGGRESSION SCORE
  BY SEX

        CASES

            12  SEX = 1
            12  SEX = 2
            --
            24  TOTAL
                                                      EXACT
                          RUNS            Z       1-TAILED P
EXACT NUMBER OF RUNS:       4         -3.5481          .0001

                NO INTER-GROUP TIES ENCOUNTERED.

WALD-WOLFOWITZ, SIEGEL, P. 142

- - - - - WALD-WOLFOWITZ RUNS TEST

    TRIALS     RELEARNING TRIALS REQUIRED
  BY TYPE

        CASES

             8  TYPE = 0
            21  TYPE = 1
            --
            29  TOTAL
                                                      EXACT
                          RUNS            Z       1-TAILED P
    MINIMUM POSSIBLE:       4         -3.8635          .0001
    MAXIMUM POSSIBLE:       6         -2.9079          .0023

    WARNING -- THERE ARE    1 INTER-GROUP TIES INVOLVING     3 CASES.
```

37.22 Moses Test of Extreme Reactions

Subcommand MOSES performs the Moses test of extreme reactions. This test arranges the scores from the groups in a single ascending sequence. The span of the control group is computed as the number of cases in the sequence containing the lowest and highest control score. The exact significance level can be computed for the span. Chance outliers can easily distort the range of the span. To minimize this problem, you can specify that a certain number of outliers be trimmed from each end of the span. No adjustments are made for tied observations.

The MOSES subcommand has the following general form:

NPAR TESTS MOSES [(*n*)] = *varlist* BY *var(value1,value2)*

where *n* is the number of cases trimmed from each end. If you do not specify *n*, MOSES automatically trims 5% of the cases from each end. *Value1* corresponds to the control group.

The following example tests SCORE by SECTION. The first test uses SECTION=1 as the control group. The second uses SECTION=2 as the control group.

```
TITLE  NPAR TESTS
SUBTITLE  'MOSES TEST, EXTREME REACTION, SIEGEL, P. 149'
DATA LIST  /SCORE 1-2 SECTION 4
VAR LABELS  SCORE 'ATTRIBUTION OF AGGRESSION'
NPAR TESTS  MOSES = SCORE BY SECTION (1,2)/
   MOSES = SCORE BY SECTION (2,1)
BEGIN DATA
25 2
 5 2
14 2
  ...
10 1
10 1
11 1
END DATA
```

Figure 37.22 is the output produced by the MOSES subcommand. For each test, the display shows the number of cases in each group, the span of the control group and its significance level for the full set of cases, and the span of the control group after outliers are removed.

Figure 37.22 Moses test of extreme reaction

```
MOSES TEST, EXTREME REACTION, SIEGEL, P. 149

- - - - - MOSES TEST OF EXTREME REACTIONS

     SCORE      ATTRIBUTION OF AGGRESSION
  BY SECTION


                    CASES

       (CONTROL)    9  SECTION = 1
  (EXPERIMENTAL)    9  SECTION = 2
                   --
                   18  TOTAL

 1-TAILED P       SPAN OF CONTROL GROUP
    .1471           14   OBSERVED
    .0767            9   AFTER REMOVING 1 OUTLIER(S) FROM EACH END

- - - - - MOSES TEST OF EXTREME REACTIONS

     SCORE      ATTRIBUTION OF AGGRESSION
  BY SECTION


                    CASES

       (CONTROL)    9  SECTION = 2
  (EXPERIMENTAL)    9  SECTION = 1
                   --
                   18  TOTAL

 1-TAILED P       SPAN OF CONTROL GROUP
   1.0000           18   OBSERVED
    .9588           15   AFTER REMOVING 1 OUTLIER(S) FROM EACH END
```

37.23 Tests for *k* Independent Samples

Tests for *k* independent samples compare *k* groups of cases on one variable. These tests have the following general form:

NPAR TESTS *testname* = *varlist* BY *var*(*value1*,*value2*)/

You must specify the name of the test and one or more variables to be tested. Each variable in the list produces one test. The variable following the keyword BY splits the file into *k* groups. *Value1* and *value2* specify minimum and maximum values for the grouping variable. For example,

```
NPAR TESTS  K-W = SCORE BY CLASS (1,5)
```

specifies five samples or groups. This syntax resembles that used for the two-independent-sample tests. However, for *k*-sample tests, *value1* and *value2* are interpreted as a range of categories, whereas for two-sample tests, they are interpreted as the two categories.

The following tests are available for *k* independent samples:

MEDIAN *k-sample median test.* This is an extension of the two-sample median test and determines whether *k* groups are drawn from populations with the same median (see Section 37.24).

K-W *Kruskal-Wallis one-way analysis of variance test.* K-W tests whether all *k* samples are from the same population (see Section 37.25).

37.24 *k*-Sample Median Test

Subcommand MEDIAN performs the *k*-sample median test, an extension of the two-sample median test. MEDIAN tabulates a 2 × *k* contingency table with counts of the number of cases greater than the median and less than or equal to the median for the *k* groups. You can specify a value as a cutting point or use the calculated median from the data. A chi-square statistic for the table is computed.

The MEDIAN subcommand has the following general form:

NPAR TESTS MEDIAN [(value)] = *varlist* BY *var*(*value1*,*value2*)

The value in parentheses following the keyword MEDIAN is the test median. If you omit that value, the calculated median is used. Note that the two-sample and *k*-sample MEDIAN subcommands are requested with the same subcommand. The particular test performed is actually determined from the (*value1*,*value2*) specification. If (*value2* − *value1* + 1) is greater than 2, the *k*-sample median test is performed. For example, in

```
NPAR TESTS  MEDIAN = A BY B (1,3)/MEDIAN = A BY B (3,1)
```

the first test is a *k*-sample median test with three groups, while the second is a two-sample median test for Groups 1 and 3.

The following example produces a median test for six groups, then recodes the grouping variable, VISITS, and produces the same test for four groups.

```
TITLE  NPAR TESTS
SUBTITLE  'K-SAMPLE MEDIAN TEST, SIEGEL, P.182'
DATA LIST  /VISITS 1 EDUC 3
VAR LABELS  VISITS 'VISITS TO SCHOOL'/
   EDUC 'LEVEL OF EDUCATION'
NPAR TESTS  MEDIAN = VISITS BY EDUC (1,6)
BEGIN DATA
4 1
3 1
0 1
  ...
2 5
2 6
6 6
END DATA
RECODE  EDUC (4 THRU 6=4)
NPAR TESTS  MEDIAN = VISITS BY EDUC (1,4)
```

Figure 37.24 is the output produced by the MEDIAN subcommand. For each test, the display shows the 2 × *k* table, the chi-square statistic, the degrees of freedom, and the significance level for the chi-square.

Figure 37.24 A *k*-sample median test

```
K-SAMPLE MEDIAN TEST, SIEGEL, P.182

- - - - - MEDIAN TEST

    VISITS     VISITS TO SCHOOL
  BY EDUC      LEVEL OF EDUCATION

                                           EDUC
                         1          2          3          4          5
             I----------I----------I----------I----------I----------I
   GT MEDIAN I        5 I        4 I        7 I        3 I        2 I
VISITS       I----------I----------I----------I----------I----------I
   LE MEDIAN I        5 I        7 I        6 I        1 I        2 I
             I----------I----------I----------I----------I----------I

                    EDUC
                         6
             I----------I
   GT MEDIAN I        1 I
VISITS       I----------I
   LE MEDIAN I        1 I
             I----------I

WARNING - CHI-SQUARE STATISTIC IS QUESTIONABLE HERE.
   6 CELLS HAVE EXPECTED FREQUENCIES LESS THAN 5.
MINIMUM EXPECTED CELL FREQUENCY IS        1.0

         CASES          MEDIAN    CHI-SQUARE     D.F.  SIGNIFICANCE
          44             2.5        1.8951         5        .8635

K-SAMPLE MEDIAN TEST, SIEGEL, P.182

- - - - - MEDIAN TEST

    VISITS     VISITS TO SCHOOL
  BY EDUC      LEVEL OF EDUCATION

                                      EDUC
                         1          2          3          4
             I----------I----------I----------I----------I
   GT MEDIAN I        5 I        4 I        7 I        6 I
VISITS       I----------I----------I----------I----------I
   LE MEDIAN I        5 I        7 I        6 I        4 I
             I----------I----------I----------I----------I

         CASES          MEDIAN    CHI-SQUARE     D.F.  SIGNIFICANCE
          44             2.5        1.2951         3        .7303
```

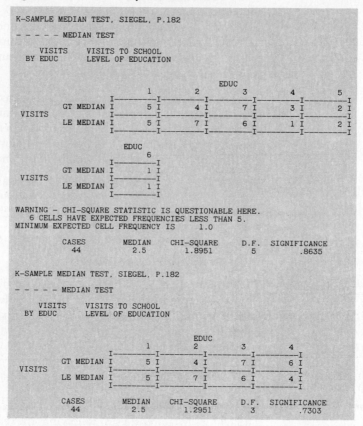

37.25 Kruskal-Wallis One-Way Analysis of Variance

Subcommand K-W performs the Kruskal-Wallis test. It ranks all cases from the *k* groups in a single series, computes the rank sum for each group, and computes the Kruskal-Wallis *H* statistic, which has approximately a chi-square distribution.

The K-W subcommand has the following general form:

NPAR TESTS K-W = *varlist* BY *var(value1,value2)*/

Every value in the range *value1* to *value2* forms a group.

The following example first analyzes AUTSCORE by GROUP and then analyzes WEIGHT by LITTER.

```
TITLE  NPAR TESTS
SUBTITLE  'KRUSKAL-WALLIS, SIEGEL, P. 187'
DATA LIST  /AUTSCORE 1-3 GROUP 5
VAR LABELS  AUTSCORE 'AUTHORITARIANISM SCORE'
NPAR TESTS  K-W = AUTSCORE BY GROUP (1,3)
BEGIN DATA
 96 1
128 1
 83 1
 61 1
101 1
 82 2
124 2
132 2
135 2
109 2
115 3
149 3
166 3
147 3
END DATA
SUBTITLE  'KRUSKAL-WALLIS, SIEGEL, P. 190'
DATA LIST  /WEIGHT 1-3(1) LITTER 5
VAR LABELS  WEIGHT 'BIRTH WEIGHT'
NPAR TESTS  K-W = WEIGHT BY LITTER (1 8)
BEGIN DATA
2.0 1
2.8 1
3.3 1
 ...
2.4 8
3.0 8
1.5 8
END DATA
```

Figure 37.25 is the output produced by the K-W subcommand. For each test, the display shows the mean rank for each group, the number of cases in each group, the chi-square statistic and its significance level uncorrected for ties, and the chi-square statistic and its significance level corrected for ties.

Figure 37.25 Kruskal-Wallis one-way analysis of variance

```
KRUSKAL-WALLIS, SIEGEL, P. 187

- - - - - KRUSKAL-WALLIS 1-WAY ANOVA

   AUTSCORE  AUTHORITARIANISM SCORE
  BY GROUP

     MEAN RANK     CASES

          4.40         5   GROUP = 1
          7.40         5   GROUP = 2
         11.50         4   GROUP = 3
                      --
                      14   TOTAL

                                                         CORRECTED FOR TIES
         CASES     CHI-SQUARE  SIGNIFICANCE       CHI-SQUARE  SIGNIFICANCE
            14         6.4057        0.0406           6.4057        0.0406

KRUSKAL-WALLIS, SIEGEL, P. 190

- - - - - KRUSKAL-WALLIS 1-WAY ANOVA

     WEIGHT     BIRTH WEIGHT
  BY LITTER

     MEAN RANK     CASES

         31.70        10   LITTER = 1
         27.06         8   LITTER = 2
         41.40        10   LITTER = 3
         34.69         8   LITTER = 4
         17.58         6   LITTER = 5
         30.50         4   LITTER = 6
         11.92         6   LITTER = 7
         18.00         4   LITTER = 8
                      --
                      56   TOTAL

                                                         CORRECTED FOR TIES
         CASES     CHI-SQUARE  SIGNIFICANCE       CHI-SQUARE  SIGNIFICANCE
            56        18.4639        0.0100          18.5654        0.0097
```

37.26 Optional Statistics

In addition to the statistics provided for each test, you may also obtain two types of summary statistics for variables named on each of the subcommands. Use the associated STATISTICS command to request the following statistics for NPAR TESTS:

STATISTIC 1 *Univariate statistics.* Prints the mean, maximum, minimum, standard deviation, and number of nonmissing cases for each variable named on the combined subcommands.

STATISTIC 2 *Quartiles and number of cases.* Prints values corresponding to the 25th, 50th, and 75th percentiles for each variable named on the combined subcommands.

The following example produces the Kruskal-Wallis test shown in the lower half of Figure 37.25 and requests both statistics:

```
SUBTITLE   'KRUSKAL-WALLIS, SIEGEL, P. 190'
DATA LIST  /WEIGHT 1-3(1) LITTER 5
VAR LABELS  WEIGHT 'BIRTH WEIGHT'
NPAR TESTS  K-W = WEIGHT BY LITTER (1 8)
STATISTICS  1 2
BEGIN DATA
2.0 1
2.8 1
3.3 1
  ...
2.4 8
3.0 8
1.5 8
END DATA
```

Figure 37.26 displays these statistics.

Figure 37.26 Statistics available in NPAR TESTS

```
KRUSKAL-WALLIS, SIEGEL, P. 190

               N        MEAN     STD DEV  MINIMUM  MAXIMUM    LABEL

WEIGHT        56      2.7214       .6695      1.1      4.4    BIRTH WEIGHT
LITTER        56      3.8571      2.2192      1.0      8.0


                               (MEDIAN)
                    25TH         50TH         75TH
               N  PERCENTILE  PERCENTILE  PERCENTILE    LABEL

WEIGHT        56      2.325       2.800       3.200     BIRTH WEIGHT
LITTER        56      2.000       3.500       5.750
```

37.27 Missing Values

By default, NPAR TESTS deletes cases with missing values on a test-by-test basis. For subcommands where you can specify several tests, it evaluates each test separately for missing values. For example,

```
NPAR TESTS  MEDIAN = A B BY GROUP (1,5)/
```

specifies two tests, A by GROUP and B by GROUP. A case missing for GROUP is excluded from both tests, but a case missing for A is not excluded for the test for B if it is not missing for B. Two missing-value options are available:

OPTION 1 *Include missing values.* User-defined missing values are treated as if they were not missing.

OPTION 2 *Exclude missing values listwise.* Cases missing on any variable named on any subcommand are excluded from all analyses.

37.28 Random Sampling

NPAR TESTS must store cases in memory. You may not have sufficient computer resources to store all the cases to produce the tests requested. Option 4 selects a random sample of cases when there is not enough space to store all the cases.

OPTION 4 *Random sampling.* If NPAR TESTS runs out of space when storing the cases, it randomly samples cases. Because sampling would invalidate a runs test, this option is ignored when you use the RUNS subcommand.

37.29 Aliases for Subcommand Names

Subcommand names have been chosen which are short and easy to enter. However, some of them do not describe the test being performed. For this reason, some of the subcommands have aliases which are usually longer but may be more meaningful. Table 37.29 lists the subcommands for which aliases are accepted.

Table 37.29 Subcommands and their aliases

Subcommand	Alias
CHISQUARE	CHI-SQUARE
K-S	KOLMOGOROV-SMIRNOV
M-W	MANN-WHITNEY
W-W	WALD-WOLFOWITZ
K-W	KRUSKAL-WALLIS

37.30 LIMITATIONS

The following limitations apply to NPAR TESTS:

- A maximum of 100 subcommands.
- A maximum of 500 variables total per NPAR TESTS command.
- A maximum of 200 values for subcommand CHISQUARE.

```
BOX-JENKINS VARIABLE = varlist
   subcommands controlling identification and model specification
   subcommands controlling estimation
   subcommands controlling forecasting
   subcommands controlling display

   / {IDENTIFY
      ESTIMATE    } at least one is required
      FORECAST}

subcommands controlling identification and model specification:

  [/ {LOG [ = {0
               constant}]
      POWER = (power [, {0
                         constant}])  } ]

  [/DIFFERENCE = m [THRU n [BY {1
                                i}]]]

  [/SDIFFERENCE = m [THRU n [BY {1
                                 i}]]  /PERIOD = {1
                                                  n}]

  [/LAG = {25
           n}]

  [/ {P
      Q
      SP
      SQ} = {0
             m [THRU n]}]   [/ {MALAG
                                ARLAG} = n,n, . . . ]

subcommands controlling estimation:

  [/ {CONSTANT
      NCONSTANT}]   [/ {NCENTER
                        CENTER}]   [/ITERATE = {40
                                                n}]

  [/FPR = {5
           n}]   [/BFR = {0
                          n}]   [/ {NTEST
                                    TEST}]

  [/ {TCON
      PCON
      ICON} = (n)]        {conditional upon CONSTANT

  [/ {TP
      PP
      IP                  {conditional upon P
      TQ
      PQ
      IQ                  {conditional upon Q
      TSP
      PSP
      ISP                 {conditional upon SP
      TSQ
      PSQ
      ISQ} = (n, . . . )] {conditional upon SQ

subcommands controlling forecasting:

  [/ORIGIN = m [THRU n]]   [/LEAD = {12
                                     n}]   [/CIN = {95
                                                    n}]

  [/FCON = (n)]           conditional upon CONSTANT

  [/ {FP                  conditional upon P
      FQ                  conditional upon Q
      FSP = (n, . . . )]  conditional upon SP
      FSQ}                conditional upon SQ

subcommands controlling display:

  [/PRINT = [ACF]  [PACF]  [ACVF]  [SER]  [TSER]
            [DSER]  [RESID]  [RACF]]

  [/PLOT = [ACF]  [PACF]  [SER]  [TSER]  [FCF]  [FLF]  [CIN]
           [DSER]  [RESID]  [RACF]]
```


OVERVIEW, **38.1**

OPERATION, **38.2**

- The VARIABLE Subcommand, **38.3**
- Step-of-Analysis Subcommands, **38.4**
  - Plotting the Series, **38.5**
- Transformation Subcommands, **38.6**
  - The LOG and POWER Subcommands, **38.7**
- Differencing Subcommands, **38.8**
  - The DIFFERENCE Subcommand, **38.9**
  - The SDIFFERENCE and PERIOD Subcommands, **38.10**
- The LAG Subcommand, **38.11**
- Parameters Subcommands, **38.12**
- Estimation Subcommands, **38.13**
  - Keywords CONSTANT and NCONSTANT, **38.14**
  - Keywords CENTER and NCENTER, **38.15**
  - The ITERATE Subcommand, **38.16**
  - The BFR Subcommand, **38.17**
  - Keywords TEST and NTEST, **38.18**
  - The FPR Subcommand, **38.19**
  - Perturbation Increment Subcommands, **38.20**
  - Tolerance Subcommands, **38.21**
  - Initial Estimates Subcommands, **38.22**
- Forecast Subcommands, **38.23**
  - The ORIGIN Subcommand, **38.24**
  - The LEAD Subcommand, **38.25**
  - The CIN Subcommand, **38.26**
  - Final Estimates Subcommands, **38.27**
- The PRINT Subcommand, **38.28**
- The PLOT Subcommand, **38.29**

Chapter 38 BOX-JENKINS

The BOX-JENKINS procedure can be used to fit and forecast time series data by means of a general class of statistical models (Box & Jenkins, 1976). An observation at a given time is modeled as a function of its past values and/or current and past values of the random shocks, both at nonseasonal and seasonal lags. BOX-JENKINS will model a variable with observations equally spaced in time and no missing values. Sometimes it may be necessary before modeling the series to transform the data by taking the log or power transformation of the series or differencing the series on a seasonal or nonseasonal basis.

38.1 OVERVIEW

The modeling of time series data is usually done in three steps. First, *identify* a tentative model for a series. Second, *estimate* the parameters and examine diagnostic statistics and plots. Third, if the model is deemed acceptable, *forecast* using the model. If the model is inadequate, other models may be examined until an acceptable fit is obtained, at which time forecasts can be computed. Thus, fitting and forecasting of a given time series typically entails several computer runs. For this reason, SPSS^{X} BOX-JENKINS syntax is designed for flexibility so that you can request sufficient information easily and efficiently.

Specifying the Time Series. The time series data must be organized with each time point coded on a separate case. Specify the variable containing the time series measurement using the VARIABLE subcommand. (See Section 38.3.)

Specifying the Step of Analysis. Three subcommands specify the step of the analysis. At least one of these subcommands is required. (See Section 38.4.)

Transforming the Time Series. You can specify a log or power transformation of your series. (See Sections 38.6 and 38.7.)

Differencing the Series. You can difference the series at different degrees or for a seasonal component at specified periods. (See Sections 38.8 through 38.10.)

Specifying the Parameters. You can specify any number of autoregressive parameters, moving average parameters, seasonal autoregressive parameters, and seasonal moving average parameters to be fit. (See Section 38.12.)

Controlling the Estimation. You can control the number of iterations and the number of backforecasts used for the parameter estimation, the perturbation increments and convergence tolerances for each parameter estimated, and a check against invertibility conditions. You can also enter initial parameter estimates. (See Sections 38.13 through 38.22.)

Specifying the Forecast. You can control the origin of the forecast values, the number of leads desired, and the confidence level for the forecast values. In addition, you can enter the final parameter estimates at the forecast step rather than having BOX-JENKINS estimate the model again. (See Sections 38.23 through 38.27.)

Displaying Results. You can control the amount of printed material that BOX-JENKINS produces. Plots and printed values of the time series, transformed series, autocorrelation function, partial autocorrelation function, residual series, and residual autocorrelation function are available. You can also plot the forecast function, fixed lead-forecasts, and confidence intervals. (See Sections 38.28 and 38.29.)

38.2 OPERATION

BOX-JENKINS is a subcommand-driven procedure. There are no associated OPTIONS and STATISTICS commands. All of the specifications are given using the appropriate subcommand. The VARIABLE subcommand and one of the step of analysis subcommands are the only required subcommands. Subcommands are separated by slashes, and the equals signs following the subcommand keywords are optional. The subcommand and specification keywords can be abbreviated to the first three characters.

38.3 The VARIABLE Subcommand

Specify the variable name of your time series data using the VARIABLE subcommand, as in:

```
BOX-JENKINS  VARIABLE=AIRLINE/IDENTIFY
```

This series consists of monthly totals, in thousands, of international airline passengers from January 1949 to December 1960. The series must be measured at equally spaced intervals with each measurement recorded on a separate case. Missing values in the series are not allowed.

The VARIABLE subcommand is required and must be the first specification. You can list up to 10 variables following the VARIABLE keyword. Univariate time series analysis is performed for each variable listed.

38.4 Step-of-Analysis Subcommands

The three steps in the analysis of a time series model are specified by three subcommands in BOX-JENKINS.

IDENTIFY *Produce statistics used for model identification.*
ESTIMATE *Produce parameter estimates.*
FORECAST *Produce forecast functions.*

At least one of these keywords is required on a BOX-JENKINS command and must be the last specification on the command, as in

```
BOX-JENKINS  VARIABLE=AIRLINE/IDENTIFY
```

which requests the identification step of analysis on a variable AIRLINE. By default, the autocorrelation function is plotted and summary statistics for the series are printed when IDENTIFY is specified. The autocorrelation function plot is shown in Figure 38.4. The default number of lags for which autocorrelations are plotted is 25. To override this default, use the LAG subcommand (see Section 38.11).

Autocorrelation plots in BOX-JENKINS display the autocorrelations up to the specified number of lags and two standard error limits. The standard errors are computed on the assumption that the time series is white noise, that is, random. Standard errors are calculated using the method documented in Ling and Roberts (1980), which differs from the method documented in Box and Jenkins (1976).

Figure 38.4 Autocorrelation function plot

```
AUTOCORRELATION FUNCTION FOR VARIABLE Y
AUTOCORRELATIONS *
TWO STANDARD ERROR LIMITS .

     AUTO. STAND.
LAG  CORR.   ERR. -1  -.75 -.5  -.25  0   .25  .5   .75   1
                  :----:----:----:----:----:----:----:----:
  1  0.948  0.082                  .  :  .               *
  2  0.876  0.082                  .  :  .              *
  3  0.807  0.081                  .  :  .            *
  4  0.753  0.081                  .  :  .           *
  5  0.714  0.081                  .  :  .          *
  6  0.682  0.080                  .  :  .          *
  7  0.663  0.080                  .  :  .         *
  8  0.656  0.080                  .  :  .         *
  9  0.671  0.080                  .  :  .         *
 10  0.703  0.079                  .  :  .          *
 11  0.743  0.079                  .  :  .           *
 12  0.760  0.079                  .  :  .           *
 13  0.713  0.078                  .  :  .          *
 14  0.646  0.078                  .  :  .         *
 15  0.586  0.078                  .  :  .        *
 16  0.538  0.077                  .  :  .       *
 17  0.500  0.077                  .  :  .      *
 18  0.469  0.077                  .  :  .     *
 19  0.450  0.076                  .  :  .     *
 20  0.442  0.076                  .  :  .     *
 21  0.457  0.076                  .  :  .     *
 22  0.482  0.076                  .  :  .      *
 23  0.517  0.075                  .  :  .      *
 24  0.532  0.075                  .  :  .       *
 25  0.494  0.075                  .  :  .      *
```

38.5 Plotting the Series

In addition to the autocorrelation function plot that is printed by default with the IDENTIFY subcommand, you can also obtain the series plot to help identify the series. To request a plot of the time series, use the PLOT subcommand and specify the keyword SER, as in:

```
BOX-JENKINS  VARIABLE=AIRLINE/PLOT=SER/IDENTIFY
```

This plot, shown in Figure 38.5, exhibits three noteworthy attributes. There is an upward tendency in series values from 1949 to 1960, and the series exhibits a periodic component consisting of a regular seasonal pattern with peaks occurring in late summer months of each year. Finally, the series values show greater amplitude in recent years than in earlier ones. Thus, the series is nonstationary and heteroscedastic, and both of these characteristics ought to be taken into account in fitting a model to the series.

38.6 Transformation Subcommands

Two types of transformations of the time series, logarithmic and power, are available in BOX-JENKINS. You can take the log or power of the series to induce constant amplitude in the series over time so that residuals from the fitted model will have a constant variance. When a transformation is called for, it is more convenient to transform the series within the procedure than in the data transformation language outside the procedure, since results will be internally back-transformed and expressed in the original units whenever possible. All of the subcommands controlling transformations of the series can be used with all steps of analysis.

Figure 38.5 Series plot and summary statistics

```
GRAPHIC DISPLAY OF SERIES FOR VARIABLE Y
DATA - *
MEAN - .

 OBS     DATA                80.00     280.00    480.00    680.00    880.00
                     :---------:---------:---------:---------:---------:
    1   112.000      :           *       .
    2   118.000      :           *       .
    3   132.000      :            *      .
    4   129.000      :           *       .
    5   121.000      :           *       .
    6   135.000      :            *      .
    7   148.000      :            *      .
    8   148.000      :            *      .
    9   136.000      :            *      .
   10   119.000      -           *       .
   11   104.000      :          *        .
   12   118.000      :           *       .
   13   115.000      :           *       .
   14   126.000      :           *       .
   15   141.000      :            *      .
   16   135.000      :            *      .
   17   125.000      :           *       .
   18   149.000      :            *      .
   19   170.000      :             *     .
   20   170.000      -             *     .
   21   158.000      :             *     .
   22   133.000      :            *      .
   23   114.000      :           *       .
   24   140.000      :            *      .



  120   337.000      -                   . *
  121   360.000      :                   .  *
  122   342.000      :                   . *
  123   406.000      :                   .    *
  124   396.000      :                   .    *
  125   420.000      :                   .     *
  126   472.000      :                   .        *
  127   548.000      :                   .           *
  128   559.000      :                   .            *
  129   463.000      :                   .       *
  130   407.000      -                   .    *
  131   362.000      :                   .  *
  132   405.000      :                   .    *
  133   417.000      :                   .     *
  134   391.000      :                   .    *
  135   419.000      :                   .     *
  136   461.000      :                   .       *
  137   472.000      :                   .        *
  138   535.000      :                   .           *
  139   622.000      :                   .               *
  140   606.000      -                   .              *
  141   508.000      :                   .         *
  142   461.000      :                   .       *
  143   390.000      :                   .   *
  144   432.000      :                   .      *

MEAN VALUE OF THE PROCESS
 0.28030E 03

STANDARD DEVIATION OF THE PROCESS
 0.11955E 03
```

38.7 The LOG and POWER Subcommands

The varying amplitude (heteroscedasticity) of a series can often be removed by using a logarithmic or power transformation. Use the LOG subcommand to log transform the series, as in:

```
BOX-JENKINS  VARIABLE=AIRLINE/LOG/IDENTIFY
```

The log transform calculates the natural logorithm (base *e*) of the series. Optionally you can specify a constant that you want added to all of the values in the series before the log transformation is calculated in order to prevent taking logs of negative numbers. For example, the following command adds 10 to all of the values of AIRLINE before calculating the log:

```
BOX-JENKINS  VARIABLE=AIRLINE/LOG=10/IDENTIFY
```

Use the POWER subcommand to take the power of the values in the series, as in

```
BOX-JENKINS  VARIABLE=Y/POWER=(2)/IDENTIFY
```

which squares the values of the series Y. Optionally you can specify a constant to be added to the series values before the power transformation is calculated. For example, the following command adds 10 to the series before calculating the third power:

```
BOX-JENKINS  VARIABLE=Y/POWER=(3,10)/IDENITFY
```

You can specify either the LOG or the POWER subcommand in a given analysis, but not both.

38.8 Differencing Subcommands

Two types of differencing of the series are available in BOX-JENKINS. Nonseasonal differencing is used to convert a nonstationary series to a stationary series with a constant mean and variance. Seasonal differencing is used to model a systematic, periodic variation. The length of the period must be specified for seasonal differencing. If the series has been transformed with the LOG or POWER subcommands, the differencing is done on the transformed series.

38.9 The DIFFERENCE Subcommand

Use the DIFFERENCE subcommand to specify a nonseasonal differencing of the series. The specification for the DIFFERENCE subcommand can be a single number indicating the the degree of differencing desired, as in

```
BOX-JENKINS  VARIABLE=AIRLINE/DIFFERENCE=1/IDENTIFY
```

which specifies a single degree of differencing for the AIRLINE series. You can specify a range of differencing degrees on the DIFFERENCE subcommand by using the keyword THRU. The number before the keyword THRU indicates the lowest degree of differencing requested, and the number following the THRU indicates the highest degree. For example, the following command requests zero (none), one, and two degrees of nonseasonal differencing:

```
BOX-JENKINS  VARIABLE=AIRLINE/LOG/DIFFERENCE=0 THRU 2/
   IDENTIFY
```

By default, the differencing is done for each degree specified by the range; that is, the default increment is 1. To specify an increment other than 1, use the keyword BY followed by the desired increment. For example, the following command requests differencing of zero, two, and four degrees:

```
BOX-JENKINS  VARIABLE=AIRLINE/LOG/DIFFERENCE=0 THRU 4 BY 2/
   IDENTIFY
```

Ordinarily, no more than two or three degrees of differencing will be required to achieve stationarity and to overdifference, if variate differencing is being done.

38.10 The SDIFFERENCE and PERIOD Subcommands

The SDIFFERENCE subcommand specifies seasonal differencing. The specifications for the SDIFFERENCE subcommand are the same as for the DIFFERENCE subcommand. You can specify a single number to indicate the degree of differencing, the keyword THRU to indicate a range of degrees, and the keyword BY to indicate an increment other than one for the range.

If you request seasonal differencing, you must use the PERIOD subcommand to specify the period for differencing. The PERIOD subcommand specifies the number of observations that make up a period. The default value of PERIOD is 1. For example, the following command requests seasonal differencing of degrees zero, one, and two for the period of one year (12 months):

```
BOX-JENKINS  VARIABLE=AIRLINE/LOG/DIFFERENCE=0 THRU 2/
   SDIFFERENCE=0 THRU 2/PERIOD=12/IDENTIFY
```

This command requests three times three, or nine, combinations of seasonal and nonseasonal differencing. Nine separate autocorrelation function plots will be produced. This, in effect, implements the "variate difference" method discussed in Anderson (1976). The variate difference method, when used in conjunction with series plots and autocorrelation function plots, will often prove useful in identifying the appropriate degrees of differencing.

Note that difference ranges, using the keyword THRU on the DIFFERENCE or SDIFFERENCE subcommand, can be specified with the ESTIMATE or FORECAST keywords. However, this results in the calculation of several different models, and can lead to extra expense and voluminous output.

38.11 The LAG Subcommand

The LAG subcommand specifies the highest lag to be considered in computing the autocovariance function, the autocorrelation function, the partial autocorrelation function, and the residual autocorrelation function. The default value is 25. For example, the following command requests 49 lags for the functions:

```
BOX-JENKINS  VARIABLE=AIRLINE/LOG/DIFFERENCE=0 THRU 2/
   SDIFFERENCE=0 THRU 2/PERIOD=12/LAG=49/IDENTIFY
```

Figure 38.11 shows the autocorrelation function plot at one degree of seasonal and one degree of nonseasonal differencing. The autocorrelations are calculated for 49 lags.

38.12 Parameters Subcommands

You can fit autoregressive parameters and moving average parameters. The parameters can be fit as nonseasonal or seasonal parameters. You can request single parameters or multiple sequential or nonsequential parameters. The subcommands used to specify the desired parameters can be used with all steps of analysis.

Use the following subcommands to fit single or multiple sequential parameters:

P *Autoregressive parameters to fit.*
Q *Moving average parameters to fit.*
SP *Seasonal autoregressive parameters to fit.*
SQ *Seasonal moving average parameters to fit.*

On each subcommand, you can specify one number representing the number of parameters to be fit. For example, the following command requests one nonseasonal moving average parameter and one seasonal moving average parameter:

```
BOX-JENKINS  VARIABLE=AIRLINE/LOG/DIFFERENCE=1/PERIOD=12/
   SDIFFERENCE=1/LAG=49/Q=1/SQ=1/IDENTIFY
```

You can use the keyword THRU on any of the parameter subcommands to specify multiple models to be fit, as in

```
BOX-JENKINS  VARIABLE=AIRLINE/LOG/DIFFERENCE=1/PERIOD=12/
   SDIFFERENCE=1/LAG=49/Q=1 THRU 2/SQ=0 THRU 2/IDENTIFY
```

which specifies two times three, or six models to be fit: one model with one nonseasonal moving parameter and no seasonal parameters, one model with one nonseasonal parameter and one seasonal parameter, one model with one nonseasonal parameter and two seasonal parameters, and so forth.

Figure 38.11 Autocorrelation of series differenced at degree 1 seasonal and nonseasonal

```
VARIABLE - Y          SERIES LENGTH - 131
DEGREE OF NONSEASONAL DIFFERENCING -  1 DEGREE OF SEASONAL  DIFFERENCING -  1

MEAN VALUE OF THE PROCESS
 0.29089E-03

STANDARD DEVIATION OF THE PROCESS
 0.45673E-01


AUTOCORRELATION FUNCTION FOR VARIABLE Y
AUTOCORRELATIONS *
TWO STANDARD ERROR LIMITS .

     AUTO. STAND.
LAG  CORR.   ERR. -1  -.75  -.5 -.25  0   .25  .5   .75   1
                   :----:----:----:----:----:----:----:----:
  1 -0.341  0.086               *   .  :  .
  2  0.105  0.085                   .  : *.
  3 -0.202  0.085                   *.  :  .
  4  0.021  0.085                   .  *  .
  5  0.056  0.084                   .  :* .
  6  0.031  0.084                   .  :* .
  7 -0.056  0.084                   . *:  .
  8 -0.001  0.083                   .  *  .
  9  0.176  0.083                   .  :  .*
 10 -0.076  0.083                   .* :  .
 11  0.064  0.082                   .  :* .
 12 -0.387  0.082               *    .  :  .
 13  0.152  0.082                   .  :  *
 14 -0.058  0.081                   . *:  .
 15  0.150  0.081                   .  :  *
 16 -0.139  0.081                   *  :  .
 17  0.070  0.080                   .  :* .
 18  0.016  0.080                   .  *  .
 19 -0.011  0.079                   .  *  .
 20 -0.117  0.079                   .* :  .
 21  0.039  0.079                   .  :* .
 22 -0.091  0.078                   .* :  .
 23  0.223  0.078                   .  :  .*
 24 -0.018  0.078                   .  *  .
 25 -0.100  0.077                   .* :  .
 26  0.049  0.077                   .  :* .
 27 -0.030  0.077                   . *:  .
 28  0.047  0.076                   .  :* .
 29 -0.018  0.076                   .  *  .
 30 -0.051  0.075                   . *:  .
 31 -0.054  0.075                   . *:  .
 32  0.196  0.075                   .  :  .*
 33 -0.122  0.074                   .* :  .
 34  0.078  0.074                   .  : *.
 35 -0.152  0.073                   *  :  .
 36 -0.010  0.073                   .  *  .
 37  0.047  0.073                   .  :* .
 38  0.031  0.072                   .  :* .
 39 -0.015  0.072                   .  *  .
 40 -0.034  0.071                   . *:  .
 41 -0.066  0.071                   . *:  .
 42  0.095  0.071                   .  : *.
 43 -0.090  0.070                   .* :  .
 44  0.029  0.070                   .  :* .
 45 -0.037  0.069                   . *:  .
 46 -0.042  0.069                   . *:  .
 47  0.108  0.069                   .  : *.
 48 -0.050  0.068                   . *:  .
 49  0.105  0.068                   .  : *.
```

Note that if you use the THRU keyword on any of the parameter subcommands and request ESTIMATE or FORECAST, you will use a great deal of computer time estimating or forecasting the several models and will produce volumes of output. If you specify only IDENTIFY, you will obtain initial parameter estimates for nonseasonal parameters, along with the usual identification output.

You can specify single or multiple nonsequential parameters by using the following subcommands:

ARLAG *Autoregressive parameters to fit.*
MALAG *Moving average parameters to fit.*

For each subcommand, specify the numbers corresponding to the order or lag that you want fit. Thus, Q=3 and MALAG=1,2,3 are equivalent specifications; SQ=1/PERIOD=12 and MALAG=12 are equivalent; but Q=3 and MALAG=1,3 specify different models. The latter specification fits no moving average parameter at lag 2, whereas the former does.

The MALAG and ARLAG specifications are alternatives to the Q and P subcommands, respectively. The difference is that MALAG and ARLAG specify single or nonsequential parameters and facilitate fitting more generalized models than those specified by the Q and P subcommands. However, the program will accept both P and ARLAG or Q and MALAG subcommands in the same run. If both P and ARLAG are specified, the same number of autoregressive terms as specified by the P subcommand must be given in the ARLAG list. Similarly, the MALAG list must contain the same number of terms as specified in the Q subcommand.

38.13 Estimation Subcommands

You can control several aspects of the estimation step in BOX-JENKINS. Subcommands specify whether a constant term is to be fit or whether the values are to be centered around their mean before estimation is done. Other subcommands control the number of iterations and the number of backforecasts used for the parameter estimation, the perturbation increments and convergence tolerances for each parameter estimated, and a check against invertibility conditions. You can also enter the initial estimates of the parameters derived from the identification of the model in a previous BOX-JENKINS run. All of these subcommands can be used only with the ESTIMATE keyword.

38.14 Keywords CONSTANT and NCONSTANT

By default, BOX-JENKINS fits a constant during the estimation step. In general, when differencing is used, the level of the series will be approximately zero and the constant can be constrained to equal zero. Use the keyword NCONSTANT to indicate that no constant term is to be fit, as in:

```
BOX-JENKINS  VARIABLE=AIRLINE/LOG/DIFFERENCE=1/PERIOD=12/
   SDIFFERENCE=1/LAG=49/Q=1/SQ=1/NCONSTANT/ESTIMATE
```

To explicitly request the default, estimation of a constant term, specify the CONSTANT keyword.

38.15 Keywords CENTER and NCENTER

The keyword CENTER is used to center values around their mean before estimation is done, as in:

```
BOX-JENKINS  VARIABLE=AIRLINE/LOG/DIFFERENCE=1/PERIOD=12/
   SDIFFERENCE=1/LAG=49/Q=1/SQ=1/NCONSTANT/CENTER/ESTIMATE
```

Ordinarily, if CENTER is chosen, the implication is that you do not wish to search on the overall constant during final parameter estimation. The default is NCENTER.

38.16 The ITERATE Subcommand

The estimation routine is an iterative search algorithm. The ITERATE subcommand indicates the maximum number of iterations for use by the estimation routine in parameter estimation. The default number of iterations is 40. The following command requests 100 iterations:

```
BOX-JENKINS  VARIABLE=AIRLINE/LOG/DIFFERENCE=1/PERIOD=12/
   SDIFFERENCE=1/LAG=49/Q=1/SQ=1/NCONSTANT/ITERATE=100/ESTIMATE
```

It is unlikely that 100 iterations will be required before convergence. The default of 40 iterations will usually be enough for convergence. Failure to converge may indicate model misspecification, and you will need to investigate this possibility. In general, if you want to avoid failure to converge, specify a relatively large number of iterations; if you want to avoid a lot of costly iterations for what may be a misspecified model, then accept the default or specify a number smaller than 40. You can also specify the convergence tolerences for the parameters (see Section 38.21).

38.17 The BFR Subcommand

The BFR subcommand specifies the number of backforecasts to be generated for use in the estimation step. The default number is 0. For example, the following command requests 13 backforecasts to be used in estimation:

```
BOX-JENKINS  VARIABLE=AIRLINE/LOG/DIFFERENCE=1/PERIOD=12/
   SDIFFERENCE=1/LAG=49/Q=1/SQ=1/NCONSTANT/ITERATE=100/BFR=13/
   ESTIMATE
```

In general, a nonzero backforecast specification will be slightly more expensive than zero backforecasts, but it will often lead to a final model with a smaller residual variance. There is no program limit on the maximum number of backforecasts that can be specified.

38.18 Keywords TEST and NTEST

Box and Jenkins (1976) discuss a set of simultaneous inequalities that constitute invertibility conditions for models with up to three moving average parameters. The keyword TEST instructs BOX-JENKINS to check the estimated parameters at each iteration against these invertibility conditions. The default is NTEST.

38.19 The FPR Subcommand

The FPR subcommand specifies the interval of iterations for printing current estimated values from iterative estimation. The default is 5, which implies that you will get printed results at every fifth iteration. The following command prints estimated values after every tenth iteration:

```
BOX-JENKINS  VARIABLE=AIRLINE/LOG/DIFFERENCE=1/PERIOD=12/
   SDIFFERENCE=1/LAG=49/Q=1/SQ=1/NCONSTANT/ITERATE=100/BFR=13/
   FPR=10/ESTIMATE
```

38.20 Perturbation Increment Subcommands

You can use the following subcommands to specify perturbation increments that are used by the estimation routine in final parameter estimation:

PCON=(number) *Perturbation increment for the constant term.*

PP=(number,...,number) *Perturbation increments for autoregressive parameters.*

PQ=(number,...,number) *Perturbation increments for moving average parameters.*

PSP=(number,...,number) *Perturbation increments for seasonal autoregressive parameters.*

PSQ=(number,...,number) *Perturbation increments for seasonal moving average parameters.*

These subcommands must have matching P, Q (or ARLAG, MALAG), SP, and SQ subcommands. If you specify NCONSTANT, you cannot specify the PCON subcommand. You cannot use these subcommands if you have used the THRU keyword to specify a range of models on the matching P, Q (or ARLAG, MALAG), SP, or SQ subcommands. If you do not specify the perturbation increment, BOX-JENKINS will use the default value of 0.1.

If you do not want to search on a particular parameter because it has some known a priori value, declare its value using the relevant initial estimates subcommand (Section 38.22) and set its perturbation increment to zero.

ANNOTATED EXAMPLE FOR BOX-JENKINS

The example illustrating BOX-JENKINS analyzes the Series G time series from Box and Jenkins (1976). This series consists of monthly totals, in thousands, of international airline passengers from January 1949 to December 1960.

Identifying the Model

The first BOX-JENKINS job requests a plot of the series.

```
FILE HANDLE SERIESG/ file specifications
DATA LIST FILE=SERIESG/AIRLINE 5-7
BOX-JENKINS  VARIABLE=AIRLINE/PLOT=SERIES/IDENTIFY
```

- The FILE HANDLE command defines the file containing the Series G data, and the DATA LIST defines the variable AIRLINE containing the total number of airline passengers (see Chapter 3).
- The BOX-JENKINS command requests the IDENTIFY step of analysis on AIRLINE and the PLOT subcommand requests a plot of the series. By default, the autocorrelation function plot and summary statistics for the series are printed when IDENTIFY is specified. The autocorrelation function plot is shown in Figure 38.4 and the series plot in Figure 38.5.

  The series plot shows that the series is both nonstationary and heteroscedastic. Nonstationarity of the series is also suggested by the autocorrelation function since the early autocorrelations remain large rather than dying out quickly. A periodicity of 12 is suggested by the autocorrelation of 0.760 at the 12th lag, which is larger than the neighboring lags.

The second BOX-JENKINS job log-transforms the series to correct for the heteroscedasticity and tries several degrees of nonseasonal and seasonal differencing to achieve a stationary series.

```
FILE HANDLE SERIESG/ file specifications
DATA LIST FILE=SERIESG/AIRLINE 5-7
BOX-JENKINS  VARIABLE=AIRLINE/LOG/DIFFERENCE=0 THRU 2/PERIOD=12/
   SDIFFERENCE=0 THRU 2/LAG=49/PLOT=DSE,PAC/IDENTIFY
```

- The LOG subcommand requests log-transformation of the series (see Section 38.7).
- The DIFFERENCE subcommand requests zero, one, and two degrees of differencing (see Section 38.9).
- The SDIFFERENCE subcommand and the PERIOD subcommands request annual differencing of the series since the series is measured monthly (see Section 38.10).
- The LAG subcommand requests that 49 lags be calculated for the autocorrelation and partial autocorrelation functions (see Section 38.11).
- The PLOT subcommand requests plots of the differenced series and partial autocorrelation function plots for each of the combinations of differencing (see Section 38.29).

  Nine separate autocorrelation function plots also are printed for each combination of differencing. The smallest standard deviation is for the series with one degree of seasonal differencing and one degree of nonseasonal differencing. Figure 38.11 shows this autocorrelation function plot. By comparison, other combinations of differencing are not as good. The plot of the series differenced at one degree seasonal and nonseasonal is shown in Figure A. This plot shows that stationarity has been obtained. The autocorrelation and partial autocorrelation function plots (Figure 38.11 and Figure B) suggest fitting a model with one moving average parameter and one seasonal moving average parameter.

A Differenced series plot

```
GRAPHIC DISPLAY OF DIFFERENCED SERIES FOR VARIABLE Y
DEGREE OF NONSEASONAL DIFFERENCING -  1 DEGREE OF  SEASONAL DIFFERENCING  1
DATA - *
MEAN - .

 OBS     DATA                -0.15     -0.05      0.05      0.15      0.25
                     :---------:---------:---------:---------:---------:
    1  0.391645E-01  :                        .   *
    2  0.360489E-03  :                        *
    3 -0.204954E-01  :                      * .
    4 -0.129395E-01  :                       *.
    5  0.661488E-01  :                        .      *
    6  0.399141E-01  :                        .   *
    7  0.0           :                        *
    8  0.113535E-01  :                        .*
    9 -0.387144E-01  :                    *   .
   10 -0.194168E-01  -                      * .
   11  0.791492E-01  :                        .       *
   12  0.608444E-01  :                        .     *
   13 -0.574493E-01  :                  *     .
   14  0.586710E-01  :                        .     *
   15 -0.445480E-01  :                    *   .
   16  0.130706      :                        .            *
   17 -0.141345      :          *             .
   18 -0.203295E-01  :                      * .
   19  0.0           :                        *
   20 -0.516605E-02  -                       *.
   21  0.449066E-01  :                        .   *
   22  0.501604E-01  :                        .    *
   23 -0.770626E-01  :                *       .
   24 -0.541496E-02  :                       *.


  120 -0.368214E-01  -                    *   .
  121 -0.130854E-01  :                       *.
  122 -0.102379      :              *         .
  123  0.120465      :                        .           *
  124 -0.352592E-01  :                    *   .
  125  0.856400E-02  :                        .*
  126  0.137711E-02  :                        *
  127 -0.459347E-01  :                   *    .
  128  0.120239E-01  :                        .*
  129  0.318298E-01  :                        .  *
  130 -0.500813E-01  -                   *    .
  131 -0.996399E-02  :                       *.

MEAN VALUE OF THE PROCESS
 0.29089E-03

STANDARD DEVIATION OF THE PROCESS
 0.45673E-01
```

B Partial autocorrelation function plot

```
PARTIAL AUTOCORRELATIONS *
TWO STANDARD ERROR LIMITS .

    PR-AUT STAND.
LAG  CORR.   ERR. -1  -.75  -.5 -.25   0   .25  .5   .75   1
                   :----:----:----:----:----:----:----:----:
  1 -0.341  0.087               *   .  :  .
  2 -0.013  0.087                   .  *  .
  3 -0.193  0.087                  *.  :  .
  4 -0.125  0.087                   *  :  .
  5  0.033  0.087                   .  :* .
  6  0.035  0.087                   .  :* .
  7 -0.060  0.087                   . *:  .
  8 -0.020  0.087                   .  *  .
  9  0.226  0.087                   .  :  . *
 10  0.043  0.087                   .  :* .
 11  0.047  0.087                   .  :* .
 12 -0.339  0.087               *   .  :  .
 13 -0.109  0.087                   .* :  .
 14 -0.077  0.087                   .* :  .
 15 -0.022  0.087                   .  *  .
 16 -0.140  0.087                   *  :  .
 17  0.026  0.087                   .  :* .
 18  0.115  0.087                   .  : *.
 19 -0.013  0.087                   .  *  .
 20 -0.167  0.087                   *  :  .
 21  0.132  0.087                   .  :  *
 22 -0.072  0.087                   . *:  .
 23  0.143  0.087                   .  :  *
```

Estimating the Model

The model is estimated with the following BOX-JENKINS command:

```
BOX-JENKINS    VARIABLE=Y/LOG/DIFFERENCE=1/SDIFFERENCE=1/
               PERIOD=12/LAG=49/Q=1/SQ=1/NCONSTANT/
               BFR=13/PLOT=RAC,RES/ESTIMATE
```

- The LOG subcommand requests a log-transformation of the series. The DIFFERENCE subcommand requests one degree of nonseasonal differencing, and the SDIFFERENCE and PERIOD subcommands request one degree of seasonal differencing at period 12. The LAG subcommand requests that 49 lags be calculated for the functions.
- The Q and SQ subcommands specify the parameters to be fit; one nonseasonal moving average parameter and one seasonal moving average parameter (see Section 38.12).
- The NCONSTANT keyword indicates that no constant term is to be fit (see Section 38.14).
- The BFR subcommand requests that 13 backforecasts be used in estimation (see Section 38.17).
- The PLOT subcommand requests a plot of the residual series values and a plot of the residual autocorrelation function (see Section 38.29). If the specified model is a good fit, the residual series should be white noise (random) and therefore uncorrelated for all lags. Except for sampling variation, values of the autocorrelations of the residual should not be statistically different from zero. The residual autocorrelation function plot is shown in Figure C.
- The ESTIMATE keyword requests estimation of the model.

The intermediate iteration results include the "Function value" which is the sum of squares function, described in Box and Jenkins (1976). For Series G, convergence criteria are met after 19 iterations. Final estimation results are shown in Figure D. The results include

- Estimated final parameter values and their standard errors.
- Residual variance, equal to the mean squared error.
- Variance-covariance matrix of estimated parameters.
- Correlation matrix of estimated parameters. High correlations may indicate model inadequacies such as over-parameterization or insufficient differencing.
- Mean, standard deviation, and variance of the residual series; chi-square statistic associated with the residual autocorrelation function.

C Residual autocorrelation function plot

```
RESIDUAL AUTOCORRELATION FUNCTION FOR VARIABLE Y
AUTOCORRELATIONS *
TWO STANDARD ERROR LIMITS .

     AUTO. STAND.
LAG  CORR.   ERR.            -1  -.75  -.5 -.25   0   .25  .5   .75   1
                              :----:----:----:----:----:----:----:----:
  1  0.017  0.086                              .  *  .
  2  0.019  0.085                              .  *  .
  3 -0.126  0.085                              *  :  .
  4 -0.142  0.085                              *  :  .
  5  0.050  0.084                              .  :* .
  6  0.062  0.084                              .  :* .
  7 -0.073  0.084                              . *:  .
  8 -0.038  0.083                              . *:  .
  9  0.103  0.083                              .  : *.
 10 -0.078  0.083                              .* :  .
 11  0.025  0.082                              .  *  .
 12 -0.010  0.082                              .  *  .
 13  0.032  0.082                              .  :* .
 14  0.043  0.081                              .  :* .
 15  0.048  0.081                              .  :* .
 16 -0.156  0.081                              *  :  .
 17  0.025  0.080                              .  *  .
 18 -0.001  0.080                              .  *  .
 19 -0.106  0.079                              .* :  .
 20 -0.102  0.079                              .* :  .
 21 -0.032  0.079                              . *:  .
 22 -0.027  0.078                              . *:  .
 23  0.220  0.078                              .  :  .*
 24  0.032  0.078                              .  :* .
```

D Final estimated values

```
NONLINEAR ESTIMATION RESULTS

PAR  LAG    ESTIMATE    STD ERROR     T RATIO

 MA    1  0.39531       0.80474E-01    4.9123
SMA   12  0.61406       0.69522E-01    8.8327

VARIANCE OF RESIDUALS   0.13423E-02

COVARIANCE MATRIX OF THE ESTIMATES

PAR  LAG
 MA    1  0.64760E-02 -0.32702E-03
SMA   12 -0.32702E-03  0.48333E-02

CORRELATION MATRIX OF THE ESTIMATES

PAR  LAG
 MA    1  1.00000 -0.05845
SMA   12 -0.05845  1.00000

MEAN VALUE OF RESIDUAL SERIES
 0.34489E-03

STANDARD DEVIATION OF RESIDUAL SERIES
 0.36227E-01

VARIANCE OF RESIDUAL SERIES
  0.13124E-02

DIAGNOSTIC CHI-SQUARE STATISTICS FOR RESIDUAL SERIES  1

LAG  CHI-SQ.  D.F.  PROB.
  6     5.90    4   0.2064
 12     9.36   10   0.4984
 18    13.92   16   0.6050
 24    25.52   22   0.2727
 30    28.74   28   0.4260
 36    35.63   34   0.3916
 42    41.39   40   0.4099
 48    44.33   46   0.5424
 49    48.64   47   0.4067
```

Forecasting the Model

BOX-JENKINS can now be used to forecast the series.

```
BOX-JENKINS       VARIABLE=Y/LOG/DIFFERENCE=1/SDIFFERENCE=1/PERIOD=12/
                  Q=1/SQ=1/FQ=(.39531)/FSQ=(.61406)/
                  ORIGIN=-24/PLOT=FCF,FLF,CIN/FORECAST
```

- The command syntax through the SQ subcommand is the same as used for the estimation step.
- The FQ and FSQ subcommands input the final values for the nonseasonal and seasonal moving average parameters that were obtained in the ESTIMATE job shown in Figure D (see Section 38.27).
- The ORIGIN subcommand requests that the forecast origin be the observation in the data 24 back from the last series observation (see Section 38.24).
- The PLOT subcommand requests a plot of the forecast function, fixed lead forecasts, and associated confidence intervals.
- The FORECAST keyword requests the forecast step of analysis.

BOX-JENKINS first prints the parameter estimates that it is using. The augmented autoregressive matrix contains information on both differencing and autoregressive parameters, if any, used in the model. In our example, the augmented autoregressive matrix contains information solely on differencing. The forecast error summary table gives the forecast variance and forecast standard error for increasing leads, as well as the impulse response function, which corresponds to Box and Jenkins' psi weights.

The forecast function is summarized in a table that can be read: (1) horizontally, to compare forecasts from past observations with a given series observation; (2) diagonally, to obtain increasing lead forecasts from a given origin; and (3) vertically, to obtain fixed lead forecasts from consecutive observations. The table of forecast functions is displayed in Figure E.

E Summary table of forecast functions

FORECASTS AT INCREASING LEAD FOR VARIABLE Y
STARTING ORIGIN AT 120

LEAD OBS	TIME DATA	1	2	3	4	5	6	7	8	9	10	11	12
120	337.000												
121	360.000	350.025											
122	342.000	340.275	334.543										
123	406.000	394.962	393.756	387.123									
124	396.000	390.939	384.477	383.304	376.846								
125	420.000	403.543	400.416	393.798	392.596	385.982							
126	472.000	486.893	475.265	471.583	463.788	462.373	454.583						
127	548.000	534.437	544.571	531.566	527.448	518.729	517.146	508.434					
128	559.000	545.396	537.193	547.380	534.308	530.168	521.405	519.813	511.056				
129	463.000	468.815	461.883	454.936	463.563	452.493	448.987	441.565	440.218	432.801			
130	407.000	407.755	410.844	404.769	398.681	406.241	396.539	393.467	386.963	385.782	379.283		
131	362.000	355.442	355.840	358.536	353.234	347.922	354.519	346.053	343.372	337.696	336.665	330.994	
132	405.000	399.073	394.686	395.128	398.122	392.235	386.335	393.661	384.260	381.283	374.981	373.836	367.538
133	417.000	418.444	414.730	410.171	410.631	413.741	407.624	401.493	409.106	399.336	396.242	389.693	388.503
134	391.000	398.169	399.002	395.461	391.114	391.552	394.518	388.685	382.839	390.098	380.782	377.832	371.587
135	419.000	460.233	465.317	466.291	462.153	457.072	457.585	461.051	454.234	447.402	455.886	444.999	441.551
136	461.000	423.617	448.356	453.309	454.258	450.226	445.277	445.776	449.153	442.511	435.856	444.121	433.515
137	472.000	462.841	439.768	465.450	470.593	471.577	467.392	462.254	462.772	466.278	459.383	452.474	461.054
138	535.000	541.713	535.332	508.645	538.350	544.297	545.436	540.596	534.652	535.252	539.307	531.332	523.341
139	622.000	610.063	614.680	607.440	577.158	610.864	617.613	618.905	613.413	606.668	607.349	611.950	602.901
140	606.000	623.974	616.705	621.372	614.053	583.442	617.515	624.337	625.643	620.091	613.274	613.961	618.613
141	508.000	514.737	523.916	517.813	521.732	515.586	489.884	518.493	524.221	525.318	520.656	514.932	515.509
142	461.000	448.040	451.624	459.677	454.322	457.760	452.369	429.818	454.919	459.945	460.907	456.817	451.795
143	390.000	400.727	393.877	397.027	404.107	399.399	402.422	397.682	377.857	399.924	404.342	405.188	401.592
144	432.000	439.001	446.263	438.635	442.143	450.027	444.785	448.151	442.872	420.794	445.369	450.289	451.231
145		450.195	454.592	462.113	454.213	457.846	466.010	460.582	464.067	458.601	435.739	461.186	466.281
146			426.503	430.669	437.794	430.310	433.752	441.486	436.343	439.646	434.467	412.808	436.916
147				482.031	486.740	494.792	486.334	490.224	498.965	493.153	496.885	491.032	466.554
148					492.168	496.976	505.198	496.562	500.533	509.458	503.524	507.334	501.359
149						508.212	513.176	521.666	512.748	516.850	526.066	519.938	523.873
150							583.240	588.938	598.681	588.447	593.153	603.730	596.697
151								668.039	674.565	685.724	674.002	679.393	691.508
152									665.766	672.269	683.391	671.708	677.082
153										558.657	564.114	573.446	563.644
154											496.579	501.430	509.725
155												430.125	434.326
156													478.014

The final printed table consists of forecasted values from the end of the series along with 95% confidence limits for the forecasts. Unlike some other forecast routines, SPSS[X] BOX-JENKINS, when possible, prints forecasts in the original scale of the series instead of in transformed units because internal transformation was used. The plot of the forecast function shows

- Series values (data).
- One-step-ahead forecasts for series values along with confidence bounds on the forecast values.
- Forecasts from the end of the series along with their confidence bounds.

The table of forecasted values and the plot of forecasts for Series G is shown in Figure F.

F Forecasted values and plot

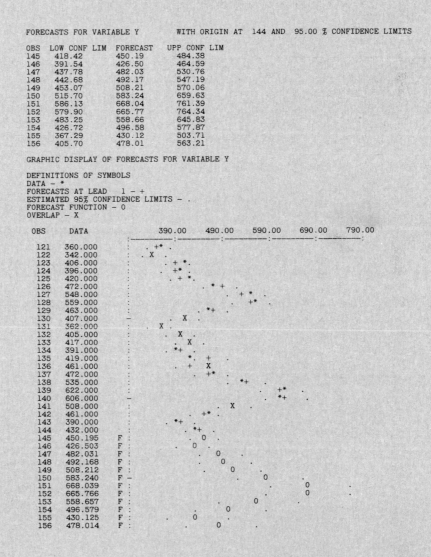

FORECASTS FOR VARIABLE Y WITH ORIGIN AT 144 AND 95.00 % CONFIDENCE LIMITS

OBS	LOW CONF LIM	FORECAST	UPP CONF LIM
145	418.42	450.19	484.38
146	391.54	426.50	464.59
147	437.78	482.03	530.76
148	442.68	492.17	547.19
149	453.07	508.21	570.06
150	515.70	583.24	659.63
151	586.13	668.04	761.39
152	579.90	665.77	764.34
153	483.25	558.66	645.83
154	426.72	496.58	577.87
155	367.29	430.12	503.71
156	405.70	478.01	563.21

GRAPHIC DISPLAY OF FORECASTS FOR VARIABLE Y

DEFINITIONS OF SYMBOLS
DATA - *
FORECASTS AT LEAD 1 - +
ESTIMATED 95% CONFIDENCE LIMITS - .
FORECAST FUNCTION - 0
OVERLAP - X

```
 OBS    DATA              390.00    490.00    590.00    690.00    790.00
                    :---------:---------:---------:---------:---------:
 121   360.000      :    . +* .
 122   342.000      :  . X  .
 123   406.000      :        . + *.
 124   396.000      :       .  +* .
 125   420.000      :         . + *.
 126   472.000      :                . * +   .
 127   548.000      :                      . + *  .
 128   559.000      :                       .  +*   .
 129   463.000      :               . *+   .
 130   407.000      -        .  X  .
 131   362.000      :    . X .
 132   405.000      :       .  X  .
 133   417.000      :         .  X  .
 134   391.000      :       . *+  .
 135   419.000      :             *.  +    .
 136   461.000      :          .  +   X
 137   472.000      :                .  +*
 138   535.000      :                     .  *+    .
 139   622.000      :                            .   +*    .
 140   606.000      -                             .  *+    .
 141   508.000      :                   .   X    .
 142   461.000      :              .  +* .
 143   390.000      :       . *+  .
 144   432.000      :           . *+   .
 145   450.195   F  :             .  0   .
 146   426.503   F  :          .  0   .
 147   482.031   F  :              .    0    .
 148   492.168   F  :              .    0     .
 149   508.212   F  :               .     0     .
 150   583.240   F  -                      .     0       .
 151   668.039   F  :                            .        0       .
 152   665.766   F  :                            .        0       .
 153   558.657   F  :                   .        0       .
 154   496.579   F  :            .       0       .
 155   430.125   F  :       .      0      .
 156   478.014   F  :            .        0       .
```

38.21 Tolerance Subcommands

You can use the following subcommands to specify the convergence tolerances used by the search algorithm when estimating parameters:

TCON=(number) *Convergence tolerance for the constant term.*

TP=(number,...,number) *Convergence tolerances for autoregressive parameters.*

TQ=(number,...,number) *Convergence tolerances for moving average parameters.*

TSP=(number,...,number) *Convergence tolerances for seasonal autoregressive parameters.*

TSQ=(number,...,number) *Convergence tolerances for seasonal moving average parameters.*

These subcommands must have matching P, Q (or ARLAG, MALAG), SP, and SQ subcommands. If you specify NCONSTANT, you cannot specify the TCON subcommand. You cannot use these subcommands if you have used the THRU keyword to specify a range of models on the matching P, Q (or ARLAG, MALAG), SP, or SQ subcommands.

Default convergence tolerances are equal to 0.001. This means that when estimated parameters in two consecutive iterations differ by no more than 0.001, the search algorithm will stop.

38.22 Initial Estimates Subcommands

You can use the following subcommands to set initial parameter estimates for the estimation step of BOX-JENKINS:

ICON=(number) *Initial estimate for the constant term.*

IP=(number,...,number) *Initial estimates for autoregressive parameters.*

IQ=(number,...,number) *Initial estimates for moving average parameters.*

ISP=(number,...,number) *Initial estimates for seasonal autoregressive parameters.*

ISQ=(number,...,number) *Initial estimates for seasonal moving average parameters.*

You can use the initial estimates from a previous BOX-JENKINS IDENTIFY run or from any other source. These subcommands must have matching P, Q (or ARLAG, MALAG), SP, and SQ subcommands. If you specify NCONSTANT, you cannot specify the ICON subcommand. You cannot use these subcommands if you have used the THRU keyword to specify a range of models on the matching P, Q (or ARLAG, MALAG), SP, or SQ subcommands. By default, the initial values are set to zero for all parameters unless both the IDENTIFY and ESTIMATE keywords are specified.

38.23 Forecast Subcommands

By default, the forecast step of BOX-JENKINS analysis prints a table of forecast values. The forecast origin is the last case in the file, and values are forecast for 12 leads. You can use the ORIGIN subcommand to specify the series values to be used as forecast origins (Section 38.24) and the LEAD subcommand to specify the highest lead desired (Section 38.25). You can also use the CIN subcommand to specify the confidence level that you want used for the forecasted values (Section 38.26) and the final parameter estimate subcommands to set the final estimates derived from a previous BOX-JENKINS ESTIMATE run (Section 38.27).

38.24 The ORIGIN Subcommand

Use the ORIGIN subcommand to specify the series values to be used as forecast origins. You can specify a single positive or negative number. A positive number begins counting from the first series value; a negative number counts back from the end of the series. For example, the following command uses the last 24 series values as the forecast origins:

```
BOX-JENKINS  VARIABLE=AIRLINE/LOG/DIFFERENCE=1/PERIOD=12/
   SDIFFERENCE=1/Q=1/SQ=1/
   ORIGIN=-24/FORECAST
```

You can use the keyword THRU to specify a range of series values. You can specify two positive numbers that correspond to sequential case numbers, as in

```
ORIGIN=130 THRU 144
```

which specifies the 130th through the 144th cases as forecast origins. You can use negative numbers to count back from the end of the series, as in

```
ORIGIN=-24 THRU -12
```

which uses the 24th case from the end of the series through the 12th case from the end of the series as the forecast origins. The default forecast origin is the last case in the file.

38.25 The LEAD Subcommand

Use the LEAD subcommand to specify the highest lead for the forecasted values. The default lead is 12. The following command requests forecasts for 24 leads:

```
BOX-JENKINS  VARIABLE=AIRLINE/LOG/DIFFERENCE=1/PERIOD=12/
   SDIFFERENCE=1/Q=1/SQ=1/
   ORIGIN=-24/LEAD=24/FORECAST
```

38.26 The CIN Subcommand

The CIN subcommand specifies the forecast confidence level expressed as a percentage. The default level is 95. The following command requests a 99% confidence interval for the forecasts:

```
BOX-JENKINS  VARIABLE=AIRLINE/LOG/DIFFERENCE=1/PERIOD=12/
   SDIFFERENCE=1/Q=1/SQ=1/
   ORIGIN=-24/CIN=99/FORECAST
```

38.27 Final Estimates Subcommands

Use the following subcommands to input final parameter estimates into the forecast step of BOX-JENKINS.

FCON=(number) *Final estimate for the constant term.*

FP=(number,...,number) *Final estimates for autoregressive parameters.*

FQ=(number,...,number) *Final estimates for moving average parameters.*

FSP=(number,...,number) *Final estimates for seasonal autoregressive parameters.*

FSQ=(number,...,number) *Final estimates for seasonal moving average parameters.*

You can use the final estimates from a previous BOX-JENKINS ESTIMATE run or from any other source. For example, the following command uses the final estimates shown in Figure D in the annotated example:

```
BOX-JENKINS  VARIABLE=AIRLINE/LOG/DIFFERENCE=1/PERIOD=12/
   SDIFFERENCE=1/Q=1/SQ=1/FQ=(.39531)/FSQ=(.61406)/
   ORIGIN=-24/FORECAST
```

These subcommands must have matching P, Q (or ARLAG, MALAG), SP, and SQ subcommands. If you specify NCONSTANT, you cannot specify the

FCON subcommand. You cannot use these subcommands if you have used the THRU keyword to specify a range of models on the matching P, Q (or ARLAG, MALAG), SP, or SQ subcommands.

38.28 The PRINT Subcommand

Use the PRINT subcommand to print the values of various functions and series. Table 38.28 shows the keywords available with the PRINT subcommand and the step of analysis when each can be used.

Table 38.28 Keywords for PRINT subcommand

Keyword	Display	Stage
ACF	Autocorrelation function	IDENTIFY
PACF	Partial autocorrelation function	IDENTIFY
ACVF	Autocovariance function	IDENTIFY
SER	Time series	IDENTIFY
TSER	Log- or power-transformed series	IDENTIFY
DSER	Differenced series	IDENTIFY
RESID	Values of the residual series	ESTIMATE
RACF	Residual autocorrelation function	ESTIMATE

By default, the FORECAST step prints forecast results. Thus, no keywords for FORECAST are available on the PRINT subcommand.

38.29 The PLOT Subcommand

The PLOT subcommand requests plots of the values of various functions and series. You can specify all the keywords available on the PRINT subcommand except ACVF, the autocovariance function. If you use the PLOT subcommand, the PRINT subcommand is not necessary because printed values are either in the plot or contiguous to it. Three additional PLOT keywords can be used with the FORECAST keyword.

FCF *Forecast function.*
FLF *Fixed lead forecasts.*
CIN *Confidence intervals.*

If the forecast origin is other than the end of the series, then one-step-ahead forecasts are plotted for all series values starting with the forecast origin, and increasing lead forecasts are plotted from the end of the series. If the origin is not specified, one-step-ahead forecasts are plotted from the beginning of the series.

RELIABILITY VARIABLES = varlist

```
  [/FORMAT = {input } ([m] / [c])]
             {output}

  /SCALE (scalename) = varlist [/SCALE . . . ]

             {ALPHA          }
             {SPLIT [(n)]    }
  /MODEL =   {GUTTMAN        } [/VARIABLES . . . ]
             {PARALLEL       }
             {STRICTPARALLEL }
```

OPTIONS:

1 Include missing values.
3 Suppress variable labels.
4 Read a square covariance matrix.
5 Read vector of standard deviations followed by a square correlation matrix.
6 Read a triangular correlation or covariance matrix.
7 A vector of means precedes other matrix materials.
8 Write a triangular covariance matrix.
9 Index matrices using the dictionary.
10 Skip scale analyses.
11 Write means.
12 Read triangular matrix formatted as a vector.
13 Write triangular covariance matrix formatted as a vector.
14 Alternative solution method using covariance matrices.
15 Friedman's analysis of variance for ranks.
16 Cochran's *Q* analysis of variance for dichotomous data.
17 *N* of cases follows matrix.

STATISTICS:

1 Item means and standard deviations.
2 Inter-item variance-covariance matrix.
3 Inter-item correlations.
4 Scale mean, scale variance.
5 Summary statistics for item means.
6 Summary statistics for item variances.
7 Summary statistics for inter-item covariances.
8 Summary statistics for inter-item correlations.
9 Item-total statistics.
10 Analysis of variance table.
11 Tukey test for additivity.
12 Hotelling's T^2.

INTRODUCTION TO RELIABILITY MODELS, **39.1**
OVERVIEW, **39.2**
OPERATION, **39.3**
- The VARIABLES Subcommand, **39.4**
- The SCALE Subcommand, **39.5**
- The MODEL Subcommand, **39.6**
- Optional Statistics, **39.7**
- Analysis of Variance, **39.8**
  - Tests for the Violation of Assumptions, **39.9**
  - Friedman's Analysis of Variance for Ranked Data, **39.10**
  - Analysis of Variance of Dichotomous Data, **39.11**
- Matrix Materials, **39.12**
  - Matrix Input, **39.13**
  - Matrix Output, **39.14**
  - The FORMAT Subcommand, **39.15**
- Alternative Computing Methods, **39.16**
- Missing Values, **39.17**
- Suppressing Variable Labels, **39.18**

LIMITATIONS, **39.19**

Chapter 39 RELIABILITY

Procedure RELIABILITY performs an item analysis on the components of additive scales by computing commonly used coefficients of reliability. RELIABILITY also prints basic summary statistics including item means, standard deviations, inter-item covariance and correlation matrices, scale means, and item-to-item correlations. You can also use RELIABILITY to perform a repeated measures design analysis of variance, a two-way factorial analysis of variance with one observation per cell, Tukey's test for additivity, Hotelling's T^2 test for equality of means in repeated measures designs, and Friedman's two-way analysis of variance on ranks. For more complex repeated measures designs, see MANOVA (Chapter 28).

RELIABILITY accepts data in the form of cases, correlation matrices, or covariance matrices. It reads matrix materials in a variety of formats including lower-triangular matrices or matrices entered as a vector. In addition, it also writes matrix materials in a variety of formats.

39.1 INTRODUCTION TO RELIABILITY MODELS

Procedure RELIABILITY provides a number of reliability coefficients for multiple-item scales, using a number of different approaches to reliability definition and estimation. The choice of approach depends upon the assumptions. In general, the computations performed are designed for those situations where the goal is to assess the reliability of a sum or weighted sum across variables as an estimate of a case's true score.

RELIABILITY does not actually compute composite or scale scores. However, once you have analyzed a set of items, you can construct scores using the transformations available with SPSS^X (see Chapter 6).

Five different models are available in procedure RELIABILITY. (For a discussion of their use and the underlying assumptions, see Cronbach, 1951; Guttman, 1945; and Kristof, 1963.)

Alpha Model. The ALPHA model computes Cronbach's α and standardized item α (Cronbach, 1951). If the data are in dichotomous form, α is equivalent to reliability coefficient KR-20 (Kuder-Richardson-20). Coefficient α is the maximum likelihood estimate of the reliability coefficient if the parallel model is assumed to be true. If only two items are used, α is also equal to Guttman's split-half coefficient. This is the default model in procedure RELIABILITY.

Split Model. The SPLIT model partitions the variables in the scale into two subsets. The sum is computed for each subset and the reliability calculations make use of only the information contained in the two sums for each case. RELIABILITY calculates the correlation between the two sums, the Spearman-Brown split-half coefficient, the unequal length Spearman-Brown coefficient, and the Guttman split-half coefficient. In addition, it also calculates coefficient α for each part.

Guttman Model. The GUTTMAN model computes the six coefficients proposed by Guttman (1945).

Parallel Model. The PARALLEL model computes a correction for the bias of α using the correction proposed by Kristof (1963). In addition, RELIABILITY prints the estimated true score variance of an individual item, the estimated error variance of an individual item, and the reliability of an individual item.

Strictly Parallel Model. The STRICTPARALLEL model computes the same measures of reliability as for the parallel model with the additional assumptions that items have the same means, the same true score variances over a set of objects being measured, and the same error variance over replications (Kristof, 1963).

39.2 OVERVIEW

To use RELIABILITY you must specify a set of variables from which an intermediate matrix is computed, a scale which references variables in the matrix, and a particular model (if you do not want the default of ALPHA). You can specify multiple sets of variables, multiple scales, and multiple models.

VARIABLES Subcommand. The VARIABLES subcommand is required and is used to specify all variables from which one or more scales are evaluated. Use multiple VARIABLES subcommands to specify multiple intermediate matrices. (See Section 39.4.)

SCALE Subcommand. The SCALE subcommand is required and specifies the set of variables forming the scale. You can specify multiple SCALE subcommands. (See Section 39.5.)

MODEL Subcommand. The optional MODEL subcommand specifies the model being tested and defaults to ALPHA. (See Section 39.6.)

Descriptive Statistics. Optional item and scale statistics include item means and standard deviations, obtained with the associated STATISTICS command. (See Section 39.7.)

Analysis of Variance. Several analysis of variance models can be requested with the STATISTICS command. These include a repeated measures model with no between-subjects factors, a factorial design with one observation per cell, a two-way randomized block design, an analysis of variance upon ranks, and an analysis of variance upon dichotomous data. (See Section 39.8.)

Matrix Input and Output. Use the OPTIONS command to control the type of matrix materials (correlation or covariance), their format (rectangular, lower-left triangular, or single vector), and whether they are being read or written. The optional FORMAT subcommand specifies nondefault formats for reading and writing matrix materials. (See Section 39.12.)

Computational Methods. Two different solution methods for obtaining coefficients are available. RELIABILITY chooses the method depending upon the types of models and statistics you request. Since these solution methods differ in the way they handle items with zero variance, you can force the solution method requiring more space. (See Section 39.16.)

Missing Values. By default, RELIABILITY excludes cases with missing values listwise from the construction of the matrix. Optionally, you can request that missing values be handled as if they were valid. (See Section 39.17.)

39.3 OPERATION

The RELIABILITY procedure operates via subcommands, OPTIONS, and STATISTICS commands. There are four different subcommands. The VARIABLES and SCALE subcommands are required. Each subcommand begins with a subcommand keyword followed by an equals sign and subcommand specifications, and terminates with a slash.

39.4 The VARIABLES Subcommand

The VARIABLES subcommand specifies all the variables to be named on one or more SCALE subcommands. Each VARIABLES subcommand builds a triangular covariance matrix and vector of means. The SCALE subcommands which follow select submatrices from the larger matrix. The variable list on the VARIABLES subcommand follows the usual SPSS^X conventions for variable lists. For example,

```
RELIABILITY  VARIABLES=ITEM1 ITEM2 ITEM3 ITEM4 ITEM5/
   SCALE (TESTSCOR) = ITEM1 TO ITEM5
```

computes one matrix to be used for the scale referenced on the SCALE command. The keyword TO can be used to name a contiguous set of variables. Only numeric variables can be used, and cases with missing values are deleted from the computation of the matrix. A case missing from one or more variables named on the VARIABLES subcommand is not used in the computation of the intermediate matrix.

39.5 The SCALE Subcommand

The SCALE subcommand specifies the scale to be tested. The SCALE subcommand has an arbitrary scale name in parentheses followed by the set of variables composing the scale, as in:

```
RELIABILITY  VARIABLES=ITEM1 ITEM2 ITEM3 ITEM4 ITEM5/
   SCALE(RATING)=ITEM1 TO ITEM5/
```

The scale name identifies the particular analysis in the display. It can be a maximum of eight characters and must be composed of the letters A to Z and digits 0 to 9. All variables named on the SCALE subcommand must be named on the preceding VARIABLES subcommand. You can use the keyword TO on the SCALE subcommand only to imply a set of adjacent variables whose order is determined by the order in which they were named on the VARIABLES subcommand. You can also use the keyword ALL to reference all variables named on the VARIABLES subcommand.

The following example produces the default display shown in Figure 39.5:

```
TITLE  'WINER, PAGE 294'
DATA LIST  /ITEM1 TO ITEM5 1-10
RELIABILITY  VARIABLES=ITEM1 TO ITEM5/
   SCALE (TESTSCOR) = ITEM1 TO ITEM5
BEGIN DATA
 1 1 1 1 1
 1 1 1 1 0
 1 1 1 0 1
 1 1 0 1 0
 1 1 1 0 0
 1 1 0 0 1
 1 1 0 0 0
 0 1 1 0 0
 1 0 1 0 0
 1 0 0 0 0
END DATA
FINISH
```

With no other specifications, this display lists the variables in the scale and their associated labels (if defined) and prints the number of valid cases, number of items, and Cronbach's α.

Figure 39.5 RELIABILITY default display

```
* * * * * * * * R E L I A B I L I T Y   A N A L Y S I S   F O R   S C A L E   (T E S T S C O R ) * * * * * * * * *

          1.     ITEM1
          2.     ITEM2
          3.     ITEM3
          4.     ITEM4
          5.     ITEM5

 RELIABILITY COEFFICIENTS

N OF CASES =     10.0              N OF ITEMS =  5

ALPHA =  0.36822
```

You can specify several SCALE subcommands following one VARIABLES subcommand, as in

```
RELIABILITY  VARIABLES=ITEM1 TO ITEM10/
   SCALE(VERBAL)=ITEM1 ITEM3 ITEM5 ITEM7 ITEM9/
   SCALE(MATH)=ITEM2 ITEM4 ITEM6 ITEM8 ITEM10
```

which specifies two analyses using the matrix computed from the VARIABLES subcommand. If missing data are present, specifying the analyses in this manner can produce different results than using two VARIABLES subcommands. For example,

```
RELIABILITY  VARIABLES=ITEM1 ITEM3 ITEM5 ITEM7 ITEM9/
             SCALE(VERBAL)=ITEM1 TO ITEM9/
             VARIABLES=ITEM2 ITEM4 ITEM6 ITEM8 ITEM10/
             SCALE(MATH)=ITEM2 TO ITEM10
```

deletes missing values listwise on the first VARIABLES subcommand only for ITEM1, ITEM3, ITEM5, ITEM7, and ITEM9 (see Section 39.17). The covariance matrix is not affected by missing values on the other variables. The second VARIABLES subcommand creates a new matrix that uses only ITEM2, ITEM4, ITEM6, ITEM8, and ITEM10.

39.6 The MODEL Subcommand

By default, RELIABILITY uses model ALPHA which computes Cronbach's α and standardized item α. The MODEL subcommand specifies the type of reliability analysis and follows the SCALE subcommand to which it applies. Specify the keyword MODEL, an equals sign, and one of the keywords listed below. For example, the command

```
RELIABILITY  VARIABLES=ITEM1 ITEM2 ITEM3 ITEM4 ITEM5/
   SCALE(RATING)=ITEM1 TO ITEM5/
   MODEL=SPLIT
```

results in a split-half coefficient analysis. The following types of reliability analyses are available in procedure RELIABILITY:

ALPHA *Cronbach's α and standardized item α.* Standardized item α is not computed if solution method 1 (the default for ALPHA) is used. (See Section 39.16.)

SPLIT(n) *Split-half coefficients.* If you specify SPLIT with no specification for *n*, the items are split into the two halves by their order on the SCALE subcommand, with the first *n*/2 items named in the first part and the remaining items in the second. If the scale is composed of an odd number of variables, the first part contains the additional variable. For example, if the scale specifies five variables, the first part contains the first three named and the second part the remaining two variables.

If you want the variables to be split into unequal parts, specify the number of variables to be contained in the second part in parentheses following the keyword SPLIT. For example, MODEL=SPLIT(3) uses the last three variables named on the SCALE subcommand for the second part and uses all the other variables for the first part.

GUTTMAN *Guttman's lower bounds for true reliability.*

PARALLEL *Maximum likelihood reliability estimate under parallel assumptions.*

STRICTPARALLEL *Maximum likelihood reliability estimate under strictly parallel assumptions.*

The MODEL subcommand follows the SCALE subcommand and applies only to the immediately preceding SCALE subcommand. RELIABILITY uses the default of ALPHA if a SCALE subcommand is not followed by a MODEL subcommand.

39.7 Optional Statistics

RELIABILITY also computes descriptive statistics for variables forming the scale and summary statistics for the scale. Use the associated STATISTICS command to print these additional statistics:

STATISTIC 1 *Item means and standard deviations.*

STATISTIC 2 *Inter-item variance-covariance matrix.*

STATISTIC 3 *Inter-item correlations.*

STATISTIC 4 *Scale means and scale variances.*

STATISTIC 5 *Summary statistics for item means.* The average item mean over the number of items, the variance of the item means, the largest item mean, the smallest, the range of the item means, and the ratio of the largest to the smallest.

STATISTIC 6 *Summary statistics for item variances.* The display from this statistic is identical to Statistic 5 but is based upon item variances rather than item means.

STATISTIC 7 *Summary statistics for inter-item covariances.* The output from this statistic is identical to Statistics 5 and 6 but is based upon covariances.

STATISTIC 8 *Summary statistics for inter-item correlations.* The output from this statistic is identical to Statistics 5, 6, and 7 but is based upon correlations.

STATISTIC 9 *Item total statistics.* The display from this statistic includes five statistics dealing with the relationship between the individual items and the items as a set. For each item the following are calculated:

Scale mean if item deleted. This is the mean the scale scores would have if the particular item were deleted from the scale.

Scale variance if item deleted. This is the variance the scale scores would have if the particular item were deleted from the scale.

Corrected item total correlations. This is the correlation between that item's score and the scale scores computed from the other items in the set.

Squared multiple correlations. Each item is regressed upon the remaining items in the set making up the scale and the squared multiple correlation coefficient is computed. (This is not computed if Method 1 is used. See Section 39.16.)

Alpha if item deleted. For each item, Cronbach's α is computed from the other items in the scale.

Figure 39.7 is the display produced for item and scale statistics for the following example:

```
RELIABILITY  VARIABLES=ITEM1 TO ITEM5/
   SCALE(TESTSCOR) = ITEM1 TO ITEM5
STATISTICS  1 2 3 4 5 6 7 8 9
```

Figure 39.7 Scale and item statistics

```
* * * * * * * * * R E L I A B I L I T Y   A N A L Y S I S   F O R   S C A L E   (T E S T S C O R ) * * * * * * * * *
                    1.      ITEM1
                    2.      ITEM2
                    3.      ITEM3
                    4.      ITEM4
                    5.      ITEM5

                                           MEANS                    STD DEV                  CASES

                    1.      ITEM1           .90000                   .31623                   10.0
                    2.      ITEM2           .80000                   .42164                   10.0
                    3.      ITEM3           .60000                   .51640                   10.0
                    4.      ITEM4           .30000                   .48305                   10.0
                    5.      ITEM5           .30000                   .48305                   10.0

                 COVARIANCE MATRIX

            ITEM1       ITEM2       ITEM3       ITEM4       ITEM5

ITEM1         .1000

ITEM2       -.0222       .1778

ITEM3       -.0444       .0222       .2667

ITEM4        .0333       .0667       .0222       .2333

ITEM5        .0333       .0667       .0222       .0111       .2333

                 CORRELATION MATRIX

            ITEM1       ITEM2       ITEM3       ITEM4       ITEM5

ITEM1      1.00000

ITEM2      -.16667     1.00000

ITEM3      -.27217      .10206     1.00000

ITEM4       .21822      .32733      .08909     1.00000

ITEM5       .21822      .32733      .08909      .04762     1.00000

* * * * * * * * * R E L I A B I L I T Y   A N A L Y S I S   F O R   S C A L E   (T E S T S C O R ) * * * * * * * * *
      # OF CASES =        10.0

STATISTICS FOR            MEAN        VARIANCE      STD DEV    # VARIABLES
          SCALE          2.90000       1.43333      1.19722           5

      ITEM  MEANS         MEAN        MINIMUM       MAXIMUM         RANGE       MAX/MIN       VARIANCE
                          .58000       .30000        .90000         .60000      3.00000        .07700

      ITEM  VARIANCES     MEAN        MINIMUM       MAXIMUM         RANGE       MAX/MIN       VARIANCE
                          .20222       .10000        .26667         .16667      2.66667        .00428

  INTER-ITEM COVARIANCES  MEAN        MINIMUM       MAXIMUM         RANGE       MAX/MIN       VARIANCE
                          .02111      -.04444        .06667         .11111     -1.50000        .00113

  INTER-ITEM CORRELATIONS MEAN        MINIMUM       MAXIMUM         RANGE       MAX/MIN       VARIANCE
                          .09801      -.27217        .32733         .59949     -1.20268        .03620

ITEM-TOTAL STATISTICS           SCALE         SCALE       CORRECTED
                                 MEAN        VARIANCE       ITEM-        SQUARED          ALPHA
                                IF ITEM       IF ITEM       TOTAL        MULTIPLE         IF ITEM
                                DELETED       DELETED    CORRELATION    CORRELATION       DELETED

                     ITEM1      2.00000       1.33333       .00000        .29293           .42222
                     ITEM2      2.10000        .98889       .31800        .30921           .20974
                     ITEM3      2.30000       1.12222       .04062        .12500           .44884
                     ITEM4      2.60000        .93333       .28571        .23077           .22222
                     ITEM5      2.60000        .93333       .28571        .23077           .22222
```

39.8 Analysis of Variance

You can use procedure RELIABILITY to perform a single-factor repeated measures design analysis of variance, a two-way factorial design with one observation per cell, a complete randomized block design analysis of variance, and Friedman's analysis of variance on ranks. Table 39.8 gives the basic relationship between the organization of data within SPSS^X and the terminology usually used by statistical texts discussing these procedures. If your data are organized according to Table 39.8, Statistic 10 produces the analysis of variance table and labels it with repeated measures design terminology.

STATISTIC 10 *Analysis of variance table.*

Table 39.8 Data organization for analysis of variance

SPSS^X processing	Repeated measures	Two-way factorial	Randomized blocks
case(row)	person(object)	treatment A	block
variable(column)	measure(judge)	treatment B	treatment

The following commands produce an analysis of variance for a repeated measures design involving the effects of four successive drug treatments:

```
TITLE  'WINER, PAGE 268'
DATA LIST /DRUG1 TO DRUG4 1-12
RELIABILITY  VARIABLES=DRUG1 TO DRUG4/
   SCALE (REACTION) = DRUG1 TO DRUG4/
STATISTICS  10
BEGIN DATA
 30 28 16 34
 14 18 10 22
 24 20 18 30
 38 34 20 44
 26 28 14 30
END DATA
```

Figure 39.8 A repeated measures design

```
* * * * * * * * R E L I A B I L I T Y   A N A L Y S I S   F O R   S C A L E   (R E A C T I O N ) * * * * * * * * *

                  1.      DRUG1
                  2.      DRUG2
                  3.      DRUG3
                  4.      DRUG4

               ANALYSIS OF VARIANCE

SOURCE OF VARIATION                SS          DF      MEAN SQUARE          F          PROBABILITY

  BETWEEN PEOPLE                 680.80000      4       170.20000
   WITHIN  PEOPLE                811.00000     15        54.06667
     BETWEEN MEASURES            698.20000      3       232.73333       24.75887        0.00002
     RESIDUAL                    112.80000     12         9.40000
   TOTAL                        1491.80000     19        78.51579

  GRAND MEAN =          24.90000
    END OF JOB.
```

See Figure 39.8 for the output from these commands.

39.9 Tests for the Violation of Assumptions

RELIABILITY optionally provides a test for the violation of the assumption of additivity and a test for the equality of multivariate means.

Tukey's test for additivity is used to detect the presence of interaction effects. The underlying model for analysis of variance designs within RELIABILITY does not contain a term for interaction. Tukey's test provides a test to decide if a transformation is necessary to achieve additivity and suggests a suitable transformation. To obtain Tukey's test, specify Statistic 11 on the associated STATISTICS command.

Hotelling's T^2 tests the assumption of the equality of means for repeated measures designs involving more than two variables. To obtain Hotelling's T^2 test, specify Statistic 12 on the associated STATISTICS command. This statistic uses a great deal of extra computation time because it requires an inversion of the matrix of order $k-1$, where k is the number of variables in the scale.

STATISTIC 11 *Tukey test for additivity.*
STATISTIC 12 *Hotelling's* T^2.

The following commands produce an analysis of variance table, Tukey's test, and Hotelling's T^2 for a repeated measures design:

```
RELIABILITY  VARIABLES=DRUG1 TO DRUG4/
   SCALE(REACTION) = DRUG1 TO DRUG4
STATISTICS   10 11 12
```

The analysis of variance table appears in Figure 39.8. Figure 39.9 shows Tukey's test and Hotelling's T^2.

Figure 39.9 Tests for the violation of assumptions

```
TUKEY ESTIMATE OF POWER TO WHICH OBSERVATIONS MUST BE RAISED TO ACHIEVE ADDITIVITY =          -0.1691306

   HOTELLINGS T-SQUARED =           170.47385              F =           28.41231
     DEGREES OF FREEDOM * *   NUMERATOR =       3      DENOMINATOR=        2      PROBABILITY = 0.03419
```

39.10 Friedman's Analysis of Variance for Ranked Data

If you have a repeated measures design in which the data are already in the form of ranks, you can obtain Friedman's chi-square statistic for the analysis of variance rather than the usual F statistic, and Kendall's coefficient of concordance. To obtain the coefficient specify Option 15 on the associated OPTIONS command and Statistic 10. The data must be in the form of ranks. When data are entered in the form of ranks, the determinant of the covariance matrix is zero and many of the reliability coefficients are not computable.

OPTION 15 *Friedman's chi-square and Kendall's coefficient of concordance.* This option affects only Statistic 10 (the analysis of variance table). Data must be in the form of ranks. If both Options 15 and 16 are specified, Option 16 is used (see Section 39.11).

Figure 39.10 is an example of the use of Option 15 in conjunction with Statistic 10. The following commands produce this output:

```
TITLE 'WINER, PAGE 301'
DATA LIST   /METHOD1 TO METHOD4 1-8
RELIABILITY  VARIABLES = METHOD1 TO METHOD4/
   SCALE (RANKS) = ALL
STATISTICS  10
OPTIONS  15
BEGIN DATA
 3 2 1 4
 4 3 1 2
 2 4 1 3
 1 3 2 4
 2 3 1 4
 1 4 2 3
 2 3 1 4
 1 4 2 3
END DATA
```

Friedman's chi-square statistic and Kendall's coefficient are also available in procedure NPAR TESTS (see Chapter 37). NPAR TESTS does not require that the data be in the form of ranks, but the number of cases which can be analyzed is limited by the available workspace.

Figure 39.10 Analysis of variance on ranks

```
* * * * * * * * * R E L I A B I L I T Y   A N A L Y S I S   F O R   S C A L E   (R A N K S        ) * * * * * * * * *

               1.      METHOD1
               2.      METHOD2
               3.      METHOD3
               4.      METHOD4

     # OF CASES =         8.0

                    ANALYSIS OF VARIANCE

 SOURCE OF VARIATION              SS          DF      MEAN SQUARE      CHI-SQUARE      PROBABILITY

  BETWEEN PEOPLE                0.00000       7        0.00000
   WITHIN PEOPLE               40.00000      24        1.66667
    BETWEEN MEASURES             22.75000      3        7.58333        13.65000         0.00342
    RESIDUAL                     17.25000     21        0.82143
   TOTAL                       40.00000      31        1.29032

  GRAND MEAN =           2.50000

  COEFFICIENT OF CONCORDANCE W =     0.56875
```

39.11 Analysis of Variance of Dichotomous Data

If the data in an analysis of variance model are in the form of dichotomies (having only two possible values), RELIABILITY can be used to obtain Cochran's *Q*. Cochran's *Q* tests the hypothesis of no change in the proportion of sucessful outcomes over time. To obtain Cochran's *Q* in place of the usual *F* test, specify Option 16 on the associated OPTIONS command and Statistic 10.

OPTION 16 *Cochran's* Q.

Figure 39.11 is an example of analysis of variance of dichotomous data. The following commands produce this display:

```
TITLE  'WINER, Page 304'
DATA LIST  /TIME1 TO TIME5 1-10
RELIABILITY  VARIABLES=TIME1 TO TIME5/
   SCALE(OVERTIME)=ALL/
STATISTICS  10
OPTIONS  16
BEGIN DATA
 0 0 0 0 0
 0 0 1 1 0
 0 0 1 1 1
 0 1 1 1 1
 0 0 0 0 1
 0 1 0 1 1
 0 0 1 1 1
 1 0 0 1 1
 1 1 1 1 1
 1 1 1 1 1
END DATA
```

Figure 39.11 Analysis of variance on dichotomous data

```
* * * * * * * * * R E L I A B I L I T Y   A N A L Y S I S   F O R   S C A L E   (O V E R T I M E ) * * * * * * * * *

               1.      TIME1
               2.      TIME2
               3.      TIME3
               4.      TIME4
               5.      TIME5

                    ANALYSIS OF VARIANCE

 SOURCE OF VARIATION              SS          DF      MEAN SQUARE          Q            PROBABILITY

  BETWEEN PEOPLE                4.58000       9        0.50889
   WITHIN  PEOPLE                7.60000     40        0.19000
    BETWEEN MEASURES              2.08000      4        0.52000        10.94737         0.02716
    RESIDUAL                      5.52000     36        0.15333
   TOTAL                       12.18000      49        0.24857

  GRAND MEAN =           0.58000
```

ANNOTATED EXAMPLE FOR RELIABILITY

The following example demonstrates the use of RELIABILITY to analyze an attitude scale of confidence in institutions in the United States. The data come from a 500-case sample of the 1980 General Social Survey. Respondents were asked how much confidence they have in the people running the following instutions: banks and financial insitutions, major companies, organized religion, education, the executive branch of the federal government, organized labor, the press, medicine, television, the United States Supreme Court, the scientific community, Congress, and the military. The $SPSS^X$ commands are

```
FILE HANDLE  GSS80/ file specifications
GET  FILE=GSS80/KEEP CONFINAN TO CONARMY
RELIABILITY  VARIABLES=ALL/
   SCALE(CONFIND)= ALL/
   MODEL=STRICTPARALLEL
STATISTICS  9 10 11 12
FINISH
```

- The FILE HANDLE identifies the GSS80 data file and gives the operating-system specifications (see Chapter 3).
- The GET command defines the data to $SPSS^X$ and selects the variables needed for analysis (see Chapter 5).
- The RELIABILITY command analyzes the scale named CONFIND formed from the 13 confidence variables and uses the STRICTPARALLEL model (see Sections 39.4, 39.5, and 39.6).
- The STATISTICS command produces item-total statistics, the analysis of variance table, the Tukey test for additivity, and Hotelling's T^2 (see Sections 39.7, 39.8, and 39.9).

RELIABILITY display

* * * * * * * * * R E L I A B I L I T Y   A N A L Y S I S   F O R   S C A L E   (C O N F I N D   ) * * * * * * * * *

1.	CONFINAN	BANKS & FINANCIAL INSTITUTIONS
2.	CONBUS	MAJOR COMPANIES
3.	CONCLERG	ORGANIZED RELIGION
4.	CONEDUC	EDUCATION
5.	CONFED	EXECUTIVE BRANCH OF FEDERAL GOVERNMENT
6.	CONLABOR	ORGANIZED LABOR
7.	CONPRESS	PRESS
8.	CONMEDIC	MEDICINE
9.	CONTV	TELEVISION
10.	CONJUDGE	U.S. SUPREME COURT
11.	CONSCI	SCIENTIFIC COMMUNITY
12.	CONLEGIS	CONGRESS
13.	CONARMY	MILITARY

\# OF CASES = 415.0

ITEM-TOTAL STATISTICS

	SCALE MEAN IF ITEM DELETED	SCALE VARIANCE IF ITEM DELETED	CORRECTED ITEM-TOTAL CORRELATION	SQUARED MULTIPLE CORRELATION	ALPHA IF ITEM DELETED
CONFINAN	22.83614	17.89579	.45504	.29889	.78312
CONBUS	22.84096	18.63165	.35560	.24236	.79177
CONCLERG	22.85542	18.31721	.36933	.16713	.79118
CONEDUC	22.84578	18.06795	.46520	.23213	.78232
CONFED	22.45783	18.04592	.46921	.29611	.78197
CONLABOR	22.51807	18.42419	.37634	.21017	.79017
CONPRESS	22.71084	18.81474	.32146	.22199	.79465
CONMEDIC	23.10361	18.01581	.49617	.27397	.77984
CONTV	22.55181	18.59091	.36696	.19377	.79077
CONJUDGE	22.74458	17.57711	.50607	.31250	.77826
CONSCI	23.10361	18.66315	.39099	.21854	.78865
CONLEGIS	22.41446	18.07902	.52769	.34814	.77793
CONARMY	22.79518	17.73814	.49305	.29034	.77959

ANALYSIS OF VARIANCE

SOURCE OF VARIATION	SS	DF	MEAN SQUARE	F	PROBABILITY
BETWEEN PEOPLE	669.74124	414	1.61773		
WITHIN PEOPLE	1858.92308	4980	0.37328		
BETWEEN MEASURES	240.96311	12	20.08026	61.65711	0.0
RESIDUAL	1617.95996	4968	0.32568		
NONADDITIVITY	0.00408	1	0.00408	0.01253	0.91086
BALANCE	1617.95588	4967	0.32574		
TOTAL	2528.66432	5394	0.46879		

GRAND MEAN = 1.89601

TUKEY ESTIMATE OF POWER TO WHICH OBSERVATIONS MUST BE RAISED TO ACHIEVE ADDITIVITY = 0.9778486

* * * * * * * * * R E L I A B I L I T Y   A N A L Y S I S   F O R   S C A L E   (C O N F I N D   ) * * * * * * * * *

HOTELLINGS T-SQUARED = 694.59442   F = 56.34492
DEGREES OF FREEDOM * * NUMERATOR = 12   DENOMINATOR= 403   PROBABILITY = 0.00000

TEST FOR GOODNESS OF FIT OF MODEL STRICTLYPARALLEL

CHI SQUARE = 965.61859   DEGREES OF FREEDOM = 101
LOG OF DETERMINANT OF UNCONSTRAINED MATRIX = -13.6742999
LOG OF DETERMINANT OF CONSTRAINED MATRIX = -11.3189635
PROBABILITY = .00000

PARAMETER ESTIMATES

ESTIMATED COMMON MEAN= 1.89601
ESTIMATED COMMON VARIANCE = 0.4697294
ERROR VARIANCE = 0.3732777
TRUE VARIANCE = 0.0964517
ESTIMATED COMMON INTERITEM CORRELATION = 0.2036639

ESTIMATED RELIABILITY OF SCALE = .7687736
UNBIASED ESTIMATE OF RELIABILITY = .7704451

39.12 Matrix Materials

RELIABILITY accepts matrix input instead of cases and also writes matrix materials which can be used for subsequent analyses with RELIABILITY and other programs. Matrices read by RELIABILITY must be in the form of covariance or correlation matrices. RELIABILITY writes covariance matrices. Matrix input and output are controlled by the OPTIONS command and the optional FORMAT subcommand. The FORMAT subcommand specifies FORTRAN format specifications and is not required if materials are entered freefield or formatted according to the defaults RELIABILITY expects.

39.13 Matrix Input

RELIABILITY computes coefficients of reliability from correlation or covariance matrices. To read a square covariance matrix, specify Option 4. Use Option 5 to read a square correlation matrix. Each row of a square matrix must begin on a new line. With Option 6 you can read a lower-triangular correlation matrix or covariance matrix, where each matrix includes the diagonal and each row begins a new line. You can also enter a triangular matrix formatted as a single vector rather than with each row beginning on a new line by using Option 12. Correlation matrices must be preceded by a vector of standard deviations. Use Option 7 if a vector of means precedes the covariance or correlation matrix.

As in other procedures in SPSS^X, RELIABILITY accepts matrix materials entered in a freefield format provided that the keyword FREE is specified on the INPUT MATRIX command (see Chapter 17). If you do not use the FREE keyword RELIABILITY expects correlation matrices to have a format of 8F10.7; means and standard deviations accompanying the correlation matrix to have a format of 8F10.4; covariance matrices to have a format of 4D20.13; means accompanying the covariance matrix to have a format of 5D16.9; and the number of cases to have a format of F10.4. The FORMAT subcommand permits you to override the default formats (see Section 39.15).

To use matrix materials instead of cases, define variable names with the NUMERIC command inside an INPUT PROGRAM, use the INPUT MATRIX command to signal matrix input, and specify the appropriate options describing the contents of the matrix materials. You must use the FILE HANDLE command to provide a file handle for matrix materials read from a separate file. You must also specify the number of cases when using matrix input, using one of three methods. First, you can use the N OF CASES command prior to the RELIABILITY command (see Chapter 10). Second, you can include a line with the number of cases following the covariance or correlation matrix and specify Option 17. Third, if neither an N OF CASES command nor Option 17 is used, RELIABILITY uses the number of variables specified on the VARIABLES subcommand plus 1 as the number of cases. The N OF CASES command overrides Option 17. For general information on the use of matrix materials in SPSS^X, see Chapter 17.

By default, RELIABILITY uses the VARIABLES subcommand to index a matrix. If you use a square matrix that has been computed on more variables than are specified on the VARIABLES subcommand, you must specify Option 9 to insure that the matrix is indexed to the variable names on the NUMERIC command. Use Option 9 if you define the variables in a different order on the NUMERIC command compared to the VARIABLES subcommand. You cannot use Option 9 when you read a triangular matrix with Option 6 or read a matrix formatted as a single vector with Option 12.

Use the following options to control the reading of matrices with procedure RELIABILITY:

OPTION 4 *Read a square covariance matrix.*

OPTION 5 *Read a vector of standard deviations followed by a square correlation matrix.*

OPTION 6 *Read a triangular correlation or covariance matrix.*

OPTION 7 *A vector of means precedes other matrix materials.*

OPTION 9 *Index a square matrix using the SPSS^X variable dictionary rather than the order of variables specified on the VARIABLES subcommand.* This option is not available for triangular matrices or matrices read as a single vector (Options 6 and 12).

OPTION 12 *Read a triangular matrix formatted as a single vector.*

OPTION 17 *Number of cases follows matrix.*

Figure 39.13 is the display produced by the following commands, which use means and a triangular covariance matrix entered in freefield format.

```
TITLE  'REPRODUCE RELIABILITY EXAMPLES'
INPUT PROGRAM
NUMERIC  A1 TO A3 B1 TO B4
INPUT MATRIX  FILE=INLINE/FREE
N OF CASES  240
END INPUT PROGRAM
VARIABLE LABELS  A1 'ROLE PERFORMANCE INDICATOR A 1'
                 A2 'ROLE PERFORMANCE INDICATOR A 2'
                 A3 'ROLE PERFORMANCE INDICATOR A 3'
                 B1 'ROLE PERFORMANCE INDICATOR B 1'
                 B2 'ROLE PERFORMANCE INDICATOR B 2'
                 B3 'ROLE PERFORMANCE INDICATOR B 3'
                 B4 'ROLE PERFORMANCE INDICATOR B 4'
SUBTITLE  'DEMONSTRATE MATRIX INPUT'
RELIABILITY  VARIABLES=ALL/
             SCALE(RPERFO3) = ALL/
             MODEL = PARALLEL/
             SCALE(RPERFO4) = ALL/
             MODEL = SPLIT(4)
OPTIONS  4 6 7
BEGIN DATA
67.33751 74.2 115.35 69.0833 90.0 76.91667 66.5125
3257.3339
283.5 5111.5833
-179.5617 863.9046 2445.6678
-153.2504 1231.1465 973.9367 1962.584
397.5941 1796.046 643.4728 1053.0738 2566.9456
112.681 4069.9916 1228.0470 1620.2452 1729.2887 5785.0642
-110.5923 784.2276 412.9705 634.6816 576.3808 903.4613 731.8074
END DATA
```

Figure 39.13 Matrix input

```
* * * * * * * * * * R E L I A B I L I T Y   A N A L Y S I S   F O R   S C A L E   (R P E R F 0 3   ) * * * * * * * * *
                    1.      A1                 ROLE PERFORMANCE INDICATOR A 1
                    2.      A2                 ROLE PERFORMANCE INDICATOR A 2
                    3.      A3                 ROLE PERFORMANCE INDICATOR A 3
                    4.      B1                 ROLE PERFORMANCE INDICATOR B 1
                    5.      B2                 ROLE PERFORMANCE INDICATOR B 2
                    6.      B3                 ROLE PERFORMANCE INDICATOR B 3
                    7.      B4                 ROLE PERFORMANCE INDICATOR B 4

      # OF CASES =      240.0

   TEST FOR GOODNESS OF FIT OF MODEL          PARALLEL

   CHI SQUARE =       566.47977          DEGREES OF FREEDOM =          26
     LOG OF DETERMINANT OF UNCONSTRAINED MATRIX =        52.8963200
     LOG OF DETERMINANT OF CONSTRAINED MATRIX =         55.2929258
     PROBABILITY = 0.0

        PARAMETER ESTIMATES


     ESTIMATED COMMON VARIANCE =   3122.9980286
          ERROR VARIANCE =     2224.3672952
           TRUE VARIANCE =      898.6307333
     ESTIMATED COMMON INTERITEM CORRELATION =          0.2877462


   ESTIMATED RELIABILITY OF SCALE = .7387640
    UNBIASED ESTIMATE OF RELIABILITY = .7409501

* * * * * * * * * * R E L I A B I L I T Y   A N A L Y S I S   F O R   S C A L E   (R P E R F 0 4   ) * * * * * * * * *
                    1.      A1                 ROLE PERFORMANCE INDICATOR A 1
                    2.      A2                 ROLE PERFORMANCE INDICATOR A 2
                    3.      A3                 ROLE PERFORMANCE INDICATOR A 3
                    4.      B1                 ROLE PERFORMANCE INDICATOR B 1
                    5.      B2                 ROLE PERFORMANCE INDICATOR B 2
                    6.      B3                 ROLE PERFORMANCE INDICATOR B 3
                    7.      B4                 ROLE PERFORMANCE INDICATOR B 4

      # OF CASES =      240.0

        RELIABILITY COEFFICIENTS              7  ITEMS

        CORRELATION BETWEEN FORMS =    .64981            EQUAL LENTH SPEARMAN-BROWN =    .78774

        UNEQUAL-LENGTH SPEARMAN-BROWN =    .79057        GUTTMAN SPLIT-HALF =    .76413

        ALPHA FOR PART 1 =    .22772                     ALPHA FOR PART 2 =    .72170

           3 ITEMS IN PART 1                                4 ITEMS IN PART 2
```

39.14 Matrix Output

RELIABILITY can produce means and covariance matrix materials for its own use and for use by other programs. Specify Option 8 to write out a triangular covariance matrix. Specify Option 11 to write a vector of means. The means will always precede the covariance matrix. One set of matrix materials is written for every VARIABLES subcommand. By default, RELIABILITY writes means with a format of 5D16.9 and writes covariance matrices with a format of 4D20.13. You can use the optional FORMAT subcommand to specify alternative output formats (see Section 39.15). Specify Option 13 to write covariance matrices as a single vector. If you use RELIABILITY solely to produce matrix materials, specify Option 10 to avoid further computations.

To write matrix materials, use the FILE HANDLE and PROCEDURE OUTPUT commands prior to the RELIABILITY command to define the file containing the matrix materials. The following options apply to the writing of matrix materials:

OPTION 8 *Write a triangular covariance matrix.* One covariance matrix is written for each VARIABLES subcommand.

OPTION 10 *Stop analyses after matrix materials are written.* All scales are bypassed.

OPTION 11 *Write means.*

OPTION 13 *Write covariance matrix formatted as a single vector.*

The following example demonstrates the use of RELIABILITY to write out a covariance matrix and means to the file referenced by RELMAT:

```
FILE HANDLE  TESTSCOR/ file specifications
GET  FILE=TESTSCOR
FILE HANDLE  RELMAT/ file specifications
PROCEDURE OUTPUT  FILE=RELMAT
RELIABILITY  VARIABLES=Q1 TO Q25/
   SCALE(TESTS) = ALL
OPTIONS  8 10 11
```

39.15 The FORMAT Subcommand

RELIABILITY reads and writes matrix materials using default formats. It assumes that the number of cases and standard deviations have a format of 8F10.4, that the correlation matrix has a format of 8F10.7, that the vector of means has a format of 5D16.9, and that the covariance matrix has a format of 4D20.13. If you are entering matrix materials freefield, these formats do not apply. Several alternative formats for formatted matrix materials are available. The FORMAT subcommand is used to specify alternative formats. The keyword INPUT defines an alternative format for the reading of matrix materials, and the keyword OUTPUT controls the writing of matrix materials. Following the keyword INPUT or OUTPUT in parentheses is a set of format selection numbers separated by a slash, as in:

```
RELIABILITY  FORMAT=OUTPUT(1/2)/
   VARIABLES=Q1 TO Q25/
   SCALE (TESTS) = ALL
OPTIONS  8 10 11
```

The first format number specifies the format for means (and standard deviations if a correlation matrix is being entered or written). The second format number specifies the format for the correlation or covariance matrix. Each format number represents a specific format. Five are available. Table 39.15 lists the format numbers and their corresponding formats. If you want to modify one but not both of the default formats, the corresponding number may be omitted, but the slash must appear.

Table 39.15 Format options

Selection number	Format
1	(8F10.0)
2	(8F10.4)
3	(8F10.7)
4	(5D16.9)
5	(4D20.13)

39.16 Alternative Computing Methods

RELIABILITY uses one of two different computing methods, depending upon the model specified and the options and statistics requested. Method 1 does not compute a covariance matrix. It is faster than Method 2 and, for large problems, requires less workspace. However, Method 1 can only compute coefficients for models ALPHA and SPLIT, and does not compute a number of optional statistics or read and write matrix materials. RELIABILITY uses Method 1 whenever it can.

Method 2 computes a covariance matrix for each VARIABLES subcommand. You can obtain all the optional statistics, and use any model with Method 2.

Method 1 continues processing a scale containing zero variance and leaves the item in the scale. Method 2 deletes items with zero variance and continues processing. If you want Method 2 and do not request any of the models, options, or statistics which force it, specify Option 14.

OPTION 14 *Use Method 2.* RELIABILITY uses a covariance matrix. This option should be specified if you want any of the following:

Deletion of items with zero variance from the scales in which they occur. The treatment used affects coefficient α, the Tukey test (Statistic 11), and the analysis of variance (Statistic 10).

Squared multiple correlations. These are included in the item total statistics (Statistic 9) when Method 2 is used, but not when Method 1 is used.

Standardized item α.

To summarize, Method 1 is automatically used if you specify

- Only ALPHA or SPLIT models.
- Only Options 1, 3, and 16.
- Only Statistics 1, 4, 9, 10, and 11.

Method 2 is used if you specify

- A model other than ALPHA or SPLIT.
- Any of Options 4 through 15 and 17.
- Any of Statistics 2, 3, 5, 6, 7, 8, or 12.

39.17 Missing Values

By default, RELIABILITY deletes cases with missing values on a listwise basis. A case missing on any of the variables listed on the VARIABLES subcommand is not used. Each VARIABLES subcommand is evaluated independently for missing values. To include cases with user-missing values, specify Option 1 on the associated OPTIONS command.

OPTION 1 *Include missing values.*

39.18 Suppressing Variable Labels

By default, RELIABILITY prints the variable label associated with each variable at the beginning of the display. To suppress the printing of variable labels, use Option 3.

OPTION 3 *Suppress variable labels.*

39.19 LIMITATIONS

The following limitations apply to procedure RELIABILITY:

- A maximum of 10 VARIABLES subcommands.
- A maximum of 50 SCALE subcommands.
- A maximum of 500 variables referenced on the combined VARIABLES subcommands. Each mention of a variable counts one toward this limit.
- A maximum of 500 variables referenced on one SCALE subcommand.
- A maximum of 1,000 variables referenced on the combined SCALE subcommands. Each mention of a variable counts one toward this limit.
- If insufficient workspace is available to handle multiple VARIABLES subcommands, RELIABILITY deletes them in the reverse order they were specified until the allocated workspace is sufficient.

```
SURVIVAL  TABLES = survival varlist [BY independent varlist (min, max) . . . ]
              [BY control varlist (min, max) . . . ]

 /INTERVALS = THRU n BY a [, THRU m BY b . . . ]

 /STATUS = status variable ({min, max}) FOR {ALL          }
                            {value   }      {survival varlist}

              [/STATUS = . . . ]

           {ALL     }
           {LOGSURV }
 [/PLOTS ( {SURVIVAL}) = {ALL             } BY {ALL                 }
           {HAZARD  }    {survival varlist}    {independent varlist}
           {DENSITY }

                          BY {ALL            }]
                             {control varlist}

 [/COMPARE = {ALL             } BY {ALL                 }
             {survival varlist}    {independent varlist}

              BY {ALL            }]
                 {control varlist}
```

OPTIONS:
1 Include missing values.
2 Exclude missing values casewise.
3 Compute comparisions only.
4 Suppress printing of life tables.
5 Do approximate comparisons if insufficient memory for exact comparsons.
6 Do approximate comparisons only.
7 Do pairwise comparisons only.
8 Write out survival table data records.
9 Write out survival table data records and label records.

OVERVIEW, **40.1**

OPERATION, **40.2**
- The TABLES Subcommand, **40.3**
- The INTERVALS Subcommand, **40.4**
- The STATUS Subcommand, **40.5**
- Life Table Output, **40.6**
  - Survival Functions, **40.7**
  - Suppressing Life Tables, **40.8**
- The PLOTS Subcommand, **40.9**
- The COMPARE Subcommand, **40.10**
  - Pairwise Comparisons, **40.11**
  - Approximate Comparisons, **40.12**
  - Obtaining Comparisons Only, **40.13**
- Entering Aggregated Data, **40.14**
- Missing Values, **40.15**
- Writing Out Survival Tables, **40.16**
  - Format, **40.17**
  - Record Order, **40.18**

LIMITATIONS, **40.19**

SURVIVAL was originally designed and implemented by Barry Brown, Marcus Schimek, Herman Walker, and Peggy Wright of M.D. Anderson Hospital, the University of Texas at Houston (Brown, et al., 1979). Their work was supported by the National Cancer Institute grants CA11430 and CA16672. A revised version of this procedure is available in the CDC-6000 version of SPSS distributed by Northwestern University. That version was extensively revised by Barry Brown and Herman Walker and by SPSS Inc. for inclusion in Release 8.

Chapter 40 SURVIVAL

Procedure SURVIVAL produces life tables, plots of the survival functions, and subgroup comparisons. An output file can be written for use on graphics devices or with other programs. Survival analysis is useful when the dependent variable represents the time interval between an initial event and a termination event. Although this type of analysis is performed most frequently in medical research, where the detection of a disease is the initial event and the patient's death is the termination event (hence the name survival), it can also be used to study other events such as length of time from marriage to the birth of the first child or number of years employed by the same firm.

40.1 OVERVIEW

The only restrictions in survival analysis are that the initial event must occur, the termination event must occur after the initial event, and the termination event may not occur more than once. In addition to the initial and termination events, two other concepts that are central to survival analysis are *censored observations* and *survival scores*.

Censored Observations. If the termination event has not occurred for an observation by the time data are analyzed, its survival time is the length of time between the initial event for that observation and the time of the analysis. Such observations are considered censored because the survival time is not known exactly but it is known to be of at least a certain duration. Censored observations can occur either because the termination event has not occurred by the time of the analysis or because an observation is withdrawn from the study for other reasons, such as death from other causes or inability to maintain contact. Censored observations cannot be treated as missing data. Eliminating from the analysis all patients who were still alive at the end of the study period, for example, would not yield very useful results. Survival analysis makes use of both censored and uncensored observations in calculating survival times.

Survival Score. A survival score is calculated for each observation by comparing its survival time to that of all other observations. The score starts at zero and is incremented by one for each observation whose survival time is known to be lower and decremented by one for each observation whose survival time is known to be greater. For observations with the same survival time, no change is made. If one of the observations is censored, the censored observation is considered to have a greater survival time since it is known to have survived at least as long as its survival time. Survival scores are used in comparisons to determine whether groups differ significantly in terms of survival.

Statistic D. For use in subgroup comparisons, a statistic *D* is calculated from the survival scores using the algorithm of Lee and Desu (1972). *D* is asymptotically distributed as chi-square with g−1 degrees of freedom, where g equals the number of groups, under the null hypothesis that the subgroups are samples from the same survival distribution. The larger the *D* statistic, the more likely that the subgroups come from different survival distributions. The level of significance of *D* is also printed.

SURVIVAL can analyze several survival variables in the same specification of the procedure. SURVIVAL produces a life table for each variable listed. First- and second-order control variables can be used to produce subgroup comparisons. Optionally, you can obtain plots of the survival functions and request specific subgroup comparisons. The life table can be written out to a file for use with other programs.

Life Tables. The TABLES subcommand lists the variables to be used in the analysis, including any control variables. Separate life tables are produced for each variable. The three survival functions and their standard errors are included in the life table. (See Section 40.3.)

Intervals. SURVIVAL reports on the survival history at various points, beginning with the initial event. The unit of time on which the survival variables are scaled can be grouped into intervals using the INTERVALS subcommand. (See Section 40.4.)

Survival Status. To determine whether the termination event has occurred for a particular observation, SURVIVAL checks the value of a status variable. The STATUS subcommand lists the status variable associated with each survival variable. (See Section 40.5.)

Producing Plots. To obtain plots of the survival functions for all cases or separately for various subgroups, use the PLOTS subcommand. (See Section 40.9.)

Comparisons. When control variables are listed on the TABLES subcommand, you can request subgroup comparisons using the COMPARE subcommand. Both overall and pairwise comparisons are available. For aggregated data, approximate comparisons can be specified. (See Section 40.10.)

Missing Values. By default, SURVIVAL handles missing values on a groupwise basis. Cases with a missing value on a variable are excluded from any calculation that involves that variable. Alternative missing-value treatments are listwise deletion and missing-value inclusion. Negative values on the survival variables are automatically treated as missing. (See Section 40.15.)

Writing Out a File. You can write the contents of the life tables, including the labeling information, to a file for use with other programs or with a graphics device that produces high-quality graphics. (See Section 40.16.)

40.2 OPERATION

SURVIVAL operates via subcommands and an associated OPTIONS command. The minimum syntax is a TABLES subcommand naming a survival variable, an INTERVALS subcommand setting the period to be examined, and a STATUS subcommand identifying the variable that indicates the survival status. The PLOTS and COMPARE subcommands are optional and can appear in any order but must be placed after the required subcommands. If you need to calculate the survival variables using information on individual starting dates and the study termination date, use the YRMODA function to take the difference between two dates (see Chapter 6).

40.3 The TABLES Subcommand

Use the TABLES subcommand to list the survival variables and control variables that you want to include in the analysis. To request a survival analysis on the variables ONSSURV and RECSURV with no controls, specify:

```
SURVIVAL TABLES=ONSSURV,RECSURV/
         INTERVALS = THRU 100 BY 10/
         STATUS = OUTCOME (3,4)/
```

This form of the TABLES subcommand, combined with appropriate INTERVALS and STATUS subcommands (Sections 40.4 and 40.5), produces a life table for the variable ONSSURV and a life table for the variable RECSURV. Use the BY keyword to separate the survival variables from the first-order control variables. Use a second BY keyword to separate the first- and second-order control variable lists. Each control variable must be followed by a value range in parentheses. These values must be integers separated by a comma or a blank. Noninteger values in the data are truncated and the case is assigned to a subgroup based on the integer portion of its value on the variable. To specify only one value for a control variable, use the same value for the minimum and maximum, as in TREATMNT(3,3). To request a survival analysis for ONSSURV and RECSURV with TREATMNT as a first-order control and SEX as a second-order control, specify:

```
SURVIVAL  TABLES=ONSSURV,RECSURV BY TREATMNT (1,3) BY SEX (1,2)
```

Each combination of TREATMNT and SEX produces a separate life table for each survival variable, for a total of 12 in this example.

40.4 The INTERVALS Subcommand

The survival variables are measured in units of time such as days, weeks, months, or years. The INTERVALS subcommand determines the period of time to be examined and how the time will be grouped for the analysis. For a 20-year period measured in months, the subcommand

```
SURVIVAL  TABLES = ONSSURV, RECSURV BY TREATMNT (1,3)/
          INTERVALS = THRU 240 BY 12/
          STATUS = OUTCOME (3,4)/
```

analyzes the entire 20-year period and groups the data into 1-year intervals. The first interval is 0–12 months, the second interval 12–24 months and so on.

The first interval always begins at zero. The final interval, in the above example 240+, is created automatically and includes any observations that exceed the specified range. The grouping increment, which follows the BY keyword, is relative to the units in which the survival variable is measured. If in the example above the variable were measured in weeks instead of months, the INTERVALS subcommand would group the data into 12-week intervals and cover a period of 240 weeks.

The period to be examined can be divided into intervals of varying lengths by repeating the THRU and BY keywords, as in:

```
SURVIVAL  ONSSURV, RECSURV BY TREATMNT (1,3)/
          INTERVALS = THRU 60 BY 6 THRU 240 BY 12/
          STATUS = OUTCOME (3,4)
```

If the data are recorded in months, this specification groups the first 5 years (60 months) into 6-month intervals and the remaining 15 years into yearly intervals.

The period must be divided in ascending order with no overlap of the values following multiple THRU keywords. If the value following the BY keyword does not divide evenly into the period to which it applies, the endpoint of the period is adjusted upward to the next even multiple of the BY value. For example, the subcommand

```
INTERVALS = THRU 50 BY 6/
```

results in a period of 54 with 9 intervals of 6 units each. When the period is divided into intervals of varying lengths by repeating the THRU and BY specifications, the adjustment of one period to produce even intervals changes the starting point of subsequent periods. For example,

```
INTERVALS = THRU 50 BY 6 THRU 100 BY 10 THRU 200 BY 20/
```

is automatically readjusted to result in a first period through 54 by 6, a second period through 104 by 10, and a third period through 204 by 20. If the upward adjustment of one period completely overlaps the next period, no adjustment is made and the procedure terminates with an error.

Only one INTERVALS subcommand can be used in a SURVIVAL command. The interval specifications apply to all the survival variables listed on the TABLES subcommand.

40.5 The STATUS Subcommand

For each survival variable listed on the TABLES subcommand, you must provide a variable that indicates the survival status of each case. The codes on these status variables distinguish between cases for which the terminal event has occurred and those that either "survived" to the end of the study or were dropped for some reason.

On the STATUS subcommand, specify a status variable with a value range enclosed in parentheses followed by the keyword FOR and the name of one or more of the survival variables. The value range identifies the codes that indicate the terminal event has taken place. For example,

```
SURVIVAL  ONSSURV BY TREATMNT (1,3)/
          INTERVALS = THRU 50 BY 5, THRU 100 BY 10/
          STATUS = OUTCOME (3,4) FOR ONSSURV/
```

specifies that a code of 3 or 4 on OUTCOME means the terminal event for the survival variable ONSSURV occurred. If the codes for OUTCOME are (1) alive, (2) dropped from study, (3) dead from unrelated causes, and (4) dead due to illness, all patients who died, regardless of the cause, are considered to have reached the terminal event. To indicate that only those deaths caused by the disease be treated as terminal events, specify:

```
STATUS = OUTCOME (4) FOR ONSSURV/
```

All observations that do not have a code in the value range are classified as censored cases. Only one status variable can be listed on a STATUS subcommand. Use separate STATUS subcommands for each of the survival variables or, if appropriate, list more than one survival variable after the FOR keyword. If the FOR keyword is not specified, the status variable specification applies to any of the survival variables not named on another STATUS subcommand.

40.6 Life Table Output

The TABLES, INTERVALS, and STATUS subcommands print one or more life tables depending on the number of survival and control variables specified. The command

```
SURVIVAL  TABLES = ONSSURV BY TREATMNT (1,3)/
          INTERVALS = THRU 50 BY 5 THRU 100 BY 10/
          STATUS = OUTCOME (3,4) FOR ONSSURV/
```

produces the life table in Figure 40.6. The 13 columns in the life table contain the following information: the start time of the interval; the number of cases entering the interval; the number withdrawing during the interval (the censored cases); the number exposed to risk (the number entering minus one-half the number withdrawing); the number of terminal events; the proportion of terminal events; the proportion surviving; and the three survival functions and their respective standard errors. Below the table is the median survival time for all cases.

Figure 40.6 Life table

LIFE TABLE
SURVIVAL VARIABLE ONSSURV MONTHS FROM ONSET TO DEATH
FOR TREATMNT PATIENT TREATMENT = 1 TREATMENT A

INTVL START TIME	NUMBER ENTRNG THIS INTVL	NUMBER WDRAWN DURING INTVL	NUMBER EXPOSD TO RISK	NUMBER OF TERMNL EVENTS	PROPN TERMI-NATING	PROPN SURVI-VING	CUMUL PROPN SURV AT END	PROBA-BILITY DENSTY	HAZARD RATE	SE OF CUMUL SURV-IVING	SE OF PROB-ABILTY DENS	SE OF HAZRD RATE
0.0	501.0	0.0	501.0	3.0	0.0060	0.9940	0.9940	0.0012	0.0012	0.003	0.001	0.001
5.0	498.0	1.0	497.5	16.0	0.0322	0.9678	0.9620	0.0064	0.0065	0.009	0.002	0.002
10.0	481.0	1.0	480.5	26.0	0.0541	0.9459	0.9100	0.0104	0.0111	0.013	0.002	0.002
15.0	454.0	0.0	454.0	17.0	0.0374	0.9626	0.8759	0.0068	0.0076	0.015	0.002	0.002
20.0	437.0	0.0	437.0	23.0	0.0526	0.9474	0.8298	0.0092	0.0108	0.017	0.002	0.002
25.0	414.0	1.0	413.5	25.0	0.0605	0.9395	0.7796	0.0100	0.0125	0.019	0.002	0.002
30.0	388.0	1.0	387.5	22.0	0.0568	0.9432	0.7354	0.0089	0.0117	0.020	0.002	0.002
35.0	365.0	1.0	364.5	24.0	0.0658	0.9342	0.6870	0.0097	0.0136	0.021	0.002	0.003
40.0	340.0	0.0	340.0	24.0	0.0706	0.9294	0.6385	0.0097	0.0146	0.022	0.002	0.003
45.0	316.0	1.0	315.5	14.0	0.0444	0.9556	0.6101	0.0057	0.0091	0.022	0.001	0.002
50.0	301.0	1.0	300.5	34.0	0.1131	0.8869	0.5411	0.0069	0.0120	0.022	0.001	0.002
60.0	266.0	0.0	266.0	22.0	0.0827	0.9173	0.4963	0.0045	0.0086	0.022	0.001	0.002
70.0	244.0	2.0	243.0	15.0	0.0617	0.9383	0.4657	0.0031	0.0064	0.022	0.001	0.002
80.0	227.0	3.0	225.5	24.0	0.1064	0.8936	0.4161	0.0050	0.0112	0.022	0.001	0.002
90.0	200.0	2.0	199.0	18.0	0.0905	0.9095	0.3785	0.0038	0.0095	0.022	0.001	0.002
100.0+	180.0	104.0	128.0	76.0	0.5938	0.4063	0.1538	**	**	0.019	**	**

** THESE CALCULATIONS FOR THE LAST INTERVAL ARE MEANINGLESS.

THE MEDIAN SURVIVAL TIME FOR THESE DATA IS 69.18

40.7 Survival Functions

Three survival functions are automatically calculated and included in the life table along with their standard errors. The computation of the survival functions is based on the actuarial method described by Berkson and Gage (1950).

Cumulative Proportion Surviving at End. This is the cumulative survival rate at the end of an interval. It is calculated by multiplying the probabilities of survival up to and including the current interval.

Probability Density. The probability density is the estimated probability per unit time of the terminal event occurring in the interval.

Hazard Rate. The hazard rate is an estimate of the probability per unit time that cases entering the interval will experience the terminal event in the interval.

40.8 Suppressing Life Tables

The TABLES subcommand is always required. If you are interested only in the plots and subgroup comparisons available in SURVIVAL, use Option 4 to suppress the printing of the life tables.

OPTION 4 *Suppress the printing of the life tables.* Only plots and comparisons are printed.

Options 8 and 9, used to write the life tables to a file, can be used when Option 4 is in effect (see Section 40.16).

40.9 The PLOTS Subcommand

In addition to the life tables, SURVIVAL produces plots of the three survival functions. Use the PLOTS subcommand followed by one of the five available keywords to request the plots you want.

ALL *Produce all available function plots.* ALL is the default and is used if PLOTS is specified without any keyword following.

LOGSURV *Produce a plot of the cumulative survival distribution on a logarithmic scale.*

SURVIVAL *Plot the cumulative survival distribution on a linear scale.*

HAZARD *Plot the hazard function.*

DENSITY *Plot the density function.*

You can list multiple keywords in parentheses following the PLOTS subcommand as in:

```
PLOTS (SURVIVAL,HAZARD)/
```

By default, each function requested is plotted for each survival variable. Individual values of the first-order control variables are represented by their codes in the plots. If second-order controls are used, a separate plot is generated for every value of the second-order control variables. The following specification produces the plot in Figure 40.9 as well as the life table in Figure 40.6:

```
SURVIVAL  TABLES = ONSSURV BY TREATMNT (1,3)/
          INTERVALS = THRU 50 BY 5 THRU 100 BY 10/
          STATUS = OUTCOME (3,4) FOR ONSSURV/
          PLOTS (SURVIVAL)/
```

The three treatment groups are represented by the values 1, 2, and 3 in the plot.

The available plots are defined by the specifications on the TABLES subcommand. To determine the default number of plots produced by SURVIVAL, multiply the number of functions requested by the number of survival variables times the number of first-order controls times the number of distinct values represented in all of the second-order controls. To reduce the number of plots that would be generated by default, use variable lists on the PLOTS subcommand.

The syntax for specifying the survival and control variables is the same as for the TABLES subcommand, except that you do not need to specify value ranges. Only variables that appear on the TABLES subcommand can be listed and their role as survival, first-order, and second-order control variables cannot be altered. You can use the TO keyword to refer to a group of variables and the keyword ALL to refer to an entire set of survival or control variables. Listing some of the variables from a given set (for instance the set of survival variables) automatically eliminates plots for those not listed. For example,

```
SURVIVAL  TABLES = ONSSURV, RECSURV BY TREATMNT (1,3) SEX (1,2)/
          INTERVALS = THRU 50 BY 5, THRU 100 BY 10/
          STATUS = OUTCOME (3,4)/
          PLOTS (ALL) = ONSSURV BY ALL BY ALL/
```

eliminates the plots associated with the variable RECSURV.

Since the default for any one of the three possible variable lists is ALL, the above PLOTS subcommand could have been abbreviated to:

```
PLOTS (ALL) = ONSSURV/
```

In addition, since (ALL) after PLOTS is the default,

```
PLOTS = ONSSURV/
```

would also result in the same plot.

Figure 40.9 Plot output for survival function

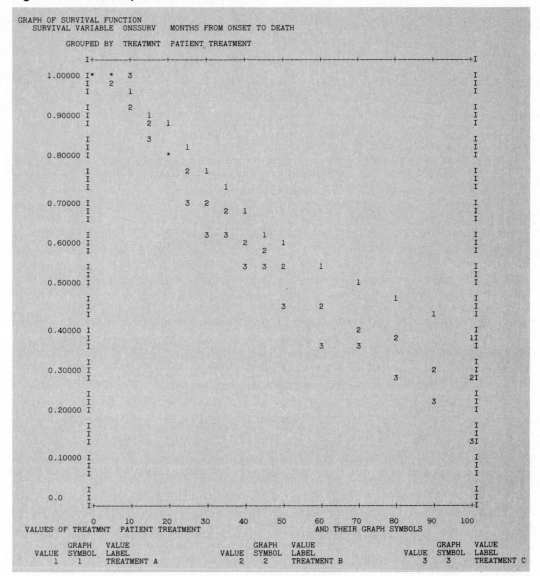

```
GRAPH OF SURVIVAL FUNCTION
   SURVIVAL VARIABLE  ONSSURV    MONTHS FROM ONSET TO DEATH

          GROUPED BY  TREATMNT  PATIENT TREATMENT

              I+-------+-------+-------+-------+-------+-------+-------+-------+-------+-------+I
      1.00000 I*   *   3                                                                        I
              I   2                                                                             I
              I        1                                                                        I
              I        2                                                                        I
      0.90000 I            1                                                                    I
              I            2   1                                                                I
              I            3                                                                    I
              I                    1                                                            I
      0.80000 I                *                                                                I
              I                    2   1                                                        I
              I                                                                                 I
              I                            1                                                    I
      0.70000 I                    3   2                                                        I
              I                            2   1                                                I
              I                                                                                 I
              I                        3   3       1                                            I
      0.60000 I                                2       1                                        I
              I                                    2                                            I
              I                                3   3   2       1                                I
              I                                                                                 I
      0.50000 I                                                        1                        I
              I                                                                1                I
              I                                        3       2                                I
              I                                                                        1        I
      0.40000 I                                                        2                        I
              I                                                                2               1I
              I                                                3       3                        I
              I                                                                                 I
      0.30000 I                                                                        2        I
              I                                                                3               2I
              I                                                                                 I
              I                                                                        3        I
      0.20000 I                                                                                 I
              I                                                                                 I
              I                                                                                 I
              I                                                                                3I
      0.10000 I                                                                                 I
              I                                                                                 I
              I                                                                                 I
              I                                                                                 I
      0.0     I                                                                                 I
              I+-------+-------+-------+-------+-------+-------+-------+-------+-------+-------+I

               0       10      20      30      40      50      60      70      80      90     100
  VALUES OF TREATMNT  PATIENT TREATMENT                          AND THEIR GRAPH SYMBOLS

          GRAPH   VALUE                             GRAPH   VALUE                             GRAPH   VALUE
  VALUE  SYMBOL  LABEL                      VALUE  SYMBOL  LABEL                      VALUE  SYMBOL  LABEL
      1    1     TREATMENT A                    2    2     TREATMENT B                    3    3     TREATMENT C
```

The variable list on the PLOTS subcommand cannot be used to plot functions both with and without control variables. To accomplish this, create a variable that has the same value for all cases using the COMPUTE command (see Chapter 6). By using this variable as a first- or second-order control (or both), you can produce plots for the entire set of cases.

40.10 The COMPARE Subcommand

To compare the survival of subgroups defined by the control variables, use the COMPARE subcommand. COMPARE with no variable list produces a default set of comparisons using the TABLES variable list. At least one survival and one first-order control variable must be specified to make comparisons possible. For example,

```
SURVIVAL  TABLES = ONSSURV BY TREATMNT (1,3)/
          INTERVALS = THRU 50 BY 5, THRU 100 BY 10/
          STATUS = OUTCOME (3,4) FOR ONSSURV/
          COMPARE/
```

produces the comparison in Figure 40.10.

Figure 40.10 Subgroup comparisons

```
COMPARISON OF SURVIVAL EXPERIENCE USING THE LEE-DESU STATISTIC

  SURVIVAL VARIABLE  ONSSURV   MONTHS FROM ONSET TO DEATH
        GROUPED BY   TREATMNT  PATIENT TREATMENT

OVERALL COMPARISON    STATISTIC          9.001  D.F.     2   PROB.  0.0111

GROUP  LABEL                  TOTAL N   UNCEN      CEN  PCT CEN  MEAN SCORE

    1  TREATMENT A                501     383      118    23.55      20.042
    2  TREATMENT B                 97      82       15    15.46     -67.412
    3  TREATMENT C                 26      24        2     7.69     -134.69
```

40.11 Pairwise Comparisons

You can obtain pairwise comparisons of survival for subgroups of cases using Option 7. Comparisons of each possible pair of values of every first-order control variable are produced along with the overall comparison. Figure 40.11 is the output produced with Option 7.

```
SURVIVAL   TABLES= ONSSURV BY TREATMNT (1,3)/
           INTERVALS = THRU 50 BY 5, THRU 100 BY 10/
           STATUS = OUTCOME (3,4) FOR ONSSURV/
           COMPARE/
OPTIONS    7
```

OPTION 7 *Perform pairwise comparisons.*

Figure 40.11 Pairwise comparisons produced using Option 7

```
COMPARISON OF SURVIVAL EXPERIENCE USING THE LEE-DESU STATISTIC

  SURVIVAL VARIABLE  ONSSURV   MONTHS FROM ONSET TO DEATH
        GROUPED BY   TREATMNT  PATIENT TREATMENT

OVERALL COMPARISON    STATISTIC          9.001  D.F.     2   PROB.  0.0111

GROUP  LABEL                  TOTAL N   UNCEN      CEN  PCT CEN  MEAN SCORE

    1  TREATMENT A                501     383      118    23.55      20.042
    2  TREATMENT B                 97      82       15    15.46     -67.412

    3  TREATMENT C                 26      24        2     7.69     -134.69

PAIRWISE COMPARISON   STATISTIC          5.042  D.F.     1   PROB.  0.0247

GROUP  LABEL                  TOTAL N   UNCEN      CEN  PCT CEN  MEAN SCORE

    1  TREATMENT A                501     383      118    23.55      13.603
    2  TREATMENT B                 97      82       15    15.46     -70.258

PAIRWISE COMPARISON   STATISTIC          4.768  D.F.     1   PROB.  0.0290

GROUP  LABEL                  TOTAL N   UNCEN      CEN  PCT CEN  MEAN SCORE

    1  TREATMENT A                501     383      118    23.55      6.4391
    3  TREATMENT C                 26      24        2     7.69     -124.08

PAIRWISE COMPARISON   STATISTIC          0.766  D.F.     1   PROB.  0.3814

GROUP  LABEL                  TOTAL N   UNCEN      CEN  PCT CEN  MEAN SCORE

    2  TREATMENT B                 97      82       15    15.46      2.8454

    3  TREATMENT C                 26      24        2     7.69     -10.615
```

40.12 Approximate Comparisons

Data can be entered into SURVIVAL on either an individual or an interval-level basis. Whether individual or aggregated data are used affects the outcome of SURVIVAL comparisons. With individual data, you can obtain exact comparisons. For exact comparisons, survival scores are calculated on the basis of the survival experience of each observation. While this method is the most accurate, it requires that all of the data be in memory simultaneously. Thus, exact comparisons may be impractical for large samples. There are also situations in which individual data are not available and data aggregated by interval must be used. See Section 40.14 for a discussion of entering aggregated data.

Option 6 requests approximate comparisons. Option 5 produces approximate comparisons only if there is insufficient memory available for exact comparisons. The approximate comparison approach assumes that all events—termination, withdrawal, and so forth—occur at the midpoint of the interval. Under exact comparisons, some of these midpoint ties can be resolved. However, if interval widths are not too great, the difference between exact and approximate comparisons should be small.

OPTION 5 *Compute approximate comparisons if memory is insufficient.*
OPTION 6 *Compute approximate comparisons only.*

40.13 Obtaining Comparisons Only

To produce only comparisons and no life tables or plots, use Option 3.

OPTION 3 *Produce comparisons only.* Survival tables specified on the TABLES subcommand are not computed and requests for plots are ignored. This allows all available workspace to be used for comparisons.

Options 8 and 9, used to write out survival tables (see Section 40.16), cannot be used when Option 3 is in effect. If they do appear on the OPTIONS command, nothing is written to the output file.

40.14 Entering Aggregated Data

When data are recorded for the entire sample at set points in time instead of on an individual basis, it is necessary to enter aggregated data into SURVIVAL. When aggregated data are used, two records are entered for each interval, one for censored cases and one for uncensored cases. The number of cases included on each record is used as the weight factor (see Chapter 10 for a discussion of the WEIGHT command). If control variables are used, there must be a pair of records (one for censored and one for uncensored cases) for each value of the control variable in each interval. These records must contain the value of the control variable and the number of cases that belong in the particular category as well as values for survival time and status. For example, the commands

```
DATA LIST   / SURVEVAR 1-2 STATVAR 4 SEX 6 COUNT 8
VALUE LABELS  STATVAR 1 'DECEASED' 2 'ALIVE'/
              SEX 1 'FEMALE' 2 'MALE'
WEIGHT  COUNT
SURVIVAL  TABLES = SURVEVAR BY SEX (1,2)/
          INTERVALS = THRU 10 BY 1/
          STATUS = STATVAR (1)/
BEGIN DATA
 1 1 1 0
 1 1 1 1
 1 2 2 2
 1 1 2 1
 2 2 1 1
 2 1 1 2
 2 2 2 1
 2 1 2 3
 and so on for all ten intervals
END DATA
```

read in aggregated data and perform a SURVIVAL analysis when a control variable with two values is used. The first data record has a code of 1 on the status variable, STATVAR, indicating it is an uncensored case and a code of 1 on SEX, the control variable. The number of cases for this subset is 0, the value of the variable COUNT. COUNT is not used in SURVIVAL but is the weight variable. In this example, each interval requires four records to provide all the data.

ANNOTATED EXAMPLE FOR SURVIVAL

The data in this example are from a study of 647 cancer patients. The variables are

- TREATMNT—the type of treatment received.
- ONSETMO, ONSETYR—month and year cancer was discovered.
- RECURSIT—indicates whether a recurrence took place.
- RECURMO, RECURYR—month and year of recurrence.
- OUTCOME—status of patient at end of study, alive or dead.
- DEATHMO, DEATHYR—month and year of death, or, for those who survived, the date the study ended.

Using these date variables and the YRMODA function, the number of months from onset to recurrence and from onset to death or survival are calculated. These new variables become the survival variables with TREATMNT as the single control variable. The SPSS^X commands are

```
FILE HANDLE  SURVDATA/ file specifications
DATA LIST  FILE = SURVDATA/ 1 TREATMNT 15 ONSETMO 19-20
           ONSETYR 21-22 RECURSIT 48 RECURMO 49-50 RECURYR 51-52
           OUTCOME 56 DEATHMO 57-58 DEATHYR 59-60
COMMENT  TRANSFORM ALL DATES TO RUNNING CALENDAR DAYS
COMPUTE  ONSDATE=YRMODA(ONSETYR,ONSETMO,15)
COMPUTE  RECDATE=YRMODA(RECURYR,RECURMO,15)
COMPUTE  DEATHDT=YRMODA(DEATHYR,DEATHMO,15)

COMMENT  NOW COMPUTE SURVIVAL VARIABLES
COMPUTE  ONSSURV = (DEATHDT-ONSDATE)/30
IF  RECURSIT EQ 0 RECSURV = ONSSURV
IF  RECURSIT NE 0 RECSURV = (RECDATE-ONSDATE)/30

VARIABLE LABELS  TREATMNT 'PATIENT TREATMENT'
                 ONSSURV 'MONTHS FROM ONSET TO DEATH'
                 RECSURV 'MONTHS FROM ONSET TO RECURRENCE'
VALUE LABELS  TREATMNT 1 'TREATMENT A' 2 'TREATMENT B'
              3 'TREATMENT C'
SURVIVAL  TABLES = ONSSURV,RECSURV BY TREATMNT(1,3)/
          STATUS = RECURSIT(1,9) FOR RECSURV/
          STATUS = OUTCOME(3,4) FOR ONSSURV/
          INTERVALS = THRU 50 BY 5 THRU 100 BY 10/
          PLOTS/
          COMPARE
OPTIONS   5,7
```

- The FILE HANDLE command identifies SURVDATA as the data file for this example and the DATA LIST command defines it (see Chapter 3).
- The onset, recurrence, and death dates are transformed to running days using the YRMODA function in the COMPUTE command (see Chapter 6). The constant 15 is used as the day argument for YRMODA since only month and year were recorded, not the actual day.

- ONSSURV, the first survival variable, is calculated by taking the difference between the date of death (or survival) and the date the cancer was discovered (ONSDATE). The difference is divided by 30 to convert it from days to months.
- RECSURV, the second survival variable, is calculated conditionally using the IF command (see Chapter 8). For cases with RECURSIT values of 0, indicating no recurrence took place, RECSURV is set equal to ONSSURV.
- The TABLES subcommand in SURVIVAL specifies two survival variables, ONSSURV and RECSURV, and one control variable, TREATMNT (see Section 40.3). The life table for ONSSURV is shown in Figure 40.6.
- The status variable for RECSURV is RECURSIT with codes 1 and 9, indicating that the termination event, recurrence, took place. OUTCOME is the status variable for ONSSURV with codes 3 and 4 signaling the terminal event, death (see Section 40.5).
- The INTERVALS subcommand groups the first 50 months into 5-month intervals and the remaining 50 months into 10-month intervals (see Section 40.4).
- The default plots are requested using PLOTS (see Section 40.9). Figure 40.9 contains the plot of the survival function for ONSSURV.
- COMPARE with no specifications requests all comparisons (see Section 40.10). The subgroup comparisons for ONSSURV are shown in Figure 40.10.
- Option 5 requests approximate comparisons if memory is insufficient for exact comparisons (see Section 40.12). Option 7 (see Section 40.11) requests the pairwise output (see Figure 40.11).

40.15 Missing Values

SURVIVAL automatically treats negative values on the survival variables as missing data. By default, SURVIVAL excludes cases with missing values on a variable from any calculation involving that variable. Also, cases outside the value range on a control variable are excluded. Two missing-value options are available.

OPTION 1 *Include missing values.* User-defined missing values are included in the analysis.

OPTION 2 *Exclude missing values listwise.* Cases missing on any variables named are excluded from the analysis.

40.16 Writing Out Survival Tables

SURVIVAL writes out a file containing the data in the survival tables. This file can be used for further analyses or to produce graphics displays. Options 8 and 9 control the output of this file.

OPTION 8 *Write out survival table data records.* All survival table statistics are written to a file.

OPTION 9 *Write out survival table data and label records.* Variable names, variable labels, and value labels are written out along with the survival table statistics.

40.17 Format

SURVIVAL writes out five types of records. Option 8 writes out record types 30, 31, and 40. Option 9 writes out record types 10, 20, 30, 31, and 40.

Record type 10, produced only by Option 9, is formatted as follows:

Columns	Content	Format
1–2	Record type (10)	F2.0
3–7	Table number	F5.0
8–15	Name of survival variable	A8
15–55	Variable label of survival variable	A40
56	Number of BY's (0, 1, or 2)	F1.0
57–60	Number of rows in current survival table	F4.0

The number (0, 1, or 2) in column 56 specifies the number of orders of control variables (none, first-order, or first- and second-order controls) that have been applied to the life table. Columns 57–60 specify the number of rows in the life table. This number is the number of intervals in the analysis that show subjects entering; intervals in which no subjects enter are not noted in the life tables. One type 10 record is produced for each life table.

Record type 20, also produced by Option 9, is formatted as follows:

Columns	Content	Format
1–2	Record type (20)	F2.0
3–7	Table number	F5.0
8–15	Name of control variable	A8
16–55	Variable label of control variable	A40
56–60	Value of control variable	F5.0
61–80	Value label for this value	A20

One type 20 record is produced for each control variable on each life table. If only first-order controls have been placed on the survival analysis, one type 20 record will be produced for each table; if second-order controls have also been applied, two type 20 records will be produced per table.

Record type 30, and its continuation 31, produced by both Options 8 and 9, are formatted as follows:

Columns	Content	Format
1–2	Record type (30)	F2.0
3–7	Table number	F5.0
8–13	Beginning of interval	F6.2
14–21	Number entering interval	F8.2
22–29	Number withdrawn in interval	F8.2
30–37	Number exposed to risk	F8.2
38–45	Number of terminal events	F8.2

Columns	Content	Format
1–2	Record type (31)	F2.0
3–7	Table number	F5.0
8–15	Proportion terminating	F8.6
16–33	Proportion surviving	F8.6
24–31	Cumulative proportion surviving	F8.6
32–38	Probability density	F8.6
40–47	Hazard rate	F8.6
48–54	S.E. of cumulative proportion surviving	F7.4
55–61	S.E. of probability density	F7.4
62–68	S.E. of hazard rate	F7.4

Each pair of type 30 and 31 records contains the information from one line of the life table. As many type 30 and 31 record pairs are output for a table as it has lines (this number is noted in columns 57–60 of the type 10 record for the table).

Record type 40, produced both under Option 8 and 9, is formatted as follows:

Columns	Content	Format
1–2	Record type (40)	F2.0

Type 40 records indicate the completion of the series of records for one life table.

40.18 Record Order

The SURVIVAL output file contains records for each of the life tables specified on the TABLES subcommand. All records for a given table are produced together in sequence.

The records for the life tables are produced in the same order as the tables themselves. All life tables for the first survival variable are written first. The values of the first- and second-order control variables rotate, with the values of the first-order controls changing most rapidly.

40.19 LIMITATIONS

The following limitations apply to procedure SURVIVAL:

- A maximum of 20 survival variables.
- A maximum of 100 control variables on the first- and second-order control variable lists combined.
- A maximum of 20 THRU . . . BY . . . specifications on the INTERVALS subcommand.
- A maximum of 35 values can appear on a plot.

REFORMAT {ALPHA / NUMERIC} = varlist [/ . . .]

SUMMARY OF CHANGES, **A.1**

DATA DEFINITION COMMANDS, **A.2**
- DATA LIST, **A.3**
  - File Definition, **A.4**
  - Variable Definition, **A.5**
  - Format Types, **A.6**
- Other Definitions, **A.7**
  - INPUT MEDIUM, **A.8**
  - VARIABLE LIST and INPUT FORMAT, **A.9**
  - PRINT FORMATS, **A.10**
  - VARIABLE LABELS and VALUE LABELS, **A.11**
  - MISSING VALUES, **A.12**
  - N OF CASES, **A.13**
  - READ INPUT DATA and END INPUT DATA, **A.14**

UTILITY COMMANDS, **A.15**
- Job Utilities, **A.16**
  - ALLOCATE, **A.17**
  - LIST ERRORS, **A.18**
  - NUMBERED, **A.19**
  - RUN NAME and TASK NAME, **A.20**
  - PAGESIZE, **A.21**
  - PRINT BACK, **A.22**
  - SEED, **A.23**
- Listing and Writing Cases, **A.24**
  - LIST CASES, **A.25**
  - WRITE CASES, **A.26**
  - WRITE FILEINFO, **A.27**
  - Print and Write Formats, **A.28**
- Sorting Cases and Splitting Files, **A.29**
  - SORT CASES, **A.30**
  - Subfiles, **A.31**
  - Automatic Sequence Variable, **A.32**

FILE UPDATE COMMANDS, **A.33**
- ADD DATA LIST and ADD VARIABLES, **A.34**
- MERGE FILES, **A.35**
- ADD CASES and ADD SUBFILES, **A.36**

SYSTEM FILE COMMANDS, **A.37**
- Reading SPSS System Files, **A.38**
- REFORMAT, **A.39**
- Other System File Commands, **A.40**
  - DELETE VARS and KEEP VARS, **A.41**
  - REORDER VARS, **A.42**
  - Archive Files, **A.43**
  - Subfiles, **A.44**
  - LIST FILEINFO, **A.45**
  - FILE NAME, **A.46**
- File Interfaces, **A.47**
  - GET SCSS, **A.48**
  - SAVE SCSS, **A.49**

DATA SELECTION COMMANDS, **A.50**
- SELECT IF, **A.51**
- N OF CASES, **A.52**
- WEIGHT, **A.53**

DATA TRANSFORMATIONS, **A.54**
- Temporary Transformations, **A.55**
- Numeric Transformations, **A.56**
  - Initialization, **A.57**
  - ASSIGN MISSING, **A.58**
  - Functions, **A.59**
  - LAG, **A.60**
  - RECODE, **A.61**
  - Recoding Blanks, **A.62**
  - COMPUTE, **A.63**
  - COUNT, **A.64**
  - DO REPEAT and END REPEAT, **A.65**
- String Transformations, **A.66**
- Conditional Transformations, **A.67**
  - Logical Expressions, **A.68**

PROCEDURE COMMANDS, **A.69**
- AGGREGATE, **A.70**
- FREQUENCIES, **A.71**
- CONDESCRIPTIVE, **A.72**
- CROSSTABS, **A.73**
  - New Options List, **A.74**
- MULT RESPONSE, **A.75**
- BREAKDOWN, **A.76**
- REPORT, **A.77**
  - Keyword Changes, **A.78**
- GRAPHICS, **A.79**
- T-TEST, **A.80**
- ANOVA, **A.81**
- ONEWAY, **A.82**
- MANOVA, **A.83**
  - WRITE and READ, **A.84**
  - Repeated Measures, **A.85**
  - Other Changes, **A.86**
- SCATTERGRAM, **A.87**
- PEARSON CORR, **A.88**
- PARTIAL CORR, **A.89**
- REGRESSION, **A.90**
- DISCRIMINANT, **A.91**
  - New Options and Statistics List, **A.92**
- NONPAR CORR, **A.93**
- NPAR TESTS, **A.94**
- FACTOR, **A.95**
- BOX-JENKINS, **A.96**
- RELIABILITY, **A.97**
- SURVIVAL, **A.98**

EXAMPLE, **A.99**

Appendix A Help for Old Friends

SPSS commands have been changed as little as possible in $SPSS^X$ in order to preserve upward compatibility of existing jobs. Though it is unlikely that an existing SPSS job will work in $SPSS^X$ with no changes, it is likely that only minor changes will be necessary.

This appendix is your reference for changing existing SPSS jobs to $SPSS^X$. Section A.1 contains important tables of nonprocedure and procedure commands, their status in $SPSS^X$, $SPSS^X$ alternatives, and the section references for this appendix. Sections A.2 through A.68 present more detailed summaries of changes for nonprocedure commands. Sections A.69 through A.98 describe differences for procedure commands. Finally, Section A.99 presents an example of a Release 9 SPSS job translated to $SPSS^X$ with highlights of differences and some advice on how to proceed.

A.1 SUMMARY OF CHANGES

The bulk of the changes between SPSS and $SPSS^X$ are in the areas of file definition and data transformation, that is, nonprocedure commands. An outline of changes to such commands is shown in Table A.1a. (See Appendix B for an explanation of how to determine the precedence order of commands in $SPSS^X$.) If a command has been replaced or rewritten, look at the section referenced in the table for summary information. If a command is obsolete, there is no need for it and it should be removed. If a command has been altered, you should look up the new syntax or function, but you probably won't need to make many changes. If a command is the same, it will work the same way in $SPSS^X$ as it did in SPSS. However, because the same commands have often been improved in $SPSS^X$, you should at least look up the commands in this appendix to see where you might be able to take advantage of new features.

Many procedures have been improved in $SPSS^X$, even though they are substantially the same as they were in SPSS. Table A.1b outlines the changes in procedures. If a procedure has been rewritten or replaced, look in this appendix for a summary of the changes and in the appropriate chapter for a complete description of the syntax and for examples. If a procedure is obsolete, it has been dropped in $SPSS^X$. If a procedure is the same, it will work in $SPSS^X$ without change in the same way it did in SPSS. However, many of the procedures have been improved, so you should consult the summaries for each procedure in this appendix.

Table A.1a Changes to nonprocedure commands

SPSS Command	Status	SPSS^X Command	Section
ADD CASES	replaced	ADD FILES	A.36
ADD DATA LIST	replaced	MATCH FILES	A.34
ADD SUBFILES	replaced	ADD FILES	A.36
ADD VARIABLES	replaced	MATCH FILES	A.34
ALLOCATE	obsolete		A.17
ASSIGN MISSING	obsolete		A.58
COMMENT	same		A.16
COMPUTE	same		A.63, A.66
COUNT	same		A.64
DATA LIST	altered		A.3
DELETE SUBFILES	obsolete		A.31
DELETE VARS	replaced	GET or SAVE	A.41
DO REPEAT	same		A.65
DOCUMENT	same		A.40
EDIT	same		A.16
END INPUT DATA	replaced	END DATA	A.14
END REPEAT	same		A.65
FILE NAME	obsolete		A.46
FINISH	same		A.16
GET ARCHIVE	obsolete		A.43
GET FILE	replaced	GET	A.38
GET SCSS	altered		A.48
IF	altered		A.67, A.68
INITIALIZE	replaced	LEAVE	A.54
INPUT FORMAT	replaced	DATA LIST	A.9
INPUT MEDIUM	replaced	FILE HANDLE	A.8
KEEP VARS	replaced	GET or SAVE	A.41
LAG	replaced	LAG function	A.60
LIST ARCHINFO	replaced	DISPLAY	A.43
LIST CASES	replaced	LIST	A.25
LIST ERRORS	obsolete		A.18
LIST FILEINFO	replaced	DISPLAY	A.45
MERGE FILES	replaced	MATCH FILES	A.35
MISSING VALUES	same		A.12
N OF CASES	altered		A.13, A.52
NUMBERED	same		A.19
OPTIONS	same		A.69
OSIRIS VARS	obsolete		A.47
PAGESIZE	replaced	SET	A.21
PRINT BACK	replaced	SET	A.22
PRINT FORMATS	altered		A.10
RAW OUTPUT UNIT	replaced	PROCEDURE OUTPUT	A.69
READ INPUT DATA	replaced	BEGIN DATA	A.14
READ MATRIX	replaced	INPUT MATRIX	A.69
RECODE	same		A.61, A.66
REORDER VARS	replaced	GET or SAVE	A.41
RUN NAME	renamed	TITLE	A.20
RUN SUBFILES	replaced	SPLIT FILE	A.31
SAMPLE	same		A.50
SAVE ARCHIVE	obsolete		A.43
SAVE FILE	replaced	SAVE	A.38
SAVE SCSS	rewritten		A.49
SEED	replaced	SET	A.23
SELECT IF	altered		A.51
STATISTICS	same		A.69
SUBFILE LIST	obsolete		A.31
TASK NAME	renamed	SUBTITLE	A.20
VALUE LABELS	same		A.11
VAR LABELS	same		A.11
VARIABLE LIST	replaced	DATA LIST	A.9
WEIGHT	same		A.53
WRITE FILEINFO	replaced	EXPORT	A.27

Table A.1b Changes to procedure commands

SPSS Command	Status	SPSS^{X} Command	Section
AGGREGATE	rewritten		A.70
ANOVA	same		A.81
BARCHART	same		A.79
BOX-JENKINS	same		A.96
BREAKDOWN	same		A.76
CANCORR	obsolete		A.69
CONDESCRIPTIVE	same		A.72
CROSSTABS	altered		A.73
DISCRIMINANT	altered		A.91
FACTOR	rewritten		A.95
FREQUENCIES	rewritten		A.71
GUTTMAN SCALE	obsolete		A.69
LINECHART	same		A.79
MANOVA	same		A.83
MULT RESPONSE	same		A.75
NEW REGRESSION	renamed	REGRESSION	A.90
NONPAR CORR	same		A.93
NPAR TESTS	same		A.94
ONEWAY	same		A.82
PARTIAL CORR	same		A.89
PEARSON CORR	same		A.88
PIECHART	same		A.79
REGRESSION	replaced	REGRESSION	A.90
RELIABILITY	same		A.97
REPORT	altered		A.77
SCATTERGRAM	same		A.87
SORT CASES	same		A.30
SURVIVAL	same		A.98
T-TEST	same		A.80
TRANSFORM	obsolete		A.69
WRITE CASES	replaced	WRITE or EXPORT	A.26

A.2 DATA DEFINITION COMMANDS

Sections A.3 through A.14 summarize changes in the data definition commands from SPSS to SPSS^{X}. See especially Sections A.3 through A.6 for a discussion of changes to the DATA LIST command. Unless otherwise indicated, consult Chapter 3 for defining files in SPSS^{X}.

Chapters 11 and 12 describe the extensions in SPSS^{X} to the file definition language which handle both complex file structures and problems with missing records.

A.3 DATA LIST

The DATA LIST command in SPSS^{X} is the only method for defining "raw" data (see Section A.9 for a discussion of changing VARIABLE LIST and INPUT FORMAT to DATA LIST). The syntax of DATA LIST has not changed very much from SPSS, so you should have little trouble updating SPSS variable definitions to SPSS^{X} syntax.

A.4 File Definition

In the file definition portion of the DATA LIST command, changes are

- The FILE subcommand is new and required, unless your data are included in the SPSS^{X} command file. Note the need for a FILE HANDLE command to define the file handle named on the FILE subcommand.
- The RECORDS subcommand specifies the total number of records per case, but SPSS syntax is accepted.
- Keyword TABLE has been added in SPSS^{X} to control printing of the variable format table.
- Keyword FIXED is the default in SPSS^{X} and is therefore optional.

A.5 Variable Definition

The variable definition portion of the DATA LIST command for SPSS works in SPSS^X in the same manner as in SPSS. There are some differences in variable naming conventions and in format types (see below).

SPSS allowed special characters in variable names and distinguished upper from lower case. In SPSS^X, variable names must start with a letter (or the symbols $, #, @) and lower case is not distinguished from upper case. See Chapter 2 for details.

A.6 Format Types

Specifications for some of the data format types have changed, depending on what kind of machine your installation has. For example, IBM integer binary (B) is now IB; packed decimal (C) is now P; and floating point binary (R) is now RB. In addition, several new format types are available in SPSS^X. Look for documentation via the INFO command on formats available on your machine (see Chapter 2).

SPSS^X interprets values defined with the F format type (the default) differently than SPSS did. Most versions of SPSS interpreted trailing blanks and embedded blanks as zeros. SPSS^X ignores trailing blanks and interprets the number portion only. In SPSS^X, values with embedded blanks defined with the default format are considered undefined and assigned the system-missing value. See the BLANKS subcommand of the SET command in SPSS^X (see Chapter 4).

A.7 Other Definitions

Data and file definitions in SPSS^X are very similar to definitions in SPSS. The VAR LABELS, VALUE LABELS, MISSING VALUES, and N OF CASES commands will work without change, although labeling in SPSS^X has new syntax and the N OF CASES command is unnecessary. Other commands are eliminated or require changes.

A.8 INPUT MEDIUM

The INPUT MEDIUM command has been dropped from SPSS^X. Its function is replaced by the FILE subcommand on the DATA LIST command and by the FILE HANDLE command in SPSS^X.

A.9 VARIABLE LIST and INPUT FORMAT

The VARIABLE LIST and INPUT FORMAT commands in SPSS have been dropped from SPSS^X. The specification fields from VARIABLE LIST and INPUT FORMAT can be easily combined into a variable definition for the SPSS^X DATA LIST command. For example, the SPSS commands

```
VARIABLE LIST  C1 TO C3 S1 TO S5 INCORP POP70 RANK70 POP80 RANK80 AREA
INPUT FORMAT   FIXED (T6,3A4,1X,5A4,F4.0,1X,F7.0,F2.0,F8.0,F2.0,F6.1//)
```

can be translated to the SPSS^X command

```
DATA LIST          FILE=CITYDATA RECORDS=3/
                   C1 TO C3 S1 TO S5 INCORP POP70 RANK70 POP80 RANK80 AREA
                   (T6,3A4,1X,5A4,F4.0,1X,F7.0,F2.0,F8.0,F2.0,F6.1//)
```

See Chapter 3 for details.

A.10 PRINT FORMATS

The PRINT FORMATS command is no longer required. SPSS^X automatically assigns the format used on the DATA LIST command to read the data as the print format. Thus, numeric variables defined with decimal positions and string variables normally will have the print format that you want. The PRINT FORMATS command is used only to change the assigned print format (see Chapter 9).

A.11 VARIABLE LABELS and VALUE LABELS

The syntax for specifying labels has changed in SPSS^X, but SPSS syntax is generally accepted with the restrictions that appeared in SPSS, Release 9. Labels that spanned command lines in SPSS will cause errors in SPSS^X. You are advised not to mix SPSS and SPSS^X syntax on the same command.

VAR LABELS is accepted as an alias for VARIABLE LABELS. In SPSS^X if you assign value labels to any variable that already has value labels assigned to it, the new assignment completely replaces the old assignment. The VALUE LABELS command is not additive for a variable.

A.12 MISSING VALUES

The MISSING VALUES command has not changed. You can declare missing values for short strings (defined by the double word length on your machine), but not for long strings.

A.13 N OF CASES

The N OF CASES command is no longer necessary for input data files. Its only function in SPSS^X is to limit the number of cases defined from a file to the first *n* cases. In SPSS, the N OF CASES limited the number of cases read; in SPSS^X, it limits the number of cases created, which makes a difference when you are sampling or selecting cases (see Chapter 10).

Keyword UNKNOWN is accepted but has no effect.

A.14 READ INPUT DATA and END INPUT DATA

The READ INPUT DATA and END INPUT DATA commands in SPSS have been changed in SPSS^X to BEGIN DATA and END DATA, respectively. The SPSS commands are not recognized as aliases for BEGIN DATA and END DATA.

A.15 UTILITY COMMANDS

The number of job-related facilities over which you have control has increased in SPSS^X, and the number of utility tasks you can accomplish in one job has expanded. The following sections describe how you control various features of an SPSS^X job; how to take a look at your actual cases before, during, and after creating or transforming them; and how to sort and define subsets of cases for display or analysis.

A.16 Job Utilities

A number of general utility commands have been changed. The RUN NAME and TASK NAME commands in SPSS have been renamed in SPSS^X and some SPSS commands have been made into subcommands of the SET command in SPSS^X. Unless otherwise noted, consult Chapter 4 for a description of the SPSS^X job utilities.

- The COMMENT command has not changed, but there is a new method of embedding comments in command lines using the /* and */ symbols to enclose the text.
- The EDIT command has not changed.
- The FINISH command has not changed and is always optional.

A.17 ALLOCATE

The ALLOCATE command in SPSS has been dropped in SPSS^X which uses memory dynamically.

A.18 LIST ERRORS

The LIST ERRORS command in SPSS has been dropped in SPSS^X. Warning and error messages in SPSS^X appear when the error is encountered.

A.19 NUMBERED

The NUMBERED command has not changed. Whether the default is NUMBERED or UNNUMBERED is an installation-specific option. See the SHOW command for local documentation.

A.20 RUN NAME and TASK NAME

The RUN NAME and TASK NAME commands in SPSS have been replaced by the TITLE and SUBTITLE commands in SPSS^X. The new syntax accepts the title as a literal within quotation marks or apostrophes. The SPSS command names are accepted and the SPSS syntax omitting the apostrophes or quotation marks is also accepted. If the literal is not enclosed in apostrophes or quotation marks, embedded apostrophes and quotation marks are taken literally, and doubling those characters will yield double characters in the title or subtitle.

The maximum length of the title is reduced from 64 characters to 60; titles or subtitles longer than 60 characters are truncated and a warning message is issued.

A.21 PAGESIZE

The PAGESIZE command in SPSS has been replaced by the LENGTH subcommand of the SET command in SPSS^X. SET LENGTH=NONE is the equivalent of the command PAGESIZE NOEJECT in SPSS. The default value for LENGTH is an installation-specific option. See the INFO command for local documentation (see Chapter 2).

A.22 PRINT BACK

The PRINT BACK command in SPSS has been replaced by the PRINTBACK subcommand on the SET command and by the NOTABLE subcommand on the DATA LIST command. The SET PRINTBACK command in SPSS^X controls the printing back of commands and the NOTABLE subcommand controls the printing of the format table from the DATA LIST command.

A.23 SEED

The SEED command in SPSS has been replaced by the SEED subcommand on the SET and SHOW commands in SPSS^X.

A.24 Listing and Writing Cases

There are a number of ways to look at your data on a case-by-case listing. The LIST command and the PRINT and WRITE commands are discussed below. In addition, the REPORT procedure can now be used to produce case listings; summaries are no longer required and you can specify NOBREAK. LIST, PRINT, and WRITE are documented in Chapter 9 and REPORT is documented in Chapter 23.

A.25 LIST CASES

The LIST CASES command in SPSS has been replaced by the LIST command in SPSS^X. The PRINT, PRINT EJECT, and PRINT SPACE commands have been added in SPSS^X to supplement case listing.

A.26 WRITE CASES

The WRITE CASES command in SPSS has been replaced by the WRITE command in SPSS^X. WRITE CASES is no longer needed to transport files across machine types (see the EXPORT command in Chapter 16).

A.27 WRITE FILEINFO

The function of the WRITE FILEINFO command in SPSS (in conjunction with the WRITE CASES command) has been replaced in SPSS^X by the EXPORT command (see Chapter 16).

A.28 Print and Write Formats

In SPSS, one format associated with each variable was used both to print and to write values to a file. The format defaulted to numeric with no decimal places unless changed by a PRINT FORMATS command.

In $SPSS^X$, there are two formats associated with each variable: a print format and a write format. The print format is used by the PRINT and LIST commands and most $SPSS^X$ procedures. The write format is used by the WRITE command. If you define your variables using a DATA LIST command, the print and write formats are generally the format specified on the variable definition portion of the DATA LIST command. You can use the PRINT FORMATS, WRITE FORMATS, and FORMATS to change only the print format, only the write format, or both formats for any variable.

A.29 Sorting Cases and Splitting Files

Sorting cases has not changed substantially, but $SPSS^X$ defines subsets of cases through file splits rather than a subfile structure.

A.30 SORT CASES

The number of variables that can be named on the SORT CASES command depends on the sort package used at your installation. The order of ties is always preserved in $SPSS^X$. The keyword BY is accepted, but optional, for compatibility with the WEIGHT and SPLIT FILE commands.

A.31 Subfiles

Subfiles are totally replaced by file splits in $SPSS^X$. Therefore, the SUBFILE LIST, ADD SUBFILES, DELETE SUBFILES, and RUN SUBFILES commands have been dropped. Likewise, the SUBFILES subcommand has been dropped from the SORT CASES command in $SPSS^X$.

File splits in $SPSS^X$ do not become a part of the system file; they must be respecified for each job.

A.32 Automatic Sequence Variable

The automatic variable SEQNUM in SPSS has been replaced by the \$CASENUM system variable in $SPSS^X$ (see Chapter 6). \$CASENUM does not reinitialize for each file split.

A.33 FILE UPDATE COMMANDS

Adding data to an existing file through either additional variables or additional cases is handled via the ADD FILES and MATCH FILES commands in $SPSS^X$ (see Chapter 15). The MATCH FILES command in particular can handle nonparallel matches and lookup tables.

A.34 ADD DATA LIST and ADD VARIABLES

The ADD DATA LIST and ADD VARIABLES commands in SPSS have been replaced by the MATCH FILES command in $SPSS^X$. MATCH FILES requires that all files being combined be system files or the active file. If your files are input data files, you save them temporarily as system files before using MATCH FILES. To do this in one $SPSS^X$ job, you use a DATA LIST command to describe each input file and a SAVE command to save each file as a system file.

A.35 MERGE FILES

The MERGE FILES command in SPSS has been replaced by the MATCH FILES facility in $SPSS^X$ to match parallel files.

A.36 ADD CASES and ADD SUBFILES

The ADD CASES and ADD SUBFILES commands in SPSS have been replaced by the ADD FILES command in SPSS^X. Subfile structures cannot be defined in SPSS^X (see the SPLIT FILE command in Chapter 13). ADD FILES requires that all files being combined be system files or the active file. If your files are input data files, you save them temporarily as system files before using ADD FILES. You can accomplish this in one SPSS^X job.

A.37 SYSTEM FILE COMMANDS

System files created in SPSS can be read in SPSS^X with the cautions outlined below. System files saved with SPSS^X cannot be read by SPSS.

A.38 Reading SPSS System Files

System files created with SPSS can be read with the SPSS^X GET command as long as the file is created and read on the same type of computer. When you use the GET command to read an SPSS system file, SPSS^X prints a message informing you that the system file is an old-format file and that the variable CASWGT is used for case weighting. CASWGT contains the value 1 for all cases unless the system file was originally saved as a weighted file using the WEIGHT command. CASWGT is the first variable in the system file. It can be deleted from the file using the DROP subcommand but cannot be implicitly deleted from the file using the KEEP subcommand. The CASWGT variable can be reordered in the file.

When the SPSS file is read, all blank values for numeric variables will automatically be changed to the system-missing value or the value set with the BLANKS subcommand on the SET command (see Chapter 4).

If you used the keyword THRU on MISSING VALUES to declare a range of missing values for an alphanumeric variable on an SPSS system file, the missing values will not always be recognized by SPSS^X. You should declare the missing values in SPSS^X or change the missing-value declaration on the SPSS system file before reading it with SPSS^X. Missing values for numeric variables are always be handled correctly by SPSS^X.

If the print format for a variable was not specified correctly on the SPSS system file, SPSS^X will not handle the values correctly. This problem occurs most frequently for alphanumeric variables that have not been declared as such on the PRINT FORMATS command in SPSS. Use the REFORMAT command to change the type of the variable from alphanumeric to numeric or from numeric to alphanumeric, and use FORMATS, WRITE FORMATS, or PRINT FORMATS to change the number of decimal places for numeric variables (see Section A.39).

SPSS was more liberal in allowing special characters in variable names and it distinguished upper from lower case. SPSS^X is more restrictive. Variable names must start with a letter (or the symbols $, #, @) and lower case is not distinguished from upper case. Therefore, when an SPSS system file is read, lower case is changed to upper case and special characters are changed to periods. Duplicate names generated in this way are changed to SYS1, SYS2, and so forth, skipping any names that already exist. SPSS^X tells you what has happened.

System files created with SPSS are stored in a different format from system files saved with SPSS^X, and more processing time is required to read SPSS system files. Therefore, if you intend to execute SPSS^X several times on your file, you should save the system file with SPSS^X.

A.39 REFORMAT

In SPSS, all variables were printed as integers unless you used a PRINT FORMATS command to specify that the variable was alphanumeric or to specify the number of decimal places. If you did not use a PRINT FORMATS command when you saved a system file with SPSS, the print formats for alphanumeric and decimal variables are indicated incorrectly on the SPSS system file as integer. When you read an SPSS system file using SPSS^X, these variables have dictionary print and write formats of F8.0. The missing-value specifications are also expressed as integers.

To change the print formats, write formats, and missing-value specifications for variables from alphanumeric to numeric, or from numeric to alphanumeric, use ALPHA and NUMERIC subcommands of the REFORMAT command, as in:

```
REFORMAT ALPHA=NAME1 TO NAME6/ NUMERIC=HOURLY79 TO HOURLY82
```

This command declares NAME1 to NAME6 as alphanumeric variables with dictionary print and write formats of A4. HOURLY79 TO HOURLY82 are declared to be numeric variables with dictionary print and write formats of F8.2 (or the format you specify using the SET command described in Chapter 4). Missing-value specifications for variables named with both the ALPHA and NUMERIC keywords are also changed to conform to the new formats.

After you have reformatted variables from your SPSS system file, you should create an SPSS^X system file by using a SAVE command. This will save you the time and trouble of having to reformat these variables each time you wish to use them. See Chapter 5 for a discussion of the SAVE command.

REFORMAT always assigns the print and write format F8.2 (or the format specified using the SET command) to variables specified after the NUMERIC keyword, and A4 to variables specified after the ALPHA keyword. However, you might want to declare a different total length for the variable or a different number of decimal places. For numeric variables, use the PRINT FORMATS, WRITE FORMATS, or FORMATS commands to change the format specifications. See Chapter 9 for a discussion of these commands.

You cannot use the PRINT FORMATS, WRITE FORMATS, or FORMATS commands to change the length of string variables in SPSS^X. To change the length of string variables, you must declare new string variables and use the COMPUTE command to assign the values of the original variable to the new variable. The following commands declare formats of A2 for the variable MMN and A3 for VISDAY.

```
FILE HANDLE R9FILE/ file specifications
GET FILE R9FILE
STRING XMMN (A2)/XVISDAY (A3)
COMPUTE XMMN=MMN
COMPUTE XVISDAY=VISDAY
FILE HANDLE NEWXFILE/ file specifications
SAVE OUTFILE=NEWXFILE/DROP=MMN VISDAY/
    RENAME=(XVISDAY=VISDAY) (XMMN=MMN)
```

The above commands do the following:

- GET accesses the SPSS system file.
- STRING declares XMMN as a string variable with two positions and XVISDAY as a string variable with three positions.
- COMPUTE commands are used to transfer the information from the old system-file variables MMN and VISDAY to the SPSS^X string variables XMMN and XVISDAY.

- The SAVE command saves a new SPSS^X system file. The DROP subcommand drops the SPSS system-file variables with the inappropriate formats. RENAME renames the new SPSS^X string variables to the original names, MMN and VISDAY.

A.40 Other System File Commands

Deleting, retaining, and reordering variables is now done on the GET or SAVE commands, and there is no need for archiving system files.

The DOCUMENT command has not changed.

A.41 DELETE VARS and KEEP VARS

The DELETE VARS and KEEP VARS commands in SPSS have been replaced by the KEEP and DROP subcommands on the GET and SAVE commands in SPSS^X.

A.42 REORDER VARS

The REORDER VARS command in SPSS has been replaced by the KEEP subcommand on the GET and SAVE commands in SPSS^X.

A.43 Archive Files

Because the number of variables allowed in SPSS^X is essentially unlimited, there is no need for archive files. Therefore, the GET ARCHIVE, SAVE ARCHIVE, and LIST ARCHINFO commands have been dropped. Existing archive files can be read as ordinary SPSS system files, and MATCH FILES can be used in SPSS^X to combine files (see Chapter 15).

A.44 Subfiles

System files in SPSS^X cannot be defined with a subfile structure. The SPLIT FILE command defines subsets of cases in a system file (see Chapter 13).

A.45 LIST FILEINFO

The LIST FILEINFO command in SPSS has been replaced by the DISPLAY command in SPSS^X. The LIST ARCHINFO command has been dropped.

A.46 FILE NAME

The FILE NAME command in SPSS has been dropped. No name is stored on SPSS^X system files. The label specification on the FILE NAME command in SPSS is replaced by the FILE LABEL command in SPSS^X.

A.47 File Interfaces

SPSS^X reads and writes SCSS masterfiles (see below). SPSS^X also reads and writes a transportable file (see the EXPORT command in Chapter 16). The OSIRIS VARS command has been dropped in SPSS^X, but considerations are under way for interfaces to various software packages and data bases. See the INFO command described in Chapter 2 for the latest information.

A.48 GET SCSS

The GET SCSS command in SPSS^X reads an SCSS masterfile or workfile/masterfile combination. The VARIABLES subcommand operates the same as the VARIABLES= specification in SPSS. The MIS= specification in SPSS is no longer valid. SPSS^X automatically recodes problem numeric values to the system-missing value, recodes problem alphabetic values to blanks, and informs you what has been done.

A.49 SAVE SCSS

The SAVE SCSS command has been completely revised for SPSS^X. The minimum specification requires that you name the file handle of the masterfile to be saved. With optional subcommands, you can reorder, keep, drop, or rename variables.

A.50 DATA SELECTION COMMANDS

Case selection, sampling, and weighting are basically the same in $SPSS^X$ as in SPSS. The SAMPLE command has not changed.

A.51 SELECT IF

Missing expressions are false in $SPSS^X$. In SPSS, logical expressions were not checked for missing values.

The parentheses enclosing logical expressions are optional in $SPSS^X$.

A.52 N OF CASES

The N OF CASES command used as a case selection command controls the building of cases in $SPSS^X$, not the reading of records as in SPSS. This means that the exact number of cases specified on N OF CASES will be built in $SPSS^X$ (assuming a sufficient number of input records).

A.53 WEIGHT

The keyword BY precedes the variable name in $SPSS^X$. To turn off weighting use the keyword OFF.

A.54 DATA TRANSFORMATIONS

Data transformations in $SPSS^X$ have changed in a number of ways. In $SPSS^X$, the active file can be rewritten to the scratch disk more than once, which means that permanent data transformations can occur anywhere including after the first procedure. In fact, unless you use the TEMPORARY command (see below), transformations are assumed to be permanent and the data are rewritten.

Extensions to the transformation language in $SPSS^X$ include scratch variables, the LEAVE command (replacing the undocumented INITIALIZE command), automatic missing-value propagation, expanded manipulation of string variables, and a number of new functions. Unless otherwise noted, data transformations are discussed in Chapters 6 through 8.

A.55 Temporary Transformations

There are no asterisked transformation commands in $SPSS^X$. Temporary transformations in $SPSS^X$ are those that follow a TEMPORARY command and precede the next procedure.

A.56 Numeric Transformations

Numeric variables are manipulated principally through the COMPUTE, RECODE, and COUNT commands in $SPSS^X$. This has not changed much from SPSS. The main additions to the language concern missing-value propagation and additional syntax to handle the system-missing value (see Chapter 6).

A.57 Initialization

New numeric variables are initialized to system-missing (except when specified on the LEAVE command). In SPSS, new numeric variables were initialized to zero.

A.58 ASSIGN MISSING

The ASSIGN MISSING command in SPSS has been dropped. Propagation of missing values in SPSS^X is similar to the ASSIGN MISSING command, except that the value propagated is always the system-missing value.

A.59 Functions

SPSS^X functions ANY and RANGE substitute for implied operators in logical expressions which were accepted in SPSS but are not accepted in SPSS^X. There are many new functions in SPSS^X, particularly statistical and logical functions.

A.60 LAG

The LAG command in SPSS is replaced by the LAG function in SPSS^X. This is not an exact replacement because LAG as a function in SPSS^X has different implications from LAG as a command in SPSS.

- LAG as a function in SPSS^X does not reset for file splits whereas LAG as a command in SPSS resets for subfiles.
- When the result of a LAG operation is missing, the system-missing value is returned, whereas SPSS had a more complicated procedure for determining the missing value.
- In SPSS^X, a lag function may be placed anywhere in relation to data selection or sampling, whereas a lag function in SPSS was executed where it was encountered, which made a difference with commands such as SELECT IF, for example.

If you have an SPSS job that assumes that a SELECT IF takes place after a LAG operation, you should probably look at the LEAVE command as an alternative to the LAG function in SPSS^X. If you assume that lagging takes place on selected cases, then the transition to SPSS^X should be easier.

A.61 RECODE

The RECODE command has been enhanced in SPSS^X. New keyword INTO recodes a variable's values by storing them into a new variable. SPSS^X keyword COPY copies values unchanged. SPSS^X keywords MISSING and SYSMIS recode input values, and keyword SYSMIS is an output value. Keyword BLANK has been dropped; see the SET command (see Chapter 4). Keyword CONVERT does not convert 11 and 12 "punches" automatically as it did in SPSS.

A.62 Recoding Blanks

The BLANK keyword on the RECODE command in SPSS is replaced by the BLANKS subcommand on the SET command in SPSS^X. SET BLANKS affects all numeric variables, so if you want to treat blanks differently for different variables, use the RECODE command for the variables in question.

A.63 COMPUTE

The COMPUTE command is basically the same. See the comments on missing-value propagation in Section A.58.

A.64 COUNT

The COUNT command is basically the same. New keywords are MISSING and SYSMIS. SPSS keyword BLANK has been dropped.

A.65 DO REPEAT and END REPEAT

The DO REPEAT facility is basically the same. The END REPEAT command in $SPSS^X$ accepts the PRINT subcommand to print the commands that are generated. END REPEAT does not therefore accept the rest of the command line as a comment, as it did in SPSS.

A.66 String Transformations

New string (alphanumeric) variables in $SPSS^X$ must be declared on a STRING command before they can be altered using data transformations such as COMPUTE, IF, or RECODE. New string variables are initialized to blanks. Only short strings (up to the double word length on your machine) can have missing values. String variables can be up to 255 characters long. (See Chapter 7.)

A.67 Conditional Transformations

The IF command is largely unchanged. However, it is supplemented by the DO IF structure for more complex conditional transformations. (See Chapter 8.)

A.68 Logical Expressions

Parentheses enclosing logical expressions are optional in $SPSS^X$ for commands such as IF, SELECT IF, and DO IF.

There are no implied operators or expressions in $SPSS^X$. Be very cautious: the command

```
IF (X EQ 0 OR 1) Y=5
```

does not have a syntax error because 1 is a valid numeric expression (logical in this case) that evaluates as true. Thus, this command always sets Y equal to 5. See the ANY and RANGE functions in Chapter 6 for alternatives to implied operators.

There are exceptions to the general rule in $SPSS^X$ that missing values found in logical expressions cause the expression to be evaluated as missing: Missing AND true yields true, missing OR false yields false.

A logical expression on an IF command that evaluates as missing has the same result as if it were false.

Optional relational symbols are ¬= and <> for NE, < and > for LT and GT, <= and >= for LE and GE, and = for EQ.

A.69 PROCEDURE COMMANDS

Some procedures have been brought over to $SPSS^X$ unchanged, some have undergone minor or major changes, and some have been completely rewritten.

- Procedures GUTTMAN SCALE and CANCORR have been dropped completely (see the MANOVA procedure for an alternative to CANCORR).
- Procedure LOGLINEAR is completely new in $SPSS^X$.
- The OPTIONS and STATISTICS commands have not changed. However, some options and statistics for specific procedures have been altered, added, or deleted. New procedures do not use these commands at all.
- The RAW OUTPUT UNIT command in SPSS has been replaced by the PROCEDURE OUTPUT command in $SPSS^X$.
- The READ MATRIX command in SPSS has been replaced by the INPUT MATRIX command in $SPSS^X$.

Otherwise, see the specifics on each procedure in the sections below.

A.70 AGGREGATE

AGGREGATE has been completely redesigned for SPSS^{X}. Since its syntax completely differs from SPSS AGGREGATE, see Chapter 14 for a discussion of the AGGREGATE syntax. Substantively SPSS^{X} AGGREGATE differs from SPSS AGGREGATE in the following respects:

- AGGREGATE produces a completely defined system file that can be analyzed in the same execution of SPSS^{X}. SPSS AGGREGATE produced a data file that required complete definition (i.e., DATA LIST, N OF CASES, MISSING VALUES, VAR LABELS, VALUE LABELS, etc.) before further processing with SPSS.
- AGGREGATE now contains the FIRST and LAST functions and functions producing fraction results as well as percentages. The percentage functions can now be requested more than once for a given source variable.
- The skewness and kurtosis functions have been dropped.
- The compositional file has been dropped. Its function has been replaced in SPSS^{X} by the TABLES subcommand in the MATCH FILES facility. (See Chapter 15 for details.)
- AGGREGATE no longer prints the contents of aggregate cases. Instead use the PRINT or LIST commands (see Chapter 9).

A.71 FREQUENCIES

FREQUENCIES syntax has been completely revised (see Chapter 18). Options and statistics are requested with keywords on subcommands. Subcommands INTEGER and GENERAL have been replaced by the VARIABLES subcommand, although they are still recognized. FREQUENCIES uses the presence or absence of a range specification to determine which mode is used. If the GENERAL subcommand is used and ranges are given, integer mode is in effect. If the INTEGER subcommand is used but no ranges are given, general mode is in effect. The default format for the frequency table has been changed. Multiple tables can be printed on one page and categories are single spaced. The following enhancements have been made:

- Both histograms and bargraphs are available. You can control the formatting of either in a variety of ways.
- You can superimpose the normal curve on a histogram.
- You can suppress the printing of tables having more categories than a specified limit.

The following changes have been made to statistics available in FREQUENCIES:

- Standard errors for the skewness and kurtosis are available.
- A new formula is used for the calculation of the median.
- The sum is available.

For the sake of upward compatibility, FREQUENCIES recognizes both SPSS syntax and options and statistics numbers. If you use the GENERAL or INTEGER keywords to specify variable names, you can also use the OPTIONS and STATISTICS commands to request nondefault displays. Table A.71 shows the correspondence between keywords and options and statistics numbers. Statistics and options marked with a double asterisk (**) were not available in SPSS but are recognized in SPSS^{X}.

Table A.71 Correspondence between keywords, options, and statistics for FREQUENCIES

SPSS	SPSS^X
Option 1	MISSING=INCLUDE
Option 2	FORMAT=NOLABELS
Option 3	Default
Option 4	FILE=handle
Option 5	FORMAT=CONDENSE
Option 6	FORMAT=ONEPAGE
Option 7	FORMAT=NOTABLE
Option 8	BARCHART
Option 9	FORMAT=INDEX
Option 10	FORMAT=DVALUE
Option 11	FORMAT=DFREQ
Option 12	FORMAT=AFREQ
Option 13**	FORMAT=DOUBLE
Option 14**	FORMAT=NEWPAGE
Option 15**	HISTOGRAM
Statistic 1	STATISTICS=MEAN
Statistic 2	STATISTICS=SEMEAN
Statistic 3	STATISTICS=MEDIAN
Statistic 4	STATISTICS=MODE
Statistic 5	STATISTICS=STDDEV
Statistic 6	STATISTICS=VARIANCE
Statistic 7	STATISTICS=KURTOSIS
Statistic 8	STATISTICS=SKEWNESS
Statistic 9	STATISTICS=RANGE
Statistic 10	STATISTICS=MINIMUM
Statistic 11	STATISTICS=MAXIMUM
Statistic 12	STATISTICS=SUM
Statistic 13**	STATISTICS=SEKURT
Statistic 14**	STATISTICS=SESKEW

A.72 CONDESCRIPTIVE

The following changes have been made to CONDESCRIPTIVE in SPSS^X (see Chapter 19):

- The default formatting style has been changed. To obtain the old format, use Option 6.
- A narrow formatting option is now available.
- *Z*-scores are automatically saved on the active file with Option 3. It automatically provides names and variable labels for the variables saved. You may also provide your own names for the *Z*-scored variables.
- Listwise deletion of missing data is available.
- Default statistics are mean, standard deviation, minimum, and maximum.
- Standard errors are reported for skewness and kurtosis.

A.73 CROSSTABS

The following changes have been made to CROSSTABS in SPSS^X (see Chapter 20):

- Equals signs are optional following subcommand keywords in integer mode.
- The keyword TABLES is optional in general mode.
- The format of statistical output has been changed, but the list of available statistics remains the same.
- Joint specification of Option 12 plus a STATISTICS command produces statistical results without the tabular output. Before, the result would be no output.

- Table percentages are printed with the percent sign when requested along with expected values or residuals (see below).
- Blanks are printed instead of zeros for counts and percentages when printed without expected values or residuals (see below).

A.74 New Options List

Several options have changed and several have been added. In SPSS^{X}, if you execute CROSSTABS with no options, tables will include cell counts only. The changes are

OPTION 3 *Print row percentages.* Changed from suppress row percentages.
OPTION 4 *Print column percentages.* Changed from suppress column percentages.
OPTION 5 *Print total percentages.* Changed from suppress total percentages.
OPTION 6 *Suppress value labels.* Now works in general mode.
OPTION 8 *Print rows ordered on highest to lowest values.* Now works in general mode.
OPTION 13 *Suppress cell counts.* New in SPSS^{X}.
OPTION 14 *Print expected frequencies.* New in SPSS^{X}.
OPTION 15 *Print residuals.* New in SPSS^{X}.
OPTION 16 *Print standardized residuals.* New in SPSS^{X}.
OPTION 17 *Print adjusted standardized residuals.* New in SPSS^{X}.
OPTION 18 *Print all cell information.* New in SPSS^{X}.

A.75 MULT RESPONSE

No substantial changes have been made to MULT RESPONSE in SPSS^{X}. MULT RESPONSE does follow the SPSS^{X} conventions for assigning labels to variables (i.e., they are enclosed in apostrophes); however, the SPSS syntax is accepted (see Chapter 21).

A.76 BREAKDOWN

The following changes have been made to BREAKDOWN in SPSS^{X} (see Chapter 22):

- Equals signs are optional following subcommand keywords.
- The keyword TABLES is optional in general mode.
- CROSSBREAK no longer prints statistics 3 through 12.

A.77 REPORT

Many changes have been made to REPORT in SPSS^{X} (see Chapter 23). In particular, see the keyword changes in Table A.78. General changes are

- Apostrophes are permitted within column heads, footnotes, and titles.
- Equals signs following subcommand keywords are optional.
- Keywords can be abbreviated to their first three characters.
- Long string variables can be specified on the STRING, VARS, and BREAK subcommands.

The FORMAT Subcommand.

- The FORMAT subcommand is now optional. If used, it must be the first subcommand.
- The MISSING specification on the FORMAT subcommand can be used to change any missing values in listings, break listings, and summaries to any one-character string.

- The maximum line width has been set to the maximum systemwide page width.
- The SUMSPACE keyword on the FORMAT subcommand controls spacing between summaries at different levels.

The STRING Subcommand.

- Keyword BLANK on the STRING subcommand left fills numeric variables with blanks rather than zeros.

The VARIABLES Subcommand.

- Column titles for columns with strings and the labels in the columns are left-justified. Column titles for columns of numbers are right-justified.
- The OFFSET keyword on the VARIABLES subcommand offsets column contents under the column heading.
- The default column width for numeric variables or dummy columns is now 8. The default column width for string variables is the maximum of the dictionary width or 8, which ever is larger.
- If LABEL is specified for a variable and some but not all values are labeled, unlabeled values are printed as strings and are left-justified within the column.

The BREAK Subcommand.

- The NOBREAK keyword on the BREAK subcommand specifies no breaks.
- The TOTAL parameter is used on the BREAK subcommand.
- A summary can be placed on the same line as the break value (BRKSPACE(−1)).
- Break titles for columns with strings and the labels in the columns are left-justified. Break titles for columns of numbers are right-justified.
- The OFFSET keyword on the BREAK subcommand offsets column contents under the break heading.
- If LABEL is specified for a variable and some but not all values are labeled, unlabeled values are printed as strings and are left-justified within the column.

The SUMMARY Subcommand.

- The SUMMARY subcommand is now optional.
- Each line of a summary is specified with a SUMMARY subcommand. CONTINUE is no longer used to place one summary group with another on the same line.
- The keyword SKIP on the SUMMARY commands controls spacing between summary lines at the same break level.
- The default target for a composite is the leftmost VARS variable named as an argument to the composite function.
- Keywords DOLLAR, COMMA, and PLAIN on the SUMMARY subcommand print the statistic in dollar format, comma format, or F format, respectively.
- Variables used as arguments in composite functions do not have to be declared on the VARS subcommand.
- MULTIPLY has been added as a new composite function. It takes up to 100 arguments and has a default print format of 2.

- By default, a blank line is inserted between the summary at the lowest level and the next highest summary. See the SUMSPACE keyword on the FORMAT subcommand to control spacing between summaries at different levels.
- VALIDN on strings and alphanumeric variables is allowed.
- Commas between arguments to functions are required in SPSS^X.

A.78 Keyword Changes

Table A.78 shows the keyword changes in REPORT syntax between SPSS and SPSS^X.

Table A.78 REPORT keyword changes

SPSS	SPSS^X
HEAD	TITLE
CHEAD	CTITLE
LHEAD	LTITLE
RHEAD	RTITLE
FOOT	FOOTNOTE
CFOOT	CFOOTNOTE
LFOOT	LFOOTNOTE
RFOOT	RFOOTNOTE
HDSPACE	TSPACE
TITLE	NAME
NOTITLE	NONAME
PCTLT	PCLT
PCTGT	PCGT
PCTBTN	PCIN

A.79 GRAPHICS

All PIECHART, BARCHART, and LINECHART jobs that run correctly under Release 9 should continue to do so under SPSS^X. Three additional subcommands are available in all three procedures.

- XPAGE sets the width of the page in inches (default 11).
- YPAGE sets the height of the page in inches (default 8½).
- FONT establishes the type style to be used when FORMAT=FANCY. Choices are DUPLEX (the default), COMPLEX, TRIPLEX, and GOTHIC.
- The maximum number of colors in addition to black (the COLORS subcommand) is now seven. The maximum specification to the ORDERS subcommand is now 28.
- The postprocessor now asks additional, device-specific questions to take advantage of characteristics of individual devices.
- The GRAPHICS OUTPUT command is required to specify where the intermediate file is to be written.

A.80 T-TEST

The following changes have been made to T-TEST in SPSS^X (see Chapter 25):

- T-TEST now provides a narrow formatting option for short-carriage terminals.
- T-TEST no longer recognizes GROUPS=n1,n2.
- TTEST is accepted as an alias.

A.81 ANOVA

The following changes have been made to ANOVA in SPSS^X (see Chapter 26):

- The maximum number of independent variables that can be specified is 10, and the maximum number of covariates that can be specified is 10, whereas in SPSS the maximum for both was five. Note that although the maximums have been increased, interaction effects greater than five-way are always ignored.
- The page headers have been simplified.
- All calculations are done in double precision on short-word machines.

A.82 ONEWAY

The following changes have been made to ONEWAY in SPSS^X (see Chapter 27):

- Both homogeneous subsets and paired comparisons are available for range tests on balanced designs or when the harmonic mean is used. Previously, paired comparisons were printed only for unbalanced designs in which homogeneous subsets might provide erroneous results.
- Equals signs are optional.
- Subcommands POLYNOMIAL, CONTRASTS, and RANGES can be entered in any order following the design specification. If more than one POLYNOMIAL subcommand is used, the last named is in effect for the analysis.

A.83 MANOVA

MANOVA in SPSS^X remains largely the same as in SPSS, with changes falling into three categories: WRITE and READ, repeated measures, and others.

A.84 WRITE and READ

The WRITE subcommand in SPSS^X MANOVA replaces the PUNCH subcommand in SPSS MANOVA. The READ subcommand reads summary materials produced by the WRITE subcommand.

A.85 Repeated Measures

There are five changes in the way SPSS^X MANOVA handles repeated measures designs.

- The new MEASURE subcommand names multivariate pooled results.
- The TRANSFORM keyword on the PRINT and NOPRINT subcommands requests printing or suppression of printing of the transformation matrix.
- The SIGNIF(AVONLY) keyword on the PRINT and NOPRINT subcommands requests printing or suppression of printing of pooled results only.
- You can specify a variable list on ANALYSIS(REPEATED).
- The MWITHIN statement specifies simple effects on DESIGN and WSDESIGN statements.

MEASURE. In SPSS MANOVA, you could test the assumption of symmetry which the univariate approach requires and you could obtain univariate and multivariate results using the multivariate setup. In SPSS^X MANOVA, this feature has been extended to the class of doubly multivariate repeated measures designs. The name "doubly multivariate" refers to two dimensions of complexity. That is, you have measured subjects on two or more attributes and on two or more occasions. In this situation, use the MEASURE subcommand to name the multivariate pooled results. Finally, the MEASURE subcommand is optional in SPSS^X.

TRANSFORM. In SPSS MANOVA, the program automatically printed the transformation matrix. In SPSS^X MANOVA, the program does not automatically print this matrix. Instead, you can specify:

```
PRINT = TRANSFORM/
```

AVONLY. In singly multivariate or doubly multivariate repeated measure analysis, the program default is to print the multivariate approach results. You requested that the program additionally print pooled results corresponding to univariate mixed model by specifying the SPSS keyword:

```
PRINT = SIGNIF(AVERF)/
```

In SPSS^X, to print only the pooled results corresponding to the univariate approach, specify:

```
PRINT = SIGNIF(AVONLY)/
```

ANALYSIS(REPEATED). In SPSS^X, you can specify variables on the ANALYSIS(REPEATED) subcommand. This allows you to examine many models in the same MANOVA invocation. Named variables can be either dependent variables or covariates, but you must first name them in the initial MANOVA specification.

MWITHIN. Use the MWITHIN keyword in SPSS^X to obtain partitioned simple effects for either within-subject factors or between-subjects factors. Thus, you can specify MWITHIN on either the WSDESIGN subcommand or the DESIGN subcommand.

A.86 Other Changes

Other changes include the following:

- You can specify more than one TRANSFORM statement in an invocation of MANOVA.
- You can specify more than one WSDESIGN statement in an invocation of MANOVA.
- You must specify a DESIGN statement between two ANALYSIS statements; failure to do so produces a fatal error.

There are many minor cosmetic changes; generally, MANOVA issues more messages about what it is doing.

A.87 SCATTERGRAM

No changes have been made to SCATTERGRAM in SPSS^X (see Chapter 30).

A.88 PEARSON CORR

No changes have been made to PEARSON CORR in SPSS^X (see Chapter 31). See Chapter 17 for a discussion of matrix input and output.

A.89 PARTIAL CORR

No substantative changes have been made to PARTIAL CORR in SPSS^X (see Chapter 32). The number of orders has been increased to 100. See Chapter 17 for a discussion of matrix input and output.

A.90 REGRESSION

The NEW REGRESSION command in SPSS has been renamed REGRESSION in SPSS^X (see Chapter 33). REGRESSION in SPSS has been dropped.

REGRESSION saves casewise materials (residuals, predictors, etc.) on the active file in SPSS^{X}. See Chapter 17 for a discussion of matrix input and output.

A.91 DISCRIMINANT

The following changes have been made to DISCRIMINANT in SPSS^{X} (see Chapter 34):

- Equals signs are optional following subcommand keywords.
- Slashes are optional for all subcommands except VARIABLES and ANALYSIS.
- The SAVE subcommand saves casewise classification information rather than Options 17, 18, and 19.
- Casewise materials are saved on the active file, rather than written to an external file.
- Two new options are available: classify only unselected cases (Option 9), and classify only unclassified cases (Option 10).
- Statistics and Options numbers have been reorganized. See the table in the following section.

See Chapter 17 for a discussion of matrix input and output.

A.92 New Options and Statistics List

The options and statistics for the DISCRIMINANT procedure have been reorganized in SPSS^{X}. Many of the so-called options in SPSS have been made statistics in SPSS^{X} and the options associated with writing DISCRIMINANT results are now obtained with the SAVE subcommand. Use Table A.92 for to convert any current DISCRIMINANT jobs from SPSS to SPSS^{X}.

Table A.92 Correspondence between SPSS and SPSS^{X} options and statistics for DISCRIMINANT

Description	SPSS^{X}	SPSS
Include missing data	Option 1	Option 1
Include missing during classification	Option 8	Option 2
Suppress step output	Option 4	Option 3
Suppress summary table	Option 5	Option 4
Classification results table	Statistic 13	Option 5
Casewise materials	Statistic 14	Option 6
Combined plot	Statistic 15	Option 7
Separate plot	Statistic 16	Option 8
Suppress classification for unclassified cases	Default	Option 9
Territorial map	Statistic 10	Option 10
Unstandardized discriminant function coefficients	Statistic 11	Option 11
Classification function coefficients	Statistic 12	Option 12
Varimax rotation of discriminant function matrix	Option 6	Option 13
Individual covariance matrices for classification	Option 11	Option 14
Write matrix materials	Option 2	Option 15
Read matrix materials	Option 3	Option 16
Write discriminant scores	SAVE	Option 17
Write membership probabilities	SAVE	Option 18
Write actual and classified group numbers	SAVE	Option 19
Varimax rotation of structure matrix	Option 7	N.A.
Classify only unselected cases	Option 9	N.A.
Classify only unclassified cases	Option 10	N.A.
Means	Statistic 1	Statistic 1
Standard deviations	Statistic 2	Statistic 2
Pooled within-groups covariance matrix	Statistic 3	Statistic 3
Pooled within-groups correlation matrix	Statistic 4	Statistic 4
Matrix of pairwise F ratios	Statistic 5	Statistic 5
Univariate F ratios	Statistic 6	Statistic 6
Box's M	Statistic 7	Statistic 7
Group covariance matrices	Statistic 8	Statistic 8
Total covariance matrix	Statistic 9	Statistic 9
Structure matrix	Default	Statistic 10

A.93 NONPAR CORR

The following changes have been made to NONPAR CORR in SPSS^X (see Chapter 36):

- The default printing format for variable lists without the keyword WITH is a lower-triangular matrix. A rectangular matrix is printed for lists using WITH.
- Option 8 prints matrices without *n*'s and exact significance levels. Significant correlations are flagged with one or two asterisks corresponding to the .01 or .001 level.
- Option 9 prints matrices in the old-style serial format.
- NPAR CORR is accepted as an alias.

A.94 NPAR TESTS

The following changes have been made to NPAR TESTS in SPSS^X (see Chapter 37):

- Subcommands BINOMIAL and KENDALL are now explicitly supported.
- Printing formats have been changed to produce clearer output. Virtually every test prints in a narrow page format. For this reason, Option 5 is redundant.
- Additional summary statistics are available. Quartiles are printed with Statistic 2.
- NONPAR TESTS is accepted as an alias.

A.95 FACTOR

FACTOR has been completely redesigned for SPSS^X. Consult Chapter 35 for the new syntax. Briefly, the following significant enhancements have been made:

- The limitation of 100 variables has been removed.
- Mean substitution has been added to the missing-value options.
- Additional statistics include the reproduced correlation matrix, anti-image covariance matrix, and the Kaiser-Meyer-Olkin measure of sampling adequacy.
- Formatting options include sorting the factor loadings and blanking correlations and loadings below a user-specified threshold.
- Three new extraction methods are available: unweighted least squares, generalized least squares, and maximum likelihood.
- A plot of eigenvalues is available.
- Factor scores are saved on the active file. Two new methods of computing factor scores are available: Bartlett and Anderson-Rubin.
- The width of the printed output is subject to user control.

See Chapter 17 for a discussion of matrix input and output.

A.96 BOX-JENKINS

The VARIABLES subcommand must be the first subcommand and a maximum of 10 variables can be specified (see Chapter 38).

A.97 RELIABILITY

Option 15 now automatically turns on Option 14 (see Chapter 39). Also, see Chapter 17 for a discussion of matrix input and output.

A.98 SURVIVAL

No changes have been made to survival in SPSS^X (see Chapter 40).

A.99 EXAMPLE

The first step you will want to take is to translate your SPSS job or jobs into SPSS^X syntax. While this appendix, the examples in this section, and SPSS^X error messages are all designed to aid you in translating your jobs, you will probably gain in the long run if you take some time to read through the relevant sections of this manual before you begin. SPSS^X is a significant upgrade of SPSS, and you should consider taking advantage of many of the new features instead of merely translating your jobs.

Figure A.99a is a fairly typical job constructed to execute on CMS Release 9 of SPSS. This job reads raw data, lists several variables for the first 25 cases, and calculates some univariate statistics for another list of variables. Figure A.99b is that same job translated to execute on CMS SPSS^X with the absolute minimum number of changes. The highlighted lines in Figure A.99b indicate the following changes:

- SPSS^X uses the TITLE command instead of RUN NAME.
- The FILE HANDLE command identifies the raw data file, CITYDATA, and replaces the INPUT MEDIUM command.
- The FILE subcommand on the DATA LIST command refers to the raw data file. The rest of the DATA LIST command needs no changes.
- The PRINT FORMATS command is not required in an SPSS^X job. The formats specified with the DATA LIST command are used for the print formats.
- The LIST command in SPSS^X replaces LIST CASES in SPSS.

No other changes are necessary. Although SPSS^X does not require that you indent specification fields to column 16, you can do so and it will have no effect on your job. However, if any commands use columns 73 through 80 and your installation has set NUMBERED as the default, use the UNNUMBERED command at the beginning of your job to allow SPSS^X to read the entire line.

Figure A.99c shows a job that performs the same tasks as the first two jobs while taking advantage of some of the features in SPSS^X:

- The FILE TYPE command defines the CITYDATA file in more detail. The RECORD TYPE and DATA LIST commands specify the variables and their formats for each record. The END FILE TYPE command completes the file definition.
- SPSS^X reads the variables CITY, STATE, AND COUNTY as three string variables.
- You can use the keywords VARIABLE LABELS instead of VAR LABELS. When the labels are enclosed in single quotation marks, no slashes are necessary.
- By default the LIST command prints the values for all cases in the file so the CASES subcommand is not necessary.
- By default, CONDESCRIPTIVE calculates the mean, standard deviation, minimum, and maximum in SPSS^X. The STATISTICS command is not necessary to request these statistics.
- All the commands require only one blank between the command name and the specifications. Continuation lines must be indented at least one space.

Figure A.99a An SPSS job

```
RUN NAME        DEFINE DATA FOR THE 25 LARGEST CITIES IN THE UNITED STATES

DATA LIST       FIXED (3) /1 C1 TO C3 6-17 (A) S1 TO S5 19-38 (A) INCORP 39-42
                POP70 44-50 RANK70 51-52 POP80 53-60 RANK80 61-62 AREA 63-68(1)
                /2 ELEV 6-9 CHURCHES 10-13 PARKS 14-17 PHONES 18-25 TVS 26-32
                RADIOST 33-35 TVST 36-38 VALUE 39-51 TAXRATE 52-57 (2)
                DEBT 58-67 REVENUE 68-79
                /3 EXPEND 6-16 CTY1 TO CTY9 18-53 (A)

INPUT MEDIUM    DISK

PRINT FORMATS   C1 TO S5, CTY1 TO CTY9 (A)/ AREA (1)/ TAXRATE (2)

MISSING VALUES  PARKS (9999)

VAR LABELS      INCORP YEAR OF INCORPORATION/
                AREA LAND AREA IN SQUARE MILES/
                RADIOST NUMBER OF RADIO STATIONS/
                TVST NUMBER OF TELEVISION STATIONS/
                VALUE ASSESSED VALUATION/
                TAXRATE CITY TAX RATE PER $1000/

LIST CASES      CASES=25/VARIABLES=C1 TO S5 POP80 RANK80

CONDESCRIPTIVE  AREA TO TVS
STATISTICS      1, 5, 10, 11
```

Figure A.99b Translation to SPSS^X

```
TITLE           DEFINE DATA FOR THE 25 LARGEST CITIES IN THE UNITED STATES

FILE HANDLE     CITYDATA/NAME='ALMANAC1 DATA'

DATA LIST       FILE=CITYDATA
                FIXED (3) /1 C1 TO C3 6-17 (A) S1 TO S5 19-38 (A) INCORP 39-42
                POP70 44-50 RANK70 51-52 POP80 53-60 RANK80 61-62 AREA 63-68(1)
                /2 ELEV 6-9 CHURCHES 10-13 PARKS 14-17 PHONES 18-25 TVS 26-32
                RADIOST 33-35 TVST 36-38 VALUE 39-51 TAXRATE 52-57 (2)
                DEBT 58-67 REVENUE 68-79
                /3 EXPEND 6-16 CTY1 TO CTY9 18-53 (A)

MISSING VALUES  PARKS (9999)

VAR LABELS      INCORP YEAR OF INCORPORATION/
                AREA LAND AREA IN SQUARE MILES/
                RADIOST NUMBER OF RADIO STATIONS/
                TVST NUMBER OF TELEVISION STATIONS/
                VALUE ASSESSED VALUATION/
                TAXRATE CITY TAX RATE PER $1000/

LIST            CASES=25/VARIABLES=C1 TO S5 POP80 RANK80

CONDESCRIPTIVE  AREA TO TVS
STATISTICS      1, 5, 10, 11
```

Figure A.99c Taking advantage of SPSS^X features

```
TITLE  DEFINE DATA FOR THE 25 LARGEST CITIES IN THE UNITED STATES

FILE HANDLE CITYDATA /NAME='ALMANAC1 DATA'

FILE TYPE GROUPED FILE=CITYDATA RECORD=#RECID 4 CASE=#CASEID 1-2
RECORD TYPE 1
DATA LIST
   /CITY 6-18 (A) STATE 19-38 (A) INCORP 39-42
    POP70 44-50 RANK70 51-52 POP80 53-60 RANK80 61-62 AREA 63-68 (1)
RECORD TYPE 2
DATA LIST
   /ELEV 6-9 CHURCHES 10-13 PARKS 14-17 PHONES 18-25 TVS 26-32
    RADIOST 33-35 TVST 36-38 VALUE 39-51 TAXRATE 52-57 (2)
    DEBT 58-67 REVENUE 68-79
RECORD TYPE 3
DATA LIST
   /EXPEND 6-16 COUNTY 18-53 (A)
END FILE TYPE

MISSING VALUES  PARKS (9999)

VARIABLE LABELS  INCORP 'YEAR OF INCORPORATION'
   AREA 'LAND AREA IN SQUARE MILES'
   RADIOST 'NUMBER OF RADIO STATIONS'
   TVST 'NUMBER OF TELEVISION STATIONS'
   VALUE 'ASSESSED VALUATION'
   TAXRATE 'CITY TAX RATE PER $1000'

LIST  VARIABLES=CITY STATE POP80 RANK80

CONDESCRIPTIVE  AREA TO TVS
```

Appendix B Command Order

Command order in $SPSS^X$ is determined only by the system's need to know and do certain things in logical sequence. One overriding rule that occurs throughout the system is that a variable must exist before it can be mentioned for labeling, transformation, analysis, and so forth. Likewise, a file handle must be defined before it can be mentioned for input or output. Otherwise, command order is a matter of your own style and of your understanding of how $SPSS^X$ works. This appendix describes the program states $SPSS^X$ goes through as it reads your command groups and executes them.

You can use this appendix to construct your $SPSS^X$ command file if you wish, but you will find that putting your commands together in an order that seems logical to you is probably the best method. However, this appendix will help you considerably if you encounter a problem and are trying to determine why $SPSS^X$ doesn't seem to want to accept your command order or seems to be carrying out your instructions incorrectly.

B.1 PROGRAM STATES

You should assemble your commands in groups that define your active file, transform the data, and analyze it. This order conforms very closely to the order of tasks $SPSS^X$ must go through as it processes your commands. Specifically, $SPSS^X$ checks command order according to the *program state* through which it passes. The program state is a characteristic of the program before and after a command is encountered. There are four program states. Each $SPSS^X$ job starts in the *initial state*. The *input program state* enables $SPSS^X$ to read data. The *transformation state* allows data modifications. The *procedure state* enables the program to begin executing a procedure. Figure B.1a shows how $SPSS^X$ moves through these states. $SPSS^X$ determines the current state from the commands that it already has encountered and then identifies which commands are allowed in that state. For example, after a FILE HANDLE command, the program is in the initial state and can accept a GET command.

Figure B.1a Program states

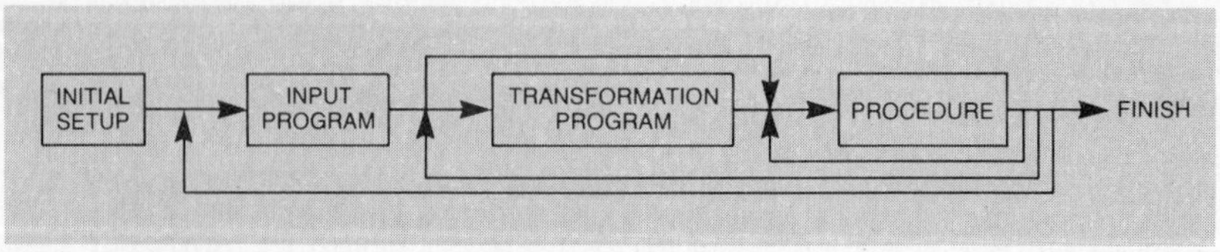

An SPSS^X job must go through initial, input program, and procedure steps to be a complete job. Since all jobs start in the initial state, you need to be concerned primarily with what commands you need to define your active file and to analyze the data. The following commands define a very minimal job:

```
FILE HANDLE DATAIN/ file specifications
GET FILE=DATAIN
FREQUENCIES VARIABLES=ALL
```

The FILE HANDLE and GET commands define the active file and the FREQUENCIES command reads the data file and analyzes it. Thus, SPSS^X goes through the required three states: initial, input, and procedure.

Typically, an SPSS^X job also goes through the transformation state, but it can be skipped as shown in the example above and in the diagram in Figure B.1a. Consider the example SPSS^X job used in Chapter 6 to illustrate the RECODE command (see Figure B.1b). SPSS^X starts in the initial state, where it processes the TITLE and FILE HANDLE commands. It then moves into the input state upon encountering the DATA LIST command. SPSS^X can then move into either the transformation or procedure state once the DATA LIST command has been processed.

Figure B.1b An SPSS^X job

```
TITLE  PILOT FOR COLLEGE SURVEY
FILE HANDLE TESTDATA/ file specifications

DATA LIST  FILE=TESTDATA
  /AGE 1-3 ITEM1 TO ITEM3 5-7

VARIABLE LABELS  ITEM1 'OPINION ON LEVEL OF DEFENSE SPENDING'
  ITEM2 'OPINION ON LEVEL OF WELFARE SPENDING'
  ITEM3 'OPINION ON LEVEL OF HEALTH SPENDING'
VALUE LABELS  ITEM1 TO ITEM3 -1 'DISAGREE' 0 'NO OPINION' 1 'AGREE'
MISSING VALUES  AGE(-99,-98) ITEM1 TO ITEM3 (9)
RECODE  ITEM1 TO ITEM3 (0=1) (1=0) (2=-1) (9=9) (ELSE=SYSMIS)
RECODE  AGE (MISSING=9) (18 THRU HI=1) (LO THRU 18=0) INTO VOTER
PRINT /$CASENUM 1-2 AGE 4-6 VOTER 8-10
VARIABLE LABELS  VOTER 'ELIGIBLE TO VOTE'
VALUE LABELS  VOTER 0 'UNDER 18' 1 '18 OR OVER'
MISSING VALUES  VOTER (9)
PRINT FORMATS  VOTER(F1.0)

FREQUENCIES VARIABLES=VOTER,ITEM1 TO ITEM3
```

In this example, SPSS^X remains in the transformation state after processing each of the commands from VARIABLE LABELS through PRINT FORMATS. SPSS^X then moves into the procedure state to process the FREQUENCIES command. As shown in Figure B.1a, SPSS^X can repeat the procedure state if it encounters a second procedure. SPSS^X can return to the transformation state if it encounters additional transformation commands following the first procedure. Finally, in some jobs SPSS^X can return to the input program state upon encountering commands such as FILE TYPE or MATCH FILES.

B.2 DETERMINING COMMAND ORDER

Table B.2 shows where specific commands can go in the command file in terms of program states and what happens when SPSS^X encounters a command in each of the four program states. If a column contains a dash, the command is accepted in that program state and it leaves the program in that state. If one of the words INPUT, TRANS, or PROC appears in the column, the command is accepted in the program state indicated by the column heading but it moves the program into the state shown in the column. Asterisks in a column indicate errors when SPSS^X encounters the command in that program state. Commands marked with the dagger in the column for the procedure state clear the active file.

The table shows six groups of commands: utility commands (which can go anywhere), file definition commands, input program commands, data transformation commands, restricted transformations, and procedure commands. These groups are discussed in Sections B.3 through B.8.

Table B.2 Commands and program states

	INIT	INPUT	TRANS	PROC
UTILITY COMMANDS				
EDIT	—	—	—	—
FILE HANDLE	—	—	—	—
FILE LABEL	—	—	—	—
FINISH	—	—	—	—
INFO	—	—	—	—
INPUT MATRIX	—	—	—	—
N OF CASES	—	—	—	TRANS
NUMBERED, UNNUMBERED	—	—	—	—
PROCEDURE OUTPUT	—	—	—	—
SET, SHOW	—	—	—	—
TITLE, SUBTITLE	—	—	—	—
FILE DEFINITION COMMANDS				
ADD FILES	TRANS	**	—	TRANS
DATA LIST	TRANS	—	**	TRANS †
FILE TYPE	INPUT	**	**	INPUT †
GET	TRANS	**	**	TRANS †
GET SCSS	TRANS	**	**	TRANS †
IMPORT	TRANS	**	**	TRANS †
INPUT PROGRAM	INPUT	**	**	INPUT †
MATCH FILES	TRANS	**	—	TRANS
INPUT PROGRAM COMMANDS				
END CASE	**	—	**	**
END FILE	**	—	**	**
END FILE TYPE	**	TRANS	**	**
END INPUT PROGRAM	**	TRANS	**	**
RECORD TYPE	**	—	**	**
REPEATING DATA	**	—	**	**
REREAD	**	—	**	**
TRANSFORMATION COMMANDS				
COMPUTE	**	—	—	TRANS
COUNT	**	—	—	TRANS
DISPLAY	**	—	—	—
DO IF—END IF	**	—	—	TRANS
DO REPEAT—END REPEAT	**	—	—	TRANS
DOCUMENT	**	—	—	TRANS
FORMATS	**	—	—	TRANS
IF	**	—	—	TRANS
LEAVE	**	—	—	TRANS
LOOP—END LOOP, BREAK	**	—	—	TRANS
MISSING VALUES	**	—	—	TRANS
NUMERIC	**	—	—	TRANS

PRINT	**	—	—	TRANS
PRINT EJECT	**	—	—	TRANS
PRINT FORMATS	**	—	—	TRANS
PRINT SPACE	**	—	—	TRANS
RECODE	**	—	—	TRANS
SPLIT FILE	**	—	—	TRANS
STRING	**	—	—	TRANS
VALUE LABELS	**	—	—	TRANS
VARIABLE LABELS	**	—	—	TRANS
VECTOR	**	—	—	TRANS
WEIGHT	**	—	—	TRANS
WRITE	**	—	—	TRANS
WRITE FORMATS	**	—	—	TRANS
RESTRICTED TRANSFORMATIONS				
REFORMAT	**	**	—	TRANS
SAMPLE	**	**	—	TRANS
SELECT IF	**	**	—	TRANS
TEMPORARY	**	**	—	TRANS
PROCEDURES				
BEGIN DATA	**	**	PROC	—
EXECUTE	**	**	PROC	—
EXPORT	**	**	PROC	—
LIST	**	**	PROC	—
SAVE	**	**	PROC	—
SAVE SCSS	**	**	PROC	—
SORT CASES	**	**	PROC	—
procedures	**	**	PROC	—

To read the table, first locate the command that concerns you. If you simply want to know where in the SPSS^X command stream it can go, look for columns without asterisks. For example, the COMPUTE command can be used when the program is in the input program state, the transformation state, or the procedure state, but it will cause an error if you try to use it in the initial state. If you want to know what can follow a command, look at each of the four columns next to the command. If the column is dashed, any commands not showing asterisks in the column for that program state can follow the command. If the column contains one of the words INPUT, TRANS, or PROC, any command not showing asterisks in the column for the program state indicated by that word can follow the command. For example, if you are concerned with what commands can follow the INPUT PROGRAM command (Chapter 12), note first that it is allowed only in the initial or procedure states. Then note that INPUT PROGRAM puts SPSS^X into the input program state wherever it occurs legally. This means that commands with dashes or words in the INPUT column can follow the INPUT PROGRAM command. This includes all the utility commands, the DATA LIST command, input program commands, and transformation commands like COMPUTE. Commands that are not allowed after the INPUT PROGRAM command are most of the file definition commands like GET that are their own input program, restricted transformations like SELECT IF, and procedures.

B.3 Unrestricted Utility Commands

The utility commands can appear in any state. Table B.2 shows this by the absence of asterisks in the columns next to the EDIT through TITLE commands. For example, the EDIT command can appear at any point in the command file.

The dashed lines indicate that after a utility command is processed, the program remains in the same state it was in before the command. The only exception is the N OF CASES command. If SPSS^X is in the procedure state, N OF CASES moves the program to the transformation state. The FINISH command terminates the job wherever it appears. Any commands appearing after FINISH will not be read and therefore will not cause an error.

B.4 File Definition Commands

You can use all the file definition commands in the initial state and in the procedure state. Most of these commands cause errors if you try to use them in the input program state or the transformation state. However, you can use ADD FILES and MATCH FILES in the transformation state because they can name the active file as one of the specifications on the FILE subcommand. You can use DATA LIST in the input program state since there can be and often are multiple DATA LIST commands in input programs.

After they are read, the system file commands (ADD FILES, GET, GET SCSS, IMPORT, and MATCH FILES) move SPSS^X directly to the transformation state since these commands are the entire input program. FILE TYPE and INPUT PROGRAM both move SPSS^X into the input program state and require input program commands to complete the input program. Commands in Table B.2 marked with a dagger clear the active file.

B.5 Input Program Commands

The commands associated with the complex file facility (Chapter 11) and commands associated with INPUT PROGRAM (Chapter 12) are allowed only in the input program state.

The RECORD TYPE command for the complex file facility and END CASE, END FILE, REPEATING DATA, and REREAD for specially written input programs leave SPSS^X in the input program state. The two that move SPSS^X on to the transformation state are END FILE TYPE for input programs initiated with FILE TYPE and END INPUT PROGRAM for those initiated with INPUT PROGRAM.

B.6 Transformation Commands

The entire set of transformation commands from COMPUTE to WRITE can appear in the input program state as part of an input program, in the transformation state, or in the procedure state.

When you use transformation commands in the input program state or the transformation state, SPSS^X remains in the same state it was in before the command. When the program is in the procedure state, these commands move SPSS^X back to the transformation state. When you use DISPLAY, the program always remains in the same state it was in before the command.

B.7 Restricted Transformations

Commands REFORMAT, SAMPLE, SELECT IF, and TEMPORARY are restricted transformation commands because they are allowed in either the transformation state or the procedure state but cannot be used in the input program state.

If you use restricted transformation commands in the transformation state, the program remains in the transformation state. If you use them in the procedure state, they move SPSS^X back to the transformation state.

B.8 Procedures

The procedures and the procedure-like commands (BEGIN DATA, EXECUTE, EXPORT, LIST, SAVE, SAVE SCSS, and SORT CASES) cause the data to be read. These commands, including all procedures, are allowed in either the transformation state or the procedure state.

When the program is in the transformation state, these commands move SPSS^X to the procedure state. When you use these commands in the procedure state, the program remains in that state.

Appendix C IMPORT/EXPORT Character Sets

POSITION	GRAPHIC	IBM EBCDIC	BURROUGHS EBCDIC	ASCII 7-BIT	ISO 8-BIT	CDC DISPLAY CODE	HIS 6-BIT	ASCII 6-BIT
0	NUL	0	0	0	0			
1	SOH	1	1	1	1			
2	STX	2	2	2	2			
3	ETX	3	3	3	3			
4	SEL	4			156			
5	HT	5	5	9	9			
6	RNL	6			134			
7	DEL	7	7	127	127			
8	GE	8			151			
9	SPS	9			141			
10	RPT	10			142			
11	VT	11	11	11	11			
12	FF	12	12	12	12			
13	CR	13	13	13	13			
14	SO	14	14	14	14			
15	SI	15	15	15	15			
16	DLE	16	16	16	16			
17	DC1	17	17	17	17			
18	DC2	18	18	18	18			
19	DC3	19	19	19	19			
20	DC4	60	60	20	20			
21	NL	21	21		133			
22	BS	22	22	8	8			
23	DOC	23			135			
24	CAN	24	24	24	24			
25	EM	25	25	25	25			
26	UBS	26			146			
27	CU1	27			143			
28	(I)FS[1]	28	28	28	28			
29	(I)GS	29	29	29	29			
30	(I)RS	30	30	30	30			
31	SM,SW	42			138			
32	DS	32			128			
33	SOS	33			129			
34	FS[2]	34			130			
35	WUS	35			131			
36	CSP	43			139			
37	LF	37	37	10	10			
38	ETB	38	38	23	23			
39	ESC	39	39	27	27			
40	(I)US	31	31	31	31			

[1]file separator
[2]field separator

POSITION	GRAPHIC	IBM EBCDIC	BURROUGHS EBCDIC	ASCII 7-BIT	ISO 8-BIT	CDC DISPLAY CODE	HIS 6-BIT	ASCII 6-BIT
41	BYP	36			132			
42	RES	20			157			
43	ENQ	45	45	5	5			
44	ACK	46	46	6	6			
45	BEL	47	47	7	7			
46	SYN	50	50	22	22			
47	IR	51			147			
48	PP	52			148			
49	TRN	53			149			
50	NBS	54			150			
51	EOT	55	55	4	4			
52	SBS	56			152			
53	IT	57			153			
54	RFF	58			154			
55	CU3	59			155			
56	NAK	61	61	21	21			
57	SUB	63	63	26	26			
58	SA	40			136			
59	SFE	41			137			
60	MFA	44			140			
61	reserved							
62	reserved							
63	reserved							
64	0	240	240	48	48	27	0	16
65	1	241	241	49	49	28	1	17
66	2	242	242	50	50	29	2	18
67	3	243	243	51	51	30	3	19
68	4	244	244	52	52	31	4	20
69	5	245	245	53	53	32	5	21
70	6	246	246	54	54	33	6	22
71	7	247	247	55	55	34	7	23
72	8	248	248	56	56	35	8	24
73	9	249	249	57	57	36	9	25
74	A	193	193	65	65	1	17	33
75	B	194	194	66	66	2	18	34
76	C	195	195	67	67	3	19	35
77	D	196	196	68	68	4	20	36
78	E	197	197	69	69	5	21	37
79	F	198	198	70	70	6	22	38
80	G	199	199	71	71	7	23	39
81	H	200	200	72	72	8	24	40
82	I	201	201	73	73	9	25	41
83	J	209	209	74	74	10	33	42
84	K	210	210	75	75	11	34	43
85	L	211	211	76	76	12	35	44
86	M	212	212	77	77	13	36	45
87	N	213	213	78	78	14	37	46
88	O	214	214	79	79	15	38	47
89	P	215	215	80	80	16	39	48
90	Q	216	216	81	81	17	40	49
91	R	217	217	82	82	18	41	50
92	S	226	226	83	83	19	50	51
93	T	227	227	84	84	20	51	52
94	U	228	228	85	85	21	52	53
95	V	229	229	86	86	22	53	54
96	W	230	230	87	87	23	54	55
97	X	231	231	88	88	24	55	56
98	Y	232	232	89	89	25	56	57
99	Z	233	233	90	90	26	57	58

POSITION	GRAPHIC	IBM EBCDIC	BURROUGHS EBCDIC	ASCII 7-BIT	ISO 8-BIT	CDC DISPLAY CODE	HIS 6-BIT	ASCII 6-BIT
100	a	129	129	97	97			
101	b	130	130	98	98			
102	c	131	131	99	99			
103	d	132	132	100	100			
104	e	133	133	101	101			
105	f	134	134	102	102			
106	g	135	135	103	103			
107	h	136	136	104	104			
108	i	137	137	105	105			
109	j	145	145	106	106			
110	k	146	146	107	107			
111	l	147	147	108	108			
112	m	148	148	109	109			
113	n	149	149	110	110			
114	o	150	150	111	111			
115	p	151	151	112	112			
116	q	152	152	113	113			
117	r	153	153	114	114			
118	s	162	162	115	115			
119	t	163	163	116	116			
120	u	164	164	117	117			
121	v	165	165	118	118			
122	w	166	166	119	119			
123	x	167	167	120	120			
124	y	168	168	121	121			
125	z	169	169	122	122			
126	space	64	64	32	32	45	16	0
127	.	75	75	46	46	47	27	14
128	<	76	76	60	60	58	30	28
129	(	77	77	40	40	41	29	8
130	+	78	78	43	43	37	48	11
131	|	79	79					
132	&	80	80	38	38	55	26	6
133	[	173	74	91	91	49	10	59
134	]	189	90	93	93	50	28	61
135	!	90	208	33	33	54	63	61
136	$	91	91	36	36	43	43	4
137	*	92	92	42	42	39	44	10
138	)	93	93	41	41	42	45	9
139	;	94	94	59	59	63	46	27
140	¬ or ^ or ↑	95	95	94	94	62	32	62
141	−	96	96	45	45	38	42	13
142	/	97	97	47	47	40	49	15
143	¦	106		124	124			
144	,	107	107	44	44	46	59	12
145	%	108	108	37	37	51*	60	5
146	_	109	109	95	95	53	58	63
147	>	110	110	62	62	59	14	30
148	?	111	111	63	63	57	15	31
149	`	121		96	96			
150	:	122	122	58	58	0|51	13	26
151	£	123	123	35	35	48	11	3
152	@	124	124	64	64	60	12	32
153	´	125	125	39	39	56	47	7
154	=	126	126	61	61	44	61	29
155	“	127	127	34	34	49	62	2

POSITION	GRAPHIC	IBM EBCDIC	BURROUGHS EBCDIC	ASCII 7-BIT	ISO 8-BIT	CDC DISPLAY CODE	HIS 6-BIT	ASCII 6-BIT
156	≤	140	140					
157	□	156	156					
158	±	158	158					
159	■	159	159					
160	°		161					
161	†	143						
162	~	161		126	126			
163	−	160	160					
164	└	171	171					
165	┌	172	172					
166	≥	174	174					
167	^{0}	176	176					
168	^{1}	177	177					
169	^{2}	178	178					
170	^{3}	179	179					
171	^{4}	180	180					
172	^{5}	181	181					
173	^{6}	182	182					
174	^{7}	183	183					
175	^{8}	184	184					
176	^{9}	185	185					
177	┘	187	187					
178	┐	188	188					
179	≠	190	190					
180	—	191	191					
181	$^($	141	141					
182	$^)$	157	157					
183	⊥	142	192					
184	{	192	139	123	123			
185	}	208	155	125	125			
186	\	224		92	92	61	31	
187	¢	74	224					
188	•	175	175					
189-255 reserved								

Appendix D Writing User Programs

In the second release of the $SPSS^X$ System, two new facilities will allow you to incorporate your own analysis program into $SPSS^X$ so that you can apply $SPSS^X$ data management and transformation facilities to your own programs. The MATRIX procedure provides a complete matrix language for performing a wide variety of matrix manipulations and calculations. In addition, the MATRIX procedure reads and writes data files and $SPSS^X$ system files. The USERPROC facility allows you to add your own procedure to $SPSS^X$. These facilities are not available in the first release of $SPSS^X$ and therefore are not documented in this *$SPSS^X$ User's Guide*. To see if the facilities are available on your version of $SPSS^X$, print the documentation available with the OVERVIEW keyword on the INFO command (see Chapter 2). The overview document will tell you how to get the complete documentation for these facilities if they are available on your version of $SPSS^X$.

D.1 THE MATRIX PROCEDURE

The MATRIX procedure provides arithmetic operators and matrix functions for constructing computational expressions that resemble standard matrix algebra notation. You can use the transformation control structures such as LOOP—END LOOP and DO IF—ELSE IF to construct your MATRIX "program," and you can read a data file or an $SPSS^X$ system file or write result matrices to an output data file or a $SPSS^X$ system file. You can read the matrix materials written by other $SPSS^X$ procedures and use them to calculate additional statistics. For example, you could read the matrix of correlation coefficients and means and standard deviations written by REGRESSION and calculate a variance-covariance matrix or weighted sums of squares.

The basic statement in the MATRIX procedure is the COMPUTE command, which operates much like the COMPUTE command in the $SPSS^X$ transformation language except that the results can be a complete matrix. Arithmetic operators available are matrix transposition, exponentiation, multiplication, subtraction, addition, and elementwise exponentiation, multiplication, and division. A large number of special matrix functions are also available to calculate the inverse of a matrix, create matrices with known characteristics such as block diagonal matrices, identity matrices, design matrices, and matrices of uniform random numbers. Other functions calculate eigenvalues of a symmetric matrix, the determinant of a matrix, column and row sums of squares, column and row sums, column and row maximum and minimum values, and so forth. Another category of functions performs calculations on the elements of a matrix such as sines, cosines, absolute values, and logarithms.

You can use the relational operators (greater than, less than, not equal to, etc.) to perform elementwise compares on two matrices. The logical operators, AND, OR, XOR, and NOT, are also available to form complete logical expressions.

You can print intermediate results or final results within the MATRIX procedure or save the results to use later in your SPSS^X job with any SPSS^X procedure. If you print results in the MATRIX procedure, you can assign headings, row and column labels, and printing formats for the display.

The following example demonstrates some of the facilities in the MATRIX procedure. There may be a few changes to the syntax before the release of the procedure. Check the documentation available with the INFO command for the exact syntax. This example reads a symmetric matrix, computes eigenvalues and eigenvectors, and prints the eigenvectors for eigenvalues greater than or equal to 1. The matrix is read from a data file in freefield format. The first record contains a single value giving the order of the matrix.

```
MATRIX
READ ORDER                          /* read the order value */
     /FILE=INMAT
     /SIZE=1
READ DATA                           /* read the n by n matrix */
     /FILE=INMAT
     /SIZE=ORDER
     /MODE=SYMMETRIC

  /* compute eigenvalues and eigenvectors */
CALL EIGEN(DATA,EIGENVAL,EIGENVEC)
COMPUTE FLAG=0
  /* print eigenvectors whose eigenvalues are >= 1 */
LOOP J=1 TO ORDER
+ DO IF (EIGENVAL(:,J) >= 1)
+ COMPUTE FLAG=1
+ PRINT EIGENVAL(J)
        /TITLE="Eigenvalue:"
        /SPACE=4
+ PRINT EIGENVEC(:,J)
        /TITLE="Eigenvector:"
        /SPACE=2
+ END IF
END LOOP
DO IF (FLAG=)
+ PRINT TITLE="No eigenvalues greater or equal to 1"
        /SPACE=4
END IF
END MATRIX
```

D.2 ADDING USER PROCEDURES

The second release of SPSS^X will also allow you to add your own procedure to SPSS^X. For example, you might want to calculate a statistic or do a type of data analysis that is not available in SPSS^X. The USERPROC command will access an executable module of your program and run it as an SPSS^X procedure. The USERPROC command can also include specifications to be used by your procedure. For example, a list of variable names will usually be specified. And, depending on the procedure other specifications for the design, criteria, and so forth, may also be included on the command record.

Many programs will need only minor modifications to run with SPSS^X. However, with a bit more work you will be able to use many SPSS^X features with your program. The variable names and pointers to each variable in the active file will be available. The values of several system variables and SPSS^X subroutines for accessing labels and other dictionary information, parsing your specifications on the USERPROC command, and handling missing values will also be available. A complete list of the arrays and routines in SPSS^X available to you and detailed information on how to use them with your program will be published in a separate Technical Applications document. The overview documentation available with the INFO command will tell you when this facility and document are available.

References

Anderson, O. D. 1976. *Time series analysis and forecasting—The Box-Jenkins approach.* Boston: Butterworth.

Andrews, F., J. Morgan, J. Sonquist, and L. Klein. 1973. *Multiple classification analysis.* 2d ed. Ann Arbor: University of Michigan.

Bancroft, T. A. 1968. *Topics in intermediate statistical methods.* Ames, Iowa: The Iowa State University Press.

Belsley, D. A., E. Kuh, and R. E. Welsch. 1980. *Regression diagnostics.* New York: John Wiley & Sons.

Berk, K. N. 1977. Tolerance and condition in regression computation. *Journal of the American Statistical Association* 72:863-66.

Berkson, J., and R. Gage. 1950. Calculation of survival rates for cancer. *Proceedings of the Mayo Clinic* 25:270.

Bock, R. D. 1975. *Multivariate statistical methods in behavioral research.* New York: McGraw-Hill.

Box, G. E. P., and G. M. Jenkins. 1976. *Time series analysis: Forecasting and control.* Rev. ed. San Francisco: Holden-Day.

Brown, B. W., H. Walker, M. Schimek, and P. R. Wright. 1979. A life table analysis package for SPSS. *American Sociological Review* 33:225-27.

Cattell, R. B. 1966. The meaning and strategic use of factor analysis. In *Handbook of multivariate experimental psychology,* ed. R. B. Cattell. Chicago: Rand McNally.

Cochran, W. G., and G. M. Cox. 1957. *Experimental design.* 2d ed. New York: Wiley.

Conover, W. J. 1973. *Practical nonparametric statistics.* New York: Wiley.

Cook, R. D. 1977. Detection of influential observations in linear regression. *Technometrics* 19:15-18.

Cooley, W. W., and P. R. Lohnes. 1971. *Multivariate Data Analysis.* New York: Wiley.

Cronbach, L. J. 1951. Coefficient alpha and the internal structure of tests. *Psychometrika* 16:297-334.

Davies, O. L. 1954. *Design and analysis of industrial experiments.* New York: Hafner.

Dineen, L. C., and B. C. Blakesley. 1973. Algorithm AS 62: A generator for the sampling distribution of the Mann-Whitney *U* statistic. *Applied Statistics* 22:269-73.

Dixon, W. J. and M. B. Brown. 1979. *BMDP-79.* Berkeley: University of California Press.

Elashoff, J. D. 1981. Data for the panel session in software for repeated measures analysis of variance. *Proceedings of the Statistical Computing Section.* American Statistical Association.

Everitt, B. S. 1978. *Graphical techniques for multivariate data.* New York: North-Holland.

Finn, J. D. 1974. *A general model for multivariate analysis.* New York: Holt, Rinehart and Winston.

Fisher, R. A. 1936. The use of multiple measurements in taxonomic problems. *Annals of Eugenics* 7:179-88.

Fuller, W. A. 1976. *Introduction to statistical time series.* New York: Wiley.

Goodman L. A. 1972. Measures of association for cross classifications, IV: Simplification of asymptotic variances. *Journal of the American Statistical Association* 67:415-421.

Goodman, L. A. 1978. *Analyzing qualitative/categorical data.* Cambridge: Abt Books.

Guttman, L. 1945. A basis for analyzing test-retest reliability. *Psychometrika* 10:255-82.

Haberman, S. J. 1978. *Analysis of qualitative data,* Vol. 1. New York: Academic Press.

Haberman, S. J. 1979. *Analysis of qualitative data,* Vol. 2. New York: Academic Press.

Haberman, S. J. 1982. Analysis of dispersion of multinomial responses. *Journal of the American Statistical Association* 77:568-80.

Harman, H. H. 1967. *Modern factor analysis.* 2d ed. Chicago: University of Chicago Press.

Harman, H. H., and W. H. Jones. 1966. Factor analysis by minimizing residuals (Minres). *Psychometrika* 31:351-68.

Harris, C. W. 1967. On factors and factor scores. *Psychometrika* 32:363-79.

Heck, D. L. 1960. Charts of some upper percentage points of the distribution of the largest characteristic root. *Annals of Mathematical Statistics* 31:625-42.

Hicks, C. R. 1973. *Fundamental concepts in the design of experiments.* 2d ed. New York: Holt, Rinehart and Winston.

Hoaglin, D. C., and R. E. Welsch. 1978. The hat matrix in regression and ANOVA. *American Statistician* 32:17-22.

Huynh, H., and G. K. Mandevill. 1979. Validity conditions in repeated measures designs. *Psychological Bulletin* 86:964-73.

Jennrich, R. I., and P. F. Sampson. 1966. Rotation for simple loading. *Psychometrika* 31:313-23.

Jöreskog, K. G. 1977. Factor analysis by least-squares and maximum likelihood methods. In *Statistical Methods for Digital Computers*, Vol. 3, ed. K. Enslein, A. Ralston, and H. S. Wilf. New York: Wiley.

Jöreskog, K. G., and D. N. Lawley. 1968. New methods in maximum likelihood factor analysis. *British Journal of Mathematical and Statistical Psychology* 21:85-96.

Kaiser, H. F. 1958. The varimax criterion for analytic rotation in factor analysis. *Psychometrika* 23:187-200.

Kaiser, H. F. 1963. Image analysis. In *Problems in measuring change*, ed. C. W. Harris, 156-66. Madison: University of Wisconsin Press.

Kaiser, H. F. 1970. A second-generation Little Jiffy. *Psychometrika* 35:401-415.

Kaiser, H. F., and J. Caffry. 1965. Alpha factor analysis. *Psychometrika* 30:1-14.

Kristof, W. 1963. The statistical theory of speed-up reliability coefficients when a test has been divided into several equal parts. *Psychometrika* 28:221-38.

Lawley D. N., and A. E. Maxwell. 1971. *Factor analysis as a statistical method.* London: Butterworths.

Lee, E., and M. Desu. 1972. A computer program for comparing k samples with right-censored data. *Computer Programs in Biomedicine* 2:315-21.

Ling, R. F., and H. V. Roberts. 1980. *IDA: A user's guide to the IDA interactive data analysis and forecasting system.* New York: McGraw-Hill.

Meyer, L. S., and M. S. Younger. 1976. Estimation of standardized coefficients. *Journal of the American Statistical Association* 71:154-57.

Morrison, D. F. 1976. *Multivariate statistical methods.* 2d ed. New York: McGraw-Hill.

Moser, C. A. and G. Kalton. 1972. *Survey methods in social investigation.* 2d ed. New York: Basic Books, Inc.

Nelson, C. R. 1973. *Applied time series analysis for managerial forecasting.* San Francisco: Holden-Day.

Pillai, K. C. S. 1967. Upper percentage points of the largest root of a matrix in multivariate analysis. *Biometrika* 54:189-93.

Rao, C. R. 1973. *Linear statistical inference and its applications.* 2d ed. New York: Wiley.

Roy, J., and R. E. Bargmann. 1958. Tests of multiple independence and the associated confidence bounds. *Annals of Mathematical Statistics* 29:491-503.

Rummel, R. J. 1970. *Applied factor analysis.* Evanston: Northwestern University Press.

Searle, S. R. 1971. *Linear models.* New York: Wiley.

Siegel, S. 1956. *Nonparametric statistics for the behavioral sciences.* New York: McGraw-Hill.

Smirnov, N. V. 1948. Table for estimating the goodness of fit of empirical distributions. *Annals of Mathematical Statistics* 19:279-81.

Snedecor, G. W., and W. G. Cochran. 1967. *Statistical methods.* 6th ed. Ames, Iowa: The Iowa State University Press.

Speed, M. F. 1976. Response curves in the one way classification with unequal numbers of observations per cell. *Proceedings of the Statistical Computing Section.* American Statistical Association.

Stouffer, S. A., E. A. Suchman, L. C. Devinney, S. A. Star, and R. M. Williams, Jr. 1949. *The American soldier: Adjustments during army life.* Vol. 1 of *Studies in social psychology in World War II.* Princeton: Princeton University Press.

Tatsuoka, M. M. 1971. *Multivariate analysis.* New York: Wiley.

Theil, H. 1970. On the estimation of relationships involving qualitative variables. *American Journal of Sociology* 76:103-154.

Tukey, J. W. 1977. *Exploratory data analysis.* Reading, Mass.: Addison-Wesley.

Velleman, P. F., and R. E. Welsch. 1981. Efficient computing of regression diagnostics. *American Statistician* 35:234-42.

Winer, B. J. 1971. *Statistical principles in experimental design,* 2d ed. New York: McGraw-Hill.

Index

A (keyword)
SORT CASES command, 207
a priori contrasts, 455
ABFREQ (function)
REPORT command, 355
ABS (function), 92
absolute value, 92
ACF (keyword)
BOX-JENKINS command, 714
active file
defined, 7, 30-31
in ADD FILES command, 238
in MATCH FILES command, 227
in SAVE SCSS command, 246
transformations, 107
ACVF (keyword)
BOX-JENKINS command, 714
ADD (function)
REPORT command, 355
ADD CASES (obsolete), 756, see ADD FILES command
ADD DATA LIST (obsolete), 755, see MATCH FILES command
ADD FILES (command), 238-243
annotated example, 243
BY subcommand, 241
common variables, 239-240, 242-242
concatenating files, 238-241
dictionary information, 239
DROP subcommand, 240, 242
FILE subcommand, 238-239, 241-241
FIRST subcommand, 242
IN subcommand, 240-241, 242-242
interleaving files, 241-242
KEEP subcommand, 240, 242
key variables, 241
LAST subcommand, 242
MAP subcommand, 240, 242
RENAME subcommand, 239-240, 242-242
reordering variables, 240, 242
with DATA LIST command, 239
with SORT CASES command, 209
ADD SUBFILES (obsolete), 755, 756, see ADD FILES comman d
ADD VARIABLES (obsolete), 755, see MATCH FILES command
addition, 91
ADJPRED (keyword)
REGRESSION command, 612
adjusted means
in MANOVA command, 471-472
AFREQ (keyword)
FREQUENCIES command, 268
AGGREGATE (command), 215-223
annotated example, 222-223
BREAK subcommand, 217
functions, 219-220
MISSING subcommand, 220-221
missing values, 220-221
old friends, 762
OUTFILE subcommand, 216-217
variable labels, 218
with MISSING VALUES command, 221
with SORT CASES command, 209, 217
with SPLIT FILE command, 213, 217
aggregate functions, 219-220
arguments, 220
defined, 216
in REPORT command, 355
aggregated data
in graphics, 392
in SURVIVAL command, 743
aggregated file
defined, 215
aggregated statistics
in REPORT command, 354-355
AIC (keyword)
FACTOR command, 651
ALLOCATE (obsolete), 753
ALPHA (keyword)
FACTOR command, 650
MANOVA command, 489
RELIABILITY command, 720
ALPHA (subcommand)
REFORMAT (command), 757-758
alpha factoring, 650
alpha model
in RELIABILITY command, 717
alphanumeric variables
old friends, 761
ANALYSIS (subcommand)
DISCRIMINANT command, 626-627
FACTOR command, 650«
MANOVA command, 468-469, 475-476
analysis of covariance, 509-511
analysis of variance
in ANOVA command, 439
in BREAKDOWN command, 326
in ONEWAY command, 453
in RELIABILITY command, 723
analysis of variance, univariate
in MANOVA command, 499-501
AND (keyword)
logical operator, 129
ANOVA (command), 439-450
annotated example, 446-447
cell means, 441-442
covariates, 443-444
formats, 450
full factorial models, 440-441
interaction effects, 442-443
limitations, 450
missing values, 450
multiple classification analysis, 449-450
old friends, 767
sums of squares, 444-445
ANOVA (keyword)
REGRESSION command, 610
ANY (function), 93, 760
AR (keyword)
FACTOR command, 655
archive files (obsolete), 758
arcsine, 92
arctangent, 93
arguments
complex, 95
defined, 92
missing values, 96-100
arithmetic operators, 91
ARLAG (subcommand)
BOX-JENKINS command, 703
ARSIN (function), 92
ARTAN (function), 93
ASSIGN MISSING (obsolete), 760
assignment expressions
in IF command, 121
asterisk (file handle)
in ADD FILES command, 234, 238, 239
in AGGREGATE command, 216-217
in MATCH FILES command, 227
asterisk (format)
in DATA LIST command, 38
in PRINT command, 136-138
in WRITE command, 142
autocorrelation plots
in BOX-JENKINS command, 698-699
AVERAGE (function)
REPORT command, 355
averaged *F* test, 489
AVERF (keyword)
MANOVA command, 489
AVONLY (keyword)
MANOVA command, 489

backforecasts
in BOX-JENKINS command, 705
BACKWARD (keyword)
REGRESSION command, 604
BADCORR (keyword)
REGRESSION command, 607
BALANCED (keyword)
MANOVA command, 480
bar charts
in FREQUENCIES command, 269-271, 272-273
BARCHART (command), 377-378, 379-380, 392-408
aggregated data, 392
annotated example, 406
BASE AXIS subcommand, 399-401
COLORS subcommand, 404
COMMENT subcommand, 399
cross-products of variables, 396-397
FONT subcommand, 404
FOOTNOTE subcommand, 399
FORMAT subcommand, 397-399
functions, 393-394
LEGEND LABELS subcommand, 402-403
LEGEND TITLE subcommand, 402-403
MISSING subcommand, 404-407
missing values, 404-407
multiple plots per page, 391-392
multiple variables, 395-396
old friends, 766
ORDER subcommand, 403-404
patterns, 403-404
PLOT subcommand, 393-397, 407-408
SAVE subcommand, 422-425
selectors, 395
SIDE AXIS subcommand, 401-402
TITLE subcommand, 399
XPAGE subcommand, 404
YPAGE subcommand, 404
BART (keyword)
FACTOR command, 655
BARTLETT (keyword)
MANOVA command, 487
Bartlett-Box *F*
in MANOVA command, 487
in ONEWAY command, 459
Bartlett's test of sphericity, 651
BARWISE (keyword)
BARCHART command, 404
BASE AXIS (subcommand)
BARCHART command, 399-401
BASIS (keyword)
MANOVA command, 476
BCOV (keyword)
REGRESSION command, 610
BEGIN DATA (command), 43-45, 259-259
between-subjects factors
in MANOVA command, 469-473
BFR (subcommand)
BOX-JENKINS command, 705
BIAS (keyword)
MANOVA command, 488
BINOMIAL (subcommand)
NPAR TESTS command, 673, 678
binomial test, 678
bivariate plots, see SCATTERGRAM (command)
BLANK (keyword)
FACTOR command, 652
REPORT command, 346
BLANK (obsolete)
COUNT command, 760
RECODE command, 760
blanks
delimiters, 23
reading, 35-36, 53-53, 54-54
BLANKS (keyword)
SET command, 53, 54
SHOW command, 53
BOX-JENKINS (command), 697-714
annotated example, 706-711
ARLAG subcommand, 703
BFR subcommand, 705
DIFFERENCE subcommand, 701
differencing the series, 701
ESTIMATE subcommand, 698-699
estimate subcommands, 704
final estimates subcommands, 713-714
fitting parameters, 702-704
FORECAST subcommand, 698-699
forecast subcommands, 712
FPR subcommand, 705
IDENTIFY subcommand, 698-699
initial estimates subcommands, 712
ITERATE subcommand, 704
LAG subcommand, 702
LEAD subcommand, 713
LOG subcommand, 700
MALAG subcommand, 703
old friends, 770
ORIGIN subcommand, 713
P subcommand, 702
PERIOD subcommand, 701-702
perturbation increment subcommands, 705
PLOT subcommand, 714
POWER subcommand, 700-701
PRINT subcommand, 714
Q subcommand, 702
SDIFFERENCE subcommand, 701-702
SP subcommmand, 702
SQ subcommand, 702
steps of analysis, 697
tolerance subcommands, 712
transforming the series, 699
VARIABLE subcommand, 698
Box's *M* test
in DISCRIMINANT command, 633
in MANOVA command, 487
BOXM (keyword)
MANOVA command, 487
BOXPLOTS (keyword)
MANOVA command, 495
BREAK (command)
with DO IF command, 193
with LOOP command, 193
BREAK (subcommand)
AGGREGATE command, 217
REPORT command, 349-354
break groups
defined, 215-216
in AGGREGATE command, 217
in REPORT command, 335-336
break variables
in AGGREGATE command, 217
in REPORT command, 335, 335-336, 349-354
BREAKDOWN (command), 321-331
annotated example, 330-331
compared to CROSSTABS, 323
CROSSBREAK subcommand, 325-326
crosstabulation, 325-326
formats, 328
general mode, 322-324
integer mode, 324-326
limitations, 329
missing values, 327
old friends, 764
statistics, 326-327
TABLES subcommand, 322-324, 325-325
tree format, 328
VARIABLES subcommand, 324-325
BRIEF (keyword)
MANOVA command, 489
BRKSPACE (keyword)
REPORT command, 339
BY (keyword)
BARCHART command, 394
BOX-JENKINS command, 701
BREAKDOWN command, 322-324
CROSSTABS command, 288-291
LINECHART command, 410
LIST command, 146
LOGLINEAR command, 544, 545
LOOP command, 191
MANOVA command, 469
MULT RESPONSE command, 311-314
NPAR TESTS command, 684-685, 691-691
PARTIAL CORR command, 590
PIECHART command, 382-383
SORT CASES command, 207
SPLIT FILE command, 212
SURVIVAL command, 737, 737-738
BY (subcommand)
ADD FILES command, 241
MATCH FILES command, 231-232, 234-235

CANCORR (obsolete), 761, see MANOVA procedure
canonical correlation analysis, 489-490, 515-521
CASE (keyword)
FILE TYPE NESTED, 174
SET command, 53, 56
SHOW command, 53
CASE (subcommand)
FILE TYPE GROUPED, 167-168, 170-170
FILE TYPE NESTED, 173, 178
$CASENUM (system variable)
defined, 106
in LIST command, 147
in PRINT command, 138
in PRINT EJECT command, 140
in PRINT SPACE command, 140-141
with SELECT IF command, 152
cases
defined, 7
CASES (subcommand)
LIST command, 146
CASEWISE (subcommand)
REGRESSION command, 613
casewise plots
in REGRESSION command, 613

CCOUNT (function)
  BARCHART command, 393
  LINECHART command, 409
CDFNORM (function), 94
CELLINFO (keyword)
  MANOVA command, 487, 487
CELLPLOTS (keyword)
  MANOVA command, 493-494
censored observations
  defined, 735
CENTER (keyword)
  BOX-JENKINS command, 704
CFOOTNOTE (subcommand)
  REPORT command, 367-368
CFVAR (function), 93
CHA (keyword)
  REGRESSION command, 610
CHDSPACE (keyword)
  REPORT command, 339
chi-square test, 294, 673-674
CHISQUARE (subcommand)
  NPAR TESTS command, 673, 673-674
CHOLESKY (keyword)
  MANOVA command, 480
CI (keyword)
  REGRESSION command, 610
CIN (keyword)
  BOX-JENKINS command, 714
CLASS (keyword)
  DISCRIMINANT command, 641
classification options
  in DISCRIMINANT command, 639-640
classification plots, 636-637
CLUSTERED (keyword)
  BARCHART command, 398
COCHRAN (keyword)
  MANOVA command, 487
COCHRAN (subcommand)
  NPAR TESTS command, 682, 682-683
Cochran's *C*
  in MANOVA command, 487
  in ONEWAY command, 459
Cochran's *Q*
  in NPAR TESTS command, 682-683
  in RELIABILITY command, 725
COEFF (keyword)
  REGRESSION command, 610
coefficient of variation, 93
COLORS (subcommand)
  BARCHART command, 404
  LINECHART command, 417
  PIECHART command, 386-387
COLUMN (keyword)
  REREAD command, 202
COLUMNWISE (keyword)
  AGGREGATE command, 220-221
COMBINE (keyword)
  PIECHART command, 384
COMMA (keyword)
  REPORT command, 359
COMMA format, 136-137, 144-144
command file
  defined, 6
commands
  case, 19, 79-80
  order, 23-24, 258-258
  syntax, 19-23
commas
  delimiters, 23
COMMENT (command), 52
  old friends, 753
COMMENT (subcommand)
  BARCHART command, 399
  LINECHART command, 412
  PIECHART command, 384
comments in command file, 52
common variables
  in ADD FILES command, 239-240, 242-242
  in MATCH FILES command, 228, 232-233
COMPARE (subcommand)
  SURVIVAL command, 741
complete randomized block designs
  in MANOVA command, 501
COMPLEX (keyword)
  BARCHART command, 404
  LINECHART command, 418
  PIECHART command, 387
complex files
  defined, 9
  with INPUT PROGRAM command, 203-204
composite functions
  in REPORT command, 355, 359-361
COMPRESSED (keyword)
  SAVE (command), 76
compression
  scratch files, 57
COMPRESSION (keyword)
  SET command, 53, 57
  SHOW command, 53
COMPUTE (command)
  annotated examples, 98-99
  missing values, 90, 111
  numeric variables, 87-90
  old friends, 760
  string variables, 114-115
  with DO IF command, 122
CONCAT (function), 116, 119
concatenating files
  ADD FILES command, 238, 238-241
concentration statistic, 544
COND (keyword)
  REGRESSION command, 610
CONDENSE (keyword)
  FREQUENCIES command, 268
CONDESCRIPTIVE (command), 279-285
  Z scores, 281-282
  annotated example, 284-285
  compared to FREQUENCIES, 279, 281
  formats, 282-283
  limitations, 283
  missing values, 282
  old friends, 763
  statistics, 280-281
  variable list, 279-280
CONDITIONAL (keyword)
  MANOVA command, 469
confidence intervals
  in LINECHART command, 409-410
  in REGRESSION command, 610
CONSPLUS (keyword)
  MANOVA command, 471-472
CONSTANT (keyword)
  BOX-JENKINS command, 704
  MANOVA command, 472-473, 481-481, 490-491
constants, 91
CONTIN (keyword)
  MANOVA command, 470
contingency coefficient, 294
CONTINUED (subcommand)
  REPEATING DATA command, 185-186
CONTRAST (keyword)
  MANOVA command, 476
CONTRAST (subcommand)
  LOGLINEAR command, 548-549
  MANOVA command, 482-486
  ONEWAY command, 455-456
contrasts
  in MANOVA command, 482-486
CONVERGE (keyword)
  LOGLINEAR command, 554
CONVERT (keyword)
  old friends, 760
  RECODE command, 114, 118
COOK (keyword)
  REGRESSION command, 612
COPY (keyword)
  RECODE command, 87, 112
COR (keyword)
  LOGLINEAR command, 547
  MANOVA command, 487, 488, 489, 489, 49 0-490
CORR (keyword), see CORRELATION keyword
CORRELATION (keyword)
  FACTOR command, 650, 660, 660
  REGRESSION command, 607, 619, 620
COS (function), 93
cosine, 93
COUNT (command), 100-101
  MISSING keyword, 101
  missing values, 101
  old friends, 760
  SYSMIS keyword, 101
  with DO IF command, 122
  with MULT RESPONSE, 316-317
COUNT (function)
  BARCHART command, 393
  LINECHART command, 409
COUNT (keyword)
  BARCHART command, 398
  PIECHART command, 383
COV (keyword)
  MANOVA command, 487, 488, 489
  REGRESSION command, 607, 619, 620
covariates
  defined, 439
  in ANOVA command, 443-444
  in MANOVA command, 468
CPERCENT (function)
  BARCHART command, 393
  LINECHART command, 409
CPROPORTION (function)
  LINECHART command, 409
Cramer's *V*, 294
CRITERIA (subcommand)
  FACTOR command, 653-654
  LOGLINEAR command, 554
  REGRESSION command, 608-609
Cronbach's Alpha, 717, 719
CROSSBREAK (subcommand)
  BREAKDOWN command, 325-326
CROSSBREAK-like tables
  in REPORT command, 372-373

CROSSTABS (command), 287-301
  annotated example, 300-301
  cell contents, 293-294
  cell percentages, 293
  compared to BREAKDOWN, 323
  expected values, 294
  formats, 296-297
  general mode, 288-291
  indexing tables, 297
  integer mode, 291-292
  limitations, 299
  missing values, 295-296
  old friends, 763-764
  reproducing tables, 298-299
  residuals, 294
  statistics, 294-295
  TABLES subcommand, 288-291, 292-292
  VARIABLES subcommand, 291-292
  with WEIGHT command, 298-299
  writing tables, 297-298
CROSSTABS-like tables
  in REPORT command, 373-374
crosstabulation
  defined, 287
  in BREAKDOWN command, 325-326
  in CROSSTABS command, 287-292
  in MULT RESPONSE command, 305-306
CSUM (function)
  BARCHART command, 393
  LINECHART command, 409
CTITLE (subcommand)
  REPORT command, 367-368
cumulative distribution function, 94
CURVES (subcommand)
  LINECHART command, 414-415
CWEIGHT (subcommand)
  LOGLINEAR command, 545-546

D (keyword)
  SORT CASES command, 207-208
d, Somers', 294
DATA (subcommand)
  REPEATING DATA command, 184
data definition, 29-30
  annotated example, 48-49
data definitions
  with transformations, 107
data formats
  A type, 36
  default, 35-36
  E type, 36
  FORTRAN-like, 45-47
  in DATA LIST command, 35-37, 45-46
  N type, 36
  table, 46
DATA LIST (command), 31-39, 45-47
  annotated example, 48-49
  column locations, 34
  data formats, 37, 45-46
  decimal places, 35
  default data format, 35-36
  dictionary formats, 38-39
  FILE subcommand, 31
  FIXED keyword, 32
  FORTRAN-like formats, 45-47
  FREE keyword, 32
  LIST keyword, 32
  naming variables, 33-34
  NOTABLE subcommand, 32-33
  old friends, 751-752
  record specification, 33, 34
  RECORDS subcommand, 32
  TABLE subcommand, 32-33
  with ADD FILES command, 239
  with INPUT PROGRAM command, 203-205
  with MATCH FILES command, 227
  with RECORD TYPE command, 164-165, 169-169
data manipulations
  defined, 10-11
data transformations
  defined, 10-11
$DATE (system variable)
  defined, 106
)DATE (argument)
  REPORT command, 367
)PAGE (argument)
  REPORT command, 367
DECOMP (keyword)
  MANOVA command, 488
DELETE SUBFILES (obsolete), 755
DELETE VARS (obsolete), 758, see GET or SAVE
delimiters
  blanks, 23
  commas, 23
  defined, 22-23
  special, 22-23
DELTA (keyword)
  FACTOR command, 653
  LOGLINEAR command, 554
DENSITY (keyword)
  SURVIVAL command, 740
DEPENDENT (subcommand)
  REGRESSION command, 603-604
DESCRIPTIVES (subcommand)
  REGRESSION command, 606-607
DESIGN (keyword)
  LOGLINEAR command, 547
  MANOVA command, 487, 488
DESIGN (subcommand)
  LOGLINEAR command, 544
  MANOVA command, 469-473
DET (keyword)
  FACTOR command, 651
determinant, matrix
  in FACTOR command, 651
DEVIATION (keyword)
  LOGLINEAR command, 548
  MANOVA command, 476, 482-483
DFREQ (keyword)
  FREQUENCIES command, 268
DIAGONAL (subcommand)
  FACTOR command, 654
dictionary
  defined, 30-31, 65-65
  structure, 79
DICTIONARY (keyword)
  DISPLAY command, 77
dictionary formats
  defined, 9, 143-144
  in AGGREGATE command, 218
  in DATA LIST command, 38-39
  in GET SCSS command, 248
  in PRINT command, 136-137
  in REPORT command, 374
  in WRITE command, 141
  old friends, 755
  transformations, 84
DIFFERENCE (keyword)
  LOGLINEAR command, 548
  MANOVA command, 476, 483-484
DIFFERENCE (subcommand)
  BOX-JENKINS command, 701
DIGITS (subcommand)
  EXPORT command, 253
DIMENR (keyword)
  MANOVA command, 489
dimension-reduction analysis, 489
DIRECT (keyword)
  DISCRIMINANT command, 627
DISCRIM (keyword)
  MANOVA command, 487, 489-490
DISCRIMINANT (command), 623-631
  ANALYSIS subcommand, 626-627
  annotated example, 630-631
  casewise plots, 639
  classification coefficients, 640
  classification options, 639-640
  classification plots, 636-637
  classification results table, 635
  classifying cases, 634-640
  direct entry, 627
  discriminant scores, 639
  display options, 634
  FUNCTIONS subcommand, 632-633
  GROUPS subcommand, 624
  inclusion levels, 628
  limitations, 645
  matrix input, 643-644
  matrix output, 642-643
  MAXSTEPS subcommand, 628
  METHOD subcommand, 627
  missing values, 641
  old friends, 769
  PRIORS subcommand, 635
  rotation options, 634
  SAVE subcommand, 641-642
  SELECT subcommand, 634
  statistical controls, 632
  syntax rules, summary, 644-645
  tolerance, 632
  VARIABLES subcommand, 625-626
discriminant analysis
  in DISCRIMINANT command, 623
  in MANOVA command, 489-490
discriminant scores, 639
DISPLAY (command), 77-78
display file
  defined, 6
  length, 55-56
  setting case, 55, 56
  width, 55-56
distance model, 567-569
DIVIDE (function)
  REPORT command, 355
division, 91
DO IF (command), 122-126
  annotated example, 130-131
  missing values, 125
  nested, 125-126
  with IF command, 122-123
  with INPUT PROGRAM command, 204
  with PRINT command, 138
  with PRINT EJECT command, 140
  with PRINT SPACE command, 140-141
  with SAMPLE command, 158
  with SELECT IF command, 158

DO REPEAT (command), 104-106
  old friends, 761
DOCUMENT (command), 76-77
  old friends, 758
documentation
  local, 24
  new facilities, 25
  new procedures, 25
  new releases, 25-26
  update, 24
DOCUMENTS (keyword)
  DISPLAY command, 77, 78
DOLLAR (keyword)
  REPORT command, 359
DOLLAR format, 136-137, 144-144
domain errors
  defined, 100
  numeric expressions, 100
DOUBLE (keyword)
  FREQUENCIES command, 268
doubly multivariate repeated
    measures, 476, 532-535
DOWN (keyword)
  SORT CASES command, 207
DRESID (keyword)
  REGRESSION command, 612
DROP (subcommand)
  ADD FILES command, 240, 242
  EXPORT command, 252
  GET command, 68-69
  IMPORT command, 253
  MATCH FILES command, 229-230
  SAVE command, 72-73
  SAVE SCSS command, 246
DSER (keyword)
  BOX-JENKINS command, 714
DUMMY (keyword)
  REPORT command, 341
dummy variables
  in REPORT command, 335, 341
DUMP (keyword)
  BARCHART command, 399
  LINECHART command, 412
  PIECHART command, 384
DUNCAN (keyword)
  ONEWAY command, 458
Duncan's multiple range test, 458
DUPLEX (keyword)
  BARCHART command, 404
  LINECHART command, 418
  PIECHART command, 387
DUPLICATE (subcommand)
  FILE TYPE GROUPED, 168,
    170-171
  FILE TYPE NESTED, 173-174
DURBIN (keyword)
  REGRESSION command, 612
DVALUE (keyword)
  FREQUENCIES command, 268

ECONVERGE (keyword)
  FACTOR command, 653
EDIT (command), 61-62
  annotated example, 58-59
  old friends, 753
EIGEN (keyword)
  FACTOR command, 652
  MANOVA command, 489
element
  VECTOR command, 193-194
ELSE (command), 123-124
  with IF command, 123-124
ELSE (keyword)
  RECODE command, 85-86, 112-112
ELSE IF (command), 124-125
END (keyword)
  REGRESSION command, 610
END CASE (command), 196-198,
    199-199
  with END FILE command, 199
END DATA (command), 43-45,
    259-259
END FILE (command), 198-199
  with END CASE command, 199
END FILE TYPE (command),
    161-162
END IF (command), 122-126
END INPUT DATA (obsolete), 753,
    see END DATA command
END INPUT PROGRAM (command),
    195-203
  with REPEATING DATA command,
    181-182
END LOOP (command), 190-193
  IF keyword, 191
  logical expressions, 191
  missing values, 192
END REPEAT (command), 104-106
  old friends, 761
  PRINT subcommand, 106
ENTER (keyword)
  REGRESSION command, 604-605
entropy statistic, 544
EPS (keyword)
  MANOVA command, 486
EQ (keyword)
  relational operator, 128
EQUAL (keyword)
  DISCRIMINANT command, 635
  NPAR TESTS command, 674
EQUAMAX (keyword)
  FACTOR command, 654
  MANOVA command, 488, 489
equiprobability model, 545, 558-560
ERROR (keyword)
  MANOVA command, 487, 489,
    491-493, 493-493
ERROR (subcommand)
  MANOVA command, 486-487
errors
  annotated example, 58-59
  messages, 61
  setting maximum, 55
ESTIM (keyword)
  LOGLINEAR command, 547
  MANOVA command, 489, 490
ESTIMATE (subcommand)
  BOX-JENKINS command, 698-699
ESTIMATION (keyword)
  MANOVA command, 480-481
eta coefficient, 294, 326
EXECUTE (command), 258-259
EXP (function), 92
EXPECTED (subcommand)
  NPAR TESTS command, 673-674
EXPLODE (subcommand)
  PIECHART command, 385
exponent function, 92
exponentiation, 91
EXPORT (command), 251-253
  DIGITS subcommand, 253
  DROP subcommand, 252
  KEEP subcommand, 252
  MAP subcommand, 252
  OUTFILE subcommand, 251
  RENAME subcommand, 252
EXTRACTION (keyword)
  FACTOR command, 651
EXTRACTION (subcommand)
  FACTOR command, 650

F (keyword)
  REGRESSION command, 610
FACILITIES (keyword)
  INFO command, 25
FACTOR (command), 647-661
  alpha factoring, 650
  ANALYSIS subcommand, 650«
  annotated example, 656-659
  CRITERIA subcommand, 653-654
  DIAGONAL subcommand, 654
  equamax rotation, 654
  EXTRACTION subcommand, 650
  factor plots, 652
  factor scores, 655
  FORMAT subcommand, 652
  generalized least squares, 650
  image factoring, 650
  limitations, 661
  matrix input, 660
  matrix output, 660-661
  maximum likelihood, 650
  MISSING subcommand, 648-649
  missing values, 648-649
  oblimin rotation, direct, 654
  old friends, 770
  PLOT subcommand, 652-653
  principal axis factoring, 650
  principal components analysis, 650
  PRINT subcommand, 650-652
  quartimax rotation, 654
  READ subcommand, 660
  ROTATION subcommand, 654-655
  SAVE subcommand, 655
  scree plots, 652
  statistics, 650-652
  syntax summary, 661
  unweighted least squares, 650
  VARIABLES subcommand, 648
  varimax rotation, 654
  WIDTH subcommand, 649
  WRITE subcommand, 660-661
F ratio, 326
FACTOR (keyword)
  FACTOR command, 660, 660
factor plots
  in FACTOR command, 652
factor scores
  Anderson-Rubin method, 655
  Bartlett method, 655
  regression method, 655
factors
  defined, 439
FACTORS (keyword)
  FACTOR command, 653
FANCY (keyword)
  BARCHART command, 398
  LINECHART command, 412
  PIECHART command, 383
FCF (keyword)
  BOX-JENKINS command, 714
FCON (subcommand)
  BOX-JENKINS command, 713
FGT (function)
  AGGREGATE command, 219
FILE (subcommand)
  ADD FILES command, 238-239,
    241-241

DATA LIST command, 31
FILE TYPE command, 163
GET command, 66
INPUT MATRIX command, 262-263
MATCH FILES command, 226-227, 234-235
REPEATING DATA command, 184-185
file definition, 29
in DATA LIST command, 31
file handle
defined, 7, 30
in FILE HANDLE command, 30
in IBM/OS version, 30
FILE HANDLE (command), 30
FILE LABEL (command), 76
file management
defined, 11-12
FILE NAME (obsolete), 758
file specifications
in FILE HANDLE command, 30
FILE TYPE (command)
CASE subcommand, 167-168, 173-173
DUPLICATE subcommand, 168, 173-174
FILE subcommand, 163
GROUPED keyword, 162
MISSING subcommand, 168-169, 174-175
MIXED keyword, 162
NESTED keyword, 162
ORDERED subcommand, 169
RECORD subcommand, 163, 167, 172-173
summary table, 179
WILD subcommand, 164, 168, 173
with REPEATING DATA command, 181
FILE TYPE GROUPED, 166-167
CASE subcommand, 167-168, 170-170
DUPLICATE subcommand, 168, 170-171
MISSING subcommand, 168-169, 170-171
ORDERED subcommand, 169
OTHER keyword, 169-170
RECORD subcommand, 167
SKIP subcommand, 169-170
WILD subcommand, 168
with RECORD TYPE command, 169-171
FILE TYPE MIXED, 162-163
OTHER keyword, 165
RECORD subcommand, 163
SKIP subcommand, 165-166
WILD subcommand, 164
with RECORD TYPE command, 164-166
FILE TYPE NESTED, 171-172
annotated example, 176-177
CASE subcommand, 173, 178
DUPLICATE subcommand, 173-174
MISSING subcommand, 174-175
RECORD subcommand, 172-173
SPREAD (subcommand), 178-179
WILD subcommand, 173
with RECORD TYPE command, 175-179
FIN (function)
AGGREGATE command, 219
FIN (keyword)
DISCRIMINANT command, 632
REGRESSION command, 609
FINISH (command), 52
old friends, 753
FIRST (function)
AGGREGATE command, 219
FIRST (subcommand)
ADD FILES command, 242
MATCH FILES command, 235-238
Fisher's exact test, 294
FIXED (keyword)
DATA LIST command, 32
FLF (keyword)
BOX-JENKINS command, 714
flow of control
DO IF command, 126
FLT (function)
AGGREGATE command, 219
FONT (subcommand)
BARCHART command, 404
LINECHART command, 418
PIECHART command, 387
FOOTNOTE (subcommand)
BARCHART command, 399
LINECHART command, 412
PIECHART command, 384
REPORT command, 367-368
FOR (keyword)
SURVIVAL command, 738
FORECAST (subcommand)
BOX-JENKINS command, 698-699
forecast function, 714
FORMAT (keyword)
MANOVA command, 493
SET command, 53, 56-57
SHOW command, 53
FORMAT (subcommand)
BARCHART command, 397-399
FACTOR command, 652
FREQUENCIES command, 267-269
LINECHART command, 412
LIST command, 146-147
PIECHART command, 383-384
RELIABILITY command, 731
REPORT command, 338-340
FORMATS (command), 144
with AGGREGATE command, 218-219
FORTRAN-like formats
in DATA LIST command, 45-47
in PRINT command, 137
in WRITE command, 142
FORWARD (keyword)
REGRESSION command, 604
FOUT (function)
AGGREGATE command, 219
FOUT (keyword)
DISCRIMINANT command, 632
REGRESSION command, 609
FP (subcommand)
BOX-JENKINS command, 713
FPR (subcommand)
BOX-JENKINS command, 705
FQ (subcommand)
BOX-JENKINS command, 713
FRAME (keyword)
BARCHART command, 398
LINECHART command, 412
FREE (keyword)
data formats, 38
DATA LIST command, 32
INPUT MATRIX command, 262-263
variable definition, 37-38
FREQ (keyword)
FREQUENCIES command, 271, 272
LOGLINEAR command, 547
frequencies
in MULT RESPONSE command, 304-305
FREQUENCIES (command), 265-277
annotated example, 274-275
bar charts, 269-271, 272-273
compared to CONDESCRIPTIVE, 279, 281
FORMAT subcommand, 267-269
general mode, 266-267
histograms, 269-270, 271-273
indexing tables, 269
integer mode, 266-267
limitations, 277
MISSING subcommand, 276
missing values, 276
NTILES subcommand, 273
old friends, 762
PERCENTILES subcommand, 273
statistics, 276
VARIABLES subcommand, 266-267
writing tables, 269
FREQUENCIES (subcommand)
MULT RESPONSE command, 309-310
FRIEDMAN (subcommand)
NPAR TESTS command, 682, 683
Friedman's analysis of variance
in NPAR TESTS command, 683
in RELIABILITY command, 724
FROM (keyword)
LIST command, 146
FSCORE (keyword)
FACTOR command, 651
FSP (subcommand)
BOX-JENKINS command, 713
FSQ (subcommand)
BOX-JENKINS command, 713
FTSPACE (keyword)
REPORT command, 339
functions
in AGGREGATE command, 217-218
in BARCHART command, 393-394
in LINECHART command, 409-410, 411-411
in REPORT command, 355
numeric variables, 92-95
old friends, 760
string variables, 116-119
FUNCTIONS (subcommand)
DISCRIMINANT command, 632-633

gamma, 294
GE (keyword)
relational operator, 128
general linear models, 465-508
general log-linear model, 555-556
general mode
in BREAKDOWN command, 322-324
in CROSSTABS command, 288-291
in FREQUENCIES command, 266-267
GET (command), 66-70
DROP subcommand, 68-69

FILE subcommand, 66
KEEP subcommand, 69-70
MAP subcommand, 67
RENAME subcommand, 67-68
reordering variables, 69-70
SPSS system files, 756-758
VARIABLES subcommand, 78
GET FILE (obsolete), 756, see GET command
GET SCSS (command), 248-250
$ convention, 250
MASTERFILE subcommand, 249, 249
missing values, 248
old friends, 758
renaming variables, 250
reserved keywords, 250
VARIABLES subcommand, 249-250
WORKFILE subcommand, 249
GLS (keyword)
FACTOR command, 650
GOTHIC (keyword)
BARCHART command, 404
LINECHART command, 418
PIECHART command, 387
Graeco-Latin squares
in MANOVA command, 502
graphics, see BARCHART, LINECHART, and PIECHART
aggregated data, 392
intermediate file, 425
multiple plots per page, 391-392
old friends, 766
TELL-A-GRAF interface, 422-425
GRAPHICS OUTPUT (command), 425
OUTFILE subcommand, 425
graphics postprocessor, 425-428
annotated example, 426-427
ASSIGN command, 428
CONTENTS command, 428
DRAW command, 428
HELP command, 428
PREVIEW command, 428
SEND command, 428
GREAT (function)
REPORT command, 355
GRESID (subcommand)
LOGLINEAR command, 546-547
GRID (keyword)
BARCHART command, 399
LINECHART command, 412
group variables
in MULT RESPONSE command, 304-306
GROUPED (keyword), see FILE TYPE GROUPED
grouped files, 166-167
defined, 162
GROUPS (subcommand)
DISCRIMINANT command, 624
MULT RESPONSE command, 308
T-TEST command, 434
GT (keyword)
relational operator, 128
GUTTMAN (keyword)
RELIABILITY command, 721
Guttman model
in RELIABILITY command, 718
GUTTMAN SCALE (obsolete), 761
Guttman split-half coefficient, 717

half-normal plots of partial correlations, 495
H, Kruskal-Wallis
see Kruskal-Wallis *H*, 695
Hartley's *F*, 459
HAZARD (keyword)
SURVIVAL command, 740
hazard rate, 739
HELMERT (keyword)
LOGLINEAR command, 548
MANOVA command, 477, 484
HI (keyword), see HIGHEST
HIDDEN (keyword)
BARCHART command, 398
hierarchical files, see nested files
HIGHEST (keyword)
MISSING VALUES command, 40-41
RECODE command, 85
SCATTERGRAM command, 576
HISTOGRAM (keyword)
REGRESSION command, 612
histograms
in FREQUENCIES command, 269-270, 271-273
HISTORY (keyword)
REGRESSION command, 610
HOMOGENEITY (keyword)
MANOVA command, 487, 487-488
homogeneity-of-variance tests
in MANOVA command, 487-488
in ONEWAY command, 459
HORIZONTAL (keyword)
BARCHART command, 397
Hotelling's T^2, 723-724
HYPOTH (keyword)
MANOVA command, 489

ICON (subcommand)
BOX-JENKINS command, 712
ID (keyword)
REGRESSION command, 612
ID (subcommand)
REPEATING DATA (command), 186-187
IDENTIFY (subcommand)
BOX-JENKINS command, 698-699
IF (command), 121
annotated example, 130-131
old friends, 761
with DO IF command, 122-123
with ELSE command, 123-124
IMAGE (keyword)
FACTOR command, 650
image factoring, 650
IMPORT (command), 253-254
DROP subcommand, 253
KEEP subcommand, 253
MAP subcommand, 254
RENAME subcommand, 254
IN (subcommand)
ADD FILES command, 240-241, 242-242
MATCH FILES command, 233
INCLUDE (keyword)
FACTOR command, 649
FREQUENCIES command, 276
REGRESSION command, 606
incomplete randomized block designs
in MANOVA command, 501-502
INCREMENT (keyword)
FREQUENCIES command, 272

increment value
in LOOP command, 191
indentation
commands, 20
continuation, 20
INDEX (function), 116, 117, 118-119
INDEX (keyword)
DISPLAY command, 77
FREQUENCIES command, 269
REGRESSION command, 619
indexing clause
in LOOP command, 190-191
indexing strings, 117
indexing variable
in LOOP command, 190-191
INFO (command), 24-26
local documentation, 24
new facilities, 25
new procedures, 25
new releases, 25-26
OUTFILE (subcommand), 26
update documentation, 24
INITIAL (keyword)
FACTOR command, 650
initial state
defined, 774-775
initial value
in LOOP command, 190-191
initialization
LEAVE command, 101
numeric variables, 87-90
old friends, 759
scratch variables, 103
string variables, 110
INITIALIZE (obsolete), 759, see LEAVE command
INLINE (handle), 30, 43
INPUT (keyword)
RELIABILITY command, 731
input data
freefield format, 32
inline, 43-45
input data file
defined, 6
INPUT FORMAT (obsolete), 752, see DATA LIST command
INPUT MATRIX (command), 262-263
FILE subcommand, 262-263
FREE keyword, 262-263
matrix input, 263
with N OF CASES command, 263
with NUMERIC command, 262-263
INPUT MEDIUM (obsolete), 752, see FILE HANDLE command
input program, 195-196, 197-198
INPUT PROGRAM (command), 195-203
annotated example, 200-201
with DATA LIST command, 203-205
with INPUT MATRIX command, 262-263
with LOOP command, 204-205
with REPEATING DATA command, 181-182
input state, 196
defined, 774-775
integer mode
in BREAKDOWN command, 324-326
in CROSSTABS command, 291-292
in FREQUENCIES command, 266-267

interleaving files
ADD FILES command, 238, 241-242
INTERVALS (subcommand)
SURVIVAL command, 737-738
INTO (keyword)
RECODE command, 86-87, 112-114
INV (keyword)
FACTOR command, 651
inverse, matrix
in FACTOR command, 651
IP (subcommand)
BOX-JENKINS command, 712
IQ (subcommand)
BOX-JENKINS command, 712
ISP (subcommand)
BOX-JENKINS command, 712
ISQ (subcommand)
BOX-JENKINS command, 712
item analysis, see RELIABILITY (command)
ITERATE (keyword)
FACTOR command, 653
ITERATE (subcommand)
BOX-JENKINS command, 704
ITERATION (keyword)
LOGLINEAR command, 554
I90 (function)
LINECHART command, 409
I95 (function)
LINECHART command, 409
I99 (function)
LINECHART command, 409

$JDATE (system variable)
defined, 106

K-S (subcommand)
NPAR TESTS command, 673, 674-676, 685-685, 687-688
K-W (subcommand)
NPAR TESTS command, 691, 692-693
KAISER (keyword)
FACTOR command, 653
Kaiser-Meyer-Olkin test, 651
KEEP (subcommand)
ADD FILES command, 240, 242
EXPORT command, 252
GET command, 69-70
IMPORT command, 253
MATCH FILES command, 229-230
SAVE command, 72-73
SAVE SCSS command, 246
KEEP VARS (obsolete), 758, see GET or SAVE
KENDALL (subcommand)
NPAR TESTS command, 682, 684
Kendall's *W* (coefficient of concordance)
in NPAR TESTS command, 684
in RELIABILITY command, 724
Kendall's tau-*b*, 294, 665
Kendall's tau-*c*, 294
key variables
in ADD FILES command, 241
in MATCH FILES command, 230, 231-232, 234-235
keywords
defined, 19-20, 21-21
reserved, 21
truncation, 21
KMO (keyword)
FACTOR command, 651
Kolmogorov-Smirnov *Z* (test), 674-676, 687-688
Kruskal-Wallis *H*, see Kruskal-Wallis one-way analysis of variance
Kruskal-Wallis *H* (one-way analysis of variance), 692-693
KURTOSIS (function)
REPORT command, 355
KURTOSIS (keyword)
FREQUENCIES command, 276

LABEL (keyword)
REGRESSION command, 610
REPORT command, 340-341, 350-350
LABELED (keyword)
BARCHART command, 399
LINECHART command, 413
labels
case, 79-80
LABELS (keyword)
DISPLAY command, 77
LAG (function), 93
LAG (obsolete command), 760, see LAG function
LAG (subcommand)
BOX-JENKINS command, 702
lambda, 294
LAST (function)
AGGREGATE command, 219
LAST (subcommand)
ADD FILES command, 242
MATCH FILES command, 235-238
LASTRES (keyword)
MANOVA command, 481
Latin squares
in MANOVA command, 502
LE (keyword)
relational operator, 128
LEAD (subcommand)
BOX-JENKINS command, 713
LEAST (function)
REPORT command, 355
least squares, generalized
in FACTOR command, 650
least squares, unweighted
in FACTOR command, 650
LEAVE (command), 101-102
annotated example, 200-201
LEGEND LABELS (subcommand)
BARCHART command, 402-403
LINECHART command, 415-416
LEGEND TITLE (subcommand)
BARCHART command, 402-403
LINECHART command, 415-416
LENGTH (keyword)
REPORT command, 339
SET command, 53-54, 55-56
SHOW command, 53-54
LENGTH (subcommand)
REPEATING DATA command, 185
$LENGTH (system variable)
defined, 106
LEVER (keyword)
REGRESSION command, 612
LFOOTNOTE (subcommand)
REPORT command, 367-368
LG10 (function), 92
life table analysis, see SURVIVAL (command)
life tables
in SURVIVAL command, 738-739
LIMIT (keyword)
FREQUENCIES command, 269
limitations, see entries under individual procedures
LINE (keyword)
REGRESSION command, 610
LINEAR (keyword)
BARCHART command, 400, 401
LINECHART command, 413, 414
linear logit model, 549, 560-561
LINECHART (command), 377-378, 380-381, 408-422
aggregated data, 392
annotated example, 424
applications, 420-422
COLORS subcommand, 417
COMMENT subcommand, 412
CURVES subcommand, 414-415
FONT subcommand, 418
FOOTNOTE subcommand, 412
FORMAT subcommand, 412
functions, 409-410, 411-411
LEGEND LABELS subcommand, 415-416
LEGEND TITLE subcommand, 415-416
MISSING subcommand, 418-419
missing values, 418-419
multiple plots per page, 391-392
old friends, 766
ORDER subcommand, 416-417
patterns, 416-417
PLOT subcommand, 408-412, 419-420
SAVE subcommand, 422-425
selectors, 410-411
superimposing line charts, 411-412
TITLE subcommand, 412
X AXIS subcommand, 413
Y AXIS subcommand, 414
LINEWISE (keyword)
LINECHART command, 418
LIST (command), 144-148
$CASENUM system variable, 147
CASES subcommand, 146
VARIABLES subcommand, 145
with SELECT IF, 147-148
with SPLIT FILE command, 146, 147
LIST (keyword)
data formats, 38
DATA LIST command, 32
REPORT command, 338-339, 368-368
variable definition, 37-38
LIST ARCHINFO (obsolete), 758, see DISPLAY command
LIST CASES (obsolete), 754, see LIST command
LIST ERRORS (obsolete), 753
LIST FILEINFO (obsolete), 758, see DISPLAY command
listing cases
in REPORT command, 338-339
LISTWISE (keyword)
FACTOR command, 649
REGRESSION command, 606
literals
case, 79-80
defined, 22, 110-111
in COMPUTE command, 110

in PRINT command, 138-139
in RECODE command, 110
in REPORT command, 342, 347
in VALUE LABELS command, 42
in VARIABLE LABELS command, 42
in WRITE command, 142
LN (function), 92
LO (keyword), see LOWEST
LOCAL (keyword)
INFO command, 25
local documentation
INFO command, 24
LOG (keyword)
BARCHART command, 401
LINECHART command, 413, 414
LOG (subcommand)
BOX-JENKINS command, 700
logarithm
base *e*, 92
base 10, 92
logical expressions, 95-96, 114-114, 127-133
defined, 127
implied operators, 761
in COMPUTE, 128
in DO IF command, 122
in ELSE IF (command), 124-125
in END LOOP, 127-128
in END LOOP command, 191
in IF command, 121
in LOOP, 127-128
in LOOP command, 192
in SELECT IF, 127
in SELECT IF command, 151-152
missing values, 132, 152
old friends, 761
order of evaluation, 129-132
string variables, 115
logical functions, 93, 94
missing values, 94
logical operators, 129
defined, 129
missing values, 132-133
logical variables
defined, 128
logistic regression model, 549, 562-563
logit model, 544, 550-552
multinomial, 556-557
simultaneous linear, 545
LOGLINEAR (command), 541-569
annotated example, 550-552
cell frequencies, 547
cell weights, 545-546
CONTRAST subcommand, 548-549
covariates, 544, 545
CRITERIA subcommand, 554
CWEIGHT subcommand, 545-546
design matrix, 547
DESIGN subcommand, 544
dispersion, analysis of, 544
distance model, 567-569
equiprobability model, 545, 558-560
factor, defined, 548
frequency table models, 558-560
general log-linear model, 542-543, 555-556
GRESID subcommand, 546-547
interactions, 545
log-linear time-trend model, 558-560
logistic regression model, 549, 562-563
logit model, 544, 550-552
logit model, linear, 549, 560-561
logit model, multinomial, 549, 556-557
main effects model, 544-545
measures of association, 544
minimum required syntax, 542-543
missing values, 554
multinomial response models, 564-566
NOPRINT subcommand, 547
parameter estimates, 547
PLOT subcommand, 547-548
PRINT subcommand, 547
residuals, 547
simultaneous linear logit model, 545
single-degree-of-freedom partitions, 545
statistics, 547
structural zeros, 546
variable specification, 542-543
WIDTH subcommand, 554
LOGSURV (keyword)
SURVIVAL command, 740
long string, see string variables
LOOP (command), 190-193
BREAK command, 193
IF keyword, 192
indexing clause, 190-191
logical expressions, 192
missing values, 192
nested, 193
with INPUT PROGRAM command, 204-205
with SET MXLOOPS command, 55, 190
with VECTOR command, 193-194
lower case, 79-80
LOWEST (keyword)
MISSING VALUES command, 40-41
RECODE command, 85
SCATTERGRAM command, 576
LPAD (function), 116, 117, 119
LSD (keyword)
ONEWAY command, 458
LSDMOD (keyword)
ONEWAY command, 458
LTITLE (subcommand)
REPORT command, 367-368
LTRIM (function), 116, 119

M-W (subcommand)
NPAR TESTS command, 685, 686-687
MAHAL (keyword)
DISCRIMINANT command, 627
REGRESSION command, 612
main effects model
in LOGLINEAR, 544-545
MALAG (subcommand)
BOX-JENKINS command, 703
Mann-Whitney *U* test, 686-687
MANOVA (command), 465-539
analysis of covariance, 509-511
ANALYSIS subcommand, 468-469, 475-476
annotated example, 539-508
between-subjects factors, 469-473
boxplots, 495
canonical correlation analysis, 515-521
cell statistics, 493-494
complete randomized block designs, 501
CONTRAST subcommand, 482-486
covariate list, 468
degrees-of-freedom partitions, 481-482
dependent variable list, 467
DESIGN subcommand, 469-473
doubly multivariate repeated measures, 476, 532-535
ERROR subcommand, 486-487
error term, 472
factor list, 467
Graeco-Latin squares, 502
half-normal plots of partial correlations, 495
homogeneity-of-variance tests, 487-488
incomplete randomized block designs, 501-502
interaction terms, 469
interactions, specification of, 470-471
Latin squares, 502
lumped effects, 471
main effects model, 469
matrix input, 498-499
matrix output, 497-498
MEASURE subcommand, 476
METHOD subcommand, 480-481
minimum required syntax, 466-468
missing values, 499
multivariate multiple regression, 515-521
multivariate one-way ANOVA, 511-515
multivariate setup, 475-476
nested designs, 471, 502-503
NOPRINT subcommand, 487-493
normal plots, 495
observed means, 490-491
old friends, 767-768
parameter estimates, 490
parameter estimation, 480-481
PARTITION subcommand, 469-470, 481-482
PLOT subcommand, 493-496
plots, 493-496
polynomial transformations, 477-478
predicted means, 491-493
predicted means plots, 496
predicted values, 493
principal components analysis, 488-489
PRINT subcommand, 487-493
profile analysis, 535-539
randomized block designs, 501-502
READ subcommand, 498-499
RENAME subcommand, 479-480
repeated measures analysis, 473-476, 521-531, 539-508
repeated measures multivariate ANCOVA, 475-476
repeated measures, doubly multivariate, 476, 532-535
residuals, 493
SETCONST subcommand, 486
single-degree-of-freedom partition, 469-470

statistics, 487-493
stem-and-leaf plots, 495
sums of squares partitions, 481
TRANSFORM subcommand, 476-479
transformation matrix, 493
transformations, 476-479
univariate analysis of variance, 499-501
variable specification, 466-468
within-subjects factors, 473-474
within-subjects model, 474-475
WRITE subcommand, 497-498
WSDESIGN subcommand, 474-475
WSFACTORS subcommand, 473-474
MAP (subcommand)
ADD FILES command, 240, 242
EXPORT command, 252
GET command, 67
IMPORT command, 254
MATCH FILES command, 228
SAVE command, 71
MARGINS (keyword)
REPORT command, 339
MARKERS (keyword)
LINECHART command, 415
MASTERFILE (subcommand)
GET SCSS command, 249, 249
MATCH FILES (command), 225-238
active file, 227
annotated example, 236-237
BY subcommand, 231-232, 234-235
common variables, 228, 232-233
dictionary information, 232
DROP subcommand, 229-230
FILE subcommand, 226-227, 234-235
FIRST subcommand, 235-238
IN subcommand, 233
KEEP subcommand, 229-230
key variables, 230, 231-232, 234-235
LAST subcommand, 235-238
MAP subcommand, 228
missing values, 231-232
nonparallel files, 230-233
RENAME subcommand, 228-229
reordering variables, 230
table lookup files, 234-238
TABLE subcommand, 234-235
with DATA LIST command, 227
with SORT CASES command, 209, 232
with TEMPORARY command, 227
matrices
anti-image covariance, 651
cell sums of squares and cross-products, 487
correlation, 487, 579-582, 593-593, 619-620, 620-621, 650 -650,651, 660, 660-661, 728-729
covariance, 487, 584, 619-620, 620-621, 728-729, 730-731
factor loadings, 660, 660-661
matrices, correlation, 663-669
matrix files
missing values, 261
reading, 262-263
writing, 261
matrix output
with SPLIT FILE command, 213
MAX (function), 93
AGGREGATE command, 219
REPORT command, 355
MAX (keyword)
FREQUENCIES command, 271, 272
MAXIMUM (keyword)
FREQUENCIES command, 276
maximum function, 93
maximum likelihood
in FACTOR command, 650
MAXMINF (keyword)
DISCRIMINANT command, 627
MAXSTEPS (keyword)
REGRESSION command, 609
MAXSTEPS (subcommand)
DISCRIMINANT command, 628
MCNEMAR (subcommand)
NPAR TESTS command, 679
McNemar test, 679-680
MEAN (function), 93
AGGREGATE command, 219
BARCHART command, 393
LINECHART command, 409
REPORT command, 355
MEAN (keyword)
FREQUENCIES command, 276
NPAR TESTS command, 676
REGRESSION command, 607, 619, 620
MEANS (keyword)
MANOVA command, 487
MEANSUB (keyword)
FACTOR command, 649
MEANSUBSTITUTION (keyword)
REGRESSION command, 606
MEASURE (subcommand)
MANOVA command, 476
median, 276
MEDIAN (function)
REPORT command, 355
MEDIAN (keyword)
FREQUENCIES command, 276
NPAR TESTS command, 676
MEDIAN (subcommand)
NPAR TESTS command, 685, 685-686, 691-691, 691-692
median test, 685-686, 691-692
MENEMAR (subcommand)
NPAR TESTS command, 679-680
MERGE FILES (obsolete), 755, see MATCH FILES command
messages
errors, 60, 61
notes, 60, 60
warnings, 60, 60-61
METHOD (subcommand)
DISCRIMINANT command, 627
MANOVA command, 480-481
MIN (function), 93
AGGREGATE command, 219
REPORT command, 355
MIN (keyword)
FREQUENCIES command, 271, 272
MINEIGEN (keyword)
FACTOR command, 653
MANOVA command, 488
MINIMUM (keyword)
FREQUENCIES command, 276
minimum function, 93
MINRESID (keyword)
DISCRIMINANT command, 627
MISSING (function), 93
SELECT IF command, 152
MISSING (keyword)
COUNT command, 101
RECODE command, 86, 112
REPORT command, 339
MISSING (subcommand)
AGGREGATE command, 220-221
BARCHART command, 404-407
FACTOR command, 648-649
FILE TYPE GROUPED, 168-169, 170-171
FILE TYPE NESTED, 174-175
FREQUENCIES command, 276
LINECHART command, 418-419
PIECHART command, 387-390
REGRESSION command, 606
REPORT command, 368-369
missing values, see entries under individual procedures
defined, 8, 39
functions, 93
in AGGREGATE command, 220-221
in arguments, 96-100
in COMPUTE command, 90
in COUNT command, 101
in DO IF command, 125
in END LOOP command, 192
in logical expressions, 132, 152
in logical functions, 94
in LOOP command, 192
in numeric expressions, 96
in REPORT command, 368-369
in SELECT IF command, 152
in string expressions, 111
MISSING function, 93
NMISS function, 93
old friends, 760
suffix, 93
SYSMIS function, 93
system-missing, 39
user-missing, 39
VALUE function, 93
with logical operators, 132-133
MISSING VALUES (command), 39-41
old friends, 753
redefining missing values, 41
string variables, 41
value range, 40-41
with AGGREGATE command, 221
MIXED (keyword), see FILE TYPE MIXED
mixed files, 162-163
defined, 162
ML (keyword)
FACTOR command, 650
MOD (function), 92
MODE (function)
REPORT command, 355
MODE (keyword)
FREQUENCIES command, 276
NPAR TESTS command, 676
MODEL (subcommand)
RELIABILITY command, 720-721
MODELTYPE (keyword)
MANOVA command, 480
modulo, 92
MONTHLY (keyword)
BARCHART command, 400
LINECHART command, 413
MOSES (subcommand)
NPAR TESTS command, 685, 690

Moses test of extreme reactions, 690
MULT RESPONSE (command), 303-319
  annotated example, 318-319
  cell percentages, 315
  crosstabulation, 305-306
  formats, 316
  FREQUENCIES subcommand, 309-310
  group variables, 304-306
  GROUPS subcommand, 308
  limitations, 317
  missing values, 315-316
  multiple response items, 303-306
  old friends, 764
  PAIRED keyword, 313-314
  statistics, 315
  stub and banner tables, 316-317
  TABLES subcommand, 311-314
  VARIABLES subcommand, 309
  with COUNT command, 316-317
multinomial logit model, 549, 556-557
multinomial response models, 564-566
multiple classification analysis
  in ANOVA command, 449-450
multiple comparisons between means, 456-458
multiple response items
  defined, 303
  in MULT RESPONSE command, 303-306
multiplication, 91
MULTIPLY (function)
  REPORT command, 355
MULTIV (keyword)
  MANOVA command, 489
multivariate *F* tests, 489
multivariate analysis of variance, 465-508
multivariate multiple regression, 515-521
multivariate one-way ANOVA, 511-515
MWITHIN (keyword)
  MANOVA command, 473
MXERRS (keyword)
  SET command, 54, 55
  SHOW command, 54
MXLOOPS (keyword)
  SET command, 54, 55
  SHOW command, 54
  with LOOP command, 190
MXWARNS (keyword)
  SET command, 54, 55
  SHOW command, 54
M90 (function)
  LINECHART command, 409
M95 (function)
  LINECHART command, 409
M99 (function)
  LINECHART command, 409

N (function)
  AGGREGATE command, 219
N (keyword)
  REGRESSION command, 607, 619, 620
  SHOW command, 54
N OF CASES (command), 154
  old friends, 753, 759
  with FILE TYPE command, 154
  with INPUT MATRIX command, 263
  with REPORT command, 371
NAME (keyword)
  BARCHART command, 400, 401
  LINECHART command, 413, 414
  REPORT command, 350
names
  defined, 20
NCENTER (keyword)
  BOX-JENKINS command, 704
NCOMP (keyword)
  MANOVA command, 488
NCONSTANT (keyword)
  BOX-JENKINS command, 704
NE (keyword)
  relational operator, 128, 128
NEGSUM (keyword)
  MANOVA command, 490
NESTED (keyword), see FILE TYPE NESTED
nested designs
  in MANOVA command, 471, 502-503
nested files, 171-172
  annotated example, 176-177
  defined, 162
NEW REGRESSION (obsolete), 768-769, see REGRESSION command
NEWPAGE (keyword)
  FREQUENCIES command, 268
Newton-Raphson algorithm, 554
NMISS (function), 93
  AGGREGATE command, 219
NO (keyword)
  FILE TYPE GROUPED, 169
  FILE TYPE NESTED, 178-179
NOBALANCED (keyword)
  MANOVA command, 480
NOBREAK (keyword)
  REPORT command, 350, 352-354
NOCONSTANT (keyword)
  MANOVA command, 481
NOEJECT (obsolete), 754, see LENGTH keyword
NOKAISER (keyword)
  FACTOR command, 653
NOLABELS (keyword)
  FREQUENCIES command, 268
NOLASTRES (keyword)
  MANOVA command, 481
NONAME (keyword)
  REPORT command, 350
NONORMAL (keyword)
  FREQUENCIES command, 272
NONPAR CORR (command), 663-669
  annotated example, 666
  formats, 668
  limitations, 669
  matrix output, 669
  missing values, 665
  old friends, 770
  random sampling, 668-669
  significance tests, 665
  with WEIGHT command, 155
nonparallel files
  defined, 225
  MATCH FILES command, 230-233
nonparametric tests, 671
NOORIGIN (subcommand)
  REGRESSION command, 611
NOPRINT (subcommand)
  LOGLINEAR command, 547
  MANOVA command, 487-493
NORMAL (function), 94
NORMAL (keyword)
  FREQUENCIES command, 272
  MANOVA command, 495
  NPAR TESTS command, 675
NORMPROB (keyword)
  LOGLINEAR command, 547
  REGRESSION command, 612
NOROTATE (keyword)
  FACTOR command, 654
  MANOVA command, 488
NOT (keyword)
  logical operator, 129
NOTABLE (keyword)
  FREQUENCIES command, 269
NOTABLE (subcommand)
  DATA LIST command, 32-33
  PRINT command, 139
  REPEATING DATA command, 184
  WRITE command, 142-143
notes
  display file messages, 60
NOTOTAL (keyword)
  REPORT command, 350
NOWARN (keyword)
  FILE TYPE GROUPED, 168-169, 170-171
  FILE TYPE MIXED, 164
  FILE TYPE NESTED, 173, 174, 174-175
NPAR TESTS (command), 671-695
  k independent samples, 691-693
  k related samples, 682-684
  aliases, 695
  BINOMIAL subcommand, 673, 678
  CHISQUARE subcommand, 673, 673-674
  COCHRAN subcommand, 682, 682-683
  EXPECTED subcommand, 673-674
  FRIEDMAN subcommand, 682, 683
  K-S subcommand, 673, 674-676, 685-685, 687-688
  K-W subcommand, 691, 692-693
  KENDALL subcommand, 682, 684
  limitations, 695
  M-W subcommand, 685, 686-687
  MCNEMAR subcommand, 679, 679-680
  MEDIAN subcommand, 685, 685-686, 691-691, 691-692
  missing values, 694
  MOSES subcommand, 685, 690
  old friends, 770
  random sampling, 695
  RUNS subcommand, 673, 676-677
  SIGN subcommand, 679, 680-681
  statistics, 694
  two independent samples, 684-690
  two related samples, 678-682
  W-W subcommand, 685, 688-689
  WILCOXON subcommand, 679, 681-682
  with WEIGHT command, 155
NTEST (keyword)
  BOX-JENKINS command, 705
NTILES (subcommand)
  FREQUENCIES command, 273

NU (function)
  AGGREGATE command, 219
NUMBER (function), 117, 118
NUMBERED
  old friends, 754
NUMBERED (command), 53
NUMBERED (keyword)
  LIST command, 147
NUMERIC (command), 104
  with INPUT MATRIX command, 262-263
NUMERIC (subcommand)
  REFORMAT (command), 757-758
numeric expressions, 90-100
  COMPUTE command, 87-90
  defined, 87, 90
  missing values, 96
numeric variables
  defined, 8
  storage, 79, 80
NUMISS (function)
  AGGREGATE command, 219
NVALID (function), 93

OBLIMIN (keyword)
  FACTOR command, 654
OCCURS (subcommand)
  REPEATING DATA command, 183
OFF (keyword)
  SPLIT FILE command, 212-213
OFFSET (keyword)
  REPORT command, 342, 350
OMEANS (keyword)
  MANOVA command, 487, 490-491
ONEPAGE (keyword)
  FREQUENCIES command, 268
ONEWAY (command), 453-462
  analysis list, 454
  annotated example, 462
  CONTRAST subcommand, 455-456
  harmonic means, 458
  limitations, 461
  matrix input, 461
  matrix output, 460
  missing values, 459
  old friends, 767
  POLYNOMIAL subcommand, 454-455
  RANGES subcommand, 456-458
  ranges, user-specified, 458
  statistics, 459
  variable and value labels, 459-460
ONEWAY (keyword)
  MANOVA command, 488
OPTIONS (command), 259
  old friends, 761
OR (keyword)
  logical operator, 129
ORDER (subcommand)
  BARCHART command, 403-404
  LINECHART command, 416-417
  PIECHART command, 385-386
order of commands, 23-24
  defined, 775-776
  file definition commands, 778
  input programs, 778
  procedure commands, 258, 779
  program states, 775-777
  restricted transformation commands, 778-779
  transformation commands, 778
  unrestricted utility commands, 778
order of operations
  numeric expressions, 91-92
ORDERED (subcommand)
  FILE TYPE GROUPED, 169
ORIGIN (subcommand)
  BOX-JENKINS command, 713
  REGRESSION command, 611
ORTHO (keyword)
  MANOVA command, 490
ORTHONORM (keyword)
  MANOVA command, 476
OSIRIS VARS (obsolete), 758
OTHER (keyword)
  FILE TYPE GROUPED, 169-170
  FILE TYPE MIXED, 165
OUTFILE (subcommand)
  AGGREGATE command, 216-217
  EXPORT command, 251
  GRAPHICS OUTPUT command, 425
  INFO command, 26
  PRINT command, 139
  PRINT SPACE command, 141
  PROCEDURE OUTPUT command, 260-261
  SAVE command, 71
  SAVE SCSS command, 246
  WRITE command, 142
OUTLIERS (keyword)
  REGRESSION command, 612, 613
OUTPUT (keyword)
  RELIABILITY command, 731
output file
  defined, 6
OUTS (keyword)
  REGRESSION command, 610
OVERALL (keyword)
  MANOVA command, 488
OVERVIEW (keyword)
  INFO command, 25

P (subcommand)
  BOX-JENKINS command, 702
PACF (keyword)
  BOX-JENKINS command, 714
padding strings, 117
PAF (keyword)
  FACTOR command, 650
PAGE (keyword)
  REPORT command, 350
page layout
  in REPORT command, 334-335
page size, see SET command
PAGESIZE (obsolete), 754, see SET command
PAIRED (keyword)
  MULT RESPONSE command, 313-314
paired crosstabulations
  in MULT RESPONSE command, 313-314
PAIRWISE (keyword)
  FACTOR command, 649
  REGRESSION command, 606
PARALLEL (keyword)
  RELIABILITY command, 721
parallel files
  defined, 225
  MATCH FILES command, 226
parallel model
  in RELIABILITY command, 718
parameter estimates
  in MANOVA command, 490
PARAMETERS (keyword)
  MANOVA command, 487, 490
PARTIAL CORR (command), 589-599
  annotated example, 598-599
  control variables, 591
  correlation list, 590-591
  formats, 594-595
  limitations, 597
  matrix input, 595-597
  matrix output, 597
  missing values, 594
  old friends, 768
  order values, 591
  significance tests, 593
  statistics, 593
partial correlation coefficient, see PARTIAL CORR
partial residual plots
  in REGRESSION command, 615
PARTIALPLOT (subcommand)
  REGRESSION command, 615
PARTITION (subcommand)
  MANOVA command, 481-482
patterns
  in BARCHART command, 403-404
  in LINECHART command, 416-417
  in PIECHART command, 385-386
PA1 (keyword)
  FACTOR command, 650
PA2 (keyword)
  FACTOR command, 650
PC (keyword)
  FACTOR command, 650
PCGT (function)
  REPORT command, 355
PCIN (function)
  REPORT command, 355
PCLT (function)
  REPORT command, 355
PCON (subcommand)
  BOX-JENKINS command, 705
PCT (function)
  REPORT command, 355
PEARSON CORR (command), 579-586
  annotated example, 582
  formats, 584-585
  limitations, 586
  matrix output, 585-586
  missing values, 584
  old friends, 768
  significance tests, 581
  statistics, 581-584
Pearson correlation coefficient, 294, 326, see also PEARSON CORR
PERCENT (function)
  BARCHART command, 393
  LINECHART command, 409
PERCENT (keyword)
  FREQUENCIES command, 271, 272
  PIECHART command, 383
PERCENTILES (subcommand)
  FREQUENCIES command, 273
PERIOD (subcommand)
  BOX-JENKINS command, 701-702
period missing value specification
  AGGREGATE command, 221
  suffix, 93
PGT (function)
  AGGREGATE command, 219
phi coefficient, 294

PIECHART (command), 377-378, 378-379, 381-392
  aggregated data, 392
  annotated example, 389
  COLORS subcommand, 386-387
  COMMENT subcommand, 384
  EXPLODE subcommand, 385
  FONT subcommand, 387
  FOOTNOTE subcommand, 384
  FORMAT subcommand, 383-384
  MISSING subcommand, 387-390
  missing values, 387-390
  multiple plots per page, 391-392
  old friends, 766
  ORDER subcommand, 385-386
  patterns, 385-386
  PLOT subcommand, 382, 390-391
  SAVE subcommand, 422-425
  SEGMENT LABELS subcommand, 384-385
  selectors, 383
  TITLE subcommand, 384
  XPAGE subcommand, 387
  YPAGE subcommand, 387
PIEWISE (keyword)
  PIECHART command, 387
PIN (function)
  AGGREGATE command, 219
PIN (keyword)
  DISCRIMINANT command, 632
  REGRESSION command, 609
PLAIN (keyword)
  REPORT command, 359
PLOT (keyword)
  REGRESSION command, 613
PLOT (subcommand)
  BARCHART command, 393-397, 407-408
  BOX-JENKINS command, 714
  FACTOR command, 652-653
  LINECHART command, 408-412, 419-420
  LOGLINEAR command, 547-548
  MANOVA command, 493-496
  PIECHART command, 382, 390-391
  SURVIVAL command, 740-741
PLOTWISE (keyword)
  BARCHART command, 404
  LINECHART command, 418
  PIECHART command, 388
PLT (function)
  AGGREGATE command, 219
PMEANS (keyword)
  MANOVA command, 487, 491-493, 496-496
POBS (keyword)
  MANOVA command, 487, 493, 496
POINTS (keyword)
  LINECHART command, 415
POISSON (keyword)
  NPAR TESTS command, 675
POLYNOMIAL (keyword)
  LOGLINEAR command, 548
  MANOVA command, 477, 477-478, 484-485
POLYNOMIAL (subcommand)
  ONEWAY (command), 454-455
POOLED (keyword)
  REGRESSION command, 612
portable files
  defined, 250-251
postprocessor
  graphics, 425-428
POUT (function)
  AGGREGATE command, 219
POUT (keyword)
  DISCRIMINANT command, 632
  REGRESSION command, 609
POWER (subcommand)
  BOX-JENKINS command, 700-701
PP (subcommand)
  BOX-JENKINS command, 705
PQ (subcommand)
  BOX-JENKINS command, 705
precedence of commands, see order of commands
PRED (keyword)
  REGRESSION command, 612
PREVIOUS (keyword)
  REPORT command, 365-366
principal axis factoring, 650
principal components analysis, 488-489, 650-650
PRINCOMPS (keyword)
  MANOVA command, 487, 488-489
PRINT (command)
  $CASENUM system variable, 138
  formats, 136-137
  line specifications, 137
  literals, 138-139
  missing values, 140
  NOTABLE subcommand, 139
  OUTFILE subcommand, 139
  TABLE subcommand, 139
  variable list, 136-137
  with DO IF command, 138
  with REPORT command, 375
  with SORT CASES command, 209
PRINT (subcommand)
  BOX-JENKINS command, 714
  END REPEAT command, 106
  FACTOR command, 650-652
  LOGLINEAR command, 547
  MANOVA command, 487-493
PRINT BACK (obsolete), 754, see SET command
PRINT EJECT (command)
  $CASENUM system variable, 140
  with DO IF command, 140
print formats
  in LIST command, 145
  in PRINT command, 135
  in REPORT command, 358-359
  setting default, 56-57
PRINT FORMATS (command
  with LIST command, 145
  with PRINT command, 135
PRINT FORMATS (command), 144
  old friends, 752, 755
  with AGGREGATE command, 218-219
  with REPORT command, 374
PRINT SPACE (command)
  $CASENUM system variable, 140-141
  number of lines, 141
  OUTFILE subcommand, 141
  with DO IF command, 140-141
PRINTBACK (keyword)
  SET command, 54, 56
  SHOW command, 54
PRIORS (subcommand)
  DISCRIMINANT command, 635
PROBIT (function), 94
PROBS (keyword)
  DISCRIMINANT command, 641
procedure
  defined, 257
PROCEDURE OUTPUT (command), 260-261
  matrix output, 261, 263
  OUTFILE subcommand, 260-261
procedure state
  defined, 774-775
procedures
  creating new variables, 260
  matrix files, 261-263
  order of commands, 258
  output files, 260
  update documentation, 25
PROCEDURES (keyword)
  INFO command, 25
profile analysis, 535-539
program states
  defined, 774-775
  order of commands, 775-777
PROPORTION (function)
  LINECHART command, 409
PSP (subcommand)
  BOX-JENKINS command, 705
PSQ (subcommand)
  BOX-JENKINS command, 705

Q (subcommand)
  BOX-JENKINS command, 702
QR (keyword)
  MANOVA command, 480
Q, Cochran's, 682-683
quartiles, 694
QUARTIMAX (keyword)
  FACTOR command, 654
  MANOVA command, 488, 489

r, see Pearson correlation coefficient
R (keyword)
  MANOVA command, 472, 486-487
  REGRESSION command, 610
RACF (keyword)
  BOX-JENKINS command, 714
random numbers
  setting seed, 57
randomized block designs
  in MANOVA command, 501-502
range, see value range
RANGE (function), 93, 760
RANGE (keyword)
  BARCHART command, 401
  FREQUENCIES command, 276
  LINECHART command, 413, 414
RANGES (subcommand)
  ONEWAY command, 456-458
rank-order correlation coefficients, see NONPAR CORR
RAO (keyword)
  DISCRIMINANT command, 627
RAW (keyword)
  MANOVA command, 489
RAW OUTPUT UNIT (obsolete), 761, see PROCEDURE OUTPUT command
RCONVERGE (keyword)
  FACTOR command, 653
READ (subcommand)
  FACTOR command, 660
  MANOVA command, 498-499
  REGRESSION command, 619-620
READ INPUT DATA (obsolete), 753, see BEGIN DATA command

READ MATRIX (obsolete), 761, see INPUT MATRIX command
RECODE (command)
  annotated example, 88-89
  CONVERT keyword, 114
  COPY keyword, 87, 112
  ELSE keyword, 85-86, 112-112
  INTO keyword, 86-87, 112-114
  MISSING keyword, 86, 112
  numeric variables, 84-87
  old friends, 760
  string variables, 111-114
  SYSMIS keyword, 86
  value range, 85, 86
  with DO IF command, 122
RECORD (subcommand)
  FILE TYPE GROUPED, 167
  FILE TYPE MIXED, 163
  FILE TYPE NESTED, 172-173
RECORD TYPE (command)
  CASE subcommand, 170, 178
  DUPLICATE subcommand, 170-171
  MISSING subcommand, 170-171
  OTHER keyword, 165, 169«
  SKIP subcommand, 165-166, 169-170
  SPREAD subcommand, 178-179
  with FILE TYPE GROUPED, 169-170
  with FILE TYPE MIXED, 164-166
  with FILE TYPE NESTED, 175-179
RECORDS (subcommand)
  DATA LIST command, 32
rectangular file
  defined, 8
REFERENCE (keyword)
  BARCHART command, 401
  LINECHART command, 413, 414
REFORMAT (command), 757-758
REG (function)
  LINECHART command, 409
REG (keyword)
  FACTOR command, 655
REGRESSION (command), 601-621
  annotated example, 616
  backward elimination, 604
  CASEWISE subcommand, 613
  CRITERIA subcommand, 608-609
  DEPENDENT subcommand, 603-604
  DESCRIPTIVES subcommand, 606-607
  forced entry, 604-605
  forced removal, 605
  forward entry, 604
  matrix input, 619-620
  matrix output, 620-621
  method subcommands, 604-605
  minimum required syntax, 602
  MISSING subcommand, 606
  missing values, 606
  NOORIGIN subcommand, 611
  old friends, 768-769
  ORIGIN subcommand, 611
  PARTIALPLOT subcommand, 615
  READ subcommand, 619-620
  RESIDUALS subcommand, 612-613
  SAVE subcommand, 618
  SCATTERPLOT subcommand, 613-614
  SELECT subcommand, 607-608
  STATISTICS subcommand, 609-610
  stepwise selection, 604
  VARIABLES subcommand, 602-603
  WIDTH subcommand, 621
  WRITE subcommand, 620-621
relational operators, 128
  defined, 128
  in BARCHART command, 395
  in LINECHART command, 410-411
  in PIECHART command, 383
RELFREQ (function)
  REPORT command, 355
RELIABILITY (command), 717-732
  alternative computing methods, 731-732
  analysis of variance, 723, 725
  annotated example, 726
  format selection numbers, 731
  FORMAT subcommand, 731
  Friedman's analysis of variance, 724
  limitations, 732
  matrix input, 728-729, 731-731
  matrix output, 730-731, 731-731
  missing values, 732
  MODEL subcommand, 720-721
  old friends, 770
  repeated measures analysis, 723
  scale name, 719
  SCALE subcommand, 719-720
  statistics, 721-722
  tests for violation of assumptions, 723-724
  variable labels, 732
  VARIABLES subcommand, 719
remainder, 92
REMOVE (keyword)
  REGRESSION command, 605
RENAME (subcommand)
  ADD FILES command, 239-240, 242-242
  EXPORT command, 252
  GET command, 67-68
  IMPORT command, 254
  MANOVA command, 479-480
  MATCH FILES command, 228-229
  SAVE command, 72
  SAVE SCSS command, 246-247
REORDER VARS (obsolete), 758, see GET or SAVE
reordering variables
  in ADD FILES command, 240, 242
  in GET command, 69-70
  in MATCH FILES (command), 230
  in SAVE command, 73
REPEATED (keyword)
  LOGLINEAR command, 548
  MANOVA command, 475-476, 477-477, 477-477, 485-485
repeated measures analysis, 473-476, 521-531, 723-723
repeated measures multivariate ANCOVA, 475-476
repeated measures, doubly multivariate, 476, 532-535
REPEATING DATA (command), 179-181
  CONTINUED subcommand, 185-186
  DATA subcommand, 184
  FILE subcommand, 184-185
  ID subcommand, 186-187
  LENGTH subcommand, 185
  NOTABLE subcommand, 184
  OCCURS subcommand, 183
  STARTS subcommand, 182-183
  with DATA LIST command, 181
  with END INPUT PROGRAM command, 181-182
  with FILE TYPE command, 181
  with INPUT PROGRAM command, 181-182
REPORT (command), 333-375
  aggregate functions, 355
  annotated example listing cases, 344-345
  annotated example with summaries, 362-363
  BREAK subcommand, 349-354
  breaks defined, 335-336
  column contents, 340-341, 342-342, 349-351
  column heads, 341-342, 349-351
  column widths, 341, 349-351
  columns defined, 335
  compared with other procedures, 372
  composite functions, 355, 359-361
  CROSSBREAK-like tables, 372-373
  CROSSTABS-like tables, 373-374
  default report, 337-338
  FORMAT subcommand, 338-340
  intercolumn spacing, 342
  limitations, 370
  MISSING subcommand, 368-369
  missing values, 368-369
  no break reports, 352-354, 369-369
  old friends, 764-766
  page layout, 334-335, 339-339
  repeating summary specifications, 365-366
  rows defined, 335
  STRING subcommand, 346-348
  subcommand order, 370
  summaries on one line, 364-365
  summary line spacing, 357
  summary print formats, 358-359
  SUMMARY subcommand, 354-367
  summary titles, 356, 357-358
  titles and footnotes, 367-368
  VARIABLES subcommand, 340-343
  with N OF CASES command, 371
  with PRINT command, 375
  with PRINT FORMATS command, 374
  with SAMPLE command, 371
  with SORT CASES command, 209, 371
  with SPLIT FILE command, 371
  with VARIABLE LABELS command, 374-375
  with WRITE command, 375
report variables
  in REPORT command, 335
REPR (keyword)
  FACTOR command, 651
REREAD (command), 202
  COLUMN keyword, 202
reserved keywords, 21
  in GET SCSS command, 250
  in SAVE SCSS command, 246
RESID (keyword), see RESIDUAL keyword
RESIDUAL (keyword)
  BOX-JENKINS command, 714
  LOGLINEAR command, 547, 547
  MANOVA command, 472, 486-487
  REGRESSION command, 612

residual variables
  in REGRESSION command, 612, 618
RESIDUALS (subcommand)
  REGRESSION command, 612-613
residuals analysis
  in REGRESSION command, 612-618
result files
  in ADD FILES command, 238
  in MATCH FILES command, 225-226
RFOOTNOTE (subcommand)
  REPORT command, 367-368
RND (function), 92
ROOT (keyword)
  BARCHART command, 401
ROTATE (keyword)
  MANOVA command, 488, 489
ROTATION (keyword)
  FACTOR command, 651, 652
ROTATION (subcommand)
  FACTOR command, 654-655
rotation options
  in DISCRIMINANT command, 634
round, 92
Roy-Bargmann step-down *F* test, 489
RPAD (function), 116
RTITLE (subcommand)
  REPORT command, 367-368
RTRIM (function), 116, 116, 117
RUN NAME (obsolete), 754, see TITLE command
RUN SUBFILES (obsolete), 755, see SPLIT FILE command
RUNS (subcommand)
  NPAR TESTS command, 673, 676-677
runs test, 676-677
RW (keyword)
  MANOVA command, 472, 486-487

SAMPLE (command), 153
  exact-sized sample, 153
  old friends, 759
  placement, 157
  proportional sample, 153
  with DO IF command, 158
  with other transformations, 158
  with REPORT command, 371
  with TEMPORARY command, 157
SAVE (command), 70-76
  annotated example, 74-75
  COMPRESSED keyword, 76
  DROP subcommand, 72-73
  KEEP subcommand, 72-73
  MAP subcommand, 71
  OUTFILE subcommand, 71
  RENAME subcommand, 72
  reordering variables, 73
  UNCOMPRESSED keyword, 76
SAVE (subcommand)
  BARCHART command, 422-425
  DISCRIMINANT command, 641-642
  FACTOR command, 655
  LINECHART command, 422-425
  PIECHART command, 422-425
  REGRESSION command, 618
SAVE FILE (obsolete), 756, see SAVE command
SAVE SCSS (command), 245-248
  DROP subcommand, 246
  KEEP subcommand, 246
  missing values, 246
  old friends, 758-759
  OUTFILE subcommand, 246
  RENAME subcommand, 246-247
  reserved keywords, 246
SCALE (subcommand)
  RELIABILITY command, 719-720
scale analysis, see RELIABILITY (command)
scale name
  in RELIABILITY command, 719
SCATTERGRAM (command), 571-577
  annotated example, 574
  default plot, 573
  grid lines, 577
  limitations, 577
  missing values, 577
  old friends, 768
  regression statistics, 576-577
  scaling, 573-576
  variable labels, 577
  variable list, 572-573
  with WEIGHT command, 155
SCATTERPLOT (subcommand)
  REGRESSION command, 613-614
scatterplots
  in REGRESSION command, 613-614
SCHEFFE (keyword)
  ONEWAY command, 458
Scheffe's test, 458
SCORES (keyword)
  DISCRIMINANT command, 641
scratch files
  compression, 57
scratch variables
  defined, 102-103
scree plots
  in FACTOR command, 652
SCSS, see GET SCSS or SAVE SCSS
SD (function), 93
  AGGREGATE command, 219
SDIFFERENCE (subcommand)
  BOX-JENKINS command, 701-702
SDRESID (keyword)
  REGRESSION command, 612
SD1 (function)
  LINECHART command, 409
SD2 (function)
  LINECHART command, 409
SD3 (function)
  LINECHART command, 409
SEED (keyword)
  SET command, 54, 57
  SHOW command, 54
SEED (obsolete), 754, see SET command
SEGMENT LABELS (subcommand)
  PIECHART command, 384-385
SEKURT (keyword)
  FREQUENCIES command, 276
SELECT (subcommand)
  DISCRIMINANT command, 634
  REGRESSION command, 607-608
SELECT IF (command), 151-153
  annotated example, 156
  MISSING function, 152
  missing values, 152
  old friends, 759, 761
  placement, 157
  VALUE function, 152
  with $CASENUM, 152
  with DO IF command, 158
  with LIST command, 147-148
  with other transformations, 158
  with TEMPORARY command, 157
SEMEAN (keyword)
  FREQUENCIES command, 276
SEPRED (keyword)1-
  REGRESSION command, 612
SEQNUM (obsolete), 755, see $CASENUM
SEQUENTIAL (keyword)
  MANOVA command, 481
SER (keyword)
  BOX-JENKINS command, 714
series plots
  in BOX-JENKINS command, 699
SES (keyword)
  REGRESSION command, 610
SESKEW (keyword)
  FREQUENCIES command, 276
SET (command), 53-57
  annotated example, 58-59
SETCONST (subcommand)
  MANOVA command, 486
SHADE (keyword)
  LINECHART command, 412
short string, see string variables
SHOW (command), 53-57
  annotated example, 58-59
SIDE AXIS (subcommand)
  BARCHART command, 401-402
SIG (keyword)
  FACTOR command, 651
  REGRESSION command, 607
SIGN (subcommand)
  NPAR TESTS command, 679, 680-681
sign test, 680-681
SIGNIF (keyword)
  MANOVA command, 487, 489
SIMPLE (keyword)
  BARCHART command, 398
  LINECHART command, 412
  LOGLINEAR command, 548
  MANOVA command, 477, 484
  PIECHART command, 383
SIN (function), 93
SINCE (keyword)
  INFO command, 25-26
sine, 93
SINGLE (keyword)
  LIST command, 147
SINGLEDF (keyword)
  MANOVA command, 489
SIZE (keyword)
  DISCRIMINANT command, 635
  MANOVA command, 496
  REGRESSION command, 612, 613
SKEWNESS (function)
  REPORT command, 355
SKEWNESS (keyword)
  FREQUENCIES command, 276
SKIP (keyword)
  REPORT command, 350, 357
SKIP (subcommand)
  FILE TYPE GROUPED, 170
  FILE TYPE MIXED, 165-166
SMEAN (function)
  LINECHART command, 409
SNK (keyword)
  ONEWAY command, 458
SOLUTION (keyword)
  MANOVA command, 488

Somers' *d*, 294
SORT (keyword)
  FACTOR command, 652
  PIECHART command, 383
SORT CASES (command), 207-209
  annotated example, 210-211
  BY keyword, 207
  old friends, 755
  specifying order, 207-208
  string variables, 208-209
  with ADD FILES command, 209
  with AGGREGATE command, 209, 217
  with MATCH FILES command, 209, 232
  with PRINT command, 209
  with REPORT command, 209, 371
  with SPLIT FILE command, 212
SORTED (keyword)
  DISPLAY command, 77-78, 78-78
source variables
  in AGGREGATE command, 217-218
SP (subcommand)
  BOX-JENKINS command, 702
Spearman-Brown split-half coefficient, 717
Spearman's rho, 665
SPECIAL (keyword)
  LOGLINEAR command, 548
  MANOVA command, 477, 478, 485-486
SPLINE (keyword)
  LINECHART command, 415
SPLIT (keyword)
  RELIABILITY command, 720-721
SPLIT FILE (command), 212-213
  annotated example, 210-211
  with AGGREGATE command, 213, 217
  with LIST command, 146, 147
  with matrix input and output, 263
  with REPORT command, 371
  with SORT CASES command, 212
  with TEMPORARY command, 212
split model
  in RELIABILITY command, 717
SPREAD (subcommand)
  FILE TYPE NESTED, 178-179
SQ (subcommand)
  BOX-JENKINS command, 702
SQRT (function), 92
square root, 92
SRESID (keyword)
  REGRESSION command, 612
SSCP (keyword)
  MANOVA command, 487, 489
SSTYPE (keyword)
  MANOVA command, 481
STACKED (keyword)
  BARCHART command, 398
STAN (keyword)
  MANOVA command, 489
stand-in variable
  DO REPEAT command, 104
standard deviation function, 93
STARTS (subcommand)
  REPEATING DATA command, 182-183
states, see program states
statistic *D*
  defined, 735-736
STATISTICS (command), 259
  old friends, 761
STATISTICS (subcommand)
  REGRESSION command, 609-610
STATUS (subcommand)
  SURVIVAL command, 738
STDDEV (keyword)
  FREQUENCIES command, 276
  REGRESSION command, 607, 619, 620
STDEV (function)
  REPORT command, 355
STDV (keyword)
  MANOVA command, 489
stem-and-leaf plots, 495
STEMLEAF (keyword)
  MANOVA command, 495
STEP (keyword)
  LINECHART command, 415
STEPDOWN (keyword)
  MANOVA command, 489
STEPWISE (keyword)
  REGRESSION command, 604
STRAIGHT (keyword)
  LINECHART command, 415
STRICTPARALLEL (keyword)
  RELIABILITY command, 721
strictparallel model
  in RELIABILITY command, 718
STRING (command), 110
STRING (function), 116, 118, 119
STRING (subcommand)
  REPORT command, 346-348
string expressions
  defined, 114, 115
string functions, 116-119
string variables
  defined, 8, 109
  in DATA LIST command, 36
  in logical expressions, 115
  in MISSING VALUES command, 41
  in SAVE SCSS command, 246
  in SORT CASES command, 208-209
  missing values, 111
  storage, 79, 80
stub and banner tables
  in MULT RESPONSE command, 316-317
Student-Newman-Keuls test, 458
Student's *t*, see T-TEST
subcommands
  defined, 19-20
SUBFILE LIST (obsolete), 755, see SPLIT FILE command
subfiles (obsolete), 755, 758, see SPLIT FILE command
SUBSTR (function), 117
substrings, 117
SUBTITLE (command), 52
SUBTRACT (function)
  REPORT command, 355
subtraction, 91
suffix
  missing values, 93, 97-100
SUM (function), 93
  AGGREGATE command, 219
  BARCHART command, 393
  LINECHART command, 409
  REPORT command, 355
SUM (keyword)
  FREQUENCIES command, 276
SUMMARY (subcommand)
  REPORT command, 354-367
summary titles
  in REPORT command, 356
SUMSPACE (keyword)
  REPORT command, 339
SURVIVAL (command), 735-747
  aggregated data, 743
  annotated example, 744-745
  COMPARE subcommand, 741
  comparisons only, 743
  comparisons, approximate, 742-743
  comparisons, pairwise, 742
  INTERVALS subcommand, 737-738
  life tables, 738-739
  limitations, 747
  missing values, 746
  old friends, 771
  output file, 746-747
  PLOTS subcommand, 740-741
  STATUS subcommand, 738
  survival functions, 739
  TABLES subcommand, 737
  value range, 738
SURVIVAL (keyword)
  SURVIVAL command, 740
survival scores
  defined, 735
syntax, 19-23
  diagrams, 23
  with EDIT command, 61-62
SYSMIS (function), 93
SYSMIS (keyword)
  COUNT command, 101
  RECODE command, 86
  SHOW command, 54
$SYSMIS (system variable)
  defined, 106
system files
  annotated example, 74-75
  binary data, 79
  case, 79-80
  compressed, 79
  defined, 65
  limitations, 80
  old friends, 756-758
  structure, 79
system variables, 106
  in SHOW command, 57
system-missing values, 39

t statistic, 455
t test, see T-TESTT-TEST (command), 431-433
  annotated example, 432-433
  formats, 436
  GROUPS subcommand, 434
  independent samples, 431-434
  limitations, 436
  missing values, 435-436
  old friends, 766
  paired samples, 434-435
  significance tests, 435
  VARIABLES subcommand, 434
TABLE (subcommand)
  DATA LIST command, 32-33
  MATCH FILES command, 234-235
  PRINT command, 139
  WRITE command, 142-143
table lookup files
  defined, 225
  MATCH FILES (command), 234-238

TABLES (keyword)
MANOVA command, 490-491, 491-493
TABLES (subcommand)
BREAKDOWN command, 322-324, 325-325
CROSSTABS command, 288-291, 292-292
MULT RESPONSE command, 311-314
SURVIVAL command, 737
target variables
in AGGREGATE command, 217-218
in COMPUTE command, 87-90, 115-115
in COUNT command, 101
in RECODE command, 86-87, 112-112
TASK NAME (obsolete), 754, see SUBTITLE command
tau statistics, 294, 665
TCON (subcommand)
BOX-JENKINS command, 712
TELL-A-GRAF interface, 422-425
TEMPORARY (command), 103-104
with MATCH FILES command, 227
with SPLIT FILE command, 212
temporary transformations
old friends, 759
temporary variables, 103
terminal value
in LOOP command, 190-191
TEST (keyword)
BOX-JENKINS command, 705
REGRESSION command, 605
test of linearity, 326
THRU (keyword)
BOX-JENKINS command, 701
RECODE command, 85
SURVIVAL command, 737-738
time series analysis, see BOX-JENKINS (command)
TITLE (command), 51-52
TITLE (subcommand)
BARCHART command, 399
LINECHART command, 412
PIECHART command, 384
REPORT command, 367-368
TO (keyword)
DATA LIST command, 35
LIST command, 146
LOOP command, 190-191
variable lists, 20-21
TOL (keyword)
REGRESSION command, 610
tolerance
in REGRESSION command, 608
TOLERANCE (keyword)
DISCRIMINANT command, 632
REGRESSION command, 609
TOTAL (keyword)
REPORT command, 350, 352
TP (subcommand)
BOX-JENKINS command, 712
TQ (subcommand)
BOX-JENKINS command, 712
TRANSFORM (keyword)
MANOVA command, 487, 487, 493
TRANSFORM (subcommand)
MANOVA command, 476-479
transformation state
defined, 774-775
transformations
active file, 107
execution, 107
in MANOVA command, 476-479
old friends, 759-761
with data definitions, 107
treatment effects, defined, 449
trimming strings, 117
TRIPLEX (keyword)
BARCHART command, 404
LINECHART command, 418
PIECHART command, 387
TRUNC (function), 92
truncate, 92
truncation of keywords, 21
TSER (keyword)
BOX-JENKINS command, 714
TSP (subcommand)
BOX-JENKINS command, 712
TSPACE (keyword)
REPORT command, 339
TSQ (subcommand)
BOX-JENKINS command, 712
TUKEY (keyword)
ONEWAY command, 458
Tukey's test for additivity, 723-724
TUKEYB (keyword)
ONEWAY command, 458

U, Mann-Whitney, 686-687
ULS (keyword)
FACTOR command, 650
uncertainty coefficient, 294
UNCOMPRESSED (keyword)
SAVE command, 76
UNCONDITIONAL (keyword)
MANOVA command, 469
UNDEFINED (keyword)
SET command, 54, 54-55
SHOW command, 54
undefined data values
with DATA LIST command, 38
UNIFORM (function), 94
UNIFORM (keyword)
NPAR TESTS command, 675
UNIQUE (keyword)
MANOVA command, 481
UNIV (keyword)
MANOVA command, 489
UNIVARIATE (keyword)
FACTOR command, 650
UNKNOWN (obsolete)
old friends, 753
UNNUMBERED
old friends, 754
UNNUMBERED (command), 53
UNNUMBERED (keyword)
LIST command, 146-147
UP (keyword)
SORT CASES command, 207
update documentation
INFO command, 24
upper case, 79-80
user-missing values, 39
utilities
defined, 12-13
general run control, 51-59
system files, 76

***V*, Cramer's, 294**
VALIDN (function)
REPORT command, 355
VALUE (function), 93
SELECT IF command, 152
VALUE (keyword)
REPORT command, 341, 350
value labels, 41-43
case, 56
VALUE LABELS (command), 41-42, 42-43
old friends, 753
value range
RECODE command, 85, 86
VALUES (function)
LINECHART command, 409
VAR (keyword)
REPORT command, 368
VAR LABELS (command)
old friends, 753
VARIABLE (subcommand)
BOX-JENKINS command, 698
variable definition, 29-30
in DATA LIST command, 33
variable labels, 41-42
case, 56
in AGGREGATE command, 218
VARIABLE LABELS (command), 41-42
with REPORT command, 374-375
VARIABLE LIST (obsolete), 752, see DATA LIST command
variable lists
TO keyword, 20-21
variable names
defined, 20
rules for assigning, 33
variable selection methods
in DISCRIMINANT command, 627
in REGRESSION command, 604-605
variables
defined, 7
VARIABLES (keyword)
DISPLAY command, 77
MANOVA command, 490-491, 491-493
VARIABLES (subcommand)
BREAKDOWN command, 324-325
CROSSTABS command, 291-292
DISCRIMINANT command, 625-626
FACTOR command, 648
FREQUENCIES command, 266-267
GET command, 78
GET SCSS command, 249-250
LIST command, 145
MULT RESPONSE command, 309
REGRESSION command, 602-603
RELIABILITY command, 719
REPORT command, 340-343
T-TEST command, 434
VARIANCE (function), 93
REPORT command, 355
VARIANCE (keyword)
FREQUENCIES command, 276
REGRESSION command, 607, 619, 620
VARIMAX (keyword)
FACTOR command, 654
MANOVA command, 488, 489
$VARS (keyword)
SHOW command, 54

vector
  VECTOR command, 193-194
VECTOR (command), 193-195
  annotated example, 200-201
  short form, 194-195
VERTICAL (keyword)
  BARCHART command, 397
VIN (keyword)
  DISCRIMINANT command, 632

W (keyword)
  MANOVA command, 472, 486-487
W-W (subcommand)
  NPAR TESTS command, 685, 688-689
W, Kendall's, see Kendall's *W*
Wald-Wolfowitz runs test, 688-689
WARN (keyword)
  FILE TYPE GROUPED, 168-169, 170-171
  FILE TYPE MIXED, 164
  FILE TYPE NESTED, 173, 174, 174-175
warnings
  messages, 60-61
  setting maximum, 55
  suppressing messages, 54-55
WEIGHT (command), 154-157
  annotated example, 156
  BY keyword, 154-155
  changing weights, 155
  OFF keyword, 155
  old friends, 759
  placement, 157
  with CROSSTABS, 298-299
  with NONPAR CORR, 155
  with NPAR TESTS, 155
  with SCATTERGRAM, 155
  with TEMPORARY command, 157
WEIGHT (keyword)
  SHOW command, 54
weighted marginals
  in MANOVA command, 471-472
weighting data, 154-157
  changing weights, 155
  effects on tests of significance, 157
  noninteger weights, 155
  turning off weights, 155
WIDTH (keyword)
  SET command, 54, 56
  SHOW command, 54
WIDTH (subcommand)
  FACTOR command, 649
  LOGLINEAR command, 554
  REGRESSION command, 621
$WIDTH (system variable)
  defined, 106
WILCOXON (subcommand)
  NPAR TESTS command, 679, 681-682
Wilcoxon matched-pairs signed-ranks test, 681-682
WILD (subcommand)
  FILE TYPE GROUPED, 168
  FILE TYPE MIXED, 164
  FILE TYPE NESTED, 173
WILKS (keyword)
  DISCRIMINANT command, 627
WITH (keyword)
  BARCHART command, 393-394
  LINECHART command, 409-410
  LOGLINEAR command, 544, 545
  NONPAR CORR command, 664, 669
  NPAR TESTS command, 679
  PARTIAL CORR command, 591
  PEARSON CORR command, 580, 585-586
  SCATTERGRAM command, 573
  T-TEST command, 435
WITHIN (keyword)
  MANOVA command, 469-470, 471-471, 472-472, 486-487
within-subjects factors
  in MANOVA command, 473-474
within-subjects transformation matrix
  in MANOVA command, 474-475
words
  data storage, 79
WORKFILE (subcommand)
  GET SCSS command, 249
WR (keyword)
  MANOVA command, 472, 486-487
WRAP (keyword)
  LIST command, 146-147
WRITE (command), 141-143
  formats, 142
  literals, 142
  NOTABLE subcommand, 142-143
  OUTFILE subcommand, 142
  record specifications, 142
  TABLE subcommand, 142-143
  with REPORT command, 375
WRITE (keyword)
  FREQUENCIES command, 269
WRITE (subcommand)
  FACTOR command, 660-661
  MANOVA command, 497-498
  REGRESSION command, 620-621
WRITE CASES (obsolete), 754, see WRITE command
WRITE FILEINFO (obsolete), 754, see EXPORT command
write formats
  setting default, 56-57
WRITE FORMATS (command), 144
  with AGGREGATE command, 218-219
WSDESIGN (subcommand)
  MANOVA command, 474-475
WSFACTORS (subcommand)
  MANOVA command, 473-474

X AXIS (subcommand)
  LINECHART command, 413
XGRID (keyword)
  LINECHART command, 412
XPAGE (subcommand)
  BARCHART command, 404
  PIECHART command, 387
XPROD (keyword)
  REGRESSION command, 607
XTX (keyword)
  REGRESSION command, 610

Y AXIS (subcommand)
  LINECHART command, 414
Yates corrected chi-square test, 294
YES (keyword)
  FILE TYPE GROUPED, 169
  FILE TYPE NESTED, 178-179
YGRID (keyword)
  LINECHART command, 412
YPAGE (subcommand)
  BARCHART command, 404
  PIECHART command, 387
YRMODA (function), 94, 95

Z, Kolmogorov-Smirnov, 687-688, see Kolmogorov-Smirnov *Z*
Z scores
  in CONDESCRIPTIVE command, 281-282ZCORR (keyword)
  MANOVA command, 495
ZETA (keyword)
  MANOVA command, 486
ZPP (keyword)
  REGRESSION command, 610
ZPRED (keyword)
  REGRESSION command, 612
ZRESID (keyword)
  REGRESSION command, 612